St. Mary's Catholic Church Records 1818-1900

Hagerstown
Washington County
Maryland

Marsha Lynne Fuller, CGRS

HERITAGE BOOKS
2006

HERITAGE BOOKS
AN IMPRINT OF HERITAGE BOOKS, INC.

Books, CDs, and more—Worldwide

For our listing of thousands of titles see our website
at
www.HeritageBooks.com

Published 2006 by
HERITAGE BOOKS, INC.
Publishing Division
65 East Main Street
Westminster, Maryland 21157-5026

Copyright © 2001 Washington County Free Library

Other books by Marsha Lynne Fuller:

African American Manumissions of Washington County, Maryland

Family Bible Records in the Washington County Free Library, Hagerstown, Maryland

Naturalizations of Washington County, Maryland, Prior to 1880

All rights reserved. No part of this book may be reproduced or transmitted in any form or by any means, electronic or mechanical, including photocopying, recording or by any information storage and retrieval system without written permission from the author, except for the inclusion of brief quotations in a review.

International Standard Book Number:978-1-58549-770-3

To my sister, Leah Ann Fuller

who knows that dreams really do come true

Table of Contents

Introduction

St. Mary's Catholic Church History & Cemetery

Father Abram J. Ryan, Poet Priest

C & O Canal

Gazeteer

Key & Definitions

Samples of Church Records

Priests' Journal 1786 – 1911

Baptisms 1818 – 1900

Marriages 1818 – 1900

Confirmations 1852 – 1871

Deaths 1853 – 1900

Endnotes

Index

Acknowledgements:

The Chesapeake and Ohio Canal in Maryland was constructed largely by Irish immigrants. Construction on the upper portion of the C&O Canal took place from 1830 until its completion in Cumberland in 1850. The Irish Catholic workers were served during that period by the priests of St. Mary's. Contractors were responsible for various portions of the canal; their names were recorded but not the names of their workers. These records, kept by the priests, are the only known published records relating to these Canal workers. That makes this work very valuable, not only for genealogical research, but for historical research as well.

One can notice a difference in the church records as the number of baptisms increased dramatically during this construction time. As the construction process moved on into Allegany County, the numbers decreased accordingly. In the entry dated June 20, 1841, Father Guth has noted that there have been 764 baptisms in the previous four years – far greater than the 179 baptisms performed during the four years prior to 1822.

The reader will also note the large number of widows remarrying in the mid-1830s. There was a massive cholera epidemic in 1832 which killed many canal workers, leaving these women without husbands.

A special thanks to Father George A. Limmer for making the records available and for assisting with the translation of them, and to Marsha Fuller for doing all the work, and to the Friends of the Western Maryland Room for funding the production of this book.

                              John C. Frye, Director
                              Western Maryland Room

I would like to add my thanks to: Tobin Bakner, Computer Systems Engineer, Washington County Free Library, for the database design and page layout; Mary Graff, Church Secretary of St. Mary's Catholic Church; Gertrude Sacchett, deceased member, St. Mary's Catholic Church Congregation; Charles S. Schmeltzer, Family Historian, Spokane, Washington; and to Kathleen Mary O'Connell, Assistant Director, Washington County Free Library, for her inspiration and encouragement.

                              Marsha L. Fuller, CGRS

Introduction

This project began through a genealogical research request I received from Charles S. Schmeltzer of Spokane, Washington. He was trying to locate the exact birth date of his ancestor, a child of John & Rosana Roof, whom he knew to be of the Catholic faith. To fill this request, I went to see Mary Graff at St. Mary's Catholic Church, and she assisted me in locating the requested records.

After viewing the array of information in these old record books, I was intrigued by the possibility of publishing this information for the use of other researchers. Father George A. Limmer graciously granted me permission to abstract the records.

To secure funding for this project, I next visited John C. Frye, Director of the Western Maryland Room at the Washington County Free Library. John believed this to be such a worthwhile project that he ensured its support by the Friends of the Western Maryland Room. The vision and foresight of these two men has made this project possible.

People

It should be noted that there is a great deal of information in these church records on the slaves in Washington County as well as on the Chesapeake & Ohio Canal workers. Apparently, the St. Mary's churchgoers were quite sincere in their belief that all persons should receive the sacraments of baptism, marriage, and last rites and made sure that their slaves did so. Even though the State of Maryland recorded marriages as early as the 1790s, there do not appear to be any Washington County marriage licenses for slaves. Thus, these church records may be the only written mention of these marriages.

RECORDS

The record books I worked from were, apparently, hardbound at some point in the 20th century. Unfortunately, this caused many of the records to run into the binding but, in most cases, I was able to gently move the paper back far enough to read the words. The researcher will note that these words, however, are not always visible on the microfilm.

The earliest record book, "Sacrament Records 1818 - 1847," has the following words handwritten on the inside back cover: *"The Deed of the three lots contained in the Catholic grave yard Dated 16 Augst 1786, No. 319-320-321 Recorded in Liber E folio 38 Tmy Ryan"*

In 1834, a Washington County deed, recorded on December 20th, shows that Rev. Timothy Ryan bought lots #31 and 32 in Rohrer's Addition from William D. and Susan Bell. The land was 102 ft. in breadth and running back from Walnut St. 98½ ft., along an alley on the north side to 8 ft. alley on the east, houses, bldgs, $180; annual rent 50 cents, due March 1st to Samuel Rohrer, proprietor of addition.[1]

---

[1] Washington County Land Records, Liber PP:491, Washington County Courthouse, Hagerstown, Maryland.

The watermark on the paper in this volume reads, "GIORMAGNANTI" and has a crest which is topped by a bird with outstretched wings. The inside front page reads:

> "On Sunday Feby 14th 1864, Rev. Frs Eming[?] & Dounough gave a spiritual retreat to the people of this Parish. It Commensed on the above Sunday and ended on the Sunday following. 325 approached the Sacraments of Penance & the Eucharist. On Pentecost, Sunday the 40 hours devotion commenced, and ended on the Tuesday following. 250 approached the above holy Sacraments. Rev. Fr. Uchul[?] S.I. helped with the devotion."

HANDWRITING AND SPELLING

The abstracting of these records was made truly difficult by the handwriting, the ink, and the spelling of the writers. The handwriting was often illegible, with loops of letters overlapping the words above and below. On some pages, the ink is faded so badly that the original pages will, likely, become illegible as the years pass. I have made every effort to abstract these pages in absolute detail because I realize that the abstraction may, ultimately, be the only surviving record of these entries.

The spelling of names in the records was always unique and, often, interesting. When doing research into 19th century records, it is important to understand that the majority of the people could not read or write. Therefore, they did not always know how their names were spelled. If the priest didn't know the spelling of a name, he just spelled it phonetically. Thus, we have such spellings as "Ellon", "Elon," and "Elen" for the name we spell today as "Ellen."

Here is an example of the spelling in the original records: 12 May 1836 - "I babtesee [baptize] Anna Maria Daughter to Mich[1] [Michael] Gibbell & Catherine, Sprs [Sponsors] Casper Metz & Elizabeth D⁰ [D⁰ = Ditto, which meant that Elizabeth had the same last name as Casper Metz]"

Words were capitalized - or not - depending on different rules than we use today. Many of the names were not capitalized in the original records; however, I have capitalized all names to make for consistency and ease of reading.

The majority of the records were written in Latin. Although I studied a number of foreign languages during my school years, Latin wasn't one of them. Whenever I got stumped, Father Limmer sat patiently beside me, helping me to work it out. Our method was for me to tell him what I thought the letters were…if that didn't seem logical, he would counter with a comment such as, "There's no such word in Latin but if the second letter was…then it could be…" I would look at it again and agree or deny that the second letter was what he suggested. This process took many hours and didn't always yield successful results; some phrases or words were simply indecipherable. In those cases, I have so noted in the record, and the reader is advised to check the microfilm of the original records.

The reader will note many question marks throughout the records. Any word or letter that shows a bracketed question mark indicates that I was unsure of the spelling.

CHRONOLOGICAL ORDER

Entries are, occasionally, out of chronological order. This is due to the fact that the record book stayed at the church but many of the baptisms and marriages took place at sites away from the church. The priest would write the information on pieces of paper as he traveled, and transcribe them into the record book whenever he had time.

VARIANCES IN RECORDING STYLES

Each priest chose to register different types of information, thus, the records vary somewhat in different time periods. For example, Father Ryan recorded the specific location of the marriage ceremony - even going so far as to mention that it took place "in my own room," i.e., in his living quarters - and Father Guth listed all the witnesses to a marriage, while other priests did not.

- Father James Redmond's handwriting was beautiful and fully legible. His baptismal records from 1818-1820 list whether the parents of a child were married; after that point, he did not so list. Due to the fact that he listed the mother's maiden name in all records, it is difficult to tell after this date whether the parents were married or not.

- Father Henry Myers' handwriting in the Marriages section was very good, but was less good in the Baptisms section. The brown ink he used was fully readable. Several of his letters were indistinguishable - "Z", "J", and "I" were alike, "R" and "B" were alike; lower-case "y" and "g" were alike, and "N" and "W" were almost alike.

- Father Michael Guth wrote very small and very poorly. He spelled both English and Latin poorly, wrote the first line over top of and running into the second line, and the ink he used is fading into illegibility. He spelled last names phonetically, often used Latin terms in a somewhat obscure way, and spelled the same names differently within the same entry. His "n" and "v" were completely alike, his "j" and "i" were exactly alike (since he almost always used lower-case letters, words such as "January" and "Isaac" appear to begin with the same letter, and he seldom capitalized first or last names.

- Father Js. Cotting, S.J., did not record if the parents of a baptized child were married or not as did most of the other priest.

- Father Edmund Didier used curlicues at the end of words, so that the last letter is sometimes indistinguishable. His "L" and "S" are alike, even in the same entry.

- Father Timothy Ryan's handwriting was extremely poor throughout his records. As were Father Myers', several of his letters were indistinguishable - "L", and "S" were alike, "S" and "A" were sometimes identical; and the lower-case "n" and "w" at the end of a word were identical. Washington County Court records show a naturalization record for Timothy Ryan in 1834 with the following information: Timotheus Ryan, from County Tipperary, Ireland, aged 42 years, who arrived in New York in 1816, and made his naturalization report in Washington County court on 21 Nov 1827.[2] The published indexes for the federal census records for Washington County for 1820-1840 show only one T. Ryan in the area.[3] It is possible that this 1827 naturalization report record was for Father Timothy Ryan.

CHOLERA AND HOSPITAL HILL

The reader will note a higher-than-average number of marriages listing widows in the mid 1830s. This was due to the cholera epidemics of 1832-1834 that killed large numbers of canal workers. Father Timothy Ryan was pastor during that time and served these workers. When the time came that their bodies could no longer be buried at St. Mary's Cemetery due to fear of further cholera infection, Father Ryan was instrumental in purchasing land for a cemetery near Williamsport.

According to the minutes of the Williamsport Town Council for July 10, 1833, a solicitation was taken among the citizens of the town to build a hospital on that land for the use of the cholera victims. The minutes of November 1, 1833 further note that the

---

[2] Marsha Lynne Fuller, *Naturalizations of Washington County, Maryland Prior to 1880* (Hagerstown, Maryland: Desert Sheik Press, 1998), unpaginated.
[3] Ronald Vern Jackson, David Schaefermeyer, & Gary Ronald Teeples, ed. *Maryland 1820 Census Index.* Bountiful, Utah: Accelerated Indexing Systems, Inc., 1977; Ronald Vern Jackson, David Schaefermeyer, & Gary Ronald Teeples, ed. *Maryland 1830 Census Index.* Bountiful, Utah: Accelerated Indexing Systems, Inc., 1978; Ronald Vern Jackson, and Gary Ronald Teeples, ed. *Maryland 1840 Census Index.* Bountiful, Utah: Accelerated Indexing Systems, Inc., 1977.

hospital was later moved to the "Market House lot" and used as a school building.[4]

History of Washington County reports, "When the cholera became epidemic among the operatives in the construction of the C. & O. Canal along the line at Williamsport, in 1831-2, Father Ryan was indefatigable in his efforts to relieve and comfort the afflicted and dying. It was then that he established a hospital on the old "Friend" farm near Williamsport on the Clearspring road where a log-house served as the hospital and the surrounding ground as a burying ground."[5] This later became known as Hospital Hill and is located on Clear Spring Road a short distance from the tannery.

On July 5, 1833, *The Hagerstown Mail* reported that,

> "Persons dying of Cholera, along the line of the Canal, have generally been brought to the Catholic burying ground in this place, for interment. This practice has heretofore been tolerated, because there was no other burying ground belonging to that sect, in the neighborhood. This is not now the case. A piece of ground has been purchased and set apart as a burying ground, near the line of the Canal, in the neighborhood of Williams-port, in which it is the request of the Rev. Mr. Ryan, that future interments of those dying along the Canal, may be made. And, it may be proper to say, that if this reasonable request be

---

[4] Williamsport Town Council Minutes, Williamsport Town Hall, Williamsport, Maryland.
[5] Thomas T.J. Williams. *History of Washington County, Maryland* (1906; reprint, Baltimore: Regional Publishing Company, 1968), 480.

disregarded, prompt measures will be adopted, by the authorities of our town, to put a stop to a practice, for the continuance of which no reasonable excuse longer exist. Agents of the Canal Company, Contractors, and others interested, will be so good as to give to this subject the attention to which its importance entitles it."[6]

One week later, on July 12, 1833, *The Hagerstown Mail* reported that,

"The cholera re-appeared among the laborers on the Canal near this place on Monday last, owing probably to the intense heat of that day. The attacks were of the most malignant character, and resulted almost invariably in death after a few hours. We are unable to state precisely their number, but they might be put down at fifteen or twenty in all. The disease abated so far, that on Thursday no new case occurred. Yesterday, however, there was a rumor of three new cases in one shantee. It has caused considerable dispersion among the hands, and must materially delay the progress of the work, if it continue. We learn that the cases have generally been attended with the usual premonitory symptoms, which have been neglected until incipient collapse, too late for relief from medical aid. They are also but slightly attended with cramps or spasms. The

---

[6] *The Hagerstown Mail*. Hagerstown, Maryland, 5 Jul 1833, page 3, column A.

citizens of the town continue to enjoy uninterrupted good health."[7]

Many other newspaper articles on the building of the C & O Canal can be located by using the series *An Index to Hagerstown Newspapers,* available at the Washington County Free Library.[8]

---

[7] *The Hagerstown Mail*. Hagerstown, Maryland, 12 Jul 1833, page 2, column A.
8 Linda C. Clark. *An Index to Hagerstown Newspapers* (Hagerstown, MD: Washington County Free Library, 1982-1988).

ST. MARY'S CATHOLIC CHURCH

For readers interested in the history of St. Mary's Catholic Church, Rita Clark Hutzell has written an excellent book entitled, *St. Mary Church 1758-2000: A History for the Millennium*. It is available at the church and at the Washington County Free Library. In it, she relates,

> **DEDICATION.**
>
> St. Mary's Church, in Hagers-town, was dedicated to the honor and glory of God, on Sunday last, by the Rt. Rev. Dr. *Whitfield*, Archbishop of Baltimore, assisted by the Revds. *F. M'Gerry, T. Purcell, F. M'Cosker*, and the Rev. Mr. *Ryan*, pastor of the Hagerstown Congregation—as also the choir under the direction of Mr. *Gegan*, Professor of Music at Mount St. Mary's, in Frederick county.
>
> This Church is a large and elegant building, finished with much taste—owing its completion, under God, in a great measure to the untiring zeal and active industry of the very worthy pastor who has charge of it and its congregation. It was filled to overflowing on the day of dedication—the ceremonies connected with which were solemn and impressive.
>
> The rite of Confirmation was administered to a considerable number of young persons by the Rev. *Archbishop*, after the dedication—at 4 o'clock in the afternoon Vespers were celebrated; and an elegant discourse was delivered by the Rev. Mr. *Purcell*.

The Torch Light, Hagerstown, Maryland
October 9, 1828

"For over 240 years there has been a Catholic congregation in Hagerstown. The present church building, begun on July 4, 1826, stands on the same site as the log chapel where the first congregations joined the itinerant Jesuit missionaries to offer the holy sacrifice of the Mass in the days when St. Mary's was under the jurisdiction of the Archdiocese of London, England."[9]

---

[9] Rita Clark Hutzell. *St. Mary Church 1758-2000: A History for the Millennium* (Hagerstown, Maryland: Privately published, 2000), 3.

Further information on St. Mary's is available in *The Catholic Red Book of Western Maryland*[10] and *A Century of Growth; or, The History of the Church in Western Maryland*[11], both available in the Western Maryland Room, Washington County Free Library.

The earliest record book for St. Mary's was titled with "Sacrament Records 1818 - 1847" printed on the front of the book; its size is 7½ inches x 12¼ inches. On the inside left cover is handwritten:

> *The following is the Deed of the Catholic grave yard, recorded in the office of this town,*
> *Jonathan Hager to The Rev. James Fremback*
> *Deed Dated 16, August 1786 for Three Lots in Hagerstown Addition to Elizabeth Town*
> *No 319 - 320 – 321*
> *Recorded in Liber E folio 38*
> *The above memorandum I have here inserted to save other Priests on a future time, from similar Troubles & Difficulties which I had to contend with before I could find the above mentioned Deed or Know the Lots.*
> *- T. Ryan*

---

[10] *The Catholic Red Book of Western Maryland, including Cumberland, Frostburg, Lonaconing, Mt. Savage, Midland, Westernport, Barton, Hagerstown, Hancock, Frederick and Oakland, a Catholic directory alphabetically arranged under parochial classification* (Baltimore and Washington: The Red Book Society, 1909).

[11] Rev. Thomas J. Stanton, *A Century of Growth; or, The History of the Church in Western Maryland*, 2 volumes (Baltimore: John Murphy Company, 1900).

Pasted onto the bottom of this inside cover is the following paper:

> Jonathan Hagers
> to
> The Revd James Frumback
> Deed Dated 16th August 1786
> for three Lotts in Hagers Addition to
> Elizabeth Town
> Nos. 319, 320 & 321
> Recorded in Liber E folio 38

Mooresville Church

Begun in 1848, St. Thomas Church at Mooresville was constructed by C&O Canal laborers. These laborers journeyed from the Four Locks area along the Potomac River through the Indian Springs district to a point just south of the Pennsylvania line to attend services on Sunday mornings. The cornerstone of this church  was laid in August of 1852 by Archbishop Kenrich. Built out of native stone in a simple Gothic style, huge oaken logs formed the main joists, and its well-constructed slate roof was still intact in the 1950s.

Dahlgren Chapel

 From *A History of Washington County*, we read, "Among the additional edifices erected [under the direction of Father J. Alphonse Frederick] was the Dahlgren Memorial Chapel on the summit of the South Mountain in '81-'82 [1881-1882]. This chapel which is located about two miles from Boonsboro on the turnpike leading to Frederick and in Washington County near the Frederick County line was built out of native mountain stone by Mrs. Madaline Vinton Dahlgren in memory of her deceased husband, Admiral Dahlgren, of the U.S. Navy...Near this place in 1863 [1862], during our great Civil War, was fought a battle by a part of the contending armies. The chapel is supplied by pastors

from Washington and other places during the hot and sultry months of summer when this place is cooled by the mountain zephyrs."[1]

> Later Catholic churches in the Washington County area were:
>
> - St. Michael's, Clear Spring, started in 1866
> - St. Patrick's, Little Orleans, started in 1860
> - St. Peter's, Hancock, started in 1834
> - St. Augustin's, Williamsport, started in 1864

---

[1] Williams. *A History of Washington County, Maryland*, page 482.

THE CATHOLIC CEMETERY

This record of a burial in St. Mary's Cemetery is from a record of deaths in Sharpsburg kept by local residents: Joseph Reel, died Jan. 25, 1831, buried in the Hagerstown Catholic Yard.[2]
There are ten pages of gravestone listings from St. Mary's Cemetery listed in records probably kept by members of the Spielman family.[3] *Other gravestone listings may be found in the published cemetery records of Washington County.*[4] *All of these books are available at the Washington County Free Library.*
The following listings of gravestones in the old Catholic cemetery are from a county history that was published in 1906.[5] *The cemetery originally sat at the corner of Randolph and Prospect Avenue. The graves and gravestones have since been removed to Rose Hill Cemetery in Hagerstown.*

Susan McLaughlin, died Dec. 1, 1846, aged 70 years.
Elizabeth Brooks, died ___[sic], in her 85th year.
William Conden, born in Queen's County, Ireland, died March 14, 1822, in his 52d year.
Francis McBride, died Feb. 25, 1874, in his 60th year.
Bridget, wife of Francis McMullin, died Nov. 20, 1863, in her 75th year.
Thomas McCardell, died Oct. 26, 1843, aged 66 years, 8 months; and his wife, Ann, died March 24, 1861, aged 84 years, 3 months.
Joseph Reel, died Jan. 17, 1831, aged 76 years, 30 days.
Elizabeth Reel, died Feb. 16, 1822, aged 54 years, 4 months.

---

[2] Rosamund Ann Ball, indexer, *Index for Registser of persons hwo have died in Sharpsburg, Wahsington County, Maryland and surrounding neighborhood from the year 1831* (Hagerstown, Maryland: privately printed, 1992).
[3] Rosamund Ann Ball, indexer, *Cemetery, Death, and Miscellaneous Records from Hagerstown and Washington County, Maryland Probaby Compiled by Members of the Spielman Family* (Hagerstown, Maryland: privately printed, 1994).
[4] Dale W. Morrow, *Washington County, Maryland Cemetery Records*, 7 volumes (Westminster, Maryland: Family Line Publications, 1992-1994).
[5] J. Thomas Scharf. *History of Western Maryland*, 2 volumes (Philadelphia: Louis H. Everts, 1882), pages 1098-99.

Hugh McKusker, died Dec. 14, 1867, aged 64 years, 9 months; and his wife, Margaret, died March 13, 1879, aged 74 years, 1 month.

James Adams, died in 1836, aged 56 years; and his wife, Elizabeth, died Feb. 5, 1836, aged 52 years.

Patrick Mooney, died Nov. 24, 1838, aged 65 years.

Margaret Adams, died Aug. 21, 1846, aged 63 years, 3 days.

Patrick Donnelly, died May 27, 1837, in his 54th year; and his wife, Margaret, died March 29, 1852, in her 59th year.

Richard Welsh, died Nov. 9, 1828, in his 61st year.

James McGonigle, native of Londonderry, Ireland, died Oct. 13, 1838, aged 70 years.

Jeremiah Lyons, died May 16, 1876, in his 75th year.

Mary Roach, native of Limerick, Ireland, died Sept. 6, 1876, aged 80 years.

Philip Bradley, native of Londonderry, Ireland, died March 1, 1875, aged 63 years.

Hugh Murphy, born in County Carlow, Ireland, died March 9, 1878, in his 71st year.

George Moore, died March 8, 1865, aged 77 years, 7 months.

William E. Doyle, died June 28, 1865, in his 64th year; and his wife, Margaret, died Dec. 15, 1860, in her 57th year.

Thomas Shirvan, died Oct. 17, 1868, in his 84th year; and his wife, Isabella, died July 29, 1867, aged 67.

Casper Schwab, died Feb. 22, 1855, aged 77 years.

Rev. Joseph J. Maguire, died Sept. 18, 1852, in the 36th year of his age.

Christopher Murphy, born in Armagh, Ireland, aged 61.

Adam Crist, died Aug. 13, 1852, aged 50.

Margaret, wife of Richard Barry, of County Limerick, Ireland, died Feb. 11, 1858, aged 68.

Thomas Drinen, a native of Queen's County, Ireland, died Oct. 17, 1857, aged 51.

Martha, wife of Isaac Rowland, born Dec. 17, 1808, died June 4, 1869, aged 60.

Julia, wife of Robert Lewis, died Dec. 20, 1856, in her 47th year.

Joachim Shilling, died March 8, 1859, in his 52d year; and his wife, Francesca, died Feb. 11, 1852, aged 42.

Jacob Butts, died May 16, 1861, aged 54.

FATHER ABRAM J. RYAN
POET PRIEST OF THE CONFEDERACY

Father Abram J. Ryan, known as the" Poet Priest of the Confederacy," was born in Hagerstown, Maryland on February 5, 1838. He was baptized in St. Mary's Catholic Church as "Matheus Abraham," (Latin for "Matthew Abraham"), the legitimate son of Mathei Ryan. Additional information about the life of Father Ryan can be found in the Western Maryland Room at the Washington County Free Library.

The original baptismal record was so faded that a copy could not be made. Father Dominic Manley had circled the baptismal record in ink and made the notation: "The poet priest – A.J. Ryan – died April 1886 – D. Manley"

Following are three letters from the first quarter of the 20th century written in reference to Father Ryan that were found in the first record book:

BISHOP'S HOUSE
800 CATHEDRAL PLACE
RICHMOND, VA.

July 28. 1910,
Rev. dear Father:

    I appreciate the courtesy in lending me the enclosed but I return them thinking better at home in Hagerstown. The time may come when the people will wake up to an appreciation of the glory that belongs to them.

I first told and wrote your predecessor - that the Poet priest was born in your parish and the information came from the lips of the Father himself in a conversation with Rev. Hugh McKeery of Norfolk, Va. I also added a small contribution in the note - that it might start the work. Maryland Catholics have not written much of their hidden treasures.

I am happy to send you the diocesan faculties and I am sure you can use them in good peace with your Va. neighbors.

With best wishes for your success I remain
Very sincerely yours in Christ,
D. J. O'Connell, Bishop of Record
Rev. C. Carroll Ken
Hagerstown, Md
P.S. The "Sister Rose" mentioned in Father Hoe's [?] letter is the Sister Servant at our St. Joseph's Orphan Asylum here. O'C.

ST. VINCENT DE PAUL'S RECTORY
PRICE STREET
CONGREGATION OF THE MISSION
Germantown, Phila. April 1st, 1918.
FOUNDED BY ST. VINCENT DE PAUL

My dear Sisters home,
The peace of Our Lord be ever with us!
F^r Abe Ryan was, according to our records, born in Hagerstown, Md. Feby 5th 1838. He entered the novitiate in 1854, made his vows Nov. 1st 1856, and left the Community Sept. 1st 1862.
Those are all the facts we have recorded about him.
With best wishes I am,
Jan[?] Jones SP
                    P. Mc___ can[?]

BISHOP'S HOUSE
800 CATHEDRAL PLACE
RICHMOND, VA.

February 18, 1925.

Rev. dear Father:

    Before passing away I should like to leave on record that I heard from the Rev. Hugh McKeefry, late pastor of St. Patrick's Church Richmond, Va. that the Revd Abram J Ryan, the "poet priest of the South" was born in your parish of Hagerstown, Md. When asked for his authority he replied that he heard it from Father Ryan himself. Father Ryan was then preaching Mission at St. Mary's Church, Norfolk, Va. where Father McKeefy was assistant and at night when the sermon was over and Father O'Keefe had retired the preacher was entertain[ed] till late at night by the assistant, Father McKeefry. It was, Father McKeefry told me, during those long conversation[s] that Father Ryan, in answer to a question, said he had been born at Hagerstown, MD. I communicated this information some years ago to Father Hurlbert, your predecessor, who later told me that he found in his early book of Baptism some entries there of baptism of Fr Ryan. Just to mark the event I gave Father a small offering for I thought the fame of the poet made him worthy at least of a tablet in your baptistry. It is a glory for your parish and the statement ends all doubt about the poet's birth-place.

                With reverant [?] memories
                   Recorder [?]
                         Sincerely yours in Xrs [Christ]
                         Bp of Rd. [Bishop of Record?]

Building the C & O Canal

C&O Canal Stones Worked by Irish Catholic Immigrants

Williamsport, Maryland

Photographs by Marsha Lynne Fuller

Gazeteer

Lane(s) Run	Branch of Licking Creek in Washington County located west of Clear Spring and east of Hancock
Sir John's Run	Branch of Potomac river in Morgan County, WV located west of Berkeley Springs
Fifteen Mile Creek	Tributary of Potomac river in eastern Allegany County
Paw Paw Tunnel	C&O Canal Tunnel located across the Potomac River from Paw Paw, WV
Parkhead	Post village on National Pike west of Licking Creek; post office here from 1825 through 1852; also known as Park Head Level
Bakersville	Crossroads village north of Sharpsburg; post office here from 1830 through 1903
Four Locks	Located at Prather's Neck on C&O Canal west of Clear Spring; canal locks 47, 48, 49, and 50 located here; post office and school once located here; post office operated from 1858 through 1903
Sideling Hill	Mountain west of Hancock
Sideling Hill Creek	Tributary of Potomac River; forms boundary between Washington and Allegany Counties
South Mountain	Ridge separating Washington and Frederick Counties; extends along east side of the Great

	Valley
Dahlgren Chapel	Catholic Chapel built by Madelin V. Dahlgren on top of South Mountain in Turner's Gap along National Pike; located between Boonsboro and Middletown
7 Mile Bottom	Near Clear Spring
Dam No. 4	Feeder dam for C&O Canal on Potomac River 15 miles below Williamsport
Dam No. 6	Feeder dam for C&O Canal on Potomac River 10 miles above Hancock; village of Great Cacapon, WV is located here
The Pike	Most likely the Baltimore extension of the National Pike linking the City of Baltimore with Cumberland – the present-day Route 40

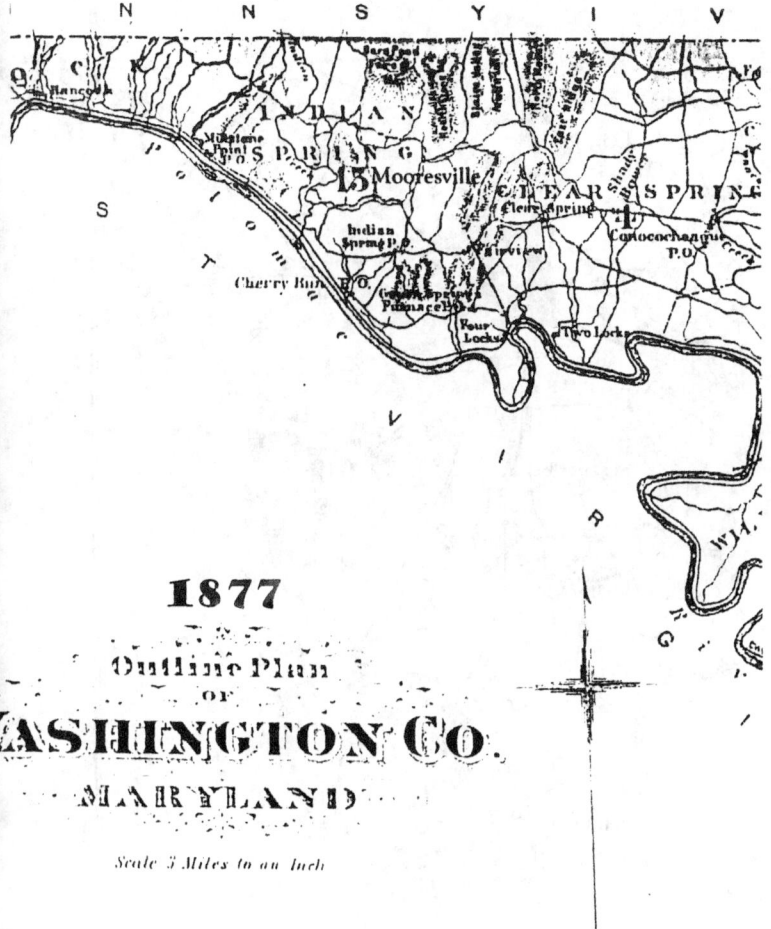

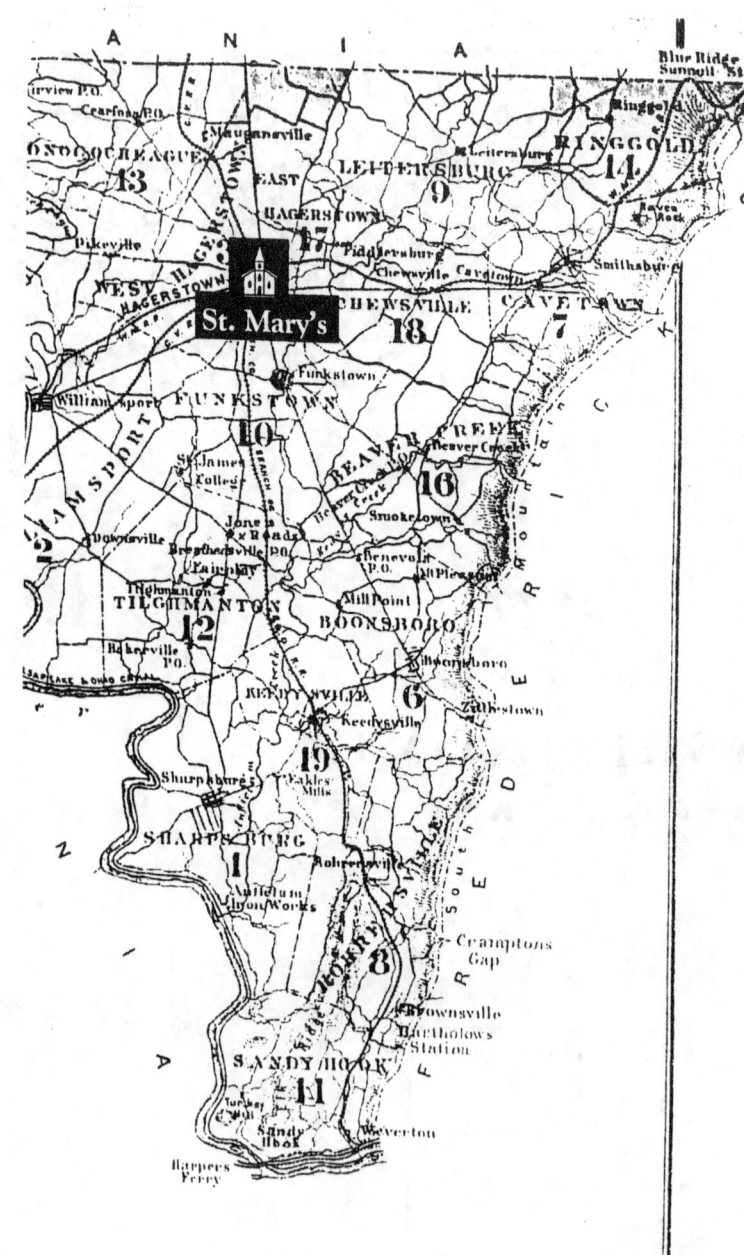

KEY & DEFINITIONS

A microfilm of the original records is available at the Washington County Free Library

GENERAL EXPLANATION:

- All available records have been abstracted with the exception of the confirmations from 1871 to 1900. Due to the fact that neither their ages nor their parents' names were given, there did not appear to be sufficient information to warrant the time necessary to abstract them.
- Please note that the index at the back of this book is referenced according to entry number and not by page number. Each entry from the original records has been assigned a sequential number and this has been used in the index.
- Where I have put a question mark after the spelling of the name, it would be wise for researchers to check the microfilm of the records to verify the spelling for themselves.
- Readers who use the microfilmed records will note that some dates are written as "bris" or "ber." Father Albert Ledoux informs us that, "Until the late 16th century, the year started on the Feast of the Annunciation, March 25th. The twelfth month was, therefore, February, the eleventh, January…September as the 7th month, October as the 8th, November as the 9th, and December as the

10th. When an old priest wrote "7ber," he meant September, and not July."⁶

- Everything in quotation marks " ", is an exact quotation from the original record.
- Everything in brackets [ ], is a note that I made in order to clarify a word or record.
- Throughout the 1871-1900 Baptism book, the married name of the woman is used but her maiden name is also, frequently, given.
- On rare occasions, there was a third witness to a marriage or a third sponsor to a baptism – these names have been included in the Notes section.
- Father Guth referred to the C & O Canal's tunnel at Paw Paw, West Virginia, as the "significat Tunnel." The word "significat" in Latin can mean "that which is to come." The tunnel, although started in 1836, was not completed until 1850, thus, "the tunnel which is to come."
- Between the 3 Feb 1840 and the 15 Feb 1840 entries, several pages have been torn out, Pages 110-117, inclusive, are missing according to the handwritten page numbers – only the torn stub of one page remains

KEY TO THE LAYOUT OF BAPTISMS 1818-1871:

- INDEX – sequential index number
- CODE 1 - information about the child (Black, Slave, etc.)
- CHILD – first name of the child
- PRIEST – the priest who recorded the entry and performed the baptism

---

⁶ Father Albert Ledoux, "Re: FW: Latin," e-mail message from frledoux@yahoo.com to author, 24 Sep 2001.

- 1ˢᵗ SPONSOR FIRST – first name of the sponsor (godfather or godmother)
- 1st SPONSOR LAST - last name of the sponsor (godfather or godmother)
- BAP DATE – baptism date
- CODE 2 – information about the father (Black, Slave, etc.)
- FATHER – first name of the father
- LAST NAME – last name of the father
- 2ⁿᵈ SPONSOR FIRST – first name of the 2ⁿᵈ sponsor
- 2ⁿᵈ SPONSOR LAST – last name of the 2ⁿᵈ sponsor
- BIRTH DATE – birth date of the child
- CODE 3 – information about the mother (Black, Slave, etc.)
- MOTHER – first name of the mother
- MAIDEN – maiden name of the mother
- LOCATION OF CEREMONY AND NOTES – location where the baptism took place; various notes made by the priest

KEY TO THE LAYOUT OF BAPTISMS 1871-1900:

- INDEX – sequential index number
- CHILD – first name of the child
- PRIEST – the priest who recorded the entry
- 1ˢᵗ SPONSOR FIRST – first name of the sponsor (godfather or godmother)
- 1st SPONSOR LAST - last name of the sponsor (godfather or godmother)
- BAP Date – baptism date
- FATHER – first name of the father
- LAST NAME – last name of the father
- FATHER FROM – father's place of origin
- 2ⁿᵈ SPONSOR FIRST – first name of the 2ⁿᵈ sponsor

- 2nd SPONSOR LAST – last name of the 2nd sponsor
- BIRTH DATE – birth date of the child
- MOTHER – first name of the mother
- MAIDEN – maiden name of the mother
- MOTHER FROM – mother's place of origin
- LOCATION OF CEREMONY - location where the baptism took place
- NOTES – various notes made by the priest

KEY TO THE LAYOUT OF MARRIAGES 1818-1871:

- INDEX – sequential index number
- DATE – date of the marriage ceremony [this may differ from the date the marriage license was taken out from the Washington County Court]
- GROOM FIRST – groom's first name
- GROOM LAST – groom's last name
- BRIDE FIRST – bride's first name
- BRIDE LAST – bride's last name
- PRIEST – the priest who recorded the entry
- 1st WITNESS FIRST – first name of the 1st witness
- 1st WITNESS LAST - last name of the 1st witness
- 2nd WITNESS FIRST – first name of the 2nd witness
- 2nd WITNESS LAST – last name of the 2nd witness
- NOTES – various notes made by the priest

KEY TO THE LAYOUT OF MARRIAGES 1871-1900:

- INDEX – sequential index number
- DATE – date of the marriage ceremony [this may differ from the date their marriage license was taken out from the Washington County Court]
- GROOM 1st – groom's first name
- GROOM LAST – groom's last name
- GROOM FROM – place where the groom resides
- GROOM'S FATHER – first name of father of the groom

- FATHER LAST – last name of father of the groom
- BRIDE 1st – bride's first name
- BRIDE LAST – bride's last name
- BRIDE FROM – place where bride resides
- BRIDE'S FATHER – first name of the father of the bride
- BRIDE'S FATHER LAST – last name of the father of the bride
- PRIEST – the priest who recorded the entry
- 1st WITNESS FIRST – first name of the 1st witness
- 1st WITNESS LAST - last name of the 1st witness
- 2nd WITNESS FIRST – first name of the 2nd witness
- 2nd WITNESS LAST – last name of the 2nd witness
- LOCATION OF CEREMONY – location where the marriage ceremony took place
- NOTES – various notes made by the priest

NOTES COLUMN:

DDC	A dispensation (special permission) was granted to the couple to be married because either the bride or the groom had never been baptized - a dispensation from disparity of cult
DMR	A dispensation (special permission) was granted to the couple to be married because either the bride or the groom was not Catholic (Dispensation Mixta Religione, i.e., a "mixed marriage")
BA	Bride is not Catholic
BN	Bride was never baptized
GA	Groom is not Catholic
GN	Groom was never baptized
SA	One of the sponsors/witnesses is

	not Catholic
SN	One of the sponsors/witnesses was never baptized
B	Black (African American)
FB	Free Black (Free African American)
S	Slave
P	Protestant
C	Convert – converted to the Catholic faith
BC	Conditional Baptism - this was done if it was unclear whether or not the person had ever been baptized - if they had, this baptism becomes, simply, a ceremonial reminder of baptism. If they had not, it was the baptism.
MA	Mother is not Catholic
FA	Father is not Catholic
BP	Baptized in "periculo mortis" – simple baptismal ceremony performed because the person was in danger of death; full ceremonies were performed later if the person lived
CS	Baptismal ceremonies supplied - "ceremonies supplied" meant that the baby has previously been "baptized privately" either by a family member or by the priest when the person was in danger of death, and was now being officially baptized
PB	Baptized privately - meant the baby or adult had been baptized at home by someone other than the priest

	because the baby or adult was in danger of dying.
AB	Absolute baptism
HB	Witnesses/Sponsors are husband and wife
WC	Without a certificate
DB	With dispensation from publications of banns
PN	Parents of baptized child were not married

PRIESTS COLUMN:

1	J. Smith
2	Theodore D. Mead
3	Sebastian Rabbia
4	J. Alphonse Frederick
5	Thos. Bevyduct [?]
6	B.J. Bradley
7	J. Card. Gibbons
8	Thos. E. Stapleton
9	Dominic Manley
10	Henry R. Volz
11	John M. Jones
12	Charles H. Stonestreet
13	Desiderius C. DeWulf
14	H. T. B. Tarr, S.J.
15	Joseph H. Plunkett
16	Michael Guth
17	Timothy Ryan
18	James M. Redmond
19	Henry Myers
20	Joseph John Maguire
21	J. Carney
22	Thomas A. McCaffrey
23	J.S. Cotting
24	William H. Elder

25	George Flautt
26	Edmund C. Didier
27	John Gloyd
28	Malachy Moran
29	Thomas W. McDonough
30	Aloysius Janaleck
31	F. Sorvin [?]
32	W.H. Gross
33	W. Wayrich
34	Charles Dammer
35	F. Boetzkes [?]
36	Nicholas D. Young
37	Father McCosker
38	John Healy
39	M. Shiel
40	Rev. Barynier
41	Bishop R.V. Whelan (Baltimore)
42	J.P. Carey
43	T.D. Revillé
44	H.T. Tarr
45	Edward T. Field
46	Alfred B. Leeson
47	Father Gereiman (Chambersburg)
48	Fr. Peck

TRANSLATION OF LATIN FIRST NAMES

Adam	*Adami*
Albert	*Albertus*
Alexander	*Alexandri*
Anne	*Anna, Annae*
Antony	*Antonii*
Arthur	*Arturus*
Augustine	*Augustinus*
Bernard	*Bernardi, Bernardus*
Bridget	*Birgittae*
Catharine	*Catharinae*
Cecil	*Caecilius*

Cecilia	*Caecilia*
Charles	*Carolus*
Clement	*Celmens*
Constance	*Constantia*
Cyril	*Cyrillus*
Dorothy	*Dorotheae*
Edmund	*Edmundus*
Edward	*Eduardus, Edwardi*
Ellen, Eleanor	*Helena*
Elnora	*Ellionorae*
Emily	*Aemilia*
Florence	*Florentia*
Francis, Frank	*Franciscus*
Frederic	*Fredericus*
George	*Georgius, Georgii*
Gregory	*Gregorius*
Helen	*Helena*
Henry	*Henrici*
Hilary	*Hilarius*
Hugo	*Hugonis*
Jacob or James	*Jacobus*
John	*Johannes, Joannes, Joannis*
Joseph	*Josephi*
Lawrence	*Laurentius*
Lewis	*Ludovicus*
Lucy	*Lucia*
Margaret	*Margaretae*
Mary	*Mariae*
Michael	*Michaelelis*
Miriam	*Mariam*
Patrick	*Patricius*
Paul	*Paulus*
Peter	*Petrus, Petri*
Philip	*Philippii*
Rebecca	*Rebeccae*
Richard	*Ricardus*

Robert	*Robertus, Roberti*
Stephen	*Stephanus*
Susanna	*Susannae*
Theresa	*Therisae*
Thomas	*Thomae*
Timothy	*Timothei*
Vincent	*Vincentius*
William	*Gulielmus*

St. Mary's Catholic Church from 1850 Map of Hagerstown

Copy of full map available at the
Washington County Free Library

Samples of

St. Mary's Catholic Church Records

1818

August 3rd 117 24

Baptisms & Marria[ges]
of Hagerstown and its vicinity Martinsb[urg]
Winchester Cumberland & its vicinity &c &[c]

Ann Eliza born the 19th last November [of]
Thomas Johnson and Mary McGraw [&]
Sponsors Bennet Peak & Elizabeth Pe[ak]
baptised the 3rd day of August 1818 b[y]

James Red[mond]

Septemr 16
Mary Elizabeth born the 17 December [of]
Ryan and Elizabeth McCanna Spouses;
Patrick McCristal & Mrs Catharine McC[ristal]

By James
Pastor of

Marriages

In the opposite of Font there are some Marriages intermixed with the Baptisms

May 18th 1819   Flora by permission

Samuel Noells to Nancy Flora by permission of the Court or rather of the laws of this State in presence of Mrs Flora mother of the above Sam[ue]l

1820

October 19th

Married Michael McAbny to Mary Ann Monahan agreably to the laws of this State, Maryland

Witnesses present
John McSherry
Leonard McCartin

By James Redmond
OfficRey McSherey
May John Monahan

October 24th

Married John O'Donnill to Susanna Stanel by Licens from the Court of Washington County Md at the Dwelling house of Mr Christopher Murphy in his & his Wife's presence & in presence of Many others

By James Redmond

December 19th

Married Denis L. McSherry to Miss Susania Whitwell of Jefferson County Va in presence of many Witnesses at the Dwelling of Captn Whitwell in the said County

Jas Richmond

1824
January 16

Married Robt A Slye of Georgetown D.C. to Miss Amanda M. F. Gwynn of Jefferson County Va at the Dwelling of Mr B Sanders in said County in presence of Ignatius Drury James Kings, Mary Slye and many others

Jas Richmond

Harris — Dan Titus to the McCoy Charity Oct. 27, 1833 also
La ticinis from the Court in the [?] Persons
Jerry Wilson — on they're the Donalds and
Jonathan Contract Jacob Ash   By [signature]

Harris William Steele to Br. Sept
Steele, who leave, from the Counts in the
[?] of many Persons on the Cattles
Church   Oct 26, 1833 —   By [signature]

Malli & Canada Steele to Sophia Smith

3° Januarii Meus baptizatos Joannes filius legitimus Josephi
Duly et Gertrudis Jutty 13 Januarii 1840 Patrini Josephus
Arthur Claude et Anna Megerly. J. B. Gatty

1° Martii Baptizatus est Joannes Petrus legitimus Michaelis
Wybolff et Eleonorae natus 3° Februarii 1840 Patrini
Bernardus Smarmy et Anna Maria Laeplin. J. B. Gatty

1° Maye baptizato est Brigan filius legitimus Antonii
Sandaef et Anae natus 13 Februarii 1840 Patrini
Dominicus Baret et Maria Sabot. J. B. Gatty

1° Aug. baptisata est Anna filia legitima Patricii Judy et
Anna nata 15 Januarii 1840 Patrini Georgius Potter
et Maria Boolan. J. B. Gatty

1° No baptisata est Maria filia legitima Marci ovenroler
et Catharinae nata 28 Novembris 1839. Patrini Henrik
F. Maria [illegible]

1640

4 juli: Junx in Matrimonium conjuncti sunt Joannes
Lollinger et Anna Eva todts[wergn] ft. Math: Bole
Brigitta Byan Mater [Laura] et M: J. Gutty.

5 juli: in Matrimonium conjuncti sunt eorum plurimi
Mathiaes ad Mayinger ft. Margareta Lauchy
Testibus Laurentio ad Mayinger ft. Margareta Lauchy
M: J. Gutty

13 juli: Junx in Matrimonium conjuncti sunt Joannes
pasenibus tolbus testibus Chrofes et Joan Anna
Me Gietzly
M: J. Gutty

13 juli: Junx in Matrimonium conjuncti sunt Joannes
plurimo . Testes Carolus Katharina Donnally
M: Gutty

22 juli: Junx in Matrimonium conjuncti sunt eorum plurimi
Joannes Rudly St. Maria Horae . M. Gutty
R.D. Gufstl me in Matrimonium conjunxit coram
te testes St. Maria Anna Corp. #

April 1849.

21st Married at the Parsonage, Mr. John Hanlan to Miss Mary Hornbeck. Witnessed sr H. Barnitz & Catharina Taney his wife.
H. Ebaugh

June 1849.

10th Married in Hancock, Mr James W.

Registrum Baptizatorum in Ecclesia Sanctae Mariae

Hagerstown, Washington Co. Dioecesis Baltimorensis

Nomen Famil.	A.D. 1871. Die Mensis.	REGISTRUM BAPTISMORUM.	Observanda.
Shehan Maria Kinney	10 Feb.	5. Ego infrascriptus baptizavi Mariam Theresiam Sheehan natam circ. 8 Febr. ex Gulielmo Shehan ex loco Cork et Antonia et Catharina Sarath ex loco Cork Hibernia conjugibus. Patrini fuerunt {Placidus Buchan Leland {Margaretta Loreto Dens C. McCoy	Ingressum
Haus Heine Schadenberg	1° Fer.	6. Ego infrascriptus baptizavi Elizabetham Haus Heine natam die 15 Feb. 1871 ex Gulielmo Hauslieine ex loco Brunsbüttel Han. Ha. C.R.	Sept. 52.

Death Records

Aug 2, 1853 [illegible] [illegible] is [illegible] a 42. Williamsport

Dec 4, 1853 John Stonebraker aged 76. Clearspring

2, 6 of [crossed out] 1854 Elmy Doodley - wife of Edward Doodley. Williamsport

8 of April 1854 Margaret Snider (col) Convict.

9 of April 1854 Thomas, son of Edward & Mary Doodley. Williamsport.

20 April 1854 Margaret Taggart aged 19 Hagerstown.

1 of June 1854 Barbara McCole aged 7 years Fairplay.

11 of Aug 1854 Patrick Cronin aged about 44 Clearspring

12 of Sep 1854. Christopher Drenner aged 16. Lock No. 4.

7 of Sep 1854. Michael King. aged 28. Lock No. 4

17 of Sept 1854 Owen King aged 36 Lock No. 4.

19 of Sept 1854 Henry Welsh aged 35. Fairplay

25 of Nov 1854 John Doolley aged 24 Williamsport

Feb 1 a
Feb 20 do
Feb 24 do
April 7 a
May 28 an
1857 [illegible]
1857 do
-off
1857 July
1857 Sept 2

1857 Sept 2

St. Mary's Catholic Church Records

1818 - 1900

Hagerstown, Washington County Maryland

St. Mary's Catholic Church Records

Priests' Journal 1786 – 1911

Priests' Journal

[*Note: The cover of the Priests' Journal reads, "1786 Church Record from 1868."*]

Page 1
1786 Aug. 16th. Deed of the catholic grave yard, Hagerstown. Jonathan Hager to Rev. James Brumback[?] for three lots in Hagers' addition to Elizabeth Town Nos. 319, 320, 321. Deed dated August 16th 1786, and recorded in Liber C. folio 38. 1794 May 5th. Deed for the property where the church and home now stand. Adam Miller of Bedford Co. Pa. to Luke Tieman of Baltimore Co, Charles Carroll, Dennis Cahill, James McClean, John Adams, James McCardell, Joseph Clark, and William Clark of Washington Co., and to the survivor and survivors, and the heirs of such survivors in trust. Deed dated May 5th 1794, and recorded Liber N. folios 847, 848, 849. This property was given for the nominal sum of five shillings. Subject to a ground rent of 50¢ a year of which sum 25¢ is now collected annually by the Misses Lawrence.

Rev. Denis Cahill whose name appears above was here in as early as 1791. He is the same who figures in the Wizard Clip accounts. He returned to Ireland about 1800. The Chapel, a log structure, was Erected on the site of the present pastoral residence; in the Chapel Tos. Cahill, Framback Galligin & other missionaries offered the holy sacrifice

The first Entry made by Fr. Redmond on record is date Aug. 3, 1818, the last Oct. 27, 1822

1845 During this year Rev. H. Myers was Taken seriously ill and received the last sacraments from Rev. C. Amestreet[?], L.L.[?]. Rev. H. Myers recovered.

1857 Rev. Geo Flant came here in Nov. 1857 & left Jun 1858

1854 Deed of the Williamsport Church recorded Liber I.N. No. 10 folio 110. Deed from Robert Lemen exc. of Peter Light to F.P. Neurick & his successors for the sum of $1000. Recorded Dec. 8th 1854. Deed delivered to Father Myers, Sept. 4th 1856.

1818 Rev. James Redmond seems to have taken charge in Hagerstown about the summer of 1818.

1822 November of this year Rev. Timothy Ryan took charge of the congregation. He moved[?] the old log-church, which stood where the main building of the "presbytery" now stands, and built the new church - laying the corner stone July 4th, 1826. He attended the congregation while the canal was building and labored during the cholera plague of 1833. He died June 2nd, 1837, and was succeeded by Rev. M. Guth.

He (Rev. M. Guth) left towards the end of 1844, and was succeeded by Rev. Henry Myers, who writes in the register as follows. "I took charge of Hagerstown and the missions served from this place on the 15th August (the Assumption of the B. Virgin) 1845." Rev. Joseph Maguire came as assistant in 1851 and died Sept. 18th, 1852. Rev. Henry Myers left about Nov. 1857, and was succeeded by Rev. George Flaut. Rev. G. Flaut left July 1858 and was succeeded by Rev. Edmund Lidies[?]. Rev. C. Lidus[?] left in Sept. 1861. Rev. John Floyd[?] from Hancock attended Hagerstown until December of the same year when Rev. Malachy[?] Moran[?] took charge of Hagerstown. Rev. M. Moran C.S.B. left the middle of 1864, and his place was Rev. Thomas McDonough, S.I., who attended from Frederick, and then by Rev. Aloyeuis Sss[?]analick S.I., who left in the summer of 1865. He was succeeded by the Rev. Edmund Dicher, who remained until May 7th, 1868.

On Sunday Feby. 14, 1864 Frs. Emig & McDonnough began a mission which ended on following Sunday 325 Comns[?] Fr. Myers attended Hagerstown Williamsport

Clearspring Hancock Fifteen Mile Creek Tunnel Indian Spring

Deed from Charles Tieman and Gay R. Tieman, his wife to Rev. C. Lidier, James J. Hurley, Jacob A. Wright, Terence[?] B. McClery, Jacob A. Wills, and Johon Cck[?] Trustees St. Mary's Roman Catholic Church at Hagerstown, dated Aug. 17th, 1867.

This deed includes the church proper and priests' house. The survivir [sic] of the original trustees of May 5th, 1794 was Luke Tieman and from him the legal title descended to Charles Tieman. This deed is recorded in [Liber H, folios 847, 848, 849 crossed out] Liber I.N. as below.

Deed from Dennis Galvin[?] and Margaret Galvin of St. Lewis to Rev. C. Lidier and other trustees, dated Aug. 21st, 1867. This deed comprises the school house. (This school property was afterwards sold to the C.V[?]. R.R. for their depot in Hagerstown.

Deed from the same trustees to Mist. Rev. M.I. Spalding and his successors, arch-bishops of Baltimore, conveying the church, priests house, school property and grave-yard. These three deeds are recorded in Liber I.N. number 18 folios 693, 694, 695 and 696.

The first deed of incorporation was recorded in liber No. 1 of church regulations and incorporations folios 7. 8 and 9. Aug. 13th 1867. The church property became vested in Rev. C. Lidier and five trustees according to Article 26 sections 88 - 101 Public General Laws. The number of trustees was afterwards changed to seven and the pastor. See Liber No. 1. Church Regulations and incorporations for agreement of March 25th, 1875. Under this agreement Rev. I.M. Tines, Josiah F. Smith, Jacob A. Wright, P.M. Johns, H.H. Keedy, James J. Hurley C.B. Boyle and W.F. Orndorf became trustees.

Record of matters connected with St. Marys' Church, Hagerstown, from May 7th, 1868.

Rev. John M. Jones came as pastor to Hagerstown on the 7th May 1868. Rev. E. Lidier, the former pastor, went the next day to St. Peters', Baltimore as assistant. Rev. Henry Myers, the pastor of St. Vincents', Baltimore, accompanied the new pastor, and introduced him on the following sunday [sic] at high mass to the people. The church-house was much out of repairs and almost destitute of furniture, which however was remedied by degrees. The mission consists of Williamsport and Hagerstown, besides Boonsboro and Smithsburg, where there are no churches. Clearspring, which formerly belonged to the mission, was given when Rev. J.N. Jones came, to Rev. M. Saush of Hancock. The first fair held by St. Marys' congregation took place at Lyceum Hall, Hagerstown during the month of November, 1868. The proceeded were applied to repairing church and church house and furnishing the same. The amount cleared was about $1900. Gas was put into the church in May 1869.

1869 June 6th. Fathers Wayrich, Gross, and O'Donohue, redemptorists, began a mission. It lasted one week and did much good. Fr. Wayrich a very eloquent speaker, but FF. Gross and O'Donohue better liked by the people. Fr. Wayrich frequently preached two houses in the evening. The congregation gave the missionaries $180 on their departure. Several converts were received into the church, and there were 320 communions. Rev. Michael Laush left Hancock in the spring of 1869, and Archbishop Spalding gave Rev. J.M. Jones the whole county. Rev. C. Beeman of Cumberland took Little Orleans.
In July 1869 Rev. Charles Samer came to Hagerstown as assistant having been recently ordained at St. Marys' Seminary, Baltimore. The mission consisted of Hagerstown, Hancock, Moorsville, Williamsport, Little Orleans (afterwards attached to Cumberland) Clearspring and Boonsboro. All these towns had churches in them. The

Boonsboro church was built by Fr. Josiah Smith with money left by Fr.[?] Otho Smith.

Aug. 22nd Devotion of the 40 hrs. Father S. Lee and John Kane of Harpers Ferry assisted and preached. During this month a festival was held for three nights in Willliamsport. The amount cleared was about $175. This was spent partly in buying an organ for the Williamsport church, and partly in paying an organist, as the congregation is small and poor.

Dec. 22nd The Jubilee began in Hagerstown and lasted till wednesday. [sic] Father Richard Barry of Harrisburg and F. Fields of Chambersburg assisted and preached. There were 280 communions. The Jubilee followed at Hancock, where there were 180 communions, and at Clearspring where there were 49.

1870 June 16th Corpus Christi. The addition to the church in Hagerstown was begun today. Frederick of Baltimore is architect and Oliver is contractor. The old school-house and lot were sold to the Cumberland Valley R.R. for $3000. The rest of the money will be raised by subscription. For November of this year the mission was again divided. Father Ryan took the Hancock missions and Rev. J.M. Jones the Hagerstown ones.

1871 January. The church in Hagerstown dedicated to-day. Father Myers dedicated it and sang the high mass. Rev. S. Lyman preached. The 40 hrs followed and F.F. Ryan and John Kain preached and assisted. While the repairs were going on in the church mass was celebrated at the house of Miss Eliza Monahan in Franklin St.

On Easter morning this year 105 communions in Hagerstown.

1871 September. September 28th Rev. J.M. Jones moved to St. Peters, Baltimore. Rev. S.S. Wult appointed pastor of Hagerstown. Father S.F. Ryan was removed about this time from Hancock to Cumberland, and Rev. C. Samer appointed to Hancock.

1873   September 21th   Archbishop Bayley gave confirmation in Hagerstown.

1874 January 25th & 29th Rev. J.S. Kain of Harpers Ferry gave a mission in Williamsport. Rev. John Boetzher of Chambersburg assisted and there were 72 communions.

1873 July 21 July 21st 1873. Father Myers for many years pastor in Hagerstown died at St. Vincents, Baltimore. Buried July 24th, Thursday, 1873.

1873. Oct. 14 Oct. 14th 1873 Rev. J.M. Jones returned to Hagerstown as pastor, and Rev. S.S. Wultz left the next day to go to St. Matthews', Washington.
1874. January   Jany. 12th & 13th   Fr. Chapelle of St. Joseph's, Baltimore gave two lectures for the altar society.
The sisters of St. Joseph came to Hagerstown to open a school. A small house owned by Mr. Kurl, had been rented for them, and they took immediate possession.
Four sisters came to make the foundation. Mother Ligueri, superior, Sister Angela, Sister Basil, Sister Winifred. The latter a lay sister. They are all strangers to each other and to us. Sister Angela teaches the head school; Sister Bassil the smaller children, and Mother Ligueri the small boys. The congregation furnished the house. We pay $200 rent for the house: $700 to the sisters and $200 to Chestnut Hill for the novitiate. The priest has all the responsibility of collecting the money and attending to the material prosperity of the school. This was the arrangement made by Mother St. John, and approved by Archbishop Bayley.

1874 Oct. 13th The fair (second one) began in Hagerstown tuesday [sic] 18th Oct. and lasted till the following saturday week. The amount cleared was $1089.05. This went to pay part of the debt of $1300 remaining from the repairs of the church. (1)
1875 Jany. 19th Father F. J. Boyle of Washington gave a lecture in the church for the school.

March 31st The sisters of St. Joseph moved into their new home, which was purchased for them of Mr. Ogilby. The house cost $6750. The following summer (1875) an addition was put by building a new dormitory in the back building. Property held in name of the Trustees.

Sept. 17th Archbishop Bayley confirmed[?] here friday [sic], Sept. 17th, and the next day in Williamsport.

The up-stairs of the church-house was papered and painted during September of this year (1875), and finished on the 15th

Sept. 19th to 26th Sept. 19th to 26th. Fathers Wayrich and Oberhard. C.S.S.R. gave a mission in Hagerstown.

(1) Nov. 1874 Miss Eliza Monahan died and left $1000 to put up an altar in Hagerstown Church.

1875 Dec. 23rd The fair in Williamsport opened the 23rd Dec. and closed Jany. 1st 1876. amount cleared $700. To this Archbishop Bayley added $100 and the congregation began immediately to tear down the church, as the walls had begun to give way. The men very kindly gave their laborer gratis in taking down the walls asserting[?] the brick &.c. For the mean time mass is said on sundays [sic] in the public Hall. The 4th sunday of July the church was sufficiently completed to have mass in it for the first time. Mr. Elie Stake acted most generously and undertook the building of the church, giving his own services gratis during the whole period and working every day. The other members of the congregation also worked well and gave according to their means.

1876 Jany. 1st Jany. 1st Church bell rung from 12 to 1 to welcome in the Centennial.

May 10th Corner stone laid in Williamsport. Fr. Tyan present.

June 10th 12th. 13th. 14th. Strawberry festival in Hagerstown for four nights. Amount cleared $145.04. This was the first strawberry festival and not very pleasant nor successful on account of disagreement between two or three ladies.

1876 July 4th Bell rung for the Centennial, and High mass at 10 A.M.

July 19th Pic-nic at Berry's woods for the Williamsport church. Amount cleared $147.97.

July 23rd Seventh sunday [sic] after Pentecost. mass for the first time in the new church at Williamsport. Dedication however deferred till the spring of 1877, owing to want of funds.
August. During this month an addition was made to the school house in Hagerstown by putting a second and third story over the kitchen. Heil contractor: cost $300.

1876. November. December. Preparations for fair in Williamsport. The fair opened Dec. 23rd, saturday, and lasted till the following wednesday week, Jany. 4th 1877. The tables were arranged in the new church. $562. was cleared - a considerable amount for the times and place. There was a table from Williamsport, one from Clearspring, one from Hagerstown and one by Mrs. Barry, who obtained all the articles herself. The order
during the fair was excellent, and there was no disagreement at any of the tables.

1876 At Christmas Mr. James I. Hurley presented the church in Hagerstown with a very handsome pair of candelabra holding 12 lights each.
1877 April 1st Easter. Easter 1877 Repository and high altar very handsome. A great many flowers (all natural) and about 140 lights. Easter sunday 106 communions.
April 2nd Easter sunday Concert in Hagerstown directed by Dr. Dielman of Emmitsburg. Total received $75.35 clear $42.25. The concert went off very well, and all present were pleased.

April 29th   Williamsport Church dedicated by Rt. Rev. J.J. Kain of Wheeling. Mass sung by Rev. Désiré Le Wulf. Deacon Rev. S.F. Ryan and deacon Rev. Thomas Fleming. There were present Rev. J. O'Sullivan, Rev. C. Lamer. Mercadantes' mass in C. flat was sung. Rt. Rev. J.J. Kain preached from Hebrews XII. 22.23.24. Tickets 50 cts. For the evening Rev. J. O'Sullivan of Westernport preached in Hagerstown from Luke I. 46-48.
Church well filled morning and evening.

1877. May 6th   Devotion of the 40 hrs. commenced in Hagerstown. Father Waterson of Mt. St. Marys' preached morning and evening on sunday, and on monday Very Rev. C.P. O'Connor from Overbrook and F.F. Gloyd and Kaelin came to help. Devotion closed at night May 8th with benediction.

1876   Mortgage on School house recorded on Mch. 23rd 1876, Liber No. 74 folio 1448 for $1100 to Rev. J.M. Jones guardian of Mary C. Hanan.

1875   Mortgage to Dr. J. Smith for $370.63   April 22nd 1875. on school house.

1877 Nov. 25th   St. Catharines' Day. Great flood on the Potomac. Water higher at Williamsport than any time since 1852. Houses, barns, &.c. washed away. Bridge of the C.V.R.R. destroyed near Williamsport.

1877 October 3rd wednesday. Abp. Bayley died to-day at 10.50 A.M. The bell was tolled in Hagerstown from 9 to 10 P.M. as the news did not reach here till evening. Collected and paid the last of September $100 on the Williamsport Church. The debt now is $300.
October 9th   Archbishop Bayley buried to-day in Baltimore. Funeral from 8 to 1 P.M. All the Office recited. Mass sung by Abp. Wood.
13th   High mass of requiem for Abp. Bayley in Hagerstown at 8 A.M.

November 27th Fair began in Hagerstown for the sisters school. Almost all the articles came from Very Rev. C.P. O'Connor; or from the Visitation Convent, Georgetown; or from the sisters of St. Joseph. The articles were very handsome. The first few nights very little was realized.
December 8th. Last night of the fair for the school. We did quite well. Cleared about $700. Several unpleasant things took place, but, all things considered, we got along quite well.

1877 See 25th. Rev. J.M. Jones too unwell to say mass. Rev. F. Fowler sang mass at 5 and 10 1/2 A.M.

1878 Rev. James P. Carey came as assistant at St. Marys' on saturday, March 2nd and left April 22nd 1878.

Rev. John M. Jones went to Europe May 4th and returned Sept. 20th.
Rev. Charles Stonestreet S.J. took charge of the missions during the absence of Rev. J.M. Jones.
October New Missah[?] brought from Puslet[?] New York: cost $22.
November new cope and white vestment arrive from Toulouse, France: bought of L. Michel. Simer in Williamsport on Thanksgiving: cleared $67.
December. Rev. Levitt S.J. from Frederick assisted at Christmas and sang the 10.30 mass preaching on the Nativity. new vestments and cope worn for the first time.
Dec. 23rd Concert in Williamsport for furnace. Cleared.
Furnace bought of Oscar Bellman: put up Dec 20 and 21st: cost $90 Furnace worked very well on Dec. 22nd sunday, and Dec. 23rd, concert tonight. Pipes &.c. cost about $20 more.
1879. Jany. 1st. Mass as usual at 7 and 9. Weather warm and slight snows all days. No bells rung in ____ at midnight.

March 11th The 40 hours began in Williamsport, and closed Thursday the 13th. 68 communions. Weather pleasant. F.F. Fleming and Lamer assisted.

May 4th Sunday The Most Rev. Archbishop of Baltimore, James Gibbons, gave confirmation in Hagerstown to 61 persons - 23 of whom were converts. His Grace preached in the evening at 7:30 vespers a very good sermon on the Infallibility of the church. The church was crowded both morning and evening. The confirmation took place at 10.30 high mass, sunday, May 4th. About 500 persons were present. At vespers about 700 were present. Many of the leading people of this city. Sixteen persons were entertained at dinner on that day by the Rector, Very Rev. C.O'Connor [?]maanaug[?]

May 5th Monday Confirmation in Williamsport by Most Rev. James Gibbons. 19 were confirmed, 5 of whom were converts. Mr. Victor Cushwa gave a dinner to the Archbishop and Rev. clergy.

1879 May 11th Sunday The devotion of the 40 hours began in Hagerstown. Rev. C. Samer preached in the evening. Rev. O'Sullivan of St. Peters Washington, preached monday and tuesday nights, and Rev. S. Lee wednesday night: as the Jubilee was continued after the 40 hours. Rev. J Kaelin finished the Jubilee on thursday morning with high mass and sermon in german. All went off well. About 300 communions.

May 29th Thursday Great fire in Hagerstown. The Washington House burned and several killed and injured. Fire broke out about 2 A.M. A magnificent but terrible scene. Only one catholic seriously injured.

October New pair of candelabra bought from Kreuzer. Price 70. Freight packing, &,c. 8.85. To be used for the first time at Christmas. During this month the Rev. John M. Jones resigned the charge of the Hagerstown mission on account of ill health. The Archbishop accepted the resignation to take effect the 1st February.

1880. Rev. J. A. Frederick appointed to To [sic] succeed Rev. J.M. Jones.

December 25th Rev. C. Stonestreet, S.J. assisted, and sang the last mass. Large number of communicants and altar handsomely decorated. Weather warm and rainy. New candelabra used for first time.

Dec. 28th Mass in Hagerstown and Williamsport. Rev. C. Stonestreet, S.J. delivered a fine sermon on the immortality of the soul at Hagerstown during the vesper service.

1883 Jan'ry 25th Rev. H. Volz succeeded Rev. J. A. Frederick in charge of St. Mary's Church, Hagerstown.

28th Introduced myself to my new Parishioners, and announced my platform.

March 25 Easter Sunday. Over 100 Communions; splendid music; altars handsomely dedicated; very large attendance at both High Mass & vespers.

May 20th Opening of the Fourty Hours Devotion. Assisted on Monday by Fathers Gloyd, Delaney, Mead & McKeefry. About 230 Communions.

June 28th Commencement of St. Joseph's Academy at 4 P.M. The children generally acquitted themselves very well.

July 15th Began the work of putting an additional story on the School Building. Albert Heil, contractor

Sept. 4th Opening of the Fair for the benefit of the Sister's School. A large variety of useful articles were presented, and very little expense was incurred, and the lady managers worked hard and faithfully.

18th Close of the Fair. The net proceeds were over fifteen hundred dollars. Very few Protestants attended. Many thanks to the members of the Congregation, and especially to the managers.

Oct 5th Dr. Josias Smith, one of the leading members of the Congregation and one of the Trustees of the School died. He was buried on Sunday Oct. 7th. The funeral was attended by an immense concourse of people, including the principal men of the town. RJ.P.

1884 Feb'ry 16th Opening of the Mission by the Lazanist[?] Fathers Lefevre and Krably.

17th Close of the Mission. This mission was a very successful one; all of the exercises were well attended, and about 400 persons received Holy Communion.

April 10th & 11th Holy Thursday & Good Friday. Office of the Tenebrae performed for the first time in many years.

April 13th Easter Sunday. 128 Communions; fine music; large attendance at all the services.

After High Mass, about 30 gentlemen met in the Pastor's Parlor to discuss the improvements to be made to the Church and Pastoral Residene[?]. it was decided to put a new roof on the Church, to add another story to the Residence and to change the stairway therein.

The improvements mentioned above were begun in the month of May, and completed about the middle of July. The Pastoral Residence is now quite convenient and comfortable. Much opposition was manifested by some few, and a very verbose petition sent to the Most Rev. Archbishop against the improvements, but the Pastor gained his point.

July 27th Most Rev. Archbishop Gibbons preached High Mass, and gave confirmation in the Evening at 7 o'clock. The Church was crowded on both occasions.

1885 Jan 7 The Rev. Henry Volz left Hagestown on the 16th of Jan.

His successor D. Manley, arrived on the Evening of the same day to take charge of this mission. Rev. Geo. Devins, Chancellor of the diocese, introduced the new rector to the Congregation on the following Sunday. Rev. H. Volz at his departure left quite a number of debts standing which amounted in all to about two thousand two hundred dollars. To meet the most pressing obligation of the Church a loan was secured from the Metropolitan Bank of Balt. After Easter preparations were begun for a fair which we proposed holding in the month of September for the purpose of raising funds to pay off the Church debt. In the early part of July of this year the Sisters of St. Joseph left their mission not to return again. The step that led to their withdrawal was the refusal of the Mother Superior, Mother Mary John, to release the congregation from the obligation of sending two hundred dollars ($200.) annually to the Mother house at Chesnut Hill, Philada. With rather limited means at his disposal, the rector of the Church was not inclined to continue an arrangement that had not proved satisfactory to either side. The sisters were not satisfied because they did not receive all that they were entitled to from the congregation; and many of the latter thought that they were taxed too heavily for the support of the school.

Such being the state of affairs, the rector of the church deemed it expedient to procure the services of another order Sisters who would agree to take charge of the school on terms more favorable to the congregation. He accordingly applied to the Mother Superior of the Sisters of Notre Dame at Govonstown[?] MD. for three teachers to conduct his school. His request was immediately granted. The Mother Supr. agreed to send three teaching sisters before the first of the following September. The terms of agreement are as follows: the rector of the Church will pay to the Sisters five hundred & fifty dollars annually for their services as teachers; he will also provide fuel for house & school; the Sister Supr. will collect dues for tuition from the pupils & will render an account of the same to the rector at stated times; the profit on school books &c. accrues to the sisters; the tuition for instrumental music also belongs to the sisters.

Ven. Mother M. Theophila Supr. de Notre Dame together with four sisters arrived here on the 10th of August to take charge of the school. The sisters of St. Joseph left shortly before. The names of the newly arrived sisters are: Sr. M. Ignatia Supr. Sr. M. Germain, Sr. M. Geralda, & St. Falconieri.

The agreement made with Mother Superior of the Notre Dame Sisters, above referred to, has the approval of the Most. Rev. Archbishop.

Towards the close of September a fair was held in the Hose Opera Hall, for the purpose of raising money to pay Church debts. About fourteen hundred dollars were realized. Previous to the fair and during its progress, the ladies in charge worked very energetically & harmoniously. financially, the fair was quite a success, considering the hard times.

> ST. MARY'S FAIR.—The fair at the Opera House for the benefit of St. Mary's R. C. church is still under full headway and has been a great success. Monday night the First Hose Company visited it and presented a receipted bill for that night's rent of the hall. Next night Antietam Fire Company paid a visit and presented a handsome silver pitcher and two drinking cups, Mr. J. A. Mason making the presentation and Mr. R. J. Halm responding. To-night the Hagerstown Light Infantry were to have gone in full uniform, and to-morrow night the Junior Fire Company will pay their visit.

An 1885 newspaper article was written about the church fair:

"St. Mary's Fair – The fair at the Opera House for the benefit of St. Mary's R.C. church is still under full headway and has been a great success. Monday night the First Hose Company visited it and presented a receipted bill for that night's rent of the hall. Next night Antietam Fire Company paid a visit and presented a handsome silver pitcher and two drinking cups, Mr. J.A. Mason making the presentation and Mr. R.J. Halm responding. To-night the Hagerstown Light Infantry were to have gone in full uniform, and to-morrow night the Junior Fire Company will pay their visit."[1]

---

[1] *The Mail.* Hagerstown, Maryland, 2 Oct 1885, page3, column A.

1885 The school opened this year with an attendance of about one hundred children. The number gradually increased until it reached one hundred and twenty five at Christmas.

1885 During the summer of this year five members of the board of trustees of St. Joseph's Academy resigned viz. W.F. Orndorff, M. Happel, Michl. White, P.M. John & A. Heil. Their resignation was accepted.

1885 In November the church was repainted on the outside. Some other improvements were also made at this time.

1886 March. Mr. James J. Hurley, after recovering from a severe illness, presented a set of stations to the church. These stations were bought from Benziyer Bros. at a cost of $230.00.

May 16th On this day a meeting of the male members of the congregation was called for the purpose of electing trustees. The following named men were elected viz. James J. Hurley, J.B. Cushwa, Michael Dillon, R.J. Halm, Dr. C.B. Boyle, Thos. Moore and John B. Sweeney.

August - During this month a steam heating apparatus was put into the school building at a cost of $550.00. Nearly all of this amount was raised by subscription. The apparatus was procured from Moore and Frick of Waynesboro Pa.

November - In accordance with a decree of the last Plenary Council, two auditors were appointed viz. Messsrs. J.B. Cushwa and R.J. Halm. This appointment was duly confirmed by his Eminence the Cardinal.

1887 Jan'y During the first days of the new year a festival was held for several nights in the Hundrick building on Washington St. for the purpose of raising money to pay balance on Steam Heater & to meet other expenses.. The amount realized was $220.00

About the middle of this month, the pastor went south for the benefit of his health, & Fr. Rabbia supplied his place until he returned in May.

June About the 20th of this month Fr. Stapleton who had been attending the missions of Williamsport Clearspring & Boonsboro for some time from Hagerstown, was taken to Balt. and the pastor of Hag. was left to look after the missions for the time being.

Sept. About the first of this month Fr. Mead came back to Washington Co. to resume the care of his former missions.

October The Pastor, Revd. D. Manley being obliged, on account of ill health to relinquish the charge of this congregation, Rev. J Nabbia was appointed his successors arriving here Oct. 8th and Fr. Manley left the next day.

1888 May 20th Forty Hour Devotion 196 Communions 300 people made the Carter Communion.

June 3rd - 20 children made their First Commun.

Sept. Sister Ignatia was (at her request) released of the charge of the School, and Sister Theofora was sent to take her place.

1889 June - The rector of Williamsport & Boonsboro (Fr. Meade) having been appointed to Hancock & surrounding missions, by order of the Archbishop, The Rector of Hagerstown assumed charge of Williamsport & Boonsboro missions, appointing the 2nd Sunday of each month to say one mass in Hagestown, at 8 o'clock, & the late mass at Williamsport; attending Boonsboro occasionally on weekdays.

Novemb. - A steam apparatus (Moore & _) was placed in this Church for $460.00. Dollars.

1890 In June a bath-room and other improvements & repairs were made on the pastoral residence costing about 240 Dollars, paid by the Pastor out of his own pocket, the congregation not being much inclined to attend to the comfort of the Pastor.

1891 In November the steam apparatus was extended & Connected with the Pastoral residence at the cost of 205

Dollars and this also was paid by the Pastor, without the concurrence of the Congregation.

1893 The Congregation feeling unable to renew the bargains with the Sisters for the stipulated annual salary[?] of $550.00 an agreement was entered into approved by the Cardinal between the Sisters of Notre Dame and the Congregation that the Sisters conduct the School at their own risk, collecting whatever tuitions they can from the school, without any responsibility resting on the Pastor or the Congregation for any deficit, provided, however, that the Congregation be bound to supply The School & The Sisters with fuel & gas; and pay for any and all repairs necessary to the School building. The Trustees with the Pastor agreed to said conditions. Said agreement went in force August 1893.

1893 Nov. 2nd - A Fair was held (at Hose Hall) closing Nov. 9th) to raise funds to pay off the School debt, which amounted to $ [blank space] The net proceeds of the Fair _____ to $ [blank]

1908 Oct 21 Rev. L. Rabbia having asked for Rev Albert E. Lueth[?] as assistant, he was appointed arriving on Oct. 21 1908. Was in rality[?] appointed by Bishop Corrigan, Auxiliary to the Cardinal.

Nov 29 This was Fr. Rabbia's 68th birthday. An entertainment was held in the Josephs Hall and Fr. Rabbia presented with a fine chair and flowers.

1909 At the beginning of this year announcement was made that new windows for the church and a new organ being needed efforts to obtain the same would be made. On May 2nd Bishop Corrigan came to confirm. At that date two windows were already installed - one by Mrs. J.B. Cushwa and the other in honor of [blank]

The others were placed in by Sept. The children raised money for their window by a Lower[?] Festival held in the Sisters Yard in the summer.

Oct. The organ was installed to night. A concert was held in the church. Prof Clark, assisted by the choir. The organ was built by Möller Organ Co., this city. Cost $2500 - $500 given by Möller - $1--- by Andrew Carnegie and sent by congregation.

*Christmas Day 1908 The electric chandelier were used for first time. The electrical arrangement was paid for by Mrs. Kealafer.

1909 Concrete walks were laid about church & school in July. Concrete on front of Church paid for by Mrs. Sweeney. Fence improved and paid for by Mr. Jno Sweeney - School and Convent painted.

1909 Aug. [nothing]

Nov 16, 17, 18 Bazaar and Supper held at St. Joseph's Hall. The affair was successful socially and financially. Cleared $408.

1910 Jan. 14 Miss Mollie McLaughlin aged 56 a member of St. Mary's died to day. By her will the church & school are made sharers in many bequests.

Jan 16 - Mrs. Keblofer gave the hos pontiers[?] on each side of the altar. Cost $37.00

Jan. 20th Albert Hill 80 years of age died today. He put the third story on old school building and I think 3rd story on Rectory.

July Public sale of the Catholic Cemetery - was had to day in front of the court. The same was withdrawn at a bid of $5300. On the 26th of this month however it was offered a second time & sold for above sum. The cemetery is unused and located next to Möller Organ Factory.

Aug 29 Division of the estate of Mollie McLaughlin was made to day.
Church $2000 - Mance[?] $1219.93. School, St. Charles College & Little[?] Sisters of the Poor $1219.93.

Dec 23, 1910 Ratification of sale of Cemetery - Purchasers - John B. Sweeney & Thomas Georg.

March 27th 1911 - Rev. Sebastian Robbia died to day Monday at 10 Am. Suddenly and alone. I was in the Rectory but in the office. Funeral held here Wed. 10 Am. Celebrant Rt. Rev OB Corrigan. Deacon Rev. Geo. Fragesser - Emmitsburg - Sub.[?] D[?] Rev. James McDermatt, Sstulton[?] Pa. Preacher Rev. Febin[?] Tarro. Remains taken to Wash at 2.15 Mass in St. Peters Church 1030 Thurs. in presence of His Eminence Celebrant Rev. AE Smith. Deacon Rev. Debuis McCormick. sub. D Rev. Hugh Curley. Preacher Mgr. MacKin - Interment Mt. Olive Cemetery Wash DC On Day of funeral in Wash March 30th Cardinal informed me that he had appointed Rev. L.L. Hurllbut, then at Clarksville, MD to succeed Rev. J. Robbia. Rev. AE Smith to go to Clarksville. Saltter[?] appointment Ehayad, Immaning[?] here as Assistant.

[The text ends on page 38 of the journal. The following text was written in the last few pages of the journal.]

September 1876
Furniture in Church House, Hagerstown, which belongs to Rev. J.M. Jones.
Parlor - Desk, 3 bookcases, two easy chairs, one carpet chair, [one rocking chair crossed out], 1 marble top table, curtains, 2 foot stools, [one rug crosse dout], all the books, pictures and parlor ornaments. 1 waste paper basket. 1 cane chair with suckers[?]
Hall [blank]
Dining Room - 1 Extension dinner table, seven dining room chairs, water cooler, chandelier, 6 pictures. All the china, glass, silver and plated ware contained in the new cup-board, which is in the side of the wall next to the hall. Also the tin-

ware in the old cup-board, and the table linen in the sideboard. 1 clock, 1 1/2 doz. knives and Carver.

Kitchen - The tin-ware, one picture, 3 flat irons, one large gallery board[?], one small do[ditto], [and the rag carpet crossed out], (Pd out of church funds for making carport Nov. 76

Cellar - 1 Ice-cream freezer.

The amount realized from this Fair was a little over $1400. fourteen hundred dollars.

2nd Floor

Slice - 4 barhots[?], china jar

Room over Dining Room - [1 hair ___ ___ crosssed out] Pd by church , blankets, spreads, sheets and bed linen in the closest.

Library Room - 3 pictures

Small Room - Pictures, vases; curtains.

Front Room - Rocking chair, bureau, pictures and ornaments, towel rack, 2 lace curtains at the front windows.

Housekeepers room - The bed, bedding and bureau belong to the housekeeper as well as the pictures and ornaments. The housekeeper is Miss Maggie Shemin[?], and she brought these articles with her.

The Church contains belonging to Rev. J.M. Jones - 1 Chair, three surplices, one alb.

The Garden - contains belonging to the same. The hot bed frames, 1 wheel-barrow, 1 set garden Tools

Hagerstown, September 13th, 1876.

I affirm the above List to be a correct account of what belongs to me personally in the Church, and Church House, and I claim the same as my property.

John M. Jones

In accordance with the statutes of the Archdiocese.

Personal property left in charge of Rev. J.A. Frederick, by Rev. J.M. Jones. 1 picture, 1 desk, 3 book-cases, books in two book cases

John M. Jones

St. Marys' Church, Jay 27th 1880.

[The following newspaper articles were found pasted into the back of the journal:

"The Catholic Fair.
The Ladies Fair opened on Tuesday evening under the most favorable auspices, not withstanding a rain interrupted their brighter anticipations. The ladies have made great efforts to hold a fair that would not only help them to pay of the debt of their church, but at the same time would give great credit to them for the fine display of rare and beautiful articles. The price of admission is ten cents with a chance of the holder of the lucky ticket drawing a prize of *Twenty Dollars in Gold*. The lunch table is in charge of Mrs. Milton Ewers, assisted by Mrs. Downin, Mrs. Clayborn, Mrs. Cushwa, and Miss Martin where will be found "oysters in every style" fried children, ham &c.

Catholic Fair.
Wednesday night was one of those pleasant evenings that make a fair really enjoyable. The visitors were not so many as on other nights, but all seemed happy, and money slipped through their fingers so easily that all the tables did well.
The contest for the Chair for railroad agent and the doctor's medicine chest polled many votes. The voting for the agent's chair closes to-night at 10.30 o'clock. The friends of the agents must vote for their favorites before that hour.
The Valley Grey Band, Capt. H. Winter, leader, favored the fair with their choice music.
To-night the Western Enterprise Fire Company will visit the fair, in uniform, with music, and a good time is expected.

The Catholic Fair
The ladies of St. Mary's Catholic church will hold a fair in Hose Hall, commencing on Tuesday evening, September 22d. This will be one of the most attractive fairs ever held in this city, as donations have been made from Boston, New York, St. Louis, Norfolk, Philadelphia, Baltimore, St. Joseph and other distant points, comprising very many rare and beautiful articles never before seen on exhibition in

Hagerstown. The ladies invite their friend sand the public generally to visit the fair, and in their kindness and generosity help them in their efforts to pay off the debt on their church. Fancy articles, as also domestic and useful goods, will be sold cheap, since they cost the management nothing, being all donated. The lunch and refreshment tables will be most tempting in their supplies, and the most delicate palate sumptuously gratified at a small cost.

The Refreshment table, in charge of Mrs. Michael White, assisted by Mrs. W.F. Orndorf, Mrs. Nierman, and Misses Moore, Fellinger and Morrison will furnish ice cream, fruits and everything that is nice.

The Cigar Stand is in charge of Miss Maggie Garey, assisted by Misses Sullivan and Heimel, where will be found cigars and smokers - articles to please taste and purse.

The First Fancy Table is presided over by Mrs. Morrison, assisted by Mrs. Zook, Misses Taggart, Shirwin and Fechtig, they display a handsome knit quit, Embroidered Plush Wall Pocket, and many very pretty and useful articles.

The Second Fancy Table is presided over by Mrs. Dillon, assisted by Misses Hurley, Schlotterbeck and Happel, on their table will be found a china tea set, oil painting of flowers on glass, handsome embroidered table scarf and many fancy and domestic articles. They have for raffle a barrel of flour, a fine hog, good heavy weight.

The Third Fancy Table, in charge of Miss Eva McCleery, assisted by Misses Mollie McLaughlin, Katie Moore and Manne [sic] Cramer. They exhibit a beautiful lamp, lovely pincushions, &C and have for a raffle a rag carpet and a half ton of coal.

The Fruit Stand, in charge of Mrs. Riordan, assisted by Mrs. Miller, and Misses Mobley and Orndorf, while they sell delicious fruits offer for raffle a fine silk quilt, handsome lamp, oil paintings &c.

There is a contest by votes for a very fine office chair between the agents of the railroads centering here, Mr. Koehler of the Western Maryland, Mr. Zeigler of the B. & O. and Mr. Feldman of the C.V. The friends of the gentlemen are invited to come and vote for their choice.

The ladies deserve success for their efforts, and here is a nice opportunity for "charity the greatest of all virtues."

St. Joseph's School
Commencement Exercises - Award of Premiums.
The annual commencement exercises of St. Joseph's School of this city, took place on Friday, in Hose Opera House, a very large audience being present and apparently highly delighted.

In cases like this it is sometimes thought necessary to give particular mention to some of the pupils who excel, but in this case where all did so very well it is useless. We would only say that the performance of the very little ones gave more real pleasure than any other part of the entertainment. The proficiency of the whole school speaks volumes for the teachers. It shows how painstaking and faithful they were to their charge. The following programme [sic] was observed, with Miss Giacomini, a pupil of Notra Dame, at the piano:

PROGRAMME:
Entrance March.
Chorus - Ave Maria.
Welcome.
Die Hydropaten Waltzer.
Recitation - Barbara Frietchie.
Trammy Galop.
Woodland Treasures.
Song - The Little Wild Birds.
Declamation - Keeping his Word.
Calisthentics - WAnds.
chorus - Distant Chimes.
October's Party - Recitatio followe dby Free Gymnastics.
Declamation - The Inquiry.
chorus and Solo - O be Joyful in the Lord.
Distributio of Premiums.
March Finale.

Premiums were awarded for the various studies, deportment, attendance, &c., to the following named scholars, the distribution being made by Rev. Father Reardon:

1st Class. - Mary Dillon, Annie White, Cecilia McLaughlin, Mary Ewers, Maggie Wills, Mary Wills, Nina Cramer, Mary Geiger, Frank White, Fred Cushwa, Frank Cushwa, Charles Orndorf, William Lawrence.

2d Class. - Kate Happel, Mary Full, Carrie Wills, Mary Orndorf, Nettie Heil, Violet Morrison, William Floyd.

SECOND DEPARTMENT.

Gertie Wills, Daisy Earhart, Genevieve McLaughlin, Mary Suter, Lizzie Schlotterbeck, Ethel Beaumont, George Fechtig, William Schlotterbeck, Thomas Battle, Robert Case, Joseph Eagan, Gussie Nierman, John Full, Frank Case.

THIRD DEPARTMENT

1st Class. - Annie Shehan, Rose Fechtig, Ella Eagan, Mary Davis, Isabael Sweitzer, Nettie Bellman, Nora Earhart, Oscar Bellman, Ammen Beaumont, Charles Suter.

2d Class. - Clarence Keedy.

Premiums for reading and spelling awarded to John Beaumont, Mary Nierman, Nora Cearfoss, Mary Grady, Cora Lorshbaugh, Maggie Fallar, Nora Geary.

Premiums for regular attendance and learning to read and spell awarded to Harry Heil, Alvie McCardell, Nellie Battle, Mary Battle.

Premiums for being good little children awarded to Clarence Gardner, Franklin Kreitz, Lizzie Full, Rose Happel, Venie Kirshner.

The following pupils deserve honorary mention; their irregular attendance, however, deprives them of premiums: Grace Cunningham, Louise Orndorf, Clara Heleine, Stella Cramer, Thoams Geary, Clyde Mayhew, Gussie Clayburn.

The exercises closed with some very appropriate remarks by Father Manly, of St. Marys' Catholic Church, this city."

The Catholic Fair

Though closed on Saturday night in Hose Hall, the remnant of this fair is being closed out in the store room of Mr. A.D. Bennett, and will continue this Tuesday afternoon and night, and also Wednesday night. Go and secure some nice article, or buy some useful or fancy goods, as there are many things yet to dispose of at very low prices.

The Catholic Fair
The closing out of this fair continued on Tuesday afternoon and night. Miss Jennie Martin won the silver pitcher. Master Fred Cushwa the extension table, and number 210 the handsome clock.
To-night, Wednesday, an auction will be held in A.D. Bennett's store room, which will finally close the fair. Go and get bargains, as this is the last chance.

The Catholic Fair
Thursday night was an interesting night at the fair, the crowd was large and in their largeness of hart spent their money liberally. Several articles were raffled off and among the lucky persons wee Misses Heimel, Happel and Taggart, each winning some fancy article, Mr. Clinton Grove won a very nice quilt.
A fine rag carpet is on raffle at ten cents a chance, and a good sized hog weighing about two hundred pounds at ten cents a chance.
A box of fine cigars raffled at the cigar stand was won by Mr. Coughlin of Brooklyn.
The refreshment and lunch tables are well supplied with good things at low prices. The lunch table offers oysters in every style, with all the requisites to tickle the palate.

Catholic Fair Notes
The Hagerstown Light Infantry Company will attend to-night in a body, and the Junior Cornet [sic] Band will also be present.
The voting for the railroad agent's chair closed last night with the following result: Mr. Chas. Feldman, 630 1/2 votes; M. Edgar Zeigler, 120; Mr. H.C. Koehler, 44.

The Catholic Fair
Hose Hall was one season of delight last night. The Junior Cornet Band rendered most excellent music, and the

Hagerstown Light Infantry added life and pleasure to the occasion. Capt. Lane in a neat speech presented for the company a handsome clock to the fair. Rev. Father Manley received their present in words of welcome and gratitude, when Col. H.K. Douglas beautifully responded in such eloquent languages as only falls from the Colonel's lips.

The voting contest for the medicine chest closed at 10:30 o'clock. Messrs. Halm and Morrison were appointed judges, and Mesrs. Reynolds, Flynn, Murts and Zinkand as tellers. When the votes were counted it was found that Dr. Geo. Fechtig had received 286 votes, Dr. C.B. Boyle 284 1/2, blank and scattering, 109.

The fair closes to-night. A pleasant evening is anticipated.

Catholic Church Fair

A fair will be held by the ladies of St. Mary's Catholic church of this city, commencing on Tuesday 22d inst., in the Hose Hall, South Potomac street. The hall will be attractively decorated, a tastful [sic] display of fancy articles will be made, and other features introduced to insure an enjoyable time to every visitor.

In addition to its merits in other respects, the fair will be held for the purpose of raising funds to assist in defraying the debt of the church property, and we have no doubt will be as it deserves, liberally patronized by our citizens.

The Western Enterprise Fire Company attended in a body last night and presented the management with a barrel of patent roller flour. Mr. J.C. Braumgart made the presentation speech, to which Rev. Father Manly responded.

March 29, 1886.

A Handsome Donation.

A new set of *Statons of the Cross* were erected with suitable ceremonies yesterday afternoon in St. Mary's church, by Father Manley, assisted by Father Reardon. The Stations comprise fourteen oil paintings representing different scenes in the passion of the Savior, beginning with the death sentence in the hall of Pilate, and ending with His burial. The paintings are ate the celebrated German artist, Deschwanden, executed in Paris, and they are splendid works of art. It is understood that they have been donated by Mr. Jas. I. Hurley, to St. Mary's church, in which he has worshipped for more than fifty years.

"Easter, MONDAY, APRIL 26, 1886 ST. MARY'S CATHOLIC.

Services were held at seven o'clock and at half past ten in the morning, and at seven o'clock in the evening. The First service was a low mass, during which over one hundred and twenty-five members received communion. At the second services, high mass was celebrated and a sermon upon the resurrection preached by Dr. McSweeney of Mt. St. Mary's church, Emmittsburg, who kindly came to the assistance of the Rev. Manley, the latter just having risen from a bed of sickness. At this service Weber's Mass was sung by the choir. The Vesper services were sung after the gregorian sick chant manner, with Werner's Regina Coeli, and selected O Salutaris and Tantum Eergo. The altar at all the services was most tastefully decorated, and presented a mass of light tapers and flowers."

St. Mary's Catholic Church. *["1887" was handwritten beside this]*

The sacrament of confirmation was administered at this church during High Mass, yesterday (June 3rd), by his Eminence the most Rev. James Gibbons, Cardinal Archbishop of Baltimore who also preached an effective sermon on the stability and unchangeableness of the Church, that was founded upon the rock "Peter." There were about fifty confirmed, amongst whom were several adults and converts. The church was densely filled, and the weather oppressively warm. A Rev. Father from Emmitsburg, whose name has escaped us, was the celebrant of the Mass, assisted by Rev. D. Manly, the resident pastor. The services lasted from 10 a.m. until after 12m.

Funeral of W. F. Orndorf.
The funeral of the late W.F. Orndorf took place yesterday morning from St. Mary's Catholic church. An eloquent and feeling tribute was paid to the memory of deceased by rev. Father Manly, the resident priest. A mass was said for the purpose of the soul, a large congregation being present and participating. The interment was made in Rose Hill cemetery. The pall bearers were Buchanan Schley, A.A.Clapp, Dr. S.J. Wishard, J.U. Adams, J.B. Sweeny, R.J. Halm, O.D. McCardell and Martin Happel. The funeral cortege was a very large one, considering the early hour, and was an evidence of the popularity of the deceased, and the public estimate of his worth. The fame have the sincere sympathy of the community in their sorrow.

CURIOUS RELIC - THE HAGERSTOWN CHURCH.
The following communication appeared in the *United States Catholic Miscellany*, of Charleston, S.C., October 18, 1828. The communication which we give below in full is appended to an editorial in the above journal upon Archbishop Whitfield, in which it is said:
"To his zeal our Church is likely to owe the commencement of that system of regulation of energy and of union which it was too early to expect in the period of Archbishop Carroll's administration , but which, for reasons which we suppose

must have been sufficient and powerful, his two immediate successors have left to Doctor Whitfield to confer."

"OPENING OF THE NEW CATHOLIC CHURCH AT HAGERSTOWN.

"On Sunday, 5th of October, the Roman Catholic church lately erected in Hagerstown, Maryland, was dedicated to the Almighty God, under the invocation of the Blessed Virgin Mary, by the Most Rev. James Whitfield, Archbishop of Baltimore. The church is 95 by 50 feet, and measures 35 feet from the floor to the ceiling. It is built with an attention to taste and convenience, which have seldom been more happily combined; and the difficulties necessarily encountered in the erection of a building of such magnitude, and to which the resources of the Catholic congregation of the place were altogether inadequate, could have been overcome only by the most confiding zeal and indefatigable industry. Happily these qualities were found united in Rev. J. Ryan, the present pastor of Hagerstown; and it gives us much pleasure to state, that while his efforts were met and seconded to the extent of their means by his own flock, every appeal addressed to the liberal-minded Protestants of the town and its immediate vicinage was promptly and generously responded to. On few occasions, too, it is believed, have the religious ceremonies prescribed in the Roman Ritual for the consecration or the blessing of churches been witnessed with more manifestations of respect by an assembly, of which by far the greater number professed different religious creeds from those of the Catholic communion: and the liberality with which many of them had contributed to aid their Catholic fellow-citizens in the erection of a church more worthy than that to which they had been hitherto confined, of the rapidly increasing respectability of the town, the number that now frequent the church, and, above all, of the holy and august Victim to be offered in it, was surpassed only by the eagerness they afterwards evinced to assist at the sacred mysteries performed, and the divine truths announced there for the first time. Notwithstanding the unavoidable pressure of the crowd during the procession o the outside of the church, the whole was conducted with a silence and a sacredness which religion alone could have inspired. The High Mass was sung by the Most Rev. Archbishop, assisted by Rev. J. McGerry, vice-president of Mount St. Mary's Seminary, and Rev. J. Purcell, professor of moral philosophy in the same institution, as deacon and subdeacon. The other assisting officers were likewise from the seminary at Emmitsburg, as well as the choir, which, under the direction of Mr. Joseph Gegan, contributed in a high degree to the solemnity of the occasion and to the impressions it was calculated to excite.

"The morning instruction was delivered by the archbishop, and the matter and manner of his address were truly worthy of a father anxious to break to a beloved family the bread of life. Thirty-two persons were confirmed during the High Mass, of whom six were converts, and all, apparently, fully impressed with the obligations they contracted and the necessary grace and strength imparted to them for their fulfillment by this sacrament. In the evening, after the singing of the *Magnificat* at Vespers, the Rev. J. Purcell ascended the pulpit. His text, from the second Book of Chronicles, seventh chapter, eleventh and twelfth verses, we though happily selected for the subject which he chose to treat. After recapitulating the substance of the instruction by the Most Rev. Archbishop, he proceeded to prove that a temple built for the purpose of a religion, of which that of the Hews was but a type, was in reality, although the bystanders beheld not the cloud descending from heaven, and fire flashing forth to consume the victims, and the holocaust far more especially honored by the presence of the Deity than that for which the greatest and wisest of kins[?] stript[?] Ophir of its purest god, and lebanon of its cedars. The discourse lasted an hour a a-half, and was listened to throughout with the most marked attention. A collection to a considerable amount was made at each of the instructions. Several of the principal Protestants of the town having invited and solicited to their houses the assisting clergymen; the fact speaks much for their unprejudiced and kindly feeling towards Catholics. The next Sunday, however, we

make the closing remark with regret, such is still the scarcity of priests in the archdiocese, that there shall be no clergyman to officiate in a church which the Sunday before had been resorted to by nearly 3,000 persons."
- HIS SUCCESSOR.

Distribution of Premiums. [*Note: "June 25, 1888" was handwritten beside this article*]
The Sunday school of St. Mary's Catholic church closed for the summer with yesterday's session. Premiums were distributed to the scholars before they were dismissed, as follows:
First honors for regular attendance, good conduct, christian doctrine - Misses Mary Dillon, Cecelia McLaughlin, Genevieve McLlaughlin, Isabelle Switzer, Maggie Faller, Rose Happle.
First premiums, Misses Annie Switzer, Grace Cunningham, Mary Nierman, Nellie Battle, Lizzie Fisher.
Second premiums, Misses Mary Malone, Lizzie Schlotterbeck, Gertie Cunningham and Master Frank Case.
Third premiums, Misses Clara Nierman, Mary Full and Master Thomas Battle. The following pupils received silver medals for good conduct and application: Misses Fannie Bryan, Nora Geary, Ella Eagan, Mary Davis, Mary Battle, Lizzie Boyle, Virgie Alexander, Rose Nierman, Ida Lizer, Rena Smith.

St. Mary's Catholic Church Records

Baptisms
1818 - 1900

ST. MARY'S CATHOLIC CHURCH
HAGERSTOWN, MARYLAND, BAPTISMS:
Index, Bap Date, Child, Last Name, Father, Mother,
Birth Date, Code1, Code2, Code3,
1st Sponsor First, 1st Sponsor Last,
2nd Sponsor First, 2nd Sponsor Last, Location,
Notes, Maiden Name, Priest

1, 03 Aug 1818, Ann Eliza, Johnson, Thomas, Mary, 19 Nov 1817, -, -, -, Bennet , Peak, Elizabeth , Peak, -, McGeehaw, 18

2, 16 Sep 1818, Mary Elizabeth, Ryan, John, Elizabeth, 17-Dec, -, -, -, Patrick , McCristal, Catharine (Mrs.), McClaskey, -, McCanna, 18

3, 16 Sep 1818, Edward, Crossen, Edward, Catha[rine?]*, 06 Sep 1818, -, -, -, Hugh , Friel, Mary, Crossen, *Catha[rine? - page is broken off], Conahan, 18

4, 17 Sep 1818, Ann , Ward, Aquella, Eleanor , 13 Aug 1818, -, -, -, Mary, Davis, Philip, Mains, See Endnote 9, -, 18

5, 20 Sep 1818, Joseph N., Abil, Vulgerinan, Julian, 27 Aug 1818, -, -, -, Ann (Miss), McLain, -, -, -, -, 18

6, 20 Sep 1818, John, Giles, William, Anna , 07 July 1818, PN, -, - , Eleanor (Miss), Monahan, -, -, -, McGinley, 18

7, 20 Sep 1818, Terasa, -, Arnold, Nelly, 02 Dec 1817, PN, S, S, S, _elly [page broken off] , -, -, -, Family and sponsors are slaves of Mr. Mason, -, 18

8, 20 Sep 1818, _rma[?] Mary, -, Jesse, _ay, 15 weeks, -, S, S, Mary, -, -, -, all Slaves of Mr. Mason [name runs into binding], -, 18

9, 30 Aug 1818, Julian, Glanville, John, Frances , 24 ___ 1816, -, -, -, Edmond , Smith, James, McAdams, 3rd witness is Elizabeth McAllister, Hartnet, 18

10, 23 Sep 1818, Martha, McGee, Hugh, Anna Maria , 25 Aug 1818, -, -, -, Peter , McGee , Ellen, Monahan, -, Miller, 18

11, 04 Oct 1818, William, Mitchel, Ignatius, Caroline , 16 Jul 1818, -, -, -, John , Jackson, John (Mrs.), Jackson [HB], -, Kohlenberg, 18

12, 04 Oct 1818, Ann, Tenley [or Teuley], Thomas, Cloe , 06 Mar 1818*, -, -, -, Mary , Lawler, -, -, PB; birth date is 06 [or 2 or 8] Mar 1818, Havis, 18

13, 02* Oct 1818, Arthur John, Johnston, William, Mary , 06 Sep 1817, -, -, -, William , Burk, Elizabeth , Burk [HB], PB; *[or 6 or 8 Oct 1818] , Halfpenny, 18

14, 30 Nov 1818, Eleanor, Tolan, John, "Alice or Else" , 15 days , -, -, -, Geo , McLaughlin, Grce, Harkan, "lawfully married in the Kingdom of Ireland", Harkin, 18

ST. MARY'S CATHOLIC CHURCH
HAGERSTOWN, MARYLAND, BAPTISMS:
Index, Bap Date, Child, Last Name, Father, Mother,
Birth Date, Code1, Code2, Code3,
1st Sponsor First, 1st Sponsor Last,
2nd Sponsor First, 2nd Sponsor Last, Location,
Notes, Maiden Name, Priest

15, 04 Jan 1819, Margaret, Keefe, Patrick, Sarah , 07 Nov 1818, -, -, -, Bridget , Tool, -, -, -, Crowley, 18

16, 10 Jan 1819, John, McDonald, Richard, Nancy , 23 May 1818, PN, S, S, Harriet , Shorter, -, -, parents are slaves to Daniel Schnebly, Gant, 18

17, 10 Jan 1819, Jane Rebecca , Fox, Geo, Mary Magdalene , 20 Aug 1818, -, -, -, Eleanor , Murphy, -, -, -, Stoss, 18

18, 07 Mar 1819, Louisa Ann, Butler, James, Lucy, 21 Jan 1819, -, FB, S, B, -, -, Peggy, Chase (slave), Lucy is a slave of Jno. Harry, Green, 18

19, 07 Mar 1819, Sarah, Justis, Andre, Mary* , 27 Dec 1818, -, -, -, Mary , Hines, -, -, *Mary [Martha crossed out] , Russel, 18

20, 07 Mar 1819, July Ann, Golsberry, Saml., Dianna , 22 Oct 1818, -, -, -, Ann Maria (Mrs.), McGee, Charles, Monahan, -, McCawley, 18

21, 20 May 1819, Basil, Carter, Jacob, Milly, 27 Sep 1818, -, S, S, John, Hensley, Sarah Ann, Wilson, "not as yet married Slaves to David Newcomber", Ronalds, 18

22, 23 May 1819, John, Hemsley, Paul, Mary , 25 Mar 1819, -, S, -, John , Hemsley, Ellen, Monahan, father is slave of Dr. Dausey, Smith, 18

23, 20 Jul 1819*, Mary Ann, O'Brien, Laurence, Mary, 01 Mar 1817, -, -, -, Thomas, Kerrney, Ann , Kearney, *20 [or 28] Jul 1819, Clougherty, 18

24, 20 Jul 1819, James, O'Brien, Laurence, Mary, 15 ___ 1819, -, -, -, -, John, Mangen, -, -, -, Clougherty, 18

25, 09 Aug 1819, Elizabeth, Purl, Charles, Nancy , 18 Jun 1810, -, -, -, Fr. , Redmond, -, -, live in Allegany Co.; BC; Both these mothers were married to Charles Purl, Grimes, 18

26, 09 Aug 1819, Charles, Purl, Charles, Nancy , 19 Oct 1811, -, -, -, Fr. , Redmond, -, -, live in Allegany Co.; BC; Both these mothers were married to Charles Purl, Grimes, 18

27, 09 Aug 1819, James Philip, Purl, Charles, Catharine Elizabeth , 31 Jan 1814, -, -, -, Fr. , Redmond, -, -, live in Allegany Co.; BC; Both these mothers were married to Charles Purl, Stindor [?], 18

ST. MARY'S CATHOLIC CHURCH
HAGERSTOWN, MARYLAND, BAPTISMS:
Index, Bap Date, Child, Last Name, Father, Mother,
Birth Date, Code1, Code2, Code3,
1st Sponsor First, 1st Sponsor Last,
2nd Sponsor First, 2nd Sponsor Last, Location,
Notes, Maiden Name, Priest

28, 09 Aug 1819, Thomas, Purl, Charles , Catharine Elizabeth , 15 Dec 1812, -, -, -, Fr., Redmond, -, -, live in Allegany Co.; BC; Both these mothers were married to Charles Purl, Stindor [?], 18

29, 06 Apr 1820 , Henry, Mouse, Philip, Catharine, 20 years, PN, -, -, Thomas, Mains, Jane, Mouse, -, Sackenhour, 18

30, 06 Apr 1820, Philip Compton, Mouse, Philip, Catharine , 34 months, PN, -, -, Thomas, Mains, Jane, Mouse, -, Sackenhour, 18

31, 06 Apr 1820, John Andrew, Quigly, Moses A., Margaret, 7 weeks, -, -, -, Alexander , Moor, Lucy, Corbet, -, Bevens , 18

32, 06 Apr 1820, John, Bevens, Leonard, Ann , 10 weeks , -, -, -, James , Hoey, Mary, Mahony, -, -, 18

33, 06 Apr 1820, Joseph, -, Philip, Darcas , 7 weeks , PN, S, S, Philip , Mains, Isabella, Corbet, Slaves to Messieurs Mains, -, 18

34, 10 Jun 1819, John, Rockhole, John, Elizabeth, 25 Apr 1820, -, -, -, Thos , Mains, Lucy, Corbet, -, Stuart, 18

35, 20 Jun 1819, Alexander, Chesley, Oliver, Clary , 22 Mar 1818, S, PN, S, S, Dolly , Wharton, -, -, The priest recorded "easter Monday" for the birthdate - research shows that date to be March 22nd in 1818., -, 18

36, 20 Jun 1819, Elizabeth, Wharton, Joe, Dolly , 26 Mar 1820, S, PN, S, S, Sarah Ann , Wilson, -, -, -, Shorter, 18

37, 20 Jun 1819, Louisa, Gates, Michael, Betsy , 18 months , PN, -, -, Oliver , Chisley, -, -, -, Allen, 18

38, 20 Jun 1819, Mary, Bevans , Edward, Betsy , 6 years , PN, -, -, Oliver , Chisley, -, -, -, Allen, 18

39, 20 Jun 1819, Henrietta, Stopps [?], Peter, Mary Ellen , 01 Apr 1819, PN, -, -, Eleanor , Monahan, -, -, -, -, 18

40, 20 Jun 1819, Elizabeth, Miller, Tobias, Elizabeth , 12 Mar 1819, PN, -, -, Elizabeth , Walsh, -, -, -, Macginty , 18

41, 07 Aug 1819, Edward Charles, Sengstack, Henry, Eliza Mary, 29 Jul 1819, -, -, -, James (Rev.), Redmond, Francis (Mrs.), Milton, this baptism was entered into the Marriages section of the record book, Dyer, 18

42, 19 Sep 1819, Andrew, Maher, Patk., Christina, 27 Sep 1818, -, -, -, Wm , Walsh, Elizabeth, Walhs, -, Mashuk, 18

43, 19 Sep 1819, David, -, Basil, Hanna, 16 Aug 1819, -, S, S, Mary , Monahan, -, -, Slaves to Thos. McArdele, -, 18

ST. MARY'S CATHOLIC CHURCH
HAGERSTOWN, MARYLAND, BAPTISMS:
Index, Bap Date, Child, Last Name, Father, Mother,
Birth Date, Code1, Code2, Code3,
1st Sponsor First, 1st Sponsor Last,
2nd Sponsor First, 2nd Sponsor Last, Location,
Notes, Maiden Name, Priest

44, 19 Sep 1819, James, Simmon*, Jacob, Elizabeth, 19 Jul 1820**, -, -, -, Ann, Bauls, -, -, *name ran into edge of page and priest ran out of room - might be an "s" on the end; See Endnote 14., Drury, 18

45, 19 Sep 1819, Judith, Chase, Henry, Cloi, 4 weeks, -, S, S, Harriet, Shorter, -, -, mother is slave to Wm. McCurdy; father is slave to Captn Lewis, Thomas, 18

46, 19 Sep 1819, Joseph, Galloway, Samuel, Judith, eight years, PN, S, S, -, -, -, -, BC;, Hemsley, 18

47, 19 Sep 1819, Catharine, Hall, Thomas, Terresa, Oct 1818, PN, S, -, Margaret, Chase, -, -, "born about the middle of Oct 1818"; mother is a slave to Stull tavern Keeper, Lucas, 18

48, 19 Oct 1819, Mary Ann, Gile, George, Hanna, 22 May 1819, -, -, -, John, Henry, Frances (Mrs.), Melton [Moltone crossed out], original signatures of witnesses in this entry, Jackson, 18

49, 19 Mar 1820, Helena, Hammond, Wm., Eleanor, 14 Jun 1819, PN, -, -, Ann, Bowls, -, -, -, Friends, 18

50, 13 Jun 1819, John, Roarke, Daniel, Elizabeth, 19 May 1819, -, -, -, Patrick, Redmond, Jane, Bevens, -, Garlock, 18

51, 14 Jun 1819, Mary Ann, Sinon, Henry, Honora, 24 May 1819, PN, -, -, John, Boyse, Mary, Dolan, -, Reidy, 18

52, 15 Mar 1819, Michael James, Kearney, Martin, Anne, 15 Mar 1819, PN, -, -, Wm., Harris, Eleanor, Bevens, -, Begs, 18

53, 1820, Philip, McClosky, Charles, Catharine [Anna crossed out], 15 Jan 1820, PN, -, -, Bernard, Devin, Gracey, Dougherty, -, Dougherty, 18

54, 18 Jun 1819, Margaret, McCarthy, Jerome, Margaret, few months, -, -, -, Thomas, Mains, Catharine, Davis, -, -, 18

55, 18 Jun 1819, Margaret, McCarthy, -, -, -, -, -, -, -, -, -, -, she is "reputed wife of Jerome McCarthy", -, 18

56, 18 Jun 1819, Eleanor, Bevens, Thomas, Ann, a few months, -, -, -, Leonard, Bevens, Ann, Reddy, -, Parsons, 18

57, 18 Jun 1819, Richard, -, -, -, -, S, -, -, Philip, Mains, Jane, Corbe, Slave of Mr. Mains, -, 18

58, 18 Jun 1819, Eliza Ann, -, -, -, -, S, -, -, Philip, Mains, Jane, Corbe, Slave of Mr. Mains, -, 18

ST. MARY'S CATHOLIC CHURCH
HAGERSTOWN, MARYLAND, BAPTISMS:
Index, Bap Date, Child, Last Name, Father, Mother,
Birth Date, Code1, Code2, Code3,
1st Sponsor First, 1st Sponsor Last,
2nd Sponsor First, 2nd Sponsor Last, Location,
Notes, Maiden Name, Priest

59, 18 Jun 1819, Jane, -, -, -, -, B, -, -, P., Mains, Margt., Quegh*, she is described as "Jane of Free Bl[ac]k People"; *See Endnote 15., -, 18

60, 21 May 1820, Harriet, Brown, Isaac, Phebe, four weeks, -, B, B, Sarah Ann [?], Wilson, -, -, "belongin [sic] to the estate of Mr. Drury deceased" , Bryan, 18

61, 21 May 1820, Elizabeth, Shirley, Joseph, Elizabeth, 22 Jan 1820, -, -, -, Catharine (Mrs.), Justis, -, -, -, Bartol, 18

62, 21 May 1820, Ann Christianna, Hussong, John, Elizabeth, 30 May 1819, -, -, -, George , Hussong, Christianna , Hussong [HB], -, Robinson, 18

63, 21 May 1820, John, Smyth, Edwd., Elizb, 20 Apr 1820, -, -, -, Dennis , Kerney, Jane, Toland, -, Power, 18

64, 24 May 1820, Benjamin, Maloon, Wm, Catharine , 24 Mar 1820, -, -, -, Elizb (Mrs.), Greenwell, John, McClain, -, Bowers, 18

65, 25 May 1820, Lucretia, McClain, John, Elizab, 05 Apr 1820, -, -, -, James , McClain, James (Mrs.), McClain, -, Core, 18

66, 25 May 1820, William, Jackson, John, Elizab , 07 Feb 1820, -, -, -, Maria , McClain, -, -, -, McClain, 18

67, 25 May 1820, Michael, Tailor, Nathaniel, Terry , 25 Feb 1820, -, S, S, Elizab* , Jackson, -, -, parents are married and slaves of John McClain; *[Martha McClain crossed out] , -, 18

68, 25 May 1820, Benjamin, Tarry, Hanna , Martha , 10 Mar 1820, -, S, -, -, -, -, -, -, McClain, 18

69, 25 May 1820, Phobe, Taylor, Jordan , Terry, 01 Jul 1819, -, S, -, -, -, -, -, -, -, 18

70, 07 Apr 1820, Jane, Connolly, James, Rose , 13 Mar 1820, -, -, -, James , Logan, Margaret, Logan, parents are married , -, 18

71, 12 Apr 1820, James, Crosby, Mathew, Mary, 12 Feb 1820, -, -, -, Patrick , Lynch, Jane, Lynch, -, Flood, 18

72, 27 Apr 1820, Henry, Compton, -, -, 21 years, -, -, -, -, -, -, -, Baptised at the House of the Misters Mains on Thursday after Easter 1820, -, 18

73, 18 Jun 1820, Michael, Jones, Abram, Mary , 9 weeks, -, -, S, Maria , Haris, -, -, mother is slave to Mr. Wise of Hagerstown, Harriss , 18

ST. MARY'S CATHOLIC CHURCH
HAGERSTOWN, MARYLAND, BAPTISMS:
Index, Bap Date, Child, Last Name, Father, Mother,
Birth Date, Code1, Code2, Code3,
1st Sponsor First, 1st Sponsor Last,
2nd Sponsor First, 2nd Sponsor Last, Location,
Notes, Maiden Name, Priest

74, 25 Jun 1820 , Philip, Money, Thos., Elizabeth, 28 years, -, -, -, James, Adams, -, -, -, Jones, 18

75, 25 Jun 1820, Helena, Adams, James, Margaret, 04 May 1820, -, -, -, Michael , Smith, Mary (Mrs.), Lover, -, Smith, 18

76, 25 Jun 1820, Henry, Pile, Naas, Catharine, 11years, B, PN, S, -, -, Hanna, -, -, -, slave to David Clegit, Hawkins, 18

77, 25 Jun 1820, Jenny, Pile, Naas, Catharine, 10 years, B, PN, S, -, -, Elizabeth, Shorter, -, -, slave to David Clegit, Hawkins, 18

78, 25 Jun 1820, James, Pile, Naas, Catharine, 8 years, B, PN, S, -, -, Harriet, Shorter, -, -, slave to David Clegit, Hawkins, 18

79, 25 Jun 1820, Jesse, Shorter, Jesse, Catharine, 2 1/2 years, B, PN, S, -, -, Mary, Homsley, -, -, slave to David Clegit, Hawkins, 18

80, 25 Jun 1820, Mary Ann, Shorter, Jesse, Catharine, 11 months, B, PN, S, -, -, Winny, Brown, -, -, slave to David Clegit, Hawkins, 18

81, 07 Aug 1820, Edward Charles, Sengstack, Henry, Eliza Mary, 29 Jul 1820, -, -, -, Revd James , Redmond, Francis (Mrs.), Milton, -, Dyer, 18

82, 20 Nov 1819, Elizabeth Ann, Ray, Joseph, Ann, 01 Jul 1816, -, -, -, Leonard , Drury, Susanna, Murry, -, Drury, 18

83, 20 Nov 1819, William, Ray, Joseph, Ann, 20 Sep 1818, -, -, -, Leonard , Bevens, Jane, Corbit, -, Drury, 18

84, 15 Nov 1818, Thomas, McAtee, Walter, Mary , 14 Jul 1817, -, -, -, blank, -, -, -, -, Morrow, 18

85, 20 Aug 1820, Henry Peter, Ward, Aquila, Mary , 7 weeks , PN, -, -, Philip , Mains, Mary, Mahoney, -, Davis , 18

86, 13 Aug 1820, George Thomas, Hawken, Wm, Catharine , 7 weeks , PN, -, -, Thos, McArdell, Thos (Mrs.), McArdell, -, Stake, 18

87, 13 Aug 1820, Lucy, -, Henny, Elizabeth , 11 months, B, PN, S, S, -, -, -, -, parents are slaves of Mr. Shingle, Shorter, 18

88, 27 Aug 1820, William, Ryan, James, Margaret, 7 weeks , PN, -, -, Wm, Durnin, Honora, McQuade, Shepherdstown, McAnulty , 18

89, 10 Jul 1820, John, Turney, John, Mary, 14-Jun, -, -, -, Jno , Broghal, Mrs., Lamasney, -, Doolan, 18

ST. MARY'S CATHOLIC CHURCH
HAGERSTOWN, MARYLAND, BAPTISMS:
Index, Bap Date, Child, Last Name, Father, Mother,
Birth Date, Code1, Code2, Code3,
1st Sponsor First, 1st Sponsor Last,
2nd Sponsor First, 2nd Sponsor Last, Location,
Notes, Maiden Name, Priest

90, 10 Jul 1820, Eleanor, Lamasney, Garratt, Bridget , 1-Jun, PN, - , -, Robert , Grady, Mrs., Tierney, -, Fitzgerald, 18

91, 12 Jul 1820, Rosanna, Gallagher, Wm, Martha , 1-May, -, -, -, James , Connor, Mary, Crosby, -, Carragan, 18

92, 17 Jul 1820, Thomas, Butler, Sandy, Mary , 1-Jun, PN, -, -, James , Drumgold, Frances C., Lane, -, McGamley , 18

93, 10 Sep 1820, Ignatius Joseph Wm, Little, David, Eliza, 4-Aug, -, -, -, Charles T. , Monahan, Frances, Milton, -, Hardgrove, 18

94, 10 Sep 1820, William, Moher, Patrick, Christianna, 10 Jul 1820, -, -, -, Thos , McLoughlin, Mrs., McCardell, -, Shoup, 18

95, 29 Nov 1820, Wm, Thomson, Elias, Ann , 07 May 1817, PN, -, -, George , Gale, Junior, Polly, McAtee, -, McAtee , 18

96, 29 Nov 1820, Bennet, Thomson, Elias, Ann, 07 Jul 1819, PN, - , -, Waltr. , McAtee, Mrs., Gale, -, McAtee , 18

97, 10 Dec 1820, Michael, Pine, Wm, Ann, 10 weeks, -, -, -, James , Drumgould, Ann, Timmonds, -, Cutshaw, 18

98, 07 Oct 1820, Elizabeth Ann, Freshoure, Matthias , Eleanor, 04 Mar 1820, PN, -, -, William, Burk, William (Mrs.), Burk [HB], -, Burk, 18

99, 22 Oct 1820, Mary, Donnelly, Patrick, Margaret, 1 Oct 1820, PN, -, -, William , Condon, *, -, *sponsors are "William Condon & his lady", O'Neale, 18

100, 22 Oct 1820, Catharine, Miller, Tobias, Elizabeth, 21 Aug 1820, PN, -, -, William , Condon, *, -, *sponsors are "William Condon & his lady", McGinty, 18

101, 22 Oct 1820, Wm Henry, Ridout, Wm, Sarah, 11 months , PN, S, S, Mary , Holland, -, -, -, Butler, 18

102, 22 Oct 1820, Rachel, Ridout, Wm, Sarah, 4 years 3 months, PN, S, S, Cloe, Chase, -, -, -, Butler, 18

103, 22 Oct 1820, Ann Carlisle, Ridout, Wm, Sarah, 6 years 3 months, PN, S, S, Sarah, Galloway, -, -, -, Butler, 18

104, 11 Nov 1820, Ambrose, -, Jesse, Lucy, 4 years, -, S, S, Salley, Lee, -, -, "at the residence of John T. Mason Washington County Md"; slaves to Mr. J.T. Mason, -, 18

105, 11 Nov 1820, Hanna, -, Jesse, Lucy, 4 months , -, S, S, Mary , Johnson, -, -, "at the residence of John T. Mason Washington County Md"; slaves to Mr. J.T. Mason, -, 18

ST. MARY'S CATHOLIC CHURCH
HAGERSTOWN, MARYLAND, BAPTISMS:
Index, Bap Date, Child, Last Name, Father, Mother,
Birth Date, Code1, Code2, Code3,
1st Sponsor First, 1st Sponsor Last,
2nd Sponsor First, 2nd Sponsor Last, Location,
Notes, Maiden Name, Priest

106, 11 Nov 1820, Rachel, -, Ralph, Celia, 5 months , -, S, S, Mary , Johnson, -, -, "at the residence of John T. Mason Washington County Md"; slaves to Mr. J.T. Mason, -, 18

107, 11 Nov 1820, Otho James, Boyd, William, Margaret , 5 months , -, -, -, James (Rev.), Redmond, -, -, -, McCumssy , 18

108, 31 Dec 1820, Alice, Curnin, Murtough, Libby , 23 Dec 1820, -, -, -, Mary (Mrs.), McAnulty, -, -, -, Keany , 18

109, 04 Jan 1821, Ultan, McCardell, Thomas, Anna , 17 Dec 1820, -, -, -, Jas. (Rev.), Redmond, Lucretia, McCardell, -, Nagle, 18

110, 13 Jan 1821, James, Metzs, Henry, Mary , 29 May 1820, -, -, - , Dennis, McGafferty, Maria, Greenwell, -, Kingan , 18

111, 13 Jan 1821, James Joseph, McGafferty, Dennis, Margaret, 27 Nov 1820, -, -, -, James, McClain, Eleanor (Mrs.), Stake, -, Dougherty , 18

112, 28 Jan 1821, Ultan, McClain, James, Margaret, 09 Dec 1820, -, -, -, Eli, Stake, Ellen, Stake [HB], -, Brown, 18

113, 11 Feb 1821, Charles, -, Jesse, Peggy, 4 months , -, S, S, Cloe "of John Harry", -, -, -, parents are married slaves of the Widow Rench, -, 18

114, 01 Apr 1821, Henrietta, Johnson, Thomas, Mary, 14 May 1820, -, -, -, Edwd, McCartin, Ellen, Hughes *, *"Elizab Marshall" crossed out, McGeeher [?] , 18

115, 01 Apr 1821, Catharine, Kenny, John, Mary, 04 Jan 1820, -, -, -, William, Condon, William (Mrs.), Condon [HB], -, Myers, 18

116, 22 Oct 1821, Augustus, Carter, Jacob, Milly, 22 Oct 1820, -, S, S, Dolly, Wharton, -, -, Slaves to Dr. Newcomber, Rollins, 18

117, 23 Apr 1821, Hester, Lucket, John, Eliza , 6 months, -, S, S, Elizab., Marshall, -, -, father is slave of Col. McPherson; mother is slave of Joseph Shirley, Shorter, 18

118, 23 Apr 1821, Judith, Abbenton, Danl , Hanna, 05 Mar 1821, -, S, S, Elizabeth, Shorter, -, -, parents are slaves of Thos. McCardell, Taylor, 18

119, 29 Apr 1821, Susanna, Joy, John, Eleanor, 8 Dec 1820, -, -, -, Sarah B. , Lynch, -, -, -, Armsey, 18

120, 23 Apr 1821, Mary Ann, Kain, Ishman, Susanna, 7 months, -, B, B, Sarah , Galloway, -, -, -, Johnson, 18

ST. MARY'S CATHOLIC CHURCH
HAGERSTOWN, MARYLAND, BAPTISMS:
Index, Bap Date, Child, Last Name, Father, Mother,
Birth Date, Code1, Code2, Code3,
1st Sponsor First, 1st Sponsor Last,
2nd Sponsor First, 2nd Sponsor Last, Location,
Notes, Maiden Name, Priest

121, 11 May 1821, Susanna, Blacken, Joseph, Clarissa , 25 Nov 1820, -, -, -, Henry , Black, Cath, Howard, -, Paw [?], 18

122, 26 May 1821, Peter, O'Farrell, John, Alice , 24 Oct 1820, -, -, -, Margaret , Shirkey, -, -, -, McKearnan, 18

123, 26 May 1821, Mary Ann, Murray, Rd., Ann, 23 Mar 1821, -, -, -, John , Brady, Mary, Parsons, -, Ross, 18

124, 06 Jun 1821, Geo Alexander, Smith, Esau, Henny, 7 weeks , FB, -, -, J. , Redmond, -, -, -, Coleman, 18

125, 09 Jun 1821, Jacob, Mouse, Peter, Jane, 20 Dec 1820, -, -, -, Geo , Redmond, Lucy, Corbet, -, Corbet, 18

126, 09 Jun 1821, Joseph, Trueman, John, Sarah , 24 Jan 1821, -, -, -, Thomas , Mains, Susanna, Murray, -, Bevens, 18

127, 09 Jun 1821, William Peter, Graham, William, Anne , 07 Mar 1814, -, -, -, Philip , Mains, Sarah, Brannan, -, Duggan, 18

128, 09 Jun 1821, John, Paten, Chambers, Mary , 04 Jul 1817, -, -, -, Sarah , Brannan, -, -, -, Brannan, 18

129, 09 Jun 1821, Louisa, Paten, Chambers, Mary , 23 Dec 1818, -, -, -, Sarah , Brannan, -, -, -, Brannan, 18

130, 09 Jun 1821, Rosanna, Paten, Chambers, Mary , 29 Nov 1820, -, -, -, Sarah, Brannan, -, -, -, Brannan, 18

131, 09 Jun 1821, Mary, McCarty, Alexr, Catharine , 29 Nov 1820, -, -, -, John , Clark, Mary, Paten, -, Weller, 18

132, 09 Jun 1821, Catharine, McCarty, Alexr, Catharine , Apr 1807, -, -, -, John , Clark, Mary, Paten, -, Weller, 18

133, 10 Jun 1821, Basil, Bevens, Barnabas, Elizab , *, -, -, -, -, -, -, -, *birthdate could read "6 1/2 months" , Hull, 18

134, 11 Jun 1821, Rosanna, Volgomet, John, Juliann , 6 weeks , -, -, -, Mary Magdalene , Fox, -, -, -, Abel, 18

135, 11 Jun 1821, Melinda Ann, Fox, Geo, Mary Magdalene , 05 Apr 1821, -, -, -, Frances , Milton, -, -, -, Stopps, 18

136, 11Jun 1821, Marymagdalene, Chase, Harry, Cloe , 6 weeks , -, B, B, Hanna , Abbenton, -, -, -, Thomas, 18

137, 13 Jun 1821, Patrick, Campbell, Pk, Catharine , 12 May 1821, -, -, -, Patrick , Heven [or Keven], Rosanna, McDermott, -, Mullen, 18

ST. MARY'S CATHOLIC CHURCH
HAGERSTOWN, MARYLAND, BAPTISMS:
Index, Bap Date, Child, Last Name, Father, Mother,
Birth Date, Code1, Code2, Code3,
1st Sponsor First, 1st Sponsor Last,
2nd Sponsor First, 2nd Sponsor Last, Location,
Notes, Maiden Name, Priest

138, 17 Jun 1821, James, Hemmensley, John, Mary , 08 Apr 1821, S, B, -, -, Mary, Holland, -, -, child is a slave to Doctor Dorsey, Smith, 18

139, 21 Jun 1821, Catharine, Fritz, Frederick, Margaret , 24 Apr 1821, -, -, -, Mrs. Frances , Milton, -, -, -, Bevens, 18

140, 24 Jun 1821, Richard , Waters, Jefrey, Maria , one year , B, -, -, Betsy , Gates, -, -, -, Joken [or Zoken], 18

141, 24 Jun 1821, Mary , Thomas, Barney, Alenda , ten years, B, S, S, Winny , Brown, -, -, parents are slaves to Mr. Wheeler, -, 18

142, 24 Jun 1821, Sarah, -, -, -, 37 years, B, -, -, Prud, Shipton, -, -, "baptised only", -, 18

143, 22 July 1821, Ann, -, Thomas, Alinda, 13 years, -, -, -, Nathaniel , Taylor, -, -, -, -, 18

144, 22 Jul 1821, William , -, Thomas, Alinda, 7 years, -, -, -, "a Coloured Man by name", -, -, -, BC, -, 18

145, 31 Jul 1821, John, Noose, John, Mary, 10 Nov 1820, -, -, -, Susanna , Murphy, Archibald, Ritchie, -, McKessick, 18

146, 07 Aug 1821, Frances Ann, McAleny, Michael, Mary, 01 Aug 1821, -, -, -, Thomas , McLoughlin, Prudentia , Shipton, -, Monahan, 36

147, 10 Aug 1821, Henry, Reid, John, Catharine , 3 months, -, -, -, John , Clark, Eleanor , Davis, -, Sackenhour, 18

148, 23 Aug 1821, Thomas Hierom, Stake, Elei, Alice E., 02 Jul 1821, -, -, -, Thomas , McArdell, Ann , McArdell, -, Monahan, 18

149, 27 Aug 1821, Charles, McClosker, Fargus, Rosanna, 15 Aug 1821, -, -, -, Edward , McAnulty, Margaret , Maheny, -, McDermott, 18

150, 11 Sep 1821, Evelina, Bevens, Thomas, Ann , 06 Sep 1821, -, -, -, Margaret , Bevens, -, -, -, Parsons , 17

151, 07 Oct 1821, Edward , Creek, George, Catharine, 7 weeks, B, -, -, Saml , Galloway, Nancy , Butler, -, Boothe , 18

152, 18 Oct 1821, John , Connolly, James, Rosanna , 11 Aug 1821, -, -, -, James , Connor, -, -, -, McAntere [?] , 18

153, 25 Oct 1821, Peter (twin), McMullen, Frances, Bridget , 10 Oct 1821, -, -, -, James , Redmond, -, -, -, Rice, 18

154, 25 Oct 1821, John (twin), McMullen, Frances, Bridget , 10 Oct 1821, -, -, -, James , Redmond, -, -, -, Rice, 18

ST. MARY'S CATHOLIC CHURCH
HAGERSTOWN, MARYLAND, BAPTISMS:
Index, Bap Date, Child, Last Name, Father, Mother,
Birth Date, Code1, Code2, Code3,
1st Sponsor First, 1st Sponsor Last,
2nd Sponsor First, 2nd Sponsor Last, Location,
Notes, Maiden Name, Priest

155, 04 Nov 1821, Catharine, Jack, John, Ann , 28 May 1821, -, -, -, Hierom , Stake, Eleanor, Willace, -, Duggan , 18

156, 18 Nov 1821, Elizabeth, Moore, Alexander, Elizabeth ., 19 Oct 1821, -, -, -, Philip , Mains, Susan, Murray, -, Bevins , 18

157, 20 Nov 1821, Philip, Garretty, Patrick, Nancy , 10 Nov 1821, PN, -, -, James , O'Donnell, Ann, Murray, -, Fox, 18

158, 16 Dec 1821, Eli , Myers, Stephen, Peggy, six months , B, PN, -, -, Nelly , Shilton, -, -, -, Fenwick, 18

159, 16 Dec 1821, George W., Harrison, Sam , Phebe, 1 yr. 5 mos., B, PN, B, B, Nelly , Shilton, -, -, -, Taylor, 18

160, 16 Dec 1821, Terry, Harrison, Sam, Phebe, 3 months, PN, -, -, Terry, Taylor, -, -, -, Taylor, 18

161, 07 Jan 1822, Henry, Donnely, Patrick, Margaret, 01 Jan 1822, PN, -, -, Patrick , McKern, Rosanna, McKosker, -, O'Nealle , 18

162, 13 Jan 1822, Rachel, Logue, William, Martha , 03 May 1821, PN, -, -, James , McGunnigle, Macilla, McGunnigle, -, Brislan , 18

163, 03 Mar 1822, Thomas H., Johnson, Thomas, Elizabeth , 05 Jan 1822, PN, -, -, Richard , McCardell, Elizabeth, Marshall, -, McGeehee, 18

164, 07 Mar 1822, John, O'Donnell, Jno, Susanna , 25 Feb 1822, PN, -, -, Jno , Duffy, Mary, Toland, -, Toland , 18

165, 23 Mar 1822, Rebecca , -, Jesse, Lucy, Six weeks , S, PN, S, S, Arnold , -, -, -, all slaves to John T. Mason, -, 18

166, 24 Mar 1822, William, Tenley, Dennis, Nancy, 13 Sep 1815, PN, -, -, Thos , Mains, Cath, Davis, -, Burk , 18

167, 24 Mar 1822, Mary Ann, Smith, Michael, Catharine , 25-Feb, -, -, -, Philip , Main, Susanna, Murray, -, Mains, 18

168, 27 Mar 1822, Ann Eliza, Gibson, Henry , Philis , 21 Mar 1822, PN, S, S, Cath. (Mrs.), Goulding, John, Brady, -, Sewel , 18

169, 27 Mar 1822, Margaret, Karr, John, Hanna , 07 Oct 1821, PN, -, -, Jas , O'Connor, Susanna, Brady, -, Good , 18

170, 28 Mar 1822, Mary, Taylor, -, Phebe, 4 years, PN, S, -, -, -, -, -, mother is slave to Sophia Smith, -, 18

171, 08 Apr 1822, Catharine, Mulryan, James, Margaret, 08 Apr 1822, -, -, -, Margaret , Donnelly, -, -, -, McAnulty, 18

172, 14 Apr 1822, Lucy , McClain, Peter (of John), Henny , 13 Dec 1821, B, PN, -, -, Terry , Taylor, -, -, -, -, 18

ST. MARY'S CATHOLIC CHURCH
HAGERSTOWN, MARYLAND, BAPTISMS:
Index, Bap Date, Child, Last Name, Father, Mother,
Birth Date, Code1, Code2, Code3,
1st Sponsor First, 1st Sponsor Last,
2nd Sponsor First, 2nd Sponsor Last, Location,
Notes, Maiden Name, Priest

173, 14 Apr 1822, Ignatius , -, Naas, Sally, 30 June 1821, B, S, S, S, Celia, -, -, -, all are slaves to J.T. Mason, Lee , 18

174, 14 Apr 1822, Jacob, Painter, Jacob, Mary , 14 Sep 1821, PN, -, -, James (Mrs.), McClain, -, -, -, Abell , 18

175, 23 Apr 1822, Joseph, Shirley, Joseph, Elizabeth, 21 Mar 1822, PN, -, -, Anna , Condon, -, -, -, Bartell , 18

176, 25 Apr 1822, Jerome, Brown, Isaac, Phebe , 11 Feb 1822, B, S, PN, B, S, B, S, Henny, Jordan, -, -, Family and sponsor are Black & Slaves to Mrs. Drury, Bryan , 18

177, 26 Apr 1822, Maria , McLoughlin, Thos, Peggy, 16 Jul 1821, PN, -, -, Mrs. (widow), Smith, -, -, -, Sands, 18

178, 27 Apr 1822, Catharine , Butler, Leonard, Charity, 6 months, B, PN, S, S, Philis , Gibson, -, -, -, Campbell , 18

179, 28 Apr 1822, Eliza, Rockhole, John, Elizab, 03 Apr 1822, PN, -, -, Thos , Mains, Eleanor, Davis, -, Stewart , 18

180, 05 May 1822, Mary Ann, Stopps, Peter, Mary, 04 Dec 1821, PN, -, -, Mrs. , Fox, -, -, -, Eller , 18

181, 09 Jun 1822, Abraham, Johnston, Jack, Mary , 18 months, S, PN, S, S, Basil, Lile, Dianna, Lile, Family and sponsors are slaves to John T. Mason, Knight , 18

182, 02 Oct 1822, Michael, Reel, Joseph, Elizabeth , 06 Mar 1798, PN, -, -, -, -, -, -, -, Newcummer, 18

183, 02 Oct 1822, Daniel, Reel, Joseph, Elizabeth , 07 Jan 1805, PN, -, -, -, -, -, -, -, Newcummer, 18

184, 02 Oct 1822, Barbara, Reel, Joseph, Elizabeth , 24 Mar 1808, PN, -, -, -, -, -, -, -, Newcummer, 18

185, Fall 1821, Elizabeth, Newcummer, -, -, 4 Oct 1767, -, -, -, -, -, -, -, "Also Baptised in the fall of 1821 the mother of the above three Children." , -, 18

186, 13 Oct 1822, Susanna Cassandra, Tarton, Edmond , Teresa , 07 Feb 1822, -, -, -, Ann, Bouls, -, -, -, Bean, 18

187, 27 Oct 1822, Lucretea Elizabeth, Shorter, Charles , Hurriet , 12 Aug 1822, S, S, S, Mary, Holland, -, -, Family and sponsors are slaves to Thomas McCardell, Lucket, 18

188, 02 Nov 1822, Henry, O'Forbes , Edward, Catherine , 10 Nov 1821, -, -, -, John, Smidy, Margaret, Donnelly, -, -, 17

ST. MARY'S CATHOLIC CHURCH
HAGERSTOWN, MARYLAND, BAPTISMS:
Index, Bap Date, Child, Last Name, Father, Mother,
Birth Date, Code1, Code2, Code3,
1st Sponsor First, 1st Sponsor Last,
2nd Sponsor First, 2nd Sponsor Last, Location,
Notes, Maiden Name, Priest

189, 03 Nov 1822, Wilfred, Hawkins, William, Catherine, 26 Jul 1822, -, -, -, Mary, Lawber, -, -, -, -, 17

190, 20 Dec 1822, Sarah Anna, McClane, James, Margret, 02 Dec 1822, -, -, -, Anna, McClane, -, -, -, -, 17

191, 20 Dec 1822, Milly Anna, Drury, T. [or F.], Mary , 25 Sep 1822, -, -, -, -, -, -, -, -, McClane, 17

192, 20 Dec 1822, Sofia, -, -, -, 20 Nov 1822, -, -, -, -, -, -, -, -, -, 17

193, 25 Dec 1822, Elisabeth, Maher, Patrick , Christina, 28 Sep 1822, -, -, -, Patrick , O'Donnelly, Margaret, O'Donnelly [HB], -, -, 17

194, 31 Dec 1822, Elisabeth Naoma, Doile, Adam*, Rebecca, 26 Dec 1822, -, -, -, Mrs., Fox, -, -, *Adam & [Joab crossed out] , -, 17

195, 04 Jan 1823, James, Armstrong, -, -, 24 years, -, -, -, -, -, -, -, -, -, 17

196, 26 Jan 1823, Teresa, Ourey [?], Peter, Mary, 08 Jan 1823, -, -, -, Aree [?], Laly [?], -, -, -, -, 17

197, 26 Jan 1823, Jacob*, Boranar [?], Jacob , Anastasia, 02 Jan 1823, -, -, -, Teresa, Stump, -, -, *[Joseph crossed out] Jacob, -, 17

198, 22 Feb 1823, John, Miller, Tobias , Elisabeth, 02 Dec 1822, -, -, -, Mrs., McGusker, -, -, -, -, 17

199, 16 Mar 1823, John Francis, McCafferty, [blank], [blank], 25 Nov 1822, -, -, -, Magy [?], McGonnagal, Trms [?], McGonnagal , -, -, 17

200, 26 Apr 1823, Jacob, Hammon, Wilson , Elender [?], 29 Jan 1822, -, -, -, Susan [or Anna] (Miss), Boles, -, -, -, -, 17

201, 28 Apr 1823, Mary Elisa, McIlheny, Micl., Mary, 3-Apr, -, -, -, -, -, -, -, -, -, 17

202, 24 May 1823, Charles, Cammel, Patrick, Catherine, 14 May 1823, -, -, -, Mrs., Carney, James, Dignen, -, -, 17

203, 24 May 1823, Mary, Collagan, James, Catherine, 03 Apr 1823, -, -, -, Mrs., Mason, -, -, -, -, 17

204, 24 May 1823, Joseph, Warthen [?], Joseph, Dolley, 03 Dec 1819, -, -, -, Elisa, Shorter, -, -, -, -, 17

205, 25 May 1823, Charles, Rider, Wel[?] , Sarah, 10 Jan 1823, -, -, -, Nancy, Butler, -, -, -, -, 17

ST. MARY'S CATHOLIC CHURCH
HAGERSTOWN, MARYLAND, BAPTISMS:
Index, Bap Date, Child, Last Name, Father, Mother,
Birth Date, Code1, Code2, Code3,
1st Sponsor First, 1st Sponsor Last,
2nd Sponsor First, 2nd Sponsor Last, Location,
Notes, Maiden Name, Priest

206, 24 May 1823, Ellon, Waters, Jeffrey , Mary, 15 Aug 1823, -, - , -, Mary, Lover, -, -, -, -, 17

207, 25 May 1823, Henrieetta, Bey [?], Henry , Catherine, 01 Jan 1822, -, -, -, Hanna, Appleton, -, -, -, -, 17

208, 24 May 1823, Prisilla, Roser, Garrott[?] , Mary, 01 Sep 1822, -, -, -, Winfred, Brower [?], -, -, -, -, 17

209, 25 May 1823, Rebecca, Abbenton, Basil, Hanna, 27-Apr, -, -, -, Lucreatia, Belordol [?], -, -, -, -, 17

210, 27 May 1823, William, Duffy [?], John , Mary, 13 May 1823, -, -, -, Mrs., Milton, -, -, -, -, 17

211, 22 Jun 1823, John, Bieser [?], Joseph, Mitelda, 15 Mar 1820, -, -, -, Evy, Laby, Antony , Stump, -, -, 17

212, 26 Jun 1823, Mary Anna, Fitzpatrick, Edward, Juliana, 28 May 1823, -, -, -, Mrs., Milton, -, -, -, -, 17

213, 24 Aug 1823, Elisa Anne, Mong, Jacob, Anne, 13 Mar 1823, -, -, -, Mary Anne (Miss), O'Boyle, -, -, -, -, 17

214, 24 Aug 1823, Elonar, Boarman, Ralph, Cecela, 21 Jun 1823, -, -, -, Mary, Jonson, Basil , [blank], -, -, 17

215, 24 Aug 1823, James, Monsil, Philip, Mary, 17-Nov, -, -, -, Mary (Mrs.), Doherty, -, -, -, -, 17

216, 24 Aug 1823, Wilm , Monsil, Philip, Mary, 20 Sep 1819, -, -, -, -, -, -, -, -, -, 17

217, 26 Aug 1823, George, Stump, Antony, Teresa, 25 Aug*, -, -, - , Gorge, Hasan, Mary, Hyenes, *birthdate is [26 crossed out] 25 Aug, -, 17

218, 22 Aug 1823, Phile , McGloughlen, Willm, Catherine, 21-Jun, -, -, -, T., Ryan, -, -, -, -, 17

219, 22 Aug 1823, Henry, McGloughlen, Willm, Catherine, 08 Jul 1823, -, -, -, Mary, McGloughlen, -, -, -, -, 17

220, 22 Aug 1823, Wilm, Monsey, Phillip, Mary, __ __ 1820, -, -, -, Cornls, Brosy [?], -, -, -, -, 17

221, 22 Aug 1823, James, Monsy, Philip, Mary, __ __ 1822, -, -, - , -, -, -, -, -, -, 17

222, 22 Aug 1823, John, Halbert, Archoobald, Catherine, __ __ 1821, -, -, -, Margret, McCloughlen, -, -, -, -, 17

223, 22 Aug 1823, Margret, Habbert, Archl., Catherine, 10 Aug 1823, -, -, -, Timothy, Ryan, -, -, -, -, 17

ST. MARY'S CATHOLIC CHURCH
HAGERSTOWN, MARYLAND, BAPTISMS:
Index, Bap Date, Child, Last Name, Father, Mother,
Birth Date, Code1, Code2, Code3,
1st Sponsor First, 1st Sponsor Last,
2nd Sponsor First, 2nd Sponsor Last, Location,
Notes, Maiden Name, Priest

224, 31 Aug 1823, Barnar[?], Rosier, -, -, 38 years , -, -, -, -, -, -, -, -, -, 17

225, [blank], Sarah, -, -, -, 15 years , S, -, -, -, -, -, -, "The two belong to Genl Ringgold.", -, 17

226, 30 Aug 1823, James, Caffry, James, Mary, 28-Aug, -, -, -, Robert, Lonny, Mrs., [blank], -, -, 17

227, 02 Sep 1823, Wilm, Hemsley, Jjohn, Mary, 30-Jul, -, -, -, Sarah, Galloy, -, -, -, -, 17

228, 29 Sep 1823, Catherine, Boden, James, Susana, 26-Sep, -, -, -, John, Burns, Mary, Donnelly, -, -, 17

229, 02 Oct 1823, Margret, Donnelly, Patrick, Margret, 30-Sep, -, -, -, Corneleus, Bradly, Mrs., McGlouglen, -, -, 17

230, 26 Oct 1823, Wilm, Bradly, Jacob, Milley, 14 Jun 1823, -, -, -, Monica Anna, [no last name], -, -, -, -, 17

231, 24 Oct 1823, Sofia, Benins, Bernard, Elisa, 01 Oct 1822, -, -, -, George, Redmond, Mrs., Bevins, -, -, 17

232, 30 Nov 1823, Peter, Henry[?], Peter, Henny, 03 Feb 1823, -, -, -, Lucy, [blank], -, -, -, -, 17

233, 02 Dec 1823, Wilm, Donnelly, Henry, Elon, 25-Nov, -, -, -, Arter, McTigert, Mrs., McDeomoth, -, -, 17

234, 21 Dec 1823, Mary, Creamer, Thomas, Mary, 9-Dec, -, -, -, Sarah (Miss), Donnelly, Hugh, McLee, -, -, 17

235, 09 Jan 1824, John, Mouse, Peter , Jane, 09 Nov 1823, -, -, -, Elonar (Miss), Davis, Patrick, Tojan, -, -, 17

236, 09 Jan 1824, Elisa, Trueman, John, Sarah, 15 Jul 1823, -, -, -, Mrs., Mouse, Thom, Meanes [?], -, -, 17

237, 09 Jan 1824, Elisa, Read [?], John, [blank], 29 Oct 1823, -, -, -, Mrs., Rockhold, George, Redmond, -, Secondhour, 17

238, 07 Jan 1824, Emilia Elisa, Murry, Richard, Nancy, 17 Dec 1823, -, -, -, Elisa, Murry, Owen, Tray, -, -, 17

239, 11 Jan 1824, John, Lee, Ignatius, Sarah, 09 Oct 1823, -, -, -, James, Thomas, Cicilia, Borman, -, -, 17

240, 19 Jan 1824, Mary, Donnelly, Henery, Mary, 14 Jan 1821, -, -, -, Mary, Donnelly, Timy., McClane, -, -, 17

241, 18 Jan 1824, Joseph Henery, Magee, Hugh, Mary, 14 Dec 1823, -, -, -, Mrs., Murphy, -, -, -, -, 17

ST. MARY'S CATHOLIC CHURCH
HAGERSTOWN, MARYLAND, BAPTISMS:
Index, Bap Date, Child, Last Name, Father, Mother,
Birth Date, Code1, Code2, Code3,
1st Sponsor First, 1st Sponsor Last,
2nd Sponsor First, 2nd Sponsor Last, Location,
Notes, Maiden Name, Priest

242, 27 Jan 1824, Elisa Magdallen, Velslager, Saml, Mary, 03 Jan 1824, -, -, -, Elisa, Walsh, -, -, -, -, 17

243, 08 Feb 1824, John Mills, Thomson, -, Mary, 08 Oct 1823, -, -, -, Thomas , McGarvey [?], -, -, -, -, 17

244, 09 Feb 1824, Mary Anna, McMullen, Francis, Bridget, 2-Feb, -, -, -, Maygor [?] N., Gonnegal, -, -, -, -, 17

245, 10 Feb 1824, Phillip Henery, Doherty, James, [blank], 05 Feb 1824, -, -, -, Mich M., Gloughlen, -, -, -, -, 17

246, 10 Feb 1824, Catherine, McGrath, James, Sarah, 05 Feb 1824, -, -, -, Hanah, Banner, Hugh, McGonnegal, -, -, 17

247, 21 Feb 1824*, John, Stake, Elia, Ellon, 23 Jan 1824, -, -, -, Elisa (Miss), Monahan, -, -, *21 [or24] Feb 1824, -, 17

248, 11 Mar 1824, Joseph Solomon, Rockhole, John, Elisa, 20-Jan, -, -, -, Elonora (Miss), Devis, Thomas, Mains, -, -, 17

249, 11 Mar 1824, George, Cole, Henry, Mary, 01 Sep 1823, -, -, -, Easter (Miss), Corney, -, -, -, -, 17

250, 17 May 1824, Arthur, McCallesten, Arahy?, Catharine, [blank], -, -, -, James, Leamey [?], -, -, -, -, 37

251, 30 Jun 1824, Joseph, Rosier, Jarret, Mary, 15 Apr 1821, -, -, -, Miss Lucreatia , McCardal, -, -, -, -, 17

252, 30 Jun 1824, Milly, Barber, Joseph, Lucy, 13 years, -, -, -, Catherine, Key, -, -, -, -, 17

253, 02 Jun 1824, Hanna , -, -, -, Convert, B, -, -, -, -, -, -, "an Old B.[Black] Lady", -, 17

254, 06 Jun 1824, Andrew, Brown, Isac, Feby, 27-Apr, -, -, -, Anna, Chester, -, -, -, -, 17

255, 06 Jun 1824, Wilm, Rideout, -, -, 28 years, B, -, -, -, -, -, -, C, -, 17

256, 06 Jun 1824, Francesa , Cole, -, -, 14 years, B, -, -, -, -, -, -, C, -, 17

257, 24 Jun 1822, Jacob, Painter, Jacob, Mary Anna, 24 Sep 1821, -, -, -, Mrs., McClane, -, -, -, -, 17

258, 09 Jun 1824, Rosana, Painter, Jacob, Mary Anna, 19 Apr 1824, -, -, -, Mrs., Walgamoth, -, -, -, -, 17

259, 21 Jun 1824, Mary Anna, O'Donnel, John, Susanna, 08 Mar 1824, -, -, -, Tany (Miss), Thomas, John, Tollen, -, -, 17

ST. MARY'S CATHOLIC CHURCH
HAGERSTOWN, MARYLAND, BAPTISMS:
Index, Bap Date, Child, Last Name, Father, Mother,
Birth Date, Code1, Code2, Code3,
1st Sponsor First, 1st Sponsor Last,
2nd Sponsor First, 2nd Sponsor Last, Location,
Notes, Maiden Name, Priest

260, 25 Jun 1824, Anna, Mundy, Patrick, M____, 17-Jun, -, -, -, Mrs., Colligan, Tho., McDermoth, -, -, 17

261, 11 Aug 1824, Thomas, Franklin, -, -, -, -, -, -, Michael, Feorde [?], Eliza, Abel, -, -, 37

262, 11 Aug 1824, Matilda, Forbis, -, -, -, -, -, -, James, McGonnegal, Mrs., McGonnagal, -, -, 17

263, 30 Aug 1824, Lucenda, McCann, Frances , Sarah, 12 Mar 1821, -, -, -, Hugh, McCann, -, -, -, -, 17

264, 30 Aug 1824, Jane, McCann, Francis, Sarah, 26 Jul 1820, -, -, -, Timy, Ryan, -, -, -, -, 17

265, 02 Sep 1824, Mary Hanna, McCann, Francis, Sarah, 1-Sep, -, -, -, Patrick, Donnelly, Catherine, Po [rest blank], -, -, 17

266, 08 Oct 1824, Winfred, Callahen, Michal , Mary, 28 Sep 1824*, -, -, -, P., Conlogue, Ellonora, McGonnagal, *birthdate reads 28 [Oct crossed out]Sep 1824, -, 17

267, 09 Oct 1824, David, Bey, Henery, Catherine, 22-Feb, -, -, -, Anna, Appleton, -, -, -, -, 17

268, 05 Nov 1824, Wilm, Lough, Wilm, Martha, 10 Sep 1824, -, -, -, Mr. [or Mrs.], Sherley, Francis, McMullen, -, -, 17

269, 08 Nov 1824, Margret, Mourer, -, -, 15 years, -, -, -, Mrs., Melton, -, -, C, -, 17

270, 10 Nov 1825*, Sarah (Mrs.), McCan, -, -, 25 years, -, -, -, Timy, Ryan, -, -, baptismal date is entered between 08 Nov 1824 and 12 Dec 1824 - perhaps it occurred in 1824 rather than 1825?, -, 17

271, 12 Dec 1824, Mary, Tigart, Hugh, Margret, 10-Nov, -, -, -, Susanna, McGloughlen, -, -, -, -, 17

272, 12 Dec 1824, Elisa, Teoney, John, Mary, 28-Nov, -, -, -, Mrs., Duffy [?], Hugh, McLeer, -, -, 17

273, 12 Dec 1824, Marcella, Shorter, Charles, Hareetta, 16-Nov, -, -, -, -, -, Mrs., Conden, -, -, 17

274, 14 Dec 1824, George Henery, Doyle, John, Rebecca, 24 Oct 1824, -, -, -, Elisa (Miss), Able, -, -, -, -, 17

275, 26 Dec 1824, Mary, Brooks, James, Margret, 20 Oct 1824, -, -, -, Mary, Counts, -, -, -, -, 17

276, 27 Dec 1824, Catherine , [blank], -, -, 25 years, C, -, -, -, -, -, -, -, -, 17

ST. MARY'S CATHOLIC CHURCH
HAGERSTOWN, MARYLAND, BAPTISMS:
Index, Bap Date, Child, Last Name, Father, Mother,
Birth Date, Code1, Code2, Code3,
1st Sponsor First, 1st Sponsor Last,
2nd Sponsor First, 2nd Sponsor Last, Location,
Notes, Maiden Name, Priest

277, 01 Jan 1825, James, Sherven, Thomas, Isabela, 10 Jan 1821, -, -, -, Margret, McGonnegal, -, -, -, -, 17

278, 01 Jan 1825, Henry, Sherven, Thomas, Isabela, 06 Nov 1824, -, -, -, J. Sherty (Mr.), McGonnagal, *, -, *can't read this name because ink is smeared, -, 17

279, 01 Jan 1825, Rose, Sherven, Thomas, Isable, 08 Feb 1823, -, -, -, Elon, McGonnagal, Thomson, [blank], -, -, 17

280, 01 Jan 1825, Michal, Warther, Joseph, Dolly, 30 Aug 1824, -, -, -, Elonora, Digs [?], -, -, -, -, 17

281, 09 Feb 1825, Richard, -, Samll, Dianna, 19 Apr 1824, -, -, -, Mary, Jonson, -, -, -, -, 17

282, 09 Feb 1825, James, Jonson, John, Mary, 16 Dec 1824, -, -, -, Dianna, [blank], -, -, -, -, 17

283, __ Feb 1825, Dianna , -, -, -, 21 years, C, -, -, -, -, -, -, -, -, 17

284, 16 Feb 1825, Lawrence, Wallas, Otho, Ellon, 26 Aug 1824, -, -, -, Mrs., Shirley, -, -, -, -, 17

285, 28 Feb 1825, Thomas, McDeomoth, Patrick, Nancy, 27 Feb 1825, -, -, -, Saly, Donnely, -, -, -, -, 17

286, 13 Mar 1825, Mary Elissa, Hawkins, Wilm, Catherine, 01 Dec 1824, -, -, -, Lucreatia (Miss), McCardel, Harim, Stake , -, -, 17

287, 07 Apr 1825, John Owen, Taylor, Peter, Henny, 10 Jan 1825, B, B, B, Terresa, -, -, -, -, -, 17

288, 07 Apr 1825, Nathanial, Frueman [or Foreman], Matt, Elisa, 02 Jan 1825, -, -, -, Nathal, Taylor, -, -, -, -, 17

289, 17 Apr 1825, Sasake[?] Anna, McQuade, James, Hanna, 13 Apr 1825, -, -, -, Peter , McCosker, -, -, -, -, 17

290, 07 May 1825, John, -, John, Juliann, 13 Apr 1825, -, -, -, Anna (Miss), Chester, -, -, -, -, 17

291, 07 May 1825, Elisa, Ourough [?], Peter, Mary, 30 Mar 1825, -, -, -, John (Mrs.), Roof*, John, Roof, *"Waltmyer" [?] was crossed out beside the name "Roof", -, 17

292, [blank], Telientas [?] , -, -, -, 7 years, B, -, -, -, -, -, -, -, -, 17

293, 13 Jun 1825, James, McKelecker, James, Catherine, 11-Jun, -, -, -, Ellon, McGonnagal, -, -, -, -, 17

294, 14 Jun 1825, Thomas, Mong, Jacob, Anna, 24-Apr, -, -, -, James ["J" crossed out], Kelly, -, -, -, -, 17

ST. MARY'S CATHOLIC CHURCH
HAGERSTOWN, MARYLAND, BAPTISMS:
Index, Bap Date, Child, Last Name, Father, Mother,
Birth Date, Code1, Code2, Code3,
1st Sponsor First, 1st Sponsor Last,
2nd Sponsor First, 2nd Sponsor Last, Location,
Notes, Maiden Name, Priest

295, 16 Jun 1825, Catherine, Swisser, George, Peggy, 08 Mar 1825, -, -, -, Margret, McGonnagal, -, -, -, -, 17

296, 10 Jul 1825, Christofor, Chinescides [?], -, Sally, 19-May, PN, -, S, -, -, -, -, Sally is "a bad girrel and Slave of Genrl. Ringgolds", -, 17

297, 10 Aug 1825, James, Sanders, James, Jane, 05 Aug 1824, -, -, -, Mary (Mrs.), Williams, -, -, -, -, 17

298, 12 Aug 1825, Henritta Maria, McGloughlen, Michal, Jane, 27-Jul, -, -, -, Nancy (Miss), McDeomath, John, McGloughlen, -, -, 17

299, 15 Aug 1825, Mary (Miss), McCord, James, Nancy, 19 years, C, -, -, Timy, Ryan, -, -, -, -, 17

300, 22 Aug 1825, Mary (Miss), Ward, -, -, 19 years, -, -, -, -, -, -, -, -, "The Father's & Mother's names I now forget."; C, -, 17

301, 01 Sep 1825, John , Snell, John, Rachel, 08 Feb 1814, C, -, -, Mrs., Milton, -, -, -, -, 17

302, 23 Oct 1825, Joseph Jackson, Stoss, Peter, Mary, 24 Nov 1825, -, -, -, Mr. , Fox, -, -, -, -, 17

303, 23-Oct, John, Couk, -, Catherine, 01 Aug 1825, -, -, -, Sarah, Gallaway, -, -, -, -, 17

304, 29 Oct 1825, Mary, Deiff, John, Mary, 25-Oct, -, -, -, Susanna, McGloughlen, -, -, -, -, 17

305, 14 Jan 1826, Wilm, Watson, Donold, Anna, 04 Nov 1825, -, -, -, Mrs. [?], Thomas, -, -, -, -, 17

306, 17 Jan 1826, Thomas (Mrs.), Coramer, -, -, 26 years, -, -, -, Timy, Ryan, -, -, -, -, 17

307, 16 Feb 1826, Mary Elisa, Jones, James, Mary, 11 Feb 1826, -, -, -, Elisa, Addams, -, -, -, -, 17

308, 26 Feb 1826, Andrew , Cole, Henry, Mary, 02 Aug 1825, -, -, -, Mrs., Thomson, -, -, -, -, 17

309, 23 Feb 1826, Ellon, Cocamer, Thomas, Mary, 14-Feb, -, -, -, Mrs., McCann, Michael, Reerden, -, -, 17

310, 20 Mar 1826, Emmilia Corolina, Wellesleger, Saml, Mary, 7-Jan, -, -, -, Elisa (Miss), Walsh, -, -, -, -, 17

311, 20 Mar 1826, John, Moge [?], Hugh, Mary, 26-Feb, -, -, -, Peter, Mager, -, -, -, -, 17

ST. MARY'S CATHOLIC CHURCH
HAGERSTOWN, MARYLAND, BAPTISMS:
Index, Bap Date, Child, Last Name, Father, Mother,
Birth Date, Code1, Code2, Code3,
1st Sponsor First, 1st Sponsor Last,
2nd Sponsor First, 2nd Sponsor Last, Location,
Notes, Maiden Name, Priest

312, 26 Mar 1826, John , Barber, -, -, 18 years, B, -, -, -, -, -, -, John [Belong to crossed out] Genr Ringgold, -, 17
313, 26 Mar 1826, A[?] Ellon, McMullen, Francis, Bridget, 13 Feb 1826, -, -, -, Susan (Miss), McGloughlen, Charly, Bolen [?], -, -, 17
314, 26 Mar 1826, Charles Aughtan[?], Stake, Elia, Sllsn[?], 14 Feb 1826, -, -, -, Prudy (Miss), Hifton [?], -, -, -, -, 17
315, 26 Mar 1826, Mary, -, -, Henny, 03 Dec 1825, -, -, B, -, -, -, -, -, -, 17
316, 26 Mar 1826, Jacob, Stabues [?], -, -, 21 years, -, -, -, -, -, -, -, -, -, 17
317, 28 May 1826, Joseph Henry, Roof, John, Rosanna, 09 Apr 1826, -, -, -, John, Boussenner, Regina, Stump, -, -, 17
318, 28 May 1826, Anna, O'Donnel, John, Susanna, 18 May 1826, -, -, -, Mrs., Conden, -, -, -, -, 17
319, 23 May 1826, Isac?, Moore, Alx, Elisa, 2-Apr, -, -, -, Thomas, Moore, -, -, -, -, 17
320, 28 May 1826, Edward, Dodson, Huly [?], Hanna, 15-Apr, -, -, -, Betsey, Liones, -, -, -, -, 17
321, 28 May 1826, Rosan, Waters, Jeffery, Mary, 14-Apr, -, -, -, Elisa, Shorter, -, -, -, -, 17
322, 03 Jun 1826, Margret, Bradly, Wilm, Susan, 28 Jul1825, -, -, -, Margret (Miss), McLeer, -, -, -, -, 17
323, 16 Jun 1826, J. (Mr.), Doyd, -, -, [blank], -, -, -, -, -, -, -, C, -, 17
324, 03 Jul 1826, Mr., Richey, -, -, -, -, -, -, -, -, -, -, C, -, 17
325, 05 Jul 1826, Susanna, Baringer, Jacob, Annastaia, 04 Oct 1824, -, -, -, Mrs., Milton, -, -, -, -, 17
326, 03 Aug 1826, Levi, Taylor, Saml, Teaby, 02 Mar 1825, B, -, -, Julianna, [blank], -, -, -, -, 17
327, 03 Aug 1826, Mary, Brown, Alrnd [?] [or Alrm?], Julianna, 07 Feb 1826, B, -, -, Terresa, [blank], -, -, -, -, 17
328, 16 Aug 1826, John, Butter, Leonard, Patience , 06 Mar 1825, -, -, B, Elonora, Landers, -, -, -, -, 17
329, 20 Aug 1826, Jane, Bord [?] , Isac, Harietta, 1-Jul, -, B, -, Elisa (Miss), Mortial [?], -, -, -, -, 17
330, 20 Aug 1826, Saml , McDonnol, Richard, Nancy, 17 Sep 1823, B, -, -, Nancy, Butler, -, -, -, -, 17

ST. MARY'S CATHOLIC CHURCH
HAGERSTOWN, MARYLAND, BAPTISMS:
Index, Bap Date, Child, Last Name, Father, Mother,
Birth Date, Code1, Code2, Code3,
1st Sponsor First, 1st Sponsor Last,
2nd Sponsor First, 2nd Sponsor Last, Location,
Notes, Maiden Name, Priest

331, 20 Aug 1826, Mary Anna, McDonnel, Richard, Nancy, 4-Jan, -, -, -, Mary, Hatain [?] [or Adla__], -, -, -, -, 17

332, 03 Sep 1826, Shexious? , Thoms, Bernard, Mary, 24-Jun, B, -, -, Sarah, Gallaway, -, -, -, -, 17

333, 10 Sep 1826, Edward , Corey, James, Harietta, 10 Aug 1826, B, -, -, Mrs., Conder, -, -, -, -, 17

334, 04 Oct 1826, Jane , Smith, Jacob, Betsey, 17 Sep 1824, B, -, - , Nelly, Lander [or Sander], -, -, -, -, 17

335, 08 Oct 1826, Daniel, Pembrooke, Basil, Nelly, 05 Oct 1825, -, -, -, Margret (Miss), Matheyly [?], -, -, -, -, 17

336, 11 Oct 1826, Saml, Lemon, Saml, Jane, 15 Feb 1826, -, -, -, Fr., McCosker, -, -, -, -, 17

337, 17 Oct 1826, Lethsia, McElhener, Michal, Mary, 30 Sep 1826, -, -, -, Mrs., Donnellen, -, -, -, -, 17

338, 22 Oct 1826, Lucinda , Key, Henry, Catherine, 01 Jun 1826, B, B, B, Saley, Ambrose, -, -, Family and sponsor are Black, -, 17

339, 07 Nov 1826, Elisa, Doyel , Lawrence, Catherine, 09 Aug 1826, -, -, -, Mrs., McCafferty, Eli, Stake, -, -, 17

340, 09 Nov 1826, Henry*, Bearinger, Jacob, Anna, 06 Nov 1826, -, -, -, Mrs., Lidy, -, -, *[Jacob crossed out] Henry, -, 17

341, 10 Nov 1826, Mary Anna, Holbert, Archibol , Catherine, 25 Jul 1826, -, -, -, Mary, McGloughlen, -, -, -, -, 17

342, 12 Oct 1826, Anna Elisa, Gocen [?], *, Mary, 28 Dec 1825, -, -, -, "Old Mrs.", McCosker, -, -, *"Father not to be mentioned", -, 17

343, 25 Dec 1826, William, Hawkins, Wilm, Catherine, 11 Oct 1826, -, -, -, Mrs., Lover, -, -, -, -, 17

344, 06 Jan 1827, John, Cole, Henry, Mary, 22 Dec 1826, -, -, -, Mrs., Thomas, -, -, -, -, 17

345, 01 Jan 1827, Jacob , N[?]egal, -, -, -, -, -, -, -, -, -, -, C, -, 17

346, 01 Jan 1827, Catherine (Mrs.), Smith, -, -, -, -, -, -, -, -, -, -, C, -, 17

347, 19 Jan 1827, Belend, Weaver, David, Anna, 20 May 1827, -, - , -, Catherine (Miss), Crow, Hugh, McCosker, this record mistakenly entered into Marriage section, -, 17

ST. MARY'S CATHOLIC CHURCH
HAGERSTOWN, MARYLAND, BAPTISMS:
Index, Bap Date, Child, Last Name, Father, Mother,
Birth Date, Code1, Code2, Code3,
1st Sponsor First, 1st Sponsor Last,
2nd Sponsor First, 2nd Sponsor Last, Location,
Notes, Maiden Name, Priest

348, 29 Jan 1827, Leonides, Tygert, Hugh, Margret, 19 Jun 1827, -, -, -, Micl, Reriden, -, -, this record mistakenly entered into Marriage section, -, 17

349, 26 Feb 1827, John, Sogee [or Logee], Wilm, Martha, 03 Sep 1826, -, -, -, Mrs., McGonnagal, -, -, -, -, 17

350, 27 Feb 1827, George, Wheeler, "unknown", Louisa, 25 Nov 1826, -, -, -, Mrs., Clapsadel, -, -, -, -, 17

351, 28 Feb 1827, Leonidas, tooney, John, Mary, 12-Feb, -, -, -, Elisa (Miss), Adams, -, -, -, -, 17

352, 28 Feb 1827, Anna Virginia, Doyle, John, Rrebecca, 17 Feb 1826, -, -, -, Mary [Mrs. Abel Crossed out], Mathinging [?]* , -, -, * name runs into binding - difficult to read, -, 17

353, 28 Feb 1827, Thomas , Goans, Joscee [?], Sophia, 04 Dec 1826, B, -, -, Betsy, Leoles, -, -, -, -, 17

354, 28 Feb 1826, Henry , Boon, Isac, Feby, 02 Dec 1826, B, -, -, Mrs., Chester, -, -, -, -, 17

355, 28 Feb 1827, Sarah, Hemsley, John Paul, Mary, 05 Aug 1826, -, -, -, Sarah, Galloway, -, -, -, -, 17

356, 28 Mar 1827, Jeremy , Page, Augustin, Catherine, 28 Oct 1826, B, -, -, Margret (Miss), Bevens, -, -, -, -, 17

357, 26 Mar 1827, Margret Matilda, Murry, Richard, Alma, 17 Dec 1827, -, -, -, Tammy (Miss), Garber [?], Peter, Stephey [?], -, -, 17

358, 16 Apr 1827, Henry James, James, Sam [?], Rachel, 25 Jan 1827, B, B, B, Barbary, Worth, -, -, -, -, 17

359, 18 Apr 1827, Mary Ellon, Sweeney, Charley, Elisa, 17 ___, -, -, -, Mary (Miss), Tollen, -, -, -, -, 17

360, 11 May 1827, Margret, Mundy, Patrick, Catherine, 26 Apr 1827, -, -, -, Sarah (Miss), Donnelly, Francis, Donnelly, -, -, 17

361, 20 May 1827, Belend, Weaver, David, Anna, 19 Jan 1827, -, -, -, Cathren (Miss), Crow, Hugh, McCosker, This record mistakenly entered into Marriage section., -, 17

362, 25 May 1827, Washington, Jonson, Jack, Mary, 26 Apr 1827, -, -, -, Nelly, Jones, -, -, -, -, 17

363, 25 May 1827, Elisa M. O. Jane, Borinan [?], Ralph, Sarah, 05 Mar 1827, -, -, -, George, Jones, Mary, Jones [HB], -, -, 17

ST. MARY'S CATHOLIC CHURCH
HAGERSTOWN, MARYLAND, BAPTISMS:
Index, Bap Date, Child, Last Name, Father, Mother,
Birth Date, Code1, Code2, Code3,
1st Sponsor First, 1st Sponsor Last,
2nd Sponsor First, 2nd Sponsor Last, Location,
Notes, Maiden Name, Priest

364, 26 May 1827, Nancy , Coleman, Eausa, Henny, 22 May 1827, B, -, -, Lucy, Smith, Philips, Smith [HB], -, -, 17

365, 21 Jun 1827, Upton, McClane, Jessey [?], Elisa, 04 Feb 1827, -, -, -, Mrs., McClane, -, -, -, -, 17

366, 21 Jun 1827, Margret, Painter, Jacob, Mary, 03 Aug 1826, -, -, -, Micl (Mrs.), Smith, -, -, -, -, 17

367, 23 Jun 1827, Mary, Merlight, James, Susanna, 07 Jun 1827, -, -, -, Mary (Miss), Mattingly, -, -, -, -, 17

368, 27 Jun 1827, Sarah Anna, McGloughlen, Mechal, Jane, 10 Jun 1827, -, -, -, Thomas, Rooney, Cathurine, Donnlly, -, -, 17

369, 29 Jun 1827, Leonides, Tigert, Hugh, Margret, 19 Jun 1827, -, -, -, Mich., Reriden, -, -, This record mistakenly entered into Marriage section., -, 17

370, 02 Aug 1827, Arch John , Aullert [?], -, -, -, -, -, -, -, -, -, -, C, -, 17

371, 31 Aug 1827, Thomas, Able, Saml, Anna, 29-Aug, -, -, -, Mrs., Able, -, -, -, -, 17

372, 09 Sep 1827, Mary Anna, Carrol, James, Margret, 10 Mar 1827, -, -, -, Patrick, Donnelly, Mrs., Conden, -, -, 17

373, 11 Nov 1827, Joseph, Ocpherin[?]*, Peter, Mary, 16 Oct 1827, -, -, -, John (Mrs.), Roof, -, -, *Ocpherin[?] ink is blurred, -, 17

374, 11 Nov 1827, Augustin, Butler, Leonard , Patience, 02 Oct 1827, -, -, -, Barbary, Worley, -, -, -, -, 17

375, 11 Nov 1827, Wilm, Deggs, Jacob, Rache[l? into binding], 16-Oct, -, -, -, Mrs., Gallaway, -, -, -, -, 17

376, [blank], Maria , Weynih [?], -, -, 24 years, C, -, -, -, -, -, -, -, 17

377, 31 Mar 1828, Catherine, Juvet [?], Edmond , Caroline, 02 Mar 1828, -, -, -, Mrs., Shirley [?], -, -, -, -, 17

378, 09 Jan 1828, Ambrose, Jordan, Wilm, Leady [?], 03 Nov 1827, -, -, -, Mrs., Brown, -, -, -, -, 17

379, 06 Apr 1828, Margret Anna, Early, James, Anna, 04 May 1828, -, -, -, Mr., Stake, Mrs., Stake, could the priest have reversed the birth and baptism dates?; this record mistakenly entered into Marriage section, -, 17

ST. MARY'S CATHOLIC CHURCH
HAGERSTOWN, MARYLAND, BAPTISMS:
Index, Bap Date, Child, Last Name, Father, Mother,
Birth Date, Code1, Code2, Code3,
1st Sponsor First, 1st Sponsor Last,
2nd Sponsor First, 2nd Sponsor Last, Location,
Notes, Maiden Name, Priest

380, 06 Apr 1828, Sophia, Bird, Esias, Harietta, 23 Dec 1827, -, -, -, Sarah, Riedout, -, -, -, -, 17
381, 17 Apr 1828, Augusten, Wolgumoth, John, Julianna, 02 May 1828, -, -, -, Mrs., Thoms, -, -, -, -, 17
382, 17 May 1828, Leonidas, Donnelly, Patrick, Margret, 16-May, -, -, -, Mrs., McGloughlen, -, -, -, -, 17
383, 19 May 1828, John, McGrath, John, Rose, 18 Mar 1828, -, -, -, "Old Tery [?]", McCosker, Easter, Carney, -, -, 17
384, 25 May 1828, Francis Horris, -, Basil, Pembrooke , 01 Sep 1827, -, -, -, Henney, Brown, -, -, -, -, 17
385, 26 May 1828, Cloey, Chisel, Oliver, Clare, 15 Mar 1822, -, -, -, Betsy, Silas, -, -, -, -, 17
386, 26 May 1828, Joseph, Flinn, Patrick, Nancy, 07 Mar 1828, -, -, -, John, Terney, -, -, -, -, 17
387, 10 May 1827*, Bernard, McCosker, Peter, Sarah, 06 Apr 1827, -, -, -, Hugh, McCosker, Mary, Sulbert, in the baptismal date of 10 May 1827, could the priest have written 1827 by mistake but meant 1828?, -, 17
388, 27 May 1828, Wilm, Weaver, David, Anna, 12-Apr, -, -, -, Mrs. , McCafferty, James , McQuade, -, -, 17
389, 27 May 1828, Mary Jane, McCosker, Peter, Sarah, 26 May 1827, -, -, -, Mrs., Lover, -, -, -, -, 17
390, 27 May 1828, Anna, McCosker, Peter, Sarah, 26-May, -, -, -, Charley, Donnelly, Mrs., McQuade, -, -, 17
391, 27 May 1828, John, Shorter, Charles, Harietta, 6-Feb, -, -, -, Elisabeth , Shorter, -, -, -, -, 17
392, 27 May 1828, George, Shorter, "not known", Matilda, 28 Apr 1828, -, -, -, Mrs., D[?]ance, -, -, -, -, 17
393, 06 Jun 1828, Edward, Kelley, Edward, Julianna, 26 Mar 1828, -, -, -, Mr., Belgold, Mrs., Belgold [HB], -, -, 17
394, 06 Jul 1828, Elias Jana, Staulbert, Arch John, Catherine, 03 May 1828, -, -, -, Anna (Miss), Chester, -, -, -, -, 17
395, 20 Jul 1828, Wilm Henry, Cole, Micl, Mary, 24-May, -, -, -, Joseph, Cooms, Sally Lour (Miss), Beer, -, -, 17
396, 31 Aug 1828, Elias Anna, Joy, Wilm, Jain, 6-Jul, -, -, -, Mrs., Conden, Fergus, McCosker, -, -, 17

ST. MARY'S CATHOLIC CHURCH
HAGERSTOWN, MARYLAND, BAPTISMS:
Index, Bap Date, Child, Last Name, Father, Mother, Birth Date, Code1, Code2, Code3, 1st Sponsor First, 1st Sponsor Last, 2nd Sponsor First, 2nd Sponsor Last, Location, Notes, Maiden Name, Priest

397, 14 Sep 1828, Catherine Anna, Stake, Atariane [or Stasiane], Catherine, 05 Aug 1828, -, -, -, Eli, Stake, Eli (Mrs.), Stake [HB], -, -, 17

398, 21 Sep 1828, James Lawrence, Doyel, Lawrence, Catherine, 27 Jul 1828, -, -, -, Charles, Donnelly, Bridgett, Donnelly [HB], -, -, 17

399, 21 Sep 1828, Mary , Hemlsly, Peter, Nancy, 27 Mar 1828, B, -, -, Sarah, Galloway, "Old John", Stembly, -, -, 17

400, 11 Dec 1828, Peter Wilem, Mundy, Patrick, Catherine, 01 Dec 1828, -, -, -, Catherine, Mundy, Denis, Mundy [HB], -, -, 17

401, 25 Dec 1828, John, Sweeney, Charley, Elisa, 21-Oct, -, -, -, John, Terney, John (Mrs.), Terney [HB], -, -, 17

402, 08 Mar 1829, John Ormand, Dollen, Charley, Catherine, 01 Jan 1829, -, -, -, Charley , Donnelley, Mary , McGoughlen, -, -, 17

403, 08 Mar 1829, Henry, Cole, Henry, Mary, 01 Jan 1829, -, -, -, Mrs., Talbott, -, -, -, -, 17

404, 08 Mar 1829, John, Power, George, Catherine, 22 Nov 1829, -, -, -, John , Roof, Mary Anna , Coufher [?], -, -, 17

405, 31-Mar, Leo Ruben , O Taly [sic], Isiac, Henerietta, 15 Mar 1829, B, -, -, -, -, -, -, -, -, 17

406, 2-Apr, Edward, McQuade, James, Anna, 11 Mar 1829, -, -, -, Mrs., McCafferty, -, -, -, -, 17

407, 17-Apr, Catherine Emmilia, Lambert, John, Catherine, 07 Mar 1829, -, -, -, T., Ryan, -, -, -, -, 17

408, 21 May 1829, Sarah Anna, Deins, Isiac, Magdallen, 28 Feb 1828, -, -, -, John, Roof, Mrs., Conden, -, -, 17

409, 22-Apr, Elisa Francis, Stake, Eli, Ellon , 19 Apr 1829 "Easter Sunday", -, -, -, Hiram, Stake, Hiram (Mrs.), Stake [HB], -, -, 17

410, 06 Jun 1829, Michal, Terney, John, Mary, 7-May, -, -, -, Mrs. Conden, Conden, -, -, -, -, 17

411, 09 Ju 1829, John Michal, Smith, Michl, Catherine, 12-May, -, -, -, Sofia Smith, Smith, -, -, -, -, 17

412, 09 Jun 1829, Jacob , Smith, Josia, Anastia, 29-Mar, B, B, B, Terresa, [no last name], -, -, -, -, 17

ST. MARY'S CATHOLIC CHURCH
HAGERSTOWN, MARYLAND, BAPTISMS:
Index, Bap Date, Child, Last Name, Father, Mother,
Birth Date, Code1, Code2, Code3,
1st Sponsor First, 1st Sponsor Last,
2nd Sponsor First, 2nd Sponsor Last, Location,
Notes, Maiden Name, Priest

413, 10 Jun 1829, Emmelia , Shorter*, Charles, Catherine, 21-Mar, B, -, -, "Old Mrs.", Shorter, -, -, *"Hister" crossed out before "Shorter", -, 17

414, 09 Jun 1829, John Michl, Smith, Michl, Catherine, 12-May, -, -, -, Sophia , Smith, -, -, -, -, 17

415, 09 Jun 1829, Jacob, __, Joe, Anastasia, 29-Mar, -, -, -, Terresa , Smith, -, -, -, -, 17

416, 5-Jul, O'[?]George, Rideout [or Ridount], Wilm, Sarah, 05 Jan 1829, -, -, -, Salley , Steamer, -, -, -, -, 17

417, 2-Jul, Elias , Burd, Isiac, Harrietta, 15 Apr 1829, B, -, -, Terresa , Green, -, -, -, -, 17

418, 02 Jul 1829, John , H[?]eary, James, Harrietta, 26 Oct 1828, B, -, -, Nancy , Butler, -, -, -, -, 17

419, 09 Aug 1829, John, Dygs, Jacob, Rachel, 16 Jul 1829, -, -, -, Saml , Gallaway, Terresa, Green, -, -, 17

420, 16 Aug 1829, James Wilm, Doyle, John, Rebecca, 23-Jul, -, -, -, Mrs. , Conden, -, -, -, -, 17

421, 28-Aug, Henrietta, Brierer, Joseph, Mitilda , 07 Mar 1829, -, -, -, David , Dafenthal, Barbary, Dafenthal, -, -, 17

422, 06 Sep 1829, Margret , Hemsley, Jack, Mary, 20 Feb 1829, B, -, -, Betty , Camel, Saml , Gallaway, -, -, 17

423, 09 Sep 1829, George , Tilghman, Thomas, Mary, 29 Aug 1829, B, -, -, Mrs. , Shirley, -, -, -, -, 17

424, 04 Sep 1829, James, McGrath, John, Rose, 04 Aug 1829, -, -, -, "Old Mrs." , McCosker, -, -, -, -, 17

425, 15 Nov 1829, Mary Elosia, Vincendeeffner[?], Vincen, Anastasa, 11 Oct 1829, -, -, -, Peter, Borgantz [?], Peter (Mrs.), Borgantz [?] [HB], -, Vincendeefnir [?], 17

426, 28 Dec 1829, Martha , Waters, Jeffery, Maria, 27 Aug 1828, B, -, -, Wefred , Brown, -, -, -, -, 17

427, 04 Jan 1830, Ambrose, McClain, Josiah, Elisa, 14 Sep 1829, -, -, -, Margret (Mrs.), McClain, -, -, -, -, 17

428, 07 Jan 1830, Otho, Clapsaddle, "unknown", "Clapsaddle's Daughter", 29 Jul 1829, -, -, -, -, -, -, -, -, -, -, 17

429, 14 Apr 1830, Catherine, McCosker, Peter, Sally, 04 Mar 1830, -, -, -, Bridget , Donnelly, Edw., McQuade, -, -, 17

ST. MARY'S CATHOLIC CHURCH
HAGERSTOWN, MARYLAND, BAPTISMS:
Index, Bap Date, Child, Last Name, Father, Mother,
Birth Date, Code1, Code2, Code3,
1st Sponsor First, 1st Sponsor Last,
2nd Sponsor First, 2nd Sponsor Last, Location,
Notes, Maiden Name, Priest

430, 14 Apr 1830, John, Truman, Matt, Betty, 10 Jun 1829, -, -, -, Nancy , Hopewell, -, -, -, -, 17

431, 19 Mar 1830, Louisa, Donnlley, Patrick, Margret, 18-Mar, -, , -, Anna (Mrs.), Mundy, -, -, -, -, 17

432, 11 Apr 1830, Elie, Tollen, John, Ellonora, 02 Apr 1830, -, -, -, Michl , McGloughlen, Margret, McCosker, -, -, 17

433, 13 Apr 1830, Otho, Tice, John, Maria, 27 Aug 1829, -, -, -, -, -, , -, -, -, -, 17

434, 15 May 1830, Leonard , Butler, Leonard, Patience, 31 May 1829, B, B, B, Mary , Holland (Black), -, -, -, -, 17

435, 02 Jun 1830, Emmilia, Stake, Hiram, Catharine, 25 May 1830, -, -, -, Eli , Stake, Eli (Mrs.), Stake [HB], -, -, 17

436, 01 Jun 1830, Benedict, Berener , Jacob, Anastasi, 26 May 1828, -, -, -, George , Gale, Mary Anna , Bevens, -, -, 17

437, 02 Jun 1830, John Harrison, Bradly, Wilm, Susanna, 21 Mar 1830, -, -, -, Upton , Begold, Sophia (Miss), Smith, -, -, 17

438, 13 Jun 1830, John Henery, Hemsley, Peter, Nancy, 18 Feb*, -, -, -, "Old Jack" , Hemsley, Betsey , Cammel, *birthdate reads 18 Feb [looks like 2 is written over 1, so it could be 28 Feb], -, 17

439, 04 July 1830, Mary Anna Catherine, Roof, John, Rosanna, 22-Jun, -, -, -, Mary Anna , Beirguntz [?], -, -, -, -, 17

440, 04 Jul 1830, Philip, Mcloughlen , Michal, Jane, 20-Jun, -, -, -, Ellon (Mrs.), McGonnagal, -, -, -, -, 17

441, 04 Jul 1830, Wilm, Aulbert, Arcibol, Catherine, 30-Jun, -, -, -, Mrs. , Gilmore, -, -, -, -, 17

442, 18-Aug, Mary Ellon, Stake, Lem , Elisa, 18 Jun 1830, -, -, -, Mrs. , Lover, -, -, -, -, 17

443, 19 Aug 1830, Margret, McGonnagal, James, Susanna, 18-Aug, -, -, -, Wilm , McLoughlen, Margret (Mrs.), Kelley, -, -, 17

444, 26 Aug 1830, Tobias John, Coile, Edward, Elisa, 10 Dec 1829, -, -, -, Catherine , Cane, Thos, Moore, this record mistakenly entered into marriage section, -, 17

445, 30 Aug 1830, Thomas, Mundy, Denis, Anna, 14 Aug 1830, -, -, -, Mary (Mrs.), Corns, -, -, -, -, 17

446, 06 Sep 1830, Mary Eloisa, Ford, John, Mary, 26 Jan 1830, -, -, , -, Jenny , Ford, Catherine, Aulbert, -, -, 17

ST. MARY'S CATHOLIC CHURCH
HAGERSTOWN, MARYLAND, BAPTISMS:
Index, Bap Date, Child, Last Name, Father, Mother,
Birth Date, Code1, Code2, Code3,
1st Sponsor First, 1st Sponsor Last,
2nd Sponsor First, 2nd Sponsor Last, Location,
Notes, Maiden Name, Priest

447, 08 Sep 1830, Mary Anna, Mundy, Patrick, Catherine, 19 Aug 1830, -, -, -, Mrs. , Conden, -, -, -, -, 17

448, 15 Sep 1830, Catherine, FitzPatrick, Edward, Julianna, 13-Sep, -, -, -, Anna (Miss), Chester, -, -, -, -, 17

449, 29 Sep 1830, Emmilia, Windle, John, Sarah, 01 May 1829, -, -, -, Anna, Moore, -, -, this record mistakenly entered in to marriage section, -, 17

450, 29 Sep 1830, Rose, Haule, James, Lucy, Dec 1822, B, -, -, Mr. , Moore, -, -, this record mistakenly entered in to marriage section, -, 17

451, 29 Sep 1830, Richard, Haule, James, Lucy, 12 Mar 1826, B, -, -, Mrs., McGoath, -, -, this record mistakenly entered in to marriage section, -, 17

452, 29 Sep 1830, Mary, Haule, James, Lucy , 26 Feb 1828, B, -, -, Mrs., Murry, -, -, this record mistakenly entered in to marriage section, -, 17

453, 03 Oct 1830, Anna, Cole, Henery, Mary, 20 Aug 1830, -, -, -, Mary (Mrs.), Cole, -, -, -, -, 17

454, 20 Oct 1830, Catherin Terresa* , Gilmore, George, Elisa, 12-Oct, -, -, -, Mary , Darcy, -, -, *Catherin Terresa Francesca, -, 17

455, 03 Nov 1830, Isaac Thomas, Windle, John, Sarah, 23 Dec 1821, -, -, -, Alx., Moore, -, -, -, -, 17

456, 05 Nov 1830, Mittilda , Beargentz, Peter, Victoria, 15 Sep 1830, -, -, -, Sabastian , Bacller, Cecelia , White, -, -, 17

457, 05 Nov 1830, James Barnet, McDevt, James, Mary Anna, 23 Oct 1830, -, -, -, Eli, Stake, Eli (Mrs.), Stake [HB], -, -, 17

458, 05 Dec 1830, Richard, Pembrook, Basil, Nelley, 10 Jan 1830, -, -, -, Sarah , Rideout, -, -, -, -, 17

459, 05 Dec 1830, Catherine, Chase, John, Peggy, 17 Oct 1830, -, -, -, Mary , Jordan, -, -, -, -, 17

460, 22 Jan 1831, Elisa , Stake, -, -, 26 years, -, -, -, -, -, -, -, C, -, 17

461, 24 Jan 1831, Wilm, Adams, "unknown", Nancy, 24 Dec 1830, PN, -, -, Mrs., Adams, -, -, -, -, 17

462, 20 Jan 1831, John, McEnulty, Danl., Bridget, 2 Jan 1831, -, -, -, Hugh, McCosker, Catherine, Mundy, -, -, 17

ST. MARY'S CATHOLIC CHURCH HAGERSTOWN, MARYLAND, BAPTISMS:
Index, Bap Date, Child, Last Name, Father, Mother, Birth Date, Code1, Code2, Code3, 1st Sponsor First, 1st Sponsor Last, 2nd Sponsor First, 2nd Sponsor Last, Location, Notes, Maiden Name, Priest

463, 22 Mar 1831, Mary Elisa, Walsh, Richard, Margret., 17 Oct 1830, -, -, -, Mrs., Walshlear, -, -, -, -, 17

464, 3 Apr 1831, Evelina, Borden [?], Esiae [?], Mariettae, 12 Jan 1831, -, -, -, Sopha, Smith, -, -, -, -, 17

465, 27 Apr 1831, Joseph, Shorter, Charls, Catherine, 15 Mar 1831, -, -, -, "Old Elisabeth", Shorter, -, -, -, -, 17

466, 12 May 1831, Rosanna, Bower, George, Catherine, 25 Sep 1830, -, -, -, John (Mrs.), Roof, -, -, -, -, 17

467, 23 May 1831, Ellon, Tigert, Hugh, Margret, 15 May 1831, -, -, -, Chotf [?], Murphy, Choft [?] (Mrs.), Murphy [HB], -, -, 17

468, [blank], Joseph Francus, Deshet [?], Saml., Lousa, 14 Mar 1831, -, -, -, George, Gilmore, George (Mrs.), Gilmore [HB], -, -, 17

469, [blank], Maria Eliza, Ellott, James, Elisa, 15 May 1831, -, -, -, Bent (Mrs.), Peake, -, -, -, -, 17

470, 18 Jul 1831, Margret Eliza, McDonnal, Charles, Lovenia Anna, 4 Jun 1831, -, -, -, Mrs., Fox, -, -, -, -, 17

471, 24 Jul 1831, Michal, Lamber, John, Catherine, 8 Jun 1831, -, -, -, Mary (Mrs.), Null, -, -, -, -, 17

472, 29 Jun 1831, Mary Anna, Smith, Mechl [?], Catherine, 12 Jun 1831, -, -, -, Sophia (Miss), Smith, -, -, -, -, 17

473, 24 Jul 1831, John, Palmer, Richard, Marietta, 12 Nov 1830, -, -, -, John (Mrs.), Lamber, -, -, -, -, 17

474, 25 Jul 1831, Anna Allosius, McGlenan, Patrick, Sarah, 27 Jun 1831, -, -, -, James, Carrigan, Catherine, Mundy, -, -, 17

475, 26 Jul 1831, Wilm Henery, McGonnagal, James, Susanna, 25 Jul 1831, -, -, -, John, McLaughlen, Wilm (Mrs.), Doherty, -, -, 17

476, 5 Sep 1831, Rose Anna, Kiamp, John, Rose Ann, 24 May 1831, -, -, -, John (Mrs.), Roof, -, -, -, -, 17

477, 20 Nov 1831, Luise [?], Dygs, Jacob, Rachel, 9 Aug 1831, -, -, -, Sally, Cramer, James, Brooks, -, -, 17

478, 20 Nov 1831, Thomas, Tilghman, Thomas, Mary, 17 Oct 1831, -, -, -, Saml., Galaway, -, -, -, -, 17

479, 31 Dec 1831, Margret, Tollen [or Follen], John, Ellon, 16 Dec 1831, -, -, -, Ellon (Mrs.), McGonnagal, -, -, -, -, 17

480, 11 Feb 1832, Thomas Edward, Hardy, George, Edith [?], 10 Oct 1828, -, -, -, Pryrilla [?], Hardy, -, -, -, -, 17

ST. MARY'S CATHOLIC CHURCH
HAGERSTOWN, MARYLAND, BAPTISMS:
Index, Bap Date, Child, Last Name, Father, Mother,
Birth Date, Code1, Code2, Code3,
1st Sponsor First, 1st Sponsor Last,
2nd Sponsor First, 2nd Sponsor Last, Location,
Notes, Maiden Name, Priest

481, 11 Feb 1832, Eliza Ellon, Hardy, George, Edith, 10 Dec 1830, -, -, -, Elizabeth (Miss), Hardy, -, -, -, -, 17

482, 2 Mar 1832, Tho., McClain, Josia, Elesa [?], 31 Jan 1832, -, -, -, Margrt. (Mrs.), McClain, -, -, -, -, 17

483, 2 Mar 1832, Sophia, McClain, Josia, Eliaza [?], 31 Jan 1832, -, -, -, Mechl. (Mrs.), Smith, -, -, -, -, 17

484, 15 Mar 1832, Pantos [?] [or Fanios], McCosker, Hugh, Ellon, 18 Feb 1832, -, -, -, Mrs., McCafferty, -, -, -, -, 17

485, 28 Mar 1832, Sarah Anna, -, Jose, Anasastia, 1 Feb 1832, B, B, B, Upton (Mrs.), Bolo [?], -, -, -, -, 17

486, 2 May 1832, Margret, McCosker, Peter, Sally, 1 May 1832, -, -, -, Daniel, McAnulty [?], P. (Mrs.), Donnelly, -, -, 17

487, [blank], Thoms. Faulen [?], Clapsaddal, -, -, 19 years, -, -, -, -, -, -, -, -, -, 17

488, 7 May 1832, Mary Anna, Shergan [?], Wilm, Maria, 11 Sep 1830, -, -, -, Catherine (Mrs.), Greenwell, -, -, -, -, 17

489, 12 May 1832, Charles, Walsh, Richard, Margret, 31 Mar 1832, -, -, -, Mrs., Walshler, -, -, -, -, 17

490, 12 May 1832, Anna Cecilia, Walshler, Saml., Mary, 18 Jan 1832, -, -, -, Mary Anna, Shirley, -, -, -, -, 17

491, 31 May 1832, Francis, Justice, Joseph, Lucratia, 17 Feb 1832, -, -, -, Mrs., Fox, -, -, -, -, 17

492, 19 Sep 1832, James, Sullen [?], Archy, Catherine, 15-Aug, -, -, -, Elisa, Adams, Wilm, McGlaughlen, -, -, 17

493, 2 Sep 1832, Mathew, Bowers, Nick, Mitilda, 20 Jul 1832, -, -, -, Mat [?], Coorad [or Coonad], Barbary, Coorad [or Coonad], -, -, 17

494, 10 Sep 1832, Margret, Sweney [?], Charly, Eliza, 5 Sep 1832, -, -, -, Mrs., Tollen, Hugh, Tigert, -, -, 17

495, 5 Oct 1832, Nichlas, Gapney, James, Jane, 27 Sep 1832, -, -, -, Richard, Gibbs, Anna, Gibbs [HB], -, -, 17

496, 5 Oct 1832, Nichls., McKenny [?], Edward, Elizabeth, 24 Sep 1832, -, -, -, Julian, Moran, Wilm, Moran, -, -, 17

497, 5 Oct 1832, Cahterine, LaStrange, Patrick, Bridget, 16 Sep 1832, -, -, -, Thoms., LaStrange, Mrs., Moran, -, -, 17

498, 10 Oct 1832, Bridge, Fogerty, Michl., Jane, 10 Oct 1832, -, -, -, Simon, Dyre, Honora (Mrs.), McCarty, -, -, 17

ST. MARY'S CATHOLIC CHURCH
HAGERSTOWN, MARYLAND, BAPTISMS:
Index, Bap Date, Child, Last Name, Father, Mother,
Birth Date, Code1, Code2, Code3,
1st Sponsor First, 1st Sponsor Last,
2nd Sponsor First, 2nd Sponsor Last, Location,
Notes, Maiden Name, Priest

499, 11 Oct 1832, Charles E., Shaffer, Jonathan, Eliza, 12 Aug 1832, -, -, -, Margret (Mrs.), Shaffer, T., Ryan, -, -, 17

500, 11 Oct 1832, Josaphean, Mong, Jacob, Anna, 15 May 1832, -, -, -, Eliza (Mrs.), Shaffer, -, -, -, -, 17

501, 9 Dec 1832, Sarah Anna, Mosthial [?], Michl., Louisa, 24 Nov 1832, -, -, -, Mrs., Clapsadal, -, -, -, -, 17

502, 23 Dec 1832, John Robert, McGonnal, James, Susan, 16 Dec 1832* , -, -, -, James, McGonnigal, Mary, McLoughlen, *"23" Dec has been overwritten by "16"], -, 17

503, 25 Dec 1832, Sophia Regia, Gillyer, George, Elisa [?], 13 Dec 1832, -, -, -, Sophia, Smith, Josia, Smith [HB], -, -, 17

504, 26 Dec 1832, Henrietta, McLoughlen, Michl., Jane [?], 22 Nov 1832, -, -, -, John (Mrs.), Tollen, Barney, McKenny, -, -, 17

505, 20 Jan 1833, Wilm, McCartney, Edward, Catherine, 18 Dec 1832, -, -, -, Mrs. , McShenney, -, -, -, -, 17

506, 18 Sep 1831, Mary Anna, Kelley, Henery, Margret, 15 Sep 1831, -, -, -, James, McGonnegal, James (Mrs.), McGonnegal [HB], -, -, 17

507, 26 Jan 1833, Wilm Edward, Kelley, Henery, Margret, 25 Jan 1833, -, -, -, Ellon (Mrs.), Daugherty, -, -, -, -, 17

508, 03 Feb 1833, Edward Ignatis, FitzPatrick, Edward, Julian, 01 Feb 1833, -, -, -, Mrs., Milton, -, -, -, -, 17

509, 17 Mar 1833, James Patrick, Wall, David, Mary, 05 Mar 1833, -, -, -, Honora, McGret [?], John, Sweeney, -, -, 17

510, 17 Mar 1833, Mary, FitzGerrald, Garrett, Bridget, 28 Feb 1833, -, -, -, Danl, Grady, Mary, Wall, -, -, 17

511, 24 Mar 1833, Mary Catherine, Bird, Isacc, Harrietta, 02 Nov 1832, -, -, -, Johnathen (Mrs.) , Shaffer, -, -, this record mistakenly entered in to Marriage section, -, 17

512, 26 Mar 1833, Catherine, Barret, James, Margret, 19 Mar 1833, -, -, -, Denis, Donavan, Honora, Barret, -, -, 17

513, 26 May 1833, Mida Anastatia, Anderson, Saml, Susanna, 31 Jan 1833, -, -, -, Eliza (Miss), FitzGerrald, -, -, -, -, 17

514, 09 Jun 1833, John , Moyers [?], -, -, 27 years, C, -, -, -, -, -, -, A Servant of Mr. John Stonebraker, -, 17

515, 09 Jun 1833, Joseph, Dygs [or Deggs], Jacob, Rachel, 28 Apr 1833, -, -, -, Mary , Hollan, John, Truman, -, -, 17

ST. MARY'S CATHOLIC CHURCH
HAGERSTOWN, MARYLAND, BAPTISMS:
Index, Bap Date, Child, Last Name, Father, Mother,
Birth Date, Code1, Code2, Code3,
1st Sponsor First, 1st Sponsor Last,
2nd Sponsor First, 2nd Sponsor Last, Location,
Notes, Maiden Name, Priest

516, 21 Jun 1833, John, Miller, Sickfriet, Apolona, 15 Jun 1833, -, -, -, George , Gilmore, Barbary , Eiler, -, -, 17

517, 07 Jul 1833, John Adam, Doyle, John Adam, Anna Rebecca, 25 Dec 1832, -, -, -, Mrs. , Shirley, -, -, -, -, 17

518, 09 Aug 1833, Elisa Anna, Walsh, Patrick, Ellon, 17 May 1832, -, -, -, Anna (Mrs.), McGinley, -, -, -, -, 17

519, 07 Aug 1833, Sophia Milia, Cole, Michl, Mary, 27 Jun 1833, -, -, -, Sarah (Miss), Cole, -, -, -, -, 17

520, 09 Sep 1833, Catherine, Shorter, Charles, Catherine, 14 Jul 1833, -, B, B, "Old Eiza" [Eliza?], Shorter, -, -, -, -, 17

521, 12 Sep 1833, James Alois , Smith, Michl, Catherine, 11-Sep, -, -, -, Sophia (Miss), Smith , -, -, -, -, 17

522, 06 Sep 1833, James, Galvin, Denis, Margaret [?], 02 Sep 1833, -, -, -, Mrs., Bury, James, Becky [?], -, -, 17

523, 15 Nov 1833, Sarah Ellon, McIlhenney, Michl, Mary, 01 Nov 1833, -, -, -, John (Mrs.), Duffey, -, -, -, -, 17

524, 27 Dec 1833, Alexander , Provert [or Provent], -, -, blank, C, -, -, Timotheus , Ryan, -, -, Canal Contractor, -, 17

525, 09 Feb 1834, James, McGonnagal, James, Susan, 8-Feb, -, -, -, Mrs., McGonnagal, H., Kelly, -, -, 17

526, 09 Feb 1834, David , Tihlman, Thos, Mary, 20 Dec 1833, B, -, -, Charles [or Charlot], Truman, -, -, -, -, 17

527, 27 Feb 1834, John, Duffey, John, Bridget, 11 Feb 1834, -, -, -, Mrs., Conden, -, -, -, -, 17

528, 27 Feeb 1834, Margret, Tigert, Hugh, Margret, 23 Feb 1834, -, -, -, Magert (Miss), Carney, -, -, -, -, 17

529, 27 Feb 1834, Susan, Cline, *, -, 26 Jul 1831, PN, -, -, -, -, -, -, *"Baseborn", -, 17

530, 27 Feb 1834, Mary Elisabeth, Clegett, "Unknown", Elisa, 15 Nov 1833, -, -, -, -, -, -, -, -, -, 17

531, 23 Mar 1834, Charles, Tollen, John, Ellon, 13 Mar 1834, -, -, -, Patrick, Jefrey, Julian , Teeny, -, -, 17

532, 27 Apr 1834, Saml., Marellues, -, -, 21 years, -, -, -, -, -, -, -, C, -, 17

533, 27 Apr 1834, Anna, Cole, Philip, Sophia, 18 Apr 1832*, -, -, -, Charles, Sweeney, Anna , Doyel, *birthdate has [22 crossed out] 18 Apr 1832, -, 17

ST. MARY'S CATHOLIC CHURCH
HAGERSTOWN, MARYLAND, BAPTISMS:
Index, Bap Date, Child, Last Name, Father, Mother,
Birth Date, Code1, Code2, Code3,
1st Sponsor First, 1st Sponsor Last,
2nd Sponsor First, 2nd Sponsor Last, Location,
Notes, Maiden Name, Priest

534, 27 Apr 1834, Catherine, Cole, Philip, Sophia, 14 Mar 1834, -, -, -, Barney , Borys [or Borjs or Boys], Julian , Teeney, -, -, 17

535, 28 Apr 1834, Joseph Garret, Ford, John, Margret, 28 Mar 1832, -, -, -, N. (Mrs.), Stake, -, -, -, -, 17

536, 28 Apr 1834, John, Ford, John, Margret, 11 Feb 1834, -, -, -, Mrs., Lover, -, -, -, -, 17

537, 01 May 1834, John, Smith, Owen, Eliza, 23 Mar 1834, -, -, -, Eliza, Adams, -, -, -, -, 17

538, 28 Apr 1834, Wilm, Thomson, Isacc [or Dfeu], Rebecca, 11 Apr 1834, -, -, -, Catherine, Hawkins, -, -, -, -, 17

539, 04 May 1834, John, Collens, Mechl, Margret, 01 May 1834, -, -, -, Julian (Mrs.), Griffen, John, Murrey, -, -, 17

540, 08 May 1834, Thoms, Wolgamoth, John, Julian, 05 Feb 1833, -, -, -, Mary Anna, Shirley, -, -, -, -, 17

541, 10 May 1834, Sophia Mary (Mrs.), -, -, -, 30 years, -, -, -, T., Ryan, -, -, C, -, 17

542, 29 Apr 1834, Wilm (Mrs.), McClane, -, -, 28 years, -, -, -, -, -, -, -, C, -, 17

543, [blank], Mrs., Arnold, -, -, [blank], -, -, -, -, -, -, -, C; "Baptized on the missions and forgot to have their names inserted in Regular places", -, 17

544, [blank], Wilm, Elvord [?], -, -, 28 years, -, -, -, -, -, -, -, C; "Baptized on the missions and forgot to have their names inserted in Regular places", -, 17

545, 11 May 1834, Edward, McCartey, Edward, Catherine, 14 Mar 1834, -, -, -, James (Mrs.), McGonnagal, -, -, -, -, 17

546, 11 May 1834, Rebecca, Chambers, -, -, -, 03 Dec 1829, -, -, -, Mary (Mrs.), Stout, -, -, "an orphan in care of Sponsor", -, 17

547, 11 May 1834, Hariettea, Colmons, Alx, Metildas, 17 Mar 1834, B, B, B, Mary, Tilhman, -, -, -, -, 17

548, 18 May 1834, John Jacob, Justice, Jacob, Lucretia, 14 Mar 1834, -, -, -, Catherine, Justice, -, -, -, -, 17

549, 30 May 1834, Robert, Mitchel, Augustus, Elisabeth, 10 Apr 1833, -, -, -, John, Walsh, -, -, -, -, 17

550, 8 Jun 1834, Richard Thomas, Well Slager [?], Saml., Mary, 18 Apr 1834, -, -, -, Sarae [?], McGlannan, [Bridget Donnelly crossed out], -, -, -, 17

ST. MARY'S CATHOLIC CHURCH
HAGERSTOWN, MARYLAND, BAPTISMS:
Index, Bap Date, Child, Last Name, Father, Mother,
Birth Date, Code1, Code2, Code3,
1st Sponsor First, 1st Sponsor Last,
2nd Sponsor First, 2nd Sponsor Last, Location,
Notes, Maiden Name, Priest

551, 8 Jun 1834, Edward, Shaffer, Jonnathan, Eliza, 5 May 1834, -, -, -, Mrs., Conden, -, -, -, -, 17

552, 8 Jun 1834, Wilm Charls., Wallslager , Saml, Mary, 18 Apr 1834, -, -, -, Easter, Carney, -, -, -, -, 17

553, 8 Jun 1834, Susanna, Walsh, Richard, Margret, 19 Jan 1834, -, -, -, Bridget, Donnelly, -, -, -, -, 17

554, 10 Aug 1834, Catherine, Hurley, James, Sophia, 15 Aug 1834, -, -, -, John [possible middle name but illegible], Oppe [?], E. (Mrs.), Stashn [?], -, -, 17

555, 11 Aug 1834, John, Green [?], Patrick, Mary, 17 Jul 1834, -, -, -, Patrick, Mundy, Cath., Balry [?], -, -, 17

556, 27 Sep 1834, James, Kelly, Henery, Margret, 22 Sep 1834, -, -, -, E. (Mrs.), Doherty, -, -, -, -, 17

557, 27 Sep 1834, Carolina, Routh, Joe, Theodora, 22 Sep 1834, -, -, -, Garret, Otte, Margret, Stymmates [?], -, -, 17

558, 13 Oct 1834, Anna Elisabaeth, Metz, Casper, Elisabeth, 8 Oct 1834, -, -, -, Elisabeth, Hessberrgar, -, -, -, -, 17

559, 2 Nov 1834, Catherine, McClenlen, John, Anna, 6 Oct 1834, -, -, -, Archobold (Mrs.), Sulbert [?], -, -, -, -, 17

560, 16 Nov 1834, Cecilia, Gilmore, George, Elisabeth, 9-Nov, -, -, -, John [middle initial illegible], Hoppyse [?], Easter, Carney, -, -, 17

561, 30 Nov 1834, Henery Francis, Sulbert [or Aulbert], Archobold, Catherine, 19-Nov, -, -, -, Mrs., Jones, -, -, -, -, 17

562, 7 Dec 1834, Elizabeth, Barrowskae, Joseph, Christena, 4 Oct 1834, -, -, -, John Igna[runs in to margin], Hoppo, Margret, Carney, -, -, 17

563, 14 Dec 1834, Isabell, McGlennan, Patrick, Sarah, 30 Oct 1834, -, -, -, Easter, Carney, John, Dealy, -, -, 17

564, 4 Jan 1835, James Wilm., Kelly, Joseph, Catherine, 4 Nov 1834, -, -, -, James (Mrs.), McGonnagal, -, -, -, -, 17

565, 6 Jan 1835, Henrietta, Gallaspey, Antony, Catherine, 4 Jan 1835, -, -, -, Easter, Carney, -, -, -, -, 17

566, 1 Mar 1835, Wilm. Peter, Stabb [?], Olatius [?], Maria, 1 Jun 1834, -, -, -, Easter, Kenney, -, -, -, -, 17

567, 1 Mar 1835, Cornelius, McDermott, Michl, Maria, 6 Feb 1835, -, -, -, Catherine (Mrs.), Hawkens, -, -, -, -, 17

ST. MARY'S CATHOLIC CHURCH
HAGERSTOWN, MARYLAND, BAPTISMS:
Index, Bap Date, Child, Last Name, Father, Mother,
Birth Date, Code1, Code2, Code3,
1st Sponsor First, 1st Sponsor Last,
2nd Sponsor First, 2nd Sponsor Last, Location,
Notes, Maiden Name, Priest

568, 26 Mar 1835, Leonard [?] Joseph, Sheling, Jochim, Francis, 2 Aug 1834, -, -, -, G. (Mrs.), Gilender [?], -, -, -, -, 17

569, 29 Mar 1835, Charles, Bird [?], Isaac, Marietta, 20 Nov 1834, -, -, -, Margret, Carney, -, -, -, -, 17

570, 11 Apr 1835, Anna Eliza, Davis, John, Mary Anna, 8 Ajpr 1835, -, -, -, Mrs., Shirley, -, -, -, -, 17

571, 20 Apr 1835, James, Sweeney, Charly, Elisabeth, 17 Apr 1835, -, -, -, Patrick (Mrs.), Doyle, -, -, -, -, 17

572, 17 May 1835, Saml., Deggs, Jacob, Rachel, 24 Mar 1835, -, -, -, George, Gilmore [?], -, -, -, -, 17

573, 17 May 1835, Daniel, Diggs, Jacob, Rachel, 24 Mar 1835, -, - , -, Charl., Donnelly, -, -, -, -, 17

574, 18 May 1835, Elizabeth, McClane, -, -, -, -, -, -, -, -, -, -, widow of Jasias McClane, -, 17

575, 25 May 1835, Richard, Doyel , John Adam, Rebecca, 25-Mar, -, -, -, Christophor ("Old Mrs."), Murphy, -, -, -, -, 17

576, 13 Jun 1835, Danial , Mitx , Antony, Clare, 24 Oct 1833, -, - , -, John, Merko, Elizabeth , Hessberger, -, -, 17

577, 13 Jun 1835, Mary Ellon, McCane, Thos, Sarah, 03 Nov 1834, -, -, -, Mrs., Fox, -, -, -, -, 17

578, 21 Jun 1835, Louisa, Clemons, Alex, Matilda, 02 Apr 1835, -, -, -, Cather, Shorter, -, -, -, -, 17

579, 06 Jul 1835, Elizabeth (Mrs.), Mettegin?, -, -, 26 years, -, -, -, -, -, -, -, C, -, 17

580, 07 Jul 1835, Charlotte (Mrs.), Makay [or Nakay], -, -, 28 years, -, -, -, -, -, -, -, C; from Hancock, -, 17

581, 29 Jul 1835, Anna Adelin [?], Messmann, Henery, Adelin [?], 26-Jul, -, -, -, Garret F., Pool, Adelin T , Shockert, -, -, 17

582, 30 Aug 1835, Augustin, McGonnagal, James, Susan, 28 Aug 1835, -, -, -, Chrty ("Old Mrs."), Murphy, -, -, -, -, 17

583, [blank], Terresa Anna , Root, -, -, 26 years, C, -, -, -, -, -, -, -, -, 17

584, 7-Nov, Maria, Pridy?, Thos, Mary, 01 Sep 1835, -, -, -, Patrick , Monohan, Mrs. , Conden, -, -, 17

585, 10 Dec 1835, Catherine, Ryan, Wilm, Mary, 29-Nov, -, -, -, Andy [?] (Mrs.), Cohrin [?], -, -, -, -, 17

ST. MARY'S CATHOLIC CHURCH
HAGERSTOWN, MARYLAND, BAPTISMS:
Index, Bap Date, Child, Last Name, Father, Mother,
Birth Date, Code1, Code2, Code3,
1st Sponsor First, 1st Sponsor Last,
2nd Sponsor First, 2nd Sponsor Last, Location,
Notes, Maiden Name, Priest

586, 12 Dec 1835, Isabele , Conrod, -, -, 27 years, C, -, -, -, -, -, -, Baptized at Old Mrs. Bevans, Fifteen Mile Creek, -, 17
587, 12 Dec 1835, Mary Jane , Anderson, -, -, 8 years, C, -, -, -, -, - , -,Baptized at Old Mrs. Bevans, Fifteen Mile Creek, -, 17
588, 12 Dec 1835, Elisa, Cavender, -, -, 9 years, -, -, -, -, -, -, -, Baptized at Old Mrs. Bevans, Fifteen Mile Creek, -, 17
589, 21 Dec 1835, Bridget, Keough, John, Mary, 15 Oct 1835, -, -, -, "Vare [?] or Wire", Gough, -, -, -, -, 17
590, 28 Dec 1835, Catherine, Murphy, Wm, Margaret , 15 months, -, -, -, Danl., Hagan [or Hagar], Mary, Casey, -, Doolan, 38
591, 29 Dec 1835, James, Ellis, -, -, 28 years, -, -, -, -, -, -, -, "a native of Wales England. At the upper Dam - or Charley O'Brien's big Shantee in the vicinity of Mr. Michl. Smith"; C, -, 17
592, 1 Jan 1836, Mary Mercy , May, -, -, 12 years, -, -, -, John (Rev.), Healy, -, -, C, -, 17
593, 31 Jan 1836, James Demetrius, Hurley, James, Sophia, -, -, -, -, James , Bury, Eliza, Monaghan, -, Smyth, 38
594, 10 Feb 1836, Mary, Higgins, -, -, 20 years, -, -, -, -, -, -, -, at her Brother's house in Virginia near the Catholic Church at Fifteen Mile Creek, Maryland, -, 17
595, 22 Feb 1836, Mary (Mrs.), Tidball , -, -, 40 years, -, -, -, Timotheus , Ryan, -, -, C, -, 17
596, 22 Feb 1836, Mary Catherine, Mindrum?, Henery, Mary Catherine, 19 Feb 1836, -, -, -, Mrs. , Gilmore, John (Fr.), Healy, -, -, 17
597, 28 Feb 1836, Simean [or Simcan], Tighlman, Thoms, Mary, 21 Jan 1836, B, -, -, Judy , Gallawy, -, -, -, -, 17
598, 28 Mar 1836, Simon Saml , Barker, Hambelton, Nancy, 9 years, B, -, -, Janck , Truman, -, -, -, -, 17
599, 28 Mar 1836, Mary Frances, Truman, Jack, Sarah, 11-Mar, -, -, -, Judy , Gallowe, -, -, -, -, 17
600, 02 Apr 1836, Mary, Renner, Ignatis, Mary, 25 Oct 1835, -, -, - , John , Morco, Elizabeth , Marshbay, -, -, 17
601, 03 Apr 1836, Margret , Seffer[?], Jonnothan, [blank], 13, C, -, -, T., Ryan, -, -, -, -, 17
602, 03 Apr 1836, Upton Otho, Sheffer, Jonothen, Elizabeth, 06 Feb 1836, -, -, -, Margret. , Leffer, -, -, -, -, 38

ST. MARY'S CATHOLIC CHURCH
HAGERSTOWN, MARYLAND, BAPTISMS:
Index, Bap Date, Child, Last Name, Father, Mother,
Birth Date, Code1, Code2, Code3,
1st Sponsor First, 1st Sponsor Last,
2nd Sponsor First, 2nd Sponsor Last, Location,
Notes, Maiden Name, Priest

603, 26 Jan 1836, Philip , Prinston, -, -, 25 years, B, -, -, -, -, -, -, C, -, 17

604, [blank], Antony, Shilling, Dnacum, Francesca, 2 months, -, -, -, Mary, Miller, -, -, -, -, 17

605, 17 Apr 1836, Elizabeth (Mrs.) (widow), Ward, -, -, 28 years, - , -, -, Mr., Kelley, Mrs., Kelley [HB], C; "in Mr. Kelleys Shantee on John Gormans Contract near Round top", -, 17

606, 23 Apr 1836, John, McCartney, Edward, Catherine, 27 Jun 1835, -, -, -, Mary , McLouhlen, -, -, -, -, 17

607, 27 Apr 1836, Ellenora, Galvin, Davis , Margret, 24 Apr 1836, -, -, -, Mrs. Bury, Bury, James, Bury [son of Mrs. Bury], -, -, 17

608, 12-May, Anna Maria, Gibbell, Michl, Catherine, [blank], -, -, -, Casper , Metz, Elizabeth , Metz, -, -, 38

609, 04 May 1836, Rebecca , O'Riely, -, -, 36 years, -, -, -, P. (Mrs.), Fitzpatrick, T., Ryan, C; she is described as "formerly the widow FitzSimmons, in Hancock", -, 17

610, 22 May 1836, Margaret Catherine, Walsh, Richard, Margaret, [blank], -, -, -, Mary, Welsleider, -, -, -, Gower, 38

611, 27-Jun, Sally , Sterling, Wm, Maria, 16 years, C, -, -, J., Healy, Mrs., Conson [?], -, Myers, 38

612, [blank], Auguston , Mitchel, -, -, 7 years, C, -, -, Old Tergus , McCosker, -, -, -, -, 17

613, 17 Jul 1836, Edward Joseph, Kelley, Joseph [Henry crossed], Catherin, 18-Jun, -, -, -, James (Mrs.), McGonnagal, -, -, -, -, 17

614, 17 Jul 1836, Elizabeth , May [or Hay], -, -, -, C, -, -, T., R. [Father Ryan], -, -, -, -, 17

615, 07 Aug 1836, Tho. (Mrs.), Corbitt, -, -, 30 years, C, -, -, -, -, -, -, -, -, 17

616, 08 Aug 1836, [male], Apernathy, -, -, 34 years, -, -, -, -, -, -, -, C, -, 17

617, 01 Aug 1836, Mary, Walsh, Martin, Mary, 27 Jul 1836, -, -, -, James, Dce, Sophia (Mrs.), Jones, -, -, 17

618, 22 Aug 1836, John , Lambert, -, -, 45 years, C, -, -, -, -, -, -, -, -, -, 17

619, 02 Oct 1836, Catherine Alousa, Aulbert, Archey, Catherene, 30 Sep 1836, -, -, -, Eliza , Adams, -, -, -, -, 17

ST. MARY'S CATHOLIC CHURCH
HAGERSTOWN, MARYLAND, BAPTISMS:
Index, Bap Date, Child, Last Name, Father, Mother,
Birth Date, Code1, Code2, Code3,
1st Sponsor First, 1st Sponsor Last,
2nd Sponsor First, 2nd Sponsor Last, Location,
Notes, Maiden Name, Priest

620, 20 Nov 1836, Mary Sophia, Davis, John, Mary Anna, 13-Nov, -, -, -, Anna (Miss), Chester, -, -, -, -, 17

621, 25 Dec 1836, Michl, Hilldebrand, Michl, Apolinia, 23 Apr 1836, -, -, -, Mech, Sprout, -, -, -, -, 17

622, -, -, -, -, -, -, -, -, -, -, -, -, -, This entry intentionally left empty., -, 17

623, 15 Jan 1837, Robert, Mills, -, -, 14 years, -, -, -, Patrick, McMannany [?], -, -, John Myers Contract; C, -, 17

624, 15 Jan 1837, [male], Mills, -, -, -, -, -, -, -, -, -, -, "and some months prior - two younger brothers" of Patrick were baptized, -, 17

625, 16 Jan 1837, [male], Mills, -, -, -, -, -, -, -, -, -, -, "and some months prior - two younger brothers" of Patrick were baptized, -, 17

626, 21 Jan 1836*, Mary, Roach, -, -, 30 years, -, -, -, Upt. C. [?], Byolos [?], -, -, C; *in baptismal date of 21 Jan 1836, could the priest have meant 1837?, -, 17

627, 23 Jan 1837, Martin, Meades, Terrencr, Margret, 3 months, -, -, -, Miss , McElroy, Micl , McCosker, -, -, 17

628, 19 Mar 1837, Sarah Jane, Gilmore, George, Eisabeth, 09 Mar 1837, -, -, -, James , Hurley, Eliza , FitzGerald, -, -, 17

629, 20 Apr 1837, children, -, -, -, -, -, -, -, -, -, -, -, "at the widow Peter McCosker's Wilmsport"; See Endnote 16, -, 17

630, 12 Apr 1837, Mary, Baker, -, -, 25 years, -, -, -, -, -, -, -, Mr. O'Herrens Shanty; C, -, 17

631, 13 Apr 1837, Jane E. , Pickens, -, -, 24 years, -, -, -, -, -, -, -, "married the same day to Thos. Kelly"; C, -, 17

632, 14 Apr 1837, [male], -, -, -, -, B, -, -, -, -, -, -, "Baptized a Coloured Man whose name I forget and was married the same evening to to [sic] Capt Jonsons' Colourd woman"; Hancock; C , -, 17

633, 19 Apr 1837, James, Farr, -, -, 35 years, -, -, -, -, -, -, -, C; "died in an hour afterwards", -, 17

634, 14 Apr 1837, James (Capt.), Hook, -, -, 46 years, -, -, -, -, -, -, -, C; "from Hancock", -, 17

635, 07 May 1837, Mary Elizabeth, Fisher, Joseph, Mary, 08 Apr 1837, -, -, -, Mary (Mrs.), Shopaerd, -, -, -, -, 17

ST. MARY'S CATHOLIC CHURCH
HAGERSTOWN, MARYLAND, BAPTISMS:
Index, Bap Date, Child, Last Name, Father, Mother,
Birth Date, Code1, Code2, Code3,
1st Sponsor First, 1st Sponsor Last,
2nd Sponsor First, 2nd Sponsor Last, Location,
Notes, Maiden Name, Priest

636, 17 Jun 1837, Susana Catharina, Gonter, Johenis, Annae, 5 years, -, -, -, -, -, -, -, -, -, 16

637, 17 Jun 1837, Johannes, Gonter, Johannis, Annae, 2 years, -, -, -, -, -, -, -, -, -, 16

638, 17 Jun 1837, Guillelmus, Fisher, Christophori, Mariae, 02 Jun 1837, -, -, -, A., McManus, Rosa , McDonnel, -, Luttman, 16

639, 18 Jun 1837, Maria, Egan, Petri, Catharinae, -, -, -, -, Joannes M. , Longstaff, Maria , McEvoy, -, -, 16

640, 18 Jun 1837, Catharina, Murray, Henrii, Catharinae, -, -, -, -, Hugo , Shue, Catharina , Clarke, -, Raynalds, 16

641, 18 Jun 1837, Catharina, Clarke, Joannis, Catharinae, 05 Jun 1837, -, -, -, Christophors , Lann, -, -, -, Carr, 16

642, 18 Jun 1837, Maria, Scot, Patricii, Mariae, 05 Jun 1837, -, -, -, Antonius , Degan, Anna , Cassidy [or Cannidy], -, Williams, 16

643, 20 Jun 1837, Joannes, Colvin, Andreae, Hellenae, 9 Jun 1837, -, -, -, Joanne, Hughes, Rosa, McCabe, Clear Spring, -, 16

644, 01 Jul 1837, Guillellarus, Maxwell, Guillelini, Catharinae, 29 Jun 1837, -, -, -, -, -, -, -, -, Hancock, -, 16

645, 04 Jul 1837, Maria, Hawkens, Joannis, -, -, -, -, -, -, -, -, -, -, Hancock; parents are married; appears to read "jus saror Aimeca Catharina", -, 16

646, 04 Jul 1837, Anna Catharina, Hawkens, Joannis, -, -, -, -, -, -, -, -, -, Hancock; sister of the above; parents are married, -, 16

647, 07 Jul 1837, Catharina, Maus, Petri, Joannae, 26 May 1837, -, -, -, -, -, -, -, -, Corbet, 16

648, 07 Jul 1837, Mathildis Anna, Lewis, Joannis, Elisabeth, 27 Apr 1837, -, -, -, Thomas, Means, Anna, Moor, -, Doxè, 16

649, 21 Jul 1837, Carolina, Marks , Joannis, Carolina, 1 year, -, -, - , M., Stake, -, -, Williamsport, Schultz, 16

650, 21 Jul 1837, Birgitta, O'Brian, -, -, 19 Jul 1837, -, -, -, -, -, -, -, -, -, 16

651, 04 Aug 1837, Guillelimus, Nevel, Michaelis, Rosae, 24-Jul, -, -, -, -, -, -, -, -, -, 16

652, 04 Aug 1837, Catharina Anna, Murray, Danienil, [blank], 31-Jul, -, -, -, -, -, -, -, -, -, 16

653, 06 Aug 1837, Joannes, Golden, Michaelis , [blank], 12-Jul, -, -, -, -, -, -, -, -, -, 16

ST. MARY'S CATHOLIC CHURCH
HAGERSTOWN, MARYLAND, BAPTISMS:
Index, Bap Date, Child, Last Name, Father, Mother,
Birth Date, Code1, Code2, Code3,
1st Sponsor First, 1st Sponsor Last,
2nd Sponsor First, 2nd Sponsor Last, Location,
Notes, Maiden Name, Priest

654, 08 Aug 1837, Henricus, Shuhe, Hugonis, [blank], 14-Jul, -, -, -, -, -, -, -, -, -, 16

655, 08 Aug 1837, Cornelius, Gallagham, Petri, [blank], Jul, -, -, -, -, -, -, -, -, -, 16

656, 12 Aug 1837, Catharina, Hegan, Terentii, Catharinae, 28 Feb 1837, -, -, -, -, -, -, -, -, -, 16

657, 20 Aug 1837, Elisabeth Hellena, [blank], Joannis, Mariae, -, -, -, -, Eli, Adams, -, -, Hagerstown, -, 16

658, 23 Aug 1837, Joannia, Morearty, Thomae, Margarethae, 15-Aug, -, -, -, -, -, -, -, Canal, -, 16

659, 23 Aug 1837, Danielis, Condon, A. [or R.], Joannae, 20-Aug, -, -, -, -, -, -, -, Canal, -, 16

660, 23 Aug 1837, Joannes, Ledan, Joannis, [blank], 2 years, -, -, -, -, -, -, -, Canal, -, 16

661, 23 Aug 1837, Maria Ludovica, Ledan, Joannis, Annae, 2 years, -, -, -, -, -, -, -, Canal, -, 16

662, 23 Aug 1837, Maria, Drennan, Thomae, Catharinae, 20-Aug, -, -, -, -, -, -, -, Canal, -, 16

663, 25 Aug 1837, Carolina, Kaisert, Jacobi Frediria, Theresiae, 2 years, -, -, -, -, -, -, -, Williamsport, Luthringer [?], 16

664, 30 Aug 1837, Anna, Gelaspe, Anthonii, Catharinae, 22-Aug, -, -, -, -, -, -, -, Above Hancock, -, 16

665, 31 Aug 1837, Jacobus, Smith, Michaelis, Brigitae, 22-Aug, -, -, -, -, -, -, -, Hancock, -, 16

666, 31 Aug 1837, Maria, McNulty, Henrici, Margaretae, 20-Aug, -, -, -, -, -, -, -, Hancock, -, 16

667, 01 Sep 1837, Joannes, Clofy, Charoli, Estheris, 16-Aug, -, -, -, -, -, -, -, -, -, 16

668, 01 Sep 1837, Joannes, Bauman, Georgii, Mariae, 07 Aug 1836, -, -, -, -, -, -, -, -, -, 16

669, 03 Sep 1837, Anna, Dexson, Thomas, Mariae, 8-Aug, -, -, -, -, -, -, -, -, -, 16

670, 04 Sep 1837, Maria Anna, Manuel, Thomas, Mariae, 11 Jan 1837, -, -, -, -, -, -, -, -, -, 16

671, 05 Sep 1837, Patricius, Munday, Patricii, Catharinae, 1-Sep, -, -, -, -, -, -, -, Hancock, -, 16

ST. MARY'S CATHOLIC CHURCH
HAGERSTOWN, MARYLAND, BAPTISMS:
Index, Bap Date, Child, Last Name, Father, Mother,
Birth Date, Code1, Code2, Code3,
1st Sponsor First, 1st Sponsor Last,
2nd Sponsor First, 2nd Sponsor Last, Location,
Notes, Maiden Name, Priest

672, 05 Sep 1837, Catharina Sophia, Conneling, Joannis, Sophias, -, -, -, -, -, -, -, -, -, -, 16

673, 05 Sep 1837, Elisabetha, Fallen, Michaelis, Susannae, -, -, -, -, -, -, -, -, -, -, 16

674, 05 Sep 1837, Catharina, Catharinae, Joannis, Catharine, 31-Aug, -, -, -, -, -, -, -, -, -, -, 16

675, 17 Sep 1837, Margareta, Heverle, Nicolai, Christinae, 27 Sep 1836, -, -, -, -, -, -, -, -, -, -, 16

676, 17 Sep 1837, Joannae Rebecca, Schoeffer, Joannis, Catharinae, 13 months, -, -, -, -, -, -, -, -, -, -, 16

677, 24 Sep 1837, Sophia, Clemens, Alexander, Matildis, 01 May 1837, -, -, -, -, -, -, -, -, -, -, 16

678, 12 Sep 1837, Joannes, Marren [?], Patricii, [blank], 5-Sep, -, -, -, -, -, -, -, -, -, 16

679, 12 Sep 1837, Maria, Degan, Antonii, Maria, 11-Sep, -, -, -, -, -, -, -, -, -, 16

680, 12 Sep 1837, Joannes Daniel, Boxter, Danieli, Maria, 4-Sep, -, -, -, -, -, -, -, -, -, 16

681, 12 Sep 1837, Joanna* , Kelley, Mias[?], Mariae, -, -, -, -, -, -, -, -, -, *Joanna [Margaretha crossed out], -, 16

682, 13 Sep 1837, Jacob, Coyle, Marei[?], Elisabeth, 5 years, -, -, -, -, -, -, -, -, -, 16

683, 13 Sep 1837, Jacob, Coyle, Marei[?], Elisabeth, 3 years, -, -, -, -, -, -, -, -, -, 16

684, 13 Sep 1837, Elisabeth, Coyle, Marei[?], Elisabeth, 14 months, -, -, -, -, -, -, -, -, -, 16

685, 13 Sep 1837, Hellena, Day, Michaelis, H [rest blank], 11 Sep 1837, -, -, -, -, -, -, -, -, -, 16

686, 13 Sep 1837, Catharina Maria, Draper, Georgii, Mariae, 20 Aug 1837, -, -, -, -, -, -, -, -, -, 16

687, 26 Sep 1837, Guillemas, Sullivan, Timothiei, Hellenae, 19-Sep, -, -, -, -, -, -, -, -, -, 16

688, 27 Sep 1837, Thomas, Coashman [first or last name?], Coashman [first or last name?], Birg, 14-Sep, -, -, -, -, -, -, -, -, -, 16

689, 01 Oct 1837, Teresia, Bevans, Walter, Mariae Annae, 29 Sep 1837, -, -, -, -, -, -, -, -, Fifteen Mile Creek , -, 16

**ST. MARY'S CATHOLIC CHURCH
HAGERSTOWN, MARYLAND, BAPTISMS:
Index, Bap Date, Child, Last Name, Father, Mother,
Birth Date, Code1, Code2, Code3,
1st Sponsor First, 1st Sponsor Last,
2nd Sponsor First, 2nd Sponsor Last, Location,
Notes, Maiden Name, Priest**

690, 01 Oct 1837, Thomas, Sharidan, Mathei, Joannae, 15 Sep 1837, -, -, -, -, -, -, -, Tunnel [Paw Paw Tunnel on C & O Canal], -, 16

691, 01 Oct 1837, A. Maria, Collon, Jacobi, Adelaidis, 8 Sep 1837, -, -, -, -, -, -, -, Tunnel [Paw Paw Tunnel on C & O Canal], -, 16

692, 05 Oct 1837, Matheldis, McCormick, Martini, Annae, 28 ___ 1837, -, -, -, -, -, -, -, -, -, 16

693, 10 Oct 1837, Helena, Stake, Eliae, Helena, Aug, -, -, -, -, -, -, -, -, -, 16

694, 10 Oct 1837, Helena Catharina, McDermott, [blank], Mariae, 1-Aug, -, -, -, -, -, -, -, -, -, 16

695, 16 Oct 1837, Jacobus, Dormor, Martini, Juliae, 2-Oct, -, -, -, -, -, -, -, -, -, 16

696, 17 Oct 1837, Maria Helena, McCarty, Michaelis, Catharinae, 10-Aug, -, -, -, -, -, -, -, -, -, 16

697, 22 Oct 1837, Petrus, Smith, Joshae, Eustasiae, 2 months, -, -, -, -, -, -, -, -, -, 16

698, 23 Oct 1837, Michael, McDonnel, Michaelis, Annae, 20-Oct, -, -, -, -, -, -, -, -, -, 16

699, 24 Oct 1837, Julia, Brit?, Joannis, Winifred, 19-Oct, -, -, -, -, -, -, -, -, -, 16

700, 30 Oct 1837, Bernardus Thomas, Hughes, Henriei, Mariae, 25 Oct 1837, -, -, -, -, -, -, -, -, -, 16

701, 30 Oct 1837, Michael, Shoise, Michaelis, Mariae, 29, -, -, -, -, -, -, -, -, -, 16

702, 05 Nov 1837, Thomas, Smith, Henrici, Mariae, 05 Nov 1837, -, -, -, -, -, -, -, -, -, 16

703, 06 Nov 1837, Birgita, Byrne, Pierce, Franciscae, 02 Nov 1837, -, -, -, -, -, -, -, -, -, 16

704, 07 Nov 1837, Joannes* , Galvey, Bartholomei, Helenae, 06 Nov 1837, -, -, -, -, -, -, -, *Joannes [Bartholomew is crossed out], -, 16

705, 17 Nov 1837, Maria, Farrel, Jacobi, Catharinae, 16 Nov 1837, -, -, -, -, -, -, -, -, -, 16

706, 19 Nov 1837, Thomas, Curley, Patricii, Catharinae, -, -, -, -, -, -, -, -, -, -, 16

ST. MARY'S CATHOLIC CHURCH
HAGERSTOWN, MARYLAND, BAPTISMS:
Index, Bap Date, Child, Last Name, Father, Mother,
Birth Date, Code1, Code2, Code3,
1st Sponsor First, 1st Sponsor Last,
2nd Sponsor First, 2nd Sponsor Last, Location,
Notes, Maiden Name, Priest

707, 20 Nov 1837, Jacobus, Brickley, Gueillimi, Juliae, 18 Nov 1837, -, -, -, -, -, -, -, -, -, 16

708, 21 Nov 1837, Joannes, Lee, Patricii, Margaretae, 09 Nov 1837, -, -, -, -, -, -, -, -, -, 16

709, 21 Nov 1837, Maria, Drescoll, Michaelis, Carolinae, -, -, -, -, -, -, -, -, -, Laver, 16

710, 21 Nov 1837, Elisabeth, Masom, -, -, -, -, -, -, -, -, -, -, -, -, 16

711, 21 Nov 1837, Elisabeth [2nd entry], -, -, -, -, -, -, -, -, -, -, -, -, -, 16

712, 24 Nov 1837, Jacobus, O'Brian, Patricii, Margaretae, 23 Nov 1837, -, -, -, -, -, -, -, -, -, 16

713, 24 Nov 1837, Michael, Riley, Michaelis, Catharinae, 23 Nov 1837, -, -, -, -, -, -, -, -, -, 16

714, 24 Nov 1837, Patricius, Kelley, Joannis, Annae, 19 Nov 1837, -, -, -, -, -, -, -, -, -, 16

715, 29 Nov 1837, Joannes Philipus, Steinmichel, Anreas, Franciscae, 13 Nov 1837, -, -, -, -, -, -, -, -, -, 16

716, 30 Nov 1837, Timotheus, Morenam, Joannis, Joannae, 23 Nov 1837, -, -, -, -, -, -, -, -, -, 16

717, 30 Nov 1837, Guillellmus Franciscus, Dermody, Guellelini, Franciscae, 26 Nov 1837, -, -, -, -, -, -, -, -, -, 16

718, 01 Dec 1837, Jacobus, Spense, Jacobi, Anna, 19 Oct 1822, -, -, -, -, -, -, -, -, -, 16

719, 02 Dec 1837, Guillelmus, Loynes, Patricii, Catharinae, 16-Oct, -, -, -, -, -, -, -, -, -, 16

720, 03 Dec 1837, Josephus Albertus, Renner, Ignatii, Mariae Annae, 23-Nov, -, -, -, -, -, -, -, -, -, 16

721, 03 Dec 1837, Catharina Anna, Gillan, Patricii, Winefart, 23-Nov, -, -, -, -, -, -, -, -, -, 16

722, 03 Dec 1837, Joannes, Daugherty, Michaelis, blank, *, -, -, -, -, -, -, -, *the age appears to read "pausis Duobus annbia[?]", -, 16

723, 03 Dec 1837, Michael, Fallen, Guillelini, Margaretae, -, -, -, -, -, -, -, -, -, -, 16

724, 14 Dec 1837, Maria, O'Brian, Caroli, Mariae, 2 Dec 1837, -, -, -, -, -, -, -, -, 16

725, 14 Dec 1837, Philippus, Dormady [?], Philippi, Helenae, 2 Dec 1837, -, -, -, -, -, -, -, -, -, 16

ST. MARY'S CATHOLIC CHURCH
HAGERSTOWN, MARYLAND, BAPTISMS:
Index, Bap Date, Child, Last Name, Father, Mother,
Birth Date, Code1, Code2, Code3,
1st Sponsor First, 1st Sponsor Last,
2nd Sponsor First, 2nd Sponsor Last, Location,
Notes, Maiden Name, Priest

726, 14 Dec 1837, Thomas, Welsh, Martini, Birgettae, 2 Dec 1837, -, -, -, -, -, -, -, -, -, 16

727, 14 Dec 1837, Anna, Dunn, Guillelmi, Mariae, 2 Dec 1837, -, -, -, -, -, -, -, -, -, -, 16

728, 15 Dec 1837, Joannes, Doyle, Joannis, Elisabethae, 8 Dec 1837, -, -, -, -, -, -, -, -, -, -, 16

729, 15 Dec 1837, Michael, More, Joannis, Sarae, 1 Dec 1837, -, -, -, -, -, -, -, -, -, -, 16

730, 16 Dec 1837, Joannes, McCabe, Patricii, blank, 3 Dec 1837, -, -, -, -, -, -, -, -, -, 16

731, 16 Dec 1837, Margareta, Shanaham, Christophori, Birgittae, 5 Dec 1837, -, -, -, -, -, -, -, -, -, -, 16

732, 23 Dec 1837, Joannes, Golvin, Dionysii, Margaretae, 7 Dec 1837, -, -, -, Jacobus, Bury, Anna, Bury, -, -, 16

733, 23 Dec 1837, Margareta Anna, Trueman, Joannes, Sarae, 2 Dec 1837, -, -, -, -, -, -, -, -, -, 16

734, 27 Dec 1837, Anna, Ryan, Guillelini, Mariae, 19 Dec 1837, -, -, -, -, -, -, -, -, -, 16

735, 27 Dec 1837, Michael, Delay, Joannes A., Mariae, 23 Dec 1837, -, -, -, -, -, -, -, -, -, 16

736, 27 Dec 1837, Julia, Driscal, Timothei, Isabellae, 12 Dec 1837, -, -, -, -, -, -, -, -, -, 16

737, 29 Dec 1837, Joannes, Tracy, Michaelis, Annae, 27 Dec 1837, -, -, -, -, -, -, -, -, -, 16

738, 29 Dec 1837, Michael, Cardal, Martini, Mariae, 2 Dec 1837, -, -, -, -, -, -, -, -, -, 16

739, 03 Jan 1838, Ladovicus Henricus, Buttler, -, Catharinae, 25 Sep 1837, PN, -, -, -, -, -, -, -, -, 16

740, 06 Jan 1838, Maria Anna, Gatton, Jackariae, Helena Josephina, 09 Oct 1837, -, -, -, -, -, -, -, -, -, 16

741, 09 Jan 1838, Michael, Colvin, Michaelis, Joannae, 22 Dec 1837, -, -, -, -, -, -, -, -, -, 16

742, 09 Jan 1838, Joannes, O'Donnel, Joannis, Margaretae, 7 Jan 1838, -, -, -, -, -, -, -, -, -, 16

743, 09 Jan 1838, Anna, Kan , Guillelmi, Marcellae, 22 Dec 1837, -, -, -, -, -, -, -, -, -, 16

ST. MARY'S CATHOLIC CHURCH
HAGERSTOWN, MARYLAND, BAPTISMS:
Index, Bap Date, Child, Last Name, Father, Mother,
Birth Date, Code1, Code2, Code3,
1st Sponsor First, 1st Sponsor Last,
2nd Sponsor First, 2nd Sponsor Last, Location,
Notes, Maiden Name, Priest

744, 10 Jan 1838, Thomas, Cadlwell, Patricii, blank, 03 Jan 1838, -, -, -, -, -, -, -, -, -, 16

745, 10 Jan 1838, Birgitta, Holton, Michaelis, Annae, 01 Jan 1838, -, -, -, -, -, -, -, -, -, 16

746, __ Jan 1838, David, Digs, Jacobi, Rachel, 24 Nov 1837, -, -, -, -, -, -, -, -, -, 16

747, 18 Jan 1838, Jacobus Henricus, Cahill, Jacobi, Mariae, 15 Jan 1838, -, -, -, -, -, -, -, -, -, 16

748, 18 Jan 1838, Thomas, Hurley, Thomae, Mariae, 3 Jan 1838, -, -, -, -, -, -, -, -, -, 16

749, 18 Jan 1838, Maria, Browne, Murrough Graydan, Elisabeth, 18 Dec 1837, -, -, -, -, -, -, -, -, -, 16

750, 19 Jan 1838, Henricus, Lichty, Jacobi, Catharinae, 2 Jun 1837, -, -, -, -, -, -, -, -, -, 16

751, 20 Jan 1838, "Ludovicus (son of)", -, -, -, -, -, -, -, -, -, -, -, rest of the entry is blank, -, 16

752, 20 Jan 1838, Margareta, Whelan, Guillelnni, Mariae, 20 Jan 1838, -, -, -, -, -, -, -, -, -, 16

753, 27 Jan 1838, Helena, Gallagher, Michaelis, Birgettae, 10 Jan 1838, -, -, -, -, -, -, -, -, -, 16

754, 01 Feb 1838, Jacobus, Callahen, Joannis, Annae, 27 Jan 1838, -, -, -, -, -, -, -, -, -, 16

755, 02 Feb 1838, Maria, Kelly, Thomae, Joannae, 28 Jan 1838, -, -, -, -, -, -, -, -, -, 16

756, 02 Feb 1838, Joannes, -, Jareth, Elisabetha, 6 years, PN, -, -, -, -, -, -, -, -, 16

757, 03 Feb 1838, Hugo, Quigley, Patricii, Mariae, 21 Jan 1838, -, -, -, -, -, -, -, -, -, 16

758, 05 Feb 1838, Joannes, Fallan, Patricii, Birgittae, 24 Jan 1838, -, -, -, -, -, -, -, -, -, 16

759, 12 Feb 1838, Jacobus, Karbey, Francisii, Helenae, 7 Feb 1838, -, -, -, -, -, -, -, -, -, 16

760, 13 Feb 1838, Joannes, Ward, Michaelis, Annae, 1 Feb 1838, -, -, -, -, -, -, -, -, -, 16

761, 18 Feb 1838, Guillelmus, Dawling, Joannis, Margaretae, 5 Feb 1838, -, -, -, -, -, -, -, -, -, 16

ST. MARY'S CATHOLIC CHURCH
HAGERSTOWN, MARYLAND, BAPTISMS:
Index, Bap Date, Child, Last Name, Father, Mother,
Birth Date, Code1, Code2, Code3,
1st Sponsor First, 1st Sponsor Last,
2nd Sponsor First, 2nd Sponsor Last, Location,
Notes, Maiden Name, Priest

762, 18 Feb 1838, Edwardus, Byrnes, Joannis, Catharinae, 15 Feb 1838, -, -, -, -, -, -, -, -, -, 16

763, 18 Feb 1838, Anna, Byrnes, Joannis, Catharinae, 15 Feb 1838, -, -, -, -, -, -, -, -, -, 16

764, 19 Feb 1838, Henricus, Steyet, Conradi, Carolinae, 30 Jan 1838, PN, -, -, -, -, -, -, -, Wihand, 16

765, 26 Feb 1838, Joannes Thomas, Bear, -, -, -, -, -, -, -, -, -, -, -, -, 16

766, 26 Feb 1838, Catharina, Bear, -, -, -, -, -, -, -, -, -, -, -, -, 16

767, 26 Feb 1838, Joanna dau., Morearty, Jacobi, Mariae, 25 Feb 1838, -, -, -, -, -, -, -, -, -, 16

768, 27 Feb 1838, -, -, Jacobi, Elisabeth Annae, Feb 1838, -, -, -, -, -, -, -, this record has been erased almost completely , -, 39

769, 02 Mar 1838, Patricius, Daughony, Jacobi, Birgittae, 27 Feb, -, -, -, -, -, -, -, -, -, 16

770, 03 Mar 1838, Joannes, McKey , Jacobi, Annae, 27 Dec 1837, -, -, -, -, -, -, -, Dam [one of the dams on the C & O Canal], -, 16

771, 04 Mar 1838, Jacobus, Doyle, Edwardi, Eleonarae, 13 Feb, -, -, -, -, -, -, -, Tunnel [Paw Paw Tunnel on C & O Canal], -, 16

772, 04 Mar 1838, Birgitta, Barrett, Dominici, Mariae, 14 Feb, -, -, -, -, -, -, -, Tunnel [Paw Paw Tunnel on C & O Canal], -, 16

773, 05 Mar 1838, Hugo, Smith, Bernardi, Catharinae, 01 Mar, -, -, -, -, -, -, -, C & O Canal, -, 16

774, 05 Mar 1838, Michael, Mardarn, Richardi, Elisabeth, 27 Feb, -, -, -, Mardarn, -, -, -, -, -, 16

775, 05 Mar 1838, Anna, McCawly, Thomae, Annae, 25 Feb, -, -, -, -, -, -, -, Sidling Hill, -, 16

776, 05 Mar 1838, Elisabeth, Winzer, Joannis, Mariae, 13 Feb 1829, -, -, -, -, -, -, -, Sidling Hill Creek , -, 16

777, 05 Mar 1838, Helena, Thomson, Henrici, Sarae, 11 years, -, -, -, -, -, -, -, Sidling Hill Creek , -, 16

778, 05 Mar 1838, Michael, Kavanagh, Caroli , Rosae, 04 Mar, -, -, -, -, -, -, -, -, -, 16

779, 11 Mar 1838, Maria, Tilghman, Thomae, Mariae, [blank], -, -, -, -, -, -, -, -, -, 16

780, 11 Mar 1838, Joannes Otheus, Hurley, Jacobi, Sophiae, 02 Mar 1838, -, -, -, -, -, -, -, -, -, 16

ST. MARY'S CATHOLIC CHURCH
HAGERSTOWN, MARYLAND, BAPTISMS:
Index, Bap Date, Child, Last Name, Father, Mother,
Birth Date, Code1, Code2, Code3,
1st Sponsor First, 1st Sponsor Last,
2nd Sponsor First, 2nd Sponsor Last, Location,
Notes, Maiden Name, Priest

781, 12 Mar 1838, Patricius, Kerbay, Guillenmi, "Caha...", 3 Mar 1838, -, -, -, -, -, -, -, -, -, 16

782, 12 Mar 1838, Patriciius, Ryan, Joannis, Mariae, 10 Mar 1838, -, -, -, -, -, -, -, -, -, 16

783, 15 Mar 1838, Jeremias, Nicodemus, Frederici, Mariae, 18 Jan 1838, -, -, -, -, -, -, -, -, -, 16

784, 18 Mar 1838, Anna, Watson, Jacobi, Sarae, 22 Feb, -, -, -, -, -, -, -, -, -, 16

785, 21 Mar 1838, Franciscus, Johanigan, Francisii, Catharinae, "2 none", -, -, -, -, -, -, -, -, -, 16

786, 23 Mar 1838, Josephus Henricus, Elliot, Jacobi Blair, Elisabeth Annae, 20 Feb, -, -, -, -, -, -, -, -, -, 16

787, 28 Mar 1838, Theresia, Hilderbrand [or Hildenbrand], Michaelis, Appoloniae, 17 Mar 1838, -, -, -, -, -, -, -, Hagerstown, -, 16

788, 27 Mar 1838, Patricius, Murrey, Stephaninom, Richardis, 21 Mar 1838, -, -, -, -, -, -, -, -, -, 16

789, 27 Mar 1838, Thomas, Downey, Thomae, Mariae, 25 Mar 1838, -, -, -, -, -, -, -, note the birth date of 26 Mar for the other twin, -, 16

790, 27 Mar 1838, Maria, Downey, Thomae, Mariae, 26 Mar 1838, -, -, -, -, -, -, -, note the birth date of 25 Mar for the other twin in the previous record, -, 16

791, 27 Mar 1838, Joannes, Riley, Hug [or Huy], Helenae, 18, -, -, -, -, -, -, -, -, 16

792, 27 Mar 1838, Helena Catharina, Hirshberger, Joannis Sebastiani, Mariae Annae Elisabeth, 14, -, -, -, -, -, -, -, -, -, 16

793, 31 Mar 1838, Margareta, Shirdan, Jacobi, Eleonorae, 10 Feb 1838, -, -, -, -, -, -, -, -, -, 16

794, 01 Apr 1838, Thomas, Brady, Jacobi, Catharinae, 03 Mar, -, -, -, -, -, -, -, -, 16

795, 01 Apr 1838, Jacobus, Higans, Ransom, Elisabeth, 12 Jan 1838, -, -, -, -, -, -, -, -, -, 16

796, 02 Apr 1838, Anna Margareta, Merz, Georgii, Catharinae, 15 Mar, -, -, -, -, -, -, -, -, -, 16

797, 02 Apr 1838, Josua Dixson, Harrison, Joannis Thomae, Margaretae, 02 Feb 1838, -, -, -, -, -, -, -, -, -, 16

ST. MARY'S CATHOLIC CHURCH
HAGERSTOWN, MARYLAND, BAPTISMS:
Index, Bap Date, Child, Last Name, Father, Mother,
Birth Date, Code1, Code2, Code3,
1st Sponsor First, 1st Sponsor Last,
2nd Sponsor First, 2nd Sponsor Last, Location,
Notes, Maiden Name, Priest

798, 09 Apr 1838, Margareta, Falley, Dionysii, Annae, 6 Apr 1838, -, -, -, -, -, -, -, -, -, 16

799, 15 Apr 1838, Michael, Kelley, Jacobi, Honorae ["Eleono" crossed out], 14 Apr 1838, -, -, -, -, -, -, -, -, -, 16

800, 16 Apr 1838, Maria Anna, Meyer, Joannis, Theresiae, *, -, -, -, -, -, -, -, birthdate appears to read "amun [?] annaun [?]", -, 16

801, 21 Apr 1838, -, -, -, -, -, -, -, -, -, -, -, -, -, This entry intentionally left blank., -, 16

802, 22 Apr 1838, Maria, Endaunn , Joses Conradi, Catharinae, 6 Apr 1838, -, -, -, -, -, -, -, -, -, 16

803, 22 Apr 1838, Anna , Morgan, Jacobi, Annae, 14 Apr 1838, -, -, -, -, -, -, -, -, -, 16

804, 22 Apr 1838, Catharina, Morgan, Jacobi, Annae, 14 Apr 1838, -, -, -, -, -, -, -, -, -, 16

805, 22 Apr 1838, Elisabeth Joanna, Buckman, Phineas, Helenae, 13 Mar 1836, -, -, -, -, -, -, -, -, -, 16

806, 22 Apr 1838, Maria, Clarke, Chareli, Margaretae, 09 Apr, -, -, -, -, -, -, -, -, -, 16

807, 22 Apr 1838, Maria, Upton, Joannis, Elisabaeth, 14 Apr 1838, -, -, -, -, -, -, -, -, -, 16

808, 29 Apr 1838, Maria Anna, Witsin [?], Alberti, Margaretae, 23 Jun 1836, -, -, -, -, -, -, -, -, -, 16

809, 30 Apr 1838, Dionisius , Luay, Cornelii, Mariae, 15 Apr 1838, -, -, -, -, -, -, -, -, -, 16

810, 30 Apr 1838, Michael, Hurley, Joannis, Annae, 27 Apr 1838, -, -, -, -, -, -, -, -, -, 16

811, 30 Apr 1838, Dionisius, Cranler, Caroli, Carolinae, 14 Apr 1838, -, -, -, -, -, -, -, -, -, 16

812, 7 Apr 1838, Anna, Haukins, -, -, 22 Feb 1838, -, -, S, -, -, -, -, mother is servant or slave of Henrici Bevans, -, 16

813, 7 May 1838, Letitia [?], Roberson, Joannis, Eleonorae, 06 Apr 1838, -, -, -, -, -, -, -, -, Tunnel [Paw Paw Tunnel on C & O Canal], -, 16

814, 7 May 1838, Anna, Mortaugh, Michaelis, Catharinae, 29 Apr 1838, -, -, -, -, -, -, -, -, Tunnel [Paw Paw Tunnel on C & O Canal], -, 16

ST. MARY'S CATHOLIC CHURCH
HAGERSTOWN, MARYLAND, BAPTISMS:
Index, Bap Date, Child, Last Name, Father, Mother,
Birth Date, Code1, Code2, Code3,
1st Sponsor First, 1st Sponsor Last,
2nd Sponsor First, 2nd Sponsor Last, Location,
Notes, Maiden Name, Priest

815, 7 May 1838, Patricius, Coners, Thomae, Catharinae, 29 Apr 1838, -, -, -, -, -, -, -, Tunnel [Paw Paw Tunnel on C & O Canal], -, 16

816, 7 May 1838, Michael, Cashon, Christophori, Elisabeth, 06 May 1838, -, -, -, -, -, -, -, Tunnel [Paw Paw Tunnel on C & O Canal], -, 16

817, 8 Apr 1838*, Jacobus, Green, Patricii, Annae, 07 Apr 1838, -, -, -, -, -, -, -, Tunnel [Paw Paw Tunnel on C & O Canal]; *baptismal date could be in April or May, -, 16

818, 9 Apr 1838*, Thomas, Dawd, Patricii, Rosae, 25 Apr 1838, -, -, -, -, -, -, -, Aquaduct [on C & O Canal]; baptismal date could be in April or May, -, 16

819, 9 May 1838, Matheus, Jonston, Jacobi, Judith, 30 Apr 1838, -, -, -, -, -, -, -, Aquaduct [on C & O Canal], -, 16

820, 10 May 1838, Thomas, Farrel, Michaelis, Mariae, 07 May 1838, -, -, -, -, -, -, -, -, -, 16

821, 10 May 1838, Georgius, Anton, Georguii, Mariae, 05 Apr 1838, -, -, -, -, -, -, -, -, -, 16

822, 14 May 1838, Joannes, Calnam, Joannis, Mariae, 06 May 1838, -, -, -, -, -, -, -, -, -, 16

823, 14 May 1838, Joannes* , Moran, Patricii, Eleonorae, 06 May 1838, -, -, -, -, -, -, -, * "Cornelius" was crossed out beside "Joannes", -, 16

824, 14 May 1838, Thomas, Norton, Thomae, Mariae, 11 May 1838, -, -, -, -, -, -, -, -, -, 16

825, 14 May 1838, Joannes, Lively, Jacobi, Catharinae, 11 May 1838, -, -, -, -, -, -, -, -, -, 16

826, 14 May 1838, Jeremias, Lary, Dionysii, Helenae, 02 May 1838, -, -, -, -, -, -, -, -, -, 16

827, 15 May 1838, Joannes, Jordan, Michaelis, Annae, 14 May 1838, -, -, -, -, -, -, -, "twins" written in margin, -, 16

828, 15 May 1838, Timotheus, Jordan, Michaelis, Annae, 14 May 1838, -, -, -, -, -, -, -, -, -, 16

829, 16 May 1838, Edwardus, Burning, Guillilmi Alexandri, Francisiae, 02 Dec 1838, -, -, -, -, -, -, -, -, -, 16

830, 16 May 1838, Catharina, Dougherty, Danielis, Mariae Annae, 23 Apr 1838, -, -, -, Patricius, Hagan, -, -, -, -, 16

ST. MARY'S CATHOLIC CHURCH
HAGERSTOWN, MARYLAND, BAPTISMS:
Index, Bap Date, Child, Last Name, Father, Mother,
Birth Date, Code1, Code2, Code3,
1st Sponsor First, 1st Sponsor Last,
2nd Sponsor First, 2nd Sponsor Last, Location,
Notes, Maiden Name, Priest

831, 18 May 1838, Maria Anna, Rush?, Martini, Eleonorae, 10 May 1838, -, -, -, -, -, -, -, -, -, 16

832, 24 May 1838, Carolus Augustus, Doyle, Joannis Adarni [?], Anna Rebeccae, 21 Mar 1838, -, -, -, -, -, -, -, -, -, -, 16

833, 26 May 1838, Maria Catharina, Kelly, Joseph, Catharinae, 18 Feb 1838, -, -, -, -, -, -, -, -, -, -, 16

834, 29 May 1838, Anna, Dimond, Jacobi, Eleonora, 24 May 1838, -, -, -, -, -, -, -, -, -, -, 16

835, 29 May 1838, Henricus Guillelmus, Rehmeier, Guillelenni Hermanis, Mariae, 19 Feb 1838, -, -, -, -, -, -, -, -, -, -, 16

836, 29 May 1838, Joannes , -, -, -, -, -, -, -, -, -, -, -, parents are married; nothing else is written - entire entry is crossed out, -, 16

837, 29 May 1838, Maria, Shelling, Joannis, Mariae, 27 May 1838, -, -, -, -, -, -, -, -, -, 16

838, 29 May 1838, Joannes, Dougherty, Hugonus, Catharinae, 12 May 1838, -, -, -, -, -, -, -, -, -, 16

839, 30 May 1838, Maria, Kennedy, Cornelisi, Bergittae, 27 May 1838, -, -, -, -, -, -, -, -, -, 16

840, 30 May 1838, Rosa, Riley, Philippi, Mariae, 18 May 1838, -, -, -, -, -, -, -, -, -, 16

841, 30 May 1838, Maria Cecilia, Stakenius?, Godfried, Wilhelminae, 29 May 1838, -, -, -, -, -, -, -, -, -, 16

842, 03 Jun 1838, Henricus, Schilling, Joachim, Franciscae, 10 Dec 1838, -, -, -, -, -, -, -, -, -, 16

843, 04 Jun 1838, Lucia, Lee, Thomae, Rebeccae, 06 Nov 1838, -, -, -, -, -, -, -, -, -, 16

844, 04 Jun 1838, Matheus Abraham, Ryan, Mathei, [blank], [blank], -, -, -, -, -, -, -, a different color of ink circles this entry with the notation: "The poet priest - A.J. Ryan - died April 1886 - D. Manly", -, 16

845, 04 Jun 1838, Henrietta, Johnson, Benjamini, Mariae, 7 Jan 1838, -, -, -, -, -, -, -, -, -, 16

846, 04 Jun 1838, Joannes, Shorter, Edwardi, Annae, Jan 1838, -, -, -, -, -, -, -, -, -, 16

847, 04 Jun 1838, Nicholaeus, Casey, Mathei, Annae, 03 Mar 1838, -, -, -, -, -, -, -, -, -, 16

ST. MARY'S CATHOLIC CHURCH
HAGERSTOWN, MARYLAND, BAPTISMS:
Index, Bap Date, Child, Last Name, Father, Mother,
Birth Date, Code1, Code2, Code3,
1st Sponsor First, 1st Sponsor Last,
2nd Sponsor First, 2nd Sponsor Last, Location,
Notes, Maiden Name, Priest

848, 04 Jun 1838, Jesse, Floid [?], -, Annae, 2 years, PN, -, -, -, -, -, -, the parents are not described as being married as the priest has done in the other entries, -, 16

849, 07 Jun 1838, Guillelinus, Hughes, Guillelini, Margaretus, 04 Jun 1838, -, -, -, -, -, -, -, -, -, 16

850, 10 Jun 1838, Joannes, Quinn, Thomae, Rosae, 19 Feb 1838, -, -, -, -, -, -, -, -, -, -, 16

851, 10 Jun 1838, Anna, Forieter, Caroli, Mariae, 07 Jun 1838, -, -, -, -, -, -, -, -, -, 16

852, 19 Jun 1838, Jacobus, Cahoe, Thomae, Annae, 18 Jun 1838, -, -, -, -, -, -, -, -, -, 16

853, 19 Jun 1838, Anna, Migham [or Meyham], Patricii, Mariae, 17 Jun 1838, -, -, -, -, -, -, -, -, -, 16

854, 19 Jun 1838, Eleonora, Brady, Hugh, Annae, 12 Jun 1838, -, -, -, -, -, -, -, -, -, 16

855, 20 Jun 1838, Anna, Kelly, Thomae, Mariae, 12-Jun, -, -, -, -, -, -, -, -, -, 16

856, 01 Jul 1838, Anna Caecilia, Crommel, Samuelis, Catharinae, 07 Jan 1833, -, -, -, -, -, -, -, -, -, 16

857, 06 Jul 1838, Anna, Blanshefield, Jacobi, Catharinae, 27 Jun 1838, -, -, -, -, -, -, -, -, -, 16

858, 08 Jul 1838, Fredericus, Moellenkamp, Frederici, Mariae Catharinae, 19 Jan 1838, -, -, -, -, -, -, -, -, -, 16

859, 08 Jul 1838, Birgitta, Moran, Thomae, Catharinae, 01 Jul 1838, -, -, -, -, -, -, -, -, -, 16

860, 14 Jul 1838, Anna, Gorman, Bernardi, Catharinae, 10 Jul 1838, -, -, -, -, -, -, -, -, -, 16

861, 16 Jul 1838, Maria, Green, Richardi, Birgittae, 03 Jul 1838, -, -, -, -, -, -, -, -, -, 16

862, 16 Jul 1838, Sara, Moore, Guillelini, Birgitae, several days, -, -, -, -, -, -, -, -, -, 16

863, 16 Jul 1838, Dionysius*, McMullen, Joannis, Annae, 10 Jul 1838, -, -, -, -, -, -, -, *[Joan crossed out] Dionysius, -, 16

864, 16 Jul 1838, Dorothea, McDonnel, Morgan, Juliae, 15 Jul 1838, -, -, -, -, -, -, -, -, -, 16

865, 17 Jul 1838, Jacobus, Landrigan[runs into margin], Charoli, Mariae, 13 Jul 1838, -, -, -, -, -, -, -, -, -, 16

ST. MARY'S CATHOLIC CHURCH
HAGERSTOWN, MARYLAND, BAPTISMS:
Index, Bap Date, Child, Last Name, Father, Mother,
Birth Date, Code1, Code2, Code3,
1st Sponsor First, 1st Sponsor Last,
2nd Sponsor First, 2nd Sponsor Last, Location,
Notes, Maiden Name, Priest

866, 17 Jul 1838, Catharina, Bigan [or Rigan]*, Rick, Catharinae, 11 Jul 1838, -, -, -, -, -, -, -, -, * name runs into margin, -, 16

867, 19 Jul 1838, Joannes, Schäffer , Joannis, Catharinae, 13 Jul 1838, -, -, -, -, -, -, -, -, -, -, 16

868, 22 Jul 1838, Therisia, Witt, Melchiori, Mariae, 16 Jul 1838, -, -, -, -, -, -, -, -, -, 16

869, 23 Jul 1838, Maria Anna, Tice, Danielis, Margaretae, 11 Mar 1836, -, -, -, -, -, -, -, -, -, 16

870, 01 Aug 1838, Anna Catharina, Hughes, -, -, -, -, -, -, -, -, -, -, parents are married, -, 16

871, 04 Aug 1838, Joannes, Benet, Mc [sic], Birgittae, 27 Jul 1838, -, -, -, -, -, -, -, -, -, 16

872, 06 Aug 1838, Joannes, McGovern, Thomae, Annae, 05 Aug 1838, -, -, -, -, -, -, -, -, -, 16

873, 06 Aug 1838, Maria, Raynolds, Francisci, Catharinae, 02 Aug 1838, -, -, -, -, -, -, -, -, -, 16

874, 06 Aug 1838, Josephus, O'beca [?], Ferdinandi, Agathae, 04 Aug 1838, -, -, -, -, -, -, -, -, -, 16

875, 07 Aug 1838, Elisabeth, Franz, Joannis, Susannae, 05 Aug 1838, -, -, -, -, -, -, -, -, -, 16

876, 07 Aug 1838, Maria, Coghlin, Petri, Annae, 06 Aug 1838, -, -, -, -, -, -, -, -, 16

877, 18 Aug 1838, Guillelmus, Welsh, Michaelis, Ellen, 14 Aug 1838, -, -, -, -, -, -, -, -, Tunnel [Paw Paw Tunnel on C & O Canal], -, 16

878, 18 Aug 1838, Patricius, Oldman, Own [Owen?], Mariae, 09 Aug 1838, -, -, -, -, -, -, -, -, Tunnel [Paw Paw Tunnel on C & O Canal], -, 16

879, 19 Aug 1838, Anna, Daudelet, Joannis, Catharinae, 17 Aug 1838, -, -, -, -, -, -, -, -, Tunnel [Paw Paw Tunnel on C & O Canal], -, 16

880, 19 Aug 1838, Thomas, Clark, Jacobi, Catharinae, 19 Aug 1838, -, -, -, -, -, -, -, -, Tunnel [Paw Paw Tunnel on C & O Canal], -, 16

881, 19 Aug 1838, Maria, Spolan, Michaelis, Margaretae, 19 Aug 1838, -, -, -, -, -, -, -, -, Tunnel [Paw Paw Tunnel on C & O Canal], -, 16

ST. MARY'S CATHOLIC CHURCH
HAGERSTOWN, MARYLAND, BAPTISMS:
Index, Bap Date, Child, Last Name, Father, Mother,
Birth Date, Code1, Code2, Code3,
1st Sponsor First, 1st Sponsor Last,
2nd Sponsor First, 2nd Sponsor Last, Location,
Notes, Maiden Name, Priest

882, 19 Aug 1838, Maria, Griffon, Guillelini, Catharinae, 04 Aug 1838, -, -, -, -, -, -, -, -, "Tunnel infra" [could be Latin for "below" or "beneath" or "on the underside of" the Tunnel - possibly "south of the tunnel"], -, 16

883, 19 Aug 1838, Anna, McDonnel, Augusti, Sarae, 20 Jul 1836, -, -, -, -, -, -, -, Tunnel [Paw Paw Tunnel on C & O Canal] on the West Virginia side of the river, -, 16

884, 20 Aug 1838, Maria, Dowyre [?], Henrici, Birgittae, 18 Aug 1838, -, -, -, -, -, -, -, -, Fifteen Mile Creek, -, 16

885, 24 Aug 1838, Elisabeth Victorina, Shaffer, -, -, -, -, -, -, -, -, -, -, -, Boonsboro; parents are married, -, 16

886, 26 Aug 1838, Jacobus, McCosker, Hugh, Mariae, 22 Aug 1838, -, -, -, -, -, -, -, -, Hancock, -, 16

887, 31 Aug 1838, David, Flinn, Michaelis, Mariae, 20 Aug 1838, -, -, -, -, -, -, -, -, Tunnel [Paw Paw Tunnel on C & O Canal], -, 16

888, 31 Aug 1838, Elisabeth, Larkin, Guillelini, Birgittae, 24 Aug 1838, -, -, -, -, -, -, -, -, Tunnel [Paw Paw Tunnel on C & O Canal], -, 16

889, 01 Sep 1838, Bernardus, Sheridan, Bernardi, Ellan, 27 Aug 1838, -, -, -, -, -, -, -, -, Fifteen Mile Creek, -, 16

890, 02 Sep 1838, Anna, Cavanaugh, Thomae, Mariae, 20 Aug 1838, -, -, -, -, -, -, -, -, -, 16

891, 02 Sep 1838, Thomas, Heart, Joannis, Elisabeth, 26 Jul 1838, -, -, -, -, -, -, -, -, -, 16

892, 02 Sep 1838, Rosa Anna, McEvoy, Patricii, Mariae, 01 Sep 1838, -, -, -, -, -, -, -, -, -, 16

893, 09 Sep 1838, Jacobas, McCartney, Edwardi, Catharinae, 27 Jul 1838, -, -, -, -, -, -, -, -, -, 16

894, 11 Sep 1838, Margareta, Kennys, Thomae, Catharinae, 03 Sep 1838, -, -, -, -, -, -, -, -, -, 16

895, 12 Sep 1838, Anna, Force, -, Serenae, 10 Aug 1838, PN, -, -, -, -, -, -, -, -, 16

896, 15 Sep 1838, William, Quin, Diyonysii, Annae, 10 Sep 1838, -, -, -, -, -, -, -, -, Tunnel [Paw Paw Tunnel on C & O Canal], -, 16

897, 15 Sep 1838, Jacobus, Rodgers, Patricii, Catharinae, 09 Sep 1838, -, -, -, -, -, -, -, -, -, 16

ST. MARY'S CATHOLIC CHURCH
HAGERSTOWN, MARYLAND, BAPTISMS:
Index, Bap Date, Child, Last Name, Father, Mother,
Birth Date, Code1, Code2, Code3,
1st Sponsor First, 1st Sponsor Last,
2nd Sponsor First, 2nd Sponsor Last, Location,
Notes, Maiden Name, Priest

898, 17 Sep 1838, Catharina, Trenner, Joannis, Rosae, 09 Sep 1838, -, -, -, -, -, -, -, -, -, 16

899, 30 Sep 1838, Eleonora, McAlister, Patricii, Margaretae, 26 Jul 1838, -, -, -, -, -, -, -, -, -, 16

900, 01 Oct 1838, Andrias, McWilliams, Michaelis, Annae, 29 Sep 1838, -, -, -, -, -, -, -, Tunnel [Paw Paw Tunnel on C & O Canal], -, 16

901, 01 Oct 1838, Anna, Brogan, Thomae, Mariae, 19 Sep 1838, -, -, -, -, -, -, -, -, -, 16

902, 07 Oct 1838, Henricus, Wittmüller, Henrici, Catharinae, 29 Aug 1838, -, -, -, -, -, -, -, -, -, 16

903, 07 Oct 1838, Lucia, Lynch, Philippi, Susannae, a few days*, -, -, -, -, -, -, -, -, *birthdate reads "paucus dies ante" meaning "a few days before", -, 16

904, 07 Oct 1838, Margareta, Mells, Arthur, Annae, 26 Sep 1828, -, -, -, -, -, -, -, -, -, 16

905, 07 Oct 1838, Guillelmus, Schuh, Hugoni, Catharinae, 16 Aug 1838, -, -, -, -, -, -, -, -, -, 16

906, 08 Oct 1838, Jacobus, Terry, Jacobi, Birgittae, 01 Sep 1838, -, -, -, -, -, -, -, -, -, 16

907, 08 Oct 1838, Joannes, Curran, Jacobi, Eleonorae, 06 Oct 1838, -, -, -, -, -, -, -, -, -, 16

908, 14 Oct 1838, Guillelmus Henricus, Shorter, Aaroli [or Naroli or Maroli], Catharinae, 15 Sep 1838, -, -, -, -, -, -, -, -, -, 16

909, 20 Oct 1838, Joannes, Harkins, Joannis, Catharinae, 16 Oct 1838, -, -, -, -, -, -, -, -, -, 16

910, 20 Oct 1838, Richardis, Power [or Pawer], Richardis, Anastasiae, 07 Oct 1838, -, -, -, -, -, -, -, -, -, 16

911, 21 Oct 1838, Michael, Spoilan, Petrii, Catharinae, 04 Oct 1838, -, -, -, -, -, -, -, Tunnel [Paw Paw Tunnel on C & O Canal], -, 16

912, 21 Oct 1838, Carolus, Kannon, Jacobi, Annae, 19 Sep 1838, -, -, -, -, -, -, -, -, -, 16

913, 22 Oct 1838, Maria, Branan, Joannis, Mariae, 10 Oct 1838, -, -, -, -, -, -, -, -, -, 16

ST. MARY'S CATHOLIC CHURCH
HAGERSTOWN, MARYLAND, BAPTISMS:
Index, Bap Date, Child, Last Name, Father, Mother,
Birth Date, Code1, Code2, Code3,
1st Sponsor First, 1st Sponsor Last,
2nd Sponsor First, 2nd Sponsor Last, Location,
Notes, Maiden Name, Priest

914, 22 Oct 1838, -, -, Develbis [?], -, -, -, -, -, -, -, -, -, This entry, other than date in ink, is written in pencil. "Develbis Black [?] girl" is total entry; Guth's handwriting., -, 16

915, 22 Oct 1838, Anastasia, Whealan, Jacobi, Johannae, 22 Oct 1838, -, -, -, -, -, -, -, -, -, 16

916, 27 Oct 1838, Guillelmus Joannes, Cooney, Laurentii, Birgittae, 20 Oct 1838, -, -, -, -, -, -, -, -, -, 16

917, 28 Oct 1838, Carolina, Kelly, Patricii, Annae, 28 Sep 1838, -, -, -, -, -, -, -, -, -, 16

918, 09 Nov 1838, Catharina Elisabeth, Stake, H___ (rest of the name is blank), Catharinae, 04 Nov 1838, -, -, -, -, -, -, -, -, -, 16

919, 10 Nov 1838, Guillelmus, Hath, Thomae, Birgittae, 01 Nov 1838, -, -, -, -, -, -, -, -, -, 16

920, 11 Nov 1838, Joannes, Green, Jacobi, Annae Catharinae, 22 Oct 1838, -, -, -, -, -, -, -, -, -, 16

921, 11 Nov 1838, Catharinae, Bell, Stephani, Catharinae, 31 Oct 1838, -, -, -, -, -, -, -, -, -, 16

922, 11 Nov 1838, Carolus M., Bevans, Josephi Ignati, Annae K., 24 Aug 1838, -, -, -, -, -, -, -, -, -, 16

923, 13 Nov 1838, Michael, Cunningham, Timothei, Margarethae, 01 Nov 1838, -, -, -, -, -, -, -, -, -, 16

924, 22 Nov 1838, Maria, Lewis?, Joannis, Elisabeth, 20 Jul 1838, -, -, -, -, -, -, -, -, -, 16

925, 23 Nov 1838, Eleonora, Carrol, Guillelmi, Maria, 15 Nov 1838, -, -, -, -, -, -, -, -, -, 16

926, 26 Nov 1838, Hugo, McKarnan, Huyonis, Margaretae, 20 Nov 1838, -, -, -, -, -, -, -, -, -, 16

927, 03 Dec 1838, Ludovica Catharina, Davis, Joannis, Mariae Annae, 14 Nov 1838, -, -, -, -, -, -, -, -, -, 16

928, 09 Dec 1838, Georgeris Alexander Fox, McCane?, Thomae, Sarae, 16 May 1838, -, -, -, -, -, -, -, -, -, 16

929, 2 Dec 1838, Michael, Dinger, Georgii Michaelis, Elisabeth, 22 Nov 1838, -, -, -, -, -, -, -, -, -, 16

930, 7 Dec 1838, Joannes, Nilis [or Silis], Georgii, Annae, 29[?] Nov 1838, -, -, -, -, -, -, -, -, -, 16

931, 3 Dec 1838, Josephus, Lee, Guillelini, Silviae, 23 Nov 1838, -, -, -, -, -, -, -, -, -, 16

ST. MARY'S CATHOLIC CHURCH
HAGERSTOWN, MARYLAND, BAPTISMS:
Index, Bap Date, Child, Last Name, Father, Mother,
Birth Date, Code1, Code2, Code3,
1st Sponsor First, 1st Sponsor Last,
2nd Sponsor First, 2nd Sponsor Last, Location,
Notes, Maiden Name, Priest

932, 17 Dec 1838, Catharina, Raynolds, Jacobi, Mariae, Dec 1838, -, -, -, -, -, -, -, -, -, 16

933, 20 Dec 1838, Francise , McLoughlin, Joannis, Birgittae, 18 Dec 1838, -, -, -, -, -, -, -, -, -, -, 16

934, 22 Dec 1838, Catharina, Cavanaugh, Thomae, Rosae Annae, 19 Nov 1838, -, -, -, -, -, -, -, -, -, 16

935, 31 Dec 1838, Martha, McLaughlin, Patricii, Sarae, 10 Dec 1838, -, -, -, -, -, -, -, -, -, 16

936, 06 Jan 1839, Lucia Joanna, Corbit, Petri, Annae, 12 Mar 1828*, -, -, -, -, -, -, -, *birthdate reads 12 Mar 1828. This appears to be 1828 but is in the midst of the 1838s., -, 16

937, 08 Jan 1839, Benjaminus, Fisher, Joannis, Elisabeth, 15 Sep 1838, -, -, -, -, -, -, -, -, -, 16

938, 10 Jan 1839, Margareta, Fritz, Frederici, Margaretae, 22 May 1838, -, -, -, -, -, -, -, -, -, 16

939, 10 Jan 1839, Franciscis Michael, McCormick, Guillelmi, Rebeccae, 10 Dec 1838, -, -, -, -, -, -, -, -, -, 16

940, 12 Jan 1839, Margareta, Carney, Michaelis, Birgittae, 10 Dec 1838, -, -, -, -, -, -, -, -, -, 16

941, 15 Jan 1839, Patricias, Teirnan [?], Jacobi, Mariae, 09 Jan 1839, -, -, -, -, -, -, -, -, -, 16

942, 15 Jan 1839, Birgitta, Caine, Jacobi, Mariae, 30 Dec 1838, -, -, -, -, -, -, -, -, -, 16

943, 15 Jan 1839, Anna, McCormick, Patricii, Mariae, 17 Jan 1839, -, -, -, -, -, -, -, -, -, 16

944, 17 Jan 1839, Guillelmus, Murphey, Guilllmi [sic], Margaretae, 18 Dec 1838, -, -, -, -, -, -, -, -, -, 16

945, 17 Jan 1839, Anna, Callon, Richardi, Annae, 15 Jan 1839, -, -, -, -, -, -, -, -, 16

946, 19 Jan 1839, Maria, Morrison, Patricii, M [rest blank], 10 Jan 1839, -, -, -, -, -, -, -, -, -, 16

947, 26 Jan 1839, Margareta, Weighand, Adam, Helenae, 23 Jan 1839, -, -, -, -, -, -, -, -, -, 16

948, 09 Jan 1839, Thomas E., Bradley, Guillelmi, Susannae, 02 Jun 1838, -, -, -, -, -, -, -, -, -, 16

949, 13 Jan 1839, Thomas G. [or J.], McCardell, Richardi, Mariae, 1838, -, -, -, -, -, -, -, -, -, 16

ST. MARY'S CATHOLIC CHURCH
HAGERSTOWN, MARYLAND, BAPTISMS:
Index, Bap Date, Child, Last Name, Father, Mother,
Birth Date, Code1, Code2, Code3,
1st Sponsor First, 1st Sponsor Last,
2nd Sponsor First, 2nd Sponsor Last, Location,
Notes, Maiden Name, Priest

950, 19 Jan 1839, Jacobus, Hughes, Edwardi, Mariae, 03 Dec 1838, -, -, -, -, -, -, -, -, -, -, 16

951, 19 Jan 1839, C. Elisabeth, Meads, Jeremiae, Margaretae, 10 Nov 1838, -, -, -, -, -, -, -, -, -, -, 16

952, 19 Jan 1839, Maria, O'Donnel, Paatricii, Margaretae, 03 Jul 1835, -, -, -, -, -, -, -, -, -, -, 16

953, 27 Jan 1839, Samuel, Coyle, Edwardi, Ludovicas, 12 Dec 1838, -, -, -, -, -, -, -, -, -, -, 16

954, 31 Jan 1839, Lucretia Anna, McLenny, -, Attiliae, 10 Oct 1837, PN, -, -, -, -, -, -, -, -, -, 16

955, 03 Feb 1839, Carolus , Abernaty [?], Thomae, Charolinae, blank, -, -, -, -, -, -, -, -, -, -, 16

956, 03 Feb 1839, Rosa, Quigley [?], Petrii, Mariae, 03 Feb 1839, -, -, -, -, -, -, -, -, -, -, 16

957, 03 Feb 1839, Birgitta, Linch, Own[Owen?], Rosae, 24 Jan 1839, -, -, -, -, -, -, -, -, -, -, 16

958, 05 Feb 1839, Maria Anna, McCoskar, Hugonis, Margaretae, 28 Jan 1839, -, -, -, -, -, -, -, -, -, -, 16

959, 08 Feb 1839, Maria Joanna, Fox, -, Elleonorae, *, PN, -, -, -, -, -, -, *age appears to read "alleguat heldamadar[?]", -, 16

960, 08 Feb 1839, Angelina, Bragonier, -, Elisabeth, 30 Sep 1837, -, -, -, -, -, -, -, parents are married, -, 16

961, 10 Feb 1839, Elisabeth, Conely, Petri, Maria, 04 Feb 1839, -, -, -, -, -, -, -, -, -, 16

962, 10 Feb 1839, Carolina, Sedon, -, -, 20 years, -, -, -, -, -, -, -, -, -, -, 16

963, 10 Feb 1839, Edwardus Richardus, Shipply, Richardi, Elisabeth, 31 Dec 1837, -, -, -, -, -, -, -, -, -, -, 16

964, 10 Feb 1839, Sara Anna, Wigus, -, -, 20 years, -, -, -, -, -, -, -, -, -, -, 16

965, 18 Feb 1839, Thomas, Whelan, Michaelis, Birgittae, 13 Feb 1839, -, -, -, -, -, -, -, -, -, -, 16

966, 18 Feb 1839, Anna, Welsh, Petri, Rosae, 01 Feb 1839, -, -, -, -, -, -, -, -, -, 16

967, 20 Feb 1839, Patricius, Manwarren?, Richardi, Elisabeth, 16 Feb 1839, -, -, -, -, -, -, -, -, -, -, 16

ST. MARY'S CATHOLIC CHURCH HAGERSTOWN, MARYLAND, BAPTISMS:
Index, Bap Date, Child, Last Name, Father, Mother,
Birth Date, Code1, Code2, Code3,
1st Sponsor First, 1st Sponsor Last,
2nd Sponsor First, 2nd Sponsor Last, Location,
Notes, Maiden Name, Priest

968, 16 Feb 1839, Catharina, McGovern, Michaelis, Elisabeth, 06 Feb 1839, -, -, -, -, -, -, -, -, -, -, 16

969, 16 Feb 1839, Birgetta, Lalley, Guillelini, Mariae, 16 Feb 1839, -, -, -, -, -, -, -, -, -, -, 16

970, 17 Feb 1839, Anna, Monahan, Michaelis, Margaretae, 01 Feb 1839, -, -, -, -, -, -, -, -, -, -, 16

971, 17 Feb 1839, Joannes Bernardus, Knapp, Henrici, Catharinae, 09 Feb 1839, -, -, -, -, -, -, -, -, -, -, 16

972, 25 Feb 1839, Daniel, Murray, Henriei, Catharinae, 25 Feb 1839, -, -, -, -, -, -, -, -, -, -, 16

973, 28 Feb 1839, Franciscus, McRainey, Patricii, Annae, 26 Feb 1839, -, -, -, -, -, -, -, -, -, -, 16

974, 28 Feb 1839, Maria Anna, Codelon, Andreas, Mariae, 26 Feb 1839, -, -, -, -, -, -, -, -, -, -, 16

975, 28 Feb 1839, Thomas Wilson, Watkins, Roberti White, Elleonorae, 18 Feb 1839, -, -, -, Dominius Augustus, O'Donnel, Anna, Bevans, -, -, 16

976, 03 Mar 1839, Joanna, Linch, Hiram, Catharinae, 22 Oct 1821, -, -, -, -, -, -, -, -, -, 16

977, 03 Mar 1839, Sara, Linch, Hiram, Catharinae, 22 Nov 1824, -, -, -, -, -, -, -, -, -, 16

978, 03 Mar 1839, Eleonora, Linch, Hiram, Catharinae, 23 Sep 1827, -, -, -, -, -, -, -, -, -, 16

979, 03 Mar 1839, Rosa Anna, Linch, Hiram, Catharinae, 27 Apr 1829, -, -, -, -, -, -, -, -, -, 16

980, 03 Mar 1839, Elisabeth, Linch, Hiram, Catharinae, 28 Jul 1831, -, -, -, -, -, -, -, -, -, 16

981, 03 Mar 1839, Jacobus Patricius, Linch, Hiram, Catharinae, 17 Mar 1834, -, -, -, -, -, -, -, -, -, 16

982, 22 Feb 1839, Elisabeth, Galvin, Dionysis, "Marga.", 21 Feb 1839, -, -, -, -, -, -, -, -, -, 16

983, 10 Mar 1839, Anna, Atwel, Joannis, Mariae, 01 Mar 1839, -, -, -, -, -, -, -, -, -, 16

984, 13 Mar 1839, Elisabeth, Murray, Brown, Elisabeth, 19 Feb 1839, -, -, -, -, -, -, -, -, -, 16

985, 13 Mar 1839, Anna, McEnerny, Patricii, Annae, 05 Mar 1839, -, -, -, -, -, -, -, -, -, 16

ST. MARY'S CATHOLIC CHURCH HAGERSTOWN, MARYLAND, BAPTISMS:
Index, Bap Date, Child, Last Name, Father, Mother,
Birth Date, Code1, Code2, Code3,
1st Sponsor First, 1st Sponsor Last,
2nd Sponsor First, 2nd Sponsor Last, Location,
Notes, Maiden Name, Priest

986, 16 Mar 1839, Maria, Duffey, Jacobi, Mariae, 14 Mar 1839, -, -, -, -, -, -, -, -, -, 16

987, 16 Mar 1839, Catharina, Welsh, Patricii, Mariae, 20 Feb 1839, -, -, -, -, -, -, -, -, -, 16

988, 16 Mar 1839, Eleonora, Hughes, Terrentii, Mariae, 08 Mar 1839, -, -, -, -, -, -, -, -, -, 16

989, 16 Mar 1839, Bernardus, McAnaly, Thomae, Joannae, 07 Mar 1839, -, -, -, -, -, -, -, -, -, 16

990, 19 Mar 1839, Guillelmus, Bell, -, -, 28 years, -, -, -, -, -, -, -, -, -, 16

991, 19 Mar 1839, Anna, Gallagher, Thomae, Mariellae, 14 Mar 1839, -, -, -, -, -, -, -, -, -, 16

992, 24 Mar 1839, Sara, Gormely, -, Mariae, 27 Feb 1839, PN, -, -, -, -, -, -, -, -, 16

993, 24 Mar 1839, Agnes Emelina, Marshal, Joannis, Agnetis Emelinae, 01 Mar 1839, -, -, -, -, -, -, -, -, -, 16

994, 31 Mar 1839, Joannes, Carrol, Guillelini, Eleonorae, 25 Dec 1839, -, -, -, -, -, -, -, -, -, 16

995, 31 Mar 1839, Catharina Elisabeth, Jegel, Jonnis, Elisabeth, 22 Mar 1839, -, -, -, -, -, -, -, -, -, 16

996, 31 Mar 1839, Joannes Edwardus, Fixpatrick [?], Philippi, Eleonorae, 28 Mar 1839, -, -, -, -, -, -, -, -, -, 16

997, 01 Apr 1839, Birgittai, Welsh, Martini, Birgittae, 05 Mar 1839, -, -, -, -, -, -, -, -, -, 16

998, 01 Apr 1839, Joannes, Conedy, Thimotheis, Catharinae, 19 Mar 1839, -, -, -, -, -, -, -, -, -, 16

999, 07 Apr 1839, Maria Anna, Curley, Patricii, Catherinae, 15 Mar 1839, -, -, -, -, -, -, -, -, -, 16

1000, 08 Apr 1839, Joannes, McAafferty, Joannis, Annae, 08 Apr 1839, -, -, -, -, -, -, -, -, -, 16

1001, 08 Apr 1839, Martha, Daugherty, Michaelis, Mariae, 07 Apr 1839, -, -, -, -, -, -, -, -, -, 16

1002, 08 Apr 1839, Jacobus, Monaghan, Joannis, Catharinae, 31 Mar 1839, -, -, -, -, -, -, -, -, -, 16

1003, 08 Apr 1839, Catharina, Sonner [or Sanner], Thomas, Margaretae, 03 Apr 1839, -, -, -, -, -, -, -, -, -, 16

ST. MARY'S CATHOLIC CHURCH
HAGERSTOWN, MARYLAND, BAPTISMS:
Index, Bap Date, Child, Last Name, Father, Mother,
Birth Date, Code1, Code2, Code3,
1st Sponsor First, 1st Sponsor Last,
2nd Sponsor First, 2nd Sponsor Last, Location,
Notes, Maiden Name, Priest

1004, 11 Apr 1839, Jacobus, Degnan, Michaelis, Elisabeth, 06 Apr 1839, -, -, -, -, -, -, -, -, -, 16

1005, 15 Apr 1839, Joannes, Tim, Thomae, Catharinae, 15 Apr 1839, -, -, -, -, -, -, -, -, -, 16

1006, 20 Apr 1839, Franciscus, Daugherty, Patricii, Judith, 16 Apr 1839, -, -, -, -, -, -, -, -, -, 16

1007, 21 Apr 1839, Anna, Sheridan, Joannis, Annae, 19 Apr 1839, -, -, -, -, -, -, -, -, -, 16

1008, 22 Apr 1839, Elisabeth, McCloskey, Petrii, Catharinae, 28 Feb 1839, -, -, -, -, -, -, -, -, -, 16

1009, 23 Apr 1839, Rosa, Lulain [or Lularn], Hugonis, Catharenae, 18 Apr 1839, -, -, -, -, -, -, -, -, -, 16

1010, 23 Apr 1839, Hilarius, blank, Joannis, Henriettae, 23 Apr 1839, -, -, -, -, -, -, -, -, -, 16

1011, 28 Apr 1839, Eleonora, Hughes, Antonii, Mariae, 26 Apr 1839, -, -, -, -, -, -, -, -, -, 16

1012, 12 May 1839, Franciscus, McAnneny, Francisa, Mariae, 06 May 1839, -, -, -, -, -, -, -, -, -, 16

1013, 14 May 1839, Bernardus, Kerbey, Francisci, Eleonorae, 05 May 1839, -, -, -, -, -, -, -, -, -, 16

1014, 14 May 1839, Bernardus, O'Donnell, -, Mariae, 09 May 1839, PN, -, -, -, -, -, -, -, -, 16

1015, 17 May 1839, Anna, McDermott, Patricii, Margaretae, 17 May 1839, -, -, -, -, -, -, -, -, -, 16

1016, 18 May 1839, Birgitta, McGerry, Patricii, Margaretae, 09 May 1839, -, -, -, -, -, -, -, -, -, 16

1017, 18 May 1839, Joannes, Flood, Joannius, Catharinae, 27 Apr 1839, -, -, -, -, -, -, -, -, -, 16

1018, 25 May 1839, Birgitta, Keltey, Guillelmi, Catharinae, 21 May 1839, -, -, -, -, -, -, -, -, -, 16

1019, 30 May 1839, Anna, Carlan, Joannis, Eleonorae, 28 May 1839, -, -, -, -, -, -, -, -, -, 16

1020, 02 Jun 1839, Philippus, Moore, Levy, Catharinae, 08 Apr 1839, -, -, -, -, -, -, -, -, -, 16

1021, 02 Jun 1839, Catharina Maria, Mous, Petri, Joannae, 10 May 1839, -, -, -, -, -, -, -, -, -, 16

ST. MARY'S CATHOLIC CHURCH
HAGERSTOWN, MARYLAND, BAPTISMS:
Index, Bap Date, Child, Last Name, Father, Mother,
Birth Date, Code1, Code2, Code3,
1st Sponsor First, 1st Sponsor Last,
2nd Sponsor First, 2nd Sponsor Last, Location,
Notes, Maiden Name, Priest

1022, 02 Jun 1839, Catharina Anna, Mills, Guillelmi, Mariae, 27 Apr 1837, -, -, -, -, -, -, -, -, -, -, 16

1023, 30 May 1839, Maria Elisabeth, Thornbury, Georgii, Elisabeth , 01 Oct 1837, PN, -, -, -, -, -, -, the word "legitimate" daughter crossed out, Criner, 16

1024, 08 Jun 1839, Maria Anna, Devoy, Guillelmi, Elisabeth, 25 May 1839, -, -, -, -, -, -, -, -, -, -, 16

1025, 10 Jun 1839, Michael, McDonnel, Anis, Mariae, 02 Jun 1839, -, -, -, -, -, -, -, -, -, -, 16

1026, 10 Jun 1839, Maria Wilhelmina, Hassmann, Guillelmi, Elisabeth, 26 Apr 1839, -, -, -, -, -, -, -, -, -, -, 16

1027, 21 Jun 1839, Andreas, Hughes, Guillelmi, Margaretae, 21 Jun 1839, -, -, -, -, -, -, -, -, -, -, 16

1028, 25 Jun 1839, Joannes, McAnnis, Joannis, Mariae, 24 Jun 1839, -, -, -, -, -, -, -, -, -, -, 16

1029, 06 Jul 1839, Michael, Finighty [?], Jacobi, Mariae, 04 Jul 1839, -, -, -, -, -, -, -, -, -, -, 16

1030, 07 Jul 1839, Margareta, Conley, Jacobi, Barbarae, 01 Jul 1839, -, -, -, -, -, -, -, -, -, -, 16

1031, 07 Jul 1839, Simon, blank, Ebberts, Apolinae, 25 Mar 1839, PN, -, -, -, -, -, -, -, -, -, 16

1032, 11 Jul 1839, Maria, McGary, Guillelmi, Sarae, 02 Jul 1839, -, -, -, -, -, -, -, -, -, -, 16

1033, 14 Jul 1839, Joannes, Farrel, Thomae, Juliae, 06 Jul 1839, -, -, -, -, -, -, -, -, -, -, 16

1034, 20 Jul 1839, Anna, Dolan, Brian, Mariae, 04 Jul 1839, -, -, -, -, -, -, -, -, -, 16

1035, 28 Apr 1839, Maria, Mooney, -, -, 13 years, -, -, -, -, -, -, -, -, -, -, 16

1036, 23 Jun 1839, Elisabeth, Sweaney, Caroli, Elisabeth, 15 Jun 1839, -, -, -, -, -, -, -, -, -, -, 16

1037, 23 Jun 1839, Marias (son), Bury, Jacobi, Annae, 18 Jun 1839, -, -, -, -, -, -, -, -, -, -, 16

1038, 25 Jun 1839, Joannes , Myer, Joannis, Theresae, 27 Nov 1839, -, -, -, -, -, -, -, note discrepancy between birth and baptisms dates, -, 16

ST. MARY'S CATHOLIC CHURCH
HAGERSTOWN, MARYLAND, BAPTISMS:
Index, Bap Date, Child, Last Name, Father, Mother,
Birth Date, Code1, Code2, Code3,
1st Sponsor First, 1st Sponsor Last,
2nd Sponsor First, 2nd Sponsor Last, Location,
Notes, Maiden Name, Priest

1039, 08 Jun 1839, Anna, Clement, Alexandri, Matildis, 27 May 1838, -, -, -, -, -, -, -, -, -, 16

1040, 08 Jun 1839, Charolus, Clement, Alexandri, Matildas, 08 Jun 1839, -, -, -, -, -, -, -, -, -, 16

1041, 27 Jul 1839, Joannes , Paton, Joannis, Mariae, 26 May 1839, -, -, -, -, -, -, -, -, -, 16

1042, 07 Mar 1839, Anna Elisabeth, Puffenburger, Samuelis, Annae Elisabeth, 03 Aug 1833, -, -, -, -, -, -, -, -, -, 16

1043, 07 Mar 1839, Sara Anna, Puffenburger, Samuelis, Annae Elisabeth, 07 Aug 1835, -, -, -, -, -, -, -, -, -, 16

1044, 07 Mar 1839, Guillelmus Henricus, Puffenburger, Samuelis, Annae Elisabeth, 14 Jun 1838, -, -, -, -, -, -, -, -, -, 16

1045, 15 Apr 1839, Catharina, Fellinger, Frederici, Rosae Annae, 31 May 1839, -, -, -, -, -, -, -, -, -, 16

1046, 15 Apr 1839, Guillelmus Henricus, Lauber, Henrici, Annae, 19 Jun 1838, -, -, -, -, -, -, -, -, -, 16

1047, 19 Apr 1839, Maria Anna, Conneley, Davidis, Joannae, 24 Feb 1839, -, -, -, -, -, -, -, -, -, 16

1048, 19 Apr 1839, Joannes (son), Rogan*, Patricii, Catharinae, 23 Mar 1839, -, -, -, -, -, -, -, *Rogan [or Brogan or Bogan], -, 16

1049, 10 Apr 1839, Guillelmes Edwardus, Smith, Michaelis, Catharinae, 08 Apr 1839, -, -, -, -, -, -, -, -, -, 16

1050, 09 Jun 1839, Elisabeth, Smith, Josias, Laetitiae, 25 May 1839, -, -, -, -, -, -, -, -, -, 16

1051, 20 Jul 1839, Maria, Doyle, Terrentii, Annae, 27 Jun 1839, -, -, -, -, -, -, -, -, -, 16

1052, 31 Jul 1839, Catharina, Shannon, Edwardi, Catharinae, 15 Jul 1839, -, -, -, -, -, -, -, -, -, 16

1053, 06 Aug 1839, Catharina, Grailey [?], Dionysii, Mariae, 14 Jul 1839, -, -, -, -, -, -, -, -, -, 16

1054, 12 Aug 1839, Georgius, -, -, -, 36 years., -, -, -, -, -, -, -, -, -, 16

1055, 15 Aug 1839, Elisabeth Anna, O'Brian, Edwardi, Eleonorae, 10 Aug 1839, -, -, -, -, -, -, -, -, -, 16

1056, 16 Aug 1839, Birgitta, Claffey, Charoli, Esther, 11 Aug 1839, -, -, -, -, -, -, -, -, -, 16

ST. MARY'S CATHOLIC CHURCH
HAGERSTOWN, MARYLAND, BAPTISMS:
Index, Bap Date, Child, Last Name, Father, Mother,
Birth Date, Code1, Code2, Code3,
1st Sponsor First, 1st Sponsor Last,
2nd Sponsor First, 2nd Sponsor Last, Location,
Notes, Maiden Name, Priest

1057, 18 Aug 1839, Maria, Tosman [or Tasman], Michaelis, Birgittae, 15 Aug 1839, -, -, -, -, -, -, -, -, -, 16

1058, 19 Aug 1839, Jacobus, Driscoll, Michaelis, Carolinaae, 02 Jul 1839, -, -, -, -, -, -, -, "Josephi Dooley" crossed out in section for father's name, -, 16

1059, 19 Aug 1839, Matheus, Daley , Joannis ["Michaelis" crossed out], Mariae, 16 Jul 1839, -, -, -, -, -, -, -, -, -, -, 16

1060, 29 Aug 1839, Margareta (twin), Dermady , Guillelini, Franciscae, 27 Aug 1839, -, -, -, -, -, -, -, -, -, -, 16

1061, 29 Aug 1839, Sophia (twin), Dermady , Guillelini, Franciscae, 27 Aug 1839, -, -, -, -, -, -, -, -, -, -, 16

1062, 29 Aug 1839, Maria, McGirr, Patricii, Mariae, 26 Aug 1839, -, -, -, -, -, -, -, -, -, -, 16

1063, 29 Aug 1839, Jacobus, Hughes, Henrici, Mariae, 27 Aug 1839, -, -, -, -, -, -, -, -, -, -, 16

1064, 01 Sep 1839, Thomas, Shevan, Thomae, Isabellae, 01 Feb 1839, -, -, -, Patricius, Kelly, Sara, Kelly, -, -, 16

1065, 09 Sep 1839, Margareta, Garoghty , Patricii, Margaretae, 03 Sep 1839, -, -, -, -, -, -, -, -, -, -, 16

1066, 09 Sep 1839, Fredericus, Stuckart, Philippi, Carolinae, 19 May 1839, -, -, -, -, -, -, -, -, -, -, 16

1067, 15 Sep 1839, Thomas, Kane [or Sane], Guillelmi, Markellae, 01 Sep 1839, -, -, -, -, -, -, -, -, -, -, 16

1068, 15 Sep 1839, Guillelmus, Cruise, Arthur, Elleonorae, 15 Sep 1839, -, -, -, -, -, -, -, -, -, 16

1069, 15 Sep 1839, Jacobus, Tigh, Jacobi, Birgittae, 13 Sep 1839, -, -, -, -, -, -, -, -, -, -, 16

1070, 19 Sep 1839, Joannes , Shnenick, Michaelen, Mariae, 11 Sep 1839, -, -, -, -, -, -, -, -, -, -, 16

1071, 19 Sep 1839, Thomas, Raynolds, Francisci, Catharinae, 16 Sep 1839, -, -, -, -, -, -, -, -, -, -, 16

1072, 22 Sep 1839, Birgitta, Hines, Thomae, Annae, 09 Sep 1839, -, -, -, -, -, -, -, -, -, -, 16

1073, 22 Sep 1839, Maria, Laghty, Jacob, Catharinae, 15 Aug 1839, -, -, -, -, -, -, -, -, -, -, 16

1074, 28 Sep 1839, Guillelmus, Holbert , Archebald, Catharinae, 20 Sep 1839, -, -, -, -, -, -, -, -, -, -, 16

ST. MARY'S CATHOLIC CHURCH
HAGERSTOWN, MARYLAND, BAPTISMS:
Index, Bap Date, Child, Last Name, Father, Mother,
Birth Date, Code1, Code2, Code3,
1st Sponsor First, 1st Sponsor Last,
2nd Sponsor First, 2nd Sponsor Last, Location,
Notes, Maiden Name, Priest

1075, 30 Sep 1839, Anna Elisabeth, Nicodemus, Frederici, Mariae Annae, 26 Sep 1839, -, -, -, -, -, -, -, -, -, 16
1076, 02 Oct 1839, Maria, Barrett, Dominici, Mariae, 19 Sep 1839, -, -, -, -, -, -, -, -, -, 16
1077, 02 Oct 1839, Michael, Coffey, Thomae, Judith, 25 Sep 1839, -, -, -, -, -, -, -, -, -, 16
1078, 03 Oct 1839, Dyonisius, O'Brian, Patricii, Margaretae, 30 Sep 1839, -, -, -, -, -, -, -, -, -, 16
1079, 03 Oct 1839, Catharina, Calory, Michaelis, Elisabeth, 26 Sep 1839, -, -, -, -, -, -, -, -, -, 16
1080, 03 Oct 1839, Franciscus, McCabe, Patricii, Juliae, 28 Sep 1839, -, -, -, -, -, -, -, -, -, 16
1081, 03 Oct 1839, Jacobus, Kelly, Thomaae, Joannae, 01 Oct 1839, -, -, -, -, -, -, -, -, -, 16
1082, 06 Oct 1839, Maria Eleonora, Tany, Ethelbert, Elisabeth, 18 Aug 1839, -, -, -, -, -, -, -, -, -, 16
1083, 08 Oct 1839, Jacobus, Jonston, Beryarnini, Mariae, 01 Jun 1839, -, -, -, -, -, -, -, -, -, 16
1084, 11 Oct 1839, Catharina, Cronley, Jacobi, Mariae, 09 Oct 1839, -, -, -, -, -, -, -, -, -, 16
1085, 15 Oct 1839, Joannes, Gorman, Joannis, Juliae Annae, 13 Oct 1839, -, -, -, Andrias, McMahon, Maria, Dennys, -, -, 16
1086, 16 Oct 1839, Gullillmus Henricus, McEnrue [?], Terrentii, Rosae Annae, 06 Oct 1839, -, -, -, Hugo, Sloe, Anastasia, Murphey, -, -, 16
1087, 16 Oct 1839, Maria Elisabeth Anna, Lewis, Perry, Annae, 20 Aug 1837, -, -, -, Terrentis, McEenrue, -, -, -, -, 16
1088, 19 Oct 1839, Thomas, Daily, Joannis, Catharinae, 27 Sep 1839, -, -, -, Patricius, McCormick, Anna, Made, -, -, 16
1089, 19 Oct 1839, Jacobus, Roach, Michaelis, Joannae, 09 Oct 1839, -, -, -, Joannis, Diamond, Maria, Conley, -, -, 16
1090, 21 Oct 1839, Sara, Gallagher, Michaelis, Birgittae, 08 Oct 1839, -, -, -, Catharina, Smith, -, -, -, -, 16
1091, 26 Oct 1839, Michael, Heverty, Petri, Mariae, 16 Oct 1839, -, -, -, Timotheus, Corbet, Eleonora, Corbet, -, -, 16
1092, 27 Oct 1839, Thomas, Crenner, Owen, Annae, 24 Oct 1839, -, -, -, Thomas, Keenan, Elisea [?], Powers, -, -, 16

ST. MARY'S CATHOLIC CHURCH
HAGERSTOWN, MARYLAND, BAPTISMS:
Index, Bap Date, Child, Last Name, Father, Mother,
Birth Date, Code1, Code2, Code3,
1st Sponsor First, 1st Sponsor Last,
2nd Sponsor First, 2nd Sponsor Last, Location,
Notes, Maiden Name, Priest

1093, 27 Oct 1839, Anna, Flanigan, Francisci, Mariae Annae, 10 Sep 1839, -, -, -, Thomas, McDermot, Catharina, Garighan, -, -, 16

1094, 03 Nov 1839, Sara Catherina, Farrel, Jacobi, Catharinae, 28 Oct 1839, -, -, -, Maria, Garaghty, Guillelmus, Byrnast [?], -, -, 16

1095, 11 Nov 1839, Patricius, Flagherty, Michaelis, Catharinae, 31 Oct, -, -, -, Birgitta , Cavanaugh, Owen, Daily, -, -, 16

1096, 11 Nov 1839, Augusta C.G. , Scott, Augusti W., Eisabeth [sic], 03 Dec 1839, -, -, -, M., Guth, Maria, More, note discrepancy between birth and baptism dates, -, 16

1097, 09 Nov 1839, Thomas Joannes B., Reinhard, Samuelis, Elisabeth, 07 Nov 1839, -, -, -, Evelina , Bevans, Michael, Guth, -, -, 16

1098, 10 Nov 1839, Daniel, McDonnell, Morgan, Juliae, 05 Nov 1839, -, -, -, Birgitta , Grey, Joannes, Grey, -, -, 16

1099, 10 Nov 1839, Joannes, Moran, Jacobi, Mariae, 29 Oct 1839, -, -, -, Rosa Anna , Sweeny, Thomas, Moran, -, -, 16

1100, 15 Nov 1839, Stephanus, Stephan, Antonii, Magdalenae, 18 Oct 1839, -, -, -, -, -, Joannes, Jägel, -, -, 16

1101, 15 Nov 1839, Guillelinus, Braungart, Gasparis, Mariae Annae, 28 Aug 1839, -, -, -, Maria, Renner, Guillelmus, Renner, -, -, 16

1102, 17 Nov 1839, Guellelinus Josephus, Gauger, Josephi, Julianae, 28 Sep 1839, -, -, -, Ludovica Anna , Coyle, Edwardus , Coyle, -, -, 16

1103, 23 Nov 1839, Jacobus, Riley, Petri, Johannae, 21 Nov 1839, -, -, -, Sara , Brisco, Georgius, Kerby, -, -, 16

1104, 25 Nov 1839, Johanna , Colens, Joannis, Mariae, 24 Nov 1839, -, -, -, Jeremiah, Sullivan, Johanna Murphey, Murphey, -, -, 16

1105, 10 Dec 1839, Joannes Alexander, Clarck, -, Mariae, 05 Oct 1839, PN, -, -, -, -, -, -, -, -, 16

1106, 16 Dec 1839, Margareta, Duffey, Michaelis, Annae, 30 Nov 1839, -, -, -, Elisabeth , Kelly, Owen, Bannon, -, -, 16

1107, 01 Jan 1840, Maria, Brogan, Thomae, Mariae, 30 Dec 1839, -, -, -, Maria , Daugherty, Thomas, Monaghan, -, -, 16

ST. MARY'S CATHOLIC CHURCH
HAGERSTOWN, MARYLAND, BAPTISMS:
Index, Bap Date, Child, Last Name, Father, Mother,
Birth Date, Code1, Code2, Code3,
1st Sponsor First, 1st Sponsor Last,
2nd Sponsor First, 2nd Sponsor Last, Location,
Notes, Maiden Name, Priest

1108, 22 Dec 1839, Guillelmas J., Gillmeyer, Georgie, Elisabeth, 22 Dec 1839, -, -, -, Maria , Muller, Sebastianas, Gillmeyer, -, -, 16

1109, 02 Jan 1840, Birgitta, Welsh, Jacobi, Joannae, 21 Dec 1840*, -, -, -, Anastasia , Power, Patricus, Tigh, *birthdate reads 21 Dec 1840, but the priest might have meant 1839, -, 16

1110, 02 Jan 1840, Catharina, Loghan, Joannis, Mariae, 31 Dec 1839, -, -, -, Anna , Duffey, Patricus, Bannon, -, -, 16

1111, 02 Jan 1840, Georgius, Mullen, Jacobi, Mariae Annae, 27 Oct 1839, -, -, -, Maria Elisabeth , McDonnell, Thomas, Beer, -, -, 16

1112, 05 Jan 1840, Chirstophorus, Drennan [?], Thomae, Catharinae, 25 Dec 1839, -, -, -, Sara , Carr, Jacobus, Carr, -, -, 16

1113, 06 Jan 1840, Martinus, Quin, Jacobi, Eleonorae, 11 Nov 1839, -, -, -, Maria, McGury, Thomas, Nugent, -, -, 16

1114, 06 Jan 1840, Joannes Richardus, Hayden, Guillelmi, Henriettae, 27 Dec 1839, -, -, -, Maria Anna , Harris, Richardus, Hayden, -, -, 16

1115, 19 Jan 1840, Maria Anna, McCauley, Caroli, Annae, 29 Dec 1839, PN, -, -, -, -, -, -, -, Pleek, 16

1116, 19 Jan 1840, Maria Anna, McCann, Joannis, Annae, 04 Jan 1840, -, -, -, Catharina , Garrighan, Jacobis, Riley, -, -, 16

1117, 20 Jan 1840, Franciscus, Henroty, Owen, Mariae, 21 Dec 1839, -, -, -, Catharina , Sleet [?], Jacobus, Dugan, -, -, 16

1118, 21 Jan 1840, Margereta Isabella, Shane, Joannis, Margaretae, 16 Dec 1839, -, -, -, Maria , Clarck, Michael, Guth, -, -, 16

1119, 27 Jan 1840, Guillelmus Franciscus, McGonigle, Jacobi, Margaretae, 24 Jan 1840, -, -, -, Eleonora, Murphey, -, -, -, -, 16

1120, 3 Feb 1840, Joannes, Daly, Josephi, Gratiae, 12 Jan 1840, -, -, -, Anna, Meginly, Arthur, Roads, -, -, 16

1121, 04 Feb 1840, Joannes, Welsh, Michaelis, Ellionorae, 03 Feb 1840, -, -, -, Rosa , McLaughlin, Bernardus, Sweeney, -, -, 16

1122, 04 Feb 1840, Bryan, Stanlan [or Scarrlan], Antonii, Sarae, 03 Feb 1840, -, -, -, Maria , Barret, Dominicus, Barret, -, -, 16

1123, 04 Feb 1840, Anna, Fealy, Patricii, Annae, 04 Feb 1840, -, -, -, Maria , Doulan, Arthur, Cruie [or Crure], -, -, 16

ST. MARY'S CATHOLIC CHURCH
HAGERSTOWN, MARYLAND, BAPTISMS:
Index, Bap Date, Child, Last Name, Father, Mother,
Birth Date, Code1, Code2, Code3,
1st Sponsor First, 1st Sponsor Last,
2nd Sponsor First, 2nd Sponsor Last, Location,
Notes, Maiden Name, Priest

1124, 04 Feb 1840, Maria, Wewerler [or Wenerler or Werverler], Marci, Catharinae, 28 Nov 1839, -, -, -, Maria , Witt, Michael, Witt, -, -, 16

1125, 04 Feb 1840, Edwardus, Doyle, Edwardi, Elleonorae, 02 Feb 1840, -, -, -, Birgitta , Doyle, Thomas, Turner, -, -, 16

1126, 05 Feb 1840, Maria Anna, Loghan , Joannis, Birgittae, 23 Jan 1840, -, -, -, Margareta , Clarck, Jacobus, Weight, -, -, 16

1127, 05 Feb 1840, Maria, Byrn, Patricii, Annae, 27 Jan 1840, -, -, -, Catharina , Sullivan, Joannes, Beer, -, -, 16

1128, 06 Feb 1840, Conrardus, Antony, Georgii, Mariae, 22 Jan 1840, -, -, -, Conrardus, Antony, -, -, -, -, 16

1129, 09 Feb 1840, Catharina, MaKenzy, Eliae, Elisabeth, 18 Sep 1839, -, -, -, Maria Anna , Brehm, Bernardus, Kraus, -, -, 16

1130, 03 Feb 1840, Josephus, Menkey [?], Joannis Josephi, Angelinae, 28 Jan 1840, -, -, -, -, -, -, -, -, -, -, 16

1131, 15 Feb 1840, Maria, Mauricy, David, Annae, 04 Jan 1840, -, -, -, Catharina , Spollen , Edwardus, Henney , -, -, 16

1132, 18 Feb 1840, Andrias , Whealen, Jacobi, Judith, 25 Jan 1840, -, -, -, Birgitta , McGee, Jacobus, Conlon, -, -, 16

1133, 19 Feb 1840, Winey [female], Connor, Joannis, Mariae, 08 Feb 1840, -, -, -, Patricius, Monaghan, Birgitta Matton, Matton, -, - , 16

1134, 20 Feb 1840, Maria Anna, Harrison, Joannis Thomae, Margaretae, 22 Dec 1830, -, -, -, -, -, -, -, -, -, 16

1135, 20 Feb 1840, Theresia, Renner, Ignatii, Mariae Annae, 27 Jan 1840, -, -, -, Maria Anna , Brauergarden, Michael, Garner, -, -, 16

1136, 23 Feb 1840, Robert, McCarty, Edwardi, Catharinae, 03 Oct 1839, -, -, -, Margareta, Tigert, -, -, -, -, 16

1137, 26 Feb 1840, Maria, Kelly, Patricii, Sarae, 25 Feb 1840, -, -, -, Maria , Mooney, Danniel, Coffee, -, -, 16

1138, 26 Feb 1840, Christophorus, Tilghman, Thomas, Maria, 19 Feb 1840, -, -, -, Sara, Trueman, -, -, -, -, 16

1139, 26 Feb 1840, Sara Joanna, Wetzel, Albertus, Margaretae, 02 Jan 1840, -, -, -, Maria Magdalena, Fox, -, -, -, -, 16

1140, 08 Mar 1840, Josephina, Hurley, Jacobi, Sophiae, 27 Feb 1840, -, -, -, Francisca , Melton, M., Guth, -, -, 16

ST. MARY'S CATHOLIC CHURCH
HAGERSTOWN, MARYLAND, BAPTISMS:
Index, Bap Date, Child, Last Name, Father, Mother,
Birth Date, Code1, Code2, Code3,
1st Sponsor First, 1st Sponsor Last,
2nd Sponsor First, 2nd Sponsor Last, Location,
Notes, Maiden Name, Priest

1141, 09 Mar 1840, Maria Anna, Cane, Jacobi, Annae, 20 Feb 1840, -, -, -, Gratia , Daly , Joannes, Steward, -, -, 16

1142, 09 Mar 1840, Thomas Antonius, Riley, Joannis, Mariae, 13 Jan 1840, -, -, -, Eleonora , Sanderson, Antonius, Riley, -, -, 16

1143, 11 Mar 1840, Catharina, Radger, Patricii, Catharinae, 28 Feb 1840, -, -, -, Margareta , Spollen, N., Spollen, -, -, 16

1144, 12 mar 1840, Rosa Anna, Byrns, Patricii, Joannae, 02 Mar 1840, -, -, -, Joannae , Rodger, Michael, Murray, -, -, 16

1145, 12 Mar 1840, Catharina, Lyons, Nicolai, Mariae, 05 Mar 1840, -, -, -, Margareta , Kelly, Jacobus, McCoane, -, -, 16

1146, 13 Mar 1840, Jacobus, Keenan, Andreas, Annae, 23 Feb 1840, -, -, -, Jacobus, Tremble, Anna , Munday, -, -, 16

1147, 15 Mar 1840, Margareta, Quicgley, Patricii, Mariae, 25 Feb 1840, -, -, -, Joanna , Farrell, Patricius , Farrel, -, -, 16

1148, 17 Mar 1840, Patricius, Murray, Timothei, Juliae, 12 Mar 1840, -, -, -, Mariae , Kelly, Thomas, Grant, -, -, 16

1149, 17 Mar 1840, Patricius, Griffon, Guillelmi, Catharinae, 14 Mar 1840, -, -, -, Anna , Tigue, Joannes , Kelly, -, -, 16

1150, 18 Mar 1840, Maria, Conley, Thomae, Birgettae, 14 Mar 1840, -, -, -, Robertus, Meloy, Catharina, Timple, -, -, 16

1151, 18 Mar 1840, Birgitta, McLaughlin, Martini, Birgettae, 17 Mar 1840, -, -, -, Anna , Doyle, Patricius , Kildogf [?], -, -, 16

1152, 18 Mar 1840, Elisabeth, Cox, Michaelis, Catharinae, 02 Mar 1840, -, -, -, Maria , Belton, Patricius , Cane, -, -, 16

1153, 19 Mar 1840, Margareta, More, Joannis, Sarae, 19 Mar 1840, -, -, -, Sara , Madan, Patricius , Fealy, -, -, 16

1154, 19 Mar 1840, Maria Anna, Murray, Laurentii, Sarae, 20 Oct 1839, -, -, -, Anna , Kelly, Joannes , Reader, -, -, 16

1155, 19 Mar 1840, Catharina, Morgan, Guillelini, Mariae, 16 Mar 1840, -, -, -, Birgitta , Mitchel, Patricius , Mitchel, -, -, 16

1156, 20 Mar 1840, Anna, Tigh, Jacobi , -, -, -, -, -, -, -, -, -, entry crossed out. nothing else written except that her parents were married, -, 16

1157, 20 Mar 1840, Caecilia (dau), McDonnell, Michaelis, Annae, 17 Mar 1840, -, -, -, Jacobus, Tigh, Maria, Copman, -, -, 16

1158, 26 Mar 1840, Birgitta, Demsey, Petri, Margaretae, 10 Mar 1840, -, -, -, Anna , Halter, Michael, Stauntan, -, -, 16

ST. MARY'S CATHOLIC CHURCH
HAGERSTOWN, MARYLAND, BAPTISMS:
Index, Bap Date, Child, Last Name, Father, Mother,
Birth Date, Code1, Code2, Code3,
1st Sponsor First, 1st Sponsor Last,
2nd Sponsor First, 2nd Sponsor Last, Location,
Notes, Maiden Name, Priest

1159, 05 Apr 1840, Anna Lucia, Shorter, -, Lucretiae, 22 Feb 1840, PN, -, -, Lucia Anna, Wilson, -, -, -, -, 16

1160, 03 Mar 1840, Anna Catharina, Gross, Caroli, Abehelam [?], 12 Oct 1839, -, -, -, -, -, -, -, -, -, 16

1161, 08 Apr 1840, Michael, Scott, Patricii, Mariae, 27 Mar 1840, -, -, -, N., Breine, Guillelmus , Denison, -, -, 16

1162, 10 Apr 1840, Joannes, Whealan, Guillelmi, Mariae, 25 Feb 1840, -, -, -, Catharina , Yasuxor [?], Patricius, Clark, -, -, 16

1163, 19 Apr 1840, Adelina?, Cossy, Matheii, Hanorae, 13 Mar 1840, -, -, -, Jeremias, Johnes, -, -, -, -, 16

1164, 19 Apr 1840, Joannes (son), Shiller, Joachim, Franciscae, 18 Jun 1839, -, -, -, Joannes, Eisler, -, -, -, -, 16

1165, 19 Apr 1840, Matheus, Hildenbrand, Michaelis, Apollinae, 08 Feb 1840, -, -, -, Matheus , Sreiner, -, -, -, -, 16

1166, 20 Apr 1840, Petrus, Fitzwilliam, Petri, Anna , 03 May 1839, -, -, -, Guillermus , Byrns, Maria , McEvoy, -, -, 16

1167, 20 Apr 1840, Georgius, Antony, Conradi [?], Catharinae, 24 Mar 1840, -, -, -, Georgius, Antony, -, -, -, -, 16

1168, 21 Apr 1840, Ally* , Hail , Roberti, Annae, 05 Apr 1840, -, -, -, Antonius, Hughes, Criso? , Carny, *Ally ["Alice" written under it] , -, 16

1169, 21 Apr 1840, Anna, Teff, Peetri, Birgittae, 10 Apr 1840, -, -, -, Michael, McLaughlin, Maria , Duffey, -, -, 16

1170, 21 Apr 1840, Edwardus, Maddon, Joannis, Sarae, 10 Apr 1840, -, -, -, Joannes, Moore, Maria , Gerner, -, -, 16

1171, 21 Apr 1840, Patricius, Mallery, Patricii, Sarae, 18 Apr 1840, -, -, -, Honora , McLaughlin, Joannes , Kelly, -, -, 16

1172, 23 Apr 1840, Guillelmus, Sullivan, Guillelimi, Sarae, 02 Mar 1840, -, -, -, Maria , Welsh, Brian , Sweeny, -, -, 16

1173, 24 Apr 1840, Michael, Dealon, Joannis, Birgittae, 21 Apr 1840, -, -, -, Margareta , Power, McNamora, Power [HB], -, 16

1174, 24 Apr 1840, Maria, Lee, Cornelii, Eleonora, 23 Apr 1840, -, -, -, Margareta , Dee, Timotheus , Morarty, -, -, 16

1175, 24 Apr 1840, Joannes , Donovan, Joannes, Catharinae, 14 Apr 1840, -, -, -, Elisabeth , Donovan, David, Sullivan, -, -, 16

1176, 24 Apr 1840, Catharina, Cray, Petrii, Margaretae, 08 Apr 1840, -, -, -, Naty , Mulligan, Owen , Heslan [?], -, -, 16

ST. MARY'S CATHOLIC CHURCH
HAGERSTOWN, MARYLAND, BAPTISMS:
Index, Bap Date, Child, Last Name, Father, Mother,
Birth Date, Code1, Code2, Code3,
1st Sponsor First, 1st Sponsor Last,
2nd Sponsor First, 2nd Sponsor Last, Location,
Notes, Maiden Name, Priest

1177, 25 Apr 1840, Christophorus, Mulvana, Thomae, Annae, 23 Apr 1840, -, -, -, Patricus, Murray, Elisabeth, Ryan, -, -, 16
1178, 25 Apr 1840, Michael, Cuningham, Joannis, Cathorinae, 10 Apr 1840, -, -, -, Elisabeth , Cambel, Jacobus , Cambel, -, -, 16
1179, 26 Apr 1840, Georgius, McAtee, Samuelis, Sarae, 29 Aug 1837, -, -, -, Stephanus , Laughlin, -, -, -, -, 16
1180, 26 Apr 1840, Walterius, McAtee, Samuelis, Sarae, 24 Jul 1839, -, -, -, Michael , Laughlin, -, -, -, -, 16
1181, 26 Apr 1840, Flora, Schlick, Joannis, Elisabeth, 22 Oct 1839, -, -, -, Elisabeth , Jiegner, Jacobus , Sneider, -, -, 16
1182, 26 Apr 1840, Maria Johanna, Quin, Thomae, Rosa Annae, 28 Mar 1840, -, -, -, Catharina , Farrel, Thomas , McDermot, -, -, 16
1183, 26 Apr 1840, Anna Elisabeth, Tarrel [or Hunter if using mother's name], Jacobi, Elisabeth , 02 Aug 1839, PN, -, -, Catharina , McLaughlin, Thomas, Kelly, -, Hunter, 16
1184, 28 Apr 1840, Anna, Kelly, Jacobi, Birgittae, 27 Apr 1840, -, -, -, Maria , Loghan [or Laghan], Michael , Kelly, -, -, 16
1185, 28 Apr 1840, Daniel, Sullivan, Danielis, Catharinae, 26 Apr 1840, -, -, -, Johanna , Cuny [?], Joannes , Sullivan, -, -, 16
1186, 10 Apr 1840*, Maria Elisabeth, McClosky, Petri, Marthae, 04 Apr 1840, -, -, -, Catharinae , Hapelty [?], Cornelius , McGron [?], in bapatismal date, it was unclear whether the date was 10 April or 10 May, -, 16
1187, 06 May 1840, Theresia, Primas, Basilie , Dianae, 27 Nov 1839, -, -, -, Elisabeth , Shorter, -, -, -, -, 16
1188, 06 May 1840, Eleonora, Ambushe, Jorck, Appoloniae, 02 Oct 1839, -, -, -, Elisabeth , Barn, -, -, -, -, 16
1189, 06 May 1840, Maria, Roberson, Joannis, Franciscae, 27 Apr 1840, -, -, -, Emma , Floy, -, -, -, -, 16
1190, 08 May 1840, Maria, Kerman, Joannis, Mariae, 20 Apr 1840, -, -, -, G., Sweeny, Birgitta, Sweeny, -, -, 16
1191, 08 May 1840, Catharina, Jacson , Henriei, Elisabeth, 06 Feb 1840, -, -, -, Catharina , Mauricy, -, -, -, -, 16
1192, 08 May 1840, Franciscus Thomas, Maynon, Patricii, Eleonorae, 21 Mar 1840, -, -, -, Francisia , McEntier, Patricius , Kelly, -, -, 16

ST. MARY'S CATHOLIC CHURCH
HAGERSTOWN, MARYLAND, BAPTISMS:
Index, Bap Date, Child, Last Name, Father, Mother,
Birth Date, Code1, Code2, Code3,
1st Sponsor First, 1st Sponsor Last,
2nd Sponsor First, 2nd Sponsor Last, Location,
Notes, Maiden Name, Priest

1193, 14 May 1840, Birgitta, Clark, Laurentii, Birgittae , 26 Nov 1838, -, -, -, -, -, -, -, -, Mauricy, 16

1194, 16 May 1840, Anna, Tygh, Patricii, Annae, 26 Apr 1840, -, -, -, Maria , Rogan, Michael , Rogan, -, -, 16

1195, 17 May 1848, Joannes , Linch, Owen, Rosae, 07 May 1840, -, -, -, Anna , Meath, Petras , Daud, -, -, 16

1196, 18 May 1840, Catharina, Kelly, Patricii, Birgittae, 01 Apr 1840, -, -, -, Maria , Smith, Patricius , Mullen, -, -, 16

1197, 18 May 1840, Henricus, Welsh, Petri, Rosae, 01 May 1840, -, -, -, Judith , O'Brian, Maatheus , McCormick, -, -, 16

1198, 21 May 1840, Juliana, Stake, Hugonis, Cathrinae, 20 Apr 1840, -, -, -, Maria Anna , Braungard, Gaspar , Braungard, -, -, 16

1199, 26 May 1840, Birgitta, Goff, Joannis, Birgittae, 09 May 1840, -, -, -, Catharina , Green, Jacobus , Kenny, -, -, 16

1200, 28 May 1840, Baltasar, Forbeck, Casimiri, Evae, 03 May 1840, -, -, -, Baltasar, Fayetter, -, -, -, -, 16

1201, 31 May 1840, Franciscus [twin], Halton, Michaelis, Annae, 30 May 1840, -, -, -, Birgitta , McEntye, Robertus , Small, -, -, 16

1202, 31 May 1840, Joannes [twin], Halton, Michaelis, Annae, 30 May 1840, -, -, -, Margareta , Demsey, Michael , Masterson, -, -, 16

1203, 03 Jun 1840, Catharina, Coleus, Petri, Rosae, 24 May 1840, -, -, -, Maria , Brogan, Joannes , McGuire, -, -, 16

1204, 03 Jun 1840, Margareta, Flinn, Michaelis, Mariae, 24 May 1840, -, -, -, Catharina , Kelly, Garret , Hogan, -, -, 16

1205, 04 Jun 1840, Margareta, Clarck, Jacobi, Catharinae, 30 May 1840, -, -, -, Anna , Linam, Loghan , Clarck, -, -, 16

1206, 04 Jun 1840, Julia, Fallon, Patricii, Birgettae, 17 May 1840, -, -, -, Maria , Allam [?], Michael , Farrell, -, -, 16

1207, 04 Jun 1840, Joannis , Lolley [?], Michaelis, Birgittae, 03 May 1840, -, -, -, Marias , Dixon, John , Dixon, -, -, 16

1208, 04 Jun 1840, Jacobus, Shanaghan, Christopheri, Birgittae, 30-May, -, -, -, Emilia , Christopher, Ludovicus, Bertolet [?], -, -, 16

1209, 04 Jun 1840, Margareta, Kelly, Joannis, Annae, 21 May 1840, -, -, -, Sara , Gellin, Bernardus , Duga, -, -, 16

ST. MARY'S CATHOLIC CHURCH
HAGERSTOWN, MARYLAND, BAPTISMS:
Index, Bap Date, Child, Last Name, Father, Mother,
Birth Date, Code1, Code2, Code3,
1st Sponsor First, 1st Sponsor Last,
2nd Sponsor First, 2nd Sponsor Last, Location,
Notes, Maiden Name, Priest

1210, 04 Jun 1840, Thomas, Mehlman , -, Mariae, -, PN, -, -, Guellelmina , Stekenius [?], -, -, -, -, 16

1211, 14 Jun 1840, Henricus , Dicks, -, -, -, -, -, -, -, -, -, -, "primi parents habueri Dicks, et postumam Dicks - In quorum fidem", -, 40

1212, 14 Jun 1840, Benjaminus, Dicks, -, -, -, -, -, -, -, -, -, -, -, -, 40

1213, 14 Jun 1840, Mariam Elizabetham, Dicks, -, -, -, -, -, -, -, -, -, -, -, -, -, 40

1214, 07 Jun 1840, Sara Anna, Smith, John K., Elisabeth, 04 Feb 1840, -, -, -, Maria, Paton, -, -, -, -, 16

1215, 08 Jun 1840, Catharina, Caudey, Dionysiius, Matildis, 23 May 1840, -, -, -, Maria, Berry, -, -, -, -, 16

1216, 08 Jun 1840, Elleonora, Thomson, Isaac, Rebeccae, 02 May 1840, -, -, -, Maria, Hackey, -, -, -, -, 16

1217, 11 Jun 1840, Thomas, Mills, Guillelmi, Mariae, 25 Oct 1840, -, -, -, Catharina , Moore, Thomas , Maines, -, -, 16

1218, 13 Jun 1840, Maria, Monaghan, Joannis, Catharinae, 04 Jun 1840, -, -, -, Catharina , Bernard, Joannes , Skelly, -, -, 16

1219, 21 Jun 1840, Johanna Rebecca, Matheus, Jannis, Henriettae, 24 May 1840, -, -, -, Rebecca, Galloway, -, -, -, -, 16

1220, 22 Jun 1840, Catharina, Noon, Joannis, Mariae, 16 Jun 1840, -, -, -, Johanna , Carl, Patricius , Carl, -, -, 16

1221, 22 Jun 1840, Joannes son, Green, Francisca, Abelonae, 22 Jun 1840, -, -, -, Birgitta , Gray, Joannes , Gray, -, -, 16

1222, 28 Jun 1840, Joannes Henricus, Kelly, Josephi, Catharinae, 15 Jan 1840, -, -, -, Maria Anna, Davis, Maria Anna , -, -, -, 16

1223, 29 Jun 1840, Margareta, Kelly, Morgan, Mariae, 22 Jun 1840, -, -, -, Margareta , Clarke, Carolus, Clarck, -, -, 16

1224, 05 Jul 1840, Carolus McG [sic], Futterer, Aloyisii, Catharinae, 15 Mar 1840, -, -, -, Jacob, Pultz, -, -, -, -, 16

1225, 12 Jul 1840, Ludavicus, Burgey, Shederick, Rebeccae, 30 Mar 1840, -, -, -, Sara , Ley, Franciscus, Johnson, -, -, 16

1226, 14 Jul 1840, Jacobus Henricus, Corbutt, Petri, Annaae, 26 Jun 1840, -, -, -, Anna , McFadden, Joannes, McFadden, -, -, 16

1227, 14 Jul 1840, [female], Means, -, -, -, -, -, -, -, -, -, -, legitimate female daughter is the only information in this entry, -, 16

ST. MARY'S CATHOLIC CHURCH
HAGERSTOWN, MARYLAND, BAPTISMS:
Index, Bap Date, Child, Last Name, Father, Mother,
Birth Date, Code1, Code2, Code3,
1st Sponsor First, 1st Sponsor Last,
2nd Sponsor First, 2nd Sponsor Last, Location,
Notes, Maiden Name, Priest

1228, 17 Jul 1840, Matheus, Renny [or Benny], Patricii, Mariae, 09 Jul 1840, -, -, -, Joannes, Fenley, Anna, Fenley [HB], -, -, 16

1229, 17 Jul 1840, Dionysius, Sweany, Miles, Julianae, 27 Jun 1840, -, -, -, Johanna , Mullen, Jeremias, Murphey, -, -, 16

1230, 19 Jul 1840, Eleonora, Madden, Joannis, Mariae, 15 Jul 1840, -, -, -, Birgitta , Philipps, Joannes, Barry, -, -, 16

1231, 19 Jul 1840, Edwardus, Paterson, Caroli, Mariae Anarr , 06 May 1840, -, -, -, Anna , McLaughlin, Jacobus, McGovenor, -, -, 16

1232, 19 Jul 1840, Philippus, Carkaron , Jacobi, Annae, 02 Jul 1840, -, -, -, Catharina , Burns, Philippus, Caldwell, -, -, 16

1233, 19 Jul 1840, Joannes son, Murphey, Patricii, Birgittae, 23 Jun 1840, -, -, -, Anna , Riley, Patricius, McDermott, -, -, 16

1234, 19 Jul 1840, Jacobus, Murphey, Guilelini, Mariae, 10 Jul 1840, -, -, -, Elisabeth , Caloury, Timothius, Hennesy, -, -, 16

1235, 21 Jul 1840, Catharina, Lasley, Richardi, Catharinae, 02 Jul 1840, -, -, -, Johanna , Daugherty, Thomas, Ferley, -, -, 16

1236, 21 Jul 1840, Joannes son, Mannon, Richardi, Elisabeth, 25 Jun 1840, -, -, -, Catharina , McGrane, Guilelinus, Ledwidge, -, -, 16

1237, 22 Jul 1840, Joannes , Skelly [or Hoarse if using mother's name], Jannis, Mariae, 2 Apr 1840, PN, -, -, Petrus, Spollen, Anna, Maurice, See Endnote 17 , Hoarse, 16

1238, 22 Jul 1840, Matheus, Hoy, Petri, Rosae, 15 Jul 1840, -, -, -, Birgitta , Caine, Stephanus, Laughlin, -, -, 16

1239, 22 Jul 1840, Anna, Cashon, Christiani, Elisabeth, 13 Jul 1840, -, -, -, Birgitta , Henry, Georgius, Henry, -, -, 16

1240, 22 Jul 1840, Maria, Conors, Thomae, Catharinae, 22 Jun 1840, -, -, -, Anna , Mulvana [?], Bernardus, King, -, -, 16

1241, 23 Jul 1840, Jacobus, Doyle, Terrentii, Annae, 22 Jul 1840, -, -, -, Maria Anna , Doyle, Owen, Quin, -, -, 16

1242, 24 Jul 1840, Jacobus, Kurley, Patricii, Catharinae, 28 Jun 1840, -, -, -, Anna , Moore, Jacobus, Karney, -, -, 16

1243, 02 Aug 1840, Rosa Anna, Karr, Jacobi, Sarae, 01 Aug 1840, -, -, -, Margareta , Taylor, Charolus, McEntey *, *["Georgius Mc" crossed out and "McEntey" written in], -, 16

ST. MARY'S CATHOLIC CHURCH
HAGERSTOWN, MARYLAND, BAPTISMS:
Index, Bap Date, Child, Last Name, Father, Mother,
Birth Date, Code1, Code2, Code3,
1st Sponsor First, 1st Sponsor Last,
2nd Sponsor First, 2nd Sponsor Last, Location,
Notes, Maiden Name, Priest

1244, 04 Aug 1840, Guilelmus, Paulus, N. *, -, 4 years, -, -, -, -, -, -, -, -, "praenomina patris & matris ignota" [translates as "the previously named father and mother unknown"]; Endnote 66, -, 16

1245, 08 Aug 1840, Theresa, Singer, Isaac, Mariannae, 04 Jan 1840, -, -, -, Elisabeth, Gilmeyer, -, -, -, -, 16

1246, 15 Aug 1840, Elisabeth, Kelly, Thomae, Mariae, 11 Aug 1840, -, -, -, Anna , Dealon, Christophorus, Casy, -, -, 16

1247, 15 Aug 1840, Catharina, Corbett, Timothei, Eleonorae, born about 08 Aug 1840, -, -, -, Elisabeth , Kelly, Joannes, Naughton, -, -, 16

1248, 15 Aug 1840, Birgitta, McGnee , Martini, Elionorae, 14 Aug 1840, -, -, -, Maria , Sheghran, Owen, Carney, -, -, 16

1249, 17 Aug 1840, Eleonora Elisabeth, Shipley, Richardi, Elisabeth, 28 Jan 1840, -, -, -, Elisabeth Johanna, Bevans, -, -, -, -, 16

1250, 17 Aug 1840, Anna, Douckry , Thomae, Eleonora, 11 Aug 1840, -, -, -, Patricius, McCormick, Mariae, McCormick [HB], -, -, 16

1251, 23 Aug 1840, Maria, Putz?, Jacobi, Margaretae, 29 Jul 1840, -, -, -, Maria , Germen , Ludovicus, Futterer, -, -, 16

1252, 27 Aug 1840, Maria Christina, Hicky, Henrici, Catharinae, 11 Aug 1840, -, -, -, -, -, -, -, -, -, 16

1253, 27 Aug 1840, Joannes , McLaughlin, Patricii, Eleonorae, 27 Aug 1840, -, -, -, Eleonora , Donnely, Michael, McLaughlin, -, -, 16

1254, 27 Aug 1840, Maria, McGerry, Patricii, Margaretae, 221 Aug 1840, -, -, -, Maria , Lalley, Patricius, Coin, -, -, 16

1255, 08 Sep 1840, Joannes, Halpin, Michaelis, Annae, 05 Aug 1840, -, -, -, Guillelimus, Coony, -, -, -, -, 16

1256, 14 Sep 1840, W. Edwardus, Bavert, David, Melindae, 14 Jul 1840, -, -, -, Michael, Martin, Catharina [crossed out], Craig [crossed out], -, -, 16

1257, 16 Sep 1840, W. Thomas, Nichols, -, Johannae, 2 years and 2 months, PN, -, -, -, -, -, -, -, -, 16

1258, 17 Sep 1840, Patricius, Chopman?, N., Mariae, 01 Sep 1840, -, -, -, Honora , McDonnell, Michael, Tyrney, -, -, 16

ST. MARY'S CATHOLIC CHURCH
HAGERSTOWN, MARYLAND, BAPTISMS:
Index, Bap Date, Child, Last Name, Father, Mother,
Birth Date, Code1, Code2, Code3,
1st Sponsor First, 1st Sponsor Last,
2nd Sponsor First, 2nd Sponsor Last, Location,
Notes, Maiden Name, Priest

1259, 18 Sep 1840, Joannes , Mausfield, Joannis, Eleonorae, 19 Aug 1840, -, -, -, Maria , Morarty, Jacobus, Morarty, -, -, 16

1260, 18 Sep 1840, Jacobus, Clark, Joannis, Margaritae, 11 Sep 1840, -, -, -, Honora , Welsh, Thomas, Garret, -, -, 16

1261, 18 Sep 1840, Patricius, Carlos, Patricii, Elisabeth, 08 Sep 1840, -, -, -, Anna , Duffey, Patricius , Condery, -, -, 16

1262, 18 Sep 1840, Catharina, Smith, William, Mariae, 29 Aug 1840, -, -, -, Dionysius, Graily, Maria, Graily [HB], -, -, 16

1263, 20 Sep 1840, Joannes, Mulligan, Jacobi, Birgittae, 26 Aug 1840, -, -, -, N., Winslon, Maria, Winslon [HB], -, -, 16

1264, 20 Sep 1840, Jacobus, Connelly, Jacobi, Sophiae, about 15 Jul 1840, -, -, -, Ellen , Quin, Patricius , Quin, -, -, 16

1265, 21 Sep 1840, Patricius, Dimsey, Thomae, Annaae, 28 Aug 1840, -, -, -, Maria , Raney [or Baney], Patricius , Coffee, -, -, 16

1266, 23 Sep 1840, Patricius, Haly, Joannis, Mariae, 21 Sep 1840, -, -, -, Catharina , Dronan, Thomas , Dronan, -, -, 16

1267, 24 Sep 1840, Elisabeth Maria, Delauny, John C., Sussannaae, 01 Sep 1838, -, -, -, Maria Rosalia, Delauny, -, -, -, -, 16

1268, 24 Sep1 840, Joannes, Leixner, Philippi, Doratheae, 10 Jun 1840, -, -, -, Gertrudis , Exkert, Joannes , Exkert, -, -, 16

1269, 01 Oct 1840, Catharina, Naughton, Joannis, Honorae, 27 Sep 1840, -, -, -, Morgan, McDonnell, Julia, McDonnell, -, -, 16

1270, 01 Oct 1840, Birgitta, Lanon, Mathei, Honorae, 29 Sep 1840, -, -, -, Catharina , McGovern, Michael , Naughton, -, -, 16

1271, 01 Oct 1840, Birgitta, Condry, Joannis, Anna, 24 Sep 1840, -, -, -, Maria , Coffile, Philippus , Lawet [or Lanet], -, -, 16

1272, 01 Oct 1840, Jacobus, Klüh , Jacobi, Florae, 27 Sep 1840, -, -, -, Jacobus, Sneidor , -, -, -, -, 16

1273, 02 Oct 1840, Jacobus Alexander, O'Brian, Edwardi, Eleonorae, 01 Sep 1840, -, -, -, Anna , Mulharon, Andreas , Colvin, -, -, 16

1274, 02 Oct 1840, Joannes Thomas, Taylor, -, Sarae Anna, 03 Aug 1840, PN, -, -, -, -, -, -, -, -, 16

1275, 19 Oct 1840, Rosa Anna, O'Neal, Hugonis, Birgittae, 20 Sep 1840, -, -, -, Margaretae , Marken, Joanes , Brown, -, -, 16

ST. MARY'S CATHOLIC CHURCH
HAGERSTOWN, MARYLAND, BAPTISMS:
Index, Bap Date, Child, Last Name, Father, Mother,
Birth Date, Code1, Code2, Code3,
1st Sponsor First, 1st Sponsor Last,
2nd Sponsor First, 2nd Sponsor Last, Location,
Notes, Maiden Name, Priest

1276, 19 Oct 1840, Bernardus, Doyle, Joannis, Elisabeth, 16 Oct 1840, -, -, -, Honora , Healy, Bernardus , Healy, -, -, 16

1277, 19 Oct 1840, Joannes, Dolen, Patricii, Annae, 03 Oct 1840, -, -, -, Catharina , Doyle, Jacobus , Cuningham, -, -, 16

1278, 19 Oct 1840, Petrus, Hayden, Joannis, Eleonorae, 24 Sep 1840, -, -, -, Margareta , Handley, Michael , Collen, -, -, 16

1279, 19 Oct 1840, Susanna, Cruse, Arthuris, Eleonorae, 18 Oct 1840, -, -, -, Margareta , McGerry, Timotheus , Garner, -, -, 16

1280, 01 Nov 1840, Carolina Matild, Dr, Danielis, Mariae, 22 Oct 1840, -, -, -, Birgita, Maurice, Birgita , Maurice, -, -, 16

1281, 10 Nov 1840, Daniel, Sullivan, Timothei, Margaretae, 31 Oct 1840, -, -, -, Maria Anna , Kerby, Timotheas , Sullivan, -, -, 16

1282, 10 Nov 1840, Margareta, Cutter, Timothei, Mariae, 14 Aug 1840, -, -, -, Jacobus, Connors, Maria, Beers, -, -, 16

1283, 10 Nov 1840, Anna, Kenden [or Renden], Mauricii, Annae, 25 Oct 1840, -, -, -, Daniel , Morarty, Maria, Collighan, -, -, 16

1284, 11 Nov 1840, Sophia, Bruskey, Ernesti, Mariae Catharina, 2 Oct 1840, -, -, -, Maria Catharina, Benskey, -, -, -, , 16

1285, 12 Nov 1840, Catharina, Kelly, Christophori, Mariae, 5 Nov 1840, -, -, -, Robertus, Meloy, Anna, Wallasse, -, -, 16

1286, 12 Nov 1840, Rosa Anna, Riley, Joannis, Mariae, 31 Oct 1840, -, -, -, Robertus, Harman, Anna, Skelly, -, -, 16

1287, 12 Nov 1840, Catharina Maria, Wetmüller , Dyonisii, Catharinae, 6 Nov 1840, -, -, -, Catharina Elisabeth, Fisbeck, -, -, -, -, 16

1288, 12 Nov 1840, Catharina, Russell, Christophori, Johannae, 7 Nov 1840, -, -, -, Miles, Downs, Birgitta, Mooty, -, -, 16

1289, 13 Nov 1840, Joannes, Finney, Caroli, Mariae, 20 Oct 1840, -, -, -, Guillelmus , Daily, Maria, Daily, -, -, 16

1290, 13 Nov 1840, Maria Elisabeth, Krauss, Bernardy, Mariae Annae, 26 Oct 1840, -, -, -, Jacobus , Hornbach , Maria , Hornbach , -, -, 16

1291, 14 Nov 1840, Susanna, Qucggley, Joannis, Annae, 18 Aug 1840, -, -, -, Patricius , Colerty, Mariae , Quicgley, -, -, 16

1292, 15 Nov 1840, Joannis, Brady, Hugonis, Annae, 22 Oct 1840, -, -, -, Patricius, Cofelly, Eleonora , Coltiel [?], -, -, 16

ST. MARY'S CATHOLIC CHURCH
HAGERSTOWN, MARYLAND, BAPTISMS:
Index, Bap Date, Child, Last Name, Father, Mother,
Birth Date, Code1, Code2, Code3,
1st Sponsor First, 1st Sponsor Last,
2nd Sponsor First, 2nd Sponsor Last, Location,
Notes, Maiden Name, Priest

1293, 16 Nov 1840, Elisabeth, Mallon, Neale, Birgettae, 12 Nov 1840, -, -, -, Hugo , McCoshar, Anna , Mulharon, -, -, 16

1294, 25 Nov 1840, Thomas, McQuigan, Terentii, Mariae, 17 Nov 1840, -, -, -, Hugo, McCoskar, Margarita, McCoskar [HB], -, -, 16

1295, 26 Nov 1840, Maria , Donovan, Dyoinysii, Elisabeth, 23 Nov 1840, -, -, -, Joannes , Donovan, Mariae , Donovan, -, -, 16

1296, 26 Nov 1840, Thomas, Caden, Jacobi, Elisabeth, 14 Nov 1840, -, -, -, Hugo , Prier, Margareta , Gray, -, -, 16

1297, 27 Nov 1840, Edwardus, McCue, Patricii, Elisabeth, 3 Nov 1840, -, -, -, Thomas , McCue, Judith , Johnson, -, -, 16

1298, 13 Dec 1840, Agnes Johanna, Trueman, Joannis , Sarae, 21 Nov 1840, -, -, -, David, Trueman, Sara, Rideout, -, -, 16

1299, 15 Dec 1840, Josephus, Baker, Jacobi, Angelinae, 20 Oct 1840, -, -, -, Franciscus Josephus, Albert, Barbara, Albert, -, -, 16

1300, 15 Dec 1840, Jacobus, Albert, Francisii Josephi, Barbara, 1 Aug 1840, -, -, -, Jacobus , Baker, Angelina, Baker [HB], -, -, 16

1301, 17 Dec 1840, Henricus, Daily, Joannis, K., 29 Nov 1840, -, - , -, Andreas , Colvin, Eleonora, Colvin [HB], -, -, 16

1302, 17 Dec 1840, Jacobus, Clark, Patricii, Catharinae, 23 Nov 1840, -, -, -, Joannes , Ryan, Elisabeth , Dant, -, -, 16

1303, 18 Dec 1840, Thomas, Ambrose, Joannis , Norae, 9 Dec 1840, -, -, -, Matheus , Kheler, Nora , Brian, -, -, 16

1304, 18 Dec 1840, Michael, Ellove [or Ellood], Francisci, Catharinae, 27 Nov 1840, -, -, -, Patricius, Coffeel, Catharina , Bearn, -, -, 16

1305, 18 Dec 1840, David Timotheus, Fling, Edwardi, Johannae, 2 Dec 1840, -, -, -, Jacobus , Mathew, Elleonora , Condon, -, -, 16

1306, 20 Dec 1840, Anna, McGovern, Michaelis, Birgittae, 2 Dec 1840, -, -, -, Patricii , McGovern, Birgitta, Dolan, -, -, 16

1307, 20 Dec 1840, Maria , Dolan, Patricii, Birgittae, 23 Nov 1840, -, -, -, Antonius , Fitzpatrick, Anna, Riley, -, -, 16

1308, 20 Dec 1840, Petrus, McGurg, Guillelini, Sarae, 23 Nov 1840, -, -, -, Patricius, Mighan, Anastasia, Murphey, -, -, 16

1309, 29 Dec 1840, Ambrosius, Barn, -, Elisabeth, 5 Sep 1840, PN, -, -, S. , Burgie, Rebecca, Burgie, -, -, 16

1310, 30 Dec 1840, Fredericus, -, -, -, -, -, -, -, -, -, -, -, rest of entry is blank, -, 16

ST. MARY'S CATHOLIC CHURCH
HAGERSTOWN, MARYLAND, BAPTISMS:
Index, Bap Date, Child, Last Name, Father, Mother,
Birth Date, Code1, Code2, Code3,
1st Sponsor First, 1st Sponsor Last,
2nd Sponsor First, 2nd Sponsor Last, Location,
Notes, Maiden Name, Priest

1311, 30 Dec 1840, Jacobus, Fellinger, Frederici, Rosae, 5 Nov 1839, -, -, -, Rubertus , Wanner, Francisca, Wanner [HB], -, -, 16

1312, 1 Jan 1841, Carolus Dominicus, Clark, Caroli, Margaretae, 20 Dec 1840, -, -, -, Hugo , McCoskar, Birgitta , Gallagher, -, -, 16

1313, 3 Jan 1841, Catharina, Lawless [or Lanless], Patricii, Annae, 25 Dec 1840, -, -, -, Michael , Linam, Birgitta, Higgens, -, -, 16

1314, 5 Jan 1841, Guillelmus Franciscus, Gatton, Zachariae, Eleonorae Josephinae, 17 Dec 1840, -, -, -, Augustinus Dominicus, O'Donnell, Mathilda, Murray, -, -, 16

1315, 5 Jan 1841, Sara, McDote?, Patricii, Susannae, 20 Dec 1840, -, -, -, Timotheus , Naughton, Anna, Naughton [HB], -, -, 16

1316, 5 Jan 1841, Michael, Toohy, -, Birgittae, about the 10 Nov 1840, PN, -, -, Arthur, McNulty, Maria, O'Donnel, -, -, 16

1317, 6 Jan 1841, Elisabeth, Brannon, Patricii, Birgittae, 3 Jan 1840, -, -, -, Thomas , Gallace, Elisabeth, Branigan, -, -, 16

1318, 13 Jan 1841, Thomas, McGovern, Michaelelis, Annae, 29 Dec 1840, -, -, -, Thomas , Mulligan, Margareta, Kelly, -, -, 16

1319, 14 Jan 1841, Johanna, Holland, Dyonisii, Juliae, 2 Dec 1840, -, -, -, Cornelius, Buckley, Honora, Crauley, -, -, 16

1320, 16 Jan 1841, Eleonora, Kelley, Guillelmi, Mariae, 14 Dec 1840, -, -, -, Maria, Fsany, -, -, -, -, 16

1321, 16 Jan 1841, Maria , Ranney [or Runney], Patricii, Mariae, 17 Dec 1840, -, -, -, McNickels , Fenny, Anna, Fenny, -, -, 16

1322, 28 Jan 1841, Daniel, Kelley, Joannis, Honorae, 22 Jan 1841, -, -, -, Michael , Conouhgt [?], Catharina, Griffon, -, -, 16

1323, 3 Feb 1841, Jacobus, McCormick, Patricii, Mariae, 16 Jan 1841, -, -, -, Jacobus, Brannon, Catharina, McDonnell, -, -, 16

1324, 3 Feb 1841, Michael, Spollen, Michaelis, Margaretae, 17 Jan 1841, -, -, -, Patricius, McAnnally, Anna, Dalon, -, -, 16

1325, 3 Feb 1841, Franciscus, McAnaney, Thomae, Johannae, 3 Feb 1841, -, -, -, Patrick, Casy, Catharina, Smith, -, -, 16

1326, 3 Feb 1841, Joannes H., Durnmermann [?], Frederici Henrici, Catharinae, 31 Jan 1841, -, -, -, Henry, Knapp, -, -, -, -, 16

1327, 3 Feb 1841, Andrias Franciscus, Sternner [or Stemmer], Eberhardi, Magdalenae, 26 Dec 1840, -, -, -, Henricus, Knapp, -, -, -, -, 16

ST. MARY'S CATHOLIC CHURCH
HAGERSTOWN, MARYLAND, BAPTISMS:
Index, Bap Date, Child, Last Name, Father, Mother,
Birth Date, Code1, Code2, Code3,
1st Sponsor First, 1st Sponsor Last,
2nd Sponsor First, 2nd Sponsor Last, Location,
Notes, Maiden Name, Priest

1328, 4 Feb 1841, Michael, Daugherty, Michaelis, Margaretae, 17 Jan 1841, -, -, -, James, Whealan, Maria, Murphey, -, -, 16

1329, 19 Feb 1841, Jacobus, McAffrey, Arthur, Birgittae, 24 Jan 1841, -, -, -, Jacobus, Byrns, Maria, Sleets, -, -, 16

1330, 20 Feb 1841, Guillelmus, Wallace, Joannis, Annae, 7 Feb 1841, -, -, -, Guillilmus, Ganley, Maria, Rodger, -, -, 16

1331, 20 Feb 1841, Jacobus, Raynolds, Francisa, Catharinae, 15 Feb 184_*, -, -, -, Arthur, Daugherty, Elisabeth, Raynolds, *birthdate is 15 Feb 184_ [last number is blank], -, 16

1332, 21 Feb 1841, Maria, O'Harran, Danielis, Johannae, 16 Feb 1841, -, -, -, Joannes, O'Brien, Maria, Shonecx, -, -, 16

1333, 21 Feb 1841, Jacobus, Grey, Joannis, Birgittae, 12 Feb 1841, -, -, -, Joannes, McCarthy, Birgitta, Loghan, -, -, 16

1334, 21 Feb 1841, Margaretta Anna, "Mo...", Henria, Birgittae, 1 Feb 1841, -, -, -, Terrentius, _____ [blank], Anna, Whealan, -, -, 16

1335, 21 Feb 1841, Morgan Patricius, McDonnel, Morgan, Juliae, 13 Feb 1841, -, -, -, Patricius, Corral, Hanora, Naughton, -, -, 16

1336, 21 Feb 1841, Joannes*, Bohan, Jacobi, Catharinae, 7 Feb 1841, -, -, -, Patricius, Flynn, Elisabeth, Ladden, *Joannes ["Jacobus" crossed out], -, 16

1337, 21 Feb 1841, Franciscus, Keeffer, Georgii, Mariae Elisabeth, 12 Feb 1841, -, -, -, Franciscus, Feoser [or Fedser], Elisabeth, Power, -, -, 16

1338, 21 Feb 1841, Joannes, Jonston, Jacobi, Judith, 19 Feb 1841, -, -, -, Patricius, Dolan, Birgitta, McCue, -, -, 16

1339, 21 Feb 1841, Daniel Philippus, Fitzpatrick, Philippi, Eleonorae, 19 Feb 1841, -, -, -, Jacobus, McAdams, Maria, Mulharron, -, -, 16

1340, 28 Feb 1841, Catharina Elisabeth, Berger, Franciscii, Bernardinae, 1 Nov 1840, -, -, -, Henricus P. [?], Crammer, Elisabeth, Berger, -, -, 16

1341, 02 Mar 1841, Franciscus Thomas, Stake, Hiram, Catharinae, 3 Sep 1840, -, -, -, Catharina, Stallon, -, -, -, -, 16

1342, 02 Mar 1841, Richardus Whealan, Stallon, Abrahami, Catharinae, 11 Jan 1841, -, -, -, Maria, Gorlet, -, -, -, -, 16

1343, 4 Mar 1841, Catharina , Terry, Roberti, Brigittae, 17 Feb 1841, -, -, -, Bernardus, Mahon, Hanora, Egan, -, -, 16

ST. MARY'S CATHOLIC CHURCH
HAGERSTOWN, MARYLAND, BAPTISMS:
Index, Bap Date, Child, Last Name, Father, Mother,
Birth Date, Code1, Code2, Code3,
1st Sponsor First, 1st Sponsor Last,
2nd Sponsor First, 2nd Sponsor Last, Location,
Notes, Maiden Name, Priest

1344, 9 Mar 1841, Margareta, Finley, Joannis, Annae, 26 Feb 1841, -, -, -, Patricius, Byrn, Maria, Rayney, -, -, 16

1345, 10 Mar 1841, Michael, Cambel, Michaelis, Rebeccae, 14 Feb 1841, -, -, -, Gaspar, Brownyard [or Browngard], Birgitta, Conneley, -, -, 16

1346, 10 Mar 1841, Josephus, Gayon [or Gagon], Joannis, Isabellae, 15 Feb 1841, -, -, -, Hugo, Schuh, Rebecca, Combel, -, -, 16

1347, 18 Mar 1841, Margareta, Drescol, Michaelis, Carolinae, 15 Dec 1840, -, -, -, Thomas, Stonton, Anna Catharina, Lon, -, -, 16

1348, 18 Mar 1841, William, Upton, Joannis, Elisabeth, 7 Jan 1841, -, -, -, Michael, Drescol, Sara, McLaughlin, -, -, 16

1349, 20 Mar 1841, Michael, Hughes, Antonii, Mariae , 28 Feb 1841, -, -, -, Patricius, Coany, Hanora, Quin, -, -, 16

1350, 20 Mar 1841, Catharina , Donnelly, William, Mariae, 2 Mar 1841, -, -, -, Jacobus, Bean, Maria, Hughes, -, -, 16

1351, 20 Mar 1841, Thomas, Kilroy, Patricii, Catharinae, 24 Feb 1841, -, -, -, Thomas, Follen, Anna, McCarty, -, -, 16

1352, 20 Mar 1841, Edwardus, Byrns, Edwardi, Eleonorae, 23 Feb 1841, -, -, -, Robertus, Hunt, Anna, Mahon, -, -, 16

1353, 20 Mar 1841, Elisabeth, Raynolds, Jacobi, Mariae , 21 ___ 1841*, -, -, -, Joannes, Gannely, Catharina, Raynolds, *birth month is blank, -, 16

1354, 21 Mar 1841, Maria, Quicgley, Petri, Mariae, 5 Feb 1841, -, -, -, Patriciis, Follen, Maria, Daugherty, -, -, 16

1355, 21 Mar 1841, Joannes, Powers, Richardi, Anastasiae, 11 Mar 1841, -, -, -, Patricius, Chapman, Maria, Sharen, -, -, 16

1356, 23 Mar 1841, Laura Birgitta, Shane, Joannis, Maria, -, -, -, -, M. [Father Michael], Guth, Birgitta, Gallagher, -, -, 16

1357, 25 Mar 1841, Bernardus, Crauley, Bernardi, Margaretae, 20 Feb 1841, -, -, -, Caroles, O'Brian, Maria, Hargan, -, -, 16

1358, 26 Mar 1841, Jacobus, Farrel, Thomae, Juliae, 7 Feb 1841, -, -, -, Daniel, Lee, Birgitta, Cox, -, -, 16

1359, 27 Mar 1841, Michael, Murphey, Thomae, Birgittae, 11-Mar, -, -, -, Joannes, Hennegan, Birgitta, Madden, -, -, 16

1360, 27 Mar 1841, Joannes, Ranney, Michaelis, Margaretae, 12 Mar 1841, -, -, -, Bernardus, Hannon, Maria, Smith, -, -, 16

ST. MARY'S CATHOLIC CHURCH
HAGERSTOWN, MARYLAND, BAPTISMS:
Index, Bap Date, Child, Last Name, Father, Mother,
Birth Date, Code1, Code2, Code3,
1st Sponsor First, 1st Sponsor Last,
2nd Sponsor First, 2nd Sponsor Last, Location,
Notes, Maiden Name, Priest

1361, 27 Mar 1841, Eleonora, Runney, Michaelis, Margaretae, 12* Mar 1841, -, -, -, John, Lyon, Catharina, Connelly, *birthdate is 12[or 18] Mar 1841, -, 16

1362, 28 Mar 1841, Maria, Coffee, Thomae, Judith, 20 Feb 1841, -, -, -, Joannes, Ferra?, Birgitta , Coffieb, -, -, 16

1363, 30 Mar 1841, Maria, Mighan, Patricii, Mariae , 21 Mar 1841, -, -, -, Jacobus, McGow, Catharina, Mulharon, -, -, 16

1364, 30 Mar 1841, Birgitta, McEvoy , Patricii, Mariae , 26 Mar 1841, -, -, -, Patricius, Little, Elisabeth, Fisher, -, -, 16

1365, 11 Apr 1841, [female], Watson, -, -, -, -, -, -, -, -, -, -, -, legitimate daughter, -, 16

1366, 11 Apr 1841, Petrus, Huslein, Michaelis, Catharinae, 17___ 1840*, -, -, -, Paulus, Paulus [sic], -, -, *birthdate reads 17 [month is blank] 1840, -, 16

1367, 18 Apr 1841, Joannes, McCue, Jacobi, Mariae , 2 Apr 1841, -, -, -, William, Hannon, Birgitta, McKey, -, -, 16

1368, 18 Apr 1841, Birgitta, McLafferty, Joannis, Franciscae, 7 Apr 1841, -, -, -, Andreas, Clarke, Maria, Donnely, -, -, 16

1369, 23 Apr 1841, Thomas, Morarty, Jacobi, Mariae , 13 Apr 1841, -, -, -, Joannes, Mansfield[?] *, Ellen, Mansfield, *The last name runs into the margin and is difficult to read., -, 16

1370, 23 Apr 1841, Hanora, Fitzgerald, David, Mariae , 22 Apr 1841, -, -, -, Daniel, McMahon, Maria, Bears, -, -, 16

1371, 23 Apr 1841, Patricius, Grayley, Dionysii, Mariae , 17 Apr 1841, -, -, -, Patricius, Grayly, Hanora, Lanan, -, -, 16

1372, 24 Apr 1841, Joannes W., McLaughlin, Joannis, Birgittae, 23 Apr 1841, -, -, -, Silvester, Murray, Johanna, Flinn, -, -, 16

1373, 25 Apr 1841, Ellen, Shortan [or Shordan], Bernardi, Ellen, 27 Mar 1841, -, -, -, Jacobus, Higgens, Catharina, Bannon, -, -, 16

1374, 25 Apr 1841, "Joannes Bop (Owen)", McAnony, Patricii, Annae, 3 Mar 1841, -, -, -, Fredericus, McLeod, Margareta, Travers, -, -, 16

1375, 26 Apr 1841, Maria Anna, Mills, Arthur, Annae, 18 Apr 1841, -, -, -, Patricius, Linch, Maria Anna, Murphey, -, -, 16

1376, 26 Apr 1841, Margareta Elisabeth, Harrison, Joannis Thomae, Margaretae, 23 Mar 1841, -, -, -, Thomas, Reed, Elisabeth, Caloary [or Caloury], -, -, 16

ST. MARY'S CATHOLIC CHURCH
HAGERSTOWN, MARYLAND, BAPTISMS:
Index, Bap Date, Child, Last Name, Father, Mother,
Birth Date, Code1, Code2, Code3,
1st Sponsor First, 1st Sponsor Last,
2nd Sponsor First, 2nd Sponsor Last, Location,
Notes, Maiden Name, Priest

1412, 20 Jun 1841, Guillelmus, Beck, Georgii, Annae, 4 Jun 1841, PN, -, -, N., Kelly, N., Farrel, -, Kelly, 16

1413, 20 Jun 1841, Jacobus, Cambell, -, Catharinae, 27 Jun 1840, PN, -, -, Thomas, Keenan, Johanna , Keenan, -, -, 16

1414, 20 Jun 1841, Anna , Hughes, Jacobi, Maria, 28 May 1841, -, -, -, Daniel, Daugherty, Maria, Daugherty, -, -, 16

1415, 20 Jun 1841, Edwardus Ignatius, Schuh ["Shove" crossed out], Hugonis, Catharinae, 7 Jun 1841, -, -, -, Ignatius, Renner, Maria Anna, Braungard, -, -, 16

1416, 21 Jun 1841, Josephus, Jarifert [?], -, Serinae, 3 Feb 1841, PN, -, -, Peter, Munday, Elisabeth, Reinhand, -, -, 16

1417, 5 Jul 1841, Joannes, Fallon, Thomae, Mariae, 28 Jun 1841, -, -, -, Jacobus, Kany, Hanora, Kelly, -, -, 16

1418, 5 Jul 1841, Michael, Casars, Jacobi, Margaritae, 23 Jun 1841, -, -, -, Joannis, Grady, Birgitta, Madden, -, -, 16

1419, 6 Jul 1841, Eleonora, Dec [or Dee], Jeremiae, Margaritae, 28 Jun 1841, -, -, -, Joannis, Decarsy, Margareta, Dee, -, -, 16

1420, 6 Jul 1841, Michael, Foley, Michaelis, Elleonorae, 28 Jun 1841, -, -, -, Jeremias, Clansey, Margareta, Condan, -, -, 16

1421, 6 Jul 1841, Margareta, Condon, Thomae, Margaretae, 21 Jun 1841, -, -, -, Patricius, Fitzgerald, Julia, Condon, -, -, 16

1422, 6 Jul 1841, Joannes, Frantz, Janannis, Susannae, 21 Jun 1841, -, -, -, Michael, Gardner, Magdalina, Gardner, -, -, 16

1423, 11 Jul 1841, Walter, Ringold, Georgeihe, Mariae, 11 Jan 1839, -, -, -, Michael, Guth, Rebecca, Ringold, -, -, 16

1424, 11 Jul 1841, Mary Antoinette, Ringold, Georgii, Mariae, 11 Jan 1841, -, -, -, John J. Fayette, Ringold, Maria Ann, Tidball, -, -, 16

1425, 17 Jul 1841, Elleonora, Nolan, Michaelis, Elleonorae, 28 Mar 1841, -, -, -, Thomas, Kelly, Judith, Coffee, -, -, 16

1426, 18 Jul 1841, Margareta, McGeeve?, Martini, Elleonorae, 15 Jul 1841, -, -, -, Michael, McDonnel, Catharina, Ready, -, -, 16

1427, 20 Jul 1841, Susanna, Clitner, Josephi, Sarae Joannae, 29 Jun 1840, -, -, -, Joannes, McFadden, Anna, McFadden, -, -, 16

1428, 23 Jul 1841, Eva Catharina, Paulus, Petry, Doretheae, 7 May 1841, PN, -, -, Eva Catharina, Guender, -, -, -, Guender, 16

ST. MARY'S CATHOLIC CHURCH
HAGERSTOWN, MARYLAND, BAPTISMS:
Index, Bap Date, Child, Last Name, Father, Mother,
Birth Date, Code1, Code2, Code3,
1st Sponsor First, 1st Sponsor Last,
2nd Sponsor First, 2nd Sponsor Last, Location,
Notes, Maiden Name, Priest

1429, 1 Aug 1841, William, Quig, Jacobi, Margaretae, 26 Jul 1841, -, -, -, Joannes, Ragan, Birgitta, Ragan, -, -, 16

1430, 15 Aug 1841, Eleonora, Mathews, Joannis, Henriettae, 12 Jun 1841, -, -, -, Georgius, Gray, Hippolita, Bevans, -, -, 16

1431, 15 Aug 1841, Thomas, Byrn , Patricii, Annae, 23 Jul 1841, -, -, -, Joannis, Shirlagh, Maria, Beers, -, -, 16

1432, 15 Aug 1841, Elisabeth, Laughlin, Jacobi, Birgittae, 3 Aug 1841, -, -, -, Joannes, Lanret [or Laweet], Maria, Noonan, -, -, 16

1433, 16 Aug 1841, Birgitta, Hughes, Terrentii, Mariae, 28 Jul 1841, -, -, -, Thomas, McFarrel, Margareta, Canah, -, -, 16

1434, 16 Aug 1841, Michael, Welsh, Michaelis, Eleonorae, 30 Jul 1841, -, -, -, Christophorus, Cashon, Maria, Daugherty, -, -, 16

1435, 17 Aug 1841, Petrus, Cardell, Martini, Mariae, 4 Jul 1841, -, -, -, Thomas, Cochran, Birgitta, Cochran, -, -, 16

1436, 22 Aug 1841, Guillelmus, Daugherty, Daniel , Joannae, 6 Jul 1841, -, -, -, Jacobus, Kelly, Maria, Tidball, -, -, 16

1437, 2 Sep 1841, Maria, Stonebreak , -, -, 43 years, -, -, -, -, -, -, -, -, -, 16

1438, 2 Sep 1841, Michael, McCan, Joanni, Annae, 7 Aug 1841, -, -, -, Garret, Sweany, Birgitta, Sweany, -, -, 16

1439, 3 Sep 1841, Maria Susanna, Wallace, Danielis, Elisabeth, 15 years, -, -, -, Augustus Upton, Bigold, Maria Anna, Nicodemus, -, - , 16

1440, 3 Sep 1841, Catharina, Gallagher, Michaelis, Birgittae, 7 Aug 1841, -, -, -, Michael, Smith, Catharina, Smith, -, -, 16

1441, 23 Aug 1841, Eugenius [male], McCardell, Richardi, Mariae, 24 Nov 1840, -, -, -, Franciscus B., Jamison, Anna, McCardell, -, -, 16

1442, 7 Sep 1841, Anna , Egan, Petri, Catharinae, 28 Aug 1841, -, -, -, Michael, Guth, Catharina, Byrns, -, -, 16

1443, 7 Sep 1841, Edwardus, Doyle, Thomae, Sarae , 2 Sep 1841, -, -, -, Terrentius, Doyle, Anna, Doyle, -, -, 16

1444, 7 Sep 1841, Julia, Dolan, Michaelis, Mariae, 6 Sep 1841, -, - , -, Patricius, Mallon, Susanna, Freeman, -, -, 16

1445, 7 Sep 1841, Joannes, O'Donnal, Joannis, Margaretae, 12 months, -, -, -, Thomas, Coffee, Eleonora, Murphey, -, -, 16

ST. MARY'S CATHOLIC CHURCH
HAGERSTOWN, MARYLAND, BAPTISMS:
Index, Bap Date, Child, Last Name, Father, Mother,
Birth Date, Code1, Code2, Code3,
1st Sponsor First, 1st Sponsor Last,
2nd Sponsor First, 2nd Sponsor Last, Location,
Notes, Maiden Name, Priest

1446, 7 Sep 1841, Guillelmas, Murphy, Guillelmi, Eleonorae, 20 Aug 1841, -, -, -, Dominicus, Barrett, Eleonorae, Noran, -, -, 16

1447, 7 Sep 1841, Maria, Nathan, Petri, Margaratae, 28 Aug 1841, -, -, -, Joannes, Drake, Maria, Byrns, -, -, 16

1448, 7 Sep 1841, Laurentius, Ronan, Mauritii, Honarae, 6 Aug 1841, -, -, -, Patricius, Desman [or Deoman], Maria, Beers, -, -, 16

1449, 7 Sep 1841, Joannes, Kerby, Joannis, Margaretae, 21 Aug 1841, -, -, -, Joannes, Harley [or Hurley], Anna, Donavan, -, -, 16

1450, 7 Sep 1841, Michael, Hines, Thomae, Annae, 28 Aug 1841, -, -, -, Joannes, Gray, Birgitta, Gray, -, -, 16

1451, 7 Sep 1841, Joannes, Land, Michaelis, Judith, 20 Aug 1841, -, -, -, Daniel, Power, Maria, Burck, -, -, 16

1452, 7 Sep 1841, Maria, Burck, Ulick, Mariae, 24 Aug 1841, -, -, -, Joannes, Gilfoile, Maria, Rafter, -, -, 16

1453, 18 Sep 1841, Maria Johanna, Quin, Jacobi, Birgittae, 26 Aug 1841, -, -, -, Patricius, McLane, Birgitta, Cavanaugh, -, -, 16

1454, 19 Sep 1841, Patricius, Tafe, Petri, Birgittae, 9 Sep 1841, -, -, -, Bernardus, King, Johanna, McAnally, -, -, 16

1455, 19 Sep 1841, Patricius, Mahon, Jacobi, Annae, 10 Sep 1841, -, -, -, Eugenius, Mernmigh [or Memmigh], Elleonora, Bern, -, -, 16

1456, 19 Sep 1841, Elleonora, Brown, Thomae, Eleonorae, 15 Aug 1841, -, -, -, Joannes, Sullivan, Maria, Kelly, -, -, 16

1457, 19 Sep 1841, Jacobus, Claffey, Caroli, Ester, 9 Sep 1841, -, -, -, Patricius, Egan, Anna, Culliam, -, -, 16

1458, 19 Sep 1841, Michael, Flanigan, Francisci, Mariae Annae, 22 Aug 1841, -, -, -, Patricias, Linch, Birgitta, Linch, -, -, 16

1459, 19 Sep 1841, Patricius, Loghan, Joannis, Mariae, 8 Sep 1841, -, -, -, Petrus, Loghan, Anna, [no last name], -, -, 16

1460, 20 Sep 1841, Joannes, McEntee, Jonathan, Cassandrae, 4 Jan 1841, -, -, -, Michael, Smith, Emilia, McAlister, -, -, 16

1461, 20 Sep 1841, Maria Anna, Smith, Michaelis, Birgittae, 16 Sep 1841, -, -, -, Henrius, McKenn, Birgitta, Bean, -, -, 16

1462, 20 Sep 1841, Dionysius, Canedy, Timothei, Catharinae, 15 Sep 1841, -, -, -, Thomas, Nugent, Birgitta, Canedy, -, -, 16

1463, 20 Sep 1841, Margareta, Drock, Joannis, Mariae, 20 Sep 1841, -, -, -, Patricius, Lusk, Margareta, Nathan, -, -, 16

ST. MARY'S CATHOLIC CHURCH
HAGERSTOWN, MARYLAND, BAPTISMS:
Index, Bap Date, Child, Last Name, Father, Mother,
Birth Date, Code1, Code2, Code3,
1st Sponsor First, 1st Sponsor Last,
2nd Sponsor First, 2nd Sponsor Last, Location,
Notes, Maiden Name, Priest

1464, 20 Sep 1841, Margareta, Naughton, Timothei, Honorae, 18 Sep 1841, -, -, -, Patricius, Farey, Catharina, Connor, -, -, 16
1465, 21 Sep 1841, Anna, Brady, Patricii, Annae, 15 Sep 1841, -, -, -, Petrus, Kerney, Elisabeth , Donn, -, -, 16
1466, 22 Sep 1841, [female], Holbert, -, -, -, -, -, -, -, -, -, -, parents are married, -, 16
1467, 29 Sep 1841, Francisca Virginia, Ribley, Joannis, Mariae Annae, 14 Sep 1840, -, -, -, Alexander, Ribley, Maria Anna, Sullivan, -, -, 16
1468, 1 Oct 1841, Thomas Benjaminus, Coyle, Edwardi, Annae, 21 Aug 1841, -, -, -, Thomas, Fecker, Barbara I.[?], Gouker, -, -, 16
1469, 1 Oct 1841, Sara Joanne, Gouker, David, Sophiae, 6 Aug 1841, -, -, -, Joseph, Gouger, Julia, Gouker, -, -, 16
1470, 21 Oct 1841, Joannes, Connelly, Joannis, Mariae, 27 Sep 1841, -, -, -, Thomas, Cassidy, Maria, Kelly, -, -, 16
1471, 21 Oct 1841, Joannes, Kelly, Joannis, Hanorae, 6 Oct 1841, -, -, -, Michael, Rehenny, Hanora, Crasby, -, -, 16
1472, 21 Oct 1841, Margareta, Barrett, Dominici, Mariae, 8 Oct 1841, -, -, -, Joannes, Linch, Birgitta, Melony, -, -, 16
1473, 21 Oct 1841, Michael, Linch, Joannis, Birgittae, 23 Sep 1841, -, -, -, Patricius, Madden, Maria, Murray, -, -, 16
1474, 22 Oct 1841, Catharina, Mulligan, Joannis, Birgittae, 5 Oct 1841, -, -, -, Petrus, Gray, Francisca, Dermady, -, -, 16
1475, 22 Oct 1841, Jacobus, Whealan, Jacobi, Johannae, 6 Oct 1841, -, -, -, Wm., McGuire, Maria, Farrell, -, -, 16
1476, 22 Oct 1841, Joannes, Whealan, Jacobi, Johannae, 6 Oct 1841, -, -, -, C., Sullivan, Sara, McGurke, -, -, 16
1477, 22 Oct 1841, Anna, McCabe, Terrentii, Mariae, 14 Oct 1841, -, -, -, Jacobus, McKanah, Maria, Sleete, -, -, 16
1478, 22 Oct 1841, Michael, Shannon, Edwardi, Catharinae, 10 Oct 1841, -, -, -, Patricius, McMahon, Rosa Anna, Sweany, -, -, 16
1479, 24 Oct 1841, Petrus, Conroy, Petri, Annae, 6 Oct 1841, -, -, -, Patricius, O'Donnell, Anna, Carlin, -, -, 16
1480, 25 Oct 1841, Georgius Albertus, Draper, Georgii, Mariae, 5 Jul 1841, -, -, -, Joannes, Upton, Sara, McLaughlin, -, -, 16
1481, 25 Oct 1841, Rebecca, McLaughlin, Patricii, Sarae, 23 Sep 1841, -, -, -, Joannes, Steward, Maria, Draper, -, -, 16

ST. MARY'S CATHOLIC CHURCH
HAGERSTOWN, MARYLAND, BAPTISMS:
Index, Bap Date, Child, Last Name, Father, Mother,
Birth Date, Code1, Code2, Code3,
1st Sponsor First, 1st Sponsor Last,
2nd Sponsor First, 2nd Sponsor Last, Location,
Notes, Maiden Name, Priest

1482, 5 Oct 1841, Jonathan, Schafer, Jonathan, Elisabeth, 1841, -, -, -, Jacobus, Hurley, Elisabeth , Lawrence, -, -, 16
1483, 10 Dec 1841, Maria Anna, Smith, -, Annae, 6 Apr 1841, PN, -, -, -, -, -, -, -, -, 16
1484, 11 Dec 1841, Jacobus, Corrighan, Joannis, Birgittae, 7 Nov 1841, -, -, -, Joannes, Tims, Maria, McGurg, -, -, 16
1485, 12 Dec 1841, Martha Eugenia, Moore, Leonardi, Elisabeth, 9 Dec 1841, -, -, -, Jacobus, McAdams, Helena Eugenia, Mattingly, -, -, 16
1486, 13 Dec 1841, Maria, Connely, Patricii, Juliae, 28 Nov 1841, -, -, -, Patricius, Whily, Maria, Dwire , -, -, 16
1487, 12 Dec 1841, Jacobus, O'Brian, Patricii, Margaretae, 16 Nov 1841, -, -, -, Carolus, Claffey, Ester, Claffey, -, -, 16
1488, 12 Dec 1841, Margareta, Lee, Joannis, H [sic], 3 Dec 1840, -, -, -, Patricius, O'Brian, Lucenta, Lee, -, -, 16
1489, 16 Dec 1841, Anna, McCarrol, -, Mariae, 16 Jun 1841, PN, -, -, Birgitta, Smith, -, -, -, -, 16
1490, 16 Dec 1841, Anna, McGinnis, Danielis, Mariae, 25 Oct 1841, -, -, -, Joannes, Linch, Birgitta, Linch, -, -, 16
1491, 16 Dec 1841, Caecilia, Fargusson, Jacobi, Maria, 29 Nov 1841, -, -, -, Joannes, Joice, Maria, Dixon, -, -, 16
1492, 24 Nov 1841, Michael J. [or I.], Welsh, Jacobi, Joannae, 20 Oct 1841, -, -, -, Patricius, Carlosk, Margareta, Baninghan, -, -, 16
1493, 25 Nov 1841, Jacobus, Mulvana [?], Thomae, Anna, 9 Nov 1841, -, -, -, Patricius, McCormack, Catharina, Monagham, -, -, 16
1494, 25 Nov 1841, Anna, Shaneck, Michaelis, Mariae, 7 Nov 1841, -, -, -, Joannes, Donovan, Honora, Ambroes, -, -, 16
1495, 25 Nov 1841, Helena, McDonnell, Patricii, Mariae, 25 Oct 1841, -, -, -, William, McLaughlin, Anna, Carlosk, -, -, 16
1496, 1 Jan 1842, Antonius, Sprig, -, -, 80 years, -, -, -, -, -, -, -, BC, -, 16
1497, 4 Jan 1842, William B., Broderick, Richardi, Mariae, 17 Oct 1841, -, -, -, Edwardus, Hughes, Francisca, McIlhenney, -, -, 16
1498, 5 Jan 1842, Joannes, Fellinger, Fredererici, Rosalia, 17 Jun 1841, -, -, -, Nicholaus, Hurerley [or Hererley], -, -, -, -, 16
1499, 5 Jan 1842, Daniel, Tranan, Thomae, Catharinae, 2 Dec 1841, -, -, -, Jacobus, Cane, Birgitta, Riley, -, -, 16

ST. MARY'S CATHOLIC CHURCH
HAGERSTOWN, MARYLAND, BAPTISMS:
Index, Bap Date, Child, Last Name, Father, Mother,
Birth Date, Code1, Code2, Code3,
1st Sponsor First, 1st Sponsor Last,
2nd Sponsor First, 2nd Sponsor Last, Location,
Notes, Maiden Name, Priest

1500, 5 Jan 1842, Henricus, Baker, Gustavi, Elisabeth, 14 Feb 1841, -, -, -, Henricus, Kerker, -, -, -, -, 16

1501, 13 Jan 1842, Maria Anna, Garvey, Michaelis, Margaretae, 2 Jan 1842, -, -, -, Joannes, Daugherty, Maria Anna, Colvin, -, -, 16

1502, 15 Jan 1842, H. Maria, Carrol, D. Williamson, Melaniae, 3 Aug 1841, -, -, -, William , Carrol, Henrietta Maria, Carrol, -, -, 16

1503, 15 Jan 1842, Honora, Moore, Joannis, Sarae, 14 Jan 1842, -, -, -, Lucas, Doyle, Catharina, Doyle, -, -, 16

1504, 16 Jan 1842, Christophorus, Cox ["Doyle" crossed out], Michaelis, Catharinae, 6 Nov 1841, -, -, -, Jacobus, Brannon, Catharina, Brannon, -, -, 16

1505, 16 Jan 1842, Thomas , Connelly, Thomaes, Birgittae, 16 Dec 1841, -, -, -, Timotheus, McLaughlin, Catharina, Spolen, -, -, 16

1506, 16 Jan 1842, Rosa Anna, Harber [or Larber], Philippi, Sophiae, 8 Jul 1841, -, -, -, Rosa Anna, Burghard, -, -, -, -, 16

1507, 16 Jan 1842, William , Clei [or Cley], Jacobi, Florae, 24 Dec 1841, -, -, -, William, Cunterenann, -, -, -, -, 16

1508, 16 Jan 1842, Elisabeth, Grey, Petris, Margaretae, 19 Dec 1841, -, -, -, Patricius, Dolan, Maria, Adam, -, -, 16

1509, 16 Jan 1842, Michael, Muladoon, Michaelis, Annae, 20 Dec 1841, -, -, -, Richardis, Collon [or Callon], Maria, Harrigan, -, -, 16

1510, 16 Jan 1842, Michael, Carlosk [runs into binding], Patricii, Birgittae, 14 Jan 1842, -, -, -, Michael, Tyrnan, Birgitta, Corlosk, -, -, 16

1511, 16 Jan 1842, Catharina, Colens, Joannis, Mariae, 25 Dec 1841, -, -, -, Joannes, Colens, Helena , Murray, -, -, 16

1512, 17 Jan 1842, Helena, McLaughlin, -, Annae, 10 Oct 1841, PN, -, -, Hugo, Pryer, Rosa, Pryer, -, -, 16

1513, 17 Jan 1842, Catharina, Pryer, Hugonis, Rosae, 28 Oct 1841, -, -, -, Anna, McLaughlin, -, -, -, -, 16

1514, 17 Jan 1842, Maria Anna, Tigh, Danielis, Margaretae, 7 Jan 1842, -, -, -, Catharina, Kanoh, -, -, -, -, 16

1515, 17 Jan 1842, Johanna, O'Hay, Thomae, Catharinae, 31 Dec 1841, -, -, -, Margareta, Tigh, -, -, -, -, 16

1516, 17 Jan 1842, Catharina, Renner, Ignatii, Mariae, 2 Dec 1841, -, -, -, Carolina, Renner, -, -, -, -, 16

ST. MARY'S CATHOLIC CHURCH
HAGERSTOWN, MARYLAND, BAPTISMS:
Index, Bap Date, Child, Last Name, Father, Mother,
Birth Date, Code1, Code2, Code3,
1st Sponsor First, 1st Sponsor Last,
2nd Sponsor First, 2nd Sponsor Last, Location,
Notes, Maiden Name, Priest

1517, 22 Jan 1842, Elisabeth, Kelly, Patricii, Sarae, 17 Jan 1842, -, -, -, Sebastianus, Gilmeyer, Elisabeth, Shirley, -, -, 16

1518, 19 Feb 1842, Joannes, Haiden, Joannis, Helenae, 20 Jan 1842, -, -, -, Michael, Doyle, Birgitta, Doyle, -, -, 16

1519, 19 Feb 1842, Margareta, Daukery, Thomae, Eleonorae, 29 Jan 1842, -, -, -, Joannes, Doyle, Anna, Doyle, -, -, 16

1520, 19 Feb 1842, Patricius, Murphey, Patricii, Birgittae, 12 Feb 1842, -, -, -, Joannes, Doman, Anna, Cahoo, -, -, 16

1521, 19 Feb 1842, Jacobus, Killdoff, Patricii, Rosae, 1 Feb 1842, -, -, -, Terrentius, Brady, Elisabeth, Brown, -, -, 16

1522, 19 Feb 1842, Michael, Nonan, Danielis, Elisabeth, 20 Oct 1841, -, -, -, Philippus, Curran, Francisca, McLofferty, -, -, 16

1523, 20 Feb 1842, Catharina, McCormack, Joannis, Mariae, 22 Jan 1842, -, -, -, Robertus, Maloy, Maria, Kelly, -, -, 16

1524, 20 Feb 1842, Antonius, Linch, Patricii, Catharinae, 1 Nov 1841, -, -, -, Jacobus, Kelly, Maria, McCormack, -, -, 16

1525, 20 Feb 1842, Birgitta, Coning, Michaelis, Catharinae, 18 Feb 1842, -, -, -, Thomas, Donnelly, Rosa , Coleus, -, -, 16

1526, 20 Feb 1842, Catharina, Dolan, Thomae, Mariae, 12 Jan 1842, -, -, -, Jacobus, Dolan, Catharina, Riley, -, -, 16

1527, 20 Feb 1842, Sara Anna, Murray, Jeremiae, Eleonorae, 5 Feb 1842, -, -, -, Thomas, Clarke, Maria, Long, -, -, 16

1528, 21 Feb 1842, Maria Anna, Evret, -, Appolloniae, 9 Feb 1842, PN, -, -, Franciscus, O'Donnell, Margareta, Breene [or Briene], -, -, 16

1529, 21 Feb 1842, Maria, Slowe, Hugonis, Mariae, 20 Feb 1842, -, -, -, Thomas, Reed, Maria, Farrell, -, -, 16

1530, 21 Feb 1842, Juliana, Welsh, M. Franklin, M. Elisabeth, 2 Feb 1842, -, -, -, Judith, Johnson, -, -, -, -, 16

1531, 21 Feb 1842, Magdalena, -, -, -, -, -, -, -, Maria, Renner, -, -, parents are married, -, 16

1532, 28 Feb 1842, Catharina, Lewis, Joannis, Elisabeth, 8 Feb 1842, -, -, -, Thomas, Maines, Catharina, Moore, -, -, 16

1533, 11 Mar 1842, Joannes G., Robertson, Joannis, Franciscae, 5 Nov 1841, -, -, -, W., Cupper, Elisobeth, Barn, -, -, 16

1534, 12 Mar 1842, Eleonora, McMahon, Andreae, Mariae, 1 Mar 1842, -, -, -, Joannes, McMahon, Catharina, Garreghan, -, -, 16

ST. MARY'S CATHOLIC CHURCH
HAGERSTOWN, MARYLAND, BAPTISMS:
Index, Bap Date, Child, Last Name, Father, Mother,
Birth Date, Code1, Code2, Code3,
1st Sponsor First, 1st Sponsor Last,
2nd Sponsor First, 2nd Sponsor Last, Location,
Notes, Maiden Name, Priest

1535, 14 Mar 1842, Michael J. [or I.], Crauss, Bernardi, Mariae, 13 Feb 1842, -, -, -, Michael J. [or I.], Hambach, Josephina, Hambach [HB], -, -, 16

1536, 14 Mar 1842, Amia [?], Brady, Hugonis, Annae, 22 Feb 1842, -, -, -, Patricius, Brady, Maria, McCue, -, -, 16

1537, 14 Mar 1842, Maria, Smith, Donnielis, Mariae, 16-Feb, -, -, -, Edwardus, Hany, Johann, Hany [HB], -, -, 16

1538, 14 Mar 1842, Patricius, Cunningham, Joannis, Catharinae, 8 Mar 1842, -, -, -, William, [blank], Josephina, Hornbach, -, -, 16

1539, 14 Mar 1842, Maria, Doyle, Terrentii, Annae, 13 Mar 1842, -, -, -, Miles, Riley, Sara, Doyle, -, -, 16

1540, 14 Mar 1842, [female], Stickenius, Godfried, Wilhelminae, 17 Apr 1840, -, -, -, Elisabeth, Mehlmann, -, -, -, -, 16

1541, 14 Mar 1842, Anna, Stickenius, Godfried, Wilhelminae, 8 Mar 1842, -, -, -, Anna, Kelly, -, -, -, -, 16

1542, 14 Mar 1842, Patricius, Coonnely, Joannes, Annae, 28 Feb 1842, -, -, -, Thomas, Groghan, Ninney , Byr_ [lost in binding], -, -, 16

1543, 15 Mar 1842, Jacobus, Collighan, Jacobi, Margaretae, 10 Mar 1842, -, -, -, Martinus, Magher [or Mayher], Sara, Sullivan, -, -, 16

1544, 15 Mar 1842, Maria, Murray, Joannis, Annae, 10 Mar 1842, -, -, -, John, Clarke, Maria, Cosgriff, -, -, 16

1545, 15 Mar 1842, Catharina, Donavan, Joannis, Catharinae, 28 Feb 1842, -, -, -, Dionysius, Donavan, Johanna, Lorgy[?], -, -, 16

1546, 15 Mar 1842, Patricius, Conner, Joannis, Mariae, 2 Mar 1842, -, -, -, Thomas, Hines, Maria, Hines [HB], -, -, 16

1547, 15 Mar 1842, Maria Anna, Havard, Thomae, Catharinae, 20 Feb 1842, -, -, -, Morgan, McDonnell, Julia, McDonnell [HB], -, -, 16

1548, 15 Mar 1842, Maria Anna, Connelly, Jacobi, Babarae, 28 Feb 1842, -, -, -, Hugo, McCoskar, Margareta, McCoskar [HB], -, -, 16

1549, 16 Mar 1842, Edgart Augustinus, Watkins, Roberti W. , Helenae, 14 Mar 1842, -, -, -, Michael, Guth, Elisabeth, Reinhard, -, -, 16

ST. MARY'S CATHOLIC CHURCH
HAGERSTOWN, MARYLAND, BAPTISMS:
Index, Bap Date, Child, Last Name, Father, Mother,
Birth Date, Code1, Code2, Code3,
1st Sponsor First, 1st Sponsor Last,
2nd Sponsor First, 2nd Sponsor Last, Location,
Notes, Maiden Name, Priest

1550, 20 Mar 1842, Anna Elisabeth, Makens, Eliae, Elisabeth, 23 Aug 1841, -, -, -, Jacobus, Mesisinger, Margareta, Mesisinger, -, -, 16

1551, 17 Mar 1842, Ludovicus Edwardus, Gillmeyer, Georgii, Elisabeth, 16 Mar 1842, -, -, -, Michael, Guth, Elisabeth, Monaghan, -, -, 16

1552, 27 Mar 1842, Joannes T., Smith, Joannis, Elisobeth, 14 Feb 1842, -, -, -, Carolus, McIlhenny, Maria, Caton, -, -, 16

1553, 10 Apr 1842, Michael, Hasland, Michaelis, Catharinae, 25 Feb 1842, -, -, -, Michael, Weber, -, -, -, -, 16

1554, 15 Apr 1842, Joannes, Cain, Jacobi, Annae, 8 Apr 1842, -, -, -, Michael, Quin, Sara, McLaughlin, -, -, 16

1555, 16 Apr 1842, Eleonora, Daughonvy, Jacobi, Birgittae, 25 Mar 1842, -, -, -, Michael, Raynolds, Margareta, Chaldon, -, -, 16

1556, 17 Apr 1842, Dominicus Augustinus, McCormack, Thomae, Catharinae, 26 Mar 1842, -, -, -, Antonius, Loftus, Elisabeth J. [or I.], Bevans, -, -, 16

1557, 18 Apr 1842, Hugo, Fitzpatrick, Antonii, Annae, 2 Apr 1842, -, -, -, Patricius , Dolan, Anna, Dolan, -, -, 16

1558, 18 Apr 1842, Edwardus, Donnelly, Patricii, Mariae, 31 Mar 1842, -, -, -, Andreas, Clarke, Eleonora, McLaughlin, -, -, 16

1559, 18 Apr 1842, Samuel, Casy, Patricii, Birgittae, 6 Apr 1842, -, -, -, Patricius, Casy, Elisabeth, Cashon, -, -, 16

1560, 19 Apr 1842, Thomas , Clarke, Joannis, Margaritae, 17 Apr 1842, -, -, -, Thomas, Clarke, Hanora, Murray, -, -, 16

1561, 19 Apr 1842, Catharina, Backley, Corneliei, Johannae, 17 Mar 1842, -, -, -, Richardus, Beers, Maria Anna, Dermard, -, -, 16

1562, 24 Apr 1842, Guillemnus, Dempsy, Petri, Margaretae, 25 Feb 1842, -, -, -, Jacobus, Carr, Sara, Carr, -, -, 16

1563, 1 May 1842, Joannes, Weber, Michaelis, Mariae, 24 Mar 1842, -, -, -, Joanne, Fox, -, -, -, -, 16

1564, 1 May 1842, Dorothea Elisabeth, Eckert, Joannis, Gertudis, 27 Sep 1842, -, -, -, Dorothea, Leixner, -, -, -, -, 16

1565, 5 May 1842, Hieronimus Franciscus, Kelly, Josephi, Catharinae, 6 Mar 1842, -, -, -, Joannes, McGonigle, Maria A., Sullivan, -, -, 16

ST. MARY'S CATHOLIC CHURCH
HAGERSTOWN, MARYLAND, BAPTISMS:
Index, Bap Date, Child, Last Name, Father, Mother,
Birth Date, Code1, Code2, Code3,
1st Sponsor First, 1st Sponsor Last,
2nd Sponsor First, 2nd Sponsor Last, Location,
Notes, Maiden Name, Priest

1566, 10 May 1842, Anna, Green, Francisci, Naby, 6 May 1842, -, -, -, Bernardus, Whealan, Anna, Whealan, -, -, 16

1567, 10 May 1842, Thomas, Morgan, Guillelmi, Mariae, 8 May 1842, -, -, -, Patricius, Casgro, Margareta, Garaghty, -, -, 16

1568, 10 May 1842, Honora, Crauley, Patricii, Johannae, 2 May 1842, -, -, -, Joannes, Donavin, Anna, Kerby, -, -, 16

1569, 10 May 1842, Maria Anna, McLaughlin, Michaelis, Julianae, 22 Apr 1842, -, -, -, Owen, Loftus, Maria, Donnelly, -, -, 16

1570, 15 May 1842, Thomas, Cambel, Thomae, Catharinae, 11 May 1842, -, -, -, Jacobus, Byrns, Anna, Souders, -, -, 16

1571, 15 May 1842, Matilda, Latmann, Georgii, Serinae, 3 Nov 1841, -, -, -, Thomas, Cambel, Catharina, Cambel [HB], -, -, 16

1572, 15 May 1842, Margareta Anna, McAnany, Francisci, Mariae, 8 May 1842, -, -, -, Owen, Byrns, Catherina, Byrns [HB], -, -, 16

1573, 15 May 1842, Edwardus, Murphey, Guillelumi, Margaretae, 25 Apr 1842, -, -, -, Joannes, Francis, Birgitta, Maurice , -, -, 16

1574, 15 May 1842, Michael Henricus, Riley, Joannis, Mariae, 6 May 1842, -, -, -, Thomas, Fealy, Catharina, Mauricy, -, -, 16

1575, 28 May 1842, Adam, Forbeck, Casimiri, Evae, 2 May 1842, -, -, -, Josephus, Kleinmeyer, Maria Anna, Fayette, -, -, 16

1576, 29 May 1842, Joannes, Daly, Joannis, [blank], 18 Apr 1842, -, -, -, Hugo, McCoskar, Margareta, McCoskar, "Philbert Tomy" crossed out in sponsor section, -, 16

1577, 29 May 1842, Maria Catharina, Hohenstein, Leinfard, Margaretae, 28 Feb 1842, -, -, -, Philbert, Tanny, Maria Elisabeth, Tanny [HB], -, -, 16

1578, 5 Jun 1842, Maria Anna, McCartney, Edwardi, Catharinae, 14 Feb 1842, -, -, -, Joannes, Gorman, Susan , McGonicle, -, -, 16

1579, 19 Jun 1842 - "at or around that time", Helena, Flinn, Edmundi, Johannae, 4 May 1842, -, -, -, Michael, Gorman, Catharina, Curren, -, -, 16

1580, 19 Jun 1842, Maria, McSweany, Miles, Juliae, 4 Jun 1842, -, -, -, Dyonisius, Hothel [or Hohel], Margareta, Day, -, -, 16

1581, 19 Jun 1842, Patricius, McDonnell, Michaelis, Annae, 29 Mar 1842, -, -, -, Michael, Copply, Sophia, McKnight, -, -, 16

ST. MARY'S CATHOLIC CHURCH
HAGERSTOWN, MARYLAND, BAPTISMS:
Index, Bap Date, Child, Last Name, Father, Mother,
Birth Date, Code1, Code2, Code3,
1st Sponsor First, 1st Sponsor Last,
2nd Sponsor First, 2nd Sponsor Last, Location,
Notes, Maiden Name, Priest

1582, 19 Jun 1842, Jacobus, Scantling [?], Mauricii, Annae, 15 May 1842, -, -, -, Jacobus, Moriarty, Maria, Moriarty, -, -, 16

1583, 19 Jun 1842, Danniel, Nolan, Martini, Mariae, 28 May 1842, -, -, -, Dyonisius, Grayley [or Grayly], Birgitta, Bannan, -, -, 16

1584, 19 Jun 1842, Honoro, Gatty, Patricii, Birgitae, 16 Jun 1842, -, -, -, Guillelmus, Morgan, Maria, Morgan, -, -, 16

1585, 19 Jun 1842, Joannes, Shanaghan, Christophori, Birgittae, 25 May 1842, -, -, -, Jacobus, Dan, Birgitta, Hughes, appears to read "vell circuter Atempu", -, 16

1586, 20 Jun 1842, Carolus Henricus, Cross, Samuel, Ludovicae, [blank], -, -, -, Jacobus, Bevans, Elisabeth, Cross, -, -, 16

1587, 20 Jun 1842, Margareta, Linch, Patricii, Birgittae, 10 Jun 1842, -, -, -, Joannes, Schannon, Birgitta, McCue, -, -, 16

1588, 20 Jun 1842, Guiellelmus, Riley, Petri, Johannae, 3 Jun 1842, -, -, -, Patricius, Purcel, Catharina, Shannon, -, -, 16

1589, 2 Jul 1842, Joannes, Bevans[?], Joannis, Helenae, J 1842 [sic], -, -, -, Birgitta, Kelly, -, -, -, -, 16

1590, 12 Jul 1842, Margareta, [blank], Dominii, Judith, 1842, -, -, -, Joannes, Daugherty, -, -, -, -, 16

1591, 12 Jul 1842, Joannes, Moran, Petri, M [rest of name is blank], 27-May, -, -, -, Joannes, [blank], Judith, [blank], -, -, 16

1592, 24 Jul 1842, Maria, Keller, Josephi, Mariae, 7 Feb 1842, -, -, -, Gaspar, Broungarden [?], Mari Anna, Broungarden, -, -, 16

1593, 24 Jul 1842, Anna, Gauger, Joannes, Helenae, 12 Apr 1842, -, -, -, Theresia, Gauger, -, -, -, -, 16

1594, 31 Jul 1842, Georgeus, Shane, Joannis, Margaretae, 23-Jul, -, -, -, Josephus, Waese, Caecilia, Waese, -, -, 16

1595, 7 Aug 1842, Joannes, Burgey, Shederic, Rebeccae, 20 Nov 1841, -, -, -, M., Guth, Maria A., Sullivan, -, -, 16

1596, 7 Aug 1842, W. Henricus, Clemens, Alexandri, Matildis, 13 Jun 1842, -, -, -, M., Guth, Elisabeth, Elliot, -, -, 16

1597, 9 Aug 1842, Levi, Fritz, Frederici, Margertae, 10 Feb 1840, -, -, -, Levi, Moore, Maria, Ward, -, -, 16

1598, 9 Aug 1842, Evelina, Fritz, Frederici, Margaretae, 26 Apr 1842, -, -, -, Levi, Moore, Anna, Rody, -, -, 16

1599, 9 Aug 1842, [male], Fritz, -, -, 6 Sep 1839, -, -, -, -, -, -, -, See Endnote 8, -, 16

ST. MARY'S CATHOLIC CHURCH
HAGERSTOWN, MARYLAND, BAPTISMS:
Index, Bap Date, Child, Last Name, Father, Mother,
Birth Date, Code1, Code2, Code3,
1st Sponsor First, 1st Sponsor Last,
2nd Sponsor First, 2nd Sponsor Last, Location,
Notes, Maiden Name, Priest

1600, 11 Aug 1842, Georges, Thomson, Isaak, Rebeccae, 27 May 1842, -, -, -, Jacobus, McGee, Maria, Lover, -, -, 16

1601, 11 Aug 1842, Georges, Stake, Guillelmi, Mariae, 11 Feb 1842, -, -, -, Michael, Guth, Maria, Hausley [or Hounay], -, -, 16

1602, 15 Aug 1842, W. Henricus, Bishop, Abner, Elisabeth, 14 Feb 1842, -, -, -, Michael, Stanton, Eleonora, Colvin, -, -, 16

1603, 15 Aug 1842, Catharina, Dolan, Francisci, Mariae, 1 Aug 1842, -, -, -, Patricius, Grady, Sara, Conroy, -, -, 16

1604, 15 Aug 1842, Maria Elleonora, Clarke, Patricii, Catharinae, 15 Aug 1842, -, -, -, Carolus, Clarke, Margareta, Clark, -, -, 16

1605, 20 Aug 1842, Thomas, Keenan, Michaelis, Catharinae, 18 Aug 1842, -, -, -, Thomas, Keenan, Anna, McCauley, -, -, 16

1606, 20 Aug 1842, Joanna, McCauley, Charoli, Annae, 1 May 1842, -, -, -, Michael, Keenan, Anna, McDonnell, -, -, 16

1607, 21 Aug 1842, Franciscus, McAttie, Jonathan, Casanae, 19-Apr, -, -, -, Joannes, Donavan, Maria, Mulharon, -, -, 16

1608, 21 Aug 1842, Margareta, Brannon, Patricii, Elleonorae, 21 Jun 1842, -, -, -, Jacobus, Kelly, Margareta, Kelly, -, -, 16

1609, 20 Jun 1842, Margareta, Linch, Patricii, Birgittae, 10 Jun 1842, -, -, -, Joannes, Shannon, Birgitta, McCue, entry crossed out, -, 16

1610, 20 Jun 1842, Guillelmas, Riley, Petri, Johannae, 3 Jun 1842, -, -, -, Patricius, Purcel, Catharina, Shannon, entry crossed out, -, 16

1611, 21 Aug 1842, Maria, Dolan, Brian, Mariae, 10 Aug 1842, -, -, -, Joannes, Welsh, Johannae, Welsh, -, -, 16

1612, 4 Sep 1842, Maria Regina, Ehwald, Gasperis, Barbarae, 2 Aug 1842, -, -, -, M. Regina, Menge, -, -, -, -, 16

1613, 12 Sep 1842, Jacobus, [blank], [blank], [blank], 9 years, -, -, -, -, -, -, -, parents married, -, 16

1614, 12 Sep 1842, Daniel, [blank], [blank], [blank], 6 years, -, -, -, -, -, -, -, parents married, -, 16

1615, 12 Sep 1842, Cathurina, [blank], [blank], [blank], 4 years, -, -, -, -, -, -, -, parents married, -, 16

1616, 12 Sep 1842, Anna Elisabeth, [blank], [blank], [blank], [blank], -, -, -, -, -, -, -, parents married, -, 16

ST. MARY'S CATHOLIC CHURCH
HAGERSTOWN, MARYLAND, BAPTISMS:
Index, Bap Date, Child, Last Name, Father, Mother,
Birth Date, Code1, Code2, Code3,
1st Sponsor First, 1st Sponsor Last,
2nd Sponsor First, 2nd Sponsor Last, Location,
Notes, Maiden Name, Priest

1617, 22 Sep 1842, Michael Henricus, Griffon, Guillelmi, Catharinie, 15 Sep 1842, -, -, -, Cornelius, Monagham, Griffith, Curry, -, -, 16

1618, 22 Sep 1842, Francisca Emilia, Smith, Caroli, Catharinae, 10 Jul 1842, -, -, -, Elisabeth, Monaghan, -, -, -, -, 16

1619, 1 Oct 1842, Joseph, Carr, Jacobi, Sarae, 24 Sep 1842, -, -, -, Joannes, McCarthy, Rosa Anna, McCabe, -, -, 16

1620, 13 Oct 1842, Anna, Miller, Jacobi, Annae, 22 years, -, -, -, -, -, -, -, -, -, 16

1621, 14 Oct 1842, Joannes Alexander, Moore, Levi, Catharinae, 10 Oct 1842, -, -, -, Thomas, Mains, Anna, Moore, -, -, 16

1622, 15 Oct 1842, William C., Elicot, Benjamini, Mariae, 13 Oct 1842, -, -, -, Williamson , Carroll, Henrietta, Carroll [HB], -, -, 16

1623, 15 Oct 1842, Rosa, Bell, Stephani, Catharinae, 3 Aug 1842, -, -, -, Maria Anna, Bell, -, -, -, -, 16

1624, 16 Oct 1842, Elisabeth, Fallon, Patricii, Birgittae, 29 Sep 1842, -, -, -, Michael, Nugent, Margareta, Grey, -, -, 16

1625, 30 Oct 1842, Barbara, Fayette, Joannes, Barbarae, 12 Aug 1842, -, -, -, Barbara, Leiner, -, -, -, -, 16

1626, 30 Oct 1842, Georgius Hubert, Adamie, Margaretae, 22 Jun 1842, -, -, -, Georgius, Vogt, -, -, -, -, 16

1627, 6 Nov 1842, Sara Anna, Baker, Jacobi, Angelinae, 17 Sep 1842, -, -, -, Jacobus, Carr [or Karr], Sara, Karr [Carr crossed out], -, -, 16

1628, 13 Nov 1842, Theresa, Schuber, Laurentii, Anna Josephinae, 9 Oct 1842, -, -, -, Theresa, Braungarden, -, -, -, -, 16

1629, 19 Nov 1842, Anna Elisabeth, Smith, Michaelis, Catharinae, 5 Nov 1842, -, -, -, Joseph, Smith, Catharina, Smith, -, -, 16

1630, 19 Nov 1842, Henricus, Smith, Josua, Anastasiae, 10 Nov 1842, -, -, -, Josephus, Smith, Martha, McLaine, -, -, 16

1631, 19 Nov 1842, Thomas Edwardus, McGrow, Jacobi, Elisabeth, 17 Oct 1842, -, -, -, Philippas, Fitzpatrick, Margareta, Cunningham, -, -, 16

1632, 20 Nov 1842, Maria, Moran, Henrici, Birgittae, 4 Nov 1842, -, -, -, Bernardus, Whealan, Maria, Smith, -, -, 16

1633, 20 Nov 1842, Maria, Hail, Roberti, Annae, 13 Oct 1842, -, -, -, Patricius, Riley, Margareta, Hail , -, -, 16

ST. MARY'S CATHOLIC CHURCH
HAGERSTOWN, MARYLAND, BAPTISMS:
Index, Bap Date, Child, Last Name, Father, Mother,
Birth Date, Code1, Code2, Code3,
1st Sponsor First, 1st Sponsor Last,
2nd Sponsor First, 2nd Sponsor Last, Location,
Notes, Maiden Name, Priest

1634, 20 Nov 1842, Michael , Trainor, Owen, Annae, 29 Mar 1842, -, -, -, Thomas, Reed, -, -, -, -, 16

1635, 20 Nov 1842, Jacobus, Cadam [?], Jacobi, Elisabeth, 22 Oct 1842, -, -, -, Jacobus, Kerry, Elisabeth, Gray, -, -, 16

1636, 21 Nov 1842, Jacobus Leonardus, Reinhard, Samuelis, Elisabeth, 17 Nov 1842, -, -, -, Thomas, Bevans, Anna, Bevans, -, -, 16

1637, 14 Dec 1842, Maria Catharina, Hurley, Jacobi, Sophiae, 4 Dec 1842, -, -, -, Michael, Guth, Elisabeth, Monaghahn, -, -, 16

1638, 13 Dec 1842, Theresa, Sshuber, Laurentii, Annae, 9 Oct 1842, -, -, -, Theresa, B [rest of name is blank], -, -, -, -, 16

1639, 18 Dec 1842, Guillelmus, Sutter, Thomai, Catharenae, 10 Dec 1842, -, -, -, Daniel, Tyrne, Catharina, Dunn, -, -, 16

1640, 18 Dec 1842, Alexander, Lenis [?], -, Mariae, 16 Oct 1842, PN, -, -, -, -, -, -, -, -, 16

1641, 19 Dec 1842, Jeremias, Sullivan, Guillelmus, Sarae, 13 Nov 1842, -, -, -, Jeremias, Garraghan, Margareta, Garraghan, -, -, 16

1642, 19 Dec 1842, Richardus, Beers, Joannis, Mariae, Dec 1842, -, -, -, Jeremias, Murray, Francisca, Dermady, -, -, 16

1643, 19 Dec 1842, Joannes, White, Mauricii, Mariae, 12 Dec 1842, -, -, -, Danniel, Sullivan, Maria, Sullivan, -, -, 16

1644, 1 Jan 1843, Jacobus Sebastainus, Clarke, Guillelmi, Margaretae, 13 Aug 1842, -, -, -, Guillelmus , McLain, Sara, McLain, -, -, 16

1645, 3 Jan 1843, Elisabeth Johanna, Smith, -, Annae, 2 months, PN, -, -, Anastasia, Smith, -, -, -, -, 16

1646, 4 Jan 1843, Andreas, Swop, Gasparis, [blank], 9 Sep 1842, -, -, -, Andreas, Blaurock, Margareta, Blonrock , -, -, 16

1647, 15 Jan 1843, Alexander, McDonnell, Patricii, Mariae, 3 Jan 1843, -, -, -, Edwardus, Cuningham, Maria, Welsh, -, -, 16

1648, 15 Jan 1843, Thomas, Bougham, Jacobi, Catharinae, 7 Jan 1843, -, -, -, Henricus, Moran, Birgitta, Moran, -, -, 16

1649, 16 Jan 1843, Joannes, Degnan, Joannis, [blank], 16 Oct 1842, -, -, -, Jacobus, Murray, Anna, O'Donnell, -, -, 16

1650, 16 Jan 1843, Elisabeth, Quigly, Joannis, Annae, 4 Dec 1842, -, -, -, Michael , Dooly, Maria, Dooly, -, -, 16

ST. MARY'S CATHOLIC CHURCH
HAGERSTOWN, MARYLAND, BAPTISMS:
Index, Bap Date, Child, Last Name, Father, Mother,
Birth Date, Code1, Code2, Code3,
1st Sponsor First, 1st Sponsor Last,
2nd Sponsor First, 2nd Sponsor Last, Location,
Notes, Maiden Name, Priest

1651, 16 Jan 1843, Maria, Brofy, Carnelii, Elisabeth, 14 Jan 1843, -, -, -, Thomas, [blank], Catharina, Kannedy, -, -, 16

1652, 16 Jan 1843, Maria, Farley, Patricii, Annae, 15 Jan 1843, -, -, -, Antonius, Hughes, Elisabeth, Hays, -, -, 16

1653, 21 Jan 1843, Mina Anna, Antony, Conrad, Catharinae, 16 Jan 1843, -, -, -, Mina, Stexenius, -, -, -, -, 16

1654, 26 Jan 1843, Carolina Regina, Trueman, Joannis, Sarae, 14 Feb 1843, -, -, -, Sara, Rideout, -, -, -, -, 16

1655, 8 Mar 1843, Jacobus, Paton, Joannis, Mariae, 20 Jan 1843, -, -, -, Michael, Guth, Anna, Davis [Adams crossed out], -, -, 16

1656, 18 Mar 1843, Alice Johanna, McArdele, Richardi, Mariae, 11 Oct 1842, -, -, -, Anna, McArdell, -, -, -, -, 16

1657, 19 Mar 1843, Maria Catharina, Watson, Jacobi, Sarae, 1 Mar 1843, -, -, -, Susanna, Shane, -, -, -, -, 16

1658, 31 Mar 1843, George, Shane, Joannis, Margaretae, 23 Mar 1843, -, -, -, Josephus, Waise, Cecilia, Waise, entire entry crossed out, -, 16

1659, 2 Mar 1843, Joannes, Rhodes, Arthuri, Rosa Annae, 13 Feb 1843, -, -, -, Josephus, Dooly, Catharina, Clarke, -, -, 16

1660, 3 Mar 1843, Jacobus Patricius, Clarke, ["Patricii" crossed out] Caroly, Margaretae, 16 Feb 1843, -, -, -, Patricius, Clarke, Maria Anna, Gorman, -, -, 16

1661, 3 Mar 1843, William Henricus, Breslin, Michaelis, Catharinae, 24 Jan 1843, -, -, -, Michael, Smith, Maria Anna, Colvin, -, -, 16

1662, 11 Mar 1843, Maria Ludovica, Griech, Guellilmii [?], Margaretae, 9 Aug 1842, -, -, -, Joannes, Griech, Catharina, Smith, -, -, 16

1663, 12 Mar 1843, Petrus, Schow [or Schour or Shour], Hugonis, Catharinae, 10 Dec 1842, -, -, -, Petrus, N. [rest of name is blank], Petrus & Anna Margareta, N. [rest of name is blank], -, -, 16

1664, 12 Mar 1843, Maria Magdalena, Francis, Joannis, Susannae, 26 Feb 1843, -, -, -, Michael, Gardener, Maria, Gardener [HB], -, -, 16

1665, 22 Mar 1843, Margareta Johanna, McCoskar, Hugonis, Margaretae, 15 Jan 1842, -, -, -, Margareta, Donnelly, -, -, -, -, 16

ST. MARY'S CATHOLIC CHURCH
HAGERSTOWN, MARYLAND, BAPTISMS:
Index, Bap Date, Child, Last Name, Father, Mother,
Birth Date, Code1, Code2, Code3,
1st Sponsor First, 1st Sponsor Last,
2nd Sponsor First, 2nd Sponsor Last, Location,
Notes, Maiden Name, Priest

1666, 16 Mar 1843, Barbara Anna, Gouker, Josephi, Juliae Annae, 31 Oct 1842, -, -, -, Jacob, Maysinger, Margareta, Maysinger [HB], -, -, 16

1667, 16 Mar 1843, Margareta, McCartin, Edwardi, Catharinae, 9 Mar 1843, -, -, -, Francisca, McEntire, -, -, -, -, 16

1668, 19 Apr 1843, Edwardus, McGuigan, Terrentii, Mariae, 29 Mar 1843, -, -, -, Michael, Garvey , Catharina, McCoskar, -, -, 16

1669, 23 Apr 1843, Lucas, Kelly, Jacobi, Margaretae, 23 Mar 1843, -, -, -, Joannes, Logan, Elisabeth, Corlosk [?], -, -, 16

1670, 23 Apr 1843, Richardus Leonidas, Murray, Laurentii, Sarae, 2 Feb 1841, -, -, -, R. [blank], Murray, Elisabeth, Haughens [?], -, -, 16

1671, 23 Apr 1843, Thomas, Kelly, Christophori, Mariae, 23 Dec 1842, -, -, -, Thomas, Kelly, Maria, Raynolds, -, -, 16

1672, 24 Apr 1843, Jacobus, Skelly, Joannis, Mariae, 8 Feb 1842, -, -, -, Joannes, Mooty, Catharina, Spollen, -, -, 16

1673, 24 Apr 1843, Michael Henricus, Quicgly , Petrii, Mariae, 18 Apr 1843, -, -, -, Joannis, Quiegly, Anna, Quiegly, -, -, 16

1674, 24 Apr 1843, Anna, Spollen, Michaelis, Margaretae, 18 Apr 1843, -, -, -, Andreas , Clarke, Margareta, Clarke [HB], -, -, 16

1675, 24 Apr 1843, Jacobus, Shirren, Edwardi, Susannae, 18 Dec 1842, -, -, -, Joannes, McLary, Maria, Quiegly, -, -, 16

1676, 24 Apr 1843, Margareta, Shannon, Dominici, Juliae, 23 Apr 1843, -, -, -, Patricius, Donnelly, Birgetta, Follen, -, -, 16

1677, 24 Apr 1843, Anna Virginia, Parker, Thomae, Susannae, 17 Dec 1842, -, -, -, Thomas, Gale, Catharina, Allen, -, -, 16

1678, 24 Apr 1843, Joannes Thomas, Boony [or Roony], Patricii, Mariae, 29 Jan 1843, -, -, -, Michael, Spollen, Catharina, Tipper, -, -, 16

1679, 25 Apr 1843, Elleonora, McDonnell, Morgan, Juliae, 8 Apr 1843, -, -, -, Patricius, Garaghty, Margareta, Garaghty, -, -, 16

1680, 29 Apr 1483, Elisabeth, Janner, Godlieb, Rosannae, 15 Mar 1843, -, -, -, Fredericus, Fellinger, Elisabeth, [blank], -, -, 16

1681, 29 Apr 1843, Josephus Ludovicus, Tice, Danielis, Margaretae, 12 Feb 1843, -, -, -, Michael , Smith, Catharina, Smith [HB], -, -, 16

ST. MARY'S CATHOLIC CHURCH
HAGERSTOWN, MARYLAND, BAPTISMS:
Index, Bap Date, Child, Last Name, Father, Mother,
Birth Date, Code1, Code2, Code3,
1st Sponsor First, 1st Sponsor Last,
2nd Sponsor First, 2nd Sponsor Last, Location,
Notes, Maiden Name, Priest

1682, 29 Apr 1843, William, Forus, -, Serenae, 16 Mar 1843, PN, - , -, -, -, -, -, -, -, 16

1683, 29 Apr 1843, Michael , Carley, Patricii, Catharinae, 19 Feb 1843, -, -, -, Joannes, Egan, Anna, Curley, -, -, 16

1684, 30 Apr 1843, Jeremias, Ambush, William, Appoloniae, 28 Apr 1842, -, -, -, [blank], [blank], [blank], [blank], -, -, 16

1685, 30 Apr 1843, Elisabeth, Johnson, -, Theresae, 6 Feb 1843, PN, -, -, -, -, -, -, -, -, 16

1686, 21 May 1843, Jacobus, Ziegler, Adami, Elisabeth, 2 Feb 1843, -, -, -, Jacobus, Klueh, -, -, -, -, 16

1687, 21 May 1843, William, Hughes, Jacobi, Mariae, 2 Apr 1843, -, -, -, Williamson , Mattingly, Henrietta, Mattingly [HB], 3rd witness - Anna Mulhargan, -, 16

1688, 22 May 1843, Patricius, Murphey, Jacobi, Mariae Ambo[?], 5 May 1843, -, -, -, Jacobus, M. [blank], Maria, Donnelly, -, -, 16

1689, 22 May 1843, Rosa Anna, Murphey, Jacobi, Mariae Ambo[?], 5 May 1843, -, -, -, Joannes , Bern, Elleonora, Bern [HB], -, -, 16

1690, 23 May 1843, Jacobus, Shannon, Edwardi, Catharinae, 5 May 1843, -, -, -, Carolus , Kern, Maria, Kern [HB], -, -, 16

1691, 25 May 1843, Johanna, Delay, Joannis, Mariae, 9 Apr 1843, -, -, -, Dionysius , Hurley, Maria, Hurley [HB], -, -, 16

1692, 25 May 1843, Susanna, Kelly, Morgan, Mariae, 10 Feb 1843, -, -, -, Patricius A. [?], Clarke, Catharina, Clarke, -, -, 16

1693, 4 Jun 1843, Jacobus, Lachenmeyer, Josiphi, Eleonorae, 7 Mar 1843, -, -, -, Jacobus, Putz, -, -, -, -, 16

1694, 4 Jun 1843, Maria, Shelling, Joachim, Franciscae, 5 Feb 1843, -, -, -, Maria, Müller, -, -, -, -, 16

1695, 15 Jun 1843, Bernardus, Whealan, Bernardi, Annae, 8 Jun 1843, -, -, -, Frannciscus , Green, "A...", Green, -, -, 16

1696, 17 Jun 1843, Guilelmus, Gallagher, Michaelis, Birgittae, 19 May 1843, -, -, -, Thomas, Dranan, Catharina, Dranan, -, -, 16

1697, 18 Jun 1843, Joannes, [Kelly crossed out] Connor, Joannis, Johannae, 23 May 1843, -, -, -, Joannes, Kelly, Johanna, Lively, -, - , 16

1698, 18 Jun 1843, Anna, Kennedy, Guillelim, Mariae, 17 Apr 1843, -, -, -, Thomas , Crady, Maria, Crady [HB], -, -, 16

ST. MARY'S CATHOLIC CHURCH
HAGERSTOWN, MARYLAND, BAPTISMS:
Index, Bap Date, Child, Last Name, Father, Mother,
Birth Date, Code1, Code2, Code3,
1st Sponsor First, 1st Sponsor Last,
2nd Sponsor First, 2nd Sponsor Last, Location,
Notes, Maiden Name, Priest

1699, 18 Jun 1843, Maria Anna, Doyle, Jacobi, Elisabeth, 5 Apr 1843, -, -, -, Johanna, Carrol, -, -, -, -, 16

1700, 18 Jun 1843, Margareta, Carrol, Patricii, Johanna, 11 May 1842, -, -, -, Maria, McBride, -, -, -, -, 16

1701, 18 Jun 1843, Elisabeth, Miller, -, Annae, 27 ___ 1841*, PN, -, -, Birgitta, Ryan, -, -, *birthdate is 27 ___[blank] 1841, -, 16

1702, 18 Jun 1843, Maria Anna, Sweany, Francisci, Annae, 28 May 1843, -, -, -, Sarah, McLaughlin, -, -, -, -, 16

1703, 16 Jul 1843, Elleonora, McKneeve, Martini, Ellionorae, 12 Jul 1843, -, -, -, Patricius, Brannon, Birgitta, Gleanan, -, -, 16

1704, 16 Jul 1843, Maria, Donovan, Joannis, Birgittae, 11 [that's all], -, -, -, Thomas, Britt, Elleonora, Murray, -, -, 16

1705, 16 Jul 1843, Joannes Henricus, Fox, -, Mariae Annae, 13 Mar 1843, PN, -, -, Bernardus, Wingelman, -, -, -, -, 16

1706, 23 Jul 1843, Guillelmus, Cuningham, Joannis, Margaretae, 1 Aug 1842, -, -, -, Joannes , Holbert, Maria Anna, Holbert [HB], -, -, 16

1707, 30 Jul 1843, Samuel Henricus, Meyer, Joannis, Theresiae, 24 Dec 1842, -, -, -, Antonius, Kappler, -, -, -, -, 16

1708, 13 Aug 1843, Samuel Eccleston, Shervan, Thom, Isabellae, 4 May 1842, -, -, -, Joannes, Tyerney [or Tierney], Maria, Tigert, -, -, 16

1709, 17 Aug 1843, Henricus Thomas, Sneider, Henrici, Elisabeth, 22 Jun 1843, -, -, -, Thomas, Means, Margareta, England, -, -, 16

1710, 18 Aug 1843, Thomas, McCurdy, -, Mariae Annae, 20 Jul 1842, PN, -, -, -, -, -, -, -, -, 16

1711, 20 Aug 1843, Isabella, Dugan, -, -, 19 yrs. , -, -, -, -, -, -, -, -, -, 16

1712, 20 Aug 1843, Terrentius Joannes, McEvoy, Patricii, Mariae, 31 Jul 1843, -, -, -, Hugo, Egan, Margarita, Tims [or Tirns?], -, -, 16

1713, 21 Aug 1843, Elisabeth, McCarr, Joannis, Annae, 27 Jun 1843, -, -, -, Bernardus, Quin, Maria, Quin, -, -, 16

1714, 22 Aug 1843, Isaak, Gehr, -, -, 20 years, -, -, -, -, -, -, -, -, -, 16

1715, 26 Aug 1843, Alfrid B , Smith, Joannis K , Elisabeth, Apr 1843, -, -, -, Elisabeth, Shirley, -, -, -, -, 16

ST. MARY'S CATHOLIC CHURCH
HAGERSTOWN, MARYLAND, BAPTISMS:
Index, Bap Date, Child, Last Name, Father, Mother,
Birth Date, Code1, Code2, Code3,
1st Sponsor First, 1st Sponsor Last,
2nd Sponsor First, 2nd Sponsor Last, Location,
Notes, Maiden Name, Priest

1716, 3 Sep 1843, Maria, Keley, Francisci, Theodorae, 7 Aug 1843, -, -, -, Maria Evae, Mesman, -, -, -, -, 16

1717, 9 Sep 1843, Catharina, Bauer, Jacobi, Mariae Anae, 31 Aug 1842, -, -, -, Catharina, Bauer, -, -, -, -, 16

1718, 10 Sep 1843, Maria, Older, Georgiin, Mariae, 15 Aug 1843, -, -, -, Maria, Cauber, -, -, -, -, 16

1719, 16 Sep 1843, Anna Dorothea, Blourock, Andreae, Margaretae, 16 Aug 1843, -, -, -, Anna Dorothea, Swab, -, -, -, -, 16

1720, 17 Sep 1483, Gaspar, Ulerich, -, -, Aug 1843, -, -, -, Gaspar, Müller, -, -, -, -, 16

1721, 27 Sep 1843, Joannes, McAnally, Joannis, Maria, 26 Aug 1843, -, -, -, Edward, McCormack, Anna, Lawless, -, -, 16

1722, 8 Oct 1843, Maria, Kauker, Joannis, Mariae, 15 Aug 1843, -, -, -, Georges, Walder, Maria, Cauber, -, -, 16

1723, 13 Oct 1843, Joannes, Grey, Petri, Margaretae, 25 Sep 1843, -, -, -, Hugo, Brady, Birgitta, Mullegan, -, -, 16

1724, 13 Oct 1843, Josephus, Smith, Patricii, Mariae, 17 Sep 1843, -, -, -, William, Riley, Catharina, Bugho, -, -, 16

1725, 13 Oct 1843, Joannes*, Philips, Jeremiae [Philippi crossed out], Mariae, 24 Sep 1843, -, -, -, Robertus, Philips, Maria Anna, Dormady, *Joannes [Jeremias crossed out], -, 16

1726, 13 Oct 1843, Michael, Cronly, Jacobi, Mariae, 13 Sep 1843, -, -, -, Thomas, Brady, Rosa, Dolan, -, -, 16

1727, 13 Oct 1843, Anna, Brann[s?], Patricii, Elleonorae, 27 Aug 1843, -, -, -, Martinus, Nolan, Anna, McGnives [sic], -, -, 16

1728, 13 Oct 1843, Jacobus, Morearty, Jacobi, Mariae, 2 Oct 1843, -, -, -, Bernardus, McGrow, Margareta, Kerby, -, -, 16

1729, 13 Oct 1843, Elleonora, Proer, Hugonis, Rosae, 26 Sep 1843, -, -, -, Jacobus, Cadden, Elisabeth, Cadden, -, -, 16

1730, 15 Oct 1843, Daniel, Harkins, Joannis, Catharinae, 23 Aug 1843, -, -, -, Patricius, Riley, Anna, Barbary, -, -, 16

1731, 16 Oct 1843, Maria, McCabe, Terrenticie, Mariae, 1 Oct 1843, -, -, -, Carolus, Kerny, Elisabeth, McCue, -, -, 16

1732, 15 Oct 1843, Joannes, Riley, Petri, Johannae, 2 Oct 1843, -, -, -, Wm., Caho, Margareta, Tims, -, -, 16

1733, 16 Oct 1843, Jacobus, Quitney, Patricii, Hanorae, 3 months, -, -, -, -, -, -, -, -, -, 16

ST. MARY'S CATHOLIC CHURCH
HAGERSTOWN, MARYLAND, BAPTISMS:
Index, Bap Date, Child, Last Name, Father, Mother,
Birth Date, Code1, Code2, Code3,
1st Sponsor First, 1st Sponsor Last,
2nd Sponsor First, 2nd Sponsor Last, Location,
Notes, Maiden Name, Priest

1734, 25 Oct 1843, Ezechias, Adams, Amos, Catharinae, 28 May 1843, -, -, -, Upton, Bigold, Elisabeth, Timmons, -, -, 16

1735, 25 Oct 1843, Zeru Elisabeth, Draper, Georgis, Mariae, 6 Aug 1843, -, -, -, matrina fuit Maria, McLaughlin, -, -, -, -, 16

1736, 1 Nov 1843, Catharina Ludovica, Smith, Michaelis, Birgittae, 27 Oct 1843, -, -, -, Philippus, Fitzpatrick, Catharina, Clarke, -, -, 16

1737, 19 Nov 1843, Jacobus, Dolan, Michaelis, Mariae, 24 Oct 1843, -, -, -, Petrus, Conroy, Maria, Conroy, -, -, 16

1738, 19 Nov 1843, Catharina, Coffer [or Coffee], Thomae, Judith, 11 Jul 1843, -, -, -, Patricius, Cada[?], Maria , Handley, -, -, 16

1739, 19 Nov 1843, Georgius, Keeffer, Georgii, Elisabeth, 17 Jun 1843, -, -, -, Michael, McDonnal, Catharina, Harkins, -, -, 16

1740, 19 Nov 1843, Catharina, Cambel, Thomae, Catharinae, 19 Nov 1843, -, -, -, Alexander, McGuire, Catharina, Gorighan, -, -, 16

1741, 19 Nov 1843, Daniel, Ragan, Patricii, Catharinae, 14 Nov 1843, -, -, -, Patricius, Crauley, Elleonora, Sullivan, -, -, 16

1742, 19 Nov 1843, Catharina, Welsh, Jacobi, Johannae, 13 Nov 1843, -, -, -, Thomas, Garighan, Birgitta, Carlosk, -, -, 16

1743, 20 Nov 1843, Maria Anna, Carnbel, Michaelis, Rebeccae, 4 Sep 1843, -, -, -, Petrus, Riley, Johanna, Riley [HB], -, -, 16

1744, 24 Nov 1843, Margareta, Huslein, Michaelis, Catharinae, 13 Oct 1843, -, -, -, Margareta, Riegel, -, -, -, -, 16

1745, 24 Nov 1843, Anna Margareta, Keller, Joseph, Catharinae, 22 Oct 1843, -, -, -, Margareta, Diederich, -, -, -, -, 16

1746, 3 Dec 1843, Petrus Henricus, Gauker, Joannis, Elleonorae, 14 Sep 1843, -, -, -, Josephus , Gauker, Julia, Gauker [HB], -, -, 16

1747, 5 Dec 1843, Sara* , Graffy, Jacobi, Clarae, 29 Nov 1841, -, -, -, Theresia, Berger, -, -, *Sara [Theresia crossed out], -, 16

1748, 5 Dec 1843, Theresia, Graffy, Jacobi, Clarae, 17 Sep 1843, -, -, -, Evelina, Renner, -, -, -, -, 16

1749, 12 Dec 1843, Joannes Richardus, Davis, Joannis, Mariae Annae, 29 Nov 1843, -, -, -, Joannes , Dinkel, Scholastica, Dinkel [HB], -, -, 16

1750, 19 Dec 1843 , Samuel, Tippet, Georgii, Sarae, 11 Dec 1843, -, -, -, Hugo, McCoskar, Maria Anna, Colvin, -, -, 16

ST. MARY'S CATHOLIC CHURCH
HAGERSTOWN, MARYLAND, BAPTISMS:
Index, Bap Date, Child, Last Name, Father, Mother,
Birth Date, Code1, Code2, Code3,
1st Sponsor First, 1st Sponsor Last,
2nd Sponsor First, 2nd Sponsor Last, Location,
Notes, Maiden Name, Priest

1751, 27 Dec 1843, Ludavicus, Clarke, William, Margaretae, 30 Nov 1843, -, -, -, Jacobus, McGee, Sara, McLane, -, -, 16

1752, 29 Dec 1843, Joannes Richardus, G [rest of name is blank], Richardi, Mariae, 21 Aug 1843, -, -, -, William, Thomson, Elisabeth, McEntire, -, -, 16

1753, 31 Dec 1843, Michael, Mighan, Patricii, Mariae, 10 Oct 1843, -, -, -, Michael, Garvey, Honora, Kelly, -, -, 16

1754, 31 Dec 1843, Joannes, Rogan, Patricii, Annae, 20 Oct 1843, -, -, -, Petrus, Annys, Maria, Mighan, -, -, 16

1755, 31 Dec 1843, Allis Sophia, Lambride, William, Mariae, 11 Aug 1843, -, -, -, Joseph, Bevans, Margareta, Cuningham, -, -, 16

1756, 7 Jan 1844, Hugo, Kelly, Patrici, Sarae, 28 Dec 1843, -, -, -, Joannes, Dinkel, Birgitta, McGonigal, -, -, 16

1757, 7 Jan 1844, Alfredus Petrus, Clemens, Alexandri, Matildis, 12 Oct 1843, -, -, -, Joannes, Dinkel, Margareta, Messer, -, -, 16

1758, 2_ Jan 1844*, Margareta, Agan, Petri, Catharinae, 2 Jan 1844, -, -, -, Elisabeth, Agan, -, -, in baptismal date, 2_ Jan 1844, the ink is smeared on second number, -, 16

1759, 22 Jan 1844, Maria Johanna, Terry, Roberti, Birgittae, 19 Jan 1844, -, -, -, Thomas, Lestrange, Anna, McFadden, -, -, 16

1760, 22 Jan 1844, Rosa Anna, Clitner, Josephi, Sarae Joannae, 23 Oct 1843, -, -, -, Joannes , McFadden, Anna, McFadden [HB], -, -, 16

1761, 22 Jan 1844, Josephus, Drennan, Thomae, Catharinae, 28 Dec 1843, -, -, -, Guillelimus, Magher, Maria, Galligher, -, -, 16

1762, 13 Feb 1844, Michael, Browngarden, Gasparis, Mariae Annae, 6 Dec 1843, -, -, -, Michael, Eck, -, -, -, -, 16

1763, 16 Feb 1844, Charolus Basileus, Abdon, -, Susannae, 9 Jan 1844, PN, -, -, Joannes Michael, Smith, -, -, -, -, 16

1764, 24 Feb 1844, Anna, Brannon, Patricii, Birgittae, 1 Feb 1844, -, -, -, Petrus, Kerney, Anna, Brady, -, -, 16

1765, 25 Feb 1844, Alys Virginia, Mathews, Joannis, Henriettae, 12 Dec 1843, -, -, -, Margareta , Cuningham, -, -, -, -, 16

1766, 26 Feb 1844, Birgitta, McGinys, Daniel, Mariae, 26 Dec 1843, -, -, -, Patricius, Carrol, Sara Johanna, Connor, -, -, 16

1767, 26 Feb 1844, E. Maria Ludovica, Higgens, Ransom, Elisabeth, 4 Feb 1844, -, -, -, Maria, Bevans, -, -, -, -, 16

ST. MARY'S CATHOLIC CHURCH HAGERSTOWN, MARYLAND, BAPTISMS:
Index, Bap Date, Child, Last Name, Father, Mother, Birth Date, Code1, Code2, Code3, 1st Sponsor First, 1st Sponsor Last, 2nd Sponsor First, 2nd Sponsor Last, Location, Notes, Maiden Name, Priest

1768, 27 Feb 1844, Martha Susanna, Maclain, Upton, Annae Elisabeth, 12 Jan 1844, -, -, -, Martha, MaClain, -, -, -, -, 16

1769, 3 Mar 1844, Georgius S., Watkins, Ed W [sic], Helenae, 22 Feb 1844, -, -, -, Thomas, Bevans, Elisabeth K.[?], Reinhard, -, -, 16

1770, 3 Mar 1844, Carolus Henricus, Watkins, E W [sic], Helenae, 22 Feb 1844*, -, -, -, Jacobus, Bevans, Evelina, Bevans, *beside this date is written "hic est junior", -, 16

1771, 3 Mar 1844, Maria Anna, Gilice [?], Thomae, Catharinae, 29 Jan 1844, -, -, -, Patricius, Gilice, Catharina, Dornion, -, -, 16

1772, 3 Mar 1844, Michael Henricus, Connelly, Jacobi, Barbarae, 25 Dec 1844, -, -, -, Terrentius, McGuigan, Elisabeth, Calory, -, -, 16

1773, 3 Mar 1844, Catharina Elleonora, Garvey, Michaelis, Margaretae, 12 Feb 1844, -, -, -, Terrentius Jacobus, Connelly, Eleonora, Colvin, -, -, 16

1774, 10 Mar 1844, Joannes D., Shonor [or Shover], Laurentii, Annae Josephinae, 30 Jan 1844, -, -, -, Joannes, Dinkel, Scholastica, Dinkel, -, -, 16

1775, 8 Apr 1844, Maria, Degnan, Michaelis, Elisabeth, 24 Dec 1843, -, -, -, Bernardus, Mahon, Birgitta, Sweany, -, -, 16

1776, 13 Apr 1844, Andreas Aloysius, Renner, Aloysii, Mariae, 6 Jan 1844, -, -, -, Michael, Gardner, Carolina, Renner, -, -, 16

1777, 13 Apr 1844, Johanna, Sweany, Joannis, Catharinae, 17 Mar 1844, -, -, -, Edwardus, Johston, Judith, Johnston, -, -, 16

1778, 14 Apr 1844, Lucinda, Henry, Joannis, blank, 8 Jan 1844, -, -, -, Upton & Anna, Jones , -, -, This entire entry was crossed out, -, 16

1779, 14 Apr 1844, Lucinda Francisca, Weaver, Georgius, Patientia, 3 Mar 1840, -, -, -, -, -, -, -, -, -, 16

1780, 14 Apr 1844, Joannes Henricus, Weaver, Georgius, Patientia, 18 Jan 1842, -, -, -, -, -, -, -, -, -, 16

1781, 14 Apr 1844, Upton A., Weaver, Georgius, Patientia, 28 Dec 1843, -, -, -, -, -, -, -, -, -, 16

1782, 14 Apr 1844, Jacobus, Flanigan, Francisci, Miae [sic] Annae , 8 Apr 1844, -, -, -, Joannus, Carrighan, Catharina, McAdam, -, -, 16

ST. MARY'S CATHOLIC CHURCH
HAGERSTOWN, MARYLAND, BAPTISMS:
Index, Bap Date, Child, Last Name, Father, Mother,
Birth Date, Code1, Code2, Code3,
1st Sponsor First, 1st Sponsor Last,
2nd Sponsor First, 2nd Sponsor Last, Location,
Notes, Maiden Name, Priest

1783, 14 Apr 1844, Elisabeth, Kluh, Jacobi, Florae, 4 Mar 1844, -, -, -, Elisabeth, Siegler, -, -, -, -, 16
1784, 15 Apr 1844, Catharina, Fargerson, Jacobi, [blank], 11 Apr 1844, -, -, -, Cornelius, Monagham, Maria, Hughes, -, -, 16
1785, 15 Apr 1844, Jacobus, Casy, Patricii, Elisabeth, 2 Mar 1844, -, -, -, Patricius, Mahon, Gratia, Curry, -, -, 16
1786, 15 Apr 1844, Edwardus, McAltee, Walter, Mariae, 16 Nov 1843, -, -, -, Thomas, Gale, -, -, -, -, 16
1787, 13 Apr 1844, Joannes, Rodger, Patricii, Catharinae, 17 Aug 1843, -, -, -, -, -, -, -, -, -, -, 16
1788, 13 Apr 1844, Petrus, Hoy, Petri, Rosae Annae, 1844, -, -, -, John, Loftus, Maria, McAltee, -, -, 16
1789, 15 Apr 1844, Richardus Leonidas, Murray, Richardi, Sarae, 2 Feb 1841, -, -, -, -, -, -, -, -, -, -, 16
1790, 15 Apr 1844, Charolus, Murray, Richardi, Sarae, 8 May 1844, -, -, -, -, -, -, -, -, -, 16
1791, 20 Apr 1844, Joannes, Scheiner, Josephi, Barborae, 2 Oct 1844, -, -, -, Joannes, Fayette, Barbara, Hoffman, -, -, 16
1792, 21 Apr 1844, Josephus, Whealan, Jacobi, Johannae, 18 Mar 1844, -, -, -, Edwardus, Whealan, Emilia, Murray, -, -, 16
1793, 14 May 1844, William, Robertson, Joannis, Franciscae, 31 May 1843, -, -, -, Arnorld, Johnes, Theresia, Jones, -, -, 16
1794, 14 May 1844, Sara A.R., Lee, Roberti, Caeciliae, 3 Nov 1843, -, -, -, Joannes, Robertson, Sara, Lee, -, -, 16
1795, 16 May 1844, Dionysius, Grady, Patricii, Catharinae, 23 Apr 1844, -, -, -, Joannes, Fallon, Maria, Brady, -, -, 16
1796, 17 May 1844, Jacobus, McAttee, Samuel, Sara, 1 Aug 1841, -, -, -, Thomas, Gale, Maria, McAttee, -, -, 16
1797, 17 May 1844, Maria, McAttee, Samuel, Sara, 3 Oct 1843, -, -, -, Thomas, Gale, Maria, McAttee, -, -, 16
1798, 17 May 1844, Sara Elmira, McDonnel, Angus, Sarae, 15 Apr 1844, -, -, -, Maria Virginia, McDonnal, -, -, -, -, 16
1799, 19 May 1844, Maria, Kelly, Joannis, K. [sic], 26 Aug 1843, -, -, -, Philippus, Milton, Elisabeth M., Tanny, -, -, 16
1800, 19 May 1844, Maria Anna, Gardner, Georgii, Magdalenae, 19 Apr 1844, -, -, -, Michael, Gardner, Maria, Renner, -, -, 16

ST. MARY'S CATHOLIC CHURCH
HAGERSTOWN, MARYLAND, BAPTISMS:
Index, Bap Date, Child, Last Name, Father, Mother,
Birth Date, Code1, Code2, Code3,
1st Sponsor First, 1st Sponsor Last,
2nd Sponsor First, 2nd Sponsor Last, Location,
Notes, Maiden Name, Priest

1801, 26 May 1844, Jacobus, Leixner, Philippi, Dorotheae, 5 Oct 1843, -, -, -, Jacobus, Putz, -, -, -, -, 16

1802, 26 May 1844, Sara, Hohenstein, Leonardi, Margaretae, 22 Apr 1844, -, -, -, Sara, Brown, -, -, -, -, 16

1803, 26 May 1844, Anna Maria, Albert, Josephi, Barbarae, 18 Feb 1844, -, -, -, Sara, Brown, -, -, -, -, 16

1804, 27 May 1844, Sara, Ambush, York, Appolinae, 28 Aug 1843, -, -, -, Theresia, Johnes, -, -, -, -, 16

1805, 18 Jun 1844, Joannes M., Swope, Gasparis, Dorotheae, 18 Apr 1844, -, -, -, -, -, -, -, -, -, 16

1806, 18 Jun 1844, Sara Anna, Scott, Josue, Emma, 15 Apr 1839, -, -, -, -, -, -, -, -, -, 16

1807, 18 Jun 1844, Josue B., Scott, Josue, Emma, 26 Jun 1842, -, -, -, -, -, -, -, -, -, 16

1808, 16 Jul 1844, Guillelimus, Bell [or Baker if using mother's name], Joannis, Elisabeth, 9 Jan 1844, PN, -, -, Joseph, Bevans, Maria, Bevans [HB], -, Baker, 16

1809, 19 Jul 1844, Matheus, McLeary [?], Timothei, -, -, -, -, -, -, -, -, -, -, -, 16

1810, 21 Jul 1844, Henricus C., Shane, Joannis, Margaritae, 9 Jul 1844, -, -, -, Jacobus, Peck, Sara, Tippet, -, -, 16

1811, 21 Jul 1844, Paulus, Weber, Michaelis, Mariae, 23 May 1844, -, -, -, Paulus, Paulus [sic], -, -, -, -, 16

1812, 7 Aug 1844, Ludovica A., Adam, Jacobi, Elisabeth, 10 Apr 1844, -, -, -, Maria Ann, Sullivan, -, -, -, -, 16

1813, 11 Aug 1844, Silvestra [dau.], Johnson, Henrici, I [?] C, 7 Jun 1844, -, -, -, Joannes, Trueman, Dorethea, Warton, -, -, 16

1814, 15 Aug 1844, Jacobus, Fitzpatrick, Philippi, Helenae, 10 Aug 1844, -, -, -, Patricius, Mathews, Margareta, McCoskar, -, -, 16

1815, 15 Aug 1844, Adolphus, Dorsey, -, Rachel, 20 Feb 1844, PN, -, -, -, -, -, -, -, -, 16

1816, 18 Aug 1844, Elisabeth, McCue, Patricii, Elisabeth, 31 Jul 1843, -, -, -, Catharina, Sweany, -, -, -, -, 16

1817, 19 Aug 1844, Joannes Theophilus, Janner, Georgii, Franciscae, 31 Jul 1844, -, -, -, Fredericus , Fellinger, Rosalia, Fillinger [HB], -, -, 16

ST. MARY'S CATHOLIC CHURCH
HAGERSTOWN, MARYLAND, BAPTISMS:
Index, Bap Date, Child, Last Name, Father, Mother,
Birth Date, Code1, Code2, Code3,
1st Sponsor First, 1st Sponsor Last,
2nd Sponsor First, 2nd Sponsor Last, Location,
Notes, Maiden Name, Priest

1818, 28 Aug 1844, Eleonora Elisabeth, Shaffer, Joannis, Catharinae, 19 Jan 1844, -, -, -, -, -, -, -, -, Fox, 16

1819, 8 Sep 1844, Joannes, Smith, Josua , Anastasia, 27 Aug 1844, -, -, -, -, -, -, -, -, -, 16

1820, 27 Sep 1844, Thomas, Mathews, Patricii, Elleonorae, 22 Sep 1844, -, -, -, Antonius, McMahon, Sara, McLaughlin, -, -, 16

1821, 8 Oct 1844, Elisabeth, Karr, Jacobi, Sarae, 25 Sep 1844, -, -, -, Maria, Taggar, -, -, -, -, 16

1822, 14 Oct 1844, Maria Anna P., McKanah, Hugonis, Mariae, 14 Aug 1844, -, -, -, Franciscus, Sweany, Lorretta, Martin, -, -, 16

1823, 14 Oct 1844, Anna Elisabeth, Corbett, Petris, Annae, 27 Apr 1844, -, -, -, Hugo, McKanah, Maria, McKanah, -, -, 16

1824, 16 Oct 1844, Ludovicus M., Kelley, Josephi, Catharinae, 20 Aug 1844, -, -, -, Ludovicus, Kelley, Scholastica, Dinkel, -, -, 16

1825, 29 Jun 1845, Susan, McGonnigle, James, Susan, 26 Jun 1845, -, -, -, James, Hughes, Magey, Devlin, -, McLouglin, 15

1826, 30 Jun 1845, James, McGee, James, Bridget, 7 Jun 1845, -, -, -, James, Hughes, Sophia A. (Mrs.), Hurley, -, St. John, 15

1827, 7 Jul 1845, James Edward, Hevend, James, May, 16 Jan 1845, -, -, -, Thomas, Dean, Anastasia, Berringer, -, Corbett, 19

1828, 7 Jul 1845, Sophia, Paulus, Peter, Magdalen, 30 Sep 1844, -, -, -, Sophia, Done, Lewis, Done, -, Done, 19

1829, 7 Jul 1845, Mary Eva, Gley, Francis, Charlotte, 1 Jan 1845, -, -, -, Mary Eva, Messman, -, -, -, Ginder, 19

1830, 7 Jul 1845, Le the [Lethe?]Ann, Brown, Loyd, Rosetta , 9 months, B, S, S, Nancy, Butler, -, -, parents are married and slaves of George Schley, -, 19

1831, 9 Jul 1845, John William, Curley, Patrick, Catharine, 1 year, -, -, -, Ulton, More, Ann, More, -, -, 19

1832, 9 Jul 1845, John, Coleman, -, Eliza, blank, FB, -, -, Mary, Ward, -, -, -, -, 19

1833, 10 Jul 1845, Catharine Elmira, Anthony, Conrad, Catharine, 24 Mar 1845, -, -, -, Ulton, More, -, -, -, Schilling, 19

1834, 10 Jul 1845, Ann Eugenia, Anthony, Conrad, Catharine, 24 Mar 1845, -, -, -, Catharine, Geleese, -, -, -, -, 19

ST. MARY'S CATHOLIC CHURCH
HAGERSTOWN, MARYLAND, BAPTISMS:
Index, Bap Date, Child, Last Name, Father, Mother,
Birth Date, Code1, Code2, Code3,
1st Sponsor First, 1st Sponsor Last,
2nd Sponsor First, 2nd Sponsor Last, Location,
Notes, Maiden Name, Priest

1835, 10 Jul 1845, Thomas Jefferson, Daley, John, Kesiah, 20 Jan 1845, -, -, -, Thomas, Clingan *, Dorothea, Clingan, *[this man's name was crossed out], Rowland, 19

1836, 10 Jul 1845, John Adam, Miller, Valentine, Margaret, 8 Jan 1845, -, -, -, Joseph, Shine, Kesiah, Rowland, -, Veifel, 19

1837, 10 Jul 1845, Mary, Daley, John, Kesiah, 2 years , -, -, -, Philip, Melton, Elizabeth, Faney, -, Rowland, 19

1838, 10 Jul 1845, Adeline, Wilkinson, -, Catharine, 5 Jan 1845, PN, B, -, S, Ellen, Watkins, -, -, mother is a slave of Ellen Watkins, -, 19

1839, 13 Jul 1845, Martha Angelina, Truman, John, Sarah Ann, 18 Dec 1844, -, FB, FB, Juda, Galloway *, -, -, *["Dalaney" is crossed out with pencil and "Galloway" written in pencil], -, 19

1840, 18 Jul 1845, William Henry, Moates, Samuel, Helena, 2 Mar 1845, -, P, P, Henry, Shervin, Isabella, Shervin, -, Hammond, 19

1841, 20 Jul 1845, John Wesley Jacob, Gauger, John, Ellen, 19 Apr 1845, -, -, -, John Wesley, Volke[?], Barbara, Gauger, -, Huntman, 19

1842, 20 Jul 1845, David, Dempsey, Peter, Margaret, 4 Aug 1844, -, -, -, Bridget, McGonnigle, -, -, -, Fitzsimmons, 19

1843, 20 Jul 1845, Dominick, Dempsey, Peter, Margaret, 4 Aug 1844, -, -, -, Fanny, McIntire, -, -, -, Fitzsimmons, 19

1844, 20 Jul 1845, William, Creigh, -, -, -, -, -, -, -, -, -, "was received into the church and made his first Communion"; C, -, 19

1845, 28 Sep 1845, John P., Donelson, -, -, -, -, -, -, -, -, -, See Endnote 18, -, 19

1846, 28 Sep 1845, Joseph, Walter, George, Maria, 4 wks. , -, -, -, -, -, -, -, -, Matthews, 19

1847, 16 Oct 1845, Barbara Catharine, Shilling, Joachim, Frances, 22 Feb 184_*, -, -, -, Mary, Miller, -, -, *birthdate is 22 Feb 184[ink blot makes the last number illegible but it appears to be 1844], Shaffer, 19

1848, 14 Nov 1845, John, Carey, Joseph, Catharine, 29 May 1843, -, -, -, John H., Rohe[?], Maria, McCleary, -, -, 19

1849, 15 Nov 1845, John Jackson, Murray, Stephen, Agatha, Feb 1831, -, P, P, -, -, -, -, PB, -, 19

ST. MARY'S CATHOLIC CHURCH
HAGERSTOWN, MARYLAND, BAPTISMS:
Index, Bap Date, Child, Last Name, Father, Mother,
Birth Date, Code1, Code2, Code3,
1st Sponsor First, 1st Sponsor Last,
2nd Sponsor First, 2nd Sponsor Last, Location,
Notes, Maiden Name, Priest

1850, 15 Nov 1845, Martin Van Buren, Murray, Stephen, Agatha, 19 Mar 1839, -, P, P, -, -, -, -, PB, -, 19

1851, 15 Nov 1845, Mary Ann, Murray, Stephen, Agatha, 7 Dec 1840, -, P, P, -, -, -, -, PB, -, 19

1852, 16 Nov 1845, John, Forbeck, Carimirus, Eva, 11 Oct 1844, -, -, -, Baltis, Feidt, -, -, -, -, 19

1853, 16 Nov 1845, William, Whelan, James, Johanna, 25 May 1845, -, -, -, Thomas, Geleese, Mary, Kelly, -, Welsh, 19

1854, 16 Nov 1845, John, Burgoyne, -, -, 35 years, P, -, -, -, -, -, -, C; "an English Protestant", -, 19

1855, 16 Nov 1845, Sarah Wheeler, Garighty, James, Sarah, 1 Sep 1845, -, -, -, James, Lee, Sarah, Garighty, -, Garighty, 19

1856, 17 Nov 1845, John, Little, Patrick, Isabella, 18 Apr 1845, -, -, -, Conrad, Anthony, Margaret, McCosker, -, -, 19

1857, 22 Nov 1845, Jane, Shannon, Edward, Catharine, 31 Jul 1845, -, -, -, John, Haydon, Elizabeth, McCue, -, McGirr, 19

1858, 24 Nov 1845, Maurice, Dixon, John, -, 5 years , S, S, -, Catharine , Collier, -, -, "slaves of Mr. H. Bevans, -, 19

1859, 24 Nov 1845, Harret Agnes, Dixon, John, -, 5 months , S, S, -, Catharine , Collier, -, -, "slaves of Mr. H. Bevans, -, 19

1860, 26 Nov 1845, Matthew, Fagan, Richard, Phebe, 7 Nov 1845, -, -, -, Jacob, Peck, Eliza, Peck, -, -, 19

1861, 2 Dec 1845, William Edward, Gannon, Michael, Sarah Ann Caroline, 21 Aug 1845, -, -, -, H., Myers [the priest], Caroline, Hall, -, Murphy, 19

1862, 23 Dec 1845, Peter Henry, Creigh, William, Margaret, 5 Dec 1845, -, -, -, Henry, Myers [the priest], -, -, -, -, 19

1863, 27 Dec 1845, Eva, Hayet, John, Barbara, 2 Dec 1845, -, -, -, Eva, Forbeck, -, -, -, -, 19

1864, 28 Dec 1845, Catharine, Moriarty, James, Mary, 9 Dec 1845, -, -, -, John, McNamarcy, Mary, McNamarcy, -, -, 19

1865, 28 Dec 1845, Elizabeth, McCabe, Tevens [sic], Mary, 28 Dec 1845*, -, -, -, John, Brannon, Bridget, Murphy, * born at 4 o'clock, -, 19

1866, 28 Dec 1845, Nicholas, Renner, Ignatius, Mary, 24 Dec 1845, -, -, -, Hugo, Schuck, Eveline, Renner, -, -, 19

ST. MARY'S CATHOLIC CHURCH
HAGERSTOWN, MARYLAND, BAPTISMS:
Index, Bap Date, Child, Last Name, Father, Mother,
Birth Date, Code1, Code2, Code3,
1st Sponsor First, 1st Sponsor Last,
2nd Sponsor First, 2nd Sponsor Last, Location,
Notes, Maiden Name, Priest

1867, 28 Dec 1845, Charles, Schuck, Hugo, Catharine, 20 Nov 1845, -, -, -, William, Renner, Catharine, Gelespy, -, -, 19

1868, 21 Dec 1845, Ellen, Conokey, Patrick, Ann, 6 wks. , -, -, -, James, Schields, Bridget, Dayhoney, -, Dayhoney, 19

1869, 21 Dec 1845, Susan, Carrol, Patrick, Jane, 15 Feb 1844, -, -, -, James, Conelly, Eva, Forbeck, -, -, 19

1870, 15 Jan 1846, James, McGee, Patrick, Nancy, 12 yrs. , -, -, -, Honorius, Schircliff, -, -, -, -, 19

1871, 4 Jan 1846, Abraham, Harrison, Samuel, -, -, S, P, S, P, -, -, -, -, -, "all slaves of Mr. Dellinger, Protestant - all joined the church", -, 19

1872, 4 Jan 1846, Lawrence, Harrison, Samuel, -, -, S, P, S, P, -, -, -, -, -, "all slaves of Mr. Dellinger, Protestant - all joined the church", -, 19

1873, 4 Jan 1846, Henry, Harrison, Samuel, -, -, S, P, S, P, -, -, -, -, -, "all slaves of Mr. Dellinger, Protestant - all joined the church", -, 19

1874, 4 Jan 1846, Benjamin, Harrison, Samuel, -, -, S, P, S, P, -, -, -, -, -, "all slaves of Mr. Dellinger, Protestant - all joined the church", -, 19

1875, 4 Jan 1846, Amos, Harrison, Samuel, -, -, S, P, S, P, -, -, -, -, -, "all slaves of Mr. Dellinger, Protestant - all joined the church", -, 19

1876, 4 Jan 1846, Maria, Harrison, Samuel, -, -, S, P, S, P, -, -, -, -, -, "all slaves of Mr. Dellinger, Protestant - all joined the church", -, 19

1877, 4 Jan 1846, Catharine, Harrison, Samuel, -, -, S, P, S, P, -, -, -, -, -, "all slaves of Mr. Dellinger, Protestant - all joined the church", -, 19

1878, 4 Jan 1846, Mary, Harrison, Samuel, -, -, S, P, S, P, -, -, -, -, -, "all slaves of Mr. Dellinger, Protestant - all joined the church", -, 19

1879, 4 Jan 1846, Clara, Harrison, Samuel, -, -, S, P, S, P, -, -, -, -, -, "all slaves of Mr. Dellinger, Protestant - all joined the church", -, 19

**ST. MARY'S CATHOLIC CHURCH
HAGERSTOWN, MARYLAND, BAPTISMS:**
Index, Bap Date, Child, Last Name, Father, Mother,
Birth Date, Code1, Code2, Code3,
1st Sponsor First, 1st Sponsor Last,
2nd Sponsor First, 2nd Sponsor Last, Location,
Notes, Maiden Name, Priest

1880, 4 Jan 1846, Louisa, Harrison, Samuel, -, -, S, P, S, P, -, -, -, -, -, "all slaves of Mr. Dellinger, Protestant - all joined the church", -, 19

1881, 4 Jan 1846, James, Harrison, Samuel, -, -, S, P, S, P, -, -, -, -, -, "all slaves of Mr. Dellinger, Protestant - all joined the church", -, 19

1882, 5 Feb 1846, Ann Elizabeth, Tice, Daniel, Margaret, 6 mos. , -, -, -, Michael, Smith, May [Mary?] Ann, Smith, -, More, 19

1883, 5 Feb 1846, Adrian Ceolfrid, McCardle, Wilfrid D., Catharine, 29 Dec 1835, -, -, -, Ann, McCardle, -, -, -, Humbrickhouse, 19

1884, 15 Feb 1846, Margaret, -, -, Syrena , 3 mos. , PN, FB, -, FB, Cornelius, Bowie (Black), Eliza, Rhinehart (white), mother from Hancock, -, 19

1885, 16 Feb 1846, Sarah Ann, Coyle, Mark, [blank] *, 4 yrs. , -, -, -, Ann, McFadden, -, -, * in space for mother's name is written "his wife dead", -, 19

1886, 16 Feb 1846, Margaret Ann, McCartey, Barnay, Harriet, 20 Jan 1846, -, -, -, Levi, More, Levi (Mrs.), More [HB], -, Cutchall, 19

1887, 16 Feb 1846, Sarah Jane, Steele, John S., Ann, 25 yrs. , -, -, -, -, -, -, -, C, -, 19

1888, 16 Feb 1846, Sarah Jane, Gletner, Joseph, Sarah Jane, 14 Jan 1846, -, -, -, Jane, Mouse, -, -, The couple received their marriage contract., Steele, 19

1889, 4 Mar 1846, Sophia Janette, Hurley, James I., Sophia Antoinette, 15 Feb 1846, -, -, -, Michael, Smith, Catharine E., Smith, -, Smith , 19

1890, 20 Mar 1846, Mary Catharine, Gehr, Isaac, Cecelia, 7 Mar 1846, -, -, -, Catharine , Harrett, -, -, -, Harritt, 19

1891, 25 Mar 1846, Michael, Shields, James, Elizabeth, 22 Jan 1846, -, -, -, Margaret, Daughaney, -, -, -, Green, 19

1892, 25 Mar 1846, Mary Elizabeth, Ludders, Thomas, Catharine, 9 weeks, -, -, -, Mary, Gunshehan, -, -, -, McGinnis, 19

1893, 12 Apr 1846, William Henry, Bird, -, Emeline, -, B, S, PN, -, B, S, Harriet, Bird, -, -, -, -, 19

ST. MARY'S CATHOLIC CHURCH
HAGERSTOWN, MARYLAND, BAPTISMS:
Index, Bap Date, Child, Last Name, Father, Mother,
Birth Date, Code1, Code2, Code3,
1st Sponsor First, 1st Sponsor Last,
2nd Sponsor First, 2nd Sponsor Last, Location,
Notes, Maiden Name, Priest

1894, 11 Apr 1846, Catharine Laura, Tierny, -, -, 21 years, -, -, -, -, -, -, -, C; "(conditionally) and received her into the church - made her 1st communion on the following day. Easter Sunday", -, 19

1895, 13 Apr 1846, Elizabeth, Richards, -, -, -, -, -, -, -, -, -, -, See Endnote 19 , -, 19

1896, 15 Apr 1846, Joseph, Miller, -, Margaret, 24-Apr, PN, -, -, Thomas , Deehan, -, -, Margaret is "a white german girl"; no explanation for the baptimsal and birth date conflict, -, 19

1897, 17 Apr 1846, Edward, Davis, John G., Mary Ann, 22 Mar 1846, -, -, -, Daniel, O'Leary, Judy, Johnson, -, Shirley, 19

1898, 25 Apr 1846, Michael, Egan, Peter, Catharine, 8 Apr 1846, -, -, -, Mary, Egan, -, -, -, -, 19

1899, 27 Apr 1846, Ann, Matthews, John, Harriet, 9 Feb 1846, B, FB, FB, Mary Ann, Shircliff (white), -, -, -, -, 19

1900, 29 Apr 1846, Lucy Ann, Miller, -, -, 54 years, S, -, -, -, -, -, -, "never been baptized.", -, 19

1901, 29 Apr 1846, Lucy Ann, Miller, -, Lucy Ann, 14 years, S, -, -, -, -, -, -, "never been baptized."; Lucy Ann is the daughter of the above listed Lucy Ann, -, 19

1902, 30 Apr 1846, Margaret, Shane, Edward, Frances, 1 month, -, -, -, Lotitia, McIlhaney, -, -, -, -, 19

1903, 03 May 1846, Joseph , Clay [or Ginter if using mother's name], Francis, Charlotte, 09 Mar 1846, PN, -, -, Joseph, Messman, Maria Eva, Messman, -, Ginter, 19

1904, 17 May 1846, William Wallace, Cunningham, John, Margaret, 02 Apr 1846, -, -, -, John, Daley, Margaret, Clark, -, Halbert, 19

1905, 22 May 1846, Ann Maria, Swain, -, Nancy, 13 Mar 1846, -, -, S, -, -, -, -, PB; "twins"; mother is a slave of Henry Bevans, -, 19

1906, 22 May 1846, Charlotte, Swain, -, Nancy, 13 Mar 1846, -, -, S, -, -, -, -, PB; "twins"; mother is a slave of Henry Bevans, -, 19

1907, 24 May 1846, Terence, McCavoy, Patrick, Mary, 20 Apr 1846, -, -, -, Mary, McCavoy, John, O'Brien, -, Griffin, 19

1908, [no date], Henry , Diggs, Thomas, -, -, B, FB, -, -, -, -, -, Henry "of Thomas Diggs (Free) who died since.", -, 19

1909, 21 May 1846, Ellen Jane, Cover, John, Jane, 01 May 1846, -, -, -, Timothy, Cover, Ann, Murray, -, Daley, 19

ST. MARY'S CATHOLIC CHURCH
HAGERSTOWN, MARYLAND, BAPTISMS:
Index, Bap Date, Child, Last Name, Father, Mother,
Birth Date, Code1, Code2, Code3,
1st Sponsor First, 1st Sponsor Last,
2nd Sponsor First, 2nd Sponsor Last, Location,
Notes, Maiden Name, Priest

1910, 28 Jun 1846, Mary , May, James, Elizabeth, 3 years, PN, -, - , James, Cadden, Elizabeth, Cadden [HB], -, Whigfield , 19
1911, 28 Jun 1846, Simon , May, James, Elizabeth, 02 Jul 1845, PN, -, -, John, Hayden, Mrs., McQuickgan, -, Whigfield , 19
1912, 19 Jul 1846, Mary Elizabeth, Hook, James, Mary, 05 Oct 1842, -, -, -, Eliza, Rhinehart, -, -, -, Davy, 19
1913, 21 Jul 1846, Sarah Jane, Rooney, Bartholomew, Bridget, 05 Jul 1846, -, -, -, Margaret, Rooney, -, -, -, McGinnis, 19
1914, 22 Jul 1846, Teresa, McGraw, John, Maria, 17 Oct 1844*, -, -, -, Patrick , McGar, Rosa , Freeman, *birthdate reads 17 [or 19] Oct 1844, -, 19
1915, 29 Jul 1846, Susanna, Snyder, Henry, Elizabeth, 13 Jan 1846, -, -, -, Leonard More, More, Mary Ward, Ward, -, Reid, 19
1916, 29 Jul 1846, Martha Ellen, Sweeney, Francis, Ann, 30 Jan 1846, -, -, -, Peter , MacCoskey, Sophia , Mouse, -, Miller, 19
1917, 12 Aug 1846, Mary Virginia Seaton, Tierney, John, Laura C., 11-Jul, -, -, -, Edward, Tierney, Mary or Elizabeth *, Kelly, * "Mary" crossed out and "Elizabeth" written over in pencil, Kershner, 19
1918, 13 Aug 1846, Anna Virginia, McCardle, Simon W., Belinda, 13 May 1846, -, -, -, Eliza F. , Stake, -, -, -, Weaver, 19
1919, 14 Aug 1846, Mary Charlotte, Goddard, Richard, Mary, 31 Jul 1845, -, -, -, Margaret , McCusker, -, -, -, Berry, 19
1920, 15 Aug 1846, Anna Margaret, Gardener, George, Magdalen, 5 weeks , -, -, -, Anna Margaret , Feidt, -, -, -, -, 19
1921, 18 Aug 1846, Helen Jenette, Smith, Otho, Jenette, 07 Aug 1839, -, -, -, Catharine , Smith, Joseph , Smith, mother is deceased; both sponsors are described as "of M. Smith" - perhaps they were the children of M. Smith, Blackford , 41
1922, 23 Aug 1846, John, Conelly, Patrick, Caroline, 28 Apr 1846, -, -, -, Patrick , Gradey, Mary , Henley, -, Hartley, 19
1923, 23 Aug 1846, Daniel, McGinnis, Daniel, Mary, 16 Aug 1846, -, -, -, John , Fallon, Frances , Dermody, -, Hamilton, 19
1924, 23 Aug 1846, Ellen, McGinnis, Daniel, Mary, [blank], -, -, -, John , Dermody, Hannah , Dermody, -, Hamilton, 19
1925, 23 Aug 1846, Michael, Norton, Timothy, Honora, 13 Jun 1846, -, -, -, Michale , Laikin, Mary , Laikin, -, McLaughlin, 19

ST. MARY'S CATHOLIC CHURCH
HAGERSTOWN, MARYLAND, BAPTISMS:
Index, Bap Date, Child, Last Name, Father, Mother,
Birth Date, Code1, Code2, Code3,
1st Sponsor First, 1st Sponsor Last,
2nd Sponsor First, 2nd Sponsor Last, Location,
Notes, Maiden Name, Priest

1377, 27 Apr 1841, Henricus Jacobus, Pulmann, Frederici, Catharinae, 24 Jan 1841, -, -, -, Jacobus, Sneider, -, -, -, -, 16

1378, 27 Apr 1841, Flora M., Zieler, Adami, Elisabeth, 19 Apr 1841, -, -, -, Flora, Klüh, -, -, -, -, 16

1379, 27 Apr 1841, Elisabeth, Götz, Antonii, Mariae Annae, 27 Feb 1841, -, -, -, Elisabeth, Zieler, -, -, -, -, 16

1380, 29 Apr 1841, Johanna, Tigh, Jacobi, Birgittae, 29 Apr 1841, -, -, -, Richardus, Power, Maria, McDonnell, -, -, 16

1381, 3 May 1841, Catharina Geneva, Stake, Eliae, Ellen, 13 Apr 1841, -, -, -, Michael, Guth, Francisca, McIlhenny, -, -, 16

1382, 3 May 1841, Sara Adelaidis, Meats [or Moats], Jeremiae, Margaretae, 9 Mar 1841, -, -, -, Maria, Donnelly, -, -, -, -, 16

1383, 9 May 1841, Anna Maria, Gauker, Joannis, Ellen, 13 Feb 1841, -, -, -, Margareta, Meisonner, -, -, -, -, 16

1384, 9 May 1841, Joannes Upton, Clemens , Alexandre, Mathildis, 13 Feb 1840, -, -, -, M. [Michael?], Guth, Catharina, Shorter, -, -, 16

1385, 9 May 1841, Joannes W., Clarke, Guillelmi, Margaretae, 30 Jan 1841, -, -, -, William, McLane, Sara, McLane, -, -, 16

1386, 10 May 1841, Maria, Smith, Joachim, Anastasiae, 31 Dec 1840, -, -, -, Catharina, Smith, -, -, -, -, 16

1387, 9 May 1841, Jacobus, Smith, -, Marie, 18 Feb 1838, PN, -, -, Jacobus, McLaughlin, Sara, McLaughlin, -, -, 16

1388, 10 May 1841, Joannes Thomas, Tice, Danielis, Margaretae, 28 Mar 1841, -, -, -, Michael , Smith, Anna, Moore, -, -, 16

1389, 12 May 1841, Daniel , Cronley, Jacobi, Mariae, 5 May 1841, -, -, -, Joannes, Man , Johanna, Connelly, -, -, 16

1390, 15 May 1841, Joannes, Monaghan, Joannis, Catharinae, 1 May 1841, -, -, -, Thomas, Mulharon, Maria, Riley, -, -, 16

1391, 15 May 1841, Petrus, Planaet [or Plunke or Planke], Patricii, Catharinae, 10 May 1841, -, -, -, Thomas, Dunbar, Catharina, Kilroy, -, -, 16

1392, 23 May 1841, Josephus, Doyle, Adami, Rebeccae, 24 Mar 1841, -, -, -, Elisabeth, Shirley, -, -, -, -, 16

1393, 27 May 1841, Elisabeth Johanna, Maus, -, Margaretae, 14 Feb 1841, PN, -, -, Johanna, Corbett, -, -, -, -, 16

ST. MARY'S CATHOLIC CHURCH
HAGERSTOWN, MARYLAND, BAPTISMS:
Index, Bap Date, Child, Last Name, Father, Mother,
Birth Date, Code1, Code2, Code3,
1st Sponsor First, 1st Sponsor Last,
2nd Sponsor First, 2nd Sponsor Last, Location,
Notes, Maiden Name, Priest

1394, 29 May 1841, Michael, Degnan, Michaelis, Elisabeth, 23 Feb 1841, -, -, -, Bernardus, Quin, Maria, Horn, -, -, 16

1395, 30 May 1841, Guillelmus, Meyer, Joannis, Therisae, 19 Oct 1841 , -, -, -, Matheus, Mütter, -, -, -, -, 16

1396, 31 May 1841, Catharina, Lee, Roberti, Caeciliae, 17 Dec 1841*, -, -, -, Catharina, Craig, -, -, *birthdate is not compatible with baptismal date, -, 16

1397, 2 Jun 1841, Dionysius, Witney, Patricii, Johannae, 10 Aug 1840, -, -, -, Michael, Quin, Elisabeth, Degnan, -, -, 16

1398, 3 Jun 1841, Edwardus, Shirran, Edwardi, Susannae, 17 May 1841, -, -, -, Jacobus, Gainer, Maria, Dolan, -, -, 16

1399, 4 Jun 1841, Carolus, Ross [or Rose], Arthur , Rosae Annae, 30 Apr 1841, -, -, -, Carolus, Brady, Maria, Riley, -, -, 16

1400, 9 Jun 1841, Jacobus, McKenna, Hugonis, Mariae, 29 May 1841, -, -, -, Petrus, McClosky, Anna, McFadden, -, -, 16

1401, 10 Jun 1841, John Thomas, Brannon, Joannis, [blank], 22 Apr 1841, -, -, -, Jacobus, McGrow, Elisabeth, Dant, -, -, 16

1402, 19 Jun 1841, Jacobus, Britt, Jacobi, Mariae, 16 Jun 1841, -, -, -, Matheus, Flahavan, Anna, Welsh, -, -, 16

1403, 19 Jun 1841, Jacobus, Whealan, Bernardi, Annae, 29 May 1841, -, -, -, Henricus , Moran, Catharina, Bohan, -, -, 16

1404, 19 Jun 1841, Joannes, Raynolds, Patricii, Birgittae, 16 Jun 1841, -, -, -, Michael, Madden, Hanora, Madden, -, -, 16

1405, 20 Jun 1841, Elisabeth, Rodger, Patricii, Cathainae, 6 Jun 1841, -, -, -, Christophorus, Russel, Johanna, Russel, -, -, 16

1406, 20 Jun 1841, Maria , Garoghty, Patricii, Margaretae, 26 May 1841, -, -, -, Guillelmus, Morgan, Maria, Morgan, -, -, 16

1407, 20 Jun 1841, Richardus, Crovan, Richardi, Marianae, 21 Apr 1841, -, -, -, N., Galley, Birgitta, Galley, -, -, 16

1408, 20 Jun 1841, Carolus, Harkins, Joannis, Catharinae, 12 Jun 1841, -, -, -, Joannes, Harkins, Anna, Mulharon, -, -, 16

1409, 20 Jun 1841, Anna , McCauley, Caroli, Annae, 16 May 1841, -, -, -, Joannes, McKann, Catharina, McLaughlin, -, -, 16

1410, 20 Jun 1841, Maria, Read, Antonii, Catharinae, 7 Jun 1841, -, -, -, Thomas, Lovell, Anna, McKneff, -, -, 16

1411, 20 Jun 1841, Thomas, Green, Jacobi, Catharinae, 14 Jun 1841, -, -, -, Joannes, Bulger, Anna, Munday, -, -, 16

ST. MARY'S CATHOLIC CHURCH
HAGERSTOWN, MARYLAND, BAPTISMS:
Index, Bap Date, Child, Last Name, Father, Mother,
Birth Date, Code1, Code2, Code3,
1st Sponsor First, 1st Sponsor Last,
2nd Sponsor First, 2nd Sponsor Last, Location,
Notes, Maiden Name, Priest

1926, 24 Aug 1846, Mary Eliza Virginia, Barnett, Henry, Catharine, 14 Aug 1846, -, -, -, Eliza , Taney "Mother of Catherine", -, -, PB, Taney, 19

1927, 11 Aug 1846, Margaret, Bluecoat, Andrew, Margaret, 16 Jul 1846, -, -, -, Rosetta , Failinger, -, -, -, Kavelin [or Ravelin], 19

1928, 11 Aug 1846, Margaret Elizabeth, Gallagher, Michael, Bridget, 12 Jul 1846, -, -, -, William , Makes, Rebecca , Dugan, -, - , 19

1929, 20 Sep 1846, Jerome, Wise, Peter, Mary Ann, 29 Nov 1845, -, -, -, Emelia , Murray, James D. , Hook, -, Norris, 19

1930, 24 Sep 1846, Peter, McKenney, Hugh, Mary, 05 Aug 1846, - , -, -, Levi , More, Jane , Mouse, -, -, 19

1931, 17 Oct 1846, Elizabeth, Butz, Jacob, Margaret Elizabeth, 24 Aug 1846, -, -, -, H., Myers, -, -, -, Shafer, 19

1932, 25 Oct 1846, John Edward, Rodgers, Joseph, Maria, 12 Aug 1846, -, -, -, Hugh , Murphey, Rosanna , McCabe, -, Artison, 19

1933, 11 Nov 1846, Mary Ann, Cain, Denis S. [?], Lavinia, 24 Sep 1846, -, -, -, Levi , More, Catharine , More, -, Mills, 19

1934, 17 Nov 1846, Michael, Furgerson, James, Mary, 27 Oct 1846, -, -, -, Mary , Mehan, -, -, -, Hughs, 19

1935, 17 Nov 1846, Edward Ross, Murray, Laurence, Sarah, 13 Sep 1846, -, -, -, Mary , Furgerson, -, -, -, Hawkens, 19

1936, 17 Nov 1846, James Edward, Mehan, Patrick, Mary, 13 Sep 1846, -, -, -, Anthony , Hughs, -, -, -, Hubart, 19

1937, 18 Nov 1846, John, McQuichan, Terence, Mary, 07 Oct 1846, -, -, -, Francis , Flannagan, Eliza , McMahan, -, -, 19

1938, 18 Nov 1846, William Henry, Flannagan, Francis, Mary Ann, 25 Sep 1846, -, -, -, Jeremiah , Nolan, Rachel, Bell, -, -, 19

1939, 18 Nov 1846, Ignatius, Leuxner, Philip, Dorothea, 07 Jan 1835* , -, -, -, Ignatius , Renner, -, -, *birthdate reads 07 Jan 1835 , -, 19

1940, 18 Nov 1846, John, Brannan, Patrick, Bridget, 01 Sep 1846, -, -, -, Charles , Brady, Rosa , Sweeney, -, -, 19

1941, 18 Nov 1846, Susanna, Clay, Jacob, Flora, 28 Jul 1846, -, -, - , Susan , Francey, -, -, -, 19

ST. MARY'S CATHOLIC CHURCH
HAGERSTOWN, MARYLAND, BAPTISMS:
Index, Bap Date, Child, Last Name, Father, Mother,
Birth Date, Code1, Code2, Code3,
1st Sponsor First, 1st Sponsor Last,
2nd Sponsor First, 2nd Sponsor Last, Location,
Notes, Maiden Name, Priest

1942, 18 Nov 1846, Harriet Ann , Matthews, John, Harriet , 09 Feb 1846, FB, -, -, Mary Ann , Shircliff, -, -, PB; "The ceremonies of Baptism were supplied"; parents are married, -, 19

1943, 10 Dec 1846, Jane, Dignan, Michael, Elizabeth, 11 Jul 1846, -, -, -, Joseph , Carey, Margaret , Creigh, -, Deacon, 19

1944, 10 Dec 1846, Mary Elizabeth, Rohe, John Henry, Ann, 20 Sep 1846, -, -, -, Vesley , Volkey, Mary Elizabeth , Robe?, -, Wyland, 19

1945, 09 Dec 1846, Edward Thomas , Clemens, Charles, Matilda , 3 months, B, S, S, Margaret , McCusker, -, -, parents are married and slaves of James White near Williamsport, -, 19

1946, 22 Dec 1846, Frederick Charles, Doyle, William, Margaret, 24 Nov 1835 , -, -, -, Henry , Myers, -, -, -, Byers, 19

1947, 22 Dec 1846, Margaret, Doyle, Williams, Margaret, 18 Oct 1838 , -, -, -, Cath. (Miss), Gilmeyer, -, -, -, Byers, 19

1948, 22 Dec 1846, Louisa Harriet, Doyle, William, Margaret, 14 Apr 1840, -, -, -, Mary S. (Miss), Maguire, -, -, -, Byers, 19

1949, 25 Dec 1846, George, McCann *, John, Rosanna, 15 Sep 1846, -, -, -, Joseph , Smith, Margaret , Shervin, * [M'han crossed out in different ink color], Shervin, 19

1950, 31 Dec 1846, John, Garvey, Michael, Margaret, 07 Dec 1846, -, -, -, Francis , McNamee, Mary , McQuickgan, -, Conner, 19

1951, 21 Jan 1847, Thomas, Reynolds, Sylvester, Ann, 27 Oct 1846, -, -, -, John, Kelly, Mary , Moore [or Moine], -, Tyler, 19

1952, 23 Jan 1847, Margaret Jane, Prior, Hugh, Rosa, 15 Jan 1847, -, -, -, Thomas , Keenan, Jane , Keenan, -, Prior, 19

1953, 20 Feb 1847, Robert, Terry, Robert, Bridget, 04 Feb 1847, -, -, -, Ann , McFadden, -, -, -, Farrel, 19

1954, 02 Mar 1847, Michael Tilgman, Furlong, William, Susan, 7 years, -, -, -, James , Furlong, Jane , Mouse, -, Cletner, 19

1955, 02 Mar 1847, Ann Elizabeth, Bear, Isaac, Ann, 01 Sep 1846, -, -, -, Eliza (Miss), Kelly, -, -, -, Donohoe, 19

1956, 14 Mar 1847, Susan, Myers, John, Teresa, 07 Jan 1846, -, -, - , Mary , Freeze, -, -, -, Miller, 19

1957, 21 Mar 1847, Ellen Virginia, Stekenius, Frederick, Amelia, 08 Mar 1847, -, -, -, Eliza (Mrs.), Rinehart, -, -, -, -, 19

ST. MARY'S CATHOLIC CHURCH
HAGERSTOWN, MARYLAND, BAPTISMS:
Index, Bap Date, Child, Last Name, Father, Mother,
Birth Date, Code1, Code2, Code3,
1st Sponsor First, 1st Sponsor Last,
2nd Sponsor First, 2nd Sponsor Last, Location,
Notes, Maiden Name, Priest

1958, 23 Mar 1847, Anna Catharine, Weaver, Philip D., Mary Ann, 24 Jan 1847, -, -, -, Bridget , McMullan, -, -, -, McMullan, 19

1959, 24 Mar 1847, Louisa, Cremer, Henry, Mary, 18 Mar 1847, -, -, -, Elizabeth (Mrs.), Shirley, -, -, -, Weaver, 19

1960, 11 Apr 1847, Charles Edward, Kelly, Patrick, Sarah, 02 Apr 1847, -, -, -, Charles , McIntire, Frances , McIntire, -, Mooney, 19

1961, 11 Apr 1847, Catharine, Egle, George, Cunegunda , 11 Feb 1847, -, -, -, John, Eck, Catharine , Eck, -, Seifert, 19

1962, 22 Apr 1847, Anna, Welch, Peter, Rosa, 13 Apr 1847, -, -, -, Bridget, Brannan, -, -, -, -, 19

1963, 07 Jul 1847, Jacob Caspar, Bromgart, Caspar, Mary Ellen, 25 Sep 1846, -, -, -, Sarah, Kelly, -, -, -, Renner, 19

1964, 09 Jul 1847, Jacob, Diggs, Solomon, Leva [or Lena], 10 Oct 1845, -, -, -, Cath., Shorter, -, -, -, Johnson , 19

1965, 25 Apr 1847, James Monroe, Shipley, Richard, Elizabeth, 28 Oct 1846, -, -, -, Joseph, Bevans, Mary, Bevans, Fifteen Mile Creek, Allegany Co., -, 19

1966, 25 Apr 1847, James Walter, McAtee, Jonathan, Cassandra, 7 Jan 1847, -, -, -, Patrick, McCadden, Mary, Hughes, Fifteen Mile Creek, -, 19

1967, 13 May 1847, William Francis, Geleese, Thomas, Catharine, 3 May 1847, -, -, -, John, Daley, Mary C., Clarke, Hancock, Brady, 19

1968, 14 May 1847, George Valentine, Miller, Valentine, Margaret, 9 May 1847, -, -, -, Frederick, Stekenius [sic], -, -, Hancock, Weaver, 19

1969, 14 May 1847, Joseph, -, -, Rachel Ann, 3 months, B, PN, S, -, S, William, Dorsey, [Unnamed] "Slave of E. Taney", -, Hancock; mother is "slave of Mr. E. Taney", -, 19

1970, 15 May 1847, Ellen Alice, Clarke, Charles, Margaret, 3 May 1847, -, -, -, Miss Mary E., Clingam, -, -, Hancock, Gallagher, 19

1971, 16 May 1847, Michael, Forbeck, Casimirus, Eva, 3 weeks, -, -, -, Michael, Gardner, -, -, Hancock, -, 19

1972, 16 May 1847, Casimirus, Feidt, Adam, Mary, 26 Jan 1847, -, -, -, Casimirus, Forbeck, -, -, Hancock, Norris, 19

1973, 16 May 1847, Thomas, Whelan, James, Judith, 4 Mar 1847, -, -, -, John, Daley, [blank], Kelley, Hancock, Welch, 19

ST. MARY'S CATHOLIC CHURCH
HAGERSTOWN, MARYLAND, BAPTISMS:
Index, Bap Date, Child, Last Name, Father, Mother,
Birth Date, Code1, Code2, Code3,
1st Sponsor First, 1st Sponsor Last,
2nd Sponsor First, 2nd Sponsor Last, Location,
Notes, Maiden Name, Priest

1974, 16 May 1847, Ellenora Jane, Carroll, Patrick, Jane, 24 Jan 1847, -, -, -, Judith, Whelan, -, -, Hancock, -, 19

1975, 18 May 1847, Anna Margaret, Swope, Caspar, Dorothea, 4 Aug 1846, -, -, -, Margaret , Blurock, -, -, Clear Spring, Gabler, 19

1976, [blank], Maria Eva, Shiremon, -, Emelia, 18 May 1846, PN, -, -, Maria Eva, Messman, -, -, -, -, 19

1977, 27 May 1847, Julianna, Fagan, Richard, Phebe, 28 Feb 1847, -, -, -, Peter, McCloskey, Catharine, Garbin [or Garlin], Clear Spring, O'Brian, 19

1978, 29 May 1847, George William, Lambright, William, Mary, 5 May 1847*, -, -, -, Joseph, Bevans, Mary, Bevans, Fifteen Mile Creek; *See Endnote 20 , Barry, 19

1979, 30 May 1847, Bridget, Moriartey, James, Mary, 4 wks. Ago, -, -, -, Maria, Cready, -, -, Fifteen Mile Creek, -, 19

1980, 30 May 1847, Mary Ellen, Wi[?]nkelman, Henry, Elizabeth, 10 Jun 1846, -, -, -, Bernard   , Wi[?]nkelman, Margaret, McNamara, Fifteen Mile Creek; PB, -, 19

1981, 31 May 1847, James Dallas, Ottman, John, Frances E.C. [or E.E.], 29 Apr 1847, -, -, -, Lethey Ann, Jarboe, -, -, Hancock, Jarboe, 19

1982, 15 Jun 1847, Sylvester, Smith, -, Anaslusia, 14 Dec 1846, PN, -, FB, Sarah, Hemsley, -, -, -, -, 19

1983, 19 Jun 1847, Mary Ann, Carey, Joseph, Catharine, 15 Jun 1846, -, -, -, W., Creigh, Betty, Dignan, Clear Spring, -, 19

1984, 20 Jun 1847, David Wilson, Daley, John, Resiah, 25 May 1847, -, -, -, Thomas, Bevans, Ellen A., Lynch, Hancock, Rowland, 19

1985, 1 Jan 1847, Andrew, Renner, Valentine, Barbara, 12 Feb 1846, -, -, -, Andrew, Regel [?], Margaret, Regle [?], -, -, 19

1986, 27 Jun 1847, Thomas, Cready, Patrick, Catharine, 1 Jun 1847, -, -, -, William, McCready, Bridget, Hughes, Fifteen Mile Creek, -, 19

1987, 27 Jun 1847, Aloysius, Renner, Syriacus, Aloysia Ernest, 22 May 1847, -, -, -, Michael, Gardner, Caroline, Renner, Fifteen Mile Creek near Washington Co., -, 19

ST. MARY'S CATHOLIC CHURCH
HAGERSTOWN, MARYLAND, BAPTISMS:
Index, Bap Date, Child, Last Name, Father, Mother,
Birth Date, Code1, Code2, Code3,
1st Sponsor First, 1st Sponsor Last,
2nd Sponsor First, 2nd Sponsor Last, Location,
Notes, Maiden Name, Priest

1988, 27 Jun 1847, Aloysia Walburg, Renner, Ignatius, Mary Anna, 16 Jul 1847, -, -, -, Syriacus, Renner, Catharine, Shue, Fifteen Mile Creek near Washington Co., Fultz, 19

1989, 18 Jul 1847, Bernard, Conelly, James, Barbara, 18 May 1847, -, -, -, John, Daley, Eliza M., Clarke, Hancock, Gross, 19

1990, 18 Jul 1847, John, Feidt, Joseph, Catharine, 6 May 1847, -, -, -, John , Feidt, Ann, Murray, Hancock, Hagel, 19

1991, 18 Jul 1847, Margaret, Murray, Thomas, Mary, 7 Jul 1847, -, -, -, James, Danheney, Elizabeth, Shields, Hancock, Lynch, 19

1992, 25 Jul 1847, James R. Polk, Nolan, Michael, Ellen, 25 Jan 1847, -, -, -, Daniel, McGinnis, Mary, Scanlin, Hancock, -, 19

1993, 25 Jul 1847, Mary, Kerkert, George, Elizabeth, 22 Jun 1847, -, -, -, James, Cadden, Mary, McGinnis, Hancock, -, 19

1994, 25 Jul 1847, Ellenora Jane, Farrell, Thomas, Judith, 2 May 1847, -, -, -, Laurence, Cosgrove, Margaret, Bannan, Hancock, -, 19

1995, 25 Jul 1847, James Herbert, Doyle, James, Elizabeth, 30 Feb 1847, -, -, -, Hugh, Egan, Catharine, Gelespey, Washington Co.. near Fifteen Mile Creek, -, 19

1996, 25 Jul 1847, Rosa, Doyle, James, Elizabeth, [blank], -, -, -, Thomas, McCavoy, Jane, McCavoy, Washington Co. near Fifteen Mile Creek, -, 19

1997, 11 Aug 1847, Adam, Moody, William, Maria, 3 wks. Ago, PN, FB, S, Bridget, Gallagher ** , -, -, Clear Spring. **described as "white", i.e., not Black; See Endnote 21, Smith, 19

1998, [blank], Margaret, -, Jortue [sic], Anastasia, 7 weeks, -, S, S, Catharine, Drennen*, -, -, * described as "white", i.e., not Black; Clear Spring. See Endnote 22, -, 19

1999, 29 Aug 1847, Mary, McCartey, Barnay, Harriet, 10 Jun 1847, -, -, -, Levi, Moore, Mary, Ward, Indian Spring, -, 19

2000, 29 Aug 1847, Francis, Curley, Patrick, Catharine, 15 Jun 1847, -, -, -, Michael, Doutel, Ann, McFadden, Parkhead, Lynch, 19

2001, 30 Aug 1847, James William Taylor, Adams, Amos, Catharine, 2 Dec 1846, -, -, -, John, Stonebraker, -, -, Clear Spring, Clarke, 19

ST. MARY'S CATHOLIC CHURCH
HAGERSTOWN, MARYLAND, BAPTISMS:
Index, Bap Date, Child, Last Name, Father, Mother,
Birth Date, Code1, Code2, Code3,
1st Sponsor First, 1st Sponsor Last,
2nd Sponsor First, 2nd Sponsor Last, Location,
Notes, Maiden Name, Priest

2002, 30 Aug 1847, Margaret, Adams, Amos, Catharine, 6 Sep 1844, -, -, -, Mary Ann, Nicodemus, -, -, Clear Spring, Clarke, 19

2003, 5 Sep 1847, Joseph Peter, Shilling, Joachim, Francisca, 14 Oct 1846, -, -, -, Matthew, Miller, -, -, Hagerstown, Shaffer, 19

2004, 9 Sep 1847, Jacob Peter, Gauger, Joseph, Julian, 26 Jul 1847, -, -, -, Augustine, Coyle, Mary, Coyle, Cavetown, Wyman, 19

2005, 9 Sep 1847, Mary Mandilla Catharine, Gauger, David, Sophia, 17 Oct 1842, -, -, -, Margaret, Misener, -, -, Cavetown, Barkdol, 19

2006, 18 Sep 1847, Mary Jane, Feidt, -, -, 18 years, P, -, -, -, -, -, -, Hancock. Sister of Catharine Lucinda Norris. , -, 19

2007, 18 Sep 1847, Catharine Lucinda, Norris, -, -, 16 years, P, -, -, -, -, -, -, Hancock. Sister of Mary Jane Feidt. , -, 19

2008, 18 Sep 1847, Charles Albert, Little, Patrick, Isabella, 28 May 1847, -, -, -, Patrick, Morissey, Catharine, Clarke, Hancock, Dugan, 19

2009, 13 Oct 1847, Charlotte Eugenia, Allen, James, Charlotte, 19 Nov 1846, -, P, P, Ellen, Stake, -, -, Williamsport, Ensmenger, 19

2010, 13 Oct 1847, Clarenda Jane, Allen, James, Charlotte, 7 months, -, P, P, Mary, Lauber, -, -, Williamsport, Ensmenger, 19

2011, 13 Oct 1847, Jeremias, Meade, Jeremias, Margaret, 4 weeks, -, -, -, Mary S., Oliver, -, -, Williamsport, -, 19

2012, 24 Oct 1847, Thomas, Noeton [or Nocton], Timothy, Honora, 18 Sep 1847, -, -, -, Daniel, McNamara, Henrietta, Bevans, Fifteen Mile Creek. Beside Henrietta Bevans name is written "dead" in a different color of ink, McLaughlin, 19

2013, 24 Oct 1847, James, Cosgrove, Lawrence, Teresa, 30 Sep 1847, -, -, -, Hugh, Phillips, Honora, Fallon, Fifteen Mile Creek, Cosgrove [sic], 19

2014, 24 Oct 1847, Jacob, France, John, Susanna, two wks. ago, -, -, -, Jacob, Clay, -, -, Fifteen Mile Creek, Sunding, 19

2015, 25 Oct 1847, Mary Anna, Hughes, Anthony, Mary, 3 Sep 1847, -, -, -, Cornelias, Monahan, Catharine, Gready, Fifteen Mile Creek, Brogan, 19

2016, 25 Oct 1847, Henry William, Brinkman, William, Maria Sophia, 15 Jul 1847, -, -, -, William, Bevans, Henrietta, Bevans,

ST. MARY'S CATHOLIC CHURCH
HAGERSTOWN, MARYLAND, BAPTISMS:
Index, Bap Date, Child, Last Name, Father, Mother,
Birth Date, Code1, Code2, Code3,
1st Sponsor First, 1st Sponsor Last,
2nd Sponsor First, 2nd Sponsor Last, Location,
Notes, Maiden Name, Priest

Fifteen Mile Creek. Beside both of the sponsors' names is written "dead" in a different color of ink., Peters, 19

2017, 27 Oct 1847, John, Clay, Jacob, Flora, a few months, -, -, -, Mrs., Brady, -, -, Fifteen Mile Creek, -, 19

2018, 27 Oct 1847, John, Sweeney, John, Catharine, 27 ___ 1847*, -, -, -, Thomas, McCue, -, -, Fifteen Mile Creek; *birthdate month is blank, O'Brian, 19

2019, 11 Nov 1847, Margaret, Nerman, -, Elizabeth, 4 Nov 1846, PN, -, -, Margaret, Regel, -, -, Hagerstown. "said to be Caspar's Swope child", -, 19

2020, 6 Dec 1847, Anna Rebecca, Zinkant, Andrew, Catharine, 7 Oct 1847, -, -, -, Josephina, Schober, -, -, Hagerstown, Metzler, 19

2021, 8 Dec 1847, James Summerille, Cremer, Jonathan H., Mary, 5 years, -, -, -, James, McGonigle, -, -, Hagerstown, -, 19

2022, 8 Dec 1847, Mary Monterey, Cremer, Jonathan H., Mary, 26 Oct 1847, -, -, -, Sarah, Carr, -, -, Hagerstown, -, 19

2023, 12 Dec 1847, Anna, Dorsey, -, Mary, [blank], PN, B, -, S, Mary Ellen, Taney, -, -, Hancock. Mother is "a slave belonging to Ethelbert Taney.", -, 19

2024, 30 Dec 1847, Mary Ann, Moore, Ulton, Elizabeth, 29 Oct 1847, -, -, -, Miss Ann, Bevans, -, -, Parkhead, Myers, 19

2025, 8 Jan 1848, Praxedes [?], Moore, James, Mary Jane, 12 Dec 1847, -, -, -, Levi, Moore, Susan, Logan, Indian Spring, Logan, 19

2026, 8 Jan 1848, John Daniel, Higgs, John, Margaret, 20 Aug 1847, -, -, -, Denis, Cain, Mary, Corbett, Indian Spring, Mouse, 19

2027, 24 Jan 1848, Philip, Snyder, Henry, Elizabeth, -, -, -, -, -, -, -, -, this entry crossed out, Read [or Reed], 19

2028, 9 Jan 1848, Thomas Edward William, McCordel, Wilfred, Catharine, 7 Oct 1847, -, -, -, Thomas C., McCordel, Mercy, May, Hagerstown, Humerickhouse, 19

2029, 30 Jan 1848, Hugh, McCann, John, Ann, 12 Jan 1848, -, -, -, Hugh, Murphey, Elizabeth, Dignan, Clear Spring, Quin, 19

2030, 28 Feb 1848, David Albertus, Barnet, Henry S., Catharine, -, -, -, -, -, -, -, -, entire entry crossed out, Taney, 19

2031, 21 Feb 1848, William , Knave, Jacob, [blank], 3 years, -, -, -, Sarah, McCusker, -, -, "Jacob Knave deceased". Williamsport, -, 19

ST. MARY'S CATHOLIC CHURCH
HAGERSTOWN, MARYLAND, BAPTISMS:
Index, Bap Date, Child, Last Name, Father, Mother,
Birth Date, Code1, Code2, Code3,
1st Sponsor First, 1st Sponsor Last,
2nd Sponsor First, 2nd Sponsor Last, Location,
Notes, Maiden Name, Priest

2032, 12 Feb 1848, John Patrick, Sheehan, Edward, Frances, 24 Jan 1848, -, -, -, Latitia, McIlhenney, -, -, Williamsport, McIlhenney, 19

2033, 28 Feb 1848, David Albertus, Barnet, Henry S., Catharine, 8 Feb 1848, -, -, -, Amelia, Murray, -, -, Hancock, Taney, 19

2034, 11 Mar 1848, Mary Ellen, Murphey, William, Margaret, 8 Mar 1848, -, -, -, Mary, Bradey, -, -, Fifteen Mile Creek, Dolan, 19

2035, 13 Mar 1848, Margaret, Trunpour [Trumpower?], George, Mary, 6 Oct 1847, -, -, -, Isaac, Moore, Anna, Martin, Indian Spring, -, 19

2036, 13 Mar 1848, Ann Jane, Shedrick, Michael, Sophia, 11 Dec 1847, -, -, -, Loretta, Martin, David, Marten, Indian Spring, Mouse, 19

2037, 13 Mar 1848, Martha Ann, McClain, James, Clarissa, 27 Feb 1848, -, -, -, Rachel Ann, McClain, -, -, Williamsport, Medcalf, 19

2038, 31 Mar 1848, Edward, Gillmeyer, Sebastian, Mary Elizabeth, 18 Mar 1848, -, -, -, H., Myers, Cecilia, Gillmeyer, Hagerstown, Maguire, 19

2039, 12 Apr 1848, Rosanna, Hannan, Dominick, Julia, 30 Mar 1848, -, -, -, John, Traner, Rosanna, Traner, See Endnote 23, Maguire, 19

2040, 16 Apr 1848, John Henry, Bevans, John, Margaret, 1 Apr 1848, -, -, -, Eliza, Higgins, -, -, See Endnote 24, Catlett, 19

2041, 17 Apr 1848, Catharine Josephina, Cain, Dennis, Lavinia, 19 Mar 1848, -, -, -, Miss Ann, Bevans, -, -, Indian Spring, Mills, 19

2042, 17 Apr 1848, Philip, Snyder, Henry, Elizabeth, 24 Jan 1848, -, -, -, Jacob, Peck, Margaret, England, Indian Spring, Reed, 19

2043, 23 Apr 1848, Joseph, Waner, Michael, Mary, 16 Feb 1848, -, -, -, George, Walder, Maria, Walder, Hagerstown, -, 19

2044, Apr 1848*, [blank], Truman, John, -, -, -, B, -, -, -, -, -, Child has "died since." Hagerstown; * baptismal date could be in April or May, -, 19

2045, 7 May 1848*, Henry, McCartney, Edward, Catharine, 14 Feb 1848, -, -, -, John, McGonigal, Margaret, McGonigal, Hagerstown; * "May" is not written in here but the birth date is consistant with the entry being in May, McLaughlin, 19

ST. MARY'S CATHOLIC CHURCH
HAGERSTOWN, MARYLAND, BAPTISMS:
Index, Bap Date, Child, Last Name, Father, Mother,
Birth Date, Code1, Code2, Code3,
1st Sponsor First, 1st Sponsor Last,
2nd Sponsor First, 2nd Sponsor Last, Location,
Notes, Maiden Name, Priest

2046, 12 May 1848*, George Francis, Evans, Thomas T., Catharine, 13 Feb 1848, -, -, -, Francis, Dugan, Catharine, Smith, Virginia near M. Smith; * "May" is not written in here but the birth date is consistant with the entry being in May, Dugan, 19

2047, 12 May 1848*, Mary Catharine, Donelly, Terence, Bridget, 19 Apr 1848, -, -, -, Edward, Hughes, Mary, Hughes, Clear Spring; * "May" is not written in here but the birth date is consistant with the entry being in May, Traner, 19

2048, 12 May 1848*, Daniel Weisel, Trice, Thomas, Mary, Oct 1847, -, -, -, Ellen, Stake, -, -, Williamsport; * "May" is not written in here but the birth date is consistant with the entry being in May, Snyder, 19

2049, 12 May 1848*, Mary Laura, McCardel, Williby, Belinda, 7 Apr 1848, -, -, -, Mary E., McDermott, -, -, Williamsport; * "May" is not written in here but the birth date is consistant with the entry being in May, Weaver, 19

2050, 10 Jun 1848, William, Getz, -, -, -, -, -, -, -, -, -, -, Hancock. "all converts received conditional Baptism", -, 19

2051, 10 Jun 1848, Elizabeth, Moore, -, -, -, -, -, -, -, -, -, -, Hancock. "all converts received conditional Baptism", -, 19

2052, 10 Jun 1848, Magdalen, Gardner, -, -, -, -, -, -, -, -, -, -, Hancock. "all converts received conditional Baptism", -, 19

2053, 11 Jun 1848, James Patrick, Braderick, Patrick, Margaret, 6 Jun 1848, -, -, -, Brook, Taney, Mary Malvina A., Ryan, Hancock, McCavoy, 19

2054, 24 Jun 1848, John Baptist, Egan, Peter, Catharine, 8 Jun 1848, -, -, -, John, Egan, Mary, Egan, Fifteen Mile Creek, -, 19

2055, 25 Jun 1848, James Henry, May, James, Elizabeth, 13 Feb 1848, -, -, -, Thomas, Donegan, Chloe, Shirchlify [?], Fifteen Mile Creek. See Endnote 25., -, 19

2056, Jun 1848, George Willoughby, McCardell, Richard P., Ann Maria, 16 Jun 1848, -, -, -, Belinda, McCardell, -, -, Williamsport, Eichelberger, 19

2057, 1 Jul 1848, Mary Alice, Riley, Philip, Mary, 5 weeks, -, -, -, Mary, Robinson, -, -, Hagerstown, Carr, 19

2058, 16 Jul 1848, Mary Catharine, Freeze, Peter, Mary, 30 May 1848, -, -, -, Sarah, Brown, -, -, Hagerstown, Miller, 19

ST. MARY'S CATHOLIC CHURCH
HAGERSTOWN, MARYLAND, BAPTISMS:
Index, Bap Date, Child, Last Name, Father, Mother,
Birth Date, Code1, Code2, Code3,
1st Sponsor First, 1st Sponsor Last,
2nd Sponsor First, 2nd Sponsor Last, Location,
Notes, Maiden Name, Priest

2059, 23 Jul 1848, Andrew, Dolan, James, Matilda, 1845, -, -, -, James, Clarke, Catharine, Barnett, Tunnel [Paw Paw Tunnel on C & O Canal], -, 19

2060, 27 Jul 1848, Anna, Dolan, James, Matilda, 20 Nov 1846, -, -, -, Bridget, Murth [runs off page], -, -, Tunnel [Paw Paw Tunnel on C & O Canal], Middleton, 19

2061, 27 Jul 1848, [blank], Dolan, James, Matilda, 1 year, -, -, -, Michael, Mooney, -, -, Tunnel [Paw Paw Tunnel on C & O Canal], Middleton, 19

2062, 30 Jul 1848, George Howard, Hansucker, Henry, Elizabeth, 29 Jun 1848, -, -, -, John, Daley, Mary Ann, Gorman, Fifteen Mile Creek, Chamberlan, 19

2063, 30 Jul 1848, Anna Rebecca, Hansucker, Henry, Elizabeth, 12 Jul 1844, -, P, P, Patrick, Clark, Sophia, McKnight, Fifteen Mile Creek, Chamberlan, 19

2064, 30 Jul 1848, Mary Frances, Hansucker, Henry, Elizabeth, 1 Nov 1848, -, -, -, Charles, Clark, Ann, Gallagher, Fifteen Mile Creek , Chamberlan, 19

2065, 13 Aug 1848, Charles McGill, Hook, James, Mary, 19 Apr 1848, -, -, -, H., Myers, -, -, Hancock, Rowland, 19

2066, 27 Aug 1848, Thomas Jefferson, McAtee, Jonathan, Casandra, 5 Jul 1848, -, -, -, James, Reynolds, Honora, Nocton, Tunnel [Paw Paw Tunnel on C & O Canal], Twigg, 19

2067, 28 Aug 1848, Alexander Warford, Hart, William, Anna, 26 Jun 1848, -, -, -, Michael, Garvey, Rosanna, Prior, Fifteen Mile Creek, Harris, 19

2068, 19 Sep 1848, Catharine, Hawken, Wilfred, Mary, 9 Aug 1848, -, -, -, Mary, Hawken, -, -, Williamsport, Long, 19

2069, 19 Sep1 848, Catharine Virginia, Goddard, Richard, Mary, 21 Apr 1848, -, -, -, Rosanna, McCusker, -, -, Williamsport, -, 19

2070, 24 Sep 1848, Bridget, McCondres[?], Mark, Bridget, 16 Aug 1848, -, -, -, Frances, Figus, -, -, Tunnel [Paw Paw Tunnel on C & O Canal], -, 19

2071, 25 Sep 1848, Catharine, Michan [or Miehan], Patrick, Mary, 4 Sep 1848, -, -, -, Thomas, Hunt, Eliza, Higgins, Tunnel [Paw Paw Tunnel on C & O Canal], -, 19

ST. MARY'S CATHOLIC CHURCH
HAGERSTOWN, MARYLAND, BAPTISMS:
Index, Bap Date, Child, Last Name, Father, Mother,
Birth Date, Code1, Code2, Code3,
1st Sponsor First, 1st Sponsor Last,
2nd Sponsor First, 2nd Sponsor Last, Location,
Notes, Maiden Name, Priest

2072, 25 Sep 1848, Elizabeth, Kehoe, Thomas, Ann, 14 Sep 1848, -, -, -, Hugh, Brady, Ellen, Traner, Tunnel [Paw Paw Tunnel on C & O Canal], -, 19

2073, 25 Sep 1848, Thomas, McAvoy, Patrick, Mary, 7 Sep 1848, -, -, -, John, Egan, Mary, Egan, Hancock, -, 19

2074, 1 Oct 1848, Anna Eccleston, Tierney, John, Laura, 1848, -, -, -, George, Gillmeyer, Eliza, Gillmeyer, 3rd sponsor is Archbishop Eccleston, Kershner, 19

2075, 22 Oct 1848, John, Coffey, Thomas, Anna, 7 Oct 1848, -, -, -, William, Nalley, Catharine, Barnett, -, Chapman, 19

2076, 19 Nov 1848, Mary, -, -, -, -, -, -, -, -, -, -, -, Hagerstown. Rest of entry is blank., -, 19

2077, 21 Nov 1848, Anna Mercy, Halbert, Archibald, Catharine, 16 Nov 1848, -, -, -, Mercy, May, -, -, Hagerstown, McLaughlin, 19

2078, 27 Nov 1848, John Francis, Dunn, Denis, Mary, 23 Nov 1848, -, -, -, Mary Ann, Donovan, -, -, Fifteen Mile Creek, Murphey, 19

2079, 10 Dec 1848, Michael, Whelan, James, Johanna, 16 Oct 1848, -, -, -, Patrick, Carrol, Jane, Kelly, Hancock, Welsh, 19

2080, 10 Dec 1848, Caroline, Gardner, George, Magdalen, 4 Oct 1848, -, -, -, Caroline, Renner [or Kenner], -, -, Hancock, Feather, 19

2081, 17 Dec 1848, Joseph William, Baughman, Lewis, Mary Elizabeth, 25 Nov 1848, -, -, -, George, Gilmeyer, Mary, Baughman, Hagerstown, Schleigh, 19

2082, 23 Dec 1848*, Mary Catharine, McCann, John, Rosanna, 24 Aug 1848, -, -, -, Henry, Shervin, Rebecca, Judey, Hagerstown; See Endnote 26, Shervin, 19

2083, 25 Dec 1848, Sarah Ann, Rohe, John, Ann, 7 Aug 1848, -, -, -, William, Creigh, Mary, Creigh, Hagerstown, Wyland, 19

2084, 3 Jan 1849, Mary Alice, Cunningham, John, Margaret, 3 Feb 1848, -, -, -, Margaret, McGonigle, -, -, Hagerstown, Halbert, 19

2085, 28 Jan 1849, William, Curran, Thomas, Mary, 12 Jan 1849, -, -, -, William, Curran, Ann, McFadden, Fifteen Mile Creek, Rafferty, 19

ST. MARY'S CATHOLIC CHURCH
HAGERSTOWN, MARYLAND, BAPTISMS:
Index, Bap Date, Child, Last Name, Father, Mother,
Birth Date, Code1, Code2, Code3,
1st Sponsor First, 1st Sponsor Last,
2nd Sponsor First, 2nd Sponsor Last, Location,
Notes, Maiden Name, Priest

2086, [blank], Jacob, Hersberger, John S., Mary Ann E., 10 Jan 1849, -, -, -, Henry, Turner, -, -, Tunnel [Paw Paw Tunnel on C & O Canal], -, 19

2087, [blank], William, Mink[?], Michael, Dorothea, 25 Dec 1848, -, -, -, H., Turner, -, -, Tunnel [Paw Paw Tunnel on C & O Canal], Liberman, 19

2088, 29 Jan 1849, Ignatius, Renner, Herman, Caroline, 28 Jan 1849, -, -, -, Eveline, Renner, -, -, Fifteen Mile Creek, -, 19

2089, 3 Feb 1849, May Jane, Swope, Casper, Dorothea, 24 Sep 1848, -, -, -, Maria, Feidt, -, -, Clear Spring, -, 19

2090, 3 Feb 1849, Mary Ellen, Feidt, Adam, May Jane, 24 Dec 1848, -, -, -, Maria, Feidt, -, -, Clear Spring, Norris, 19

2091, 4 Feb 1849, John Peter, Dempsey, Peter, Margaret, 10 Oct 1848, -, -, -, George, Gillmeyer, Elizabeth, Gillmeyer, Hagerstown, Fitzsimmons, 19

2092, 11 Feb 1849, Catharine, Fresh, Michael, Catharine, 6 Feb 1849, -, -, -, John, France, Eveline, Renner, Fifteen Mile Creek, -, 19

2093, 25 Feb 1849, John, Coners, John, Josephine, 20 Feb 1849, -, -, -, Peter, Coners, Lavinia, Hornbeck, Tunnel [Paw Paw Tunnel on C & O Canal], Hornbeck, 19

2094, 25 Feb 1849, Patrick, Curley, John, Ann, 16 Feb 1849, -, -, -, Michael, Rabbit, Catharine, Borlow [?], Tunnel [Paw Paw Tunnel on C & O Canal], Barlow, 19

2095, 26 Feb 1849, Maria, McMahon, deceased, Mary, 15 Feb 1849, -, -, -, James, Behan, Bridget, Daley, Tunnel [Paw Paw Tunnel on C & O Canal]; mother is described as a widow, -, 19

2096, 27 Feb 1849, John Patrick, McAneny, Francis, Mary, 16 Feb 1849, -, -, -, John T., McLaughlin, Mary Ann, McLaughlin, Fifteen Mile Creek, Mulligan, 19

2097, 1 Apr 1849, Mary Frances, Miller, Valentine, Margaret, 30 Mar 1849, -, -, -, Conrad, Anthony, Mary C., Anthony, Hancock, -, 19

2098, 1 Apr 1849, Francis, Sweeney, deceased, Ann, 10 Mar 1849, -, -, -, Conrad, Anthony, Mary C., Anthony, Hancock; the mother is described as "widow (lately)", , 19

ST. MARY'S CATHOLIC CHURCH
HAGERSTOWN, MARYLAND, BAPTISMS:
Index, Bap Date, Child, Last Name, Father, Mother,
Birth Date, Code1, Code2, Code3,
1st Sponsor First, 1st Sponsor Last,
2nd Sponsor First, 2nd Sponsor Last, Location,
Notes, Maiden Name, Priest

2099, 16 Apr 1849, Mary Ellen, Stake, John M., Susan, 23 Mar 1849, -, -, -, Eli, Stake, Ellen, Stake [HB], Williamsport, Fullalove, 19

2100, 20 Apr 1849, Mrs. May, Hawken, -, -, -, -, -, -, Mrs., Starling, -, -, Williamsport; "Baptized conditionally Mrs. Mary Hawken and received her into the Church", -, 19

2101, 24 Apr 1849, Eliza Jane, Flannagan, Francis, Mary Ann, 21 Apr 1849, -, -, -, Terence , Donelly, Bridget, Donelly [HB], Fifteen Mile Creek; entire entry is crossed out, Bell, 19

2102, 1 May 1849, Mary Ann, Fellinger, Frederick, Rosanna, 14 Feb 1849, -, -, -, Mrs., Kreigh, -, -, Clear Spring; entire entry is crossed out, -, 19

2103, 1 May 1849, Henrietta, -, Joshua, Estatia , 26 Feb 1849, -, S, S, Rebecca (Miss), Dugan, -, -, Clear Spring; both parents are "slaves of Mr. Smith"; entire entry is crossed out, -, 19

2104, 20 May 1849, Isaac, Thompson, Isaac, Rebecca, 15 Apr 1849, -, -, -, Catharine, Starling, -, -, Williamsport, -, 19

2105, 24 May 1849, James Henry, McCullogh, William, Sarah Jane, Dec 1847, -, -, -, W., Shircliff, -, -, Fifteen Mile Creek, Keper, 19

2106, 24 May 1849, Sarah Elizabeth, McCullogh, William, Sarah Jane, 1846, -, -, -, Elizabeth, McCullogh, -, -, Fifteen Mile Creek, Keper, 19

2107, 24 May 1849, Eliza Jane, Flannagan, Francis, Mary Ann, 22 Apr 1849, -, -, -, Terence, Donnelly, Bridget, Donelley, Fifteen Mile Creek, Bell, 19

2108, 1 May 1849, Mary Ann, Fellinger, Frederick, Rosanna, 14 Feb 1849, -, -, -, Margaret, Kreigh, -, -, Clear Spring, -, 19

2109, 1 May 1849, Henrietta, -, Joshua, Eustatia*, 26 Feb 1849, -, S, S, Rebecca, Dugan, -, -, Clear Spring; parents both "slaves of M. Smith"; *Eustatia [the top loop of the capital "E" is very light but clearly visible., -, 19

2110, 12 May 1849, Anna Frances, Gerh, Isaac, Cecelia, 19 Nov 1848, -, -, -, M., Smith, Sr., Cath., Smith, Sr., Clear Spring, -, 19

2111, 13 May 1849, Bernard Thomas, Cox, Bernard, Bridget, 8 Apr 1849, -, -, -, Patrick, McDonel, Bridget, Gunshaw, Hancock, -, 19

ST. MARY'S CATHOLIC CHURCH
HAGERSTOWN, MARYLAND, BAPTISMS:
Index, Bap Date, Child, Last Name, Father, Mother,
Birth Date, Code1, Code2, Code3,
1st Sponsor First, 1st Sponsor Last,
2nd Sponsor First, 2nd Sponsor Last, Location,
Notes, Maiden Name, Priest

2112, 10 ___ 1849*, Eliza Jane, Bell, Henry, Mary, 19 Feb 1849, B, -, -, Mercy , May, -, -, 10 ___ 1847* - no month listed; Hagerstown; priest writes "I do not know what month I baptized Eliza Jane...", Smith, 19

2113, 27 May 1849, John, McGran, Patrick, Catharine, 5 May 1849, -, -, -, James, McDermet, Rosa, Traner, Tunnel [Paw Paw Tunnel on C & O Canal], -, 19

2114, 27 May 1849, Lucy, Reynolds, deceased, Ann (widow), 4 Jul 1842, -, -, -, John, Kennedy, Elizabeth, Cadden *, Tunnel [Paw Paw Tunnel on C & O Canal]; * or Cadders or Caddes, -, 19

2115, 28 May 1849, Philip, Sigler * , Adam, Elizabeth, 7 weeks, -, -, -, Philip, Lenner, Dorothea, Lenner, Fifteen Mile Creek; * "Ziegler" written in pencil to the side, -, 19

2116, 28 May 1849, Ellen, Day, John, Catharine, 11 May 1849, -, -, -, Maurice, Cain, Ann, Kelly, Fifteen Mile Creek, Kelly, 19

2117, 10 Jun 1849, Joseph Marian Campbell, Ottman, John, Frances, 7 Jun 1849, -, -, -, Thomas, Galeese, Eliza, Rinehart, Hancock, Jarboe, 19

2118, 12 Jun 1849, Regina, Moore, James, Mary Jane, 1849, -, -, -, Isaac, Moore, Ann, Bevans, Indian Spring, Logan, 19

2119, 23 Jun 1849, Margaret Ann, Collins, Michael, Mary Jane, 16 May 1849, -, -, -, John, [blank], Bridget, [blank], Tunnel [Paw Paw Tunnel on C & O Canal], Lively, 19

2120, 24 Jun 1849, Bridget, Farrel, Thomas, Judy, 16 May 1849, -, -, -, Matthew, Maguire, Bridget, Sullivan, Tunnel [Paw Paw Tunnel on C & O Canal], -, 19

2121, 24 Jun 1849, Margaret Matilda, Murray, Lawrence, Sarah, 4 May 1849, -, -, -, Michael, Collins, Bridget, Hughes, Tunnel [Paw Paw Tunnel on C & O Canal], Hawkens, 19

2122, 25 Jun 1849, Joseph, Keefer, Joseph, Elizabeth, 2 Apr 1849, -, -, -, Joseph, Pecker, Catharine, McGinnis, Fifteen Mile Creek, -, 19

2123, 25 Jun 1849, Mary Ann, Welsh, James, Fanney, 15 Jun 1849, -, -, -, William, Painey, Bridget, McKnight, Fifteen Mile Creek, Brown, 19

ST. MARY'S CATHOLIC CHURCH HAGERSTOWN, MARYLAND, BAPTISMS:
Index, Bap Date, Child, Last Name, Father, Mother, Birth Date, Code1, Code2, Code3, 1st Sponsor First, 1st Sponsor Last, 2nd Sponsor First, 2nd Sponsor Last, Location, Notes, Maiden Name, Priest

2124, 22 Jul 1849, John , Gallagher, Daniel, Ann, 15 Jun 1849, -, -, -, Daniel, McNamara, Catharine, Gradey, Fifteen Mile Creek, Tracey, 19

2125, 22 Jul 1849, Catharine, May, James, Elizabeth, 12 May 1849, -, -, -, Francis, Flannagan, Mary, Morarty, Fifteen Mile Creek, -, 19

2126, 22 Jul 1849, Mary Martha, Matthews, John, Harriet, 14 Mar 1849, -, FB, FB, Patrick, Clarke, Catharine, Clarke, Fifteen Mile Creek; parents are married, -, 19

2127, 22 Jul 1849, Ann Maria, Bevans, John, Ann, 12 Jul 1849, -, -, -, Leonidas, Bevans, -, -, Fifteen Mile Creek, Catlett, 19

2128, 28 Jul 1849, Jacob, Rubey, Isaac (widower), deceased, 14 Feb 1845, -, P, -, William, Shircliff, Ann, Shircliff, Fifteen Mile Creek, -, 19

2129, 28 Jul 1849, James Henry, Bevans, Walter, Martha, 10 Jul 1849, -, -, -, Ambrose, Bevans, -, -, Fifteen Mile Creek, Ridgely, 19

2130, 3 Aug 1849, William Henry, Lewis, Robert, Julian, 19 Jul 1849, -, -, -, John, Johnston, Margaret, McGonigle, Hagerstown, -, 19

2131, 3 Aug 1849, Levi, Bird, -, Mary Catharine, [blank], PN, -, S, B, Harriet, Bird, -, -, Hagerstown; mother is "slave of Mr. Clagett", -, 19

2132, 12 Aug 1849, William, -, -, Rachel, 7 months, -, -, S, B, Catharine , Barnett, -, -, Hancock; mother is "slave of E. Taney", -, 19

2133, 12 Aug 1849, Mary Bridget, Crokett [?], Isaias, Rosanna, 16 Aug 1847, -, -, -, Conrad, Anthoney, Mary, Shubll [or Stubel], Hancock, Marten, 19

2134, 14 Aug 1849, Joseph Edmund, Adams, Amos, Catharine Ann, 23 Apr 1849, -, -, -, Upton, Bigold, Cecelia, Gehr, Clear Spring, Clark, 19

2135, 15 Aug 1849, George, Corbett, Peter, Ann, 24 Mar 1848, -, -, -, Jacob, Peck, Jane, Mouse, Indian Spring, -, 19

2136, 15 Aug 1849, Isabella Agnes, Shedrick, Michael, Sophia, 24 May 1849, -, -, -, Thomas, Moore, Isabella, Mouse, Indian Spring, Mouse, 19

**ST. MARY'S CATHOLIC CHURCH
HAGERSTOWN, MARYLAND, BAPTISMS:
Index, Bap Date, Child, Last Name, Father, Mother,
Birth Date, Code1, Code2, Code3,
1st Sponsor First, 1st Sponsor Last,
2nd Sponsor First, 2nd Sponsor Last, Location,
Notes, Maiden Name, Priest**

2137, 15 Aug 1849, John Alexander, McCartey, Barnay, Harriet, 9 Dec 1848, -, -, -, Levi, Moore, Elizabeth, Moore, Indian Spring, -, 19

2138, 16 Aug 1849, Patrick, Crowley, Jeremias, May, 3 Aug 1849, -, -, -, Patrick, Crawley, Mary Jane, Collins, Tunnel, Reardon, 19

2139, 19 Aug 1849, Anna, Harbine, Thomas, Catharine, 10 Aug 1849, -, -, -, William, McClain, Mary Ann, Smith, Hagerstown, Smith, 19

2140, 23 Aug 1849, Rosa, Blake, Joseph, Lucy, 5 months, -, B, S, S, B, Maria, Oliver, -, -, Williamsport; both parents "slaves of Mr. White", -, 19

2141, 23 Aug 1849, Frances Letitia, Shehan, Edward, Frances Ann, 9 Aug 1849, -, -, -, Letitia, McIlheney, -, -, Williamsport, McIlheney, 19

2142, 25 Aug 1849, Margaret, Clark, Charles, Margaret, 4 Aug 1849, -, -, -, John, Daley, Ann, Gallagher, Fifteen Mile Creek, Gallagher, 19

2143, 26 Aug 1849, James, McCabe, Terence, Mary, 9 Aug 1849, -, -, -, Patrick, Galeese, Catharine, Clark, Fifteen Mile Creek, McGowan, 19

2144, 23 Aug 1849, James, Welsh, Henry, Mary, 5 Dec 1849, -, -, -, Margaret, Shervin, Thomas, Hennessy, Bakersville, -, 19

2145, 23 Aug 1849, Elizabeth, Welsh, Henry, Mary, 5 Nov 1847, -, -, -, Peter, Hennessy, Isabella, Shervin, Bakersville, -, 19

2146, 23 Aug 1849, Sarah, Welsh, Henry, Mary, 5 Sep 1846, -, -, -, Thomas, Shervin, Margaret, Hennessy, Bakersville, -, 19

2147, 2 Sep 1849, Maria, Renner, Valentine, Barbara, 21 Aug 1849, -, -, -, George, Walter, Maria, Walter, Hagerstown, -, 19

2148, 7 Sep 1849, Philip Emory, Washington, John, Mary Ann, 15 Jul 1849, -, FB, FB, Cornelius, Buckley, -, -, Tunnel [Paw Paw Tunnel on C & O Canal]; parents are married, -, 19

2149, 9 Sep 1849, Mary, Forbeck, Casimirus, Eva, 12 Ju 1849, -, -, -, Mary, Feidt, -, -, Hancock, -, 19

2150, 11 Sep 1849, William Albert, Tice, Daniel, Margaret, 10 Aug 1848, -, -, -, John M., Smith, Catharine, Drenan, Clear Spring, Moore, 19

ST. MARY'S CATHOLIC CHURCH
HAGERSTOWN, MARYLAND, BAPTISMS:
Index, Bap Date, Child, Last Name, Father, Mother,
Birth Date, Code1, Code2, Code3,
1st Sponsor First, 1st Sponsor Last,
2nd Sponsor First, 2nd Sponsor Last, Location,
Notes, Maiden Name, Priest

2151, 28 Sep 1849, John, Dixion [?], -, -, -, B, S, -, -, Mary, Johnson, -, -, supplied the Ceremonies of Baptism; "Slave of H. Bevans", -, 19

2152, 7 Oct 1849, William, Hurley, James, Sophia, 15 Sep 1849, -, -, -, William, Duffey, Mary, Taggart, Hagerstown, Smith, 19

2153, 13 Oct 1849, Isabella, O'Keeffe, Nicholas, Helena, 23 Oct 1848, -, -, -, Elizabeth, Timmons, -, -, Clear Spring, Adams, 19

2154, 27 Oct 1849, Ellenora, Nocton, Timothy, Honora, 6 Oct 1849, -, -, -, Eliza, Higgins, -, -, Tunnel [Paw Paw Tunnel on C & O Canal], McLaughlin, 19

2155, 28 Oct 1849, William Henry, McGann, James, Ann, 21 Oct 1849, -, -, -, William, McCartey, Elizabeth, Cadden, Tunnel [Paw Paw Tunnel on C & O Canal], Curley, 19

2156, 29 Oct 1849, Margaret Ann, Garvey, Michael, Margaret, 25 Oct 1849, -, -, -, Michael, Summers, Mary, Summers, Fifteen Mile Creek, Coners, 19

2157, 1 Nov 1849, John Francis, Brown, Lewis, Mary, Oct 1847, -, FB, FB, Isaac, Brown, Phebe, Brown, Hagerstown; parents are not listed as married, Colbert, 19

2158, 4 Nov 1849, John, Crist, Peter, Louisa, [blank], -, -, -, John, Helfrick, -, -, Hagerstown, -, 19

2159, 4 Nov 1849, George, Crist, Peter, Lousia, 2 years, -, -, -, Adam, Crist, -, -, Hagerstown; supplied the ceremonies of baptism, -, 19

2160, 4 Nov 1849, Mary Alverta, McCardel, Wilfred, Catharine, 23 Aug 1849, -, -, -, Eliza, Monahan, -, -, Hagerstown, Humerich-House, 19

2161, 4 Nov 1849, Martha Ann, Lizer, Wesley, Mary Elizabeth, 31 Jul 1849, -, -, -, Joseph, Gauger, Julian, Gaugher, Hagerstown, Gaugher, 19

2162, 9 Nov 1849, Mary Montezuma, Cremer, Jonathan H., Mary, 1 Jun 1849, -, -, -, Mary, Carr, -, -, Hagerstown, -, 19

2163, 10 Nov 1849, William Henry, Dunn, -, Harriet, 30 Sep 1849, PN, B, -, S, Jane, Mouse, -, -, Clear Spring, -, 19

2164, 11 Nov 1849, William Henry Watkins, James, John, Rosanna, 3 weeks, -, -, -, Hugh, McKusker, Margaret, McKusker, Hancock, McKusker, 19

ST. MARY'S CATHOLIC CHURCH
HAGERSTOWN, MARYLAND, BAPTISMS:
Index, Bap Date, Child, Last Name, Father, Mother,
Birth Date, Code1, Code2, Code3,
1st Sponsor First, 1st Sponsor Last,
2nd Sponsor First, 2nd Sponsor Last, Location,
Notes, Maiden Name, Priest

2165, 25 Nov 1849, Hugo, McGuigan, Terence, Mary, 2 Oct 1849, -, -, -, James, Karney, Mary, McLaughlin, Fifteen Mile Creek, -, 19

2166, 29 Nov 1849, James Albert, Stikenius, Godfrey, Margaret W., 23 Nov 1849, -, -, -, Frances E., Ottman, Albert, Hile, Hancock, Melman, 19

2167, 18 Nov 1849, Frances Elizabeth, Shilling, Joachim, Frances, 5 Jun 1849, -, -, -, Maria Anna, Singer, M., Winzfeld, Hagerstown, Shafer, 19

2168, 2 Dec 1849, Sarah Jane, Gillmeyer, Sebastian, Elizabeth M., blank, -, -, -, Daniel, O'Leary, Regina, Gillmeyer, Hagerstown, Maguire, 19

2169, 30 Dec 1849, John, Murphey, Maurice, Mary, 20 Nov 1849, -, -, -, Daniel, Byrnes, Mary Ann, Dillon, Fifteen Mile Creek, -, 19

2170, 31 Dec 1849, Peter, Donelly, Terence, Bridget, 28 Dec 1849, -, -, -, John, Martin, Sophia, McKnight, Fifteen Mile Creek, Traner, 19

2171, 1 Jan 1850, Elizabeth, Cosgrove, Laurence, Teresa, 5 wks. *, -, -, -, John, Philips, Margaret, McCusker, Fifteen Mile Creek; *"born about 5 weeks yesterday", -, 19

2172, 24 Jan 1850, James, Hunt, Robert, Margaret, 21 Jan 1850, -, -, -, George, Hunt, Charlotte, Abernethey, -, -, 19

2173, 20 Jan 1850, Alfred Henry Myers, McCardel, Timon Wetleby [?], Belinda Mary Eugenia, 26 Nov 1849, -, -, -, Thomas C., McCardel, Catharine, Robinson, Hagerstown, -, 19

2174, 20 Jan 1850, Anna Margaret, Griffey, Jacob, Clara, 6 Nov 1848, -, -, -, Margaret, Teterick, -, -, -, -, 19

2175, 13 Jan 1850, James Edgar, Rinehart, Samuel, Eliza, 21 Dec 1849, -, -, -, Thomas, Bevans, Miss Ann, Bevans, Hancock, Bevans, 19

2176, 24 Feb 1850, Eliza, Sullivan, Rodger, Catharine, 3 months, -, -, -, Patrick, Britt, Bridget, Sullevan, Tunnel [Paw Paw Tunnel on C & O Canal], -, 19

2177, 24 Feb 1850, Anna, Shearan, Edward, Anna, 15 Dec 1849, -, -, -, Daniel, McNamara, Mary, Nocton, Tunnel [Paw Paw Tunnel on C & O Canal], -, 19

ST. MARY'S CATHOLIC CHURCH
HAGERSTOWN, MARYLAND, BAPTISMS:
Index, Bap Date, Child, Last Name, Father, Mother,
Birth Date, Code1, Code2, Code3,
1st Sponsor First, 1st Sponsor Last,
2nd Sponsor First, 2nd Sponsor Last, Location,
Notes, Maiden Name, Priest

2178, 24 Feb 1850, John William, Hanlan, John, Mary, 24 Feb 1850, -, -, -, Hugh, Coners, Lavinia, Hornbeck, Tunnel [Paw Paw Tunnel on C & O Canal], -, 19

2179, 24 Feb 1850, Patrick, Francis, Patrick, Mary, 21 ___ 1850*, -, -, -, Michael, Caton, Bridget, Mehan, Tunnel [Paw Paw Tunnel on C & O Canal]; *birthdate month is blank, -, 19

2180, 24 Feb 1850, Mary Anna, Nufskel [or Nusskel], Ludwick, Eva Catharina, 5 Dec 1849, -, -, -, Bridget, Lynch, -, -, Tunnel [Paw Paw Tunnel on C & O Canal], -, 19

2181, 24 Feb 1850, Sarah Eugenia, Benton, Golan, Mary, 17 Feb 1848, -, -, -, Eva, Nusskel [or Nufskel], -, -, Tunnel [Paw Paw Tunnel on C & O Canal], -, 19

2182, 3 Mar 1850, -, Kelly, -, -, -, -, -, -, -, -, -, -, only word in this entry is "Kelly", -, 19

2183, 3 Mar 1850, Mary Eliza Augustina, Eckar, Adam, Elizabeth, 2 Sep 1849, -, -, -, George, Walder, Maria, Walder, Hagerstown, Easterday, 19

2184, 10 Mar 1850, Henry Augustine, Barnett, Henry, Catharine, 4 Jan 1850, -, -, -, James, Baxter, Mary Ellen, Taney, Hancock, Taney, 19

2185, 12 Mar 1850, Catharine, Snider, Henry, Elizabeth, 6 Feb 1850, -, -, -, Ulton, Moore, Elizabeth, Moore, Indian Spring, -, 19

2186, 17 Mar 1850, David, Barry, James, Bridget, 8 Mar 1850, -, -, -, John, O'Brian, Honora, Nocton, Tunnel [Paw Paw Tunnel on C & O Canal], Coner, 19

2187, 20 Mar 1850, George, Mahoney, William, Elmira, 25 May 1843, -, -, -, -, -, -, -, Piney Plains, -, 19

2188, 20 Mar 1850, Thomas, Mahoney, William, Elmira, 18 Jan 1850, -, -, -, L., Shircliff, -, -, Piney Plains, -, 19

2189, 20 Mar 1850, Margaret, Mahoney, William, Elmira, 23 May 1850*, -, -, -, -, -, -, -, Piney Plains; *birthdate is incompatible with baptismal date, -, 19

2190, 20 Mar 1850, Martha, Mahoney, William, Elmira, 12 Feb 1846, -, -, -, L., Shircliff, -, -, Piney Plains, -, 19

2191, 23 Mar 1850, Catharine Alice, Clarke, Patrick, Mary Catharine, 5 Mar 1850, -, -, -, Patrick, Brogan, Catharine, Clarke, Fifteen Mile Creek, -, 19

ST. MARY'S CATHOLIC CHURCH
HAGERSTOWN, MARYLAND, BAPTISMS:
Index, Bap Date, Child, Last Name, Father, Mother,
Birth Date, Code1, Code2, Code3,
1st Sponsor First, 1st Sponsor Last,
2nd Sponsor First, 2nd Sponsor Last, Location,
Notes, Maiden Name, Priest

2192, 23 Mar 1850, Mary Ann, Linn *, -, Margaret, 22 Jun 1849, PN, -, -, John, Daley, Mary Catharine, Clarke, Fifteen Mile Creek; * "Lynn" is written in pencil in margin beside the entry, -, 19

2193, 25 Mar 1850, Bridget Margaret, Coners, John, Jane, 9 Mar 1850, -, -, -, Jane, McCabe, -, -, Hancock, -, 19

2194, 31 Mar 1850, Laura Catharine, Lorsbaugh, George, Frances, 3 Oct 1849, -, -, -, Elizabeth, Jenkins, -, -, Hagerstown, McIntire, 19

2195, 14 Apr 1850, John Francis, Antoney, Conrad, Catharine, 9 Apr 1850, -, -, -, Valentine, Miller, Margaret, Miller, Hancock, -, 19

2196, 14 Apr 1850, Bridget Jemima, Crocket, Isaias, Rosanna, 25 Mar 1850, -, -, -, Frances, Ottman, -, -, Hancock, -, 19

2197, 14 Apr 1850, Charles, O'Rourke, Bernard, Hannah, 13 Jul 1848, -, -, -, H., Myers, -, -, Hancock, -, 19

2198, 14 Apr 1850, Louisa, O'Rourke, Bernard, Hannah, 8 Dec 1846, -, -, -, James, Baxter, -, -, Hancock, -, 19

2199, 14 Apr 1850, Anna, O'Rourke, Bernard, Hannah, 18 Mar 1844, -, -, -, Valentine, Miller, -, -, Hancock, -, 19

2200, 15 Apr 1850, Margaret Elizabeth, Terry, Robert, Bridget, 16 Mar 1850, -, -, -, Hugh, McKenna, Mary, McKenna, Parkhead, -, 19

2201, 16 Apr 1850, James, Hoy, Laurence, Ellen, 8 Apr 1850, -, -, -, Michael, Meyler, Johanna, Hurleyheath , Williamsport, Conlon, 19

2202, 28 Apr 1850, Thomas, McCann, Peter, Ann, 29 Mar 1850, -, -, -, Patrick, Welsh, Mary Ann, McGran, -, Miles, 19

2203, 12 May 1850, Margaret, McCann, John, Ann, 8 Apr 1850, -, -, -, Patrick, Smith, Ann, Mehan, -, -, 19

2204, 25 May 1850, Joanna, Corrigan, Owen, Julia, 1 May 1850, -, -, -, Matthew, Corrigan, Mary, McCue, -, -, 19

2205, 20 May 1850, John Joseph, Martil, Jacob, Mary, 20 Dec 1849, -, -, -, John, Eck, Catharine, Eck, Hagerstown, Miller, 19

2206, 13 Jun 1850, Anna, McDonald, -, Margaret (widow), 8 Sep 1840, -, -, -, Sophia, Devine, -, -, Williamsport, -, 19

2207, 13 Jun 1850, William, McDonald, -, Margaret (widow), 4 Mar 1842, -, -, -, David, Barry, -, -, Williamsport, -, 19

ST. MARY'S CATHOLIC CHURCH
HAGERSTOWN, MARYLAND, BAPTISMS:
Index, Bap Date, Child, Last Name, Father, Mother,
Birth Date, Code1, Code2, Code3,
1st Sponsor First, 1st Sponsor Last,
2nd Sponsor First, 2nd Sponsor Last, Location,
Notes, Maiden Name, Priest

2208, 13 Jun 1850, Rosa, McDonald, -, Margaret (widow), Aug 1844, -, -, -, Mary, Oliver, -, -, Williamsport, -, 19

2209, 13 Jun 1850, Margaret, McDonald, -, Margaret (widow), 4 Sep 1848, -, -, -, Margaret, McCusker, -, -, Williamsport, -, 19

2210, 13 Jun 1850, Susanna Emma, Stake, -, -, 21 years, -, -, -, H., Myers, -, -, Williamsport; she is "wife of John Stake…and made them renew their consent of marriage", -, 19

2211, 30 Jun 1850, Charles Henry, Hansucker, Henry, Elizabeth, 14 Jun 1850, -, -, -, Anna, Hart, -, -, Fifteen Mile Creek, -, 19

2212, Jul 1850, Mary Frances, Spor, Harrison, Mary, 23 May 1850, -, -, -, Edward, Ganshun [?], Bridget, Cox, Hancock, -, 19

2213, 14 Jul 1850, Catharine*, Daley, John, Kesiah, 9 Jun 1850, -, -, -, Morgan, Kelly, Mary, Kelly, Hancock; *[Hesikia as a second name was crossed out], Rowland, 19

2214, 28 Jul 1850, Harriet Annette, Benton, Eleven , Harriet, 9 Jul 1850, -, -, -, Catharine, Clark, Sr., -, -, Fifteen Mile Creek, -, 19

2215, 28 Jul 1850, Mary Florence Virginia, Benton, Eleven , Harriet, 1 Mar 1848, -, -, -, Eliza, Higgins, -, -, Fifteen Mile Creek, -, 19

2216, 28 Jul 1850, Amanda Jane, Benton, Eleven , Harriet, 2 Jul 1845, -, -, -, Martha, Bevans, -, -, Fifteen Mile Creek, -, 19

2217, 28 Jul 1850, Mary Virginia, Null, George, Charlotte, 13 Feb 1850, -, -, -, Sophia, McKnight, -, -, Fifteen Mile Creek, -, 19

2218, 28 Jul 1850, Mary Jane, Kane, Edward, Mary Jane, 11-Jun, -, -, -, Bridget A., McKnight, -, -, Fifteen Mile Creek, -, 19

2219, 28 Jul 1850, Mary Margaret, Shue, Hugo, Catharine, 5 Jun 1850, -, -, -, John, Frelig, Margaret, Frelig, Fifteen Mile Creek, -, 19

2220, 3 Aug 1850, Michael, Weaver, Michael, Maria, 21 May 1850, -, -, -, George, Walder, Maria, Walder, Hagerstown; he was described as being "10 weeks old on Tuesday last" which was 30 Jul 1850, Paulus, 19

2221, 8 Aug 1850, Adam, Adams, Otho, -, "about 3 weeks ago", FB, FB, -, Elizabeth M., McKusker, -, -, Williamsport, -, 19

2222, 11 Aug 1850, John Denis Howard, Cunningham, John D. H., Margaret, 25-Jun, -, -, -, Christina, Antoney, -, -, Hancock, Halbert, 19

ST. MARY'S CATHOLIC CHURCH HAGERSTOWN, MARYLAND, BAPTISMS:
Index, Bap Date, Child, Last Name, Father, Mother, Birth Date, Code1, Code2, Code3, 1st Sponsor First, 1st Sponsor Last, 2nd Sponsor First, 2nd Sponsor Last, Location, Notes, Maiden Name, Priest

2223, 11 Aug 1850, Mary Elizabeth, Siler, Echart, Nancy, 25 Aug 1849, -, -, -, Frances E., Ottman, -, -, Hancock, -, 19

2224, 11 Aug 1850, Cecelia, Connelly, James, Barbara, 20 Jun 1850, -, -, -, Mary, Kelly, -, -, Hancock, -, 19

2225, 15 Aug 1850, Elizabeth, Swope, Casimirus, Catharine, 17 Apr 1850, -, -, -, Elizabeth, Schipers, -, -, Clear Spring, -, 19

2226, 15 Aug 1850, Susanna Catharine, Nickerson, James, Sarah, 25 Apr 1850, -, -, -, Francisca, Warner, -, -, Clear Spring, -, 19

2227, 4 Aug 1850, Andrew, Turberger [or Tunberger], Adam, Elizabeth, 1 Feb 1850, -, -, -, Andrew, Regler, Margaret, Regler, Clear Spring, -, 19

2228, 15 Aug 1850, Sarah, Nickerson, James, Sarah, 27 Jul 1846 , -, -, -, Bridget, Gallegher, -, -, Clear Spring; date of 25 Apr 1850 was crossed out in birth date section, -, 19

2229, 25 Aug 1850, Lucy Ellen, Stottelmeyer, Peter, Jane, 29 May 1850, -, -, -, Ann Ellen, Hart, -, -, Fifteen Mile Creek, -, 19

2230, 28 Aug 1850, John Henry, Hasting, David, Mary Ann, 9 Dec 1845, -, -, -, Mary, Martin, -, -, Clear Spring, -, 19

2231, 28 Agu 1850, Samuel, Hasting, David, Mary Ann, 4 Dec 1847, -, -, -, Mary, Ward, -, -, Clear Spring, -, 19

2232, 28 Aug 1850, Catharine Elizabeth, Hasting, David, Mary Ann, 15 Jul 1849, -, -, -, Levi, Moore, Catharine, Moore, Clear Spring, -, 19

2233, 29 Aug 1850, David, McCartey, Barnay, Harriet, 5 Jul 1850, -, -, -, Levi, Moore, Ann, Bevans, Clear Spring, -, 19

2234, 29 Aug 1850, James Augustine, Maguire, James, Barbara, 2 May 1850, -, -, -, James, Moore, Mary Jane, Moore, Clear Spring, -, 19

2235, 31 Aug 1850, Benjamin Franklin, Tierney, John, Laura, 20 Jul 1850, -, -, -, Leo, Tierney, Margaret, McGonigle, Hagerstown, Kershner, 19

2236, [blank], Charles James, Myers, James, Margoret [sic] Ann, Mar 1847, -, -, -, -, -, -, -, "about 4 months ago these were baptized", -, 19

2237, [blank], Eliza Ilda [ILDA] [?], Myers, James, Margoret [sic] Ann, 8 Feb 1849, -, -, -, Ann E. Isabella, Myers, -, -, "about 4 months ago these were baptized", -, 19

ST. MARY'S CATHOLIC CHURCH
HAGERSTOWN, MARYLAND, BAPTISMS:
Index, Bap Date, Child, Last Name, Father, Mother,
Birth Date, Code1, Code2, Code3,
1st Sponsor First, 1st Sponsor Last,
2nd Sponsor First, 2nd Sponsor Last, Location,
Notes, Maiden Name, Priest

2238, 13 Oct 1850, Anna Catharine, Little, Patrick, Isabella, 28 Jul 1850, -, -, -, Patrick, Butler, Ann, McCann, Hancock, Dugan, 19

2239, 13 Oct 1850, Anna Catharine, Stroubel, John, Mary, 14 Sep 1850, -, -, -, Gertrude, Antoney, -, -, Hancock, -, 19

2240, 3 Nov 1850, Anna Elizabeth, Dix, John, Maria, 16 Jun 1850, -, -, -, Catharine, Craig, -, -, Hagerstown, Phenig, 19

2241, 3 Nov 1850, Sarah Eliza, Freize, Peter, Mary, 26 Dec 1849, -, -, -, Sarah, Brown, -, -, Hagerstown, Miller, 19

2242, 10 Nov 1850, Mary Ellen, Ingram, Charles, Margaret, 31 Oct 1850, -, -, -, Johanna, Broderick, Hugh, Egan, Hancock, -, 19

2243, 7 Nov 1850, Thomas Robinson, Hawken, Wilfred, Mary, 22 Aug 1850, -, -, -, Eliza, Donelly, -, -, Williamsport, Long, 19

2244, 16 Nov 1850, John Cornelius, Tinderman, Lewis, Barbara, 24 Sep 1850, -, -, -, Edward Aug. P., Coyle, Catharine, Gauger, -, Gauger, 19

2245, 19 Nov 1850, Thomas, Harris, William, Harriet, -, -, B, B, John, Truman, Catharine, Craig, Hagerstown; entire entry crossed out, -, 19

2246, 12 Jan 1851, James, Daugheney, deceased, Bridget (widow), 12 Jan 1851, -, -, -, Richard, Callan [or Callon], Margaret, Minor, Hancock, -, 19

2247, 12 Jan 1851, Maria, Daugheney, deceased, Bridget (widow), -, -, -, -, Bridget, Daugheney, -, -, Hancock, -, 19

2248, 12 Jan 1851, Edward George, Gatton, Zariah , Ellen, Sep 1847, -, -, -, Ann, Murray, Lawrence, Murray, Hancock; birth date given as "born 3 years last September 1847", Murray, 19

2249, 12 Jan 1851, Richard, Gatton, Zariah , Ellen, Apr 1844, -, -, -, Richard, Murray, -, -, Hancock , Murray, 19

2250, 12 Jan 1851, Lawrence, Gatton, Zariah , Ellen, 21 Dec 1849, -, -, -, David, McAvoy, Ann Ross, Gatton, Hancock, Murray, 19

2251, 19 Jan 1851, Victoria Elizabeth, Baughman, Lewis, Elizabeth, 27 Dec 1850, -, -, -, Mercy, May, -, -, Hagerstown, Sleighk [sic], 19

2252, 19 Jan 1851, John Thomas, Harris, William, Harriet, 3 weeks, -, B, S, S, B, John, Truman, Catharine, Craig, Hagerstown, -, 19

ST. MARY'S CATHOLIC CHURCH
HAGERSTOWN, MARYLAND, BAPTISMS:
Index, Bap Date, Child, Last Name, Father, Mother,
Birth Date, Code1, Code2, Code3,
1st Sponsor First, 1st Sponsor Last,
2nd Sponsor First, 2nd Sponsor Last, Location,
Notes, Maiden Name, Priest

2253, 8 Feb 1851, James, Shields, James, Elizabeth, 9 Nov 1850, -, -, -, James, Shields, Ann, Callan, Hancock, Green, 19

2254, 14 Feb 1851, Catharine, Moore, -, Susan, 8 Sep 1850, PN, -, -, Levi, Moore, Catharine, Moore, Indian Spring, -, 19

2255, 15 Feb 1851, Philomena, Moore, Ulton, Elizabeth, 31 Jan 1850, -, -, -, Levi, Moore, Catharine, Moore, Indian Spring, Myers, 19

2256, 15 Feb 1851, David, Hasting, -, -, 30 years, -, -, -, Alexander, Moore, -, -, Indian Spring, -, 19

2257, 15 Feb 1851, Peter, Shedrick, Michael, Sophia, -, -, -, -, Denis, Cain, Jane, Mouse, Indian Spring, -, 19

2258, 15 Feb 1851, James , Minor, -, -, 16 years, B, -, -, Philip, Dun, -, -, Indian Spring, -, 19

2259, 20 Feb 1851, Thomas Courtney, Woltz, Charles Wm., Amelia, 15 Jan 1851, -, -, -, Thomas C., McCardel, Mary, Oliver, Williamsport, Stake, 19

2260, 25 Feb 1851, Sarah Anna, Dun, -, Mary Jane, 22 Nov 1850, PN, -, B, Catharine, Harbine, -, -, -, -, 19

2261, 10 Apr 1851, James Henry, Lintz, Bernard, Louisa, 31 Jan 1851, -, -, -, James, Noonan, Catharine, Clark, Fifteen Mile Creek, Gibbs, 19

2262, 19 Apr 1851, Sarah, Woods, -, -, 70 years , B, -, -, James, Butler, Catharine, Craig, Hagerstown; BC, -, 19

2263, 19 Apr 1851, Mary, Henson, -, -, 35 years, -, -, -, Anna Josephine, Wesley, -, -, Hagerstown, -, 19

2264, 25 Apr 1851, Elizabeth Virginia, Wells, Minor Francis, Mary Elizabeth, 22 Nov 1847, -, -, -, Henry, Myers, -, -, Fifteen Mile Creek, Grant, 19

2265, 25 Apr 1851, Anna Maria, Wells, Minor Francis, Mary Elizabeth, 6 May 1849, -, -, -, Ellen, Bevans, -, -, Fifteen Mile Creek, Grant, 19

2266, 26 Apr 1851, Matthew, Cosgrove, Laurence, Teresa, 9 Apr 1851, -, -, -, Daniel, McNamara, Margaret, Bannon, Fifteen Mile Creek, -, 19

2267, 26 Apr 1851, Sarah, Farrel, Thomas, Judey, 3 Mar 1851, -, -, -, Laurence, Cosgrove, Mary, McAnaney, Fifteen Mile Creek, -, 19

ST. MARY'S CATHOLIC CHURCH
HAGERSTOWN, MARYLAND, BAPTISMS:
Index, Bap Date, Child, Last Name, Father, Mother,
Birth Date, Code1, Code2, Code3,
1st Sponsor First, 1st Sponsor Last,
2nd Sponsor First, 2nd Sponsor Last, Location,
Notes, Maiden Name, Priest

2268, May 1851, -, -, -, -, -, -, -, -, -, -, -, -, nothing in this entry except "Hancock", -, 19

2269, 13 May 1851, Isaac, Dun, Richard, Jane, 17 Oct 1850, -, -, -, Catharine, Moore, -, -, Indian Spring, Bryan, 19

2270, 13 May 1851, John Alexander, Moore, James, Mary Jane, 11 Apr 1851, -, -, -, Thomas, Moore, Bridget, Terry, Williamsport, Logan, 19

2271, 13 May 1851, Louisa Virginia, Tice, Daniel, Margaret, 2 Nov 1850, -, -, -, Ulton, Moore, Elizabeth, Moore, Williamsport, Moore, 19

2272, 19 May 1851, Rosa Rebecca, Garry, Michael M., Catharine R., 23 Oct 1849, -, -, -, Martha, McClain, -, -, Clear Spring, Dare, 19

2273, 19 May 1851, Mary Frances, Garry, Michael M., Catharine R., 29 Jan 1851, -, -, -, Martha, McClain, -, -, Clear Spring, Dare, 19

2274, 20 May 1851, Anna Ada, McCardel, Richard, Anna Maria, 5 Apr 1851, -, -, -, Louisa, Donnelly, -, -, Williamsport, Eichelberger, 19

2275, 25 May 1851, Daniel, Gallagher, Daniel, Anna, 20 Apr 1851, -, -, -, Bernard, McGran, Margaret, Gradey, -, Tracey, 19

2276, 25 May 1851, Elizabeth, Keefer, George, Elizabeth, 21 Mar 1851, -, -, -, Peter, Clayman, Elizabeth, Zickler, -, Shelburn [?], 19

2277, 26 May 1851, Mary Elizabeth, Gates, -, -, 18 years, -, -, -, Teresa, Cosgrove, -, -, BC, -, 19

2278, 19 Jun 1851, Ann, Deagan, Michael, Elizabeth, 10 Apr 1851, -, -, -, Frederick, Wesley, Catharine, Byan, "at Mr. Smith's", -, 19

2279, 25 Jun 1851, Charles William, Wilson, Joshua, Rebecca, 1 Aug 1850, -, -, -, Mary Ann, Millor [sic], -, -, Hagerstown, -, 19

2280, 29 Jun 1851, Mary, Gock, Joseph, Josepha, 17 Jun 1851, -, -, -, Joshua, Walder, Maria, Walder [HB], Hagerstown, -, 19

2281, 20 Jul 1851, Margaret, Goddard, Richard, Mary, 6 May 1851, -, -, -, Patrick, Roach, Mary, Kale, Williamsport, Barry, 19

2282, 20 Jul 1851, Catharine, Hoy, George, Bridgitt, 20 Jul 1851, -, -, -, Michael, Donovan, Mary, Hughes, Williamsport, Weldon, 19

ST. MARY'S CATHOLIC CHURCH
HAGERSTOWN, MARYLAND, BAPTISMS:
Index, Bap Date, Child, Last Name, Father, Mother,
Birth Date, Code1, Code2, Code3,
1st Sponsor First, 1st Sponsor Last,
2nd Sponsor First, 2nd Sponsor Last, Location,
Notes, Maiden Name, Priest

2283, 26 Jul 1851, Elizabeth Rebecca, McAttee, Johnathan, Cassandra, 24 Mar 1851, -, -, -, Eliza, Higgins, -, -, "at Higgins' near the Tunnell [Paw Paw Tunnell on the C & O Canal]", -, 20

2284, 4 Aug 1851, Daniel, O'Leary, Thomas, Elizabeth, 27 Apr 1851, -, -, -, Daniel, O'Leary *, Mercy (Miss), May, * This sponsor was described as "Daniel O'Leary (who was not present)", -, 20

2285, 9 Aug 1851, James Joshua, Davis, John George, Mary Ann, 26 Jul 1851, -, -, -, Catharine, Robinson, -, -, Hagerstown, Shirley, 19

2286, 9 Aug 1851, Elizabeth Ellen, Vernon, deceased, Mrs., 3 years, -, -, P, Peter, Hennessey, Bridget, Hennessey, Fairplay; mother is widow, -, 19

2287, 10 Aug 1851, Susan Elizabeth, Trumpower, George, Mary, 23 Dec 1849, -, -, -, James, Cullan, Lorretto, Martin, "at Moore's" [St. Thomas Catholic Church at Mooresville, near Clear Spring], -, 20

2288, 10 Aug 1851, James Edward, Connor, John, Catharine, 5 Jul 1851, -, -, -, Redmond, Louis, Francena, Larris [or Harrit] **, "at Moore's" [St. Thomas Catholic Church at Mooresville, near Clear Spring]; *See Endnote 46., -, 20

2289, 10 Aug 1851, John Michael, Cain, Denis, Levenia, 16 Jul 1851, -, -, -, Thomas, Moore, Susanna, Moore, "at Moore's" [St. Thomas Catholic Church at Mooresville, near Clear Spring], -, 20

2290, 17 Aug 1851, George, Myers, John, Teresa, 22 May 1851, -, -, -, Cecelia, Evehart [?], -, -, Hagerstown, Miller, 19

2291, 14 Aug 1851, Frances Catharine, Fellman, Ross, Elizabeth, 10 years, -, -, -, Catharine, Craig, -, -, Hagerstown; supplied ceremonies of baptism, -, 20

2292, 24 Aug 1851, Sarah, Lee, William, Priscilla, 17 Jun 1850, -, B, B, Sarah, Lee, -, -, Williamsport, -, 20

2293, 31 Aug 1851, Mary Louisa, Coone, Daniel, Mary, 9 months, -, B, B, Frances, Cole, -, -, Hagerstown, -, 20

2294, 31 Aug 1851, Ellen Clarissa, Bevans, John, Margaret, 1 Aug 1851, -, -, -, Ambrose, Bevans, Mary, MacDonald, 15. M. Creek, Catlett, 19

ST. MARY'S CATHOLIC CHURCH HAGERSTOWN, MARYLAND, BAPTISMS:
Index, Bap Date, Child, Last Name, Father, Mother,
Birth Date, Code1, Code2, Code3,
1st Sponsor First, 1st Sponsor Last,
2nd Sponsor First, 2nd Sponsor Last, Location,
Notes, Maiden Name, Priest

2295, 21 Sep 1851, Cornelius Cassey, Harrison, Elbert, Mary, 4 Aug 1851, PN, B, S, B, S, Harriet, Bird, -, -, Hagerstown, Bird, 19

2296, 21 Sep 1851, James Albert, Dorsey, -, Rachel, 3 months, PN, -, -, Elizabeth, Anthony, -, -, Hancock, -, 20

2297, 4 Oct 1851, Robert, Carey [?], Joseph, Catharine, 7 Apr 1847, -, -, -, Catharine, Harritt, -, -, Clear Spring, -, 19

2298, 5 Oct 1851, Frances Amelia Catharine, Stekenius, Frederick, Welhelma, 21 Sep 1851, -, -, -, Mary Catharine, Antoney, -, -, Hancock; supplied ceremonies of baptims, Melman, 19

2299, 13 Oct 1851, Samuel, McCormick, William, Rebecca, 3 Mar 1843, -, -, -, Jacob, Peck, Bridget, McComas, "at Moore's" [St. Thomas Catholic Church at Mooresville, near Clear Spring], -, 20

2300, 13 Oct 1851, Margaret, McCormick, William, Rebecca, 7 Jun 1845, -, -, -, Hughey, McKennedy, Catharine, Richard, "at Moore's" [St. Thomas Catholic Church at Mooresville, near Clear Spring], -, 20

2301, 13 Oct 1851, Sarah, McCormick, William, Rebecca, 4 Aug 1848, -, -, -, Mary, Branan, -, -, "at Moore's" [St. Thomas Catholic Church at Mooresville, near Clear Spring], -, 20

2302, 20 Oct 1851, John Erasmus, James, John, Rose Ann, 7 months, -, -, -, Hugh, McConster, Ann, Doyle, Hancock; entry begins with "At McCousker's house", -, 20

2303, 13 Oct 1851, Francis Xavier, Stoner, John, Cecilia, 12 Aug 1851, -, -, -, Saml., Tydrick, Alexina E., Garlin [?], "near Moore's - at Martin's " [St. Thomas Catholic Church at Mooresville, near Clear Spring], -, 20

2304, 2 Nov 1851, Charles, McDonald, Michael, Louisa, 14 Dec 1850, -, -, -, Kate, Gilmyer, -, -, Hagerstown, -, 20

2305, 27 Oct 1851, Emelia Isabella, Wells, Minor, Mary E., -, -, -, -, -, -, -, -, "on the 7 Mile Bottom"; PB, Grant, 19

2306, 27 Oct 1851, John Henry, Gay, John H., Eliza, 29 Sep 1851, -, -, -, Leonidas, Bevans, -, -, "on the 7 Mile Bottom", Miller, 19

2307, 27 Oct 1851, John William, Winkelman, John B., Ellen Mary, 25 Sep 1851, -, -, -, Henry, Winkelman, -, -, "on the 7 Mile Bottom", -, 19

ST. MARY'S CATHOLIC CHURCH
HAGERSTOWN, MARYLAND, BAPTISMS:
Index, Bap Date, Child, Last Name, Father, Mother,
Birth Date, Code1, Code2, Code3,
1st Sponsor First, 1st Sponsor Last,
2nd Sponsor First, 2nd Sponsor Last, Location,
Notes, Maiden Name, Priest

2308, 23 Nov 1851, Wilfred H., McArdle, Wilfred D., Catharine, 30 Aug 1851, -, -, -, Elizabeth, Stake, -, -, St. Augustin's Church, Williamsport, -, 20

2309, 23 Nov 1851, Mary Ann, Donelly, Edward, Mary, 2 weeks, -, -, -, Margaret, McCain, -, -, St. Augustin's Church, Williamsport, -, 20

2310, 15 Nov 1851, Martha Anna, Shilling, Joachim, Frances, 29 Jul 1851, -, -, -, Mary Ann, Miller, -, -, Cavetown, Schafner, 19

2311, 16 Nov 1851, John Pius, Truman, John, Mary, 17 Oct 1851, -, -, -, Enock, Brawn, Harriet, Brown, Hagerstown, Brown, 19

2312, 1 Dec 1851, Mary, Hurleheigh, -, Johanna, 4 weeks, PN, -, -, Owen, King, Ellen, King [HB], -, -, 20

2313, 9 Dec 1851, Martin Clarke, Adams, Amos, Catharine, 8 Oct 1851, -, -, -, John, Stonebraker, -, -, Clear Spring, Clarke [sic], 19

2314, 15 Dec 1851, George, Clarkson, Edward, Catharine, 28 Nov 1851, -, -, -, John, Chambers, Ann, Nelegan, "on the Road", -, 20

2315, 15 Dec 1851, Honora, Sullivan, Jeremia, Catharine, 7 Nov 1851, -, -, -, Daniel, Dunleary, Julia, McCarthy, "on the Road", -, 20

2316, 15 Dec 1851, William, Corbet, Roger, Margaret, 4 Dec 1851, -, -, -, Patk., Rehill, Margt., Cunningham, "on the Road", -, 20

2317, 20 Dec 1851, John Francis, Faight, Adam, Mary, 4 Nov 1851, -, -, -, Upton A., Bejold [?], Theodora, Swope, Clear Spring, -, 20

2318, 20 Dec 1851, Catharine Hester, Holland, John W., Ann E., 7 Dec 1851, -, -, -, Levi, More, Catharine, More [HB], "Above Clear Spring, on the Road", -, 20

2319, 4 Jan 1852, Mary Frances Virginia, Ottman, John, Frances E. E., 3 Dec 1851, -, -, -, Patrick, Broderick, Ann, Galeese, Hancock, Jarboe, 19

2320, 6 Jan 1852, Thomas, Harbine, Thomas, Catharine, 31 Dec 1851, -, -, -, Michael, Smith, Cathrine, Smith [HB], Hagerstown; BC, -, 20

2321, 25 Jan 1852, George Ignatius, Gillmeyer, Sebastian, Elizabeth, 2 Jan 1852, -, -, -, John, McGonigle, Mercy, May, Hagerstown, Maguire, 19

ST. MARY'S CATHOLIC CHURCH
HAGERSTOWN, MARYLAND, BAPTISMS:
Index, Bap Date, Child, Last Name, Father, Mother,
Birth Date, Code1, Code2, Code3,
1st Sponsor First, 1st Sponsor Last,
2nd Sponsor First, 2nd Sponsor Last, Location,
Notes, Maiden Name, Priest

2322, 2 Feb 1852, Mary Ann, Welsh, Henry, Mary, 4 months, -, -, -, Daniel, Hughes, Catharine, Duffy, Williamsport, -, 20

2323, 3 Feb 1852, Edward, McAvoy, Patrick, Catharine, 26 Dec 1851, -, -, -, Hugh, Murphy, Catharine, Hughes, Williamsport, -, 20

2324, 3 Feb 1852, Mary Eugene, Wolfe, Joseph, Martha, 22 Dec 1850, -, -, -, Mary, Oliver, -, -, Williamsport, -, 20

2325, 5 Feb 1852, Joseph, Boher, Adam, Catharine, 24 Oct 1851, -, -, -, Joseph, Scwope, Rosalia, Filinger, "Smith's", -, 20

2326, 5 Feb 1852, Sarah Amelia, Hasset, Thomas, Ellen, 18 Jan 1852, -, -, -, Bridget, Hasset, -, -, "at their house near the Canal", -, 20

2327, 6 Feb 1852, Patrick, Marony, Thomas, Mary, 6 weeks, -, -, -, Michael, Hasset, Catharine, Hasset, "Smith's", -, 20

2328, 8 Feb 1852, Mary Loretto, Martin, John H., Lucy, 14 Dec 1851, -, -, -, James, Curran, Mary Loretto, Martin, "Moor's", -, 20

2329, 15 Feb 1852, Catharine, Coogan, Patrick, Margaret, 6 Feb 1852, -, -, -, Patrick, Lynch, Anastasia, Chambers, Hagerstown, -, 20

2330, 24 Feb 1852, Peter, Freeze, Peter, Mary, 7 Sep 1851, -, -, -, Phil., Brown, -, -, Hagerstown, Miller, 19

2331, 21 Feb 1852, Mary, Freligh, John, Margaret, 7 Sep 1851, -, -, -, William, McAvoy, Mary, McAvoy, "Sidling Hill at McAvoy's", -, 20

2332, 29 Feb 1852, Elizabeth, Shehan, Edward, Frances Ann, 21 Feb 1852, -, -, -, Letitia, McIlhenney, -, -, Williamsport, McIlhenney, 19

2333, 25 Mar 1852, Jacob, Shaw, -, -, 42 years, -, -, -, -, -, -, -, -, Lane Run, -, 19

2334, 25 Mar 1852, Jacob, Shaw, Jacob, Elizabeth, 16 Feb 1850, -, -, -, Levi, Moore, -, -, Lane Run, Whetstone, 19

2335, 25 Mar 1852, David Silvester, Shaw, Jacob, Elizabeth, 7 Jun 1851, -, -, -, Hugh, McKenney, -, -, Lane Run, Whetstone, 19

2336, Apr 1852, Anna Amelia, Forsman, -, Barbar [sic], 1 May 1850, PN, -, -, Sarah, Brown, -, -, Hagerstown; "adopted by Mrs. Mary Henson", -, 19

ST. MARY'S CATHOLIC CHURCH
HAGERSTOWN, MARYLAND, BAPTISMS:
Index, Bap Date, Child, Last Name, Father, Mother,
Birth Date, Code1, Code2, Code3,
1st Sponsor First, 1st Sponsor Last,
2nd Sponsor First, 2nd Sponsor Last, Location,
Notes, Maiden Name, Priest

2337, 26 Apr 1852, Elizabeth, Cunningham, Christopher, Margaret, 25 Apr 1852, -, -, -, Patrick, Reihal, Elizabeth, Kennedy, "on the New Turn Pike, near Williamsport", -, 20

2338, 19 Apr 1852, Maria, Kniess, Adolphus Leopold, Emile, 10 months, -, -, -, Maria, Messman, -, -, Hagerstown, Finger , 19

2339, 2 May 1852, Sarah Anna, Rinehart, Samuel, Eliza, 12 Apr 1852, -, -, -, H., Myers, Mary, Baxter, Hancock, -, 19

2340, 2 May 1852, Thomas White, Bevans, Thomas, Elizabeth, 15 Apr 1852, -, -, -, Thomas, Plunkett, Matilda, Murray, Near Hancock, -, 19

2341, 23 May 1852, Eugene Alphonsus, Hart, William, Ann, 10 Aug 1851, -, -, -, Timothy, Naughton, Honora, Naughton [HB], Fifteen Mile Creek; supplied ceremonies, -, 20

2342, 23 May 1852, Agnes Cecilia, Noughton, Timothy, Honora, 5 Mar 1852, -, -, -, Leonidas, Bevans, Ann Josephine, Hart, Fifteen Mile Creek, -, 20

2343, 23 May 1852, Mary Ellen, Shevan, Edward, Nancy, 11 Aug 1851, -, -, -, Michael, Larkin, Bridget, McKnight, Fifteen Mile Creek, -, 20

2344, 23 May 1852, Charles Henry, Farmer, -, Bridget, 22 Mar 1851, PN, -, -, Jacob, Clay, Catharine, Murphy, "Near Dam No. 6" , -, 20

2345, 30 May 1852, Joseph J., Fouder, Aloysius, Catharine, 19 Mar 1852, -, -, -, John, Eck, Catharine, Eck, Hagerstown, Stots, 19

2346, 30 May 1852, Catharine Elizabeth, McCarthey, Barney, Harriet, 24 Feb 1852, -, -, -, Denis, Cain, Eliz., Moor, "at Moor's", -, 20

2347, 27 Jun 1852, Jacob Edward, Tinterman, Louis, Barbara, 11 May 1852, -, -, -, Edward, Coyle, Louisa Ann, Gouker, Hagerstown, -, 20

2348, 27 Jun 1852, Daniel William, Gates, -, Mary Elizabeth, a month, PN, -, -, Thomas, McGrath, Catharine, Farrel, Fifteen Mile Creek, -, 19

2349, 27 Jun 1852, Francisca Theresia, Shue, Hugo, Catharine, 26 Jan 1852, -, -, -, Jacob, Clay, Francisca, Clay, Fifteen Mile Creek, - , 19

ST. MARY'S CATHOLIC CHURCH
HAGERSTOWN, MARYLAND, BAPTISMS:
Index, Bap Date, Child, Last Name, Father, Mother,
Birth Date, Code1, Code2, Code3,
1st Sponsor First, 1st Sponsor Last,
2nd Sponsor First, 2nd Sponsor Last, Location,
Notes, Maiden Name, Priest

2350, 4 Jul 1852, Mary Laura Virginia, Fourthman, Jacob Wm., Marcellina, 28 Jun 1852, -, -, -, Eliza, Rinehart, -, -, Hancock, Blakency, 19

2351, 13 Jul 1852, Margaret, Chambers, John, Anastasia, 8 Jul 1852, -, -, -, Owen, Riley, Cath., Clarke, "on the Pike", -, 20

2352, 19 Jul 1852, Elizabeth, Martin, David, Isabel, 21 Jun 1852, -, -, -, Levi, Moor, Jane, Mouse, "near Moor's"; "Baptized, at their house, ", -, 20

2353, 25 Jul 1852, Catharine, Foxberger, Adam, Elizabeth, 11 Feb 1852, -, -, -, Catharine, Weaver, -, -, Hagerstown, -, 19

2354, 25 Jul 1852, Daniel William, Gates, -, Maly Elizabeth, 21 Mar 1852, PN, -, -, Catharine, Ferral, -, -, Fifteen Mile Creek , -, 20

2355, 7 Aug 1852, Edward, Duffy, Edward, Catharine, 2 Jul 1852, -, -, -, Mary A., Gallagher, -, -, Williamsport; supplied ceremonies, Whelan, 20

2356, 7 Aug 1852, George W., Creack, -, -, adult, -, -, -, -, -, -, -, Hagerstown; BC, -, 20

2357, 7 Aug 1852, Anna, McArdle, -, -, adult, -, -, -, -, -, -, -, Hagerstown; BC, -, 20

2358, 7 Aug 1852, Ann Maria, Rouskoulp, -, -, adult, -, -, -, -, -, -, - , Hagerstown; BC, -, 20

2359, 7 Aug 1852, Catharine Mary, Suter, -, -, adult, -, -, -, -, -, -, -, Hagerstown; BC, -, 20

2360, 8 Aug 1852, George Edward, Lorsbaugh , George, Frances, 4 Nov 1851, -, P, -, John, McGonigle, Margaret, McGonigle, Hagerstown, McIntire, 19

2361, 6 Sep 1852, Margaret, Keefe, Nicholas, Helena, 16 Nov 1851, -, -, -, Ann, McCardell, -, -, "near Hagerstown", Adams, 19

2362, 6 Sep 1852, Frances, Keefe, Nicholas, Helena, 26 Oct 1849, -, -, -, Ann, McCardell, -, -, "near Hagerstown", Adams, 19

2363, 23 Sep 1852, Joseph John, Kelly, Patrick, Sarah, 16 Sep 1852, -, -, -, Philip, Brown, Sarah, Brown, Hagerstown, Mooney, 19

2364, 28 Sep 1852, John Michael, Rudisill, George, Sarah Ann, 21 Sep 1841, -, P, P, John, Lowery, Catharine, Lowery, "near Leitersburg", Lowery, 19

ST. MARY'S CATHOLIC CHURCH
HAGERSTOWN, MARYLAND, BAPTISMS:
Index, Bap Date, Child, Last Name, Father, Mother,
Birth Date, Code1, Code2, Code3,
1st Sponsor First, 1st Sponsor Last,
2nd Sponsor First, 2nd Sponsor Last, Location,
Notes, Maiden Name, Priest

2365, 28 Sep 1852, George Washington, Rudisill, George, Sarah Ann, 21 Sep 1845, -, P, P, John, Lowery, Catharine, Lowery, "near Leitersburg", Lowery, 19

2366, 28 Sep 1852, Mary Catharine, Rudisill, George, Sarah Ann, 17 May 1843, -, P, P, John, Lowery, Catharine, Lowery, "near Leitersburg", Lowery, 19

2367, 28 Sep 1852, Sarah Ellen, Rudisill, George, Sarah Ann, 17 Jul 1849, -, P, P, John, Lowery, Catharine, Lowery, "near Leitersburg", Lowery, 19

2368, 6 Oct 1852, Mary Ann, Kennedy, Thomas, Eliza, 30 Sep 1852, -, -, -, Patrick, McGiff, Ellen, Stake, Williamsport, Dimond, 19

2369, 29 Oct 1852, John Michael, Shedrick, Michael, Sophia, 7 Oct 1852, -, -, -, Levi, Moore, Catharine, Moore, "Lane-run", Monde, 19

2370, 31 Oct 1852, Catharine Alveretto, Lizor, Wesley, Mary, 10 Aug 1852, -, P, -, Mary M. I.[?], Coyle, -, -, Hagerstown; mother's religion not specified, Gauger, 19

2371, 17 Oct 1852, Alice Virginia, McDonald, Michael, Louisa, 12 Apr 1852*, -, -, P, Anna Elizabeth, Davis, -, -, Hagerstown; j*birhtdate reads 12 Apr 1852 [Oct crossed out], Crissinger, 19

2372, 10 Oct 1852, Ann Elizabeth, Goleese, Thomas, Ann, 3 Oct 1852, -, -, -, Redmund, Galeese, Frances E., Ottman, Hancock, McCue, 19

2373, 11 Nov 1852, Mary Elizabeth , Oker, -, Caroline, 16 Jul 1852, PN, -, -, Mary A., Oker, -, -, PB; "And the Ceremonies of baptism were supplied on the 19th of May 1856" was written in the margin at a later date, -, 19

2374, 11 Nov 1852, Thomas Alvey, Creamer, Jonathan, Mary, 16 Sep 1851, -, -, -, Philip, Brown, -, -, -, Hanson, 19

2375, 14 Nov 1852, Anna Elizabeth, Ingram, Charles Wm., Margaret, 17 Oct 1852, -, -, -, Christina M., Antoney, -, -, Hancock, Tims, 19

2376, 15 Nov 1852, Mary Frances, James, John, Rosanna, 14 Aug 1852, -, -, -, Conrad, Antoney, Hugh [name crossed out], McCusker [name crossed out], Hancock, McCusker, 19

ST. MARY'S CATHOLIC CHURCH
HAGERSTOWN, MARYLAND, BAPTISMS:
Index, Bap Date, Child, Last Name, Father, Mother,
Birth Date, Code1, Code2, Code3,
1st Sponsor First, 1st Sponsor Last,
2nd Sponsor First, 2nd Sponsor Last, Location,
Notes, Maiden Name, Priest

2377, 16 Nov 1852, John Michael, Smith, William, Jane, 17 Oct 1852, B, B, S, -, Harriet, Dunn, -, -, Clear Spring; parents are married, Dunn, 19

2378, 16 Nov 1852, Anna Elizabeth, Dunn, -, Harriet, 14 Sep 1852, PN, B, -, B, Jane [Harriet crossed out], Dunn, -, -, Clear Spring, -, 19

2379, 25 Nov 1852, Catharine Lauranette, Ford, John, Catharine, 22 Oct 1847, -, -, -, Philip, Brown, -, -, Hagerstown, Buckhart, 19

2380, 25 Nov 1852, Anna Virgenia, Ford, John, Catharine, 3 Aug 1851, -, -, -, Rosa E., Ford, -, -, Hagerstown; twins, Buckhart, 19

2381, 25 Nov 1852, Mary Elizabeth, Ford, John, Catharine, 3 Aug 1851, -, -, -, Rosa E., Ford, -, -, Hagerstown; twins, Buckhart, 19

2382, 28 Nov 1852, Joseph James, Kenney, Arthur, Bridget, 16 Jul 1852, -, -, -, Thomas, Henessey, Mary, Kale, Williamsport, Henessey, 19

2383, 13 Dec 1852, Mary Jane, Kreigh, John, Margaret R., 25 Jun 1852, -, -, -, Franklin, Kreigh, Mary Ann, Kreigh, Clear Spring, Hays, 19

2384, 16 Dec 1852, Mary Emma, Woltz, Charles Wm., Emelia, 4 May 1852, -, -, -, Mary Josephine, Stake [?], -, -, -, Stake, 19

2385, 25 Dec 1852, Leo, Tierney, John, Laura, 19 Nov 1852, -, -, -, Michael, Tierney, Mercy, May, Hagerstown, Kershner, 19

2386, 26 Dec 1852, George Emory, Cole, Samuel, Catharine, 29 Nov 1852, B, FB, FB, Catharine, Brown, -, -, Hagerstown; parents are married, Shorter, 19

2387, 1 Jan 1853, Margaret, Riley, Michael, Mary, 28 Dec 1852, -, -, -, Catharine, Rehill, -, -, Williamsport, Rehill, 19

2388, 6 Jan 1853, Mary Magdalen, Trumpour, George, Mary, 22 May 1852, -, -, -, Levi, Moore, Catharine, Moore, Clear Spring; parents are "not Catholics yet", Myers, 19

2389, 6 Jan 1853, Elizabeth Mary, Bevans, -, -, 44 years, -, -, -, Mary, Waid, -, -, Clear Spring; C; she is wife of Leonard Bevans and they were married after the baptism ceremony, -, 19

2390, 20 Jan 1853, Charles Augustine, Diffendal, Samuel, Margaret Catharine, 1 Nov 1852, -, -, -, Wm., McClain, Catharine E. , Smith, Clear Spring, Haugh, 19

ST. MARY'S CATHOLIC CHURCH
HAGERSTOWN, MARYLAND, BAPTISMS:
Index, Bap Date, Child, Last Name, Father, Mother,
Birth Date, Code1, Code2, Code3,
1st Sponsor First, 1st Sponsor Last,
2nd Sponsor First, 2nd Sponsor Last, Location,
Notes, Maiden Name, Priest

2391, 23 Jan 1853, James Elie, Stake, John, Susan, 23 Jun 1852, -, -, -, Elie, Stake, Eliza, Stake, Williamsport, Fullalove, 19

2392, 25 Jan 1853, Mary Louisa, Sims, Thomas, Catharine, 7 Jul 1852, PN, B, -, -, Catharine, Brown, -, -, Hagerstown, V[?]erner, 19

2393, 25 Jan 1853, Margaret, Dias, Wm., Mary Jane, 5 Oct 1852, PN, -, -, Philip, Brown, -, -, Hagerstown, Morgan, 19

2394, 15 Feb 1853, Patrick, Dooling, Timothy, Eliza, 14 Feb 1853, -, -, -, Thomas, Chambers, Margaret, Corbitt, Williamsport, Connel, 19

2395, 6 Mar 1853, John Henry, Heil, Albert, Caroline, 14 Nov 1852, -, -, -, Philip, Brown, Sarah, Brown, Hagerstown, Blumenour, 19

2396, 6 Mar 1853, Andrew, Zinkant, Andrew, Catharine, 7 Sep 1852, -, -, P, Albert, Heil, -, -, Hagerstown, Metzler, 19

2397, 6 Mar 1853, Sophia Jennette, Hurley, James I., Sophia, 29 Jan 1853, -, -, -, Henry, Myers, Latitia, McIlheney, Hagerstown, Smith, 19

2398, 28 Mar 1853, Helena Elizabeth, Lewis, Robert, Julianna, 5 Nov 1852, -, -, -, Thomas, Henessey, Johanna, Hurleyhy, Williamsport, Hawkey, 19

2399, 29 Mar 1853, John Jacob, Smith, John, Margaret, 27 May 1852, -, -, P, Henry, Creamer, -, -, Hagerstown, Leonard, 19

2400, 2 Apr 1853, John William, Garry, Michael M., Catharine, 23 Oct 1852, -, -, P, Upton A., Begold, Rosanna, Garry, Clear Spring, Dar, 19

2401, 15 Apr 1853, Laurence Willibey, McCardell, Willibey, Belinda Mary E., 25 Nov 1852, -, -, -, Philip, Brown, -, -, Hagerstown; Philip Brown is "Sexton", Weaver, 19

2402, 27 Apr 1853, Joseph Wm., Davis, John George, Mary Ann, 30 Mar 1853, -, -, -, Margaret, McGonigle, -, -, -, Shirley, 19

2403, 15 May 1853, Mary Catharine Elizabeth, Eck, John M., Catharine, 3 Apr 1853, -, -, -, Catharine, Fouder, -, -, -, Hoffman, 19

2404, 17 May 1853, Thomas Theodore, O'Learey, Thomas, Elizabeth, 7 Apr 1853, -, -, -, John T., Kneckstet, Mary A., Kneckstet, -, Hoffman, 19

ST. MARY'S CATHOLIC CHURCH
HAGERSTOWN, MARYLAND, BAPTISMS:
Index, Bap Date, Child, Last Name, Father, Mother,
Birth Date, Code1, Code2, Code3,
1st Sponsor First, 1st Sponsor Last,
2nd Sponsor First, 2nd Sponsor Last, Location,
Notes, Maiden Name, Priest

2405, 22 May 1853, Mary, King, Owen, Ellen, 26 Apr 1853, -, -, -, Daniel, Hurleyhy, Margaret, Barry, -, Hurleyhy, 19

2406, 19 Jun 1853, Mary Clara, Griffey, Jacob, Clara Catharine, 7 Oct 1852, -, -, -, Mary, Clabaugh, -, -, Hagerstown, Eberhart, 19

2407, 19 Jun 1853, Louisa Jane, Poffenberger, Benjamin, Louisa, 5 Jun 1852, -, P, P, Catharine, Suter, -, -, Hagerstown, Gelwicks, 19

2408, 19 Jun 1853, James William, Herbert, Philip, Margaret, 13 May 1853, -, FB, FA, FB, John, Hemsley, Sarah, Rideout, Hagerstown, Hemsley, 19

2409, 26 Jun 1853, Mary Magdalen, Keefer, George, Maria Elizabeth, 28 May 1853, -, -, -, Mary M., Clay, -, -, -, Shellhouse, 19

2410, 30 Jun 1853, Michael Harrison, Wells, -, Sophia Jane, 15 Jan 1853, PN, B, -, S, Mary, Gales, -, -, mother is "slave of Thomas Gales", -, 19

2411, 7 Jul 1853, Theodore, Liberg, -, -, -, -, -, -, -, -, -, -, "parents unknown" , -, 21

2412, 2 Jul 1853, James Wm., Johnston, -, Phebe, 7 months , B, S, -, -, Cordelia, McCan, -, -, baby is "Slave of Thomas Gales", -, 19

2413, 2 Jul 1853, Elizabeth, McCan, Barnay, Cordelia, 5 Jul 1852, -, -, -, Ellen E., Gales, -, -, mother is not described as father's wife, which the priest normally did in all entries, Cooney, 19

2414, 9 Jul 1853, Eliza, Bell, Wm., Mary, 16 Jan 1853, B, -, -, Mary, Bell, -, -, -, -, 21

2415, 10 Jul 1853, Emma Eliza, Maddoc [or Maddoe], Wm., Emma, 13 Jan 1850, B, -, -, -, -, -, -, -, Briscol, 21

2416, 17 Jul 1853, Sarah Ann, Herr, John Henry, Elizabeth, 29 Oct 1852, -, -, -, Thos. A., McCaffrey, -, -, -, Little, 22

2417, 21 Jul 1853, Anna Luiza, O'Kief, Nicholas, Helena, 1 May 1853, -, -, -, Eliza, Timmons, -, -, -, Adams, 21

2418, 21 Jul 1853, Luiza, Donne, Richard, Jane, 14 Feb 1853, B, -, -, Eliza, Timmons, -, -, -, Gours, 21

2419, 21 Jul 1853, Dolly Anne, Boughner, Adam, Catherine, 13 Apr 1853, -, -, -, Dolly, Soupe, -, -, -, Soupe, 21

2420, 22 Jul 1853, Susanna Frances, Moore, James, Mary Jane, 5 Jun 1853, -, -, -, Susanna, Logan, -, -, -, Logan, 21

ST. MARY'S CATHOLIC CHURCH
HAGERSTOWN, MARYLAND, BAPTISMS:
Index, Bap Date, Child, Last Name, Father, Mother,
Birth Date, Code1, Code2, Code3,
1st Sponsor First, 1st Sponsor Last,
2nd Sponsor First, 2nd Sponsor Last, Location,
Notes, Maiden Name, Priest

2421, 22 Jul 1853, Anne, Shnider, Henry, Elizabeth, 25 Dec 1853, -, -, -, Cane, Davis, Mary, Davis [HB], -, Reed, 21

2422, 28 Jul 1853, Anna Lousa [Louisa], Able, Leonard, Louisa, 6 months , B, -, -, Sarah, Rideout, H., Myers, baptized baby "privately being sick"; parents are married; See Endnote 27, -, 19

2423, 14 Aug 1853, Jacob, Frice, Peter, Mary, -, -, -, -, Philip, Brown, -, -, -, Miller, 21

2424, 16 Aug 1853, Joseph Arnold, Lee, John, Teresa, Dec 1847, - , FB, FB, Ellenora, Jones, -, -, "Baptized conditionally and supplied the Ceremonies of baptism"; parents are not listed as married, Jones, 19

2425, 21 Aug 1853, Joseph Maguire, McCardle, Ulton F., Anne, 10-Jun, -, -, -, Wilfred D., McArdle, Mercy, May, -, Morin, 21

2426, 28 Aug 1853, Archibald Ensminger, Parker, John, Catharine, 4 years , -, -, -, Thomas, Shervin, -, -, Williamsport, Ensminger, 19

2427, 28 Aug 1853, Samuel Culberson, Parker, John, Catharine, 6 years , -, -, -, Hugh, McCusker, -, -, Williamsport, Ensminger, 19

2428, 28 Aug 1853, Anna Anderson, Parker, John, Catharine, 9 years , -, -, -, Hellen, Stake, -, -, Williamsport, Ensminger, 19

2429, 28 Aug 1853, Frances, Parker, John, Catharine, 7 years , -, -, -, Mary, Lauber, -, -, Williamsport, Ensminger, 19

2430, 31 Aug 1853, John Francis, Creamer, David, Margaret, 21 Oct 1852, -, P, P, H., Myers, -, -, -, Sands, 19

2431, 30 Sep 1853, John Robert, Moxley, Perry, Sarah, -, -, S, FB, John, Hemsley, Sarah, Hemsley, baby was baptized "privately being sick"; See Endnote 28, Hemsley, 19

2432, 2 Oct 1853, O'Dellon Dubois, McCardell, Wilfred D., Catharine Mari, 24 Jul 1853, -, -, P, James I., Hurley, Latitia, McIlheney, -, Humerickhouse, 19

2433, 14 Oct 1853, William James, McCoy, Edmond, Caroline, 8 Oct 1853, -, P, -, Margaret, Deterick, -, -, baby was baptized "privately being sick"; "The Ceremonies of baptism were supplied to the above child on the 16th.", Coch, 19

2434, 16 Oct 1853, Joseph, Helsley, Ferdinand, Anna Josephina, 9 Aug 1853, -, -, -, Maria, Messner, -, -, -, Shobe [or Shober?], 19

2435, 23 Oct 1853, Mary Ellen, Hoy, George, Bridgitt, 17 Oct 1853, -, -, -, Patrick, Clarke, Margaret, McCusker, -, -, 19

ST. MARY'S CATHOLIC CHURCH
HAGERSTOWN, MARYLAND, BAPTISMS:
Index, Bap Date, Child, Last Name, Father, Mother,
Birth Date, Code1, Code2, Code3,
1st Sponsor First, 1st Sponsor Last,
2nd Sponsor First, 2nd Sponsor Last, Location,
Notes, Maiden Name, Priest

2436, 23 Oct 1853, Sarah Jane, Hawken, William, Mary, 10 Aug 1853, -, -, -, Ellen M., Stake, -, -, -, Long, 19

2437, 30 Oct 1853, Samuel Francis Patrick, J[?]enderman [or Tenderman], Lewis Peter, Barbara, 26 Aug 1853, -, -, -, John F., Coyle, Catharine, Maguire, -, Gauger, 19

2438, 1 Nov 1853, Joseph, Carey, Joseph, Catharine, 19 Jul 1851, -, -, P, Richard, Branan, Ann, Branan, -, -, 19

2439, 8 Nov 1853, Anna Elizabeth, Null, George, Charlotte, 8 Jul 1853, -, P, P, Catharine, Clarke, -, -, -, Littleton, 19

2440, 20 Nov 1853, Mary Christina, Haurende, Martin, Christina Catharine, 24 Sep 1853, -, -, P, Sarah, Brown, -, -, -, Shuten, 19

2441, 22 Nov 1853, James Thompson, Spotts, -, -, 35 years, -, -, -, Henry, Myers, -, -, "in the Alms'-House of this place"; C, -, 19

2442, 24 Nov 1853, Mary Louisa, Doyle, John, Mary, Sep 1849, -, -, P, Evelina, Doyle, -, -, "all of Wayne Co., Ohio", Hartman, 19

2443, 5 Dec 1853, Thomas, Welsh, Henry, "name not remembered", a year, -, -, -, Peter, Henessey, Bridget, Kenney, Fairplay, -, 19

2444, 25 Dec 1853, Mary Ann, Clarke, Edward, Catharine, 25 Nov 1853, -, -, -, Michael, Kelly, Margaret, McGonigle, Newpike Toll Gate, McCartey, 19

2445, 6 Jan 1854, John Daniel, Dun, William, Margaret, 27 Aug 1853, -, FB, FB, MA, Lucinda, Smith (Black), -, -, parents are married, Brian, 19

2446, 9 Jan 1854, Mary Catharine, Lantz, David, Mary Ellen, 21 Apr 1853, -, P, P, -, -, -, -, baptized "privately in the house"; baby "very sick", Banks, 19

2447, 17 Jan 1854, John Michael, Harbine, Thomas, Catharine A., 11 Jan 1854, -, -, -, James I., Hurley, Catharine E., Smith *, * [looks like "Sr" after Smith]; "Baptized privately in the house"; See Endnote 29, Smith, 19

2448, 22 Jan 1854, Anna Jeannette, Sheehan, Edward, Frances, 16 Nov 1853, -, -, -, Mary Jane, Stake, -, -, -, McIlhenney, 19

2449, 19 Feb 1854, Robert Ellsworth, Warner, Robert, Mary Elizabeth, 13 Jan 1854, -, -, -, Peter J., McGary, -, -, -, Shafer, 19

2450, 26 Feb 1854, Thomas, Donelly, Edward, Mary, 11 Feb 1854, -, -, -, Thomas, Donelly, Bridget, Donelly, -, McCaughan, 19

ST. MARY'S CATHOLIC CHURCH HAGERSTOWN, MARYLAND, BAPTISMS:
Index, Bap Date, Child, Last Name, Father, Mother, Birth Date, Code1, Code2, Code3, 1st Sponsor First, 1st Sponsor Last, 2nd Sponsor First, 2nd Sponsor Last, Location, Notes, Maiden Name, Priest

2451, 7 Mar 1854, Regina, Clarke, Charles, Margaret Eliza, 12 Jan 1854, -, -, -, Charles, Clarke, Mary, Clarke, -, Gallagher, 19

2452, 18 Apr 1854, Zacharias, Reeder, Zacharias, Margaret Ann, 26 Jan 1853, -, -, -, Lucy A., Poffenberger, -, -, -, Poffenberger, 19

2453, 18 Apr 1854, Mary Elizabeth, Reeder, Zacharias, Margaret Ann, 30 Aug 1850, -, -, -, Lucy A., Poffenberger, -, -, -, Poffenberger, 19

2454, 18 Apr 1854, Emelia Alice, Reeder, Zacharias, Margaret Ann, 17 Jul 1851, -, -, -, Lucy A., Poffenberger, -, -, -, Poffenberger, 19

2455, 23 Apr 1854, Adam, Kline, George, Margaret, 30 Jan 1854, -, -, -, Adam, Crist, Catharine, Crist, -, Crist, 23

2456, 29 Apr 1854, Mary Catharine, Lynch, Jacob, Rebecca, 35 years , B, -, -, Catharine R., Brown, -, -, C, Jones, 23

2457, 29 Apr 1854, Anna Sarah Elizabeth, Jones, Robert, Ruth, 12 years , B, -, -, Catharine, Gillmeyer, -, -, C, Caleb, 23

2458, 29 Apr 1854, Mary Olivia, Quin, Jesse, Mary Ann, 13 years , B, -, -, Cecelia S., Gillmeyer, -, -, C; BC, Brown, 23

2459, 29 Apr 1854, Mary Agnes Virginia, Cook, John, Grace, 19 Apr 1842, B, -, -, Eva E., Doyle, -, -, C, Campbell, 23

2460, 29 Apr 1854, Mary Jane, [blank], Robert, Ruth, 13 years , B, -, -, Regina Angela, Gillmeyer, -, -, C; BC, -, 23

2461, 9 May 1854, Henry, Mullan, Gilbert, Lucy, 4 May 1854, -, -, -, Elizabeth, Mullan, -, -, -, Smith, 19

2462, 27 May 1854, John Elie, McClain, James A., Clarissa, 6 May 1854, -, -, -, Elie, Stake, Ellen, Stake, -, Midcalf, 19

2463, 4 Jun 1854, John, Foxberger, Adam, Elizabeth, 4 Apr 1854, -, -, -, Michael, Weaver, Mary, Weaver, -, Akel, 19

2464, 4 Jun 1854, Theodore Ulrick, Shilling, Joachim, Elizabeth, 11 Mar 1854, -, -, -, Ulrick, Zinkant, Mary, Messman, -, Markoe, 19

2465, 7 Jun 1854, Margaret Ann Missouri, Welsh, -, Julia, 9 May 1854*, -, -, -, H., Myers, -, -, "Baptized privately at the Alms House of this place."; See Endnote 30, -, 19

2466, 11 Jun 1854, William Edward, Furley, James, Jane, 30 Mar 1854, -, -, -, Edward, Koyle, Susan, Fessler, Cavetown, Black, 19

ST. MARY'S CATHOLIC CHURCH
HAGERSTOWN, MARYLAND, BAPTISMS:
Index, Bap Date, Child, Last Name, Father, Mother,
Birth Date, Code1, Code2, Code3,
1st Sponsor First, 1st Sponsor Last,
2nd Sponsor First, 2nd Sponsor Last, Location,
Notes, Maiden Name, Priest

2467, 16 Jul 1854, Charles Romanus, Lorsbaugh, George, Frances, 28 May 1854, -, -, -, Philip, Brown, -, -, Hagerstown, McIntire, 19

2468, 22 Jul 1854, John Henry, Nimmy, -, Louisa, about a month, B, -, -, H., Myers, -, -, Hagerstown; PB, -, 19

2469, 9 Aug 1854, Anna Elizabeth, Hasset, Thomas, Ellen, 7 Aug 1854, -, -, P, John, Hasset, Mary, Drennen, Four Locks , Silvers, 19

2470, 10 Aug 1854*, Catharine Virginia, Feidt, Adam, Mary Jane, 17 Jul 1854, -, -, -, Catharine, Boocker, -, -, Clear Spring; *10 Aug 1854 - day is unclear, might not be 10, Norris, 19

2471, 17 Aug 1854, Clara Jane, Goddard, Richard, Mary, 1 Jul 1854, -, -, -, David, Hurlehy, Margaret, Berry, Williamsport, Berry, 19

2472, 26 Aug 1854, Mary Catharine, Smith, Joseph M., Margaret, 26 Aug 1854, -, -, -, Dr. Alexander V., McNeal, Martha A., McNeal, Clear Spring, McClearey, 19

2473, 26 Aug 1854, William Patrick, Carey, Joseph, Catharine, 17 Sep 1853, -, -, -, Thomas, Drenen, Francisca, Weaver, Clear Spring, McClanahan, 19

2474, 26 Aug 1854, Catharine, McClanahan, -, -, 39 years, -, -, -, Dorothea, Swope, -, -, Clear Spring; this is the mother of the child above; See Endnote 31, -, 19

2475, 17 Sep 1854, Anna Elizabeth, McDonald, Michael, Louisa, 16 Feb 1854, -, -, P, Regina A., Gillmeyer, -, -, Hagerstown , Crissinger, 19

2476, 24 Sep 1854, Margaret, Donelly, James, Bridget, 18 Sep 1854, -, -, -, Marcus, Donelly, Bridget, Hoy, Williamsport, Monohan, 19

2477, 18 Oct 1854, Mary Louisa, McLaughlin, James [John crossed out], Kate, 16 Jun 1854, -, P, -, Louisa, Doyle, -, -, Hagerstown , Doyle, 19

2478, 5 Nov 1854, Joseph Francis, Lizor, Wesley, Mary A., 29 Jul 1854, -, P, -, Edward A., Koyle, Catharine M., Gauger, Hagerstown , Gauger, 19

2479, 19 Nov 1854, Mary Elizabeth, Weaver, Michael, Mary, about 10 weeks , -, -, -, Frances, Lorsbaugh, -, -, Hagerstown, Paulus, 19

ST. MARY'S CATHOLIC CHURCH
HAGERSTOWN, MARYLAND, BAPTISMS:
Index, Bap Date, Child, Last Name, Father, Mother,
Birth Date, Code1, Code2, Code3,
1st Sponsor First, 1st Sponsor Last,
2nd Sponsor First, 2nd Sponsor Last, Location,
Notes, Maiden Name, Priest

2480, 20 Nov 1854, Henry Rufus, Devolt, "not known", Mary Ann, Mar 1854, -, -, -, -, -, -, -, "Baptized privately in the Alms House"; mother is "Prot", -, 19

2481, 16 Dec 1854, Elizabeth Laura Virginia, Smith, William, Mary Jane, 13 Jun 1854, B, B, S, FB, Lucinda Susanna, Smith, -, -, Clear Spring; father is "slave of Joseph Smith", Dunn, 19

2482, 1 Jan 1855, George Scott, -, -, -, *, -, -, -, Thomas, Shevin, Margaret, Shevin [?], *"who died in about a week after", -, 19

2483, 5 Feb 1855, Bridget, King, Owen, Ellen, 1 Feb 1855, -, -, -, John, McCusker, Joanna, Hurlehey, Williamsport; mother is "widow of Owen King (dead)", -, 19

2484, 25 Feb 1855, William Adam, Steward, Wm., Hester Ann, 19 Sep 1854, PN, B, B, P, B, P, Ellen, Stake Sr., -, -, Williamsport, -, 19

2485, 12 Mar 1855, Josias Francis, Staub, James, Harriet, 10 Nov 1844, -, -, -, Amelia, Staub, -, -, "near Mr. Th. Shervin's", Huntsberger, 19

2486, 12 Mar 1855, Joseph Frisby Tilgman, Staub, James, Harriet, 14 Jan 1850, -, -, -, Catharine, Shervin, -, -, "near Mr. Th. Shervin's", Huntsberger, 19

2487, 12 Mar 1855, Thomas Maddox, Staub, James, Harriet, 1852, -, -, -, Amelia, Staub, -, -, "near Mr. Th. Shervin's", Huntsberger, 19

2488, 12 Mar 1855, Margaret Anna, Staub, James, Harriet, 29 Aug 1846, -, -, -, Amelia, Staub, -, -, "near Mr. Th. Shervin's", Huntsberger, 19

2489, 29 Mar 1855, Levi, McCartey, Barney, Harriet, 30 Jan 1855, -, -, -, Denis, Cain, Bridgett, McCormick, "at St. Thomas' Church", Cutsall, 19

2490, 1 Apr 1855, Mary Magdalen, Cramer, Henry, Mary, 28 Apr 1855, -, -, -, Sarah, Brown, -, -, Hagerstown, Weaver, 19

2491, 1 Apr 1855, Frederick Francis Joseph, Halm, Rinehault, Philippina, 31 Jan 1855, -, -, -, James I. , Hurley, -, -, Hagerstown, Ullepstsip [or Ullepstsih], 19

2492, 5 Jul 1917* , -, -, -, -, -, -, -, -, -, -, -, -, Appears to be the marriage record of baby boy in above entry; See Endnote 32, -, 19

ST. MARY'S CATHOLIC CHURCH
HAGERSTOWN, MARYLAND, BAPTISMS:
Index, Bap Date, Child, Last Name, Father, Mother,
Birth Date, Code1, Code2, Code3,
1st Sponsor First, 1st Sponsor Last,
2nd Sponsor First, 2nd Sponsor Last, Location,
Notes, Maiden Name, Priest

2493, 14 Apr 1855, Margaret Anna Amelia, Kneniss, -, -, 21 years, -, -, -, Maria E., Messman, -, -, Hagerstown; "Baptized conditionally"; she is wife of Adolphus Kneniss; C; See Endnote 33, -, 19

2494, 18 Apr 1855, Andrew, Shank, -, -, 22 years, -, -, -, -, -, -, -, -, C; PB, -, 19

2495, 19 Apr 1855, Laura Regina, Tierney, John G., Laura C., 2 Mar 1855, -, -, -, Henry, Myers, Regina, Gillmeyer, Hagerstown, Kershner, 19

2496, 14 May 1855, Teresa Matilda, Horenda [or Hovenda], Martin, Christina, 6 Jan 1855, -, -, P, Catharine J., Shervin, -, -, near Bakersville; mother is "Lutheran", Suckgen, 19

2497, 17 May 1855, Mary Catharine, Shank, Adam, Anna, 28 Mar 1855, -, P, -, Susan, Fessler, -, -, Cave-Town, Maguire, 19

2498, 26 May 1855, Mary Ann, Oker, -, -, 1 May 1811, -, -, -, Mary, Clabaugh, -, -, Hagerstown; C; BC, -, 19

2499, 27 May 1855, Sarah Virginia, Boucher, Adam, Catharine, 2 Mar 1855, -, -, -, Mary Jane, Feidt, -, -, Hagerstown, Swope, 19

2500, 6 Jun 1855, Alfred D., Merrick, -, -, 23 years, -, -, -, James I., Hurley, -, -, Hagerstown; C; BC, -, 19

2501, 7 Jun 1855, Joseph, Rufcut, John, Mary Ann, 28 Mar 1854, -, -, -, George, Rinebaugh, -, -, Hagerstown, Ernst, 19

2502, 7 Jun 1855, Charles D., McCardell, Willebey, Belinda, 24 May 1855, -, -, -, Margaret, McGonigle, -, -, Hagerstown, Weaver, 19

2503, 24 Jun 1855, William Blair Morin, McCardell, Ulton F., Ann E., 7 Mar 1855, -, -, -, John, McCarthy, Ellen, Stake, -, Morin, 19

2504, 1 Jul 1855, William Edward, Hyle, Albert, Caroline, 24 Jun 1854, -, -, MA, Sarah, Brown, -, -, -, Bloomingour, 19

2505, 2 Jul 1855, Charles Franklin, Virtz, -, -, -, -, -, -, -, -, -, -, PB; BP; "Parents not known", -, 19

2506, 5 Jul 1855, Cecelia Iris, Moxley, Perry, Sarah, 2 May 1855, -, -, B, Frances, Cole, -, -, -, Hemsley, 19

2507, 30 Jul 1855, Sarah Jane, Harbaugh, John C., Mary, 28 Jan 1855, -, -, MA, Samuel, Koyle, -, -, Cavetown, Tracey, 19

2508, 30 Jul 1855, Lewis Daniel, Tinderman, Lewis, Barbara, 19 Jun 1855, -, -, -, Margaret, Misiner, -, -, Cavetown, Gauger, 19

ST. MARY'S CATHOLIC CHURCH
HAGERSTOWN, MARYLAND, BAPTISMS:
Index, Bap Date, Child, Last Name, Father, Mother,
Birth Date, Code1, Code2, Code3,
1st Sponsor First, 1st Sponsor Last,
2nd Sponsor First, 2nd Sponsor Last, Location,
Notes, Maiden Name, Priest

2509, 23 Sep 1855, Edward, Sheehan, Edward, Frances, 11 Aug 1855, -, -, -, Maurie, Sheehan, Mary, Sheehan, Williamsport, McIlhenney, 19

2510, 24 Sep 1855, Adolphus, Kniess, Adolphus, Margaret, 6 Aug 1855, -, -, -, Elie, Dettleheuser, Joanna, Dettlehauser, Hagerstown, Finger, 19

2511, 24 Sep 1855, Catharine, Woltz, Wm., Amelia, 28 Feb 1855, -, -, -, Eliza, Duffy, -, -, Hagerstown, Stake, 19

2512, 27 Sep 1855, Thomas, Harbine, Thomas, Catharine, 8 Sep 1855, -, -, -, Mary A., Smith, Henry, Myers, -, Smith, 19

2513, 29 Sep 1855, Catharine Rebecca Regina, Kreigh, William, Margaret, 14 years, -, -, -, Mary, Hurley, M., O'Reilly, C; BC, McCleary, 19

2514, 4 Nov 1855, Anna Elizabeth, Midcalf, William, Sarah Ann, 20 Aug 1855, -, -, MA, Ann, McClain, -, -, -, Homersby, 19

2515, 25 Nov 1855, George, Hoy, George, Bridgitt, 13 Nov 1855, -, -, -, Margaret, McCusker, -, -, father is dead, Weldon, 19

2516, 28 Nov 1855, Dorothea Sylvesta* , Postetter, David [H crossed out after David], Rebecca, 27 Nov 1855, -, P, P, -, -, -, -, PB; BP; *Dorothea Sylvesta [or Sylvestra], Miller, 19

2517, Dec 1855, Mary Genero, Wolf, Henry, Mary Ann J., 16 Dec 1855, -, -, -, William, McClain, Martha, McClain, Williamsport, McClain, 19

2518, 1 Jan 1856, Emma Martha, Ooster [or Oaster], Lewis, Louisa, 25 Nov 1855, -, -, -, Philip, Brown, Sarah, Brown, -, Stalh, 19

2519, 9 Feb 1856, Henry Myers, Clark, Charles, Margaret, 5 Jan 1856, -, -, -, James, Clark, Catharine, Clark, -, Gallager, 19

2520, 2 Mar 1856, Bertha Regina, Herbert, Philip, Margaret, 29 Dec 1855, -, -, -, Margaret, Truman, -, -, -, Hemsley, 19

2521, 2 Mar 1855, Cecelia Irene, Truman, John (deceased), Mary (widow), 12 Feb 1856, -, -, -, Hannah, Luckett, -, -, father is dead, Brown, 19

2522, 1 Apr 1856, Mary Ann, Sullivan, Patrick, Mary, 17 Feb 1856, -, -, -, Maurice, Coffey, Mary A., McLaughlin, -, Bressnam, 19

ST. MARY'S CATHOLIC CHURCH
HAGERSTOWN, MARYLAND, BAPTISMS:
Index, Bap Date, Child, Last Name, Father, Mother,
Birth Date, Code1, Code2, Code3,
1st Sponsor First, 1st Sponsor Last,
2nd Sponsor First, 2nd Sponsor Last, Location,
Notes, Maiden Name, Priest

2523, 14 Apr 1856, Catharine, Kenney, Arthur, Bridgett, 8 Apr 1856, -, -, -, Thomas, Shervin, Ellen, Dooling, -, Hennessey, 19

2524, 15 Apr 1856, Charles Howard, Lorsbaugh, George, Frances, 14 Mar 1856, -, -, -, Margaret, Lewis, -, -, -, McIntire, 19

2525, 25 Apr 1856, William, McCormick, William, Rebecca, 18 Nov 1855, -, -, -, Hugh, McKenny, -, -, "This Baptism belongs to St. Thomas' Church", Folder, 19

2526, 27 Apr 1856, Lucretia Parthenia, McCardell, Wilfred, Catharine M., 28 Dec 1856*, -, -, -, Edward, Shehan, Mary J., Stake, *birthdate and baptismal date are incompatible, Humerickhouse, 19

2527, 13 May 1856, Mary Amelia, Adams, Amos, Catharine, 16 Jan 1855, -, -, -, Mary A., Kreigh, -, -, "were supplied the Ceremonies of Baptism", -, 19

2528, 22 May 1856, John Jacob, Nicodemus, Jacob, Elizabeth Catharine, 8 Jan 1856, -, P, -, Barbara, Nicodemus, -, -, This baptism belongs to "Waynesboro, Pa.", Eyer, 19

2529, 22 May 1856, James Sylvester, Nicodemus, Jacob, Elizabeth Catharine, 2 Feb 1848, -, P, -, Barbara, Nicodemus, -, -, This baptism belongs to "Waynesboro, Pa.", Eyer, 19

2530, 1 Jun 1856, Carolina Victoria, Shilling, Joachim, Elizabeth, 4 Feb 1856, -, -, -, Ulrick, Zincant, -, -, Cavetown, Marco, 19

2531, 8 Jun 1856, Anastatia, Ahern, James, Johanna, 28 May 1856, -, -, -, Mary, Coffey, -, -, Hagerstown, Dillon, 19

2532, 17 Jul 1856, Joseph Edward, Smith, Joseph Maines, Margaret Ann, 16 Jul 1856, -, -, -, William Adolphus, Smith, Catharine Elizabeth (Mrs.), Smith, -, McCleery, 24

2533, 3 Aug 1856, John William, Duffy, William S., Eliza F., 21 Jul 1856, -, -, -, H., Myers, Josephine A., Hurley, -, Stake, 19

2534, 3 Aug 1856, Henry Myers, Warner, Robert, Elizabeth, 22 Apr 1856, -, -, MA, Letty, McIlheney, H., Myers, -, Shafer, 19

2535, 17 Aug 1856, Anna, Kelly, Patrick, Sarah, 5 Aug 1856, -, -, -, Michael, Kelly, Catharine, Carr, -, Mooney, 19

2536, 17 Aug 1856, Margaret Agnes, Wright, Jacob A., Sarah R., 11 Jul 1856, -, -, -, James, Magonigle, Jane, Maguire, -, Bosserman, 19

ST. MARY'S CATHOLIC CHURCH
HAGERSTOWN, MARYLAND, BAPTISMS:
Index, Bap Date, Child, Last Name, Father, Mother,
Birth Date, Code1, Code2, Code3,
1st Sponsor First, 1st Sponsor Last,
2nd Sponsor First, 2nd Sponsor Last, Location,
Notes, Maiden Name, Priest

2537, 4 Sep 1856, Marcella, Zinkant, Laurence, Mary Ann, 20 Jul 1856, -, -, MA, Mary, Clabaugh, Ulrick, Zinkant, -, Swinger, 19
2538, 7 Sep 1856, Genevieve, Kramer, Henry, Mary, 17 Aug 1856, -, -, -, Catharine, Carr, -, -, -, -, 19
2539, 1 Nov 1856, Elizabeth Agnes, Baker, -, -, 28 years , -, -, -, Mrs., Fellinger, -, -, Clear Spring, -, 19
2540, 19 Nov 1856, Mary Jane, Cook, Joseph, Ellenora, 24 Oct 1856, -, -, -, John, Decrune, Rosanna, Lutz, -, Kenely, 19
2541, 9 Nov 1856, Joseph Bernard, Furley, James, Mary Jane, 13 Aug 1856, -, -, -, Samuel, Koyle, Barbara, Gauger, -, Black, 19
2542, 29 Nov 1856, William Henry, Smith, William, Mary Jane, 3 Oct 1856, -, -, -, Anastatia, Smith, -, -, -, Dunn, 19
2543, 1 Jan 1857, Anthoney, Collins, Patrick, Jane, 17 Oct 1856, -, -, -, John, Evason, Ann, Evason, -, O'Connor, 19
2544, 10 Feb 1857, Benjamin Franklin, Shedrick, Michael, Sophia, 23 Nov 1856, -, -, -, Wm., Kreigh, Margaret, Kreigh [HB], -, Mouse, 19
2545, 10 Feb 1857, Sarah, Hyder, John A., Anna Maria, 26 Dec 1856, -, -, -, Sarah, Kreigh, -, -, -, -, 19
2546, 24 Feb 1857, Catharine, Harbine, Thomas, Catharine, 20 Jan 1857, -, -, -, Catharine, Smith, Sr., -, -, "Baptized (privately in the House)"; "The Ceremonies of Baptism were supplied on the 2nd of August 1857", Smith, 19
2547, 24 Feb 1857, James Buchanan, McClain, James, Clarissa, 16 Feb 1857, -, -, -, Samuel, Koyle, -, -, "Baptized (privately in the House)", Medcalf, 19
2548, 26 Mar 1857, Anna Rebecca, Dunn, William, Margaret Ann Elizabeth, 26 Nov 1856, -, -, -, Harriet, Dunn, -, -, Clear Spring, Bryan, 19
2549, 3 May 1857, Joseph Perry, Moxley, Perry, Sarah, 26 Feb 1857, FB, -, -, Catharine, Shorter, H., Myers, Hagerstown; parents are married, Hemsley, 19
2550, 17 May 1857, Mary Catharine Elizabeth, Dettlehauser, Lewis, Johanna , 26 Jan 1857, -, -, -, John, Eck, Catharine, Eck, -, - , 19
2551, 21 May 1857, John Henry, Boucher, Adam, Catharine, 17 Mar 1857, -, -, -, Catharine, Fellinger, -, -, -, Swope, 19

ST. MARY'S CATHOLIC CHURCH
HAGERSTOWN, MARYLAND, BAPTISMS:
Index, Bap Date, Child, Last Name, Father, Mother,
Birth Date, Code1, Code2, Code3,
1st Sponsor First, 1st Sponsor Last,
2nd Sponsor First, 2nd Sponsor Last, Location,
Notes, Maiden Name, Priest

2552, 1 Jun 1857, George Buchanan, Null, George J., Charlotte, 10 Dec 1856, -, -, -, Mary, Clarke, -, -, -, Littleton, 19

2553, 19 Jul 1857, George W., Post, -, -, 43 years, -, -, -, -, -, -, -, BC; C, -, 19

2554, 19 Jul 1857, Frederick Dorsey, Herbert, Philip, Margaret, 21 May 1857, B, -, -, Rosa, Brown, -, -, parents are married, Hemsley, 19

2555, 3 Aug 1857, James Buchanan, McCardell, Ulton, Anna, 6 Feb 1857, -, -, -, Ann, McCardell * , -, -, * "Jr." crossed out and "Sr." written over it, Morne, 19

2556, 25 Aug 1857, Ellen, Hasset, Thomas, Ellen, 29 Jun 1857*, -, -, -, Patrick, Morissey, Catharine, Hasset, *birthdate reads 29 Jun 1857 [1856 crossed out], Sylvis, 19

2557, 29 Aug 1857, Mary Josephina, Smith, Dr. Josiah F., Catharine, 20 Jun 1854, -, -, -, Mary A., Smith, -, -, -, Horine, 19

2558, 29 Aug 1857, Ella Teresa, Smith, Dr. Josiah F., Catharine, 13 Dec 1855, -, -, -, Helen J., Smith, -, -, -, Horine, 19

2559, 29 Aug 1857, William Francis, Smith, Dr. Josiah F., Catharine, 18 May 1857, -, -, -, John D., Smith, -, -, -, Horine, 19

2560, 7 Sep 1857, Joachim Edward, Shilling, Joachim, Elizabeth, 3 Apr 1857, -, -, -, Samuel, Koyle, Barbara, Gauger, -, Marko, 19

2561, 17 Oct 1857, Michael Adam, Foxberger, Adam, Mary E., 7 Oct 1857, -, -, -, M., Weaver, -, -, -, Yeager, 19

2562, 24 Oct 1857, William, Wagoner, Christopher, Margaret, 7 Oct 1857, -, -, -, H., Myers, -, -, -, Iler , 19

2563, 2 Nov 1857, Ann Sophia, Shank, Adam, Ann S., 13 Sep 1857, -, -, -, Samuel, Koyle, Susan, Fessler, -, Maguire, 19

2564, 10 Nov 1857, James Francis, Futter, Lewis, Catharine, 5 Oct 1857, -, -, -, Catharine, Eck, -, -, -, -, 19

2565, 11 Nov 1857, Lawrence Clegget, Lushbaugh, George, Frances, 20 Oct 1857, -, -, -, Mary, Tagent , -, -, -, -, 25

2566, 11 Nov 1857, Mary Aloysia[?], Shervin, Henry, Catharine J., 3 Nov 1857, -, -, -, Mary A., Clarke, H., Myers, -, Clarke, 19

2567, 20 Dec 1857, Frederick Brien, McCardell, Wilfred D., Catharine, 22 Aug 1857, -, -, -, -, -, -, -, -, Mavier, 25

2568, 20 Dec 1857, William Bernard, Wolf, Henry, Mary D., 21 Nov 1857, -, -, -, Mr., McClain, Mrs., McClain, -, McClain, 25

ST. MARY'S CATHOLIC CHURCH HAGERSTOWN, MARYLAND, BAPTISMS:
Index, Bap Date, Child, Last Name, Father, Mother, Birth Date, Code1, Code2, Code3, 1st Sponsor First, 1st Sponsor Last, 2nd Sponsor First, 2nd Sponsor Last, Location, Notes, Maiden Name, Priest

2569, 25 Dec 1857, James Lewis, Medcalf, Wm., Sarah Ann, 26 Aug 1857, -, -, -, J. M., Smith, Mrs., McClaine, -, Hansbury, 25
2570, 25 Dec 1857, Albert, Heit, Albert, Caroline, 30 Aug 1857, -, -, -, Lewis, Oaster, Margaret, Heit, -, Heit, 25
2571, 25 Dec 1857, Christianna, Paster, Lewis, Luisia, 20-Oct, -, -, -, Albert, Heit, Margret, Heit, -, Oaster, 25
2572, 18 Feb 1858, Charles Aloyisius, Smith, Joseph, Margaret A., 3 Feb 1858, -, -, -, Kate, McCliery, -, -, -, McClairy, 25
2573, 24 Feb 1858, Margret Ann, Springer, -, Martha Jane, 26 Dec 1857, -, -, -, Mary, Tagert, -, -, -, -, 25
2574, 28 Mar 1858, James Isaac, Thompson, William Henry, Margret, 17 Mar 1858, -, -, -, Jesse, Thompson, Cecelia, Oliver [?], -, McGonnigal, 25
2575, 11 May 1858, Anna Maria, Wingarty, Theobold, Eve Margret, 23 Apr 1858, -, -, -, Anna Maria, Weider, -, -, "Baptized at Mr. Krieghts", -, 25
2576, 30 May 1858, Margeret Ann, Heil, Albert, Carolina, 26 May 1858, -, -, -, Elizabeth, Shirley, -, -, -, Blumenaur, 25
2577, 20 Jun 1858, John, O'Neil, Patrick, Ellen, 8 Jan 1858, -, -, -, William, Picket, Ellen, Connell, -, Mahany, 25
2578, 22 Jun 1858, Sarah Jane, Shilling, Joacam, Elizabeth, 5 Jun 1858, -, -, -, Samuel, Koyle, Mary, Gauger, "Cavetown district", -, 25
2579, 25 Jun 1858, Brazilia, McCardell, Williby, Belinda, 25 May 1858, -, -, -, Catherine, Grey, -, -, -, -, 25
2580, 28 Jun 1858, Anna, Sheridan, Patrick, Bridget, 21 Apr 1858, -, -, -, Hugh, Murphy, Mary Ann, McCloskey, Williamsport, -, 25
2581, 9 Jul 1858, Danl., Sansford, Geo. W., Susanna, 26 Apr 1858, -, -, -, -, -, -, -, B; baby baptised privately by priest, -, 26
2582, 20 Jul 1858, Margaret, Roach, Wm. , Catharine, 16 Feb 1858, -, -, -, Cath., Smith, -, -, Clear Spring District, -, 26
2583, 24 Jul 1858, Anna, Clarke, Chas. , Margaret, 15 Jun 1858, -, -, -, Mary, Clarke, Chas., Clarke [HB], Sharpsburg District, -, 26
2584, 25 Jul 1858, George Howan, Warner, Robt., Mary Eliz., 30 Apr 1858, -, -, -, Jacob, Creamer, -, -, -, -, 26
2585, 28 Jul 1858, Anne Elizabeth, Kindle, Jacob, blank, 24 Feb 1858, -, -, -, Cath., Shervin, Chas., Clarke, -, -, 26

ST. MARY'S CATHOLIC CHURCH
HAGERSTOWN, MARYLAND, BAPTISMS:
Index, Bap Date, Child, Last Name, Father, Mother,
Birth Date, Code1, Code2, Code3,
1st Sponsor First, 1st Sponsor Last,
2nd Sponsor First, 2nd Sponsor Last, Location,
Notes, Maiden Name, Priest

2586, 8 Aug 1858, James Edman [sic], Corel *, Joseph, Elizabeth, 22 Jan 1857, -, -, -, -, -, -, -, Williamsport; baptized privately by priest; * this name may be "Covel" but it is not "Coyle", -, 26

2587, 10 Aug 1858, Charles Edgar, Duffy, Wm. S., Eliza, 2 Aug 1858, -, -, -, -, -, -, -, -, "baptized, today, without ceremony", -, 26

2588, 12 Sep 1859, Charles Edgar, Duffy, Wm. S., Eliza, 2 Aug 1858, -, -, -, Mary J., Stake, -, -, "Ceremonies supplied", -, 26

2589, 28 Aug 1858, Danl., Sansford, -, -, -, -, -, -, Sophia, Davis, -, -, "The ceremonies of baptism were supplied this day to the private baptism of Danl. Sansford, which occurred July 9, 1858.", -, 26

2590, 31 Aug 1858, Sarah Jane, Carney, "unknown", Rose, 21 Nov 1852, -, -, -, -, -, -, -, baptized without ceremony, -, 26

2591, 13 Sep 1858, Anna Minerva, Woltz, John, Catharine, Aug 1852, -, -, -, Marg., McKusker Jr., -, -, -, -, 26

2592, 13 Sep 1858, Catharine, Woltz, John, Catharine, Aug 1854, -, -, -, Anna, McKusker, -, -, -, -, 26

2593, 13 Sep 1858, John Van Buren, Woltz, John, Catharine, 9 Sep 1856, -, -, -, Margaret ["Cath." crossed out], McKusker Sr., -, -, -, -, 26

2594, 30 Sep 1858, Louis Benjamin, Tinterman, Louis, Barbara, about 1 Aug 1858, -, -, -, Jacob, Meisner, Rabecca, Meisner, Cavetown District, -, 26

2595, [blank], Louis Edmund, Creamer, Henry, Mary, 22 Sep 1858, -, -, -, -, -, -, -, PB, -, 26

2596, 29 Aug 1859, Louis Edmund, Creamer, Henry, Mary, 23 Sep 1858, -, -, -, Ellen, Taggarty, -, -, "Ceremonies supplied", -, 26

2597, 26 Oct 1858, Geo. Wm., Kemp, D., Margaret, 15 Sep 1858, -, -, -, Mary A., Oker, -, -, -, -, 26

2598, 27 Oct 1858, Wm. Thos. Alexander, Cameron, Thos. M., Sarah, about 9 mos., -, -, -, -, -, -, -, -, Jumper, 26

2599, 31 Oct 1858, Mary, Kennedy, Thos., Cath., 26 Oct 1858, -, -, -, Michael, Holehen, Ellen, Holehen [HB], -, -, 26

2600, 1 Dec 1858, Jno. Adam Theobald, Hyder, Adam, Mary, 27 Nov 1858, -, -, -, Theobald, Winortgy [?], -, -, -, -, 26

2601, 12 Dec 1858, Ann Eliza, Wright, J.A., Sarah R., 4-5 wks.*, -, -, -, Cath., Maguire, -, -, *4 or 5 weeks, "27 Oct" written beside it in another color ink, -, 26

ST. MARY'S CATHOLIC CHURCH
HAGERSTOWN, MARYLAND, BAPTISMS:
Index, Bap Date, Child, Last Name, Father, Mother, Birth Date, Code1, Code2, Code3, 1st Sponsor First, 1st Sponsor Last, 2nd Sponsor First, 2nd Sponsor Last, Location, Notes, Maiden Name, Priest

2602, 25 Dec 1858, Clagett Nelson, McCameron, Nelson, Ellen, about 4 weeks , -, -, -, Julia, McCann, -, -, -, Bostick, 26

2603, 19 Jan 1859, Emory Edwd., Stouffer, Andrew, Kate, 28 May 1858, -, -, -, Joseph, Gonker, -, -, -, -, 26

2604, 2 Feb 1859, Mary, Harbine, Thos., Kate, Dec 1858, -, -, -, Jerome B., McCleary, Mary J.[?], Pith [?], -, -, 26

2605, 2 Feb 1859, Mary Damanda [sic], Watson, Jno. , Mary J., 1 Apr 1855, -, -, -, Ellen, Stake, -, -, -, -, 26

2606, 8 Feb 1859, Patrick, Riley, Thos., Ellen, 25 Jan 1859, -, -, -, Jas., Dolan, Margaret, Welsh, -, -, 26

2607, 8 Feb 1859, Michael Joachim, Laurence, Michael, Anna, 22 Jan 1859, -, -, -, Andrew, Laurence, Mary, Laurence [HB], -, -, 26

2608, 8 Feb 1859, Mary Ellen, Green, Henry, Bridget, 25 Jan 1859, -, -, -, Cath., Togan, Michael, Shannen [or Shannan], -, 26

2609, 11 Feb 1859, Margaret Eva, Cushwa, Victor, Mary Ann, 8 Jan 1859, -, -, -, Morgan, Hunter, Sallie, Krigh, -, -, 26

2610, 18 Feb 1859, Maria Louisa, Kelly, Patrick [Michael crossed out], Sarah P., 15 Jan 1859 , -, -, -, Cath., O'Brien, -, -, -, -, 26

2611, 27 Feb 1859, Anold , Collman, -, -, 85 years, -, -, -, Somerset, Ballett, Mary, Hemsley, C; he is "called Naasen[?] Lee", -, 26

2612, 12 Mar 1859, Joseph, Diffelhonset, Louis, Johanna, 4 Dec 1858, -, -, -, -, -, -, -, PB, -, 26

2613, 25 Mar 1860, Joseph, Diffelhonset, Louis, Johanna, 5 Dec 1858, -, -, -, Jos., Quirellan [?], -, -, "Ceremonies supplied", -, 26

2614, 25 Mar 1859, Sallie, Martiny, -, -, 18 years, -, -, -, Belinda, McCardell, Edm., Didier, BC; C, -, 26

2615, 29 Mar 1859, Johanna, Aherine, James, Johanna, 2 weeks , -, -, -, Johanna, Collins, -, -, -, -, 26

2616, 3 Apr 1859, Elizabeth, Murray, -, -, 18 years , -, -, -, Elizabeth, Sherley, -, -, BC; a convert from Protestantism, -, 26

2617, 17 Apr 1859, Jno, O'Connor, Michael, Elleen [sic], about 1 week , -, -, -, Ellen, O'Connor * , -, -, Ellen O'Connor is described as the "sister of the father", -, 26

2618, 24 Apr 1859, James, Henry, Geo., Kahleen [sic], 22 Nov 1858, PN, -, -, Annie, Rister, -, -, -, Rister, 26

ST. MARY'S CATHOLIC CHURCH
HAGERSTOWN, MARYLAND, BAPTISMS:
Index, Bap Date, Child, Last Name, Father, Mother,
Birth Date, Code1, Code2, Code3,
1st Sponsor First, 1st Sponsor Last,
2nd Sponsor First, 2nd Sponsor Last, Location,
Notes, Maiden Name, Priest

2619, 28 Apr 1859, James Elie, Wooltz [?], Jno., Kate, 24 Nov 1858, -, -, -, Mary, McKusker, -, -, Williamsport, -, 26

2620, 18 May 1859, David Willibee, Sheehan, Marten, Ann Elizabeth, 9 Aug 1858, -, -, -, Mary, Coyle, -, -, Cavetown, -, 26

2621, 19 May 1859, Lucinda, Smith, Wm., Mary Jane, 15 Mar 1859, -, -, -, "The grandmother", -, -, -, B, -, 26

2622, 20 May 1859, Victor, Cushwa, -, -, *, -, -, -, Wm., Kreigh, Margaret, Kreigh [HB], *about 30 years is crossed out and "1839" is written in a different color of ink beside it, -, 26

2623, 30 May 1859, Georginna, Saunders, Saml., Nancy, 29 Jun 1857, PN, -, -, Margaret, Riddle, -, -, -, Saunders, 26

2624, 19 Jun 1859, Mary Elizabeth, Lizor, Wesley, Mary, 2 May 1859, -, -, -, Mary, Coyle, -, -, -, -, 26

2625, 10 Jul 1859, Laetitiae, Barber, Geo., Mary, 25 May 1859, -, -, -, -, -, -, -, PB; BP, -, 26

2626, 20 Jul 1859, Edwd. M. , Nicodemus, Fred. [?], Mary A., 1 Aug 1857, -, -, -, Frank, Kreigh, Clara, McClain, -, -, 26

2627, 20 Jul 1859, James B., McClain, Jas., Clara, 16 Feb 1856, -, -, -, Ellen, Dockenny, Aug., Coyle, -, -, 26

2628, 7 Aug 1859, Mary Elizabeth, Warner, -, -, 25 years, -, -, -, Cillie M., Dickers [or Dickens], -, -, C; baptized conditionally and received into the church, -, 26

2629, 7 Aug 1859, Anna Virginia, Byas, Wm., Emily, about 2 mos., -, -, -, Julia [sic] M., Didier, -, -, -, Brown, 26

2630, 14 Aug 1859, Sarah Catharine, Fredk. [sic], Jno., Sarah Ann, 23 Aug 1857, -, -, -, -, -, -, -, PB, Munson, 26

2631, 15 Aug 1859, Margaret, Gary, Eugene, Cath., 1 Aug 1859, -, -, -, Thos., Kennedy, Cath., Kennedy [HB], -, -, 26

2632, 5 Sep 1859, Adalaide, Teirnan, L., Virginia, about 2 months, -, -, -, Rebecca, Somerville, -, -, -, Brien, 26

2633, 12 Sep 1859, Mary Ellen, Duffy, Wm. S., Eliza, 10 Aug 1859, -, -, -, Ellen, Stake, -, -, twins, -, 26

2634, 12 Sep 1859, Frances McKearnan, Duffy, Wm. S., Eliza, 10 Aug 1859, -, -, -, Eliza, Monahan, -, -, twins, -, 26

2635, 18 Sep 1859, Michael, Dowd, Jno., Johanna, 5 days , -, -, -, Lawrence, Handehon, Ellen, Connor, -, -, 26

ST. MARY'S CATHOLIC CHURCH
HAGERSTOWN, MARYLAND, BAPTISMS:
Index, Bap Date, Child, Last Name, Father, Mother,
Birth Date, Code1, Code2, Code3,
1st Sponsor First, 1st Sponsor Last,
2nd Sponsor First, 2nd Sponsor Last, Location,
Notes, Maiden Name, Priest

2636, 2 Oct 1859, Geo. Edwd., Foxburgh, Adam, Elizabeth, 28 Aug 1859, -, -, -, Martin, Weaver, -, -, -, -, 26

2637, 5 Oct 1859, Jacob Ulroy, Sheddrick, Michael, Sophia, 19 May 1859, -, -, -, Catharine, Fellinger, -, -, -, -, 26

2638, 5 Oct 1859, Mary Amanda, Mouse, Thos., Mary Catharine, 23 Jan 1859, -, -, -, Mrs., Bear, -, -, -, -, 26

2639, 16 Oct 1859, Albertus Melito, McCardell, Wilfrid, Catharine, 21 Jun 1859, -, -, -, Mary L. [or Q.], Stake, -, -, -, -, 26

2640, 29 Nov 1859, Theodore Adolphus, Diffendal, Saml., Margaret C., 4 Aug 1859, -, -, -, Saml. , Coyle, Mary, Coyle [HB], Cavetown District, -, 26

2641, 30 Nov 1859, Thos. McCleary, Smith, Jos. M., Margaret A., 17 Nov 1859, -, -, -, Rose, McGary, -, -, Clear Spring District, -, 26

2642, 8 Jan 1860, Jacob Henry, Clarkson, Edwd., Cath., 19 Nov 1859, -, -, -, Richd., Hurlehe [?], Mary J., Stake, Williamsport, -, 26

2643, 15 Jan 1860, Sarah Helen, Zonk, Jacob A., Margaret, 31 Oct 1859*, -, -, -, Jane, Maguire, -, -, *birthdate has "Oct" crossed out, -, 26

2644, 29 Jan 1860, Thos., Carsner [or Carener?], Donald, Mary, 26 Jan 1860, -, -, -, Mary, Herr [?], Mich., Hurlehan, -, -, 26

2645, 12 Feb 1860, John Wm., Thompson, Wm., Margaret, 12 Jan 1860, -, -, -, Whelan, Sterling, Ellen, Oliver, -, -, 26

2646, 19 Feb 1860, Thomas, Hennessy, Peter, Ellen, 17 Jan 1860, -, -, -, John, Barry, Kate, Hassett, -, -, 26

2647, 27 Feb 1860, John William, Wooltz, Am., Amelia, 12 Jan 1860, -, -, -, Mary, Julius, -, -, -, -, 26

2648, 11 Mar 1860, Elias, Malot, Jno. , Margaret Ann, 8 Feb 1860, -, -, -, Lucy, Poffinbarger, -, -, -, -, 26

2649, 11 Mar 1860, Jas. Edwd., Lake, Saml., Kate, 2 Sep 1859, -, -, -, Maria, Oliver, -, -, "col" [Black] is written after wife's name but could refer to both parents, -, 26

2650, 12 Mar 1860, Wm. Hy Myers, Medcalff, Wm., Sarah Ann, 21 Dec 1859, -, -, -, Sallie, Martiny, -, -, -, -, 26

2651, 8 Apr 1860, John, Kenny, Simon, Bridget, 27 Mar 1860, -, -, -, Jno., Flynn, Kate, Toben, -, -, 26

ST. MARY'S CATHOLIC CHURCH
HAGERSTOWN, MARYLAND, BAPTISMS:
Index, Bap Date, Child, Last Name, Father, Mother,
Birth Date, Code1, Code2, Code3,
1st Sponsor First, 1st Sponsor Last,
2nd Sponsor First, 2nd Sponsor Last, Location,
Notes, Maiden Name, Priest

2652, 8 Apr 1860, Jane Agora, Shank, Adam, Ann, 22 Nov 1859, -, -, -, Jane, Maguire, -, -, -, -, 26

2653, 22 Apr 1860, Sarah Virginia, Wise, Richard, Mary, 11 Feb 1860, -, -, -, Lettie, McIlhenny, Edm., Didier, -, -, 26

2654, 25 Apr 1860, Mary, Daley, Patr., Margaret, 8 Mar 1860, -, -, -, Michael, Shannon, Mary, McClane, -, -, 26

2655, 25 Apr 1860, Martha Eliza Jane, McClane, Patr. Jas. Hogan, Mary, 3 Jan 1860, -, -, -, Patr., Daley, Mary, Martin, -, -, 26

2656, 6 May 1860, Lilly Josephine, McCardell, Willabee, Belinda, 11 Apr 1860, -, -, -, Josephine, Hurley, -, -, -, -, 26

2657, 10 May 1860, John Thos., Flynn, Jas., Mary, 10 Feb 1860, -, -, -, Jno., Hassett, Mary, Flynn, -, -, 26

2658, 10 May 1860, Nancy, Walsh, Wm., Marg., 8 Feb 1860, -, -, -, Jas., Flynn, Marg., Walsh, -, -, 26

2659, [blank], Kate, Walsh, Robt., Marg., 13 Apr 1860, -, -, -, Ellen, Knox, Wm., Roach, -, -, 26

2660, 11 May 1860, Lyda Belle, Hassett, Thos., Ellen, 19 Apr 1860, -, -, -, Mary Ann, Hassett, Edm., Didier, -, -, 26

2661, 1 Aug 1860, Margaret, Russell, Jno., Ellen, 27 Jun 1860, -, -, -, Richd., Hurlehan, Mary, Russell, -, -, 26

2662, 8 Aug 1860, Geo. Wm., Watson, Jno. Joseph, Jane, 15 Apr 1860, -, -, -, Ann, Lawrence, -, -, -, -, 26

2663, 8 Aug 1860, Robt, Lewis, Robt., Isabella, 4 Nov 1859, -, -, -, Hugh, Murphyq, Bridget, Donnelly, -, -, 26

2664, 22 Aug 1860, Mary Ann, Mahony, Patr., Johanna, 8 Aug 1860, -, -, -, Thos., Hennessy, Mary, Collins, -, -, 26

2665, 12 Aug 1860, Patrick, Connor, Jas., Bridget, 9 Aug 1860, -, -, -, Patrick, Nerejan [?], May [or Mary], Connor, -, -, 26

2666, 9 Aug 1860, Elizabeth, Dietrich, Dr., -, 20 years , -, -, -, -, -, -, -, C; "Being very ill, she was received into the church, by private Baptism", -, 26

2667, 23 Aug 1860, Margaretha, Wolf, Hy, Mary, Aug 1860, -, -, -, Wm., Hawken, Martha, McClain, -, -, 26

2668, 5 Sep 1860, Julia, Warner, Robt., Mary, 28 Aug 1860, -, -, -, Julia, Didier, -, -, -, -, 26

2669, 17 Oct 1860, Joseph , Gillis, -, -, 35 years, -, -, -, -, -, -, -, -, BC; "convert from Protestantism"; B., -, 26

ST. MARY'S CATHOLIC CHURCH
HAGERSTOWN, MARYLAND, BAPTISMS:
Index, Bap Date, Child, Last Name, Father, Mother, Birth Date, Code1, Code2, Code3, 1st Sponsor First, 1st Sponsor Last, 2nd Sponsor First, 2nd Sponsor Last, Location, Notes, Maiden Name, Priest

2670, 23 Oct 1860, Michael, Lyons, Michael, Kate, 3 Oct 1860, -, -, -, Mary, O'Brien, -, -, -, -, 26

2671, 23 Oct 1860, Hannora, Lyons, Michael, Kate, 3 Oct 1860, -, -, -, Mary, Cavener [or Carener], -, -, -, -, 26

2672, 20 Oct 1860, Cath., Smith, -, -, 50 years, -, -, -, -, -, -, -, -, BC; convert from Protestantism, -, 26

2673, 20 Oct 1860, Lizzie, Dietrick, -, -, -, -, -, -, Jospehine, Hurley, -, -, "supplied ceremonies"; "baptized some months before", -, 26

2674, 13 Nov 1860, Danl. Florence, Smith [?], Wm., Mary, 26 Sep 1860, -, -, -, E. (Rev.), Didier, Ella, Broderick, -, Donovan, 26

2675, 16 Nov 1860, Sarah Ann, Hoover, Jos., Lucinda, 9 Sep 1860, -, -, -, Sarah R., Wright, -, -, -, Motter, 26

2676, 9 Dec 1860, Sarah Catharine, Cushwa, Victor, Mary, 18 Nov 1860, -, -, -, Ellen, Stake, -, -, -, Kreigh, 26

2677, 16 Dec 1860, Louisa , McDonald, -, -, -, -, -, -, -, -, -, -, BC; PB; "convert to the holy Faith", -, 26

2678, 14 Dec 1860, Mrs., Doyle, -, -, -, -, -, -, -, -, -, -, She was "baptized conditionally and privately she, on her death bed, wishing to be recd. Into the Church. She died the next day.", -, 26

2679, 19 Dec 1860, Mary Louisa, Davis, [blank], Louisa, 25 Sep 1860, PN, -, -, -, -, -, -, "Being sick, was baptized privately." , -, 26

2680, 27 Dec 1860, Ellen, Aherin, Jas., Johanna, 18 Dec 1860, -, -, -, Jas., O'Brien, Ellen, Long, -, Dillon, 26

2681, 31 Jan 1861, Mary Elizabeth, Sheridan, Patrick, Bridget, 28 Dec 1860, -, -, -, Maggie, Barry, Philip, Bradley, -, Hoy, 26

2682, 2 Feb 1861, Florence, Ford, John, Catharine, 13 May 1858, -, -, -, -, -, -, -, PB, -, 26

2683, 15 Feb 1861, Danl., Carls, -, -, 60 years, -, -, -, -, -, -, -, Williamsport District; baptized privately; "he being at the time very ill", -, 26

2684, 5 Mar 1861, Jos. Danl., Tinterman, Lewis, Barbary [sic], 15 Dec 1860, -, -, -, Saml., Coyle, Mary, Gonker, Cavetown District, -, 26

2685, 15 Mar 1861, Allen Perry, Barber, Geo., Mary, 4 Mar 1861, -, -, -, -, -, -, -, -, -, Fald [?], 26

ST. MARY'S CATHOLIC CHURCH
HAGERSTOWN, MARYLAND, BAPTISMS:
Index, Bap Date, Child, Last Name, Father, Mother,
Birth Date, Code1, Code2, Code3,
1st Sponsor First, 1st Sponsor Last,
2nd Sponsor First, 2nd Sponsor Last, Location,
Notes, Maiden Name, Priest

2686, 28 Apr 1861, Joseph S., Duffy, Wm. S., Eliza, 5 Feb 1861, -, -, -, Jas. I., Hurley, Sophia, Hurley [HB], -, Stake, 26

2687, 19 May 1861, Chrissontia, Difflehonser [sic], Lewis, Johanna, 22-Mar, -, -, -, Chrissontia, Neberlen, -, -, -, -, 26

2688, 19 May 1861, Johanna, Neberlen, Joseph, Chrissintia, 2 Mar 1861, -, -, -, Johanna, Dittlehonser [or Difflehonser], -, -, "supplied ceremonies", -, 26

2689, 2 Jun 1861, Saml. W., Lyzer [or Lzzer], Wesley, Mary, 8 Feb 1861, -, -, -, Edmund, Didier, -, -, -, Gouker, 26

2690, 6 Jun 1861, John Michael, Smith, Jos. M., Margaret, 28 Ajpr 1861, -, -, -, Cath., Smith, -, -, -, McCleary, 26

2691, 10 Jun 1861, Laura Millicent, Kemp, David, Margaret, 10 Feb 1861, -, -, -, Mrs., Eck, -, -, -, Day, 26

2692, 18 Jun 1861, Wm. Henry, Haurande[?], Martin, Christina, 21 Nov 1860, -, -, -, Jno., Eck, -, -, "Supplied ceremonies"; "Baptized privately at home when sick", Shaten, 26

2693, 30 Jun 1861, Frances Elizabeth, Lorschbaugh, Geo., Frances [See Notes], 27 Jan 1861, -, -, -, Lizzie, Sherley, -, -, See Endnote 13 after Death section , -, 26

2694, 8 Jul 1861, Mary Elizabeth, Dorsey, Ignatius B., Anna R., 29 Aug 1860, -, -, -, -, -, -, -, PB, Andrews, 26

2695, 14 Jul 1861, Mary Elizabeth, Hawken, Jas. E., Mary S., 9 Mar 1861, -, -, -, Mary E.[?], Hawken, Wm. H., Hawken, -, Mendenhall, 26

2696, 14 Jul 1861, Anna Cecilia, McCardell, Chas., Kate, 13 Jun 1861, -, -, -, Cecilia, Oliver, Jesse, Thompson, -, -, 26

2697, 19 Jul 1861, Chas. Patrick, Coogan, Mark [?], Eliz., 1 Jul 1861, -, -, -, Bridget, Coogan, -, -, -, Kelly, 26

2698, 3 Aug 1861, Margaret, Houser, Hiram, Mary, 18 Jul 1861, -, -, -, Margaret, Riddle [or Riddler or Riddles], -, -, -, Walter, 26

2699, 3 Aug 1861, [blank], Barry, John, Mary, 10 Jul 1861, -, -, -, -, -, -, -, PB; BP, Collins, 26

2700, 16 Aug 1861, Francis, Hyles, Albert, Mrs., 2 years , -, -, -, -, -, -, -, PB, -, 26

2701, 8 Sep 1861, Edwd. Oscar, Covell, Jos., Eliz., 15 Aug 1859, -, -, -, Mary, Barry, -, -, Williamsport, -, 26

ST. MARY'S CATHOLIC CHURCH
HAGERSTOWN, MARYLAND, BAPTISMS:
Index, Bap Date, Child, Last Name, Father, Mother,
Birth Date, Code1, Code2, Code3,
1st Sponsor First, 1st Sponsor Last,
2nd Sponsor First, 2nd Sponsor Last, Location,
Notes, Maiden Name, Priest

2702, 30 Sep 1861, John, Geary, Eugene, Catherine, 30-Sep, -, -, -, John, Sullivan, Mary, Sullivan [HB], Hagerstown, Sullivan, 27

2703, 20 Oct 1861, Anna Mary, Ryan, Timothy, Ann, 26 Oct 1860, -, -, -, John, Barry, Mary, Barry, Williamsport, McAnany, 27

2704, 16 Nov 1861, Ella Mary, Doran, Charles, Anna E., 27-Sep, -, -, -, Jerome B., McClery, Mary I. [or J.], Pitt, Hagerstown, Dodson, 27

2705, 16 Nov 1861, Sarah, Mealene, Hugh, Mary, 11-Nov, -, -, -, Alescius, Cratin, Ellen, Cratin, Hagerstown, Kelly, 27

2706, 7 Jan 1862, Joseph Benedict, Hennessy, Peter, Ellen, 5 Jan 1862, -, -, -, Arthur, Kenny, Briget, Kenny, Hagerstown, Dolan, 28

2707, 21 Jan 1862, Thomas, Sullivan, Thos., Mary, 21 Dec 1861, -, -, -, John, Glison, M., Cleary, Hagerstown, Rabit, 28

2708, 26 Jan 1862, Regina Virginia, Kelly, Patrick, Sally, 9 Jan 1862, -, -, -, Hugh, Taggart, Eliz [?], Taggart [HB], Hagerstown, Moony, 28

2709, 9 Feb 1862, Sarah Ellen, Campbell, Manley, Grace, [blank], -, -, -, Wm., Failinger, ["Mary" crossed out] Catherine, Failinger [HB], Clear Spring, Tadden, 28

2710, 10 Feb 1862, Sarah Scholastica, Kriegh, George Wm., Christina, [blank], -, -, -, P., Moran, Miss, Kreigh, Clear Spring, Martin, 28

2711, 16 Feb 1862, George, Quick, Jacob, Margaret, [blank], -, -, -, Mr., Wright, Mrs., Wright [HB], -, -, 28

2712, 18 Feb 1862, Joanna Eva Cristina, Bridenburgh, Geo., Margaret, 23-Jan, -, -, -, Joanna, Delhouser, -, -, -, Arnold, 28

2713, 9 Mar 1862, Anne Elisabeth, Duncan, Levi, Mary Catherine, 18 Jan 1859, -, -, -, Theresa, Germans, -, -, BC, Lewis, 28

2714, 25 Mar 1862, Sarah Agnes, Murray, Andrew, Pollie, 24 Jun 1847, -, -, -, Eva, Doyle, -, -, C; BC; "natural child" crossed out - "natural child" was a term which was used to mean an illegitimate child, Loudeslager, 28

2715, 25 Mar 1862, Eliza, Stewart, Henry, Eliza, "born about a year ago", -, B, B, -, -, -, -, PB, -, 28

2716, 27 Mar 1862, John, Warner, Robert, Mary Elisabeth, 24 Mar 1862, -, -, -, Samuel, Eck, Mary, Cremer, -, Chephur, 28

ST. MARY'S CATHOLIC CHURCH
HAGERSTOWN, MARYLAND, BAPTISMS:
Index, Bap Date, Child, Last Name, Father, Mother,
Birth Date, Code1, Code2, Code3,
1st Sponsor First, 1st Sponsor Last,
2nd Sponsor First, 2nd Sponsor Last, Location,
Notes, Maiden Name, Priest

2717, 4 Apr 1862, Mary Enna, Wolse [?], John, Catherine, "born about a year ago", -, -, -, Mary, McCoskey, -, -, BP; PB, McCoskey, 28

2718, 5 Apr 1862, Charlotte Susanna, Barger, -, -, 13 years, -, -, -, Josephine, Hurley, -, -, "convert from Protestantism", -, 28

2719, 20 Apr 1862, Susan Margaret, Furley, James, Mary Jane, 18 Aug 1861, -, -, -, Mary, Coyle, -, -, baptized "without ceremonies"; "Supplied ceremonies 21st July 1862", Black, 28

2720, 21 Apr 1862, Ceceilia, Powell, Wm., Cecilia, 25-Mar, -, -, -, Eva, Doyle, -, -, "Baptized (without cermonies)"; "I suppied ceremonies 16th May", Gilmeyer, 28

2721, 21 Apr 1862, -, -, -, -, -, -, -, -, -, -, -, -, only text in this entry is "I Baptized (without ceremonies)", -, 28

2722, 11 May 1862, James, McGonigle, John, Sarah, 25-Apr, -, -, -, Joseph, Gonigle, Mary, Taggaret, -, -, 28

2723, 11 May 1862, Meargaret [sic], Coogan, Michael [sic], Briget, 23-Apr, -, -, -, Elisabeth, Coogan, -, -, -, -, 28

2724, 24 May 1862, Mary Alphonsus Theresia, Harne, -, -, 21 years, -, -, -, Mary, Coyle, -, -, C; "never before baptized", -, 28

2725, [blank], [blank], Gumpurt [?], South, Mary, -, PN, -, -, -, -, -, -, "I baptized (privately an illegitimate child of Mary Gumpurt[?] and one South the parents being of no religion.", -, 28

2726, 9 Jun 1862, Joseph Herman, Hiel, Albert, Carlisle, 15-Mar, -, -, -, Mrs., Brown, -, -, -, -, 28

2727, 15 Jun 1862, Elisabeth Ellen, Kenney, Arthur, Bridget, 20-May, -, -, -, Thos., Dolan, Elisabeth, Walsh, -, -, 28

2728, 15 Jun 1862, Daniel Patrick, Gouer, Joseph, Mary, 7-Mar, -, -, -, Aug., Coyle, Mary, Coyle [HB], Cavetown; BC, -, 28

2729, 22 Jun 1862, Aloysius, Flyn, Jas., Mary, 20-May, -, -, -, Thos., Drinnin, M., Hanna, Dam No. 4, -, 28

2730, 21 Jul 1862, Marry [sic] Cahterine, Bouer, Michel, Anne, "born 29. 1862", -, -, -, Julia Anne, Gouker, -, -, -, -, 28

2731, 21 Jul 1862, Anne Mary, Diffendel, Samuel, Mary, 15 Oct 1861, -, -, -, Susan, [blank], -, -, -, -, 28

2732, 7 Aug 1862, Jas. Wm., Cogle [?], Joseph, Elisabeth, 3-Jul, -, -, -, Margaret, McCosker, -, -, -, -, 28

ST. MARY'S CATHOLIC CHURCH
HAGERSTOWN, MARYLAND, BAPTISMS:
Index, Bap Date, Child, Last Name, Father, Mother,
Birth Date, Code1, Code2, Code3,
1st Sponsor First, 1st Sponsor Last,
2nd Sponsor First, 2nd Sponsor Last, Location,
Notes, Maiden Name, Priest

2733, 17 Aug 1862, Edmund Didier, McCardel, Ulton, Ann E., about a month , -, -, -, Evelina, McCardel, -, -, -, Mevrin [?], 28

2734, 24 Aug 1862, Elisabeth Mary, Roach, Wm., Catherine, 23 Dec 1861, -, -, -, Wm., Brown, Marg., Walsh, Clear Spring, -, 28

2735, 31 Aug 1862, Mary Geneva, Wright, Jacob, Sarah R., 5 Aug 1862, -, -, -, Jane B., Maguire, -, -, Hagerstown, Bosserman, 19

2736, 25 Aug 1862, Mary Catharine, Wolf, Henry, Mary Ann, 15 Aug 1862, -, -, -, William, McClain, Martha, McClain, Williamsport, McClain, 19

2737, 7 Aug 1862, Sarah Ellen, Sterling, William, Matilda, 1 Oct 1861, -, -, -, Cecelia, Oliver, -, -, Williamsport, Murray, 19

2738, 12 Sep 1862, Donnel, Kavanagh, Donnel, Mary, 1 Sep 1862, -, -, -, Thos., Sullivan, Mary, Sullivan [HB], Hagerstown, -, 28

2739, 25 Sep 1862, Mary Eliza, Needy, Isaac, Catherine, Jul, -, -, -, Sarah, Griffith, -, -, Hagerstown, Griffith, 28

2740, 5 Oct 1862, John Richard, Barry, John, Mary, 12 Sep 1862, -, -, -, John, Goddard, Catherine, Barry, Williamsport, -, 28

2741, 14 Oct 1862, Catherine, Smith, Josiah, Catherine, 15-Jun, -, -, -, Julia, Lane, -, -, Boonsboro, -, 28

2742, 14 Oct 1862, Elizabeth, Smith, Josiah, Catherine, 11 Apr 1861, -, -, -, Susan, Weast, -, -, Boonsboro, -, 28

2743, 22 Oct 1862, Maria Angela, Wise, Richard, Mary, 5 Oct 1862, -, -, -, Mrs., Hoskinson, -, -, Hagerstown, -, 28

2744, 27 Oct 1862, George Wm.* , Tinderman, Leuis [Lewis?], Barbary [sic], 15 Sep 1862, -, -, -, Augustine, Coyle, Mary, Gouker, Cavetown; * "McC" is crossed out beside "George Wm.", -, 28

2745, 6 Nov 1862, Louisa, Rodes [?], -, -, 26 years, -, -, -, Laetitia, McAlleny, -, -, Hagerstown; C; BC, -, 28

2746, 14 Nov 1862, Margaret Elisabeth, Coogan, Mathew, Elisabeth, 28 Oct 1862, -, -, -, Margaret, Doyle, -, -, Hagerstown, -, 28

2747, 24 Nov 1862, Mary Theresa, Crauley, John, Mary Theresa, 21 Nov 1862, -, -, -, Eva (Miss), Doyle, -, -, Hagerstown, -, 28

2748, 24 Nov 1862, Elisabeth, South, Benjamin, Catherine, 19 Sep 1862, -, -, -, Jerome, McCleary, Eva, Doyle, Fungstown [Funkstown], -, 28

ST. MARY'S CATHOLIC CHURCH
HAGERSTOWN, MARYLAND, BAPTISMS:
Index, Bap Date, Child, Last Name, Father, Mother,
Birth Date, Code1, Code2, Code3,
1st Sponsor First, 1st Sponsor Last,
2nd Sponsor First, 2nd Sponsor Last, Location,
Notes, Maiden Name, Priest

2749, 25 Nov 1862, Mary Louisa, Cushwa, Victor, Mary Anne, 2-Nov, -, -, -, Elisabeth, Kriegh, -, -, Williamsport, -, 28

2750, 1 Dec 1862, George , Shank, Adam, Anne Sophia, 20-Aug, -, -, -, Mary, Tierney, -, -, Hagerstown, -, 28

2751, 11 Dec 1862, Margaret Elisabeth, Prior, Jacob, Mary, 15-Sep, -, -, -, Ellen, Murphy, -, -, Fifteen Mile Creek, -, 28

2752, 18 Jan 1863, Alice Margaret, Clarkson, Edward, Ellen, about a month , -, -, -, Michel, O'Brien, Elisabeth, Clarkson, Hagerstown, -, 28

2753, 18 Jan 1863, Ellen, Clarkson, Edward, Ellen, about a month , -, -, -, Morris, O'Connor, Catherine, Hossett, Hagerstown, -, 28

2754, 24 Jan 1863, Jas. Clarke, Shervin, Henry, Catherine, 31 Dec 1862, -, -, -, Jas., Clarke, Mary, Parker, Bakersville, -, 28

2755, 26 Jan 1863, Henry Stanislaus, Smith, Joseph, Margaret, 21 Jan 1862, -, -, -, Evaline, Doyle, -, -, Clear Spring, -, 28

2756, 19 Mar 1863, Emma Florence, Smith, John, Theresa, 28 Jan 1863, -, -, -, Elisabeth, Deiterich, -, -, -, -, 28

2757, 3 May 1863, Augustine, Stewart, Henry, Eliza, 3 Apr 1863, -, -, -, Hanna, Lucket, -, -, Hagerstown, -, 28

2758, 4 Jun 1863, Mary Cecilia, Cretin, Alexius, Mary Ellen, 13-May, -, -, -, Jerome, McCleary, Miss, Burke, Hagerstown, Corbin, 28

2759, 20 Jun 1863, Anastasia, Kemp, David, Margaret, 29-Mar, -, -, -, Mary, Eck, -, -, -, Day, 28

2760, 16 Jul 1863, Geo. Edward, Green, Martin, Susan, 16 May 1863, -, -, -, G.[?] A. (Mrs.), Smith, -, -, -, Smith, 28

2761, 30 Jul 1863, Genevef Regina, McCardell, Willebee, Belinda, 28 Jun 1863, -, -, -, Jane, Magguire, -, -, -, -, 28

2762, 8 Sep 1863, Ellen, Duffey, Wm., Eliza, 20 Aug 1863 , -, ?, -, Letitia, McAlleaney [?], -, -, Hagerstown, Stake, 28

2763, 14 Sep 1863, Anne, Govern, Pat, Margaret, 5 Feb 1863, PN, -, -, Catherine, McCleary, James, Dunne, Potomac Landing , Walsh, 28

2764, 4 Oct 1863, Charles William, Mahony, William, Arrabella Frances, "born on Easter day", -, -, -, Hanna, Lucket, -, -, Hagerstown, -, 28

ST. MARY'S CATHOLIC CHURCH HAGERSTOWN, MARYLAND, BAPTISMS:
Index, Bap Date, Child, Last Name, Father, Mother, Birth Date, Code1, Code2, Code3, 1st Sponsor First, 1st Sponsor Last, 2nd Sponsor First, 2nd Sponsor Last, Location, Notes, Maiden Name, Priest

2765, 15 Oct 1863, Theresa, Coyle, Thos., Eda, 4 Oct 1863, -, -, -, Mrs., Coyle, -, -, Cavetown, Hearn, 28

2766, 2 Nov 1863, John Augustine, Voud [?], John, Teresa Rebecca, 13-Jun, PN, -, -, Mary Ann, Schofer, -, -, Hagerstown , Schoeffer, 28

2767, 4 Nov 1863, William Charles, Pouer, William, Cecilia, "4th inst.", -, -, -, Catherine, Gray, -, -, Hagerstown, Gilmeyer, 28

2768, [blank], Mary C., Flynn, James, Mary, 19-Oct, -, -, -, Thos., Hasset, Jane, Mouse, Potomac Landing, Drennan, 28

2769, [blank], Clarence Regina [sic], Hasset, Thos., Ellen, 30-Mar, -, -, -, John, Flynn, -, -, Potomac Landing, Silvers, 28

2770, 6 Dec 1863, Joseph, Griffin, Jacob H., Mary, 31 Oct 1863, -, -, -, Jacob, Griffin, -, Jos, Hagerstown, Walk, 28

2771, 16 Dec 1863, Robt., Kriegh, Georg, Cristina, 28-Nov, -, -, -, Wm., Kriegh, Sarah, Cushwa, Avondale, Martin, 28

2772, [blank]*, David Franklin, Cushwa, William, Margaret, 7-Nov, -, -, -, Judge [John T.], Mason, Miss, Kriegh, Avondale; baptismal date is blank - could be 16 Dec 1863, Kriegh, 28

2773, 10 Feb 1864, Mary Alice, South, [blank], [blank], -, -, -, -, M. (Rev., Moran, -, -, -, -, 28

2774, 14 Feb 1864, Joseph, Oner [or Over], [blank], [blank], -, -, -, -, Frank, Hoover, Mary, Eck, -, -, 28

2775, 6 Mar 1864, Mary , Tierney, Martin, Johnna [sic], 29 Feb 1864, -, -, -, Mr. [?], McLeary, Mrs., Gray, Hagerstown, Sullivan, 28

2776, 6 Mar 1864, William, Geary, Eugene, Catherine, 4 Mar 1864, -, -, -, Martin, Tierney, Catherine, Hulahan, Hagerstown, Sullivan, 28

2777, 13 Mar 1864, John Frederick, Warner, Robert, Elisabeth, 2 Mar 1864, -, -, -, Samuel, Eck, Samuel (Mrs.), Eck [HB], Hagerstown, Chephar, 28

2778, 13 Mar 1864, William Edgar, Sterling, John F., Anna, 29 Apr 1863, -, -, -, William, Hawken, Tanny [Fanny?], Thompson, Williamsport, -, 28

2779, 14 Mar 1864, John Jas., Turner, Joseph, Margaret, 10 May 1863, -, -, -, Miss, Faelinger, Mr. [?], Suoup [Swope?], Potomac Landing, -, 28

ST. MARY'S CATHOLIC CHURCH
HAGERSTOWN, MARYLAND, BAPTISMS:
Index, Bap Date, Child, Last Name, Father, Mother,
Birth Date, Code1, Code2, Code3,
1st Sponsor First, 1st Sponsor Last,
2nd Sponsor First, 2nd Sponsor Last, Location,
Notes, Maiden Name, Priest

2780, 18 Apr 1864, Mary, Sullivan, Thos., Mary, 12 Apr 1864, -, -, -, Mrs., Tierney, -, -, Hagerstown, Rabit, 28

2781, 8 May 1864, Anne, Roach, William, Catherine, 29 Dec 1863, -, -, -, John, Flynn, Rose (Miss), McLeary, Potomac Landing, -, 28

2782, 8 May 1864, Timothy Trane [?], Dunne, Jas., Magaret [sic], 29 Feb 1864, -, -, -, Thos., Hapet, Sally (Miss), McLeary, Potomac Landing, -, 28

2783, 16 May 1864, Richard, Dounin, S. S.[?], Martha, about 6 years , -, -, -, E. (Miss), Taggart, -, -, Hagerstown, -, 28

2784, 16 May 1864, Edina, Dounin, S. S.[?], Martha, 8 years , -, -, -, Ellen (Miss), Taggart, -, -, Hagerstown, -, 28

2785, 16 May 1864, Flora, O'Conner [?], James, Mary, 26 Jun 1859, -, -, -, Jennie (Mrs.), Celuflin, -, -, -, -, 28

2786, 14 Aug 1864, Caroline, Wooltz, William, Amelia, 18 May 1864, -, -, -, Letitia, McIlhenny, -, -, Hagerstown, -, 29

2787, 14 Aug 1864, Jeremiah, Hennessy, Peter, Ellen, 6 weeks , -, -, -, Elizabeth, Welch, Richard W., Sterling, Tilmington [Tilghminton], -, 29

2788, 28 Aug 1864, Mary Cooper, Claflin, Ira W., Jane, 7 Jun 1864, -, -, -, Mary, Hurley, -, -, Hagerstown, -, 29

2789, 28 Aug 1864, Francis Ruiston [?], Doran, Charles, Anne A., 15 Jun 1864, -, -, -, R. (Mrs.), Gray, -, -, Hagerstown, -, 29

2790, 10 Sep 1864, Julian Lee, South, Benjamin, Catharine, 4-Aug, -, -, -, Emma J., Malony, -, -, Hagerstown; "reside at Funkstown", Donovan, 29

2791, 11 Sep 1864, Frederick Augustus, Tasea [?], Julias, Rachel, 2 Sep 1864, -, -, -, Sarah, Reidout, -, -, Hagerstown, -, 29

2792, 11 Sep 1864, William David, Barry, John, Mary, 11 Aug 1864, -, -, -, Mary, Goddard, -, -, Williamsport, -, 29

2793, 25 Sep 1864, Mary, Downing, Samuel S., Mary, 10 Sep 1864, -, -, -, Mary, Burke, -, -, Hagerstown, -, 29

2794, 26 Sep 1864, Anne Lee, Smith, Joseph N. [or M.], Margaret, 15 Aug 1864, -, -, -, Eliza, McGeary, -, -, -, -, 29

2795, 16 Oct 1864, Mary Catharine, Heil, Albert, Caroline, 5 Apr 1864, -, -, -, Mary, Eck, -, -, -, -, 26

ST. MARY'S CATHOLIC CHURCH
HAGERSTOWN, MARYLAND, BAPTISMS:
Index, Bap Date, Child, Last Name, Father, Mother,
Birth Date, Code1, Code2, Code3,
1st Sponsor First, 1st Sponsor Last,
2nd Sponsor First, 2nd Sponsor Last, Location,
Notes, Maiden Name, Priest

2796, 20 Oct 1864, Thos. Hiram, Barber, Geo., Mary, 10 Jul 1863, -, -, -, Hugh, Taggart, -, -, -, -, 26

2797, [blank]*, Letitia, Barber, Geo., Mary, -, -, -, -, Mrs., Warner, -, -, "supplied ceremonies"; baptismal date is blank-appears to be 20 Oct 1864, -, 26

2798, [blank]*, Harvey, Barber, Geo., Mary, -, -, -, -, Hugh, Taggart, -, -, "supplied ceremonies"; baptismal date is blank-appears to be 20 Oct 1865, -, 26

2799, [blank]*, Allen Perry, Barber, Geo., Mary, -, -, -, -, [no sponsor listed for this 3rd child], -, -, -, "supplied ceremonies"; baptismal date is blank-appears to be 20 Oct 1866, -, 26

2800, 23 Oct 1864, David Thomas, Herlehy, Richard, Ellen, 16 Sep 1864, -, -, -, David, Herlehy, Mary, Barry, Williamsport, Desmond, 30

2801, 6 Nov 1864, George Kyper, Bauer, John, Christianna, 31 Dec 1815, -, -, -, Richard, Starling, -, -, BC; C, -, 30

2802, 21 Nov 1864, Thomas Benton, Cushwa, David, Susan, 12 Sep 1846, -, -, -, William, Doyle, Eva, Doyle [HB], C; Hagerstown, Zuck, 30

2803, 15 Dec 1864, Lucinda Margaret, Motter, George, Mary, 8 Mar 1820, -, -, -, Al., Pilz, -, -, C; BC, Kraft, 30

2804, 31 Dec 1864, Charles Henry, Zuck, Jacob, Margaret, 9 Nov 1864, -, -, -, Jacob P., Wright, Sarah, Wright, Hagerstown; "Died soon afterwards"; baptized without ceremony, Lewis, 30

2805, 1 Jan 1864, Mary, Cavin, Daniel, Mary, 27 Dec 1864, -, -, -, Thomas, Griffin, Ann, McCulloff, Hagerstown, Sullivan, 30

2806, 2 Jan 1865, Mary, Stuk, C.[?] F., Jane C., 30 Apr 1835, -, -, -, Catharine (Mrs.), Grey, -, -, Hagerstown; C; BC; in the margin is written "Mary Stuck (Owner)" - perhaps her married name is Owner?, Cooper, 30

2807, 4 Jan 1865, Mary A. Catharine, Turner, Joseph, Marg., 5 Oct 1864, -, -, -, Mary, Whitney, -, -, Clear Spring, Saners, 30

2808, 9 Jan 1865, William, Cushwa, David, Susan, 1 Mar 1839, -, -, -, William, Doyle, -, -, C; Hagerstown, Zuck, 30

2809, 1 Mar 1865, Charles Jessie, Smith, William, Emily, 3 Feb 1865, -, -, -, Margaret, Smith, -, -, Clear Spring, McLaughlin, 30

ST. MARY'S CATHOLIC CHURCH
HAGERSTOWN, MARYLAND, BAPTISMS:
Index, Bap Date, Child, Last Name, Father, Mother,
Birth Date, Code1, Code2, Code3,
1st Sponsor First, 1st Sponsor Last,
2nd Sponsor First, 2nd Sponsor Last, Location,
Notes, Maiden Name, Priest

2810, 27 Feb 1865, Eve, Farrensworth, Will., Marg., 21 Feb 1865, -, -, -, Margar., McCusker, -, -, Williamsport, McCusker, 30

2811, 12 Mar 1865, David, Hurlehy, David, Cathar., 29 Dec 1864, -, -, -, Richard, Hurlehy, Mary, Hassett, Williamsport, Hassett, 30

2812, 11 Mar 1865, Jesse F., Thompson, Fannis M., Leo, 27 Feb 1865, -, -, -, Helen (Mrs.), Stake [Thompson crossed out], -, -, Williamsport, Duhanell, 30

2813, 11 Mar 1865, Harry Lee*, Ardinger, Benjamin, Susan, 26 Nov 1864, -, -, -, Mrs., Thompson, -, -, Williamsport; *Harry Lee [Benjamin crossed out], Thompson, 30

2814, 14 Mar 1865, Victor Monroe, Cushwa, Victor, Mary, 12 Mar 1865, -, -, -, H. Angelo, Powell, Sallie, Cushwa, Williamsport, Creigh, 30

2815, 31 Mar 1865, Virginia, Ward, Samuel, Elis., 23 Jan 1843, -, -, -, Louisa, Doyle, -, -, Hagerstown; C, Shaw, 30

2816, 8 Apr 1865, Rolin Eugene, McArdle, Ambrose D., Cecilia, 28 Mar 1865, -, -, -, Ellen S., Oliver, -, -, Williamsport, Oliver, 30

2817, 25 Apr 1865, Ellen Genevieve, Sheridan, Patr., Bridget, 11 Apr 1865, -, -, -, Ellen, Stake, -, -, Williamsport, -, 30

2818, 26 Apr 1865, Charles Malachy, Coyle, Thomas, Mary, 1 Mar 1865, -, -, -, Sarah, Kelly, -, -, Cavetown, Harne, 30

2819, 27 Apr 1865, Annie, Souers, Daniel, Mary, 20 years, -, -, -, Kate, Gray, -, -, Hagerstown; B; Annie is described as "an infidel"; C, Hall, 30

2820, 28 Apr 1865, James Augustus, Furley, James A., Mary I.[?], 30 Dec 1864, -, -, -, Cathar., Maguire [?], -, -, Hagerstown, Hack [?], 31

2821, 28 Apr 1865, Cecilia Jane, Gaugher, Joseph, Mary I.[?], 23 Sep 1864, -, -, -, Mary, Levin *, -, -, Hagerstown; * "(3)" is written after her name, Maten [?], 31

2822, 14 May 1865, Samuel Frederick, Green, Martin V., Susan R., 27 Mar 1865, -, -, -, Martha, Griffey, -, -, Williamsport; father is "infidel" and mother is "catholic", Smith, 30

2823, 28 May 1865, Edmund Didier, Smith, John, Teresa, 9 Feb 1865, -, -, -, Rose, McGeary, -, -, Funkstown, Griffin, 30

ST. MARY'S CATHOLIC CHURCH
HAGERSTOWN, MARYLAND, BAPTISMS:
Index, Bap Date, Child, Last Name, Father, Mother,
Birth Date, Code1, Code2, Code3,
1st Sponsor First, 1st Sponsor Last,
2nd Sponsor First, 2nd Sponsor Last, Location,
Notes, Maiden Name, Priest

2824, 28 May 1865, Mary Elis., Hipner, Thomas, Mary, 1 Jun 1864, -, -, -, Elisabeth, Schloterbeck, -, -, St. James College, Selmer, 30

2825, 9 Jun 1865, Sarah Elis., Covel, Joseph, Elis., 5 Apr 1865, -, -, -, Mary, Paddon, -, -, Williamsport, Paddon, 30

2826, 4 Aug 1865, Emilla [?] Hugheshew [?], Newsome, Augustus, Mary Olivia, 20 Dec 1864, B, -, -, Kitty, Shorter, -, -, Hagerstown , -, 26

2827, 13 Aug 1865, [female], Byroads, -, -, 20 years, -, -, -, -, -, -, -, BP; "She died two days afterwards.", -, 26

2828, 3 Sep 1865, Geo. Adrian, McCardell, Ulton, Ann, 29 Jan 1865, -, -, -, Annie , McCardell, Edmund, Didier, -, -, 26

2829, 12 Sep 1865, Nathanael Joseph, Braxten, -, -, 16 years, -, -, -, Rose, McGary, -, -, B, -, 26

2830, 12 Sep 1865, Kate, Hassett, Thos., Ellen, 14 Feb 1865, -, -, -, Jas., Flynn, -, -, -, -, 26

2831, 18 Sep 1865, Jas. Day, Kemp, David, Margt., 16 Jun 1865, -, -, -, Anna, Floyd, -, -, -, -, 26

2832, 17 Sep 1865, Jas. Zellers, Thompson, Wm., Margt., 16 Jun 1865, -, -, -, -, -, -, -, WC, -, 26

2833, 23 Sep 1865, Ida Kate, Little, Chs., Rebecca, 4 Sep 1864, -, -, -, Jane, Maguire, -, -, -, -, 26

2834, 26 Sep 1865, Wm. David, Clarkson, Edwd., Cath., 25 Aug 1865, -, -, -, Mary, Clabaugh, Geo., Clarkson, -, -, 26

2835, 26 Sep 1865, Nelly Lee, Hawken, Jas., Mary Susan, 8 Mar 1864, -, -, -, Rosa, McAvoy, -, -, -, -, 26

2836, 8 Oct 1865, Wm. Hy., Leffleman, Geo., Lucretia, 13 Aug 1865, -, -, -, Eli, Stake, Eli (Mrs.), Stake [HB], -, -, 26

2837, 8 Oct 1865, Florence, Bowman, Jno., Sybilla [?], Jun 1862, -, -, -, Nelly, Stake, -, -, -, Newcomer, 26

2838, 9 Oct 1865, Wm., Shervin, Hy., Kate, 10 Feb 1865, -, -, -, Thos., Shervin, Mar., Clark, -, Clark, 26

2839, 10 Oct 1865, Ellen, Collins, Patr., Jane, 2 Jul 1865, -, -, -, Margt., Clark [or Clarke], -, -, -, -, 26

2840, 26 Oct 1865, Wm. Carroll, Martiny, -, Sally, 14 Jan 1862, -, -, -, Ellen, Oliver, -, -, CS, -, 26

ST. MARY'S CATHOLIC CHURCH
HAGERSTOWN, MARYLAND, BAPTISMS:
Index, Bap Date, Child, Last Name, Father, Mother,
Birth Date, Code1, Code2, Code3,
1st Sponsor First, 1st Sponsor Last,
2nd Sponsor First, 2nd Sponsor Last, Location,
Notes, Maiden Name, Priest

2841, 26 Oct 1865, John, Marlot ["Covell" crossed out], Jno. Stillwell, Margt., 4 Jan 1861, -, -, -, Bridget, Rodgers, -, -, -, -, 26

2842, 2 Nov 1865, Wm. Edwd. Chas., Richter, Chas., Caroline, 19 Jul 1865, -, -, -, Eliz., Rickter, -, -, -, -, 26

2843, 1 Dec 1865, Ida Kate, Lyttle, Hy., Mary, May 1865, -, -, -, Cecie, Lyttle, -, -, -, -, 26

2844, 10 Dec 1865, Fanny Eliz. Julia, Smith, Jno. W., Sarah A., 4 Nov 1865, -, -, -, Julia, Pritner [?], -, -, -, -, 26

2845, 11 Dec 1865, Jno. W., Hetzer, Chas., Cath., 3 Aug 1865, -, -, -, Eliz., Covell, -, -, -, -, 26

2846, 1 Jan 1866, Henry Stanislaw, Wolf, Hy., Mary Ann, 15 Nov 1865, -, -, -, Wm. B., McClain, Wm. B. (Mrs.), McClain [HB], -, -, 26

2847, 5 Jan 1866, Hy Clay Morris, Henneberger, Hiram[?], M. Eliz., 1 Oct 1865, -, -, -, Lucinda, Hoover, -, -, -, -, 26

2848, 28 Jan 1918, Henry C., Henneberger, -, -, -, -, -, -, -, -, -, -, [this entry is written in a darker ink between the margins of the entry above]; See Endnote 34., -, 26

2849, 6 Jan 1866, Wm. Flora, Ryan, Mich. H., -, 6 years, -, -, -, Richd., Sterling, -, -, "adopted child", -, 26

2850, 2 Feb 1866, Mary Eliz., Warner, Robt., Mary, 9 weeks, -, -, -, Kate, Gray, -, -, -, -, 26

2851, 2 Apr 1866, Reuben, Hornsby, -, -, 23 years, -, -, -, -, -, -, -, baptized in a simple manner before marriage ceremony, -, 26

2852, 10 Apr 1866, Francis Matthew, Dellen, Mich., Martha, 16 Mar 1866, -, -, -, R., Sterling, -, -, See Endnote 35. , McCalleen, 26

2853, 12 Apr 1866, Edwd., Williams, -, -, -, -, -, -, -, -, -, -, WC; baptized "just before marriage with Eliza Lewis"; B, -, 26

2854, 14 Apr 1866, Clara Ellen, Shorter, Nathan, Frances, 25 Feb 1866, -, -, -, Mary, Galloway, -, -, B, -, 26

2855, 13 Apr 1866, Kate, Justice, -, -, -, -, -, -, -, -, -, -, WC; "a convert to our holy faith", -, 26

2856, 22 Apr 1866, Chs. Francis, Foller, Jno, Mary, 19 Mar 1866, -, -, -, Lucinda, Hoover, Wm., Orndorff, -, Orndorff, 26

2857, 22 Apr 1866, Robt. Franklin, Shank, Adam, Ann, 8 Dec 1865, -, -, -, Jane, Maguire, -, -, -, Maguire, 26

ST. MARY'S CATHOLIC CHURCH
HAGERSTOWN, MARYLAND, BAPTISMS:
Index, Bap Date, Child, Last Name, Father, Mother,
Birth Date, Code1, Code2, Code3,
1st Sponsor First, 1st Sponsor Last,
2nd Sponsor First, 2nd Sponsor Last, Location,
Notes, Maiden Name, Priest

2858, 27 Apr 1866, Thos. Henry, Flynn, Jas., Louisa, 11 Jul 1865, -, -, -, Rd., Sterling, -, -, "near Downsville, Md.", -, 26

2859, 29 Apr 1866, Jos. Hy., Flynn, Jas., Mary, 30 Mar 1866, -, -, -, Wm. B., McClain, Sarah, Brannan, -, Drennan, 26

2860, 29 Apr 1866, Wm. Francis, Smith, Jos. M., Margt., 11 Apr 1866, -, -, -, Fred., Doyle, Kate, McCleary, -, McCleary, 26

2861, 30 Apr 1866, Martha Eliz., Mouse, Thos., Mary Catharine, 20 Aug 1863, -, -, -, Lizzie, Fellinger, -, -, -, -, 26

2862, 30 Apr 1866, Ann Jane, Mouse, Thos., Mary Catharine, 17 Sep 1865, -, -, -, Ann, Baer, -, -, -, -, 26

2863, 20 May 1866, Charles Emmanuel, Holmes, Jno., Margt., 8 May 1866, -, -, -, Danl., Mouse, -, -, -, Dugan, 26

2864, 10 Jun 1866, Denis Henry, Barry, John, Mary, 1 May 1866, -, -, -, Denis, Collins, Margt., Collins [HB], -, Collins, 26

2865, 10 Jun 1866, Norman Eugene, Cleyburne, Jno., Sally, 25 Mar 1866, -, -, -, Mary, Cushwa, -, -, -, Martiny, 26

2866, 24 Jun 1866, Clara Virginia, Needy, Isaac, Kate, 13 Dec 1865, -, -, -, Margt., Griffey, -, -, -, -, 26

2867, 8 Jul 1866, Wm. Baker, Morrison, Brown, Mary, 8 May 1866, -, -, -, Lon. [?], Brazelle, -, -, -, McKusker, 26

2868, 25 Jul 1866, Miles[?] Benedict, O'Brien, Matthew, Rebecca, 1 Dec 1863, -, -, -, Letty, McIlhenny, -, -, -, O'Brien, 26

2869, 31 Jul 1866, May [or Mary] Ellen, Ryan, Jas., [wife], -, -, -, -, -, -, -, -, BP, -, 26

2870, 5 Aug 1866, Wm. Doyle, Fechtig, Geo., Louisa, 10 Jul 1866, -, -, -, Eva, McCleary, -, -, -, Doyle, 26

2871, 10 Feb 1866, Caroline, Dolan, Wm., Mary, 19 Jan 1866, -, -, -, Peter, Hennessy, Johann, Lewis [or Lewin], -, Smith, 47

2872, 13 Aug 1866, Percy Costello, Oliver, -, Kate, 3 months , PN, -, -, Maria, Oliver, -, -, -, -, 26

2873, 13 Aug 1866, Jno. Parker, Creamer, -, -, a few days, -, -, -, -, -, -, -, PB, -, 26

2874, 19 Aug 1866, Mary Eliz. Frances, Green, Martin, Susan, 7 Jul 1866, -, -, -, May [or Mary], Smith, -, -, -, Smith, 26

2875, 2 Sep 1866, Clara, Alsip, [blank], [blank], 26 Jul 1866, -, -, -, Mrs., Creamer, -, -, -, -, 26

ST. MARY'S CATHOLIC CHURCH HAGERSTOWN, MARYLAND, BAPTISMS:
Index, Bap Date, Child, Last Name, Father, Mother,
Birth Date, Code1, Code2, Code3,
1st Sponsor First, 1st Sponsor Last,
2nd Sponsor First, 2nd Sponsor Last, Location,
Notes, Maiden Name, Priest

2876, 2 Sep 1866, Joseph Ellsworth, Alsip, [blank], [blank], 17 Oct 1864, -, -, -, Eug. [Eugene], Gary, -, -, -, -, 26
2877, 2 Sep 1866, Mary Eliz., Barber, Geo., Mary, 20 Mar 1866, -, -, -, Barbara, Fate, -, -, -, Fald, 26
2878, 10 Sep 1866, Bertrand, Sterling, Jno., Anna, 27 Dec 1865, -, -, -, -, -, -, -, PB; WC, Menall, 26
2879, 16 Sep 1866, Jno. Eugene, Gary, Eugene, Cath., 1 Sep 1866, -, -, -, Thos., Gray, Ellen, Kelly, -, Sullivan, 26
2880, 23 Sep 1866, Thos., Green, Thos., Margt., 17 Jul 1866, -, -, -, Bridget, Reilly, Jas., Duigman[?] [or Dujman], -, Armstrong, 26
2881, 22 Nov 1866, Ann Josephine, Dittelhouser, Lewis [?], Johanna, 10 Jul 1866, -, -, -, Mrs., Helzele [or Helgele], -, -, -, -, 26
2882, 22 Nov 1866, Mary Ann, Shover, -, Theresa, 9 Jun 1866, -, -, -, Johanna, Dittelhouser, -, -, -, -, 26
2883, 2 Dec 1866, Chs. Elias, Byers, M., Barbara, 3-Jul, -, -, -, Mary, Gouker, -, -, -, Gouker, 26
2884, 21 Dec 1866, Chas., Hornback, Wm., [wife], 15 Nov 1866, -, -, -, -, -, -, -, WC, -, 26
2885, 23 Dec 1866, Mary Otilia, Evers [or Ewers], Milling [?], Susan, 26 May 1866, -, -, -, Mary, Eck, -, -, -, Futterer, 26
2886, 1 Jan 1867, Geo. Wm., Wooltz, Jno., Kate, 19 Dec 1866, -, -, -, -, -, -, -, WC, McKusker, 26
2887, 14 Jan 1867, Anna Laucenia [?], Wolff, Henry, Mary Ann, 17 Dec 1866, -, -, -, Wm. B., McClain, Wm. B. (Mrs.), McClain, -, -, 26
2888, 25 Jan 1867, Anestine [?] Rosa, Coyle, Thos., Ada, 18 Dec 1866, -, -, -, -, -, -, -, -, Harne, 26
2889, 26 Jan 1867, Geo. Hyner [?], Woltz, Chs. W., Amelia, 20 Nov 1866, -, -, -, Mary, Coyle, -, -, -, Stake, 26
2890, 3 Feb 1867, Sarah Berry, Lorschbaugh, Geo., Fanny, 2 Nov 1866, -, -, -, Bridget, Rodgers, -, -, -, -, 26
2891, 25 Feb 1867, Emma Etta, Stewart, [blank], [bland], 5 years, -, -, -, -, -, -, -, WC, -, 26
2892, 26 Feb 1867, Peter, Hennessy, Peter, Mary, 11-Feb, -, -, -, Barney, Halpin, Widow, Walsh, Widow Walsh is listed as the wife of Barney Halpin, -, 26

ST. MARY'S CATHOLIC CHURCH
HAGERSTOWN, MARYLAND, BAPTISMS:
Index, Bap Date, Child, Last Name, Father, Mother,
Birth Date, Code1, Code2, Code3,
1st Sponsor First, 1st Sponsor Last,
2nd Sponsor First, 2nd Sponsor Last, Location,
Notes, Maiden Name, Priest

2893, 10 Mar 1867, Benj. Francis, Hornesby, Reuben, Margt., 22 Oct 1866, -, -, -, Sally, Cleybarne, -, -, -, Marlot, 26
2894, 10 Mar 1867, Danl. Wm., Hurlehee, Rich., Ellen, 8 Feb 1867, -, -, -, Mary, Donnelly, Hugh, Murphy, -, Desmond, 26
2895, 10 Mar 1867, Netty Amelia, Thompson, Jesse, Fanny, 16 Feb 1867, -, -, -, Ella, Oliver, -, -, -, Oliver, 26
2896, 11 Mar 1867, Kate Clark, Shervin, Henry, Kate, 3 Feb 1867, -, -, -, Chs., Clark, Margt., Clark [HB], -, Clark, 26
2897, 19 Mar 1867, Wm. Benj., Ordner, Geo., Anna, 8 Feb 1867, -, -, -, Ann [?], Walton [?], -, -, -, Snyder, 26
2898, 25 Mar 1867, Jno. , Douglass, -, -, 77 years, B, -, -, Ellen , Stake, Th., Donnelly, -, -, 26
2899, 4 Apr 1867, Margt. Alice, Stouffer, Andr., Kate, 13 Feb 1867, -, -, -, Mary, Coyle, -, -, -, Gouker, 26
2900, 31 Mar 1867, Jacob Wm., Dunn, Jas., Margt., 19 Sep 1866, -, -, -, Margt., Dunn, -, -, -, -, 26
2901, 14 Apr 1867, Sarah Washington, Smith, Jno. W., Sarah A., 22 Feb 1867, -, -, -, Julia, Britner* , -, -, * name could be Butner or Bulner, Britner/Britmer[?], 26
2902, 5 May 1867, Owen, McDevitt, Brosnin [?], Cath., 26 Apr 1867, -, -, -, Wm., Heapley [?], Cathe., Gar [?], -, -, 26
2903, 12 May 1867, Mary Cath., Eliz., Jos., Covell, 23 Mar 1867, -, -, -, Charlotte, Goddard, -, -, -, -, 26
2904, 15 May 1867, Casper Swope, Jno., Nelly, 15 Feb 1867, -, -, -, Casper, Swope, Dolly, Swope [HB], -, Clare [or Clane], 26
2905, 19 May 1867, Henry Edwd., Smith, Edwd., Jenny, 15 Feb 1867, -, -, -, Mary, Coyle, -, -, -, -, 26
2906, 19 May 1867, John Elmer, Dick, Geo., Sarah, 11 Mar 1867, -, -, -, Jno., Peters, Jno. (Mrs.), Peters, -, -, 26
2907, 6 Jun 1867*, Mary Eliz., Malone, Hugh, Mary, 20 May 1867, -, -, -, Chs., Kelly, Ella, Taggart, *baptismal date is 6 [or 7] Jun 1867, Kelly, 26
2908, 8 Jun 1867, Eliz. May, South, Benj., Cath., 14 May 1867, -, -, -, Mary, Broderick, Edmund, Didier, -, -, 26
2909, 10 Jun 1867, Mary Ann, Heil, Albert, Caroline, 10 Jan 1866, -, -, -, Mary, Koppler, -, -, -, -, 26

ST. MARY'S CATHOLIC CHURCH
HAGERSTOWN, MARYLAND, BAPTISMS:
Index, Bap Date, Child, Last Name, Father, Mother,
Birth Date, Code1, Code2, Code3,
1st Sponsor First, 1st Sponsor Last,
2nd Sponsor First, 2nd Sponsor Last, Location,
Notes, Maiden Name, Priest

2910, 20 Jun 1867, Ann Amanda, Leffleman, Geo., Lucretia, 27 Mar 1867, -, -, -, Wm. B., McClain, "lady" ["Wm. B. McClain & lady"], -, -, Wolford, 26

2911, 30 Jun 1867, Geo. Franeir [?], Dick, Jno., Ann, 13 May 1867, -, -, -, Peter, Dick, Harriet, Dick [HB], -, Poper, 26

2912, 14 Jul 1867, Ellen Stake, Cushwa, Victor, Mary Ann, 24 Jun 1867, -, -, -, Wm., Kreigh, Ellan, Stake, -, Kreigh, 26

2913, 25 Jul 1867, Honora, Hurlehee, David, Kate, 24 Apr 1867, -, -, -, Maggy [?], Goddard, -, -, -, Hassett, 26

2914, 25 Jul 1867, Mary Magdella [?], Goddard, Wm., Cath., 13 Jun 1867, -, -, -, Magt., Barry, -, -, -, -, 26

2915, 25 Jul 1867, Thos., Downin, S.S., Mary, 14 Jul 1867, -, -, -, -, -, -, -, PB, McEvoy, 26

2916, 28 Jul 1867, Mary Jeanette, Fellenger, Phil, Lizzie, 4 Jul 1867, -, -, -, Lizzy, Fellinger, -, -, -, -, 26

2917, 9 Aug 1867, Sarah, Turner, Joseph, Ann, 15 Oct 1862, -, -, -, Cath., Smith, -, -, -, -, 26

2918, 9 Aug 1867, Joseph Edwd., Turner, Joseph, Ann, 1 May 1867, -, -, -, Cath., Smith, -, -, -, -, 26

2919, 23 Aug 1867, Jno., Barry, J.[?] M., Alice, 16 Aug 1867, -, -, -, M. G.[?], Barry, Eliz., Barry, -, -, 26

2920, 30 Aug 1867, Indiana Blanche, Young, Jos., Barbara, 5 Feb 1867, -, -, -, Susan, Fessler, -, -, See Endnote 36. , Pass [or Pap], 26

2921, 1 Sep 1867, Mary Cath., Mayberry, Peter, Margt., 13 Jul1867, -, -, -, Eva, McCleary, -, -, -, Doyle, 26

2922, 15 Sep 1867, Susan, Happell, M., Rosinse, 7 Aug 1867, -, -, -, Mrs., Futterer, -, -, -, -, 26

2923, 15 Sep 1867, Jonas Spielman, McCardell, Ultin, Anne, 2 Aug 1867, -, -, -, Mary, Coyle, -, -, -, -, 26

2924, 29 Sep 1867, Jesse Sorrel [?], McCardell, Thos., Alice, 28 Jun 1867, -, -, -, Anna, McCardell, -, -, -, -, 26

2925, 21 Oct 1867, Cath. Clarke, Collins, Pat, Jane, 9 Sep 1867, -, -, -, Ann, Ryan, Harry, Clarke, -, -, 26

2926, 1 Nov 1867, Margaret, Sheely, M., Margaret, 25 Oct 1867, -, -, -, Dan., Callaham, Anna, Talbott, -, -, 26

2927, 24 Nov 1867, Joseph, McKee, Jas., Rebecca, 5 Nov 1867, -, -, -, Michael, Chambers, Mary, Chambers [HB], -, -, 26

ST. MARY'S CATHOLIC CHURCH
HAGERSTOWN, MARYLAND, BAPTISMS:
Index, Bap Date, Child, Last Name, Father, Mother,
Birth Date, Code1, Code2, Code3,
1st Sponsor First, 1st Sponsor Last,
2nd Sponsor First, 2nd Sponsor Last, Location,
Notes, Maiden Name, Priest

2928, 30 Nov 1867, Mary Susan, Fechtig, Geo., Lou., 10 Sep 1867, -, -, -, Mary, Hurley, -, -, -, Doyle, 26

2929, 1 Dec 1867, James, Donnelly, Pat., Mary, 7 Nov 1867, -, -, -, Wm., Dugan, Bridget, Dugan [HB], -, McNealy, 26

2930, 9 Dec 1867, Jas. Demetris, Duffy, Wm., Eliza, 6 Nov 1867, -, -, -, Eliza, Meraban [?], -, -, -, Stake, 26

2931, 14 Dec 1867, Loutto Jane, Furley, Jas. A., Mary I.[?], 8 Oct 1867, -, -, -, M. Cath., Furley, -, -, -, -, 26

2932, 25 Dec 1867, Jno. Wm., Orndorf, Wm., Mary Jane, 25 Nov 1867, -, -, -, Lucinda, Horret, -, -, -, -, 26

2933, 25 Dec 1867, Nicholas, Hackett, Mich., Mary Ann, 23 Dec 1867, -, -, -, Mary, Hackett, Edwd., Whalen, -, -, 26

2934, 22 Jan 1868, George M., Kyper, Geo., Margt., 3 Dec 1867, -, -, -, -, -, -, -, PB, Moore, 26

2935, 3 May 1868, George M., Kyper, Geo., Margt., 3 Dec 1867, -, -, -, Jno., Eck, Jno. (Mrs.), Eck, supplied ceremonies, Moore, 26

2936, 30 Jan 1868, Geo. Francis Bernard, Diffendal, Saml., Margt., 26 Dec 1867, -, -, -, Thos., Coyle, Ada, Coyle [HB], -, -, 26

2937, 16 Feb 1868, John Edmund, Grady, Thos., Cath., 9 Feb 1868, -, -, -, Mary, Eck, Jno., Halpin, -, -, 26

2938, 16 Feb 1868, Bridget, Lyons, Danl., Eliza, 5 Feb 1868, -, -, -, Jno., Lyons, Bridget, Callahan, -, -, 26

2939, 1 Mar 1868, Joanna, Barry, Jno., Mary, 24 Jan 1868, -, -, -, Joanna, Roach, Jas., Ahorrin [?], -, -, 26

2940, 1 Mar 1868, John, Fininy [or Fining], Simon, Mary, 3 Feb 1868, -, -, -, Mike, Sheedy, Fanny, Sheedy [HB], -, -, 26

2941, 8 Mar 1868, Edward, O'Neill, Thos., Kate, 8 Feb 1868, -, -, -, Edwd., Donnelly, Mary, Donnelly [HB], -, Hughes, 26

2942, 13 Mar 1868, James, Malone, Jas., Ellen, 17 Feb 1868, -, -, -, Mich., Barry, Regina, McGran [?], -, McGrakin [?], 26

2943, 30 Mar 1868, David, Kemp, David, Margt., 16 Dec 1867, -, -, -, Cath., Smith, -, -, -, -, 26

2944, 19 Apr 1868, Francis Ernest, McCardell, Ambr. [Ambrose], Cecilia, 15 Mar 1868, -, -, -, Ella, Oliver, -, -, -, Oliver, 26

2945, 26 Apr 1868, Benedict James, Boswell, F. C., Anna M., 21 Mar 1868, -, -, -, Jas., Flynn, Cath., White, -, Fasnacht, 26

ST. MARY'S CATHOLIC CHURCH
HAGERSTOWN, MARYLAND, BAPTISMS:
Index, Bap Date, Child, Last Name, Father, Mother,
Birth Date, Code1, Code2, Code3,
1st Sponsor First, 1st Sponsor Last,
2nd Sponsor First, 2nd Sponsor Last, Location,
Notes, Maiden Name, Priest

2946, 27 Apr 1868, Wm. Kreigh, Cushwa, Wm., Margt., 25 Mar 1868, -, -, -, Mary, Cretin, -, -, -, Kreigh, 26

2947, 28 Apr 1868, Chas. Edmund, Hoover, Jos., Lucinda M., 27 Mar 1868, -, -, -, Mary J., Orndorff, -, -, -, Motter, 26

2948, 28 Apr 1868, Albert Roney, Doran, Chs. R., Anna, 19 Feb 1868, -, -, -, Emily, Pomme De Terre [sic], -, -, -, Dodson, 26

2949, 1 May 1868, Emily Jane, Heil, Alb. [Albert], Caroline, 19 Mar 1868, -, -, -, Rosanna, Heppel, -, -, -, Bloominoor, 26

2950, 2 May 1868, Catharine V., Deeds, -, -, 24 years, -, -, -, Cath., Gray, -, -, C; "never baptized before and never had the long ceremony", -, 26

2951, 2 May 1868, Sarah Ellen, Dusang, -, -, 21 years, -, -, -, -, -, -, -, BC; WC; "had been baps. Long ago, in Lutheran Church", -, 26

2952, 3 May 1868, Mary Ann, Shahen, Cornelius, Ellen, 1 Mar 1868, -, -, -, Eliz., Schilling, Dan., Long, -, Long, 26

2953, 5 May 1868, Clara Virginia, Dusang, Geo., Eliz., 6 Dec 1867, -, -, -, Tim., Doolin, Sarah E., Dusang, -, Dooling, 26

2954, May 1868, Ann Rosella, Green, Martin, susan, 10-Apr, -, -, -, -, -, -, -, -, Smith, 11

2955, 1 Jun 1868, Henry Lee, Shehan, Martin, Ann, 24 Oct 1863, -, -, -, Cornelius, Shehan, Elizabeth, Shillen, -, Hasset, 11

2956, 14 Jun 1868, Robert Eli, Lennon, Peter, Helan, 19-May, -, -, -, Eli, Stake, Louisa, Brazelle, -, Stake, 11

2957, 6 Jul 1868, William, Smith, John H., Theresa, 13-May, -, -, -, Mary, South, -, -, -, Griffey, 11

2958, 17 Jul 1868, Wm. Henry, Ryan, James, Julia, 24 Apr 1867, -, -, -, -, -, -, -, -, White, 11

2959, 19 Jul 1868, Elizabeth, Aheren [sic], James, Joanna, 29 Jun 1868, -, -, -, Catherine, Dillon, -, -, -, Dillon, 11

2960, 23 Jul 1868, James Wm., Loyd, John, Sarah, 19 months, -, -, -, Mary, Clabaugh, -, -, Hagerstown, Fox, 11

2961, 2 Aug 1868, Mary Daisy, Morrison, G. W. Brown[?], Mary, 5-Jul, -, -, -, Mary, McCuskery, -, -, Hagerstown, McCuskery, 11

2962, 8 Sep 1868, Margaret Ann, Wlaker, Allan, Ann, 6 months, B, B, B, John, Sweeny, -, -, Hagerstown; sponsor is Black; See Endnote 37, Brown [?], 11

**ST. MARY'S CATHOLIC CHURCH
HAGERSTOWN, MARYLAND, BAPTISMS:**
Index, Bap Date, Child, Last Name, Father, Mother,
Birth Date, Code1, Code2, Code3,
1st Sponsor First, 1st Sponsor Last,
2nd Sponsor First, 2nd Sponsor Last, Location,
Notes, Maiden Name, Priest

2963, 21 Sep 1868, Ann Cath., Mundy, George, Mary, 3 Jul 1858, -, -, -, John, Sweeny, -, -, Hagerstown, McCartin, 11

2964, 27 Sep 1868, Mary Theresa, Ewers, Milton, Susan, 11-Feb, -, -, -, Frank, Futterer, Mary, Clarbaugh, Hagerstown, Futterer, 11

2965, 5 Oct 1868, Owen Andrew, Hanson, -, Ann, 25-Sep, PN, -, -, Mrs., Helzele, -, -, Harristown – could be referring to Harry's Town, a part of Hagerstown, -, 11

2966, 14 Oct 1868, Alice Elizabeth, McDonald, Aaron [?], Anna, 31-Aug, -, -, -, Hugh, McKune, Elizabeth, McKune [HB], Hagerstown, Dunne [or Derme] ??, 11

2967, 29 Oct 1868, Charles Frederick, White, Mich., Cath., 19-Oct, -, -, -, Rosa, Fillinger, -, -, Rohrsville [Rohrersville], Fillinger, 11

2968, 29 Oct 1868, John, Conlan, Denis, Bridget, 3-Oct, -, -, -, Mich., White, -, -, Eakles Mill, Cunningham, 11

2969, 22 Nov 1868, Ann Eliza, Dilworth, Jeremiah, [blank], 17-Nov, -, -, -, Patrick, duffey, [blank], Dilworth, -, Murray, 11

2970, 6 Jan 1869, Charles Ragan, Yohn, Philip, Frances, [blank], -, -, -, Katherine, Gray, -, -, -, Wright, 11

2971, 13 Jan 1869, Alverta Gertrude, Little, Charles, Rebecca, 6 Jul 1868, -, -, -, Alverta, Shank, -, -, -, Laurence, 11

2972, 24 Jan 1868, Ellen Catherine, Geary, Owen, Catherine, 9-Jan, -, -, -, Michael, Battle, Mary, Chambers, -, Sullivan, 11

2973, 14 Feb 1869, Catherine, Hurlehey, David, Catherine, two months, -, -, -, May, Barry, -, -, Williamsport, -, 11

2974, 14 Feb 1869, Margaret Ann, Covell, Joseph, Elizabeth, [blank], -, -, -, Ann, O'Neil, -, -, Williamsport, -, 11

2975, 20 Feb 1869, Daniel, Dore, Pat., Mary, 11-Feb, -, -, -, Mary Ann, Halpin, Pat., Neville, -, Shehan, 11

2976, 19 Nov 1918, Anna, Harter, -, -, -, -, -, -, -, -, -, Married on 19 Nov 1918 to Anna Harter, Revd. W.E. Martin, Lebanon, PA, -, 11

2977, 3 Mar 1869, Charles, Smith, Edw., Jennie, 21 Sep 1868, -, -, -, Margaret, Kyper, -, -, -, Ward, 11

2978, 4 Mar 1869, Hugh Francis, McKuskery, John, Martha, 17-Feb, -, -, -, Margaret, McKuskery, -, -, "At Mrs. McKuskery's toll gate", Randall, 11

ST. MARY'S CATHOLIC CHURCH
HAGERSTOWN, MARYLAND, BAPTISMS:
Index, Bap Date, Child, Last Name, Father, Mother,
Birth Date, Code1, Code2, Code3,
1st Sponsor First, 1st Sponsor Last,
2nd Sponsor First, 2nd Sponsor Last, Location,
Notes, Maiden Name, Priest

2979, 4 Mar 1869, Martha Ann, Randall, Isaac, Martha, 29 years, -, -, -, Margaret, McKuskery, -, -, -, -, 11

2980, 7 Mar 1869, Francis Marshall, Mahoney, Wm., Arabella Frances, 4 Sep 1868, B, B, B, Rachel, Tasker (Black), -, -, -, -, 11

2981, 8 Mar 1869, John Edward, Fillinger, Philip, Elizabeth, 22-Jan, -, -, -, John, Fillinger, -, -, -, Garman, 11

2982, 14 Mar 1869, John Franklin, Leffermann, George, Lucretia, 3 Sep 1868, -, -, -, John, Barry, Ann, Laurence, Williamsport, -, 11

2983, 16 Mar 1869, Richard Bond, Fechtig, George, Louisa, 19-Jan, -, -, -, Josaphine, Hurley, -, -, -, Doyle, 11

2984, 18 Mar 1869, David Kreigh, Cushwa, Victor, Mary, 14-Mar, -, -, -, Elizabeth, Thompson, -, -, Williamsport, Kreigh, 11

2985, 20 Mar 1869, Catherine, Downin, Samuel, Mary, 16-Mar, -, -, -, Lilly, Downin, -, -, -, McCrey [?], 11

2986, 28 Mar 1869, Jacob Henry, Needy, Isaac, Catherin, 14-Jan, -, -, -, Jacob, Griffey, -, -, -, Griffey, 11

2987, 4 Apr 1869, Matthew Augustine, Dillon, Michael, Martha, "born end of March", -, -, -, Augustin, McCallen, Ellen, Sheehan, -, McCallen, 11

2988, 10 Apr 1869, Hugh, McDevitt, Moses, Catherine, 1-Apr, -, -, -, Thomas, Grady, -, -, -, Griffiin, 11

2989, 11 Apr 1869, Charles Edward, Kershner, Cyrus, Sarah, 15-Feb, -, -, -, Elizabeth, Brittner, -, -, -, Brittner, 11

2990, 18 Apr 1869, Francis Theodore*, Coyle, Thomas, Ada, 16-Nov, -, -, -, Samuel, Diffendal, -, -, * Francis Theodore Augustus, Harn, 11

2991, 15 May 1869, Catherine May, Powell, [blank[, Cecilia, Nov 1868, -, -, -, Catherine, Gray, -, -, "Rites supplied"; PB, Gillmeyer, 11

2992, 16 May 1869, Harriet Elizabeth, Dick, George, Sarah, 27-Jan, -, -, -, Wilhelmina, May, -, -, -, Syphon [?], 11

2993, 16 May 1869, Laura Bell, Flegel, Philip, Mary, 6-May, -, -, -, Rosa, Hipple, -, -, -, Adams, 11

2994, 6 Jun 1869, Mary Susan, Sanders, Wm., Margaret, 5 Jun 1868, -, -, -, Lizzie, Shirley, -, -, -, Topper, 11

2995, 6 Jun 1869, Mary Ann Elizabeth, Gauger, Joseph, Mary, 3-Sep, -, -, -, Ann, Laurence, -, -, -, Gauger [sic], 11

ST. MARY'S CATHOLIC CHURCH
HAGERSTOWN, MARYLAND, BAPTISMS:
Index, Bap Date, Child, Last Name, Father, Mother,
Birth Date, Code1, Code2, Code3,
1st Sponsor First, 1st Sponsor Last,
2nd Sponsor First, 2nd Sponsor Last, Location,
Notes, Maiden Name, Priest

2996, 6 Jun 1869, Mary Irene, Mayhugh, Clement, Francis, 2 Dec 1868, -, -, -, Michael, Curran, Laura, Ford, -, Miller, 11

2997, 11 Jun 1869, Stonewall Jackson, Loyd, John, Sarah, 29-Apr, -, -, -, Letty, McIlhany, -, -, -, Fox, 11

2998, 11 Jun 1869, Charlotte Magdalene, Gross, Jacob, Magd., 1 Jan 1845, -, -, -, Josephine, Hurly, -, -, "convert from Luthernism", -, 32

2999, 11 Jun 1869, Frances , Whipp, -, -, -, -, -, -, -, -, -, BC; "convert from Lutheranism", -, 33

3000, 12 Jun 1869, Henry Horatio, Keedy , -, -, -, -, -, -, -, -, -, -, convert from Lutheranism, -, 33

3001, 12 Jun 1869, Caroline Hile, Blumnar, Michael, Annie, 27 Apr 1833, -, -, -, Let., McIlhenny, -, -, convert from Lutheranism, -, 32

3002, 12 Jun 1869, Jacob Milton, Ewers, Jonathan, Rosanna, 25 Dec 1844, -, -, -, Jacob H., Wills, -, -, convert from Lutheranism, -, 33

3003, 12 Jun 1869, James R., McLaughlin, James, Amelia, 4 Sep 1830, -, -, -, Thomas, Futterer, -, -, appears to read: "conv. Ex Leck[?] Reform.", -, 33

3004, 13 Jun 1869, Lawrence, Middlekoff, Elias, Martha M., 25 May 1857, -, -, -, Let. , McIlhenny, -, -, -, -, 32

3005, 13 Jun 1869, Margarite, Middlekoff, E., M. M., 22 Sep 1861, -, -, -, Let., McIlhenny, -, -, -, -, 32

3006, 13 Jun 1869, Anna, Middlekoff, Elias, Martha M., 25 Sep 1850, -, -, -, Let., McIlhenny, -, -, convert from Methodism, -, 32

3007, 13 Jun 1869, Sarah, Tyler -, -, 10 years, -, -, -, Sarah, Rideout, -, -, parents are unknown, -, 32

3008, 25 Jul 1869, Edward Pierce, Gouker, Samuel, Mary Ann, 15 Dec 1858, -, -, -, Daniel, Lizor, -, -, -, Hose, 34

3009, 25 Jul 1869, Margareth Alice* , Bowers, Michael, Barbara, 18 Apr 1868, -, -, -, Martha A., Lizor, -, -, *Margareth Alice Elisabeth, Gouker, 34

3010, 25 Jul 1869, Mary, Lyons, John, Rosa Anna, 24-Jun, -, -, -, Edward, Clark, Catherine, Clark, -, Gregory, 34

3011, 25 Jul 1869, Charles Henry, Dunn, James, Margaret, 10-Feb, -, -, -, Charles, Clarke, Mary, Clarke, -, Bulliard, 11

ST. MARY'S CATHOLIC CHURCH
HAGERSTOWN, MARYLAND, BAPTISMS:
Index, Bap Date, Child, Last Name, Father, Mother,
Birth Date, Code1, Code2, Code3,
1st Sponsor First, 1st Sponsor Last,
2nd Sponsor First, 2nd Sponsor Last, Location,
Notes, Maiden Name, Priest

3012, 25 Jul 1869, Joseph Motter, Thompson, Jesse, Fannie, 25-May, -, -, -, Mary, Oliver, -, -, -, Oliver, 11

3013, 25 Jul 1869, Josiah, Meeds, Benedict, Amelia, 31 Mar 1862, -, -, -, Ellen, Stake, -, -, -, McLain, 11

3014, 31 Jul 1869, Charles Adam, Full, Michael, Ann, 26-Jun, -, -, -, Ann (Mrs.), McCardell, -, -, -, Price, 11

3015, 15 Aug 1869, Charles, Middlekauff, Elias, Martha, 21 Jul 1862, -, -, -, Mary, Eck, -, -, BC, Ford, 11

3016, 15 Aug 1869, Mary Janet, Taylor, Andrew, Lucinda, 27-May, PN, -, -, Josephine, Hurley, -, -, -, Jones [sic], 11

3017, 15 Aug 1869, Anna Amelia, Taylor, Andrew, Lucinda, 27-May, PN, -, -, Letty, McIlhany, -, -, -, Jones [sic], 11

3018, 22 Aug 1869, Catherine, Malone, Hugh, Mary, 7-Aug, -, -, -, James, Malone, Bridget, Rodgers, -, Kelly, 11

3019, 29 Aug 1869, John Roy Larcunbe[?], McCardell, Thomas, Alice Eve, 30-Jun, -, -, -, Ann (Mrs.), McCardell, -, -, -, -, 11

3020, 26Sep1869, Mary, Foronsworth, William, Margareth, 15 Aug 1868, -, -, -, Cath., Woltz, -, -, -, McCloskery, 34

3021, 26 Sep 1869, William Thomas, Waters, James, Eliza, 20 Aug 1848, -, -, -, Edward, Donelly, M., Donelly, "Received private baptism, only the ceremonies supplied", McLain, 34

3022, 4 Oct 1869, Bridget, Grady, Daniel, Julia, 9-Sep, -, -, -, Daniel, Hurley, -, -, -, Conner, 11

3023, 14 Oct 1869, Mary, Reilly, John, Sarah, 15 Sep 1847, -, -, -, Anastasia, Faller, -, -, C, jones, 11

3024, 16 Oct 1869, Catherine, Williams, George, Mary, 25-Jul, -, -, -, James, Gleesen, Kate, Halpine, -, Henser [?], 11

3025, 17 Oct 1869, John, Hennessey, John, Ellen, 6-Aug, -, -, -, Joseph, McKenny, Lizzie, Dusany, -, Doolan, 11

3026, 9 Oct 1869, Grace, McHenry, James, [blank], [blank], -, -, -, Charles, Boyle, -, -, "baptized at house in danger of death", -, 11

3027, 17 Nov 1869, Bridget, Cunningham, Michael, Catherine, 11-Oct, -, -, -, James, Cunningham, Mary Ellen, Halpine, BC; "baptized privately before", Shea, 11

3028, 23 Nov 1869, Edgar Thomas, Smith, Toho, Anne, 6 Aug 1860, -, -, -, Susan, Weast, -, -, -, Thomas, 11

ST. MARY'S CATHOLIC CHURCH
HAGERSTOWN, MARYLAND, BAPTISMS:
Index, Bap Date, Child, Last Name, Father, Mother,
Birth Date, Code1, Code2, Code3,
1st Sponsor First, 1st Sponsor Last,
2nd Sponsor First, 2nd Sponsor Last, Location,
Notes, Maiden Name, Priest

3029, 23 Nov 1869, Julia Kate, Smith, John, Kate, 16-Jun, -, -, -, Josaphine, Hurley, -, -, Boonsboro, Hagan, 11

3030, 11 Nov 1869, Eliza Monahan, Lemen [or Lennen], Peter, Helen, [blank], -, -, -, Mary, Clark, -, -, Williamsport, Stake, 11

3031, 27 Nov 1869, Patrick, Nebbles, Patrick, Elizabeth, 17-Aug, PN, -, -, James, Gleeson, Catherine, Halpine, -, Con [or Cew?], 11

3032, 28 Nov 1869, Mary Agnes, Laurence, Jerome M., Catherine, 31 Oct 1869, -, -, -, Andrew C., Laurence, Bridget, Dononghue, Williamsport, Dononghue, 34

3033, 22 Dec 1869, John Michael, Shehan, Sm., Catherine, 16-Dec, -, -, -, Peter, Shehan, Catherine, Kane, -, Barrett, 11

3034, 6 Jan 1870, Hugh Edward, Corgan [or Covgan], Mathew, Elizabeth, 24 Dec 1869, -, -, -, Charles, Kelly, Nettie, Hurley, -, -, 11

3035, 23 Jan 1870, Emelia, Flynn, James, Louisa, 26 Dec 1869, -, -, -, [blank], Wooltz, -, -, -, Brooks, 34

3036, 23 Jan 1870, Jerome Jacob, Brown, John, Jinnie, 24Sep 1869, -, -, -, Mary, Clabaugh, -, -, -, Hyskins [?], 34

3037, 23 Jan 1870, Mary Elizabeth, Walker, Allen, Annie, 8 Oct 1869, -, -, -, Ginnie [or Jinnie], Brown, -, -, -, Brown, 34

3038, 23 Jan 1870, James, Anderson, -, -, -, -, -, -, Louisa, Brazille, -, -, C; Williamsport, -, 11

3039, 2 Feb 1870, Elizabeth Lane, Keedy, Henry, Julia, 26 Nov 1869, -, -, -, Mollie, Hurley, -, -, -, Lane, 11

3040, 8 Mar 1870, Leo, Warner, Robert, Mary, 26-Jan, -, -, -, Louisa, Cramer, -, -, -, Shafer, 11

3041, 26 Mar 1870, Joseph, Brennan, Francis, Mary, 16 Jan 1870, -, -, -, Lettie, McIlheney, Felig, McFaul , -, Coil, 34

3042, 26 Mar 1870, James, Brennan, Francis, Mary, 16 Jan 1870, -, -, -, Josephine, Hurley, Thomas, McFaul, -, Coil, 34

3043, 29 Mar 1870, Clara Elizabeth, Nierman, August, Philamena, 22-Mar, -, -, -, Elizabeth, Frendhoff [?], -, -, -, Spechman [?], 11

3044, 10 Apr 1870, Sophia Agnes, Sanders, Wm., Margaret, 14 Mar 1870, -, -, -, Josephine, Hurley, -, -, -, Topper, 11

3045, 25 Apr 1870, Margaret, Kerrigan, Patrick, Catherine, 12-Feb, -, -, -, Charles, Duffy, -, -, -, O'Hara, 11

ST. MARY'S CATHOLIC CHURCH
HAGERSTOWN, MARYLAND, BAPTISMS:
Index, Bap Date, Child, Last Name, Father, Mother,
Birth Date, Code1, Code2, Code3,
1st Sponsor First, 1st Sponsor Last,
2nd Sponsor First, 2nd Sponsor Last, Location,
Notes, Maiden Name, Priest

3046, 1 May 1870, Martin Henry, Green, Martin B., Susan R., 7 Nov 1869, -, -, -, Mary, Coy, -, -, -, Smith, 34

3047, 1 May 1870, Lilien Catherine, Eisiminger, Albert, Mary G. [or J.], 5 Mar 1870, -, -, -, Susan, Green, -, -, -, Smith, 34

3048, 18 Jun 1870, Peter, Conlen [?], Denis, Bridget, 3-May, -, -, -, Mary, Clabaugh, -, -, -, Cunningham, 11

3049, 19 Jun 1870, Mary Elizabeth*, Chambers, Thomas, Emmeline, 23 Aug [sic], -, -, -, Mary, Mundey, -, -, ["Theresa" crossed out] before Mary Elizabeth, -, 11

3050, 26 Jun 1870, James Eli, Barry, John, Mary, 8 Jun 1870, -, -, -, James, Doyle, Maggie, Godgart [?], -, Collins, 34

3051, 27 Jun 1870, Elisabeth, Geary, Owen, Catherine, 11 Jun 1870, -, -, -, Patrick, Sullivan, Mary C., Toben [?], -, Sullivan, 34

3052, 10 Jul 1870, Charles William, Flynn, James, Mary C., [blank], -, -, -, -, -, -, -, -, Drennan, 11

3053, 22 Jul 1870, Francis Daniel, McFadden, Daniel, Mary, 4-Mar, -, -, -, Jacob, Wills, Letitia, McIlhany, -, Dichas [?], 11

3054, 22 Jul 1870, Leila May, McFadden, Daniel, Mary, 16 May 1867, -, -, -, -, -, -, -, -, Dichas [?], 11

3055, 28 Jul 1870, Margareth, Collins, Patrick, Jane, 17-May, -, -, -, Maggie, Clark, -, -, "baptized privately, ceremonies supplied."; Williamsport, O'Connor, 34

3056, 28 Jul 1870, Anna, Collins, Patrick, Jane, 17-May, -, -, -, Regina, Clark, -, -, Williamsport, O'Connor, 34

3057, 1 Aug 1870, Sarah Jane, Needy, Isaac, Catherine, 30-Apr, -, -, -, Mary, Clabaugh, -, -, -, Griffy, 34

3058, 7 Aug 1870, John Wm., Fleigle, [blank], Mary, 24-Jul, -, -, -, Louis, Smith, Cornelia, Smith [HB], parents are married, Adams, 11

3059, 21 Aug 1870, Clara May, Hornbach, William D., Virginia, 19 Jun 1870, -, -, -, Sallie, Cushwa, -, -, -, Lambert, 34

3060, 20 Aug 1870, Sarah, Mahon, John, Catherine, 11 Jun 1870, -, -, -, William, Mahon, Ellen, Mahon [HB], Brownsville, Brady, 34

3061, 28 Aug 1870, Marian, Waters, William, Mary, 24 Aug 1870, -, -, -, Mary, Reed, -, -, Williamsport, Donelly, 34

ST. MARY'S CATHOLIC CHURCH HAGERSTOWN, MARYLAND, BAPTISMS:
Index, Bap Date, Child, Last Name, Father, Mother,
Birth Date, Code1, Code2, Code3,
1st Sponsor First, 1st Sponsor Last,
2nd Sponsor First, 2nd Sponsor Last, Location,
Notes, Maiden Name, Priest

3062, 28 Aug 1870, Laura Anna, Clayburn, John, Sallie, 25 Sep 1870*, -, -, -, Clara, Goddart, -, -, Williamsport; *note discrepancy between birthdate and baptismal date, Martini, 34

3063, 20 Sep 1870, Charles Augustine, Futterer, Charles, Otella, [blank], -, -, -, Daniel, Sweeny, Catherine, Futterer, -, -, 11

3064, 2 Oct 1870, Michael Amos, Lefferman, George, Lucretia, 15-Jul, -, -, -, Edward, Clarkson, Catherine, Futterer, -, -, 11

3065, 14 Oct 1870, John Henry, Barry, John, Mary, 5-Oct, -, -, -, Patrick, Nelligan, Ellen, Nelligan, -, -, 11

3066, 23 Oct 1870, John Thomas, O'Brien, Timothy, Mary, 16-Oct, -, -, -, James, Doyle, Eliza, Barrett, -, -, 11

3067, 13 Nov 1870, Joseph Wm., Green, George, Mary, 5-Sep, -, B, B, Margaret, Smith, -, -, Clear Spring, -, 11

3068, 27 Nov 1870, Wm. Arthur, Kimble, Wm., Alice, 8 months, -, -, -, Margaret, Hornsby, -, -, Williamsport, Reeder, 11

3069, 27 Nov 1870, Mary Loreta [?], Little, Wm., Kate, 1-Oct, -, -, -, Wm., Hawkins, Ellen, Olvier, Williamsport, Hawkins, 11

3070, 30 Jan 1871, Mary Elizabeth, Smith, Edward, Jane, 8-Aug, -, -, -, Mary, Coyle, -, -, -, -, 11

3071, 5 Mar 1871, Margaret, Shehan, Cornelius, Ellen, 18-Feb, -, -, -, Mr., Dillon, Mrs., Dillon, -, -, 11

3072, 16 Apr 1871, Aloysius David Eugene, Gouker [or Gonker], Joseph, Mary, 9-Feb, -, -, -, Mary, Coyle, -, -, Cavetown, Gouker [or Gonker], 11

3073, 17 May 1871, Laura Jane, Baker, -, -, 15 years, -, -, -, Letitia, McIlhany, Sarah, Cushwa, C, -, 11

3074, 17 May 1871, Emily, Baker, -, -, 16 years, -, -, -, Letitia, McIlhany, Sarah, Cushwa, C, -, 11

3075, 13 May 1871, George, Smith, John, [blank], [blank], -, -, -, Mrs., Kyper, -, -, -, Griffey, 11

3076, 18 May 1871, Wm. Henry, Little, Charles, Rebecca, 12 Jul 1870, -, -, -, Jane, Maguire, -, -, Funkstown, -, 11

3077, 24 May 1871, Anna Mary, Miller, -, -, adult, -, -, -, David, Sweeny, -, -, "from Waynesboro, Pa.", -, 35

3078, 4 Jun 1871, Mary Elizabeth, McDevitt, Moses, Catherine, 5-Apr, -, -, -, Owen, Geary, Mary, Geary [HB], -, -, 11

**ST. MARY'S CATHOLIC CHURCH
HAGERSTOWN, MARYLAND, BAPTISMS:
Index, Bap Date, Child, Last Name, Father, Mother,
Birth Date, Code1, Code2, Code3,
1st Sponsor First, 1st Sponsor Last,
2nd Sponsor First, 2nd Sponsor Last, Location,
Notes, Maiden Name, Priest**

3079, 8 Jun 1871, Ida [Ada?] Cecilia, Kemp, David, Margaret, 28-Mar, -, -, -, Philamena, Nierman, -, -, -, Day, 11

3080, 15 Jun 1871, Mary Elizabeth, Ford, Franklin, Ann, 9-Feb, -, -, -, Margaret, Shervin, -, -, -, Jacobs, 11

3081, 25 Jun 1871, James, O'Neil, Thomas, Catherine, [blank], -, -, -, Mark, Donelly, Miss, O'Neil, Williamsport, -, 11

3082, 17 Aug 1871, Charles William Franklin, Cushwa, Victor, Mary, 15-Aug, -, -, -, Kate, Hoy, -, -, Williamsport, -, 11

3083, 20 Aug 1871, Nina Gertrude, Cramer, Jacob, Martha, 16-Jul, -, -, -, Felix, Curran, Laura, Ford, -, -, 11

3084, 10 Sep 1871, John Thomas, Brown, John, Virginia, 15-Apr, -, -, -, David, Sweeney, -, -, B, -, 11

3085, 10 Sep 1871, John Vincent, Ewers, Milton, Susan, 18 months, -, -, -, David, Sweeney, Josephine, Hurley, -, Futterer, 11

3086, 17 Sep 1871, John Henry, Happle, Martin, Rosine, 19-Jul, -, -, -, Philip, Fleigle, -, -, -, -, 11

3087, 21 Sep 1871, Mary Gertrude, Baker, Daniel, Mary Ann, 20-May, -, -, -, Sally, Cushwa, -, -, -, -, 11

3088, 23 Sep 1871, Ada, Himes, -, Bell, 7 years, PN, B, -, B, Harriet, Lynch, -, -, BC, -, 11

3089, 24 Sep 1871, James, Reid, Wm., Mary, 16-Sep, -, -, -, James, Donelley, Mary, Waters, Williamsport, -, 11

3090, 24 Sep 1871, Ella Honora [?], Hurlehey, Richard, Ellen, 30-Aug, -, -, -, James, Cunningham, Mary, King, Williamsport, -, 11

3091, 24 Sep 1871, James Richard, Doyle, James, Charlotte, 28-Aug, -, -, -, Thomas, Brandon, Margaret, Goddard, Williamsport, -, 11

3092, 27 Sep 1871, Mary Ellen, McDermott, Richard, Mary Ellen, 24-Sep, -, -, -, Miss, Chambers, M., Conway, PB, Halpine, 11

ST. MARY'S CATHOLIC CHURCH
HAGERSTOWN, MARYLAND, BAPTISMS:
Index, Baptism Date, Child, Last Name, Father from, Mother, Mother from, Birth Date, 1st Sponsor First, 1st Sponsor Last, 2nd Sponsor First, 2nd Sponsor Last, Location, Notes, Maiden Name, Priest

3425, 31 Jan 1879, Mariam Genovesam [?], Battles, Michaele, Hagerstown, Anna, Hagerstown, 23-Jan, Birgitta, Rogers, -, -, Hagerstown, -, Barrett, 11

3426, 1 Feb 1879, Annam (Mrs.), Full*, Jacob, Washington County, Susan, St. James College, -, -, -, -, -, "Near Hagerstown", BP; C; *father's last name is Price; C, Moreland, 11

3427, 23 Mar 1879, Albertum [?], Cheney, Johanne, Williamsport, Barbara, Williamsport, 19 years, -, -, -, -, Williamsport, C; BP, [blank], 11

3428, 30 Mar 1879, Giorgium, McCarthy, Joseph, Hagerstown, Maria, Hagerstown, 2 Jan 1842, Margaretta, Shervin, -, -, Hagerstown, C, [blank], 11

3429, 6 Apr 1879, Annam Laviniam, Kershner, Joseph, Hagerstown, Helena, Hagerstown, 2 Feb 1879, Lucinda (Mrs.), Hoover, -, -, Hagerstown, -, Hoover, 11

3430, [no date], Augustum Aloysium, Clayburn, Johanne, Hagerstown, Sallie, Hagerstown, 14 Mar 1879, Catharina, Ahern, -, -, Hagerstown, -, [blank], 11

3431, 19 Apr 1879, Sarah, Zellers*, Raisin, -, Maria, -, 19 Mar 1828, Maria, McGrath, -, -, Hagerstown, C; BC; *fathers last name is Adams [or Storm?], [blank], 11

3432, 26 Apr 1879, J. Forrese [?] Morgan, Fox, Henrico S., Hagerstown, Catharina C., Hagerstown, 4 Apr 1854, Henricus, Cramer, -, -, Hagerstown, -, [blank], 11

3433, 30 Apr 1879, Johannem Fredericum, Fechtig, Georgio, Hagerstown, Lousia, Hagerstown, 30 Dec 1878, Eva, McCleery, -, -, Hagerstown, -, Doyle, 11

3434, 5 May 1879, -, Cheney, -, Williamsport, -, Williamsport, -, -, -, -, -, Williamsport, C, -, 11

3435, 4 May 1879, J. Upton, Wolf [mother's name], -, -, Maria, Hagerstown, 6-Mar, Wilhelmus, Eyler, Maria, Eyler [HB], Hagerstown, -, Wolf, 11

3436, 11 May 1879, Ricardum Carolum, Bennett, Ricardo S., Hagerstown, Maria, Hagerstown, 28-Apr, Anna, Jourdain, -, -, Hagerstown, -, Cretin, 11

3437, 1 Jun 1879, Jacob L., Addlesperger, -, Waynesboro, Susan, Waynesboro, 4 Jun 1851, Michael, McDonald, -, -,

ST. MARY'S CATHOLIC CHURCH
HAGERSTOWN, MARYLAND, BAPTISMS:
Index, Baptism Date, Child, Last Name, Father from, Mother, Mother from, Birth Date, 1st Sponsor First, 1st Sponsor Last, 2nd Sponsor First, 2nd Sponsor Last, Location, Notes, Maiden Name, Priest

Hagerstown, C; PN, Addlesperger [or Adelsperger in column], 11

3438, 9 Jun 1879, Johannesm, Fox, Fernando, Hagerstown, Jennie, Hagerstown, 5-Jun, Isaac, Feighley, Mrs., Cramer, Hagerstown, -, Nicely, 11

3439, 15 Jun 1879, Othonem, Hull, N. B., VA, Mathilda, MD, 19 Jul 1850, -, -, -, -, Hagerstown, C; BC, Wade, 11

3093, 25 Feb 1872, Margt Louisa, Fechtig, George, -, Louisa H., -, 18 Feb 1872, Eva (Mrs.), McCleary, -, -, Hagerstown, "this baptism was not recorded", Doyle, 13

3094, 29 Sep 1871, Gulielmum Harman, Fall, Michaele, -, Anna Amelia, -, 20 Jul 1871, Maria, Fall, -, -, Hagerstown, born in Hagerstown, Price, 13

3095, 31 Oct 1871, Saram Alicem, Lemon, Petro L., Berkeley Co., WV, Helena M., Washington Co., 11 Oct 1871, Elias, Stake, Letitia, McElhenny, Williamsport, born in Williamsport, Stake, 13

3096, 1 Nov 1871, Georgium P., Clayborne, Joanne B., Chambersburg, Sara, Hagerstown, 20 Jul 1871, Henricus, Clarke, Margaritta, Clarke, Williamsport, born in Williamsport, Martinez, 13

3097, 1 Nov 1871, Josephum Marcellum, Coyle, Thoma B., Cavetown, Maria, Smithsburg, 5 Apr 1871, W. F., Orndorff, Maria, Hughes, Hagerstown, born in Cavetown, Horn, 13

3098, 10 Nov 1871, Mariam Honoram, Sheehan, Eulichmo, Cork Co., Ireland, Catharina, Cork Co., Ireland, 23 Oct 1871, Patricius, Sheehan *, Margaritta, Barrett, Hagerstown, * Sheehan is absent from baptism, Barrett, 13

3099, 17 Nov 1871, Gertrudam May, Hunsteine, Gulielmo, Waynesboro, Maria D., Waynesboro, 16 Oct 1871, Georgius H., Laird, Lucia, Rider, Waynesboro, -, Rider, 13

3100, 17 Nov 1871, Jacobus Samuel, Smith, Gulielmo H., Adams Co., PA, Catharina, Adams Co., PA, 7 Mar 1871, Henricus, Creighton, Maria, Wassum, Waynesboro, -, Sanders, 13

3101, 17 Nov 1871, Edgar S., Rider, Gulielmo, Waynesboro, Maria, Waynesboro, 11 May 1871, David, Rider, Louisa, Rider, Waynesboro, -, Scheller, 13

ST. MARY'S CATHOLIC CHURCH HAGERSTOWN, MARYLAND, BAPTISMS:
Index, Baptism Date, Child, Last Name, Father from, Mother, Mother from, Birth Date, 1st Sponsor First, 1st Sponsor Last, 2nd Sponsor First, 2nd Sponsor Last, Location, Notes, Maiden Name, Priest

3102, 17 Nov 1871, Maria, Grace, Samueli L., Waynesboro, Catharina, Waynesboro, 23 Oct 1871, Joanna, Smith, -, -, Waynesboro, -, Rider, 13

3103, 19 Nov 1871, Maria Cathar., Schwitzer, Samuele, Washington Co., Maria Josephina, Adams Co., PA, 10 Nov 1871, Michael, Laurens, Maria Anna, Laurens, Williamsport, -, Laurens, 13

3104, 19 Nov 1871, Thomas, Barry, Joanne, Limerick Co., Ireland, Maria, Limerick Co., Ireland, 26 Oct 1871, Philippus, Bradley, Maria, Claybaugh, Williamsport, -, Collins, 13

3440, 17 Jun 1879, Margaret Ann, Gross [?], [blank], Smithsburg, Catharine, Smithsburg, 20 Jul 1851, Laura, Wills, -, -, Hagerstown, C, [blank], 11

3441, 26 Jun 1879, Laurentium Sylvestrem, Mundey, Giorgio, Washington County, Maria, Washington Co., 3 Dec 1878, Margaret, Shervin, -, -, Hagerstown, -, McCarthy, 11

3442, 11 May 1879, Johannem Guglielmum, Woods, Johanne F., Hagerstown, Ann E., Hagerstown, 17 Dec 1878, Jennie, Bayley, -, -, Hagerstown, Family and sponsors are Black., Hines, 11

3443, 8 Jul 1879, Gracie Lee, Barber, Carolo B., Zittlestown, Anna Elizabeth, "eodem vel vicino", 14 Sep 1864, M. V., Dahlgren, -, -, South Mountain House, C, [blank], 11

3444, 8 Jul 1879, Percy Poffinbarger, Barber, Carolo B., Zittlestown, Anna E., Zittlestown, 4 Feb 1869, Mrs., Dahlgren, -, -, South Mountain House, C, [blank], 11

3445, 8 Jul 1879, Bradley Townsend, Barber, Carolo B., "Zittlestown vel vicino", Anna E., "Zittlestown vel vicino", 14 Dec 1874, Mrs., Dahlgren, -, -, South Mountain House, -, [blank], 11

3446, 8 Jul 1879, Emmerikas [?] Mariam, Washington, Abraham Lincoln, South Mountain, Harriet, "incognito" [unknown], 1859, Mrs., Smith, -, -, South Mountain House, C; B, [blank], 11

3447, 29 Jul 1879, Georgium Mertin, Ryan, Michaele, "Downsville neighborhood", Maria, "Downsville neighborhood", 5-Jan, Georgius, Ryan, -, -, Hagerstown, -, Kroon [?], 11

ST. MARY'S CATHOLIC CHURCH
HAGERSTOWN, MARYLAND, BAPTISMS:
Index, Baptism Date, Child, Last Name, Father from, Mother, Mother from, Birth Date, 1st Sponsor First, 1st Sponsor Last, 2nd Sponsor First, 2nd Sponsor Last, Location, Notes, Maiden Name, Priest

3448, 19 Aug 1879, Rosam, Furley, Jacobo A., Washington County, Maria, Washington Co., 12 Mar 1870, Maria, Riordan, -, -, "Hagerstown (near).", -, Black, 11

3449, 6 Oct 1879, Danielem Deurie [?], Strite, Daniel, Washington County, Jennie, Washington Co., 2 Apr 1878, A., Condry, Emma, Young, St. James College, -, Young, 11

3450, 10 Oct 1879, Columbum Leonem, Allan, Johanne, Hagerstown, Maria, Hagerstown, 19 Sep, Rachael, Allan, -, -, Hagerstown, Family and sponsors are Black, Stewart, 11

3451, 12 Oct 1879, Jacobum Franklin, Coxson, Wm., Hagerstown, Margaretta, Hagerstown, January, Isaac, Feighley, -, -, Hagerstown, Adopted by Wm. Coxson, Street, 11

3452, 13 Oct 1879, Joseph Alvey, St. Clair, Henri, Washington County, Martha Ellen, Washington Co., 28 Jun 1876, Madeleine, Dahlgren, -, -, South Mountain, -, Lapole, 11

3453, 13 Oct 1879, David Vinton, St. Clair, Henri, Washington County, Martha E., Washington Co., 28-Jul, Madeleine, Dahlgren, -, -, South Mountain, -, Lapole, 11

3454, 13 Oct 1879, Carolum Guglielmum, Lapole, Guglielum, Washington County, Lena Catherina, Washington Co., 18 Sep 1875, Madeleine, Dahlgren, -, -, South Mountain, -, Rent, 11

3455, 13 Oct 1879, Harry Rutherford, Lapole, Guglielmo, Washington County, Lena C., Washington Co., 27 Feb 1878, Madeleine, Dahlgren, -, -, South Mountain, -, Rent, 11

3456, 13 Oct 1879, Sarah Ellen, Harper, Meredith, Washington County, Eliza Jane, Washington Co., 31 Jan 1870, Madeleine, Dahlgren, -, -, South Mountain, B, Perkins, 11

3457, 13 Oct 1879, Eric Ludovicum, Jones, Ludovico, Washington County, Maria, Washington Co., 8-Oct, Eric, Dahlgren, -, -, South Mountain, -, Kaufman, 11

3458, Aug 1879, Mariam, Williams, F. C., Hagerstown, Ellen, Hagerstown, 18-Aug, -, -, -, -, -, Baptized in danger of death by Mrs. Kelley, a holy and Catholic woman, [blank],

3459, Aug 1879, Jennie, Williams, F. C., Hagerstown, Ellen, Hagerstown, 19-Aug, -, -, -, -, -, Baptized in danger of death by Mrs. Kelley, a holy and Catholic woman, [blank],

ST. MARY'S CATHOLIC CHURCH
HAGERSTOWN, MARYLAND, BAPTISMS:
Index, Baptism Date, Child, Last Name, Father from, Mother, Mother from, Birth Date, 1st Sponsor First, 1st Sponsor Last, 2nd Sponsor First, 2nd Sponsor Last, Location, Notes, Maiden Name, Priest

3460, 25 Oct 1879, Johannem Martinum, Laurence, Johanne, Washington County, Sarah, Washington Co., 6-Oct, Michael, Laurence, Maria, Laurence [HB], Hagerstown, -, Baker, 11

3461, 27 Oct 1879, Margaret Gertrudem, Cullins, Jacobo, "near Williamsport", Maria, "near Williamsport", 13-Sep, Elie, Stake, Johanna, Gallagher, Williamsport, -, McKenna, 11

3462, 28 Oct 1879, Jacobus Clifton, Gruber, Johanne, Hagerstown, Julia, Hagerstown, 19-Oct, Jennie, Bayley, -, -, Hagerstown, Family and sponsors are Black, Sprague, 11

3463, 2 Nov 1879, Johannem Guglielmum, Fagan, Johanne, Hagerstown, Sarah, Hagerstown, 20-Sep, Johannes, Hellane, Luisa, Ogle, Hagerstown, -, Daley, 11

3464, 8 Nov 1879, Bernardum Simmons, Addlesperger, Luthero, Waynesboro, Anna, Hagerstown, 3-Nov, -, -, -, -, Hagerstown, BP, McDonald, 11

3465, 24 Nov 1879, Nancy (Mrs.), Carr, -, -, -, -, *, Mrs., Barry, -, -, Williamsport, BP; from Williamsport; * "age unknown - probably 80", -, 11

3105, 19 Nov 1871, Joannem Patricium, Downin, Samuele, Washington County, Maria, Hancock, 16 Oct 1871, Sara, Hoskinson, -, -, Hagerstown, -, McAvoy, 13

3106, 3 Dec 1871, Franciscus, Helene, Philippo, Hagerstown, Louisa Catharina, Hagerstown, 11 Nov 1870, Helena, Taggart, -, -, Hagerstown, -, Davis, 13

3107, 13 Dec 1871, Ludovicus, Walker, Allen, Franklin, VA, Anna, Washington Co., 8 Oct 1871, Lotitia, McElhenny, -, -, Hagerstown, father is described as "Etiopus" [Black?], Brown, 13

3108, 17 Dec 1871, David Clemens, Kushner, Cyro, Berkley Co., WV, Sara Agneto [?], Berkeley Co., WV, 4 Nov 1871, Clemens, Brittner, Elisabeth, Brittner, Williamsport, -, Brittner, 13

3109, 24 Dec 1871, Jacobus Patricius, Malone, Hugone, Cavan, Ireland, Maria, Hagerstown, 15 Dec 1871, Gulielmus, Hurley, Eleanora, Kelly, Hagerstown, -, Kelly, 13

3110, 3 Jan 1872, Anna Elisabeth, Gipe, Isaac, Franklin Co., PA, Maria, Franklin Co., PA, 11 Nov 1871, Johannes, Spalding, Sara, Spalding, Waynesboro, -, Honodel, 13

ST. MARY'S CATHOLIC CHURCH
HAGERSTOWN, MARYLAND, BAPTISMS:
Index, Baptism Date, Child, Last Name, Father from, Mother, Mother from, Birth Date, 1st Sponsor First, 1st Sponsor Last, 2nd Sponsor First, 2nd Sponsor Last, Location, Notes, Maiden Name, Priest

3111, 1 Sep [1871?], Carolus E., Martz, Benjamin, Funkstown, Anna, Funkstown, 13-Aug, Jno. (Mrs.), Broderick, -, -, Hagerstown, -, Martz, 13

3112, 21 Jan 1872, Anges, Thompson, Jesse, Washington County, Frances, Crawford Co., Ark., 12 Jan 1872, Edwardus, Donnelly, Ellen, Oliver, Williamsport, -, Oliver, 13

3113, 3 Mar 1872, Maria Ameliam, Nierman, Augusto, Prussia, Philomena, Cincinnati, OH, 19 Feb 1872, Michael, Dillon, Martha, Dillon, Hagerstown, -, Speckman, 13

3114, 19 Mar 1872, Johannam Albertam, McKusker, Th. Jno., Washington County, Anna Martha, Washington Co., 7 Apr 1870, Maria, McKusker, -, -, Hagerstown, -, Rowland, 13

3115, 19 Mar 1872, Sara Anna, McKusker, Joanne Thoma, Washington County, Anna Martha, Washington Co., 9 Dec 1871, Maria, McKusker, -, -, Hagerstown, -, Rowland, 13

3116, 25 Mar 1872, Annam Margarittam, Conlan, Dionysis, Clare, Ireland, Brigitta, Clare, Ireland, 25 Dec 1871, Maria, Hughes, -, -, Hagerstown, -, Cunningham, 13

3117, 30 Mar 1872, Mariam Caeiliam, McLaughllin, Ludovico, Washington County, Maria, Hagerstown, 19 Mar 1872, Josias, Smith, Suzanna, Weast [?], Hagerstown, -, Hurley, 13

3118, 31 Mar 1872, Joannem F., Wills, Jacobo H., Adams Co., PA, Martha S., Williamsport, 4 Mar 1872, S., Cushwa, -, -, Hagerstown, -, McClain, 13

3119, 10 Apr 1872, Franciscum B., Orndorf, Gulielmo F., Conewago, PA, Maria J., Conewago, 11-Mar, J. A., Wright, Sara R., Wright, Hagerstown, -, Toy, 13

3120, 13 Apr 1872, Joannem, Lloyd, Joanne, Clarke Co., VA, Sara, Washington Co., 1 Apr 1872, Virginia, Fox, -, -, Hagerstown, -, Fox, 13

3121, 13 Apr 1872, Mariam Catharinam, Lloyd, Joanne, Clarke Co., VA, Sara, Washington Co., 1 Apr 1872, Maria C., Fox, -, -, Hagerstown, -, Fox, 13

3122, 25 May 1872, Henricum H., Keedy, Henrico H., Boonsboro, Julia, Boonsboro, 26-Jan, F., Whipple, -, -, Hagerstown, -, Lane, 13

ST. MARY'S CATHOLIC CHURCH HAGERSTOWN, MARYLAND, BAPTISMS:
Index, Baptism Date, Child, Last Name, Father from, Mother, Mother from, Birth Date, 1st Sponsor First, 1st Sponsor Last, 2nd Sponsor First, 2nd Sponsor Last, Location, Notes, Maiden Name, Priest

3123, 23 Jun 1872, Gulielmum, Green, Martino, Funkstown, Suzanna, Funkstown, 17-Jun, Maria, Coyle, -, -, Hagerstown, -, Smith, 13

3124, 21 May 1872, Helena Flora, Cretin, Henrico, Emmittsburg, Maria A., Emmittsburg, 22-Jan, David, Ryder, Louisa, Ryder, Waynesboro, -, Harbaugh, 13

3125, 28 May 1872, George Anne, Williams, -, -, -, -, 1856, Sara, Cushwa, -, -, Williamsport, convert from Methodism; from Williamsport, -, 13

3126, 27 Jul 1872, Catharinam, Lymbach, -, -, Francisca, -, 1870, Maria, Roach, -, -, Hagerstown, PN, Lymbach, 13

3127, 21 Jul 1872, Richardum, McGuchen, Jacobo, Philadelphia, PA, Johanna, Franklin Co., PA, 12 Jun 1872, J.J., McGeaham, Margaritta, Moran, Williamsport, -, Willard, 13

3128, 30 Jul 1872, Joannem Michaelem, Bowers, Lebam, Frederick Co., MD, Sara Joanna, Frederick Co., MD, 10 May 1872, Sab [?], Cushwa, -, -, Hagerstown, -, Murphy, 13

3129, 5 Aug 1872, Albertum C., Smith, Joanne, Waynesboro, Joanna, Waynesboro, 14 Jul 1872, Gulielmus, Rider, Maria, Cretin, Waynesboro, -, Rider, 13

3130, 18 Aug 1872, Margarittam S., Cushwa, Clinton Geo., Washington County, Ella, Williamsport, 4 Jul 1872, Ben., Cushwa, Maria, Clarke, Williamsport, -, Clarke, 13

3131, 6 Oct 1872, Rosam Annam, Heigel, Philippo, Adams Co., PA, Maria, Adams Co., 23 Sep 1872, Martinus, Happle, Rosa, Happle, Hagerstown, -, Adams, 13

3132, 17 Oct 1872, Philippum, Mahon, Joanne, Mayo, Ireland, Catharina, Mayo, Ireland, 22 Sep 1872, Arthur, Kenny, Mary, Kenny, Hagerstown, -, Brady, 13

3133, 19 Oct 1872, Henricum C., Gehr, Isaac, Smithsburg, Elisabeth, Waynesboro, 31 Jul 1837, Arnorldus [?], Condy, Josephina, Hurley, Hagerstown, C; BC, Funk, 13

3134, 19 Oct 1872, Joannem, Moorhead, Jacobo, Greencastle, Anna, Greencastle, 10 years, Arnoldus, Condy, Josephina, Hurley, Hagerstown, C; BC, Moorhead, 13

ST. MARY'S CATHOLIC CHURCH HAGERSTOWN, MARYLAND, BAPTISMS:
Index, Baptism Date, Child, Last Name, Father from, Mother, Mother from, Birth Date, 1st Sponsor First, 1st Sponsor Last, 2nd Sponsor First, 2nd Sponsor Last, Location, Notes, Maiden Name, Priest

3135, 19 Oct 1872, Catharina, Tinken, Andrea, Germany, Cathrine, Germany, 15 Dec 1847, Martha, Wolls, -, -, Hagerstown, C; BC, Metzer, 13

3136, 19 Oct 1872, Carolum, Smith, Joanne, Massachusetts, Catharina, Hagerstown, 21 Apr 1869, Martha, Wolls, -, -, Hagerstown, C, Zinken, 13

3137, 19 Oct 1872, Elisabeth, Smith, Joanne, Massachusetts, Catharina, Hagerstown, 28 Apr 1867, Martha, Wills, -, -, Hagerstown, C, Tinken [sic], 13

3138, 19 Oct 1872, Danielem, Baker, Gulielmo, PA, Maria, PA, 1832, Josephina, Hurley, -, -, Hagerstown, C; BC, Hurley, 13

3139, 19 Oct 1872, Mariam Annam, Hoover, Benjamin, Leitersburg, Emilia, Leitersburg, 1832, Josephina, Hurley, -, -, Hagerstown, C, Harrison, 13

3140, 19 Oct 1872, Danielem, Baker, Daniele, PA, Mariam Anna, Leitersburg, 12 years, Josephina, Hurley, -, -, Hagerstown, C, Hoover, 13

3141, 19 Oct 1872, Joannem, Baker, Daniele, PA, Maria Anna, Leitersburg, 16 years, Josephina, Hurley, -, -, Hagerstown, C, Hoover, 13

3142, 19 Oct 1872, Mariam Henriettam, Baker, Daniele, PA, Maria Anna, Leitersburg, 14 years, Josephina, Hurley, -, -, Hagerstown, C, Hoover, 13

3143, 19 Oct 1872, Helenam, Baker, Daniele, PA, Maria Anna, Leitersburg, 10 years, Josephina, Hurley, -, -, Hagerstown, C, Hoover, 13

3144, 19 Oct 1872, Obediam, Baker, Daniele, PA, Maria Anna, Leitersburg, 4 years, Josephina, Hurley, -, -, Hagerstown, C, Hoover, 13

3145, 19 Oct 1872, Annam Cath., Baker, Daniele, PA, Maria Anna, Leitersburg, 7 years, Josephina, Hurley, -, -, Hagerstown, C, Hoover, 13

3146, 20 Oct 1872, Catharinam, Trussell, Ebenezer, Berkeley Co., WV, Savannah, Jefferson Co., WV, 12 Jan 1843, Carolus, Clark, Sara, Kushner, Williamsport, C, Fleming, 13

3147, 20 Oct 1872, Josephum W., Brittner, Clemente, Berkeley Co., WV, Catharina, Jefferson Co., WV, 27 Sep

ST. MARY'S CATHOLIC CHURCH
HAGERSTOWN, MARYLAND, BAPTISMS:
Index, Baptism Date, Child, Last Name, Father from, Mother, Mother from, Birth Date, 1st Sponsor First, 1st Sponsor Last, 2nd Sponsor First, 2nd Sponsor Last, Location, Notes, Maiden Name, Priest

1872, Carolus, Clark, Sara, Kushner, Williamsport, -, Trussell, 13

3148, 20 Oct 1872, Gertrudam Agatham, Ford, Joanne, -, Catharine, -, 15 Aug 1866, W. L., May, -, -, Hagerstown, MA, Burkett, 13

3149, 20 Oct 1872, Emmam Catharinam, Fellinger, Philippo, Hessen, Germany, Elisabeth, Hagerstown, 15 Jul 1870, Josephine, Hurley, -, -, Hagerstown, MA, Garman, 13

3150, 20 Oct 1872, Elisabeth Tinam, Dusang, George, Frederick, MD, Elisabeth, Ireland, 10 Jun 1870, Helena, Kelly, -, -, Hagerstown, -, Doolan, 13

3151, 20 Oct 1872, Helenam Joannam, Hyle, Alberto, Germany, Carolina, Funkstown, 8 Aug 1872, Margaritta, O'Connor, -, -, Hagerstown, -, Blumenour, 13

3152, 20 Oct 1872, Elisabeth, -, -, -, Teresia, Hagerstown, 6 Feb 1870, Josephina, Hurley, -, -, Hagerstown, PN, Shover, 13

3153, 20 Oct 1872, Carolum Alphonsum, Little, Carolo, Franklin Co., PA, Rebecca, Germany, Europe, 4 Oct 1872, -, -, -, -, Hagerstown, -, Laurens, 13

3154, 4 Nov 1872, Mariam Catharinam, Dillon, Michaele, Kerry, Ireland, Martha, Adams Co., PA, 3 Nov 1872, Augustus, Nierman, Philomena, Nierman, Hagerstown, -, McCallion, 13

3155, 8 Dec 1872, Gulielmum, Allen, Joanne, Washington County, Maria E., Frederick Co., MD, 28 Sep 1872, Rachel, Allen, -, -, Hagerstown, both parents are Black, Stewart, 13

3156, 15 Dec 1872, Richardum Vincentium *, Hawken, Gulielmo W., Williamsport, Anna A., Williamsport, 29 Oct 1872, Joannes, O'Neill, Catharina, Little, Williamsport, * full name is "Richardum Vincentium Whelan P.", Parker, 13

3157, 6 Jan 1873, Catharinam, Smith, -, -, -, -, -, -, -, -, -, Hagerstown, she was Catharina Horine and married Jesse Smith; from Boonsboro; PB, -, 13

3158, 20 Jan 1873, Helenam, Gallagher, Gulielmo, Washington County, Catharina, Arkansas, 7 Jan 1873, Edwardus, Donnelly, Helena, Oliver, Williamsport, -, Oliver, 13

ST. MARY'S CATHOLIC CHURCH HAGERSTOWN, MARYLAND, BAPTISMS:
Index, Baptism Date, Child, Last Name, Father from, Mother, Mother from, Birth Date, 1st Sponsor First, 1st Sponsor Last, 2nd Sponsor First, 2nd Sponsor Last, Location, Notes, Maiden Name, Priest

3159, 23 Jan 1873, Mariam E., Anderson, -, -, -, -, 4 Jul 1826, Josephina, Hurley, -, -, -, convert from Anglicanism; from Loundon Co., VA, -, 13

3160, 25 Jan 1873, Anitam Eulaliam, Wroe, Joanne, Washington, DC, Martha, Hagerstown, 12 Jul 1855, Helena, Taggart, -, -, -, convert from paganism, Barr, 13

3161, 21 Feb 1873, Mariam, Dore, Patricio, Limerick, Ireland, Marias, Limerick, Ireland, 15 Dec 1872, Dan., Riordan, Marg., Kennedy, Hagerstown, -, Sheehan, 13

3162, 25 Mar 1873, Josephum Patricium, Sheehan, Gulielmo, Cork, Ireland, Catharina, Cork, Ireland, 16 Mar 1873, Michael, Battle, Maria, Gehry, Hagerstown, -, Barrett, 13

3163, 6 Apr 1873, Annam Reginam, Yohn, Philippo, PA, Maria Francisca, PA, 23 Mar 1873, Carolus B., Boyle, Josephine, Hurley, Hagerstown, -, Wright, 13

3164, 6 Apr 1873, Margaritta Letitia, Wills, Joanne F., Adams Co., PA, Martha S. [?], Williamsport, 26 Mar 1873, Thomas B., Cushwa, Letitia, McElhenny, Hagerstown, -, McClain, 13

3165, 5 Apr 1873, Jacobum Franciscum, White, Michaele, Ireland, Catharina, Clear Spring, 21 Jan 1873, Elisabeth, Fellinger, -, -, Hagerstown, -, Fellinger, 13

3166, 27 Apr 1873, Mariam Suzannam, Fall, Michaele A., Washington County, Anna A., Washington Co., 30 Mar 1873, Maria Johenna, Fall, -, -, Hagerstown, -, Price, 13

3167, 18 May 1873, Davidem Patricium, Hurleyhy, Davide, Limerick, Ireland, Catharina, Clare, Ireland, 26 Mar 1873, David, Hurleyhy, Maria, King, Williamsport, -, Hassett, 13

3168, 6 Jun 1873, Hugonem Alexandrum, Rose, Allen, New York, Anna, Canada [the next word has been overwritten and is illegible], 30 Mar 1873, Josephina, Hurley, -, -, Hagerstown, FA, Lefevere, 13

3169, 8 Jun 1873, Joannem, Cunningham, Joanne, Harpers Ferry, WV, Sarah, Sandy Hook, 26 Jan 1873, Thos., Egan, -, -, Hagerstown, -, Montaigue, 13

3170, 15 Jul 1873, Edmundum Franklin, Smith, Edw., Hagerstown, Genoveffa, Hagerstown, 16 Jun 1873, Maria, Coyle, -, -, Hagerstown, -, Ward, 26

ST. MARY'S CATHOLIC CHURCH HAGERSTOWN, MARYLAND, BAPTISMS:
Index, Baptism Date, Child, Last Name, Father from, Mother, Mother from, Birth Date, 1st Sponsor First, 1st Sponsor Last, 2nd Sponsor First, 2nd Sponsor Last, Location, Notes, Maiden Name, Priest

3171, 30 Jun 1873, Louisam Elisabeth, Conlan, Dionysis, Clare, Ireland, Brigitta, Clare, 13 Apr 1873, Maria, Coyle, -, -, Hagerstown, -, Cunningham, 13

3172, 21 Jul 1873, Mariam Helenam, Barry, Joanne, Limerick, Ireland, Maria, Limerick, Ireland, 10 Jul 1873, Joannes R., Barry, Cath., Hoy, Williamsport, -, Collins, 13

3173, 26 Jul 1873, Cletum Patricium, Coyle, Thoma B., Cavetown, Maria, Cavetown, 23 Mar 1873, Josephina, Hurley, -, -, Hagerstown, -, Horn, 13

3174, 27 Jul 1873, Annam Virginiam, Fox, Fernando J. [or I.], Washington County, Virginia Anna, Rockingham Co., VA, 23 Jul 1873, Maria, Coyle, -, -, Hagerstown, -, Nicely, 13

3175, 10 Aug 1873, Joannem Everitt, Needy, Isaac, Hagerstown, Catharina, Hagerstown, 13 May 1873, Margarita, Griffin, -, -, Hagerstown, -, Griffin, 2

3176, 19 Aug 1873, Carolus R. E., Sheehan, Martino, Kerry, Ireland, Elisabeth, Germany, 4 May 1873, Arnoldus, Condy, Lucinda, Hoover, Hagerstown, -, Shilling, 13

3177, 24 Aug 1873, Mariam Helenam, Leman [or Lemen], Petro, Berkeley Co., WV, Helena, Williamsport, 6 Aug 1873, Hugo, Clarke, Helena, Oliver, Williamsport, -, Stake, 13

3178, 21 Sep 1873, Joannes Edwardus, Stoner, Roberto, PA, Margaritta, Emmittsburg, MD, 7 Sep 1873, Carolus B., Boyle, Anna, Tierney, Hagerstown, -, Webb, 13

3179, 5 Oct 1873, Maria Francisca, Gher, Henrico, Smithsburg, Cora, Hagerstown, 8 Sep 1873, Arnoldus, Condey, Josephina, Hurley, Hagerstown, -, Shank, 13

3180, 25 Oct 1873, Giergiee [?] Winter, Fechtig, Georgio, Hagerstown, Louisa, Hagerstown, 6 weeks, Maria, McLoughlin, -, -, Hagerstown, -, Doyle, 11

3181, 25 Oct 1873, Daniel, McDeritt [?], Cornelio, Donegal Co., Margaret, Donegal Co., 24-Oct, Daniel, O'Donohue, -, -, Hagerstown, -, O'Donohue, 11

3182, 26 Oct 1873, Mariam Aliciam, Reid, Guglielmo, w, Maria Ellen, Williamsport, 29-Sep, Jacobus, Hughes, Regina, Clark, Williamsport, -, Donelly, 11

ST. MARY'S CATHOLIC CHURCH
HAGERSTOWN, MARYLAND, BAPTISMS:
Index, Baptism Date, Child, Last Name, Father from,
Mother, Mother from, Birth Date, 1st Sponsor First,
1st Sponsor Last, 2nd Sponsor First, 2nd Sponsor Last,
Location, Notes, Maiden Name, Priest

3183, 26 Oct 1873, Hester Virginiam, Cevell [or Covell?], Joseph, w, Elizabeth, Williamsport, 11-Jun, Clara, Goddard, -, -, Williamsport, -, Paden, 11

3184, 2 Nov 1873, Mariam Jane Rebeccam, Taylor, Otho, Hagerstown, Francis, Hagerstown, 5 years, Jennie, Bayley, -, -, Hagerstown, Family and sponsors are Black., Smith, 11

3185, 22 Nov 1873, Carolum Eduardem, Davis, Georgio, Hagerstown, Anna, Hagerstown, 8 Jan 1873, Mrs., Hippner, -, -, Hagerstown, -, Hansen [?], 11

3186, 23 Nov 1873, Carolum Benton, Cushwa, Clinton, w, Ella, Williamsport, 15-Nov, T. Benten, Cushwa, Maria, Shervin, Williamsport, -, Clark, 11

3187, 23 Nov 1873, Lemem Predestin, Brittner, Clemente, WV, Elizabeth, WV, 21-Oct, Johannes, Laurence, -, -, Williamsport, -, Trexell, 11

3188, 14 Dec 1873, Andream Johnsen, Jones, David, Hagerstown, Margareta A., Hagerstown, 27 Jun 1866, Fredericus, Halm, Belinda, McCardell, Hagerstown, -, Wolf, 11

3189, 28 Dec 1873, Annam Mariam, Hoy, Laurentio, Williamsport, Kate, Williamsport, "about the" 20 Dec, Georgianna, Williams, -, -, Williamsport, -, Donn, 11

3190, 28 Dec 1873, Annam Isabellam, Reeder, -, -, -, -, Dec 1872, Clara, Goddard, -, -, Williamsport, PN, -, 11

3191, 1 Jan 1874, Margaretam, Wolf, John, Hagerstown, -, -, 35 years, Belinda, McCardell, -, -, Hagerstown, C; wife of David Jones, -, 11

3192, 8 Jan 1874, Martinum Henricus, Flegel, Philippo, PA, Maria M., PA, 3-Jan, Wm., Schlotterbeck, Elizabeth, Schlotterbeck [HB], Hagerstown, -, Adams, 11

3193, 25 Jan 1874, Gingunn [?] Albertum, Kershner, Ezro, VA, Sara, VA, 5-Nov, Clement, Brittner, Julia A., Brittner, Williamsport, -, Brittner, 11

3194, 9 Feb 1874, Annam Elizabeth, Sweitzer, Samuel, Washington County, Mary J., Adams Co., PA, 22-Jan, Andrew C., Laurence, Anna M., Laurence, Hagerstown, -, Laurence, 11

ST. MARY'S CATHOLIC CHURCH
HAGERSTOWN, MARYLAND, BAPTISMS:
Index, Baptism Date, Child, Last Name, Father from, Mother, Mother from, Birth Date, 1st Sponsor First, 1st Sponsor Last, 2nd Sponsor First, 2nd Sponsor Last, Location, Notes, Maiden Name, Priest

3195, 19 Feb 1874, Joannam Francescam, Cushwa, Victore, Williamsport, Maria Anna, Williamsport, 5-Feb, Evalina, Cushwa, Sarah, Cushwa, Williamsport, Evalina Cushwa stood proxy for Sarah Cushwa, Kreigh, 11

3196, 24 Feb 1874, Hermione Moffatt, Young, Jerome, VA, Maria, VA, 30 years, Josephine, Hurley, -, -, Hagerstown, C; BC, Young, 11

3197, 24 Feb 1874, Emmam, Young, Jerome, VA, Maria, VA, 21 years, Julia, Keedy, -, -, Hagerstown, C; BC, Young, 11

3198, 4 Mar 1874, Annam Catharinam, Häpple, Martino, Westphalia, Germany, Rosina, Westphalia, Germany, 9-Feb, Mrs., Schlotterbeck, -, -, Hagerstown, -, Beckman, 11

3199, 25 Mar 1874, Mariam Protis, Shank [father's name is Lord], Elie, Smithsburg, Maria, Smithsburg, 31-Oct, Susan, Fessler, -, -, Hagerstown, PN, Shank, 11

3200, 29 Mar 1874, Ludvicum [?], Downs, Cristophero, Downsville, [blank], Downsville, "about" 21 years, Georgius, Kyper [?], -, -, Hagerstown, C, Downs, 11

3201, 7 Apr 1874, Benjamin, Welsh, -, -, -, -, "about" 80 years, -, -, -, -, Cavetown, C; BC; from Cavetown, -, 11

3202, 3 May 1874, Hammond [?], Dern, Isaac, Union Mills, Delilah, Union Mills, 26 Aug 1855, Benton, Cushwa, Sallie, Cushwa [HB], Hagerstown, C; Hammond is described as "infidelitate", Andersen, 11

3203, 6 May 1874, Henricum Franklin, Stein, Jacob, Washington County, Catharine, Washington Co., 4 Mar 1874, Ann, Lizer, -, -, Hagerstown, -, Lizer, 11

3204, 17 May 1874, Mariam, Maffatt, Isaac, Philadelphia, Hermione [?], Washington Co., 14 Mar 1871, Mrs., Anderson, -, -, Hagerstown, BC; married Cornelio Dougherty, St. Joseph's Church, Philadelphia, 21 Jun 1911, Rev. Father Thoma A. Reid, S.J., Young, 11

3205, 17 May 1874, Hermione Virginiam, Maffatt, Isaac, Philadelphia, Hermione, Washington Co., 4 Jan 1869, Mrs., Anderson, -, -, Hagerstown, BC, Young, 11

3206, 17 May 1874, Joanne Franciscum, -, -, -, Anna, Hagerstown, about the 15 of the month, Sarah, Rideout, -, -, Hagerstown, PN; Family and sponsors are Black, Walker, 11

ST. MARY'S CATHOLIC CHURCH
HAGERSTOWN, MARYLAND, BAPTISMS:
Index, Baptism Date, Child, Last Name, Father from,
Mother, Mother from, Birth Date, 1st Sponsor First,
1st Sponsor Last, 2nd Sponsor First, 2nd Sponsor Last,
Location, Notes, Maiden Name, Priest

3207, 17 May 1874, Georgium Albertem, Brown [?], Joanni, Hagerstown, Jennie, Hagerstown, 28-Apr, Sarah, Rideout, -, -, Hagerstown, Family and sponsors are Black, Brown, 11

3208, 17 May 1874, Mariam Grace Reginam, Tayler, Ottone [?], Hagerstown, Frances, Hagerstown, 5 Mar 1866, Jennie, Bayley, -, -, Hagerstown, Family and sponsors are Black, Taylor, 11

3209, 31 May 1874, Helena Cindry [?], Watts, John W., Hagerstown, Jennie, Hagerstown, 12 Apr 1874, Sarah, Cushwa, -, -, Hagerstown, Family and sponsors are Black, King, 11

3210, 14 Jun 1874, Carolum Franciscum, Allen, Johanne, Hagerstown, Maria, Hagerstown, 27-Apr, Jennie, Bayley, -, -, Hagerstown, Family and sponsors are Black, Stewart, 11

3211, 14 Jun 1874, Franciscum Thomam, Grady, Thoma, Hagerstown, Catharina, Hagerstown, 6-Jun, Jacobus, O'Conner [?], Margarrita, O'Conner [?] [HB], Hagerstown, -, Lynch, 11

3212, 24 Jun 1874, Patritium Guglielmum, Gilleece, Patritio, Mill Stone Point, Rachel, Mill Stone Point, 24-May, Margaret, Rigney, -, -, Hagerstown, -, Gilleece, 11

3213, 25 Jun 1874*, Michaelem Themain, Geary, Eugenis, Hagerstown, Catharina, Hagerstown, 19-Jun, Maria, Reordan, -, -, Hagerstown, *baptismal date is 25 [or 27] Jun 1874, Sullivan, 11

3214, 8 Jul 1874, Thomam Henricum, Ford, Franklin, Washington County, Maria, Washington Co., 8 May 1873, Belle, Shervin, -, -, Hagerstown, -, Jacobs, 11

3215, 19 Jul 1874, Carolum Guglielnum, Baker, Daniele, Washington County, Maria A., Washington Co., 20-May, Wilhelmina, May, -, -, Hagerstown, -, Hoover, 11

3216, 27 Aug 1874, Mariam Helenam, Orndorf, Guglieluco, Hagerstown, Romanus [?], Hagerstown, 17-Aug, Carolus, Boyle, Sally, Cushwa, Hagerstown, -, Schilling, 11

3217, 30 Aug 1874, Claran Louisam, Wills, Jacob, Hagerstown, Matilda, Hagerstown, 18 Aug 1874, Guglielmus, McClain, Anna, McClain [HB], Hagerstown, -, McClain, 11

ST. MARY'S CATHOLIC CHURCH
HAGERSTOWN, MARYLAND, BAPTISMS:
Index, Baptism Date, Child, Last Name, Father from,
Mother, Mother from, Birth Date, 1st Sponsor First,
1st Sponsor Last, 2nd Sponsor First, 2nd Sponsor Last,
Location, Notes, Maiden Name, Priest

3218, 14 Sep 1874, Helenam May, Mobley, Carver, Hagerstown, Anna, Hagerstown, 20-Aug, Belinda, McCardell, -, -, Hagerstown, -, McCardell, 11

3219, 13 Sep 1874, Carolinam, Futterer, -, -, -, -, -, Margareta, [blank], -, -, Hagerstown, wife of John Futterer; from Washington Co.; C; BC, -, 11

3220, 4 Oct 1874, Mariam Catharinam, Lewis, Georgio, Washington County, Elizabeth, Washington Co., 18-Aug, Margaret, Lewis, -, -, Hagerstown, -, [blank], 11

3221, 27 Sep 1874, Susan, Hurlehey, Ricardo, sc, Ellen, Washington Co., 12-Aug, Maria, Barry, -, -, Williamsport, -, Desmend, 11

3222, 25 Oct 1874, Frances, Hawkins, Wm., Williamsport, Ann, Williamsport, 3 mos. *, Ellen, Stake, -, -, Williamsport, * "about 3 months", Parkes, 11

3223, 5 Nov 1874, Georgium Martinum, Davis, Georgio, Hagerstown, Anna, Hagerstown, 2-Sep, Bell, Shervin, -, -, Hagerstown, -, Hänson, 11

3224, 30 Nov 1874, Mariam Genevieve, McLoughlin, Ludovico [?], Hagerstown, Maria, Hagerstown, 4-Nov, Jacobus, McLoughlin, Letitia, McIlhany, Hagerstown, -, Hurley, 11

3225, 30 Dec 1874, Mariam Joseph, Malone, Hugh, Hagerstown, Maria, Hagerstown, 9-Dec, Ella, Taggart, -, -, Hagerstown, -, Kelly, 11

3226, 10 Jan 1875, Nettie Virginia, Strite, Daniele, Grand Junction, Iowa, Jennie, Grand Junction, Iowa, 15 Jan 1873, Mrs., Anderson, -, -, Hagerstown, -, Young, 11

3227, 17 Jan 1875, Carrery [?] Bernardum, Cramer, Jacob, Hagerstown, Martha, Hagerstown, 10 Dec 1874, Maria, Cramer, -, -, Hagerstown, -, Jacobs, 11

3228, 25 Jan 1875, William Walsh, McCardle, Ambrose, Williamsport, Cecilia, Williamsport, 12 Dec 1874, Ellen, Oliver, -, -, Williamsport, -, Olvier, 11

3229, 25 Jan 1875, James Percy, McCardle, Ambrose, Williamsport, Cecilia, Williamsport, 12 Dec 1874, Fanny, Thompson, -, -, Williamsport, -, Olvier, 11

ST. MARY'S CATHOLIC CHURCH
HAGERSTOWN, MARYLAND, BAPTISMS:
Index, Baptism Date, Child, Last Name, Father from, Mother, Mother from, Birth Date, 1st Sponsor First, 1st Sponsor Last, 2nd Sponsor First, 2nd Sponsor Last, Location, Notes, Maiden Name, Priest

3230, 14 Feb 1875, Jesse Franciscum, Clayburn, Jahanne, Hagerstown, Sallie, Hagerstown, 21 Oct 1874, Sallie, Cushwa, -, -, Hagerstown, -, Martini, 11

3231, 1 Mar 1875, Ezechiel, Chaney, Joanne, Williamsport, Barbara, Williamsport, 26 Oct 1843, Elie, Stake, -, -, Williamsport, C, Demande [?], 11

3232, 21 Mar 1875, Eleanora Ligusi [?], Gehr, Harry, Hagerstown, Cora, Hagerstown, 5 Feb 1875, Auguste, Nearman, L. Margaret, Hoover, Hagerstown, -, Shank, 11

3233, 25 Mar 1875, Josephum Patritium, Eagan, Thoma, Hagerstown, Margareta, Hagerstown, 18 Mar 1875, Caroles, Boyle, Margareta, Keiper, Hagerstown, -, O'Conner, 11

3234, 27 Mar 1875, Henricum Simon, Fox, Fernardo, Hagerstown, Virginia, Hagerstown, 8 Mar 1875, Wilhelmina Louisa, May, -, -, Hagerstown, -, Nicely, 11

3235, 28 Mar 1875, Guglielmum Weston [?], Preston, Samuel, Williamsport, Maria, Williamsport, 22-Jan, Clara, Goddard, -, -, Williamsport, -, Reeder, 11

3236, 28 Mar 1875, Catharinam, Edwards, Roberto, Paw Paw, Md., Margareta, Paw Paw, Md., 9 Dec 1874, Margaret, Barry, -, -, Williamsport, -, Goddard, 11

3237, 1 Apr 1875, Mariam Ceciliam Jane, Bowers, Michaele, "Cavetown Mountains", Barbara, "Cavetown Mountains", 26-Aug, Maria, Gauger, -, -, "Cavetown at Mrs. Coyles", -, Gauger, 11

3238, 10 Apr 1875, Annam Ceciliam, Shehan, Cornelis, Hagerstown, Ellen, Hagerstown, 21-Mar, Alfred, McCardell, Anna, Ahern, Hagerstown, -, Long, 11

3239, 22 Apr 1875, Margaretam May, Full, Michaele, Hagerstown, Anna, Hagerstown, 30-Jan, Margareta, Rigney, -, -, Hagerstown, -, Price, 11

3240, 22 Apr 1875, Jacob Michael, Mishner, -, Cavetown, -, Cavetown, 63 years, -, -, -, -, Cavetown, BP; "Neo-conversus at Mrs. Mishners'.", -, 11

3241, 25 Apr 1875, Jacobum Elie, Donelley, Edwardo, Williamsport, Catharina, Williamsport, 1-Apr, Franciscus, Gallagher, Maria, Reid, Williamsport, Married 16 Sept. 1916,

ST. MARY'S CATHOLIC CHURCH HAGERSTOWN, MARYLAND, BAPTISMS:
Index, Baptism Date, Child, Last Name, Father from, Mother, Mother from, Birth Date, 1st Sponsor First, 1st Sponsor Last, 2nd Sponsor First, 2nd Sponsor Last, Location, Notes, Maiden Name, Priest

in St. Aloysii Church, Washington, D.C., to Catharina Moran.", Hoy, 11

3242, 13 Jun 1875, Augustum Henricum, Nierman, Augusto, Hagerstown, Philomena, Hagerstown, 6-Jun, T.B., Cushwa, Sallie, Cushwa, Hagerstown, -, Spechman, 11

3243, 23 Jul 1875, Grace, Cumming, Johanne, Hagerstown, Sarah, Hagerstown, 11 Dec 1874, Martha, Montague, -, -, Hagerstown, -, Montague, 11

3244, 25 Jul 1875, Hugh Clinton, Cushwa, Clinton, Cherry Run, Md., Ella, Cherry Run, Md., 19-Jun, Hugh, Clark, Regina, Clark [HB], Williamsport, -, Clark, 11

3245, 25 Jul 1875, Andream, Blair, Andrea, Williamsport, Amanda, Williamsport, 2 years, Tim, Hughes, Kate, Little, Williamsport, -, Watson, 11

3246, 25 Jul 1875, Franciscum, Blair, Andrea, Williamsport, Amanda, Williamsport, 1 year, Mary, Barry, -, -, Williamsport, -, Watson, 11

3247, 8 Aug 1875, Johannem Franciscum, Moxley, Johanne, Hagerstown, Julia, Hagerstown, 1-Aug, Rachel, Spriggs, -, -, Hagerstown, Family and sponsors are Black, Spriggs, 11

3248, 22 Aug 1875, Ricardum Eugenium, Cushwa, Guglielmo, Williamsport, Modie [sic], Williamsport, 22-Jul, Fred., Halm, Eva, McCleery, Williamsport, -, Kreigh, 11

3249, 22 Aug 1875, Guglielmum, Jessup, [blank], Williamsport, Maria, Williamsport, 4 years, John, Barry, Lillie, Williams, Williamsport; PN, PN, Bourgoyne, 11

3250, 7 Sep 1875, Lauran Beatricum, Taylor, Charlie, Williamsport, Lizzie, Williamsport, 11 years, Georgiana, Williams, -, -, Williamsport, B; C, Taylor, 11

3251, 12 Sep 1875, Isaac, Feigley, -, -, Elizabeth, -, 28 Jun 1844, -, -, -, -, Hagerstown, C, Feigley, 11

3252, 21 Sep 1875, Edwardum Linum, Coyle, Thoma, Smithsburg, Ada, Smithsburg, 29-Jan, Susan, Fessler, -, -, Hagerstown, -, Horn, 11

3253, 25 Spe 1875, Idam [sic] Robertam, Weirich [father's last name is Miller], Isaac, VA, Lucretia, Charlestown, VA, 12 Jan 1874, Maria, Weirich, -, -, Hagerstown, "The husband left and the wife goes by her maiden name.", Weirich, 11

ST. MARY'S CATHOLIC CHURCH
HAGERSTOWN, MARYLAND, BAPTISMS:
Index, Baptism Date, Child, Last Name, Father from, Mother, Mother from, Birth Date, 1st Sponsor First, 1st Sponsor Last, 2nd Sponsor First, 2nd Sponsor Last, Location, Notes, Maiden Name, Priest

3254, 30 Sep 1875, Michaelem Aloysium, Reardon, Daniele, Hagerstown, Maria, Hagerstown, 17-Sep, Elizabeth, Reordan, -, -, Hagerstown, -, Farrelly, 11

3255, 2 Oct 1875, Nellie Regina, Grimm, Thoma, Hagerstown, Ada, Hagerstown, 19-Sep, Wilhelmina Maria Louisa, May, -, -, Hagerstown, -, Spangler, 11

3256, 17 Oct 1875, Edwardum Ludovicum, Needy, David, Washington County, Maria, Washington Co., 3-Jul, Maggie, Griffey, -, -, Hagerstown, PN, Griffey, 11

3257, 25 Oct 1875, Ellen, Reid, Guglielmo, Williamsport, Maria, Williamsport, 13-Oct, Kate, Donelley, -, -, Williamsport, -, Donelley, 11

3258, 6 Nov 1875, Gertrude, Wills, Jacob, Hagerstown, Martha, Hagerstown, 13-Oct, Kate, Gray, -, -, Hagerstown, -, McClain, 11

3259, 30 Oct 1875, Danielem, Laesure, -, -, -, -, -, -, -, -, -, Hagerstown, "Baptised when very ill at the pen [?] house." C; from Mill Stone Point., -, 11

3260, 27 Nov 1875, Mariam Emmam, Schweitzer, Samuele, Washington County, Maria, Washington Co., 14-Nov, Sallie, Cushwa, -, -, Hagerstown, -, Laurence, 11

3261, 28 Nov 1875, Annam Elizabeth, Busch, David, Williamsport, Margaret, -, 15-Oct, Charles, Clark, Margaret, Clark, Williamsport, -, Snovell [?], 11

3262, 26 Dec 1875, Georgium Guglielmum, Johnson, David, Williamsport, Maria, Franklin Co., PA, 46 years, Edwardus, Donelley, -, -, Williamsport, C, Johnson, 11

3263, 6 Jan 1876, Lauram Virginiam, Hose, Johanne, Hagerstown, Jennie, Hagerstown, 17 Oct 1875, Schilling (Mrs.), Shehan, -, -, Hagerstown, -, Schilling, 11

3264, 23 Jan 1876, Johannem, McKusker, Johanne, Toll Gate, Martha, Toll Gate, 29 Oct 1875, Mrs., McKusker, -, -, Toll Gate, -, Roland, 11

3265, 24 Jan 1876, Harriet Louisam, Orndorf, Guglielmus [?], Hagerstown, Romanus, Hagerstown, 14-Jan, Benton, Cushwa, Josephine, Hurley, Hagerstown, -, Schilling, 11

3266, 27 Jan 1876, Guglielmum Thomam, Little, -, -, -, -, 10 Jul 1870, -, -, -, -, Williamsport, from Williamsport; C, -, 11

ST. MARY'S CATHOLIC CHURCH
HAGERSTOWN, MARYLAND, BAPTISMS:
Index, Baptism Date, Child, Last Name, Father from, Mother, Mother from, Birth Date, 1st Sponsor First, 1st Sponsor Last, 2nd Sponsor First, 2nd Sponsor Last, Location, Notes, Maiden Name, Priest

3267, 13 Feb 1876, Thomam Michaelem, Battles, Michaele, Hagerstown, Nannie, Hagerstown, 4-Feb, Jacobus, Malone, Maria, Malone [HB], Hagerstown, -, Barrett, 11

3268, 26 Mar 1876, Bertham Aloysiam, Hoy, Laurentio, Williamsport, Catharina, Williamsport, 21-Jan, Ann, Sheridan, -, -, Williamsport, -, Doran [?], 11

3269, 26 Mar 1876, Danielem Gregorium, Kershner, Ezro, Williamsport, Sarah, Williamsport, 20 Nov 1875, Miss, Brittner, -, -, Williamsport, -, Brittner, 11

3270, 8 Apr 1876, Helenam Agnetem, Fechtig, Georgio, Hagerstown, Louisa, Hagerstown, 25 Nov 1875, Sallie, Cushwa, -, -, Hagerstown, -, Doyle, 11

3271, 30 Apr 1876, Georgium Guglielmums, Kershner, Joseph, Hagerstown, Helen, Hagerstown, 12-Apr, Georgius, Hoover, Maria, Eck, Hagerstown, -, Hoover, 11

3272, 7 May 1876, Mabel Virginiam, Brown, Johanne, Hagerstown, Jennie, Hagerstown, 8 months, Josephina, Hurley, -, -, Hagerstown, Child is Black, Hipkins, 11

3273, 9 May 1876, Mariam Catharinam, Schlotterbeck, Guglielmus, Hagerstown, Elizabeth, Hagerstown, 4 May 1867, Mrs., Hippner [?], -, -, Hagerstown, BC, [blank], 11

3274, 11 May 1876, Johannem Michaelem, Full, Michaele, Washington County, Anna, Washington Co., 24-Mar, Wilhelmina Amelia Louisa, May, -, -, Hagerstown, -, Price, 11

3275, 12 May 1876, Jonathan, Kershner, -, -, -, -, 85 years, -, -, -, -, Hagerstown, "Baptised conditionally on his death-bed.", -, 11

3276, 14 May 1876, Edwardem Howard, Bateman [or Cramer], Isaac, unknown, Theresa, unknown, 20-Jan, Maria, Cramer, -, -, Hagerstown, PN, Cramer, 11

3277, 11 Jun 1876, Claram Reginam, Coon [or Scott], Guglielmo, Hagerstown, Henrietta, Hagerstown, 11-May, Jennie, Cook, -, -, Hagerstown, family and sponsors are Black; PN; father's last name is Scott, Coon, 11

3278, 14 Jun 1876, Giorgium, Ebert, -, -, -, -, 18 Mar 1821, -, -, -, -, Hagerstown, from Carroll Co.; "Conditionally baptized when very ill." C, -, 11

ST. MARY'S CATHOLIC CHURCH
HAGERSTOWN, MARYLAND, BAPTISMS:
Index, Baptism Date, Child, Last Name, Father from, Mother, Mother from, Birth Date, 1st Sponsor First, 1st Sponsor Last, 2nd Sponsor First, 2nd Sponsor Last, Location, Notes, Maiden Name, Priest

3279, 15 Jun 1876, Florence Ceciliam, Needy, Isaac, Washington County, Catharine, Washington Co., 4 months, Margaret, Griffey, -, -, Hagerstown, -, Griffey, 11

3280, 23 Jun 1876, Philippum Chester, Cumming, Johanne, Hagerstown, Sarah, Hagerstown, 12 Jun *, Mrs., Battles, -, -, Hagerstown, BP; PB; * "about 12 Jun", Montague, 11

3281, 28 Jun 1876, Susan, Johnson [father's name is Schneider], Jacob, Williamsport, Margaret, Williamsport, 2 Mar 1844, -, -, -, -, Williamsport, Johnson is her married name.; C; "Baptized privately when ill.", [blank], 11

3282, [no date], Mariam Catharina, Johnson, George W., Williamsport, Susannah, Williamsport, 17 Aug 1866, Frank, Gallagher, Maria, Barry, Williamsport, C, Schneider, 11

3283, 4 Jul 1876, Mariam Elizabeth, Woods, Joseph, Washington Co., Anna, Washington Co., 8-May, Jennie, Bayley, -, -, Hagerstown, B; parents' residence listed as "mountains" of Washington Co., Woods, 11

3284, 9 Aug 1876, Martham J. [or I.], Wroe, -, -, -, -, 50 years, -, -, -, -, Hagerstown, C; from Hagerstown, -, 11

3285, 9 Aug 1876, Johannem L., Wroe, Dr., Hagerstown, Martha J. [or I.], Hagerstown, 23 years, W. L., May, -, -, Hagerstown, C, Barr, 11

3286, 9 Aug 1876, Ricardem E., Wroe, Dr., Hagerstown, Martha J. [or I.], Hagerstown, 22 years, W.L., May, -, -, Hagerstown, C, Barr, 11

3287, 9 Aug 1876, Samuel C., Wroe, Dr., Hagerstown, Martha J. [or I.], Hagerstown, 15 years, W.L., May, -, -, Hagerstown, C, Barr, 11

3288, 9 Aug 1876, Daisy Paulitam, Wroe, Dr., Hagerstown, Martha J. [or I.], Hagerstown, 13 years, Annita, Wroe, -, -, Hagerstown, C, Barr, 11

3289, 9 Aug 1876, Ninam Carlotam, Wroe, Dr., Hagerstown, Martha J. [or I.], Hagerstown, 8 years, Wilhelmina L., May, -, -, Hagerstown, C; "Married at St. Mary Rockville, Md to Anthony Polito on June 7, 1957 by Re. H. Perkinson", Barr, 11

ST. MARY'S CATHOLIC CHURCH
HAGERSTOWN, MARYLAND, BAPTISMS:
Index, Baptism Date, Child, Last Name, Father from, Mother, Mother from, Birth Date, 1st Sponsor First, 1st Sponsor Last, 2nd Sponsor First, 2nd Sponsor Last, Location, Notes, Maiden Name, Priest

3290, 10 Sep 1876, Mariam Elizabeth, Grady, Thoma, Hagerstown, Catharina, Hagerstown, 30-Aug, Guglielmus, Geary, Johanna, Geary [HB], Hagerstown, -, Lynch, 11

3291, 10 Sep 1876, Guglielmum Arthurum, Thomas, -, -, Susan, -, 12 May 1873, Jennie, Bayley, -, -, Hagerstown, B; PN, Thomas, 11

3292, 24 Sep 1876, Carolum Eduardem, Donelley, Edwardo, Williamsport, Kate, Williamsport, 31-Aug, Ellen, Oliver, -, -, Williamsport, -, Hoy, 11

3293, 1 Oct 1876, Guglielmum Michaelem, Flynn, Johanne, Hagerstown, Catharina, Hagerstown, 17-Sep, J.B., Sweeney, Maria, Smith, Hagerstown, -, [blank], 11

3294, 27 Dec 1876, Guglielmum Thomam, Schlotterbeck, Guglielmo, Hagerstown, Elizabetha, Hagerstown, 2 years, Maria, Hipner, -, -, Hagerstown, BC, Selner, 11

3295, 27 Dec 1876, Rosinam Elizabetham, Schlotterbeck, Guglielmo, Hagerstown, Elizabetha, Hagerstown, 27-Sep, Rosina, Happle, -, -, Hagerstown, -, Selner, 11

3296, 7 Jan 1877, Catharinam, Gabriel, Guglielmo, Alsatia, B., Germany, 20 Aug 1874, Otho, Duffy, -, -, Hagerstown, -, Coniger [?], 11

3297, 7 Jan 1877, Augustam, Gabriel, Guglielmo, Alsatia, B., Germany, 26 Aug 1876, Johannes, Dillon, -, -, Hagerstown, -, Conniger [?], 11

3298, 1 Feb 1877, Sarah Catharina, Baker, David, Washington County, Mary, Washington Co., 3 Feb 1856, Wilhelmina, May, -, -, Hagerstown, C; mother is deceased, Baker, 11

3299, 3 Feb 1877, Josephina Agnestem, Fox, Fernando, Hagerstown, Jennie, Hagerstown, 12 Jan 1877, Josephine, Hurley, -, -, Hagerstown, -, Nicely, 11

3300, 4 Feb 1877, Mariam Claram, Johnson, Johanne, Hagerstown, Pricilla, Hagerstown, 20 years, Josephina, Hurley, -, -, Hagerstown, C, [blank], 11

3301, 4 Feb 1877, Albertam Gertrude, Clayburn, Johanni, Hagerstown, Sarah, Hagerstown, 21-Jan, Martha, Dillen [or Dillon], -, -, Hagerstown, -, [blank], 11

ST. MARY'S CATHOLIC CHURCH
HAGERSTOWN, MARYLAND, BAPTISMS:
Index, Baptism Date, Child, Last Name, Father from, Mother, Mother from, Birth Date, 1st Sponsor First, 1st Sponsor Last, 2nd Sponsor First, 2nd Sponsor Last, Location, Notes, Maiden Name, Priest

3302, 11 Feb 1877, Eliza Mariam, Hare, Jacob, Hagerstown, Philemena, Hagerstown, 27-Jan, Margaret, Zook, -, -, Hagerstown, -, Altorff [?], 11

3303, 11 Feb 1877, Guglielmum, Walker, Allen, Hagerstown, Anna, Hagerstown, 30 Sep 1875, Sallie, Cushwa, -, -, Hagerstown, Child and parents are Black., Brown [?], 11

3304, 27 Feb 1877, Annam Theresam, Fagan, Johanni, Hagerstown, Sarah, Hagerstown, 22-Feb, J.B., Sweeney, Maria, Tierney, Hagerstown, -, Daley, 11

3305, 13 Mar 1877, Edwardum Guistini, Wills, Jacob, Hagerstown, Martha, Hagerstown, 4-Mar, Wm., McClain, Ann, McClain [HB], Hagerstown, -, McClain, 11

3306, 11 Mar 1877, [blank], -, -, -, -, -, -, -, -, -, -, -, "Baptized a child privately, which died soon afterwards.", -, 11

3307, 13 Mar 1877, Annam Elizabeth, Reinholder, Lemuel, Williamsport, Mary E., Williamsport, 22-Feb, Frank, Gallagher, Susan, Johnson, Hagerstown, -, Schneider, 11

3308, 14 Mar 1877, Aliciam, Shorter, -, -, -, -, -, -, Kitty, Shorter, -, -, Hagerstown, C; B; from Hagerstown, -, 11

3309, 24 Mar 1877, Bernardum G., Alexander, Carolo, Hagerstown, Catharine, Hagerstown, 19 Nov 1876, Mrs., Cramer, -, -, Hagerstown, PN; DDC; DMR; "Married July - 70[?] to Laura E. Hood" "See Marriage Record #2 Page 15 [or 18].", Schilling, 11

3310, 26 Apr 1877, Giorgium D., Williamson, David, -, Sarah, -, 4 Dec 1827, Elie, Stake, -, -, Williamsport, C, [blank], 11

3311, 29 Apr 1877, Catharinam Agnetem, Cullen, Jacobo, Williamsport, Maria, Williamsport, -, Johannes, Barry, -, -, Williamsport, -, McKenna, 11

3312, 29 Apr 1877, Samuelem C., Lefferman, Geirgio, Williamsport, Lucretia, Williamsport, 2 Oct 1876, Susan, Ewers [?], -, -, Williamsport, -, [blank], 11

3313, 12 May 1877, Franciscum Henrieum, Orndorf, Guglielmo, Hagerstown, Romanus, Hagerstown, 1-May, Arnauldus, Condry, Wilhelmina L., May, Hagerstown, -, Schilling, 11

ST. MARY'S CATHOLIC CHURCH
HAGERSTOWN, MARYLAND, BAPTISMS:
Index, Baptism Date, Child, Last Name, Father from, Mother, Mother from, Birth Date, 1st Sponsor First, 1st Sponsor Last, 2nd Sponsor First, 2nd Sponsor Last, Location, Notes, Maiden Name, Priest

3314, 13 May 1877, Johannes Aloyium, Allan, Johanne, Hagerstown, Maria, Hagerstown, 25 Apr 1877, Sallie, Cushwa, -, -, Hagerstown, B, Stewart, 11

3315, 13 May 1877, Mariam Catharina Bostock, Gehr, Henrico, Hagerstown, Cora, Hagerstown, 14-Apr, Josephina, Hurley, -, -, Hagerstown, -, Shank, 11

3316, 17 May 1877, Jessi [?] Louisam, Thompson, Jesse, Williamsport, Francesca, Williamsport, 20-Apr, Louisa, Brazil, -, -, Williamsport, -, Thompson, 11

3317, 18 May 1877, Mariam Helenam, Egan, Thoma, Hagerstown, Margarita, Hagerstown, 8-May, Ella, Taggart, -, -, Hagerstown, -, O'Conner, 11

3318, 21 May 1877, Susan Catharinam, Coale, "unknown", Hagerstown, Catharina, Hagerstown, 1-Mar, Kitty, Shorter, -, -, Hagerstown, PN; Family and sponsors are Black, Coale, 11

3319, 27 May 1877, Mariam Blanche, Lancaster, Jacob, Williamsport, Anna, Williamsport, 8 years, Ella, Oliver, -, -, Williamsport, -, McCardell, 11

3320, 27 May 1877, Ricardeum McCardell, Lancaster, Jacob, Williamsport, Anna, Williamsport, 6 years, Ella, Oliver, -, -, Williamsport, -, McCardell, 11

3321, 27 May 1877, Henriettam Myers, Lancaster, Jacob, Williamsport, Anna, Williamsport, 3 years, Ella, Oliver, -, -, Williamsport, -, McCardell, 11

3322, 31 May 1877, Johanneam, Reed, Francisco, -, Jane, -, 35 years, Maria, Barry, -, -, Williamsport, C, Herbert, 11

3323, 31 May 1877, Ceciliam, Ardinger, Benjamin, Williamsport, Susan, Williamsport, 20 Sep 1873, Johanna, Gallagher, -, -, Williamsport, -, Thompson, 11

3324, 31 May 1877, Catharinam, Ardinger, Benjamin, Williamsport, Susan, Williamsport, 15 Feb 1867, Johanna, Gallagher, -, -, Williamsport, -, Thompson, 11

3325, 31 May 1877, Benjamin, Garrish, Josepho, Williamsport, Gingetta, Williamsport, 24 Dec 1872, Maria, Barry, -, -, Williamsport, -, Ardinger, 11

3326, 31 May 1877, Elie Dixon, Garrish, Josepho, Williamsport, Georgietta, Williamsport, 9 Oct 1870, Maria, Barry, -, -, Williamsport, -, Ardinger, 11

ST. MARY'S CATHOLIC CHURCH
HAGERSTOWN, MARYLAND, BAPTISMS:
Index, Baptism Date, Child, Last Name, Father from, Mother, Mother from, Birth Date, 1st Sponsor First, 1st Sponsor Last, 2nd Sponsor First, 2nd Sponsor Last, Location, Notes, Maiden Name, Priest

3327, [blank], Reinam May, Hose, Johanni, Hagerstown, Jennie, Hagerstown, 6 Oct 1876, Sally, Kelly, -, -, Hagerstown, -, Schilling, 11

3328, 23 Jul 1877, Elizabeth, Johnson, Geirgio W., Hagerstown, -, -, 19 years, -, -, -, -, Hagerstown, C; BC, -, 11

3329, 12 Aug 1877, Margaritam Helenam, Brown, Johanne, Hagerstown, Jennie, Hagerstown, -, Jennie, Bayley, -, -, Hagerstown, "Privately baptized when ill."; family and sponsors are Black; PN, Hipkins, 11

3330, 15 Aug 1877, Margaret Eve, Schatzer, Francisco, Williamsport, Catharina, Williamsport, 1-Aug, Elie, Stake, -, -, Williamsport, -, Anderson, 11

3331, 15 Aug 1877, Catharinam, Schatzer [father's name is Anderson], Roberto, Williamsport, Eva, Williamsport, 30 years, Elie, Stake, -, -, Williamsport, C; Catharine is described as "Infidelitate"; Schatzer appears to be her married name., Ensminger, 11

3332, 19 Aug 1877, Mariam Veronicam, Coyle, Thoma, Washington County, Maria, Washington Co., 8 Apr 1877, Jennie, Smith, -, -, Hagerstown, She married Henrico Brunsdey, in St. Joseph's Church, Emmitsburg, MD, 6 Sept. 1917, by Rev. J.O. Hayden., Horn, 11

3333, 26 Aug 1877, Annam, Poole, Jacobo F., Williamsport, Maria, Williamsport, 1-Feb, -, -, -, -, Williamsport, "Baptized at home in danger of death.", Rauthraff [?], 11

3334, 25 Sep 1877, Stellam Anna Loffam, Cramer, Jake, Hagerstown, Martah, Hagerstown, 16 Sep 1877, Martha, Wills, -, -, Hagerstown, -, Jacbos, 11

3335, 30 Sep 1877, Fredericum, Gruber, Johanni, Hagerstown, Julia, Hagerstown, 28-Aug, Lucinda, Smith, -, -, Hagerstown, B, Sprigg, 11

3336, 1 Oct 1877, Margaret (Mrs.), McKaig, -, -, -, -, -, -, -, -, -, Hagerstown, See Endnote 67, -, 11

3337, 1 Oct 1877, Nina, McKaig, -, -, -, -, -, -, -, -, -, Hagerstown, -, -, 11

3338, 1 Oct 1877, Tilgman, McKaig, -, -, -, -, -, -, -, -, -, Hagerstown, -, -, 11

ST. MARY'S CATHOLIC CHURCH
HAGERSTOWN, MARYLAND, BAPTISMS:
Index, Baptism Date, Child, Last Name, Father from, Mother, Mother from, Birth Date, 1st Sponsor First, 1st Sponsor Last, 2nd Sponsor First, 2nd Sponsor Last, Location, Notes, Maiden Name, Priest

3339, 6 Oct 1877, Mariam Teresiam, Nierman, Augusto, Hagerstown, Philemena, Hagerstown, 1 Oct 1877, J., Sweeney, Josephina, Hurley, Hagerstown, "Marriage Record #1 Pg. 165", Spechman, 11

3340, 7 Oct 1877, Samuel Johannem Joseph, -, -, -, -, -, -, C.B., Boyle, Josephina, Hurley, Hagerstown, B; C; does not appear to have a last name - none written in the left-hand column., -, 11

3341, 17 Oct 1877, Mariam Helenam, Jones, Jeremiah, Zittlestown, Wash. Co., MD, Helena, Zittlestown, Wash. Co., MD, 15 years, M.V., Dahlgren, -, -, "At Mrs. Dahlgren's, South Mountain", C, Caughman, 11

3342, 17 Oct 1877, Geirgium, Jones, Jeremiah, Zittlestown, Wash. Co., MD, Helena, Zittlestown, Wash. Co., MD, 7 Aug 1870, M.V., Dahlgren, -, -, "At Mrs. Dahlgren's, South Mountain", -, Caughman, 11

3343, 17 Oct 1877, Carolum Eduardum, Jones, Jeremiah, Zittlestown, Wash. Co., MD, Helena, Zittlestown, Wash. Co., MD, 2 Dec 1871, M.V., Dahlgren, -, -, "At Mrs. Dahlgren's, South Mountain", -, Caughman, 11

3344, 17 Oct 1877, Letitiam Madelinam, Jones, Jeremiah, Zittlestown, Wash. Co., MD, Helena, Zittlestown, Wash. Co., MD, 6 Apr 1873, M.V. (Mrs.), Dahlgren, -, -, "At Mrs. Dahlgren's, South Mountain", -, Caughman, 11

3345, 17 Oct 1877, Lilliam Mariam, Jones, Jeremiah, Zittlestown, Wash. Co., MD, Helena, Zittlestown, Wash. Co., MD, 7 Sep 1877, M.V., Dahlgren, -, -, "At Mrs. Dahlgren's, South Mountain", -, Caughman, 11

3346, 17 Oct 1877, Guglielmum Albertum, Jones, Ludovico, Zittlestown, Wash. Co., MD, Maria, Zittlestown, Wash. Co., MD, 28 Oct 1863, M.V., Dahlgren, -, -, "At Mrs. Dahlgren's, South Mountain", -, Caughman, 11

3347, 17 Oct 1877, Samuel L.C., Jones, Ludovico, Zittlestown, Wash. Co., MD, Maria, Zittlestown, Wash. Co., MD, 26 Feb 1868, M.V., Dahlgren, -, -, "At Mrs. Dahlgren's, South Mountain", -, Caughman, 11

3348, 17 Oct 1877, Johannem Hardie, Jones, Ludovico, Zittlestown, Wash. Co., MD, Maria, Zittlestown, Wash. Co.,

ST. MARY'S CATHOLIC CHURCH HAGERSTOWN, MARYLAND, BAPTISMS:
Index, Baptism Date, Child, Last Name, Father from, Mother, Mother from, Birth Date, 1st Sponsor First, 1st Sponsor Last, 2nd Sponsor First, 2nd Sponsor Last, Location, Notes, Maiden Name, Priest

MD, 29 Jan 1870, M.V. (Mrs.), Dahlgren, -, -, "At Mrs. Dahlgren's, South Mountain", -, Caughman, 11

3349, 17 Oct 1877, Annam Mariam, Jones, Ludovico, Zittlestown, Wash. Co., MD, Maria, Zittlestown, Wash. Co., MD, 6 May 1873, M.V., Dahlgren, -, -, "At Mrs. Dahlgren's, South Mountain", -, Caughman, 11

3350, 17 Oct 1877, Pearliam Agnetem, Jones, Ludovico, Zittlestown, Wash. Co., MD, Maria, Zittlestown, Wash. Co., MD, 18 Sep 1877, Madeleine Sarah Vinton [?], Dahlgren, -, -, "At Mrs. Dahlgren's, South Mountain", -, Caughman, 11

3351, 17 Oct 1877, Jesse, Hight, "unknown", Washington, DC, Maria Helena, Washington, DC, 70 years*, M.V., Dahlgren, -, -, "At Mrs. Dahlgren's, South Mountain", B; "Colored gentleman"; Endnote 68, -, 11

3352, 18 Oct 1877, Carolem Joseph, Kershner, Joseph, Hagerstown, Helena, Hagerstown, 3-Oct, Geirgie [?], Hoover, Maria, Hoover, Hagerstown, -, Hoover, 11

3353, 19 Oct 1877, Margaret, McKaig, -, -, -, -, -, -, -, -, -, Hagerstown, BC; C, -, 11

3354, 19 Oct 1877, Frisby Tilghman, McKaig, Gen., Washington County, Margaret, Washington Co., -, -, -, -, -, Hagerstown, BC; C, Tilghman, 11

3355, 19 Oct 1877, Ninam, McKaig, Gen., Washington County, Margaret, Washington Co., -, -, -, -, -, Hagerstown, BC; C, Tilghman, 11

3356, 23 Oct 1877, Joseph Minor Elmor, Bowles [?], Flavius Josephus, Welsh Run, Wash. Co., Florence, Canada, 10-May, M., Shervin, -, -, Hagerstown, -, Elmer, 11

3357, [no date], [child], -, -, -, -, -, -, -, -, -, -, -, "Two children in articulo mortis" [in danger of death], -, 11

3358, [no date], [child], -, -, -, -, -, -, -, -, -, -, -, "Two children in articulo mortis" [in danger of death], -, 11

3359, 28 Oct 1877, Johannem Guglielmum, Mundey, Georgio, Williamsport Pike, Maria, Williamsport Pike, 21 May 1873*, -, -, -, -, "Baptized at the house", *birthdate is 21 [or 22 or 29] May 1873, McCarthy, 11

ST. MARY'S CATHOLIC CHURCH
HAGERSTOWN, MARYLAND, BAPTISMS:
Index, Baptism Date, Child, Last Name, Father from, Mother, Mother from, Birth Date, 1st Sponsor First, 1st Sponsor Last, 2nd Sponsor First, 2nd Sponsor Last, Location, Notes, Maiden Name, Priest

3360, 28 Oct 1877, Norman Scott, Mundey, Giergio, Williamsport Pike, Maria, Williamsport Pike, 27 Jan 1875, -, -, -, -, "Baptized at the house", -, McCarthy, 11

3361, 28 Oct 1877, Bernardum, Mundey, Georgio, Williamsport Pike, Maria, Williamsport Pike, Apr 1877, -, -, -, -, "Baptized at the house", -, McCarthy, 11

3362, 17 Nov 1877, Harriet Rosam, Fechtig, Georgio, Hagerstown, Louisa, Hagerstown, 1 Sep 1877, Maria, McLaughlin, -, -, Hagerstown, -, Doyle, 11

3363, 16 Nov 1877, [child], Mundey, Georgio, Williamsport Pike, Maria, Williamsport Pike, -, -, -, -, -, -, "Mrs. Laurence baptized a child of George Munday on the Williamsport Pike. The child died soon after.", McCarthy, 11

3364, 18 Nov 1877, Mariam Isabel, Schweitzer, Samuele, Washington County, Maria, Washington Co., 12-Nov, Johannes, Laurence, Magdalen, Laurence [HB], Hagerstown, -, Laurence, 11

3365, 18 Nov 1877, Clyde Vincintium, Mayhew, Clement, Hagerstown, Frances, Hagerstown, 7 Nov 1877, Ann, Miller, -, -, Hagerstown, -, Miller, 11

3366, 21 Nov 1877, Johannem Michaelem, Jacobs, T. R., Washington County, [blank], Washington Co., 22 Aug 1875, Theodoria, Jacobs, -, -, Hagerstown; "At Mr. McCauleys house 4 miles from town.", -, Sleight, 11

3367, 21 Nov 1877, Annam Elizabeth, Jacobs, Thoma R., Washington County, [blank], Washington Co., 6-Feb, Matilda, Jacobs, -, -, Hagerstown; "At Mr. McCauley's.", -, Sleight, 11

3368, 21 Nov 1877, Florence May, Jacobs, T. R., Washington County, [blank], Washington Co., 26 Feb 1870, Matilda, Jacobs, -, -, Hagerstown; "At Mr. McCauley's near town.", -, Sleight, 11

3369, 9 Jan 1878, Gregorium Sylvestrem, Laurence, Johanne, Williamsport Pike, Sarah, Williamsport Pike, 27 Nov 1877, Andreas, Laurence, Anna, Laurence [HB], Hagerstown, -, Baker, 11

3370, 18 Jan 1878, Edith Olivia, Baker, Daniele, Washington County, Maria, Washington Co., 31 May 1877, Margaret,

ST. MARY'S CATHOLIC CHURCH
HAGERSTOWN, MARYLAND, BAPTISMS:
Index, Baptism Date, Child, Last Name, Father from, Mother, Mother from, Birth Date, 1st Sponsor First, 1st Sponsor Last, 2nd Sponsor First, 2nd Sponsor Last, Location, Notes, Maiden Name, Priest

Shervin, -, -, Hagerstown, "This is the first baptized in the new font.", Hoover, 11

3371, 10 Mar 1878, Guglielmum, Eyler, -, Frederick Co., -, Frederick Co., 21 years, Mr., Laurence, -, -, Hagerstown, BC; C, -, 11

3372, 11 Mar 1878, Mariam Catharinam Gertrude, Fiery, Alberto, Washington County, Maria C., Washington Co., 4 Dec 1877, Catharina, Shervin, -, -, Hagerstown, -, Ball, 11

3373, 13 Mar 1878, Agnetem, Gibson, Joshua G., Virginia, Susan, Virginia, -, -, -, -, -, Williamsport, BC; C, Waters, 11

3374, 14 Mar 1878, Mariam Susan, Cushwa, Guglielmo, Washington County, Maud, Washington Co., 10-Mar, Mary, Cushwa, -, -, "Canal near Williamsport", -, Kreigh, 11

3375, 19 Mar 1878, Annam Ligueri [?], Dillon, Michaele, Hagerstown, Martha, Hagerstown, 16-Mar, Otho, Duffey, Anna, Ahern, Hagerstown, -, McCallon, 11

3376, 13 Apr 1878, Henricum Augustinum, Wright, Wilfred G., Hagerstown, Elizabeth, Hagerstown, 2 Apr 1878, Wilhelmina, May, -, -, Hagerstown, -, Johnson, 11

3377, 13 Apr 1878, Louisam, Schlotterbeck, Guglielmo, Hagerstown, Elizabeth, Hagerstown, 7 Mar 1865, Maria, McGrath, -, -, Hagerstown, BC, [blank], 11

3378, 18 Apr 1878, Dionysium, Tyler, -, -, -, -, 25 years, Moses, Butler, Rachel, Riley, Hagerstown, B; C; BC, -, 42

3379, 28 Apr 1878, Guglielmum Edwin, Dugan, Johanne, VA, Maria, Williamsport, 22 Apr 1878, Carolus, Duffey, Agnes, Gibson, Williamsport, -, Stake, 11

3380, 28 Apr 1878, Mary Jane, McKuskar, Johanne, Toll Gate, Wash. Co., Martha, Toll Gate, Wash. Co., 21-Feb, Margaretta, McKuskar, -, -, "Williamsport Toll-gate", -, Rowland, 11

3381, 28 Apr 1878, Noram, Gerry, Owen, Washington County, Catharina, Washington Co., 28 Apr 1878, Maria, Sullivan, -, -, Washington Co., BC, Sullivan, 12

3382, 12 May 1878, Robertum Carrole, Orndorf, Gulielmo F., Hagerstown, Dna Romana, Hagerstown, 4 May 1878, Jacobus R., McLaughlin, Jannette, Hurley, Hagerstown, -, Broderick, 12

ST. MARY'S CATHOLIC CHURCH
HAGERSTOWN, MARYLAND, BAPTISMS:
Index, Baptism Date, Child, Last Name, Father from, Mother, Mother from, Birth Date, 1st Sponsor First, 1st Sponsor Last, 2nd Sponsor First, 2nd Sponsor Last, Location, Notes, Maiden Name, Priest

3383, 9 Jun 1878, Floyd Sprigg, Hollyday, Gullielmo, MD, Louisa, -, 30 years, -, -, -, -, Hagerstown, C; BC; in the vicinity of Rockland, Washington Co., Lamar, 12

3384, 16 Jun 1878, Adam Dellam, Warner, Roberto, Hagerstown, Maria E., Hagerstown, 3 months, Maria, Smith, -, -, Hagerstown, -, Shaker, 12

3385, 18 Jun 1878, Joseph, Henniberger, Hiram, Hagerstown, Maria E., Hagerstown, 8 weeks, Lucinda, Hoover, -, -, Hagerstown, -, Hoover, 12

3386, 23 Jun 1878, Georgium Edwardum, Garish, Joseph, Williamsport, Georgietta, Williamsport, 9 Oct 1877, Wilhelmey, Barry, Joanna M., Duddy, Williamsport, -, Ardinger, 12

3387, 23 Jun 1878, Wilhelmam Edwinum, Hawkins, Wilhelmo H., Portu [or Podrter] Gulielmico, Anna A., Portu [or Podrter] Gulielmico, 6 May 1876, Michael F., Gallagher, Joanna M., Duddy, Williamsport, -, Parker, 12

3388, 30 Jun 1878, Georgium Alvey, McCardle, Blair, Hagerstown, Bettie, Hagerstown, 6 weeks, Dne Anna, McCardle, -, -, Hagerstown, -, Stouck, 12

3389, 1 Jul 1878, Clarentium Lane, Keady, Henrico H., Hagerstown, Julia M., Hagerstown, 6 weeks, Betty, Smith [?], -, -, Hagerstown, -, Lane, 12

3390, 9 Jul 1878, Davidem Cadwile, Young, Davide, South Mountain, Maria, South Mountain, 1877*, Madeleine**, Dahlgren, -, -, South Mountain, * birthdate is "Dni 1877"; **she is described as "Domina [lady of the house] Magdeleine", Dimalins [?], 12

3391, 9 Jul 1878, Helenam Misouri, Young, Davide, South Mountain, Maria, South Mountain, "'Dni 1874", Madeleine*, Dahlgren, -, -, South Mountain, *she is named as "Domina [lady of the house] Magdeleine", Dimalins [?], 12

3392, 22 Jul 1878, Mariam Cecilliam, Martin, Emery, -, Josephina, *, 29 Jun 1877, Sara, Fagan [?], -, -, Hagerstown, * [looks as if it reads "now adeo constat"], Davis, 12

3393, 5 Aug 1878, Gulielmum, Needy, Isaac, *, Catharina, *, Oct 1877, Jacob, Griffith **, -, -, Hagerstown, FA; *

ST. MARY'S CATHOLIC CHURCH HAGERSTOWN, MARYLAND, BAPTISMS:
Index, Baptism Date, Child, Last Name, Father from, Mother, Mother from, Birth Date, 1st Sponsor First, 1st Sponsor Last, 2nd Sponsor First, 2nd Sponsor Last, Location, Notes, Maiden Name, Priest

countryside near Hagerstown; ** [grandfather of the child], Griffith, 12

3394, 18 Aug 1878, Henricum Jacobum, Hennessy, Thoma, near Hagerstown, Helena, near Hagerstown, *, Tilghman, McKaig, Nina, McKaig, -, * "about" 1 Nov 1877, Dolan [?], 12

3395, 1 Sep 1878, Catharinam, Schealer, -, -, -, -, 5 weeks, Maggie, Sherbown, Alice, Shorter, -, "Maggie Sherbown vel [Latin for 'one or the other'] Alice Shorter", -, 12

3396, 14 Jul 1878, Mariam Franciscam, Ryan, -, -, -, -, 4 yrs, 6 mos, Maria Margarita Josephina, McGratte, -, -, -, appears to read "Filiam adoptivam aliunde acceptam", -, 12

3397, 18 Sep 1878, Josephum, Hutzell, Samuele, South Mountain, Elizabeth C., South Mountain, 20 Jun 1870, Madeleine v. (Mrs.), Dahlgren, -, -, South Mountain, -, Lepold, 43

3398, 18 Sep 1878, Florentiam Virginiam, Hutzell, Samuele, South Mountain, Elizabeth C., South Mountain, 20 Dec 1872, M.V. (Mrs.), Dahlgren, -, -, South Mountain, -, Lepold, 43

3399, 18 Sep 1878, Catharinam Helenam, Hutzell, Samuele, South Mountain, Elizabeth C., South Mountain, 28 May 1875, M.V. (Mrs.), Dahlgren, -, -, South Mountain, -, Lepold, 43

3400, 18 Sep 1878, Johannem Francis, Horine, Johanne, Boonsboro, Emma, Boonsboro, 18 years, M. V. (Mrs.), Dahlgren, -, -, South Mountain, -, Smith, 43

3401, 18 Sep 1878, Eugeniam Franciscam, Horine, Johanne, Boonsboro, Emma, Boonsboro, 19 years, M. V. (Mrs.), Dahlgren, -, -, South Mountain, -, Smith, 43

3402, 22 Sep 1878, Carolum Eduardum, Mills, Eduardo, Williamsport, Sally, Williamsport, 9-Sep, Mary, Barry, -, -, Williamsport, PN, White, 12

3403, 15 Oct 1878, Claram Melissam Violam J., Zittle, Samuele, South Mountain, Lydia, South Mountain, 2 Apr 1869, M. V. (Mrs.), Dahlgren, -, -, South Mountain, -, [blank], 11

3404, 15 Oct 1878, Georguim Henricum, Mitchell, Johanne R., South Mountain, Lydia, South Mountain, 15 Jan 1867, M. V. (Mrs.), Dahlgren, -, -, South Mountain, -, [blank], 11

ST. MARY'S CATHOLIC CHURCH
HAGERSTOWN, MARYLAND, BAPTISMS:
Index, Baptism Date, Child, Last Name, Father from, Mother, Mother from, Birth Date, 1st Sponsor First, 1st Sponsor Last, 2nd Sponsor First, 2nd Sponsor Last, Location, Notes, Maiden Name, Priest

3405, 15 Oct 1878, Carolum W., Mitchell, Johanne R., South Mountain, Lydia, South Mountain, 29 Jul 1870, M. V. (Mrs.), Dahlgren, -, -, South Mountain, -, [blank], 11

3406, 15 Oct 1878, Archie John, Mitchell, Johanne R., South Mountain, Lydia, South Mountain, 11 Mar 1872, M. V. (Mrs.), Dahlgren, -, -, South Mountain, -, [blank], 11

3407, 15 Oct 1878, Carleton Eugene Smith, Mitchell, Johanne R., South Mountain, Susan, South Mountain, 4 Nov 1873, M. V. (Mrs.), Dahlgren, -, -, South Mountain, -, [blank], 11

3408, 15 Oct 1878, Mariam Sally, Mitchell, Johanne R., South Mountain, Lydia, South Mountain, 5 Dec 1875, M. V. (Mrs.), Dahlgren, -, -, South Mountain, -, [blank], 11

3409, 15 Oct 1878, Guglielmum C., Young, David, South Mountain, Maria, South Mountain, 13-Oct, M. V. (Mrs.), Dahlgren, -, -, South Mountain, -, Lepold, 11

3410, 15 Oct 1878, Jacob P. E., Hutzell, Samuele, South Mountain, E. C., South Mountain, 25-Sep, M. V. (Mrs.), Dahlgren, -, -, South Mountain, -, Lepold, 11

3411, 27 Oct 1878, Eduardum, Hughes, Jacobo, Williamsport, Margaret, Williamsport, 26-Sep, Franciscus, Gallagher, Johanna, Doody, Williamsport, -, Clark, 11

3412, 17 Nov 1878, Margaret, Grady, Thoma, Hagerstown, Catharine, Hagerstown, 3 Nov 1878, Jacobus, Malone, Jacobus (Mrs.), Malone, Hagerstown, -, Lynch, 11

3413, 24 Nov 1878, Franciscum Eduardum, Donelley, Eduardo, Williamsport, Katarina, Williamsport, 10 Nov 1878, Mrs., Gallagher, -, -, Williamsport, -, Hoy, 11

3414, 25 Nov 1878, Lulam [?] Reginam, Tritch, Franklin, Funkstown, Alicia, Hagerstown, 12-Aug, Ella, Taggart, -, -, Hagerstown, -, McDonald, 11

3415, 27 Nov 1878, Johannem Hampton, Shervin, Samuele, Washington County, Elizabeth, Washington Co., 2 years, Bell, Shervin, -, -, Hagerstown, -, Knodle, 11

3416, 1 Dec 1878, Joseph Victorum, Stine, Jacob L., Washington County, Catherina, Washington Co., 19 Sep 1878, Joseph, Lizer, Josephini, Hurley, Hagerstown, -, Lizer, 11

ST. MARY'S CATHOLIC CHURCH HAGERSTOWN, MARYLAND, BAPTISMS:
Index, Baptism Date, Child, Last Name, Father from, Mother, Mother from, Birth Date, 1st Sponsor First, 1st Sponsor Last, 2nd Sponsor First, 2nd Sponsor Last, Location, Notes, Maiden Name, Priest

3417, 22 Dec 1878, Sarah Agnetem, Reed, Guglielmo, Williamsport, Maria, Williamsport, 18 Nov 1878, Eduardus, Donelley, Johanna, Doody, Williamsport, -, Donelley, 11

3418, 26 Jan 1879, Helenam Catharinam, Hoy, Laurentio, Williamsport, L. Cath., Williamsport, 25 Dec 1878, Ellen, Oliver, -, -, Williamsport, -, Dorn [or Dom], 11

3419, 27 Jan 1879, Lauram Catharinam, Hoy [father's name is Dorn], -, Williamsport, -, -, 25 years, -, -, -, -, Williamsport, C; BP, -, 11

3420, 16 Feb 1879, Mariam Johannam, Louman, Jacobo, Washington County, Louisa, Washington Co., 23 Jun 1860, Maria, McGrath, -, -, Hagerstown, C, [blank], 11

3421, 23 Feb 1879, Agnetem Catharinam, Busch, David, Williamsport, Margaretta, Williamsport, 21 Jan 1879, Mr., Gallagher, Johanna, Doody, Williamsport, -, Busch, 11

3422, 9 Mar 1879, Johannem, Watts, -, -, -, -, -, -, Mrs. Benton, Cushwa, -, -, Hagerstown, C; B; from Hagerstown, -, 11

3423, 11 Mar 1879, Sarah, Chaney, Johanne, Williamsport, Barbara, Williamsport, 9 Oct 1866, Johanna, Doody, -, -, Williamsport, C, [blank], 11

3424, 31 Jan 1879, Helenam Liguori, Battles, Michaele, Hagerstown, Anna, Hagerstown, 23-Jan, Michael, White, Kate (Mrs.), White [HB], Hagerstown, -, Barrett, 11

3466, 7 Dec 1879, Mariam Bernardum, -, -, -, -, -, -, Jennie, Bayley, -, -, Hagerstown, Family and sponsors are Black, -, 11

3467, 31 Dec 1879, Helenam, Schnell, -, -, -, -, *, Eva (Mrs.), McCleery, -, -, at the Poor House Hagerstown, BP; from Hagerstown; * "age unknown - about 80", -, 11

3468, 11 Jan 1880, Norman Bruce, Schafer, Jahanne, Hagerstown, Elizabeth B., Hagerstown, 22 Dec 1879, Georgius, McCarter, Elizabeth, Shehan, Hagerstown, -, Kelly, 11

3469, 24 Jan 1880, Ceciliam Virginiam, Sweitzer, Samuele, Hagerstown, Maria, Hagerstown, 8 Dec 1879, Maria, Laurence, -, -, Hagerstown, -, Laurence, 11

3470, 2 Feb 1880, Benjamin Franciscum, Banks, Josepho, Rockingham Co., VA, Maria Francesca, Smithsburg, Oct

ST. MARY'S CATHOLIC CHURCH
HAGERSTOWN, MARYLAND, BAPTISMS:
Index, Baptism Date, Child, Last Name, Father from, Mother, Mother from, Birth Date, 1st Sponsor First, 1st Sponsor Last, 2nd Sponsor First, 2nd Sponsor Last, Location, Notes, Maiden Name, Priest

1870, Maria Agnes Regina, Bayley, -, -, Hagerstown, FA; B, Madison, 4
3471, 2 Feb 1880, Elizabeth Annam, Banks, Josepho, Rockingham Co., VA, Maria Francesca, Smithsburg, 22 Feb 1873, Maria Agnes Reg., Bayley, -, -, Hagerstown, FA; B, Madison, 4
3472, 14 Feb 1880, Cornelium Jeremiam, Flynn, Joanni, Kerry Co., Ireland, Catharina, Kerry Co., Ireland, 8 Feb 1880, Wm., Geary, Johanna, Geary, Hagerstown, -, O'Connor, 4
3473, 21 Feb 1880, Rosam Bernadettam, Niermann, Augusto, Germany, Philomena, Cincinnati, OH, 19 Feb 1880, Joannes, Dillen, Hannah, Breen [?], Hagerstown, -, Speckmann, 4
3474, 2 Mar 1880, Mariam Josephnam, Nikirk, Silas A., Washington County, Maria Agneto, Washington Co., 15 Oct 1879, Catherina E., Smith, -, -, Boonsboro, FA, Walter, 4
3475, 21 Mar 1880, Franciscum David, Futterer, Jacobo, Washington County, Maria Francesca, Wheeling, WV, 28 Feb 1880, Francisous, Futterer, Lydia, Mayhugh, Hagerstown, -, Kaiser, 4
3476, 9 Apr 1880, Elizabeth Ameliam, Full, Michael, Germany, Anna Amelia, Washington Co., 18 Jan 1880, Martha, Wroe, -, -, Hagerstown, -, Price, 4
3477, 24 Apr 1880, Mariam Florentiam, suman, Alberto H., Frederick Co., MD, Barbara A., "near Blue Ridge", 27 Aug 1857, Agnes Maria, Gibson, -, -, Hagerstown, BC, Hamburg, 4
3478, 25 Apr 1880, Mariam, Hughes, Jacobo, Williamsport, Margaritta, Williamsport, 10 Apr 1880, Emmet, Cullen, Anna, Sheridan, Williamsport, "married 14 Apr 1909 in Balt. St. Anne Church", Clark, 4
3479, 22 Mar 1880, Margaretam Virginiam, Banks, Joseph, Rockingham Co., VA, Maria Francesca, Emmitsburg, MD [?], 1 Mar 1880, -, -, -, -, Hagerstown, Baptized privately in the home, in danger of death, Madison, 4
3480, 22 May 1880, Louisam Rosam, Happel, Martino, Germany, Rosa, Germany, 13 May 1880, Louisa Regina, Schlotterbeck, -, -, -, -, Beckmann, 4
3481, 23 May 1880, Mariam Elizabeth, Gallagher [fathers name is Gower], Guielmo, Washington County, Catherina,

ST. MARY'S CATHOLIC CHURCH
HAGERSTOWN, MARYLAND, BAPTISMS:
Index, Baptism Date, Child, Last Name, Father from, Mother, Mother from, Birth Date, 1st Sponsor First, 1st Sponsor Last, 2nd Sponsor First, 2nd Sponsor Last, Location, Notes, Maiden Name, Priest

Washington Co., 17 Nov 1877, Jacobus, Hughes, Domina, Barry, Williamsport, Endnote 69, Reid, 4

3482, 24 May 1880, Edith Elizabeth, Fiery, Alberto, Washington County, Maria, Washington Co., 15 Sep 1879, Elizabeth, Ball, -, -, Hagerstown, FA, Ball, 4

3483, 27 May 1880, Elizabeth Reginam, Wright, Wilfred Gergory, Waynesboro, Elizabeth, Hagerstown, 6 May 1880, Rosa, Marsh, -, -, Hagerstown, -, Johnson, 4

3484, 6 Jun 1880, Upton Franciscum, McCardle, -, -, -, -, -, Mrs., Condry, -, -, -, -, -, 34

3485, 6 Jun 1880, Gulielmum Earl, McCardle, Blair, Hagerstown, Bettie, Washington Co., 13 Apr 1880, Anna V., Mobley, -, -, Hagerstown, MA, Stock [?], 4

3486, 6 Jun 1880, Gulielmum Francis, Mayhue, Clemento, Hagerstown, Francesca, Waynesboro, 24 May 1880, Anna E., McCardle, -, -, Hagerstown, MA, Mills, 4

3487, 10 Jun 1880, Mariam Agnetem, Murphy, Joanne, New York, Clara J., Washington Co., 9 Apr 1880, Otho B., Smith, Mary F., Deaner, Boonsboro, MA, Brining, 4

3488, 10 Jun 1880, Daisy Agnetem, Young, David, Washington County, Maria E., Washington Co., 12 Mar 1880, Catherina, Smith, M.V., Dahlgren, Boonsboro, MA; FA, Duncan, 4

3489, 11 Jun 1880, Ericum Vinton, Lapole, Gulielmo L., Washington County, Anna C., Frederick Co., 18 Feb 1880, Mad. V., Dahlgren, -, -, South Mountain, MA; FA, Rent, 4

3490, 4 Jul 1880, Annam Mariam, Laurence, Jerenimo, -, Catharina, -, 29 May 1880, [blank], Laurence, Maria F., Sumann, Hagerstown, -, Donohue, 4

3491, 1 Sep 1880, Gertrudem Rush, Jones, Laurentio Scott, Hagerstown, Maria, Pittsburg, Pa., 21 May 1880, Margaretha, Jones, -, -, Hagerstown, MA; FA, McKee, 4

3492, 7 Sep 1880, Thomam Porter, Blair, [blank], -, Georgia, Williamsport, 7 Aug 1880, Lilia, Williams, -, -, Williamsport, Private baptism was done earlier because child was in danger of death, Williams, 4

ST. MARY'S CATHOLIC CHURCH
HAGERSTOWN, MARYLAND, BAPTISMS:
Index, Baptism Date, Child, Last Name, Father from, Mother, Mother from, Birth Date, 1st Sponsor First, 1st Sponsor Last, 2nd Sponsor First, 2nd Sponsor Last, Location, Notes, Maiden Name, Priest

3493, 13 Sep 1880, Josephum, Kelly, Josepho M., Hagerstown, Amelia, Harrisburg, Pa., 20 Jul 1880, Patricius, Kelly, Johanna, Geary, Harrisburg, MA, Pentz, 4

3494, 18 Sep 1880, Petrum Horatium, Coyle, Thoma, Washington County, Maria Alphonsa, Washington Co., 18 Mar 1879, Johanna, Kelly, -, -, Hagerstown, -, Harn, 4

3495, 2 Oct 1880, Irenam Agnetem, Smith, Eugenio Eduardo, Hagerstown, Geneveva, Clear Spring, 25 Jul 1880, Catharina, Eck, -, -, Hagerstown, FA, Ward, 4

3496, 8 Oct 1880, Gulielmum Thomam, Fellinger, Philippo, Hessen, Germany, Elizabeth, Hagerstown, 6 months, Catharina, Fellinger, -, -, Hagerstown, MA, Garmann, 4

3497, 9 Oct 1880, Gulielmum Laurentium, Bryan, Georgio M., Washington, DC, Theresia, Hagerstown, 3 May 1876, Anna Jos., Hilsle, -, -, Hagerstown, PA, Schover, 4

3498, 10 Oct 1880, Gulielmum A. Ludovicam, Woolrich, Joanni, Franklin Co., Emma F., Franklin Co., 5 Mar 1878, Birgitta, Schaefer, -, -, Hagerstown, MA; FA, Angle, 4

3499, 10 Oct 1880, Mariam Rebeccam, Woolrich, Joanni, Franklin Co., Emma F., Franklin Co., 30 Jan 1876, Birgitta, Schaefer, -, -, -, -, Angle, 4

3500, 10 Oct 1880, Florentiam Violam, Woolrich, Joanni, Franklin Co., Emma F., Franklin Co., 17 Jun 1880, Birgitta, Schaefer, -, -, -, -, Angle, 4

3501, 10 Oct 1880, Claram Virgeniam, -, -, -, Maria Elizabeth, Franklin Co., 22 Sep 1873, Birgitta, Schaefer, -, -, Hagerstown, note reads "Parens" not Catholic - this could mean one or both parents; PN, Kerr, 4

3502, 10 Oct 1880, Elizabeth Mariam, -, -, -, Maria Elizabeth, Franklin Co., 3 Nov 1877, Birgitta, Schaefer, -, -, Hagerstown, FA; PN, Kerr, 4

3503, 11 Oct 1880, Virginiam Beatricem, Alexander, Carolo, -, Carrie, -, 14 Aug 1880, Mrs., Sheehan, -, -, Hagerstown, FA, Shilling, 4

3504, 11 Oct 1880, Mariam Elizabeth, Alexander, Carolo, -, Carrie, -, -, -, -, -, -, Hagerstown, FA; CS, -, 4

ST. MARY'S CATHOLIC CHURCH
HAGERSTOWN, MARYLAND, BAPTISMS:
Index, Baptism Date, Child, Last Name, Father from,
Mother, Mother from, Birth Date, 1st Sponsor First,
1st Sponsor Last, 2nd Sponsor First, 2nd Sponsor Last,
Location, Notes, Maiden Name, Priest

3505, 10 Oct 1880, Elizabeth Mary, Boyle, Carolo, Carroll Co., MD, Maria, Boonsboro, 19 Oct 1879, Elizabeth, Smith, -, -, -, CS, Smith, 4

3506, 23 Oct 1880, Sharam [?] Annam Matildam, Lens, Jacobo, Harrisburg, Susanna, Gettysburg, 17 Jan 1854, Martha, Wills, -, -, Hagerstown, C, Geis, 4

3507, 31 Oct 1880, Michaelem, Battle, Michaeli, Mayo, Ireland, Anna, Cork Co., Ireland, 13 Oct 1880, Mary, Battle, -, -, Hagerstown, -, Barrett, 4

3508, 31 Oct 1880, Danielem, Battle, Michaeli, Mayo, Ireland, Anna, Cork Co., Ireland, 13 Oct 1880, Catherine, Sheean, -, -, Hagerstown, -, Barrett, 4

3509, 2 Nov 1880, Gulielmum Henricum, Hose, Joanni P., Hagerstown, Sara Johanna, Cavetown, 6 Apr 1878, J. Demetrius, Duffy, -, -, Hagerstown, FA, Shiller, 4

3510, 2 Nov 1880, Carolum Eduardum, Hose, Joanni P., Hagerstown, Sara Johanna, Cavetown, 18 Apr 1879, J. Demetrius, Duffy, -, -, Hagerstown, -, Shiller, 4

3511, 30 Dec 1880, Catherinam Elizabeth, Johnson, Wm. A., Sharpsburg, Margatha, Massachuset, 14 Jun 1879, Maria, Claibaugh, -, -, Hagerstown, FA, Kennedy, 4

3512, 22 Jan 1881, Carolum Bruce, boyle, Carolo F., Carroll Co., Maria J., Boonsboro, 16 Jan 1881, Joseph B., Boyle, Maria Brook, Boyle, Hagerstown, -, Smith, 4

3513, 30 Jan 1881, Natham Wilson Bayley, Feigley, Isaac Kent, Hagerstown, Emma Cath., Martinsburg, 14 Jan 1881, A. S., Condry, Josephina, Hurley, [blank], MA, Armstrong, 4

3514, 17 Apr 1881, Howard Benjamin, Stein, Jacobo L., -, Catharina A., -, 10 Feb 1881, Otho, Duffy, -, -, [balnk], FA, Lizer, 4

3515, 9 May 1881, Fridericum [?] Carolum Eduardum, Banks, Joseph, Rockingham Co., VA, Maria Francesca, Emmittsburg, MD, 17 Apr 1881, M.A. Regina, Bayley, -, -, [blank], Prior to this day was baptised privately, in danger of death, by M.A. Reg. Bayley, Madison, 4

3516, 22 May 1881, David Edgar, Busch, David, Baltimore, Margaretta, Taneytown, MD, 8 Mar 1881, Ludovica, Cushwa, -, -, Williamsport, FA, Snevel [?], 4

ST. MARY'S CATHOLIC CHURCH
HAGERSTOWN, MARYLAND, BAPTISMS:
Index, Baptism Date, Child, Last Name, Father from, Mother, Mother from, Birth Date, 1st Sponsor First, 1st Sponsor Last, 2nd Sponsor First, 2nd Sponsor Last, Location, Notes, Maiden Name, Priest

3517, 22 May 1881, Victorem Franciscum, Reid, Gulielmo, Funkstown, Maria, Williamsport, 26 Apr 1881, Catharina, Woltz, -, -, Williamsport, FA, Donelly, 4

3518, 26 May 1881, Alexandrum Christianum, Fechtig, Georgio, -, Ludovica, -, 23 Mar 1881, Helena, Taggart, -, -, Hagerstown, FA, Doyle, 4

3519, 5 Jun 1881, Mariam Elizabeth, Walters, Georgio, PA, Adleid, Hagerstown, 25 Dec 1864, Miss [?], May, -, -, Hagerstown, -, Giles [?], 4

3520, 18 Jun 1881, Mabel Ceciliam, Fiery, Alberto, Washington County, Maria, Washington, DC, 24 Jan 1881*, Elizabeth, Ball, -, -, Hagerstown, FA; *birthdate is 24 [26 crossed out] Jan 1881, Ball, 4

3521, 8 Jun 1881, Daisy Magdelenam P., Barber, Carolo, -, Anna E., -, 23 Mar 1878, M. V., Dahlgren, -, -, South Mountain, MA; FA, Riddlemoser, 4

3522, 4 Jul 1881, Joannem Henson, Davis, Giorgio, Hagerstown, Anna, Hagerstown, 2 Nov 1877, Maria, Malone, -, -, Hagerstown, FA, Henson, 4

3523, 4 Jul 1881, Franciscum Burton, Davis, Georgio, Hagerstown, Anna, Hagerstown, 26 Feb 1881, Maria, Malone, -, -, Hagerstown, FA, Henson, 4

3524, 24 Jul 1881, Evam Aureliam, Hoy, Laurentio, Williamsport, Laura C., Williamsport, 21 Jun 1881, Margaretha, Malone, -, -, Williamsport, -, Dorn, 4

3525, 27 Jul 1881, Hubertum Russel, Lapole, David, -, Laura, -, 16 Jun 1881, M. V., Dahlgren, -, -, South Mountain, MA; FA, Drill, 4

3526, 27 Jul 1881, Daisie Johannam, Ford, Henrico, -, Johanna, -, "about" 1875, M. V., Dahlgren, -, -, South Mountain, MA; FA, Zittle, 4

3527, 29 Jul 1881, Catharinam Estellam, Heil, Joanni, Hagerstown, Clara, -, 5 Apr 1881, Catharina, Heil, -, -, Hagerstown, MA; Baptized privately at home, in danger of death, Gross, 4

3528, 14 Aug 1881, Henricum Milford, Heil, Joanni H., Hagerstown, Clara, Hagerstown, 26 Jun 1879, Emma, Heil, -, -, Hagerstown, MA, Gross, 4

ST. MARY'S CATHOLIC CHURCH
HAGERSTOWN, MARYLAND, BAPTISMS:
Index, Baptism Date, Child, Last Name, Father from, Mother, Mother from, Birth Date, 1st Sponsor First, 1st Sponsor Last, 2nd Sponsor First, 2nd Sponsor Last, Location, Notes, Maiden Name, Priest

3529, 14 Aug 1881, Gulielmum Richard, Henessy, Thoma, Co. Kildare, Ireland, Helena, Co. Cork, Ireland, 7 Mar 1881, Tilghman F., McKaig, Nina L., McKaig, Hagerstown, -, Doolan, 4

3530, 21 Aug 1881, Margaretham Franciscam, Fox, Ferdinando, Hagerstown, Johanna, VA, 17 Aug 1881, Michael, White, Helena, Kelly, Hagerstown, -, Nicely, 4

3531, 30 Aug 1881, Gulielmum Edmund, Bennet, Richardo S., Hagerstown, Maria C., Hagerstown, 21 Jul 1881, Maria M., Cretin, -, -, Hagerstown, FA, Cretin, 4

3532, 28 Aug 1881, Daisie Mariam, McKusker, Joanni, "Hagerst. (Wmpt.[Williamsport] Road)", Martha, "Hagerst. (Wmpt. Road)", 25 May 1881*, Mrs., Woltz, -, -, Williamsport, MA; *birthdate is 25 [or 26] May 1881*, Roland, 4

3533, 17 Sep 1881, Ludovicam Helenam, Hull [Holloran is fathers name], Joanni Wm., VA, Amanda L., VA, 21 Jun 1860, Cecilia, Frederick, -, -, Hagerstown, BC; Hull appears to be her married name, Johnson, 4

3534, 17 Sep 1881, Victorem Franciscum, Cullen, Emmet, Washington County, Eva, Williamsport, 5 Sep 1881, Munroe V., Cushwa, Sarah, Cushwa, FunkstoWilliamsportn, -, Cushwa, 4

3535, 18 Sep 1881, Carolum Bernardum, Fagan, Joanni, -, Sara, Baltimore, 21 Aug 1881, Joseph, Croner [?], Anna S. [or E.], Tierny, Hagerstown, -, Daily, 4

3536, 25 Sep1 881, Agnetem Teresiam, Kershner, Cyro, Berkeley Co., WV, Sara A., Berkeley Co., WV, 13 Jul 1881, Mrs., Brittner, -, -, Williamsport, FA; BC, Brittner, 4

3537, 25 Sep 1881, Carolum Foster, Hawken, Wm. W., Williamsport, Anna A., Williamsport, 6 Oct 1880, Francesca, Thompson, -, -, Williamsport, MA, Parker, 4

3538, 5 Oct 1881, Pearli Ireniam Placidiam, Mitchell, -, -, Susan, Zittlestown, Md., 7 Sep 1881, M. V., Dahlgren, -, -, South Mountain, MA; PN, "Mitchell (Zittle)", 4

3539, 16 Oct 1881, Carolum Matth. Bern., Miles, Joanni, Hagerstown, Lucia, Hagerstown, 29 Jun 1881, Joannes W., Watts, Jennie, Watts, Hagerstown, FA; B; PN, Smith, 4

ST. MARY'S CATHOLIC CHURCH
HAGERSTOWN, MARYLAND, BAPTISMS:
Index, Baptism Date, Child, Last Name, Father from, Mother, Mother from, Birth Date, 1st Sponsor First, 1st Sponsor Last, 2nd Sponsor First, 2nd Sponsor Last, Location, Notes, Maiden Name, Priest

3540, 16 Oct 1881, Joannem Thomam Sandford, Miles, Joanni, Hagerstown, Lucia, Hagerstown, 29 Jun 1881, Joannes W., Watts, Jennie, Watts, Hagerstown, FA; B; PN, Smith, 4

3541, 24 Oct 1881, Elizabeth Francescam, McCardell, -, -, -, -, 29 years, Ella, Oliver, -, -, Williamsport, C; BC, -, 4

3542, 10 Nov 1881, Claram A.[?] Ednam [?], Young, David, Washington County, Maria E., Washington Co., 17 Jun 1881, Catharina, Smith, M. V., Dahlgren, Boonsboro, MA; FA; Catharina Smith was the sponsor in place of M.V. Dahlgren, Duncan, 4

3543, 3 Dec 1881, Gulielmum Everest, Wordon, Richardo, -, Julia, -, 29 May 1881, Mrs., Reardon, -, -, Hagerstown, FA; MA; BP, Alexander, 4

3544, 18 Dec 1881, Richardum Daniel, Keedy, Henrico H., Keedysville, Julia, -, 22 Oct 1881, J. Alph., Frederick, Ella, Smith, Hagerstown, -, Lane, 4

3545, 1 Jan 1882, Clarentium Carolum, Neikirk, Silas, Boonsboro, Maria Agnete [?], Boonsboro, 21 Oct 1881, Catharina, Smith, -, -, Boonsboro, FA, Walters, 2

3546, 16 Jan 1882, Jacobum Sheridan, Smith, -, -, -, -, 16 Apr 1879, Mrs., Smith, -, -, Hagerstown, Baptized privately at home, in danger of death., -, 4

3547, 29 Jan 1882, Jacobum Henricum, Zook, -, -, -, -, 1835, Thomas, Taggart, -, -, Hagerstown, BC, -, 4

3548, 29 Jun 1882, Franciscum Roy Clayton, Gruber, Joanni, Hagerstown, Julia, Frederick Co., 1 Jan 1882, Jennie, Bailey, -, -, Hagerstown, FA, Sprague, 4

3549, 3 Feb 1882, Tilghman Bernadum, Full, Michael, Germany, Anna, Washington Co., 14 Nov 1881, Anna E., McCardell, -, -, -, -, Price, 4

3550, 4 Feb 1882, Emma Mariem, Weast, -, -, -, -, -, Catharina, Smith, -, -, Boonsboro, BC, -, 2

3551, 8 Feb 1882, Thornton Alphonsum Pool, Deaner, Andrea M. V., Washington County, Margaretha F., Frederick Co., 1881, Cecilia, Frederick, -, -, Boonsboro, FA; "Baprizatus domi fuit caeremoniis omissis", Pool, 4

3552, 12 Feb 1882, Joannem Fridericum, Futterer, Jacobo, Washington County, Maria Francesca, Wheeling, WV, 29 Jan

ST. MARY'S CATHOLIC CHURCH HAGERSTOWN, MARYLAND, BAPTISMS:
Index, Baptism Date, Child, Last Name, Father from, Mother, Mother from, Birth Date, 1st Sponsor First, 1st Sponsor Last, 2nd Sponsor First, 2nd Sponsor Last, Location, Notes, Maiden Name, Priest

1882, Milton, Ewers, Milton (Mrs.), Ewers [HB], Hagerstown, -, Kaiser, 4

3553, 14 Feb 1882, Idam Helenam, Wood, Joseph, Emmittsburg, MD, Anna Elizabeth, Frederick Co., MD, 1881, Francesca, Wye, -, -, Hagerstown, MA, Heim, 4

3554, 5 Mar 1882, Mariam Annam Josephinam, Bryan, Georgio M., Washington, DC, Theresia R., Hagerstown, 22 Nov 1881, Maria Catharina, Schlotterbeck, -, -, Hagerstown, FA, Shover, 4

3555, 26 Mar 1882, Henricum Edmundum, Kershsner, Joseph, -, Helena, -, 19 Feb 1882, Gulielmus, Orndorf, Jr., Catharina, Maguire, Hagerstown, FA, Hoover, 4

3556, 5 Mar 1882, Henriettam Baptistem, Myers, -, Keedysville, Agneti R., Keedysville, 11 Oct 1881, Andrew (Mrs.), Deaner, -, -, -, -, Hitzelberger [?], 2

3557, 23 Apr 1882, Elizabeth Bernadettam, Hornbach, -, -, -, -, 11 Apr 1882, Mrs., Yingling, -, -, Hagerstown, -, -, 4

3558, 30 Apr 1882, Henricum Fredericum, Allen, Joanni, Frederick Co., Maria, Frederick Co., 6 Apr 1882, Joannes, Watts, Joanna, Watts [HB], Hagerstown, MA, Stewart, 4

3559, 30 Apr 1882, Henricum Wiley, Dremen [or Dreman], Josepho, Washington County, Margarita, Washington Co., 7 Dec 1881, Jos., Swope, Maria Johanna, Wiley, Clear Spring, -, Swope, 2

3560, 21 May 1882, Thomem Sylvestrem, Mahoney, Stephen, Washington County, Rebecca, Washington Co., 31 Oct 1881, Eva, McCleary, -, -, Clear Spring, "Niger", Wilson, 2

3561, 28 May 1882, Carolum Alphons, Helferstay, Carole L., Martinsburg, Rebecca A., Hagerstown, 24 Dec 1862, Timotheus, Reardon, -, -, Hagerstown, C; BC, Peltz, 4

3562, 4 Jun 1882, Mariam Catherinam, Boyle, Carolo B., Carroll Co., Maria, Washington Co., 10 Apr 1882, Infrasanptus [?], Smith, Elizabeth, Smith [HB], Hagerstown, -, Smith, 4

3563, 11 Jul 1882, Gulielmum Herman Jos., Myers [mother's name], -, -, [blank], -, Dec 1881, Margaritta, Reardon, -, -, Hagerstown, mother is a widow and not Catholic; BP, Myers, 4

ST. MARY'S CATHOLIC CHURCH HAGERSTOWN, MARYLAND, BAPTISMS:
Index, Baptism Date, Child, Last Name, Father from, Mother, Mother from, Birth Date, 1st Sponsor First, 1st Sponsor Last, 2nd Sponsor First, 2nd Sponsor Last, Location, Notes, Maiden Name, Priest

3564, 31 May 1882, Joannem Patritium, Dreman, Themate, Washington County, Margarita, Washington Co., 18 Mar 1882, Margarita, Welch, -, -, Clear Spring, -, Welch, 2

3565, 8 Jun 1882, Thomem Leonem, Donnolly, Ednardo, Washington County, Catharina, Washington Co., 25 May 1882, Monroe, Cushwa, Margarita, Hughes, Williamsport, -, Hoy, 2

3566, 18 Jun 1882, Violettam Mariam, Smith, Erasmo, Washington County, Henrietta, Washington Co., 3 May 1882, Mrs., Smith, Jos., M___ [rest blank], Clear Spring, -, Wilson, 2

3567, 23 Jul 1882, Joseph Leonem, Lawrence, Joanni Patritio, -, Sarah C., -, 16 Jul 1882, Andreas C., Lawrenc, Lucia, Lawrence, Hagerstown, -, Baker, 4

3568, 4 Aug 1882, Emory Clarence Joseph, Stoter, [blank], -, Maria Elizabeth, Washington Co., 24 Sep 1881, Margaretha, Griffy, -, -, Hagerstown, FA, Needy, 4

3569, 6 Aug 1882, Andream M., Salladé, -, -, -, -, 32 years, F. T., McKaig, -, -, Hagerstown, C, -, 4

3570, 11 Aug 1882, Theodorem, Barr, Clinton, Washington County, Ella, Washington Co., 9 Jul 1882, Ferdinadus, Fox, -, -, Hagerstown, FA; MA; priest has put a question mark beside the section which states the parents are married, Wieley, 4

3571, 13 Aug 1882, Joannem Reilly, Brophy, Synesius M., Altoona, PA, Eleanora Loretto, Altoona, PA, 9 Jul 1882, Nicholas D., Maher, Ellen Jane, McClain, Hagerstown, -, Carr, 4

3572, 17 Aug 1882, Mariam Gertrudem, Ward, -, -, -, -, 11 months, -, -, -, -, Hagerstown, Baptized at home and in danger of death; MA; FA, -, 4

3573, 21 Aug 1882, Rilam Elsie, Ryan, Mattheo, Jefferson Co., WV, Maria Eliz., Washington Co., 5 Aug 1881, Anna Maria, Ryan, -, -, Williamsport, MA, Kroone, 4

3574, 27 Aug 1882, Idam Mariam, Futterer, Joanne, Hagerstown, Carolina, St. James College, 4 Aug 1882, Josephus, Futterer, Idam M., Futterer, Shepherdstown, -, Febrey, 4

ST. MARY'S CATHOLIC CHURCH
HAGERSTOWN, MARYLAND, BAPTISMS:
Index, Baptism Date, Child, Last Name, Father from,
Mother, Mother from, Birth Date, 1st Sponsor First,
1st Sponsor Last, 2nd Sponsor First, 2nd Sponsor Last,
Location, Notes, Maiden Name, Priest

3575, 10 Sep 1882, Mariam Catharinam, Egan, Thoma, Ros Common, Ireland, Margaretta, PA, 1 Sep 1882, Otho, Duffey, Anna, O'Connor, Hagerstown, -, O'Conner, 4

3576, 1 Oct 1882, Mariam Elizabeth, Keitz, Conradi, Germany, Maria Elizabeth, Frederick Co., MD, 19 Sep 1882, Wm, Sheean, Maria, Sheean, -, -, Moran, 4

3577, 4 Oct 1882, Mariam Matildam, Flegel, Martino Johnson, Emmittsburg, MD, Marg. Elfrida, Mechanicstown, MD, 9 Jul 1882, Theodesia, Lushbaugh, -, -, Pen Mar, FA, Wilhide, 4

3578, 29 Oct 1882, Laurentium Claggett, Lorshbaugh, Carolo H., Hagerstown, Margaretta V., Hagerstown, 21 May 1882, Carolus A., Helferstay, Maria, Reardon, Hagerstown, MA, Gates, 4

3579, 5 Nov 1882, Zachariam Hughes, Feigley, Isaac K., Hagerstown, Emma C., Martinsburg, 27 Oct 1882, Jacobus H., Wills, -, -, Hagerstown, MA, Armstrong, 4

3580, 20 Nov 1882, Joannem Franciscum, Lushbaugh, Joanni, Hagerstown, Theodosia, Frederick Co., 1 Nov 1882, Gulielmus, Wills, Rosa, Yingling, Hagerstown, FA, Jacobs, 4

3581, 28 Nov 1882, Agnetem Myrtle Mantz, Lane, Horatio M., Patterson, NJ, Helena V., New York, NY, 18 Jul 1882, Ellenora J., Taggart, -, -, Hagerstown, FA, Moore, 4

3582, 30 Nov 1882, Mariam Emmam, Howard, -, -, -, -, 45 years, -, -, -, -, Hagerstown, BC; BP, -, 4

3583, 14 Jan 1883, Georgius Howard, Warner, Georgio H., Hagerstown, Anna F., Greencastle, 23 Nov 1882, Robertus, Warner, -, -, Hagerstown, MA, Martin, 4

3584, 23 Jan 1883, Mariam Eliza Cath., Lecord, Wilhelm, Hagerstown, Maria Elizabeth, Hagerstown, 30 Dec 1882, Ccilia, Frederick, -, -, Hagerstown, MA; FA, Munson, 4

3585, 23 Feb 1883, Carolum Gregorium, Wright, Wilfrido G., Franklin Co., Elizabeth, Franklin Co., 20 Dec 1882, Rosa, Morris, -, -, -, -, Johnson, 10

3586, 21 Mar 1883, Elizabeth Glendening, Fox, -, -, -, -, 4 Feb 1881, -, -, -, -, -, PB; BP, -, 10

ST. MARY'S CATHOLIC CHURCH
HAGERSTOWN, MARYLAND, BAPTISMS:
Index, Baptism Date, Child, Last Name, Father from, Mother, Mother from, Birth Date, 1st Sponsor First, 1st Sponsor Last, 2nd Sponsor First, 2nd Sponsor Last, Location, Notes, Maiden Name, Priest

3587, 10 Apr 1883, Paulum, Fechtig, Joanne, Hagerstown, Louisa, Hagerstown, 10 Feb 1883, Anna, Smith, -, -, -, FA, Doyle, 10

3588, 15 Apr 1883, Annam Margaritam, McCardell, Jacobo B., Hagerstown, Helena S., Hagerstown, 1 Apr 1883, Louisa, Ford, -, -, -, -, Zook, 10

3589, 27 May 1883, Gulielmum Oliver, Heil, Jr., Alberto, Hagerstown, Carolina, -, 14 Dec 1882, Catharina, Heil, -, -, -, -, Irwin, 10

3590, 31 May 1883, Thomam McKaig, Mikle, Henrico, Baltimore, Nina, Washington Co., 24 Apr 1883, Tilghman, McKaig, Margarita, McKaig, -, Privately baptized 24 April by C.B. Boyle M.D., McKaig, 10

3591, 3 Jun 1883, Josephum, McCusker, -, -, -, -, 1850, nc; "Baptizatus est privatim in articulo mortis", -, -, -, -, -, -, 10

3592, 18 Jun 1883, Eduardum Sylvestrum, Keenan, Joanne, -, Sarah, Hagerstown, 23 Aug 1882, Helena, Kirchner, -, -, -, PN; Baptized on 23 August 1882 by C.B. Boyle M.D., Hoover, 10

3593, 20 Jun 1883, Rogerium Bernardus, Fiery, Alberto, Washington County, Maria, Georgetown, DC, 30 Nov 1883*, Elizabeth, Ball, -, -, -, FA; *birthdate is 30 Nov 1883 ["____ Januarii" crossed out], Ball, 10

3594, 8 Jul 1883, Jacobum Lee Roy, McCardle, Gulielmo Blair, Hagerstown, Elizabeth, Hagerstown, 13 Jul 1882, Maria, Malone, -, -, -, MA, Storck, 10

3595, 23 Jul 1883, Mariam Loretto, Fagan, Joanne, Baltimore, Sarah Agnes, Baltimore, 15 Jun 1883, Henricus, Volz, Anna Eccleston, Tierney, -, -, Daly, 10

3596, 7 Oct 1883, Mariam Gertrudim, Loughrey, Gulielmo, Harrisburg, PA, Anna, Carlisle, PA, 9 Sep 1883, Anna, Daniels, -, -, -, -, Thomas, 10

3597, 3 Dec 1883, Franciscam Arnold, Feigle, "unknown", -, Harriet, -, 1 Nov 1883, -, -, -, -, -, PB; PN, Feigle, 10

3598, 12 Jan 1884, Rosam Mariam, Orndorf, Gulielmo F., Conawago, PA, Romana, Washington Co., 30 Dec 1883, Fredericus, Halm, Maria, Bennett, -, -, Schilling, 10

ST. MARY'S CATHOLIC CHURCH
HAGERSTOWN, MARYLAND, BAPTISMS:
Index, Baptism Date, Child, Last Name, Father from, Mother, Mother from, Birth Date, 1st Sponsor First, 1st Sponsor Last, 2nd Sponsor First, 2nd Sponsor Last, Location, Notes, Maiden Name, Priest

3599, 13 Jan 1884, Elizabeth Mariam, Fox, Fernando, Hagerstown, Virginia, Hagerstown, 16 Dec 1883, Jacobus, McCardell, Maria, Maloney, -, -, Nicely, 10

3600, 16 Feb 1884, Vincentium Eugenium, Coyle, Thoma B., Cavetown, Maria, Smithsburg, 30 Nov 1882, Helena, Sweeney, -, -, -, -, Harne, 10

3601, 16 Feb 1884, Mariam, Rumley, Carolo, Cork, Ireland, Maria, Winchester, 16 Apr 1867, Martha, Dillon, -, -, -, C; BC, Barks, 10

3602, 12 Nov 1882, Abraham Augustimm, Long, -, -, -, -, 1857, Johannes, Barry, -, -, -, C; born in Welch Run, PA, -, 2

3603, 19 Nov 1882, Berthem Lorrettem, Ward, Jacobo A., Washington County, Catharina, Washington Co., 21 Mar 1882, Margarita, Flynn, -, -, -, FA, Dolan, 2

3604, 15 Aug 1882, Lilliem Johennem, Blair, Gulielmo, Shippensburg, Georgianna, Shippensburg, 1 Mar 1882, Emmet, Cullen, Eva, Cullen, -, FA, Williams, 2

3605, 3 Mar 1883, Mariam, O'Brien, Matheo, Boonsboro, Julia, Boonsboro, 10 Feb 1883, M., Murphy, -, -, -, -, Murphy, 2

3606, 21 Feb 1883, Danielem Josephem, -, -, -, -, -, 5 Aug 1842, Mrs., Ardinger [?], -, -, -, from Mechanicstown, Frederick Co.; nc; "Bap obsol", -, 2

3607, 18 Mar 1883, Robertum Petrem, Welch, Patritio, Clear Spring, Maria, Clear Spring, 30 Nov 1882, Thos., Drennen, Anna, McGuern [?], -, -, Donn [or Dunn], 2

3608, 25 Jul 1883, Benjamen Josephum, Hawkins, Gulielmo, Williamsport, -, Williamsport, 16 Jun 1882, Cath., Cushwa, -, -, -, -, -, 2

3609, 24 May 1883, Henricum Raymundum [?], Kershner, Cyro, Berkeley Co., WV, Sara Agneto, Berkeley Co., WV, 7 Aug 1883, Julia, Britner, -, -, -, FA, Britner, 2

3610, 4 Nov 1883, Johannesm, Anderson, -, -, -, -, 1846, M., Brennen, -, -, -, C; appears to read "Bapt abs", -, 2

3611, 16 Dec 1883, Rosam Lucindem, Hasty, Samuele, Clear Spring, Joanne, Clear Spring, 5 Feb 1870, Rosa, Wamer [?], -, -, -, -, Bridenhoff, 2

ST. MARY'S CATHOLIC CHURCH HAGERSTOWN, MARYLAND, BAPTISMS:
Index, Baptism Date, Child, Last Name, Father from, Mother, Mother from, Birth Date, 1st Sponsor First, 1st Sponsor Last, 2nd Sponsor First, 2nd Sponsor Last, Location, Notes, Maiden Name, Priest

3612, 24 May 1883, Helenem Alice, Hughes, Jacobo, Williamsport, Margarita, Williamsport, 11 May 1882, Victor, Cushwa, Mrs., Clarke, -, 3rd sponsor Ella Oliver; "Born May 11, 1882 as stated by Helen Alice Hughes. (1/10/46).", Clarke, 2

3613, 24 May 1883, Margarethem Regimam, Hughes, Jacobo, Williamsport, Margarita, Williamsport, 11 May 1882, Victor, Cushwa, Mrs., Clarke, -, 3rd sponsor Ella Oliver; "Born May 11, 1882 as stated by Helen Alice Hughes. (1/10/46).", Clarke, 2

3614, 3 Jun 1883, Joannam Catherinem, Wolfe, -, -, -, -, -, Agnes, Gobbart [?], -, -, -, C; from Boonsboro, -, 2

3615, 4 Jul 1883, Bernardum Edwardum, Lapole, Gulielmo, South Mountain, Helena Cath., South Mountain, 29 Dec 1882, Bernardde, Barros [?], Ullrica, Dahlgren, -, MA; FA, Rent, 2

3616, 19 Jul 1883, Edwardum Maremn [?], Reed, Guilielmo, Williamsport, Maria, Williamsport, 22 Jun 1883, Ella, Oliver, Jos., Anderson, -, FA; "Marriage Record #1 Pg. 162", Donnolly, 2

3617, 27 Feb 1884, Mariam Louisam, Williams, Gulielmo, Washington County, Maria, Washington Co., 9 Jan 1884, Ambrose, McCardle, Mrs., Wultz, -, FA, Wultz, 2

3618, [no date], Mariam Louisam, Hoy, Laurentio [?], Williamsport, Catharina, Williamsport, 21 Feb 1884, Latitia, McCardle, -, -, -, -, [blank], 2

3619, 4 Apr 1884, Mariam Agnetem, Cooney [or Brown], Georgio, Washington County, Sarah, Washington Co., 10 Oct 1882, Rachael, Jasco [?], -, -, -, B; PN, Brown, 10

3620, 6 Apr 1884, Fredericum, Feigley, Isaac, Hagerstown, Emma, Martinsburg, 3 Oct 1883, Jacobus, Wills, Sara, Cushwa, -, -, Armstrong, 10

3621, 5 May 1884, Mariam Stellam Irenam, Alexander, Carolo, Hagerstown, Carolina, Hagerstown, Nov 1882, Noah F., Lawrence, Maria F., Lawrence, -, FA, Schilling, 10

3622, 6 May 1884, Joannam Gertrudim, Lawrence, Hieronimo, Washington County, Catharina, Washington Co., 14 Apr 1884, Albertus, Heil, Catharina, Geary, -, -, Donoghue, 10

ST. MARY'S CATHOLIC CHURCH HAGERSTOWN, MARYLAND, BAPTISMS:
Index, Baptism Date, Child, Last Name, Father from, Mother, Mother from, Birth Date, 1st Sponsor First, 1st Sponsor Last, 2nd Sponsor First, 2nd Sponsor Last, Location, Notes, Maiden Name, Priest

3623, 25 May 1884, Helenam Juliam, McCardell, Jacobo, Hagerstown, Helena, Hagerstown, 5 May 1884, Olton F., McCardell, Catharina, Zook, -, "Married at St. Malachy's Church, N.Y. City, Mar. 1, 1930 to Nathan F. Luce", Zook, 10

3624, 2 Jun 1884, Emman Linden, Smith, Eduardo, Hagerstown, Geneviva, Clear Spring, 20 Jan 1884, Sarah, Montague, -, -, -, -, Warren [?], 10

3625, 15 Jun 1884, Mariam Urillam, Groover, Joanne, Hagerstown, Julia, Frederick Co., 6 Jun 1884, Virginia, Bayley, -, -, -, B, Spriggs, 10

3626, 22 Jun 1884, Joannem Gulielmum, Alexander, Carolo, Hagerstown, Carolina, Hagerstown, 5 Jun 1884, Noah F., Lawrence, Maria F., Lawrence, -, -, Schilling, 10

3627, 22 Jun 1884, Robertum Franciscum, Full, Michaele, Washington County, Anna, Washington Co., 1 May 1884, Georgim, McCarter, Maria Johanna, O'Connor, -, -, Price, 10

3628, 1 Jul 1884, Michaele, Battle, Jr., Michaele, Ireland, Maria, Ireland, 27 Jun 1884, Michael, Battle, Sr., Anna, Battle, -, -, Larkin, 10

3629, 1 Jul 1884, Annam, Battle, Jr., Michaele, Ireland, Maria, Ireland, 27 Jun 1884, Brigitta, Battle, -, -, -, -, Larkin, 10

3630, 14 Jul 1884, Mariam Josephinam, Boyle, Carolo B., Carroll Co., Maria, Washington Co., 13 Jun 1884, Gulielmus F., Smith, Helena, Smith, -, -, Smith, 10

3631, 27 Jul 1884, Noram Augustan, Downin, Samuele, Hagerstown, Anna, Hagerstown, 23 Sep 1877, Gulielmus, Geary, Virginia, Kelly, -, -, Kelly, 10

3632, 27 Jul 1884, Annam Mariam, Downin, Samuele, Hagerstown, Anna, Hagerstown, 16 Nov 1879, Henricus, Creamer, Maria, Creamer, -, -, Kelly, 10

3633, 27 Jul 1884, Grace Theresiam, Downin, Samuele, Hagerstown, Anna, Hagerstown, 20 Sep 1882, Hugo, Kelly, Jospehina, Geary, -, -, Kelly, 10

3634, 5 Apr 1884, Maria Josephinam, O'Brien, Matteo, Boonsboro, Julia, Boonsboro, 13 Mar 1884, Emma, Weast, -, -, -, -, Murphy, 2

ST. MARY'S CATHOLIC CHURCH
HAGERSTOWN, MARYLAND, BAPTISMS:
Index, Baptism Date, Child, Last Name, Father from, Mother, Mother from, Birth Date, 1st Sponsor First, 1st Sponsor Last, 2nd Sponsor First, 2nd Sponsor Last, Location, Notes, Maiden Name, Priest

3635, 27 May 1884, Theresam, Smith, -, -, -, -, -, Agnes, Golibart []?], -, -, Boonsboro, C; BC; Adult; from Boonsboro, -, 2

3636, 10 Aug 1884, Henricum Bernardum, Smith, Johanne [?] W., VA, Catharina, MD, 18 Jun 1884, Maria, Kirshner, -, -, Williamsport, -, Poole, 2

3637, 15 Aug 1884, Mariam Rosam, Cullen, Emmet, Williamsport, Eva, Williamsport, 11 Aug 1884, Victor, Cushwa, Maria, Cushwa, Williamsport, -, Cushwa, 2

3638, 17 Aug 1884, Eugenium Josephum, Krebs, Henrico, Washington County, Theresaq, Chambersburg, 21 Apr 1884, Sophia, Steimtmiyer [?], -, -, Clear Spring, -, Steintneyer [?], 2

3639, 14 Sep 1884, Aliciam, Kreitz, Conradio, Germany, Marion [or Marian?], Emmittsburg, 3 Sep 1884, Huronimus [?], Lawrence, Magarita, Cunningham, -, -, Moran, 10

3640, 14 Sep 1884, Robertum, Warner, Georgio H., Hagerstown, Anna, Greencastle, 20 Mar 1884, Robertus, Warner, Maria, Malone, -, -, Martin, 10

3641, 21 Sep 1884, Henricum Wesley, Arnold, Tennis [sic], Washington County, Susanna, Washington Co., 9 Jan 1883, Virginia, Bayley, -, -, -, B, Thomas, 10

3642, 21 Sep 1884, Mariam Helenam, Arnold, Tennis [sic], Washington County, Susanna, Virginia, 10 Aug 1884, Bayley, -, -, -, -, B, Thomaswc, 10

3643, 17 Oct 1884, Alfredun Earl Morrill, McCardell, Alfredo, Hagerstown, Rina [sic], Hagerstown, 30 May 1884, Anna V., Mobley, -, -, -, -, Baseford, 10

3644, 26 Oct 1884, Franciscum Eduardum, Detrich, Benjamin F., Franklin Co., Maria, Franklin Co., 1 Sep 1884, Joseph, Lizer, Helena, Clarkson, -, -, Lizer, 10

3645, 26 Oct 1884, Eleonoram Catharinam, Lizer, Joseph Francisco, Franklin Co., Susannah R., Franklin Co., 27 May 1884, Catharina, Stine, -, -, -, -, Bemisdarfe, 10

3646, 26 Oct 1884, Gulielmum David, Kershner, Joseph, Hagerstown, Helena, Hagerstown, 22 Sep 1884, Elizabeth, Hoover, -, -, -, -, Hoover, 10

ST. MARY'S CATHOLIC CHURCH
HAGERSTOWN, MARYLAND, BAPTISMS:
Index, Baptism Date, Child, Last Name, Father from,
Mother, Mother from, Birth Date, 1st Sponsor First,
1st Sponsor Last, 2nd Sponsor First, 2nd Sponsor Last,
Location, Notes, Maiden Name, Priest

3647, 9 Nov 1884, Ludovicum Bernardum, Lushbaugh, Joanne H., Hagerstown, Theodosia Virginia, Frederick Co., 8 Oct 1884, Maria, Sweitzer, -, -, -, -, Jacobs, 10

3648, 20 Nov 1884, Harold Key Mauritium, Robertson, Roberto W., Baltimore, Anna E., Hagerstown, 24 Jun 1884, Martha, Wroe, -, -, -, -, Wroe, 10

3649, 26 Nov 1884, Thomam, Gallagher, Thoma, Bedford Co., PA, Elizabeth, Berkeley Co., WV, 19 Jul 1883, Eva, Gallagher, -, -, -, -, Hoyle, 10

3650, 31 Dec 1884, Gulielmum Franciscum, Miller, Georgia W., Frederick Co., Anna, Frederick Co., 15 Oct 1860, -, -, -, -, -, C; BC, Greentree, 10

3651, 1 Jan 1885, Joannem Jones [?], Sweeney, Joanne B., Baltimore, Nettie, Hagerstown, 12 Dec 1884, Jacobus I., Hurley, Helena, Smith, -, -, Hurley, 10

3652, 4 Feb 1885, Mariam Elsie, Baker, Jr., Daniel, MD, Leila Ady, MD, 6 Jan 1885, Noah, Laurence, Maria, Laurence, -, Endnote 70, Harbaugh, 9

3653, 7 Feb 1885, Henricum Xaverium, Koehler, Mynolf, Westphalia, Germany, Cristiana, Westphalia, Germany, 13 Sep 1821, Joannes, Mauley [or Manley], Anna, Wright, -, C; note by priest reads "Erat praeco vulgo dictus dunker praedicavit evangelium 35 annos", Hundermark, 9

3654, 27 Mar 1885, Carolum Joseph, Helferstay, Carolo L., -, Maria E., -, 27 Mar 1885, -, -, -, -, -, note by priest reads "Privatim donio rative morbi postea morticus est", Riordan, 9

3655, 31 Mar 1885, Paulum Joseph, Wright, Wilfrid, PA, Elizabetha, PA, 25 Feb 1885, Anna, Goss, -, -, -, baptized privately at home by reason of danger of death; died afterwards, Johnson, 9

3656, 31 Mar 1885, Bernardum Alexium, Wright, Wilfrid, -, Elizabetha, -, 25 Feb 1885, Anna, Goss [?], -, -, -, Baptized privately at home, Johnson, 9

3657, 12 Apr 1885, Charolum Wesley, Stine, Jacobo L., PA, Catherina A., PA, 31 Jan 1885, Elizabetha, Clarkson, -, -, -, -, Lizer, 9

3658, 4 Apr 1885, Guleilmum Maxiunum, Kleineibst, Adolpho, Germany, Henrietta, Germany, 20 Jul 1856, Theo.

ST. MARY'S CATHOLIC CHURCH
HAGERSTOWN, MARYLAND, BAPTISMS:
Index, Baptism Date, Child, Last Name, Father from,
Mother, Mother from, Birth Date, 1st Sponsor First,
1st Sponsor Last, 2nd Sponsor First, 2nd Sponsor Last,
Location, Notes, Maiden Name, Priest

(Rev.), Mead, -, -, -, born in Baltimore; C; "Ex Judaismo", Bachrach, 9

3659, 20 Apr 1885, David Lucian [?], Thomson [or Thompson in margin], David, MD, Sarah, PA, 23 Sep 1882, Susanna, Thomson, -, -, -, MA, Barnhart, 9

3660, 27 Apr 1885, Gulielmum Albertum, Burger, Adamo, Germany, Wilhilmina, Germany, 13 Apr 1885, Gul., Schlotterbeck, Maria, Kemmer, -, -, Kemmer, 9

3661, 13 May 1885, Josephinam, Fisher, Joanne, Germany, Margarita, Germany, 26 Oct 1884, Elisabetha, Grosscoup, -, -, -, -, Grosscoup, 9

3662, 15 Feb 1885, Mariam Elizabeth, Welsh, Patritio, Berkeley Co., WV, Maria, Berkeley Co., WV, 1 Jan 1885, Aloysius, Flynn, Maria, Drennan, Clear Spring, -, McGerem [?], 2

3663, 23 Feb 1885, Eugeniam[?] Allen, Myers, Ricardo M., Keedysville, Agnete, Keedysville, 17 Dec 1884, Baptisto, Hitzelberger, -, -, Keedysville, -, Hitzelberger, 2

3664, 26 Apr 1885, Carolem Fredriem, Lefferman, Georgio, Washington County, -, Washington Co., 23 Oct 1881, Ricardus, Hurleyhe, Ricardus (Mrs.), Hurleyhe, Williamsport, -, -, 2

3665, 31 Aug 1885, Mariam Catharinam, Drennan, Thomati, Berkeley Co., WV, Margarita, Berkeley Co., WV, 11 Aug 1884, Maria, Flynn, -, -, Clear Spring, -, Welsh, 2

3666, 12 Oct 1885, Joannem Semmllen [Samuelem?], Kountz, Cremell, Berkeley Co., WV, Julia, Berkeley Co., WV, 21 Aug 1884, Julia, Britner, -, -, Williamsport, -, Smith, 2

3667, 8 Dec 1885, Annam Lorettam, Hennessy, Josepho, Washington County, Mary, Washington Co., 11 Oct 1883, Jno., Dulin, Jno. (Mrs.), Dulin, Williamsport, -, Tedrick, 2

3668, 25 Dec 1885, Francescam G., Hughes, Jacobo, Washington County, Margarita, Washington Co., 12 Dec 1884, H., Clark, S., Templeton, Williamsport, -, Clarke, 2

3669, 28 Jun 1885, Mariam Golden, McCardel, Guleilmo, Washington County, Elizabeth, Washington Co., 5 Nov 1884, Anna, McCardell, -, -, -, MA, Stauch, 9

ST. MARY'S CATHOLIC CHURCH
HAGERSTOWN, MARYLAND, BAPTISMS:
Index, Baptism Date, Child, Last Name, Father from, Mother, Mother from, Birth Date, 1st Sponsor First, 1st Sponsor Last, 2nd Sponsor First, 2nd Sponsor Last, Location, Notes, Maiden Name, Priest

3670, 12 Jul 1885, Ludovicum David, Kelley, Joanne, PA, Anna, Washington Co., 2 Nov 1864, Arnold, Condry, -, -, -, convert from Protestanism, Beard, 9

3671, 14 Aug 1885, Joannem Brooke, Boyle, Carolo B., Carroll Co., Maria J., Washington Co., 4 Jul 1885, Carolus F., Smith, Elizabetha, Smith, -, -, Smith, 9

3672, 16 Aug 1885, Leonem Arthur, Fahrney, Alberto, Washington County, Margarita E., Frederick Co., 1 Jun 1883, Maria J., McCarter, -, -, -, "protestantico - Jane defunct.", Zeller, 9

3673, 16 Aug 1885, Mariam Isabellam, Fahrney, Alberto, MD, Margaret E., MD, 1 May 1885, Maria J., McCarter, -, -, -, -, Zeller, 9

3674, 23 Aug 1885, Elizabetham Mabel, Davis, Gul. J., Washington County, Alicia J., VA, 17 Feb 1877, Elizabetha, Shirley, -, -, -, MA, Cruzen [?], 9

3675, 23 Aug 1885, Mariam Irene, Davis, Gul. J., Washington County, Alecia J., -, 28 Jan 1882, Elizabetha, Shirley, -, -, -, -, Cruzn [?], 9

3676, 6 Sep 1885, Xavieruim Wallace, Tarr, Frederico C., Baltimore, Maria, -, 4 Dec 1880, [blank] [female], Owner, -, -, -, -, Shoop [?], 44

3677, 10 Sep 1885, Annam Elizabeth, Riddlemoser, M.D., Josepho, MD, Marian, MD, 19 Jun 1884, Wilhelmina L., May, -, -, -, mother is Protestant, Lydy, 9

3678, 2 Oct 1885, Joannem Leonem, Kechline *, [blank], -, -, -, 11 Aug 1881, Jeremiah, Sheehan, Agnes, Sheehan, -, "orphanum parentibus orbatum & ab ejus patrinis adoptatum"; * Kechline is father's name but Sheehan is adopted name, -, 9

3679, 4 Oct 1885, Josephum Fredricum, Fagan, Joanne, Ireland, Sarah, Baltimore, 31 Aug 1885, Helena, Taggart, -, -, -, -, Daley, 9

3680, 25 Oct 1885, Charlottam Maud., Hoover, Georgio H., Washington County, Elizabetha A., Carroll Co., 20 Sep 1885, [blank], Hildebrand, Anna M., Case, -, -, Heldebrand, 9

3681, 28 Oct 1885, Agnel [?] Euladiam, Orndorf, Gulielmo, MD, Romana, MD, 22 Oct 1885, D., Manley, Eva, McCleary, -, -, Shilling, 9

ST. MARY'S CATHOLIC CHURCH HAGERSTOWN, MARYLAND, BAPTISMS:
Index, Baptism Date, Child, Last Name, Father from, Mother, Mother from, Birth Date, 1st Sponsor First, 1st Sponsor Last, 2nd Sponsor First, 2nd Sponsor Last, Location, Notes, Maiden Name, Priest

3682, 15 Nov 1885, Mariam Margaretam, Laurence, Joanne P., Washington County, Sarah Cath., Washington Co., 12 Oct 1885, Noah, Laurence, Maria F., Laurence, -, -, Baker, 9

3683, 17 Nov 1885, Isabellam, Cunning, Joanne, Washington County, Sarah, Washington Co., 12 May 1884, Maria, Montague, -, -, -, -, Montague, 9

3684, 25 Nov 1885, Joannem Henricum, Kunell, Jacobo, Germany, Josephina, PA, 23 Aug 1878, D., Manley, -, -, Edgemont, -, Andry [or Audry], 9

3685, 25 Nov 1885, Josephinam Ethel, Kunell, Jacobo, Germany, Josaphina, PA, 24 Jul 1875, D., Manley, -, -, -, -, Audry [or Andry], 9

3686, 25 Nov 1885, Catherinam Magdalenam, Kunell, Jacobo, Germany, Josephina, PA, 14 Dec 1882, D., Manley, -, -, -, -, Audry [or Andry], 9

3687, 29 Nov 1885, Rosam Bernardittam, Fellinger, Philippo, Germany, Elizabetha, Washington Co., 7 Dec 1884, Eva, McCleary, -, -, -, MA, Garman, 9

3688, 3 Dec 1885, Carlum Richardum, Alaxander, Carolo, MD, Carolina, MD, 1 Oct 1885, Sarah, Montague, -, -, -, -, Schilling, 9

3689, 24 Dec 1885, Mariam Elizabetham, Warner, Georgio H., Washington County, Anna F., Washington Co., 6 Oct 1885, Domina Sarah, Cushwa, -, -, -, -, Martin, 9

3690, 28 Dec 1885, Adron [?], Futterer, Francisco, Washington County, Anna E., Washington Co., 19 Nov 1885, Jacobus, Futterer, Susanna, Ewers, -, baptized privately at home by reason of sickness, Mayhew, 9

3691, 1 Jan 1886, Ireniam Deliam, Clements, Joanne L., MD, Irena A., VA, 25 Jul 1885, Elizabeth, Jarboe, -, -, -, -, Wright, 9

3692, 3 Jan 1886, David C., Shilling, Guleilmo, Washington County, Hannah, Washington Co., 10 Feb 1886, Martimus [?], Happol, David, Sweeney, -, appears to read "attestis [or ab testis] per fifidis"; C; "Ex methodismo", Long, 9

3693, 3 Jan 1886, Gulielmum L., Mourer, Benjamen, Franklin Co., Georgia, Franklin Co., 25 Dec 1858, David, Sweeney,

ST. MARY'S CATHOLIC CHURCH
HAGERSTOWN, MARYLAND, BAPTISMS:
Index, Baptism Date, Child, Last Name, Father from, Mother, Mother from, Birth Date, 1st Sponsor First, 1st Sponsor Last, 2nd Sponsor First, 2nd Sponsor Last, Location, Notes, Maiden Name, Priest

Martinis, Happel, -, BC; appears to read "ultestlis profidfidc[?]"; C; "Ex methodismo", Clang, 9

3694, 18 Jan 1886, Honoram Leola, Lushbaugh, Carolo, -, Margarita, -, 10 Nov 1885, -, -, -, -, -, PB, [blank], 9

3695, 31 Jan 1886, Mariam Angellam, McCardell, Jacobo, Washington County, Helena, Washington Co., 4 Nov 1885, Maria, Cramer, -, -, -, "Married Wm. R. Morganstern on Oct. 18, 1905 at St. Mary's", Zook, 9

3696, 12 Mar 1886, Mariam Francescam, Cephas, Joanne, -, Maria E., -, 6 Jul 1885, Joanne, Bailey, -, -, -, -, Cephas, 9

3697, 21 Jun 1885, Berthem Mariem, Warner, Frederico, Clear Spring, Rosa, Clear Spring, 25 May 1885, Maria, Fellinger, -, -, -, -, Felligner, 2

3698, 12 Jul 1885, Georgina Leenen [?], Thompson, Loene [?] D., Williamsport, Catharina, w, 23 Jun 1885, M., Dugen [?], Helena, Collins, -, -, Collins, 2

3699, 23 Jul 1885, Ullricam [?] Mariem, -, -, -, Susanna, Washington Co., 27 Sep 1884, M. V., Dahlgren, -, -, South Mountain, Endnote 71, Mitchell [?], 2

3700, 24 Jul 1885, Angustimam, Lapole, Guilemo [?], Washington County, Lena, Washington Co., 25 Dec 1884, M. V., Dahlgren, -, -, South Mountain, -, Lapole, 2

3701, 8 Sep 1885, Samuelen Vincentium, Reeder, Wash., Washington County, Maria A., Washington Co., 8 Nov 1875, M.V., Dahlgren, -, -, South Mountain, -, Reeder, 2

3702, 24 Sep 1885, Meoniam [?] Stepheniuem [?], Michel [or Mikle], Henrice, Washington County, Nina, Washington Co., 4 Aug 1885, T.D., Mead, Margt., McKaig, South Mountain, -, McKaig, 2

3703, 2 Oct 1885, Samuelem Hubertem [?], [blank], -, Boonsboro, -, Boonsboro, -, P., Walsh, M.V., Dahlgren, South Mountain, -, -, 2

3704, 2 Oct 1885, Ullricem [?] Mariam, -, -, South Mountain, Washington Co., -, South Mountain, Washington Co., -, P., Walsh, M.V., Dahlgren, South Mountain, -, -, 2

3705, 4 Oct 1885, Susannem Mariem, Neikirk, Silas, Boonsboro, M. Agneti, Boonsboro, 31 Aug 1885, P., Walsh, Joanne, Wolf, -, -, Walters, 2

ST. MARY'S CATHOLIC CHURCH HAGERSTOWN, MARYLAND, BAPTISMS:
Index, Baptism Date, Child, Last Name, Father from, Mother, Mother from, Birth Date, 1st Sponsor First, 1st Sponsor Last, 2nd Sponsor First, 2nd Sponsor Last, Location, Notes, Maiden Name, Priest

3706, 4 Oct 1885, Helenem Mariam, O'Brien, Mattheo, Boonsboro, Julia, Boonsboro, 10 Sep 1885, Otho, Smith, Missouri, Smith, -, -, Murphy, 2

3707, 20 Dec 1885, Helenem Elizabeth, Brown, Gulielmo, Clear Spring, Maria, Clear Spring, 11 Dec 1885, Joanne, Moriarty, Helena, King, -, -, Knox, 2

3708, 14 Jan 1886, Franciscem Albertam, Darr, Gulielmo, Williamsport, Maria, Williamsport, 4 Dec 1885, Margt., O'Neil, -, -, -, -, Coffman, 2

3709, 22 May 1886, Jacobum Holton, Sweeney, Joanne B., Baltimore, Nettie, Maryland, 9 May 1886, Jos. S., Owner, Maria C., McLaughlin, -, -, Hurley, 9

3710, 13 Jun 1886, Honoram, Lizer, Samuel, Hagerstown, Eliza, -, 1 May 1877, Joanna, Kelly, -, -, -, MA; FA, Lizer, 9

3711, 13 Jun 1886, Idam May, Lizer, Samuel, -, Elizabetha, -, 11 Mar 1879, Joanna, Kelly, -, -, -, MA; FA, Lizer, 9

3712, 13 Jun 1886, Gulielmune [?] Emory, Lizer, Samuel, -, Elizabetha, -, 11 Apr 1883, Joanna, Geary, -, -, -, MA; FA, Lizer, 9

3713, 13 Jun 1886, Gertrude, Reilly, Joanne, -, Elizabeth, -, 18 Jun 1875, Joanna, Kelly, -, -, -, MA; FA, Maurs [?], 9

3714, 13 Jun 1886, Henricum W., Boward, Jacobo, -, Catherina V., -, 28 Mar 1876, Isaac, Feigley, -, -, -, MA; FA, Boward, 9

3715, 13 Jun 1886, Malverna Teresa, Brisco, Jacobo, -, Catherina, -, 8 Jul 1881, Virginia, Bayley, -, -, -, MA; FA, Boward, 9

3716, 20 Jun 1886, Henricum, Shilling, -, MD, -, -, 27 Jan 1820, Sarah, Cushwa, -, -, -, C; former Protestant; BC, -, 9

3717, 27 Jun 1886, Helenam May, Herbert, Dorsey, -, Susanna, -, 8 Nov 1876, Joanna, Bayley, -, -, -, BC; MA; FA, Thomas, 9

3718, 15 Jul 1886, Joannem Gul., Rauth, Gulielmo, Hagerstown, Lucia, PA, 6 Jul 1886, Maria, Saur, -, -, -, -, Saur, 9

3719, 18 Jul 1886, Henricum B., Full, Michaelo, MD, Anna, MD, 6 Jul 1886, Margaret, Rigney, -, -, -, baptized privately at

ST. MARY'S CATHOLIC CHURCH
HAGERSTOWN, MARYLAND, BAPTISMS:
Index, Baptism Date, Child, Last Name, Father from, Mother, Mother from, Birth Date, 1st Sponsor First, 1st Sponsor Last, 2nd Sponsor First, 2nd Sponsor Last, Location, Notes, Maiden Name, Priest

home by reason of sickness and danger of death on 23 Jul, Price, 9

3720, 25 Jul 1886, Jacobum Aloysium, Shafer, Joanne W., MD, Brigetta, Ireland, 13 Jul 1886, Arnold, Condry, Mary Jeneatte, Fellinger, -, -, Kelly, 9

3721, 21 Aug 1886, Jacobum Dominicum, Coyle, Thoma B., Washington County, Maria, Washington Co., 6 Feb 1886, Domenicus, Manley, -, -, -, -, Harne, 9

3722, 8 Aug 1886, Luciam Elizabeth, Burger, Adam, Germany, Wilhelmina, Germany, 29 Jul 1886, Elizabetha, Hippner, -, -, -, -, Kammerer, 9

3723, 8 Sep 1886, Mariam, Egan, Thoma, Ireland, Margareta, -, 31 Aug 1886, Thomas, O'Connor, Maria, O'Connor, -, -, O'Connor, 9

3724, 26 Sep 1886, Caeciliam G., Duffie, Loyd, MD, Laura, MD, 28 Jul 1886, Louisa, Dykes, -, -, -, -, Cann, 9

3725, 24 Oct 1886, Lucindam Margaretan, Hoover, Georgeo, Washington [sic], Elizabetha, Carroll Co., MD, 7 Oct 1886, Maria V., Ecknode, -, -, -, -, Hildebrand, 9

3726, 1 Nov 1886, Aannam Bernedettam, Cooke, Joanne, -, Margareta, -, 6 Oct 1886, Jannes, Laurence, Catherina, Laurence, -, PN, Laurence, 9

3727, 7 Nov 1886, Stellam Amandam, Kreitz, Condrad, Germany, Maria, MD, 25 Oct 1886, Gul., Moran, Amanda, Moran, -, -, Moran, 9

3728, 14 Nov 1886, Mariam Selma, O'Neill, Frederico, Canada, Maria, VA, 24 Sep 1877, Amelia, Shafer, -, -, -, -, Braker, 9

3729, 28 Nov 1886, Carolum Ambrosium, Detrich, Benjamen F., PA, Maria, PA, 17 Sep 1886, Elizabeth, Clarkson, -, -, -, -, Lizer, 9

3730, 28 Nov 1886, Audream Johnson, Jones, Andrea Johnson, Hagerstown, Margareta, Hagerstown, 3 Nov 1886, Elizabetha, Hoover, -, -, -, -, Semler, 9

3731, 1 Jan 1887, Clarencum Franciscum, Rielly, Joanne, PA, Elizabetha, MD, 8 Aug 1873, Donna[?] Sarah, Cushwa, -, -, -, -, Maurs [?], 9

ST. MARY'S CATHOLIC CHURCH HAGERSTOWN, MARYLAND, BAPTISMS:
Index, Baptism Date, Child, Last Name, Father from, Mother, Mother from, Birth Date, 1st Sponsor First, 1st Sponsor Last, 2nd Sponsor First, 2nd Sponsor Last, Location, Notes, Maiden Name, Priest

3732, 17 Jan 1887, Robert Ambrose, Briscoe*, Daniele, Hagerstown, Addore [?], Hagerstown, 19 Nov 1886, Jennie, Barley, -, -, baby appears to carry father's last name, B; PN, Hines, 3

3733, 16 Feb 1887, Leila Ada, Baker [father's name is Arbaugh], Joanne L., Frederick Co., -, -, 18 Mar 1866, Mrs., Dillon, -, -, -, BC; C, -, 3

3734, 24 Mar 1887, Mariam, Ball, Bernardo M., Washington County, Thalia, Washington Co., 2 Feb 1887, Clara, Ball, -, -, -, "married to William E. Hammaker June 15, 1912 by Father Conlon Frederick", Butler, 3

3735, 3 Apr 1887, Mariam Ruth, Miller, Israel J. [or I.], PA, Sallie, Washington Co., 15 Jan 1880, Mrs., Orndorff, -, -, -, -, Zittle, 3

3736, 9 Apr 1887, Irenem Adelaidem, McCardle [father's name is Barford], John Henry, Frederick Co., Julia, Frederick Co., 19 Jul 1859, Nettie (Mrs.), Moller [sic], -, -, -, C; BC, Trout, 3

3737, 10 Apr 1887, Thomam Flynn, McCardell, Jacobo B., Washington County, Helena, Washington Co., 6 Mar 1887, Thomas, Flynn, -, -, -, -, Zooke, 3

3738, 10 Apr 1887, Samuelem Clifford, Lizor, Joseph T., Franklin Co., Susan Rebecca, -, 27 Aug 1886, Martha, Lizor, -, -, -, Married Rosa B. Tendery, 7 Jan 1909; St. Joseph's Church, Emmittsburg, MD, Binskuzy [?], 3

3739, 12 May 1887, Helenam Theresiam, Boyle, Carolo, -, Maria J., -, 22 Oct 1886, Maria, Garesha "(by proxy)", -, -, -, appears to read "jamprodem baptizata provatim ob mortis periculem"; appears to read "supplevi coeremoniag super", Smith, 3

3740, 27 May 1887, Carolum Cecilium, Cunning, Joanne, MD, Sarah, MD, 29 Dec 1885, Domincus, Manley, -, -, -, -, Montague, 9

3741, 26 Jun 1887, Ludivicum, Cookerly, Jacobo, -, Sarah, -, 30 Nov 1821, Jacobus I., Hurley, -, -, -, C; former Protestant; BC, [blank], 9

3742, 26 Jun 1887, Grace, Warner, Gorgio H., Washington County, Anna F., Washington Co., 19 Feb 1887, Margarita,

ST. MARY'S CATHOLIC CHURCH HAGERSTOWN, MARYLAND, BAPTISMS:
Index, Baptism Date, Child, Last Name, Father from, Mother, Mother from, Birth Date, 1st Sponsor First, 1st Sponsor Last, 2nd Sponsor First, 2nd Sponsor Last, Location, Notes, Maiden Name, Priest

Jones, -, -, -, "Had marriage revalidated at St. Katharine's Church Baltimore, by Rev. Jno. S.[?] Martin, Asst. Pastor.", Martin, 9

3743, 30 Jun 1887, Gulielmum Kent, Feigly, Isaac, MD, Emma, WV, 23 Feb 1885, Jacob, Wills, Catherina, Laurence, -, -, Armstrong, 9

3744, 30 Jun 1887, Raymond N., Feigley, Isaac, MD, Emma, WV, 12 Jan 1886, Jacob, Wills, Sarah, Cushwa, -, -, Armstrong, 9

3745, 2 Jul 1887, Mariam, Fields, Joanne, MD, Margareta, MD, 30 Dec 1870, Anna, Walker, -, -, -, -, Hemsly, 9

3746, 13 Jul 1887, Jacobum Henricum, Lizer, Samuel, -, Elizabetha, -, 4 Oct 1886, Isaac, Figley, Catherina, Laurence, -, parents are Protestant, Lizer, 9

3747, 11 Apr 1886, Robertum Emmitt, Cullen, Emmet, MD, Eva, MD, 1 Apr 1886, Victor, Cushwa, Helena, Cushwa, -, Williamsport, Cushwa, 9

3748, 25 Apr 1886, Gulielmum G., Reed, Wm. W., -, Marg. Ellen, -, 13 Mar 1886, Franciscus, Cushwa, Helena, Hurleyhee, -, Williamsport; "See Marriage Record #1 Pg. 171", Donnelly, 9

3749, 5 May 1886, Vinton Augusterum, Jones, Ludovico, -, Maria, -, 4 Mar 1882, Magdalena, Dahlgren, -, -, South Mountain, -, Kauffman, 9

3750, 9 May 1886, Joannane Francescam, Hughes, Jacobo, -, -, -, 188_*, Victor, Cushwa, Margarita, Hughes, Williamsport, *birthdate is 188_ [last number is blank], -, 9

3751, May 1886, Elizabetham Helenam, Ward, -, -, -, -, -, -, -, -, -, -, -, -, 9

3752, 4 Jul 1886, Paulum, Norris, Melean [or Wiliard?], -, Catherina, -, 9 Jun 1886, Domina, Walters, -, -, Boonsboro, -, Farrell, 9

3753, 17 Oct 1886, Ludivecum Victor, Drennan [or Dunnan], Thoma, -, Maria, -, 18 Seo 1886, -, -, -, -, -, -, Welsh, 9

3754, 27 Mar 1887, Jacobum Henricum, Hughes, Jacobo, -, Margareta, -, 2 Mar 1887, Joanna, Duggan, Maria, Duggan, Williamsport, -, Clark, 9

ST. MARY'S CATHOLIC CHURCH
HAGERSTOWN, MARYLAND, BAPTISMS:
Index, Baptism Date, Child, Last Name, Father from, Mother, Mother from, Birth Date, 1st Sponsor First, 1st Sponsor Last, 2nd Sponsor First, 2nd Sponsor Last, Location, Notes, Maiden Name, Priest

3755, 8 May 1887, Mariane Evam, Thompson, Ludivico, -, Catherina, -, 1 May 1887, Eugenius [?], McCardell, Helena, Collins, Williamsport, -, Collins, 9

3756, 29 May 1887, Mariom, Hastings, -, -, -, -, 29 May 1878, Maria, Fellinger, -, -, Clear Spring, -, -, 9

3757, 29 May 1887, Annam, Hastings, -, -, -, -, 23 Apr 1873, M., Roache, -, -, Clear Spring, -, -, 9

3758, 22 Jul 1887, Mariam Josephinam, Mullen, Carolo A., MD, Maria Ludivico, MD, 9 Jul 1887, David, Cushwa, Susanna, Fechtig, -, -, Cushwa, 9

3759, 30 Jul 1887, Joannem, Heil, Joanne, MD, Clara, MD, 24 Jun 1886, Catherina, Heil, -, -, -, -, Gross, 9

3760, 30 Jul 1887, Maud Genefefuen [?], Heil, Joanne, MD, Clara, MD, 4 May 1883, Cath., Hiel, -, -, -, -, Gross, 9

3761, 31 Jul 1887, Joannam *, Swink, Decatur, MD, Anna, MD, 19 Mar 1887, Margarita, Geary, -, -, -, * "Jane Erma" written in a different color ink over top, Hall, 9

3762, 14 Aug 1887, Mariam Bernardinam, Shilling, David, MD, Catherina Maria, MD, 28 Jul 1887, Elizabetha, Schlotterbeck, -, -, -, She married Joanni Dorsey, in Corporis Christi Church, Baltimore, 18 Apr. 1917, by Rev. J. A. Smith, Schlotterbeck, 9

3763, 19 Aug 1887, Bertham Josephenam, Switzer, Samuel, MD, Maria, PA, 14 Aug 1887, Maria, Switzer, -, -, -, BC, Laurence, 9

3764, 21 Aug 1887, Agnes Theresium, Baker, Joanne C., MD, Lebeda, -, 16 Feb 1887, Noah, Laurence, Maria, Laurence, -, -, Harbaugh, 9

3765, 28 Aug 1887, Mariam Motter, Kershner, Josepho, MD, Helena, PA, 4 Aug 1887, Maria E., Henneberger, -, -, -, -, Hoover, 9

3766, 15 Sep 1887, Urbanum Alphonsum, Wright, Wilfredo, PA, Elizabetha, PA, 1 Sep 1887, Maria, Tierney, -, -, -, -, Johnson, 9

3767, 18 Sep 1887, Margaretam, Lushbaugh [father's name is Gates], Windel, WV, Catherina, WV, 4 Nov 1857, Margarita, Sherwin, -, -, -, C; former Lutheran; BC, Keller, 9

ST. MARY'S CATHOLIC CHURCH HAGERSTOWN, MARYLAND, BAPTISMS:
Index, Baptism Date, Child, Last Name, Father from, Mother, Mother from, Birth Date, 1st Sponsor First, 1st Sponsor Last, 2nd Sponsor First, 2nd Sponsor Last, Location, Notes, Maiden Name, Priest

3768, 6 Oct 1887, Mariam Josephinam, Sweeney, Joanne B., Baltimore, Henrietta, Hagerstown, 27 Sep 1887, Jacobus, McLaughlin, Josephina, Hurley, -, -, Hurley, 9

3769, 9 Oct 1887, Georgium Earl, Mayhew, Clemente, -, Francisca, -, 25 Jul 1887, Irenes, Mayhew, -, -, -, -, Miller, 3

3770, 6 Nov 1887, Sararma [?] Magdalenam, Allen, Joanne, -, Maria [?], -, 15 Oct 1887, Julia, Grooms, -, -, -, child and father are Black, Stuart, 3

3771, 13 Nov 1887, Joseph Rogery, Davis, Gulielmo J., -, Alicia, -, 16 Aug 1887, Johanna, Garey, -, -, -, -, Cruzeen [?], 3

3772, 1 Nov 1887, Albertem Clarentium, Kinek [or Kouck?], Davide, Clear Spring, Elizabeth, Clear Spring, 25 Oct 1887, Jos., Swope, Maria, Flynn, Williamsport, -, Swope, 2

3773, 13 Nov 1887, Mariem Virginam, Lyddam, Joanne G., Williamsport, Anna, Williamsport, 19 Oct 1887, Cath., Donnolly, -, -, Williamsport, Maria married Alberto Bendiert in St. Caroli Church, Clarendon, VA, 30 Sept. 1917, Sheridan, 2

3774, 27 Nov 1887, Joseph Franciscum, Boyle, Carolo, Hagerstown, Maria J., Hagerstown, 31 Oct 1887, Mimika, Fareth, -, -, -, -, Smith, 3

3775, 27 Nov 1887, Mariam Mabel, Rauth, Gulielmo, -, Lucia, -, 10 Nov 1887, Jacobus, Moran, Maria, Moran, -, -, Sauer, 3

3776, 24 Dec 1887, Emma Catherinam, McGinley [father's name is Cunningham], Gulielmo H., Mechanicsburg, PA, Sarah Elis., -, 13 Apr 1868, Mrs., Shlotterbeck, -, -, -, C, Reynolds, 3

3777, 10 Oct 1887, Catharinem, Britner, -, -, -, -, -, Julia, Britner, -, -, Williamsport; she from Berkeley Co., WV, C, -, 2

3778, 1 Dec 1887, Ludovicum Vincentium, Myers, R.M., Sharpsburg, Agneti Caeilia, Sharpsburg, 12 Aug 1887, Agnes, Myers, -, -, Williamsport, -, Hitzelberger, 2

3779, 22 Jan 1888, Margaritem Caceilliam, McCardle, Eugenio, Williamsport, Effie, Williamsport, 25 Dec 1887,

ST. MARY'S CATHOLIC CHURCH
HAGERSTOWN, MARYLAND, BAPTISMS:
Index, Baptism Date, Child, Last Name, Father from,
Mother, Mother from, Birth Date, 1st Sponsor First,
1st Sponsor Last, 2nd Sponsor First, 2nd Sponsor Last,
Location, Notes, Maiden Name, Priest

Ambrosius, McCardle, Elizabeth F., McCardle, Williamsport, -, King, 2

3780, 2 Feb 1888, Francescam Joseph, Bryan, Georgio M., Hagerstown, Theresa, Hagerstown, 19 Mar 1872*, Maria (Mrs.), Condry, -, -, -, *birthdate is 19 Mar 1872 [or 1873], Shover, 3

3781, 14 Feb 1888, Thomen Edwardum, Mense, Joanne E., Four Locks, Wash. Co., Maria, Four Locks, Wash. Co., 18 Nov 1882, Elizabeth, McCardle, -, -, Williamsport, -, McClain, 2

3782, 1 Apr 1888, Carolum Fredericum, Burger, Adamo, -, Minnie, -, 8 Mar 1888, Carolus, Kammerer, Maria, Kammerer, -, -, Kammerer, 3

3783, 22 Apr 1888, Terentium Vincentum, Alexander, Carolo, Hagerstown, Carolina, Hagerstown, 16 Oct 1887, Maria, Cunningham, -, -, -, -, Schilling, 2

3784, 23 May 1888, Margaritem Elizabeth, Drennan, Thomati, Berkeley Co., WV, Margarita, Berkeley Co., WV, 14 May 1888, Margt., Roache, -, -, Williamsport, -, Welch, 2

3785, 10 Jun 1888, Joseph, Feigley, Isaac, -, Emma C., -, 28 May 1888, Jerome, Lawrence, -, -, -, Armstrong, 3

3786, 17 Jun 1888, Louis Resh, Jones, Andrea J., Hagerstown, Margarita, Hagerstown, 29 May 1888, H. (Mrs.), Kershner, -, -, -, "Married to Ruth I. Dusang July 12, 1916.", Semler, 3

3787, 15 Jan 1888, Robert E. Benedict, Fagan, Joanne, -, Sarah, -, 23 Dec 1887, Cararie, Witty [?], -, -, -, -, Daley [or Dady], 3

3788, 6 May 1888, Catharinam, Futterer, Francesio, -, Anna E., -, 27 Mar 1888, Jacob, Futterer, Susanna, Ewers, -, -, Mayhew, 3

3789, 14 Jul 1888, Henricum Jacobum, Hennessy, Thoma J., -, Catharina, -, 12 Apr 1888, Thomas, Hennessy, Ellen, Hennessy, -, MA, Ripple, 3

3790, 15 Jul 1888, Joannem Joseph, Hoover, Georgio D., Hagerstown, Elisabeth A., -, 22 Jun 1888, Mrs., Kershner, -, -, -, -, Hildebrand, 3

ST. MARY'S CATHOLIC CHURCH
HAGERSTOWN, MARYLAND, BAPTISMS:
Index, Baptism Date, Child, Last Name, Father from,
Mother, Mother from, Birth Date, 1st Sponsor First,
1st Sponsor Last, 2nd Sponsor First, 2nd Sponsor Last,
Location, Notes, Maiden Name, Priest

3791, 15 Jul 1888, David Henricum, Lawrence, Joanne P., -, Sarah C., -, 4 Jul 1888, Noah F., Lawrence, Maria, Lawrence [HB], -, -, Baker, 3

3792, 29 Jul 1888, Mariam Catharinam, Moran, Jacobo H., -, Maria A., -, 21 Jul 1888, Conradus, Kreitz, Maria [?] E., Kreitz, -, -, Hoke, 3

3793, 29 Apr 1888, Annem, Green, -, -, -, -, -, Maria, Fellenger, -, -, -, she from Clear Spring; B; C; BC; appears to read "all fidem conversa L Baptismo sub conditione fuit Reremdus or Neremdus", -, 2

3794, 23 Jul 1888, Geneveffam, O'Brien, Mattheo, Boonsboro, Julia, Boonsboro, 14 Jul 1888, Maria, Murphy, -, -, -, -, Murphy, 2

3795, 22 Jul 1888, Mariem Lucindem, Helsel, -, -, -, -, -, Margt., O'Neil, -, -, -, Endnote 72, -, 2

3796, 19 Aug 1888, Annam V., Moore, Ulton C., Washington County, Ida V., Washington Co., 21 Feb 1887, Noah, Lawrence, Noah (Mrs.), Lawrence, -, -, Tidrick, 3

3797, 26 Aug 1888, Emiliam Catharinam, Feigley [father's name is Armstrong], Joanne, -, -, -, 8 Dec 1857, Sarai, Cushwa "(by proxy)", -, -, -, C, -, 3

3798, 26 Aug 1888, Mariam Magdalenam, Heil, Joanne, Washington County, Clara, Washington Co., 5 May 1888, Elizabeth, Hopner, -, -, -, "Married to George R. Bussard at St. Mary's, Hagerstown, 6-29-46. Sanstis in radice obtained from Balto. 6-28-46" C.W. Dawdi [?]; MA, Gross, 3

3799, 15 Aug 1888, Fremciscum Allen, Templeton, Jacobo, Williamsport, Beatrice, Williamsport, 25 Jul 1888, Maria, Dugan, -, -, Williamsport, FA, Dufini, 2

3800, 30 Sep 1888, Howard Carolum, Heil, Alberto, Hagerstown, Carrie, Hagerstown, 7 Jun 1888, Catharina, Heil, -, -, -, MA, Irvin, 3

3801, 30 Sep 1888, Catharinem, Kreigh, -, -, -, -, -, Sara, Kreigh, -, -, Clear Spring, C; from Washington Co., -, 2

3802, 19 Oct 1888, Carrie May, Weedon [?], Alfredo, Frederick Co., Priscilla, Frederick Co., 18 Feb 1888, Rachel, Tasco, -, -, -, from Frederick County; child is Black, Harper, 3

ST. MARY'S CATHOLIC CHURCH
HAGERSTOWN, MARYLAND, BAPTISMS:
Index, Baptism Date, Child, Last Name, Father from, Mother, Mother from, Birth Date, 1st Sponsor First, 1st Sponsor Last, 2nd Sponsor First, 2nd Sponsor Last, Location, Notes, Maiden Name, Priest

3803, 21 Oct 1888, Juliam Vidier [female], Warner, George, Hagerstown, Anna, Hagerstown, 12 Sep 1888, Maria, Cramer, -, -, -, MA, Martin, 3

3804, 25 Oct 1888, Elisabeth, Hose, Joanne, -, Sarai J., -, 28 Jan 1885, Sara, Mantague, -, -, -, -, Shillong [?], 3

3805, 25 Oct 1888, Joseph R., Hose, Joanne, -, Sarah, -, 28 May 1883, Sara, Montague, -, -, -, "Joseph's marriage to Bertha Bawnd [?] revalidated June 4, 1924. See Marriage Record #2 Page I", Shillong [?], 3

3806, 25 Oct 1888, Mariam, Hose, Joanne, -, Sarah, -, -, Sara, Montague, -, -, -, -, Shillong [?], 3

3807, 2 Nov 1888, Evan Bernardum Joannem, Diffendel, Thoma B., Frederick Co., Maria, Frederick Co., 23 Oct 1888, Rosa, Yinglon [?], -, -, -, MA, Hobbs, 3

3808, 2 Nov 1888, Isabellam Susannam, Moore [father's name is McCrea], Adam, Washington County, -, -, 10 Apr 1855, -, -, -, -, -, C, -, 3

3809, 2 Nov 1888, Idam Virginiam, Moore [father's name is Titworth ?], Jacobo, Washington County, -, -, 25 Aug 1866, Maria F., Lawrence, -, -, -, C, -, 3

3810, 25 Nov 1888, Mary Elisabeth, Stine, Jacobo L., Franklin Co., Catherine, -, 1 Oct 1888, Josephine, Hurley, -, -, -, -, Lizer, 3

3811, 15 Oct 1888, Samuelem Ludovicum, Mouse [?], Themati [?], Clear Spring, Maria, Clear Spring, 16 Oct 1878, Benj., Boswel, -, -, -, -, Blair [?], 2

3812, 1 Nov 1888, Gulielmen Edwardum, Mouse [?], Joanne, Four Locks, Wash. Co., Maria, Four Locks, Wash. Co., 27 Jun 1885, Benj., Boswel, -, -, -, -, McClain, 2

3813, 1 Nov 1888, Mariem Catharinem, Mouse, Joanne, Four Locks, Wash. Co., Maria, Four Locks, Wash. Co., 30 Dec 1887, Margt., Roache, -, -, Williamsport, -, McClain, 2

3814, 12 Nov 1888, Annem Caceiliam, Dickerhoff, Samuele, Williamsport, Emma, Williamsport, 7 Aug 1888, Cath., Richter, -, -, Williamsport, -, Richter, 2

3815, 3 Jan 1889, Joannem Thematem [?], Murphy, Joanne, Sharpsburg, Genefeffa, Sharpsburg, 3 Jul 1888, Clara,

ST. MARY'S CATHOLIC CHURCH
HAGERSTOWN, MARYLAND, BAPTISMS:
Index, Baptism Date, Child, Last Name, Father from,
Mother, Mother from, Birth Date, 1st Sponsor First,
1st Sponsor Last, 2nd Sponsor First, 2nd Sponsor Last,
Location, Notes, Maiden Name, Priest

Highbarger, -, -, -, "confirmed St. Matthew's Cathedral D.C. 11-7-48 [the 4 is unclear]", Snayne [?], 2

3816, 10 Feb 1889, Franciscam Lillian Walsh, Cullen, M. Emmett, Williamsport, Maria Eva, Williamsport, 9 Jan 1889, C.W.F., Cushwa, Francisca De Sales, Cushwa, Williamsport, -, Cushwa, 2

3817, 6 May 1889, Victorem Bernardum, Thompson, Leone, Williamsport, Catharina, Williamsport, 11 Feb 1889, Helena, Oliver, -, -, Williamsport, -, Collins, 2

3818, 13 Jan 1889, Edmundum Ephraim [?], Provence, Ephradm [?], PA, Helena, -, 24 Nov 1888, Edmundus Jos., Burner, Maria, Provence, -, -, Floyd, 3

3819, 3 Feb 1889, Georgium Vendel, Lushbaugh, Carolo, Hagerstown, Maria Virginia, Hagerstown, 3 Dec 1888, Fannie (Mrs.), Lushbaugh, -, -, -, -, Gates, 3

3820, 3 Feb 1889, Edwardum Guliemum, McGinley, Edwardo, -, Emma Catharina, Hagerstown, 13 Jan 1889, Gulielmus, Miller, Nettie, Miller, -, -, Cuningham, 3

3821, 17 Feb 1889, Mariam Helenam, Hellane, Joanne, Hagerstown, Julia, Frostburg, MD, 5 Feb 1889, Margarita, Brady, -, -, -, Married to Ferry D. Connor, Hagerstown, 13 Aug 1913, Brady, 3

3822, 17 Mar 1889, Fredericum Spickler, Kreigh, Petro, Clear Spring, Helena, Clear Spring, 16 Feb 1889, Victor, Cushwa, Maria, Cushwa, Clear Spring, -, Spickler, 2

3823, 7 Apr 1889, Mariam, Rouskulp, Henrico W., Hagerstown, Catharina, Hagerstown, 1 Oct 1888, Maria, Downin, -, -, -, CS; PB; baptized at home in danger of death, Downin, 3

3824, 14 Apr 1889, Fredericum Gulielmum, Sweeney, Joanne B., Hagerstown, Sophia J., Hagerstown, 23 Feb 1889, Fredericus, Holm, Elisabeth (Mrs.), Kelhoffer [?], -, -, Hurley, 3

3825, 14 Apr 1889, Agnetem Catharinam, Kreiz, Conrado, -, Maria E., -, 6 Apr 1889, Gulielmus, Montague, Sarah (Mrs.), Montague, -, -, Moran, 3

ST. MARY'S CATHOLIC CHURCH
HAGERSTOWN, MARYLAND, BAPTISMS:
Index, Baptism Date, Child, Last Name, Father from, Mother, Mother from, Birth Date, 1st Sponsor First, 1st Sponsor Last, 2nd Sponsor First, 2nd Sponsor Last, Location, Notes, Maiden Name, Priest

3826, 14 Apr 1889, Luciam Barbaram, Routh, Gulielmo, Hagerstown, Lucia, -, 4 Apr 1889, Anna (Mrs.), Battle, -, -, -, -, Sauer [?], 3

3827, 21 Apr 1889, Francescum M., Boyle, Carolo, -, Maria, Hagerstown, 11 Apr 1889, Elisabeth, Kelhoffer, -, -, -, -, Smith, 3

3828, 28 Apr 1889, Lauram Lucretiam, Lawrence [or Burgonver], Jacobo, Washington County, Elisabeth, Washington Co., 1 Jan 1868, Anna, Full, -, -, -, C; father's name is Burgonver [?], Hose, 3

3829, 12 May 1889, Georgium, Reed, Gulielmo, Williamsport, Maria, Williamsport, 30 Mar 1889, Margarita, O'Neil, -, -, Williamsport, -, Donnolly, 2

3830, 2 Jun 1889, Gratiam Geneviefam, Owner, Joseph, -, Emma B., Cumberland, 15 May 1889, J.[?] B., Sweeney, Genevefa, Gonder "(by proxy)", -, -, Harding, 3

3831, 16 Jun 1889, Mariam Annam Margaritam, Burger, Adamo, -, Minnie, -, 2 Jun 1889, Maria, Kammerer, -, -, -, -, Kammerer, 3

3832, 16 Jun 1889, Mariam Geneviefam, Moore, Joanne *, -, Margareta, -, 8 Jun 1889, Mrs., Kreitz, -, -, -, * written above this name is "Zeph[?]", Martin, 3

3833, 23 Jun 1889, Helenam Matildam, Moore, Upton, Washington County, Ida Virginia, Washington Co., 25 May 1889, Noah, Lawrence, Maria F., Lawrence, -, -, Tidwick, 3

3834, 30 Jun 1889, Mariam Bertam, Shwink, Decatur, VA, Anna, -, 17 Mar 1889, Joanna, Geary, -, -, -, -, Hall, 3

3835, 13 Aug 1889, Rebeccam Lucindam, Long, Adamo A., Washington County, Catharina, Washington Co., 16 Sep1 886, Carolina (Mrs.), Richter, -, -, Williamsport, -, Andrew, 3

3836, 13 Aug 1889, Franklin Jeremiam, Long, Adamo A., Washington County, Catharina, Washington Co., 2 Dec 1888, Carolina (Mrs.), Richter, -, -, Williamsport, -, Andrew, 3

3837, 20 Aug 1889, Carolum Gulielmum, Hoover, Edwardo, Hagerstown, Lydia A., Hagerstown, 2 May 1889, Helen (Mrs.), Kershner, -, -, -, -, Porter, 3

ST. MARY'S CATHOLIC CHURCH HAGERSTOWN, MARYLAND, BAPTISMS:
Index, Baptism Date, Child, Last Name, Father from, Mother, Mother from, Birth Date, 1st Sponsor First, 1st Sponsor Last, 2nd Sponsor First, 2nd Sponsor Last, Location, Notes, Maiden Name, Priest

3838, 25 Aug 1889, Anitam Mateer, Robertson, Mauricio, -, Anna, -, 19 Jan 1889, Martha, Wroe "(by proxy)", -, -, -, -, Wroe, 3

3839, 30 Sep 1889, Ruth Helenam, Clements, Joanne, MD, Irene A., VA, 21 Jun 1889, Cornelius, O'Brien, appears to read "uxor eiry (per procuratorem)", -, -, -, Wright, 3

3840, 6 Oct 1889, Ludovicam Clementinam, Mullen, Carolo A., MD, Maria Ludovica, MD, 16 Sep 1889, Fred., Cushwa, Nellie, Cushwa, -, -, Cushwa, 3

3841, 20 Oct 1889, Leonem R., Hoover, Georgio, Hagerstown, Elisabeth, Hagerstown, 15 Sep 1889, Josephine, Hurley, -, -, -, "Married twice - widower. Second time see Marriage Record #1 Pg. 140.", Hildebrand, 3

3842, 26 Oct 1889, Joseph Omer, Hennessey, Thoma J., Washington County, Catharina, Washington Co., 7 Aug 1889, Thomas, Hennessey, Helena, Hennessey, -, MA, Ropple, 3

3843, 3 Nov 1889, Eleonoram, Reckert, Andrea, Baltimore, Ella E., Hagerstown, 23 Sep 1889, Eleonora, Recket, -, -, -, MA, Gold, 3

3844, 23 Nov 1889, Catharinam, Detrich, Benjamin, -, Maria E., -, 6 Sep 1889, Martha, Lizer, -, -, -, -, Lizer, 3

3845, 13 Dec 1889, Ednam Mariam, Martin, Clifford P., Hagerstown, Maria, Hagerstown, 9 Nov 1889, -, -, -, -, -, BP; PB, Wise, 3

3846, 22 Dec 1889, Juliam Mariam, Halm, Reinhold, Hagerstown, Francisca, Washington, DC, 8 Dec 1889, Fredericus, Halm, Julia (Mrs.), Keedy, -, "Julia married Conrado Adolpho Kuz, 5 May 1816, Annapolis, MD" with pastor's permission, Rev. P. Warren C.S.S.R. S.S. Hulbert [?]", Beaumont, 3

3847, 22 Dec 1889, Mariam C., Jones, A.J., -, Margarita, -, 24 Nov 1889, Elisabeth, Wright, -, -, -, MA, Semler, 3

3848, 25 Dec 1889, Addie Eugeniam, McCardell, Eugenio, -, Effie, -, 16 Nov 1889, Ella, Oliver, -, -, Williamsport, MA; Married to John G. Aehrl [?]; "2-17-45 convalidation", King, 3

3849, 28 Dec 1889, Thoman Alexandum, Moore, Thoma, Washington County, Isabella, Washington Co., 25 Jan 1890,

ST. MARY'S CATHOLIC CHURCH
HAGERSTOWN, MARYLAND, BAPTISMS:
Index, Baptism Date, Child, Last Name, Father from, Mother, Mother from, Birth Date, 1st Sponsor First, 1st Sponsor Last, 2nd Sponsor First, 2nd Sponsor Last, Location, Notes, Maiden Name, Priest

Maria (Mrs.), Battle, -, -, -, [This entire entry is crossed out.], McCray, 3

3850, 30 Jan 1890, Saraim Elisabeth, Fagan, Joanne R., Ireland, Sarai, Baltimore, 16 Jan 1890, Anna, Fagan, -, -, -, Sara married Roy P. Shreiner, Hagerstown, 6 Jul 1918, Daley, 3

3851, 10 Feb 1890, Carolum Victorem, McCall, Jacobo, Baltimore, Anna, Hagerstown, 7 Oct 1889, Maria, Baker, -, -, -, -, Mitchell, 3

3852, 23 Feb 1890, Nellie Pearl, Alexander, Carolo W., Washington County, Carolina, Washington Co., 25 Dec 1889, Margarita, Griffey, -, -, -, "Married Oct. 22, 1923 by Rev. M.J. Riordan, to Earle Bailey", Sheehan, 3

3853, 23 Feb 1890, Bernardum, Lizer, Samuele, -, Elisabeth, -, 19 Jan 1890, Nina, Cramer, -, -, -, MA; FA, [blank], 3

3854, 4 Mar 1890, Evam Estellam, Spielman, Henrico, Hagerstown, Cora, Hagerstown, 27 Dec 1889, Irenes, McCardell, -, -, -, MA; father is dead, Baxford, 3

3855, 7 Apr 1890, Francescum S. [male], Orndorf, Gulielmo, Hagerstown, Maria, Hagerstown, 4 Jun 1889, Elisabeth (Mrs.), Moore, -, -, -, PB; CS; baptized by the grandmother due to danger of death, Downin, 3

3856, 20 Apr 1890, Helenam Paulinam, Lawrence, Jerome, -, Catharina, -, 22 Mar 1890, Josephina, Hurley, -, -, -, -, Donohue, 3

3857, 28 Apr 1890, Thomam Alexandum, Moore, Thomas, Washington County, Elisabeth, Washington Co., 25 Jan 1890, Mary (Mrs.), Battle, -, -, -, -, McCray, 3

3858, 17 Jun 1890, Joannem Leroy, Hennessey, Petro, Tilghmanton, Maria L., Tilghmanton, 20 Mar 1890, Helena, Hennessey, -, -, -, MA, Smith, 3

3859, 6 Jul 1890, Gertrudem Mariam, Allen [or Allan], Joanne, -, Maria, -, 9 Jun 1890, Jennie, Bailey, -, -, -, father is Black, Stewart, 3

3860, 20 Jul 1890, Mariam Violam, Moore, Upton, -, Ida V., -, 25 Jun 1890, Noah, Lawrence, Mary Francy, Lawrence "his wife", -, -, Tidwick, 3

ST. MARY'S CATHOLIC CHURCH
HAGERSTOWN, MARYLAND, BAPTISMS:
Index, Baptism Date, Child, Last Name, Father from,
Mother, Mother from, Birth Date, 1st Sponsor First,
1st Sponsor Last, 2nd Sponsor First, 2nd Sponsor Last,
Location, Notes, Maiden Name, Priest

3861, 27 Jul 1890, Edgar Willm. Leonem, Wolf, Henrico, Hagerstown, Maria, Hagerstown, 16 Jul 1890, Otho, Duffy, Maria, Cramer, -, "Married to Mary K. Gossard, non-catholic, St. Martin's Rectory, Sept. 30, 1937 by Rev. R.J. Berron, Baltimore, Md.", Switzer, 3

3862, 1 Aug 1890, Georgium M., Feigley, Isaac, Hagerstown, Emma C., Hagerstown, 27 Jul 1890, Eleonora, Lizer, -, -, -, Baptized at home in danger of death, Armstrong, 3

3863, 31 Aug 1890, Annam Rosaliam, Burger, Adamo, -, Willhelmina, -, 6 Aug 1890, Elisabeth, Shlotterbeck, -, -, -, -, Kammerer, 3

3864, 7 Sep 1890, Lula Gertrudem, Conlehen, Thoma, MD, Gertrude, PA, 25 Jun 1890, Michael, Coulehan, Theresia, Hughes, -, MA, Snyder, 3

3865, 19 Sep 1890, Leonem Aloysirem [?], Wright, Wilfredo, -, Elisabeth, -, 30 Jul 1890, Irenes, Mayhew, -, -, -, -, Johnson, 3

3866, 21 Sep 1890, Mariam Ednam, Lawrence, Aaron, Hagerstown, Elisabeth, Hagerstown, 13 Nov 1888, Lewis, Kelly, Anna, Felix, -, MA, Cross, 3

3867, 21 Sep 1890, Robertum Henricum, -, isdem parentobus, -, -, -, 6 Apr 1890, isdem at supra, -, -, -, -, -, -, 3

3868, 5 Oct 1890, Joannem Cornelium, Hennessy, Joseph, Washington County, Margareta, Washington Co., 27 Sep 1890, Upton, Moore, Ida, Moore, -, -, Keedwik [?], 3

3869, 9 Oct 1890, Gulieslmum Franciscum, Rauth, Gulielmo, -, Lucia, -, 6 Sep 1890, Milton, Ewer, Milton (Mrs.), Ewer [HB], -, -, Sauer, 3

3870, 11 Oct 1890, Thomam Henricum, Cramer, Henrico, -, Felia, -, 1 Oct 1890, Nina, Cramer, -, -, -, MA, Armstrong, 3

3871, 14 Oct 1890, Adam Rebeccam, Warner, Georgio, Hagerstown, Anna, Hagerstown, 3 Aug 1890, Maria, Cramer, -, -, -, Baptized at home, Martin, 3

3872, 19 Oct 1890, Georgium Edwardum, Moore, Eduardo, Hagerstown, Elisabeth, Hagerstown, 29 Sep 1890, L. (Mrs.), Steffey, -, -, -, -, Hippner, 3

ST. MARY'S CATHOLIC CHURCH
HAGERSTOWN, MARYLAND, BAPTISMS:
Index, Baptism Date, Child, Last Name, Father from, Mother, Mother from, Birth Date, 1st Sponsor First, 1st Sponsor Last, 2nd Sponsor First, 2nd Sponsor Last, Location, Notes, Maiden Name, Priest

3873, 26 Oct 1890, Geneviefe [?], Orndorff, Gulielmo, -, Mary [?], -, 4 Oct 1890, Franciscus, Futterer, Franciscus (Mrs.), Futterer [HB], -, -, Downing, 3

3874, 4 Nov 1890, Margaritem Mariam, Boyle, Carolo, -, Maria, -, 3 Jun 1890, Anna, Cook, -, -, -, BP; PB, Smith, 3

3875, 23 Nov 1890, Gulielmum Franciscum, Kriegh, Petro, Washington County, Ella J., Washington Co., 7 Nov 1890, Victor M., Cushwa, Susanna, Cushwa [HB], -, -, Spickler, 3

3876, 8 Dec 1890, Mariam Theresiam, Lawrence, -, -, -, -, 21 Nov 1890, Ida [?] (Mrs.), Moore, -, -, -, adopted by Noah Lawrence, -, 3

3877, 10 Jan 1891, Daisy Mariam, Flynn, Jacob, Baltimore, Amilia, Germany, 27 Nov 1890, Irene, Mayhew, -, -, -, -, Spidzing, 3

3878, 1 Feb 1891, Carolum Joseph, Kershner, Joseph, Hagerstown, Helena, -, 13 Jan 1891, Lillie (Mrs.), March, -, -, -, -, Hoover, 3

3879, 1 Feb 1891, Margaritam Annam, Mullen, Carolo, -, Lutie [?], -, 1 Jan 1891, T.B., Cushwa, Sallie, Cushwa, -, "Married David Warner Fry, son of John W. Fry, 18 May 1918, Rev. M.A. Ryan, Baltimore", Cushwa, 3

3880, 8 Feb 1891, Rosam Mariam, Turner, Joseph E., Hagerstown, Mary L., Hagerstown, 10 Sep1890, Ella (Mrs.), Futterer, -, -, -, -, McDonnell, 3

3881, 11 Feb 1891, Annam Helenam, Thompson, Leone, -, Catharina, -, 6 Jan 1891, Elizabeth, McCardell, -, -, Williamsport, -, Collins, 3

3882, 24 Feb 1891, Mariam Agnetem, Myers, R.M., Sharpsburg, Agnete Cacelilia, Sharpsburg, 15 Jan 1890, M. Maria, Justice [?], -, -, Sharpsburg, sponsor is from Richmond, VA, Hitzelbarger, 2

3883, 5 Apr 1891, Annam Ceciliam, Moran, Jacobo H., Emmittsburg, Maria A., Emmittsburg, 23 Mar 1891, Mattew [?], Moran, Mrs., Montague, -, Anna married Paulo Raymundo Duffey, 29 Nov 1913, Sidney S. Hulbert [?], Hoke, 3

ST. MARY'S CATHOLIC CHURCH
HAGERSTOWN, MARYLAND, BAPTISMS:
Index, Baptism Date, Child, Last Name, Father from,
Mother, Mother from, Birth Date, 1st Sponsor First,
1st Sponsor Last, 2nd Sponsor First, 2nd Sponsor Last,
Location, Notes, Maiden Name, Priest

3884, 24 Apr 1891, Robertum Clifford, Shank, Adam Roberto, Hagerstown, Anna Lee, Hagerstown, 24 Jan 1891, Maria, Lord, -, -, -, -, Rudy, 3

3885, 30 Apr 1891, Mauritium Augustum, Senecal, Augusto, Cleveland, NY, Maria, Gettysburg, 3 Apr 1891, Carrie, Smith "(by proxy)", -, -, -, -, Redding, 3

3886, 3 May 1891, Evam Mariam, Yates, Danieles, Emmitsburg, Lea, -, 19 Mar 1869, Maria, Kreitz, -, -, -, converted to the Catholic faith and baptism was conferred absolutely, Moller [or Miller], 3

3887, 7 May 1891, Phoebem Genevefam, Wolf, Georgio H., Hagerstown, Emlia I. [orJ.], Hagerstown, 7 Oct 1890, Catharina, Rauth, -, -, -, -, Heil, 3

3888, 27 May 1891, Margaritem Louisam, Davis, Gulielmo, Hagerstown, Alice, Hagerstown, 7 Sep 1890, Maria, Davis, -, -, -, -, [blank], 2

3889, 31 May 1891, Odelia Mariam, Clopper, Jacobo A., -, Maria, -, 7 May 1891, Mrs., Kooperstine, -, -, -, -, Kooperstine, 3

3890, 10 May 1891, Paulum, Futterer, Francisco, -, Anna E., -, 24 Apr 1891, Jacob (Mrs.), Futterer, -, -, -, -, Mayhew, 3

3891, 14 Jun 1891, Mauritium Paulum, Dominici, Mauritio, Luica in Italy, Maria, -, 16 May 1891, Paulus, Bonavide [?], Maria, Bonavode [?], -, -, Loterzo, 3

3892, 28 Jun 1891, Annam Reginam, Swink [Shwink in 2nd place], Decatur, -, Anna, -, 10 Apr 1891, Bessie, Malone, -, -, -, -, Hall, 3

3893, 12 Jul 1891, Joannem Murvey, Hennessy, Thoma, Washington County, Catharina, -, 22 Apr 1891, Mrs., Kenney, -, -, -, -, Ripple, 3

3894, 23 Jul 1891, Carolinam Ceciliam, Full, Michaele, -, Anna, -, 27 Jun 1891, C. (Dr.), Boyle, Maria (Mrs.), Boyle [HB], -, -, Price, 3

3895, 28 Jul 1891, Franciscam King [?], Halm, Reinhold, -, Mrs., -, 16 Jul 1891*, Columbus, O'Donnell, Ella, Smith, -, *birthdate is 16[?] Jul 1891; Francisca married Joanni Calvin Hayes Cobb, 11 Nov 1913. Sidney S. Hulbut[?], Beaumont, 3

ST. MARY'S CATHOLIC CHURCH
HAGERSTOWN, MARYLAND, BAPTISMS:
Index, Baptism Date, Child, Last Name, Father from, Mother, Mother from, Birth Date, 1st Sponsor First, 1st Sponsor Last, 2nd Sponsor First, 2nd Sponsor Last, Location, Notes, Maiden Name, Priest

3896, 15 Aug 1891, Gabriellam Ruth, Rouskulp, Henrico W., Hagerstown, Catharina, Hagerstown, 12 Jul 1891, W. (Mrs.), Miller, -, -, -, -, Downin, 3

3897, 15 Aug 1891, Glen Joseph, Hellaine, Joanne, Hagerstown, Julia, Frostburg, 7 Aug 1891, Maria, Cramer, -, -, -, -, Brady, 3

3898, 12 Sep 1891, Lewis Benjamin, Coyle, Thoma, Washington County, Ada, -, 5 Jun 1889, Martha Anna, Lizer, -, -, -, Lewis married Eulalia Rodrigues by Rev. E. O'Flynn, Buena Vista, PA, 14 Aug 1918, Harne, 3

3899, 12 Sep 1891, Bernardum, Feigley, Isaac, -, Emma A., -, 22 Jul 1891, Eva (Mrs.), McCleary, -, -, -, -, Armstrong, 3

3900, 23 Sep 1891, Mariam Josephinam, Brooks [or Brook], Chance [?], -, Emma, -, 16 Aug 1891, Maria, Boyle, -, -, -, -, Bush, 3

3901, 25 Sep 1891, Catharinam Lucindam, Trone, Carolo, Washington County, Jennie, Washington Co., 1 Jul 1891, Susanna, Simmy [?], -, -, -, -, Wolf, 3

3902, 27 Sep 1891, Lilian Joannam, Moore, Thomas, -, Elisabeth, -, 6 Aug 1891, Ulton, Moore, Ida, Moore [HB], -, -, McCrea, 3

3903, 27 Sep 1891, Bernardinam [female], Henneberger, Henrico, -, Emma, -, 8 Sep 1891, Jesse, Cookerly, -, -, -, married to Amos F. Eves 1 Jun 1913, Cookerly, 3

3904, 28 Oct 1891*, Sophiam Joannettam, Sweeney, Joanne B., -, Sophia J., -, 16 Sep 1891, T.B., Cushwa, Sallie (Mrs.), Cushwa, -, *baptismal date is unclear - 28 [8 written over a 9] Oct 1891, Hurley, 3

3905, 8 Nov 1891, Oscar Eduardum, Burger, Adam, -, Willhelmina, -, 18 Oct 1891, Mrs., Montague, -, -, -, Oscar Burger married Elsie Tracey 23 Jun 1936, Philips and James Church, Baltimore, by Rev. Thos. J. Tee[?], Kammarer, 3

3906, 22 Nov 1891, Annam, Rauth, Gulielmo, -, Lucia, -, 19 Oct 1891, Maria (MRs.), Moran, -, -, -, -, Sauer, 3

3907, 8 Dec 1891, Jacobum Fredericum, Hoover, Georgio, -, Elisabeth, -, 28 Nov 1891, Catharina, Happel, -, -, -, -, Hildebrand, 3

ST. MARY'S CATHOLIC CHURCH
HAGERSTOWN, MARYLAND, BAPTISMS:
Index, Baptism Date, Child, Last Name, Father from,
Mother, Mother from, Birth Date, 1st Sponsor First,
1st Sponsor Last, 2nd Sponsor First, 2nd Sponsor Last,
Location, Notes, Maiden Name, Priest

3908, 13 Dec 1891, Irenem M., Switzer, Samuele, -, Maria, -, 29 Nov 1891, Maria, Wolf, -, -, -, -, Lawrence, 3

3909, 27 Dec 1891, Georgium Ludovicum, Codori, Georgio, -, Cornelia, -, 12 Dec 1891, Mrs., Codori, -, -, -, -, Florence, 3

3910, 10 Jan 1892, Thomam Benton, Cushwa, Victoria Monroe, Hagerstown, Susanna, Hagerstown, 3 Jan 1892, T.B., Cushwa, L. (Mrs.), Fechtig, -, -, Fechtig, 3

3911, 15 Jan 1892, Mariam Anastasiam, Dillon, Joanne, -, Maria, -, 5 Jan 1892, Maria, Dillon, -, -, -, -, Happel, 3

3912, 24 Jan 1892, Stellam [or Hellam] Ceciliam, Montague, Joanne, -, Anna C., Hagerstown, 31 Dec 1891, Mrs., Burger, -, -, -, MA, Wethiger [or Welhnzer?], 3

3913, 31 Jan 1892, Carlottam Annam, Kelly, Lewis, Hagerstown, Agnete, -, 6 Jan 1892, Nettie, Conrad, -, -, -, -, Conrad, 3

3914, 7 Mar 1892, Gulielmum Burns, Templeton, Jacobo, -, Beatrice, -, 7 Feb 1892, Maria, Duggan, -, -, Williamsport, -, Dufour, 3

3915, 10 Apr 1892, Ernestum Austin, Martin, Joanne D., -, Maria H., -, 29 Mar 1892, Clarence V., Martin, Sarah A., Dorsey, -, -, Haan, 3

3916, 17 Apr 1892, Joseph Cornelium, Moore, Ulton, Washington County, Ida V., -, 11 Feb 1892, Noah (Mrs.), Lawrence, -, -, -, -, Tidwick, 3

3917, 17 Apr 1892, Susannam Irenem, Carter, Patritio, -, Leteie, Hagerstown, 19 Sep 1891, Jennie (Mrs.), Moore, -, -, -, MA, Landenslager, 3

3918, 22 Apr 1892, Herman Laurentium, Abel, Grandson [?], Potomac City, VA, Maria J. [or I.], -, 31 Mar 1867, Jacobus, Malone, -, -, -, C, Handroson [?], 3

3919, 8 May 1892, David Gulielmum, Moore, Joseph, Washington County, Susanna, Washington Co., 2 Oct 1891, Rosa, McEvoy, -, -, Williamsport, -, Martin, 3

3920, 8 May 1892, Annam Helenam, McCardell, Eugenis, -, Effie, -, 10 Jan 1892, Ella, Oliver, -, -, Williamsport, -, King, 3

3921, 1 May 1892, Joseph Paulus, Clayburn, N.N., -, Anna, -, 17 Dec 1891, Sallie, Clayburn, -, -, -, -, -, 3

ST. MARY'S CATHOLIC CHURCH
HAGERSTOWN, MARYLAND, BAPTISMS:
Index, Baptism Date, Child, Last Name, Father from, Mother, Mother from, Birth Date, 1st Sponsor First, 1st Sponsor Last, 2nd Sponsor First, 2nd Sponsor Last, Location, Notes, Maiden Name, Priest

3922, 8 May 1892, Samuelem Henricum, Wolfe, Hopkin, -, Maria, -, 28 Apr 1892, Joanne, Lawrence, Mrs., Switzer, -, -, Switzer, 3

3923, 14 May 1892, Gulielmum Geary, Porter, Gulielum, Hagerstown, Joanna, -, 14 May 1892, Gulielmum, Geary, Mrs., Geary, -, Marriage Record #1 Pg. 129, Geary, 3

3924, 12 Jun 1892, Annam H. Florentiam, Petticord, Jacobo A., -, Maria E., -, 8 Jun 1892, Eduardus, Petticord, Maria, Alexander, -, Anna married Roberto W. Elliott, 6 Apr 1915, H. Patritii [?] York, PA, Gilland, 3

3925, 21 Jul 1892, Georgium B., Long, Adam A., Williamsport, Catharina, Williamsport, 28 Jan 1892, Jesse, Thompson, -, -, Williamsport, -, Andrew, 3

3926, 24 Jul 1892, Clarence Daniel, Fagan, Joanne, -, Sara, -, 1 Jul 1892, Michael, Weldon, Maria, Donohue, -, married to Bridget Mun[?]tha 16 Sep 1925, St. Patrick's Church, Youngstown, OH, Daley, 3

3927, 4 Aug 1892, Bernardum Robertum, Ball, Bernardo, -, Thalia, -, 1 Mar 1892, Mrs., Ball, -, -, -, married Olys Kesfort [?] at St. Mary's, Hagerstown, Boteler, 3

3928, 28 Aug 1892, Saraim Jennie, Mullen, Carolo, -, Lutie, -, 4 Aug 1892, V. Monroe, Cushwa, David (Mrs.), Cushwa, -, -, Cushwa, 3

3929, 15 Sep 1892, Josiah Dahlgren, Pierce, Josiah [Pierce, Jr.], St. Petersburg, Russia, Ulrica, Washington, DC, 26 Jul 1892, Eric B., Dahlgren, Helena H.[?], Squire [?], -, Endnote 73, Dahlgren, 4

3930, 20 Oct 1892, Benjamin Ernestum, Reed, Gulielmo, -, Maria, -, 11 Sep 1892, Joannes, Donnelly, Anges, Thompson, Williamsport, -, Donnelly, 3

3931, 3 Nov 1892, Carolum Clark, Hughes, Jacobo, -, Margarita, -, 9 Oct 1892, Joannes, Duggan, L. (Mrs.), McCardell, Williamsport, -, Clarke, 3

3932, 20 Nov 1892, Carolum Samuelem, Reamer, Georgio, PA, Gertrude, PA, 15 Nov 1892, Sophia, Martin, -, -, -, -, Martin, 3

3933, 18 Dec 1892, Minnie Catherinam, Burger, Adamo, -, Willelmina, -, 23 Nov 1892, Sarah (Mrs.), Montague, -, -, -,

ST. MARY'S CATHOLIC CHURCH
HAGERSTOWN, MARYLAND, BAPTISMS:
Index, Baptism Date, Child, Last Name, Father from, Mother, Mother from, Birth Date, 1st Sponsor First, 1st Sponsor Last, 2nd Sponsor First, 2nd Sponsor Last, Location, Notes, Maiden Name, Priest

married to Joseph Walter Schindle [?] 2 Apr 1934 by Rev. Terence F. Beehan? Asst. at Corpis Christi Church, Baltimore, Kammarer, 3

3934, 1 Jan 1893, Samuelem Josiah, Banks, Gulielmo, Franklin Co., -, -, 25 Dec 1862, -, -, -, -, -, C, -, 3

3935, 28 Jan 1893, Thoman, Fitzpatrick, Gulielmo A., -, Margarita, -, 10 Jan 1893, Maria, Jordan, -, -, -, -, Jordan, 3

3936, 27 Feb 1893, Genevefam Gertrudem, Alexander, Carolo, -, Carolina, -, 23 Jan 1893, Anna (Mrs.), Cunningham, -, -, -, married Norman Eugenio Clayburn 4 Jul 1914, Sidney S. Hulbut [?], Shilling, 3

3937, 12 Mar 1893, Owen Lewis, Abell, Herman L., -, Maria Agnes, -, 28 Jan 1893, Maria, McDevitt, -, -, -, -, Lawrence, 3

3938, 4 Apr 1893, Alicem Catharinam, Shank, Roberto, -, Anna L., -, Jun 1892, Maria, Shank, -, -, -, -, Rudy, 3

3939, 17 Apr 1893, Jacob Franciscum, Rauth, Gulielmo, -, Lucia, -, 8 Jan 1893, Anna (Mrs.), Battle, -, -, -, -, Sauer, 3

3940, 23 Apr 1893, Joseph Ernestum, Kreitz, Conrado, -, Maria, -, 13 Apr 1893, Joseph, Lingg, Catharina, Lingg, -, -, Moran, 3

3941, 11 May 1893, Riccardum Hurley, Sweeney, Joanne B., -, Nettie, -, 3 Apr 1893, Gulielmo J., Wills, Geneviefe, McLaughlin "(by proxy)", -, -, Hurley, 3

3942, 28 May 1893, Margaritam Rebeccam, Lechlider, Francisco A., -, Maria C., -, 28 Apr 1893, Catharina, McLaughlin, -, -, -, -, Mayberry, 3

3943, 21 May 1893, Albertum Lawrence, Moore, Ulton, -, Ida, -, 23 Apr 1893, Noah (Mrs.), Lawrence, -, -, -, -, Tidwick, 3

3944, 21 May 1893, Annam, Fenwick, Jacobo, -, Catharina, -, 12 May 1893, Emma, Marlow, -, -, -, -, Clarke, 3

3945, 25 Jun 1893, Mariam Josephinam, Moore, Edwardo, -, Elisabeth, -, 6 Jun 1893, Mrs., Hippner, -, -, -, -, Hippner, 3

3946, 6 Aug 1893, Raimundum Jeremiam, Hennessey, Thoma, Tilghmanton, Catharina, Tilghmanton, 28 Apr 1893, Lula, Fechtig, -, -, -, MA, Ripple, 3

3947, 26 Aug 1893, Joannem Alphonsum, Switzer [mother's name] [father is only listed as "N.N."], N., -, Anna,

ST. MARY'S CATHOLIC CHURCH
HAGERSTOWN, MARYLAND, BAPTISMS:
Index, Baptism Date, Child, Last Name, Father from, Mother, Mother from, Birth Date, 1st Sponsor First, 1st Sponsor Last, 2nd Sponsor First, 2nd Sponsor Last, Location, Notes, Maiden Name, Priest

Hagerstown, 28 Jan 1892, Florence (Mrs.), Lawrence, -, -, -, PN; CS; PB; BP, Switzer, 3
3948, 27 Aug 1893, Bertam Mariam, Pearl, Cornelio, -, Catharine, -, 8 Aug 1893, Patritius, O'Conner "(by proxy)", Birgitta, O'Conner "(by proxy)", -, -, O'Conner, 3
3949, 3 Sep 1893, Mariam Vincentiam, Futterer, Jacob, -, Nellie, -, 3 Aug 1893, Gulielmum, Geary, Maria, Barry, -, married Charles F. Gerry[?], 3 Jan 1932, At. Matthew's Church, Washington, DC, by Rev. Ed. Roach, Nelligan, 3
3950, 3 Sep 1893, Georgium, Rodney, David, Hagerstown, Catharina, -, 1 Nov 1892, -, -, -, -, -, C, [blank], 3
3951, 10 Sep 1893, Catharinam Hazel, Thompson, Leone, Williamsport, Catharini Agnes, Williamsport, 1 Jul 1893, Ella, Oliver, -, -, -, married Robert D. Keller 26 Jul 1957 at St. Mary's, Hagerstown, Collins, 3
3952, 24 Sep 1893, Mariam Sheridan Army[?], Craig, Gulielmo, -, Jennie, -, Dec, Jennie, Bailey, -, -, -, convert; BC; B, [blank], 3
3953, 29 Sep 1893, Clyde Franciscum, Fiegley, Isaac, -, Emma, -, 21 Aug 1893, Maria, Smith, -, -, -, -, Armstrong, 3
3954, 22 Nov 1893, Pearl Anastasiam, Shueler, Carolo F., -, Maria, -, 8 Oct 1893, Jacob, Futterer, Helen, Futterer [HB], -, -, Ewery, 3
3955, 26 Nov 1893, Paulum, Senecal, Augusto, -, Maria, PA, 3 Oct 1893, Maria, Dominici, -, -, -, -, Redding, 3
3956, 27 Nov 1893, Paulum Lesley, March, Jacobo, -, Lillie, -, 6 Jun 1893, Nettie, Miller, -, -, -, -, McCardell, 3
3957, 17 Sep 1893, Nora Elisabeth, Moore, Daniele A., -, Anna E., -, 27 Jul 1893, Florence (Mrs.), Lawrence, -, -, -, -, Rice, 3
3958, 1 Jan 1894, Maud Mariam, Barry, Jacobo Taylor, Washington, DC, Sarah H., -, 23 May 1876, -, -, -, -, -, C, [blank], 3
3959, 21 Jan 1894, Mary Louise, Cushwa, Victore Monroe, Hagerstown, Susanna, Hagerstown, 12 Jan 1894, Edward, Fechtig, Sallie, Kreigh, -, -, Fechtig, 3
3960, 2 Jan 1894, Evam Mariam, McCardell, Jacobo, -, Helena, -, Dec 1893, Mrs., Full, -, -, -, -, Zook, 3

ST. MARY'S CATHOLIC CHURCH
HAGERSTOWN, MARYLAND, BAPTISMS:
Index, Baptism Date, Child, Last Name, Father from, Mother, Mother from, Birth Date, 1st Sponsor First, 1st Sponsor Last, 2nd Sponsor First, 2nd Sponsor Last, Location, Notes, Maiden Name, Priest

3961, 7 Jan 1894, Francescam, Futterer, Francesco, -, Anna, -, 12 Nov 1893, Jacoba, Futterer, Susanna (Mrs.), Ewer, -, -, Mayhugh, 3

3962, 4 Feb 1894, Mariam Willhelminam, Montague, Oscar, -, Anna C., -, 14 Jan 1894, Margarita, Faller, -, -, -, MA, Wellinger, 3

3963, 11 Mar 1894, Joannem Thomam [male], Barry, Thoma, Williamsport, Maud Maria, Washington, DC, 24 Feb 1894, David, Cushwa, Margarita (Mrs.), O'Neill, Williamsport, -, Taylor, 3

3964, 24 Mar 1894, Gulielmum M., Cearfoss, Simone, Washington County, Margt., -, 21 Dec 1869, -, -, -, -, -, C, McGirey [?], 3

3965, 12 Apr 1894, Henricum Leonem, Moore, Joseph, -, Susanna, -, 21 Sep 1893, Helena, Duggan, -, -, Williamsport, -, Martin, 3

3966, 13 May 1894, Gulielmum Alonzo, Moatz, Georgio, -, Anna, -, 2 May 1894, Joannes, Lawrence, Sarai C., Lawrence, -, -, Switzer, 3

3967, 20 May 1894, Joannem Jacobum, Fagan, Joanne, -, Sarai, -, 24 Apr 1894, Maria, Welsh, -, -, -, married at St. Peter & Paul Byzantine Slavonic Rite, Struthers, OH, 9 Jul 1960 to Catherine Solar by Rev. Geo. Petro, Daley, 3

3968, 21 May 1894, Gulielmum J., Rouscoulp [Rouskoulp in 2nd place], Henrico, -, Catharina, -, May 1894, -, -, -, -, -, PB; BP; baby died the next day, Downin, 3

3969, 10 Jun 1894, Eduardum Hurley, Sweeney, Joanne B., -, Nettie, -, 19 May 1894, Georgio [?], Fechtig, Cecilia, McLaughlin, -, -, Hurley, 3

3970, 8 Jun 1894, Joannem H., Cotter, Patritio, -, Lutie, -, 13 May 1894, Lucia, Moore, -, -, -, PB; BP, Laudenslager, 3

3971, 25 Jun 1894, Joannem Burton, Firey, Joseph H., Hagerstown, -, -, 26 Jul 1868, John B., Sweeney, -, -, -, C, -, 3

3972, 26 Jun 1894, Georgium Albertum, Rauth, Gulielmo, -, -, -, 31 May 1894, Iva [?] (Mrs.), Moran, -, -, -, -, -, 3

3973, 26 Jun 1894, Carroll Martinum, Rauth, Gulielmo, -, Lucy [?], -, 31 May 1894, Mrs., Kreitz, -, -, -, -, Sauer, 3

ST. MARY'S CATHOLIC CHURCH
HAGERSTOWN, MARYLAND, BAPTISMS:
Index, Baptism Date, Child, Last Name, Father from, Mother, Mother from, Birth Date, 1st Sponsor First, 1st Sponsor Last, 2nd Sponsor First, 2nd Sponsor Last, Location, Notes, Maiden Name, Priest

3974, 17 Jun 1894, Mariam Catharinam, Rauth, Carolo, Hagerstown, Catharina, Hagerstown, 19 May 1894, Anne (Mrs.), Hebb, -, -, -, married at Hagerstown, 8 Jan 1930, Marriage Record p. 24, Heil, 3

3975, 29 Jul 1894, Ceciliam Liguori [?], Dillon, Joanne, -, Maria, -, 22 Jul 1894, Catharine, Happel [?], -, -, -, -, Happel [?], 3

3976, 7 Aug 1894, Albertum Harricum, Gunnell, Joanne, -, -, -, 12 Feb 1864, John B., Sweeney, -, -, -, C; AB, -, 3

3977, 12 Aug 1894, Joseph Howard, Abell, Eugenio [?], -, Agnete, -, 1 Jun 1894, Mrs., Montague, -, -, -, -, Lawrence, 3

3978, 12 Aug 1894, Margaritam Virginiam, Lingg, Joseph, Emmitsburg, Catharina, Emmitsburg, 1 Aug 1894, David, Martin, Mary (Mrs.), Martin, -, -, Bentz, 3

3979, 7 Oct 1894, Vera Margaritam, Swink [Shwink in 2nd place], Decatur, -, Anna Daley, PA, 7 Aug 1894, Edelia (Mrs.), Hall, -, -, -, -, Hall [or Daly is last name and Hall is ???], 3

3980, 21 Oct 1894, Sebastium Grant, Moore, Upton, -, Ida Virginia, -, 19 Sep 1894, Noah (Mrs.), Lawrence, -, -, -, -, Tidwick, 3

3981, 23 Dec 1894, Franciscum E., Shafer, Joanne, -, Maria, -, 14 Sep 1894, Helen, Battle, -, -, -, -, Wolf, 3

3982, 13 Jan 1895, Georgium Victorem, Cushwa, Victore Monroe, Hagerstown, Susanna, Hagerstown, 8 Jan 1895, Franciscus, Kreigh, Sallie, Cushwa, -, -, Fechtig, 3

3983, 13 Jan 1895, Franciscum Percival, Harbin, Jacobo T., Washington, DC, Jennie, Washington, Dc, 3 Jan 1895, Nathaniel J., Wilson, Catharina B., Holden, -, married to Corine [?] M. Lottersp [?], 20 Oct 1920, St. Patrick's, Washington, DC, Mitchell, 3

3984, 19 Jan 1895, Ada Maria L., Pile [or Pith or Pic] [father's name is Shorts], Henrico, Mercersburg, -, -, 18 Dec 1869, Mrs., Battle, -, -, -, C; BC; wife of Francisci Pile [or Pith or Pic], -, 3

3985, 27 Jan 1895, Catharinam, Fitzpatrick, Gulielmo, -, Margarita, -, 17 Jan 1895, Georgius, Alexander, Virginia, Alexander, -, -, Jordan, 3

ST. MARY'S CATHOLIC CHURCH
HAGERSTOWN, MARYLAND, BAPTISMS:
Index, Baptism Date, Child, Last Name, Father from, Mother, Mother from, Birth Date, 1st Sponsor First, 1st Sponsor Last, 2nd Sponsor First, 2nd Sponsor Last, Location, Notes, Maiden Name, Priest

3986, 27 Jan 1895, Nettie Frances, Codori, Francisco, -, Emma, -, 23 Jan 1895, Susanna (Mrs.), Codori, -, -, -, -, Smith [?], 3

3987, 24 Feb 1895, Mariam Margaritam, Quinn, Jacobo, -, Anna, -, 10 Dec 1894, Milton, Ewer, Milton (Mrs.), Ewer [HB], -, -, Herman, 3

3988, 3 Mar 1895, Susannam Otheliam, Futterer, Francisco, -, Anna E., -, 19 Jan 1895, Jacob, Futterer, Mrs., Battle, -, -, Mayhew, 3

3989, 19 Mar 1895, Riccardum Liton [?], Wroe, Ricardo E., -, Anna, -, 10 Oct 1887, Mrs., Kreitz, -, -, -, CS, Fessler, 3

3990, 19 Mar 1895, Ninam Eulaliam, Wroe, Ricardo, -, Anna, -, 16 Dec 1883, Daisie, Wroe, -, -, -, -, Fessler, 3

3991, 19 Mar 1895, Violettam Franciscam, -, -, -, -, -, 22 Jul 1891, Mrs., Kreitz, -, -, -, appears to read "risdem parentibus at supra", -, 3

3992, 7 Apr 1895, Mariam Reginam, Dillon, Augusto, -, Edith, -, 26 Mar 1895, Maria, Dillon, -, -, -, MA, Bennett, 3

3993, 14 Apr 1895, Frederick Alponsum, Burger, Adam, -, Minnie, -, 26 Mar 1895, Mrs., Kreitz, -, -, -, Marriage Record #1 Pg 128, Kammarer, 3

3994, 21 Arp 1895, Josephinam C., Cullen, M. Emmett, -, Eva, -, 18 hours, Jacobus, Hughes, Fannie, Thomson, Williamsport, -, Cushwa, 3

3995, 1 May 1895, Gulielmum Herman, Lorshbaugh, Jacobo, -, Dora, -, 26 Apr 1895, Gulielmus, Spalding, Maria (Mrs.), Smith, -, FA, Spalding, 3

3996, 5 May 1895, Nellie Rosalie, Mullen, Carolo, -, Lutie, -, 22 Apr 1895, Eduardus, Fechtig, Nellie, Grimm, -, -, Cushwa, 3

3997, 19 May 1895, Gratiam Catharinam, Wall, Michaele, Salem, Mass., Berta, Salem, MA, 15 May 1895, Joannes, Lawrence, Mrs., Quinn, -, -, Dempsey, 3

3998, 26 May 1895, Mariam Josephinam, Wire, Jacob, Adams Co., PA, Sarai, -, 30 Apr 1895, Mary (Mrs.), Smith, -, -, -, -, Eckenrode, 3

3999, 14 Jun 1895, Helenam Josephinam, Hebb, Ricardo J., -, Anna, -, 22 May 1895, Catharina, Rauth, -, -, -, FA, Heil, 3

ST. MARY'S CATHOLIC CHURCH
HAGERSTOWN, MARYLAND, BAPTISMS:
Index, Baptism Date, Child, Last Name, Father from, Mother, Mother from, Birth Date, 1st Sponsor First, 1st Sponsor Last, 2nd Sponsor First, 2nd Sponsor Last, Location, Notes, Maiden Name, Priest

4000, 25 Jun 1895, Mariam Catharinam Wise, White, Joseph, Frederick, MD, Rebecca, -, 1 Feb 1872, -, -, -, -, -, C, Markin [?], 3

4001, 5 Jul 1895, Edwardum F., Feigley, Isaac, -, Emma, -, 28 May 1895, Mary (Mrs.), Smith, -, -, -, -, Armstrong, 3

4002, 7 Jul 1895, Thomam Ricardum, Moore, Edwardo, -, Elsiabeth, -, 24 Jun 1895, Elisabeth, Shlotterbeck, -, -, -, -, Hippner, 3

4003, 13 Jul 1895, Ella Elisabeth, Coxon, Gulielmo, -, Jennie, -, 3 Jul 1895, Mary (Mrs.), Smith, -, -, -, MA; FA, Houp, 3

4004, 14 Jul 1895, Franciscum, Taylor, Francesco, Williamsport, Jesse, Williamsport, 11 Jun 1895, Catherine (Mrs.), Falkenstein, -, -, Williamsport, -, Thompson, 3

4005, 14 Jul 1895, Jacobum Stewart, Fenwick, Jacobo, Montgomery Co., MD, Catharina, Montgomery Co., MD, 30 Jun 1895, Rosa, Clarke, -, -, -, -, Clarke, 3

4006, 28 Jul 1895, Catharinam Louise, Rouskulp, Henrico W., -, Catharina, -, 6 Jun 1895, Maria, "Orndorf (Downin)" [perhaps Downin is her maiden name?], -, -, -, -, Downin, 3

4007, 1 Sep 1895, Mariam Josephinam, Moats [or Moatz], Georgio, -, Anna, -, 16 Aug 1895, Mrs., Switzer, -, -, -, -, Switzer, 3

4008, 8 Sep 1895, Gulielmum Ernestum, McCardell, R. Eugeneo, -, Effie [?] R. [?], -, 16 Aug 1895, Margarita (Mrs.), O'Neill, -, -, Williamsport, -, King, 3

4009, 10 Sep 1895, Carolum Jacob, Poper, Carolo, -, Maria, Illinois, 24 Aug 1892, Maria, Smith, -, -, -, -, O'Toole, 3

4010, 10 Sep 1895, Byron Henricum, Poper, Carolo J., -, Maria, -, 15 Jun 1894, Maria, Smith, -, -, -, -, O'Toole, 3

4011, 29 Sep 1895, Franciscum M., Lechliter, Francisco A., -, Maria, -, 1 Sep 1895, Mrs., Nierman, -, -, -, -, Mayberry, 3

4012, 6 Oct 1895, Mariam Elisabeth, Lizer, Joseph, -, Susanna R., -, 5 Aug 1895, Maria E. (Mrs.), Dietrich, -, -, -, -, Bemsdarfe [?], 3

4013, 6 Oct 1895, Lillie Magdalenam, March, Jacobo, -, Lillie, -, 20 Sep 1895, Mrs., Mobley, -, -, -, -, McCardell, 3

ST. MARY'S CATHOLIC CHURCH HAGERSTOWN, MARYLAND, BAPTISMS:
Index, Baptism Date, Child, Last Name, Father from, Mother, Mother from, Birth Date, 1st Sponsor First, 1st Sponsor Last, 2nd Sponsor First, 2nd Sponsor Last, Location, Notes, Maiden Name, Priest

4014, 1 Nov 1895, Ludovicum Augustinum, Martin, David, -, Henrietta, -, 29 Oct 1895, Clarence, Marton, Maria, Martin, -, -, Hann, 3

4015, 17 Nov 1895, Phoebe Laurentinam, Shueler, Carolo F., -, Maria, -, 9 Oct 1895, Jacob, Futterer, Helen, Futterer [HB], -, -, Ewers, 3

4016, 25 Dec 1895, Edgar Aloysium, Kreitz, Conrad, -, Maria, -, 11 Dec 1895, Francisus [?], Kreitz, Sarah (Mrs.), Montague, -, See Marriage Register #1 Page 150, Moran, 3

4017, 17 Jan 1896, Jesse Paulinam, Wise, Walter S., -, Elisabeth, Hagerstown, 5 Nov 1895, Sallie, Cushwa, -, -, -, -, Smith, 3

4018, 18 Jan 1896, Annam Ruth, Trone, Carolo, -, Jennie, -, 30 Jul 1895, Susanna, Simms [?], -, -, -, -, Wolf, 3

4019, 19 Jan 1896, Liza Jane, Tedrick, Jacob, Washington County, Anna, -, 15 Jan 1871, Mrs., Dolan, -, -, -, C, Tice, 3

4020, 4 Feb 1896, Carolum Gulielmum, Douglas, Carolo, -, Maria, -, 6 Oct 1895, Dm [?] (Mrs.), Boyle, -, -, -, Baptized privately at home, Foley, 3

4021, 10 Mar 1896, Joseph, McCardell, Jacobo, -, Helena, -, 21 Dec 1895, -, -, -, -, -, Baptized privately at home, Zook, 3

4022, 23 Feb 1896, Margaritam Josephinam, Moore, Ulton, -, Ida V., -, 23 Dec 1895, Josephine (Mrs.), Dolan, -, -, -, -, Tidwik, 3

4023, 15 Mar 1896, Franciscum Augustinum, Rauth, Gulielmo, -, Lucia, -, 21 Feb 1896, Mary (Mrs.), Smith, -, -, -, -, Sauer [or Sawer], 3

4024, 22 Mar 1896, Samuelem Edwardum, Basore, Georgio, -, Lucia, -, 17 Aug 1895, Catherina, Moore, -, -, -, CS; PB, Moore, 3

4025, 25 Mar 1896, Christi Annam, Cushwa, Davide K., -, Nanie, Williamsport, 23 Feb 1896, Michael E., Cullen, Eva, Cullen, Williamsport, See Marriage Record #1 Pg 144., Taylor, 3

4026, 31 Mar 1896, Hermann Russell, Elam, Carolo, -, Gertrude, -, 24 Mar 1896, Sallie (Mrs.), Smith, -, -, -, -, Riley, 3

ST. MARY'S CATHOLIC CHURCH
HAGERSTOWN, MARYLAND, BAPTISMS:
Index, Baptism Date, Child, Last Name, Father from, Mother, Mother from, Birth Date, 1st Sponsor First, 1st Sponsor Last, 2nd Sponsor First, 2nd Sponsor Last, Location, Notes, Maiden Name, Priest

4027, 8 Apr 1896, Mariam, Thompson, Leone, Williamsport, -, -, 24 Mar 1896, Ella, Oliver, -, -, Williamsport, -, -, 3

4028, 26 Apr 1896, Mariam, Liddy, Jeremiah, Ireland, Helena D.[?], Ireland, 5 Apr 1896, Conradus, Kreitz, Maria, Kreitz [HB], -, -, Parks, 3

4029, 22 Jun 1896, Ulricum Vinton Dalgreen, Pierce, Josiah, -, Ulrica, -, 18 Apr 1896, John V., Dalgreen, Romadne [?] V., Overbeck, South Mountain, -, Dalgreen, 4

4030, 14 Jun 1896, Louisam, Ramaciotti, Domenico, Italy, Ausilia [?], Italy, 22 Mar 1896, Andrea, Lazzari, note by priest written after name of Andrea Lazzari appears to read "umr. Dominci", -, -, -, Layzari [?], 3

4031, [no date], Carolem Eugenium [?], Porter, Gulielmo, -, Joanna, -, 5 Jun 1896, Thomas, Geary, Margareta, Geary, -, -, Geary, 3

4032, 23 Jun 1896, Josia Ray, Mitchell, Carlton E., Washington County, Maria Eliz., Washington Co., 9 Nov 1895, Magdalena V., Dahlgren, -, -, South Mountain, MA; FA, Zittle, 4

4033, 28 Jun 1896, Thomam Andream, Vartz [or Vantz], Jacob P., -, Berta C., -, 1 Jun 1896, Isabaella (Mrs.), Moore, -, -, -, -, Oak, 3

4034, 19 Jul 1896, Elisabeth, Noel, Jacobo H., Scranton, PA, Anna L., -, 11 Jul 1896, Thomas, Delaney, James (Mrs.), Moran, -, -, Delaney, 3

4035, 26 Jul 1896, Marion Catherinam, Firey, Joanne B., -, Susanna, -, 15 Jul 1896, Catharina, Happel [?], -, -, -, -, Happel [?], 3

4036, 17 Aug 1896, Elisabeth, Moore, Joseph, -, Susanna, -, 21 Jun 1896, Mary (Mrs.), Smith, -, -, -, -, Martin, 3

4037, 23 Aug 1896, Franciscum, Kershner, Jos., -, Helena, -, 31 Jul 1896, Mrs., Kreitzs, -, -, -, DMR; married 27 Feb 1924 to Pearl Ward of Hagerstown By Geo. B. Harrington, Hoover, 3

4038, 13 Sep 1896, Emmam Theresiam, Miller, Carolo, -, Sarai, -, 26 Jul 1896, Mrs., Kershner, -, -, Williamsport, -, Smith, 3

ST. MARY'S CATHOLIC CHURCH
HAGERSTOWN, MARYLAND, BAPTISMS:
Index, Baptism Date, Child, Last Name, Father from,
Mother, Mother from, Birth Date, 1st Sponsor First,
1st Sponsor Last, 2nd Sponsor First, 2nd Sponsor Last,
Location, Notes, Maiden Name, Priest

4039, 27 Sep 1896, Gulielmum Joseph, Duffy, Otho, -, Maria, -, 18 Sep 1896, W. (Mr.), Duffy, Eliza (Mrs.), Duffy, -, -, Cramer, 3

4040, 4 Oct 1896, Mariam Louisam, Dillon, Joanne, -, Maria, -, 28 Sep 1896, Sallie (Mrs.), Cushwa, -, -, -, -, Happel, 3

4041, 11 Oct 1896, Neormam Esther, Cearfoss, Gulielmo, -, Rosa, -, 17 Oct 1895, Josephina (Mrs.), Dolan, -, -, -, -, Hull, 3

4042, 20 Nov 1896, Helenam, Trainor [father's surname is blank], Jacobo, Frederick Co., Maria Elisab., -, 31 Aug 1861, Elisabeth, Shacy [or Shaey], -, -, -, AB; C, McDaniel, 3

4043, 26 Oct 1896, Mariam G., Kershner, Carolo, -, Catharina, -, 23 Oct 1895, Sarah (Mrs.), Kershner, -, -, -, -, James, 3

4044, 12 Nov 1896, Edward Sharp, Conley, John, -, Anne, -, 10 Oct 1896, Bertha, Hoy, -, -, -, -, McHoy, 3

4045, 11 Dec 1896, Franciscum Bennett, Dillon, Augusto, -, Edith, -, 2 Dec 1896, Joannes, Dillon, Mrs., Bennett, -, married Anna Starner, St. Andrew's Church, Waynesboro, 22 Oct 1919, Bennett, 3

4046, 20 Dec 1896, Carolum Jacob, Poper, Jacob, Franklin Co., Margareta, -, 19 Aug 1862, -, -, -, -, AB; C, Leach, 3

4047, 20 Dec 1896, Gulielmum Henricum, Switzer, Samuele, -, Mary, -, 12 Dec 1896, Joanne, Helaine, Julia, Helaine [HB], -, -, Lawrence, 3

4048, 25 Dec 1896, Mariam Ruth, Lingg, Joseph, -, Catharina, -, 16 Dec 1896, Clarence, Martin, Maria, Bently, -, -, Bently, 3

4049, 27 Dec 1896, Ceciliam Bernardinam, Burger, Adam, -, Minnie, -, 26 Nov 1896, Lizzie, Shlotterbeck, -, -, -, -, Kammarer, 3

4050, 3 Jan 1897, Mariam Violam, Young, Benjamon F., Hagerstown, M. Isabella, -, 21 Dec 1896, Joanne, Lawrence, Sarai, Lawrence [HB], -, FA, Switzer, 3

4051, 14 Feb 1897, Emmam G., Codori [father's name is Smith], Eduardo, Gettysburg, -, -, -, Mrs., Codori, Sr., -, -, -, BC; C, -, 3

4052, 16 Feb 1897, Catharinam Vincentiam, Geary, Gulielmo, Hagerstown, Maria J., Hagerstown, 27 Jan 1897, Hanora, Geary, -, -, -, MA, Seachrist, 3

ST. MARY'S CATHOLIC CHURCH
HAGERSTOWN, MARYLAND, BAPTISMS:
Index, Baptism Date, Child, Last Name, Father from,
Mother, Mother from, Birth Date, 1st Sponsor First,
1st Sponsor Last, 2nd Sponsor First, 2nd Sponsor Last,
Location, Notes, Maiden Name, Priest

4053, 27 Feb 1897, Emmam Maud, Arther [father's name is Weiser], Samuel H., Cumberland Co., PA, Rachele, -, 4 Jan 1878, Susan (Mrs.), Codori, -, -, -, BC; C, [blank], 3
4054, 14 Mar 1897, Guliemum Aloysorem, Hennessey, Jeremia, -, Elisa J., -, 6 Feb 1897, Mrs., Dolan, -, -, -, -, Tidrich, 3
4055, 21 Mar 1897, Joannem Irwin, Basore, Samuele, -, Lucia, -, 20 Mar 1897, Mrs., Moore, -, -, -, -, Moore, 3
4056, 28 Mar 1897, Adelinam Elisabeth, Moats, Georgio, -, Anna, -, 14 Feb 1897, Joannes, Lawrence, Joannes (Mrs.), Lawrence [HB], -, -, Switzer, 3
4057, 10 May 1897, Carlottam, Thompson, Henrico, Franklin Co., -, -, 1844, Mrs., Malone, -, -, -, -, C; BC, -, 3
4058, 12 May 1897, Samuelem, Basore, Georgio, Washington County, -, -, 12 Oct 1871, -, -, -, -, -, C; AB, -, 3
4059, 12 May 1897, Joseph C., Jones, Joanne, Allegany Co., Arah, -, 21 Jun 1874, John (Mrs.), Moore, -, -, -, C; AB; married Flora J. Firy [?], she a non-Catholic, 27 Dec 1908, Cumberland, MD, [blank], 3
4060, 23 May 1897, Herbert Aloysium, Henneberger, Henrico, -, Emma, -, 9 May 1897, Hella, Keller, -, -, -, -, Coskerly [?], 3
4061, 2 Jun 1897, Helenam Emiliam, Munsen, Ellsworth, Hagerstown, Maria, -, 21 Jan 1896, D. (Mrs.), Jones, -, -, -, married Tudor Davies, 12 Dec 1913, Hagerstown, Sheehan, 3
4062, 5 Jun 1897, Franciscam Magdalenam, Sigler, Henrico A., Smithsburg, Protasia, Smithsburg, 29 Nov 1896, Maria, Shank, -, -, -, -, Lord, 3
4063, 6 Jun 1897, Thomam Eduardum, Fagan, Joanne, -, Sarai, -, 5 May 1897, Daniel, Fagan, Maria, Davis, -, -, Daly, 3
4064, 13 Jun 1897, Franciscum Eugenium, McCardell, Ernesto F., Williamsport, Vertie [?], -, 14 Apr 1897, Eda, Olvier, -, -, Williamsport, -, Brown, 3
4065, 17 Jun 1897, Clarence Gulielmum, Kershner, Clemente, Falling Waters, WV, Emma, Falling Waters, WV, 13 Sep 1896, Mrs., Kershner, Sr., -, -, Williamsport, -, Trout, 3

ST. MARY'S CATHOLIC CHURCH
HAGERSTOWN, MARYLAND, BAPTISMS:
Index, Baptism Date, Child, Last Name, Father from, Mother, Mother from, Birth Date, 1st Sponsor First, 1st Sponsor Last, 2nd Sponsor First, 2nd Sponsor Last, Location, Notes, Maiden Name, Priest

4066, 27 Jun 1897, Mariam Catharinam, Bredley, Georgio S., Hagerstown, Bertha E., -, 1 Jun 1897, Mary (Mrs.), Wolf "(Switzer)", -, -, -, -, Moser, 3

4067, 18 Jul 1897, Juliam Geneviefam, Harrison, Emmert, -, Clara, -, 30 Jan 1896, Jennie, Bailey, -, -, -, parents are Black, Carey, 3

4068, 15 Aug 1897, Catharinam Margaretam, Chricton [also written Krichton], Gulielmo A., -, Maria, -, 9 Aug 1897, Franciscus, Codori, Franciscus (Mrs.), Codori, -, notation reads: "The name 'Chricton' is spelled 'Krichton'"., Grady, 3

4069, 20 Aug 1897, Carolum Augustinum, Feighley, Isaac, -, Emma, -, 22 Jul 11897, Mary (Mrs.), Smith, -, -, -, -, Armstrong, 3

4070, 15 Sep 1897, David Kreigh, Cushwa, David, Williamsport, Nannie, Williamsport, 24 Aug 1897, Victor, Cushwa, Maria, Cushwa [HB], Williamsport, See Marriage Record #1 Pg. 155., Taylor, 3

4071, 15 Sep 1897, Beatricem, Taylor, Francisco, Williamsport, Jesse, Williamsport, 29 Jul 1897, Fannie (Mrs.), Thomson, -, -, Williamsport, -, Thompson, 3

4072, 3 Oct 1897, Joseph Constanticum, Cushwa, V. Monroe, -, Susanna, -, 29 Sep 1897, Fredericus, Fechtig, Nellie, Fechtig, -, Endnote 74, Fechtig, 3

4073, 3 Oct 1897, Juliam Catharinam, Cushwa, V. Monroe, -, Susanna, -, 29 Sep 1897, Fred., Fechtig, Nellie, Fechtig [HB], -, -, Fechtig, 3

4074, 3 Oct 1897, Mariam Helenam, Carter, Patritio, -, Lutie, -, 6 Aug 1896, Mrs., Lloyd, -, -, -, -, Laudenslager, 3

4075, 22 Oct 1897, Margaritam Helenam, Lorshbaugh, Carolo, -, Maria V., -, 9 Oct 1897, -, -, -, -, -, BP; PB, Gates, 3

4076, 14 Nov 1897, Mariam Virginiam, Cushwa, Francisco, Williamsport, Gertrude, Washington, DC, 25 Oct 1897, Frederico, Cushwa, Francisca, Cushwa, -, -, Spohn, 3

4077, 14 Nov 1897, Jacobum Riorden, McCardell, Jacobo Percy, Williamsport, Anna M., Williamsport, 12 Oct 1897, Catharina, Falkerstein, -, -, -, -, Collins, 3

ST. MARY'S CATHOLIC CHURCH
HAGERSTOWN, MARYLAND, BAPTISMS:
Index, Baptism Date, Child, Last Name, Father from, Mother, Mother from, Birth Date, 1st Sponsor First, 1st Sponsor Last, 2nd Sponsor First, 2nd Sponsor Last, Location, Notes, Maiden Name, Priest

4078, 28 Nov 1897, Mariam Vincentiam, Shueler, Carolo F., -, Maria, -, 3 Oct 1897, Ella J. (Mrs.), Futterer, -, -, -, -, Ewers, 3

4079, 2 Jan 1898, Lulam May Catharinam, Nierman, Augusto, -, Daisy, -, 29 Sep 1897, Rosa, Nierman, -, -, -, -, Fry, 3

4080, 4 Jan 1898, Jacob Joseph, Winch, Jacob Jos., Washington, DC, -, -, 24 Apr 1870, -, -, -, -, -, BC; C, -, 3

4081, 16 Jan 1898, Henricum Felicem, Ertter, Joanne Eduardo, Adams Co., Maud Emma, Cumberland Co., PA, 27 Dec 1897, David (Mrs.), Martin, -, -, -, -, Weiser, 3

4082, 19 Jan 1898, Mariam, Fitzpatrick, Gulielmo, -, Margarita, -, 16 Jan 1898, Mrs., Tracy "(by proxy)", Mrs., Moore, -, ceremonies supplied 12 Jun; BP; PB, Jordan, 3

4083, 18 Feb 1898, Alphonsum F., Hetzer, Carolo H., -, Anna J., -, 27 Jul 1888, Joseph, Moore, -, -, Williamsport, -, Moore, 3

4084, 18 Feb 1898, Cleofas M [male], -, -, -, -, -, 1 Nov 1890, Jos., Moore, -, -, Williamsport, appears to read "iisdem parentibus, ist supra", -, 3

4085, 6 Mar 1898, Jacobum Willson, Lyddy, Jeremiah, -, Helenard [or Helen D.], -, 16 Feb 1898, Henricus, Willson, Ella, McCann, -, Endnote 75, Parks, 3

4086, 15 Mar 1898, Norman Rollin, McCardell, Eugenio, -, Effie, -, 31 Jan 1898, Catharina, Falkenstine, -, -, Williamsport, Endnote 76, King, 3

4087, 15 Mar 1898, Samuel Calvin [or Joseph], Dickerhoff, Samuele, -, Emma, -, 14 Nov 1894, Rosa, McEvoy, -, -, Williamsport, Endnote 77, Reichter, 3

4088, 20 Mar 1898, Jacobum R., Nowell, -, -, -, -, 13 Sep 1844, -, -, -, -, -, C, -, 3

4089, 20 Mar 1898, Mariettam, Gallagher, Eduardo F., Hagerstown, Maria, Hagerstown, 18 Feb 1898, Elisabeth, Full, -, -, -, -, Full, 3

4090, 20 Mar 1898, Augustum Leonem, Senecal, Augusto, -, Maria, -, 23 Feb 1898, Joannes, Reading, Susanna, Reading, -, -, Reading, 3

4091, 5 May 1898, Helenam Geneviefam, Dugan, Joanne Monahan, Williamsport, Helena S., Williamsport, 19 Ajpr

ST. MARY'S CATHOLIC CHURCH
HAGERSTOWN, MARYLAND, BAPTISMS:
Index, Baptism Date, Child, Last Name, Father from,
Mother, Mother from, Birth Date, 1st Sponsor First,
1st Sponsor Last, 2nd Sponsor First, 2nd Sponsor Last,
Location, Notes, Maiden Name, Priest

1898, David V., Cushwa, Helena, Dugan, Williamsport, -, Cushwa, 3

4092, 26 May 1898, Elisabeth May, Miller, Carolo, Falling Waters, WV, Sarah, Falling Waters, WV, 27 Dec 1897, Mrs., Kershner, -, -, Williamsport, -, Smith, 3

4093, 29 May 1898, Margaritam Elisabeth, Basore, Samuele E., -, Lucia S., -, 20 May 1898, Margaret (Mrs.), Moore, -, -, -, married Scott McKane 27 Jul 1927. Marriage Record #2, Moore, 3

4094, 5 June 1898, Margaritam M., Crosson, Henrico J., -, Maria, -, 29 Apr 1898, Joannes, Helaine, Julia, Helaine [HB], -, -, Srymbersly, 3

4095, 3 Jul 1898, Vivian Geneviefam, Morrison, Gulielmo, -, Ella Thoma [or Thomas], Baltimore, 26 Jun 1898, Violetta, Morrison, -, -, -, See Marriage Record #1 Pg. 154, Humes, 3

4096, 24 Jul 1898, Roscoe Vincentium, Cearfoss, Gulielmo, -, Rosa, -, 4 Nov 1897, Mrs., Hull "(grandmother)", -, -, -, -, Hull, 3

4097, 24 Jul 1898, Hannam Kennedy, Gunnell, Alberto H., -, Sallie K., -, 11 Jul 1898, Theresia, Nolan, -, -, -, Marriage Record #1 Pg. 142, Nolan, 3

4098, 31 Jul 1898, Robertum Bruce, Boyle, Carolo, -, Maria, -, 25 Jul 1898, Brook, Boyle, Catharina, Boyle, -, married Jun 1922 to Ruth Flook, a non-Catholic, by Rev. M. A. Ryan, St. Paul's Church, Ellicott City, MD; DMR, Smith, 3

4099, 7 Aug 1898, Mariam Ednam, Ramacciotti, Domenico, -, Ausilia, -, 8 Jun 1898, Petrus, Giuliani, Bianca, Ramacciotti, -, -, Lazzari, 3

4100, 25 Aug 1898, Annam Mariam, Payne, Joanne, -, Cecilia, -, 28 Jul 1898, Eva (Mrs.), Cullen, -, -, Williamsport, FA, Ardinger, 3

4101, 3 Sep 1898, Veronicam Ohiliam [?], O'Brist, Joanne R., -, Anna R., -, 19 Apr 1898, Rosa (Mrs.), Cearfoss, -, -, -, -, Hull, 3

4102, 11 Sep 1898, Irvin McKinley, Kershner, Carolo, -, Catharina, -, 18 Oct 1897, Mrs., Kershner, -, -, -, James, 3

ST. MARY'S CATHOLIC CHURCH HAGERSTOWN, MARYLAND, BAPTISMS:
Index, Baptism Date, Child, Last Name, Father from, Mother, Mother from, Birth Date, 1st Sponsor First, 1st Sponsor Last, 2nd Sponsor First, 2nd Sponsor Last, Location, Notes, Maiden Name, Priest

4103, 25 Sep 1898, Paulinam Catherinam, Lingg, Joseph, -, Catharina, -, 11 Sep 1898, Mr., Kreitzer, Mrs., Kreitzer, -, -, Bentz, 3

4104, 25 Sep 1898, Beatricem Geneviefam, Grady, Francisco, -, Jesse J. [or I.], -, 5 Sep 1898, Catharina, Grady, -, -, -, -, Moller, 3

4105, 10 Oct 1898, [blank], Boward, -, -, -, -, 7 Oct 1898, -, -, -, -, -, BP; PB, -, 3

4106, 17 Oct 1898, Robertum Guy, Conley, Joanne, Williamsport, Annamaria, Williamsport, 24 Sep 1898, -, -, -, -, Williamsport, -, Hoy, 3

4107, 12 Nov 1898, Franciscam Irenem, Wise, Walter S., Hagerstown, Elisabeth, Hagerstown, 12 Sep 1898, Mary C. (Mrs.), Smith, -, -, -, -, Smith, 3

4108, 16 Nov 1898, Joannam Franciscam, Cushwa, Francisco, -, Gertrude, -, 8 Nov 1898, Georgius, McCardell, Georgius (Mrs.), McCardell [HB], -, -, Spohn, 3

4109, 20 Nov 1898, Thomam Antonium, Anderson, Joanne, -, Maria, -, 10 Nov 1898, Cornelius, Pearl, Maria, Martin "(by proxy)", -, -, O'Brien, 3

4110, 20 Nov 1898, Danielem, O'Keefe, Thoma, -, Anna, -, 1 Nov 1898, Albertus, Watzler, Maria, Alexander, -, -, Jordan [?], 3

4111, 11 Dec 1898, Rosam, Ferguson, Francisco E., Washington, DC, Maria E., Baltimore, 12 Sep 1898, Maria, Smith, -, -, -, FA, Garret, 3

4112, 8 Jan 1899, Ceciliam Agnetem, McCardell, Ernesto F., Williamsport, Vertie, Berkeley Co., WV, 14 Dec 1898, Cecilia, Switzer, -, -, -, -, Brown, 3

4113, 8 Jan 1899, Jacobum Riccardum, Rauth, Gulielmo, -, Lucia, -, 1 Dec 1898, Mrs., Moran, -, -, -, Marriage Register #1 Pg. 150, Sawer, 3

4114, 15 Jan 1899, Annam Margaretam, Wagner, Jacobo, -, Sarah, -, 27 Dec 1898, Joseph, Marton, Ida, Bell, -,, Dorsey, 3

4115, 29 Jan 1899, Fredericum Joseph, Kammarer, Frederico, -, Maria, Allegheny Co., PA, 3 Jan 1899, Elisabeth, Moore, -, -, -, married Anna C. Ford, St. Mary's Church, Patton, PA,

ST. MARY'S CATHOLIC CHURCH
HAGERSTOWN, MARYLAND, BAPTISMS:
Index, Baptism Date, Child, Last Name, Father from, Mother, Mother from, Birth Date, 1st Sponsor First, 1st Sponsor Last, 2nd Sponsor First, 2nd Sponsor Last, Location, Notes, Maiden Name, Priest

Rev. Adrian Krakom[?] O.S.B. 10 Jul 1924, Barns [or Barry], 3

4116, 5 Feb 1899, Margaritam Catharinam, Hager, Emerson A. [Jonathan J. crossed out], Hagerstown, Anna C., Hagerstown, 13 Nov 1898, Margarita, Grady, -, -, -, -, Sheehon, 3

4117, 19 Feb 1899, Inez Ceciliam, Young, Benjamin, -, Isabella, -, 1 Feb 1899, Cecilia, Switzer, -, -, -, -, Switzer, 3

4118, 21 Feb 1899, Joannem Burton, Firey, Joanne B., -, Susanna, -, 31 Jan 1899, Rosa, Happel, -, -, -, -, Happel, 3

4119, 5 Mar 1899, Joannem Augustinum, Nierman, Augusto, -, Daisy, -, 14 Jan 1899, Amelia, Nierman, -, -, -, married Mrs. Eliz. Sell, 29 Nov 1928, St. Stephens Church, Washington, DC, Rev. Geo. B. Harrington [?], Fry, 3

4120, 5 Mar 1899, Martinum Franciscum Gualbertum, Dillon, Joanne, -, Maria, -, 11 Feb 1899, Franciscus, Futterer, Maria (Mrs.), Smith, -, -, Happel, 3

4121, 9 Apr 1899, Catharinam Reginem, Humelsine, Leonardo E., -, Catharina, -, 9 Mar 1899, Clarence, Martin, Ida, Bell, -, -, Moore, 3

4122, 23 Apr 1899, Otho Francescun Fisher, Duffy, Otho Jos. S., -, Maria M., -, 31 Mar 1899, Joannes T., Hellaine, Julia, Hellaine [HB], -, married Alice Summer of this parish, St. Mary's Church, 7 May 1923, Cramer, 3

4123, 21 May 1899, Rosam Mariam, Fenwick, Jacobo, Montgomery Co., Catharina, Montgomery Co., 15 Apr 1899, Emma, Marlow "(by proxy)", -, -, -, -, Clarke, 3

4124, 29 May 1899, Henry James, Jeffrey [?], Jacobo E., -, Catharina, Baltimore, 27 Feb 1868, Joannes, Firey, -, -, -, C, Miller, 3

4125, 21 Jun 1899, Mariam Aureliam, Taylor, Francisco, Williamsport, Jesse, Williamsport, 28 May 1899, Fannie (Mrs.), Thompson, -, -, Williamsport, See Marriage Record #1 Pg. 146, Thompson, 3

4126, 5 Jul 1899, Rosam Ethel, Adams, J.W. [or U.], Hagerstown, -, -, 28 Nov 1881, Maria (Mrs.), Smith, -, -, -, C; BC, -, 3

ST. MARY'S CATHOLIC CHURCH
HAGERSTOWN, MARYLAND, BAPTISMS:
Index, Baptism Date, Child, Last Name, Father from,
Mother, Mother from, Birth Date, 1st Sponsor First,
1st Sponsor Last, 2nd Sponsor First, 2nd Sponsor Last,
Location, Notes, Maiden Name, Priest

4127, 15 Jul 1899, Minervam Elisabeth, Hetzer, Carolo I. [or J.}, Washington County, Anne J., -, 8 Ajpr 1898, Alexandro, Moore, -, -, -, Marriage Record #1 Pg. 137, Moore, 3

4128, 23 Jul 1899, Ricardum Daly, Fagan, Joanne, -, Sarai, -, 18 Jun 1899, Maria Lauretta, Fagan, -, -, -, -, Daly, 3

4129, 30 Jul 1899, Carolum Herbertum, Vantz, Jacob R., -, Bertha C., -, 12 Nov 1898, Maria (Mrs.), Smith, -, -, -, -, Oak, 3

4130, 13 Aug 1899, Mariam Franciscam, Goddard, Gulielmo, Springfield, OH, Maria, -, 10 Sep 1875, Mrs., Shue, -, -, -, BC, Mahew, 3

4131, 17 Sep 1899, Francescum Joseph, Chrieton, Gulielmo, -, Maria, -, 21? Aug 1899, Franciscus, Grady, Catharina, Grady, -, -, Grady, 3

4132, 10 Oct 1899, Mariam Amandam, McCardell, Percey, Williamsport, Anna M., Williamsport, 18 Sep 1899, Helena, Gallagher, -, -, Williamsport, MA, Collins, 3

4133, 15 Oct 1899, Carolum Petrum, Shueler, Carolo, -, Maria, -, 27 Aug 1899, Milton, Ewers, Milton (Mrs.), Ewers [HB], -, -, Ewers, 3

4134, 15 Oct 1899, Ruth, Futterer, Francisco, Hagerstown, Anna, -, 15 Sep 1899, Jacobus, Moran, Jacobus (Mrs.), Moran [HB], -, -, Mayhew, 3

4135, 12 Nov 1899, Annam Rachelem, Matthews, Jacobo, -, Maria, -, 30 Oct 1899, Joannes, Helaine, Margarita, Brady, -, ceremonies supplied on this date; PB; BP; had been baptized at home by doctor due to danger of death, McDevitt, 3

4136, 16 Nov 1899, Aliciam Ryan, McCardell, Georgio W., Williamsport, Anna, -, 31 Oct 1899, Franklin, Cushwa, Gertrude, Cushwa [HB], -, married St. Paul's Church, Baltimore, 31 Oct 1923, Henry J. Chirick [?], Jr., Rev. W. Paul [last name unreadable], Ryan, 3

4137, 26 Nov 1899, Florentiam Catharinam, Cotter, Patritio, -, Lettie, -, 28 Jul 1899, Mrs., Lloyd, -, -, -, married 18 Dec 1921, Sts. Philip & James, Baltimore, to Preston Matthews, Rev. Hugh J. Monaghan, Del., Lauderslager, 3

ST. MARY'S CATHOLIC CHURCH
HAGERSTOWN, MARYLAND, BAPTISMS:
Index, Baptism Date, Child, Last Name, Father from, Mother, Mother from, Birth Date, 1st Sponsor First, 1st Sponsor Last, 2nd Sponsor First, 2nd Sponsor Last, Location, Notes, Maiden Name, Priest

4138, 17 Dec 1899, Leonardum Eduardum, Humelsine, Manarias, -, -, -, 28 Jan 1875, Thomas, Moore, -, -, -, BC; C, -, 3

4139, 27 Dec 1899, Jesse Virginiam, McKalvey, Jacobo N., Williamsport, Anna M., Little Orleans, Md, 6 Oct 1899, Nellie, Hughes, -, -, Williamsport, -, Shields, 3

4140, 10 Dec 1899, Franklin Michaelem, Gallagher, Eduardo F., -, Maria, -, 15 Sep 1899, Maria, Wills, -, -, -, married Mabel Kelly, validated 22 Jun 1947, S.E. Kenny [originally married outside of the church, and had marriage validated], Full, 3

4141, 7 Jan 1900, Ricardum Orndorf Antonium, Shafer, Roberto, -, Maria, -, 16 Dec 1899, Antonius, Hankey, Mrs., Hankey, -, -, Orndorf, 3

4142, 7 Jan 1900, Louisam Romaine, Shafer, Roberto, -, Maria, -, 16 Dec 1899, Antonius, Hankey, Luisa (Orndorf), Hankey [HB], -, -, Orndorf, 3

4143, 28 Jan 1900, Helenam, Tanner, Thoma H., -, Helena, -, 25 Apr 1899, Elisabeth (Mrs.), Cashman, -, -, -, FA, Cashman, 3

4144, 4 Feb 1900, Agnetem Muriel, Hoelle, Martino R., -, Elisabeth, -, 25 Dec 1899, Maria, Wills, -, -, -, -, Gephart, 3

4145, 11 Mar 1900, Gulielmum Ernestum, Basore, Samuele E., -, Lucia, -, 27-Feb 1900, Thomas, Moore, Cecilia, Moore, -, -, Moore, 3

4146, 15 Mar 1900, Joseph Kriegh, Cushwa, Franklin, -, Gertrude, -, 1-Mar 1900, David K., Cushwa, Helen S. (Mrs.), Duggan, Williamsport, -, Spohn, 3

4147, 8 Apr 1900, Eduardum Allen Alexander, Martin, Joseph, -, Virginia, -, 1-Apr 1900, Georgius, Alexander, Maria, Martin, -, Marriage Register #1 Pg 139, 174, Alexander, 3

4148, 8 Apr 1900, Juliam Lane, Clayburn [father's name is Kidwell], Joanne W., Shepherdstown, WV, -, -, 6 Nov 1866, Sallie (Mrs.), Cushwa, -, -, -, C, -, 3

4149, 8 Apr 1900, Margaret Elisabeth, Clayburn **, Davis, Leitersburg, -, -, 11 Jan 1870*, Sallie, Clayburn, -, -, -, C; BC; appears to read ""primum visca novi bpatimatos fontier"";

ST. MARY'S CATHOLIC CHURCH HAGERSTOWN, MARYLAND, BAPTISMS:
Index, Baptism Date, Child, Last Name, Father from, Mother, Mother from, Birth Date, 1st Sponsor First, 1st Sponsor Last, 2nd Sponsor First, 2nd Sponsor Last, Location, Notes, Maiden Name, Priest

*birthdate is 11 [?] Jan 1870 [or 1890]; ** father's last name is Barnhart, -, 3

4150, 22 Apr 1900, Idam Mariam, Ramacciotti, Domenico, -, Ausilia, -, 26-Feb 1900, Bianca, Rammacciotti, -, -, -, Marriage Record #1 Pg. 155, Lazzari, 3

4151, 12-Mar 1900, Henriettam Mariam, Feigly, Isaac, -, Emma, -, 23-Feb 1900, Mary (Mrs.), Smith, -, -, -, -, Armstrong, 3

4152, 6-May 1900, Gulielmum Joseph, Fitzpatrick, Gulielmo, -, Margarita, -, 19 Apr 1900*, Joseph, Martin, M. Elisabeth, Fitzpatrick [?], -, *birthdate is 11 [?] Jan 1870 [or 1890], Jordan, 3

4153, 13-May 1900, Georgium Carlton, Watzler, Carolo A., -, Maria E., -, 31-Mar 1900, Joannes Gulielmus, Alexander, Maria, Gossard, -, Marriage Record #1 Pg. 135, Alexander, 3

4154, 16-May 1900, Margaritam Agnetem, Garish, Joseph H., -, Georgetta, -, 23 Sep 1885, Mrs., Templeton, -, -, Williamsport, -, Ardinger, 3

4155, 3-Jun 1900, Franciscum Joseph, Quinn, Jacobo, -, Anna, -, 11-Apr 1900, Joseph, Lyndca [?], Maria, Domenici, -, -, Herman, 3

4156, 4-Jun 1900, Augustam Margaritam, Cearfoss, Gulielmo, -, Rosa, -, 25 Aug 1899, Anna, Obritt [?], -, -, -, -, Hull, 3

4157, 17-Jun 1900, Allen Joseph Hartzler, Mumma, Henrico C., Hagerstown, -, -, 17 Apr 1878, Thomas, Geary, -, -, -, C; BC, -, 3

4158, 20-Jun 1900, Riccardum King, McCardell, Eugenio, Williamsport, Effie, Williamsport, 17-Jan 1900, Ella, Oliver, -, -, Williamsport, -, King, 3

4159, 15-Jul 1900, Florentiam Louisam, Lawrence, Carolo L., -, Lila A., -, 16-Jun 1900, Florence (Mrs.), Lawrence, -, -, -, -, Yost [?], 3

4160, 30-Jul 1900, Agnetem Caeciliam, Thomson, Leone, Williamsport, Catharina, Williamsport, 22-Jun 1900, Ella, Gallagher, -, -, Williamsport, -, Collins, 3

4161, 30-Jul 1900, Elisabeth Catharinam, Cushwa, David K., Williamsport, Nanie, Williamsport, 23-Jul 1900, George,

ST. MARY'S CATHOLIC CHURCH
HAGERSTOWN, MARYLAND, BAPTISMS:
Index, Baptism Date, Child, Last Name, Father from, Mother, Mother from, Birth Date, 1st Sponsor First, 1st Sponsor Last, 2nd Sponsor First, 2nd Sponsor Last, Location, Notes, Maiden Name, Priest

McCardell, Fannie (Mrs.), Thomson, Williamsport, Endnote 78, Taylor, 3

4162, 12-Aug 1900, Riccardum Cole *, Willson, Walter D., -, Francisca R., -, 5-Aug 1900, John B., Sweeney, Jennette (Mrs.), Sweeney, -, * "Coale" written in pencil above the name, Aumen, 3

4163, 17-Aug 1900, Jacobum Eduardum, Simler, [blank], -, Winnie, -, 9-Aug 1900, -, -, -, -, -, BP; PB, Keegan, 3

4164, 19-Aug 1900, Mariam Reginam, Duffy, Otho, -, Maria, -, 9-Aug 1900, Jacobus, Moran, Jacobus (Mrs.), Moran [HB], -, -, Cramer, 3

4165, 2-Sep 1900, Robertum Carolum, Brezzler, Georgio, -, Bertha, -, 7-Feb 1900, Catharina (Mrs.), Pearl, -, -, -, -, Moser, 3

4166, 5-Sep 1900, Joseph Carolum, Willson, Carolo, Washington County, Bessie, Washington Co., 25-Jun 1900, Carolus, Mullen, Sallie (Mrs.), Cushwa "(by proxy)", -, -, Shnider, 3

4167, 2-Oct 1900, Rosam Rebeccam, Coxon, Gulielmo H., -, Maud, -, 18-Apr 1900, Mary (Mrs.), Smith, -, -, -, -, [blank] "his wife", 3

4168, 7-Oct 1900, Bernadettam Josephinam, Lingg, Joseph F., Emmitsburg, Catharina, Emmitsburg, 27-Sep 1900, Henricus, Martin, Ida, Bell, -, married W. K. Bower, 14 Apr 1925, St. Mary's Church, disp. mix religion, caut. Disp. cult.; Marriage Register #2, Bentz, 3

4169, 28-Oct 1900, Genevefam Catharinam, Moats, Edwin M., -, Anna E., -, 30-Sep 1900, Maria, Wolff, -, -, -, -, Switzer, 3

4170, 18-Nov 1900, Joannem Francescum, Shriner, Davide, -, Maria, -, 28-Oct 1900, Emma (Mrs.), Codori, -, -, -, "This man states that he was born in Gettysburg, PA 27 Aug 1943. J.F. Leary [?]", Codori, 3

4171, 15-Dec 1900, Helenam Dorotheam, Rauth, Gulielmo, -, Lucia, -, 25-Nov 1900, Mary (Mrs.), Smith, -, -, -, -, Sawers, 3

4172, 23-Dec 1900, Elisabeth Mariam, Kelly, Lewis, -, Agnete, -, 15-Dec 1900, Martiney, Happel, Rosa, Kappel, -, Married John R. Fitzpatrick of Dixon, PN, 27 May 1920, St.

**ST. MARY'S CATHOLIC CHURCH
HAGERSTOWN, MARYLAND, BAPTISMS:**
Index, Baptism Date, Child, Last Name, Father from,
Mother, Mother from, Birth Date, 1st Sponsor First,
1st Sponsor Last, 2nd Sponsor First, 2nd Sponsor Last,
Location, Notes, Maiden Name, Priest

Paul's Church, Washington, DC, by Rt. Rev. Mgr. Jas. Macken [?], Conrad, 3
4173, 25-Dec 1900, Doris Josephinam, Morrison, Gulielmo, -, Ella T., Baltimore, 9-Dec 1900, Lillie, Morrison, -, -, -, -, Humes, 3

St. Mary's Catholic Church Records

Marriages 1818-1900

ST. MARY'S CATHOLIC CHURCH
HAGERSTOWN, MARYLAND, MARRIAGES:
Index, Date, Groom 1st Name, Groom Last Name, Code, Bride 1st Name, Bride Last Name, Code B, Location of Ceremony, 1st Witness First, 1st Witness Last, 2nd Witness First, 2nd Witness Last, Notes, Priest

4174, 18 Nov 1818, Francis, Shercliff, -, Rosanna , Connolly, -, dwelling of Francis Connolly on Town Creek Alleghaney Co., Francis, Connelly, Francis (Mrs.), Connelly [HB], 3rd witness is Mary Ann Connelly, daughter of the two witnesses; this record was mistakenly entered into the Baptism section by the priest, 18

4175, 18 May 1819, Samuel, Abell, -, Nancy, Flora, -, house of Mr. Bradshaw, Chair Maker, Mrs., Milton, Mrs., Abell, Mrs. Abell, witness, is mother of Samuel, 18

4176, 15 Aug 1819, Henry A., Byrne, -, Margaret, Goulding, -, dwelling of Mr. John Develbiss in Alleghany County Md, -, -, -, -, bride from Berkeley Co., WV, 18

4177, 20 Nov 1819, Peter, Mass, -, Jane, Corbet, -, dwelling of Misses Mains, -, -, -, -, ceremony held after Divine Service on Saturday Nov 20 1819, 18

4178, 14 Nov 1819, James, Gallagher, -, Ann, Carr, -, in Alleghany County Md, Mr., Carr "her brother", Mr., Carr, a pedlar, License granted on the same day in Cumberland. Ceremony on Sunday., 18

4179, 29 Aug 1818, John C. W., Jackson, -, Elizabeth, McClain, -, St. Mary's, -, -, -, -, bride is daughter of Jas. McClain, 18

4180, 04 Apr 1820, William, Hawkin, -, Catharine, Stake, -, St. Mary's, Ann (Miss), Jack, Ellen, Monahan, 3rd witness is Eliza Monahan; ceremony on Easter Sunday, 18

4181, 27 Apr 1820, Henry, Compton, -, Matilda (Miss), Drury, -, bride of Blairs Valley, -, -, -, -, this record mistakenly entered into Baptism section, 18

4182, 24 Jun 1820, Ben, -, S, Henny, -, S, St. Mary's, Mrs., Milton, Elizabeth, Monahan, "Ben Slave of Charles Shaffner, Henny of Joseph Grafft"; married by written permissions from their masters, 18

4183, 18 Jun 1820, John, Jack, -, Ann, Duggan, -, Dwelling house of Col John Blackford near Shepherdstown, -, -, -, -, -, 18

4184, 06 Jan 1819, Frederick, Fitz, -, Margaret, Bevens, -, -, -, -, -, -, See Endnote 38., 18

4185, 20 Aug 1819, John, Brady, -, Susanna, Goulding, -, Hancock, Upton, Begald, Jacob, Peck, original signatures of both witnesses are in this entry; married by written consent of the parents of both parties, 18

ST. MARY'S CATHOLIC CHURCH
HAGERSTOWN, MARYLAND, MARRIAGES:
Index, Date, Groom 1st Name, Groom Last Name, Code, Bride 1st Name, Bride Last Name, Code B, Location of Ceremony, 1st Witness First, 1st Witness Last, 2nd Witness First, 2nd Witness Last, Notes, Priest

4186, 14 Sep 1819, Elie, Stake, -, Ellen, Monahan, -, dwelling house of Mr. Thomas McCardell, Thos, McCardell, Mrs., McCardell, 3rd witness is Mrs. Milton, 18

4187, 18 Jan 1820, Terrence , McOwen, -, Mary, Duggan, -, -, Edwd., FitzPatrick, Mary, Richards, 3rd witness is John Richards; original signatures of all 3 witnesses; this record mistakenly entered in to Baptism section, 18

4188, 23 Jan 1820, Ned, -, -, Delia, -, -, -, Edwd., Fitzpatrick, Richd. H., Murphy, Ned "of Michael Smith"; Delia "of Doctor Wm Hammond"; See Endnote 39., 18

4189, 19 Oct 1820, Michael, McAleny, -, Mary Ann, Monahan, -, -, John, McCleary, Mary Ann, Monahan, 3rd witness - Edward McCartin; 4th witness - Mickey McLeney; original signatures of all 4 witnesses in this entry, 18

4190, 24 Oct 1820, John, O'Donnell, -, Susanna, Toland, -, Dwelling house of Mr. Christopher Murphy, his & his wife's presence, -, -, -, -, 18

4191, 19 Dec 1820, Denis L., McSherry, -, Susanna, Abell, -, Dwelling of Captn Abell in Jefferson Co., -, -, -, -, all of Jefferson County, 18

4192, 16 Jan 1821, Robt A., Slye, -, Amanda M.F., Geoynn, -, Dwelling of Mr. B. Sanders in Jefferson Co., Ignatius, Drury, Mary, Slye, 3rd witness - James King; groom of Georgetown D.C.; bride of Jefferson Co., Va, 18

4193, 29 Jan 1821, Samuel, Galloway, -, Jude, [blank], -, -, Frances (Mrs.) , Milton, John, Monahan, 3rd witness - Mrs. Eliza Sengstack; both of Hagerstown; written permission given, 18

4194, 07 Feb 1821, Somerset, -, S, Iris, -, S, St. Mary's, Mrs., Ringgold, -, -, bride is slave of General Ringgold's; groom is slave of Thomas McCardell; by permission in writing from both owners, 18

4195, 26 Apr 1821, John, Williams, -, Maria, Greenwell, -, St. Mary's, William D., Stadt, John, Nollman, 3rd witness - James Chambers; 4th witness - Jno. Williams; 5th witness - Maria Greeneele; original signatures of all 5 witnesses in this entry, 18

4196, 08 Apr 1822, John Peter, Ulrich, -, Mary, Stump, -, St. Mary's Church after Divine Service, Johan Peter, Ulrich *, M___ [?], Lombi [or Tombi] **, * name was signed in German; ** name

ST. MARY'S CATHOLIC CHURCH HAGERSTOWN, MARYLAND, MARRIAGES:

Index, Date, Groom 1st Name, Groom Last Name, Code, Bride 1st Name, Bride Last Name, Code B, Location of Ceremony, 1st Witness First, 1st Witness Last, 2nd Witness First, 2nd Witness Last, Notes, Priest

was signed in German; "Called in the Court License Mary Stump after her father in law", 18

4197, 02 Jun 1822, Jacob, Bradley, S, Milly, Butler, -, before divine service in St. Mary's Church, Milly , Butler (Free Black), -, -, groom is slave to Jno Buchannan, 18

4198, 09 Jun 1822, Peter, Taylor , S, Henny, Lane, S, residence of the late James McClain, -, -, -, -, groom is slave of Jno McClain; bride is slave of Henry Firey; with "written and express consent of both masters", 18

4199, 22 Oct 1822, John, O'Ferrel, -, Eliza (Miss), Humrickhouse, -, Dwelling house of Mr. Humrickhouse father to the lady, Mr., Humrickhouse *, Mrs. , Humrickhouse, witnesses are the bride's father and mother, 18

4200, 29 Apr 1823, John, Duffy, -, Mary, Smith, -, Catholic Chapel in Hagerstown [St. Mary's], Mrs., Milton, -, -, marriage license reads "Dupy", 17

4201, 29 Jun 1823, Lennard, E. Turners [?], B, Patience, -, FB, -, -, -, -, -, many witnesses, 17

4202, 30 Jun 1823, John, Cerns, -, Margret, Brady, -, Catholic Chapel in Hagerstown [St. Mary's], -, -, -, -, many witnesses, 17

4203, 31 Jul 1823, James, McGee, -, Mary Anna, Flemming, -, Catholic Chapel in Hagerstown [St. Mary's], -, -, -, -, many witnesses, 17

4204, 30 Nov 1823, Peter, Mondy, -, Nancy, McClane, -, Catholic Chapel in Hagerstown [St. Mary's], -, -, -, -, many witnesses, 17

4205, 08 Jan 1824, George, Hartshoge, -, Eva, Liba, -, St. Mary's , -, -, -, -, "after been published three Sundays", 17

4206, 17 Feb 1824, Patrick, King, -, Bridget, McGlouglen, -, -, -, -, -, -, many witnesses, 17

4207, 18 Feb 1824, Timothy, Donovan, -, Mary, Lane, -, -, -, -, -, -, many witnesses, 17

4208, 18 May 1824, John, McClain, -, Mary, Smith, -, -, -, -, -, -, many witnesses, 17

4209, 01 Jun 1824, Rody, Ryan, -, Mary (Miss), Donnelly, -, -, Patrick, King, Mrs., McDev__?, original signatures of both witnesses in this entry, 17

ST. MARY'S CATHOLIC CHURCH HAGERSTOWN, MARYLAND, MARRIAGES:
Index, Date, Groom 1st Name, Groom Last Name, Code, Bride 1st Name, Bride Last Name, Code B, Location of Ceremony, 1st Witness First, 1st Witness Last, 2nd Witness First, 2nd Witness Last, Notes, Priest

4210, 20 Jun 1824, Michael, McLoughlen, -, Jane, Toland, -, Catholic Chapel in Hagerstown [St. Mary's], -, -, -, -, many witnesses, 17

4211, 27 Jun 1825, Patrick, Tagen, -, Catherine (widow), Collegan, -, -, John, Roof , John, Terney , 3rd witness is John O'Donnel; 4th witness is John (Mrs.) O'Donnel; 5th witness is John (Mrs.) Roof; 6th witness is John (Mrs.) Terney, 17

4212, 26 Dec 1825, Josue, -, -, Amanda, -, -, St. Mary's, Prudy (Miss), Shefton, Mary (Miss), Cortence [?], 3rd witness is Mr. Cox; 4th witness is Frances McMullen; both are servants to Mr. Micl Smith , 17

4213, 16 Apr 1826, Henry B., Kelley, -, Margret (Miss), McGonnagal, -, St. Mary's , -, -, -, -, -, 17

4214, 04 Aug 1827, Patrick, Londergen, -, Margret (widow), Winters, -, St. Mary's , Patrick, Redmond, Patrick, Donnelly, -, 17

4215, 04 Aug 1827, Charley, Dolen, -, Catherine (Miss), Crow, -, St. Mary's , Hugh, McCosker, Frances, Donnelly, -, 17

4216, -, -, -, -, -, -, -, -, -, -, -, -, This entry intentionally left blank., 17

4217, 16 Apr 1828, Michael, Reariden, -, Mrs., Creamer, -, St. Mary's , -, -, -, -, -, 17

4218, 08 Jun 1828, Jacob, Burk, -, Henny, Rye, -, St. Mary's, "two of Mr.D. Claget's servants", -, -, -, "with the permission of their Master, David Claget, by letter", 17

4219, 15 Jul 1828, John, Devlin, -, Margret, McGonnagal, -, St. Mary's , -, -, -, -, -, 17

4220, 25 Dec 1828, John, Chane [or Chase] , FB, Peggy, Pembrook , S, -, -, -, -, -, Peggy a Slave of Mr. F. Tilghman who had her masters permission by note", 17

4221, 31 Dec 1828, Thomas, Tilghman , S, Mary, Brown, FB, -, -, -, -, -, groom is General Ringgold's slave; Thomas "having his masters permission by note", 17

4222, 01 Jan 1829, Stephen, Tarlton, -, Margret (widow), Adams, -, -, -, -, -, -, -, 17

4223, 20 Apr 1829, Charles, Cooper, S, Betsy, Lyles, FB, -, -, -, -, - , groom is slave of Dr. T. Tilghman; received license from his master to marry , 17

ST. MARY'S CATHOLIC CHURCH HAGERSTOWN, MARYLAND, MARRIAGES:

Index, Date, Groom 1st Name, Groom Last Name, Code, Bride 1st Name, Bride Last Name, Code B, Location of Ceremony, 1st Witness First, 1st Witness Last, 2nd Witness First, 2nd Witness Last, Notes, Priest

4224, 23 Aug 1829, Peter, Burgunty, -, Victoria [?], With, -, St. Mary's , -, -, -, -, on Sunday evening after three Sundays publication, 17

4225, 05 Nov 1829, James, McGonnagal, -, Susan (Miss), McLaughlen, -, St. Mary's , -, -, -, -, -, 17

4226, 24 Nov 1829, James, Elliott, -, Elizabeth (Miss), Marshal, -, -, -, -, -, -, -, 17

4227, 01 Jan 1830*, Nn_?, -, -, Nancy, -, -, St. Mary's; *marriage date reads 01 [or 3] Jan 1830, -, -, -, -, groom is servant of Mrs. Mason; bride is servant of Mrs. Saundey; "both had written authorities"; entry has 1 Jan at top and 3 Jan at end, 17

4228, 30 Sep 1830*, Jacob, Ulgry, -, Isabella (Miss), Corbet, -, St. Mary's; *marriage date reads 30 Sep [or 1 Oct] 1830, -, -, -, -, entry has 1 Oct at top and 30 Sep at end, 17

4229, -, -, -, -, -, -, -, -, -, -, -, -, This entry intentionally left blank.,

4230, -, -, -, -, -, -, -, -, -, -, -, -, This entry intentionally left blank.,

4231, -, -, -, -, -, -, -, -, -, -, -, -, This entry intentionally left blank.,

4232, -, -, -, -, -, -, -, -, -, -, -, -, This entry intentionally left blank.,

4233, -, -, -, -, -, -, -, -, -, -, -, -, This entry intentionally left blank.,

4234, 21 Dec 1830, John, Hay, -, Margret (Miss), Morgan, -, her Brothers house, -, -, -, -, [Decmb 22 1830 written. Above the 22 is written 21st but neither crossed out], 17

4235, -, -, -, -, -, -, -, -, -, -, -, -, This entry intentionally left blank.,

4236, 05 Oct 1831, William, McClain, -, Anna (Miss), Midcalf, -, St. Mary's , -, -, -, -, -, 17

4237, 24 Oct 1831, Patrick J., McMahon, -, Catherine (Miss), McDermoth, -, St. Mary's , -, -, -, -, -, 17

4238, 15 Feb 1832, Daniel, Haller, -, Mary (Miss), McClain, -, Mr. Williams house, -, -, -, -, -, 17

4239, 08 May 1832, Robert, Lowery, -, Julian (Miss), Glamule?, -, "in my own room" [priest's dwelling], -, -, -, -, "by a License from the Court Allegany County, half after one o'clock in the morning in the presence of many witnesses", 17

4240, 17 Jun 1832, Stephen, -, -, L[?]enny, -, -, "in my own room" [priest's dwelling], -, -, -, -, groom is Dr. Hammond's servant; bride is Miss Catherine Miller's servant; both had license from the two masters, 17

ST. MARY'S CATHOLIC CHURCH
HAGERSTOWN, MARYLAND, MARRIAGES:
Index, Date, Groom 1st Name, Groom Last Name, Code, Bride 1st Name, Bride Last Name, Code B, Location of Ceremony, 1st Witness First, 1st Witness Last, 2nd Witness First, 2nd Witness Last, Notes, Priest

4241, 24 Sep 1832, Alexocess [?], Foltz, -, Eucriana, Becktel, -, St. Mary's , -, -, -, -, Sunday; "after three publica.., 17

4242, 30 Sep 1832, Seikfinth?, Keller, -, Apolonia , Mosser, -, St. Mary's , -, -, -, -, Sunday, 17

4243, 30 Sep 1832, John, Ritz [?], -, Carolina, Newhart, -, St. Mary's , -, -, -, -, Sunday, 17

4244, 18 Oct 1832, Alexander, -, S, Matilois , -, -, -, -, -, -, -, groom is slave of Mrs. Vanlear; bride is servant of Thomas McCardell; written permission, 17

4245, 23 Oct 1832, John, Panafather, -, Ellon, Paulr?, -, St. Mary's , -, -, -, -, -, 17

4246, 15 Nov 1832, James, McFadden, -, Catherine (widow), Coy, -, Town of Sharpsburg, -, -, -, -, -, 17

4247, 29 Nov 1832, Owen, Donnelly, -, Mary (Miss), Maniou, -, "in my own room" [priest's dwelling], -, -, -, -, both of Williamsport", 17

4248, 25 Dec 1832, Patrick, Chapman, -, Mary (widow), Rieley, -, St. Mary's , -, -, -, -, Mary "from the Canal", 17

4249, 12 Jan 1833, Michl, Hare, -, Mary (Miss), Roughan, -, "in my own room" [priest's dwelling]; bride from Sharpsburg, -, -, -, -, -, 17

4250, 15 Jan 1833, Aaron, Stoudt, -, Mary (Miss), Dany, -, Miss Anna Chesters [or Chietens] Room, -, -, -, -, both from Hagerstown, 17

4251, 02 Feb 1833, John, Magher, -, Anna (Mrs.), McCormick, -, "in my own room" [priest's dwelling], -, -, -, -, "both from the Dam", 17

4252, 09 Feb 1833, John, Quinlivin?, -, Margret (Mrs.), McCune, -, "in my own room" [priest's dwelling], -, -, -, -, "both from the Dam", 17

4253, -, -, -, -, -, -, -, -, -, -, -, -, This entry intentionally left blank.,

4254, -, -, -, -, -, -, -, -, -, -, -, -, This entry intentionally left blank.,

4255, 21 Apr 1833, Prince [?], -, -, Anna, -, -, -, -, -, -, -, groom is servant of Mr. Wharton; bride is servant of Mrs. Mason; entry has 1 Apr 1833 at top; written permission of Dr. Wharton, 17

4256, 05 May 1833, Isaac, Rowland, -, Martha, Adams, -, St. Mary's, -, -, -, -, Sunday, 17

ST. MARY'S CATHOLIC CHURCH HAGERSTOWN, MARYLAND, MARRIAGES:
Index, Date, Groom 1st Name, Groom Last Name, Code, Bride 1st Name, Bride Last Name, Code B, Location of Ceremony, 1st Witness First, 1st Witness Last, 2nd Witness First, 2nd Witness Last, Notes, Priest

4257, 10 May 1833, Edward, Roane, -, Honora, Murphy, -, Williamsport, -, -, -, -, 17

4258, 11 May 1833, Joseph, Bonan, -, Nancy, Fagan, -, "in my own room" [priest's dwelling], -, -, -, -, -, 17

4259, 25 May 1833, Richard, Lanagan, -, Anna, "Corrogan or Cordy", -, "in my own room" [priest's dwelling], -, -, -, -, both of Washington, 17

4260, 23 May 1835, Arthur, Tenery?, -, Nancy, Mulon* , -, Hugh McCleers [?], Sharpsburg, -, -, -, -, *Mulon [the t in Multon crossed out], 17

4261, 31 May 1833, Terrence, Monahan, -, Bridget, Early, -, St. Mary's , -, -, -, -, both of Sharpsburg, 17

4262, 01 Jun 1833, John, Murphy, -, Margaret (widow), Murphy, -, St. Mary's, -, -, -, -, -, 17

4263, 17 Jun 1833, Edward, Dumond [?], -, Catherine, Mundy, -, Catholic Church in Williamsport, -, -, -, -, -, 17

4264, 23 Jun 1833, Jeremiah, Mades [or Meades], -, Margret, McCosker, -, St. Mary's , -, -, -, -, Sunday, 17

4265, 06 Jul 1833, John, McCormick, -, Mary, McEntire, -, St. Mary's, -, -, -, -, "both from the Canal line", 17

4266, 05 Aug 1833, Thomas, Cany [or Cary], -, Mary (widow), Row, -, St. Mary's , -, -, -, -, -, 17

4267, 05 Aug 1833, Richard, Fahey, -, Mary, Ellott, -, St. Mary's , -, -, -, -, -, 17

4268, 11 Aug 1833, Patrick, Doyle, -, Nancy, "Frial or Denney", -, St. Mary's , -, -, -, -, -, 17

4269, 01 Sep 1833, Bernard, O'Conner, -, Margret (widow), McCafferty, -, St. Mary's , -, -, -, -, Sunday; both from Washington Co., 17

4270, 03 Sep 1833, Thomas, Hennesy, -, Mary (widow), Sullavan, -, St. Mary's , -, -, -, -, both from Washington Co., 17

4271, 04 Sep 1833, Charles, Lundragen, -, Mary, Willis, -, St. Mary's , -, -, -, -, -, 17

4272, 19 Sep 1833, Danal , Fitzgerald [?], -, Mary (widow), "Rice or Estill", -, Williamsport, -, -, -, -, both from Williamsport, 17

4273, 22 Sep 1833, Danial, Brosnehen, -, Catherine, Black, -, St. Mary's , -, -, -, -, both from Williamsport, 17

ST. MARY'S CATHOLIC CHURCH HAGERSTOWN, MARYLAND, MARRIAGES:
Index, Date, Groom 1st Name, Groom Last Name, Code, Bride 1st Name, Bride Last Name, Code B, Location of Ceremony, 1st Witness First, 1st Witness Last, 2nd Witness First, 2nd Witness Last, Notes, Priest

4274, 07 Oct 1833, Thoms, McDermoth, -, Fealy, Herbert, -, Patrick Mihans house, -, -, -, -, -, 17

4275, 08 Oct 1833, Cornelius, Donovan, -, Margret (widow), Barret, -, "on Mr. McKinly Contract near the upper Dam", -, -, -, -, -, 17

4276, 24 Oct 1833, Dan, Owens, -, Eliza (widow), Doherty, -, Misters McDannels and Jamason's Contract. Jacks Rock, -, -, -, -, -, 17

4277, 26 Oct 1833, William, Ferrall, -, Bridget, Ferrell, -, St. Mary's, -, -, -, -, -, 17

4278, 29 Oct 1833, James, Hurley, -, Sophia, Smith, -, Mrs. Milton's [or Melton's] house, -, -, -, -, -, 17

4279, 09 Nov 1833, Wilm, Sullavan, -, Margret, Calrol, -, St. Mary's, -, -, -, -, -, 17

4280, 25 Dec 1833, Daniel, Lahey [or Sahey], -, Catherine (Miss), Haley, -, St. Mary's, -, -, -, -, -, "Both from Harries locks", 17

4281, 04 Jan 1834, Francis, Armstrong, -, Margret, Grant, -, Wilm Coiles [?] house, Jacks Rock, -, -, -, -, entry has 1 Jan 1834 at top, 17

4282, 13 Jan 1834, John, Larguery [?], -, Catherine, Horgan [?], -, Mr. Blacks; Williamsport, -, -, -, -, -, 17

4283, 07 Jan 1834, Patrick, Rodgers, -, Sarah (Miss), Galogy [?], -, -, -, -, -, -, -, 17

4284, 07 Jan 1834, Nichous, Cusick, -, Judy (Miss), Carroll, -, St. Mary's, -, -, -, -, -, 17

4285, 08 Feb 1834, Neel, Mellon [or Mollow], -, Bridget (widow), Bradly, -, St. Mary's, -, -, -, -, -, 17

4286, 08 Feb 1834, Wilm, Mahoney, -, Ellon (widow), Cavana, -, St. Mary's, -, -, -, -, -, 17

4287, 09 Feb 1834, Yorick, Ambush, B, Polley, [blank], B, -, -, -, -, -, both Servants of M.B. Mason; received written permission to marry from him, 17

4288, 09 Feb 1834, Joseph, Kelley, -, Catherine, Dick [or Deck], -, Henry Kellies house, -, -, -, -, -, 17

4289, 11 Feb 1834, James, O'Farrell, -, Suan, Murry, -, Mr? McSherry? McIlhennys Jack's Rock", -, -, -, -, -, 17

4290, 11 Feb 1834, James, Galvin [or Golvin], -, Elisabeth, South [?], -, St. Mary's, -, -, -, -, -, 17

ST. MARY'S CATHOLIC CHURCH
HAGERSTOWN, MARYLAND, MARRIAGES:
Index, Date, Groom 1st Name, Groom Last Name, Code, Bride 1st Name, Bride Last Name, Code B, Location of Ceremony, 1st Witness First, 1st Witness Last, 2nd Witness First, 2nd Witness Last, Notes, Priest

4291, 18 Feb 1834, Lemal , Cross, -, Lidia [or Susia] (Miss), Bevans, -, her Fathers House in Allegany County, -, -, -, -, -, 17

4292, 30 Mar 1834, Ben, -, -, Maria, -, -, St. Mary's , -, -, -, -, received written permission to marry; groom is Barn Mason's servant; bride is Mr. Mason's servant, 17

4293, 30 Mar 1834, Patrick, Foy, -, Widow, Audlem* , -, St. Mary's , -, -, -, -, *Audlem [or Audlemn or Audlew], 17

4294, 31 Mar 1834, Patrick, Scott, -, Mary (widow), Kinney, -, Jack's Rock, -, -, -, -, -, 17

4295, 12 Apr 1834, John, Mason, -, Rose, McMullen, -, St. Mary's , -, -, -, -, -, 17

4296, 14 May 1834, Robert, Lewis, -, Mary, Sherran, -, at her Fathers house, on Misses Tracys & Fridens[?] Contract, -, -, -, -, -, 17

4297, 14 May 1834, Michl, McDermoth, -, Mary, Albert, -, her Mothers house in Williamsport, -, -, -, -, -, 17

4298, 21 May 1834, Lewis, McClain, -, Matilda, West, -, his Mother's house, Widow Peggy McCains", -, -, -, -, -, 17

4299, 31 May 1834, Denis, Cornneskery [?], -, Sarah (widow), Flannagan, -, Hagerstown, -, -, -, -, -, 17

4300, 03 Jun 1834, John G., Davis, -, Mary Anna, Shirley, -, at her Mother's house, -, -, -, -, John "barber by trade", 17

4301, 19 Jun 1834, Otho, McClain, -, Margaretta, Sherkery , -, at John O'Ferrels house, -, -, -, -, -, 17

4302, 19 Jul 1834, Charles, Cavan, -, Rosanna, Dempsy, -, St. Mary's , -, -, -, -, -, 17

4303, 07 Aug 1834, Richard A., Shipley, -, Ellon, Albert, -, her Mothers house in Williamsport, -, -, -, -, -, 17

4304, 22 Aug 1834, James , Hughes, -, Mary, Duffey, -, at Mr. Dan Doherty House Williamsport, -, -, -, -, "merect" is beside Hughes name (trade?), 17

4305, 07 Sep 1834, James, Brarail, -, Catherine, Slater [or Stakes], -, St. Mary's , -, -, -, -, ceremony took place "in the presence of many witnesses", 17

4306, 11 Sep 1834, Henery, McNulty[?], -, Margaret (widow), Whalen, -, "in my own room" [priest's dwelling], -, -, -, -, ceremony took place "in the presence of many witnesses", 17

ST. MARY'S CATHOLIC CHURCH HAGERSTOWN, MARYLAND, MARRIAGES:

Index, Date, Groom 1st Name, Groom Last Name, Code, Bride 1st Name, Bride Last Name, Code B, Location of Ceremony, 1st Witness First, 1st Witness Last, 2nd Witness First, 2nd Witness Last, Notes, Priest

4307, 19 Sep1 834, Wilm, McCormack, -, Rebeca, Folder, -, St. Mary's , -, -, -, -, ceremony took place "in the presence of many witnesses", 17

4308, 04 Oct 1834, Wilm, Flannagan, -, Catherine (widow), Allen, -, at the Upper Dam, -, -, -, -, -, 17

4309, 19 Oct 1834, Cornelius, McGonnogal, -, Bridget, McEntire, -, -, -, -, -, -, -, 17

4310, 09 Nov 1834, James, Jonston , -, Jdudy [sic], McCabe, -, -, -, -, -, -, McCabe lived from same town with Patrick McLoughlen before her marriage"; both from Williamsport, 17

4311, 03 Jan 1835, John, Bowler, -, Margret, Lynch, -, St. Mary's, -, -, -, -, -, 17

4312, 01 Mar 1835, James, Watson, -, Sarah, Donnelly, -, at her Fathers house in Williamsport, -, -, -, -, -, 17

4313, 02 Mar 1835, Thoms., Fealy, -, Jane, O'Donnell, -, at Dan Dahertys house, Williamsport, -, -, -, -, -, 17

4314, 19 Apr 1835, Wilim., Gell, -, Bridget, Higgins?, -, "in my own house" [priest's dwelling], -, -, -, -, -, 17

4315, 30 Apr 1835, Thoms, Gainer, -, Aanna (widow), Tengary, -, "in my own house" [priest's dwelling], -, -, -, -, -, 17

4316, 14 May 1835, Danial, Mahoney, -, Charlotte (widow), McCelollane [?], -, St. Mary's , -, -, -, -, both from Hancock, 17

4317, 22 May 1835, John, Mahon, -, Eliza (widow), Kennedy, -, St. Mary's , -, -, -, -, both from Williamsport, 17

4318, 16 Jun 1835, Robert James, Brent, -, Matilda, Lawrence, -, at her Mother's house, -, -, -, -, -, 17

4319, 11 Jul 1835, Daniel, Smith, -, Mary (widow), Donavan, -, St. Mary's , -, -, -, -, both from Williamsport, 17

4320, 18 Jul 1835, Bernard, Duncan, -, Maria, McGarry, -, St. Mary's, -, -, -, -, both from Williamsport, 17

4321, 04 Aug 1835, Philip, Colman, -, Ellon (widow), Degan, -, St. Mary's , -, -, -, -, both from the Canal, 17

4322, 10 Sep 1835, Patrick, Trenner, -, Mary (widow), Burk, -, Widow Donnavons Shantee, -, -, -, -, "both from McCobbens Contract, 17

4323, 29 Oct 1835, John, Upton, -, Elizabeth, Locher, -, St. Mary's , -, -, -, -, -, 17

ST. MARY'S CATHOLIC CHURCH
HAGERSTOWN, MARYLAND, MARRIAGES:
Index, Date, Groom 1st Name, Groom Last Name, Code, Bride 1st Name, Bride Last Name, Code B, Location of Ceremony, 1st Witness First, 1st Witness Last, 2nd Witness First, 2nd Witness Last, Notes, Priest

4324, 31 Oct 1835, David, Reagen, -, Winfred (widow), Merrick, -, St. Mary's , -, -, -, -, -, 17

4325, 09 Nov 1835, Laurence, Cosgrove, -, Terresa Hanna, Root, -, at John O'Ferrals Shantee Barney Gorman's Contract, -, -, -, -, -, 17

4326, 11 Nov 1835, Thomas, Shea, -, Margraret (widow), Garman, -, in a Shantee on John Sherlock's Contract, -, -, -, -, -, 17

4327, 22 Nov 1835, John, Paden, -, Mary (widow), Jones, -, St. Mary's , -, -, -, -, -, 17

4328, 15 Dec 1835, Patrick, McNeney, -, Nancy (widow), Mundy, -, in the Widow Burn's house Hancock, -, -, -, -, -, 17

4329, 26 Jan 1836, Wilm, Dunn [or Drum], -, Bridget (widow), Fitzgerald, -, -, -, -, -, -, entry has 20 Jan 1836 at top, 17

4330, 11 ___ 1836, Hugh, Reilly, -, Ellen, Thornton, -, -, James, Tully, Owen, Tully, there is a marriage license for this couple on 11 Feb 1836, 17

4331, 17 Apr 1836, James, Galvin, -, Mary (widow), Burns, -, in her own house, Hancock, -, -, -, -, -, 17

4332, 19 Apr 1836, James, Rynolos* , -, Maria, Kelley, -, "at her Fathers house, on Mr. John Sherlocks Contract Miller, Stone Point", -, -, -, -, *possibly Reynolds?, 17

4333, 11 Apr 1836, Owen, Dunn, -, Mary, Whealan, -, Mr. Richard Walsh's on Lyles Contract, -, -, -, -, -, 17

4334, 29 Apr 1836, John, O'Donnell, -, Harriett, Coss, -, St. Mary's , Mr., Gulmen [?], Mrs., Conden, -, 17

4335, 02 May 1836, Antony, Daily, -, Catherine, Mulholland, -, at her brother's house, near Mr Yeates", -, -, -, -, -, 17

4336, 04 May 1836, Patrick, O'Riely, -, Rebeca (widow), FitzSimmons, -, Hancock, in the house of P. Fitzpatrick, -, -, -, -, notation read, "or rather had removed an impediment, " but was crossed out, 17

4337, 14 Jun 1836, Peter, Eagan, -, Catherine (Miss), Eagan, -, "next door to James Ryan's Store, Contractor; on the Canal, Hancock", -, -, -, -, -, 17

4338, 27 May 1836, John, Foshy [?], -, Widow, Coury, -, -, John, Sherlock, Mrs., Relly, -, 17

4339, 27 Jun 1836, James, Roche, -, Margaret, Lynch, -, -, Josiah , Smith, John, Lynch, -, 17

ST. MARY'S CATHOLIC CHURCH
HAGERSTOWN, MARYLAND, MARRIAGES:
Index, Date, Groom 1st Name, Groom Last Name, Code, Bride 1st Name, Bride Last Name, Code B, Location of Ceremony, 1st Witness First, 1st Witness Last, 2nd Witness First, 2nd Witness Last, Notes, Priest

4340, 10 Jul 1836, Joe, Hypp, -, Ellen, Myres, -, near John O'Ferrals house, -, -, -, -, -, 17

4341, 16 Jul 1836, James, Manning, -, Sarah (widow), Owens, -, St. Mary's , -, -, -, -, -, 17

4342, 17 Jul 1836, Abraham, Starling, -, Catherin (widow), Hawkey, -, St. Mary's , -, -, -, -, -, 17

4343, 28 Aug 1836, Michl, Smith, -, Bridget, Donnelly, -, in Williamsport at her Fathers house, -, -, -, -, -, 17

4344, 07 Oct 1836, Antony, Dignan, -, Mary (widow), Smith, -, in John Oheras, Contractor, Shantee, -, -, -, -, groom is "Antony Dignan, Contractor", 17

4345, 16 Oct 1836, George, Draper, -, Mary, Ryan, -, St. Mary's , -, -, -, -, -, 17

4346, 09 Dec 1836, Charly, Forrester, -, Mary, O'Rourk, -, at John Gorman's Shanty, -, -, -, -, -, 17

4347, 29 Dec 1836, Edward, Brennagin, -, Elizabeth (widow), Ward, -, "in my room" [priest's dwelling], -, -, -, -, -, 17

4348, 01 Jan 1836* , Francis, Reynolds, -, Catherene (widow), Ryan, -, St. Mary's , -, -, -, -, * could be 1837, 17

4349, 14 Jan 1837, Michel, Joice, -, Mary (widow), Keough, -, -, -, -, -, -, -, 17

4350, 14 Jan 1837, Thomas, Qannen, -, Margareth, Gaul, -, -, -, -, -, -, -, 17

4351, 01 Jan 1837, John, O'Reiley, -, Bridget, O'Rieley, -, James O'Rieley's Shantee, -, -, -, -, John is Contractor, 17

4352, 02 Feb 1837, James, Farrell, -, Catherene (widow), Lice [or Suce?], -, "in my own room" [priest's dwelling], -, -, -, -, -, 17

4353, 2 Feb 1837, James, O'Rielly, -, Susan, McGovern, -, "in my own house" [priest's dwelling], -, -, -, -, -, 17

4354, 06 Feb 1837, Patrick, [Dill crossed out] Gillan, -, Winfrod (widow), Kennedy, -, Hagerstown, -, -, -, -, -, 17

4355, 06 Feb 1837, Jeremy, Mehen, -, Anna (widow), Smith, -, Hagerstown, -, -, -, -, -, 17

4356, 14 Feb 1837, Zachiah [?], Gaton, -, Ellon (Miss), Murry, -, in her Father's house near Hancock Md, Ben, Bear, Misses, Russtte, -, 17

ST. MARY'S CATHOLIC CHURCH
HAGERSTOWN, MARYLAND, MARRIAGES:
Index, Date, Groom 1st Name, Groom Last Name, Code, Bride 1st Name, Bride Last Name, Code B, Location of Ceremony, 1st Witness First, 1st Witness Last, 2nd Witness First, 2nd Witness Last, Notes, Priest

4357, 26 Mar 1837, Matthew, Cosey, B, Hannah, Floyde, B, "in my own room" [priest's dwelling], two Servants of Colonel A. Baevens Mason's, -, -, -, -, 17

4358, 13 Apr 1837, Thos, Kelley, -, Jane Elen [?], Peekins, -, near Mr. Yeates, or Tonnolloway Aqaduct, -, -, -, -, groom is a stonecutter, 17

4359, 16 Apr 1837, James, Morgan, -, Nancy (widow), Keller [or Kellen], -, "at Mr. James Hooks house Hancock", -, -, -, -, 17

4360, -, -, -, -, -, -, -, -, -, -, -, -, This entry intentionally left blank.,

4361, 16 Jun 1837, Michael, Canty, -, Margareta, Donovan , -, -, -, -, -, -, -, 16

4362, 22 Jun 1837, Jacobus, Bury, -, Anna, Chichester, -, -, -, -, -, -, -, 16

4363, 09 Jun 1837, Thomas, Brofy, -, Sara, Degne , -, -, -, -, -, -, -, 16

4364, 06 Jul 1837, Hugo, Donnelly, -, Maria, Garraghty, -, Washington County, -, -, -, -, -, 16

4365, 17 Jul 1837, Joannes, Callohan, -, Brigistta, McMahan, -, -, Fr., Gilmeyer, S., Couderon, -, 16

4366, 21 Jul 1837, Henricus, Gardner, -, Margareta, Bachus, -, -, -, -, -, -, -, 16

4367, 17 Jul 1837, Joannes, Lewis, -, Elisabetha, Doke?, -, house of Thomas Means, -, -, -, -, -, 16

4368, 07 Aug 1837, Thomas, Corner, -, Catharina, Kelly, -, Tunnel [Paw Paw Tunnel on C & O Canal], -, -, -, -, -, 16

4369, 09 Aug 1837, Thomas, Sery, -, Maria, Brady, -, in Hancock, -, -, -, -, -, 16

4370, 11 Aug 1837, Dominius Augustus, O'Donnell, -, Maria Anna, Bevans, -, near Hancock, -, -, -, -, -, 16

4371, 18 Aug 1837, Michael, Terry, -, H. , Dellon, -, near Clear Spring, -, -, -, -, -, 16

4372, 24 Aug 1837, Terrentius, Done, -, Margaretha, Fagan, -, Above Clear Spring, -, -, -, -, -, 16

4373, 03 Sep 1837, Johannes, Doyle, -, Maria, Sunderman, -, Tunnel [Paw Paw Tunnel on C & O Canal], -, -, -, -, -, 16

4374, 18 Sep 1837, Michael, Green, -, Brigittae, Smith, -, -, -, -, -, -, -, 16

ST. MARY'S CATHOLIC CHURCH
HAGERSTOWN, MARYLAND, MARRIAGES:
Index, Date, Groom 1st Name, Groom Last Name, Code, Bride 1st Name, Bride Last Name, Code B, Location of Ceremony, 1st Witness First, 1st Witness Last, 2nd Witness First, 2nd Witness Last, Notes, Priest

4375, 04 Oct 1837, Martinus, McLaughlin, -, Birgitta, Hopkins, -, -, -, -, -, -, -, 16

4376, 08 Oct 1837*, Thomas, Kiney, -, Catharina, Keting, -, Clear Spring; *marriage date reads 08 Oct [or Sep] 1837, -, -, -, -, -, 16

4377, 08 Oct 1837, Hugh, McCosker, -, Margareta, Conner, -, Clear Spring, -, -, -, -, -, 16

4378, 17 Oct 1837, Bryne, Monahan, -, Maria, Colens [?], -, Hancock, -, -, -, -, -, 16

4379, 05 Nov 1837, Joannes, O'Kerran, -, Anna, McIvoy, -, -, -, -, -, -, -, 16

4380, 12 Nov 1837, Robertus, Terry, -, Birgitta, Farrel, -, -, -, -, -, -, -, 16

4381, 18 Nov 1837, Joannes M., McConnal [?], -, Anna, Hadk [?]*, -, -, -, -, -, -, *Hadk [?] ["Has" in marriage licenses], 16

4382, 21 Nov 1837, Michael, Drescoll, -, Caroline, Lauer, -, -, -, -, -, -, -, 16

4383, 23 Nov 1837, Michael, Heart, -, Anna A., Roe, -, -, -, -, -, -, -, 16

4384, 25 Nov 1837, William, McGuire, -, Anna, Downey, -, -, -, -, -, -, -, 16

4385, 25 Nov 1837, Fredericus, Fellinger, -, Rosalia, WeissMuller*, -, -, -, -, -, -, -, *WeissMüller, 16

4386, 24 Dec 1837, Patricius, McDrade [?], -, Susanna, O'Donnel, -, -, -, -, -, -, groom's name is McKade in county marriage license, 16

4387, ____? 1837, Nicholaus, Baker, -, Catharina, Mousfeel, -, -, -, -, -, -, bride's name is Mansfield and marriage date is 20 Jan 1838 in Washington County marriage license, 16

4388, 03 Feb 1838, Michael, Delany, -, Mary, Noonan, -, -, -, -, -, -, -, 16

4389, 05 Feb 1837, Jacobus, Kane, -, Mary, McManum, -, -, -, -, -, -, -, 16

4390, 10 Feb 1838, Joannes, Eckert, -, Gertrudis, Keil, -, Hagerstown, -, -, -, -, -, 16

4391, 13 Feb 1838, Robertus W., Watkins, -, Eleonora, Bevans, -, Hancock, -, -, -, -, -, 16

4392, 16 Feb 1838, Guillelmus, Kelley, -, Maria, Smith, -, -, -, -, -, -, -, -, 16

ST. MARY'S CATHOLIC CHURCH
HAGERSTOWN, MARYLAND, MARRIAGES:
Index, Date, Groom 1st Name, Groom Last Name, Code, Bride 1st Name, Bride Last Name, Code B, Location of Ceremony, 1st Witness First, 1st Witness Last, 2nd Witness First, 2nd Witness Last, Notes, Priest

4393, 18 Feb 1838, Andreas, Conlon, -, Maria, , -, -, -, -, -, -, -, 16

4394, 18 Feb 1838, Patricius, McGrane?, -, Catharina, McQuaid, -, -, -, -, -, -, -, 16

4395, 19 Feb 1838, Conradus, Stey, -, Catharina, Wihand?, -, -, -, -, -, -, -, 16

4396, 19 Feb 1838, Carolus Guillelmus , Weiss, -, Ludovica, Hirzelan [?], -, -, -, -, -, -, -, 16

4397, 19 Feb 1838, Joannes, Neibert, -, Theresia, Roman, -, -, -, -, -, -, -, 16

4398, 27 Feb 1838, Timotheas, Sullivan, -, Helena, Healy, -, -, -, -, -, -, -, 16

4399, 27 Feb 1838, Terentius, McGuigan, -, Maria, McElroy, -, -, -, -, -, -, -, 16

4400, 24 Apr 1838, Joannes K., Smith, -, Elisabeth, Adams, -, -, -, -, -, -, -, 16

4401, 29 Apr 1838, Jacobus, Petri, -, Elisabeth, Freidhofin, -, -, -, -, -, -, -, 16

4402, 17 May 1838, Guillelmus, Lallay, -, Maria, David, -, -, -, -, -, -, -, 16

4403, 23 May 1838, Franciscus, Gallagher, -, Anna, Murray, -, -, -, -, -, -, -, 16

4404, 14 Jun 1838, Joannes, Gorman, -, Julia Anna, Denny, -, -, -, -, -, -, -, 16

4405, 17 Jun 1838, Michael, Degnan, -, Elisabeth, Deacon, -, -, -, -, -, -, -, 16

4406, 08 Jul 1838, Guillelmus, McGurk, -, Sara, Reed, -, -, -, -, -, -, -, 16

4407, 16 Jul 1838, Georgius, Protastinger, -, Elisabeth, Schilhass, -, -, -, -, -, -, -, 16

4408, 24 Jul 1838, Fredericus, Hammel, -, Julia Anna, Hofacker, -, -, -, -, -, -, -, 16

4409, 01 Aug 1838, Joannes, McCann, -, Anna, Quin, -, -, -, -, -, -, -, 16

4410, 07 Aug 1838, Henricus, Gramsie, -, Elisabeth, Meinan, -, -, -, -, -, -, -, 16

4411, 11 Aug 1838, Donel, Spelohan, -, Magareta, Luhy, -, -, -, -, -, -, -, 16

ST. MARY'S CATHOLIC CHURCH
HAGERSTOWN, MARYLAND, MARRIAGES:
Index, Date, Groom 1st Name, Groom Last Name, Code, Bride 1st Name, Bride Last Name, Code B, Location of Ceremony, 1st Witness First, 1st Witness Last, 2nd Witness First, 2nd Witness Last, Notes, Priest

4412, 12 Aug 1838, William, Clark, -, Margaretha, MacLain , -, -, -, -, -, -, -, 16

4413, 03 Sep 1838, William, Colman, -, Ellan, Mahoney, -, -, -, -, -, -, -, 16

4414, 09 Sep 1838, Robert, Lee, -, Cecelia, Wals, -, -, -, -, -, -, -, 16

4415, 15 Sep 1838, Petrus, Colens, -, Rosa, Lyands, -, -, -, -, -, -, -, 16

4416, 29 Sep 1838, Thomas, Drageser, -, Margareta, Hartmann, -, -, -, -, -, -, -, 16

4417, 29 Sep 1838, Josephus, Reinhard, -, Catharina, Kluch, -, -, -, -, -, -, -, 16

4418, 29 Sep 1838, Joannes, McCoslar, -, Sara, Bishop, -, -, -, -, -, -, -, 16

4419, 07 Oct 1838, Patrick, Mayar [or Magarn], -, Maria, Brown, -, -, -, -, -, -, -, 16

4420, 08 Oct 1838, Philippus, Tinges, -, Maria Anna, Hartmann, -, -, -, -, -, -, -, 16

4421, 14 Oct 1838, Franciscus Martinus, Zinkand, -, Joanna, Hohfacher, -, -, -, -, -, -, -, 16

4422, 29 Oct 1838, Michael, Calory, -, Elisabeth, McAfferty , -, -, -, -, -, -, -, 16

4423, 23 Oct 1838, Samuel, Reinhart, -, Elisabeth, Bevans, -, -, -, -, -, -, -, 16

4424, 11 Dec 1838, Patricius, Clark, -, Catharina, Caudy, -, -, -, -, -, -, -, 16

4425, 23 Dec 1838, Joannes, Casy, -, Maria, Rogan, -, -, -, -, -, -, -, 16

4426, 25 Dec 1838, Jacobus, Cronly, -, Maria, Hedwidge, -, -, -, -, -, -, -, 16

4427, 25 Dec 1838, Josephus, Schreiber, -, Syn, Steel, -, -, -, -, -, -, -, 16

4428, 06 Jan 1839, David, Morrison, -, Anna Elisabeth, Toohey, -, -, -, -, -, -, -, 16

4429, 07 Jan 1839, Patricius, Kelly, -, Sara, Mooney, -, -, -, -, -, -, -, 16

4430, 27 Jan 1839, Hugo, Slowie, -, Mary, Reed, -, -, -, -, -, -, -, 16

4431, 31 Jan 1839, Josephus, Galloway, -, Maria, Rideout, -, -, -, -, -, -, -, 16

ST. MARY'S CATHOLIC CHURCH
HAGERSTOWN, MARYLAND, MARRIAGES:
Index, Date, Groom 1st Name, Groom Last Name, Code, Bride 1st Name, Bride Last Name, Code B, Location of Ceremony, 1st Witness First, 1st Witness Last, 2nd Witness First, 2nd Witness Last, Notes, Priest

4432, 10 Feb 1839, Joannes, Briscoe, -, Sara Anna, Wigus, -, -, -, -, -, -, -, 16

4433, 10 Feb 1838, Bernardus, Brady, -, Carolina, Sedan, -, -, -, -, -, -, -, 16

4434, 07 Mar 1839, Guiillelmus G., Haidan, -, Henrietta, Spittler, -, -, -, -, -, -, -, 16

4435, 04 Apr 1839, Owen, Houraty, -, Mary, McCabe, -, -, -, -, -, -, -, 16

4436, 08 Apr 1839, Petrus, Steal, -, Catharina, Kasekanom [?], -, -, -, -, -, -, -, 16

4437, 05 Jun 1839, Robertus, Wilson, -, Lucia, Shorter, -, -, Joseph , Piegut [?], Michael, Stanton, -, 16

4438, 09 Aug 1839, Joannes, Mulligan, -, Margaretae, Kelly, -, -, -, -, -, -, -, 16

4439, 17 Aug 1839, Jacobus Josephus, Barrett, -, Maria Anna, O'Donnell, -, -, -, -, -, -, -, 16

4440, 18 Aug 1839, Henricus Rudolfus, Durninerman, -, Maria Catharina, Lang, -, -, -, -, -, -, -, 16

4441, 02 Sep 1839, Patricius, Murphey, -, Birgitta, McGee, -, -, -, -, -, -, -, 16

4442, 09 __? 1839, Bernardus, Crowley?, -, Margareta, Lane, -, -, -, -, -, -, -, 16

4443, 03 Oct 1839, Joannes, Daily, -, Kesia, Rowland, -, -, -, -, -, -, -, 16

4444, 10 Nov 1839, Joannes, Condry, -, Anna, Cartors [or Carlors], -, -, -, -, -, -, -, 16

4445, 17 Nov 1839, Michael, Divine, -, Sophia, May, -, -, -, -, -, -, -, 16

4446, 24 Nov 1839, Henricus, Hegert, -, Catharina, Jekel, -, -, -, -, -, -, -, 16

4447, 09 Feb 1840, Bernardus, Kraus, -, Mary Ann, Brehm, -, -, -, -, -, -, -, 16

4448, 27 Apr 1840, Bernardus, König, -, Elisabeth, Chistopher, -, -, -, -, -, -, -, 16

4449, 08 May 1840, Joannes, Beers, -, Mary, O'Brian, -, -, -, -, -, -, -, 16

4450, 11 May 1840, Daniel, Toy , -, Margareta, Maxwell, -, -, -, -, -, -, -, 16

ST. MARY'S CATHOLIC CHURCH
HAGERSTOWN, MARYLAND, MARRIAGES:
Index, Date, Groom 1st Name, Groom Last Name, Code, Bride 1st Name, Bride Last Name, Code B, Location of Ceremony, 1st Witness First, 1st Witness Last, 2nd Witness First, 2nd Witness Last, Notes, Priest

4451, 04 Jun 1840, Joannes, Roberts, -, Rosa Anna, McLauglin, -, -, Catharine, Mulhoron, Michael, McLaughlin, -, 16

4452, -, -, -, -, -, -, -, -, -, -, -, -, This entry intentionally left blank.,

4453, -, -, -, -, -, -, -, -, -, -, -, -, This entry intentionally left blank.,

4454, -, -, -, -, -, -, -, -, -, -, -, -, This entry intentionally left blank.,

4455, 04 Jul 1840, Jeremias, Sullivan, -, Anna, Tiva, -, -, Bridget, Ryan*, Arthur, Rodes, *"mother of the bride", 16

4456, 05 Jul 1840, Jacob, Maysinger, -, Margareta, Gouker, -, -, -, -, -, -, -, 16

4457, 13 Jul 1840, Arthur, Rhodes, -, Rosa Anna, McGinly, -, -, -, -, -, -, -, 16

4458, 13 Jul 1840, Lucas, Cassidy, -, Catharina, Donnelly, -, -, -, -, -, -, -, 16

4459, 22 Jul 1840, Joannes, Kelly, -, Maria, Horse, -, -, -, -, -, -, -, 16

4460, 26 Jul 1840, Daniel, Hurley, -, Maria Anna, Cross, -, -, -, -, -, -, -, 16

4461, 01 Aug 1840, Charles, McCain, -, Maria, Fealy, -, -, -, -, -, -, -, 16

4462, 02 Aug 1840, Daniel W., Gauger, -, Elisabeth, Hartmann, -, -, -, -, -, -, -, 16

4463, 16 Aug 1840, Patricius, Rogan, -, Anna, Loan, -, -, -, -, -, -, -, 16

4464, 23 Aug 1840, Hugo, Rock, -, Maria, Little, -, -, -, -, -, -, -, 16

4465, 08 Sep 1840, Patricius, Tornay, -, Johanna, Kennedy, -, -, -, -, -, -, -, 16

4466, 20 Sep 1840, Michael, Land, -, Julia, O'Brian, -, -, -, -, -, -, -, 16

4467, 20 Sep 1840, Garret, Hogan, -, Catharina, Timple, -, -, -, -, -, -, -, 16

4468, 20 Oct 1840, Antonius, Ready, -, Catharina, Barrett, -, -, -, -, -, -, -, 16

4469, 01 Nov 1840, Richardus, Godard, -, Martha, Barry, -, -, -, -, -, -, -, 40

4470, 19 Nov 1840, Joannes, Gauker, -, Elleonora, Hartmann, -, -, -, -, -, -, -, 16

4471, 26 Nov 1840, Patricius, McDonnell, -, Maria, Sharen, -, -, -, -, -, -, -, 16

ST. MARY'S CATHOLIC CHURCH
HAGERSTOWN, MARYLAND, MARRIAGES:
Index, Date, Groom 1st Name, Groom Last Name, Code, Bride 1st Name, Bride Last Name, Code B, Location of Ceremony, 1st Witness First, 1st Witness Last, 2nd Witness First, 2nd Witness Last, Notes, Priest

4472, 09 Dec 1840, Joannes, Cunningham, -, Margareta, Holbert, -, -, -, -, -, -, -, 16

4473, 18 Dec 1840, Jacobus, Conry, -, Catherina, Bearn, -, -, -, -, -, -, -, 16

4474, 19 Dec 1840, Michael, Flanigan, -, Maria, Farrel, -, -, -, -, -, -, -, 16

4475, 27 Dec 1840, Petrus, Nathan, -, Margareta, Carl, -, -, -, -, -, -, -, 16

4476, 06 Jan 1841, Anthonius, Fitzpatrick, -, Anna, Riley, -, -, -, -, -, -, -, 16

4477, 18 Jan 1841, Jacobus, Doyle, -, Elisabeth, Dugan, -, -, -, -, -, -, -, 16

4478, 03 Feb 1841, Thomas, Raynolds, -, Birgitta, Coppley, -, -, -, -, -, -, -, 16

4479, 19 Feb 1841, Leonardus, Moore, -, Elisabeth Catharinae, Mattingby, -, -, -, -, -, -, -, -, 16

4480, 21 Feb 1841, Thomas, McCormack, -, Catharina, Farrell, -, -, -, -, -, -, -, 16

4481, 23 Feb 1841, Joannes, Mallon, -, Birgitta, Philips, -, -, -, -, -, -, -, 16

4482, 12 Apr 1841, Joannes, McCauley, -, Catharina, Gormon, -, -, -, -, -, -, -, 16

4483, 06 May 1841, David, Gauker, -, Sophia, Oster, -, -, -, -, -, -, -, 16

4484, 09 May 1841, Amos, Adams, -, Catharina Anna, Clarke, -, -, -, -, -, -, -, 16

4485, 06 Jull 1841, Joannes, Bean, -, Birgitta, Gallagher, -, -, -, -, -, -, -, 16

4486, 15 Aug 1841, Eugenias, Bannon, -, Elisabeth, Rice, -, -, -, -, -, -, -, 16

4487, 15 Aug 1841, Eugenias, Carney, -, Birgitta, Carlosk, -, -, -, -, -, -, -, 16

4488, 17 Aug 1841, Thomas, Casy, -, Birgitta, Riley, -, -, -, -, -, -, -, 16

4489, 08 Sep 1841, Lienhard, Hohenstein, -, Margareta, Fayetlin, -, -, -, -, -, -, -, 16

4490, 18 Sep 1841, Patricius, Linch, -, Birgitta, Connelly, -, -, -, -, -, -, -, 16

ST. MARY'S CATHOLIC CHURCH HAGERSTOWN, MARYLAND, MARRIAGES:
Index, Date, Groom 1st Name, Groom Last Name, Code, Bride 1st Name, Bride Last Name, Code B, Location of Ceremony, 1st Witness First, 1st Witness Last, 2nd Witness First, 2nd Witness Last, Notes, Priest

4491, 09 Sep 1841, Jacobus, McGrow, -, Elisabeth, Dont, -, -, -, -, -, -, -, 16

4492, 19 Sep 1841, Joannes, Dignan, -, Julia, Donoghoe [?], -, -, -, -, -, -, -, 16

4493, 20 Nov 1841, Michael, Breslin, -, Catharina, Mulharon, -, -, -, -, -, -, -, 16

4494, 13 Dec 1841, Joannes, Largy, -, Johanna, Murphey, -, -, -, -, -, -, -, 16

4495, 17 Dec 1841, Andreas, Clarke, -, Margareta, Kelly, -, -, -, -, -, -, -, 16

4496, 12 Jul 1842, Opherebus Dominius, Hannon, -, Judith, Daugherty, -, -, -, -, -, -, -, 16

4497, 13 Oct 1842, Franciscus, Sweeny, -, Anna, Miller, -, -, -, -, -, -, -, 16

4498, 30 Oct 1842, Josephus, Hartmann, -, Anna Martha, Keilemann, -, -, -, -, -, -, -, 16

4499, 15 Jan 1843, Georgius, Gardner, -, Magdalena, Fetter, -, -, -, -, -, -, -, 16

4500, 16 Jul 1843, Patricius, Purcel, -, Birgitta, Maurice, -, -, -, -, -, -, -, 16

4501, 26 Jul 1843, Patricius, Mattewes, -, Eleonora, Colvin, -, -, -, -, -, -, -, 16

4502, 22 Aug 1843, Isaak, Gehr, -, Cecilia, Harritt, -, -, -, -, -, -, -, 16

4503, 03 Sep 1843, Henricus, Jonston, -, Carena, Hill, -, -, -, -, -, -, -, 16

4504, 20 Aug 1843, Patricius, Little, -, Isabella, Dugan, -, -, -, -, -, -, -, 16

4505, 28 ___? 1843, Henricus, Bellman, -, Henrietta, Heiser, -, -, -, -, -, -, -, 16

4506, 24 Oct 1843, Jacobus Henricus, Bevans, -, Evelina Ludovica, Bevans, -, -, -, -, -, -, the couple was married "with dispensation in the 3rd degree", 16

4507, 18 Oct 1843, Richardus, Roa, -, Catharina, Mooney, -, -, -, -, -, -, -, 16

4508, 21 Nov 1843, Edwardus, Shehan, -, Francisca, McIlhenny, -, -, -, -, -, -, -, 16

ST. MARY'S CATHOLIC CHURCH
HAGERSTOWN, MARYLAND, MARRIAGES:
Index, Date, Groom 1st Name, Groom Last Name, Code, Bride 1st Name, Bride Last Name, Code B, Location of Ceremony, 1st Witness First, 1st Witness Last, 2nd Witness First, 2nd Witness Last, Notes, Priest

4509, 30 Nov 1843, Upton, McClain, -, Anna, Wolf, -, -, -, -, -, -, -, 16

4510, 17 Dec 1843, Charolus, McCauley, -, Anna A., Black, -, -, -, -, -, -, -, 16

4511, 01 Jan 1844, Josephus Henricus, Bevans, -, Maria, Higgans, -, -, -, -, -, -, -, 16

4512, 01 Jan 1844, Joannes, Linch, -, Elleonora, Brannon, -, -, -, -, -, -, -, 16

4513, 18 Jan 1844, Loyd, Brown, -, Rosa, Dorsey, -, -, -, -, -, -, -, 16

4514, 01 Mar 1844, Richardus, Fagan, -, Phoebe, O'Brian, -, -, -, -, -, -, -, 16

4515, 18 Jun 1844, Timotheus, McLeary, -, Johanna, Donovan, -, -, -, -, -, -, -, 16

4516, 01 Aug 1844, Joannes, Hartmann, -, Margarita, Swob, -, -, -, -, -, -, -, 16

4517, 13 Oct 1845, Henry S., Barnett, -, Catharine (Miss), Tancy, -, -, Daniel, O'Learey, John, Adams, -, 19

4518, 04 Nov 1845, John, McCann, -, Rosanna (Miss), Shervin, -, -, Mr. & Mrs., Shervin, -, -, -, 19

4519, 06 Nov 1845, Denis, Cain, -, Lavinia (Miss), Mills, -, -, John Q., Adams, E. (Miss), Maguire, Lavinia baptized "she never having been baptized.", 19

4520, 02 Dec 1845, John Henry, Rohe, -, Ann (Miss), Wyland, P, -, John Q., Adams, E. (Miss), Maguire, -, 19

4521, 03 Dec 1845, Joseph, Rodgers, -, Maria (Mrs.), Artison, -, -, Mr. & Mrs., Cobler, -, -, (a widow with 3 children) and baptized her, she never having been baptized., 19

4522, 04 Jan 1846, Lewis, Baughman, -, Elizabeth (Miss), Schleigh, -, -, Mr. & Mrs., Schleigh, John, Adams, -, 19

4523, 06 Jan 1846, Robert, Hazelet, -, Sarah (Miss), Green, -, -, Mr. & Mrs. , Stover, [blank], Hurt, groom received Dispensation to marry because he was never baptized, 19

4524, 13 Jan 1846, William, Bevans, -, Henrietta (Miss), Shirley, -, -, Mr., Bevans, Mrs., Bevans [HB], -, 19

4525, 11 Nov 1846, James B., Moore, -, Mary Jane (Miss), Logun, -, Mr. Levi Moore's house, Levi, Moore, Catharine, More, -, 19

ST. MARY'S CATHOLIC CHURCH
HAGERSTOWN, MARYLAND, MARRIAGES:
Index, Date, Groom 1st Name, Groom Last Name, Code, Bride 1st Name, Bride Last Name, Code B, Location of Ceremony, 1st Witness First, 1st Witness Last, 2nd Witness First, 2nd Witness Last, Notes, Priest

4526, 06 Dec 1846, Lewis, Brown, FB, Mary, Colbert, FB, -, Isaac, Brown, John, Jordon, -, 19

4527, 08 Dec 1846, George, Tgel?, -, Kunegunda (Miss), Seyfert, -, -, E. (Miss), Maguire, C. (Miss), Gilmeyer, -, 19

4528, 02 Jan 1847, John, Skelly, -, Elizabeth (Miss), Hauss?, -, Widow Bevans house near Hancock, Mrs., Bevans, Thomas, Bevans, -, 19

4529, 14 Jan 1847, Richard, Bearsey, -, Elizabeth (Miss), Lowman, -, -, Richard (Rev.), O'Connor, John, McIntere, -, 19

4530, 14 Jan 1847, Tosmmerset, Ballad, FB, Maria, Reister, FB, -, N. (Dr.), Scott, N. (Mrs. Dr.), Scott [HB], -, 19

4531, 02 Feb 1847, James A., McClain, -, Clarissa C. (Miss), Middcalf, -, near Williamsport, Michael, Smith, Joseph, Smith, -, 19

4532, 15 Apr 1847, Charles, Karnes, -, Mrs., Munday (widow), -, St. Mary's, E. (Miss), Maguire, C. (Miss), Gilmeyer, bride from Hancock; groom from Washington Co., 19

4533, 18 May 1847, Thomas, Harbine, -, Catharine (Miss), Smith, -, Michael Smith's house, Mrs., Smith, Mr., Smith, -, 19

4534, 23 May 1847, John, Bevans, -, Margaret Ann (Miss), Catlett, -, on the Potomac-shore near Fifteen Mile Creek; groom of Allegany Co.; bride of Morgan Co., VA, Dr., Peugh, Basil, Bevans, -, 19

4535, 25 May 1847, Sebastian, Gillmeyer, -, Mary Elizabeth (Miss), Maguire, -, Hagerstown., Mr., Gillmeyer, Mrs., Gillmeyer, Mary of District of Columbia; groom from Washington Co., 19

4536, 29 Aug 1847, Ulton, Moore, -, Elizabeth, Myers, BA, near Parkhead, Levi, Moore, James, Moore, -, 19

4537, 1 Sep 1847, Nicholas, O'Keefe, -, Helena, Adams, -, St. Mary's, George, Gilmeyer, Mary Ann, Robinson, -, 19

4538, 4 Oct 1847, John William, Holland, GA, Ann E. (Miss), Moore, -, near Parkhead, Alexander, Moore, Levi, Moore, groom from Virginia; bride from Wash. Co., 19

4539, 26 Oct 1847, Michael, Shedrick, GA, Sophia (Miss), Mouse, -, "near the Indian Spring" [Indian Spring], Thomas, Maines, Peter, Mouse, -, 19

ST. MARY'S CATHOLIC CHURCH
HAGERSTOWN, MARYLAND, MARRIAGES:
Index, Date, Groom 1st Name, Groom Last Name, Code, Bride 1st Name, Bride Last Name, Code B, Location of Ceremony, 1st Witness First, 1st Witness Last, 2nd Witness First, 2nd Witness Last, Notes, Priest

4540, 21 Oct 1847, Wilfred E., Hawken, -, Mary E. (Miss), Long, -, Hagerstown, Mary, Hawken, Louisa, Donelly, both of Williamsport, 19

4541, 21 Oct 1847, John, Ford, -, Catharine (Miss), Burkhart, BA, Hagerstown, Charles, Hart, Mrs., Burkhart, both from Hagerstown, 19

4542, 4 Nov 1847, George, Lorshbough, GA, Frances (Miss), McIntire, -, Hagerstown, Mr. D., Roman, Mr., Johnston, both from Hagerstown, 19

4543, Feb 1848, Ethelbert, Taney, -, Martha (widow), Snyder, BA, near Parkhead, Ulton, Moore, Ulton (Mrs.), Moore, -, 19

4544, 29 May 1848, James V., Cook, -, Mary Ann (Miss), Shircliff, -, Fifteen M. Creek, L., Shircliff, W., Shircliff, both of Allegany Co., 19

4545, 2 Jun 1848, John Hoppin, Gardner, GA, "Widow", Debinstine, -, Fifteen M. Creek, Mr., Low, Elizabeth, Shirley, -, 19

4546, 13 Jun 1848, Frederick, Helsey, -, Ann (widow), Shober, -, Hagerstown, Valentine, Renner, Barbara, Renner, -, 19

4547, 3 Aug 1848, Joseph, Klunk, -, Mary Ann, Robinson, -, Hagerstown , E. (Mrs.), Gilmeyer, Catharine, Robinson, groom of Adams Co., PA; bride from Washington Co., 19

4548, 31 Aug 1848, Wesley, Lizer, GA, Mary E., Gauger, -, Hagerstown , her brother, his sister, -, -, groom and bride from Cavetown District, 19

4549, 27 Nov 1848, George, Graves, GA, Amelia E. (Miss), Murray, -, near Hancock, Richard, Murray, Richard (Mrs.), Murray, -, 19

4550, 19 Dec 1848, Wesley, Wolke, -, Elizabeth (Miss), Rohe, -, St. Mary's, C., Robinson, Regina, Gillmeyer, -, 19

4551, 28 Jan 1849, James, McGahan, -, Ann, Curley, -, Tunnel [Paw Paw Tunnel on C & O Canal]; Fifteen Mile Creek, Henry, Barnett, Catharine, Barnett [HB], -, 19

4552, 11 Feb 1849, Herman, Renner, -, Caroline (Miss), Renner, -, near Hancock, T [or I.] (Mr.), Renner, T [or I.]'s (Mrs.), Renner, "with a Dispensation from the Archbishop, they being first cousins", 19

ST. MARY'S CATHOLIC CHURCH
HAGERSTOWN, MARYLAND, MARRIAGES:
Index, Date, Groom 1st Name, Groom Last Name, Code, Bride 1st Name, Bride Last Name, Code B, Location of Ceremony, 1st Witness First, 1st Witness Last, 2nd Witness First, 2nd Witness Last, Notes, Priest

4553, 15 Feb 1849, Thomas, Hassett, -, Ellen (Miss), Silvers, BA, near Clear Spring, Joseph, Smith, Mary Ann, *, * no last name given - described as "Joseph Smith's sister", 19

4554, 21 Apr 1849, John, Hanlan, -, Mary (Miss), Hornbeck, -, Tunnel [Paw Paw Tunnel on C & O Canal]; Fifteen Mile Creek, H. (Mr.), Barnett, Catharine, Barnett [HB] *, * her maiden name is Taney, 19

4555, 10 Jun 1849, James W., Wolvington, GA, Catharine M. (Miss), Garlin, -, Hancock, Mr., Coudy, Mr., Harrit, -, 19

4556, 26 Jun 1849, John, Riley, -, Rosanna (Mrs.), Prior, -, Hancock, Hugh, McCosker, -, -, bride is widow, 19

4557, 22 Jul 1849, John, Dooling, -, Ann (widow), Reynolds, -, Fifteen Mile Creek, Mr., Benton, Dr., Peugh, ["Ann Reynolds - he died in a month's after." [I cannot tell if this is the old husband or the new], 19

4558, 19 Aug 1849, Lewis, Tinterman, GA, Barbara (Miss), Gauger, -, Hagerstown, W., McClain, Ed., Shehan, -, 19

4559, 1 Oct 1849, John, Hughes, -, Mary Ann, Gorman, -, Hancock, near Dam No. 6, Charles, Clarke, Charles's wife, Clarke, -, 19

4560, 28 Oct 1849, Bernard, Smith, -, Jane, Arnold, -, on Tunnel Hill [Paw Paw Tunnell on the C & O Canal], Thomas, Hunt, "several more", -, bride and groom from VA, 19

4561, 22 Jan 1850, Reuben, Streit, -, Anna (Miss), Harbaugh, -, Hagerstown, Cath., Gilmeyer, Cath., Robinson, "dead since" written in pencil, 19

4562, 17 Mar 1850, Michael, Horin, -, Ellen, Doyle, -, Hagerstown, George, Gillmeyer, C., Robinson, -, 19

4563, 23 Mar 1850, Bernard, Lynch, -, Louisa, Gibson*, -, 15 Mile Creek, Charles W., Harman, Wiliam H., Hayward, "She was baptized before the ceremony."; *Gibson ["or Baxter" crossed out in pencil], 19

4564, 16 Apr 1850, Charles W., Woltz, -, Amelia (Miss), Stake, -, Williamsport, Eli, Stake, C., McCardel, and others, 19

4565, 13 Aug 1850, Matthias C., Kyne, -, Catharine (Miss), White, -, Hagerstown, Mrs., Gillmeyer, Catharine, Robinson, bride and groom from Martinsburg, VA, 19

ST. MARY'S CATHOLIC CHURCH
HAGERSTOWN, MARYLAND, MARRIAGES:
Index, Date, Groom 1st Name, Groom Last Name, Code, Bride 1st Name, Bride Last Name, Code B, Location of Ceremony, 1st Witness First, 1st Witness Last, 2nd Witness First, 2nd Witness Last, Notes, Priest

4566, 14 Aug 1850, Adolphus Leopold, Kniess, -, Margaret Emile (Miss), Finger, -, Hagerstown , Catharine, Robinson, Mrs., "Cook her mother" *, bride and groom from Washington Co.; * it is unclear if this means she is the mother of the bride or of the other witness., 19

4567, 2 Oct 1850, Adam, Buahner, -, Catharine (Miss), Swope, -, Clear Spring, -, Swope, -, Swope, "in presence of her parents", 19

4568, 10 Oct 1850, John, Doyle, -, Bridget (Miss), Horne, -, Hagerstown , George, Gilmeyer, Catharine, Robinson, -, 19

4569, 17 Oct 1850, William H., Harrison, FB, Harriet, -, S, Hagerstown , George , Gilmeyer, Mr., Mason, bride is "a slave of Mr. John Mason" and married with his consent, 19

4570, 19 Nov 1850, John, Truman, FB, Mary, Brown, FB, Hagerstown , Mr., Brown, Mrs., Brown , the witnesses, Mr. & Mrs. Brown are the parents of the bride, 19

4571, 22 Dec 1850, John B., Winkelman, -, Mary Ann, Burds, -, Bevansville [in present-day Garrett Co., MD; would have been Allegany Co. at that time], W., Bevans, L., Bevans *, bride and groom from Allegany Co.; *the witnesses' names were written as if they were a husband and wife, 19

4572, Jan 1851, Edward, Doneley, -, Mary, McKann, -, Hancock, Mrs., Bevans, Thomas, Bevans, -, 19

4573, 5 Feb 1851, Thomas, Bevans, -, Elizabeth (Miss), Sheriff, -, Hancock, Mr., Rinehart, Mrs., Rinehart, bride and groom from Washington Co., 15

4574, 20 Feb 1851, Philip, Herbert, FB, Margaret, Hemsley, FB, Hagerstown , Mrs., Dorsey, Sebastian, Gilemeyer, -, 19

4575, 1 Apr 1851, John, Shepperd, -, Margaret (Miss), Souder, -, Hagerstown , Mr., Renner, Mrs., Renner, -, 19

4576, 27 Feb 1851, John, Fessler, -, Susan, Maguire, -, Hagerstown , Eliza, Gillmeyer, C., Robinson, See Endnote 40., 19

4577, 27 Feb 1851, John Henry, Martin, -, Lucy, Mouse, -, Indianspring, Mr., Mouse, Mrs., Mouse, See Endnote 41., 19

4578, 8 May 1851, Benjamin F., Kershner, -, Anna Rebecca, Freaner, -, Hagerstown , many witnesses, -, -, -, -, 19

4579, 13 May 1851, John D., Turner, -, Mary, McIlhenny, -, Hagerstown , Mrs., Milton, Js., Hurley, -, 19

ST. MARY'S CATHOLIC CHURCH
HAGERSTOWN, MARYLAND, MARRIAGES:
Index, Date, Groom 1st Name, Groom Last Name, Code, Bride 1st Name, Bride Last Name, Code B, Location of Ceremony, 1st Witness First, 1st Witness Last, 2nd Witness First, 2nd Witness Last, Notes, Priest

4580, 5 Jun 1851, James, Cassidy, -, Louisa* , Donelly, -, -, Mrs., Donnelly, Rev. J., Maguire, *Louisa [Mary crossed out], 19

4581, 8 Jun 1851, Otho, Gillons, B, Maria, Smith, B, S, -, Geo., Gillmeyer, Kate (Miss), Gillmyer, bride is slave of William McLain; 3rd witness is Regina (Miss) Gillmeyer, 20

4582, 9 Aug 1851, Arthur, Kenney, -, Bridget, Hennessey, -, -, Peter, Hennessey, Thomas, Hennessy, -, 19

4583, 27 Aug 1851, Thomas, Clarke, -, Catharine, Maguire, -, -, J. I.[or J.] (Rev.), Maguire, Mercy (Miss), May, -, 19

4584, 22 Nov 1851, Owen, King, -, Ellen, Heslehan [?], -, -, David, Barry, Margaret, Barry, -, 20

4585, 24 Dec 1851, Edward, McCoy, -, Caroline, Cook, -, -, bride's mother, -, many witnesses, -, -, 19

4586, 25 Dec 1851, Ulton F., McArdell, -, Ann E., Morin, -, -, Courtney, McArdell, Mercy, May, -, 19

4587, 19 Feb 1852, Henry J., Brown, -, Catharine, Craig, B , [Hagerstown crossed out], Mercy, May, John, Truman, -, 19

4588, 29 Mar 1852, David, Martin, -, Isabella, Mouse, -, -, Mr., Shedrick, Mrs., Shedrick [HB], -, 19

4589, 11 May 1852, Dr. Josiah F., Smith, -, Catharine (Miss), Horine, -, Boonsboro, Michael, Smith, Mrs. C., Smith [HB], bride and groom from Boonsboro; 3rd witness is Wm. McClain, 19

4590, 20 May 1852, Perry, Moxly, S, B, Sarah, Hemsly, -, Hagerstown , Robert, Harris, Matilda, Williamson, groom is "slave of Isaac B. Hunter", 20

4591, 7 Jun 1852, John W., Blakely, -, Marion E., Gerrard, -, Hagerstown , Thos., Bevans, Kate (Miss), Doyle, -, 20

4592, Jun 1852, William, Smith, S, Mary J., Dunn, FB, St. Mary's, Philip, Brown, Sarah, Brown [HB], groom is "slave of Michael Smith", 20

4593, 10 Jul 1852, Christian, Link, -, Anna M. (Miss), Berkley, -, St. Mary's Church, P., Brown, S., Brown, bride and groom from VA, 19

4594, 18 Nov 1852, John, Delcour, -, Mary (widow), Walder, -, St. Mary's Church, Philip, Brown, Sarah, Brown, -, 19

4595, 31 Jan 1853, Isaac, Moore, -, Matilda (Miss), Mills, P, near St. Thomas' Church, Levi, Moore, Alexander, Moore, -, 19

ST. MARY'S CATHOLIC CHURCH HAGERSTOWN, MARYLAND, MARRIAGES:

Index, Date, Groom 1st Name, Groom Last Name, Code, Bride 1st Name, Bride Last Name, Code B, Location of Ceremony, 1st Witness First, 1st Witness Last, 2nd Witness First, 2nd Witness Last, Notes, Priest

4596, 21 Feb 1853, Joachim, Shilling (widower), -, Elizabeth (Miss), Markoe, -, St. Mary's, Philip, Brown, Ellenora, Shilling, both Catholic, 19

4597, 4 Apr 1853, Daniel, Deitrick, -, Ann (Miss), Bevans, -, at Mr. Levi Moore's residence, Levi, More, John, Holland, both Catholic, 19

4598, 5 Apr 1853, Robert, Warner, -, Mary E. (Miss), Shafer, P, in Clear Spring, Rev. Th., McCaffrey, Wm. , Kreigh, -, 19

4599, 17 Apr 1853, John Theodore, Knackstedt, -, Mary A. (Mrs.), Riffsnyder, -, St. Mary's, John, Tierney, James I.[or T.], Hurley, both Catholic, 19

4600, 18 Sep 1853, George, Kline, -, Margaret, Crist, -, St. Mary's, John, Crist, Michael, Crist, both Catholic; "Married after three Publications of the Banns of marriage", 19

4601, 27 Oct 1853, Henry, Wolf, P, GA, Mary A.J. (Miss), McClain, -, Wm. McClain's house, Wm. , McClain, John, Wolfe, bride is Catholic, 19

4602, 14 Feb 1854, William S., Duffey, -, Eliza F., Stake, -, "at her Father's house Williamsport", James I. [or T.], Hurley, Dr. J., Smith, 3rd witness is Peter McGeery , 19

4603, 6 Jun 1854, William J., McBride, -, Susan (Miss) **, Snyder, -, "Mr. Protzman's Hotel of this place", Mr., Protzman, Watson, -, -, 19

4604, 16 Aug 1854, James R., McLaughlin, GA, Catharine B., Doyle, -, Mr. Wm. Doyle's Hotel, Mr., Doyle, Mrs., Doyle [HB], 3rd witness is Doctor F. Dorsey, 19

4605, 22 Aug 1854, Philip T., McDonald, -, Elizabeth, Guyer *, -, Hagerstown , Sarah, Brown, Mrs., Miller &c, -, 19

4606, 21 Oct 1854, Aloysius, Dealhauser, -, Johanna, Mitterer, -, St. Mary's Church, James, Flyn, Mary, Kreigh, "Married after three Publications of the Banns of marriage", 19

4607, 14 Nov 1854, William E., Medcalf, -, Sarah Ann, Hammersley, -, Hagerstown , Mr., Gruber, Mrs., Gruber, -, 19

4608, 12 Feb 1855, Edward, Donelly, -, Mary, Kail, -, St. Mary's Church, James, Flynn, George, Hoy, bride and groom from Williamsport, 19

ST. MARY'S CATHOLIC CHURCH
HAGERSTOWN, MARYLAND, MARRIAGES:
Index, Date, Groom 1st Name, Groom Last Name, Code, Bride 1st Name, Bride Last Name, Code B, Location of Ceremony, 1st Witness First, 1st Witness Last, 2nd Witness First, 2nd Witness Last, Notes, Priest

4609, 18 Apr 1855, Andrew, Shank, -, Ann R., Martin, -, St. Mary's Church, George, Gilmeyer, Mary, Clabaugh, bride and groom from Washington Co., 19

4610, 4 May 1856, David , Boray, -, Johanna, Hurlehey, -, St. Mary's Church, Monroe, Kreigh, Eliza, Halm, "Married after three Publications of the Banns of marriage"; See Endnote 42., 19

4611, 16 Sep 1856, Cumberland F., Dugan, -, Harriet A. (Miss), Buchanan, -, "at Dalton", John T., Mason, Dr., Ward, groom from Baltimore; bride from Washington Co., 19

4612, 20 Sep 1856, Peter, Henessy, -, Ellen (Miss), Doolan, -, St. Mary's Church, Congregation, -, -, -, -, 19

4613, 21 Sep 1856, Benjamin F., Greg, -, Catharine J. (Miss), Gillmeyer, -, at the Parsonage, Mr., Fortune, -, -, -, 19

4614, 16 Oct 1856, David, Dunning, -, Susan (Miss), Moore, -, at Moore'sville, Thomas, Moore, Mrs., Mouse, "The Bans of Marriage were published", 19

4615, Nov 1856, William H., Ryan, -, Elizabeth A. (Miss), Baker, -, in Clear Spring, Mr. Jos., Smith, P., Fellinger, -, 19

4616, 21 Dec 1856, Thomas Wm., Jones, -, Ann Mary (Mrs.), McDermott, -, at the Washington House, Hagerstown, Jos. P., Mong, C., McCardle, bride and groom from Frederick City, 19

4617, 3 Feb 1857, Henry J., Shervin, -, Catharine J. (Miss), Clarke, -, near Shepherds Town, Charles, Clarke, Margaret (Mrs.), Clarke, Endnote 78, 19

4618, 14 Apr 1857, William H., Thompson, -, Margaret, Magonigle* , -, in her Father's House, Jacob, Wright, Thomas, Taggart, "Married after one publication of the Bans of marriage and a License from the Court"; *Magonigle [McGonigle?], 19

4619, 19 Jul 1857, Patrick, Sherdan, -, Bridget, Hoy, -, -, Mary A. (Miss), Smith, Jerome, McClearey, &c.; "The Bans of Marriage were published.", 19

4620, 4 Feb 1858, Richard H., Wise, -, Mary E., McGlone, -, -, Mr., Galagan, Eveline, Doyle, -, 25

4621, 13 Apr 1858, Victor, Cushwa, -, Mary An [sic], Kreigh, -, at the house of her Father, "whole family of", Kreighs, -, -, "He unbaptized married by dispensation", 25

4622, 13 May 1858, Richard, Hurley, -, Ellen, Desmond, -, St. Mary's, -, -, -, -, -, 25

ST. MARY'S CATHOLIC CHURCH
HAGERSTOWN, MARYLAND, MARRIAGES:
Index, Date, Groom 1st Name, Groom Last Name, Code, Bride 1st Name, Bride Last Name, Code B, Location of Ceremony, 1st Witness First, 1st Witness Last, 2nd Witness First, 2nd Witness Last, Notes, Priest

4623, 22 Aug 1858, Patrick, Daily, -, Margaret, McManus, -, St. Mary's, Rich., Kelly, Lizzie, Kelly, witnesses included whole congregation; "Bans of marriage were published once.", 26

4624, 30 Sep 1858, Wm. Angelo, Powell, -, Cecilia, Gillmeyer, -, -, Mr., Gillmeyer *, William, Gillmeyer **, "by Dispensation of Archbishop Kenrick"; * bride's father; ** bride's brother, 26

4625, 7 Oct 1858, Geo., Barber, -, Mary, Fate, -, residence of Jno. Eck, Jno., Eck, Irene C., Dugan, "by Dispensation of Archb.", 26

4626, 14 Oct 1858, Michel, Whitney, -, Mary Ellen, Payne, -, Four Locks, Patrick, Ryan, John, Whitney, "by Dispensation of the Archb."; bride "not baptized", 26

4627, 14 Nov 1858, Thos., O'Conner, -, Bridget, Hurlehee, -, Hagerstown, Kate, Hassett, Saml., Coyle, 3rd witness is Fr. Julia [sic] Didier; married "after one publication of the bans", 26

4628, 23 Dec 1858, John, Strovinger, -, Sophia, Miller, -, -, Jas., Flynn, Saml., Coyle, "dispensation in disparity of worship being granted by the archbishop", 26

4629, 3 Feb 1859, Jacob A., Luck [?], -, Margaret, Lewis, -, pastoral residence, Hagerstown, Ella, Taggart, J.W., Schlosser, -, 26

4630, 19 May 1859, Richard, Knox [?], -, Ellen, King, -, "Jos. M. Smith's station", "the congregation there", -, -, -, -, 26

4631, 2 Jun 1859, Robt., Lewis, -, Isabella, Shafer, -, Williamsport, Jas., Flynn, Margaret, Barry, -, 26

4632, 15 Jun 1859, Jas., Flynn, -, Mary, Drenner [or Drennen], -, St. Mary's, John, Bolmar, Mary, Taggart, bride and groom of Four Locks, 26

4633, 25 Sep 1859, Patr., Mahony, -, Johanna, Collins, -, St. Mary's Church, Mary, Collins, -, -, -, 26

4634, 1 Jan 1860, Joseph, Gilliss, -, Maria, Gilliss, -, -, Jacob, Cram, Frances, Wright, Maria is Joseph's sister-in-law, "dispensation being granted by the Archb.", 26

4635, 21 Jun 1860, Hy., Stewart, B, S, Eliza, Robinson, B, -, Otho, Hurley, Inig [?], Taylor, groom is "a slave of Mr. Reagan", 26

4636, 8 Jul 1860, Anthony, Cook, -, Marion, Gold, -, -, G.J., Gillmeyer, Jno. M., Cook, -, 26

ST. MARY'S CATHOLIC CHURCH
HAGERSTOWN, MARYLAND, MARRIAGES:
Index, Date, Groom 1st Name, Groom Last Name, Code, Bride 1st Name, Bride Last Name, Code B, Location of Ceremony, 1st Witness First, 1st Witness Last, 2nd Witness First, 2nd Witness Last, Notes, Priest

4637, 9 Aug 1860, Jos. W., Gouker, -, Mary, Gouker, -, -, Saml., Coyle, Julier [or Julies] A., Didier, first cousins, "dispensation having been granted by the Most Rev. Archb. Of Baltimore", 26

4638, 14 Sep 1860, Hy., Brinn, -, Cath., Dillon, -, -, Jas., Dempsey, Johanna, Mahoney, "No Bans published, with permission of Archbishop.", 26

4639, 25 Sep 1860, John, Barry, -, Mary, Collins, -, St. Mary's Church, Margaret, Barry, Wm., Goddard, he of Williamsport, she of Hagerstown, 26

4640, 18 Oct 1860, Thos., Colkleper, GA, Catharine, Meads, -, -, Fannie, Wright, Bernard, McCullogh, entry is unclear as to whether both are from Williamsport or only bride, 26

4641, 16 Dec 1860, Mr., McDonald, -, Louisa, -, -, -, Jos., Hurley, Mrs., Julius , See Endnote 43., 26

4642, 24 Jan 1861, Hugh, Malone, -, Mary, Kelly, -, -, Lizzie, Kelly, Mary, Taggart, "Dispensation from bans being obtained from Archb.", 26

4643, 10 Feb 1861, Mark [?], Coogen, -, Lizzie, Kelly, -, St. Mary's Church, Hugh, Malone, Hugh (Mrs.), Malone, See Endnote 44., 26

4644, 25 Dec 1861, Julius, Tasker, GA, Rachel, Slephun, -, -, Rev. Ed., Didier, P., Moran, -, 28

4645, 28 Dec 1861, Martin V.B., Green, GA, Susan R., Smith, -, St. Mary's Church, John, Smith, -, -, both of Hagerstown, 28

4646, 14 Jan 1862, Wm. A., O'Hara, -, Elise, Sgarkotich*, -, -, Reinold, Halm, Reinold's wife, Halm, he of Cincinnati, she of Hagerstown; "after one publication of bands"; *Sgarkotich is clearly written, 28

4647, 26 Jan 1862, John R., McGonigal, -, Sarah, Eichelberger, BA, -, Mary, Bumyard, Sarah, Idelburgh, 3rd witness is the "Grandmother"; both of Hagerstown, 28

4648, 28 Jan 1862, Jesse F., Thompson, -, Mary F., Oliver, -, St. Augustine's Church, Williamsport, -, -, -, -, both of Williamsport, 28

4649, 4 Feb 1862, John H., Smith, -, Tracy, Griffith, -, -, Jerome, McCleary, Mrs., Cretin, both of Funkstown, 28

4650, 4 Feb 1862, John H., Crauly, -, Theresa, Cremer, -, St. Mary's Church, John, Foley, Margaret, Cremer, -, 28

ST. MARY'S CATHOLIC CHURCH
HAGERSTOWN, MARYLAND, MARRIAGES:
Index, Date, Groom 1st Name, Groom Last Name, Code, Bride 1st Name, Bride Last Name, Code B, Location of Ceremony, 1st Witness First, 1st Witness Last, 2nd Witness First, 2nd Witness Last, Notes, Priest

4651, 25 Jun 1862, John, Sterling, -, Ann, Mundenhall [?], BA, Williamsport, Daniel, Baxter, Ellen, Stake, -, 28

4652, 3 Dec 1862, Benjamin, Marks, GA, Anna, Smith, -, at her father's house, Martin, Green, Susan, Green [HB], -, 28

4653, 25 Dec 1862, George, Hifleman, -, Lucretia, Woeford, BA, -, M., Moran, -, -, -, 28

4654, 30 Dec 1862, Jacob H., Griffith, -, Mary, Walk, BA, -, Sarah, Griffith, -, -, -, 28

4655, 20 Jan 1863, Wm., Cushwa, -, Margaret, Kriegh, -, at her father's house, Wm., Smith, Martha, McClain, "He unbaptized was married by dispensation.", 28

4656, 27 Jan 1863, Thos., Coyle, -, Eva, Harn, -, Hagerstown, Sarah, Middlecaff, -, -, -, 28

4657, 27 Jan 1863, Ambrose, McArdell, -, Cecilia, Oliver, -, Williamsport, Mr., Stake, Mrs., Stake, -, 28

4658, 27 Jan 1863, Wm., Mahony, B, Francis, Arrabella, B, Dr. McGills House, Hagerstown, Jerome, McCleary, Dr., McGill, -, 28

4659, Apr 1863, Thos. M., Cushwa, -, Sarah, Kreigh, -, Hagerstown, Wm., Kreigh, Luisa, Kreigh *, * daughter of Wm. Kreigh, the other witness; groom non baptized; married with dispensation of the Archbishop, 28

4660, 21 Apr 1863, Era W. (Capt), Claflin [?], P, Jane C., Stuck, -, Hagerstown, Dr., McKee, Thos., Johnson, -, 28

4661, 16 Nov 1863, William, Bailey, B, Jane, Cook, B, Hagerstown, Judy, Taylor, Henry, Young, -, 28

4662, 18 Nov 1863, Alex. (Dr.), McNeal, -, Mary A., Smith, -, Potomac Landing, Mes [?], Lyons, Eva, Doyle, "dispensation granted being in the Second degree of [?] affinity", 28

4663, 17 Dec 1863*, William, Fernsworth, -, Margaret, McKusker, -, Hagerstown, Mr., Myers, Mary, McKusker, for marriage date see Endnote 1 after the Deaths section, 28

4664, Jan 1864, Wm., Bailey, P, B, Jane, Cook, B, Hagerstown, Judy, Taylor, Henry, Young, -, 28

4665, [blank], Patrick, McGaulin, -, Margaret, Welsh, -, Potomac Landing, Patr., Ryan, Joseph, Smith, -, 28

4666, 26 Apr 1864, William, Smith, -, Emily, McLaughlin, P, Clear Spring District, Jerome, McCleary, Margaret, Smith, -, 28

ST. MARY'S CATHOLIC CHURCH
HAGERSTOWN, MARYLAND, MARRIAGES:
Index, Date, Groom 1st Name, Groom Last Name, Code, Bride 1st Name, Bride Last Name, Code B, Location of Ceremony, 1st Witness First, 1st Witness Last, 2nd Witness First, 2nd Witness Last, Notes, Priest

4667, 1864, David, Herely, -, Catherine, Hupet [or Hapet], -, Hagerstown, Wm (Mr. or Mrs.[?]), Doyle, Eva (Miss), Doyle, -, 28

4668, 17 May 1864, Francis, McCormick, -, Virginia, Bryload [?], -, Hagerstown, James, Flynn, Eva, Doyle, -, 28

4669, 9 Oct 1864, James, Flynn, -, Louisa, Brooks, -, Hagerstown, Franty, Tierney, Letty, McElhany, See Endnote 45., 30

4670, 22 Nov 1864, George, Kyper, -, Louisa, Moore, -, Hagerstown, Mary, Julius, M., Moore, -, 30

4671, 17 Jan 1865, Philip J., Fellinger, -, Lizzie, German, P, Hagerstown, John, Fellinger, Mary, German, "The party are of" Clear Spring, 30

4672, 19 Jan 1865, Arthur, Stevens, P, Catharine, Riser, -, Hagerstown, Judith, Taylor, Joseph, Futter, -, 30

4673, 14 Feb 1865, Peter Justinian, Mayberry, P, Margaret Genevieve, Doyle, -, Hagerstown, Wm. E., Doyle, Louisa, Doyle, -, 30

4674, 14 Feb 1865, Michael, White, -, Kate, Fellinger, -, -, Philip J., Fellinger, Mary, Hannah, he "of Va."; she of Clear Spring, 30

4675, 15 Feb 1865, George W.B., Morrison, -, Mary P., McCusker, -, -, John H., Anderson, Fanny, Ardinger, The groom is described as "an infidel"; "The dispensation was granted by Abp. Spalding.", 30

4676, 23 Apr 1865, Arthur, Kenney, -, Mary, Hutton, -, Sharpsburg, George, Hoover, Margaret, McCusker, -, 30

4677, 15 May 1865, John B., Clayborne, -, Sarah, Martiney, -, -, Willm. C., Irving, Judith, Taylor (Black), -, 30

4678, 9 Jul 1865, Allen, Walker, -, Anna, Brown, B, -, Lewis, Whelan, Luisa, Robinson, -, 20

4679, 3 Aug 1865, Jerome B., McCleery, -, Eva E., Doyle, -, -, Fred., Doyle, Kate, McCleery, both of Hagerstown "no bans published by dispensation.", 26

4680, 14 Sep 1865, Geo., Fechtig Jr., -, Louisa, Doyle, -, -, Hy., Fingeing [?], Kate, McCleery, both of Hagerstown, 26

4681, 7 Nov 1865, Jas. Q., Lydelane, -, Margt., Lydelaine, -, -, Mary, Coyle, V., Wright, "License being obtd. And dispensation granted by Most Rev. Archb. They were first cousins", 26

4682, 28 Dec 1865, Wm. D., Hembach, -, Jenny, Lambert, P, Hagerstown, Mary, Coyle, Richd. W., Sterling, DMR, 26

ST. MARY'S CATHOLIC CHURCH
HAGERSTOWN, MARYLAND, MARRIAGES:
Index, Date, Groom 1st Name, Groom Last Name, Code, Bride 1st Name, Bride Last Name, Code B, Location of Ceremony, 1st Witness First, 1st Witness Last, 2nd Witness First, 2nd Witness Last, Notes, Priest

4683, 2 Jan 1866, Philip, Yohn, -, Fanny, Wright, -, St. Mary's Church, Mollie, Tierney, Richd., Sterling, he of Philadelphia, 26

4684, 2 Apr 1866, Reuben, Hornsby, -, Margaret A., Malott, -, -, Margaret (Mrs.), Thompson, Elizabeth, Poffenberger, "The man not having been baptized, was baptized on this occasion.", 26

4685, 10 Apr 1866, Chs. M., Futterer, -, Otilia, Brockelman, BA, -, Mrs., Post, Lou, Fechtig, DMR, 26

4686, 12 Apr 1866, Edwd., Williams, B, Eliza, Lewis, B, -, Mrs., Owner, Mary, Coyle, "woman a Catholic - the man I baptized...just before marriage.", 26

4687, 24 Apr 1866, Jno. A., Dugan, -, Mary Q., Stake, -, St. Augustin's Church, Williamsport, Helen, Stake, Dr., Johnson, 3rd witness is Fanney Thompson "plus the whole congregation"; 3rd cousins - dispensation granted. Bridal Mass with music.", 26

4688, 16 Aug 1866, Wm. B., Goddard, -, Cath. V., Gower, P, -, Charlotte, Goddard, Maggie, Goddard, -, 26

4689, 16 Aug 1866, Eugene E., Smith, P, Jennie A., Ward, -, -, Mary, Coyle, Rd., Sterling, -, 26

4690, 14 Oct 1866, Pat., Collins, -, Jane, O'Connor, -, Williamsport, R., Sterling, Reuben, Hornesby, they "were married by magistrate 12 y. before", 26

4691, 26 Dec 1866, Jno., Hoover, -, Anna, McClain, -, -, Martin [?], McClain, Ellen, Docknoy [?], "the man being non-Catholic and unbaptized (disp. From Archb)", 26

4692, 31 Jan 1867, Jno, Dick, -, Anna, Poper, BA, -, Ann, Hanley, Mary, Coyle, -, 26

4693, 14 Feb 1867, Stephen, Mahoney, B, Betty, Wilsen, B, P, home of Jos. M. Smith, F.B., McCleary, F.B. (Mrs.), McCleary, 3rd witness is Jos. M. Smith, 26

4694, 14 Mar 1867, Jno, Burkart, -, Mary, Swinger, BA, -, Thomas, H[?]ady, bride's mother, -, 3rd witness is the bride's sister; groom "late U.S.A. [Union Army, Civil War]"; bride of Hagerstown, 26

4695, 5 Jun 1867, Peter L., Lismen [?], GA, Helen M., Stake, -, Williamsport, Victor, Cushwa, Dr., Johnson, -, 26

4696, 24 Oct 1867, Geo. A., Duvamy [?], P, Lizzie A., Duling, -, -, Phil., Barry, Mike, Full [?], -, 26

ST. MARY'S CATHOLIC CHURCH
HAGERSTOWN, MARYLAND, MARRIAGES:
Index, Date, Groom 1st Name, Groom Last Name, Code, Bride 1st Name, Bride Last Name, Code B, Location of Ceremony, 1st Witness First, 1st Witness Last, 2nd Witness First, 2nd Witness Last, Notes, Priest

4697, 29 Oct 1867, Michael A., Full, -, Anna A., Price, P, -, Dr., Wroe, Mrs. Dr., Wroe, 3rd witness is Margaret Keyne [?], 26

4698, 3 Nov 1867, Cyrus, Kershner, P, Sarah A., Smith, -, -, Mary, Coyle, Rachel C., Diggs, both from Berkeley Co., Va., 26

4699, 3 Nov 1867, John [?], Whaley, -, Mary, Hackett, -, -, W.L., May, L., McIlheny, -, 26

4700, 26 Dec 1867, Jacob H., Wills, -, Martha, McClain, -, Williamsport Church, Lewis, McLaughlin, Mary, Hurley, groom from Hagerstown, 26

4701, 31 Dec 1867, Jnoss [?], Lithco [?], P, Barbara, Faley, -, -, Perry, Barber, Martha, Lizer, -, 26

4702, 14 Jan 1868, John T., McCusker, -, Martha, Rowland, -, -, Mary, Coyle, Ann, Hammersley, bride not baptized, "dispensation having been granted by the Archb.", 26

4703, 22 Jan 1868, Geo, Greene, B, P, Mary, Mahoney, B, -, Judy, Taylor, Theresa, Jones, groom baptized Protestant "at 9 years of age"; DMR granted by the Archb., 26

4704, 14 Feb 1868, Jeremiah, Murphy, -, Ellen, Dillon, -, -, Mich., Dillon *, Mich. (Mrs.), Dillon **, * father of bride; ** mother of bride; groom from Washington, DC, bride from "W.Md. R Road", 26

4705, 11 Aug 1868, Franklin, Ford, -, Ann Maria, Jacobs, P, -, John, Sweeny, Josephine, Hurley, "by dispensation, both of Washington Co.", 11

4706, 24 Jan 1869, Frederick, Houser, -, Mary, Schilemp, -, -, William, Cheelsman, Sophia, Schilemp, both of Williamsport, 11

4707, 2 Feb 1869, Uriah, Smith, B, Harriet, Wilson, B, P, -, Arabella, Harney, Louisa, Brown, "All the parties colored"; couple from Clear Spring; DDC from Most Rev. Abp. Shalding.", 11

4708, 4 Oct 1869, William, Waters, -, Mary A., Donelly, -, -, Charles, Faughan [?], Mary, Doneley, both from Williamsport, 34

4709, 10 Nov 1869, Wm., Reed, -, Mary, Donelley, -, Williamsport, Kate, Hoy, Joseph, Futterer, DDC, 11

4710, 2 Dec 1869, Martin, Shehan, -, Elizabeth, Shilling, -, -, Charles (Rev.), Samer, Mary, Clarbaugh, -, 11

4711, 4 Jan 1870, Wm., Gallagher, -, Catherine, Oliver, -, -, James, Anderson, Ella, Oliver, -, 11

ST. MARY'S CATHOLIC CHURCH
HAGERSTOWN, MARYLAND, MARRIAGES:
Index, Date, Groom 1st Name, Groom Last Name, Code, Bride 1st Name, Bride Last Name, Code B, Location of Ceremony, 1st Witness First, 1st Witness Last, 2nd Witness First, 2nd Witness Last, Notes, Priest

4712, 5 Jan 1870, Albertus, Iseminger, P, Mary, Smith, -, -, Catherine, Smith, Edward, Smith [HB], -, 11

4713, 3 Nov 1869, Alphonsus, Fallei, -, Mary, Riley, -, -, Nicholas, Dormer, Cecelia, Faller, -, 45

4714, 3 Feb 1870, Louis, McLoughlin, -, Mollie, Hurley, -, -, Charles, Biyle, Eliza, Ryan, -, 11

4715, 26 Apr 1870, Jeremiah, Hanen, -, Mary, McClain, -, "At Residence of Mr. Shervin, Washington Co.", Samuel, Shervin, Miss, Shervins, married "by dispensation";, 11

4716, 3 May 1870, John, Doyle, -, Laura, Cunningham, -, "At residence of Mr. Cunningham near Sir John's Run", John, Cunningham, Margaret, Cunningham [HB], -, 11

4717, 24 May 1870, Charles, Little, -, Mary L., Bowers, -, -, Patrick, Gilleece, Rachel, Gilleece, all of Hancock , 34

4718, 9 Jun 1870, Conrad, Halpp, P, Elizabeth A., Harsh, -, -, Jacob, Harsh, Catherine, Harsh, groom of Hancock; bride of Martinsburg, WV, 34

4719, 13 Nov 1870, James, Cunningham, -, Mary, Barry, -, Clear Spring, Wm., Burns, Mary, King, -, 11

4720, 27 Nov 1870, James, Doyle, -, Mary C., Goddard, -, Williamsport, Terry, Rierdan, Margaret, Goddard, -, 11

4721, 22 Dec 1870, Daniel, Cramer, -, Mary, Halbert, -, -, David, Sweeny, Letitia, McIlhany, -, 11

4722, 7 Feb 1871, Earnest C., Fogle, -, Jennie, Welch, -, -, David, Sweeny, Margaret, Shervin, married by dispensation, 11

4723, 3 Mar 1871, David, Needy, -, Sarah, Griffey, -, -, John, Smith * , Margaret, Griffey, * "Needy" crossed out and "Smith" written in; married by "dispensation", 11

4724, 23 May 1871, John, Donelly, -, Mary Anna, Miller, -, -, David, Sweeny, -, -, "both (quasi) catholics", 11

4725, 24 May 1871, Wm. C., Metcalf, -, Mary C., Oker, -, -, Albert (Mrs.), Shunei [?], -, -, groom "quasi catholic", bride baptized Methodist; married with dispensation, 11

ST. MARY'S CATHOLIC CHURCH
HAGERSTOWN, MARYLAND, MARRIAGES:
Index, Marriage Date, 1st and Last Name of Groom, Groom from, 1st and Last Name of Groom's Father, 1st and Last Name of Bride, Bride from, 1st and Last Name of Bride's Father, 1st and Last Name of 1st Witness, 1st and Last Name of 2nd Witness, Location of Ceremony, Notes, Priest

4726, 3 Oct 1871, Georgium Clinton, Cushwa, Cherry Run, WV, -, -, Ellam A., Clarke, Williamsport, -, -, Petro, Kreigh, Margaritta, Clarke, Williamport, -, 13

4727, 21 Nov 1871, Clementem, Brittner, Berkeley Co., WV, Henrico, Brittner, Elisabeth Sauerbeer J.A., Trussel, Jefferson Co., WV, Edm., Trussell, Josephus, Trussel, Julia, Brittner, Williamport, DDC; bride's mother is "Sav.", 13

4728, 4 Jan 1872, Gulielmum, Hawken, Williamsport, Gulielmi, Hawken, Annam A., Parker, Williamsport, Joanni, Parker, Jacobus, Hughes, Maria, Hughes, Williamport, groom's mother is Catharine (Stake) Hawken; bride's mother is Catharine Ensminger, 13

4729, 15 Jan 1872, Michaelim F., Gallagher, Salamaned [?], NY, -, -, Johannam, Reid, Williamsport, -, -, Carolo, Clarke, Margaritta, Clarke, Williamport, DMR; BA, 13

4730, 29 Jan 1872, Johannem A., Allen, Hagerstown, -, -, Mariam E., Stewart, Middleburg, -, -, Moses, Buttler, Julia, Taylor, Hagerstown, DMR; BA; Couple is Black, 13

4731, 30 Jan 1872, Samuelem, Shervin, Hagerstown, -, -, Elisabetham, Knodle, -, -, -, J., Knodle, Mary, Ball, Hagerstown, DDC; BA, 13

4732, 10 Apr 1872, Michaelem, McDonald, Baltimore, -, -, Luciam, Reppey, Hagerstown, -, -, Geo., Freanor, M., Murray, Hagerstown, DMR; BA, 13

4733, 9 Apr 1872, Carolum D., Smith, Hagerstown, -, -, Lauram L., Ford, Hagerstown, -, -, J., Ford, W., Duffy, Hagerstown, DMR; GA, 13

4734, 30 Jul 1872, Georgium A., Davis, Hagerstown, -, -, Annam A., Henson, Hagerstown, -, -, Carolo, Duffy, Maria, Burke, Hagerstown, DMR; GA, 13

4735, 24 Sep 1872, Thomam, O'Neill, Wexford, Ireland, Joannis, O'Neill, Margarite, Moran, Greenbrier, VA, Joannis, Moran, Joannes, Moran, Maria Anna, Moran, Williamport, groom's mother is Margarita (Benville) O'Neill; bride's mother is Anna (Cummings) Moran, 13

ST. MARY'S CATHOLIC CHURCH HAGERSTOWN, MARYLAND, MARRIAGES:

Index, Marriage Date, 1st and Last Name of Groom, Groom from, 1st and Last Name of Groom's Father, 1st and Last Name of Bride, Bride from, 1st and Last Name of Bride's Father, 1st and Last Name of 1st Witness, 1st and Last Name of 2nd Witness, Location of Ceremony, Notes, Priest

4736, 15 Oct 1872, Joannem M., Sims, Washington, DC, -, -, Susannam M., Weast, Boonsboro, -, -, Horine, Weast, Maria, Troupe, Boonsboro, -, 13

4737, 17 Oct 1872, Josephum W., Ott, Harpers Ferry, WV, -, -, Gertrudam, Shannon, Keedysville, -, -, M., Ault, M., Ault, Keedysville, DMR, 13

4738, 21 Sep 1872, Georgium M., Bryan, Washington, DC, -, -, Teresa, Shover, Hagerstown, -, -, Ludovicus, McLaughlin, M., Carter, Hagerstown, DMR; DB, 13

4739, 30 Apr 1873, Thomam B., Grimm, Hagerstown, -, -, Adelaide V., Spangler, Hagerstown, -, -, Arnoldus, Condry, M. L., Spangler, Hagerstown, DB, 13

4740, 6 May 1873, Georgium W., Nipe, Haynesville, WV, -, -, Martham, Kensell, Haynesville, WV, -, -, Joannes, Turner, H., Turner, Hagerstown, DDC, 13

4741, 20 Nov 1873, Guglielmum, Orndorf, Hagerstown, -, -, Romaine E., Burdrich [?], Funkstown, -, -, Frederico, Hahn, Annette, Hurley, Hagerstown, DB; appears to read "5 scutatis Archiepiscopi cancellario obtentis", 11

4742, 26 Nov 1873, Eduardum, Donelley, Williamsport, -, -, Catarinam, Hoy, Williamsport, -, -, Thoma, Donelly, Lilia, Williams, Williamport, -, 11

4743, 27 Jan 1874, Patritium, Gilleece, Hagerstown, -, -, Rachel, Gilleece, Mill Stone Point, -, -, Elie, Stake, -, -, Williamport, with dispensation of affinity in "2nd grader attiniz.[?] ad primum", 11

4744, 29 Jan 1874, Wm. H., McDonald, Washington Co., -, -, Annam , O'Neal, Williamsport, -, -, Thomas, Donelly, Maria, Rodenheiser, Williamport, -, 11

4745, 18 Mar 1874, Robert, Sherlock, Ireland, -, -, Catharine, Rafferty, Ireland, -, -, Margaret, Shervin, Mrs., Cramer, Hagerstown, "Both parties catholics, and gypsies.", 11

4746, 8 Apr 1874, Ludovicum, Downs, Downsville, Christopheri, Downs, Catharinam, Wooltz, Williamsport, Joannis, Wooltz, "The Downs, Wooltz and others", -, -, -, Williamsport, -, 11

4747, 28 May 1874, Joseph, Kershner, Hagerstown, -, -, Helen, Hoover, Hagerstown, Joseph, Hoover, Joseph, Hoover, Maria, Eck, Hagerstown, DMR, 11

ST. MARY'S CATHOLIC CHURCH
HAGERSTOWN, MARYLAND, MARRIAGES:
Index, Marriage Date, 1st and Last Name of Groom, Groom from, 1st and Last Name of Groom's Father, 1st and Last Name of Bride, Bride from, 1st and Last Name of Bride's Father, 1st and Last Name of 1st Witness, 1st and Last Name of 2nd Witness, Location of Ceremony, Notes, Priest

4748, 18 Jun 1874, Albertum, Fiery, Washington Co., Joseph, Fiery, Mariam C., Ball, Washington Co., Alberti, Ball, Mr., Ball, Mrs., Ball, -, DDC, 11

4749, 26 Nov 1874, Thomam, Eagan, Hagerstown, -, -, Margaritam, O'Conner, Hagerstown, -, -, Benton, Cushwa, Bridget, McAvoy, Hagerstown, -, 11

4750, 16 Dec 1874, Johannem P., Hose, Hagerstown, Henrici, Hose, Jennie, Schilling, Hagerstown, Joachim, Schilling, Carolo, Alexander, Caroline, Schilling, Hagerstown, -, 11

4751, 15 Apr 1875, Michaelem, Battal, Hagerstown, -, -, Nannie, Barrett, Hagerstown, -, -, Margareta, Shervin, Milton, Ewers, Hagerstown, -, 11

4752, 19 Oct 1875, Thomam, Hennessey, Tilghmanton, -, -, Ellen, Hennessey, Tilghmanton, -, -, H. (Rev.), Hoffman, Margaret, Shervin, Hagerstown, "Married his sister-in-law by dispensation from Abp. Bayley", 11

4753, 4 May 1876, Charles A., Melus, Hagerstown, -, -, Catharine, Laurence, Hagerstown, -, -, Mrs., Middlekauff, Mr., Laurence, Hagerstown, DMR, 11

4754, 13 Jun 1876, Johannem, Dougherty, Chambersburg, -, -, Mariam, Eck, Hagerstown, Johannis, Eck, Johannes, Eck, Jenni, Hoover, Hagerstown, 3rd witness is Joseph Oesterman, 11

4755, 7 Feb 1877, Laurentium "(Johannem)", Laurence, Washington Co., -, -, Sarah C., Baker, -, -, -, Johannes, Helane, M.W.L., May, Hagerstown, -, 11

4756, 23 Jul 1877, Wilfridum G., Wright, Hagerstown, Jacobi A., Wright, Elizabeth, Johnson, Hagerstown, George W., Johnson, J.B., Sweeney, Margaret, Shervin, Hagerstown, -, 11

4757, 20 Nov 1877, Johannem, Donohue, Ohio, Patrick, Donohue, Mirandam, Stipes, Harpers Ferry, WV, Ezekiel, Stipes, Anna, Tierney, Margaret, Shervin, Hagerstown, -, 11

4758, 21 Nov 1877, Samuelem, McCauley, Washington Co., -, -, Theodesia V., Jacobs, Emmitsburg, Michaelis, Jacobs, R., Jacobs, Matilda, Jacobs, M. McCauley's, Washington Co., bride's mother is Matilda Jacobs, the 2nd witness, 11

ST. MARY'S CATHOLIC CHURCH
HAGERSTOWN, MARYLAND, MARRIAGES:
Index, Marriage Date, 1st and Last Name of Groom, Groom from, 1st and Last Name of Groom's Father, 1st and Last Name of Bride, Bride from, 1st and Last Name of Bride's Father, 1st and Last Name of 1st Witness, 1st and Last Name of 2nd Witness, Location of Ceremony, Notes, Priest

4759, 21 Nov 1877, Franklin, Tritch, Funkstown, Henrici, Tritch, Aliciam, McDonald, Hagerstown, Michaelis, McDonald, Mrs., Tritch, Michael, McDonald, Hagerstown, -, 11

4760, 22 Nov 1877, Blair, McCardell, Hagerstown, Ulton F., McCardell, Elizabeth, Stout [?], Western Pike, Henrici, Stout [?], Ann, McCardell, Ann, Mobley, Hagerstown, -, 11

4761, 22 Jan 1878, Patritium, McSweeney, Tilghmanton, -, -, Sophiam, Hawtherne, Tilghmanton, -, -, R. (Rev.), Fleming, -, -, -, Dispensation from Archb. Gibbons, 11

4762, 24 Apr 1878, Ricardum, Bennett, Hagerstown, Amos D., Bennett, Mariam C., Cretin, Hagerstown, Johannis, Cretin, Joseph, Owner, Nettie, Hurley, Hagerstown, DMR, 11

4763, 20 Jun 1878, Carolum B., Boyle, M.D., Westminster, MD, Senig [?], Boyle, Mariam I. [?], Smith, Hagerstown, Dr. [?], Smith, Drs. [?] Joe, Hurley, *, -, -, * "patre Sponsi", 12

4764, 6 May 1879, Guglielmum J., Case, Carroll Co., MD, -, -, Margaritam, Kyper, Washington Co., -, -, Jack, Hellane, Nettie, Hurley, Hagerstown, -, 11

4765, 12 May 1879, Joseph L., Owner, Hagerstown, -, -, Emmam, Harding, Cumberland, MD, -, -, J.B., Sweeney, Nettie, Hurley, Hagerstown, -, 11

4766, 12 Jun 1879, Lutherum, Addlesperger, Waynesboro, -, -, Annam, McDonald, Hagerstown, Michaelis, McDonald, Fredericus, Halm, J. [or I.], Hurley, Hagerstown, groom's mother is Susan Addlesperger, 11

4767, 15 Jan 1880, Isaac A., Feigley, Hagerstown, Isaac, Feigley, Emma C., Reynolds, Hagerstown, Johanne, Armstrong, John, Farrell, Margaret, Shervin, -, DMR, 11

4768, 3 Nov 1880, Gulielmum Foster, Brown, Washington Co., Gulielmi, Brown, Mariam Ellen, King, Washington Co., Owen, King, Joanni R., Barry, Birgitta Anna, King, -, -, 4

4769, 16 Feb 1881, Emmet M., Cullen, Washington Co., -, -, Evam M., Cushwa, Williamsport, Victori, Cushwa, [blank], Mullen, Sara, Kreigh, Williamport, -, 4

4770, 28 Feb 1881, Georgium H., Warner, Washington Co., Roberti, Warner, Annam F., Martin, Greencastle, Nicolai, Martin, "parentibus & aliis", -, -, -, -, DMR, 4

ST. MARY'S CATHOLIC CHURCH
HAGERSTOWN, MARYLAND, MARRIAGES:
Index, Marriage Date, 1st and Last Name of Groom, Groom from, 1st and Last Name of Groom's Father, 1st and Last Name of Bride, Bride from, 1st and Last Name of Bride's Father, 1st and Last Name of 1st Witness, 1st and Last Name of 2nd Witness, Location of Ceremony, Notes, Priest

4771, 1 Mar 1881, Robert Morris, Robertson, Baltimore, -, -, Annam E., Wroe, Hagerstown, -, -, Francisco, Wroe, Susana, Love, -, -, 4

4772, 28 Apr 1881, Albertum, Fahrney, Hagerstown, Joannis, Fahrney, Margaretham E., Zeller, Hagerstown, Valentini, Zeller, Sara, Zeller, -, -, -, DDC, 4

4773, 26 May 1881, Carrolum H., Lorshbaugh, Hagerstown, -, -, Margarettam V., Gates, Hagerstown, -, -, Charles L., Helferolay [?], Susie, Gates, -, DMR; BA, 4

4774, 23 Jun 1881, Noah Franciscum, Lawrence, Adams Co., PA, Michaelis C., Lawrence, Mariam Florentam [?], Suman, Washington Co., Alberti H., Suman, Andreas C., Lawrence, Elizabeth, Suman, -, -, 4

4775, 23 Jun 1881, Georgium Michael, Blumenour, Frederick, Michaelis, Blumenour, Saram Agnetem, Murray, Hagerstown, Mariae H., Murray, Mrs., Wright, Mrs., Yohn, -, DMR; groom's father is not Catholic, 4

4776, 18 Aug 1881, Joannem E. W., Dillon, Hagerstown, [blank], Dillon, Mariam S., Happel, Hagerstown, Martini, Happel, Michael, Dillon, Martin, Happel, -, "Dispen. in denuntiationibus obtenta", 4

4777, 25 Oct 1881, Henricum, McGill, Boston, MA, Roberti, McGill, Josephinam, Nelligan, Hagerstown, Jeremiae, Nelligan, [blank], McGill, Anna, Nelligan, -, "Dispen. in denuntiationibus obtenta"; groom's mother is Catharinae; bride's mother is Mariae, 4

4778, 16 Nov 1881, Richardum Randolph, MacMahon, Weston, WV, Dion B., MacMahon, Emmam S., Young, Harpers Ferry, WV, Hieronimi [?] B., Young, Joanne, Schwartz, Susanna, Schwartz, -, "Dispen. in denuntiationibus obtenta", 4

4779, 31 Jan 1882, Jacobum Henricum, Zook, Hagerstown, -, -, Catharinam S., Stonesiefer, Hagerstown, -, -, Anna H., Frederick, -, -, -, -, 4

4780, 31 May 1882, Henricum, Mickle, Baltimore, Roberti, Mickle, Ninam Lamar, McKaig, Hagerstown, Thomae J., McKaig, Eduardus, Mickle, F.T., McKaig, -, groom's mother is Stephanae; bride's mother is "M.A.", 4

ST. MARY'S CATHOLIC CHURCH
HAGERSTOWN, MARYLAND, MARRIAGES:
Index, Marriage Date, 1st and Last Name of Groom, Groom from, 1st and Last Name of Groom's Father, 1st and Last Name of Bride, Bride from, 1st and Last Name of Bride's Father, 1st and Last Name of 1st Witness, 1st and Last Name of 2nd Witness, Location of Ceremony, Notes, Priest

4781, 9 Aug 1882, Jacobum B., McCardell, Hagerstown, -, -, Helenam S., Zook, Hagerstown, Jacobi A., Zook, parentibus & aliis, -, -, -, -, groom's mother is Mrs. E.A. McCardell, 4

4782, 28 Dec 1882, Joseph Franciscum, Lizer, Franklin Co., PA, Wesley, Lizer, Susanam R., Bemisdarfer, Franklin Co., PA, Samuel, Bemisdarfer, Benjamin, Detrich *, Maria Elizabeth, Lizer, -, DMR; * "Bemisdarfer" crossed out, 4

4783, 16 Jan 1883, Harry H., Mobley, Baltimore, E.M. (Col.), Mobley, Jennie T., Hoover, Hagerstown, Joseph, Hoover, "Parentibus & cognatis", -, -, -, -, DMR, 4

4784, 30 Jan 1883, Franciscum L., Brown, Winchester, VA, Gulielmi A., Brown, Annam A., Nelligan, Martinsburg, VA, Jeremiae, Nelligan, Elizabeth, Clarkson, Virginia, Kelly, -, -, 10

4785, 31 Jan 1883, Joannem L., Clements, Montgomery Co., MD, Petri, Clements, Irene A., Wright, Augusta Co., VA, Jacobi, Wright, B.F., Luschbaugh, C.H., Herbert, -, DDC; bride never baptized, 10

4786, 28 Mar 1883, J. Franciscum, Futterer, Washington Co., Jacobi, Futterer, Annam E., Mayhew, Washington Co., Clementis, Mayhew, Milton, Ewers, Jacobo, Futterer, -, DB, 10

4787, 26 Apr 1883, Jacobum A., Adams, Jefferson Co., WV, -, -, Rebeccam, Walters, Jefferson Co., WV, -, -, Gulielmo, Riley, J.M., Mause, -, DMR; BA, 10

4788, 1 Aug 1883, Carolum L., Helferstay, Hagerstown, Caroli, Helferstay, Mariam E., Riordan, Hagerstown, -, -, Maria, Riordan, Margarita, Riordan, -, with dispensation, 10

4789, 6 Nov 1883, Joannem H., Hoffman, Frederick Co., MD, Joannis H., Hoffman, Annam A., Sweitzer, Washington Co., Gulielmi H., Sweitzer, Alberto C., Flenne, Maria C., Harsh, -, DMR; BA, 10

4790, 21 Nov 1883, Benjamin F., Detrich, Franklin Co., PA, Joannis, Detrich, Mariam, Lizer, Franklin Co., PA, Wesley, Lizer, Georgio W., Stoullper, Helena, Clarkson, -, DMR; GA, 10

4791, 27 Dec 1883, Georgium A., Zook, Washington Co., Jacobi, Zook, Marian, Creager, Washington Co., Henrici, Creager, Jacobo, Zook, Catharina, Zook, -, DMR; BA, 10

ST. MARY'S CATHOLIC CHURCH
HAGERSTOWN, MARYLAND, MARRIAGES:
Index, Marriage Date, 1st and Last Name of Groom, Groom from, 1st and Last Name of Groom's Father, 1st and Last Name of Bride, Bride from, 1st and Last Name of Bride's Father, 1st and Last Name of 1st Witness, 1st and Last Name of 2nd Witness, Location of Ceremony, Notes, Priest

4792, 26 Feb 1884, Joannem B., Sweeney, Baltimore, Patritii, Sweeney, Jennette, Hurley, Hagerstown, Jacobi, Hurley, Jacobo I., Hurley, Helena, Sweeney, -, DB; groom's mother is Helenae; bride's mother is Martha, 10

4793, 18 Jun 1884, Joannem N.[or W.] H., Reese, Frederick, Joannis, Reese, Delilah, Prince, Shephardstown, WV, Ludoni [?], Prince, Jennie, Watts, Rosalie, Proctor, -, DDC; BA, 10

4794, 6 Aug 1884, Alexandrum, Knott, Frederick Co., MD, Joannis S., Knott, Annam M., Bowman, Washington Co., David, Bowman, Alberto, Heil, Sr., Rosalia, Proctor, -, DMR; BA, 10

4795, 17 Jan 1884, Joannem, McDonald, Williamsport, -, -, Annem E., Eversole, Williamsport, -, -, Jno., Eversole, Helena, Collins, -, DDC; BA, 2

4796, 30 Apr 1884, Nicholem B., Martin, Waynesboro, PA, -, -, Catharinam, Cushwa, Williamsport, Victor, Cushwa, Reinald [?] J., Halm, Louisa, Cushwa, -, -, 2

4797, 13 Aug 1884, Davidem L., Henek, Clear Spring, -, -, Elizabetha, Swope, Clear Spring, -, -, Maria, Hillman [?], Susan, Williams, -, DMR; GA, 2

4798, 4 Sep 1884, Adam, Berger, Germany, Adam, Berger, Philomenam, Kammerer, Germany, Laurentii, Kammerer, Carolo, Kammerer, Maria, Kammerer [HB], -, DB, 10

4799, 15 Oct 1884, Gulielmum V., Miller, Frederick Co., MD, Georgii, Miller, Nettie R., McCardell, Washington Co., Willoughby, McCardell, Alfredo, McCardell, Rina, McCardell, -, DMR; GA, 10

4800, 10 Nov 1884, Gulielmum W., Shoch, York Co., PA, Benjamin, Shoch, Franciscam R., Besant, Jacobi, Besant, -, Sarah, Wright, Virginia, Baifley [or Bufley], -, DMR; GA, 10

4801, 23 Apr 1885, Walter S., Boward, MD, Andrew, Boward, Loutie, Foy, VA, John, Foy, Gul., Miller, Nettie, Miller, -, with dispensation, 9

4802, 13 Nov 1884, Gulielmum, O'Neal, Williamsport, -, -, Margaritem, Maloney, Williamsport, -, -, Jno., Ryan, Anna, Sherden [?], Williamport, -, 2

ST. MARY'S CATHOLIC CHURCH
HAGERSTOWN, MARYLAND, MARRIAGES:
Index, Marriage Date, 1st and Last Name of Groom, Groom from, 1st and Last Name of Groom's Father, 1st and Last Name of Bride, Bride from, 1st and Last Name of Bride's Father, 1st and Last Name of 1st Witness, 1st and Last Name of 2nd Witness, Location of Ceremony, Notes, Priest

4803, 13 Feb 1885, Leonem, Thompson, Williamsport, -, -, Catharinam, Collins, Williamsport, -, -, Eugenio, McCardle, Helena, Collins, Williamport, DB, 2

4804, 7 Apr 1885, Carolum B., Mullem [?], Allegany Co., MD, -, -, Louisam, Cushwa, Washington Co., Victoris, Cushwa, Danl. [?], Ryan, Rosa, Bevens, Williamport, -, 2

4805, 9 Apr 1885, Simenem [?], Golibart, Cecil Co., MD, -, -, Emmem K., Weast, Boonsboro, -, -, Otho, Smith, Cath., Smith, Boonsboro, -, 2

4806, 12 Nov 1885, Bernardum M., Ball, Funkstown, Alfridi, Ball, Thaliam, Boteler, Funkstown, Roberti, Boteler, Elizabetha, Ball, May, Newcomer, -, with dispensation, 9

4807, 19 Jul 1885, Theodorem, Barnes, Washington Co., -, -, Catharinem, Faithe, Franklin Co., MD [sic] , -, -, Joanne, Faithe, -, -, -, with dispensation, 2

4808, 16 Jan 1886, Lloyd, Duffie, Washington Co., Joannis, Duffie, Lauram, Cann, Frederick Co., MD, Gulielmi, Cann, Forena [sic], Dykes, Louisa, Dykes, -, with dispensation, 9

4809, 9 Mar 1886, Joannem L., Steffey, Washington Co., Gul., Steffey, Louisam , Schlotterbeck, Washington Co., Gul., Schlotterbeck, Cyrus, Simmons, Gertrude, Steffey, -, with dispensation, 9

4810, 9 Mar 1886, Joannem W., Lyddem, Washington Co., -, -, Annam M., Sheridan, Washington Co., -, -, L., McCardle, -, -, -, with dispensation, 2

4811, 5 Jan 1886, Samuelem, Dickerhoff, Washington Co., -, -, Emmam, Richter, Washington Co., -, -, Cath., Richter, Johanne, Duncan, -, with dispensation, 2

4812, 4 May 1886, Franciscum, Stienberger, PA, Joannis, Stienberger, Sarah E., Sheppard, PA, Gul., Sheppard, James V., Sheppard, Catherine, Stienberger, -, -, 9

4813, 5 May 1886, Andream J., Jones, Hagerstown, David W. [or N.], Jones, Margaritam R., Semler, Hagerstown, Joannis F., Semler, Joseph H., Griffe, Anna M., Bowers, -, with dispensation, 9

ST. MARY'S CATHOLIC CHURCH
HAGERSTOWN, MARYLAND, MARRIAGES:
Index, Marriage Date, 1st and Last Name of Groom, Groom from, 1st and Last Name of Groom's Father, 1st and Last Name of Bride, Bride from, 1st and Last Name of Bride's Father, 1st and Last Name of 1st Witness, 1st and Last Name of 2nd Witness, Location of Ceremony, Notes, Priest

4814, 5 Jul 1886, Andream J. [or T.], Reckert, Baltimore, Georgii M., Reckert, Helenam M., Gold, Hagerstown, Joannis, Gold, Elizabetha, O'Mara, Gul., Laurence, -, DMR; BA, 9

4815, 22 Sep 1886, David, Schilling, Washington Co., Gul., Schilling, Mariam C., Schlotterbeck, Washington Co., Gul., Schlotterbeck, Gul., Mourer, Susanna, Happel, -, -, 9

4816, 28 Sep 1886, Jacobum C., McCurdy, PA, Jacobi, McCurdy, Helenam R., Gallagher, PA, Jacobi W., Gallagher, Jacobus, Gallagher, Amilia, Shafer, -, -, 9

4817, 21 Oct 1886, Jacobum, Shadrach, MD, Michaelis, Shadrack, [blank], Mung, MD, Gulielmii, Mung, Edwardus, Moore, Lucia, Moore, -, with dispensation, 9

4818, 29 Dec 1886, Fredericum J., Halm, Hagerstown, Reinhold, Halm, Mariam V., Moore, Hagerstown, -, -, Columbus, O'Donnell, Ruby, Simmons, -, with dispensation, 9

4819, 18 May 1887, Thoma ["Jacobiam" crossed out], Hennesy, Washington Co., Thomae, Hennesy, Catharinam, Ripple, Washington Co., Joannes, Ripple, Thomas, Hennesy, Alice, Rover [or Roner], -, with dispensation; bride is Protestant, 9

4820, 26 May 1887, Aaron A., Laurence, -, Michaelis, Laurence, Anna E., Cross, "M" [?], Roberti, Cross, John W., Petre, Lillie, Ellet, -, with dispensation; bride is Protestant, 9

4821, 1887, Rollini [?] Eugene, McCardell, Washington Co., Ambrosii, McCardell, Effie Rcahel, King, Washington Co., Hieminii [?], King, Conrad, Falkenstein, Catharinae, Gallagher, -, with dispensation, 8

4822, [blank], Stewart, Westenhaver, Martinsburg, WV, Jacobi, Westenhaver, Margarita, Burkhardt, Martinsburg, WV, -, -, Jacobus, Dugan, Maria, Dugan, -, with dispensation, 8

4823, 6 Sep 1887, Edwardum J., McGinley, PA, Edwardi P., McGinley, Margaritae Doherty, Cunningham, MD, Gulielmi, Cunningham, Ambrosius A., Brown, Elizabetha, Hippner, -, with dispensation; BA, 9

4824, 2 Nov 1887, Henricum W., Rouskulp, Hagerstown, Upton, Rouskulp, Catharinam, Downin, Hagerstown, Samuelis, Downin, Gulielmo, Orndorff, Maria, Downin, -, DMR; GA, 3

ST. MARY'S CATHOLIC CHURCH
HAGERSTOWN, MARYLAND, MARRIAGES:
Index, Marriage Date, 1st and Last Name of Groom, Groom from, 1st and Last Name of Groom's Father, 1st and Last Name of Bride, Bride from, 1st and Last Name of Bride's Father, 1st and Last Name of 1st Witness, 1st and Last Name of 2nd Witness, Location of Ceremony, Notes, Priest

4825, 11 Jan 1888, Petrum Henricum, Kreigh, Clear Spring, Gulielmi, Kreigh, Helenem, Spickler, Clear Spring, Frisby, Spickler, Davide, Cushwa, Helena, Cushwa, Williamport, DDC; BA, 2

4826, 7 Feb 1888, Henricum L., Henneberger, Hagerstown, Alfredi, Henneberger, Emma L., Cookerly, Hagerstown, Ludovici, Cookerly, Jacobo C., Cookerly, Jessie, Cookerly, -, DMR; GA, 3

4827, 5 Apr 1888, Jacobum A., Clopper, Washington Co., Simonis, Clopper, Mariam, Roperstein, Washington Co., Nicolas, Roberstine, Harry, Holtzapple, Lucinda , Clopper, -, DDC; GN, 3

4828, 10 Apr 1888, Joannem Thomam, Hellane, Hagerstown, Joannis, Hellane, Juliam, Brady, Frostburg, Michaelis, Brady, Otho, Duffy, Maria, Creamer, -, -, 3

4829, 23 Mar 1888, Jacobem, Whitney, Four Locks, MD, Patritii, Whitney, Margaritem, Devereux, Four Locks, MD, Joannis, Moore, B., Bernel [?] [or Bemel], Rosa, Warmir [?], Williamport, DDC; BA, 2

4830, 19 Sep 1888, Carolum Eduardum, Hoover, Hagerstown, Joseph, Hoover, Lydiam Agnetem, Porter, Hagerstown, Caroli, Porter, Gulielmo, Porter, Flora, Lout, -, DMR; BA, 3

4831, 11 Oct 1888*, Henricum A., Cramer, Hagerstown, Henrici, Cramer, Delia A., Armstrong, Hagerstown, Andreae, Armstrong, Otho, Duffy, Mary, Cramer, -, DMR; BA; *marriage date reads 11 [or 17] Oct 1888, 3

4832, 28 Nov 1888, Gulielmum J., Orndorf, Hagerstown, Gulielmi, Orndorf, Mariam C., Downin, Hagerstown, Samuelis, Downin, Gulielmo, Geary, Demetrio, Duffy, -, -, 3

4833, 17 Dec 1888, Jacobum, McCall, Baltimore, Joannis, McCall, Annam, Mitchell, Hagerstown, -, -, Jerome, Lawrence, Mrs., Baker, -, Mrs. Baker is "matre adoptiva sponsae" [adoptive mother of the bride], 3

4834, 17 Jan 1889, Jacob F., Futterer, Washington Co., Ludovici, Futterer, Nellie, Nellligan, Washington Co., Jeremae, Nelligan, Thoma, Flynn, Gulielmus, Geary, -, dispensation from banns, 3

4835, 23 Jan 1889, Clifford R., Martin, Hagerstown, Samuelis V., Martin, Mariam, Wise, Hagerstown, Ricardi, Wise, Henrico, Stouter, Gulielmo J., Boryer, -, DDC; SN, 3

ST. MARY'S CATHOLIC CHURCH
HAGERSTOWN, MARYLAND, MARRIAGES:
Index, Marriage Date, 1st and Last Name of Groom, Groom from, 1st and Last Name of Groom's Father, 1st and Last Name of Bride, Bride from, 1st and Last Name of Bride's Father, 1st and Last Name of 1st Witness, 1st and Last Name of 2nd Witness, Location of Ceremony, Notes, Priest

4836, 29 Jan 1889, Michaelem, Lawrence, Hagerstown, Michaelis, Lawrence, Lauram L., Brogunier, Washington Co., Jacobi D., Brogunier, Frederico, Stover [?], Daisie, Brogunier, -, DDC; SN, 3

4837, 6 Feb 1889, Georgium H., Wolf, Hagerstown, David, Wolf, Emiliam [?] J., Heil, Hagerstown, Alberti, Heil, Henrico A., McKewn, Anna, Bichley, -, DDC; GA, 3

4838, 29 Apr 1889, Henricum, Wolf, Hagerstown, Hopkins, Wolf, Mariam, Switzer, Hagerstown, Samuelis, Switzer, Otho J. [?], Duffy, Margarita, Lawrence, -, DMR; GA, 3

4839, 18 Aug 1889, Carolum C., Kershner, Berkeley Co., WV, Cyri, Kershner, Catharinam, James, Washington Co., Otho, James, Mrs., Garey, Jennie, Bailey, Williamport, DDC; BA, 3

4840, 3 Oct 1889, Carolum W., Rauth, Hagerstown, Georgii, Rauth, Catherinam, Heil, Hagerstown, Alberti, Heil, Francisum [?] M., Farhney, Georgory, Hoffman, -, DMR;GA, 3

4841, 30 Oct 1889, Franciscum A., Lechleider, Hagerstown, A.A., Lechleider, Mariam C., Mayberry, Hagerstown, Petri P. [?], Mayberry, Francisco S., Heard, M.C., Lechleider, -, DMR; GA, 3

4842, 11 Jan 1890, Petrum, Hennessey, Washington Co., Petri, Hennessy, Mariam L., Smith, Washington Co., Alfredi, Smith, Thoma, Hennessy, Joanne, Hennessy, -, DMR; BA, 3

4843, 4 Feb 1890, Carolum A., Frone, Washington Co., Louis, Frone, Jennie, Wolf, Washington Co., -, -, Elmire (Dr.), Fahrney, Missoura, Smith, -, DDC;BA, 3

4844, 18 Feb 1890, Levi Eduardum, Moore, Washington Co., Thomae, Moore, Mariam Elisabeth, Hipner, Hagerstown, -, -, F.P. ["Carolo" crossed out], Morton [?], Susanna, Happel, -, DDC; GA, 3

4845, 24 Apr 1890, Robertum F., Shank, Hagerstown, Adam, Shank, Annam Lee, Rudy, Hagerstown, Gulielmy, Rudy, Jerry, Earnshaw, Nettie, Neibert, -, DDC; BA, 3

4846, 27 May 1890, Joannem Henricum, Losler, Washington Co., -, -, Emmam, Washington, Washington Co., Abraham, Washington, Sallie, Williams, Anna, Kiser, -, DDC; GA; Couple is Black, 3

ST. MARY'S CATHOLIC CHURCH HAGERSTOWN, MARYLAND, MARRIAGES:
Index, Marriage Date, 1st and Last Name of Groom, Groom from, 1st and Last Name of Groom's Father, 1st and Last Name of Bride, Bride from, 1st and Last Name of Bride's Father, 1st and Last Name of 1st Witness, 1st and Last Name of 2nd Witness, Location of Ceremony, Notes, Priest

4847, 29 Oct 1890, Francescum Patritium, Murphy, Baltimore, Patritii, Murphy, Sallie, Yohn, Hagerstown, O.M., Yohn, Carolo, Yohn, J., Mohler, -, -, 3

4848, 24 Dec 1890, Patrotsum [?] E., Cotter, -, Patritii, Cotter, Letie, Loudenslager, Hagerstown, Joannis, Loudenslager, Gulielmo, Lloyd, Laura, Lowe, -, DDC; BA, 3

4849, 24 May 1891, Gulielmum, Porter, Hagerstown, Caroli, Porter, Joannam, Garey, Hagerstown, -, -, Gulielmo, Garey, Thomas, Porter, -, DMR; GA, 3

4850, 23 Sep 1891, Joannem T. [?], Hull, Washington Co., Danielis, Hull, Jennie, Martin, Washington Co., David W., Moore, Gulielmo S., Duffy, Maria, Smith, -, DMR; GA, 3

4851, 6 Oct 1891, Gulielmus F., Moran, -, Matthaei, Moran, Evam B., Yeates, -, Danielis, Yeates, Victore, Montgomery, Maria Agnes, Lawrence, -, -, 3

4852, 15 Sep 1891, Josiah , Pierce, Jr., Portland, ME, -, -, Ulrica, Dahlgren, Washington, DC, -, -, -, -, -, -, Dahlgren Chapel, South Mountain, See Endnote 2 after the Deaths section, 7

4853, 20 Jan 1892, Joannem Oscar, Montague, -, Joannis Thomas, Montague, Annam Catherinam, Wellinger, Hagerstown, Philippi Jacob, Wellinger, Newton, Farhney, Mary, Smith, -, DMR; BA, 3

4854, 16 Feb 1892, Danielem A., Moore, Washington Co., -, -, Annam C., Rice , Washington Co., Samuelis, Harnish, Francisco, Bloyer, Lillie, Rice, -, DDC; SN; bride is widow; Lillie Rice (witness) is daughter of the bride, 3

4855, 27 Apr 1892, Herman L., Abel, VA, -, -, Mariam Agnetem, Lawrence, Hagerstown, Jerome, Lawrence, Jacobo, Malone, -, -, -, -, 3

4856, 7 Jun 1892, Jacobum A., Wagner, Altoona, PA, Augustini, Wagner, Saraim A., Dorsey, Emmitsburg, Gulielmi, Dorsey, Paulo G., Corry, Maria C., Martin, -, -, 3

4857, 11 Aug 1892, Georgium D., Clayburn, Hagerstown, Joannis, Clayburn, Margaritam, Barnhart, -, David, Barnhart, Sallie (Mrs.), Clayburn, Alice, Hemmersley, -, DMR; BA, 3

4858, 7 Sep 1892, Eduardum A., Higgins, Washington Co., Patritii, Higgins, Hattie V., Berry, Washington Co., Gulielmi H., Berry, W.H., Berry, Gulielmo, Nelson, -, DDC; BN, 3

ST. MARY'S CATHOLIC CHURCH
HAGERSTOWN, MARYLAND, MARRIAGES:
Index, Marriage Date, 1st and Last Name of Groom, Groom from, 1st and Last Name of Groom's Father, 1st and Last Name of Bride, Bride from, 1st and Last Name of Bride's Father, 1st and Last Name of 1st Witness, 1st and Last Name of 2nd Witness, Location of Ceremony, Notes, Priest

4859, 6 Dec 1892, Carolum H., Ramsburg, Martinsburg, WV, David, Ramsburg, Mariam Bernardinam, Ramsburg, Martinsburg, WV, Joannis, Ramsburg, Maria, Cunningham, Maria, Smith, -, DMR; GA, 3

4860, 3-Jul, Edmun [?] M., Moatz, New Balto, OH, Georgi, Moatz, Annam E., Sweitzer, Hagerstown, Samuelis, Switzer, Henrico, Swinger, Emma, Sweitzer [?], -, Entire entry is crossed out, 3

4861, 1 Feb 1893, Joannem L., Shafer, Washington Co., Joannis, Shafer, Mariam M., Wolf, Washington Co., Alberti, Wolf, Otho B., Downin, Cora M., Lewis, -, DDC; BN, 3

4862, 16 Feb 1893, Carolum F., Schueler, Hagerstown, -, -, Mariam, Ewers, Hagerstown, Milton, Ewers, Milton, Ewers, Frank (Mrs.), Futterer, -, DMR;GA, 3

4863, 27 Apr 1893, Carolum A., Full, Hagerstown, Michaelis, Full, Fannie G., Funk, Hagerstown, Henrici, Funk, Jacob, Downin, Margarita, Funk, -, DMR; BA, 3

4864, 23 May 1893, Samuelem, Banks, -, -, -, Martham A., Lizer, -, -, -, Maria, Smith, Mrs., Anderson, -, -, 3

4865, 3 Jul 1893, Edwin M., Moatz, New Baltimore, OH, Georgii, Moatz, Annam E., Switzer, Hagerstown, Samuelis, Switzer, Henrico, Winger, Emma, Switzer, -, DMR; GA, 3

4866, 5 Jul 1893, Thomam J., Callanan, Roanoke, VA, Joannis, Callenan, Ninam, Cramer, Hagerstown, Jacobi, Cramer, Otho, Duffy, Maria, Cramer, -, DB, 3

4867, 27 Jul 1893, Richard J., Hebb, Hagerstown, Richard Joseph, [Hebb], Annam, Heil, Hagerstown, Albert, Heil, William A., Hebb, Alice, Miller, -, DMR; GA, 3

4868, 3 Aug 1893, Gulielmum Albertum, Cole, Adams Co., PA, Francisci, Cole, Minnie A., Martin, Adams Co., PA, Gulielmi A., Martin, Loretta, Cole, Anna M., Cole, -, DMR; BA, 3

4869, 28 Jun 1894, Otho J., Duffy, Hagerstown, Gulielmi, Duffy, Mariam M., Cramer, Hagerstown, -, -, William, Willy, Helena, Duffy, -, -, 3

4870, 5 Jul 1894, Thomam E., Doyle, Kelamazoo *, Jeremiah, Doyle, Catharinam E., Hamilton, Stanton, VA, Roberti, Hamilton, Maria, Fisher, Rosa, Smith [?], -, DDC; BA; *notation beside

ST. MARY'S CATHOLIC CHURCH
HAGERSTOWN, MARYLAND, MARRIAGES:
Index, Marriage Date, 1st and Last Name of Groom, Groom from, 1st and Last Name of Groom's Father, 1st and Last Name of Bride, Bride from, 1st and Last Name of Bride's Father, 1st and Last Name of 1st Witness, 1st and Last Name of 2nd Witness, Location of Ceremony, Notes, Priest

Kelamazoo, translated from Latin, reads "born there as far as we know"], 6

4871, 12 Jul 1894, Joannem B., Firey, Hagerstown, Joseph, Firey, Susan R., Happell, Hagerstown, Martin, Happell, Georgio F., Cushwa, Rosa, Happel, -, -, 6

4872, 3 Oct 1894, Jacobum Gulielmum, Matthews, Warren Co., VA, Joseph, Matthews, Mariam E., McDevitt, Hagerstown, -, -, Francisco, Matthews, Alicia, Reed, -, DMR; 1st witness SA, 3

4873, 21 Nov 1894, Henricum Scott, Wise, Hagerstown, Walter S., Wise, Elisabeth, Smith, Hagerstown, -, -, Carolo F., Johston, Clara, Semler, -, DDC; GA, 3

4874, 17 Dec 1894, Otho O., Sigler, Smithsburg, Henrici C., Sigler, Protase M., Lord, Smithsburg, -, -, Newton, Fahrney, Maria, Smith, -, DMR; GA, 3

4875, 26 Dec 1894, Samuelem E., Basore, Washington Co., Georgii, Basore, Luciam E., Moore, Washington Co., Joannis, Moore, Joseph H., Martin, Maria C., Martin, -, DDC; GA, 3

4876, 3 Jan 1895, Joannem W., Nelson, MD, Gulielmi H. [?], Nelson, Jennie A., Higgins, MD, Patritii O. [?], Higgins, Howard, Fahrney, Maria, Smith, -, DMR; GA, 3

4877, 16 Jan 1895, Gulielmum H., Lefevre, VA, Henrici, Lefevre, Helenam B., Duffy, Hagerstown, Gulielmo, Duffy, Francisco, Lefevre, Helena, Duggan, -, DMR; GA, 3

4878, 26 Feb 1895, Joannem P., Downin, Hagerstown, Samuelis, Downin, Daisy [?] V., Buhrman, Washington Co., Hiram, Burhman, H.A., Clevidence, Maria, Malone, -, DMR; BA, 3

4879, 28 Feb 1895, Jesse F., Clayburn, Hagerstown, Joannis, Clayburne, Hattie B., Stern [?], Hagerstown, Gulielmi H., Stern, Gulielmo E., Biershing, Lettie A., Clayburn, -, DMR; BA, 3

4880, 8 Jun 1895, Franciscum D., Taylor, Williamsport, Gulielmi E., Taylor, Jesse, Thompson, Williamsport, -, -, Ella, Oliver, Daisy, Taylor, -, DMR; GA, 3

4881, 26 Sep 1895, Carolum, Douglas, Frederick Co., MD, Gulielmi, Douglas, Mariam, Foley, Co. Galway, Ireland, -, -, Mary (Mrs.), Smith, Mrs., Fisher [?], -, DMR; GA, 3

ST. MARY'S CATHOLIC CHURCH HAGERSTOWN, MARYLAND, MARRIAGES:

Index, Marriage Date, 1st and Last Name of Groom, Groom from, 1st and Last Name of Groom's Father, 1st and Last Name of Bride, Bride from, 1st and Last Name of Bride's Father, 1st and Last Name of 1st Witness, 1st and Last Name of 2nd Witness, Location of Ceremony, Notes, Priest

4882, 5 Feb 1896, Jeremiam , Hennessey, Washington Co., Petri, Hennessy, Elisam [?] J., Tidrick, Washington Co., Jacob, Tidrick, Mrs., Dolan, Mrs., Dolan, -, -, 3

4883, 18 Feb 1896, Eduardum Guy, Conley, Williamsport, Joannis, Conley, Annam Mariam, Hoy, Williamsport, -, -, Ernesto, McCardell, Bertah, Hoy, -, DMR; GA, 3

4884, 8 Apr 1896, Ernestum F., McCardell, Williamsport, Ambrosii, McCardell, Vertie *, Brown, Berkeley Co., WV, Joannis, Brown, J.S., Manford, J.A., Gearhart, -, DDC; BN; * something is crossed out - could be a middle initial, 3

4885, 16 Jun 1896, Leonardum E., Humelsine, Hagerstown, -, -, Catharinam L., Moore, Hagerstown, Joannis, Moore, Mr., Beck, Mr., Delamarter, -, 3rd witness is Mrs. Elisabeth Moore; DMR; GA, 3

4886, 1 Jul 1896, Benjamin F., Young, Hagerstown, Jacob A., Young, Mariam Isabellam, Switzer, Hagerstown, Samuelis, Switzer, Noah, Lawrence, Noah (Mrs.), Lawrence [HB], -, DDC; GA, 3

4887, 26 Aug 1896, Gulielmum A., Chricton, Baltimore, Joseph, Chricton, Mariam E., Grady, Hagerstown, Thomas, Grady, Carolo, Coderi, Catharina, Grady, -, -, 3

4888, 6 Oct 1896, Georgium W., McCardell, Williamsport, Riccardi, McCardell, Annam M., Ryan, Williamsport, Timothei, Ryan, Georgio, Ryan, Mrs. [?], Boward, -, -, 3

4889, 5 Dec 1896, Gulielmum, Geary, -, Eugenii, Geary, Mariam Jane, Sechrist, Hagerstown, Israel, Sechrist, Milton R., Hawkins, Mrs., Porter, -, DMR; BA, 3

4890, 24 Dec 1896, Joannem Eduardum, Ertter, Adams Co., PA, Adam, Ertter, Maria E., Wiser, Adams Co., PA, Samuelis, Wiser, Joanne, Faller, Mrs., Codori, -, DMR; BA, 3

4891, 2 Mar 1897, Eduardum F., Gallagher, Hagerstown, Francisci [?], Gallagher, Mariam S., Full, Hagerstown, Michaelis, Full, Carolo, Full, Lizzie, Full, -, DMR; GA, 3

4892, 6 May 1897, Joannem R., Obrist, Washington Co., Joannis, Obrist, Annam R., Hull, Washington Co., David, Hull, Gulielmo, Gittinger [?], Rosa, Chearfoss, -, DMR; GA, 3

ST. MARY'S CATHOLIC CHURCH
HAGERSTOWN, MARYLAND, MARRIAGES:
Index, Marriage Date, 1st and Last Name of Groom, Groom from, 1st and Last Name of Groom's Father, 1st and Last Name of Bride, Bride from, 1st and Last Name of Bride's Father, 1st and Last Name of 1st Witness, 1st and Last Name of 2nd Witness, Location of Ceremony, Notes, Priest

4893, 6 May 1897, Franciscum J., Grady, Hagerstown, Thomae, Grady, Jesse J., Miller, -, -, -, Gulielmo A., Chricton, Catharina, Grady, -, DMR; BA, 3

4894, 13 May 1897, Eduardum J., Nolan, Patterson, NJ, Michaelis, Nolan, Emililam J., Parker, Patterson, NJ, Joseph, Parker, Martino, Happel, Mary (Mrs.), Smith, -, -, 3

4895, 3 Jun 1897, Emerson A., Hager, Hagerstown, Jonathan J., Hager, Annam C., Sheehan, Hagerstown, Cornelii, Sheehan, Jonathan, Hager, Maria, Munson, -, DMR; GA, 3

4896, 29 Sep 1897, Augustum, Nierman, Hagerstown, Augusti, Nierman, Daisy, Fry, Hagerstown, Joannis, Fry, -, -, -, -, -, DMR; BA, 3

4897, 7 Oct 1897, Jacobum Percy, McCardell, Williamsport, Ambrosii, McCardell, Annam May, Collins, Williamsport, Harrison, Collins, Georgio ["Ambrowsii" crossed out], McCardell, Anna, McCardell [HB], -, DMR; BA, 3

4898, 19 Oct 1897, Carolum Eduardum, Wiles, -, Henrici, Wiles, Margaritam Laetitiam, Wills, Hagerstown, Jacob, Wills, Jacob J. [or I.], Wills, Carrie, Wills, -, DMR; GA, 3

4899, 13 Apr 1898, Preston L., McPherson, Chambersburg, Jacobi Monroe, McPherson, Rosam E., Osterman, Chambersburg, Joannis, Osterman, Dr., Fahrney, Mary (Mrs.), Smith "(housekeeper)", -, DMR; GA, 3

4900, 11 May 1898, Joannem R., Thomas, Bryantown, MD, Gulielmi, Thomas, Bertham, Hoy, Williamsport, Laurentii, Hoy, Dr., Fahrney, Anna Maria (Mrs.), Conley "/Hoy"*, -, DMR; GA; *perhaps this means that Hoy was her maiden name?, 3

4901, 28 Aug 1898, Jacobum N., McKalving, Washington Co., Alexandri, McKalving, Annam M., Shields, Washington Co., Eduardi, Shields, Joanne, Hildebrand, Maria (Mrs.), Smith, -, GA, 3

4902, 3 Nov 1898, Robertum F., Shafer, Hagerstown, -, -, Mariam H., Orndorf, Hagerstown, -, -, John B., Sweeney, Fannie (Miss), Cushwa, -, DMR; GA, 3

4903, 10 Dec 1898, Otille, Crumbaugh, D. R.[?], Joannes, Crumbaugh, Edna L., Jacobs, Washington Co., Gulielmi, Jacobs, Gulielmus, Jacob, Dore, Crumbaugh, -, DMR; BA, 3

ST. MARY'S CATHOLIC CHURCH
HAGERSTOWN, MARYLAND, MARRIAGES:

Index, Marriage Date, 1st and Last Name of Groom, Groom from, 1st and Last Name of Groom's Father, 1st and Last Name of Bride, Bride from, 1st and Last Name of Bride's Father, 1st and Last Name of 1st Witness, 1st and Last Name of 2nd Witness, Location of Ceremony, Notes, Priest

4904, 25 Apr 1899, Carolum Albertum, Wastler, -, Caroli, Wastler, Mariam Elisabeth, Alexander, Hagerstown, Caroli, Alexander, Georgio, Alexander, Maria, Wastler, -, -, 3

4905, 31 May 1899, Henricum Jacobum, Jeffers, Baltimore, -, -, Annam Catharinam, Happel, Hagerstown, Martini, Happel, Martino, Happel, Jennie, Diggs, -, -, 3

4906, 6 Jun 1899, Joseph H., Martin, -, David, Martin, Virginia B., Alexander, Hagerstown, Caroli, Alexander, Georgio, Alexander, Maria, Martin, -, -, 3

4907, 6 Jun 1899, Carolum , Yeakle, -, -, -, Magdalenem L., Lawrence, -, -, -, Andrea, Lawrence, Edwin M., Moats, -, GA, 3

4908, 14 Jun 1899, Patritium M., Byrne, Bedford, VA, -, -, M. Daisy, Morrison, Hagerstown, -, -, Gulielmo, Wills, Lillie, Morrison, -, -, 3

4909, 5 Jul 1899, Jacobum, Leaman, Washington Co., Georgii, Leaman, Rosam Ethel, Adams, Hagerstown, Joannis N., Adams, Isaac, Moore, Maria (Mrs.), Smith, -, -, 3

4910, 12 Jul 1899, Carolum W., Gruber, Hagerstown, Martini W., Gruber, Laurettam, Shue, Hagerstown, Eduardi, Shue, Maria, Goddard, Maria, Shue, -, DMR; GA, 3

4911, 2 Aug 1899, Max, Gossard, Hagerstown, Jerry, Gossard, Mariam, Wastler, Hagerstown, Caroli, Wastler, Carolo A., Wastler, Maria, Wastler [HB], -, -, 3

4912, 6 Sep 1899, Antonium, Hankey, Philadelphia, Antonii, Hankey, L. Harriet, Orndorf, Hagerstown, Gulielmi F. [or H.], Orndorf, Walter J. (Dr.), Favence [?], Adele, Dyer, -, -, 5

4913, 21 Sep 1899, Augustum, Heimel, Hagerstown, -, -, Helenam C., Dugan, Williamsport, Joannis, Dugan, Monroe, Dugan, Sophia, Anderson, -, DMR; GA, 3

4914, 19 Jun 1900, Allen H., Mumma, Hagerstown, -, -, Heleonoram A., Geary, Hagerstown, Eugenii, Geary, Gulielmo, Middlekauff, Blanche, Mark, -, -, 3

4915, 16 Oct 1900, Carolum W., Brown, Oberlin, PA, -, -, Nettie (Mrs.), Miller, Hagerstown, -, -, Dr., Fahrney, Maria (Mrs.), Smith, -, DMR; GA, 3

ST. MARY'S CATHOLIC CHURCH
HAGERSTOWN, MARYLAND, MARRIAGES:
Index, Marriage Date, 1st and Last Name of Groom, Groom from, 1st and Last Name of Groom's Father, 1st and Last Name of Bride, Bride from, 1st and Last Name of Bride's Father, 1st and Last Name of 1st Witness, 1st and Last Name of 2nd Witness, Location of Ceremony, Notes, Priest

4916, 5 Nov 1900, Joannem J., Lindon, Coventry, England, -, -, Maria Franciscam, Goddard, Hagerstown, Gulielmi, Goddard, Francisco, Futterer, Mauritio, Domenici, -, -, 3

St. Mary's Catholic Church Records

Confirmations 1852 - 1871

ST. MARY'S CATHOLIC CHURCH
HAGERSTOWN, MARYLAND, CONFIRMATIONS:
Index, 1st Name, Last Name, Date, Ceremony, Place, Endnotes

5375, Anna, McArdle, 8 Aug 1852, Confirmed, Hagerstown, 47
5376, Francis B. F., Kerchener, 8 Aug 1852, Confirmed, Hagerstown, 47
5377, Mary C.C., Hurley, 8 Aug 1852, Confirmed, Hagerstown, 47
5378, Catharine M., Gauker, 8 Aug 1852, Confirmed, Hagerstown, 47
5379, Elizabeth, O'Leary, 8 Aug 1852, Confirmed, Hagerstown, 47
5380, Mary C., Suter, 8 Aug 1852, Confirmed, Hagerstown, 47
5381, Margaret, Doyle, 8 Aug 1852, Confirmed, Hagerstown, 47
5382, Louisa H., Doyle, 8 Aug 1852, Confirmed, Hagerstown, 47
5383, Elizabeth, Kelly, 8 Aug 1852, Confirmed, Hagerstown, 47
5384, Louisa C.J., Davis, 8 Aug 1852, Confirmed, Hagerstown, 47
5385, Teresa, Creamer, 8 Aug 1852, Confirmed, Hagerstown, 47
5386, Ann M., Rouskoulp, 8 Aug 1852, Confirmed, Hagerstown, 47
5387, George W., Creach [Creact?], 8 Aug 1852, Confirmed, Hagerstown, 47
5388, Joseph W., Gouker, 8 Aug 1852, Confirmed, Hagerstown, 47
5389, Louis, Tinterman, 8 Aug 1852, Confirmed, Hagerstown, 47
5390, John, Coyle, 8 Aug 1852, Confirmed, Hagerstown, 47
5391, Francis, McGlonagel, 8 Aug 1852, Confirmed, Hagerstown, 47
5392, Jacob, Creamer, 8 Aug 1852, Confirmed, Hagerstown, 47
5393, Mary A., Hinson, 8 Aug 1852, Confirmed, Hagerstown, 47
5394, Sophia M.R., Davis, 8 Aug 1852, Confirmed, Hagerstown, 47
5395, John, Weaver, 8 Aug 1852, Confirmed, Hagerstown, 47
5396, Samuel D., Coyle, 8 Aug 1852, Confirmed, Hagerstown, 47
5397, William, Diggs, 8 Aug 1852, Confirmed, Hagerstown, 47
5398, Caroline, Rister, 8 Aug 1852, Confirmed, Hagerstown, 47
5399, Matilda A., Brown, 8 Aug 1852, Confirmed, Hagerstown, 47
5400, Samuel, Brown, 8 Aug 1852, Confirmed, Hagerstown, 47
5401, Harriet, Brown, 8 Aug 1852, Confirmed, Hagerstown, 47
5402, William, Gilmyer, 8 Aug 1852, Confirmed, Hagerstown, 47
5403, Susan, Wright, 8 Aug 1852, Confirmed, Hagerstown, 47
5404, Catharine, Weaver, 8 Aug 1852, Confirmed, Hagerstown, 47
5405, Thomas, Chambers, 8 Aug 1852, Confirmed, Hagerstown, 47
5406, Josephene M. Agnes, Hurley, 8 Aug 1852, Confirmed, Hagerstown, 47

ST. MARY'S CATHOLIC CHURCH
HAGERSTOWN, MARYLAND, CONFIRMATIONS:
Index, 1st Name, Last Name, Date, Ceremony, Place, Endnotes

5407, Catharine, Foutre, 8 Aug 1852, Confirmed, Hagerstown, 47
5408, Mary Jane A. [or O.], Wilhyde, 8 Aug 1852, Confirmed, Hagerstown, 47; 63
5409, Charles B., Foutre, 8 Aug 1852, Confirmed, Hagerstown, 47
5410, Ellen, Doolan, 8 Aug 1852, Confirmed, Hagerstown, 47
5411, Lydia S., Boward, 8 Aug 1852, Confirmed, Hagerstown, 47
5412, Peter, Boward, 8 Aug 1852, Confirmed, Hagerstown, 47
5413, James, McCarty, 8 Aug 1852, Confirmed, Hagerstown, 47
5414, Louisa, Fitzhue, 8 Aug 1852, Confirmed, Hagerstown, 47
5415, Joseph, Swope, 8 Aug 1852, Confirmed, Hagerstown, 47
5416, Jacob, Griffith, 8 Aug 1852, Confirmed, Hagerstown, 47
5417, Lydia M.C., Miller, 8 Aug 1852, Confirmed, Hagerstown, 47
5418, Elizabeth, Dugan [or Deguan], 8 Aug 1852, Confirmed, Hagerstown, 47
5419, Catharine, Cambell, 8 Aug 1852, Confirmed, Hagerstown, 47
5420, Louisa, [no last name], 8 Aug 1852, Confirmed, Hagerstown, 47
5421, Regina, Cook, 30 Sep 1855, Confirmed, Hagerstown, 48
5422, Mary, Wright, 30 Sep 1855, Confirmed, Hagerstown, 48
5423, Rebecca, Shober, 30 Sep 1855, Confirmed, Hagerstown, 48
5424, Patrick, McCarthy, 30 Sep 1855, Confirmed, Hagerstown, 48
5425, Elizabeth, Oker, 30 Sep 1855, Confirmed, Hagerstown, 48
5426, Louisa, Wilhide, 30 Sep 1855, Confirmed, Hagerstown, 48
5427, Josephine, Kramer, 30 Sep 1855, Confirmed, Hagerstown, 48
5428, Patricia, McCartney, 30 Sep 1855, Confirmed, Hagerstown, 48
5429, Stanislaus, Koyle, 30 Sep 1855, Confirmed, Hagerstown, 48
5430, Aloysius, Clarke, 30 Sep 1855, Confirmed, Hagerstown, 48
5431, Jane, Floyd, 30 Sep 1855, Confirmed, Hagerstown, 48
5432, Ann, Griffey, 30 Sep 1855, Confirmed, Hagerstown, 48
5433, Francis, O'Brien, 30 Sep 1855, Confirmed, Hagerstown, 48
5434, Magdalena, McClain, 30 Sep 1855, Confirmed, Hagerstown, 48
5435, Augustine, Smith, 30 Sep 1855, Confirmed, Hagerstown, 48
5436, Matthew, O'Brien, 30 Sep 1855, Confirmed, Hagerstown, 48
5437, Augustine, Clarke, 30 Sep 1855, Confirmed, Hagerstown, 48

ST. MARY'S CATHOLIC CHURCH
HAGERSTOWN, MARYLAND, CONFIRMATIONS:
Index, 1st Name, Last Name, Date, Ceremony, Place, Endnotes

5438, Elizabeth, Tierney, 30 Sep 1855, Confirmed, Hagerstown, 48

5439, Anna, Shilling, 30 Sep 1855, Confirmed, Hagerstown, 48

5440, Mary, Futter, 30 Sep 1855, Confirmed, Hagerstown, 48

5441, James, Gillmeyer, 30 Sep 1855, Confirmed, Hagerstown, 48

5442, Petronella, Griffey, 30 Sep 1855, Confirmed, Hagerstown, 48

5443, Patrick, Kelly, 30 Sep 1855, Confirmed, Hagerstown, 48

5444, Regina, Kreigh, 30 Sep 1855, Confirmed, Hagerstown, 48

5445, Elizabeth, Walters, 30 Sep 1855, Confirmed, Hagerstown, 48

5446, Agnes, Brown, 30 Sep 1855, Confirmed, Hagerstown, 48

5447, Victoria, Gauger, 30 Sep 1855, Confirmed, Hagerstown, 48

5448, Michael, Hanly, 30 Sep 1855, Confirmed, Hagerstown, 48

5449, Michael, Shober, 30 Sep 1855, Confirmed, Hagerstown, 48

5450, Lucy, Gauger, 30 Sep 1855, Confirmed, Hagerstown, 48

5451, Clara, Brown, 30 Sep 1855, Confirmed, Hagerstown, 48

5452, Margaret Elizabeth, Gauger, 30 Sep 1855, Confirmed, Hagerstown, 48

5453, Charles, Kelly, 25 Dec 1856, 1st communion, -, 49

5454, Mary, Shilling, 25 Dec 1856, 1st communion, -, 49

5455, Mary Susan, Shehan, 25 Dec 1856, 1st communion, -, 49

5456, Lethe, Brown, 25 Dec 1856, 1st communion, -, 49

5457, Mary, Walters, 25 Dec 1856, 1st communion, -, 49

5458, Frances M., Wright, 25 Dec 1856, 1st communion, -, 49

5459, Frances, Smith, 25 Dec 1856, 1st communion, -, 49

5460, Catharine, Griffey, 25 Dec 1856, 1st communion, -, 49

5461, Petronilla, Griffey, 25 Dec 1856, 1st communion, -, 49

5462, William, O'Neal, 3 May 1857, 1st communion, -, 49

5463, Mark, Donnelly, 31 May 1857, 1st communion, -, 49

5464, Louisa, Kreigh, 25 Dec 1858, 1st communion, Hagerstown, 49

5465, James, Hughes, 13 Feb 1859, 1st communion, Williamsport, 49

5466, Sallie, Martiny, 10 Apr 1859, 1st communion, Hagerstown, 49

5467, Lizzie, Murray, 21 Apr 1859, 1st communion, Hagerstown, 49

5468, Mary Catharine, Lynch, 30 Apr 1854, 1st communion, Hagerstown, 50

ST. MARY'S CATHOLIC CHURCH
HAGERSTOWN, MARYLAND, CONFIRMATIONS:
Index, 1st Name, Last Name, Date, Ceremony, Place, Endnotes

5469, Anna Sarah Elizabeth, Jones, 30 Apr 1854, 1st communion, Hagerstown, 50
5470, Mary Olivia, Quinn, 30 Apr 1854, 1st communion, Hagerstown, 50
5471, May Agnes Virginia, Cook, 30 Apr 1854, 1st communion, Hagerstown, 50
5472, Mary Jane, Jones, 30 Apr 1854, 1st communion, Hagerstown, 50
5473, William, Nicodemus, 30 Apr 1854, 1st communion, Hagerstown, 50
5474, Mary, Smith, 30 Apr 1854, 1st communion, Hagerstown, 50
5475, Joseph, Swope, 30 Apr 1854, 1st communion, Hagerstown, 50
5476, Margaret, Kreigh, 25 Dec 1854, 1st communion, -, 51
5477, Anna, McCardell, 25 Dec 1854, 1st communion, -, 51
5478, Susan, Fouder, 25 Dec 1854, 1st communion, -, 51
5479, Sarah, Jones, 25 Dec 1854, 1st communion, -, 51
5480, Mary, Jones, 25 Dec 1854, 1st communion, -, 51
5481, Philip, Warner, 25 Dec 1854, 1st communion, -, 51
5482, Catharine, McCartey, 25 Dec 1854, 1st communion, -, 51
5483, Teresa, Shover, 25 Dec 1854, 1st communion, -, 51
5484, John, Shover, 25 Dec 1854, 1st communion, -, 51
5485, Hugh, Kelly, 25 Dec 1854, 1st communion, -, 51
5486, Thomas, Koyle, 25 Dec 1854, 1st communion, -, 51
5487, Lewis, Gillmeyer, 25 Dec 1854, 1st communion, -, 51
5488, Charles, Clark, 25 Dec 1854, 1st communion, -, 51
5489, James, Clark, 25 Dec 1854, 1st communion, -, 51
5490, Catharine, Wilhide, 25 Dec 1854, 1st communion, -, 51
5491, Elizabeth, Smith, 25 Dec 1854, 1st communion, -, 51
5492, Barbara, Gauger, 25 Dec 1854, 1st communion, -, 51
5493, Mary, Gauger, 25 Dec 1854, 1st communion, -, 51
5494, Samuel, Shervin, 25 Dec 1854, 1st communion, -, 51
5495, Mary, Oker, 1855, 1st communion, -, 51
5496, Alfred, Merrick, 1855, 1st communion, -, 51
5497, Lomsa, Kreigh, 25 Dec 1858, 1st communion, -, 52
5498, Annie, Louvson, 15 May 1859, 1st communion, Tennessee, 52, 64
5499, Bernard, McCullogh, -, 1st communion, Hagerstown, 52
5500, Victor, Cushwa, 29 May 1859, 1st communion, Hagerstown, 52, 64

ST. MARY'S CATHOLIC CHURCH
HAGERSTOWN, MARYLAND, CONFIRMATIONS:
Index, 1st Name, Last Name, Date, Ceremony, Place, Endnotes

5501, Jas. [James], Hughes, 13 Feb 1859, 1st communion, Williamsport, 52

5502, Sallie, Martiny , 10 Apr 1859, 1st communion, Hagerstown, 52, 64

5503, Lizzie, Murray , 21 Apr 1859, 1st communion, Hagerstown, 52, 64

5504, Uncle, Nasy [?] , 12 Jun 1859, 1st communion, Hagerstown, 52, 64

5505, Wm., Hawken, 16 Jun 1859, 1st communion, Williamsport, 52

5506, Mr. D., McDonald, 17 Jul 1859, 1st communion, Hagerstown, 52

5507, Wm., Goddreck, 18 Aug 1859, 1st communion, Williamsport, 52

5508, Mrs. Robt., Warner , 21 Aug 1859, 1st communion, Hagerstown, 52, 64

5509, Rosa, Fellinger, 5 Oct 1859, 1st communion, Clear Spring, 52

5510, Catharine, Gallagher, 5 Oct 1859, 1st communion, Clear Spring, 52

5511, Sarah Ann, Medcalff , 23 Oct 1859, 1st communion, Hagerstown, 52, 64

5512, Edward, Donnelly, 24 Nov 1859, 1st communion, Williamsport, 52

5513, Ellen, Oliver, 24 Nov 1859, 1st communion, Williamsport, 52

5514, Mrs. , Julius [?] , 29 Jan 1860, 1st communion, Hagerstown, 52, 64

5515, Fannie, Cramer, 5 Apr 1860, 1st communion, Hagerstown, 52

5516, Ginnie, Anderson , 20 May 1860, 1st communion, Hagerstown, 52, 64, 65

5517, Lizzie, Bearsay , 21 May 1860, 1st communion, Hagerstown, 52, 64

5518, Thos., Donnelly, 24 May 1860, 1st communion, Williamsport, 52

5519, Elizabeth, Dietrich , 9 Aug 1860, 1st communion, Hagerstown, 52, 64

5520, Alverta J., Shank, 8 Sep 1860, 1st communion, Hagestown, 52

ST. MARY'S CATHOLIC CHURCH
HAGERSTOWN, MARYLAND, CONFIRMATIONS:
Index, 1st Name, Last Name, Date, Ceremony, Place, Endnotes

5521, Louisa, McDonald , 26 Dec 1860, 1st communion, Hagerstown, 52, 64
5522, Danl., Carls , Jan 1861, 1st communion, Williamsport, 52, 64
5523, Sallie, Martiny, 21 Oct 1860, confirmation, Hagerstown, 53
5524, Victor, Cushwa, 21 Oct 1860, confirmation, Hagerstown, 53
5525, Sarah, Medcalff, 21 Oct 1860, confirmation, Hagerstown, 53
5526, Alfred, Merrick, 21 Oct 1860, confirmation, Hagerstown, 53
5527, M.D., McDonald, 21 Oct 1860, confirmation, Hagerstown, 53
5528, Mary, Warner, 21 Oct 1860, confirmation, Hagerstown, 53
5529, Naason, See , 21 Oct 1860, confirmation, Hagerstown, 53, 65
5530, Joseph, Gillis , 21 Oct 1860, confirmation, Hagerstown, 53, 65
5531, Virginia, Anderson , 21 Oct 1860, confirmation, Hagerstown, 53, 65
5532, Catharine, Smith, 21 Oct 1860, confirmation, Hagerstown, 53
5533, Lizzie, Dietrick, 21 Oct 1860, confirmation, Hagerstown, 53
5534, Maala, Adams, 21 Oct 1860, confirmation, Hagerstown, 53
5535, Mary Eliz., Bosey, 21 Oct 1860, confirmation, Hagerstown, 53
5536, Mary, Juluis [?], 21 Oct 1860, confirmation, Hagerstown, 53
5537, Lizzie, Murray, 21 Oct 1860, confirmation, Hagerstown, 53
5538, Wm., Thompson, 21 Oct 1860, confirmation, Hagerstown, 53
5539, Mary, Bury , 21 Oct 1860, confirmation, Hagerstown, 53, 65
5540, Louisa, Kreigh, 21 Oct 1860, confirmation, Hagerstown, 53
5541, Annie, Hanson, 21 Oct 1860, confirmation, Hagerstown, 53
5542, Louisa, Cramer, 21 Oct 1860, confirmation, Hagerstown, 53
5543, Annie, Smith, 21 Oct 1860, confirmation, Hagerstown, 53
5544, Elizabeth, Griffey, 21 Oct 1860, confirmation, Hagerstown, 53
5545, Laura, Ford, 21 Oct 1860, confirmation, Hagerstown, 53
5546, Cath., Toben, 21 Oct 1860, confirmation, Hagerstown, 53
5547, Peter, Kreigh, 21 Oct 1860, confirmation, Hagerstown, 53
5548, Thos., Donnelly, 21 Oct 1860, confirmation, Hagerstown, 53
5549, Francis, Hoover, 21 Oct 1860, confirmation, Hagerstown, 53

ST. MARY'S CATHOLIC CHURCH
HAGERSTOWN, MARYLAND, CONFIRMATIONS:
Index, 1st Name, Last Name, Date, Ceremony, Place, Endnotes

5550, Theresa, Griffey, 21 Oct 1860, confirmation, Hagerstown, 53
5551, Wm., Hurley, 21 Oct 1860, confirmation, Hagerstown, 53
5552, Theresa, Jones, 21 Oct 1860, confirmation, Hagerstown, 53, 65
5553, Jas., McGee, 21 Oct 1860, confirmation, Hagerstown, 53
5554, Charles, Wright, 21 Oct 1860, confirmation, Hagerstown, 53
5555, Jacob, Futterer, 21 Oct 1860, confirmation, Hagerstown, 53
5556, Jas., Osborn, 21 Oct 1860, confirmation, Hagerstown, 53
5557, John, Futterer, 21 Oct 1860, confirmation, Hagerstown, 53
5558, Geo., McCann, 21 Oct 1860, confirmation, Hagerstown, 53
5559, Wilfrid, Wright, 21 Oct 1860, confirmation, Hagerstown, 53
5560, Annie, Pitt, 21 Oct 1860, confirmation, Hagerstown, 53
5561, Elizabeth, Walsh, 21 Oct 1860, confirmation, Hagerstown, 53
5562, Helen, Kelly, 21 Oct 1860, confirmation, Hagerstown, 53
5563, Mary, McCann, 21 Oct 1860, confirmation, Hagerstown, 53
5564, Cath., Laurence, 21 Oct 1860, confirmation, Williamsport, 53
5565, Genevieve, Stake, 21 Oct 1860, confirmation, Williamsport, 53
5566, Ellen, Oliver, 21 Oct 1860, confirmation, Williamsport, 53
5567, Wm., Goddard, 21 Oct 1860, confirmation, Williamsport, 53
5568, Edw., Donnelly, 21 Oct 1860, confirmation, Williamsport, 53
5569, Cath., Oliver, 21 Oct 1860, confirmation, Williamsport, 53
5570, John, Laurence, 21 Oct 1860, confirmation, Williamsport, 53
5571, Mary, Donnelly, 21 Oct 1860, confirmation, Williamsport, 53
5572, Wm., Lewis, 21 Oct 1860, confirmation, Williamsport, 53
5573, Rosa, McAvoy, 21 Oct 1860, confirmation, Williamsport, 53
5574, Noah, Laurence, 21 Oct 1860, confirmation, Williamsport, 53
5575, Kate, Hawken, 21 Oct 1860, confirmation, Williamsport, 53
5576, Laurence, Hoy, 21 Oct 1860, confirmation, Williamsport, 53
5577, Kate, Hoy, 21 Oct 1860, confirmation, Williamsport, 53
5578, Laura, Nicodemus, 21 Oct 1860, confirmation, Williamsport, 53
5579, Adam, Harrison , 21 Oct 1860, confirmation, Williamsport, 53, 65

ST. MARY'S CATHOLIC CHURCH
HAGERSTOWN, MARYLAND, CONFIRMATIONS:
Index, 1st Name, Last Name, Date, Ceremony, Place, Endnotes

5580, Anna, McClain, 21 Oct 1860, confirmation, Williamsport, 53

5581, Clara, Thompson, 21 Oct 1860, confirmation, Williamsport, 53

5582, Cath., Smith, 21 Oct 1860, 1st communion, Hagerstown, 54

5583, Jos, Gillis , 21 Oct 1860, 1st communion, Hagerstown, 54, 65

5584, Maala, Adams, 21 Oct 1860, 1st communion, Hagerstown, 54

5585, Wm, Thompson, 21 Oct 1860, 1st communion, Hagerstown, 54

5586, Mary, Bury , 21 Oct 1860, 1st communion, Hagerstown, 54, 65

5587, Louisa, Cramer, 21 Oct 1860, 1st communion, Hagerstown, 54

5588, Anna, Smith, 21 Oct 1860, 1st communion, Hagerstown, 54

5589, Elizabeth, Griffey, 21 Oct 1860, 1st communion, Hagerstown, 54

5590, Laura, Ford, 21 Oct 1860, 1st communion, Hagerstown, 54

5591, Cath., Toben, 21 Oct 1860, 1st communion, Hagerstown, 54

5592, Theresa, Griffey, 21 Oct 1860, 1st communion, Hagerstown, 54

5593, Theresa, Jones , 21 Oct 1860, 1st communion, Hagerstown, 54, 65

5594, Charles, Wright, 21 Oct 1860, 1st communion, Hagerstown, 54

5595, Jas, Osborn, 21 Oct 1860, 1st communion, Hagerstown, 54

5596, Jas, Osborn [2nd entry], 21 Oct 1860, 1st communion, Hagerstown, 54

5597, Geo., McCann, 21 Oct 1860, 1st communion, Hagerstown, 54

5598, Mary, McCann, 21 Oct 1860, 1st communion, Hagerstown, 54

5599, Elizabeth, Walsh, 21 Oct 1860, 1st communion, Hagerstown, 54

5600, Sarah Agnes, Murray, 25 Mar 1862, 1st communion, Hagerstown, 55

5601, Benjamin Franklin, Tierney, 25 Mar 1862, 1st communion, Hagerstown, 55

5602, Wm., Hurley, 25 Mar 1862, 1st communion, Hagerstown, 55

ST. MARY'S CATHOLIC CHURCH
HAGERSTOWN, MARYLAND, CONFIRMATIONS:
Index, 1st Name, Last Name, Date, Ceremony, Place, Endnotes

5603, Henry, Cremer, 25 Mar 1862, 1st communion, Hagerstown, 55

5604, Annie, Tierney, 25 Mar 1862, 1st communion, Hagerstown, 55

5605, Ellen, Kelly, 25 Mar 1862, 1st communion, Hagerstown, 55

5606, Charlotta, Burger, 25 Mar 1862, 1st communion, Hagerstown, 55

5607, Annie, Hanson, 25 Mar 1862, 1st communion, Hagerstown, 55

5608, Laura, Lausburgh, 25 Mar 1862, 1st communion, Hagerstown, 55

5609, Malachy, Moran, 25 Mar 1862, 1st communion, Hagerstown, 55

5610, Mary, Eck, 28 Apr 1865, confirmation, Hagerstown, 56

5611, Ellen, Hoover, 28 Apr 1865, confirmation, Hagerstown, 56

5612, Charlotte, Barger, 28 Apr 1865, confirmation, Hagerstown, 56

5613, Nitty, Hurley, 28 Apr 1865, confirmation, Hagerstown, 56

5614, Mary Louisa, Doyle, 28 Apr 1865, confirmation, Hagerstown, 56

5615, Cath., Tasker , 28 Apr 1865, confirmation, Hagerstown, 56, 65

5616, Harriet, Tasker , 28 Apr 1865, confirmation, Hagerstown, 56, 65

5617, Mary, McLaughlin, 28 Apr 1865, confirmation, Hagerstown, 56

5618, Jenny, Hoover, 28 Apr 1865, confirmation, Hagerstown, 56

5619, Annie, McDonnell, 28 Apr 1865, confirmation, Hagerstown, 56

5620, Alice, McDonnell, 28 Apr 1865, confirmation, Hagerstown, 56

5621, Laura, Lorshbaugh, 28 Apr 1865, confirmation, Hagerstown, 56

5622, Lilly Mary, Downey, 28 Apr 1865, confirmation, Hagerstown, 56

5623, Joseph, Owner, 28 Apr 1865, confirmation, Hagerstown, 56

5624, George Edw., Ragney, 28 Apr 1865, confirmation, Hagerstown, 56

5625, Victor, Wright, 28 Apr 1865, confirmation, Hagerstown, 56

5626, Joseph, Hoeltzle, 28 Apr 1865, confirmation, Hagerstown, 56

ST. MARY'S CATHOLIC CHURCH
HAGERSTOWN, MARYLAND, CONFIRMATIONS:
Index, 1st Name, Last Name, Date, Ceremony, Place, Endnotes

5627, Will., Duffey, 28 Apr 1865, confirmation, Hagerstown, 56
5628, Mally, South, 28 Apr 1865, confirmation, Funkstown, 56
5629, Richd, South, 28 Apr 1865, confirmation, Funkstown, 56
5630, Mrs. Mary, Owner, 28 Apr 1865, confirmation, Hagerstown, 56
5631, Cath., Woolts, 28 Apr 1865, confirmation, Hagerstown, 56
5632, Benton, Cushwa, 28 Apr 1865, confirmation, Hagerstown, 56
5633, George, Kyper, 28 Apr 1865, confirmation, Hagerstown, 56
5634, Mrs. Mary, Coyle, 28 Apr 1865, confirmation, Cavetown, 56
5635, Henry, McCartney, 28 Apr 1865, confirmation, Hagerstown, 56
5636, Martha Ann, Leiser, 28 Apr 1865, confirmation, Hagerstown, 56
5637, Kate, Furley, 28 Apr 1865, confirmation, Hagerstown, 56
5638, Genevieve, Ward, 28 Apr 1865, confirmation, Hagerstown, 56
5639, Charl., Diefendal, 28 Apr 1865, confirmation, Hagerstown, 56
5640, Albert, Diefendal, 28 Apr 1865, confirmation, Hagerstown, 56
5641, Robert E., Warner, 28 Apr 1865, confirmation, Hagerstown, 56
5642, Elis., Clarkson, 28 Apr 1865, confirmation, Williamsport, 56
5643, Aaron, Lawrence, 28 Apr 1865, confirmation, Williamsport, 56
5644, Maria, Lawrence, 28 Apr 1865, confirmation, Williamsport, 56
5645, Mary Jos., Lawrence, 28 Apr 1865, confirmation, Williamsport, 56
5646, Mary, Berry, 28 Apr 1865, confirmation, Williamsport, 56
5647, Mrs. Mary A., Molatt, 28 Apr 1865, confirmation, Hagerstown, 56
5648, Verdy, Thank, 28 Apr 1865, confirmation, Smithsburg, 56
5649, Joseph James, Kenney, 28 Apr 1865, confirmation, Sharpsburg, 56
5650, Lizzie, Swab [?], 28 Apr 1865, confirmation, Clearspring, 56
5651, Cath., Leiser, 28 Apr 1865, confirmation, Hagerstown, 56
5652, Annie, Souers , 28 Apr 1865, confirmation, Hagerstown, 56, 65

ST. MARY'S CATHOLIC CHURCH
HAGERSTOWN, MARYLAND, CONFIRMATIONS:
Index, 1st Name, Last Name, Date, Ceremony, Place, Endnotes

5653, James A., Wright, 28 Apr 1865, confirmation, Hagerstown, 56

5654, Mary, Griffen, 28 Apr 1865, confirmation, Smithsburg, 56

5655, Henry, Cramer, 28 Apr 1865, confirmation, Hagerstown, 56

5656, Mary Elis., Fuchsberger, 28 Apr 1865, confirmation, Hagerstown, 56

5657, Andrew, Fuchsberger, 28 Apr 1865, confirmation, Hagerstown, 56

5658, Marg., Goddard, 28 Apr 1865, confirmation, Williamsport, 56

5659, Mary, Goddard, 28 Apr 1865, confirmation, Williamsport, 56

5660, George, Clarkson, 28 Apr 1865, confirmation, Williamsport, 56

5661, Willm., McLane, 28 Apr 1865, confirmation, Williamsport, 56

5662, Andrew, Zinke [or Zinken], 28 Apr 1865, confirmation, Hagerstown, 56

5663, James, McIlvaugh, 28 Apr 1865, confirmation, Hagerstown, 56

5664, Sarah Agnes, Murray, 28 Apr 1865, confirmation, Hagerstown, 56

5665, Charles, Furley [?], 28 Apr 1865, confirmation, Hagerstown, 56

5666, Kate, Wooltz, 3 Jun 1866, 1st communion, Hagerstown, 57

5667, Molly, McLaughlin, 3 Jun 1866, 1st communion, Hagerstown, 57

5668, Alice, McDonald, 3 Jun 1866, 1st communion, Hagerstown, 57

5669, Anna, McDonald, 3 Jun 1866, 1st communion, Hagerstown, 57

5670, Ginny, Hoover, 3 Jun 1866, 1st communion, Hagerstown, 57

5671, Anna, Creamer, 3 Jun 1866, 1st communion, Hagerstown, 57

5672, Mary, Griffey, 3 Jun 1866, 1st communion, Hagerstown, 57

5673, Mary, Smith, 3 Jun 1866, 1st communion, Hagerstown, 57

5674, Maria, Laurence, 3 Jun 1866, 1st communion, Hagerstown, 57

5675, Mary, Laurence, 3 Jun 1866, 1st communion, Hagerstown, 57

5676, Martin, Green, 3 Jun 1866, 1st communion, Hagerstown, 57

ST. MARY'S CATHOLIC CHURCH
HAGERSTOWN, MARYLAND, CONFIRMATIONS:
Index, 1st Name, Last Name, Date, Ceremony, Place, Endnotes

5677, Jos, Kenny, 3 Jun 1866, 1st communion, Hagerstown, 57
5678, Edwd., Smith, 3 Jun 1866, 1st communion, Hagerstown, 57
5679, Anna, Laurence, 3 Jun 1866, 1st communion, Hagerstown, 57
5680, Chs., Diffendal, 3 Jun 1866, 1st communion, Hagerstown, 57
5681, Albertus, Diffendal, 3 Jun 1866, 1st communion, Hagerstown, 57
5682, Richd., Broderick, 3 Jun 1866, 1st communion, Hagerstown, 57
5683, Wm., McClain, 3 Jun 1866, 1st communion, Hagerstown, 57
5684, Francis John, Futterer, 14 Oct 1868, confirmation, Hagerstown, 58
5685, Michael, Long, 14 Oct 1868, confirmation, Hagerstown, 58
5686, Michael, Termey [?], 14 Oct 1868, confirmation, Hagerstown, 58
5687, S. Daniel, Toy, 14 Oct 1868, confirmation, Hagerstown, 58
5688, Harry M., Warner, 14 Oct 1868, confirmation, Hagerstown, 58
5689, Bernard, Ball, 14 Oct 1868, confirmation, Hagerstown, 58
5690, Richard, Downey [?], 14 Oct 1868, confirmation, Hagerstown, 58
5691, John Elder, Hoover, 14 Oct 1868, confirmation, Hagerstown, 58
5692, Joseph Francis, Leizer, 14 Oct 1868, confirmation, Hagerstown, 58
5693, Isaac, Orndorf, 14 Oct 1868, confirmation, Hagerstown, 58
5694, Chas. Andrew, Duffey, 14 Oct 1868, confirmation, Hagerstown, 58
5695, Daniel, Long, 14 Oct 1868, confirmation, Hagerstown, 58
5696, Edward, Smith, 14 Oct 1868, confirmation, Hagerstown, 58
5697, Joseph John, Kelly, 14 Oct 1868, confirmation, Hagerstown, 58
5698, John, Hellane, 14 Oct 1868, confirmation, Hagerstown, 58
5699, Henry Philip, Clark, 14 Oct 1868, confirmation, Hagerstown, 58
5700, Edward John, Smith, 14 Oct 1868, confirmation, Hagerstown, 58
5701, Cath. Mary, Butler, 14 Oct 1868, confirmation, Hagerstown, 58

ST. MARY'S CATHOLIC CHURCH
HAGERSTOWN, MARYLAND, CONFIRMATIONS:
Index, 1st Name, Last Name, Date, Ceremony, Place, Endnotes

5702, Jenny Rose, Creamer, 14 Oct 1868, confirmation, Hagerstown, 58

5703, Mary, Ryder, 14 Oct 1868, confirmation, Hagerstown, 58

5704, Marg. Mary, Wright, 14 Oct 1868, confirmation, Hagerstown, 58

5705, Jennie, Humbach [?], 14 Oct 1868, confirmation, Hagerstown, 58

5706, Anna Rosina, Kelly, 14 Oct 1868, confirmation, Hagerstown, 58

5707, Mary Jos., Shervin, 14 Oct 1868, confirmation, Hagerstown, 58

5708, Ellen Anastasia, Nelligan, 14 Oct 1868, confirmation, Hagerstown, 58

5709, Christie A. Marg., Clarkson, 14 Oct 1868, confirmation, Hagerstown, 58

5710, Regina Angela, Clark, 14 Oct 1868, confirmation, Hagerstown, 58

5711, Lucy, Ryder, 14 Oct 1868, confirmation, Hagerstown, 58

5712, Mary Cath., Geary, 14 Oct 1868, confirmation, Hagerstown, 58

5713, Mary Cecilia, Creamer, 14 Oct 1868, confirmation, Hagerstown, 58

5714, Evelina Marg. [Mary.?], Cushwa, 14 Oct 1868, confirmation, Hagerstown, 58

5715, Frances, Mayhew, 14 Oct 1868, confirmation, Hagerstown, 58

5716, Mary Regina, Hearn, 14 Oct 1868, confirmation, Hagerstown, 58

5717, Ann Amelia, Turner, 14 Oct 1868, confirmation, Hagerstown, 58

5718, Caroline, Reichter [?], 14 Oct 1868, confirmation, Hagerstown, 58

5719, John William, Diffendall, 28 Jun 1871, confirmation, Hagerstown, 59

5720, Samuel, Diffendall, 28 Jun 1871, confirmation, Hagerstown, 59

5721, Thomas, Diffendall, 28 Jun 1871, confirmation, Hagerstown, 59

5722, Theodore, Diffendall, 28 Jun 1871, confirmation, Hagerstown, 59

ST. MARY'S CATHOLIC CHURCH
HAGERSTOWN, MARYLAND, CONFIRMATIONS:
Index, 1st Name, Last Name, Date, Ceremony, Place, Endnotes

5723, Otho Joseph Smith, Duffy, 28 Jun 1871, confirmation, Hagerstown, 59

5724, William John, Ball, 28 Jun 1871, confirmation, Hagerstown, 59

5725, Danial [sic], Creamer, 28 Jun 1871, confirmation, Hagerstown, 59

5726, Edward Franklin, Zwoke [?], 28 Jun 1871, confirmation, Hagerstown, 59

5727, Fernando Jackson, Fox, 28 Jun 1871, confirmation, Hagerstown, 59

5728, Joseph Philip Charles, Dillon, 28 Jun 1871, confirmation, Hagerstown, 59

5729, Michael C. I.[?], Dillon, 28 Jun 1871, confirmation, Hagerstown, 59

5730, Isaac, Gallaway, 28 Jun 1871, confirmation, Hagerstown, 59

5731, Felix Michael, O'Connor, 28 Jun 1871, confirmation, Hagerstown, 59

5732, James Remar J.[or Remard], O'Conner [?], 28 Jun 1871, confirmation, Hagerstown, 59

5733, John William, Dillon [?], 28 Jun 1871, confirmation, Hagerstown, 59

5734, Lawrence, Middlekauf, 28 Jun 1871, confirmation, Hagerstown, 59

5735, Joanna E., O'Henan [?], 28 Jun 1871, confirmation, Hagerstown, 59

5736, Ellen Emelia, O'Huran, 28 Jun 1871, confirmation, Hagerstown, 59

5737, Anna Mary V., Diffindall, 28 Jun 1871, confirmation, Hagerstown, 59

5738, Margret Jane, Gray, 28 Jun 1871, confirmation, Hagerstown, 59

5739, Helen Cecelia, J[?]uch, 28 Jun 1871, confirmation, Hagerstown, 59

5740, Annie Elisabeth, Wright, 28 Jun 1871, confirmation, Hagerstown, 59

5741, Julia Elizabeth, Warner, 28 Jun 1871, confirmation, Hagerstown, 59

5742, Annie, Middlekauff, 28 Jun 1871, confirmation, Hagerstown, 59

5743, Romana E., Zroderick [?], 28 Jun 1871, confirmation, Hagerstown, 59

ST. MARY'S CATHOLIC CHURCH
HAGERSTOWN, MARYLAND, CONFIRMATIONS:
Index, 1st Name, Last Name, Date, Ceremony, Place, Endnotes

5744, Laura Jane, Baker, 28 Jun 1871, confirmation, Hagerstown, 59

5745, Emily A., Baker, 28 Jun 1871, confirmation, Hagerstown, 59

5746, Agnes Xavier, Creamer, 28 Jun 1871, confirmation, Hagerstown, 59

5747, Carolina, Heil, 28 Jun 1871, confirmation, Hagerstown, 59

5748, Helen C., Chambers, 28 Jun 1871, confirmation, Hagerstown, 59

5749, Jennie Ann, Fox, 28 Jun 1871, confirmation, Hagerstown, 59

5750, Sarah J., Schilling, 28 Jun 1871, confirmation, Hagerstown, 59

5751, C. Mary E., Weaver, 28 Jun 1871, confirmation, Hagerstown, 59

5752, Mary Cecelia Agnes, Cretin, 28 Jun 1871, confirmation, Hagerstown, 59

5753, Mary Annie, Hoover, 28 Jun 1871, confirmation, Hagerstown, 59

5754, Mary Jane, Howard [?], 28 Jun 1871, confirmation, Hagerstown, 59

5755, Annie Cecelia, O'Huran, 28 Jun 1871, confirmation, Hagerstown, 59

5756, Catherine Lillie, O'Huran, 28 Jun 1871, confirmation, Hagerstown, 59

5757, Michael J., Collins, 27 Jun 1871, confirmation, Williamsport, 60

5758, George W., Watson, 27 Jun 1871, confirmation, Williamsport, 60

5759, Andrew J. C. R., Hemsley [?], 27 Jun 1871, confirmation, Williamsport, 60

5760, Anthony C.W., Collins, 27 Jun 1871, confirmation, Williamsport, 60

5761, Hugh C.C., Clarke, 27 Jun 1871, confirmation, Williamsport, 60

5762, Michael C.J., Lawrence, 27 Jun 1871, confirmation, Williamsport, 60

5763, Lillie C.T., Williams, 27 Jun 1871, confirmation, Williamsport, 60

5764, Janettie C.A., McCardell, 27 Jun 1871, confirmation, Williamsport, 60

5765, Ann C.M., Metcaff, 27 Jun 1871, confirmation, Williamsport, 60

ST. MARY'S CATHOLIC CHURCH
HAGERSTOWN, MARYLAND, CONFIRMATIONS:
Index, 1st Name, Last Name, Date, Ceremony, Place, Endnotes

5766, Emma C. Ann L., Richter, 27 Jun 1871, confirmation, Williamsport, 60
5767, M.C. Heston [?], King, 27 Jun 1871, confirmation, Williamsport, 60
5768, Mary S., Watson, 27 Jun 1871, confirmation, Williamsport, 60
5769, C.R. Ann, King, 27 Jun 1871, confirmation, Williamsport, 60
5770, Catherine C., Cushwa, 27 Jun 1871, confirmation, Williamsport, 60
5771, Lillie Gertrude, McCardell, 27 Jun 1871, confirmation, Williamsport, 60
5772, Sarah Josephine, Wolf, 27 Jun 1871, confirmation, Williamsport, 60
5773, Louisa C.M.A., Lawrence, 27 Jun 1871, confirmation, Williamsport, 60
5774, Elisabeth C.H., Sheridon [?], 27 Jun 1871, confirmation, Williamsport, 60
5775, Mary Ann, Donnelly, 27 Jun 1871, confirmation, Williamsport, 60
5776, Elisabeth C., Collins, 27 Jun 1871, confirmation, Williamsport, 60
5777, John, Davis, 18 Jul 1858, Holy Scapular, Hagerstown, 61
5778, Sophia, Davis, 19 Sep 1858, Holy Scapular, Hagerstown, 61
5779, Saml., Coyle, 3 Oct 1858, Holy Scapular, Hagerstown, 61
5780, Jacob, Creamer, 3 Oct 1858, Holy Scapular, Hagerstown, 61
5781, Jas. I., Hurley, 3 Oct 1858, Holy Scapular, Hagerstown, 61
5782, Robt., Warner, 3 Oct 1858, Holy Scapular, Hagerstown, 61
5783, Theresa, Creamer, 3 Oct 1858, Holy Scapular, Hagerstown, 61
5784, Lizzie, Shirley, 3 Oct 1858, Holy Scapular, Hagerstown, 61
5785, Mrs., Diggs , 3 Oct 1858, Holy Scapular, Hagerstown, 61, 65
5786, Mary, Hemsley, 3 Oct 1858, Holy Scapular, Hagerstown, 61
5787, Mary, Truman, 3 Oct 1858, Holy Scapular, Hagerstown, 61
5788, Annie, McCardle, 3 Oct 1858, Holy Scapular, Hagerstown, 61
5789, Ginnie, Cook , 3 Oct 1858, Holy Scapular, Hagerstown, 61, 65
5790, Lizzie, Kelly, 3 Oct 1858, Holy Scapular, Hagerstown, 61

ST. MARY'S CATHOLIC CHURCH
HAGERSTOWN, MARYLAND, CONFIRMATIONS:
Index, 1st Name, Last Name, Date, Ceremony, Place, Endnotes

5791, Sallie, Martiny, 25 Mar 1859, Holy Scapular, Hagerstown, 61

5792, Mrs., McGonigal, 25 Mar 1859, Holy Scapular, Hagerstown, 61

5793, Mary, Hanson, 25 Mar 1859, Holy Scapular, Hagerstown, 61

5794, Emma, Floyd , 25 Mar 1859, Holy Scapular, Hagerstown, 61, 65

5795, Mary , "of Mrs. Harbine", 25 Mar 1859, Holy Scapular, Hagerstown, 61, 65

5796, A.D., Merrick, 27 May 1860, Holy Scapular, Hagerstown, 61

5797, Any [or Ang], Coyle, 27 May 1860, Holy Scapular, Hagerstown, 61

5798, Edwd., Coyle, 27 May 1860, Holy Scapular, Hagerstown, 61

5799, Kate, Maguire, 27 May 1860, Holy Scapular, Hagerstown, 61

5800, Mary, Inlius [or Julius], 27 May 1860, Holy Scapular, Hagerstown, 61

5801, Lizzie, Bearsay, 27 May 1860, Holy Scapular, Hagerstown, 61

5802, Uncle, Naason, 27 May 1860, Holy Scapular, Hagerstown, 61

5803, Fannie, Cramer, 27 May 1860, Holy Scapular, Hagerstown, 61

5804, Bernard, McCullogh, 27 May 1860, Holy Scapular, Hagerstown, 61

5805, Sallie, Ambrose , 27 May 1860, Holy Scapular, Hagerstown, 61, 65

5806, Mary, Collens, 23 Sep 1860, Holy Scapular, Hagerstown, 61

5807, Lizzie, Murray, 4 Nov 1860, Holy Scapular, Hagerstown, 61

5808, Thos. B., Coyle, 8 May 1861, Holy Scapular, Hagerstown, 61

5809, Mrs. Mary, McMememm, Mar 1861, Holy Scapular, Hagerstown, 62

5810, Wm., Krish [?], 11 Jun 1861, Holy Scapular, Hagerstown, 62

St. Mary's Catholic Church Records

Deaths
1853 – 1900

ST. MARY'S CATHOLIC CHURCH
HAGERSTOWN, MARYLAND, DEATHS:
Index, Date, First, Last, Age, Place, Other

4917, 22 Jun 1853, Josephine, Stake, 19, Williamsport,
4918, 27 Aug 1853, Hugh, McKale, 42, Williamsport,
4919, 4 Dec 1853, John, Stonebraker, 76, Clear Spring,
4920, 26 Mar 1854, Mary, Donelly, -, Williamsport, wife of Edward Donelly
4921, 8 Apr 1854, Margaret, Snider, -, Hagerstown, C; B
4922, 9 Apr 1854, Thomas, Donelly, -, Williamsport, *See Endnote 6
4923, 20 Apr 1854, Margaret, Taggart, 19, Hagerstown,
4924, 10 Jun 1854, Barbara, Welsh, 7, Fairplay,
4925, 12 Aug 1854, Patrick, Cronin, 44 *, Clear Spring, * "about 44"
4926, -, Christopher, Drennen, 16, Lock No. 4,
4927, 7 Sep 1854, Michael, King, 22, Lock No. 4,
4928, 19 Sep 1854, Owen, King, 28, Lock No. 4, See Endnote 12
4929, -, Henry, Welsh, 35, Fairplay,
4930, 25 Nov 1854, John, Sculley, 24, Williamsport,
4931, Jan 1855, John, Goddard, 11, Dam No. 4,
4932, 24 Jan 1855, Anna, Clark, 3, Shepherdstown,
4933, 20 Feb 1855, Elizabeth Ann*, Bigold, 71, Clear Spring, * Mrs. Elizabeth Ann
4934, 22 Feb 1855, Caspar, Swope, 77, Hagerstown,
4935, 10 Mar 1855, Michael, Gallagher, -, Dam No. 5,
4936, 12 Mar 1855, Rebecca, Thompson, 50, Williamsport,
4937, 19 Apr 1855, Louisa (Miss), Fitzhugh, 25, "Montreal Ca." ,
4938, 26 Apr 1855, Thomas, Harbine, 5, Clear Spring,
4939, 12 May 1855, Andrew, Rigler, 49, Hagerstown,
4940, 15 May 1855, Mary Catharine, Smith, 8 mos., Clear Spring,
4941, 18 May 1855, Richard, Barry, 34, Williamsport *, * "and also Hagerstown"
4942, 31 May 1855, Maria, Messman, 65, Hagerstown,
4943, 3[?] Jun 1855, Peter, Delcor, 52, Hagerstown,
4944, 24 Jul 1855, Margaret, Lynch, 62, Hagerstown,
4945, 26 Aug 1855, Patrick, O'Brien, 50, Browns' Furnace,
4946, 11 Sep 1855, John A., Tierney, 33 *, Hagerstown, * "about 33"
4947, 29 Sep 1855, Old Aunt Dolley, -, 96, Hagerstown,
4948, 8 Oct 1855, John, Truman, 50, Hagerstown,
4949, 16 Nov 1855, Catharine, Craig, 75, Hagerstown, B
4950, 1 Feb 1856, Mrs., McIntire, 56 *, Hagerstown, * "about 56"
4951, 20 Feb 1856, Sarah, Jones, 14, Hagerstown, B

ST. MARY'S CATHOLIC CHURCH
HAGERSTOWN, MARYLAND, DEATHS:
Index, Date, First, Last, Age, Place, Other

4952, 24 Feb 1856, Uncle Arnold, -, 72, Hagerstown, B
4953, 7 Apr 1856, Phebe, Brown, 68, Hagerstown, B
4954, 28 May 1856, Elizabeth, Lewis, 3, Williamsport,
4955, 12 Jan 1857, Frances, Cole, 36, Hagerstown,
4956, 6 Jan 1857, Mr., Peake, 74, Hagerstown,
4957, Apr 1857, Mary F., Truman, 20, Hagerstown,
4958, 25 Jul 1857, David, Barry, 32, Williamsport,
4959, 2 Sep 1857, Ulerick, Suddenly, 49, Hagerstown,
4960, 28 Sep 1857, Peter, Ryan, 70, 4 Locks,
4961, 17 Oct 1857, Thomas, Drennen, 50, 4 Locks,
4962, 18 Oct 1857, Michael Adam, Foxberger, 11 days, Hagerstown,
4963, 27 Jul 1858, Ann, Clark, 6 wks., Sharpsburg,
4964, 16 Aug 1858, Mary, Brien, 9 mos., -, *See Endnote 7
4965, 28 Aug 1858, Aunt Sally, Lee, 60 *, Hagerstown, * "about 60"
4966, 12 Sep 1858, Sarah Jane, Carney, 6 *, Hagerstown, * "about 6 years"
4967, 13 Oct 1858, James, McGonigle, 70, Hagerstown,
4968, 14 Nov 1858, Wm. Thos. Alex., McCameron, 10 mos., Hagerstown,
4969, 23 Dec 1858, Patsy, McClain, 50, Clear Spring,
4970, 24 Jan 1859, Michael, Boyd, 90, Hagerstown,
4971, 10 Mar 1859, Joachim, Schilling, 50, Cavetown,
4972, 7 Jun 1859, Henry, Crametz, 51, Hagerstown,
4973, 17 Jun 1859, Frances, Mettony, 87, Hagerstown,
4974, 4 Jul 1859, Judy [?], Gallaway, 80, Hagerstown,
4975, 26 Nov 1859, Theresa, Gonker, 70, Cavetown,
4976, 2 Dec 1859, Louis Edmd., Cramer, 1, Hagerstown,
4977, 15 Dec 1859, Mary, Laedver [Larver?], 65, Williamsport,
4978, 18 Dec 1859, Helen, Wright, 5, Hagerstown,
4979, Dec 1859, -, Long, 5, Hagerstown,
4980, 28 Feb 1860, John, Stewart, 50, Hagerstown,
4981, 16 Mar 1860, Charles, McCardell, 5, Hagerstown,
4982, 23 Mar 1860, Uncle, Brown, 70, Hagerstown,
4983, Jul 1860, Adalaide, Brien, 1, Hagerstown,
4984, 13 Aug 1860, Mrs., Meads, 50, Williamsport,
4985, 15 Dec 1860, Mrs., Doyle, 67, Hagerstown,
4986, 8 Apr 1861, Catharine (Mrs.), Stake, 60, Hagerstown,
4987, 25 Mar 1861, Ann (Mrs.), McCardell, 84, Hagerstown,
4988, 19 Apr 1861, Edward, Coyle, 50, Cavetown,

ST. MARY'S CATHOLIC CHURCH
HAGERSTOWN, MARYLAND, DEATHS:
Index, Date, First, Last, Age, Place, Other

4989, 16 May 1861, Jacob, Bath [?], 54, Hagerstown,

4990, 1 Jun 1861, Wilfrid, McCardell, 50, Williamsport,

4991, 9 Dec 1861, William, O'Neill, 74, Williamsport,

4992, 26 Jan 1862, Esther, Mahony, 60, Hagerstown,

4993, 4 Feb 1862, Samuel, Coyle, 22, Cavetown,

4994, 8 Apr 1862, Eliza, Bell, 18, Hagerstown, B

4995, 27 May 1862, Twin Children, Duffy, 3, Hagerstown, *See Endnote 5

4996, 26 Jun 1862, Samuel Wm., Lizzer, 1, Adams Co., PA,

4997, 26 Sep 1862, Angline, Paulus, 75, Hagerstown,

4998, no date, Mary, Goddard, 15, Dam No. 5,

4999, no date, [blank], Schilling, 9, Cavetown,

5000, 10 Oct 1862, Joseph, Buley, 20, Cavetown, B

5001, 16 Oct 1862, Catherine, Smith, 3, Boonsboro,

5002, [blank], Margaret, Goddard, 15, Dam No. 5, entire entry crossed out

5003, 22 Oct 1862, Jacob, Gouker, 15, Cavetown,

5004, 11 Dec 1862, Old Uncle, Lee, 100, Hagerstown, B

5005, 14 Dec 1862, Sydney, Murray, 21, Hagerstown,

5006, 14 Dec 1862, John, Meads, 27, Hagerstown,

5007, 18 Dec 1862, Mrs., Mooney, 75, Hagerstown,

5008, 29 Dec 1862, Old Uncle, Mouse, 79, Hagerstown, B

5009, Jan 1863, Geo. B., Fox, 85, Hagerstown,

5010, 16 Mar 1863, Ed., Meads, 30, Hagerstown,

5011, 18 Mar 1863, Augustine, Coyle, 34, Cavetown,

5012, 30 May 1863, John, McGonigle, 28, Hagerstown,

5013, 7 Jul 1863, Henry, Freaner, 66, Hagerstown,

5014, Jul 1863, Phillip, Warner, 24, Gettysburg, PA,

5015, 9 Aug 1863, Mary Geneva, Wright, 1, -,

5016, 12 Aug 1863, Ros. [?], Warner, 14 mos., -,

5017, [blank], Mrs. [?], Kenney, 34, -,

5018, 4 Sep 1863, Wm., Thompson, 2, -,

5019, 12 Mar 1864, Old Aunt Nelly, -, 100 *, -, * "over one hundred"

5020, Sep 1864, Mrs., Creigh, 60, -,

5021, 8 Dec 1864, Mary (Miss), Hawken, 38, Williamsport,

5022, Mar 1865, George, Moore, 68, -,

5023, 19 May 1865, Charles, Richter, 42, Williamsport,

5024, "1866 & 1867", Mrs. Henry, Shervin, 33, -, *See Endnote 3

5025, "1866 & 1867", Mr., Gouker, 75, -,

5026, "1866 & 1867", Illsworth, Warner, 13, -,

ST. MARY'S CATHOLIC CHURCH
HAGERSTOWN, MARYLAND, DEATHS:
Index, Date, First, Last, Age, Place, Other

5027, "1866 & 1867", [blank], Diggs, 35, -, B
5028, "1866 & 1867", Mrs., Gallagher, 70, -,
5029, May 1867, Uncle, Ballett, 75, -, B
5030, May 1867, [blank], Schilling, 11, -,
5031, Jun 1867, Mrs., Curran, 64, -,
5032, 7 Jul 1867, Mr., Riedy [?], 20, -, *See Endnote 4
5033, 7 Jul 1867, Dr. Frank, Smith, 25, Boonsboro,
5034, 10 Jul 1867, Aunt Nancy, -, 85, Hagerstown,
5035, 11 Jul 1867, Uncle, Diggs, 84, Hagerstown,
5036, 29 Jul 1867, Mrs., Shervin, 66, Bakersville,
5037, 22 Dec 1867, Hugh, McKusker [?], 70, Hagerstown,
5038, 14 Jun 1868, Dr. Otho, Smith, 56, Boonsboro,
5039, 9 Jul 1868, Margaret (Mrs.), Sheedy, 33, Hagerstown,
5040, 9 Oct 1868, Marg. (Mrs.), Boward, 38, Hagerstown,
5041, 16 Oct 1868, Thomas, Shervin, 82, Bakersville,
5042, 8 Nov 1868, Mary (Mrs.), Barber, 37, Hagerstown,
5043, 6 Jun 1868, Martha, Rowland, 61, -,
5044, 16 Jun 1872, A. (Mrs.), Oliver, 59, Williamsport,
5045, 3 Jul 1872, Infant, Wills, -, Hagerstown, "Infant of Mr. Wills"
5046, 4 Jul 1872, Infant, Smith, -, Hagerstown, "Infant of Mr. R. Smith"
5047, 15 Oct 1872, Jennie, Anderson, 65, Hagerstown, B
5048, 18 Oct 1872, John, Johnson, 20, Hagerstown, B
5049, 6 Dec 1872, Gen. H. (Mrs.), Brooks, 64, -,
5050, 4 Nov 1872, Geo., Gillmyer, 71, -,
5051, 30 Jan 1873, Julia, Holm, 30, Memphis,
5052, 30 Jan 1873, M. (Mrs.), Orndorf, 29, Hagerstown,
5053, 20 Feb 1873, David, Hurlehy, 45, Williamsport,
5054, 15 Mar 1873, Judge, Mason, 59, Easton, MD,
5055, 18 Apr 1873, Mr., Sarracco, 50, Hagerstown,
5056, 18 Apr 1873, Infant, Troupe, -, Boonsboro, "Infant of Mrs. Dr. Troupe"
5057, 16 May 1873, Mrs. Dr. J., Smith, 45, Hagerstown,
5058, 13 Jul 1873, Ann (Mrs.), Turner, 49, -,
5059, 22 Jul 1873, Annie (Miss), Kramer, 22, -,
5060, 3 Aug 1873, Barbara, Sellner, 75, -,
5061, 7 Sep 1873, Sallie, Lemen, infant, Williamsport, "Infant of Mr. P. Lemen"

ST. MARY'S CATHOLIC CHURCH
HAGERSTOWN, MARYLAND, DEATHS:
Index, Death, Burial, First, Last, Birthplace, Age, Disease, Cemetery, Notes, Priest

5083, 3 Feb 1885, -, Mr., Hepner, Germany , -, pneumonia, Rose Hill, "Asked to be a Catholic on his death bed before priest came, he died",

5084, 13 Feb 1885, -, Patrick, Kelley, Ireland, 75, old age, Rose Hill, Received last sacraments, 9

5085, 21 Feb 1885, -, Robert, Lewis, Ireland, 97, old age, Old cemetery, Received last sacraments, 9

5086, 2 Mar 1885, -, Rose, Orndorf, Hagerstown, infant, -, Rose Hill, -, 9

5087, 9 Mar 1885, -, Ellen, Mobley, From Baltimore, 11, consumption, Rose Hill, Received last sacraments, 9

5088, 28 Mar 1885, -, Chas. Jos., Helferstay, Hagerstown, infant, -, Rose Hill, -, 9

5089, 2 Apr 1885, -, Infant*, Wright, Hagerstown, infant, -, Rose Hill, *Unnamed infant child of Wilfrid, 9

5090, 5 Apr 1885, -, Geo., Detrich, Germany, 90, old age, St. Mary's, Received last sacraments, 9

5091, 8 Apr 1885, -, Patrick, O'Connor, Ireland, 65, consumption, Rose Hill, Received last sacraments, 9

5092, 18 Apr 1885, -, Henry, Fox, Maryland, 86, -, St. Mary's, Received last sacraments, 9

5093, 10 Jun 1885, -, Daniel, Cramer, Maryland, 66, consumption, Rose Hill, Died Suddently, 9

5094, 11 Jun 1885, -, Nathan, Shorter, Maryland, 50, consumption, St. Mary's, B, 9

5095, 24 Jun 1885, -, Denis, Cretin, Maryland, 55, Nervous prostration, Rose Hill, -, 9

5096, 29 Aug 1885, -, Sarah, Wise, Maryland, 25, internal abscess, Rose Hill, -, 9

5097, 13 Oct 1885, -, [blank], Eagan, Maryland, 3, menenjitis, Rose Hill, -, 9

5098, 15 Nov 1885, 18 Nov 1885, J.[or I.] M., Yohn, Pennsylvania, 46, Bright's disease, Rose Hill, -, 9

5099, 15 Nov 1885, 16 Nov 1885, Dan., McCarthy, Ireland, -, consumption, St. Mary's, Alms House, 9

5100, 27 Feb 1877, -, Jesse, Thompson, Williamsport, -, -, -, -, 11
5101, 24 Mar 1877, -, Cath, Porter, Hagerstown, 70, -, -, -, 11
5102, 10 Apr 1877, -, Christie, Clarkson, Hagerstown, 26, -, -, -, 11
5103, 5 Jul 1877, -, Henry, Gehr, Hagerstown, 36, -, -, -, 11

ST. MARY'S CATHOLIC CHURCH
HAGERSTOWN, MARYLAND, DEATHS:
Index, Death, Burial, First, Last, Birthplace, Age, Disease, Cemetery, Notes, Priest

5104, 20 Jul 1877, -, Francis, Orndorf, Hagerstown, infant, -, -, -, 11
5105, 27 Jul 1877, -, Edw., Wills, Hagerstown, infant, -, -, -, 11
5106, 13 Aug 1877, -, John, Brown [?], Hagerstown, 32, -, -, B, 11
5107, 4 Sep 1877, -, Elizabeth, Gillmyer, Hagerstown *, 77, -, -, * "Leitersburg" crossed out, 11
5108, 5 Oct 1877, -, Rebecca, Little, Leitersburg, 40, -, -, -, 11
5109, 30 Oct 1877, -, Chas., Kershner, Hagerstown, infant, -, -, -, 11
5110, 8 Nov 1877, -, Elizabeth, Deitrick, Hagerstown, 40, -, -, -, 11
5111, 22 Feb 1878, -, Belinda, McCardell, Hagerstown, 46, -, -, -, 11
5112, 24 Feb 1878, -, Francis, Deitrick, Hagerstown, 90, -, -, -, 11
5113, 7 Mar 1878, -, Mary, Gehr, Hagerstown, infant, -, -, -, 11
5114, 9 Mar 1878, -, Hugh, Murphy, Williamsport, 72, -, -, -, 11
5115, 31 Mar 1878, -, Thomas, Grim, Hagerstown, 34, -, -, -, 11
5116, 31 Mar 1878, -, Sarah, Ridout, Hagerstown, -, -, -, B, 11
5117, 31 Mar 1878, -, Franklin, Ford, -, -, -, -, -, 11
5118, 30 Oct 1878, -, Joseph, Dillon, Hagerstown, 18, -, -, -, 11
5119, 30 Oct 1878, -, L.F., Gruber [?], Hagerstown, infant, -, -, -, 11
5120, 14 Nov 1878, -, Elizabeth, Busry [?], Hagerstown, 56, -, -, -, 11
5121, 5 Jan 1879, -, Henry, Happle, -, 8, -, -, -, 11
5122, 15 Feb 1879, -, Mary, Baker, -, 15, -, -, -, 11
5123, 13 Mar 1879, -, Margaret, McKusker, -, 75, -, -, -, 11
5124, 20 Mar 1879, -, Ellen, Stake, Died at Williamsport, 82, -, -, -, 11
5125, 15 Apr 1879, -, Henry, Hennesy, Died at Williamsport, infant, -, -, -, 11
5126, 12 Mar 1879, -, Domenic, Gillan, Hagerstown, 50, -, -, -, 11
5127, 31 May 1879, -, Claget, Lorsbaugh, Hagerstown, 21, -, -, -, 11
5128, 15 Jun 1879, -, John, Fox, -, infant, -, -, -, 11
5129, 4 Jul 1879, -, Mrs., Black, Smithsburg, 83, -, -, -, 11
5130, 2 Aug 1879, -, Peggy, Meisner, Cavetown, 80, -, -, -, 11
5131, 1 Sep 1879, -, Richard, Busey, Hagerstown, 75, -, -, -, 11
5132, 2 Aug 1879, -, [blank], Williams, -, infant, -, -, -, 11
5133, 26 Dec 1879, -, Gregory, Laurence, Hagerstown, 3, -, -, -, 11

ST. MARY'S CATHOLIC CHURCH
HAGERSTOWN, MARYLAND, DEATHS:
Index, Death, Burial, First, Last, Birthplace, Age, Disease, Cemetery, Notes, Priest

5134, 26 Jan 1880, -, Frances J., Banks, Hagerstown, 3, typhoid, Mt. St. Jerome, -, 4

5135, 27 Jan 1880, -, Alfreda G., Clayborne, Hagerstown, 3, pneumonia, Rose Hill, -, 4

5136, 27 Jan 1880, -, Harry, Wright, Hagerstown, -, -, Rose Hill, -, 4

5137, 27 Jan 1880, -, Jno. M., Laurence, Hagerstown, -, -, Mt. St. Jerome, -, 4

5138, 23 Mar 1880, -, Ben F., Banks, Hagerstown, 9, consumption, Mt. St. Jerome, B, 4

5139, 29 Mar 1880, -, Marg. [or Mary], Banks, Hagerstown, infant, -, Mt. St. Jerome, B, 4

5140, 21 Apr 1880, -, Nancy, Carr, Hagerstown, -, old age, Near McClains, -, 4

5141, 12 Jul 1880, -, Mary, Hanson, -, 70, paralysis, Mt. St. Jerome, -, 4

5142, 10 Sep 1880, -, Geo., Fox, Hagerstown, 70, cancer, Mt. St. Jerome, -, 4

5143, 10 Sep 1880, -, Alice, Clarkson, Hagerstown, 18, consumption, Rose Hill, -, 4

5144, 20 Sep 1880, -, Benedict, Mead, Williamsport, 70, many diseases [?], Williamsport Church, -, 4

5145, 5 Oct 1880, -, Addie, Warner, Hagerstown, 3, croup, Mt. St. Jerome , -, 4

5146, 5 Oct 1880, -, Homey, Weast, Boonsboro, -, -, -, -, 4

5147, 5 Oct 1880, -, Annie, Dellon, Hagerstown, 3, -, -, -, 4

5148, 5 Oct 1880, -, [blank], Fox, Hagerstown, infant, -, Mt. St. Jerome, -, 4

5149, 5 Oct 1880, -, Thos., O'Neill, Williamsport, 9, -, -, Died suddenly, 4

5150, 3 Jan 1881, -, Robert, Haskin, Williamsport, 40, -, Williamsport Church, -, 4

5151, 6 Jan 1881, -, Mary, McCartney, Hagerstown, 70, -, Mt. St. Jerome, insane pauper, 4

5152, 15 Feb 1881, -, Lillie F., Williams, Williamsport, 24, -, -, -, 4

5153, [no date], -, Mrs., Poffenberger, Williamsport, 70, -, -, -, 4

5154, 25 Mar 1881, -, W.A. (Dr.), Reddlemoser [?], Smithsburg, 60, consumption, Smithsburg, -, 4

5155, 30 Mar 1881, -, Mary, Hughes, Hagerstown, 70, -, -, -, 4

5156, 4 Apr 1881, -, Jos. (Mrs.), Cullan, Williamsport, -, -, -, -, 4

ST. MARY'S CATHOLIC CHURCH
HAGERSTOWN, MARYLAND, DEATHS:
Index, Death, Burial, First, Last, Birthplace, Age, Disease, Cemetery, Notes, Priest

5157, 15 May 1881, -, Jennie, McLaughlin, Hagerstown, 90, -, -, -, 4

5158, 27 May 1881, -, Mr., McCartney, -, 70, -, Mt. St. Jerome , Alms House, 4

5159, 5 Aug 1881, -, [blank], Zook, -, 45, -, -, -, 4

5160, 7 Aug 1881, -, Aloysius, Futterer, Hagerstown, 75, -, -, -, 4

5161, 7 Aug 1881, -, Mary, Galloway, Hagerstown, 45, -, -, -,

5162, Sep 1881, -, Patr, Keenan, Hagerstown, 60, -, -, -,

5163, [blank], -, Mary, Full, -, 60, -, -, -,

5164, 26 Dec 1881, -, Eliz., Walters, -, 18, -, -, -,

5165, 5 Jan 1882, -, Mary, McLaughlin, Hagerstown, 80, -, -, -,

5166, 5 Jan 1882, -, Jos., Banks, Hagerstown, 40, -, -, -,

5167, 5 Jan 1882, -, Frid, Helsely, -, 80, -, -, -,

5168, 12 Feb 1882, -, John, Miles, -, infant, -, -, -,

5169, 7 Mar 1882, -, Henry, Fagan, -, 7 [or 70], -, -, -,

5170, 12 Mar 1882, -, Willie, Allen, -, 9, -, -, -,

5171, 19 Mar 1882, -, Catherin, Shorter, Hagerstown, 90, -, -, -, 4

5172, 22 Mar 1882, -, Thos., Gibson, Hagerstown, 75, -, -, -, 4

5173, 4 Apr 1882, -, Grace, Campbell, Hagerstown, 80, -, -, -, 4

5174, 18 Apr 1882, -, Elizabeth R., Wright, Hagerstown, 2, -, -, -, 4

5175, 18 Apr 1882, -, John, Davis, Hagerstown, 6, -, -, -, 4

5176, 8 May 1882, -, Thos. J., McKaig, -, 79, -, -, -, 4

5177, 14 May 1882, -, Charles, Gross, -, 65, -, -, -, 4

5178, 17 May 1882, -, Michal, Kennedy, -, 75, -, -, -, 4

5179, 4 Jun 1882, -, T., Krugh, -, 40, -, -, -, 4

5180, 3 Jul 1882, -, Columb., Allan, -, 3, -, -, B, 4

5181, 3 Jul 1882, -, Chas., Miles, -, 1, -, -, -, 4

5182, 3 Jul 1882, -, Wm., Myers, -, infant, -, -, -, 4

5183, 15 Aug 1882, -, Owen, Flynn, Alms House, 75, -, -, -, 4

5184, 15 Aug 1882, -, Theo., Barr, -, -, -, -, -, 4

5185, 20 Aug 1882, -, Mary, Ward, -, -, -, -, -, 4

5186, 17 Oct 1882, -, Virginia, Laurence, -, 6, -, -, -, 4

5187, 14 Dec 1882, -, Ann W., Crouse, -, 58, -, -, -, 4

5188, 3 Dec 1882, -, E., Howard, -, 45, -, -, -, 4

5189, 18 Jan 1883, -, Julia A., Gauger, -, 82, -, -, -, 4

5190, 21 Jan 1883, -, John E., Geary, -, 16, -, -, -, 4

5191, 11 Jan 1886, 14 Jan 1886, Susan, Blakely, Maryland, 70, -, Old Cemetery, Died suddenly, 9

5192, 28 Jan 1886, 31 Jan 1886, Mary, Maudy, Maryland, 36, pneumonia, Old Cemetery, -, 9

ST. MARY'S CATHOLIC CHURCH
HAGERSTOWN, MARYLAND, DEATHS:
Index, Death, Burial, First, Last, Birthplace, Age, Disease, Cemetery, Notes, Priest

5193, 20 Mar 1886, 22 Mar 1886, Lucind, Hoover, Maryland, 66, dropsy of heart, Rose Hill, Died suddenly, 9

5194, 22 Mar 1886, 24 Mar 1886, Peter, Kammerer, -, 22, accident on R. Road, Old graveyard, Died in Lancaster, Pa.,

5195, 11 May 1886, 13 May 1886, Frederick, Figley, Hagerstown, 2, pneumonia, Old graveyard, -, 9

5196, 14 May 1886, 17 May 1886, Wm. F., Orndorff, Maryland, 46, consumption, Rose Hill, a prominent member of the church, 9

5197, 17 Jun 1886, 19 Jun 1886, Louisa, Ogle, Hagerstown, -, comsumption, Rose Hill, -, 9

5198, 16 Jul 1886, 19 Jul 1886, Susan (Mrs.), Schockey, Schockey Station, 67, -, Waynesboro, died suddenly,

5199, 23 Jul 1886, 19 Jul 1886, Henry, Full, Hagerstown, infant, -, Rose Hill, baptized privately, 9

5200, 12 Sep 1886, 13 Sep 1886, Agnes, Orndorf, Hagerstown, infant, -, Rose Hill, -, 9

5201, 17 Oct 1886, 19 Oct 1886, Henry, Schilling, Washington County, 67, consumption, Funkstown, convert, 9

5202, 1 Dec 1886, 3 Dec 1886, Emma, Smith, Hagerstown, 2, -, Rose Hill , -, 9

5203, 31 Dec 1886, 2 Jan 1887, Ann (Mrs.), Cookerly, Pennsylvania, -, liver disease, Rose Hill, -, 9

5204, 29 Jan 1887, 31 Jan 1887, Charles (Dr.), Wright, -, -, paralysis, Rose Hill, -, 3

5205, 8 Feb 1887, 9 Feb 1887, Alfred, Ball, -, -, paralysis, Rose Hill, convert, 3

5206, 17 Apr 1887, 19 Apr 1887, Bridget, Rodgers, Ireland, -, pneumonia, Rose Hill, -, 3

5207, 20 Apr 1887, 22 Apr 1887, Jennie (Mrs.), Smith, -, -, -, Rose Hill, Died suddenly, 3

5208, 1 May 1887, 3 May 1887, Jennie, Kelley, Hagerstown, 25, consumption, Rose Hill, -, 3

5209, 16 May 1887, 18 May 1887, Joseph, Hoover, Pennsylvania, 80, liver disease, Rose Hill, -, 9

5210, 10 Jul 1887, 12 Jul 1887, Catherine, Clarkson, Ireland, 64, disentery, Rose Hill, -, 9

5211, 10 Jul 1887, -, Robt., Brisco, Maryland, infant, -, Old graveyard, baptised,

5212, 28 Jul 1887, 31 Jul 1887, John, Curran, -, -, -, Rose Hill, Did not get Christian burial,

ST. MARY'S CATHOLIC CHURCH
HAGERSTOWN, MARYLAND, DEATHS:
Index, Death, Burial, First, Last, Birthplace, Age, Disease, Cemetery, Notes, Priest

5213, 24 Aug 1887, -, Charles, Stine, -, infant, -, Rose Hill , -, 9

5214, 19 Sep 1887, -, James, McDonald, Maryland, 56, dysentery, Rose Hill, -, 9

5215, 14 Jan 1888, 15 Jan 1888, Thom F., McCardle, Hagerstown, 10 months, croup, Rose Hill, -, 3

5216, 14 Feb 1888, -, Mrs., Fesler [or Flesler], -, *, pneumonia, Emmitsburg, * "about 65", 3

5217, 2 Mar 1888, 4 Mar 1888, Francis, Boyle, Hagerstown, 8 months, spasms, Rose Hill, -, 3

5218, 19 Mar 1888, 21 Mar 1888, Jeremiah, Nelligan, Ireland, 82, old age, Rose Hill, -, 3

5219, 29 Apr 1888, 30 Apr 1888, Andrew J. [or I.], Jones, Hagerstown, 17 mos., pneumonia, Rose Hill, -, 3

5220, 4 Sep 1888, 6 Sep 1888, Anne, Montague, -, 13, dropsy, Rose Hill , -, 3

5221, 21 Oct 1888, 22 Oct 1888, William, Mayhew, Hagerstown, 8, malaria, Rose Hill, -, 3

5222, 2 Dec 1888, 5 Dec 1888, Jacob, Wright, -, 76, paralysis, Rose Hill, -, 3

5223, 3 Dec 1888, 5 Dec 1888, Jeremia, Sullivan, Co. Cork, Ireland, *, consumption, St. Mary's, * "about 40"; Poor House, 3

5224, 16 Dec 1888, 19 Dec 1888, Michael, Dillon, Ireland, 69*, -, Rose Hill, * "about 69 [or 60]", 3

5225, 10 Jan 1889, 12 Jan 1889, Margaret (Mrs.), Mayberry, -, -, penumonia, Rose Hill, -, 3

5226, 5 Feb 1889, 7 Feb 1889, Laura (Mrs.), Fierney, -, 66, Inward[?] Cancer, Rose Hill, -, 3

5227, 30 Mar 1889, 31 Mar 1889, Fannie Elisab. (Mrs.), Warton, Maryland, 30, Childbirth, Rose Hill, -, 3

5228, 18 May 1889, 19 May 1889, Joseph, McCallion, Maryland, 55, -, Rose Hill, -, 3

5229, 24 Jun 1889, 26 Jun 1889, Thomas, Flynn, Maryland, -, consumption, Rose Hill, -, 3

5230, 9 Jul 1889, 11 Jul 1889, John, Flynn, Ireland, 70, general debility, Rose Hill, -, 3

5231, 21 Jul 1889, 22 Jul 1889, Bridget (Mrs.), Folks, Emmittsburg, 20, -, Rose Hill, -, 3

5232, 28 Jul 1889, 30 Jul 1889, Terrence, Alexander, Hagerstown, 1.5, cholera infant, Rose Hill, -, 3

ST. MARY'S CATHOLIC CHURCH
HAGERSTOWN, MARYLAND, DEATHS:
Index, Death, Burial, First, Last, Birthplace, Age, Disease, Cemetery, Notes, Priest

5233, 9 Dec 1889, 11 Dec 1889, Mary (Mrs.), Welsh, Hagerstown, 71, old age, St. Mary's, -, 3

5234, 19 Dec 1889, -, Hannah (Miss), Portel, Hagerstown, 56, -, Rose Hill, -, 3

5235, 28 Dec 1889, 31 Dec 1889, Margaret (Mrs.), Eagan, Hagerstown, 35, consumption, Rose Hill, -, 3

5236, 4 Jan 1890, 6 Jan 1890, William, Montague, Mount Savage, MD, 24, consumption, Rose Hill, -,

5237, 26 Jan 1890, -, Lewis, Gillmeyer, Hagerstown, -, -, Rose Hill, Did not get Christian burial; in Priest section was written "none",

5238, 28 Jan 1890, 30 Jan 1890, Louis, Cookerly, -, 69, heart disease, Rose Hill, -, 3

5239, 20 Mar 1890, 21 Mar 1890, Charles, Sheehan, Hagerstown, 17, Killed on railroad, Rose Hill, -, 3

5240, 26 Mar 1890, 28 Mar 1890, Mrs., Helsley, Germany, -, old age, St. Mary's, Died in Washington at Little Sist. Of Poor, 3

5241, Aug 1890, -, H.P., Lawrence, Hagerstown, 4 months, -, St. Mary's, -, 3

5242, 1 Aug 1890, 2 Aug 1890, George M., Feigley, Hagerstown, 8 days, -, St. Mary's, -, 3

5243, 10 Sep 1890, 12 Sep 1890, Louis Bernard, Lushbaugh, Hagerstown, 6, -, Rose Hill, -, 3

5244, 11 Sep 1890, 13 Sep 1890, Edw., O'Neill, Williamsport, "24?", typhoid pneumonia, Williamsport*, *Church yard at Williamsport, 3

5245, 14 Sep 1890, 16 Sep 1890, James J. [or I.], Hurley, Ireland, 79, -, Rose Hill, -, 3

5246, 17 Sep 1890, 19 Sep 1890, Mary M. (Mrs.), Lawrence, Adams Co., PA, 73, -, Rose Hill, -, 3

5247, 28 Sep 1890, 1 Oct 1890, James, McLaughlin, -, 60, congestion of the lungs, Rose Hill, -, 3

5248, 16 Oct 1890, 17 Oct 1890, John C., Hennessey, Washington County, 20 days, -, St. Mary's, -, 3

5249, 23 Oct 1890, -, Philip, McLaughlin, -, -, pneumonia, St. Mary's, Died at Poorhouse, 3

5250, 3 Nov 1890, 4 Nov 1890, John, McNamara, Co. Limmerick, Ireland, "over" 60, -, St. Mary's, -, 3

5251, 21 Nov 1890, 24 Nov 1890, Martha (Mrs.), Dillon, -, 55, consumption, Rose Hill, -, 3

ST. MARY'S CATHOLIC CHURCH
HAGERSTOWN, MARYLAND, DEATHS:
Index, Death, Burial, First, Last, Birthplace, Age, Disease, Cemetery, Notes, Priest

5252, 21 Dec 1890, 23 Dec 1890, Mary, Taggart, -, -, -, Rose Hill, -, 3

5253, 27 Dec 1890, 29 Dec 1890, Arthur, Kenney, Ireland, 73, pneumonia, Rose Hill , -, 3

5254, 6 Jan 1891, 9 Jan 1891, John H., Unseld, Harpers Ferry, WV, 50, consumption, Harpers Ferry, WV, -, 3

5255, 8 Mar 1891, 10 Mar 1891, John, Moore, -, 48, pneumonia, Rose Hill, -, 3

5256, 10 Jun 1891, 12 Jun 1891, Mary A., Richards, New York, 18, consumption, Rose Hill, -, 3

5257, 20 Sep 1891, 22 Sep 1891, Michael, Flynn, -, 72, -, Rose Hill, -, 3

5258, 11 Oct 1891, 12 Oct 1891, Nettie, Clingan, Virginia, 4, diptheria, Rose Hill, -, 3

5259, 26 Nov 1891, 27 Nov 1891, Raymond Napoleon*, Feigley, Hagerstown, **, -, St. Mary's, *"Willm. K." crossed out; ** 5 yrs., 5 mos., 3

5260, 6 Dec 1891, 8 Dec 1891, [blank], Unseld, -, 23, killed on railroad, Rose Hill, -, 3

5261, 10 Dec 1891, 13 Dec 1891, Anne, Fagan, Hagerstown, 14, heart disease, Rose Hill, -, 3

5262, 5 Jan 1892, -, Thomas H., Cramer, Hagerstown, 15 mos., -, St. Mary's, -, 3

5263, 8 Jan 1892, 11 Jan 1892, Michael C., Dillon, Hagerstown, 28, grippe, Rose Hill, -, 3

5264, 8 Jan 1892, 11 Jan 1892, Reinhold (Dr.), Halm, Austria, 71, pneumonia, Rose Hill, -, 3

5265, 30 Feb 1892, -, Bridget, Battle, -, -, -, St. Mary's, -, 3

5266, 26 Feb 1892, 29 Feb 1892, Michael, Lawrence, Adams Co., PA, 80, cancer and old age, St. Mary's, -, 3

5267, 28 Feb 1892, 1 Mar 1892, Franey [?], Whipp, Washington County, 71, -, St. Mary's, -, 3

5268, 2 Apr 1892, 2 Apr 1892, Patrik, Riley, Ireland, -, -, St. Mary's, Died at Alms House, 3

5269, 14 Apr 1892, 15 Apr 1892, Cornelius, Hurley, Ireland, 78, -, St. Mary's , Died at Alms House, 3

5270, 29 Jul 1892, 1 Aug 1892, Ely, Stake, Williamsport, 95, old age, Rose Hill, -, 3

5271, 27 Dec 1892, 29 Dec 1892, Mary E. [?], Cunningham, -, 20, consumption, Rose Hill , -, 3

ST. MARY'S CATHOLIC CHURCH
HAGERSTOWN, MARYLAND, DEATHS:
Index, Death, Burial, First, Last, Birthplace, Age, Disease, Cemetery, Notes, Priest

5272, 22 Jan 1893, 24 Jan 1893, Anne Dorothea, Rauth, Hagerstown, 15 mos., -, Rose Hill , -, 3

5273, 22 Jan 1893, 25 Jan 1893, Henry H., Keedy, Washington County, 51, -, Rose Hill, -,

5274, 7 Feb 1893, 9 Feb 1893, William, Eyler, Frederick Co., 36, pneumonia, St. Mary's, -, 1

5275, 10 Feb 1893, 11 Feb 1893, Jeannette, Sweeney, Hagerstown, 16 mos., dyptheria, Rose Hill, -, 3

5276, 5 Mar 1893, 7 Mar 1893, Jacob J., Cramer, -, 55, -, Rose Hill, -, 3

5277, 8 Mar 1893, 11 Mar 1893, James, Sherwin, -, 72, -, Rose Hill, -, 3

5278, 21 May 1893, 23 May 1893, Adam, Foxemburger, Germany, *, paralysis, Rose Hill, * "about 70", 3

5279, 30 Jul 1893, 31 Jul 1893, Mary R., Hose, Hagerstown, 10, dropsy, Rose Hill, -, 3

5280, 5 Aug 1893, 6 Aug 1893, Jacob Franc., Rauth, Hagerstown, 7 mos., -, Rose Hill, -, 3

5281, 13 Oct 1893, 16 Oct 1893, John, Barry, Ireland, 71, -, Rose Hill, -, 3

5282, 10 Nov 1893, 13 Nov 1893, Andrew, Reickert, -, -, consumption, Rose Hill, -, 3

5283, 14 Mar 1894, 17 Mar 1894, Kate, Sherwin, -, 69, -, Rose Hill, -, 3

5284, 17 Mar 1894, 19 Mar 1894, Mary (Mrs.), Clabaugh, -, 77, -, Rose Hill, -, 3

5285, 4 Apr 1894, 6 Apr 1894, Augustus, Clayburne, -, 15, -, Rose Hill, -, 3

5286, 4-Apr, 5 Apr 1894, Eva Maria, McCardell, -, 4 mos., -, Rose Hill, -, 3

5287, 12 Jul 1894, 14 Jun 1894, Saml., Diffendall, -, 64, -, Rose Hill, -, 3

5288, 14 Jun 1894, 15 Jun 1894, Saml., Harrison, -, -, -, St. Mary's , B; Died at Poor House, 3

5289, 11 Jul 1894, 13 Jul 1894, Peter, Hennessy, -, -, -, Rose Hill , -, 6

5290, 14 Jul 1894, 15 Jul 1894, John H. [?], Cother [or Cather], -, 2 mos., -, Rose Hill , -, 3

ST. MARY'S CATHOLIC CHURCH
HAGERSTOWN, MARYLAND, DEATHS:
Index, Death, Burial, First, Last, Birthplace, Age, Disease, Cemetery, Notes, Priest

5291, 21 ___ 1894*, 23 ___ 1894**, Gertrude, Cunningham, -, 15, consumption, Rose Hill , *21 ["Aug" has been crossed out] 1894; **23 ["Aug" has been crossed out] 1894, 3

5292, 13 Aug 1894, 16 Aug 1894, Jane R. (Mrs.), Boward, -, 76, -, Rose Hill , -, 3

5293, 2 Oct 1894, 5 Oct 1894, Thomas, Taggart, Ireland, 78, -, Rose Hill , -, 3

5294, 14 Jan 1895, 16 Jan 1895, Charles, Kammarer, -, 25, -, Rose Hill , -, 3

5295, 17 Jan 1895, 20 Jan 1895, Johnson (Dr.), Jones , -, 29, heart disease, Rose Hill , -, 3

5296, 16 Jan 1895, 18 Jan 1895, Josephine, Moore, Hagerstown, 19 mos., spinal meningitis, Rose Hill , -, 3

5297, 9 Feb 1895, 12 Feb 1895, Cornelius, Shehan, Ireland, -, -, Rose Hill , died suddenly without the sacraments, 3

5298, 23 Mar 1895, 25 Mar 1895, Nancy, Brewer, -, 72, hemorhage, Rose Hill , died suddenly without the sacraments, 3

5299, 2 Apr 1895, 5 Apr 1895, Clara, Wills, -, 21, typhoid fever, Rose Hill , -, 3

5300, 26 Apr 1895, 28 Apr 1895, Eugene, Geary, Ireland, 80, -, Rose Hill , -, 3

5301, 3 May 1895, 5 May 1895, George H.*, Warner, Hagerstown, 13, -, Rose Hill , * "Robert" crossed out, 3

5302, 20 Jun 1895, 22 Jun 1895, Anne, Hebb" (Heil)", Hagerstown, 29, -, Rose Hill , -, 3

5303, 27 Jul 1895, -, Michael, Battle, -, 11, -, Rose Hill , -, 3

5304, 5 Aug 1895, 7 Aug 1895, Mrs., Sheehan, -, -, -, Rose Hill , -, 3

5305, 15 Sep 1895, 18 Sep 1895, Sophia, Shadrich, Washington County, 69, -, Rose Hill , -, 3

5306, 8 Oct 1895, 10 Oct 1895, Catherine (Mrs.), Flynn, -, -, -, Rose Hill , -, 3

5307, 7 Nov 1895, 9 Nov 1895, Mr., Moran, Ireland, 80, -, Emmitsburg, -,

5308, 16 Nov 1895, 18 Nov 1895, John P., Shafer, -, 56, -, Rose Hill, -, 3

5309, 19 Dec 1895, 23 Dec 1895, Catherine (Mrs.), McLaughlin, -, 65, -, Rose Hill, -, 3

5310, 10 Jan 1896, 13 Jan 1896, Willhelmina, May, -, -, pneumonia, Reformed Church, -, 3

ST. MARY'S CATHOLIC CHURCH
HAGERSTOWN, MARYLAND, DEATHS:
Index, Death, Burial, First, Last, Birthplace, Age, Disease, Cemetery, Notes, Priest

5311, 21 Jan 1896, 24 Jan 1896, Benjamin, Dietrich, -, -, consumption, Rose Hill, -, 3

5312, 2 Feb 1896, 4 Feb 1896, Sarah (Mrs.), Kelly, -, 75, gripp, Rose Hill, -, 3

5313, 12 Feb 1896, 13 Feb 1896, Mary (Mrs.), Duglass, -, -, -, St. Mary's, -, 3

5314, 11 Feb 1896, 14 Feb 1896, Isaak, Moore, -, 65, pneumonia, Mooresville, -, 3

5315, 16 Mar 1896, 18 Mar 1896, Mary (Mrs.), Murray, -, 83, -, Rose Hill, -, 3

5316, 18 Mar 1896, 21 Mar 1896, Robert, Warner, Germany, 67, -, Rose Hill, -, 3

5317, 26 Mar 1896, 27 Mar 1896, Byron H., Poper, -, 21 mos., -, St. Mary's, -, 3

5318, Apr 1896, 3 Apr 1896, Francis A., Rauth, -, 40 days, -, Rose Hill, -, 3

5319, 16 May 1896, 18 May 1896, John, Hildebrand, Berlins, PA, 83, -, Rose Hill, -, 3

5320, 15 Jul 1896, 17 Jul 1896, Catherine E., Woltz, -, 63, -, Rose Hill, Williamsport, 3

5321, 10 Sep 1896, 12 Sep 1896, Mrs., Baker, -, -, consumption, Rose Hill, -, 3

5322, 4 Oct 1896, 7 Oct 1896, Elisabeth, Boyle, Hagerstown, 17, consumption, Rose Hill, -, 3

5323, 28 Oct 1896, 30 Oct 1896, James, Malone, Ireland, 65, explosion*, Rose Hill, *killed by dynamite explosion, 3

5324, 6 Nov 1896, 9 Nov 1896, Margaret, Sheehan, -, -, comsumption, Rose Hill, Died in Washington, 3

5325, 13 Nov 1896, 16 Nov 1896, Caroline, Futterer, Washington County, 46, dropsy, Rose Hill, -, 3

5326, 19 Dec 1896, 22 Dec 1896, Jacob, Griffe, -, 88, -, Rose Hill, -, 3

5327, 23 Dec 1896, 26 Dec 1896, Mrs., Fletcher, -, -, comsumption, Boonsboro, -, 3

5328, 5 Feb 1897, -, Augustus, Shorb, -, 63, heart failure*, Littlestown, PA, heart failure and pneumonia,

5329, 29 Apr 1897, 1 May 1897, Elisabeth (Mrs.), Hoover, -, 40, heart disease, Rose Hill, -, 3

5330, 22 May 1897, 24 May 1897, Thos. Benton, Cushwa, -, 57, apoplexy, Rose Hill, -, 3

ST. MARY'S CATHOLIC CHURCH
HAGERSTOWN, MARYLAND, DEATHS:
Index, Death, Burial, First, Last, Birthplace, Age, Disease, Cemetery, Notes, Priest

5331, 19 Aug 1897, 21 Aug 1897, Charlotte (Mrs.), Chesley, -, *, general debility, Rose Hill, B; * "about 75", 3

5332, 12 Dec 1897, 15 Dec 1897, William, Miller, -, 37, heart failure, Rose Hill, -, 3

5333, 29 Jan 1898, 1 Feb 1898, Elisabeth, Shay, -, *, -, Sharpsburg, * "about 70", 3

5334, 14 Feb 1898, 16 Feb 1898, Mary (Mrs.), Poper , -, 76, consumption, Rose Hill, -, 3

5335, 20 Feb 1898, 22 Feb 1898, Jos. P., Clayburn, -, *, -, Rose Hill, * "6 yrs., 2 mos."; "child of Anne L. Clayburn", 3

5336, 28 May 1898, -, Margaret (Mrs.), Fisher [?], Germany, 52, pneumonia, Rose Hill, -, 3

5337, 31 Jul 1898, 2 Aug 1898, Charles, Orndorfe, Hagerstown, 30, consumption, Rose Hill, -, 3

5338, 6 Sep 1898, 8 Sep 1898, Will., Dorsey, -, 72, -, Rose Hill, -, 3

5339, 30 Sep 1898, 3 Oct 1898, Mabel, Davis, Hagerstown, 22, heart disease, Rose Hill, Died in Baltimore, 3

5340, 2 Oct 1898, 5 Oct 1898, Charles, Full, Hagerstown, 29, -, Rose Hill, -, 3

5341, 16 Nov 1898, 18 Nov 1898, Anne Lavinia, Kershner, Hagerstown, 20, typhoid fever, Rose Hill, -, 3

5342, 18 Nov 1898, 19 Nov 1898, Cecilia B., Burger, Hagerstown, 2, diptheria, Rose Hill, -, 3

5343, 28 Nov 1898, 30 Ov 1898, Mary, Barrett, Ireland, 65, consumption, Rose Hill, -, 3

5344, 4 Dec 1898, 6 Dec 1898, Vera, Swink, Ireland, 4, -, Rose Hill, -, 3

5345, 4 Dec 1898, 6 Dec 1898, Mary, Malone, Ireland, 24, consumption, Rose Hill, -, 3

5346, 6 Dec 1898, 8 Dec 1898, Mary A. (Mrs.), Cramer, -, 83, -, St. Mary's , -, 3

5347, 11 Jan 1899, 12 Jan 1899, Frances, Futterer, Hagerstown, 5, diptheria, Rose Hill, -, 3

5348, 12 Jan 1899, 13 Jan 1899, Grace, Keller, Hagerstown, 6, diptheria, Rose Hill, -, 3

5349, 24 Feb 1899, 27 Feb 1899, Mary (Mrs.), Cushwa, near Clear Spring, 65, -, Rose Hill, -, 3

5350, 31 Mar 1899, 2 Apr 1899, William, Smith, Boonsboro, 42, -, Rose Hill, -, 3

ST. MARY'S CATHOLIC CHURCH HAGERSTOWN, MARYLAND, DEATHS:
Index, Death, Burial, First, Last, Birthplace, Age, Disease, Cemetery, Notes, Priest

5351, 13 Apr 1899, 16 Apr 1899, Mary (Mrs.), Boyle, Boonsboro, 45, -, Rose Hill, -, 3

5352, 9 Jun 1899, 12 Jun 1899, Samuel S. (Mrs.), Downin, Hagerstown, *, -, Rose Hill, * "about 88", 3

5353, 3 Jul 1899, 4 Jul 1899, Cather. Regina, Humelsine, Hagerstown, 3 mos., -, Rose Hill, -, 3

5354, 15Jul 1899, 17 Jul 1899, Anne M., Lawrence, Hagerstown, 19, -, Rose Hill, -, 3

5355, 2 Aug 1899, 4 Aug 1899, Clara, Nierman, Hagerstown, 29, -, Rose Hill, -, 3

5356, 2 Sep 1899, 4 Sep 1899, James, Wagner, Hagerstown, -, typhoid fever, Rose Hill, -, 3

5357, 15 Sep 1899, 16 Sep 1899, Catherine (Mrs.), O'Neill, Ireland, 75, -, Williamsport, -, 3

5358, 28 Sep 1899, -, John, Allen, -, -, -, Rose Hill , -, 3

5359, 14 Nov 1899, 17 Nov 1899, Otho, Smith, Boonsboro, -, -, Boonsboro, -, 3

5360, 15 Nov 1899, 17 Nov 1899, William, Daly, -, 21, -, Rose Hill, -, 3

5361, 28 Nov 1899, -, Mary, Liddy, Hagerstown, 3 yrs.*, diptheria, Rose Hill, *3 years and 1 [or 7] months; in Priest section was written "none",

5362, 27 Dec 1899, 29 Dec 1899, Uncle Frank, Keys, -, *, old age, Rose Hill, B; * "about 80", 3

5363, 30 Dec 1899, 1 Jan 1900, Alfred W. [?], Merrick, -, 67, -, Rose Hill, Died at Pikesville [?], 3

5364, 19 Jan 1900, 21 Jan 1900, William Carroll, Clayburn, -, 38, -, Rose Hill, -, 3

5365, 30 Jan 1900, 1 Feb 1900, Lutie (Mrs.), Boward, -, 36, -, Rose Hill, -, 3

5366, 24 Apr 1900, 26 Apr 1900, Mary (Mrs.), Rigney, -, -, -, Frederick, -, 3

5367, 19 Jun 1900, 21 Jun 1900, James P., Malone, -, 28, consumption, Rose Hill, -, 3

5368, 19 Aug 1900, 21 Aug 1900, Lutie, Mullen, -, 38, -, Rose Hill, -, 3

5369, 8 Sep 1900, 11 Sep 1900, Lawrence, Kammarer, Germany, 66, -, Rose Hill, Died in Philadelphia, 3

5370, 15 Sep 1900, 17 Sep 1900, Henry Fred., Allen, Hagerstown, 18, typhoid fever, St. Mary's, -, 3

ST. MARY'S CATHOLIC CHURCH
HAGERSTOWN, MARYLAND, DEATHS:
Index, Death, Burial, First, Last, Birthplace, Age, Disease, Cemetery, Notes, Priest

5371, 13 Oct 1900, 15 Oct 1900, Anne, O'Connell, -, 16, consumption, Rose Hill, -, 3

5372, 8 Dec 1900, 10 Dec 1900, Charles, Boyle, Hagerstown, 20, accident, Rose Hill, -, 3

5373, 12 Dec 1900, 14 Dec 1900, M. (Mrs.), Banks, Hagerstown, 65, accident, Rose Hill, B, 3

5374, 29 Dec 1900, 31 Dec 1900, Charles, Smith, Washington County, -, consumption, Rose Hill, -, 3

5062, 15 Apr 1883, 22 Apr 1883, Jacob, Clarkson, Washington County, 22, consumption, St. Mary's, -, 10

5063, 4 Jun 1883, 6 Jun 1883, Joseph, McCusker, Hancock, 33, lockjaw, Hancock, convert, 10

5064, 5 Jul 1883, 7 Jul 1883, Margt., Fox, -, 69, consumption, St. Mary's, -, 10

5065, 7 Jul 1883, 8 Jul 1883, Eliza, Williams, -, *, asthma, St. Mary's, B; * "about 65", 10

5066, 19 Jul 1883, 20 Jul 1883, John, Shephan, Germany, 80, old age, Rose Hill, pauper, 10

5067, 21 Aug 1883, 23 Aug 1883, Wm., Hurley, Washington County, 12, consumption, St. Mary's, -, 2

5068, 26 Sep 1883, 28 Sep 1883, Mollie, Geary, Hagerstown, 25, comsumption, Rose Hill, -, 10

5069, 5 Oct 1883, 7 Oct 1883, Josiah (Dr.), Smith, Washington County, 69, heart disease, Rose Hill, -, 10

5070, 30 Oct 1883, 31 Oct 1883, Cecilia (Mrs.), Gehr, Washington County, 58, pneumonia, Rose Hill, -, 10

5071, 4 Nov 1883, 5 Nov 1883, Mary (Mrs.), Cramer, Washington County, 49, heart disease, Rose Hill, -, 10

5072, 29 Nov 1883, 1 Dec 1883, Martha (Mrs.), Mills, Washington County, 39, consumption, Rose Hill, -, 10

5073, 15 May 1884, 17 May 1884, Sophia (Mrs.), Hurley, Washington County, 78, general debility, Rose Hill, -, 10

5074, 18 Jun 1884, 20 Jun 1884, John, Shanahan, Ireland, *, general debility, St. Mary's, * "about 70"; pauper, 10

5075, 10 Jul 1884, 11 Jul 1884, William, Mills, Indiana Co., PA, 38, paralysis, Indiana, PA, -, 10

5076, 12 Jul 1884, 14 Jul 1884, Mary (Mrs.), Futterer, Virginia, 33, consumption, Rose Hill, -, 10

5077, 16 Aug 1884, 18 Aug 1884, Ida, McDonald, Washington County, 18, typhoid, St. Mary's, -, 10

ST. MARY'S CATHOLIC CHURCH
HAGERSTOWN, MARYLAND, DEATHS:
Index, Death, Burial, First, Last, Birthplace, Age, Disease, Cemetery, Notes, Priest

5078, 12 Oct 1884, 14 Oct 1884, Annie (Mrs.), Brown, Washington County, 27, consumption, Rose Hill, -, 10

5079, 7 Nov 1884, 9 Nov 1884, Edw., Clarkson, Ireland, 65, apoplexy, Rose Hill, Died Suddenly,

5080, 1 Dec 1884, 3 Dec 1884, August, Nierman, Prussia, 40, consumption, Rose Hill, -, 10

5081, 11 Dec 1884, 12 Dec 1884, Francis, Coyle, Smithsburg, 15, consumption, St. Mary's, -, 10

5082, 14 Dec 1884, 17 Dec 1884, Sarah, Bush, Washington County, 26, [blank], St. Mary's, B, 46

Endnotes

ENDNOTES

Endnotes 1: it is difficult to ascertain if this date is 7 Dec or 17 Dec; I checked the license at the Washington County Courthouse and it was dated 14 Dec 1863, therefore, this entry date must be for 17 Dec 1863.

Endnote 2: notation reads, "entry of marriage made 24 Feb 1944 by J.F. Leary of certificate of marriage from Clerk of Court, Wash. Co."; Washington Co. certificate signed by the Clerk of the Court states that groom was 30 years old and white, and that bride was from Washington, DC and 25 years old and white (Marriage 15 Sep 1891)

Endnote 3: She died "Leaving 7 little children"

Endnote 4: "lab.[laborer] on W.M.R.R." [Western Maryland Railroad]

Endnote 5: "The twin Children of Wm. Duffy" [There is a baptismal record for Mary Ellen Duffy and Frances McKearnan Duffy, twin daughters of William and Eliza Duffy, born 10 Aug 1859.]

Endnote 6: son of Edward & Mary Donelly

Endnote 7: "baptized privately by family"

Endnote 8: "N.B. frater corumdem fredericus fritz baptisatus est R.do jacobo Miller anno 1841 et natus est 6 Septembri 1839" [This appears to translate as: "Note well: the brother of the same Frederick Fritz was baptized Jacob Miller year 1841 and was born 6 Sep 1839"]

Endnote 9: In the Baptismal entry for 17 Sep 1818, tape was put on the edges of this first page and some information was covered by it. I held the page up to the light to look through it and it doesn't look as if there is any name before the word "Ann." I think the priest indented this line of writing.

Endnote 12: In 1999, a woman called the Washington County Free Library and told the author that the caller's husband had worked at Moller Pipe Organs at one time. Moller sat on the original site of St. Mary's Cemetery. The caller said that her husband had found a gravestone that read,

"Owen King who emigrated from County Galway died in April 1862."

Endnote 13: the mother's name is difficult to read, so I checked the county marriage records and found a marriage between George Lorshbough and Frances McIntire in 1847.

Endnote 14: **could the priest have meant a birthdate of 19 Jul 1819?-that would be consistent with the birthdate

Endnote 15: *Quegh[runs off edge of page where a corner is missing - could be Quigly]

Endnote 16: "I Baptised two Children for Mrs. Auberts daughter. I forget the names of both children."

Endnote 17: the priest's note reads that the parents were married on the same day as the baptism. [There is a Washington County marriage license for John Skelley and Elizabeth Hose on 30 Dec 1846.]

Endnote 18: "During the illness of the Pastor of the congregation, I baptised...John P. Donelson of St. Matthews Church, City of Washington D.C."

Endnote 19: "wife of Dr. Richards in Chambersburg Pa. She was taken into the church during a severe spell of sickness and received all the rites of the church - died two weeks after."

Endnote 20: *birthdate reads 5 May 1847 [or 6 May 1847 - the 5 and 6 have been overwritten but it is unclear as to which one is on top]

Endnote 21: the mother is "a slave of Mr. Michael Smith."; child's last name is Moody or Smith, depending on whether he uses father's or mother's name

Endnote 22: Doesn't note if parents are married or not. Neither parent has a last name and both are "slaves of Mr. Michael Smith"

Endnote 23: It is unclear if the "Fifteen M. Creek" [Fifteen Mile Creek] written on the line between this entry and the following entry refers to both or not but it appears to.

Endnote 24: It is unclear if the "Fifteen M. Creek" [Fifteen Mile Creek] written on the line between this entry and the following entry refers to both or not but it appears to.

Endnote 25: "Chloe" has been written over the original name in a different color of ink; the original name is "Clo__da" [the middle letters are illegible]

Endnote 26: 23 Dec - could be 23 or 24 or 25 -the "3" has been written over as if all 3 numbers were written over each other and it is unclear which is correct

Endnote 27: "The ceremonies of Baptism were supplied on the 1st of Jan. 1854."

Endnote 28: "The Ceremonies of Baptism were supplied to the above child on the 16 of Octr. 1853."; parents are not listed as married.

Endnote 29: "The Ceremonies of Baptism were supplied on the 19th of August 1854"

Endnote 30: "the ceremonies of Baptism were supplied on the 5th of August 1854"; *birthdate reads 9 [18 crossed out] May 1854

Endnote 31: "and they also renewed their consent of marriage ["she" crossed out] he never having been baptized."

Endnote 32: Married at "St. Stepling Church, Hazelwood, Pa. To Hazel Reginia Elder by Rev. T.A. Connors, Bernard Ott and Mary Ott being witnesses."

Endnote 33: "She made her first Communion today the 15th 1855."

Endnote 34: "Henry C. Henneberger was married 28 Jan. 1918, by Right Revd. M.F. Foley, Baltimore, Md. to Nellie Smith, non catholic."

Endnote 35: written in darker ink in the margin under this entry is: "Francis took solemn vows in the Society of Jesus 16th July 1918, before V. Rev. R.A. Gleeson, S.J. Provincial, Portland, Oregon"

Endnote 36: It appears that the parents are not married because the father and mother are listed in reverse order, and because the mother is *not* described as "his wife" as the priest commonly did.

Endnote 37: The parents may not be married because the mother is not named as the father's wife as the priest did in the other entries.

Endnote 38: This entry is in Baptism section (where it is dated 05 Jan 1819) and was transferred to this section by the priest. Their marriage license was taken out on 4 Jan 1819; bride received written consent of her father to marry.

Endnote 39: married by permission of both masters in writing; original signatures of both witnesses are in this entry.

Endnote 40: although it is unclear which month this entry is in, the couple received a Washington County marriage license on 25 Feb 1851, thus, it appears that the marriage was in February.

Endnote 41: although it is unclear which month this entry is in, the couple received a Washington County marriage license on 27 Feb 1851, thus, it appears that the marriage was in February.

Endnote 42: special dispensation granted because they were 1st cousins; 3rd witness is Mary Clabaugh; bride and groom from Washington Co.

Endnote 43: Louisa was baptized this day and they "being now both Catholics, and having been married out of the Church, performed in their favor the matrimonial ceremony"

Endnote 44: "Married today, in St. Mary's Church, Hagerstown, Md, after one publication of Bans in Williamsport, Mark Coogen & Lizzie Kelly both of this Town."

Endnote 45: note inserted for this entry: "I am informed this 25th Day of April 1856[1865?], that the woman was married to some other man, whose wherabouts she ignores (according to her own statement made to me to-day), I, accordingly, obliged them to separate. Al. Janalick" [Is it possible that the priest transposed the last two numbers in the year? The ink is different from what is on this page, but is consistent with what is on the next page for his April 1865 entry.]

Endnote 46: "Larris" [or "Harrit"] has been completely overwritten with another name and neither are particularly legible

Endnote 47: These persons were confirmed, By Archbishop Kedrick[?] in Hagerstown Md. August 8th 1852. Signed by Joseph Maguire.

Endnote 48: These persons were "Confirmed by Archbishop Kenrick, in Mary's Church." Hagerstown - Sept. 30th 1855. Signed by F. Myers

Endnote 49: These persons made their first Holy Communion on the 25th of December 1856.

Endnote 50: "1st Communion in Hagerstown April 30 /54" [1854].

Endnote 51: These persons made their first Communion on Chistmas [sic] Day 1854.

Endnote 52: These persons made their 1st Communion.

Endnote 53: Confirmation was administered in St. Mary's Church, Hagerstown, and St. Augustin's Church, Williamsport, by Most Rev. Archb. Renrick[?] on Sunday Octr. 21 1860. [Signed by E. Didier Pastor]

Endnote 54: First Communion, Hagerstown, Octr. 21 1860 [signed by Edm Didier]

Endnote 55: First Communion, Hagerstown, March 25 1862.

Endnote 56: Confirmaton was administered in St. Mary's Church, Hagerstown, by the Most Rev. Archb. Spaulding, April 28th 1865. Signed by Al. Janalick, Soc. Jes.

Endnote 57: First Communion, Hagerstown, Md, 1st Sunday June (3d) 1866. [signed by Edmund Didier, Pastor]

Endnote 58: Confirmation was administered in St. Mary's Church, Hagerstown, by the Most Rev. Abp. Spalding, Wednesday, Oct. 14th 1868. Sixty two (62) persons were confirmed, of whom six were converts. [signed by John M. Jones]

Endnote 59: Confirmation was administered in St. Mary's Church, Hagerstown, by the Right Rev. Jos.[?] Gibbons, Wednesday June 28th 1871. Thirteen of these thirty-nine persons were converts.

Endnote 60: These persons were confirmed by The Rev. Bishop Gibbons at Williamsport on the 27th of June 1871. [signed by John M. Jones, Pastor of St. Mary's Church, Hagerstown. June 28th 1871]

Endnote 61: Holy Scapular - these persons received "the scapular to day"

Endnote 62: Sacred Scapular

Endnote 63: "Margaret" has been overwritten by "Mary Jane"

Endnote 64: Convert to Catholic faith

Endnote 65: Black [African American]

Endnote 66: * this may be an "N." or a ditto mark - there is a Paulus Paulus in the congregation

Endnote 67: "Received into the church at Hagerstown...They [the three McKaigs] were satisfied that they had been properly baptized, and so were not baptized conditionally, but made the profession of faith."

Endnote 68: *"die et anno menises incognito, probabiliter circa annos 70" [day and year month unknown, probably about 70 years old]

Endnote 69: Child is adopted - it would appear from the entry that she was adopted by a Gallagher family and that her birth parents are Guielmo Gower and Catherina Reid; birth parents are not married; PN

Endnote 70: The notation for "mother not a Catholic" is crossed out; "converya [?] 1887" crossed out; Married Gulielano Andrea Ligon, St. Andreae Church, Roanoke, Virginia, 29 Sept. 1916.

Endnote 71: the mother is listed in the section for father, and the section for mother has lines crossed through it, but the word for marriage has not been crossed out as was normally done if the parents are not married

Endnote 72: mother from Williamsport; appears to read "ad fidem conversa et Baptimss absolute confertus"; married Georgio Downey, 20 Feb 1912. Married by S.S. Hulbert

Endnote 73: married 26 Mar 1924 [4 is unclear] at Dahlgren Chapel to Leona Hurd by Geo. B. Harrington, Witnesses: Mrs. Josiah Pierce, Mrs. Wallace Cull

Endnote 74: "A medico privatim fuit baptizatus in partu ob mortis periculum" [appears to translate as "privately baptized by doctor at birth due to danger of death"]

Endnote 75: married 28 Aug 1931 to Helen Gruber, Rev. T.E. Parks, St. Joan of Arc Church, Hershey, PA; married 3 Nov 1942 after death of 1st wife to Catherine Collins in Holy Angels Church, Philadelphia, Rev. C.E. Parks

Endnote 76: married 24 Sep 1923, Washington, DC, Jno. H. Eckinrode[?] to Edna L. Donaldson [unreadable word in parentheses beside her name], Witnesses: R.A. Jenkins, Jean McCardell

Endnote 77: "This man states that he has always been known as Samuel Calvin Dickerhoff. Correction made 6 Feb 1943. J.F. Leary, Pastor. [name on baptism record is "Joseph" only.]; married to Catherine Cushwa 14 Jun 1943, St. Augustine's, Williamsport

Endnote 78: married William J. Kelly, 27 Aug 1977, Parish of St. Gregory, Lebanon, PA, married[?] Robert Maher [?]; married S.C. Dickerhoff [?] 14 Jun 1943, St. Augustine's, Williamsport, MD

Endnote 79: "After 3 publications of the Bans of Matrimoney"; 3rd witness is James Shervin, 4th witness is Miss Margaret Shervin; bride and groom from Washington Co.

INDEX

Index

Please note that numbers refer to entries and not to page numbers

Abbenton, Basil, 209
Abbenton, Danl, 118
Abbenton, Hanna, 136
Abbenton, Hanna, 118
Abbenton, Hanna, 209
Abbenton, Judith, 118
Abbenton, Rebecca, 209
Abdon, Charolus Basileus, 1763
Abdon, Susannae, 1763
Abel, Eliza, 261
Abel, Grandson, 3918
Abel, Herman L., 4855
Abel, Herman Laurentium, 3918
Abel, Juliann, 134
Abel, Maria J. [or I.], 3918
Abell, Jacob, 174
Abell, Mary, 174
Abell, Agnete, 3977
Abell, Eugenio, 3977
Abell, Herman L., 3937
Abell, Joseph Howard, 3977
Abell, Maria Agnes, 3937
Abell, Mrs., 4175
Abell, Owen Lewis, 3937
Abell, Samuel, 4175
Abell, Susanna, 4191
Abernaty, Carolus, 955
Abernaty, Charolinae, 955
Abernaty, Thomae, 955
Abernethey, Charlotte, 2172
Abil, Joseph N., 5
Abil, Julian, 5
Abil, Vulgerinan, 5
Able, Anna Lousa [Louisa], 2422
Able, Anna, 371
Able, Elisa (Miss), 274
Able, Leonard, 2422
Able, Louisa, 2422
Able, Mrs., 371
Able, Saml, 371
Able, Thomas, 371
Adam, Elisabeth, 1812
Adam, Jacobi, 1812
Adam, Ludovica A., 1812
Adam, Maria, 1508
Adams, "unknown", 461
Adams, Adam, 2221
Adams, Amos, 1734
Adams, Amos, 2001
Adams, Amos, 2002
Adams, Amos, 2134
Adams, Amos, 2313
Adams, Amos, 2527
Adams, Amos, 4484
Adams, Catharinae, 1734
Adams, Catharine Ann, 2134
Adams, Catharine, 2001
Adams, Catharine, 2002
Adams, Catharine, 2313
Adams, Catharine, 2527
Adams, Eli, 657
Adams, Elisa (Miss), 351
Adams, Elisa, 492
Adams, Elisabeth, 4400
Adams, Eliza, 619
Adams, Eliza, 537
Adams, Ezechias, 1734
Adams, Helena, 2153
Adams, Helena, 2361
Adams, Helena, 2362
Adams, Helena, 2417
Adams, Helena, 4537
Adams, Helena, 75
Adams, J.W. [or U.], 4126
Adams, Jacobum A., 4787
Adams, James William Taylor, 2001
Adams, James, 74
Adams, James, 75
Adams, John Q., 4519
Adams, John Q., 4520
Adams, John, 4517
Adams, John, 4522
Adams, Joseph Edmund, 2134

Adams, Maala, 5534
Adams, Maala, 5584
Adams, Margaret, 2002
Adams, Margaret, 75
Adams, Margret (widow), 4222
Adams, Maria M., 3192
Adams, Maria, 3131
Adams, Martha, 4256
Adams, Martin Clarke, 2313
Adams, Mary Amelia, 2527
Adams, Mary, 2993
Adams, Mary, 3058
Adams, Mrs., 461
Adams, Nancy, 461
Adams, Otho, 2221
Adams, Rosam Ethel, 4126
Adams, Rosam Ethel, 4909
Adams, Sarah, 3431
Adams, Wilm, 461
Addams, Elisa, 307
Addlesperger, Susan, 3437
Addlesperger, Anna, 3464
Addlesperger, Bernardum Simmons, 3464
Addlesperger, Jacob L., 3437
Addlesperger, Luthero, 3464
Addlesperger, Lutherum, 4766

Addlesperger, Susan, 3437
Aehrl, John G., 3848
Agan, Catharinae, 1758
Agan, Elisabeth, 1758
Agan, Margareta, 1758
Agan, Petri, 1758
Aheren [sic], Elizabeth, 2959
Aheren [sic], James, 2959
Aheren [sic], Joanna, 2959
Aherin, Ellen, 2680
Aherin, Jas., 2680
Aherin, Johanna, 2680
Aherine, James, 2615
Aherine, Johanna, 2615
Aherine, Johanna, 2615
Ahern, Anastatia, 2531
Ahern, Anna, 3238
Ahern, Anna, 3375
Ahern, Catharina, 3430
Ahern, James, 2531
Ahern, Johanna, 2531
Ahorrin, Jas., 2939
Akel, Elizabeth, 2463
Alaxander, Carlum Richardum, 3688
Alaxander, Carolina, 3688
Alaxander, Carolo, 3688

Albert, Anna Maria, 1803
Albert, Barbara, 1299
Albert, Barbara, 1300
Albert, Barbarae, 1803
Albert, Ellon, 4303
Albert, Franciscus Josephus, 1299
Albert, Francisii Josephi, 1300
Albert, Jacobus, 1300
Albert, Josephi, 1803
Albert, Mary, 4297
Alexander, Bernardum G., 3309
Alexander, Carolina, 3621
Alexander, Carolina, 3626
Alexander, Carolina, 3783
Alexander, Carolina, 3852
Alexander, Carolina, 3936
Alexander, Carolo, 3309
Alexander, Carolo W., 3852
Alexander, Carolo, 3503
Alexander, Carolo, 3504
Alexander, Carolo, 3621
Alexander, Carolo, 3626
Alexander, Carolo, 3783
Alexander, Carolo, 3936
Alexander, Carolo, 4750
Alexander, Carrie, 3503
Alexander, Carrie, 3504

Alexander, Catharine, 3309
Alexander, Genevefam Gertrudem, 3936
Alexander, Georgio, 4904
Alexander, Georgio, 4906
Alexander, Georgius, 3985
Alexander, Georgius, 4147
Alexander, Joannem Gulielmum, 3626
Alexander, Joannes Gulielmus, 4153
Alexander, Julia, 3543
Alexander, Maria E., 4153
Alexander, Maria, 3924
Alexander, Maria, 4110
Alexander, Mariam Elisabeth, 4904
Alexander, Mariam Elizabeth, 3504
Alexander, Mariam Stellam Irenam, 3621
Alexander, Nellie Pearl, 3852
Alexander, Terentium Vincentum, 3783
Alexander, Terrence, 5232
Alexander, Virginia B., 4906
Alexander, Virginia, 3985
Alexander, Virginia, 4147

Alexander, Virginiam Beatricem, 3503
Allam, Maria, 1206
Allan, Columb., 5180
Allan, Columbum Leonem, 3450
Allan, Johanne, 3314
Allan, Johanne, 3450
Allan, Johannes Aloyium, 3314
Allan, Maria, 3314
Allan, Maria, 3450
Allan, Rachael, 3450
Allen [or Allan], Gertrudem Mariam, 3859
Allen [or Allan], Joanne, 3859
Allen [or Allan], Maria, 3859
Allen, Betsy, 38
Allen, Betsy, 37
Allen, Carolum Franciscum, 3210
Allen, Catharina, 1677
Allen, Catherine (widow), 4308
Allen, Charlotte Eugenia, 2009
Allen, Charlotte, 2009
Allen, Charlotte, 2010
Allen, Clarenda Jane, 2010
Allen, Gulielmum, 3155
Allen, Henricum Fredericum, 3558
Allen, Henry Fred., 5370

Allen, James, 2009
Allen, James, 2010
Allen, Joanne, 3155
Allen, Joanne, 3770
Allen, Joanni, 3558
Allen, Johanne, 3210
Allen, Johannem A., 4730
Allen, John, 5358
Allen, Louisa, 37
Allen, Maria, 3770
Allen, Maria E., 3155
Allen, Maria, 3210
Allen, Maria, 3558
Allen, Mary, 38
Allen, Rachel, 3155
Allen, Sararma Magdalenam, 3770
Allen, Willie, 5170
Alsip, [blank], 2875
Alsip, [blank], 2875
Alsip, [blank], 2876
Alsip, [blank], 2876
Alsip, Clara, 2875
Alsip, Joseph Ellsworth, 2876
Altorff, Philemena, 3302
Ambroes, Honora, 1494
Ambrose, Sallie, 5805

Ambrose, Joannis, 1303
Ambrose, Norae, 1303
Ambrose, Saley, 338
Ambrose, Thomas, 1303
Ambush, Appolinae, 1804
Ambush, Appoloniae, 1684
Ambush, Jeremias, 1684
Ambush, Sara, 1804
Ambush, William, 1684
Ambush, Yorick, 4287
Ambush, York, 1804
Ambushe, Appoloniae, 1188
Ambushe, Eleonora, 1188
Ambushe, Jorck, 1188
Andersen, Delilah, 3202
Anderson, Ginnie, 5516
Anderson, Virginia, 5531
Anderson, Catharina, 3330
Anderson, James, 3038
Anderson, James, 4711
Anderson, Jennie, 5047
Anderson, Joanne, 4109
Anderson, Johannesm, 3610
Anderson, John H., 4675
Anderson, Jos., 3616
Anderson, Maria, 4109
Anderson, Mariam E., 3159

Anderson, Mary Jane, 587
Anderson, Mida Anastatia, 513
Anderson, Mrs, 3204
Anderson, Mrs., 3205
Anderson, Mrs., 3226
Anderson, Mrs., 4864
Anderson, Saml, 513
Anderson, Sophia, 4913
Anderson, Susanna, 513
Anderson, Thomam Antonium, 4109
Andrew, Catharina, 3835
Andrew, Catharina, 3836
Andrew, Catharina, 3925
Andrews, Anna R., 2694
Andry, Josephina, 3684
Andry, Josaphina, 3685
Andry, Josephina, 3686
Angle, Emma F., 3498
Angle, Emma F., 3499
Angle, Emma F., 3500
Annys, Petrus, 1754
Anthoney, Conrad, 2133
Anthony, Ann Eugenia, 1834
Anthony, Catharine Elmira, 1833
Anthony, Catharine, 1833
Anthony, Catharine, 1834

Anthony, Conrad, 1833
Anthony, Conrad, 1834
Anthony, Conrad, 1856
Anthony, Conrad, 2097
Anthony, Conrad, 2098
Anthony, Elizabeth, 2296
Anthony, Mary C., 2097
Anthony, Mary C., 2098
Anton, Georgius, 821
Anton, Georguii, 821
Anton, Mariae, 821
Antoney, Catharine, 2195
Antoney, Christina M., 2375
Antoney, Christina, 2222
Antoney, Conrad, 2195
Antoney, Conrad, 2376
Antoney, Gertrude, 2239
Antoney, John Francis, 2195
Antoney, Mary Catharine, 2298
Antony, Catharinae, 1167
Antony, Catharinae, 1653
Antony, Conrad, 1653
Antony, Conradi, 1167
Antony, Conrardus, 1128
Antony, Conrardus, 1128
Antony, Georgii, 1128
Antony, Georgius, 1167

Antony, Georgius, 1167
Antony, Mariae, 1128
Antony, Mina Anna, 1653
Apernathy, 616
Appleton, Anna, 267
Appleton, Hanna, 207
Arbaugh, Joanne L., 3733
Arbaugh, Leila Ada, 3733
Ardinger, Mrs., 3606
Ardinger, Benjamin, 2813
Ardinger, Benjamin, 3323
Ardinger, Benjamin, 3324
Ardinger, Catharinam, 3324
Ardinger, Cecilia, 4100
Ardinger, Ceciliam, 3323
Ardinger, Fanny, 4675
Ardinger, Georgetta, 4154
Ardinger, Georgietta, 3326
Ardinger, Georgietta, 3386
Ardinger, Gingetta, 3325
Ardinger, Harry Lee, 2813
Ardinger, Susan, 2813
Ardinger, Susan, 3323
Ardinger, Susan, 3324
Armsey, Eleanor, 119
Armstrong, Delia A., 4831
Armstrong, Emma A., 3899

Armstrong, Emma C., 3579
Armstrong, Emma C., 3785
Armstrong, Emma C., 3862
Armstrong, Emma Cath., 3513
Armstrong, Emma, 3620
Armstrong, Emma, 3743
Armstrong, Emma, 3744
Armstrong, Emma, 3953
Armstrong, Emma, 4001
Armstrong, Emma, 4069
Armstrong, Emma, 4151
Armstrong, Felia, 3870
Armstrong, Francis, 4281
Armstrong, James, 195
Armstrong, Margt., 2880
Arnold, Henricum Wesley, 3641
Arnold, Jane, 4560
Arnold, Margaret, 2712
Arnold, Mariam Helenam, 3642
Arnold, Mrs., 543
Arnold, Susanna, 3641
Arnold, Susanna, 3642
Arnold, Tennis [sic], 3641
Arnold, Tennis [sic], 3642
Arrabella, Francis, 4658
Arther, Emmam Maud, 4053
Arther, Rachele, 4053

Arther, Samuel H., 4053
Artison, Maria (Mrs.), 4521
Artison, Maria, 1932
Atwel, Anna, 983
Atwel, Joannis, 983
Atwel, Mariae, 983
Audlem, Widow, 4293
Audry, Josaphina, 3685
Audry, Josephina, 3686
Audry, Josephina, 3684
Aulbert, Archey, 619
Aulbert, Archobold, 561
Aulbert, Arcibol, 441
Aulbert, Catherene, 619
Aulbert, Catherine Alousa, 619
Aulbert, Catherine, 441
Aulbert, Catherine, 446
Aulbert, Catherine, 561
Aulbert, Henery Francis, 561
Aulbert, Wilm, 441
Aullert, Arch John, 370
Ault, M., 4737
Ault, M., 4737
Aumen, Francisca R., 4162
B [rest of name is blank], Theresa, 1638
Bachrach, Henrietta, 3658

Bachus, Margareta, 4366
Backley, Catharina, 1561
Backley, Corneliei, 1561
Backley, Johannae, 1561
Baciler, Sabastian, 456
Baer, Ann, 2862
Baifley, Virginia, 4800
Bailey, Earle, 3852
Bailey, Jennie, 3548
Bailey, Jennie, 3859
Bailey, Jennie, 3952
Bailey, Jennie, 4067
Bailey, Jennie, 4839
Bailey, Joanne, 3696
Bailey, William, 4661
Bailey, Wm., 4664
Baker, Angelina, 1300
Baker, Joanne L., 3733
Baker, Leila Ada, 3733
Baker, Jr., Daniel, 3652
Baker, Jr., Leila Ady, 3652
Baker, Jr., Mariam Elsie, 3652
Baker, Agnes Theresium, 3764
Baker, Angelinae, 1299
Baker, Angelinae, 1627
Baker, Annam Cath., 3145
Baker, Carolum Guglielmum, 3215

Baker, Daniel, 3087
Baker, Daniele, 3140
Baker, Daniele, 3141
Baker, Daniele, 3142
Baker, Daniele, 3143
Baker, Daniele, 3144
Baker, Daniele, 3145
Baker, Daniele, 3215
Baker, Daniele, 3370
Baker, Danielem, 3138
Baker, Danielem, 3140
Baker, David, 3298
Baker, Edith Olivia, 3370
Baker, Elisabeth, 1500
Baker, Elisabeth, 1808
Baker, Elizabeth A. (Miss), 4615
Baker, Elizabeth Agnes, 2539
Baker, Emily A., 5745
Baker, Emily, 3074
Baker, Guglielmo, 1808
Baker, Gulielmo, 3138
Baker, Gustavi, 1500
Baker, Helenam, 3143
Baker, Henricus, 1500
Baker, Jacobi, 1299
Baker, Jacobi, 1627
Baker, Jacobus, 1300

Baker, Joanne C., 3764
Baker, Joannem, 3141
Baker, Joannis, 1808
Baker, Josephus, 1299
Baker, Laura Jane, 3073
Baker, Laura Jane, 5744
Baker, Lebeda, 3764
Baker, Maria A., 3215
Baker, Maria Anna, 3141
Baker, Maria Anna, 3142
Baker, Maria Anna, 3143
Baker, Maria Anna, 3144
Baker, Maria Anna, 3145
Baker, Maria, 3138
Baker, Maria, 3370
Baker, Maria, 3851
Baker, Mariam Anna, 3140
Baker, Mariam Henriettam, 3142
Baker, Mary Ann, 3087
Baker, Mary Gertrude, 3087
Baker, Mary, 3298
Baker, Mary, 3298
Baker, Mary, 5122
Baker, Mary, 630
Baker, Mrs, 4833
Baker, Mrs., 5321
Baker, Nicholaus, 4387

Baker, Obediam, 3144
Baker, Sara Anna, 1627
Baker, Sarah C., 3567
Baker, Sarah C., 3791
Baker, Sarah C., 4755
Baker, Sarah Cath., 3682
Baker, Sarah Catharina, 3298
Baker, Sarah, 3369
Baker, Sarah, 3460
Ball, Alfred, 5205
Ball, Bernard, 5689
Ball, Bernardo M., 3734
Ball, Bernardo, 3927
Ball, Bernardum M., 4806
Ball, Bernardum Robertum, 3927
Ball, Clara, 3734
Ball, Elizabeth, 3482
Ball, Elizabeth, 3520
Ball, Elizabeth, 3593
Ball, Elizabetha, 4806
Ball, Maria C., 3372
Ball, Maria, 3482
Ball, Maria, 3520
Ball, Maria, 3593
Ball, Mariam C., 4748
Ball, Mariam, 3734
Ball, Mary, 4731

Ball, Mr., 4748
Ball, Mrs, 3927
Ball, Mrs, 4748
Ball, Thalia, 3734
Ball, Thalia, 3927
Ball, William John, 5724
Ballad, Tosmmerset, 4530
Ballett, Somerset, 2611
Ballett, Uncle, 5029
Balry, Cath., 555
Baney, Maria, 1265
Baninghan, Margareta, 1492
Banks, Ben F., 5138
Banks, Benjamin Franciscum, 3470
Banks, Elizabeth Annam, 3471
Banks, Frances J., 5134
Banks, Fridericum Carolum Eduardum, 3515
Banks, Gulielmo, 3934
Banks, Jos., 5166
Banks, Joseph, 3479
Banks, Joseph, 3515
Banks, Josepho, 3470
Banks, Josepho, 3471
Banks, M. (Mrs.), 5373
Banks, Marg. [or Mary], 5139

Banks, Margaretam Virginiam, 3479
Banks, Maria Francesca, 3470
Banks, Maria Francesca, 3471
Banks, Maria Francesca, 3479
Banks, Maria Francesca, 3515
Banks, Mary Ellen, 2446
Banks, Samuelem Josiah, 3934
Banks, Samuelem, 4864
Bannan, Birgitta, 1583
Bannan, Margaret, 1994
Banner, Hanah, 246
Bannon, Catharina, 1373
Bannon, Eugenias, 4486
Bannon, Margaret, 2266
Bannon, Owen, 1106
Bannon, Patricus, 1110
Barbary, Anna, 1730
Barber, Allen Perry, 2685
Barber, Allen Perry, 2799
Barber, Anna E., 3444
Barber, Anna E., 3445
Barber, Anna E., 3521
Barber, Anna Elizabeth, 3443
Barber, Bradley Townsend, 3445
Barber, Carolo B., 3443
Barber, Carolo B., 3444

Barber, Carolo B., 3445
Barber, Carolo, 3521
Barber, Daisy Magdelenam P., 3521
Barber, Geo., 2625
Barber, Geo., 2685
Barber, Geo., 2796
Barber, Geo., 2797
Barber, Geo., 2798
Barber, Geo., 2799
Barber, Geo., 2877
Barber, Geo., 4625
Barber, Gracie Lee, 3443
Barber, Harvey, 2798
Barber, John, 312
Barber, Joseph, 252
Barber, Laetitiae, 2625
Barber, Letitia, 2797
Barber, Lucy, 252
Barber, Mary (Mrs.), 5042
Barber, Mary Eliz., 2877
Barber, Mary, 2625
Barber, Mary, 2685
Barber, Mary, 2796
Barber, Mary, 2797
Barber, Mary, 2798
Barber, Mary, 2799

Barber, Mary, 2877
Barber, Milly, 252
Barber, Percy Poffinbarger, 3444
Barber, Perry, 4701
Barber, Thos. Hiram, 2796
Barger, Charlotte Susanna, 2718
Barger, Charlotte, 5612
Baringer, Annastaia, 325
Baringer, Jacob, 325
Baringer, Susanna, 325
Barkdol, Sophia, 2005
Barker, Hambelton, 598
Barker, Nancy, 598
Barker, Simon Saml, 598
Barks, Maria, 3601
Barley, Jennie, 3732
Barlow, Ann, 2094
Barn, Ambrosius, 1309
Barn, Elisabeth, 1188
Barn, Elisabeth, 1309
Barn, Elisobeth, 1533
Barnes, Theodorem, 4807
Barnet, Catharine, 2030
Barnet, Catharine, 2033
Barnet, David Albertus, 2030
Barnet, David Albertus, 2033
Barnet, Henry S., 2030

Barnet, Henry S., 2033
Barnett, Catharine, 4554
Barnett, Catharine, 4551
Barnett, Catharine, 2132
Barnett, Catharine, 1926
Barnett, Catharine, 2059
Barnett, Catharine, 2075
Barnett, Catharine, 2184
Barnett, H. (Mr.), 4554
Barnett, Henry Augustine, 2184
Barnett, Henry S., 4517
Barnett, Henry, 1926
Barnett, Henry, 2184
Barnett, Henry, 4551
Barnett, Mary Eliza Virginia, 1926
Barnhart, Margaritam, 4857
Barnhart, Sarah, 3659
Barns, Maria, 4115
Barr, Clinton, 3570
Barr, Ella, 3570
Barr, Martha J. [or I.], 3285
Barr, Martha J. [or I.], 3286
Barr, Martha J. [or I.], 3287
Barr, Martha J. [or I.], 3288
Barr, Martha J. [or I.], 3289
Barr, Martha, 3160
Barr, Theo., 5184

Barr, Theodorem, 3570
Barret, Catherine, 512
Barret, Dominicus, 1122
Barret, Honora, 4254
Barret, Honora, 512
Barret, James, 4254
Barret, James, 512
Barret, Margret (widow), 4275
Barret, Margret, 512
Barret, Maria, 1122
Barrett, Anna, 3424
Barrett, Anna, 3425
Barrett, Anna, 3507
Barrett, Anna, 3508
Barrett, Birgitta, 772
Barrett, Catharina, 3098
Barrett, Catharina, 3162
Barrett, Catharina, 4468
Barrett, Catherine, 3033
Barrett, Dominici, 1076
Barrett, Dominici, 1472
Barrett, Dominici, 772
Barrett, Dominicus, 1446
Barrett, Eliza, 3066
Barrett, Jacobus Josephus, 4439
Barrett, Margareta, 1472
Barrett, Margarita, 3098

Barrett, Maria, 1076
Barrett, Mariae, 1076
Barrett, Mariae, 1472
Barrett, Mariae, 772
Barrett, Mary, 5343
Barrett, Nannie, 3267
Barrett, Nannie, 4751
Barros, Bernardde, 3615
Barrowskae, Christena, 562
Barrowskae, Elizabeth, 562
Barrowskae, Joseph, 562
Barry, [blank], 2699
Barry, Alice, 2919
Barry, Bridget, 2186
Barry, Catherine, 2740
Barry, David, 2186
Barry, David, 2207
Barry, David, 4584
Barry, David, 4958
Barry, Denis Henry, 2864
Barry, Domina, 3481
Barry, Eliz., 2919
Barry, J. M., 2919
Barry, Jacobo Taylor, 3958
Barry, James Eli, 3050
Barry, James, 2186
Barry, Jno, 2919

Barry, Jno., 2939
Barry, Joanna, 2939
Barry, Joanne, 3104
Barry, Joanne, 3172
Barry, Joannem Thomam, 3963
Barry, Joannes R., 3172
Barry, Joannes, 1230
Barry, Joanni R., 4768
Barry, Johannes, 3311
Barry, Johannes, 3602
Barry, John Henry, 3065
Barry, John Richard, 2740
Barry, John, 2646
Barry, John, 2699
Barry, John, 2703
Barry, John, 2740
Barry, John, 2792
Barry, John, 2864
Barry, John, 2982
Barry, John, 3050
Barry, John, 3065
Barry, John, 3249
Barry, John, 4639
Barry, John, 5281
Barry, M. G., 2919
Barry, Maggie, 2681
Barry, Magt., 2914

Barry, Margaret, 2405
Barry, Margaret, 3236
Barry, Margaret, 4584
Barry, Margaret, 4631
Barry, Margaret, 4639
Barry, Maria, 3104
Barry, Maria, 3172
Barry, Maria, 3221
Barry, Maria, 3282
Barry, Maria, 3322
Barry, Maria, 3325
Barry, Maria, 3326
Barry, Maria, 3949
Barry, Maria, 4115
Barry, Mariam Helenam, 3172
Barry, Martha, 4469
Barry, Mary, 1978
Barry, Mary, 2281
Barry, Mary, 2699
Barry, Mary, 2701
Barry, Mary, 2703
Barry, Mary, 2740
Barry, Mary, 2792
Barry, Mary, 2800
Barry, Mary, 2864
Barry, Mary, 2939
Barry, Mary, 3050

Barry, Mary, 3065
Barry, Mary, 3246
Barry, Mary, 3402
Barry, Mary, 4719
Barry, Maud Maria, 3963
Barry, Maud Mariam, 3958
Barry, May, 2973
Barry, Mich., 2942
Barry, Mrs., 3465
Barry, Phil, 4696
Barry, Richard, 4941
Barry, Sarah H., 3958
Barry, Thoma, 3963
Barry, Thomas, 3104
Barry, Wilhelmey, 3386
Barry, William David, 2792
Bartell, Elizabeth, 175
Bartol, Joseph, 175
Bartol, Elizabeth, 61
Baseford, Rina [sic], 3643
Basore, Georgio, 4024
Basore, Georgio, 4058
Basore, Gulielmum Ernestum, 4145
Basore, Joannem Irwin, 4055
Basore, Lucia S., 4093
Basore, Lucia, 4024

Basore, Lucia, 4055
Basore, Lucia, 4145
Basore, Margaritam Elisabeth, 4093
Basore, Samuele E., 4093
Basore, Samuele E., 4145
Basore, Samuele, 4055
Basore, Samuelem E., 4875
Basore, Samuelem Edwardum, 4024
Basore, Samuelem, 4058
Bateman, Edwardem Howard, 3276
Bateman, Isaac, 3276
Bateman, Theresa, 3276
Bath, Jacob, 4989
Battal, Michaelem, 4751
Battle, Jr., Amam, 3629
Battle, Jr., Maria, 3628
Battle, Jr., Maria, 3629
Battle, Jr., Michaele, 3628
Battle, Jr., Michaele, 3629
Battle, Sr., Michael, 3628
Battle, Anna (Mrs.), 3826
Battle, Anna (Mrs.), 3939
Battle, Anna, 3507
Battle, Anna, 3508

Battle, Anna, 3628
Battle, Bridget, 5265
Battle, Brigitta, 3629
Battle, Danielem, 3508
Battle, Helen, 3981
Battle, Maria (Mrs.), 3849
Battle, Mary (Mrs.), 3857
Battle, Mary, 3507
Battle, Michael, 2972
Battle, Michael, 3162
Battle, Michael, 5303
Battle, Michaelem, 3507
Battle, Michaeli, 3507
Battle, Michaeli, 3508
Battle, Mrs., 3984
Battle, Mrs., 3988
Battles, Anna, 3424
Battles, Anna, 3425
Battles, Helenam Liguori, 3424
Battles, Mariam Genovesam, 3425
Battles, Michaele, 3267
Battles, Michaele, 3424
Battles, Michaele, 3425
Battles, Mrs., 3280
Battles, Nannie, 3267
Battles, Thomam Michaelem, 3267
Bauer, Catharina, 1717

Bauer, Catharina, 1717
Bauer, Christianna, 2801
Bauer, George Kyper, 2801
Bauer, Jacobi, 1717
Bauer, John, 2801
Bauer, Mariae Anae, 1717
Baughman, Elizabeth, 2251
Baughman, Joseph William, 2081
Baughman, Lewis, 2081
Baughman, Lewis, 2251
Baughman, Lewis, 4522
Baughman, Mary Elizabeth, 2081
Baughman, Mary, 2081
Baughman, Victoria Elizabeth, 2251
Bauls, Ann, 44
Bauman, Georgii, 668
Bauman, Joannes, 668
Bauman, Mariae, 668
Bavert, David, 1256
Bavert, Melindae, 1256
Bavert, W. Edwardus, 1256
Bawnd, Bertha, 3805
Baxford, Cora, 3854
Baxter, Daniel, 4651
Baxter, James, 2184
Baxter, James, 2198

Baxter, Mary, 2339
Bayley, Jennie, 3184
Bayley, Jennie, 3208
Bayley, Jennie, 3210
Bayley, Jennie, 3283
Bayley, Jennie, 3291
Bayley, Jennie, 3329
Bayley, Jennie, 3442
Bayley, Jennie, 3462
Bayley, Jennie, 3466
Bayley, Joanna, 3717
Bayley, M.A. Reg., 3515
Bayley, M.A. Regina, 3515
Bayley, Maria Agnes Reg., 3471
Bayley, Maria Agnes Regina, 3470
Bayley, Virginia, 3625
Bayley, Virginia, 3641
Bayley, Virginia, 3715
Bean, Birgitta, 1461
Bean, Jacobus, 1350
Bean, Joannes, 4485
Bean, Teresa, 186
Bear, Ann Elizabeth, 1955
Bear, Ann, 1955
Bear, Ben, 4356
Bear, Catharina, 766
Bear, Isaac, 1955

Bear, Joannes Thomas, 765
Bear, Mrs., 2638
Beard, Anna, 3670
Beargentz, Mittilda, 456
Beargentz, Peter, 456
Beargentz, Victoria, 456
Bearinger, Anna, 340
Bearinger, Henry, 340
Bearinger, Jacob, 340
Bearn, Catharina, 1304
Bearn, Catharina, 4473
Bearns, Maria, 1370
Bearsay, Lizzie, 5517
Bearsay, Lizzie, 5801
Bearsey, Richard, 4529
Beaumont, Francisca, 3846
Beaumont, Mrs., 3895
Beck, Annae, 1412
Beck, Georgii, 1412
Beck, Guillelmus, 1412
Beck, Mr., 4885
Beckman, Rosina, 3198
Beckmann, Rosa, 3480
Becktel, Eucriana, 4241
Becky, James, 522
Beer, Joannes, 1127
Beer, Sally Lour (Miss), 395

Beer, Thomas, 1111
Beers, Joannes, 4449
Beers, Joannis, 1642
Beers, Maria, 1282
Beers, Maria, 1431
Beers, Mariae, 1448
Beers, Mariae, 1642
Beers, Richardus, 1561
Beers, Richardus, 1642
Begald, Upton, 4185
Begold, Upton A., 2400
Begold, Upton, 437
Begs, Anne, 52
Begs, Michael James, 52
Behan, James, 2095
Beirguntz, Mary Anna, 439
Bejold, Upton A.., 2317
Belgold, Mr., 393
Belgold, Mrs., 393
Bell, Catharinae, 1623
Bell, Catharinae, 921
Bell, Catharinae, 921
Bell, Elisabeth, 1808
Bell, Eliza Jane, 2112
Bell, Eliza, 2414
Bell, Eliza, 4994
Bell, Guillelimus, 1808

Bell, Guillelmus, 990
Bell, Henry, 2112
Bell, Ida, 4114
Bell, Ida, 4121
Bell, Ida, 4168
Bell, Joannis, 1808
Bell, Maria Anna, 1623
Bell, Mary Ann, 2101
Bell, Mary Ann, 2107
Bell, Mary, 2112
Bell, Mary, 2414
Bell, Mary, 2414
Bell, Rachel, 1938
Bell, Rosa, 1623
Bell, Stephani, 1623
Bell, Stephani, 921
Bell, Wm, 2414
Bellman, Henricus, 4505
Belordol, Lucreatia, 209
Belton, Maria, 1152
Bemel, B., 4829
Bemisdarfe, Susannah R., 3645
Bernisdarfer, Susanam R., 4782
Bernsdarfe, Susanna R., 4012
Bendiert, Alberto, 3773
Benet, Birgittae, 871
Benet, Joannes, 871
Benet, Mc [sic], 871
Benins, Bernard, 231
Benins, Elisa, 231
Benins, Sofia, 231
Bennet, Gulielmum Edmund, 3531
Bennet, Maria C., 3531
Bennett, Richardo S., 3531
Bennett, Edith, 3992
Bennett, Edith, 4045
Bennett, Maria, 3436
Bennett, Maria, 3598
Bennett, Mrs., 4045
Bennett, Ricardo S., 3436
Bennett, Ricardum, 4762
Bennett, Ricardum Carolum, 3436
Benny, Mariae, 1228
Benny, Matheus, 1228
Benny, Patricii, 1228
Benskey, Maria Catharina, 1284
Bently, Catharina, 4048
Bently, Maria, 4048
Benton, Amanda Jane, 2216
Benton, Elleven, 2214
Benton, Elleven, 2215
Benton, Elleven, 2216
Benton, Golan, 2181
Benton, Harriet Annette, 2214
Benton, Harriet, 2214
Benton, Harriet, 2215
Benton, Harriet, 2216
Benton, Mary Florence Virginia, 2215
Benton, Mary, 2181
Benton, Mr., 4557
Benton, Sarah Eugenia, 2181
Bentz, Catharina, 3978
Bentz, Catharina, 4103
Bentz, Catharina, 4168
Berener, Anastasi, 436
Berener, Benedict, 436
Berener, Jacob, 436
Berger, Adam, 4798
Berger, Bernardinae, 1340
Berger, Catharina Elisabeth, 1340
Berger, Elisabeth, 1340
Berger, Franciscii, 1340
Berger, Theresia, 1747
Berkley, Anna M. (Miss), 4593
Bern, Elleonora, 1689
Bern, Elleonora, 1455
Bern, Joannes, 1689
Bernard, Catharina, 1218
Bernel, B., 4829
Berringer, Anastasia, 1827
Berron, R.J. (Rev.), 3861
Berry, Hattie V., 4858
Berry, Margaret, 2471
Berry, Maria, 1215
Berry, Mary, 1919
Berry, Mary, 2471
Berry, Mary, 5646
Berry, W.H., 4858
Bertolet, Ludovicus, 1208
Besant, Franciscam R., 4800
Bevans, Betsy, 38
Bevans, Edward, 38
Bevans, Helenae, 1589
Bevans, Joannes, 1589
Bevans, Joannis, 1589
Bevans, L., 4571
Bevans, Maria, 1808
Bevans, Mary, 38
Bevans, Mrs., 4524
Bevans, Ambrose, 2129
Bevans, Ambrose, 2294
Bevans, Ann (Miss), 4597
Bevans, Ann Maria, 2127
Bevans, Ann, 2118
Bevans, Ann, 2127
Bevans, Ann, 2233
Bevans, Anna, 1636

Bevans, Anna, 975
Bevans, Annae K., 922
Bevans, Basil, 4534
Bevans, Carolus M., 922
Bevans, Eleonora, 4391
Bevans, Elisabeth J. [or I.], 1556
Bevans, Elisabeth Johanna, 1249
Bevans, Elisabeth, 4423
Bevans, Eliza, 2175
Bevans, Elizabeth Mary, 2389
Bevans, Elizabeth, 2340
Bevans, Ellen Clarissa, 2294
Bevans, Ellen, 2265
Bevans, Evelina, 1097
Bevans, Evelina Ludovica, 4506
Bevans, Evelina, 1770
Bevans, Henrietta, 2012
Bevans, Henrietta, 2016
Bevans, Hippolita, 1430
Bevans, Jacobus Henricus, 4506
Bevans, Jacobus, 1586
Bevans, Jacobus, 1770
Bevans, James Henry, 2129
Bevans, John Henry, 2040
Bevans, John, 2040
Bevans, John, 2127
Bevans, John, 2294

Bevans, John, 4534
Bevans, Joseph, 1755
Bevans, Joseph, 1808
Bevans, Joseph, 1965
Bevans, Joseph, 1978
Bevans, Josephi Ignati, 922
Bevans, Josephus Henricus, 4511
Bevans, Leonidas, 2127
Bevans, Leonidas, 2306
Bevans, Leonidas, 2342
Bevans, Lidia [or Susia] (Miss), 4291
Bevans, Margaret, 2040
Bevans, Margaret, 2294
Bevans, Maria Anna, 4370
Bevans, Maria, 1767
Bevans, Mariae Annae, 689
Bevans, Martha, 2129
Bevans, Martha, 2216
Bevans, Mary, 1965
Bevans, Mary, 1978
Bevans, Miss Ann, 2024
Bevans, Miss Ann, 2041
Bevans, Miss Ann, 2175
Bevans, Mr., 4524
Bevans, Mrs., 4528
Bevans, Mrs., 4572

Bevans, Teresia, 689
Bevans, Thomas White, 2340
Bevans, Thomas, 1636
Bevans, Thomas, 1769
Bevans, Thomas, 1984
Bevans, Thomas, 2175
Bevans, Thomas, 2340
Bevans, Thomas, 4528
Bevans, Thomas, 4572
Bevans, Thomas, 4573
Bevans, Thos., 4591
Bevans, W., 4571
Bevans, Walter, 2129
Bevans, Walter, 689
Bevans, William, 2016
Bevans, William, 4524
Bevens, Ann, 150
Bevens, Ann, 32
Bevens, Ann, 56
Bevens, Barnabas, 133
Bevens, Basil, 133
Bevens, Eleanor, 52
Bevens, Eleanor, 56
Bevens, Elizab, 133
Bevens, Evelina, 150
Bevens, Jane, 50
Bevens, John, 32

Bevens, Leonard, 83
Bevens, Leonard, 56
Bevens, Leonard, 32
Bevens, Margaret, 139
Bevens, Margaret, 150
Bevens, Margaret, 31
Bevens, Margaret, 4184
Bevens, Margret (Miss), 356
Bevens, Mary Anna, 436
Bevens, Rosa, 4804
Bevens, Sarah, 126
Bevens, Thomas, 150
Bevens, Thomas, 56
Bevins, Elizabeth, ., 156
Bivins, Mrs., 231
Bey, Catherine, 207
Bey, Henrieetta, 207
Bey, Henry, 207
Bey, Catherine, 267
Bey, David, 267
Bey, Henery, 267
Bichley, Anna, 4837
Biershing, Gulielmo E., 4879
Bieser, John, 211
Bieser, Joseph, 211
Bieser, Mitelda, 211
Bigan, Catharina, 866

Bigan, Catharinae, 866
Bigan, Rick, 866
Bigold, Augustus Upton, 1439
Bigold, Elizabeth Ann, 4933
Bigold, Upton, 1734
Bigold, Upton, 2134
Binskuzy, Susan Rebecca, 3738
Bird, Charels, 569
Bird, Isaac, 569
Bird, Marietta, 569
Bird, Cornelius Cassey, 2295
Bird, Emeline, 1893
Bird, Esias, 380
Bird, Harieta, 380
Bird, Harriet, 1893
Bird, Harriet, 2131
Bird, Harriet, 2295
Bird, Harrietta, 511
Bird, Isacc, 4253
Bird, Isacc, 511
Bird, Levi, 2131
Bird, Mary Catharine, 2131
Bird, Mary Catherine, 511
Bird, Mary, 2295
Bird, Sophia, 380
Bird, William Henry, 1893
Bishop, Abner, 1602

Bishop, Elisabeth, 1602
Bishop, Sara, 4418
Bishop, W. Henricus, 1602
Biyle, Charles, 4714
Black, Anna A., 4510
Black, Catherine, 4273
Black, Henry, 121
Black, Jane, 2466
Black, Maria, 3448
Black, Mary Jane, 2541
Black, Mary Jane, 2719
Black, Mrs., 5129
Blacken, Clarissa, 121
Blacken, Joseph, 121
Blacken, Susanna, 121
Blackford, Jenette, 1921
Blair, Maria, 3811
Blair, [blank], 3492
Blair, Amanda, 3245
Blair, Amanda, 3246
Blair, Andrea, 3245
Blair, Andrea, 3246
Blair, Andream, 3245
Blair, Franciscum, 3246
Blair, Georgia, 3492
Blair, Georgianna, 3604
Blair, Gulielmo, 3604

Blair, Lilliem Johennem, 3604
Blair, Thomam Porter, 3492
Blake, Joseph, 2140
Blake, Lucy, 2140
Blake, Rosa, 2140
Blakely, John W., 4591
Blakely, Susan, 5191
Blakency, Marcellina, 2350
Blanshefield, Anna, 857
Blanshefield, Catharinae, 857
Blanshefield, Jacobi, 857
Blaurock, Andreas, 1646
Blonrock, Margareta, 1646
Bloomingour, Caroline, 2504
Bloominoor, Caroline, 2949
Blourock, Andreae, 1719
Blourock, Anna Dorothea, 1719
Blourock, Margaretae, 1719
Bloyer, Francisco, 4854
Bluecoat, Andrew, 1927
Bluecoat, Margaret, 1927
Bluecoat, Margaret, 1927
Blumenaur, Carolina, 2576
Blumenour, Carolina, 3151
Blumenour, Caroline, 2395
Blumenour, Georgium Michael, 4775

Blummar, Annie, 3001
Blumnar, Caroline Hile, 3001
Blumnar, Michael, 3001
Blurock, Margaret, 1975
Boarman, Cecela, 214
Boarman, Elonar, 214
Boarman, Ralph, 214
Boden, Catherine, 228
Boden, James, 228
Boden, Susana, 228
Bohan, Catharina, 1403
Bohan, Catharinae, 1336
Bohan, Jacobi, 1336
Bohan, Joannes, 1336
Boher, Adam, 2325
Boher, Catharine, 2325
Boher, Joseph, 2325
Bolen, Charly, 313
Boles, Susan [or Anna] (Miss), 200
Bolmar, John, 4632
Bolo, Upton (Mrs.), 485
Bonan, Joseph, 4258
Bonavide, Paulus, 3891
Bonavode, Maria, 3891
Boocker, Catharine, 2470
Boon, Feby, 354
Boon, Henry, 354

Boon, Isac, 354
Boony, Joannes Thomas, 1678
Boony, Mariae, 1678
Boony, Patricii, 1678
Boothe, Catharine, 151
Boranar, Anastasia, 197
Boranar, Jacob, 197
Boray, David, 4610
Bord, Harietta, 329
Bord, Isac, 329
Bord, Jane, 329
Borden, Esiae, 464
Borden, Evelina, 464
Borden, Mariettae, 464
Borgantz, Peter (Mrs.), 425
Borgantz, Peter, 425
Borinan, Elisa M. O. Jane, 363
Borinan, Ralph, 363
Borinan, Sarah, 363
Borlow, Catharine, 2094
Borman, Cicilia, 239
Boryer, Gulielmo J., 4835
Borys, Barney, 534
Bosey, Mary Eliz., 5535
Bosserman, Sarah R., 2536
Bosserman, Sarah R., 2735

Bostick, Ellen, 2602
Boswel, Benj., 3811
Boswel, Benj., 3812
Boswell, Anna M., 2945
Boswell, Benedict James, 2945
Boswell, F. C., 2945
Boteler, Thalia, 3927
Boteler, Thaliam, 4806
Boucher, Adam, 2499
Boucher, Adam, 2551
Boucher, Catharinae, 2499
Boucher, Catharine, 2551
Boucher, John Henry, 2551
Boucher, Sarah Virginia, 2499
Bouer, Anne, 2730
Bouer, Marry [sic] Cahterine, 2730
Bouer, Michel, 2730
Bougham, Catharinae, 1648
Bougham, Jacobi, 1648
Bougham, Thomas, 1648
Boughner, Adam, 2419
Boughner, Catherine, 2419
Boughner, Dolly Anne, 2419
Bouls, Ann, 186
Bourgoyne, Guglielmum, 3249
Bourgoyne, Maria, 3249
Boussenner, John, 317

Boward, [blank], 4105
Boward, Catherina V., 3714
Boward, Catherina V., 3714
Boward, Catherina, 3715
Boward, Henricum W., 3714
Boward, Jacobo, 3714
Boward, Jane R. (Mrs.), 5292
Boward, Lutie (Mrs.), 5365
Boward, Lydia S., 5411
Boward, Marg. (Mrs.), 5040
Boward, Mrs., 4888
Boward, Peter, 5412
Boward, Walter S., 4801
Bower, Catherine, 466
Bower, George, 466
Bower, Rosanna, 466
Bower, W.K., 4168
Bowers, Anna M., 4813
Bowers, Barbara, 3009
Bowers, Barbara, 3237
Bowers, Catharine, 64
Bowers, Joannem Michaelem, 3128
Bowers, Lebam, 3128
Bowers, Margareth Alice, 3009
Bowers, Mariam Ceciliam Jane, 3237
Bowers, Mary L., 4717

Bowers, Mathew, 493
Bowers, Michael, 3009
Bowers, Michaele, 3237
Bowers, Mitilda, 493
Bowers, Nick, 493
Bowers, Sara Joanna, 3128
Bowie (Black), Cornelius, 1884
Bowler, John, 4311
Bowles, Flavius Josephus, 3356
Bowles, Florence, 3356
Bowles, Joseph Minor Elmor, 3356
Bowls, Ann, 49
Bowman, Annam M., 4794
Bowman, Florence, 2837
Bowman, Jno., 2837
Bowman, Sybilla, 2837
Boxter, Danieli, 680
Boxter, Joannes Daniel, 680
Boxter, Maria, 680
Boyd, Margaret, 107
Boyd, Michael, 4970
Boyd, Otho James, 107
Boyd, William, 107
Boyle, Maria (Mrs.), 3894
Boyle, M.D., C.B., 3590
Boyle, M.D., C.B., 3592
Boyle, M.D., Carolum B., 4763

Boyle, Brook, 4098
Boyle, C. (Dr.), 3894
Boyle, C.B., 3340
Boyle, Caroles, 3233
Boyle, Carolo B., 3562
Boyle, Carolo B., 3630
Boyle, Carolo B., 3671
boyle, Carolo F., 3512
Boyle, Carolo, 3505
Boyle, Carolo, 3739
Boyle, Carolo, 3774
Boyle, Carolo, 3827
Boyle, Carolo, 3874
Boyle, Carolo, 4098
boyle, Carolum Bruce, 3512
Boyle, Carolus B., 3163
Boyle, Carolus B., 3178
Boyle, Carolus, 3216
Boyle, Catharina, 4098
Boyle, Charles, 3026
Boyle, Charles, 5372
Boyle, Dm (Mrs.), 4020
Boyle, Elisabeth, 5322
Boyle, Elizabeth Mary, 3505
Boyle, Francescum M., 3827
Boyle, Francis, 5217
Boyle, Helenam Theresiam, 3739

Boyle, Joannem Brooke, 3671
Boyle, Joseph B., 3512
Boyle, Joseph Franciscum, 3774
Boyle, Margaritem Mariam, 3874
Boyle, Maria Brook, 3512
boyle, Maria J., 3512
Boyle, Maria J., 3671
Boyle, Maria J., 3739
Boyle, Maria J., 3774
Boyle, Maria, 3505
Boyle, Maria, 3562
Boyle, Maria, 3630
Boyle, Maria, 3827
Boyle, Maria, 3874
Boyle, Maria, 3900
Boyle, Maria, 4098
Boyle, Mariam Catherinam, 3562
Boyle, Mariam Josephinam, 3630
Boyle, Mary (Mrs.), 5351
Boyle, Robertum Bruce, 4098
Boyse, John, 51
Braderick, James Patrick, 2053
Braderick, Margaret, 2053
Braderick, Patrick, 2053
Bradley, Mary, 2034
Bradley, Guillelmi, 948
Bradley, Jacob, 4197

Bradley, Philip, 2681
Bradley, Philippus, 3104
Bradley, Susannae, 948
Bradley, Thomas E., 948
Bradly, Bridget (widow), 4285
Bradly, Corneleus, 229
Bradly, Jacob, 230
Bradly, John Harrison, 437
Bradly, Margret, 322
Bradly, Milley, 230
Bradly, Susan, 322
Bradly, Susanna, 437
Bradly, Wilm, 230
Bradly, Wilm, 322
Bradly, Wilm, 437
Brady, Amia, 1536
Brady, Anna, 1465
Brady, Anna, 1764
Brady, Annae, 1292
Brady, Annae, 1465
Brady, Annae, 1536
Brady, Annae, 854
Brady, Bernardus, 4433
Brady, Carolus, 1399
Brady, Catharina, 3132
Brady, Catharinae, 794
Brady, Catharine, 1967

Brady, Catherine, 3060
Brady, Charles, 1940
Brady, Eleonora, 854
Brady, Hugh, 2072
Brady, Hugh, 854
Brady, Hugo, 1723
Brady, Hugonis, 1292
Brady, Hugonis, 1536
Brady, Jacobi, 794
Brady, Joannis, 1292
Brady, John, 123
Brady, John, 168
Brady, John, 4185
Brady, Julia, 3821
Brady, Julia, 3897
Brady, Juliam, 4828
Brady, Margarita, 3821
Brady, Margarita, 4135
Brady, Margret, 4202
Brady, Maria, 1795
Brady, Maria, 4369
Brady, Mrs., 2017
Brady, Patricii, 1465
Brady, Patricius, 1536
Brady, Susanna, 169
Brady, Terrentius, 1521
Brady, Thomas, 1726

Brady, Thomas, 794
Bragonier, Angelina, 960
Bragonier, Elisabeth, 960
Braker, Maria, 3728
Branan, Ann, 2438
Branan, Joannis, 913
Branan, Maria, 913
Branan, Mariae, 913
Branan, Mary, 2301
Branan, Richard, 2438
Brandon, Thomas, 3091
Branigan, Elisabeth, 1317
Brann[s?], Anna, 1727
Brann[s?], Elleonorae, 1727
Brann[s?], Patricii, 1727
Brannan, Bridget, 1940
Brannan, Bridget, 1962
Brannan, John, 1940
Brannan, Mary, 128
Brannan, Mary, 129
Brannan, Mary, 130
Brannan, Patrick, 1940
Brannan, Sarah, 128
Brannan, Sarah, 129
Brannan, Sarah, 127
Brannan, Sarah, 130
Brannan, Sarah, 2859

Brannon, [blank], 1401
Brannon, Anna, 1764
Brannon, Birgittae, 1317
Brannon, Birgittae, 1764
Brannon, Catharina, 1504
Brannon, Elisabeth, 1317
Brannon, Elleonora, 4512
Brannon, Elleonorae, 1608
Brannon, Jacobus, 1323
Brannon, Jacobus, 1504
Brannon, Joannis, 1401
Brannon, John Thomas, 1401
Brannon, John, 1865
Brannon, Margareta, 1608
Brannon, Patricii, 1317
Brannon, Patricii, 1608
Brannon, Patricii, 1764
Brannon, Patricius, 1703
Brarail, James, 4305
Brauergarden, Maria Anna, 1135
Braungard, Gaspar, 1198
Braungard, Maria Anna, 1198
Braungard, Maria Anna, 1415
Braungarden, Theresa, 1628
Braungart, Gasparis, 1101
Braungart, Guillelinus, 1101
Braungart, Mariae Annae, 1101

Brawn, Enock, 2311
Braxten, Nathanael Joseph, 2829
Brazelle, Lon., 2867
Brazelle, Louisa, 2956
Brazil, Louisa, 3316
Brazille, Louisa, 3038
Bredley, Bertha E., 4066
Bredley, Georgio S., 4066
Bredley, Mariam Catharinam, 4066
Breen, Hannah, 3473
Breene, Margareta, 1528
Brehm, Maria Anna, 1129
Brehm, Mary Ann, 4447
Breine, N., 1161
Brennagin, Edward, 4347
Brennan, Francis, 3041
Brennan, Francis, 3042
Brennan, James, 3042
Brennan, Joseph, 3041
Brennan, Mary, 3041
Brennan, Mary, 3042
Brennen, M., 3610
Brent, Robert James, 4318
Breslin, Catharinae, 1661
Breslin, Michaelis, 1661
Breslin, William Henricus, 1661

Bressnam, Mary, 2522
Brewer, Nancy, 5298
Brezzler, Bertha, 4165
Brezzler, Georgio, 4165
Brezzler, Robertum Carolum, 4165
Brian, Margaret, 2445
Brian, Nora, 1303
Brickley, Gueillimi, 707
Brickley, Jacobus, 707
Brickley, Juliae, 707
Bridenburgh, Geo., 2712
Bridenburgh, Joanna Eva Cristina, 2712
Bridenburgh, Margaret, 2712
Bridenhoff, Joanne, 3611
Bridget, Bridget, 1868
Brien, Adalaide, 4983
Brien, Mary, 4964
Brien, Virginia, 2632
Briene, Margareta, 1528
Brierer, Henrietta, 421
Brierer, Joseph, 421
Brierer, Mitilda, 421
Brining, Clara J., 3487
Brinkman, Henry William, 2016
Brinkman, Maria Sophia, 2016
Brinkman, William, 2016

Brinn, Hy., 4638
Brisco, Catherina, 3715
Brisco, Jacobo, 3715
Brisco, Malverna Teresa, 3715
Brisco, Robt, 5211
Brisco, Sara, 1103
Briscoe, Addore, 3732
Briscoe, Daniele, 3732
Briscoe, Robert Ambrose, 3732
Briscoe, Joannes, 4432
Briscol, Emma, 2415
Brislan, Martha, 162
Brislan, Rachel, 162
Brit?, Joannis, 699
Brit?, Julia, 699
Brit?, Winifred, 699
Britner, Julia, 2901
Britner, Catharinem, 3777
Britner, Julia, 3609
Britner, Julia, 3666
Britner, Julia, 3777
Britner, Sara Agneto, 3609
Britner/Britmer, Sarah A., 2901
Britt, Jacobi, 1402
Britt, Jacobus, 1402
Britt, Mariae, 1402
Britt, Patrick, 2176

Britt, Thomas, 1704
Brittner, Catharina, 3147
Brittner, Clemens, 3108
Brittner, Clemens, 3193
Brittner, Clemente, 3147
Brittner, Clemente, 3187
Brittner, Clementem, 4727
Brittner, Elisabeth, 3108
Brittner, Elizabeth, 2989
Brittner, Elizabeth, 3187
Brittner, Josephum W., 3147
Brittner, Julia A., 3193
Brittner, Julia, 4727
Brittner, Lemem Predestin, 3187
Brittner, Miss, 3269
Brittner, Mrs., 3536
Brittner, Sara A.., 3536
Brittner, Sara Agneto, 3108
Brittner, Sara, 3193
Brittner, Sarah, 2989
Brittner, Sarah, 3269
Brockelman, Otilia, 4685
Broderick, Dna [na is superscript] Romana, 3382
Broderick, Ella, 2674
Broderick, Jno. (Mrs.), 3111
Broderick, Johanna, 2242

Broderick, Mariae, 1497
Broderick, Mary, 2908
Broderick, Patrick, 2319
Broderick, Richardi, 1497
Broderick, Richd., 5682
Broderick, William B., 1497
Brofy, Camelii, 1651
Brofy, Elisabeth, 1651
Brofy, Maria, 1651
Brofy, Thomas, 4363
Brogan, Anna, 901
Brogan, Maria, 1203
Brogan, Maria, 1107
Brogan, Mariae, 1107
Brogan, Mariae, 901
Brogan, Mary, 2015
Brogan, Patrick, 2191
Brogan, Thomae, 1107
Brogan, Thomae, 901
Broghal, Jno, 89
Brogunier, Daisie, 4836
Brogunier, Lauram L., 4836
Bromgart, Caspar, 1963
Bromgart, Jacob Caspar, 1963
Bromgart, Mary Ellen, 1963
Brooks [or Brook], Chance, 3900
Brooks [or Brook], Emma, 3900

Brooks [or Brook], Mariam Josephinam, 3900
Brooks, Gen. H. (Mrs.), 5049
Brooks, James, 275
Brooks, James, 477
Brooks, Louisa, 3035
Brooks, Louisa, 4669
Brooks, Margret, 275
Brooks, Mary, 275
Brophy, Eleanora Loretto, 3571
Brophy, Joannem Reilly, 3571
Brophy, Synesius M., 3571
Brosnehen, Danial, 4273
Brosy, Cornls, 220
Broungarden, Gaspar, 1592
Broungarden, Mari Anna, 1592
Brower, Winfred, 208
Brown, Ann, 2962
Brown, Anna, 3303
Brown, Georgium Albertem, 3207
Brown, Jennie, 3207
Brown, Joanni, 3207
Brown, John, 5106
Brown, Sarah, 4592
Brown, Agnes, 5446
Brown, Alsw, 327
Brown, Ambrosius A., 4823

Brown, Andrew, 254
Brown, Anna, 3107
Brown, Anna, 4678
Brown, Annie (Mrs.), 5078
Brown, Annie, 3037
Brown, Carolum W., 4915
Brown, Catharine R., 2456
Brown, Catharine, 2386
Brown, Catharine, 2392
Brown, Clara, 5451
Brown, Eleonorae, 1456
Brown, Elisabeth, 1521
Brown, Elleonora, 1456
Brown, Emily, 2629
Brown, Fanney, 2123
Brown, Feby, 254
Brown, Franciscum L., 4784
Brown, Georgio, 3619
Brown, Ginnie [or Jinnie], 3037
Brown, Gulielmo, 3707
Brown, Gulielmum Foster, 4768
Brown, Harriet, 2311
Brown, Harriet, 5401
Brown, Harriet, 60
Brown, Helenem Elizabeth, 3707
Brown, Henney, 384
Brown, Henry J., 4587

Brown, Isaac, 176
Brown, Isaac, 2157
Brown, Isaac, 4526
Brown, Isaac, 60
Brown, Isac, 254
Brown, Jennie, 3207
Brown, Jennie, 3272
Brown, Jennie, 3329
Brown, Jerome Jacob, 3036
Brown, Jerome, 176
Brown, Jinnie, 3036
Brown, Joanes, 1275
Brown, Johanne, 3272
Brown, Johanne, 3329
Brown, John Francis, 2157
Brown, John Thomas, 3084
Brown, John, 3036
Brown, John, 3084
Brown, Julianna, 327
Brown, Le the [Lethe?]Ann, 1830
Brown, Lethe, 5456
Brown, Lewis, 2157
Brown, Lewis, 4526
Brown, Louisa, 4707
Brown, Loyd, 1830
Brown, Loyd, 4513
Brown, Mabel Virginiam, 3272

Brown, Margaret, 112
Brown, Margaritam Helenam, 3329
Brown, Maria, 4419
Brown, Mariam Agnetem, 3619
Brown, Mariam Agnetem, 3619
Brown, Mary (widow), 2521
Brown, Mary Am, 2458
Brown, Mary, 2157
Brown, Mary, 2311
Brown, Mary, 327
Brown, Mary, 4221
Brown, Mary, 4570
Brown, Matilda A., 5399
Brown, Mrs., 2726
Brown, Mrs., 378
Brown, P., 4593
Brown, Phebe, 176
Brown, Phebe, 2157
Brown, Phebe, 4953
Brown, Phebe, 60
Brown, Phil, 2330
Brown, Philip, 2401
Brown, Philip, 2363
Brown, Philip, 2374
Brown, Philip, 2379
Brown, Philip, 2393

Brown, Philip, 2395
Brown, Philip, 2423
Brown, Philip, 2467
Brown, Philip, 2518
Brown, Philip, 4592
Brown, Philip, 4594
Brown, Philip, 4596
Brown, Rosa, 2554
Brown, Rosetta, 1830
Brown, S., 4593
Brown, Samuel, 5400
Brown, Sara, 1802
Brown, Sara, 1803
Brown, Sarah, 2058
Brown, Sarah, 2241
Brown, Sarah, 2336
Brown, Sarah, 2363
Brown, Sarah, 2395
Brown, Sarah, 2440
Brown, Sarah, 2490
Brown, Sarah, 2504
Brown, Sarah, 2518
Brown, Sarah, 3619
Brown, Sarah, 3619
Brown, Sarah, 4594
Brown, Sarah, 4605
Brown, Thomae, 1456

Brown, Uncle, 4982
Brown, Vertie, 4064
Brown, Vertie, 4884
Brown, Vertie, 4112
Brown, Virginia, 3084
Brown, Wefred, 426
Brown, Winny, 141
Brown, Winny, 80
Brown, Wm., 2734
Browne, Elisabeth, 749
Browne, Maria, 749
Browne, Murrough Graydan, 749
Browngarden, Gasparis, 1762
Browngarden, Mariae Annae, 1762
Browngarden, Michael, 1762
Brownyard, Gaspar, 1345
Brunsdey, Henrico, 3332
Bruskey, Ernesti, 1284
Bruskey, Mariae Catharina, 1284
Bruskey, Sophia, 1284
Bryan, Jerome, 176
Bryan, Phebe, 176
Bryan, Francescam Joseph, 3780
Bryan, Georgio M., 3497
Bryan, Georgio M., 3554
Bryan, Georgio M., 3780
Bryan, Georgium M., 4738

Bryan, Gulielmum Laurentium, 3497
Bryan, Jane, 2269
Bryan, Margaret Ann Elizabeth, 2548
Bryan, Mariam Annam Josephinam, 3554
Bryan, Phebe, 60
Bryan, Theresa, 3780
Bryan, Theresia R., 3554
Bryan, Theresia, 3497
Bryload, Virginia, 4668
Buahner, Adam, 4567
Buchanan, Harriet A. (Miss), 4611
Buckhart, Catharine, 2379
Buckhart, Catharine, 2380
Buckhart, Catharine, 2381
Buckley, Cornelius, 1319
Buckley, Cornelius, 2148
Buckman, Elisabeth Joanna, 805
Buckman, Helenae, 805
Buckman, Phineas, 805
Bufley, Virginia, 4800
Bugho, Catharina, 1724
Buhrman, Daisy V., 4878
Buley, Joseph, 5000
Bulger, Joannes, 1411

Bulliard, Margaret, 3011
Bumyard, Mary, 4647
Burck, Maria, 1451
Burck, Maria, 1452
Burck, Mariae, 1452
Burck, Ulick, 1452
Burd, Elias, 417
Burd, Harrietta, 417
Burd, Isiac, 417
Burdrich, Romaine E., 4741
Burds, Mary Ann, 4571
Burger, Adam, 3722
Burger, Adam, 3905
Burger, Adam, 3993
Burger, Adam, 4049
Burger, Adamo, 3660
Burger, Adamo, 3782
Burger, Adamo, 3831
Burger, Adamo, 3863
Burger, Adamo, 3933
Burger, Annam Rosaliam, 3863
Burger, Carolum Fredericum, 3782
Burger, Cecilia B., 5342
Burger, Ceciliam Bernardinam, 4049
Burger, Charlotta, 5606
Burger, Frederick Alponsum, 3993

Burger, Gulielmum Albertum, 3660
Burger, Luciam Elizabeth, 3722
Burger, Mariam Annam Margaritam, 3831
Burger, Minnie Catherinam, 3933
Burger, Minnie, 3782
Burger, Minnie, 3831
Burger, Minnie, 3993
Burger, Minnie, 4049
Burger, Mrs., 3912
Burger, Oscar Eduardum, 3905
Burger, Wilhelmina, 3722
Burger, Wilhelmina, 3660
Burger, Willelmina, 3933
Burger, Willhelmina, 3863
Burger, Willhelmina, 3905
Burgey, Joannes, 1595
Burgey, Ludavicus, 1225
Burgey, Rebeccae, 1225
Burgey, Rebeccae, 1595
Burgey, Shederic, 1595
Burgey, Shederick, 1225
Burghard, Rosa Anna, 1506
Burgie, Rebecca, 1309
Burgie, S., 1309
Burgoyne, John, 1854

Burgunty, Peter, 4224
Burk, Elizabeth, 13
Burk, William (Mrs.), 98
Burk, Eleanor, 98
Burk, Elizabeth Ann, 98
Burk, Jacob, 4218
Burk, Mary (widow), 4322
Burk, Nancy, 166
Burk, William, 13
Burk, William, 166
Burk, William, 98
Burkart, Jno, 4694
Burke, Maria, 4734
Burke, Mary, 2793
Burke, Miss, 2758
Burkett, Catharine, 3148
Burkhardt, Margarita, 4822
Burkhart, Catharine (Miss), 4541
Burkhart, Mrs., 4541
Burner, Edmundus Jos., 3818
Burning, Edwardus, 829
Burning, Francisiae, 829
Burning, Guillilmi Alexandri, 829
Burns, Catharina, 1232
Burns, John, 228
Burns, Mary (widow), 4331
Burns, Wm., 4719

Bury, Mary, 5539
Bury, Mary, 5586
Bury, James, 607
Bury, Anna, 732
Bury, Annae, 1037
Bury, Jacobi, 1037
Bury, Jacobus, 4362
Bury, Jacobus, 732
Bury, James, 593
Bury, Marias (son), 1037
Bury, Mrs. Bury, 607
Bury, Mrs., 522
Busch, Agnetem Catharinam, 3421
Busch, Annam Elizabeth, 3261
Busch, David Edgar, 3516
Busch, David, 3261
Busch, David, 3421
Busch, David, 3516
Busch, Margaret, 3261
Busch, Margaretta, 3421
Busch, Margaretta, 3421
Busch, Margaretta, 3516
Busey, Richard, 5131
Bush, Emma, 3900
Bush, Sarah, 5082
Busry, Elizabeth, 5120
Bussard, George R., 3798

Butler, Milly, 4197
Butler, Ann Carlisle, 103
Butler, Augustin, 374
Butler, Cath. Mary, 5701
Butler, Catharine, 178
Butler, Charity, 178
Butler, James, 18
Butler, James, 2262
Butler, Leonard, 374
Butler, Leonard, 434
Butler, Leonard, 178
Butler, Leonard, 434
Butler, Louisa Ann, 18
Butler, Lucy, 18
Butler, Mary, 92
Butler, Milly, 4197
Butler, Moses, 3378
Butler, Nancy, 151
Butler, Nancy, 418
Butler, Nancy, 1830
Butler, Nancy, 205
Butler, Nany, 330
Butler, Patience, 374
Butler, Patience, 434
Butler, Patrick, 2238
Butler, Rachel, 102
Butler, Sandy, 92

Butler, Sarah, 101
Butler, Sarah, 102
Butler, Sarah, 103
Butler, Thalia, 3734
Butler, Thomas, 92
Butler, Wm Henry, 101
Butter, John, 328
Butter, Leonard, 328
Butter, Patience, 328
Buttler, Catharinae, 739
Buttler, Ladovicus Henricus, 739
Buttler, Moses, 4730
Butz, Elizabeth, 1931
Butz, Jacob, 1931
Butz, Margaret Elizabeth, 1931
Byan, Catharine, 2278
Byas, Anna Virginia, 2629
Byas, Emily, 2629
Byas, Wm., 2629
Byers, Barbara, 2883
Byers, Chs. Elias, 2883
Byers, M., 2883
Byers, Margaret, 1946
Byers, Margaret, 1947
Byers, Margaret, 1948
Byolos, Upt. C., 626
Byr_, Ninney, 1542

Byrn, Annae, 1431
Byrn, Patricii, 1431
Byrn, Thomas, 1431
Byrn, Annae, 1127
Byrn, Maria, 1127
Byrn, Patricii, 1127
Byrn, Patricius, 1344
Byrnast, Guillelmus, 1094
Byrne, Birgita, 703
Byrne, Franciscae, 703
Byrne, Henry A., 4176
Byrne, Patritium M., 4908
Byrne, Pierce, 703
Byrnes, Anna, 763
Byrnes, Catharinae, 762
Byrnes, Catharinae, 763
Byrnes, Daniel, 2169
Byrnes, Edwardus, 762
Byrnes, Joannis, 762
Byrnes, Joannis, 763
Byrns, Catherina, 1572
Byrns, Catharina, 1442
Byrns, Edwardi, 1352
Byrns, Edwardus, 1352
Byrns, Eleonorae, 1352
Byrns, Guillelmus, 1166
Byrns, Jacobus, 1329

Byrns, Jacobus, 1570
Byrns, Joannae, 1144
Byrns, Maria, 1447
Byrns, Owen, 1572
Byrns, Patricii, 1144
Byrns, Rosa Anna, 1144
Byroads, [blank], 2827
Cada, Patricius, 1738
Cadam, Elisabeth, 1635
Cadam, Jacobi, 1635
Cadden, Elizabeth, 1910
Cadden, Elizabeth, 2114
Cadden, Elisabeth, 1729
Cadden, Elizabeth, 2155
Cadden, Jacobus, 1729
Cadden, James, 1910
Cadden, James, 1993
Caddes, Elizabeth, 2114
Caddes, Elizabeth, 2114
Caden, Elisabeth, 1296
Caden, Jacobi, 1296
Caden, Thomas, 1296
Cadlwell, blank, 744
Cadlwell, Patricii, 744
Cadlwell, Thomas, 744
Caffry, James, 226

Caffry, James, 226
Caffry, Mary, 226
Cahill, Jacobi, 747
Cahill, Jacobus Henricus, 747
Cahill, Mariae, 747
Caho, Wm., 1732
Cahoe, Annae, 852
Cahoe, Jacobus, 852
Cahoe, Thomae, 852
Cahoo, Anna, 1520
Cain, Annae, 1554
Cain, Catharine Josephina, 2041
Cain, Denis S.?, 1933
Cain, Denis, 2026
Cain, Denis, 2257
Cain, Denis, 2289
Cain, Denis, 2346
Cain, Denis, 2489
Cain, Denis, 4519
Cain, Dennis, 2041
Cain, Jacobi, 1554
Cain, Joannes, 1554
Cain, John Michael, 2289
Cain, Lavinia, 1933
Cain, Lavinia, 2041
Cain, Levenia, 2289
Cain, Mary Ann, 1933

Cain, Maurice, 2116
Caine, Birgitta, 1238
Caine, Birgitta, 942
Caine, Jacobi, 942
Caine, Mariae, 942
Caldwell, Philippus, 1232
Caleb, Ruth, 2457
Callaham, Dan, 2926
Callahan, Bridget, 2938
Callahen, Annae, 754
Callahen, Jacobus, 754
Callahen, Mary, 266
Callahen, Michal, 266
Callahen, Winfred, 266
Callan, Richard, 2246
Callan, Am, 2253
Callanan, Thomam J., 4866
Callohan, Joannes, 4365
Callon, Anna, 945
Callon, Annae, 945
Callon, Richard, 2246
Callon, Richardi, 945
Callon, Richardis, 1509
Calnam, Joannes, 822
Calnam, Joannis, 822
Calnam, Mariae, 822

Caloary, Elisabeth, 1376
Calory, Catharina, 1079
Calory, Elisabeth, 1079
Calory, Michaelis, 1079
Calory, Elisabeth, 1772
Calory, Michael, 4422
Caloury, Elisabeth, 1234
Caloury, Elisabeth, 1376
Calrol, Margret, 4279
Cambel, Catharina, 1571
Cambel, Catharina, 1740
Cambel, Catharinae, 1570
Cambel, Catharinae, 1740
Cambel, Elisabeth, 1178
Cambel, Jacobus, 1178
Cambel, Michael, 1345
Cambel, Michaelis, 1345
Cambel, Rebeccae, 1345
Cambel, Thomae, 1570
Cambel, Thomae, 1740
Cambel, Thomas, 1570
Cambel, Thomas, 1571
Cambell, Catharinae, 1413
Cambell, Catharine, 5419
Cambell, Jacobus, 1413
Camel, Betty, 422
Cameron, Sarah, 2598

Cameron, Thos. M., 2598
Cameron, Wm. Thos. Alexander, 2598
Cammel, Betsey, 438
Cammel, Catherine, 202
Cammel, Charles, 202
Cammel, Patrick, 202
Campbell, Catharine, 178
Campbell, Catharine, 137
Campbell, Charity, 178
Campbell, Grace, 2459
Campbell, Grace, 2709
Campbell, Grace, 5173
Campbell, Manley, 2709
Campbell, Patrick, 137
Campbell, Pk, 137
Campbell, Sarah Ellen, 2709
Canah, Margareta, 1433
Cane, Annae, 1141
Cane, Catherine, 444
Cane, Jacobi, 1141
Cane, Jacobus, 1499
Cane, Maria Anna, 1141
Cane, Patricius, 1152
Canedy, Birgitta, 1462
Canedy, Catharinae, 1462
Canedy, Dionysius, 1462

Canedy, Timothei, 1462
Cann, Laura, 3724
Cann, Lauram, 4808
Cannidy, Anna, 642
Canty, Michael, 4361
Cany, Thomas, 4266
Cardal, Mariae, 738
Cardal, Martini, 738
Cardal, Michael, 738
Cardell, Mariae, 1435
Cardell, Martini, 1435
Cardell, Petrus, 1435
Carener, Donald, 2644
Carener, Mary, 2644
Carener, Mary, 2671
Carener, Thos., 2644
Carey, Catharine, 2297
Carey, Joseph, 2297
Carey, Robert, 2297
Carey, Catharine, 1848
Carey, Catharine, 1983
Carey, Catharine, 2438
Carey, Catharine, 2473
Carey, Clara, 4067
Carey, John, 1848
Carey, Joseph, 1943
Carey, Joseph, 1848

Carey, Joseph, 1983
Carey, Joseph, 2438
Carey, Joseph, 2438
Carey, Joseph, 2473
Carey, Mary Ann, 1983
Carey, William Patrick, 2473
Carkaron, Annae, 1232
Carkaron, Jacobi, 1232
Carkaron, Philippus, 1232
Carl, Johanna, 1220
Carl, Margareta, 4475
Carl, Patricius, 1220
Carlan, Anna, 1019
Carlan, Eleonorae, 1019
Carlan, Joannis, 1019
Carley, Catharinae, 1683
Carley, Michael, 1683
Carley, Patricii, 1683
Carlin, Anna, 1479
Carlors, Anna, 4444
Carlos, Elisabeth, 1261
Carlos, Patricii, 1261
Carlos, Patricius, 1261
Carlosk, Birgittae, 1510
Carlosk, Michael, 1510
Carlosk, Patricii, 1510
Carlosk, Anna, 1495

Carlosk, Birgitta, 1742
Carlosk, Birgitta, 4487
Carlosk, Patricius, 1492
Carls, Danl., 5522
Carls, Danl., 2683
Cambel, Maria Anna, 1743
Cambel, Michaelis, 1743
Cambel, Rebeccae, 1743
Carney, "unknown", 2590
Carney, Birgittae, 940
Carney, Easter, 383
Carney, Easter, 552
Carney, Easter, 560
Carney, Easter, 563
Carney, Easter, 565
Carney, Eugenias, 4487
Carney, Magert (Miss), 528
Carney, Margareta, 940
Carney, Margret, 562
Carney, Margret, 569
Carney, Michaelis, 940
Carney, Mrs., 202
Carney, Owen, 1248
Carney, Rose, 2590
Carney, Sarah Jane, 2590
Carney, Sarah Jane, 4966
Carny, Criso?, 1168

Carr, Jacobus, 1627
Carr, Ann, 4178
Carr, Catharinae, 641
Carr, Catharine, 2535
Carr, Catharine, 2538
Carr, Eleanora Loretto, 3571
Carr, Jacobi, 1619
Carr, Jacobus, 1112
Carr, Jacobus, 1562
Carr, Joseph, 1619
Carr, Mary, 2057
Carr, Mary, 2162
Carr, Mr., 4178
Carr, Mr., 4178
Carr, Nancy (Mrs.), 3465
Carr, Nancy, 5140
Carr, Sara, 1112
Carr, Sara, 1562
Carr, Sara, 1627
Carr, Sarae, 1619
Carr, Sarah, 2022
Carragan, Martha, 91
Carrigan, James, 474
Carrighan, Joannus, 1782
Carrol, D. Williamson, 1502
Carrol, Eleonora, 925
Carrol, Eleonorae, 994

Carrol, Guillelmi, 994
Carrol, Guillelmi, 925
Carrol, H. Maria, 1502
Carrol, Henrietta Maria, 1502
Carrol, James, 372
Carrol, Jane, 1869
Carrol, Joannes, 994
Carrol, Johanna, 1699
Carrol, Johanna, 1700
Carrol, Margareta, 1700
Carrol, Margret, 372
Carrol, Maria, 925
Carrol, Mary Anna, 372
Carrol, Melaniae, 1502
Carrol, Patricii, 1700
Carrol, Patricius, 1766
Carrol, Patrick, 1869
Carrol, Patrick, 2079
Carrol, Susan, 1869
Carrol, William, 1502
Carroll, Henriettia, 1622
Carroll, Ellenora Jane, 1974
Carroll, Jane, 1974
Carroll, Judy (Miss), 4284
Carroll, Patrick, 1974
Carroll, Williamson, 1622
Carsner, Donald, 2644

Carsner, Mary, 2644
Carsner, Thos., 2644
Carter, Augustus, 116
Carter, Basil, 21
Carter, Jacob, 116
Carter, Jacob, 21
Carter, Leteie, 3917
Carter, Lutie, 4074
Carter, M., 4738
Carter, Mariam Helenam, 4074
Carter, Milly, 116
Carter, Milly, 21
Carter, Patritio, 3917
Carter, Patritio, 4074
Carter, Susannam Irenem, 3917
Cartors, Anna, 4444
Cary, Thomas, 4266
Casars, Jacobi, 1418
Casars, Margaritae, 1418
Casars, Michael, 1418
Case, Anna M., 3680
Case, Guglielmum J., 4764
Casey, Annae, 847
Casey, Mary, 590
Casey, Mathei, 847
Casey, Nicholaeus, 847
Casgro, Patricius, 1567

Cashman, Elisabeth (Mrs.), 4143
Cashman, Helena, 4143
Cashon, Anna, 1239
Cashon, Christiani, 1239
Cashon, Christophori, 816
Cashon, Christophorus, 1434
Cashon, Elisabeth, 1239
Cashon, Elisabeth, 1559
Cashon, Elisabeth, 816
Cashon, Michael, 816
Cassidy, Anna, 642
Cassidy, James, 4580
Cassidy, Lucas, 4458
Cassidy, Thomas, 1470
Casy, Birgittae, 1559
Casy, Christophorus, 1246
Casy, Elisabeth, 1785
Casy, Jacobus, 1785
Casy, Joannes, 4425
Casy, Patricii, 1559
Casy, Patricii, 1785
Casy, Patricius, 1559
Casy, Patrick, 1325
Casy, Samuel, 1559
Casy, Thomas, 4488
Catharinae, Catharina, 674
Catharinae, Catharine, 674

Catharinae, Joannis, 674
Cather, John H., 5290
Catlett, Ann, 2127
Catlett, Margaret Ann (Miss), 4534
Catlett, Margaret, 2040
Catlett, Margaret, 2294
Caton, Maria, 1552
Caton, Michael, 2179
Cauber, Maria, 1718
Cauber, Maria, 1722
Caudey, Catharina, 1215
Caudey, Dionysiius, 1215
Caudey, Matildis, 1215
Caudy, Catharina, 4424
Caughman, Helena, 3341
Caughman, Helena, 3342
Caughman, Helena, 3343
Caughman, Helena, 3344
Caughman, Helena, 3345
Caughman, Maria, 3346
Caughman, Maria, 3347
Caughman, Maria, 3348
Caughman, Maria, 3349
Caughman, Maria, 3350
Cavan, Charles, 4302
Cavana, Ellon (widow), 4286
Cavanaugh, Anna, 890

Cavanaugh, Birgitta, 1095
Cavanaugh, Birgitta, 1453
Cavanaugh, Catharina, 934
Cavanaugh, Mariae, 890
Cavanaugh, Rosae Annae, 934
Cavanaugh, Thomae, 890
Cavanaugh, Thomae, 934
Cavener, Elisa, 588
Cavin, Daniel, 2805
Cavin, Mary, 2805
Cavin, Mary, 2805
Cearfoss, Augustam Margaritam, 4156
Cearfoss, Gulielmo, 4041
Cearfoss, Gulielmo, 4096
Cearfoss, Gulielmo, 4156
Cearfoss, Gulielmum M., 3964
Cearfoss, Margt., 3964
Cearfoss, Neormam Esther, 4041
Cearfoss, Rosa (Mrs.), 4101
Cearfoss, Rosa, 4041
Cearfoss, Rosa, 4096
Cearfoss, Rosa, 4156
Cearfoss, Roscoe Vincentium, 4096
Cearfoss, Simone, 3964

Celuflin, Jennie (Mrs.), 2785
Cephas, Joanne, 3696
Cephas, Maria E, 3696
Cephas, Maria E, 3696
Cephas, Mariam Francescam, 3696
Cerns, John, 4202
Cevell, Elizabeth, 3183
Cevell, Hester Virginiam, 3183
Cevell, Joseph, 3183
Cew, Elizabeth, 3031
Cew, Patrick, 3031
Chaldon, Margareta, 1555
Chamberlan, Elizabeth, 2062
Chamberlan, Elizabeth, 2063
Chamberlan, Elizabeth, 2064
Chambers, Mary, 2927
Chambers, Anastasia, 2329
Chambers, Anastasia, 2351
Chambers, Emmeline, 3049
Chambers, Helen C., 5748
Chambers, James, 4195
Chambers, John, 2314
Chambers, John, 2351
Chambers, Margaret, 2351
Chambers, Mary Elizabeth, 3049
Chambers, Mary, 2972
Chambers, Michael, 2927

Chambers, Miss, 3092
Chambers, Rebecca, 546
Chambers, Thomas, 2394
Chambers, Thomas, 3049
Chambers, Thomas, 5405
Chane, John, 4220
Chaney, Barbara, 3231
Chaney, Barbara, 3423
Chaney, Ezechiel, 3231
Chaney, Joanne, 3231
Chaney, Johanne, 3423
Chaney, Sarah, 3423
Chapman, Anna, 2075
Chapman, Patricius, 1355
Chapman, Patrick, 4248
Chase (slave), Peggy, 18
Chase, Catherine, 459
Chase, Cloe, 136
Chase, Cloe, 102
Chase, Cloi, 45
Chase, Harry, 136
Chase, Henry, 45
Chase, John, 4220
Chase, John, 459
Chase, Judith, 45
Chase, Margaret, 47
Chase, Marymagdalene, 136

Chase, Peggy, 459
Chearfoss, Rosa, 4892
Cheelsman, William, 4706
Cheney, Albertum, 3427
Cheney, Barbara, 3427
Cheney, Johanne, 3427
Chephar, Elisabeth, 2777
Chephur, Mary Elisabeth, 2716
Chesley, Alexander, 35
Chesley, Charlotte (Mrs.), 5331
Chesley, Clary, 35
Chesley, Oliver, 35
Chester, Anna (Miss), 290
Chester, Anna (Miss), 394
Chester, Anna (Miss), 448
Chester, Anna (Miss), 620
Chester, Anna, 254
Chester, Mrs., 354
Chichester, Anna, 4362
Chinescides, Christofor, 296
Chinescides, Sally, 296
Chirick, Henry J., 4136
Chisel, Clare, 385
Chisel, Cloey, 385
Chisel, Oliver, 385
Chisley, Oliver, 37
Chisley, Oliver, 38

Chistopher, Elisabeth, 4448
Chopman?, Mariae, 1258
Chopman?, N, 1258
Chopman?, Patricius, 1258
Chricton, Catharinam Margaretam, 4068
Chricton, Gulielmo A., 4068
Chricton, Maria, 4068
Chricton, Gulielmo A., 4893
Chricton, Gulielmum A., 4887
Chrieton, Francescum Joseph, 4131
Chrieton, Gulielmo, 4131
Chrieton, Maria, 4131
Christopher, Emilia, 1208
Clabaugh, Mary (Mrs.), 5284
Clabaugh, Mary, 2406
Clabaugh, Mary, 2498
Clabaugh, Mary, 2537
Clabaugh, Mary, 2834
Clabaugh, Mary, 2960
Clabaugh, Mary, 3036
Clabaugh, Mary, 3048
Clabaugh, Mary, 3057
Clabaugh, Mary, 4609
Clabaugh, Mary, 4610
Claffey, Birgitta, 1056
Claffey, Caroli, 1457

Claffey, Carolus, 1487
Claffey, Charoli, 1056
Claffey, Ester, 1457
Claffey, Ester, 1487
Claffey, Esther, 1056
Claffey, Jacobus, 1457
Claflin, Era W. (Capt), 4660
Claflin, Ira W., 2788
Claflin, Jane, 2788
Claflin, Mary Cooper, 2788
Claibaugh, Maria, 3511
Clane, Nelly, 2904
Clane, Georgia, 3693
Clansey, Jeremias, 1420
Clapsadal, Mrs., 501
Clapsaddal, Thoms. Faulen, 487
Clapsaddle, "unknown", 428
Clapsaddle, daughter, 428
Clapsaddle, Otho, 428
Clapsadel, Mrs., 350
Clarbaugh, Mary, 2964
Clarbaugh, Mary, 4710
Clarck, Carolus, 1223
Clarck, Catharinae, 1205
Clarck, Jacobi, 1205
Clarck, Joannes Alexander, 1105
Clarck, Loghan, 1205

Clarck, Margareta, 1126
Clarck, Margareta, 1205
Clarck, Maria, 1118
Clarck, Mariae, 1105
Clare, Nelly, 2904
Clark, Margt., 2896
Clark, Regina, 3244
Clark [or Clarke], Margt., 2839
Clark, Ann, 4963
Clark, Anna, 4932
Clark, Birgitta, 1193
Clark, Birgittae, 1193
Clark, Caroli, 1312
Clark, Carolus Dominicus, 1312
Clark, Carolus, 3146
Clark, Carolus, 3147
Clark, Catharinae, 1302
Clark, Catharinae, 880
Clark, Catharine Ann, 2134
Clark, Catharine, 2143
Clark, Catharine, 2261
Clark, Catharine, 2519
Clark, Catherine, 3010
Clark, Charles, 2064
Clark, Charles, 2142
Clark, Charles, 2519
Clark, Charles, 3261

Clark, Charles, 5488
Clark, Chs., 2896
Clark, Edward, 3010
Clark, Ella, 3186
Clark, Ella, 3244
Clark, H., 3668
Clark, Henry Myers, 2519
Clark, Henry Philip, 5699
Clark, Hugh, 3244
Clark, Jacobi, 880
Clark, Jacobus, 1260
Clark, Jacobus, 1302
Clark, James, 2519
Clark, James, 5489
Clark, Joannis, 1260
Clark, John, 131
Clark, John, 132
Clark, John, 147
Clark, Kate, 2838
Clark, Kate, 2896
Clark, Laurentii, 1193
Clark, Maggie, 3055
Clark, Mar., 2838
Clark, Margaret, 1904
Clark, Margaret, 2142
Clark, Margaret, 2142
Clark, Margaret, 2519

Clark, Margaret, 3261
Clark, Margaret, 3411
Clark, Margareta, 1604
Clark, Margareta, 3754
Clark, Margaretae, 1312
Clark, Margaritae, 1260
Clark, Margaritta, 3478
Clark, Mary, 3030
Clark, Patricii, 1302
Clark, Patricius, 1162
Clark, Patricius, 4424
Clark, Patrick, 2063
Clark, Regina Angela, 5710
Clark, Regina, 3056
Clark, Regina, 3182
Clark, Sr., Catharine, 2214
Clark, Thomas, 880
Clark, William, 4412
Clarke, Margareta, 1674
Clarke, Chas., 2583
Clarke [sic], Catharine, 2313
Clarke, Aloysius, 5430
Clarke, Andreas, 1674
Clarke, Andreas, 1368
Clarke, Andreas, 1558
Clarke, Andreas, 4495
Clarke, Anna, 2583

Clarke, Augustine, 5437
Clarke, Carolo, 4729
Clarke, Carolus, 1604
Clarke, Caroly, 1660
Clarke, Cath, 2351
Clarke, Catharina, 640
Clarke, Catharina Anna, 4484
Clarke, Catharina, 1659
Clarke, Catharina, 1692
Clarke, Catharina, 1736
Clarke, Catharina, 3944
Clarke, Catharina, 4005
Clarke, Catharina, 4123
Clarke, Catharina, 641
Clarke, Catharinae, 1604
Clarke, Catharinae, 641
Clarke, Catharine Alice, 2191
Clarke, Catharine J. (Miss), 4617
Clarke, Catharine J., 2566
Clarke, Catharine, 2001
Clarke, Catharine, 2002
Clarke, Catharine, 2008
Clarke, Catharine, 2126
Clarke, Catharine, 2191
Clarke, Catharine, 2439
Clarke, Catharine, 2444
Clarke, Chareli, 806

Clarke, Charles, 1970
Clarke, Charles, 2451
Clarke, Charles, 2451
Clarke, Charles, 3011
Clarke, Charles, 4559
Clarke, Charles, 4617
Clarke, Charles's wife, 4559
Clarke, Chas., 2583
Clarke, Chas., 2585
Clarke, Edward, 2444
Clarke, Eliza M., 1989
Clarke, Ella, 3130
Clarke, Ellam A., 4726
Clarke, Ellen Alice, 1970
Clarke, Guillelmi, 1385
Clarke, Guillelmi, 1644
Clarke, Harry, 2925
Clarke, Henricus, 3096
Clarke, Hugh C.C., 5761
Clarke, Hugo, 3177
Clarke, Jacobus Patricius, 1660
Clarke, Jacobus Sebastainus, 1644
Clarke, James, 2059
Clarke, Jas., 2754
Clarke, Joannes W., 1385
Clarke, Joannis, 1560
Clarke, Joannis, 641

Clarke, John, 1544
Clarke, Ludavicus, 1751
Clarke, Margaret (Mrs.), 4617
Clarke, Margaret Eliza, 2451
Clarke, Margaret, 1970
Clarke, Margaret, 2583
Clarke, Margareta, 1223
Clarke, Margaretae, 1385
Clarke, Margaretae, 1644
Clarke, Margaretae, 1660
Clarke, Margaretae, 1751
Clarke, Margaretae, 806
Clarke, Margaretae, 3612
Clarke, Margarita, 3613
Clarke, Margarita, 3668
Clarke, Margarita, 3931
Clarke, Margaritae, 1560
Clarke, Margaritta, 3096
Clarke, Margaritta, 4726
Clarke, Margaritta, 4729
Clarke, Maria Elleonora, 1604
Clarke, Maria, 3130
Clarke, Maria, 806
Clarke, Mary A., 2566
Clarke, Mary Ann, 2444
Clarke, Mary C., 1967
Clarke, Mary Catharine, 2191

Clarke, Mary Catharine, 2192
Clarke, Mary, 2451
Clarke, Mary, 2552
Clarke, Mary, 2583
Clarke, Mary, 3011
Clarke, Mrs., 3613
Clarke, Patricii, 1604
Clarke, Patricius A.,, 1692
Clarke, Patricius, 1660
Clarke, Patrick, 2126
Clarke, Patrick, 2191
Clarke, Patrick, 2435
Clarke, Regina, 2451
Clarke, Rosa, 4005
Clarke, Thomas, 1560
Clarke, Thomas, 1527
Clarke, Thomas, 1560
Clarke, Thomas, 4583
Clarke, William, 1751
Clarkson, Alice Margaret, 2752
Clarkson, Alice, 5143
Clarkson, Cath., 2642
Clarkson, Cath., 2834
Clarkson, Catharine, 2314
Clarkson, Catherine, 5210
Clarkson, Christie A. Marg., 5709

Clarkson, Christie, 5102
Clarkson, Edw., 5079
Clarkson, Edward, 2314
Clarkson, Edward, 2752
Clarkson, Edward, 2753
Clarkson, Edward, 3064
Clarkson, Edwd., 2642
Clarkson, Edwd., 2834
Clarkson, Elis., 5642
Clarkson, Elisabeth, 2752
Clarkson, Elizabeth, 3729
Clarkson, Elizabeth, 4784
Clarkson, Elizabetha, 3657
Clarkson, Ellen, 2752
Clarkson, Ellen, 2753
Clarkson, Ellen, 2753
Clarkson, Geo., 2834
Clarkson, George, 2314
Clarkson, George, 5660
Clarkson, Helena, 3644
Clarkson, Helena, 4790
Clarkson, Jacob Henry, 2642
Clarkson, Jacob, 5062
Clarkson, Wm. David, 2834
Clay, Charlotte, 1903
Clay, Francis, 1903
Clay, Joseph, 1903

Clay, Flora, 1941
Clay, Flora, 2017
Clay, Francisca, 2349
Clay, Jacob, 1941
Clay, Jacob, 2014
Clay, Jacob, 2017
Clay, Jacob, 2344
Clay, Jacob, 2349
Clay, John, 2017
Clay, Mary M., 2409
Clay, Susanna, 1941
Claybaugh, Maria, 3104
Clayborne, Alfreda G., 5135
Clayborne, Georgium P., 3096
Clayborne, Joanne B., 3096
Clayborne, John B., 4677
Clayborne, Sara, 3096
Clayburn, Davis, 4149
Clayburn, Joanne W., 4148
Clayburn, Juliam Lane, 4148
Clayburn, Margaret Elisabeth, 4149
Clayburn, Albertam Gertrude, 3301
Clayburn, Anna, 3921
Clayburn, Annie L., 5335
Clayburn, Augustum Aloysium, 3430
Clayburn, Georgium D., 4857
Clayburn, Jahanne, 3230
Clayburn, Jesse F., 4879
Clayburn, Jesse Franciscum, 3230
Clayburn, Johanne, 3430
Clayburn, Johanni, 3301
Clayburn, John, 3062
Clayburn, Jos. P., 5335
Clayburn, Joseph Paulus, 3921
Clayburn, Laura Anna, 3062
Clayburn, Lettie A., 4879
Clayburn, N.N., 3921
Clayburn, Sallie (Mrs.), 4857
Clayburn, Sallie, 3062
Clayburn, Sallie, 3230
Clayburn, Sallie, 3430
Clayburn, Sallie, 3921
Clayburn, Sallie, 4149
Clayburn, Sarah, 3301
Clayburn, William Carroll, 5364
Clayburne, Augustus, 5285
Clayman, Peter, 2276
Cleary, M., 2707
Clegett, "unknown", 530
Clegett, Elisa, 530
Clegett, Mary Elisabeth, 530
Clei, Florae, 1507
Clei, Jacobi, 1507
Clei, William, 1507
Clemens, Alexandre, 1384
Clemens, Joannes Upton, 1384
Clemens, Mathildis, 1384
Clemens, Alexander, 677
Clemens, Alexandri, 1596
Clemens, Alexandri, 1757
Clemens, Alfredus Petrus, 1757
Clemens, Charles, 1945
Clemens, Edward Thomas, 1945
Clemens, Matilda, 1945
Clemens, Matildis, 1596
Clemens, Matildis, 1757
Clemens, Matildis, 677
Clemens, Sophia, 677
Clemens, W. Henricus, 1596
Clement, Alexandri, 1039
Clement, Alexandri, 1040
Clement, Anna, 1039
Clement, Charolus, 1040
Clement, Matildas, 1040
Clement, Matildis, 1039
Clements, Irena A., 3691
Clements, Irene A., 3839
Clements, Ireniam Deliam, 3691
Clements, Joanne L., 3691
Clements, Joanne, 3839
Clements, Joannem L., 4785
Clements, Ruth Helenam, 3839
Clemons, Alex, 578
Clemons, Louisa, 578
Clemons, Matilda, 578
Cletner, Susan, 1954
Clevidence, H.A., 4878
Cley, Florae, 1507
Cley, Jacobi, 1507
Cley, William, 1507
Cleybarne, Sally, 2893
Cleyburne, Jno., 2865
Cleyburne, Norman Eugene, 2865
Cleyburne, Sally, 2865
Cline, Basebom, 529
Cline, Susan, 529
Clingam, Miss Mary E., 1970
Clingan, Thomas, 1835
Clingan, Dorothea, 1835
Clingan, Nettie, 5258
Clitner, Josephi, 1427
Clitner, Josephi, 1760
Clitner, Rosa Anna, 1760
Clitner, Sarae Joannae, 1427
Clitner, Sarae Joannae, 1760
Clitner, Susanna, 1427
Clofy, Charoli, 667

Clofy, Estheris, 667
Clofy, Joannes, 667
Clopper, Jacobo A., 3889
Clopper, Jacobum A., 4827
Clopper, Lucinda, 4827
Clopper, Maria, 3889
Clopper, Odelia Mariam, 3889
Clougherty, Mary, 23
Clougherty, Mary, 24
Coale, "unknown", 3318
Coale, Catharina, 3318
Coale, Susan Catharinam, 3318
Coale, Catharina, 3318
Coale, Susan Catharinam, 3318
Coany, Patricius, 1349
Coashman, Birg, 688
Coashman, Coashman, 688
Coashman, Thomas, 688
Cobb, Joanni Calvin Hayes, 3895
Cobler, Mr. & Mrs., 4521
Cocamer, Ellon, 309
Cocamer, Mary, 309
Cocamer, Thomas, 309
Coch, Caroline, 2433
Cochran, Birgitta, 1435
Cochran, Thomas, 1435
Codelon, Andreas, 974

Codelon, Maria Anna, 974
Codelon, Mariae, 974
Coderi, Carolo, 4887
Codori, Eduardo, 4051
Codori, Emmam G., 4051
Codori, Cornelia, 3909
Codori, Emma (Mrs.), 4170
Codori, Emma, 3986
Codori, Francisco, 3986
Codori, Franciscus (Mrs.), 4068
Codori, Franciscus, 4068
Codori, Georgio, 3909
Codori, Georgium Ludovicum, 3909
Codori, Maria, 4170
Codori, Mrs., 3909
Codori, Mrs., 4890
Codori, Nettie Frances, 3986
Codori, Sr, Mrs., 4051
Codori, Susan (Mrs.), 4053
Codori, Susanna (Mrs.), 3986
Cofelly, Patricius, 1292
Coffee, Danniel, 1137
Coffee, Judith, 1362
Coffee, Judith, 1425
Coffee, Maria, 1362
Coffee, Patricius, 1265

Coffee, Thomae, 1362
Coffee, Thomas, 1445
Coffeel, Patricius, 1304
Coffer [or Coffee], Catharina, 1738
Coffer [or Coffee], Judith, 1738
Coffer [or Coffee], Thomae, 1738
Coffey, Anna, 2075
Coffey, John, 2075
Coffey, Judith, 1077
Coffey, Mary, 2531
Coffey, Maurice, 2522
Coffey, Michael, 1077
Coffey, Thomae, 1077
Coffey, Thomas, 2075
Coffieb, Birgitta, 1362
Coffile, Maria, 1271
Coffman, Maria, 3708
Coghlin, Annae, 876
Coghlin, Maria, 876
Coghlin, Petri, 876
Cogle, Elisabeth, 2732
Cogle, Jas. Wm., 2732
Cogle, Joseph, 2732
Cohrin, Andy (Mrs.), 585
Coil, Mary, 3041
Coil, Mary, 3042
Coile, Edward, 444

Coile, Elisa, 444
Coile, Tobias John, 444
Coin, Patricius, 1254
Colbert, Mary, 2157
Colbert, Mary, 4526
Cole, Andrew, 308
Cole, Anna M., 4868
Cole, Anna, 453
Cole, Anna, 533
Cole, Catharine, 2386
Cole, Catherine, 534
Cole, Frances, 2293
Cole, Frances, 2506
Cole, Frances, 4955
Cole, Francesa, 256
Cole, George Emory, 2386
Cole, George, 249
Cole, Gulielmum Albertum, 4868
Cole, Henery, 453
Cole, Henry, 249
Cole, Henry, 308
Cole, Henry, 344
Cole, Henry, 403
Cole, Henry, 403
Cole, John, 344
Cole, Loretta, 4868
Cole, Mary (Mrs.), 453

Cole, Mary, 249
Cole, Mary, 308
Cole, Mary, 344
Cole, Mary, 395
Cole, Mary, 403
Cole, Mary, 453
Cole, Mary, 519
Cole, Michl, 519
Cole, Micl, 395
Cole, Philip, 533
Cole, Philip, 534
Cole, Samuel, 2386
Cole, Sarah (Miss), 519
Cole, Sophia Milia, 519
Cole, Sophia, 533
Cole, Sophia, 534
Cole, Wilm Henry, 395
Coleman, Eausa, 364
Coleman, Eliza, 1832
Coleman, Henny, 124
Coleman, Henny, 364
Coleman, John, 1832
Coleman, Nancy, 364
Colens, Maria, 4378
Colens, Catharina, 1511
Colens, Joannes, 1511
Colens, Joannis, 1104

Colens, Joannis, 1511
Colens, Johanna, 1104
Colens, Mariae, 1104
Colens, Mariae, 1511
Colens, Petrus, 4415
Colerty, Patricius, 1291
Coleus, Catharina, 1203
Coleus, Petri, 1203
Coleus, Rosa, 1525
Coleus, Rosae, 1203
Colkleper, Thos., 4640
Collagan, Catherine, 203
Collagan, James, 203
Collagan, Mary, 203
Collegan, Catherine (widow), 4211
Collen, Michael, 1278
Collens, John, 539
Collens, Margret, 539
Collens, Mary, 5806
Collens, Mechl, 539
Collier, Catharine, 1858
Collier, Catharine, 1859
Colligan, Mrs., 260
Collighan, Jacobi, 1543
Collighan, Jacobus, 1543
Collighan, Margaretae, 1543
Collighan, Maria, 1283

Collins, Margt., 2864
Collins, Anna M., 4077
Collins, Anna M., 4132
Collins, Anna, 3056
Collins, Annam May, 4897
Collins, Anthoney, 2543
Collins, Anthony C.W., 5760
Collins, Cath. Clarke, 2925
Collins, Catharina, 3698
Collins, Catharina, 3817
Collins, Catharina, 3881
Collins, Catharina, 4160
Collins, Catharinam, 4803
Collins, Catharini Agnes, 3951
Collins, Catherina, 3755
Collins, Catherine, 4085
Collins, Denis, 2864
Collins, Elisabeth C., 5776
Collins, Ellen, 2839
Collins, Helena, 3698
Collins, Helena, 3755
Collins, Helena, 4795
Collins, Helena, 4803
Collins, Jane, 2543
Collins, Jane, 2839
Collins, Jane, 2925
Collins, Jane, 3055

Collins, Jane, 3056
Collins, Johanna, 2615
Collins, Johanna, 4633
Collins, Margaret Ann, 2119
Collins, Margareth, 3055
Collins, Maria, 3104
Collins, Maria, 3172
Collins, Mary Jane, 2119
Collins, Mary Jane, 2138
Collins, Mary, 2664
Collins, Mary, 2699
Collins, Mary, 2864
Collins, Mary, 3050
Collins, Mary, 4633
Collins, Mary, 4639
Collins, Michael J., 5757
Collins, Michael, 2119
Collins, Michael, 2121
Collins, Pat, 2925
Collins, Pat, 4690
Collins, Patr., 2839
Collins, Patrick, 2543
Collins, Patrick, 3055
Collins, Patrick, 3056
Collman, Anold, 2611
Collon, Richardis, 1509
Collon, A. Maria, 691

Collon, Adelaidis, 691
Collon, Jacobi, 691
Colman, Philip, 4321
Colman, William, 4413
Colmons, Alx, 547
Colmons, Hariettea, 547
Colmons, Metildas, 547
Coltiel, Eleonora, 1292
Colvin, Eleonora, 1301
Colvin, Andreae, 643
Colvin, Andreas, 1273
Colvin, Andreas, 1301
Colvin, Eleonora, 1602
Colvin, Eleonora, 1773
Colvin, Eleonora, 4501
Colvin, Hellenae, 643
Colvin, Joannae, 741
Colvin, Joannes, 643
Colvin, Maria Anna, 1501
Colvin, Maria Anna, 1661
Colvin, Maria Anna, 1750
Colvin, Michael, 741
Colvin, Michaelis, 741
Combel, Rebecca, 1346
Compton, Henry, 29
Compton, Henry, 4181
Compton, Henry, 72

Con, Elizabeth, 3031
Con, Patrick, 3031
Conahan, Catha[rine?], 3
Condan, Margareta, 1420
Conden, Mrs., 584
Conden, Mrs., 420
Conden, Mrs., 447
Conden, Mrs. Conden, 410
Conden, Mrs., 273
Conden, Mrs., 318
Conden, Mrs., 372
Conden, Mrs., 396
Conden, Mrs., 408
Conden, Mrs., 4334
Conden, Mrs., 527
Conden, Mrs., 551
Conder, Mrs., 333
Condery, Patricius, 1261
Condey, Arnoldus, 3179
Condon, William (Mrs.), 115
Condon, A. [or R.], 659
Condon, Anna, 175
Condon, Danielis, 659
Condon, Elleonora, 1305
Condon, Joannae, 659
Condon, Julia, 1421
Condon, Margareta, 1421

Condon, Margaretae, 1421
Condon, Thomae, 1421
Condon, William, 100
Condon, William, 115
Condry, A. S., 3513
Condry, A., 3449
Condry, Anna, 1271
Condry, Arnauldus, 3313
Condry, Arnold, 3670
Condry, Arnold, 3720
Condry, Arnoldus, 4739
Condry, Birgitta, 1271
Condry, Joannes, 4444
Condry, Joannis, 1271
Condry, Maria (Mrs.), 3780
Condry, Mrs., 3484
Condy, Arnorldus, 3133
Condy, Arnoldus, 3134
Condy, Arnoldus, 3176
Condy, Catharinae, 998
Conedy, Joannes, 998
Conedy, Thimotheis, 998
Conelly, Barbara, 1989
Conelly, Bernard, 1989
Conelly, Caroline, 1922
Conelly, James, 1869
Conelly, James, 1989

Conelly, John, 1922
Conelly, Patrick, 1922
Conely, Elisabeth, 961
Conely, Maria, 961
Conely, Petri, 961
Coner, Bridget, 2186
Coners, Bridget Margaret, 2193
Coners, Catharinae, 815
Coners, Hugh, 2178
Coners, Jane, 2193
Coners, John, 2093
Coners, John, 2093
Coners, John, 2193
Coners, Josephine, 2093
Coners, Margaret, 2156
Coners, Patricius, 815
Coners, Peter, 2093
Coners, Thomae, 815
Coniger, B., 3296
Coning, Birgitta, 1525
Coning, Catharinae, 1525
Coning, Michaelis, 1525
Conlan, Annam Margarittam, 3116
Conlan, Bridget, 2968
Conlan, Brigitta, 3116
Conlan, Brigitta, 3171
Conlan, Denis, 2968

Conlan, Dionysis, 3116
Conlan, Dionysis, 3171
Conlan, John, 2968
Conlan, Louisam Elisabeth, 3171
Conlehen, Gertrude, 3864
Conlehen, Lula Gertrudem, 3864
Conlehen, Thoma, 3864
Conlen, Bridget, 3048
Conlen, Denis, 3048
Conlen, Peter, 3048
Conley, Anna Maria (Mrs.), 4900
Conley, Annamaria, 4106
Conley, Anne, 4044
Conley, Barbarae, 1030
Conley, Birgettae, 1150
Conley, Eduardum Guy, 4883
Conley, Edward Sharp, 4044
Conley, Jacobi, 1030
Conley, Joanne, 4106
Conley, John, 4044
Conley, Margareta, 1030
Conley, Maria, 1089
Conley, Maria, 1150
Conley, Robertum Guy, 4106
Conley, Thomae, 1150
Conlogue, P., 266
Conlon, Andreas, 4393

Conlon, Ellen, 2201
Conlon, Jacobus, 1132
Connel, Eliza, 2394
Conneley, Birgitta, 1345
Conneley, Davidis, 1047
Conneley, Joannae, 1047
Conneley, Maria Anna, 1047
Conneling, Catharina Sophia, 672
Conneling, Joannis, 672
Conneling, Sophias, 672
Connell, Ellen, 2577
Connelly, Mary Ann, 4174
Connelly, Babarae, 1548
Connelly, Barbara, 2224
Connelly, Barbarae, 1772
Connelly, Birgitta, 4490
Connelly, Birgittae, 1505
Connelly, Catharina, 1361
Connelly, Cecelia, 2224
Connelly, Francis, 4174
Connelly, Jacobi, 1264
Connelly, Jacobi, 1548
Connelly, Jacobi, 1772
Connelly, Jacobus, 1264
Connelly, James, 2224
Connelly, Joannes, 1470
Connelly, Joannis, 1470

Connelly, Johanna, 1389
Connelly, Maria Anna, 1548
Connelly, Mariae, 1470
Connelly, Michael Henricus, 1772
Connelly, Sophiae, 1264
Connelly, Terrentius Jacobus, 1773
Connelly, Thomaes, 1505
Connelly, Thomas, 1505
Connely, Juliae, 1486
Connely, Maria, 1486
Connely, Patricii, 1486
Conner, Joannis, 1546
Conner, Julia, 3022
Conner, Margaret, 1950
Conner, Margareta, 4377
Conner, Mariae, 1546
Conner, Patricius, 1546
Conniger, B., 3297
Connolly, James, 152
Connolly, James, 70
Connolly, Jane, 70
Connolly, John, 152
Connolly, Rosanna, 152
Connolly, Rosanna, 4174
Connolly, Rose, 70
Connor, Bridget, 2665
Connor, Catharina, 1464

Connor, Catharine, 2288
Connor, Ellen, 2635
Connor, Ferry D., 3821
Connor, James, 152
Connor, James, 91
Connor, James Edward, 2288
Connor, Jas., 2665
Connor, Joannes, 1697
Connor, Joannis, 1133
Connor, Joannis, 1697
Connor, Johannae, 1697
Connor, John, 2288
Connor, Mariae, 1133
Connor, May [or Mary], 2665
Connor, Patrick, 2665
Connor, Sara Johanna, 1766
Connor, Winey, 1133
Connors, Jacobus, 1282
Conokey, Ann, 1868
Conokey, Ellen, 1868
Conokey, Patrick, 1868
Conors, Catharinae, 1240
Conors, Maria, 1240
Conors, Thomae, 1240
Conouhgt, Michael, 1322
Conrad, Agnete, 3913
Conrad, Agnete, 4172

Conrad, Nettie, 3913
Conrod, Isabele, 586
Conroy, Annae, 1479
Conroy, Maria, 1737
Conroy, Petri, 1479
Conroy, Petrus, 1479
Conroy, Petrus, 1737
Conroy, Sara, 1603
Conry, Jacobus, 4473
Conson, Mrs., 611
Conway, M., 3092
Coogan, Bridget, 2697
Coogan, Briget, 2723
Coogan, Catharine, 2329
Coogan, Chas. Patrick, 2697
Coogan, Elisabeth, 2723
Coogan, Elisabeth, 2746
Coogan, Eliz., 2697
Coogan, Margaret Elisabeth, 2746
Coogan, Margaret, 2329
Coogan, Mark, 2697
Coogan, Mathew, 2746
Coogan, Meargaret [sic], 2723
Coogan, Michael [sic], 2723
Coogan, Patrick, 2329
Coogan, Mark, 4643
Coogen, Ginnie, 5789

Cook, Anna, 3874
Cook, Anthony, 4636
Cook, Caroline, 4585
Cook, Ellenora, 2540
Cook, Grace, 2459
Cook, James V., 4544
Cook, Jane, 4661
Cook, Jane, 4664
Cook, Jennie, 3277
Cook, Jno. M., 4636
Cook, John, 2459
Cook, Joseph, 2540
Cook, Mary Agnes Virginia, 2459
Cook, Mary Jane, 2540
Cook, May Agnes Virginia, 5471
Cook, Mrs., 4566
Cook, Regina, 5421
Cooke, Aannam Bernedettam, 3726
Cooke, Joanne, 3726
Cooke, Margareta, 3726
Cookerly, Ann (Mrs.), 5203
Cookerly, Emma L., 4826
Cookerly, Emma, 3903
Cookerly, Jacobo C., 4826
Cookerly, Jacobo, 3741
Cookerly, Jesse, 3903
Cookerly, Jessie, 4826

Cookerly, Louis, 5238
Cookerly, Ludivicum, 3741
Cookerly, Sarah, 3741
Cooms, Joseph, 395
Coon, Claram Reginam, 3277
Coon, Guglielmo, 3277
Coon, Henrietta, 3277
Coon, Claram Reginam, 3277
Coon, Henrietta, 3277
Coonad, Barbary, 493
Coonad, Mat, 493
Coone, Daniel, 2293
Coone, Mary Louisa, 2293
Coone, Mary, 2293
Cooney, Georgio, 3619
Cooney, Mariam Agnetem, 3619
Cooney, Sarah, 3619
Cooney, Birgittae, 916
Cooney, Cordelia, 2413
Cooney, Guillelmus Joannes, 916
Cooney, Laurentii, 916
Coonnely, Annae, 1542
Coonnely, Joannes, 1542
Coonnely, Patricius, 1542
Coony, Guillelimus, 1255
Cooper, Charles, 4223
Cooper, Jane C., 2806

Coorad, Barbary, 493
Coorad, Mat, 493
Copman, Maria, 1157
Coppley, Birgitta, 4478
Copply, Michael, 1581
Coramer, Thomas (Mrs.), 306
Corbe, Jane, 57
Corbe, Jane, 58
Corbet, Eleonora, 1091
Corbet, Isabella (Miss), 4228
Corbet, Isabella, 33
Corbet, Jane, 125
Corbet, Jane, 4177
Corbet, Joannae, 647
Corbet, Lucy, 125
Corbet, Lucy, 31
Corbet, Lucy, 34
Corbet, Margaret, 2316
Corbet, Roger, 2316
Corbet, Timotheus, 1091
Corbet, William, 2316
Corbett, Ann, 2135
Corbett, Anna Elisabeth, 1823
Corbett, Annae, 1823
Corbett, Catharina, 1247
Corbett, Eleonorae, 1247
Corbett, George, 2135

Corbett, Johanna, 1393
Corbett, Mary, 2026
Corbett, May, 1827
Corbett, Peter, 2135
Corbett, Petris, 1823
Corbett, Timothei, 1247
Corbin, Mary Ellen, 2758
Corbit, Annae, 936
Corbit, Jane, 83
Corbit, Lucia Joanna, 936
Corbit, Petri, 936
Corbitt, Margaret, 2394
Corbitt, Tho. (Mrs.), 615
Corbutt, Annaae, 1226
Corbutt, Jacobus Henricus, 1226
Corbutt, Petri, 1226
Cordy, Anna, 4259
Core, Elizab, 65
Corel, Elizabeth, 2586
Corel, James Edman [sic], 2586
Corel, Joseph, 2586
Corey, Edward, 333
Corey, Harietta, 333
Corey, James, 333
Corgan, Elizabeth, 3034
Corgan, Hugh Edward, 3034
Corgan, Mathew, 3034

Corlosk, Elisabeth, 1669
Corlosk, Birgitta, 1510
Corner, Thomas, 4368
Corney, Easter (Miss), 249
Cormeskery, Denis, 4299
Corns, Mary (Mrs.), 445
Corral, Patricius, 1335
Corrigan, Joanna, 2204
Corrigan, Julia, 2204
Corrigan, Matthew, 2204
Corrigan, Owen, 2204
Corrighan, Birgittae, 1484
Corrighan, Jacobus, 1484
Corrighan, Joannis, 1484
Corrogan, Anna, 4259
Corry, Paulo G., 4856
Cortence, Mary (Miss), 4212
Cosey, Matthew, 4357
Cosgriff, Maria, 1544
Cosgrove [sic], Teresa, 2013
Cosgrove, Elizabeth, 2171
Cosgrove, James, 2013
Cosgrove, Laurence, 1994
Cosgrove, Laurence, 2171
Cosgrove, Laurence, 2266
Cosgrove, Laurence, 2267
Cosgrove, Laurence, 4325

Cosgrove, Lawrence, 2013
Cosgrove, Matthew, 2266
Cosgrove, Teresa, 2013
Cosgrove, Teresa, 2171
Cosgrove, Teresa, 2266
Cosgrove, Teresa, 2277
Coskerly, Emma, 4060
Coss, Harriett, 4334
Cossy, Adelina?, 1163
Cossy, Hanorae, 1163
Cossy, Matheii, 1163
Cother, John H., 5290
Cotter, Florentiam Catharinam, 4137
Cotter, Joannem H, 3970
Cotter, Lettie, 4137
Cotter, Lutie, 3970
Cotter, Patritio, 3970
Cotter, Patritio, 4137
Cotter, Patrotsum E., 4848
Couderon, S., 4365
Coudy, Mr., 4555
Coufher, Mary Anna, 404
Couk, Catherine, 303
Couk, John, 303
Coulehan, Michael, 3864
Counts, Mary, 275

Coury, Widow, 4338
Covel, Elis., 2825
Covel, Elizabeth, 2586
Covel, James Edman [sic], 2586
Covel, Joseph, 2586
Covel, Joseph, 2825
Covel, Sarah Elis., 2825
Covell, Edwd. Oscar, 2701
Covell, Eliz., 2701
Covell, Eliz., 2845
Covell, Elizabeth, 2974
Covell, Elizabeth, 3183
Covell, Hester Virginiam, 3183
Covell, Jos., 2701
Covell, Joseph, 2974
Covell, Joseph, 3183
Covell, Margaret Ann, 2974
Cover, Ellen Jane, 1909
Cover, Jane, 1909
Cover, John, 1909
Cover, Timothy, 1909
Covgan, Elizabeth, 3034
Covgan, Hugh Edward, 3034
Covgan, Mathew, 3034
Cox, Bernard Thomas, 2111
Cox, Bernard, 2111
Cox, Birgitta, 1358

Cox, Bridget, 2111
Cox, Bridget, 2212
Cox, Catharinae, 1152
Cox, Catharinae, 1504
Cox, Christophorus, 1504
Cox, Elisabeth, 1152
Cox, Michaelis, 1152
Cox, Michaelis, 1504
Cox, Mr., 4212
Coxen, Ella Elisabeth, 4003
Coxon, Gulielmo H., 4167
Coxon, Gulielmo, 4003
Coxon, Jennie, 4003
Coxon, Maud, 4167
Coxson, Rosam Rebeccam, 4167
Coxson, Jacobum Franklin, 3451
Coxson, Margaretta, 3451
Coxson, Wm, 3451
Coy, Catherine (widow), 4246
Coy, Mary, 3046
Coyle, Ada, 2936
Coyle, Mary, 2640
Coyle, Mary, 2728
Coyle, Ada, 2888
Coyle, Ada, 2990
Coyle, Ada, 3252
Coyle, Ada, 3898

Coyle, Anestine Rosa, 2888
Coyle, Annae, 1468
Coyle, Any [or Ang], 5797
Coyle, Aug., 2627
Coyle, Aug., 2728
Coyle, Augustine, 2004
Coyle, Augustine, 2744
Coyle, Augustine, 5011
Coyle, Charles Malachy, 2818
Coyle, Cletum Patricium, 3173
Coyle, Eda, 2765
Coyle, Edward Aug. P., 2244
Coyle, Edward, 2347
Coyle, Edward, 4988
Coyle, Edwardi, 1468
Coyle, Edwardi, 953
Coyle, Edwardum Linum, 3252
Coyle, Edwardus, 1102
Coyle, Edwd, 5798
Coyle, Elisabeth, 682
Coyle, Elisabeth, 683
Coyle, Elisabeth, 684
Coyle, Elisabeth, 684
Coyle, Francis Theodore, 2990
Coyle, Francis, 5081
Coyle, Jacob, 682
Coyle, Jacob, 683

Coyle, Jacobum Dominicum, 3721
Coyle, John F., 2437
Coyle, John, 5390
Coyle, Josephum Marcellum, 3097
Coyle, Lewis Benjamin, 3898
Coyle, Ludovica Anna, 1102
Coyle, Ludovicas, 953
Coyle, Marei, 682
Coyle, Marei, 683
Coyle, Marei, 684
Coyle, Maria Alphonsa, 3494
Coyle, Maria, 3097
Coyle, Maria, 3123
Coyle, Maria, 3170
Coyle, Maria, 3171
Coyle, Maria, 3173
Coyle, Maria, 3174
Coyle, Maria, 3332
Coyle, Maria, 3600
Coyle, Maria, 3721
Coyle, Mariam Veronicam, 3332
Coyle, Mark, 1885
Coyle, Mary M. I., 2370
Coyle, Mary, 2004
Coyle, Mary, 2620
Coyle, Mary, 2624
Coyle, Mary, 2719

Coyle, Mary, 2724
Coyle, Mary, 2818
Coyle, Mary, 2889
Coyle, Mary, 2899
Coyle, Mary, 2905
Coyle, Mary, 2923
Coyle, Mary, 3070
Coyle, Mary, 3072
Coyle, Mary, 4681
Coyle, Mary, 4682
Coyle, Mary, 4686
Coyle, Mary, 4689
Coyle, Mary, 4692
Coyle, Mary, 4698
Coyle, Mary, 4702
Coyle, Mrs. Mary, 5634
Coyle, Mrs., 1885
Coyle, Mrs., 2765
Coyle, Petrum Horatium, 3494
Coyle, Saml, 2640
Coyle, Saml, 2684
Coyle, Saml, 4627
Coyle, Saml, 4628
Coyle, Saml, 4637
Coyle, Saml, 5779
Coyle, Samuel D., 5396
Coyle, Samuel, 4993

Coyle, Samuel, 953
Coyle, Sarah Ann, 1885
Coyle, Theresa, 2765
Coyle, Thoma B., 3097
Coyle, Thoma B., 3173
Coyle, Thoma B., 3600
Coyle, Thoma B., 3721
Coyle, Thoma, 3252
Coyle, Thoma, 3332
Coyle, Thoma, 3494
Coyle, Thoma, 3898
Coyle, Thomas Benjaminus, 1468
Coyle, Thomas, 2818
Coyle, Thomas, 2990
Coyle, Thos. B., 5808
Coyle, Thos., 2765
Coyle, Thos., 2888
Coyle, Thos., 2936
Coyle, Thos., 4656
Coyle, Vincentium Eugenium, 3600

Crady, Maria, 1698
Crady, Thomas, 1698
Craig, Catharina, 1256
Craig, Catharina, 1396
Craig, Catharine, 2240
Craig, Catharine, 2245
Craig, Catharine, 2252
Craig, Catharine, 2262
Craig, Catharine, 2291
Craig, Catharine, 4587
Craig, Catharine, 4949
Craig, Gulielmo, 3952
Craig, Jennie, 3952
Craig, Mariam Sheridan Army, 3952
Cram, Jacob, 4634
Cramer, Carrery Bernardum, 3227
Cramer, Daniel, 4721
Cramer, Daniel, 5093
Cramer, Edwardem Howard, 3276
Cramer, Edwardem Howard, 3276
Cramer, Fannie, 5515
Cramer, Fannie, 5803
Cramer, Felia, 3870
Cramer, Henrico, 3870
Cramer, Henricum A., 4831
Cramer, Henricus, 3432
Cramer, Henry, 2490
Cramer, Henry, 5655
Cramer, Isaac, 3276
Cramer, Jacob J., 5276
Cramer, Jacob, 3083
Cramer, Jacob, 3227

Cramer, Jake, 3334
Cramer, Louis Edmd., 4976
Cramer, Louisa, 3040
Cramer, Louisa, 5542
Cramer, Louisa, 5587
Cramer, Maria M., 4122
Cramer, Maria, 3227
Cramer, Maria, 3276
Cramer, Maria, 3695
Cramer, Maria, 3803
Cramer, Maria, 3861
Cramer, Maria, 3871
Cramer, Maria, 3897
Cramer, Maria, 4039
Cramer, Maria, 4164
Cramer, Maria, 4866
Cramer, Mariam M., 4869
Cramer, Martah, 3334
Cramer, Martha, 3083
Cramer, Martha, 3227
Cramer, Mary (Mrs.), 5071
Cramer, Mary A. (Mrs.), 5346
Cramer, Mary Magdalen, 2490
Cramer, Mary, 2490
Cramer, Mary, 4831
Cramer, Mrs., 3309
Cramer, Mrs., 3438

Cramer, Mrs., 4745
Cramer, Nina Gertrude, 3083
Cramer, Nina, 3853
Cramer, Nina, 3870
Cramer, Ninam, 4866
Cramer, Sally, 477
Cramer, Stellam Anna Loffam, 3334
Cramer, Theresa, 3276
Cramer, Theresa, 3276
Cramer, Thomam Henricum, 3870
Cramer, Thomas H., 5262
Crametz, Henry, 4972
Crammer, Henricus P., 1340
Cranler, Caroli, 811
Cranler, Carolinae, 811
Cranler, Dionisius, 811
Crasby, Hanora, 1471
Cratin, Alescius, 2705
Cratin, Ellen, 2705
Crauley, Bernardi, 1357
Crauley, Bernardus, 1357
Crauley, Honora, 1319
Crauley, Honora, 1568
Crauley, Johannae, 1568
Crauley, John, 2747
Crauley, Margaretae, 1357

Crauley, Mary Theresa, 2747
Crauley, Mary Theresa, 2747
Crauley, Patricii, 1568
Crauley, Patricius, 1741
Crauly, John H., 4650
Crauss, Bernardi, 1535
Crauss, Mariae, 1535
Crauss, Michael J. [or I.], 1535
Crawley, Patrick, 2138
Cray, Catharina, 1176
Cray, Margaretae, 1176
Cray, Petrii, 1176
Creach [Creact?], George W., 5387
Creack, George W., 2356
Cready, Catharine, 1986
Cready, Maria, 1979
Cready, Patrick, 1986
Cready, Thomas, 1986
Creager, Marian, 4791
Creamer, Agnes Xavier, 5746
Creamer, Anna, 5671
Creamer, Danial [sic], 5725
Creamer, David, 2430
Creamer, Henricus, 3632
Creamer, Henry, 2399
Creamer, Henry, 2595
Creamer, Henry, 2596

Creamer, Jacob, 2584
Creamer, Jacob, 5392
Creamer, Jacob, 5780
Creamer, Jenny Rose, 5702
Creamer, Jno. Parker, 2873
Creamer, John Francis, 2430
Creamer, Jonathan, 2374
Creamer, Louis Edmund, 2595
Creamer, Louis Edmund, 2596
Creamer, Margaret, 2430
Creamer, Maria, 3632
Creamer, Maria, 4828
Creamer, Mary Cecilia, 5713
Creamer, Mary, 234
Creamer, Mary, 234
Creamer, Mary, 2374
Creamer, Mary, 2595
Creamer, Mary, 2596
Creamer, Mrs., 2875
Creamer, Mrs., 4217
Creamer, Teresa, 5385
Creamer, Theresa, 5783
Creamer, Thomas Alvey, 2374
Creamer, Thomas, 234
Creek, Catharine, 151
Creek, Edward, 151
Creek, George, 151

Creigh, Margaret, 1943
Creigh, Margaret, 1862
Creigh, Mary, 2083
Creigh, Mary, 2814
Creigh, Mrs., 5020
Creigh, Peter Henry, 1862
Creigh, W., 1983
Creigh, William, 1844
Creigh, William, 1862
Creigh, William, 2083
Creighton, Henricus, 3100
Cremer, Henry, 1959
Cremer, Henry, 5603
Cremer, James Summerille, 2021
Cremer, Jonathan H., 2021
Cremer, Jonathan H., 2022
Cremer, Jonathan H., 2162
Cremer, Louisa, 1959
Cremer, Margaret, 4650
Cremer, Mary Monterey, 2022
Cremer, Mary Montezuma, 2162
Cremer, Mary, 1959
Cremer, Mary, 2021
Cremer, Mary, 2022
Cremer, Mary, 2162
Cremer, Mary, 2716
Cremer, Theresa, 4650

Crenner, Annae, 1092
Crenner, Owen, 1092
Crenner, Thomas, 1092
Cretin, Alexius, 2758
Cretin, Denis, 5095
Cretin, Helena Flora, 3124
Cretin, Henrico, 3124
Cretin, Maria A., 3124
Cretin, Maria C., 3531
Cretin, Maria M., 3531
Cretin, Maria, 3129
Cretin, Maria, 3436
Cretin, Mariam C., 4762
Cretin, Mary Cecelia Agnes, 5752
Cretin, Mary Cecilia, 2758
Cretin, Mary Ellen, 2758
Cretin, Mary, 2946
Cretin, Mrs., 4649
Criner, Elisabeth, 1023
Criner, Maria Elisabeth, 1023
Crissinger, Louisa, 2371
Crissinger, Louisa, 2475
Crist, Adam, 2159
Crist, Adam, 2455
Crist, Catharine, 2455
Crist, George, 2159
Crist, John, 2158

Crist, John, 4600
Crist, Louisa, 2158
Crist, Lousia, 2159
Crist, Margaret, 2455
Crist, Margaret, 4600
Crist, Michael, 4600
Crist, Peter, 2158
Crist, Peter, 2159
Crocket, Bridget Jemima, 2196
Crocket, Isaias, 2196
Crocket, Rosanna, 2196
Crokett, Isaias, 2133
Crokett, Mary Bridget, 2133
Crokett, Rosanna, 2133
Crommel, Anna Caecilia, 856
Crommel, Catharinae, 856
Crommel, Samuelis, 856
Croner, Joseph, 3535
Cronin, Patrick, 4925
Cronley, Catharina, 1084
Cronley, Daniel, 1389
Cronley, Jacobi, 1084
Cronley, Jacobi, 1389
Cronley, Mariae, 1084
Cronley, Mariae, 1389
Cronly, Jacobi, 1726
Cronly, Jacobus, 4426

Cronly, Mariae, 1726
Cronly, Michael, 1726
Crosby, James, 71
Crosby, Mary, 71
Crosby, Mary, 91
Crosby, Mathew, 71
Cross, Anna E., 4820
Cross, Carolus Henricus, 1586
Cross, Elisabeth, 1586
Cross, Elisabeth, 3866
Cross, Lernal, 4291
Cross, Ludovicae, 1586
Cross, Maria Anna, 4460
Cross, Samuel, 1586
Crossen, Catha[rine?], 3
Crossen, Edward, 3
Crossen, Edward, 3
Crossen, Mary, 3
Crosson, Henrico J., 4094
Crosson, Margaritam M., 4094
Crosson, Maria, 4094
Crouse, Ann W., 5187
Crovan, Marianae, 1407
Crovan, Richardi, 1407
Crovan, Richardus, 1407
Crow, Catherine (Miss), 347
Crow, Catherine (Miss), 4215

Crow, Cathren (Miss), 361
Crowley, Jeremias, 2138
Crowley, May, 2138
Crowley, Patrick, 2138
Crowley, Sarah, 15
Crowley?, Bernardus, 4442
Cruie, Arthur, 1123
Cruise, Arthur, 1068
Cruise, Elleonorae, 1068
Cruise, Guillelmus, 1068
Crumbaugh, Dore, 4903
Crumbaugh, Otille, 4903
Crure, Arthur, 1123
Cruse, Arthuris, 1279
Cruse, Eleonorae, 1279
Cruse, Susanna, 1279
Cruzen, Alicia, 3771
Cruzen, Alicia J., 3674
Cruzn, Alecia J., 3675
Cull, Wallace (Mrs.), 3929
Cullan, James, 2287
Cullan, Jos. (Mrs.), 5156
Cullen, Catharinam Agnetem, 3311
Cullen, Emmet M., 4769
Cullen, Emmet, 3478
Cullen, Emmet, 3534
Cullen, Emmet, 3604

Cullen, Emmet, 3637
Cullen, Emmet, 3747
Cullen, Eva (Mrs.), 4100
Cullen, Eva, 3534
Cullen, Eva, 3604
Cullen, Eva, 3637
Cullen, Eva, 3747
Cullen, Eva, 3994
Cullen, Eva, 4025
Cullen, Franciscam Lillian Walsh, 3816
Cullen, Jacobo, 3311
Cullen, Josephinam C., 3994
Cullen, M. Emmett, 3816
Cullen, M. Emmett, 3994
Cullen, Maria Eva, 3816
Cullen, Maria, 3311
Cullen, Mariam Rosam, 3637
Cullen, Michael E., 4025
Cullen, Robertum Emmitt, 3747
Cullen, Victorem Franciscum, 3534
Culliam, Anna, 1457
Cullins, Jacobo, 3461
Cullins, Margaret Gertrudem, 3461
Cullins, Maria, 3461
Cumming, Grace, 3243
Cumming, Johanne, 3243

Cumming, Johanne, 3280
Cumming, Philippum Chester, 3280
Cumming, Sarah, 3243
Cumming, Sarah, 3280
Cuningham, Cathorinae, 1178
Cuningham, Edwardus, 1647
Cuningham, Emma Catharina, 3820
Cuningham, Guillelmus, 1706
Cuningham, Jacobus, 1277
Cuningham, Joannis, 1178
Cuningham, Joannis, 1706
Cuningham, Margareta, 1765
Cuningham, Margareta, 1755
Cuningham, Margaretae, 1706
Cuningham, Michael, 1178
Cunning, Carolum Cecilium, 3740
Cunning, Isabellam, 3683
Cunning, Joanne, 3683
Cunning, Joanne, 3740
Cunning, Sarah, 3683
Cunning, Sarah, 3740
Cunningham, Margaret, 4716
Cunningham, Anna (Mrs.), 3936
Cunningham, Bridget, 2968
Cunningham, Bridget, 3027

Cunningham, Bridget, 3048
Cunningham, Brigitta, 3116
Cunningham, Brigitta, 3171
Cunningham, Catharinae, 1538
Cunningham, Catherine, 3027
Cunningham, Christopher, 2337
Cunningham, Elizabeth, 2337
Cunningham, Gertrude, 5291
Cunningham, James, 3027
Cunningham, James, 3090
Cunningham, Joanne, 3169
Cunningham, Joannem, 3169
Cunningham, Joannis, 4472
Cunningham, Joannis, 1538
Cunningham, John D. H., 2222
Cunningham, John Denis Howard, 2222
Cunningham, John, 1904
Cunningham, John, 2084
Cunningham, John, 4716
Cunningham, Laura, 4716
Cunningham, Magarita, 3639
Cunningham, Margaret, 1904
Cunningham, Margaret, 2084
Cunningham, Margaret, 2222
Cunningham, Margaret, 2337

Cunningham, Margareta, 1631
Cunningham, Margarethae, 923
Cunningham, Margaritae Doherty, 4823
Cunningham, Margt., 2316
Cunningham, Maria, 3783
Cunningham, Maria, 4859
Cunningham, Mary Alice, 2084
Cunningham, Mary E, 5271
Cunningham, Michael, 3027
Cunningham, Michael, 923
Cunningham, Patricius, 1538
Cunningham, Sarah, 3169
Cunningham, Timothei, 923
Cunningham, William Wallace, 1904
Cunterenann, William, 1507
Cuny, Johanna, 1185
Cupper, W., 1533
Curley, Ann, 2094
Curley, Ann, 2155
Curley, Ann, 4551
Curley, Anna, 1683
Curley, Catharinae, 706
Curley, Catharine, 1831
Curley, Catharine, 2000
Curley, Catherinae, 999

Curley, Francis, 2000
Curley, John William, 1831
Curley, John, 2094
Curley, Maria Anna, 999
Curley, Patricii, 706
Curley, Patricii, 999
Curley, Patrick, 1831
Curley, Patrick, 2000
Curley, Patrick, 2094
Curley, Thomas, 706
Curnin, Alice, 108
Curnin, Libby, 108
Curnin, Murtough, 108
Curran, Eleonorae, 907
Curran, Felix, 3083
Curran, Jacobi, 907
Curran, James, 2328
Curran, Joannes, 907
Curran, John, 5212
Curran, Mary, 2085
Curran, Michael, 2996
Curran, Mrs., 5031
Curran, Philippus, 1522
Curran, Thomas, 2085
Curran, William, 2085
Curran, William, 2085
Curren, Catharina, 1579

Curry, Gratia, 1785
Curry, Griffith, 1617
Cushwa, Victor, 5500
Cushwa, Gertrude, 4136
Cushwa, Maria, 4070
Cushwa, Sallie, 3202
Cushwa, Sarah, 3195
Cushwa, Susanna, 3875
Cushwa, Ben., 3130
Cushwa, Benton, 3265
Cushwa, Benton, 3202
Cushwa, Benton, 4749
Cushwa, Benton, 5632
Cushwa, C.W.F., 3816
Cushwa, Carolum Benton, 3186
Cushwa, Cath., 3608
Cushwa, Catharinam, 4796
Cushwa, Catherine C., 5770
Cushwa, Catherine, 4087
Cushwa, Charles William Franklin, 3082
Cushwa, Christi Annam, 4025
Cushwa, Clinton Geo., 3130
Cushwa, Clinton, 3186
Cushwa, Clinton, 3244
Cushwa, David (Mrs.), 3928
Cushwa, David Franklin, 2772
Cushwa, David K., 4146
Cushwa, David K., 4161
Cushwa, David Kreigh, 2984
Cushwa, David Kreigh, 4070
Cushwa, David V., 4091
Cushwa, David, 2802
Cushwa, David, 2808
Cushwa, David, 3758
Cushwa, David, 3963
Cushwa, David, 4070
Cushwa, Davide K., 4025
Cushwa, Davide, 4825
Cushwa, Domina Sarah, 3689
Cushwa, Donna Sarah, 3731
Cushwa, Elisabeth Catharinam, 4161
Cushwa, Ella, 3130
Cushwa, Ella, 3186
Cushwa, Ella, 3244
Cushwa, Ellen Stake, 2912
Cushwa, Eva, 3534
Cushwa, Eva, 3637
Cushwa, Eva, 3747
Cushwa, Eva, 3994
Cushwa, Evalina, 3195
Cushwa, Evam M., 4769
Cushwa, Evelina Marg. [Mary.?], 5714
Cushwa, Fannie (Miss), 4902
Cushwa, Francisca De Sales, 3816
Cushwa, Francisca, 4076
Cushwa, Francisco, 4076
Cushwa, Francisco, 4108
Cushwa, Franciscus, 3748
Cushwa, Franklin, 4136
Cushwa, Franklin, 4146
Cushwa, Fred., 3840
Cushwa, Frederico, 4076
Cushwa, Georgio F., 4871
Cushwa, Georgium Clinton, 4726
Cushwa, Georgium Victorem, 3982
Cushwa, Gertrude, 4076
Cushwa, Gertrude, 4108
Cushwa, Gertrude, 4146
Cushwa, Guglielmo, 3248
Cushwa, Guglielmo, 3374
Cushwa, Helena S., 4091
Cushwa, Helena, 3637
Cushwa, Helena, 4825
Cushwa, Hugh Clinton, 3244
Cushwa, Joannam Francescam, 3195
Cushwa, Joannam Franciscam, 4108
Cushwa, Joseph Constanticum, 4072
Cushwa, Joseph Kriegh, 4146
Cushwa, Juliam Catharinam, 4073
Cushwa, Louisa, 4796
Cushwa, Louisam, 4804
Cushwa, Ludovica, 3516
Cushwa, Lutie, 3879
Cushwa, Lutie, 3928
Cushwa, Lutie, 3996
Cushwa, Margaret Eva, 2609
Cushwa, Margaret, 2772
Cushwa, Margarittam S., 3130
Cushwa, Margt., 2946
Cushwa, Maria Anna, 3195
Cushwa, Maria Eva, 3816
Cushwa, Maria Ludivico, 3758
Cushwa, Maria Ludovica, 3840
Cushwa, Maria, 3637
Cushwa, Maria, 3822
Cushwa, Mariam Susan, 3374
Cushwa, Mariam Virginiam, 4076
Cushwa, Mary (Mrs.), 5349
Cushwa, Mary Ann, 2609
Cushwa, Mary Ann, 2912

Cushwa, Mary Anne, 2749
Cushwa, Mary Louisa, 2749
Cushwa, Mary Louise, 3959
Cushwa, Mary, 2676
Cushwa, Mary, 2814
Cushwa, Mary, 2865
Cushwa, Mary, 2984
Cushwa, Mary, 3082
Cushwa, Mary, 3374
Cushwa, Maud, 3374
Cushwa, Modie [sic], 3248
Cushwa, Monroe, 3565
Cushwa, Mrs. Benton, 3422
Cushwa, Munroe V., 3534
Cushwa, Nanie, 4025
Cushwa, Nanie, 4161
Cushwa, Nannie, 4070
Cushwa, Nellie, 3840
Cushwa, Ricardum Eugenium, 3248
Cushwa, S., 3118
Cushwa, Sab, 3128
Cushwa, Sallie (Mrs.), 3904
Cushwa, Sallie (Mrs.), 4040
Cushwa, Sallie (Mrs.), 4148
Cushwa, Sallie (Mrs.), 4166
Cushwa, Sallie, 2814

Cushwa, Sallie, 3059
Cushwa, Sallie, 3230
Cushwa, Sallie, 3242
Cushwa, Sallie, 3260
Cushwa, Sallie, 3270
Cushwa, Sallie, 3303
Cushwa, Sallie, 3314
Cushwa, Sallie, 3879
Cushwa, Sallie, 3982
Cushwa, Sallie, 4017
Cushwa, Sally, 3087
Cushwa, Sally, 3216
Cushwa, Sara, 3125
Cushwa, Sara, 3620
Cushwa, Sarah Catharine, 2676
Cushwa, Sarah, 2771
Cushwa, Sarah, 3073
Cushwa, Sarah, 3074
Cushwa, Sarah, 3209
Cushwa, Sarah, 3534
Cushwa, Sarah, 3716
Cushwa, Sarah, 3744
Cushwa, Sarai, 3797
Cushwa, Susan, 2802
Cushwa, Susan, 2808
Cushwa, Susanna, 3910
Cushwa, Susanna, 3959

Cushwa, Susanna, 3982
Cushwa, Susanna, 4072
Cushwa, Susanna, 4073
Cushwa, T. Benten, 3186
Cushwa, T.B., 3242
Cushwa, T.B., 3879
Cushwa, T.B., 3904
Cushwa, T.B., 3910
Cushwa, Thomam Benton, 3910
Cushwa, Thomas B., 3164
Cushwa, Thomas Benton, 2802
Cushwa, Thos. Benton, 5330
Cushwa, Thos. M., 4659
Cushwa, V. Monroe, 3928
Cushwa, V. Monroe, 4072
Cushwa, V. Monroe, 4073
Cushwa, Victor M., 3875
Cushwa, Victor Monroe, 2814
Cushwa, Victor, 2609
Cushwa, Victor, 2622
Cushwa, Victor, 2676
Cushwa, Victor, 2749
Cushwa, Victor, 2814
Cushwa, Victor, 2912
Cushwa, Victor, 2984
Cushwa, Victor, 3082
Cushwa, Victor, 3612

Cushwa, Victor, 3613
Cushwa, Victor, 3637
Cushwa, Victor, 3747
Cushwa, Victor, 3750
Cushwa, Victor, 3822
Cushwa, Victor, 4070
Cushwa, Victor, 4621
Cushwa, Victor, 4695
Cushwa, Victor, 5524
Cushwa, Victore Monroe, 3959
Cushwa, Victore Monroe, 3982
Cushwa, Victore, 3195
Cushwa, Victoria Monroe, 3910
Cushwa, William, 2772
Cushwa, William, 2808
Cushwa, Wm. Kreigh, 2946
Cushwa, Wm. 2946
Cushwa, Wm. 4655
Cusick, Nichous, 4284
Cutchall, Harriet, 1886
Cutsall, Harriet, 2489
Cutshaw, Ann, 97
Cutter, Margareta, 1282
Cutter, Mariae, 1282
Cutter, Timothei, 1282
D ance, Mrs., 392
Dafenthal, Barbary, 421

Dafenthal, David, 421
Dahlgren, Eric B., 3929
Dahlgren, Eric, 3457
Dahlgren, M. V. (Mrs.), 3400
Dahlgren, M. V. (Mrs.), 3401
Dahlgren, M. V. (Mrs.), 3403
Dahlgren, M. V. (Mrs.), 3404
Dahlgren, M. V. (Mrs.), 3405
Dahlgren, M. V. (Mrs.), 3406
Dahlgren, M. V. (Mrs.), 3407
Dahlgren, M. V. (Mrs.), 3408
Dahlgren, M. V. (Mrs.), 3409
Dahlgren, M. V. (Mrs.), 3410
Dahlgren, M. V., 3526
Dahlgren, M. V., 3538
Dahlgren, M. V., 3443
Dahlgren, M. V., 3521
Dahlgren, M. V., 3525
Dahlgren, M. V., 3542
Dahlgren, M. V., 3699
Dahlgren, M. V., 3700
Dahlgren, M.V. (Mrs.), 3344
Dahlgren, M.V. (Mrs.), 3348
Dahlgren, M.V. (Mrs.), 3398
Dahlgren, M.V. (Mrs.), 3399
Dahlgren, M.V., 3341
Dahlgren, M.V., 3342

Dahlgren, M.V., 3343
Dahlgren, M.V., 3345
Dahlgren, M.V., 3346
Dahlgren, M.V., 3347
Dahlgren, M.V., 3349
Dahlgren, M.V., 3351
Dahlgren, M.V., 3488
Dahlgren, M.V., 3701
Dahlgren, M.V., 3703
Dahlgren, M.V., 3704
Dahlgren, Mad. V., 3489
Dahlgren, Madeleine Sarah Vinton, 3350
Dahlgren, Madeleine v. (Mrs.), 3397
Dahlgren, Madeleine, 3390
Dahlgren, Madeleine, 3391
Dahlgren, Madeleine, 3452
Dahlgren, Madeleine, 3453
Dahlgren, Madeleine, 3454
Dahlgren, Madeleine, 3455
Dahlgren, Madeleine, 3456
Dahlgren, Magdalena V., 4032
Dahlgren, Magdalena, 3749
Dahlgren, Mrs., 3444
Dahlgren, Mrs., 3445
Dahlgren, Ullrica, 3615

Dahlgren, Ulrica, 3929
Dahlgren, Ulrica, 4852
Daily, Antony, 4335
Daily, Catharinae, 1088
Daily, Guillelmus, 1289
Daily, Henricus, 1301
Daily, Joannes, 4443
Daily, Joannis, 1088
Daily, Joannis, 1301
Daily, K., 1301
Daily, Maria, 1289
Daily, Owen, 1095
Daily, Patrick, 4623
Daily, Sara, 3535
Daily, Thomas, 1088
Daley, Joannis, 1059
Daley, Mariae, 1059
Daley, Matheus, 1059
Daley, Sarah, 3787
Daley, Bridget, 2095
Daley, Catharine, 2213
Daley, David Wilson, 1984
Daley, Jane, 1909
Daley, John, 1835
Daley, John, 1837
Daley, John, 1904
Daley, John, 1967

Daley, John, 1973
Daley, John, 1984
Daley, John, 1989
Daley, John, 2062
Daley, John, 2142
Daley, John, 2192
Daley, John, 2213
Daley, Kesiah, 1835
Daley, Kesiah, 1837
Daley, Kesiah, 2213
Daley, Margaret, 2654
Daley, Mary, 1837
Daley, Mary, 2654
Daley, Patr., 2654
Daley, Patr., 2655
Daley, Resiah, 1984
Daley, Sara, 3926
Daley, Sarah, 3304
Daley, Sarah, 3463
Daley, Sarah, 3679
Daley, Sarai, 3850
Daley, Sarai, 3967
Daley, Thomas Jefferson, 1835
Dalgreen, John V., 4029
Dalgreen, Ulrica, 4029
Dalon, Anna, 1324
Daly, Gratia, 1141

Daly, [blank], 1576
Daly, Gratiae, 1120
Daly, Joannes, 1120
Daly, Joannes, 1576
Daly, Joannis, 1576
Daly, Josephi, 1120
Daly, Sarah Agnes, 3595
Daly, Sarai, 4063
Daly, Sarai, 4128
Daly, William, 5360
Dan, Jacobus, 1585
Danheney, James, 1991
Daniels, Anna, 3596
Dant, Elisabeth, 1302
Dant, Elisabeth, 1401
Dany, Mary (Miss), 4250
Dar, Catharine, 2400
Darcy, Mary, 454
Dare, Catharine R., 2272
Dare, Catharine R., 2273
Darr, Franciscem Albertam, 3708
Darr, Gulielmo, 3708
Darr, Maria, 3708
Daud, Petras, 1195
Daudelet, Anna, 879
Daudelet, Catharinae, 879
Daudelet, Joannis, 879

Daughaney, Margaret, 1891
Daugheney, Bridget (widow), 2246
Daugheney, Bridget (widow), 2247
Daugheney, Bridget, 2247
Daugheney, deceased, 2246
Daugheney, deceased, 2247
Daugheney, James, 2246
Daugheney, Maria, 2247
Daugherty, Arthur, 1331
Daugherty, blank, 722
Daugherty, Daniel, 1436
Daugherty, Daniel, 1414
Daugherty, Ellon (Mrs.), 507
Daugherty, Franciscus, 1006
Daugherty, Guillelmus, 1436
Daugherty, Joannae, 1436
Daugherty, Joannes, 1501
Daugherty, Joannes, 1590
Daugherty, Joannes, 722
Daugherty, Johanna, 1235
Daugherty, Judith, 1006
Daugherty, Judith, 4496
Daugherty, Margaretae, 1328
Daugherty, Maria, 1107
Daugherty, Maria, 1354
Daugherty, Maria, 1414
Daugherty, Maria, 1434

Daugherty, Mariae, 1001
Daugherty, Martha, 1001
Daugherty, Michael, 1328
Daugherty, Michaelis, 1001
Daugherty, Michaelis, 1328
Daugherty, Michaelis, 722
Daugherty, Patricii, 1006
Daughonvy, Birgittae, 1555
Daughonvy, Eleonora, 1555
Daughonvy, Jacobi, 1555
Daughony, Birgittae, 769
Daughony, Jacobi, 769
Daughony, Patricius, 769
Daukery, Eleonorae, 1519
Daukery, Margareta, 1519
Daukery, Thomae, 1519
David, Maria, 4402
Davis, Anna, 1655
Davis, Henry Peter, 85
Davis, Mary, 85
Davis, Mary, 2421
Davis, [blank], 2679
Davis, Alecia J., 3675
Davis, Alice, 3888
Davis, Alicia J., 3674
Davis, Alicia, 3771
Davis, Anna Eliza, 570

Davis, Anna Elizabeth, 2371
Davis, Anna, 3185
Davis, Anna, 3223
Davis, Anna, 3522
Davis, Anna, 3523
Davis, Cane, 2421
Davis, Carolum Eduardem, 3185
Davis, Cath, 166
Davis, Catharine, 54
Davis, Edward, 1897
Davis, Eleanor, 147
Davis, Eleanor, 179
Davis, Elizabetham Mabel, 3674
Davis, Elonar (Miss), 235
Davis, Franciscum Burton, 3523
Davis, Georgio, 3185
Davis, Georgio, 3223
Davis, Georgio, 3523
Davis, Georgium A., 4734
Davis, Georgium Martinum, 3223
Davis, Giorgio, 3522
Davis, Gul. J., 3674
Davis, Gul. J., 3675
Davis, Gulielmo J., 3771
Davis, Gulielmo, 3888
Davis, James Joshua, 2285
Davis, Joannem Henson, 3522

Davis, Joannes Richardus, 1749
Davis, Joannis, 1749
Davis, Joannis, 927
Davis, John G., 1897
Davis, John G., 4300
Davis, John George, 2285
Davis, John George, 2402
Davis, John, 5175
Davis, John, 570
Davis, John, 5777
Davis, John, 620
Davis, Joseph Rogery, 3771
Davis, Joseph Wm., 2402
Davis, Josephina, 3392
Davis, Louisa C.J., 5384
Davis, Louisa Catharina, 3106
Davis, Louisa, 2679
Davis, Ludovica Catharina, 927
Davis, Mabel, 5339
Davis, Margaritem Louisam, 3888
Davis, Maria Anna, 1222
Davis, Maria, 3888
Davis, Maria, 4063
Davis, Mariae Annae, 1749
Davis, Mariae Annae, 927
Davis, Mariam Irene, 3675
Davis, Mary Ann, 1897

Davis, Mary Ann, 2285
Davis, Mary Ann, 2402
Davis, Mary Anna, 570
Davis, Mary Anna, 620
Davis, Mary Louisa, 2679
Davis, Mary Sophia, 620
Davis, Mary, 4
Davis, Sophia M.R., 5394
Davis, Sophia, 2589
Davis, Sophia, 5778
Davy, Mary, 1912
Dawd, Patricii, 818
Dawd, Rosae, 818
Dawd, Thomas, 818
Dawdi, C.W., 3798
Dawling, Guillelmus, 761
Dawling, Joannis, 761
Dawling, Margaretae, 761
Day, Catharine, 2116
Day, Ellen, 2116
Day, H [rest blank], 685
Day, Hellena, 685
Day, John, 2116
Day, Margaret, 2691
Day, Margaret, 2759
Day, Margaret, 3079
Day, Margareta, 1580

Day, Michaelis, 685
Dayhoney, Ann, 1868
Dce, James, 617
Deacon, Elisabeth, 4405
Deacon, Elizabeth, 1943
Deagan, Ann, 2278
Deagan, Elizabeth, 2278
Deagan, Michael, 2278
Dealhauser, Aloysius, 4606
Dealon, Anna, 1246
Dealon, Birgittae, 1173
Dealon, Joannis, 1173
Dealon, Michael, 1173
Dealy, John, 563
Dean, Thomas, 1827
Deaner, Andrea M. V., 3551
Deaner, Andrew (Mrs.), 3556
Deaner, Margaretha F., 3551
Deaner, Mary F., 3487
Deaner, Thornton Alphonsum Pool, 3551
Debinstine, Widow, 4545
Dee, Eleonora, 1419
Decarsy, Joannis, 1419
Deck, Catherine, 4288
Decrune, John, 2540
Dee, Eleonora, 1419

Dee, Jeremiae, 1419
Dee, Margareta, 1174
Dee, Margareta, 1419
Dee, Margaritae, 1419
Deeds, Catharine V., 2950
Deehan, Thomas, 1896
Degan, Antonii, 679
Degan, Antonius, 642
Degan, Ellon (widow), 4321
Degan, Maria, 679
Deggs, Jacob, 375
Deggs, Jacob, 515
Deggs, Jacob, 572
Deggs, Joseph, 515
Deggs, Rache[l?], 375
Deggs, Rachel, 515
Deggs, Rachel, 572
Deggs, Saml., 572
Deggs, Wilm, 375
Degnan, [blank], 1649
Degnan, Elisabeth, 1004
Degnan, Elisabeth, 1394
Degnan, Elisabeth, 1397
Degnan, Elisabeth, 1775
Degnan, Jacobus, 1004
Degnan, Joannes, 1649

Degnan, Joannis, 1649
Degnan, Maria, 1775
Degnan, Michael, 1394
Degnan, Michael, 4405
Degnan, Michaelis, 1004
Degnan, Michaelis, 1394
Degnan, Michaelis, 1775
Degne, Sara, 4363
Deiff, John, 304
Deiff, Mary, 304
Deiff, Mary, 304
Deins, Isiac, 408
Deins, Magdallen, 408
Deins, Sarah Anna, 408
Deiterich, Elisabeth, 2756
Deitrick, Daniel, 4597
Deitrick, Elizabeth, 5110
Deitrick, Francis, 5112
Delamarter, Mr., 4885
Delaney, Anna L., 4034
Delaney, Thomas, 4034
Delany, Michael, 4388
Delauny, Elisabeth Maria, 1267
Delauny, John C., 1267
Delauny, Maria Rosalia, 1267
Delauny, Sussannaae, 1267
Delay, Joannes A., 735

Delay, Joannis, 1691
Delay, Johanna, 1691
Delay, Mariae, 1691
Delay, Mariae, 735
Delay, Michael, 735
Delcor, Peter, 4943
Delcour, John, 4594
Delhouser, Joanna, 2712
Dellen, Francis Matthew, 2852
Dellen, Martha, 2852
Dellen, Mich, 2852
Dellon, Annie, 5147
Dellon, H., 4371
Demande, Barbara, 3231
Dempsey, Berta, 3997
Dempsey, David, 1842
Dempsey, Dominick, 1843
Dempsey, Jas., 4638
Dempsey, John Peter, 2091
Dempsey, Margaret, 1842
Dempsey, Margaret, 1843
Dempsey, Margaret, 2091
Dempsey, Peter, 1842
Dempsey, Peter, 1843
Dempsey, Peter, 2091
Dempsy, Guillemnus, 1562
Dempsy, Margaretae, 1562

Dempsy, Petri, 1562
Dempsy, Rosanna, 4302
Demsey, Birgitta, 1158
Demsey, Margareta, 1202
Demsey, Margaretae, 1158
Demsey, Petri, 1158
Denison, Guillelmus, 1161
Denney, Nancy, 4268
Denny, Julia Anna, 4404
Dennys, Maria, 1085
Deoman, Patarcicius, 1448
Dermady, Franciscae, 1060
Dermady, Franciscae, 1061
Dermady, Guillelini, 1060
Dermady, Guillelini, 1061
Dermady, Margareta (twin), 1060
Dermady, Sophia (twin), 1061
Dermady, Francisca, 1474
Dermady, Francisca, 1642
Dermard, Maria Anna, 1561
Dermel, Anna, 2966
Dermody, Frances, 1923
Dermody, Franciscae, 717
Dermody, Guellelini, 717
Dermody, Guillellmus Franciscus, 717
Dermody, Hannah, 1924

Dermody, John, 1924
Dern, Delilah, 3202
Dern, Hammond, 3202
Dern, Isaac, 3202
Deshet, Joseph Francus, 468
Deshet, Lousa, 468
Deshet, Saml., 468
Desman, Patricius, 1448
Desmend, Ellen, 3221
Desmond, Ellen, 2800
Desmond, Ellen, 2894
Desmond, Ellen, 4622
Deterick, Margaret, 2433
Detrich, Benjamin, 4782
Detrich, Benjamen F., 3729
Detrich, Benjamin F., 3644
Detrich, Benjamin F., 4790
Detrich, Benjamin, 3844
Detrich, Carolum Ambrosium, 3729
Detrich, Catharinam, 3844
Detrich, Franciscum Eduardum, 3644
Detrich, Geo., 5090
Detrich, Maria E., 3844
Detrich, Maria, 3644
Detrich, Maria, 3729

Dettlehauser, Joanna, 2510
Dettlehauser, Johanna, 2550
Dettlehauser, Lewis, 2550
Dettlehauser, Mary Catharine Elizabeth, 2550
Dettleheuser, Elie, 2510
Devereux, Margaritem, 4829
Devin, Bernard, 53
Devine, Sophia, 2206
Devis, Elonora (Miss), 248
Devlin, John, 4219
Devlin, Magey, 1825
Devolt, "not known", 2480
Devolt, Henry Rufus, 2480
Devolt, Mary Ann, 2480
Devoreux, Maria, 4393
Devoy, Elisabeth, 1024
Devoy, Guillelmi, 1024
Devoy, Maria Anna, 1024
Dexson, Anna, 669
Dexson, Mariae, 669
Dexson, Thomas, 669
Diamond, Joannis, 1089
Dias, Margaret, 2393
Dias, Mary Jane, 2393
Dias, Wm., 2393
Dichas, Mary, 3053

Dichas, Mary, 3054
Dick, Catherine, 4288
Dick, Harriet, 2911
Dick, Ann, 2911
Dick, Geo. Franeir, 2911
Dick, Geo., 2906
Dick, George, 2992
Dick, Harriet Elizabeth, 2992
Dick, Jno, 4692
Dick, Jno, 2911
Dick, John Elmer, 2906
Dick, Peter, 2911
Dick, Sarah, 2906
Dick, Sarah, 2992
Dickerhoff, Annem Caceiliam, 3814
Dickerhoff, Emma, 3814
Dickerhoff, Emma, 4087
Dickerhoff, S.C., 4161
Dickerhoff, Samuel Calvin [or Joseph], 4087
Dickerhoff, Samuele, 3814
Dickerhoff, Samuele, 4087
Dickerhoff, Samuelem, 4811
Dickers [or Dickens], Cillie M., 2628
Dicks, Benjaminus, 1212

Dicks, Henricus, 1211
Dicks, Maria Elisabeth, 1213
Didier, E. (Rev.), 2674
Didier, Edm., 2614
Didier, Edm., 2653
Didier, Edm., 2660
Didier, Edmund, 2689
Didier, Edmund, 2828
Didier, Edmund, 2908
Didier, Julia (Fr.), 4627
Didier, Julia [sic] M., 2629
Didier, Julia, 2668
Didier, Julier [or Julies] A., 4637
Didier, Rev. Ed., 4644
Diederich, Margareta, 1745
Diefendal, Albert, 5640
Diefendal, Charl., 5639
Dietrich, Elizabeth, 5519
Dietrich, Benjamin, 5311
Dietrich, Dr., 2666
Dietrich, Elizabeth, 2666
Dietrich, Maria E. (Mrs.), 4012
Dietrick, Lizzie, 2673
Dietrick, Lizzie, 5533
Diffelhonset, Johanna, 2612
Diffelhonset, Johanna, 2613
Diffelhonset, Joseph, 2612

Diffelhonset, Joseph, 2613
Diffelhonset, Louis, 2612
Diffelhonset, Louis, 2613
Diffendal, Albertus, 5681
Diffendal, Charles Augustine, 2390
Diffendal, Chs., 5680
Diffendal, Geo. Francis Bernard, 2936
Diffendal, Margaret C., 2640
Diffendal, Margaret Catharine, 2390
Diffendal, Margt., 2936
Diffendal, Saml., 2640
Diffendal, Saml., 2936
Diffendal, Samuel, 2390
Diffendal, Samuel, 2990
Diffendal, Theodore Adolphus, 2640
Diffendall, John William, 5719
Diffendall, Saml., 5287
Diffendall, Samuel, 5720
Diffendall, Theodore, 5722
Diffendall, Thomas, 5721
Diffendel, Anne Mary, 2731
Diffendel, Evan Bernardum Joannem, 3807
Diffendel, Maria, 3807

Diffendel, Mary, 2731
Diffendel, Samuel, 2731
Diffendel, Thoma B., 3807
Diffindall, Anna Mary V., 5737
Difflehonser [sic], Chrissontia, 2687
Difflehonser [sic], Johanna, 2687
Difflehonser [sic], Lewis, 2687
Difflehonser, Johanna, 2688
Diggs, Mrs., 5785
Diggs, Daniel, 573
Diggs, Henry, 1908
Diggs, Jacob, 1964
Diggs, Jacob, 573
Diggs, Jennie, 4905
Diggs, Leva [or Lena], 1964
Diggs, none, 5027
Diggs, Rachel C., 4698
Diggs, Rachel, 573
Diggs, Solomon, 1964
Diggs, Thomas, 1908
Diggs, Uncle, 5035
Diggs, William, 5397
Dignan, Antony, 4344
Dignan, Betty, 1983
Dignan, Elizabeth, 1943
Dignan, Elizabeth, 2029

Dignan, Jane, 1943
Dignan, Joannes, 4492
Dignan, Michael, 1943
Dignen, James, 202
Digs, Elonora, 280
Digs, David, 746
Digs, Jacobi, 746
Digs, Rachel, 746
Dillen, Martha, 3301
Dillen, Joannes, 3473
Dillon, John William, 5733
Dillon, Annam Ligueri, 3375
Dillon, Augusto, 3992
Dillon, Augusto, 4045
Dillon, Cath, 4638
Dillon, Catherine, 2959
Dillon, Ceciliam Liguori, 3975
Dillon, Edith, 3992
Dillon, Edith, 4045
Dillon, Ellen, 4704
Dillon, Franciscum Bennett, 4045
Dillon, Joanna, 2959
Dillon, Joanne, 3911
Dillon, Joanne, 3975
Dillon, Joanne, 4040
Dillon, Joanne, 4120
Dillon, Joannem E. W., 4776

Dillon, Joannes, 4045
Dillon, Johanna, 2531
Dillon, Johanna, 2680
Dillon, Johannes, 3297
Dillon, Joseph Philip Charles, 5728
Dillon, Joseph, 5118
Dillon, Maria, 3911
Dillon, Maria, 3911
Dillon, Maria, 3975
Dillon, Maria, 3992
Dillon, Maria, 4040
Dillon, Maria, 4120
Dillon, Mariam Anastasiam, 3911
Dillon, Mariam Catharinam, 3154
Dillon, Mariam Louisam, 4040
Dillon, Mariam Reginam, 3992
Dillon, Martha (Mrs.), 5251
Dillon, Martha, 2987
Dillon, Martha, 3113
Dillon, Martha, 3154
Dillon, Martha, 3301
Dillon, Martha, 3375
Dillon, Martha, 3601
Dillon, Martinum Franciscum Gualbertum, 4120
Dillon, Mary Ann, 2169
Dillon, Matthew Augustine, 2987

Dillon, Mich. (Mrs.), 4704
Dillon, Mich., 4704
Dillon, Michael C. I., 5729
Dillon, Michael C., 5263
Dillon, Michael, 2987
Dillon, Michael, 3113
Dillon, Michael, 4776
Dillon, Michael, 5224
Dillon, Michaele, 3154
Dillon, Michaele, 3375
Dillon, Mr., 3071
Dillon, Mrs., 3071
Dillon, Mrs., 3733
Dilworth, [blank], 2969
Dilworth, [blank], 2969
Dilworth, Ann Eliza, 2969
Dilworth, Jeremiah, 2969
Dimalins, Maria, 3390
Dimalins, Maria, 3391
Dimond, Anna, 834
Dimond, Eleonora, 834
Dimond, Eliza, 2368
Dimond, Jacobi, 834
Dimsey, Annaae, 1265
Dimsey, Patricius, 1265
Dimsey, Thomae, 1265
Dinger, Elisabeth, 929

Dinger, Georgii Michaelis, 929
Dinger, Michael, 929
Dinkel, Scholastica, 1749
Dinkel, Joannes, 1749
Dinkel, Joannes, 1756
Dinkel, Joannes, 1757
Dinkel, Joannes, 1774
Dinkel, Scholastica, 1774
Dinkel, Scholastica, 1824
Dittelhouser, Ann Josephine, 2881
Dittelhouser, Johanna, 2881
Dittelhouser, Johanna, 2882
Dittelhouser, Lewis, 2881
Dittlehonser, Johanna, 2688
Divine, Michael, 4445
Dix, Anna Elizabeth, 2240
Dix, John, 2240
Dix, Maria, 2240
Dixion, John, 2151
Dixion, Harret Agnes, 1859
Dixon, John, 1207
Dixon, John, 1858
Dixon, John, 1859
Dixon, Maria, 1491
Dixon, Marias, 1207
Dixon, Maurice, 1858
Dockenny, Ellen, 2627

Docknoy, Ellen, 4691
Dodson, Anna E., 2704
Dodson, Anna, 2948
Dodson, Edward, 320
Dodson, Hanna, 320
Dodson, Huly, 320
Doherty, E. (Mrs.), 556
Doherty, Eliza (widow), 4276
Doherty, James, 245
Doherty, Mary (Mrs.), 215
Doherty, Phillip Henery, 245
Doherty, Wilm (Mrs.), 475
Doile, Adam, 194
Doile, Elisabeth Naoma, 194
Doile, Rebecca, 194
Doke?, Elisabetha, 4367
Dolan, Helena, 3394
Dolan, [blank], 2061
Dolan, Andrew, 2059
Dolan, Anna, 1034
Dolan, Anna, 1557
Dolan, Anna, 2060
Dolan, Birgitta, 1306
Dolan, Birgittae, 1307
Dolan, Brian, 1034
Dolan, Brian, 1611
Dolan, Caroline, 2871

Dolan, Catharina, 1526
Dolan, Catharina, 1603
Dolan, Catharina, 3603
Dolan, Ellen, 2706
Dolan, Francisci, 1603
Dolan, Jacobus, 1526
Dolan, Jacobus, 1737
Dolan, James, 2059
Dolan, James, 2060
Dolan, James, 2061
Dolan, Jas., 2606
Dolan, Josephina (Mrs.), 4041
Dolan, Josephine (Mrs.), 4022
Dolan, Julia, 1444
Dolan, Margaret, 2034
Dolan, Maria, 1307
Dolan, Maria, 1398
Dolan, Maria, 1611
Dolan, Mariae, 1034
Dolan, Mariae, 1444
Dolan, Mariae, 1526
Dolan, Mariae, 1603
Dolan, Mariae, 1611
Dolan, Mariae, 1737
Dolan, Mary, 2871
Dolan, Mary, 51
Dolan, Matilda, 2059

Dolan, Matilda, 2060
Dolan, Matilda, 2061
Dolan, Michaelis, 1444
Dolan, Michaelis, 1737
Dolan, Mrs., 4019
Dolan, Mrs., 4054
Dolan, Mrs., 4882
Dolan, Mrs., 4882
Dolan, Patricii, 1307
Dolan, Patricii, 1557
Dolan, Patricius, 1338
Dolan, Patricius, 1508
Dolan, Rosa, 1726
Dolan, Thomae, 1526
Dolan, Thos., 2727
Dolan, Wm., 2871
Dolen, Annae, 1277
Dolen, Charley, 4215
Dolen, Joannes, 1277
Dolen, Patricii, 1277
Dollen, Catherine, 402
Dollen, Charley, 402
Dollen, John Ormand, 402
Dom, L. Cath., 3418
Doman, Joannes, 1520
Domenici, Maria, 4155
Domenici, Mauritio, 4916

Dominici, Maria, 3891
Dominici, Maria, 3955
Dominici, Mauritio, 3891
Dominici, Mauritium Paulum, 3891
Donaldson, Edna L., 4086
Donavan, Anna, 1449
Donavan, Catharina, 1545
Donavan, Catharinae, 1545
Donavan, Denis, 4254
Donavan, Denis, 512
Donavan, Dionysius, 1545
Donavan, Joannes, 1607
Donavan, Joannis, 1545
Donavan, Mary (widow), 4319
Donavin, Joannes, 1568
Done, Lewis, 1828
Done, Magdalen, 1828
Done, Sophia, 1828
Done, Terrentius, 4372
Donegan, Thomas, 2055
Doneley, Edward, 4572
Doneley, Mary, 4708
Donelley, Bridget, 2107
Donelley, Carolum Eduardem, 3292
Donelley, Catharina, 3241
Donelley, Eduardo, 3413

Donelley, Eduardum, 4742
Donelley, Eduardus, 3417
Donelley, Edwardo, 3241
Donelley, Edwardo, 3292
Donelley, Edwardus, 3262
Donelley, Franciscum Eduardum, 3413
Donelley, Jacobum Elie, 3241
Donelley, James, 3089
Donelley, Katarina, 3413
Donelley, Kate, 3257
Donelley, Kate, 3292
Donelley, Maria, 3257
Donelley, Maria, 3417
Donelley, Mary, 4709
Donelly, Bridget, 2101
Donelly, Bridget, 2047
Donelly, Bridget, 2170
Donelly, Bridget, 2450
Donelly, Bridget, 2476
Donelly, Edward, 2309
Donelly, Edward, 2450
Donelly, Edward, 3021
Donelly, Edward, 4608
Donelly, Eliza, 2243
Donelly, James, 2476
Donelly, John, 4724

Donelly, Louisa, 4580
Donelly, Louisa, 4540
Donelly, M., 3021
Donelly, Marcus, 2476
Donelly, Margaret, 2476
Donelly, Maria Ellen, 3182
Donelly, Maria, 3517
Donelly, Mark, 3081
Donelly, Mary A., 4708
Donelly, Mary Ann, 2309
Donelly, Mary Catharine, 2047
Donelly, Mary, 2309
Donelly, Mary, 2450
Donelly, Mary, 3061
Donelly, Mary, 4920
Donelly, Peter, 2170
Donelly, Terence, 2101
Donelly, Terence, 2047
Donelly, Terence, 2170
Donelly, Thoma, 4742
Donelly, Thomas, 2450
Donelly, Thomas, 2450
Donelly, Thomas, 4744
Donelly, Thomas, 4922
Donelson, John P., 1845
Donn, Maria, 3607
Donn, Elisabeth, 1465

Donn, Kate, 3189
Donne, Jane, 2418
Donne, Luiza, 2418
Donne, Richard, 2418
Donnellen, Mrs., 337
Donnelley, Charley, 402
Donnelley, Bridgett, 398
Donnelly, Mary, 2941
Donnelly, Bridget, 429
Donnelly, Bridget, 2663
Donnelly, Bridget, 4343
Donnelly, Bridget, 553
Donnelly, Catharina, 1350
Donnelly, Catharina, 4458
Donnelly, Charl., 573
Donnelly, Charles, 398
Donnelly, Charley, 390
Donnelly, Edw., 5568
Donnelly, Edward, 4920
Donnelly, Edward, 5512
Donnelly, Edwardus, 1558
Donnelly, Edwardus, 3112
Donnelly, Edwardus, 3158
Donnelly, Edwd., 2941
Donnelly, Elon, 233
Donnelly, Frances, 4215
Donnelly, Francis, 360

Donnelly, Henery, 240
Donnelly, Henry, 233
Donnelly, Hugo, 4364
Donnelly, James, 2929
Donnelly, Joannes, 3930
Donnelly, Leonidas, 382
Donnelly, Louisa, 2274
Donnelly, Marg. Ellen, 3748
Donnelly, Margaret, 171
Donnelly, Margaret, 188
Donnelly, Margareta, 1665
Donnelly, Margret, 229
Donnelly, Margret, 229
Donnelly, Margret, 382
Donnelly, Maria, 1382
Donnelly, Maria, 1569
Donnelly, Maria, 1688
Donnelly, Maria, 3930
Donnelly, Mariae, 1350
Donnelly, Mariae, 1558
Donnelly, Mark, 5463
Donnelly, Mary (Miss), 4209
Donnelly, Mary Ann, 5775
Donnelly, Mary, 228
Donnelly, Mary, 240
Donnelly, Mary, 240
Donnelly, Mary, 240

Donnelly, Mary, 2894
Donnelly, Mary, 2929
Donnelly, Mary, 5571
Donnelly, Mary, 99
Donnelly, Mrs., 4580
Donnelly, Owen, 4247
Donnelly, P. (Mrs.), 486
Donnelly, Pat, 2929
Donnelly, Patricii, 1558
Donnelly, Patricius, 1676
Donnelly, Patrick Donnelly, 99
Donnelly, Patrick, 229
Donnelly, Patrick, 265
Donnelly, Patrick, 372
Donnelly, Patrick, 382
Donnelly, Patrick, 4214
Donnelly, Patrick, 99
Donnelly, Sarah (Miss), 234
Donnelly, Sarah (Miss), 360
Donnelly, Sarah, 4312
Donnelly, Terence, 2107
Donnelly, Th., 2898
Donnelly, Thomas, 1525
Donnelly, Thos., 5518
Donnelly, Thos., 5548
Donnelly, William, 1350
Donnelly, Wilm, 233

Donnely, Eleonora, 1253
Donnely, Henry, 161
Donnely, Margaret, 161
Donnely, Maria, 1368
Donnely, Patrick, 161
Donnely, Saly, 285
Domlley, Louisa, 431
Domlley, Margret, 431
Domlley, Patrick, 431
Donnlly, Catharine, 368
Donnolly, Cath., 3773
Donnolly, Catharina, 3565
Donnolly, Ednardo, 3565
Donnolly, Maria, 3616
Donnolly, Maria, 3829
Donnolly, Thomem Leonem, 3565
Donoghoe, Julia, 4492
Donoghue, Catharina, 3622
Donohoe, Ann, 1955
Donohue, Catharina, 3490
Donohue, Catharina, 3856
Donohue, Johannem, 4757
Donohue, Maria, 3926
Dononghue, Bridget, 3032
Dononghue, Catherine, 3032
Donovan, Margareta, 4361
Donovan, Birgittae, 1704

Donovan, Catharinae, 1175
Donovan, Catharine, 2790
Donovan, Cornelius, 4275
Donovan, Dyoinysii, 1295
Donovan, Elisabeth, 1175
Donovan, Elisabeth, 1295
Donovan, Joannes, 1175
Donovan, Joannes, 1295
Donovan, Joannes, 1175
Donovan, Joannes, 1494
Donovan, Joannis, 1704
Donovan, Johanna, 4515
Donovan, Maria, 1295
Donovan, Maria, 1704
Donovan, Mariae, 1295
Donovan, Mary Ann, 2078
Donovan, Mary, 2674
Donovan, Michael, 2282
Donovan, Timothy, 4207
Dont, Elisabeth, 4491
Doody, Johanna, 3411
Doody, Johanna, 3417
Doody, Johanna, 3421
Doody, Johanna, 3423
Doolan, Elisabeth, 3150
Doolan, Ellen (Miss), 4612
Doolan, Ellen, 3025

Doolan, Ellen, 5410
Doolan, Helena, 3529
Doolan, Margaret, 590
Doolan, Mary, 89
Doolin, Tim, 2953
Dooling, Eliz., 2953
Dooling, Eliza, 2394
Dooling, Ellen, 2523
Dooling, John, 4557
Dooling, Patrick, 2394
Dooling, Timothy, 2394
Dooly, Josephus, 1659
Dooly, Maria, 1650
Dooly, Michael, 1650
Doran, Catharina, 3268
Doran, Albert Roney, 2948
Doran, Anna E., 2704
Doran, Anna, 2948
Doran, Anne A., 2789
Doran, Charles, 2704
Doran, Charles, 2789
Doran, Chs. R., 2948
Doran, Ella Mary, 2704
Doran, Francis Ruiston, 2789
Dore, Daniel, 2975
Dore, Mariam, 3161
Dore, Marias, 3161

Dore, Mary, 2975
Dore, Pat, 2975
Dore, Patricio, 3161
Dormady, Helenae, 725
Dormady, Philippi, 725
Dormady, Philippus, 725
Dormady, Maria Anna, 1725
Dormer, Nicholas, 4713
Dormor, Jacobus, 695
Dormor, Juliae, 695
Dormor, Martini, 695
Dorn, L. Cath., 3418
Dorn, Laura C., 3524
Dornion, Catharina, 1771
Dorsey, Adolphus, 1815
Dorsey, Anna R., 2694
Dorsey, Anna, 2023
Dorsey, F. (Dr.), 4604
Dorsey, Ignatius B., 2694
Dorsey, James Albert, 2296
Dorsey, Joanni, 3762
Dorsey, Mary Elizabeth, 2694
Dorsey, Mary, 2023
Dorsey, Mrs., 4574
Dorsey, Rachel, 1815
Dorsey, Rachel, 2296
Dorsey, Rosa, 4513

Dorsey, Sarah A., 3915
Dorsey, Sarah, 4114
Dorsey, Saraim A., 4856
Dorsey, Will, 5338
Dorsey, William, 1969
Douckry, Anna, 1250
Douckry, Eleonora, 1250
Douckry, Thomae, 1250
Dougherty, Catharina, 830
Dougherty, Catharinae, 838
Dougherty, Catharine, 53
Dougherty, Danielis, 830
Dougherty, Gracey, 53
Dougherty, Hugonus, 838
Dougherty, Joannes, 838
Dougherty, Johannem, 4754
Dougherty, Margaret, 111
Dougherty, Mariae Annae, 830
Dougherty, Philip, 53
Doughterty, Cornelio, 3204
Douglas, Carolo, 4020
Douglas, Carolum Gulielmum, 4020
Douglas, Carolum, 4881
Douglas, Maria, 4020
Douglass, Jno., 2898
Doulan, Maria, 1123

Dounin, Edina, 2784
Dounin, Martha, 2783
Dounin, Martha, 2784
Dounin, Richard, 2783
Dounin, S. S., 2783
Dounin, S. S., 2784
Doutel, Michael, 2000
Dowd, Jno., 2635
Dowd, Johanna, 2635
Dowd, Michael, 2635
Downey, Richard, 5690
Downey (clear), Maria, 790
Downey (clear), Mariae, 790
Downey (clear), Thomae, 790
Downey, Anna, 4384
Downey, Georgio, 3795
Downey, Lilly Mary, 5622
Downey, Mariae, 789
Downey, Thomae, 789
Downey, Thomas, 789
Downin, Anna, 3631
Downin, Anna, 3632
Downin, Anna, 3633
Downin, Annam Mariam, 3632
Downin, Catharina, 3823
Downin, Catharina, 3896
Downin, Catharina, 3968

Downin, Catharina, 4006
Downin, Catharinam, 4824
Downin, Catherine, 2985
Downin, Grace Theresiam, 3633
Downin, Jacob, 4863
Downin, Joannem P., 4878
Downin, Joannem Patricium, 3105
Downin, Lilly, 2985
Downin, Maria, 3105
Downin, Maria, 3823
Downin, Maria, 3855
Downin, Maria, 4006
Downin, Maria, 4824
Downin, Mariam C., 4832
Downin, Mary, 2915
Downin, Mary, 2985
Downin, Noram Augustan, 3631
Downin, Otho B., 4861
Downin, S.S., 2915
Downin, Samuel S. (Mrs.), 5352
Downin, Samuel, 2985
Downin, Samuele, 3105
Downin, Samuele, 3631
Downin, Samuele, 3632
Downin, Samuele, 3633
Downin, Thos., 2915
Downing, Mary, 3873

Downing, Mary, 2793
Downing, Mary, 2793
Downing, Samuel S., 2793
Downs, [blank], 3200
Downs, [blank], 3200
Downs, Cristophero, 3200
Downs, Ludovicum, 4746
Downs, Ludvicum, 3200
Downs, Miles, 1288
Dowyre, Birgittae, 884
Dowyre, Henrici, 884
Dowyre, Maria, 884
Doxe', Elisabeth, 648
Doyd, J. (Mr.), 323
Doyel, Catherine, 339
Doyel, Elisa, 339
Doyel, John Adam, 575
Doyel, Lawrence, 339
Doyel, Rebecca, 575
Doyel, Richard, 575
Doyel, Anna, 533
Doyel, Catherine, 398
Doyel, James Lawrence, 398
Doyel, Lawrence, 398
Doyle, Eva, 2802
Doyle, Mrs., 4604
Doyle, Adami, 1392

Doyle, Ann, 2302
Doyle, Anna, 1151
Doyle, Anna Rebecca, 517
Doyle, Anna Rebeccae, 832
Doyle, Anna Virginia, 352
Doyle, Anna, 1443
Doyle, Anna, 1519
Doyle, Annae, 1051
Doyle, Annae, 1241
Doyle, Annae, 1539
Doyle, Bernardus, 1276
Doyle, Birgitta, 1125
Doyle, Birgitta, 1518
Doyle, Carolus Augustus, 832
Doyle, Catharina, 1277
Doyle, Catharina, 1503
Doyle, Catharine B., 4604
Doyle, Charlotte, 3091
Doyle, Edwardi, 1125
Doyle, Edwardi, 771
Doyle, Edwardus, 1125
Doyle, Edwardus, 1443
Doyle, Eleonarae, 771
Doyle, Elisabeth, 1276
Doyle, Elisabeth, 1699
Doyle, Elisabethae, 728
Doyle, Elizabeth, 1995

Doyle, Elizabeth, 1996
Doyle, Ellen, 4562
Doyle, Elleonorae, 1125
Doyle, Eva (Miss), 2747
Doyle, Eva (Miss), 4667
Doyle, Eva E., 2459
Doyle, Eva E., 4679
Doyle, Eva, 2714
Doyle, Eva, 2720
Doyle, Eva, 2748
Doyle, Eva, 4662
Doyle, Eva, 4668
Doyle, Evaline, 2755
Doyle, Evelina, 2442
Doyle, Eveline, 4620
Doyle, Fred, 2860
Doyle, Fred, 4679
Doyle, Frederick Charles, 1946
Doyle, George Henery, 274
Doyle, Jacobi, 1699
Doyle, Jacobus, 1241
Doyle, Jacobus, 4477
Doyle, Jacobus, 771
Doyle, James Herbert, 1995
Doyle, James Richard, 3091
Doyle, James Wilm, 420
Doyle, James, 1995

Doyle, James, 1996
Doyle, James, 3050
Doyle, James, 3066
Doyle, James, 3091
Doyle, James, 4720
Doyle, Joannes, 1519
Doyle, Joannes, 728
Doyle, Joannis Adami, 832
Doyle, Joannis, 1276
Doyle, Joannis, 728
Doyle, Johannes, 4373
Doyle, John Adam, 517
Doyle, John Adam, 517
Doyle, John, 2442
Doyle, John, 274
Doyle, John, 352
Doyle, John, 420
Doyle, John, 4568
Doyle, John, 4716
Doyle, Josephus, 1392
Doyle, Kate (Miss), 4591
Doyle, Lou., 2928
Doyle, Louisa H., 3093
Doyle, Louisa H., 5382
Doyle, Louisa Harriet, 1948
Doyle, Louisa, 2477

Doyle, Louisa, 2815
Doyle, Louisa, 2870
Doyle, Louisa, 2983
Doyle, Louisa, 3180
Doyle, Louisa, 3270
Doyle, Louisa, 3362
Doyle, Louisa, 3587
Doyle, Louisa, 4673
Doyle, Louisa, 4680
Doyle, Lousia, 3433
Doyle, Lucas, 1503
Doyle, Ludovica, 3518
Doyle, Margaret Genevieve, 4673
Doyle, Margaret, 1946
Doyle, Margaret, 1947
Doyle, Margaret, 1948
Doyle, Margaret, 2746
Doyle, Margaret, 5381
Doyle, Margt., 2921
Doyle, Maria Anna, 1241
Doyle, Maria Anna, 1699
Doyle, Maria, 1051
Doyle, Maria, 1539
Doyle, Mary Louisa, 2442
Doyle, Mary Louisa, 5614
Doyle, Mary, 2442

Doyle, Michael, 1518
Doyle, Mr., 4604
Doyle, Mrs., 2678
Doyle, Mrs., 4985
Doyle, Patrick (Mrs.), 571
Doyle, Patrick, 4268
Doyle, Rebecca, 274
Doyle, Rebecca, 420
Doyle, Rebeccae, 1392
Doyle, Rosa, 1996
Doyle, Rrebecca, 352
Doyle, Sara, 1539
Doyle, Sarae, 1443
Doyle, Terrentii, 1051
Doyle, Terrentii, 1241
Doyle, Terrentii, 1539
Doyle, Terrentius, 1443
Doyle, Thomae, 1443
Doyle, Thomam E., 4870
Doyle, William, 1946
Doyle, William, 1948
Doyle, William, 2802
Doyle, William, 2808
Doyle, Williams, 1947
Doyle, Wm (Mr. or Mrs.), 4667
Doyle, Wm. E., 4673
Dr, Carolina Matild, 1280

Dr, Danielis, 1280
Dr, Mariae, 1280
Drageser, Thomas, 4416
Drake, Joannes, 1447
Dranan, Catharina, 1696
Dranan, Thomas, 1696
Draper, Catharina Maria, 686
Draper, George, 4345
Draper, Georgii, 1480
Draper, Georgii, 686
Draper, Georgis, 1735
Draper, Georgius Albertus, 1480
Draper, Maria, 1481
Draper, Mariae, 1480
Draper, Mariae, 1735
Draper, Mariae, 686
Draper, Zeru Elisabeth, 1735
Dreman, Joannem Patritium, 3564
Dreman, Margarita, 3564
Dreman, Themate, 3564
Dremen [or Dreman], Henricum Wiley, 3559
Dremen [or Dreman], Josepho, 3559
Dremen [or Dreman], Margarita, 3559
Drenan, Catharine, 2150

Drenen, Thomas, 2473
Drennan, Catharinae, 1112
Drennan, Chirstophorus, 1112
Drennan, Ludivecum Victor, 3753
Drennan, Maria, 3753
Drennan, Thoma, 3753
Drennan, Thomae, 1112
Drennan, Catharinae, 1761
Drennan, Catharinae, 662
Drennan, Josephus, 1761
Drennan, Margarita, 3665
Drennan, Margarita, 3784
Drennan, Margaritem Elizabeth, 3784
Drennan, Maria, 3662
Drennan, Maria, 662
Drennan, Mariam Catharinam, 3665
Drennan, Mary C., 3052
Drennan, Mary, 2768
Drennan, Mary, 2859
Drennan, Thomae, 1761
Drennan, Thomae, 662
Drennan, Thomati, 3665
Drennan, Thomati, 3784
Drennen, Catharine, 1998
Drennen, Christopher, 4926

Drennen, Mary, 2469
Drennen, Thomas, 4961
Drennen, Thos., 3607
Drenner, Mary, 4632
Drescol, Carolinae, 1347
Drescol, Margareta, 1347
Drescol, Michael, 1348
Drescoll, Michaelis, 1347
Drescoll, Carolinae, 709
Drescoll, Maria, 709
Drescoll, Michael, 4382
Drescoll, Michaelis, 709
Dril, Laura, 3525
Drinnin, Thos., 2729
Driscal, Isabellae, 736
Driscal, Julia, 736
Driscal, Timothei, 736
Driscoll, Carolinaae, 1058
Driscoll, Jacobus, 1058
Driscoll, Michaelis, 1058
Drock, Joannis, 1463
Drock, Margareta, 1463
Drock, Mariae, 1463
Dronan, Catharina, 1266
Dronan, Thomas, 1266
Drum, Wilm, 4329
Drumgold, James, 92

Drumgould, James, 97
Drury, Ann, 82
Drury, Ann, 83
Drury, Elizabeth, 44
Drury, Ignatius, 4192
Drury, Leonard, 82
Drury, Mary, 191
Drury, Matilda (Miss), 4181
Drury, Milly Anna, 191
Drury, T. [or F.], 191
Duddy, Joanna M., 3386
Duddy, Joanna M., 3387
Duffey, Anna, 1110
Duffey, Annae, 1261
Duffey, Annae, 1106
Duffey, Bridget, 527
Duffey, Carolus, 3379
Duffey, Chas. Andrew, 5694
Duffey, Eliza, 2762
Duffey, Ellen, 2762
Duffey, Jacobi, 986
Duffey, John (Mrs.), 523
Duffey, John, 527
Duffey, John, 527
Duffey, Margareta, 1106
Duffey, Maria, 1169
Duffey, Maria, 986

Duffey, Mariae, 986
Duffey, Mary, 4304
Duffey, Michaelis, 1106
Duffey, Otho, 3375
Duffey, Otho, 3575
duffey, Patrick, 2969
Duffey, Paulo Raymundo, 3883
Duffey, Will., 5627
Duffey, William S., 4602
Duffey, William, 2152
Duffey, Wm., 2762
Duffie, Caeciliam G., 3724
Duffie, Laura, 3724
Duffie, Lloyd, 4808
Duffie, Loyd, 3724
Duffy, John, 210
Duffy, Mary, 210
Duffy, Mrs., 272
Duffy, William, 210
Duffy, Carolo, 4734
Duffy, Catharine, 2322
Duffy, Catharine, 2355
Duffy, Charles Edgar, 2587
Duffy, Charles Edgar, 2588
Duffy, Charles, 3045
Duffy, Demetrio, 4832
Duffy, Edward, 2355

Duffy, Edward, 2355
Duffy, Eliza (Mrs.), 4039
Duffy, Eliza F., 2533
Duffy, Eliza, 2511
Duffy, Eliza, 2587
Duffy, Eliza, 2588
Duffy, Eliza, 2633
Duffy, Eliza, 2634
Duffy, Eliza, 2686
Duffy, Eliza, 2930
Duffy, Frances McKearnan, 2634
Duffy, Guielmo S., 4850
Duffy, Gulielmum Joseph, 4039
Duffy, Helena, 4869
Duffy, Helenam B., 4877
Duffy, J. Demetrius, 3509
Duffy, J. Demetrius, 3510
Duffy, Jas. Demetris, 2930
Duffy, Jno, 164
Duffy, John William, 2533
Duffy, John, 4200
Duffy, Joseph S., 2686
Duffy, Maria M., 4122
Duffy, Maria, 4039
Duffy, Maria, 4164
Duffy, Mariam Reginam, 4164
Duffy, Mary Ellen, 2633

Duffy, Otho Francescun Fisher, 4122
Duffy, Otho J., 4838
Duffy, Otho J., 4869
Duffy, Otho Jos. S., 4122
Duffy, Otho Joseph Smith, 5723
Duffy, Otho, 3296
Duffy, Otho, 3514
Duffy, Otho, 3861
Duffy, Otho, 4039
Duffy, Otho, 4164
Duffy, Otho, 4828
Duffy, Otho, 4831
Duffy, Otho, 4866
Duffy, Twin Children, 4995
Duffy, W. (Mr.), 4039
Duffy, W., 4733
Duffy, William S., 2533
Duffy, Wm. S., 2587
Duffy, Wm. S., 2588
Duffy, Wm. S., 2633
Duffy, Wm. S., 2634
Duffy, Wm. S., 2686
Duffy, Wm., 2930
Dufini, Beatrice, 3799
Dufour, Beatrice, 3914
Duga, Bernardus, 1209

Dugan, Bridget, 2929
Dugan [or Deguan], Elizabeth, 5418
Dugan, Catharine, 2046
Dugan, Cumberland F., 4611
Dugan, Elisabeth, 4477
Dugan, Francis, 2046
Dugan, Guglielmum Edwin, 3379
Dugan, Helena S., 4091
Dugan, Helena, 4091
Dugan, Helenam C., 4913
Dugan, Helenam Geneviefam, 4091
Dugan, Irene C., 4625
Dugan, Isabella, 1711
Dugan, Isabella, 2008
Dugan, Isabella, 2238
Dugan, Isabella, 4504
Dugan, Jacobus, 1117
Dugan, Jacobus, 4822
Dugan, Jno. A., 4687
Dugan, Joanne Monahan, 4091
Dugan, Johanne, 3379
Dugan, Margt., 2863
Dugan, Maria, 3379
Dugan, Maria, 3799
Dugan, Maria, 4822

Dugan, Monroe, 4913
Dugan, Rebecca (Miss), 2103
Dugan, Rebecca, 1928
Dugan, Rebecca, 2109
Dugan, Wm., 2929
Dugen, M., 3698
Duggan, Ann, 155
Duggan, Ann, 4183
Duggan, Anne, 127
Duggan, Helen S. (Mrs.), 4146
Duggan, Helena, 3965
Duggan, Helena, 4877
Duggan, Joanna, 3754
Duggan, Joannes, 3931
Duggan, Maria, 3754
Duggan, Maria, 3914
Duggan, Mary, 4187
Duglass, Mary (Mrs.), 5313
Duhanell, Leo, 2812
Duigman [or Dujman], Jas., 2880
Dulin, Jno. (Mrs.), 3667
Dulin, Jno, 3667
Duling, Lizzie A., 4696
Dumond, Edward, 4263
Dun, Isaac, 2269
Dun, Jane, 2269
Dun, John Daniel, 2445

Dun, Margaret, 2445
Dun, Mary Jane, 2260
Dun, Philip, 2258
Dun, Richard, 2269
Dun, Sarah Anna, 2260
Dun, William, 2445
Dunbar, Thomas, 1391
Duncan, Anne Elisabeth, 2713
Duncan, Bernard, 4320
Duncan, Johanne, 4811
Duncan, Levi, 2713
Duncan, Maria E., 3488
Duncan, Maria E., 3542
Duncan, Mary Catherine, 2713
Dunleary, Daniel, 2315
Dunn, Wilm, 4329
Dunn, Anna Elizabeth, 2378
Dunn, Anna Rebecca, 2548
Dunn, Anna, 727
Dunn, Catharina, 1639
Dunn, Charles Henry, 3011
Dunn, Denis, 2078
Dunn, Guillelmi, 727
Dunn, Harriet, 2163
Dunn, Harriet, 2377
Dunn, Harriet, 2378
Dunn, Harriet, 2548

Dunn, Jacob Wm, 2900
Dunn, James, 3011
Dunn, Jane [Harriet crossed out], 2378
Dunn, Jane, 2377
Dunn, Jas., 2900
Dunn, John Francis, 2078
Dunn, Margaret Ann Elizabeth, 2548
Dunn, Margaret, 3011
Dunn, Margt, 2900
Dunn, Margt, 2900
Dunn, Maria, 3607
Dunn, Mariae, 727
Dunn, Mary J., 4592
Dunn, Mary Jane, 2481
Dunn, Mary Jane, 2542
Dunn, Mary, 2078
Dunn, Owen, 4333
Dunn, William Henry, 2163
Dunn, William, 2548
Dunnan, Ludivecum Victor, 3753
Dunnan, Maria, 3753
Dunnan, Thoma, 3753
Dunne, Anna, 2966
Dunne, James, 2763
Dunne, Jas., 2782

Dunne, Margaret [sic], 2782
Dunne, Timothy Trane, 2782
Dunning, David, 4614
Durnin, Wm, 88
Durninerman, Henricus Rudolfus, 4440
Durnmermann, Catharinae, 1326
Durnmermann, Frederici Henrici, 1326
Durnmermann, Joannes H., 1326
Dusang, Clara Virginia, 2953
Dusang, Elisabeth Tinam, 3150
Dusang, Elisabeth, 3150
Dusang, Eliz., 2953
Dusang, Geo, 2953
Dusang, George, 3150
Dusang, Ruth I., 3786
Dusang, Sarah E., 2953
Dusang, Sarah Ellen, 2951
Dusany, Lizzie, 3025
Duvamy, Geo. A., 4696
Dwire, Maria, 1486
Dyer, Adele, 4912
Dyer, Eliza Mary, 41
Dyer, Eliza Mary, 81
Dygs, Jacob, 419
Dygs, Jacob, 477

Dygs, Jacob, 515
Dygs, John, 419
Dygs, Joseph, 515
Dygs, Luise, 477
Dygs, Rachel, 419
Dygs, Rachel, 477
Dygs, Rachel, 515
Dykes, Forena [sic], 4808
Dykes, Louisa, 3724
Dykes, Louisa, 4808
Dyre, Simon, 498
E. Turners, Lennard, 4201
Eagan, [blank], 5097
Eagan, Catherine (Miss), 4337
Eagan, Josephum Patritium, 3233
Eagan, Margaret (Mrs.), 5235
Eagan, Margareta, 3233
Eagan, Peter, 4337
Eagan, Thoma, 3233
Eagan, Thomam, 4749
Early, Anna, 379
Early, Bridget, 4261
Early, James, 379
Early, Margret Anna, 379
Earnshaw, Jerry, 4845
Easterday, Elizabeth, 2183
Eberhart, Clara Catharine, 2406

Ebert, Giorgium, 3278
Eccleston, Archbishop, 2074
Eck, Samuel (Mrs.), 2777
Eck, Catharina, 3495
Eck, Catharine, 1961
Eck, Catharine, 2205
Eck, Catharine, 2345
Eck, Catharine, 2403
Eck, Catharine, 2550
Eck, Catharine, 2564
Eck, Jno. (Mrs.), 2935
Eck, Jno., 2692
Eck, Jno., 2935
Eck, Jno., 4625
Eck, Johannes, 4754
Eck, John M., 2403
Eck, John, 1961
Eck, John, 2205
Eck, John, 2345
Eck, John, 2550
Eck, Maria, 3271
Eck, Maria, 4747
Eck, Mariam, 4754
Eck, Mary Catharine Elizabeth, 2403
Eck, Mary, 2759
Eck, Mary, 2774

Eck, Mary, 2795
Eck, Mary, 2885
Eck, Mary, 2937
Eck, Mary, 3015
Eck, Mary, 5610
Eck, Michael, 1762
Eck, Mrs., 2691
Eck, Samuel, 2716
Eck, Samuel, 2777
Eckar, Adam, 2183
Eckar, Elizabeth, 2183
Eckar, Mary Eliza Augustina, 2183
Eckenrode, Sarai, 3998
Eckert, Dorothea Elisabeth, 1564
Eckert, Gertudis, 1564
Eckert, Joannes, 4390
Eckert, Joannis, 1564
Eckinrode, Jno. H., 4086
Ecknode, Maria V., 3725
Edwards, Catharinam, 3236
Edwards, Margareta, 3236
Edwards, Roberto, 3236
Egan, Anna, 1442
Egan, Catharinae, 1442
Egan, Catharinae, 639
Egan, Catharine, 1898
Egan, Catharine, 2054

Egan, Hanora, 1343
Egan, Hugh, 1995
Egan, Hugh, 2242
Egan, Hugo, 1712
Egan, Joannes, 1683
Egan, John Baptist, 2054
Egan, John, 2054
Egan, John, 2073
Egan, Margareta, 3723
Egan, Margaretta, 3575
Egan, Margarita, 3317
Egan, Maria, 639
Egan, Mariam Catharinam, 3575
Egan, Mariam Helenam, 3317
Egan, Mariam, 3723
Egan, Mary, 1898
Egan, Mary, 2054
Egan, Mary, 2073
Egan, Michael, 1898
Egan, Patricius, 1457
Egan, Peter, 1898
Egan, Peter, 2054
Egan, Petri, 1442
Egan, Petri, 639
Egan, Thoma, 3317
Egan, Thoma, 3575
Egan, Thoma, 3723

Egan, Thos., 3169
Egle, Catharine, 1961
Egle, Cunegunda, 1961
Egle, George, 1961
Ehwald, Barbarae, 1612
Ehwald, Gasperis, 1612
Ehwald, Maria Regina, 1612
Eichelberger, Ann Maria, 2056
Eichelberger, Anna Maria, 2274
Eichelberger, Sarah, 4647
Eiler, Barbary, 516
Eisiminger, Albert, 3047
Eisiminger, Lilien Catherine, 3047
Eisiminger, Mary G. [or J.], 3047
Eisler, Joannes, 1164
Elam, Carolo, 4026
Elam, Gertrude, 4026
Elam, Hermann Russell, 4026
Elicot, Benjamini, 1622
Elicot, Mariae, 1622
Elicot, William C., 1622
Eliz., Covell, 2903
Eliz., Jos., 2903
Eliz., Mary Cath., 2903
Eller, Mary Ann, 180
Eller, Mary, 180
Ellet, Lillie, 4820

Elliot, Elisabeth Annae, 786
Elliot, Elisabeth, 1596
Elliot, Jacobi Blair, 786
Elliot, Josephus Henricus, 786
Elliott, James, 4226
Elliott, Roberto W., 3924
Ellis, James, 591
Ellood, Catharinae, 1304
Ellood, Francisci, 1304
Ellood, Michael, 1304
Ellott, Elisa, 469
Ellott, James, 469
Ellott, Maria Eliza, 469
Ellott, Mary, 4267
Ellove, Catharinae, 1304
Ellove, Francisci, 1304
Ellove, Michael, 1304
Elmer, Florence, 3356
Elvord, Wilm, 544
Endaunn, Catharinae, 802
Endaunn, Joses Conradi, 802
Endaunn, Maria, 802
England, Margaret, 2042
England, Margareta, 1709
Ensmenger, Charlotte, 2009
Ensmenger, Charlotte, 2010
Ensminger, Catharine, 2426

Ensminger, Catharine, 2427
Ensminger, Catharine, 2428
Ensminger, Catharine, 2429
Ensminger, Eva, 3331
Ernst, Mary Ann, 2501
Ertter, Henricum Felicem, 4081
Ertter, Joanne Eduardo, 4081
Ertter, Joannem Eduardum, 4890
Ertter, Maud Emma, 4081
Estill, Mary (widow), 4272
Evans, Catharine, 2046
Evans, George Francis, 2046
Evans, Thomas T., 2046
Evason, Ann, 2543
Evason, John, 2543
Evehart, Cecelia, 2290
Evers, Mary Otilia, 2885
Evers, Milling, 2885
Evers, Susan, 2885
Eversole, Annem E., 4795
Eversole, Jno., 4795
Eves, Amos F., 3903
Evret, Appolloniae, 1528
Evret, Maria Anna, 1528
Ewer, Milton (Mrs.), 3869
Ewer, Milton (Mrs.), 3987
Ewer, Milton, 3869

Ewer, Milton, 3987
Ewer, Susanna (Mrs.), 3961
Ewers, Susan, 3312
Ewers, Milton (Mrs.), 3552
Ewers, Milton (Mrs.), 4133
Ewers, Jacob Milton, 3002
Ewers, John Vincent, 3085
Ewers, Jonathan, 3002
Ewers, Maria, 4015
Ewers, Maria, 4078
Ewers, Maria, 4133
Ewers, Mariam, 4862
Ewers, Mary Otilia, 2885
Ewers, Mary Theresa, 2964
Ewers, Milling, 2885
Ewers, Milton, 2964
Ewers, Milton, 3085
Ewers, Milton, 3552
Ewers, Milton, 4133
Ewers, Milton, 4751
Ewers, Milton, 4786
Ewers, Milton, 4862
Ewers, Rosanna, 3002
Ewers, Susan, 2885
Ewers, Susan, 2964
Ewers, Susan, 3085
Ewers, Susanna, 3690

Ewers, Susanna, 3788
Ewery, Maria, 3954
Exkert, Gertrudis, 1268
Exkert, Joannes, 1268
Eyer, Elizabeth Catharine, 2528
Eyer, Elizabeth Catharine, 2529
Eyler, Maria, 3435
Eyler, Guglielmum, 3371
Eyler, Wilhelmus, 3435
Eyler, William, 5274
Faelinger, Miss, 2779
Fagan, Sara, 3392
Fagan, Anna, 3850
Fagan, Amam Theresam, 3304
Fagan, Anne, 5261
Fagan, Carolum Bernardum, 3535
Fagan, Clarence Daniel, 3926
Fagan, Daniel, 4063
Fagan, Henry, 5169
Fagan, Joanne R., 3850
Fagan, Joanne, 3595
Fagan, Joanne, 3679
Fagan, Joanne, 3787
Fagan, Joanne, 3926
Fagan, Joanne, 3967
Fagan, Joanne, 4063
Fagan, Joanne, 4128

Fagan, Joannem Jacobum, 3967
Fagan, Joanni, 3535
Fagan, Johanne, 3463
Fagan, Johannem Guglielmum, 3463
Fagan, Johanni, 3304
Fagan, Josephum Fredricum, 3679
Fagan, Julianna, 1977
Fagan, Margaretha, 4372
Fagan, Maria Lauretta, 4128
Fagan, Mariam Loretto, 3595
Fagan, Matthew, 1860
Fagan, Nancy, 4258
Fagan, Phebe, 1860
Fagan, Phebe, 1977
Fagan, Ricardum Daly, 4128
Fagan, Richard, 1860
Fagan, Richard, 1977
Fagan, Richardus, 4514
Fagan, Robert E. Benedict, 3787
Fagan, Sara, 3535
Fagan, Sara, 3926
Fagan, Sarah Agnes, 3595
Fagan, Sarah, 3304
Fagan, Sarah, 3463
Fagan, Sarah, 3679
Fagan, Sarah, 3787

Fagan, Sarai, 3850
Fagan, Sarai, 3967
Fagan, Sarai, 4063
Fagan, Sarai, 4128
Fagan, Saraim Elisabeth, 3850
Fagan, Thomam Eduardum, 4063
Fahey, Richard, 4267
Fahrney, Alberto, 3672
Fahrney, Alberto, 3673
Fahrney, Albertum, 4772
Fahrney, Dr., 4899
Fahrney, Dr., 4900
Fahrney, Dr., 4915
Fahrney, Elmire (Dr.), 4843
Fahrney, Howard, 4876
Fahrney, Leonem Arthur, 3672
Fahrney, Margaret E., 3673
Fahrney, Margarita E., 3672
Fahrney, Mariam Isabellam, 3673
Fahrney, Newton, 4874
Faight, Adam, 2317
Faight, John Francis, 2317
Faight, Mary, 2317
Failinger, Catherine, 2709
Failinger, Rosetta, 1927
Failinger, Wm., 2709
Faithe, Catharinem, 4807

Faithe, Joanne, 4807
Fald, Mary, 2685
Fald, Mary, 2877
Faley, Barbara, 4701
Falkenstein, Catherine (Mrs.), 4004
Falkenstein, Conrad, 4821
Falkenstine, Catharina, 4086
Falkerstein, Catharina, 4077
Fall, Anna A., 3166
Fall, Anna Amelia, 3094
Fall, Gulielmum Harman, 3094
Fall, Maria Johenna, 3166
Fall, Maria, 3094
Fall, Mariam Suzannam, 3166
Fall, Michaele A., 3166
Fall, Michaele, 3094
Fallan, Birgittae, 758
Fallan, Joannes, 758
Fallan, Patricii, 758
Fallei, Alphonsus, 4713
Fallen, Elisabetha, 673
Fallen, Guillelini, 723
Fallen, Margaretae, 723
Fallen, Michael, 723
Fallen, Michaelis, 673
Fallen, Susannae, 673
Faller, Anastasia, 3023

Faller, Cecelia, 4713
Faller, Joanne, 4890
Faller, Margarita, 3962
Falley, Annae, 798
Falley, Dionysii, 798
Falley, Margareta, 798
Fallon, Birgittae, 1206
Fallon, Birgittae, 1624
Fallon, Elisabeth, 1624
Fallon, Honora, 2013
Fallon, Joannes, 1417
Fallon, Joannes, 1795
Fallon, John, 1923
Fallon, Julia, 1206
Fallon, Mariae, 1417
Fallon, Patricii, 1206
Fallon, Patricii, 1624
Fallon, Thomae, 1417
Faney, Elizabeth, 1837
Fareth, Mimika, 3774
Farey, Patricius, 1464
Fargerson, blank, 1784
Fargerson, Catharina, 1784
Fargerson, Jacobi, 1784
Fargusson, Caecilia, 1491
Fargusson, Jacobi, 1491
Fargusson, Maria, 1491

Farhney, Francisum M., 4840
Farhney, Newton, 4853
Farley, Annae, 1652
Farley, Maria, 1652
Farley, Patricii, 1652
Farmer, Bridget, 2344
Farmer, Charles Henry, 2344
Farr, James, 633
Farrel, Birgitta, 4380
Farrel, Bridget, 1953
Farrel, Bridget, 2120
Farrel, Catharina, 1182
Farrel, Catharinae, 1094
Farrel, Catharinae, 705
Farrel, Catharine, 2348
Farrel, Jacobi, 1094
Farrel, Jacobi, 705
Farrel, Jacobus, 1358
Farrel, Joannes, 1033
Farrel, Judey, 2267
Farrel, Judy, 2120
Farrel, Juliae, 1033
Farrel, Juliae, 1358
Farrel, Maria, 4474
Farrel, Maria, 705
Farrel, Mariae, 820
Farrel, Michaelis, 820

Farrel, N., 1412
Farrel, Patricius, 1147
Farrel, Sara Catherina, 1094
Farrel, Sarah, 2267
Farrel, Thomae, 1033
Farrel, Thomae, 1358
Farrel, Thomas, 2120
Farrel, Thomas, 2267
Farrel, Thomas, 820
Farrell, Catharina, 4480
Farrell, Catharina, 3752
Farrell, Ellenora Jane, 1994
Farrell, James, 4352
Farrell, Joanna, 1147
Farrell, John, 4767
Farrell, Judith, 1994
Farrell, Maria, 1475
Farrell, Maria, 1529
Farrell, Michael, 1206
Farrell, Thomas, 1994
Farrelly, Maria, 3254
Farrensworth, Eve, 2810
Farrensworth, Marg., 2810
Farrensworth, Will., 2810
Fasnacht, Anna M., 2945
Fate, Barbara, 2877
Fate, Mary, 4625

Faughan, Charles, 4708
Favence, Walter J. (Dr.), 4912
Fayetlin, Margareta, 4489
Fayette, Barbara, 1625
Fayette, Barbarae, 1625
Fayette, Joannes, 1625
Fayette, Joannes, 1791
Fayetter, Maria Anna, 1575
Fayetter, Baltasar, 1200
Fealy, Anna, 1123
Fealy, Annae, 1123
Fealy, Maria, 4461
Fealy, Patricii, 1123
Fealy, Patricius, 1153
Fealy, Thomas, 1574
Fealy, Thoms., 4313
Feather, Magdalen, 2080
Feb, Margaritae, 1419
Febrey, Carolina, 3574
Febrey, Nellie, 4073
Fechtig Jr., Geo., 4680
Fechtig, Alexandrum Christianum, 3518
Fechtig, Eduardus, 3996
Fechtig, Edward, 3959
Fechtig, Fred, 4073
Fechtig, Fredericus, 4072

Fechtig, Geo., 2870
Fechtig, Geo., 2928
Fechtig, George, 2983
Fechtig, George, 3093
Fechtig, Georgio, 3969
Fechtig, Georgio, 3180
Fechtig, Georgio, 3270
Fechtig, Georgio, 3362
Fechtig, Georgio, 3433
Fechtig, Georgio, 3518
Fechtig, Giergiee Winter, 3180
Fechtig, Harriet Rosam, 3362
Fechtig, Helenam Agnetem, 3270
Fechtig, Joanne, 3587
Fechtig, Johannem Fredericum, 3433
Fechtig, L. (Mrs.), 3910
Fechtig, Lou, 4685
Fechtig, Lou, 2928
Fechtig, Louisa H., 3093
Fechtig, Louisa, 2870
Fechtig, Louisa, 2983
Fechtig, Louisa, 3180
Fechtig, Louisa, 3270
Fechtig, Louisa, 3362
Fechtig, Louisa, 3587
Fechtig, Lousia, 3433

Fechtig, Ludovica, 3518
Fechtig, Lula, 3946
Fechtig, Margt Louisa, 3093
Fechtig, Mary Susan, 2928
Fechtig, Nellie, 4072
Fechtig, Paulum, 3587
Fechtig, Richard Bond, 2983
Fechtig, Susanna, 3758
Fechtig, Susanna, 3910
Fechtig, Susanna, 3959
Fechtig, Susanna, 3982
Fechtig, Susanna, 4072
Fechtig, Susanna, 4073
Fechtig, Wm. Doyle, 2870
Fecker, Thomas, 1468
Fedser, Franciscus, 1337
Feidt, Adam, 1972
Feidt, Adam, 2090
Feidt, Adam, 2470
Feidt, Anna Margaret, 1920
Feidt, Baltis, 1852
Feidt, Casimirus, 1972
Feidt, Catharine Virginia, 2470
Feidt, Catharine, 1990
Feidt, John, 1990
Feidt, John, 1990
Feidt, Joseph, 1990

Feidt, Maria, 2089
Feidt, Maria, 2090
Feidt, Mary Ellen, 2090
Feidt, Mary Jane, 2006
Feidt, Mary Jane, 2470
Feidt, Mary Jane, 2499
Feidt, Mary, 1972
Feidt, Mary, 2149
Feidt, May Jane, 2090
Feighley, Carolum Augustinum, 4069
Feighley, Emma, 4069
Feighley, Isaac, 3438
Feighley, Isaac, 3451
Feighley, Isaac, 4069
Feigle, "unknown", 3597
Feigle, Franciscam Arnold, 3597
Feigle, Franciscam Arnold, 3597
Feigle, Harriet, 3597
Feigle, Harriet, 3597
Feigley, Elizabeth, 3251
Feigley, Emiliam Cathariam, 3797
Feigley, Elizabeth, 3251
Feigley, Joanne, 3797
Feigley, Bernardum, 3899
Feigley, Edwardum F., 4001
Feigley, Elizabeth, 3251

Feigly, Emma A., 3899
Feigly, Emma C., 3579
Feigly, Emma C., 3785
Feigly, Emma C., 3862
Feigley, Emma Cath., 3513
Feigley, Emma, 3620
Feigley, Emma, 3744
Feigley, Emma, 4001
Feigley, Fredericum, 3620
Feigley, George M., 5242
Feigley, Georgium M., 3862
Feigley, Isaac, 3862
Feigley, Isaac A., 4767
Feigley, Isaac K., 3579
Feigley, Isaac Kent, 3513
Feigley, Isaac, 3620
Feigley, Isaac, 3714
Feigley, Isaac, 3744
Feigley, Isaac, 3785
Feigley, Isaac, 3899
Feigley, Isaac, 4001
Feigley, Joseph, 3785
Feigley, Natham Wilson Bayley, 3513
Feigley, Raymond N., 3744
Feigley, Raymond Napoleon, 5259
Feigley, Zachariam Hughes, 3579

Feigly, Emma, 3743
Feigly, Emma, 4151
Feigly, Gulielmum Kent, 3743
Feigly, Henriettam Mariam, 4151
Feigly, Isaac, 3743
Feigly, Isaac, 4151
Felix, Anna, 3866
Fellenger, Lizzie, 2916
Fellenger, Maria, 3793
Fellenger, Mary Jeanette, 2916
Fellenger, Phil, 2916
Felligner, Rosa, 3697
Fellinger, Catharina, 1045
Fellinger, Catharina, 3165
Fellinger, Catharina, 3496
Fellinger, Catharine, 2551
Fellinger, Catharine, 2637
Fellinger, Elisabeth, 3149
Fellinger, Elisabeth, 3165
Fellinger, Elizabeth, 3496
Fellinger, Elizabetha, 3687
Fellinger, Emmam Catharinam, 3149
Fellinger, Fredererici, 1498
Fellinger, Frederici, 1045
Fellinger, Frederici, 1311
Fellinger, Frederick, 2102

Fellinger, Frederick, 2108
Fellinger, Fredericus, 1817
Fellinger, Fredericus, 1680
Fellinger, Fredericus, 4385
Fellinger, Gulielmum Thomam, 3496
Fellinger, Jacobus, 1311
Fellinger, Joannes, 1498
Fellinger, John, 4671
Fellinger, Kate, 4674
Fellinger, Lizzie, 2861
Fellinger, Lizzy, 2916
Fellinger, Maria, 3697
Fellinger, Maria, 3756
Fellinger, Mary Ann, 2102
Fellinger, Mary Ann, 2108
Fellinger, Mary Jeneatte, 3720
Fellinger, Mrs., 2539
Fellinger, P., 4615
Fellinger, Philip J., 4671
Fellinger, Philip J., 4674
Fellinger, Philippo, 3149
Fellinger, Philippo, 3496
Fellinger, Philippo, 3687
Fellinger, Rosa, 5509
Fellinger, Rosae Annae, 1045
Fellinger, Rosae, 1311

Fellinger, Rosalia, 1498
Fellinger, Rosam Bernardittam, 3687
Fellinger, Rosanna, 2102
Fellinger, Rosanna, 2108
Fellman, Elizabeth, 2291
Fellman, Frances Catharine, 2291
Fellman, Ross, 2291
Fenley, Anna, 1228
Fenley, Joannes, 1228
Fenny, Anna, 1321
Fenny, McNickels, 1321
Fenwick, Annam, 3944
Fenwick, Catharina, 3944
Fenwick, Catharina, 4005
Fenwick, Catharina, 4123
Fenwick, Eli, 158
Fenwick, Jacobo, 3944
Fenwick, Jacobo, 4005
Fenwick, Jacobo, 4123
Fenwick, Jacoburn Stewart, 4005
Fenwick, Peggy, 158
Fenwick, Rosam Mariam, 4123
Feorde, Michael, 261
Feoser, Franciscus, 1337
Ferguson, Francisco E., 4111
Ferguson, Maria E., 4111

Ferguson, Rosam, 4111
Ferley, Thomas, 1235
Fernsworth, William, 4663
Ferra?, Joannes, 1362
Ferral, Catharine, 2354
Ferrall, William, 4277
Ferrell, Bridget, 4277
Fesler, Mrs., 5216
Fessler, Anna, 3989
Fessler, Anna, 3990
Fessler, John, 4576
Fessler, Susan, 3199
Fessler, Susan, 2466
Fessler, Susan, 2497
Fessler, Susan, 2563
Fessler, Susan, 2920
Fessler, Susan, 3252
Fetter, Magdalena, 4499
Fiegley, Clyde Franciscum, 3953
Fiegley, Emma, 3953
Fiegley, Isaac, 3953
Fields, Joanne, 3745
Fields, Mariam, 3745
Fields, Mariam, 3745
Fiemey, Laura (Mrs.), 5226
Fiery, Alberto, 3372
Fiery, Alberto, 3482

Fiery, Alberto, 3520
Fiery, Alberto, 3593
Fiery, Albertum, 4748
Fiery, Edith Elizabeth, 3482
Fiery, Mabel Ceciliam, 3520
Fiery, Maria C., 3372
Fiery, Maria, 3482
Fiery, Maria, 3520
Fiery, Maria, 3593
Fiery, Mariam Catharinam Gertrude, 3372
Fiery, Rogerium Bernardus, 3593
Figley, Frederick, 5195
Figley, Isaac, 3746
Figus, Frances, 2070
Fillinger, Rosalia, 1817
Fillinger, Rosalia, 2325
Fillinger, Cath, 2967
Fillinger, Elizabeth, 2981
Fillinger, John Edward, 2981
Fillinger, John, 2981
Fillinger, Philip, 2981
Fillinger, Rosa, 2967
Fingeing, Hy, 4680
Finger, Emile, 2338
Finger, Margaret Emile (Miss), 4566

Finger, Margaret, 2510
Finghty?, Jacobi, 1029
Finghty?, Mariae, 1029
Finghty?, Michael, 1029
Fining, John, 2940
Fining, Mary, 2940
Fining, Simon, 2940
Fininy, John, 2940
Fininy, Mary, 2940
Fininy, Simon, 2940
Finley, Annae, 1344
Finley, Joannis, 1344
Finley, Margareta, 1344
Finney, Caroli, 1289
Finney, Joannes, 1289
Finney, Mariae, 1289
Firey, Joanne B., 4035
Firey, Joanne B., 4118
Firey, Joannem B., 4871
Firey, Joannem Burton, 3971
Firey, Joannem Burton, 4118
Firey, Joannes, 4124
Firey, Joseph H., 3971
Firey, Marion Catherinam, 4035
Firey, Susanna, 4035
Firey, Susanna, 4118
Fisbeck, Catharina Elisabeth, 1287

Fisher, Margaret (Mrs.), 5336
Fisher, Mrs., 4881
Fisher, Benjaminus, 937
Fisher, Christophori, 638
Fisher, Elisabeth, 1364
Fisher, Elisabeth, 937
Fisher, Guillelmus, 638
Fisher, Joanne, 3661
Fisher, Joannis, 937
Fisher, Joseph, 635
Fisher, Josephinam, 3661
Fisher, Margarita, 3661
Fisher, Maria, 4870
Fisher, Mariae, 638
Fisher, Mary Elizabeth, 635
Fisher, Mary, 635
Fitz, Frederick, 4184
Fitzgerald, Danal, 4272
Fitzgerald, Bridget (widow), 4329
Fitzgerald, Bridget, 90
Fitzgerald, David, 1370
Fitzgerald, Eleanor, 90
FitzGerald, Eliza, 628
Fitzgerald, Hanora, 1370
Fitzgerald, Mariae, 1370
Fitzgerald, Patricius, 1421
FitzGerrald, Bridget, 510

FitzGerrald, Eliza (Miss), 513
FitzGerrald, Garrett, 510
FitzGerrald, Mary, 510
Fitzhue, Louisa, 5414
Fitzhugh, Louisa (Miss), 4937
Fitzpatrick, M. Elisabeth, 4152
Fitzpatrick, Annae, 1557
Fitzpatrick, Anthonius, 4476
Fitzpatrick, Antonii, 1557
Fitzpatrick, Antonius, 1307
Fitzpatrick, Catharinam, 3985
FitzPatrick, Catherine, 448
Fitzpatrick, Daniel Philippus, 1339
FitzPatrick, Edward Ignatis, 508
Fitzpatrick, Edward, 212
FitzPatrick, Edward, 448
Fitzpatrick, Edward, 508
FitzPatrick, Edwd, 4187
Fitzpatrick, Edwd., 4188
Fitzpatrick, Eleonorae, 1339
Fitzpatrick, Gulielmo A., 3935
Fitzpatrick, Gulielmo, 3985
Fitzpatrick, Gulielmo, 4082
Fitzpatrick, Gulielmo, 4152
Fitzpatrick, Gulielmum Joseph, 4152
Fitzpatrick, Helenae, 1814

Fitzpatrick, Hugo, 1557
Fitzpatrick, Jacobus, 1814
Fitzpatrick, John R., 4172
FitzPatrick, Julian, 508
Fitzpatrick, Juliana, 212
FitzPatrick, Julianna, 448
Fitzpatrick, Margarita, 3935
Fitzpatrick, Margarita, 3985
Fitzpatrick, Margarita, 4082
Fitzpatrick, Margarita, 4152
Fitzpatrick, Mariam, 4082
Fitzpatrick, Mary Anna, 212
Fitzpatrick, P. (Mrs.), 609
Fitzpatrick, Philippas, 1631
Fitzpatrick, Philippi, 1339
Fitzpatrick, Philippi, 1814
Fitzpatrick, Philippus, 1736
Fitzpatrick, Thoman, 3935
Fitzsimmons, Margaret, 1842
Fitzsimmons, Margaret, 1843
Fitzsimmons, Margaret, 2091
FitzSimmons, Rebeca (widow), 4336
Fitzwilliam, Anna, 1166
Fitzwilliam, Petri, 1166
Fitzwilliam, Petrus, 1166
Fixpatrick?, Eleonorae, 996

Fixpatrick?, Joannes Edwardus, 996
Fixpatrick?, Philippi, 996
Flagherty, Catharinae, 1095
Flagherty, Michaelis, 1095
Flagherty, Patricius, 1095
Flahavan, Matheus, 1402
Flanigan, Anna, 1093
Flanigan, Francisci, 1093
Flanigan, Francisci, 1458
Flanigan, Francisci, 1782
Flanigan, Jacobus, 1782
Flanigan, Mariae Annae, 1093
Flanigan, Mariae Annae, 1458
Flanigan, Miae [sic] Annae, 1782
Flanigan, Michael, 1458
Flanigan, Michael, 4474
Flannagan, Eliza Jane, 2101
Flannagan, Eliza Jane, 2107
Flannagan, Francis, 1937
Flannagan, Francis, 1938
Flannagan, Francis, 2101
Flannagan, Francis, 2107
Flannagan, Francis, 2125
Flannagan, Mary Ann, 1938
Flannagan, Mary Ann, 2101
Flannagan, Mary Ann, 2107
Flannagan, Sarah (widow), 4299
Flannagan, William Henry, 1938
Flannagan, Wilm, 4308
Flegel, Laura Bell, 2993
Flegel, Marg. Elfrida, 3577
Flegel, Maria M., 3192
Flegel, Mariam Matildam, 3577
Flegel, Martino Johnson, 3577
Flegel, Martinum Henricus, 3192
Flegel, Mary, 2993
Flegel, Philip, 2993
Flegel, Philippo, 3192
Fleigle, [blank], 3058
Fleigle, John Wm., 3058
Fleigle, Mary, 3058
Fleigle, Philip, 3086
Fleming, R. (Rev.), 4761
Fleming, Savannah, 3146
Flemming, Mary Anna, 4203
Flenne, Alberto C., 4789
Flesler, Mrs., 5216
Fletcher, Mrs., 5327
Fling, David Timotheus, 1305
Fling, Edwardi, 1305
Fling, Johannae, 1305
Flinn, David, 887
Flinn, Edmundi, 1579
Flinn, Helena, 1579
Flinn, Johanna, 1372
Flinn, Johannae, 1579
Flinn, Joseph, 386
Flinn, Margareta, 1204
Flinn, Mariae, 1204
Flinn, Mariae, 887
Flinn, Michaelis, 1204
Flinn, Michaelis, 887
Flinn, Nancy, 386
Flinn, Patrick, 386
Floid, Annae, 848
Floid, Jesse, 848
Flood, Catharinae, 1017
Flood, Joannes, 1017
Flood, Joannius, 1017
Flood, Mary, 71
Flook, Ruth, 4098
Flora, Nancy, 4175
Florence, Cornelia, 3909
Floy, Emma, 1189
Floyd, Emma, 5794
Floyd, Anna, 2831
Floyd, Helena, 3818
Floyd, Jane, 5431
Floyde, Hannah, 4357
Flyn, Aloysius, 2729
Flyn, James, 4606
Flyn, Jas., 2729
Flyn, Mary, 2729
Flynn, Aloysius, 3662
Flynn, Amilia, 3877
Flynn, Catharina, 3293
Flynn, Catharina, 3472
Flynn, Catherine (Mrs.), 5306
Flynn, Charles William, 3052
Flynn, Cornelium Jeremiam, 3472
Flynn, Daisy Mariam, 3877
Flynn, Emelia, 3035
Flynn, Guglielmum Michaelem, 3293
Flynn, Jacob, 3877
Flynn, James, 2768
Flynn, James, 3035
Flynn, James, 3052
Flynn, James, 4608
Flynn, James, 4668
Flynn, James, 4669
Flymn, Jas., 2657
Flymn, Jas., 2658
Flymn, Jas., 2830
Flymn, Jas., 2858
Flymn, Jas., 2859
Flymn, Jas., 2945

Flynn, Jas., 4628
Flynn, Jas., 4631
Flynn, Jas., 4632
Flynn, Jno., 2651
Flynn, Joanni, 3472
Flynn, Johanne, 3293
Flynn, John Thos., 2657
Flynn, John, 2769
Flynn, John, 2781
Flynn, John, 5230
Flynn, Jos. Hy., 2859
Flynn, Louisa, 2858
Flynn, Louisa, 3035
Flynn, Margarita, 3603
Flynn, Maria, 3665
Flynn, Maria, 3772
Flynn, Mary C., 2768
Flynn, Mary C., 3052
Flynn, Mary, 2657
Flynn, Mary, 2657
Flynn, Mary, 2768
Flynn, Mary, 2859
Flynn, Michael, 5257
Flynn, Owen, 5183
Flynn, Patricius, 1336
Flynn, Thoma, 4834
Flynn, Thomas, 3737

Flynn, Thomas, 5229
Flynn, Thos. Henry, 2858
Fogerty, Bridge, 498
Fogerty, Jane, 498
Fogerty, Michl., 498
Fogle, Earnest C., 4722
Folder, Rebeca, 4307
Folder, Rebecca, 2525
Foley, Elleonorae, 1420
Foley, John, 4650
Foley, Maria, 4020
Foley, Mariam, 4881
Foley, Michael, 1420
Foley, Michaelis, 1420
Folks, Bridget (Mrs.), 5231
Follen, Birgetta, 1676
Follen, Ellon, 479
Follen, John, 479
Follen, Margret, 479
Follen, Patriciis, 1354
Follen, Thomas, 1351
Foller, Chs. Francis, 2856
Foller, Jno, 2856
Foller, Mary, 2856
Foltz, Alexocess, 4241
Forbeck, Adam, 1575
Forbeck, Baltasar, 1200

Forbeck, Carimirus, 1852
Forbeck, Casimiri, 1200
Forbeck, Casimiri, 1575
Forbeck, Casimirus, 1971
Forbeck, Casimirus, 1972
Forbeck, Casimirus, 2149
Forbeck, Eva, 1852
Forbeck, Eva, 1863
Forbeck, Eva, 1869
Forbeck, Eva, 1971
Forbeck, Eva, 2149
Forbeck, Evae, 1200
Forbeck, Evae, 1575
Forbeck, John, 1852
Forbeck, Mary, 2149
Forbeck, Michael, 1971
Forbis, Matilda, 262
Force, Anna, 895
Force, Serenae, 895
Ford, Ann, 3080
Ford, Anna C., 4115
Ford, Anna Virginia, 2380
Ford, Catharine Lauranette, 2379
Ford, Catharine, 2379
Ford, Catharine, 2380
Ford, Catharine, 2381
Ford, Catharine, 2682

Ford, Catharine, 3148
Ford, Daisie Johannam, 3526
Ford, Florence, 2682
Ford, Franklin, 4705
Ford, Franklin, 3080
Ford, Franklin, 3214
Ford, Franklin, 5117
Ford, Gertrudam Agatham, 3148
Ford, Henrico, 3526
Ford, J., 4733
Ford, Jenny, 446
Ford, Joanne, 3148
Ford, Johanna, 3526
Ford, John, 2379
Ford, John, 2380
Ford, John, 2381
Ford, John, 2682
Ford, John, 446
Ford, John, 4541
Ford, John, 535
Ford, John, 536
Ford, John, 536
Ford, Joseph Garret, 535
Ford, Laura, 2996
Ford, Laura, 3083
Ford, Laura, 5545
Ford, Laura, 5590

Ford, Lauram L., 4733
Ford, Louisa, 3588
Ford, Margret, 535
Ford, Margret, 536
Ford, Maria, 3214
Ford, Martha, 3015
Ford, Mary Elizabeth, 2381
Ford, Mary Elizabeth, 3080
Ford, Mary Eloisa, 446
Ford, Mary, 446
Ford, Rosa E, 2380
Ford, Rosa E, 2381
Ford, Thornam Henricum, 3214
Foreman, Elisa, 288
Foreman, Matt, 288
Foreman, Nathanial, 288
Forieter, Anna, 851
Forieter, Caroli, 851
Forieter, Mariae, 851
Foronsworth, Margareth, 3020
Foronsworth, Mary, 3020
Foronsworth, William, 3020
Forrester, Charly, 4346
Forsman, Anna Amelia, 2336
Forsman, Barbar [sic], 2336
Fortune, Mr., 4613
Forus, Serenae, 1682

Forus, William, 1682
Foshy?, John, 4338
Fouder, Aloysius, 2345
Fouder, Catharine, 2345
Fouder, Catharine, 2403
Fouder, Joseph J., 2345
Fouder, Susan, 5478
Fourthman, Jacob Wm., 2350
Fourthman, Marcellina, 2350
Fourthman, Mary Laura Virginia, 2350
Foutre, Catharine, 5407
Foutre, Charles B., 5409
Fox, [blank], 5148
Fox, Annam Virginiam, 3174
Fox, Catharina C., 3432
Fox, Catharinae, 1818
Fox, Elizabeth Glendening, 3586
Fox, Elizabeth Mariam, 3599
Fox, Elleonorae, 959
Fox, Ferdinadus, 3570
Fox, Ferdinando, 3530
Fox, Fernando J. [or I.], 3174
Fox, Fernando Jackson, 5727
Fox, Fernando, 3299
Fox, Fernando, 3438
Fox, Fernando, 3599

Fox, Fernardo, 3234
Fox, Geo, 135
Fox, Geo, 17
Fox, Geo. B., 5009
Fox, Geo, 5142
Fox, Henrico S., 3432
Fox, Henricum Simon, 3234
Fox, Henry, 5092
Fox, J. Forrese Morgan, 3432
Fox, Jane Rebecca, 17
Fox, Jennie Ann, 5749
Fox, Jennie, 3299
Fox, Jennie, 3438
Fox, Joanne, 1563
Fox, Joannes Henricus, 1705
Fox, Johanna, 3530
Fox, Johannesm, 3438
Fox, John, 5128
Fox, Josephina Agnestem, 3299
Fox, Margaretham Franciscam, 3530
Fox, Margt., 5064
Fox, Maria C., 3121
Fox, Maria Joanna, 959
Fox, Maria Magdalena, 1139
Fox, Mariae Annae, 1705
Fox, Mary Magdalene, 135

Fox, Mary Magdalene, 134
Fox, Mary Magdalene, 17
Fox, Melinda Ann, 135
Fox, Mr., 302
Fox, Mrs., 180
Fox, Mrs., 194
Fox, Mrs., 470
Fox, Mrs., 491
Fox, Mrs., 577
Fox, Nancy, 157
Fox, Philip, 157
Fox, Sara, 3120
Fox, Sara, 3121
Fox, Sarah, 2960
Fox, Sarah, 2997
Fox, Virginia Anna, 3174
Fox, Virginia, 3120
Fox, Virginia, 3234
Fox, Virginia, 3599
Foxberger, Adam, 2353
Foxberger, Adam, 2463
Foxberger, Adam, 2561
Foxberger, Catharine, 2353
Foxberger, Elizabeth, 2353
Foxberger, Elizabeth, 2463
Foxberger, John, 2463
Foxberger, Mary E., 2561

Foxberger, Michael Adam, 2561
Foxberger, Michael Adam, 4962
Foxburgh, Adam, 2636
Foxburgh, Elizabeth, 2636
Foxburgh, Geo. Edwd., 2636
Foxemburger, Adam, 5278
Foy, Loutie, 4801
Foy, Patrick, 4293
France, Jacob, 2014
France, John, 2014
France, John, 2092
France, Susanna, 2014
Francey, Susan, 1941
Francis, Joannes, 1573
Francis, Joannis, 1664
Francis, Maria Magdalena, 1664
Francis, Mary, 2179
Francis, Patrick, 2179
Francis, Patrick, 2179
Francis, Susannae, 1664
Franklin, Thomas, 261
Frantz, Janannis, 1422
Frantz, Joannes, 1422
Frantz, Susannae, 1422
Franz, Elisabeth, 875
Franz, Joannis, 875
Franz, Susannae, 875

Freaner, Anna Rebecca, 4578
Freaner, Henry, 5013
Freanor, Geo., 4732
Frederick, Anna H., 4779
Frederick, Ccilia, 3584
Frederick, Cecilia, 3533
Frederick, Cecilia, 3551
Frederick, Conlon (Rev.), 3734
Frederick, J. Alph., 3544
Fredk. [sic] Jno., 2630
Fredk. [sic], Sarah Ann, 2630
Fredk. [sic], Sarah Catharine, 2630
Freeman, Rosa, 1914
Freeman, Susanna, 1444
Freeze, Mary, 1956
Freeze, Mary Catharine, 2058
Freeze, Mary, 2058
Freeze, Mary, 2330
Freeze, Peter, 2058
Freeze, Peter, 2330
Freeze, Peter, 2330
Freidhofin, Elisabeth, 4401
Freize, Mary, 2241
Freize, Peter, 2241
Freize, Sarah Eliza, 2241
Frelig, John, 2219
Frelig, Margaret, 2219

Freligh, John, 2331
Freligh, Margaret, 2331
Freligh, Mary, 2331
Frendhoff, Elizabeth, 3043
Fresh, Catharine, 2092
Fresh, Catharine, 2092
Fresh, Michael, 2092
Freshoure, Eleanor, 98
Freshoure, Elizabeth Ann, 98
Freshoure, Matthias, 98
Frial, Nancy, 4268
Frice, Jacob, 2423
Frice, Mary, 2423
Frice, Peter, 2423
Friel, Hugh, 3
Friends, Eleanor, 49
Friends, Helena, 49
Fritz, 1599
Fritz, Catharine, 139
Fritz, Evelina, 1598
Fritz, Frederici, 1597
Fritz, Frederici, 1598
Fritz, Frederici, 938
Fritz, Frederick, 139
Fritz, Levi, 1597
Fritz, Margaret, 139
Fritz, Margareta, 938

Fritz, Margaretae, 1598
Fritz, Margaretae, 938
Fritz, Margertae, 1597
Frone, Carolum A., 4843
Frueman, Elisa, 288
Frueman, Matt, 288
Frueman, Nathanial, 288
Fry, Daisy, 4079
Fry, Daisy, 4119
Fry, Daisy, 4896
Fry, David Warner, 3879
Fry, John W., 3879
Fsany, Maria, 1320
Fuchsberger, Andrew, 5657
Fuchsberger, Mary Elis., 5656
Full, Annam (Mrs.), 3426
Full, Jacob, 3426
Full, Mike, 4696
Full, Susan, 3426
Full, Ann, 3014
Full, Anna Amelia, 3476
Full, Anna, 3239
Full, Anna, 3274
Full, Anna, 3549
Full, Anna, 3627
Full, Anna, 3719
Full, Anna, 3828

Full, Anna, 3894
Full, Carolinam Ceciliam, 3894
Full, Carolo, 4891
Full, Carolum A., 4863
Full, Charles Adam, 3014
Full, Charles, 5340
Full, Elisabeth, 4089
Full, Elizabeth Ameliam, 3476
Full, Henricum B., 3719
Full, Henry, 5199
Full, Johannem Michaelem, 3274
Full, Lizzie, 4891
Full, Margaretam May, 3239
Full, Maria, 4089
Full, Maria, 4140
Full, Mariam S., 4891
Full, Mary, 5163
Full, Michael A., 4697
Full, Michael, 3014
Full, Michael, 3476
Full, Michael, 3549
Full, Michaele, 3239
Full, Michaele, 3274
Full, Michaele, 3627
Full, Michaele, 3894
Full, Michaelo, 3719
Full, Mrs., 3960

Full, Robertum Franciscum, 3627
Full, Tilghman Bernadum, 3549
Fullalove, Susan, 2099
Fullalove, Susan, 2391
Fultz, Mary Anna, 1988
Funk, Elisabeth, 3133
Funk, Fannie G., 4863
Funk, Margarita, 4863
Furgerson, James, 1934
Furgerson, Mary, 1935
Furgerson, Mary, 1934
Furgerson, Michael, 1934
Furley, Charles, 5665
Furley, Jacobo A., 3448
Furley, James A., 2820
Furley, James Augustus, 2820
Furley, James, 2466
Furley, James, 2541
Furley, James, 2719
Furley, Jane, 2466
Furley, Jas. A., 2931
Furley, Joseph Bernard, 2541
Furley, Kate, 5637
Furley, Loutto Jane, 2931
Furley, M. Cath, 2931
Furley, Maria, 3448
Furley, Mary I., 2820

Furley, Mary I., 2931
Furley, Mary Jane, 2541
Furley, Mary Jane, 2719
Furley, Rosam, 3448
Furley, Susan Margaret, 2719
Furley, William Edward, 2466
Furlong, James, 1954
Furlong, Michael Tilgman, 1954
Furlong, Susan, 1954
Furlong, William, 1954
Futter, Catharine, 2564
Futter, James Francis, 2564
Futter, Joseph, 4672
Futter, Lewis, 2564
Futter, Mary, 5440
Futter, Franciscus (Mrs.), 3873
Futterer, Helen, 3954
Futterer, Helen, 4015
Futterer, Adron, 3690
Futterer, Aloyisii, 1224
Futterer, Aloysius, 5160
Futterer, Anna E., 3690
Futterer, Anna E., 3788
Futterer, Anna E., 3890
Futterer, Anna E., 3988
Futterer, Anna, 3961
Futterer, Anna, 4134

Futterer, Carolina, 3574
Futterer, Carolinam, 3219
Futterer, Caroline, 5325
Futterer, Carolus McG [sic], 1224
Futterer, Catharinae, 1224
Futterer, Catharinam, 3788
Futterer, Catherine, 3063
Futterer, Catherine, 3064
Futterer, Charles Augustine, 3063
Futterer, Charles, 3063
Futterer, Chs. M., 4685
Futterer, Ella (Mrs.), 3880
Futterer, Ella J. (Mrs.), 4078
Futterer, Frances, 5347
Futterer, Francescam, 3961
Futterer, Francesco, 3961
Futterer, Francesio, 3788
Futterer, Francis John, 5684
Futterer, Francisco, 3690
Futterer, Francisco, 3890
Futterer, Francisco, 3988
Futterer, Francisco, 4134
Futterer, Francisco, 4916
Futterer, Franciscum David, 3475
Futterer, Franciscus, 3873
Futterer, Franciscus, 4120
Futterer, Francisous, 3475

Futterer, Frank (Mrs.), 4862
Futterer, Frank, 2964
Futterer, Idam M., 3574
Futterer, Idam Mariam, 3574
Futterer, J. Franciscum, 4786
Futterer, Jacob (Mrs.), 3890
Futterer, Jacob F., 4834
Futterer, Jacob, 3788
Futterer, Jacob, 3949
Futterer, Jacob, 3954
Futterer, Jacob, 3988
Futterer, Jacob, 4015
Futterer, Jacob, 5555
Futterer, Jacoba, 3961
Futterer, Jacobo, 3475
Futterer, Jacobo, 3552
Futterer, Jacobo, 4786
Futterer, Jacobus, 3690
Futterer, Joanne, 3574
Futterer, Joannem Fridericum, 3552
Futterer, John, 3219
Futterer, John, 5557
Futterer, Joseph, 4709
Futterer, Josephus, 3574
Futterer, Ludovicus, 1251
Futterer, Maria Francesca, 3475

Futterer, Maria Francesca, 3552
Futterer, Mariam Vincentiam, 3949
Futterer, Mary (Mrs.), 5076
Futterer, Mrs., 2922
Futterer, Nellie, 3949
Futterer, Otella, 3063
Futterer, Paulum, 3890
Futterer, Ruth, 4134
Futterer, Susan, 2885
Futterer, Susan, 2964
Futterer, Susan, 3085
Futterer, Susannam Otheliam, 3988
Futterer, Thomas, 3003
G [rest of name is blank], Joannes Richardus, 1752
G [rest of name is blank], Mariae, 1752
G [rest of name is blank], Richardi, 1752
Gabler, Dorothea, 1975
Gabriel, Augustam, 3297
Gabriel, B., 3296
Gabriel, B., 3297
Gabriel, Catharinam, 3296
Gabriel, Guglielmo, 3296
Gabriel, Guglielmo, 3297
Gagon, Isabellae, 1346

Gagon, Joannis, 1346
Gagon, Josephus, 1346
Gainer, Jacobus, 1398
Gainer, Thoms, 4315
Galagan, Mr., 4620
Galaway, Saml., 478
Gale, George, 436
Gale, Junior, George, 95
Gale, Mrs., 96
Gale, Thomas, 1677
Gale, Thomas, 1786
Gale, Thomas, 1796
Gale, Thomas, 1797
Galeese, Ann, 2319
Galeese, Patrick, 2143
Galeese, Redmund, 2372
Galeese, Thomas, 2117
Gales, Ellen E., 2413
Gales, Mary, 2410
Gallace, Thomas, 1317
Gallager, Margaret, 2519
Gallagham, [blank], 655
Gallagham, Cornelius, 655
Gallagham, Petri, 655
Gallagher, Bridget, 1997
Gallagher, Catherina, 3481
Gallagher, Guielmo, 3481

Gallagher, Mariam Elizabeth, 3481
Gallagher, Ann, 2064
Gallagher, Ann, 2124
Gallagher, Ann, 2142
Gallagher, Anna, 2275
Gallagher, Anna, 991
Gallagher, Birgettae, 753
Gallagher, Birgitta, 1312
Gallagher, Birgitta, 1356
Gallagher, Birgitta, 4485
Gallagher, Birgittae, 1090
Gallagher, Birgittae, 1440
Gallagher, Birgittae, 1696
Gallagher, Bridget, 1928
Gallagher, Catharina, 1440
Gallagher, Catharina, 3158
Gallagher, Catharinae, 4821
Gallagher, Catharine, 5510
Gallagher, Daniel, 2124
Gallagher, Daniel, 2275
Gallagher, Daniel, 2275
Gallagher, Eduardo F., 4089
Gallagher, Eduardo F., 4140
Gallagher, Eduardum F., 4891
Gallagher, Elizabeth, 3649
Gallagher, Ella, 4160
Gallagher, Eva, 3649

Gallagher, Franciscus, 3241
Gallagher, Franciscus, 3411
Gallagher, Franciscus, 4403
Gallagher, Frank, 3282
Gallagher, Frank, 3307
Gallagher, Franklin Michaelem, 4140
Gallagher, Guilelmus, 1696
Gallagher, Gulielmo, 3158
Gallagher, Helena, 4132
Gallagher, Helena, 753
Gallagher, Helenam R., 4816
Gallagher, Helenam, 3158
Gallagher, Jacobus, 4816
Gallagher, James, 4178
Gallagher, Johanna, 3323
Gallagher, Johanna, 3324
Gallagher, Johanna, 3461
Gallagher, John, 2124
Gallagher, Margaret Eliza, 2451
Gallagher, Margaret Elizabeth, 1928
Gallagher, Margaret, 1970
Gallagher, Margaret, 2142
Gallagher, Maria, 4089
Gallagher, Maria, 4140
Gallagher, Mariellae, 991

Gallagher, Mariettam, 4089
Gallagher, Martha, 91
Gallagher, Mary A., 2355
Gallagher, Michael F., 3387
Gallagher, Michael, 1928
Gallagher, Michael, 4935
Gallagher, Michaelim F., 4729
Gallagher, Michaelis, 1090
Gallagher, Michaelis, 1440
Gallagher, Michaelis, 1696
Gallagher, Michaelis, 753
Gallagher, Mr., 3421
Gallagher, Mrs., 3413
Gallagher, Mrs., 5028
Gallagher, Rosanna, 91
Gallagher, Sara, 1090
Gallagher, Thoma, 3649
Gallagher, Thomae, 991
Gallagher, Thomam, 3649
Gallagher, Wm, 91
Gallagher, Wm, 4711
Gallaspey, Antony, 565
Gallaspey, Catherine, 565
Gallaspey, Henrietta, 565
Gallaway, Isaac, 5730
Gallaway, Judy, 4974
Gallaway, Mrs., 375

Gallaway, Saml, 422
Gallaway, Saml, 419
Gallaway, Sarah, 303
Gallaway, Sarah, 332
Gallawy, Judy, 597
Gallegher, Bridget, 2228
Galley, Birgitta, 1407
Galley, N., 1407
Galligher, Maria, 1761
Galloway, Juda, 1839
Galloway, Joseph, 46
Galloway, Josephus, 4431
Galloway, Judith, 46
Galloway, Mary, 2854
Galloway, Mary, 5161
Galloway, Rebecca, 1219
Galloway, Saml, 151
Galloway, Samuel, 4193
Galloway, Samuel, 46
Galloway, Sarah, 120
Galloway, Sarah, 103
Galloway, Sarah, 355
Galloway, Sarah, 399
Gallowe, Judy, 599
Galloy, Sarah, 227
Galogy, Sarah (Miss), 4283
Galvey, Bartholomei, 704

Galvey, Helenae, 704
Galvey, Joannes, 704
Galvin [or Golvin], James, 4290
Galvin, Davis, 607
Galvin, Denis, 522
Galvin, Dionysis, 982
Galvin, Elisabeth, 982
Galvin, Ellenora, 607
Galvin, James, 4331
Galvin, James, 522
Galvin, Marga, 982
Galvin, Margaret, 522
Galvin, Margret, 607
Ganley, Guillilmus, 1330
Gannely, Joannes, 1353
Gannon, Michael, 1861
Gannon, Sarah Ann Caroline, 1861
Gannon, William Edward, 1861
Ganshun, Edward, 2212
Gant, John, 16
Gant, Nancy, 16
Gapney, James, 495
Gapney, Jane, 495
Gapney, Nichlas, 495
Gar, Cathe, 2902
Garaghty, Margareta, 1567
Garaghty, Margareta, 1679

Garaghty, Maria, 1094
Garaghty, Patricius, 1679
Garber, Tammy (Miss), 357
Garbin, Catharina, 1977
Gardener, Maria, 1664
Gardener, Anna Margaret, 1920
Gardener, George, 1920
Gardener, Magdalen, 1920
Gardener, Michael, 1664
Gardener, Caroline, 2080
Gardner, George, 2080
Gardner, Georgii, 1800
Gardner, Georgius, 4499
Gardner, Henricus, 4366
Gardner, John Hoppin, 4545
Gardner, Magdalen, 2052
Gardner, Magdalen, 2080
Gardner, Magdalenae, 1800
Gardner, Magdalina, 1422
Gardner, Maria Anna, 1800
Gardner, Michael, 1422
Gardner, Michael, 1776
Gardner, Michael, 1800
Gardner, Michael, 1971
Gardner, Michael, 1987
Garesha, Maria, 3739
Garey, Gulielmo, 4849

Garey, Joannam, 4849
Garey, Johanna, 3771
Garey, Mrs., 4839
Garighan, Catharina, 1093
Garighan, Thomas, 1742
Garighty, James, 1855
Garighty, Sarah Wheeler, 1855
Garighty, Sarah, 1855
Garighty, Sarah, 1855
Garighty, Sarah, 1855
Garish, Georgietta, 4154
Garish, Georgietta, 3386
Garish, Georgium Edwardum, 3386
Garish, Joseph H., 4154
Garish, Joseph, 3386
Garish, Margaritam Agnetem, 4154
Garlin, Alexina E., 2303
Garlin, Catharine M. (Miss), 4555
Garlin, Catharine, 1978
Garlock, Elizabeth, 50
Garman, Elisabeth, 3149
Garman, Elizabeth, 2981
Garman, Elizabetha, 3687
Garman, Margaret (widow), 4326
Garmann, Elizabeth, 3496
Garner, Michael, 1135
Garner, Timotheus, 1279

Garoghty, Margareta, 1065
Garoghty, Margaretae, 1065
Garoghty, Patricii, 1065
Garoghty, Margaretae, 1406
Garoghty, Maria, 1406
Garoghty, Patricii, 1406
Garraghan, Jeremias, 1641
Garraghan, Margareta, 1641
Garraghty, Maria, 4364
Garreghan, Catharina, 1534
Garret, Maria E., 4111
Garret, Thomas, 1260
Garretty, Nancy, 157
Garretty, Patrick, 157
Garretty, Philip, 157
Garrighan, Catharina, 1116
Garrish, Benjamin, 3325
Garrish, Elie Dixon, 3326
Garrish, Georgietta, 3326
Garrish, Gingetta, 3325
Garrish, Josepho, 3325
Garrish, Josepho, 3326
Garry, Catharine R., 2272
Garry, Catharine R., 2273
Garry, Catharine, 2400
Garry, John William, 2400
Garry, Mary Frances, 2273

Garry, Michael M., 2272
Garry, Michael M., 2273
Garry, Michael M., 2400
Garry, Rosa Rebecca, 2272
Garry, Rosanna, 2400
Garvey, Michael, 1668
Garvey, Catharina Elleonora, 1773
Garvey, John, 1950
Garvey, Margaret Ann, 2156
Garvey, Margaret, 1950
Garvey, Margaret, 2156
Garvey, Margaretae, 1501
Garvey, Margaretae, 1773
Garvey, Maria Anna, 1501
Garvey, Michael, 1753
Garvey, Michael, 1950
Garvey, Michael, 2067
Garvey, Michael, 2156
Garvey, Michaelis, 1501
Garvey, Michaelis, 1773
Gary, Cath., 2631
Gary, Cath., 2879
Gary, Eug. [Eugene], 2876
Gary, Eugene, 2631
Gary, Eugene, 2879
Gary, Jno. Eugene, 2879
Gary, Margaret, 2631

Gates, Betsy, 140
Gates, Betsy, 37
Gates, Daniel William, 2348
Gates, Daniel William, 2354
Gates, Louisa, 37
Gates, Maly Elizabeth, 2354
Gates, Margaretta V., 3578
Gates, Margarettam V., 4773
Gates, Maria V., 4075
Gates, Maria Virginia, 3819
Gates, Mary Elizabeth, 2277
Gates, Mary Elizabeth, 2348
Gates, Michael, 37
Gates, Susie, 4773
Gatton, Zachiah?, 4356
Gatton, Ann Ross, 2250
Gatton, Edward George, 2248
Gatton, Eleonorae Josephinae, 1314
Gatton, Ellen, 2248
Gatton, Ellen, 2249
Gatton, Ellen, 2250
Gatton, Guillelmus Franciscus, 1314
Gatton, Helena Josephina, 740
Gatton, Jackariae, 740
Gatton, Lawrence, 2250
Gatton, Maria Anna, 740
Gatton, Richard, 2249
Gatton, Zachariae, 1314
Gatton, Zariah, 2248
Gatton, Zariah, 2249
Gatton, Zariah, 2250
Gatty, Birgitae, 1584
Gatty, Honoro, 1584
Gatty, Patricii, 1584
Gauger [sic], Mary, 2995
Gauger, Anna, 1593
Gauger, Barbara (Miss), 4558
Gauger, Barbara, 1841
Gauger, Barbara, 2244
Gauger, Barbara, 2437
Gauger, Barbara, 2508
Gauger, Barbara, 2541
Gauger, Barbara, 2560
Gauger, Barbara, 3237
Gauger, Barbara, 5492
Gauger, Catharine M., 2478
Gauger, Catharine, 2244
Gauger, Daniel W., 4462
Gauger, David, 2005
Gauger, Ellen, 1841
Gauger, Guellelimus Josephus, 1102
Gauger, Helenae, 1593
Gauger, Jacob Peter, 2004
Gauger, Joannes, 1593
Gauger, John Wesley Jacob, 1841
Gauger, John, 1841
Gauger, Joseph, 2004
Gauger, Joseph, 2161
Gauger, Joseph, 2995
Gauger, Josephi, 1102
Gauger, Julia A., 5189
Gauger, Julian, 2004
Gauger, Julianae, 1102
Gauger, Lucy, 5450
Gauger, Margaret Elizabeth, 5452
Gauger, Maria, 3237
Gauger, Mary A., 2478
Gauger, Mary Ann Elizabeth, 2995
Gauger, Mary E., 4548
Gauger, Mary Mandilla Catharine, 2005
Gauger, Mary, 2370
Gauger, Mary, 2578
Gauger, Mary, 2995
Gauger, Mary, 5493
Gauger, Sophia, 2005
Gauger, Theresia, 1593
Gauger, Victoria, 5447
Gaugher, Cecilia Jane, 2821
Gaugher, Joseph, 2821
Gaugher, Julian, 2161
Gaugher, Mary Elizabeth, 2161
Gaugher, Mary I., 2821
Gauker, Julia, 1746
Gauker, Anna Maria, 1383
Gauker, Catharine M., 5378
Gauker, David, 4483
Gauker, Ellen, 1383
Gauker, Elleonorae, 1746
Gauker, Joannes, 4470
Gauker, Joannis, 1383
Gauker, Joannis, 1746
Gauker, Josephus, 1746
Gauker, Petrus Henricus, 1746
Gaul, Margareth, 4350
Gay, Eliza, 2306
Gay, John H., 2306
Gay, John Henry, 2306
Gayon, Isabellae, 1346
Gayon, Joannis, 1346
Gayon, Josephus, 1346
Gearhart, J.A., 4884
Geary, Johanna, 3290
Geary, Mary, 3078
Geary, Catharina, 3213

Geary, Catharina, 3622
Geary, Catharinam Vincentiam, 4052
Geary, Catherine, 2702
Geary, Catherine, 2776
Geary, Catherine, 2972
Geary, Catherine, 3051
Geary, Elisabeth, 3051
Geary, Ellen Catharine, 2972
Geary, Eugene, 2702
Geary, Eugene, 2776
Geary, Eugene, 5300
Geary, Eugenis, 3213
Geary, Guglielmus, 3290
Geary, Gulielmo, 4052
Geary, Gulielmo, 4832
Geary, Gulielmum, 3923
Geary, Gulielmum, 3949
Geary, Gulielmum, 4889
Geary, Gulielmus, 3631
Geary, Gulielmus, 4834
Geary, Hanora, 4052
Geary, Heleonoram A., 4914
Geary, Joanna, 3712
Geary, Joanna, 3834
Geary, Joanna, 3923
Geary, Joanna, 4031

Geary, Johanna, 3472
Geary, Johanna, 3493
Geary, John E., 5190
Geary, John, 2702
Geary, Jospehina, 3633
Geary, Margareta, 4031
Geary, Margarita, 3761
Geary, Maria J., 4052
Geary, Mary Cath, 5712
Geary, Michaelem Themain, 3213
Geary, Mollie, 5068
Geary, Mrs., 3923
Geary, Owen, 2972
Geary, Owen, 3051
Geary, Owen, 3078
Geary, Thomas, 4031
Geary, Thomas, 4157
Geary, William, 2776
Geary, Wm, 3472
Gehr, Cecelia, 1890
Gehr, Cecelia, 2134
Gehr, Cecilia (Mrs.), 5070
Gehr, Cora, 3232
Gehr, Cora, 3315
Gehr, Eleanora Ligusi, 3232
Gehr, Elisabeth, 3133
Gehr, Harry, 3232

Gehr, Henrico, 3315
Gehr, Henricum C., 3133
Gehr, Henry, 5103
Gehr, Isaac, 1890
Gehr, Isaac, 3133
Gehr, Isaak, 1714
Gehr, Isaak, 4502
Gehr, Mariam Catharina Bostock, 3315
Gehr, Mary Catharine, 1890
Gehr, Mary, 5113
Gehry, Maria, 3162
Geis, Susanna, 3506
Gelaspe, Anthonii, 664
Gelaspe, Catharinae, 664
Gelcese, Catharine, 1834
Gelcese, Catharine, 1967
Gelcese, Thomas, 1853
Gelcese, Thomas, 1967
Gelcese, William Francis, 1967
Gelespey, Catharine, 1995
Gelespy, Catharine, 1867
Gell, Wilim, 4314
Gellin, Sara, 1209
Gelwicks, Louisa, 2407
Geoynn, Amanda M.F., 4192

Gephart, Elisabeth, 4144
Gerh, Anna Frances, 2110
Gerh, Cecelia, 2110
Gerh, Isaac, 2110
German, Lizzie, 4671
German, Mary, 4671
Germans, Theresa, 2713
Germen, Maria, 1251
Gerner, Maria, 1170
Gerrard, Marion E., 4591
Gerry, Catharina, 3381
Gerry, Noram, 3381
Gerry, Owen, 3381
Getz, William, 2050
Gher, Cora, 3179
Gher, Henrico, 3179
Gher, Maria Francisca, 3179
Gibbell, Anna Maria, 608
Gibbell, Catherine, 608
Gibbell, Michl, 608
Gibbs, Anna, 495
Gibbs, Louisa, 2261
Gibbs, Richard, 495
Gibson, Louisa, 4563
Gibson, Agnes Maria, 3477
Gibson, Agnes, 3379
Gibson, Agnetem, 3373

Gibson, Ann Eliza, 168
Gibson, Henry, 168
Gibson, Joshua G., 3373
Gibson, Philis, 168
Gibson, Philis, 178
Gibson, Susan, 3373
Gibson, Thos., 5172
Gile, George, 48
Gile, Hanna, 48
Gile, Mary Ann, 48
Gilemeyer, Sebastian, 4574
Gilender, G. (Mrs.), 568
Giles, Adleid, 3519
Giles, Anna, 6
Giles, John, 6
Giles, William, 6
Gilfoile, Joannes, 1452
Gilice, Catharinae, 1771
Gilice, Maria Anna, 1771
Gilice, Thomae, 1771
Gilice, Patricius, 1771
Gillan, Catharina Anna, 721
Gillan, Domenic, 5126
Gillan, Patricii, 721
Gillan, Patrick, 4354
Gillan, Winefart, 721
Gilland, Maria E., 3924

Gilleece, Patrick, 4717
Gilleece, Patritio, 3212
Gilleece, Patritium Guglielmum, 3212
Gilleece, Patritium, 4743
Gilleece, Rachel, 3212
Gilleece, Rachel, 3212
Gilleece, Rachel, 4717
Gilleece, Rachel, 4743
Gillis, Jos, 5583
Gillis, Joseph, 5530
Gillis, Joseph, 2669
Gilliss, Joseph, 4634
Gilliss, Maria, 4634
Gillmeyer, William, 4624
Gillmeyer, bride's father, 4624
Gillmeyer, Catharine J. (Miss), 4613
Gillmeyer, Catharine, 2457
Gillmeyer, Cecelia S., 2458
Gillmeyer, Cecilia, 2038
Gillmeyer, Cecilia, 2991
Gillmeyer, Cecilia, 4624
Gillmeyer, Edward, 2038
Gillmeyer, Elisabeth, 1108
Gillmeyer, Elisabeth, 1551
Gillmeyer, Eliza, 2074

Gillmeyer, Eliza, 4576
Gillmeyer, Elizabeth M., 2168
Gillmeyer, Elizabeth, 2091
Gillmeyer, Elizabeth, 2321
Gillmeyer, G.J., 4636
Gillmeyer, Geo., 4581
Gillmeyer, George, 2074
Gillmeyer, George Ignatius, 2321
Gillmeyer, George, 2091
Gillmeyer, George, 4562
Gillmeyer, Georgie, 1108
Gillmeyer, Georgii, 1551
Gillmeyer, Guillelmas J., 1108
Gillmeyer, James, 5441
Gillmeyer, Lewis, 5237
Gillmeyer, Lewis, 5487
Gillmeyer, Ludovicus Edwardus, 1551
Gillmeyer, Mary Elizabeth, 2038
Gillmeyer, Mr., 4535
Gillmeyer, Mrs., 4535
Gillmeyer, Mrs., 4565
Gillmeyer, Regina (Miss), 4581
Gillmeyer, Regina A., 2475
Gillmeyer, Regina Angela, 2460
Gillmeyer, Regina, 2168
Gillmeyer, Regina, 2495

Gillmeyer, Regina, 4550
Gillmeyer, Sarah Jane, 2168
Gillmeyer, Sebastian, 2038
Gillmeyer, Sebastian, 2168
Gillmeyer, Sebastian, 2321
Gillmeyer, Sebastian, 4535
Gillmeyer, Sebastianas, 1108
Gillmyer, Elizabeth, 5107
Gillmyer, Geo., 5050
Gillmyer, Kate (Miss), 4581
Gillons, Otho, 4581
Gillyer, Elisa, 503
Gillyer, George, 503
Gillyer, Sophia Regia, 503
Gilmeyer, C. (Miss), 4527
Gilmeyer, C. (Miss), 4532
Gilmeyer, Cath. (Miss), 1947
Gilmeyer, Cath., 4561
Gilmeyer, Cecilia, 2720
Gilmeyer, Cecilia, 2767
Gilmeyer, E. (Mrs.), 4547
Gilmeyer, Elisabeth, 1245
Gilmeyer, Fr., 4365
Gilmeyer, George, 4569
Gilmeyer, George, 2081
Gilmeyer, George, 4537
Gilmeyer, George, 4568

Gilmeyer, George, 4609
Gilmeyer, Sebastianus, 1517
Gilmore, George, 572
Gilmore, George (Mrs.), 468
Gilmore, Catherin Terresa, 454
Gilmore, Cecilia, 560
Gilmore, Eisabeth, 628
Gilmore, Elisa, 454
Gilmore, Elisabeth, 560
Gilmore, George, 516
Gilmore, George, 454
Gilmore, George, 468
Gilmore, George, 560
Gilmore, George, 628
Gilmore, Mrs., 596
Gilmore, Mrs., 441
Gilmore, Sarah Jane, 628
Gilmyer, Kate, 2304
Gilmyer, William, 5402
Ginder, Charlotte, 1829
Ginter, Charlotte, 1903
Ginter, Joseph, 1903
Gipe, Anna Elisabeth, 3110
Gipe, Isaac, 3110
Gipe, Maria, 3110
Gittinger, Gulielmo, 4892
Giuliani, Petrus, 4099

Glamule?, Julian (Miss), 4239
Glanville, Frances, 9
Glanville, John, 9
Glanville, Julian, 9
Gleanan, Birgitta, 1703
Gleesen, James, 3024
Gleeson, James, 3031
Gletner, Joseph, 1888
Gletner, Sarah Jane, 1888
Gletner, Sarah Jane, 1888
Gley, Charlotte, 1829
Gley, Francis, 1829
Gley, Mary Eva, 1829
Glison, John, 2707
Gloughlen, Mich M., 245
Goans, Joscee, 353
Goans, Sophia, 353
Goans, Thomas, 353
Gobbart, Agnes, 3614
Gocen, 342
Gocen, Anna Elisa, 342
Gocen, Mary, 342
Gock, Josephi, 2280
Gock, Josepha, 2280
Gock, Mary, 2280
Godard, Richardus, 4469
Goddard, Cath., 2914

Goddard, Catharine Virginia, 2069
Goddard, Charlotte, 2903
Goddard, Charlotte, 4688
Goddard, Clara Jane, 2471
Goddard, Clara, 3183
Goddard, Clara, 3190
Goddard, Clara, 3235
Goddard, Gulielmo, 4130
Goddard, John, 2740
Goddard, John, 4931
Goddard, Maggie, 4688
Goddard, Maggy, 2913
Goddard, Marg, 5658
Goddard, Margaret, 2281
Goddard, Margaret, 3091
Goddard, Margaret, 4720
Goddard, Margaret, 5002
Goddard, Margareta, 3236
Goddard, Maria Franciscam, 4916
Goddard, Maria, 4130
Goddard, Maria, 4910
Goddard, Mariam Franciscam, 4130
Goddard, Mary C., 4720
Goddard, Mary Charlotte, 1919
Goddard, Mary Magdella, 2914
Goddard, Mary, 1919

Goddard, Mary, 2069
Goddard, Mary, 2281
Goddard, Mary, 2471
Goddard, Mary, 2792
Goddard, Mary, 4998
Goddard, Mary, 5659
Goddard, Richard, 1919
Goddard, Richard, 2069
Goddard, Richard, 2281
Goddard, Richard, 2471
Goddard, Wm. B., 4688
Goddard, Wm, 2914
Goddard, Wm, 4639
Goddard, Wm, 5567
Goddart, Clara, 3062
Goddreck, Wm., 5507
Godgart, Maggie, 3050
Goff, Birgitta, 1199
Goff, Birgittae, 1199
Goff, Joannis, 1199
Gold, Ella E., 3843
Gold, Helenam M., 4814
Gold, Marion, 4636
Golden, [blank], 653
Golden, Joannes, 653
Golden, Michaelis, 653
Goleese, Ann Elizabeth, 2372

Goleese, Ann, 2372
Goleese, Thomas, 2372
Golibart, Agnes, 3635
Golibart, Simenem, 4805
Golsberry, Dianna, 20
Golsberry, July Ann, 20
Golsberry, Saml., 20
Golvin, Dionysii, 732
Golvin, Joannes, 732
Golvin, Margaretae, 732
Gonder, Genevefa, 3830
Gonigle, Joseph, 2722
Gonker, Aloysius David Eugene, 3072
Gonker, Joseph, 2603
Gonker, Joseph, 3072
Gonker, Mary, 2684
Gonker, Mary, 3072
Gonker, Theresa, 4975
Gonnegal, Maygor N., 244
Gonter, Annae, 636
Gonter, Annae, 637
Gonter, Johannes, 637
Gonter, Johannis, 637
Gonter, Johenis, 636
Gonter, Susana Catharina, 636
Good, Hanna, 169

Good, Margaret, 169
Gorighan, Catharina, 1740
Gorlet, Maria, 1342
Gorman, Anna, 860
Gorman, Bernardi, 860
Gorman, Catharinae, 860
Gorman, Joannes, 1085
Gorman, Joannes, 1578
Gorman, Joannes, 4404
Gorman, Joannis, 1085
Gorman, Juliae Annae, 1085
Gorman, Maria Anna, 1660
Gorman, Mary Ann, 2062
Gorman, Mary Ann, 4559
Gorman, Michael, 1579
Gormely, Mariae, 992
Gormely, Sara, 992
Gormon, Catharina, 4482
Goss, Anna, 3656
Goss, Anna, 3655
Gossard, Maria, 4153
Gossard, Mary K., 3861
Gossard, Max, 4911
Gotz, Antonii, 1379
Gotz, Elisabeth, 1379
Gotz, Mariae Annae, 1379
Gouer, Daniel Patrick, 2728

Gouer, Joseph, 2728
Gouer, Mary, 2728
Gouger, Joseph, 1469
Gough, Vare[?] or Wire, 589
Gouker, Aloysius David Eugene, 3072
Gouker, Joseph, 3072
Gouker, Mary, 3072
Gouker, Barbara Anna, 1666
Gouker, Barbara I., 1468
Gouker, Barbara, 2883
Gouker, Barbara, 3009
Gouker, David, 1469
Gouker, Edward Pierce, 3008
Gouker, Jacob, 5003
Gouker, Jos. W., 4637
Gouker, Joseph W., 5388
Gouker, Josephi, 1666
Gouker, Julia Anne, 2730
Gouker, Julia, 1469
Gouker, Juliae Annae, 1666
Gouker, Kate, 2899
Gouker, Louisa Ann, 2347
Gouker, Margareta, 4456
Gouker, Mary Ann, 3008
Gouker, Mary, 2689
Gouker, Mary, 2744

Gouker, Mary, 2883
Gouker, Mary, 4637
Gouker, Mr., 5025
Gouker, Samuel, 3008
Gouker, Sara Joanne, 1469
Gouker, Sophiae, 1469
Goulding, Cath. (Mrs.), 168
Goulding, Margaret, 4176
Goulding, Susanna, 4185
Gours, Jane, 2418
Govern, Anne, 2763
Govern, Margaret, 2763
Govern, Pat, 2763
Gower, Cath. V., 4688
Gower, Margaret, 610
Gower, Mariam Elizabeth, 3481
Grace, Catharina, 3102
Grace, Maria, 3102
Grace, Samueli L., 3102
Gradey, Catharine, 2124
Gradey, Margaret, 2275
Gradey, Patrick, 1922
Grady, Beatricem Geneviefam, 4104
Grady, Bridget, 3022
Grady, Cath, 2937
Grady, Catharina, 3211

Grady, Catharina, 3290
Grady, Catharina, 4104
Grady, Catharina, 4131
Grady, Catharina, 4887
Grady, Catharina, 4893
Grady, Catharinae, 1795
Grady, Catharine, 3412
Grady, Daniel, 3022
Grady, Danl, 510
Grady, Dionysius, 1795
Grady, Francisco, 4104
Grady, Franciscum J., 4893
Grady, Franciscum Thomam, 3211
Grady, Franciscus, 4131
Grady, Jesse J. [or I.], 4104
Grady, Joannis, 1418
Grady, John Edmund, 2937
Grady, Julia, 3022
Grady, Margaret, 3412
Grady, Margarita, 4116
Grady, Maria, 4068
Grady, Maria, 4131
Grady, Mariam E., 4887
Grady, Mariam Elizabeth, 3290
Grady, Patricii, 1795
Grady, Patricius, 1603
Grady, Robert, 90

Grady, Thoma, 3211
Grady, Thoma, 3290
Grady, Thoma, 3412
Grady, Thomas, 2988
Grady, Thos., 2937
Graffy, Clarae, 1747
Graffy, Clarae, 1748
Graffy, Jacobi, 1747
Graffy, Jacobi, 1748
Graffy, Sara, 1747
Graffy, Theresia, 1748
Graham, Anne, 127
Graham, William Peter, 127
Graham, William, 127
Grailey, Catharina, 1053
Grailey, Dionysii, 1053
Grailey, Mariae, 1053
Graily, Maria, 1262
Graily, Dionysius, 1262
Gramsie, Henricus, 4410
Grant, Margret, 4281
Grant, Mary E., 2305
Grant, Mary Elizabeth, 2264
Grant, Mary Elizabeth, 2265
Grant, Thomas, 1148
Graves, George, 4549
Gray, Birgitta, 1221

Gray, Birgitta, 1450
Gray, Cath., 2950
Gray, Catherine, 2767
Gray, Catherine, 2991
Gray, Elisabeth, 1635
Gray, Georgius, 1430
Gray, Joannes, 1221
Gray, Joannes, 1450
Gray, Kate, 2819
Gray, Kate, 2850
Gray, Kate, 3258
Gray, Katherine, 2970
Gray, Margareta, 1296
Gray, Margret Jane, 5738
Gray, Mrs., 2775
Gray, Petrus, 1474
Gray, R. (Mrs.), 2789
Gray, Thos., 2879
Grayley [or Grayly], Dyonisius, 1583
Grayley, Dionysii, 1371
Grayley, Mariae, 1371
Grayley, Patricius, 1371
Grayly, Patricius, 1371
Gready, Catharine, 2015
Green, John, 555
Green, Mary, 555

Green, Patrick, 555
Green, Susan, 4652
Green, A...., 1695
Green, Abelonae, 1221
Green, Ann Rosella, 2954
Green, Anna, 1566
Green, Annae Catharinae, 920
Green, Annae, 817
Green, Annem, 3793
Green, Birgittae, 861
Green, Bridget, 2608
Green, Catharina, 1199
Green, Catharinae, 1411
Green, Elizabeth, 1891
Green, Elizabeth, 2253
Green, Francisca, 1221
Green, Francisci, 1566
Green, Framnciscus, 1695
Green, Geo. Edward, 2760
Green, George, 3067
Green, Gulielmum, 3123
Green, Henry, 2608
Green, Jacobi, 1411
Green, Jacobi, 920
Green, Jacobus, 817
Green, Joannes son, 1221
Green, Joannes, 920

Green, Joseph Wm., 3067
Green, Lucy, 18
Green, Margt., 2880
Green, Maria, 861
Green, Martin B., 3046
Green, Martin Henry, 3046
Green, Martin V., 2822
Green, Martin V.B., 4645
Green, Martin, 2760
Green, Martin, 2874
Green, Martin, 2954
Green, Martin, 4652
Green, Martin, 5676
Green, Martino, 3123
Green, Mary Eliz. Frances, 2874
Green, Mary Ellen, 2608
Green, Mary, 3067
Green, Michael, 4374
Green, Naby, 1566
Green, Patricii, 817
Green, Richardi, 861
Green, Samuel Frederick, 2822
Green, Sarah (Miss), 4523
Green, Susan R., 2822
Green, Susan R., 3046
Green, Susan, 2760
Green, Susan, 2874

Green, susan, 2954
Green, Susan, 3047
Green, Suzanna, 3123
Green, Terresa, 417
Green, Terresa, 419
Green, Thomas, 1411
Green, Thos., 2880
Green, Thos., 2880
Greene, Geo, 4703
Greeneele, Maria, 4195
Greentree, Anna, 3650
Greenwell, Catherine (Mrs.), 488
Greenwell, Elizb (Mrs.), 64
Greenwell, Maria, 110
Greenwell, Maria, 4195
Greg, Benjamin F., 4613
Gregory, Rosa Anna, 3010
Grey, Birgitta, 1098
Grey, Birgittae, 1333
Grey, Catharine (Mrs.), 2806
Grey, Catherine (Mrs.), 2579
Grey, Elisabeth, 1508
Grey, Jacobus, 1333
Grey, Joannes, 1098
Grey, Joannes, 1723
Grey, Joannis, 1333
Grey, Margareta, 1624

Grey, Margaretae, 1508
Grey, Margaretae, 1723
Grey, Petri, 1723
Grey, Petris, 1508
Griech, Guelilmii, 1662
Griech, Joannes, 1662
Griech, Margaretae, 1662
Griech, Maria Ludovica, 1662
Griffe, Jacob, 5326
Griffe, Joseph H., 4813
Griffen, Julian (Mrs.), 539
Griffen, Mary, 5654
Griffey, [blank], 3075
Griffey, Ann, 5432
Griffey, Anna Margaret, 2174
Griffey, Catharine, 3279
Griffey, Catharine, 5460
Griffey, Catherin, 2986
Griffey, Clara Catharine, 2406
Griffey, Clara, 2174
Griffey, Edwardum Ludovicum, 3256
Griffey, Elizabeth, 5544
Griffey, Elizabeth, 5589
Griffey, Jacob, 2174
Griffey, Jacob, 2406
Griffey, Jacob, 2986

Griffey, Maggie, 3256
Griffey, Margaret, 3279
Griffey, Margaret, 4723
Griffey, Margarita, 3852
Griffey, Margt., 2866
Griffey, Maria, 3256
Griffey, Martha, 2822
Griffey, Mary Clara, 2406
Griffey, Mary, 5672
Griffey, Petronella, 5442
Griffey, Petronilla, 5461
Griffey, Sarah, 4723
Griffey, Theresa, 2957
Griffey, Theresa, 5550
Griffey, Theresa, 5592
Griffin, Catharine, 2988
Griffin, Catharina, 3175
Griffin, Jacob H., 2770
Griffin, Jacob, 2770
Griffin, Joseph, 2770
Griffin, Margarita, 3175
Griffin, Mary, 1907
Griffin, Mary, 2770
Griffin, Teresa, 2823
Griffin, Thomas, 2805
Griffith, Catharina, 3393
Griffith, Catherine, 2739

Griffith, Jacob H., 4654
Griffith, Jacob J., 3393, 5416
Griffith, Sarah, 2739
Griffith, Sarah, 4654
Griffith, Tracy, 4649
Griffon, Catharina, 1322
Griffon, Catharinae, 882, 1149, 1617
Griffon, Guillelini, 882
Griffon, Guillelmi, 1149, 1617
Griffon, Maria, 882
Griffon, Michael Henricus, 1617
Griffon, Patricius, 1149
Griffy, Catherine, 3057
Griffy, Margaretha, 3568
Grim, Thomas, 5115
Grimes, Nancy, 25
Grimes, Nancy, 26
Grimm, Ada, 3255
Grimm, Nellie Regina, 3255
Grimm, Nellie, 3996
Grimm, Thoma, 3255
Grimm, Thomam B., 4739
Groghan, Thomas, 1542
Grooms, Julia, 3770
Groover, Joanne, 3625
Groover, Julia, 3625

Groover, Mariam Urillam, 3625
Gross, [blank], 3440
Gross, Catharine, 3440
Gross, Margaret Ann, 3440
Gross, Abehelam, 1160
Gross, Anna Catharina, 1160
Gross, Barbara, 1989
Gross, Caroli, 1160
Gross, Charles, 5177
Gross, Charlotte Magdalene, 2998
Gross, Clara, 3527
Gross, Clara, 3528
Gross, Clara, 3759
Gross, Clara, 3760
Gross, Clara, 3798
Gross, Jacob, 2998
Gross, Magd., 2998
Grosscoup, Elisabetha, 3661
Grosscoup, Margarita, 3661
Gruber, L.F., 5119
Gruber, Carolum W., 4910
Gruber, Franciscum Roy Clayton, 3548
Gruber, Fredericum, 3335
Gruber, Helen, 4085
Gruber, Jacobus Clifton, 3462
Gruber, Joanni, 3548

Gruber, Johanne, 3462
Gruber, Johanni, 3335
Gruber, Julia, 3335
Gruber, Julia, 3462
Gruber, Julia, 3548
Gruber, Mr., 4607
Gruber, Mrs., 4607
Guender, Doretheae, 1428
Guender, Eva Catharina, 1428
Gulmen, Mr., 4334
Gumpurt, [blank], 2725
Gumpurt, Mary, 2725
Gumpurt, South, 2725
Gunnell, Alberto H., 4097
Gunnell, Albertum Harricum, 3976
Gunnell, Hannam Kennedy, 4097
Gunnell, Joanne, 3976
Gunnell, Sallie K., 4097
Gunshaw, Bridget, 2111
Gunshehan, Mary, 1892
Guth, M. [Father Michael], 1356
Guth, M., 1096, 1140, 1384, 1595, 1596
Guth, Michael, 1097, 1118, 1381, 1423, 1442, 1549, 1551
Guth, Michael, 1601, 1637, 1655
Guyer, Elizabeth, 4605

Haan, Maria H., 3915
Habbert, Archl., 223
Habbert, Catherine, 223
Habbert, Margret, 223
Hack, Mary I., 2820
Hackett, Mary Ann, 2933
Hackett, Mary, 2933
Hackett, Mary, 4699
Hackett, Mich., 2933
Hackett, Nicholas, 2933
Hackey, Maria, 1216
Hadk, Anna, 4381
Hady, Thomas, 4694
Hagan, Danl., 590
Hagan, Kate, 3029
Hagan, Patricius, 830
Hagar, Danl., 590
Hagel, Catharine, 1990
Hager, Anna C., 4116
Hager, Emerson A. [Jonathan J. crossed out], 4116
Hager, Emerson A., 4895
Hager, Jonathan, 4895
Hager, Margaritam Catharinam, 4116
Hahn, Frederico, 4741
Haidan, Guillelmus G., 4434

Haiden, Helenae, 1518
Haiden, Joannes, 1518
Haiden, Joannis, 1518
Hail, Ally, 1168
Hail, Annae, 1168
Hail, Margareta, 1633
Hail, Roberti, 1168
Hail, Annae, 1633
Hail, Maria, 1633
Hail, Roberti, 1633
Halbert, Anna Mercy, 2077
Halbert, Archibald, 2077
Halbert, Archoobald, 222
Halbert, Catherine, 2077
Halbert, Catherine, 222
Halbert, John, 222
Halbert, Margaret, 1904
Halbert, Margaret, 2084
Halbert, Margaret, 2222
Halbert, Mary, 4721
Haley, Catherine (Miss), 4280
Halfpenny, Mary, 13
Hall, Anna Daley, 3979
Hall, Anna, 3761
Hall, Anna, 3834
Hall, Anna, 3892
Hall, Caroline, 1861

Hall, Catharine, 47
Hall, Edelia (Mrs.), 3979
Hall, Mary, 2819
Hall, Terresa, 47
Hall, Thomas, 47
Haller, Daniel, 4238
Halm, Eliza, 4610
Halm, Francisca, 3846
Halm, Franciscam King, 3895
Halm, Fred., 3248
Halm, Frederick Francis Joseph, 2491
Halm, Fredericum J., 4818
Halm, Fredericus, 3188
Halm, Fredericus, 3598
Halm, Fredericus, 3846
Halm, Fredericus, 4766
Halm, Juliam Mariam, 3846
Halm, Mrs., 3895
Halm, Philippina, 2491
Halm, Reinald J., 4796
Halm, Reinhold (Dr.), 5264
Halm, Reinhold, 3846
Halm, Reinhold, 3895
Halm, Reinold, 4646
Halm, Reinold's wife, 4646
Halm, Rinehault, 2491

Halpin, Annae, 1255
Halpin, Barney, 2892
Halpin, Jno., 2937
Halpin, Joannes, 1255
Halpin, Mary Ann, 2975
Halpin, Michaelis, 1255
Halpine, Catherine, 3031
Halpine, Kate, 3024
Halpine, Mary Ellen, 3027
Halpine, Mary Ellen, 3092
Halpp, Conrad, 4718
Halter, Anna, 1158
Halton, Annae, 1201
Halton, Annae, 1202
Halton, Franciscus [twin], 1201
Halton, Joannes [twin], 1202
Halton, Michaelis, 1201
Halton, Michaelis, 1202
Haly, Joannis, 1266
Haly, Mariae, 1266
Haly, Patricius, 1266
Hambach, Josephina, 1535
Hambach, Michael J. [or I.], 1535
Hamburg, Barbara A., 3477
Hamilton, Catharinam E., 4870
Hamilton, Mary, 1923
Hamilton, Mary, 1924

Hammaker, William E., 3734
Hammel, Fredericus, 4408
Hammersley, Ann, 4702
Hammersley, Sarah Ann, 4607
Hammon, Elender, 200
Hammon, Jacob, 200
Hammon, Wilson, 200
Hammond, Eleanor, 49
Hammond, Helena, 1840
Hammond, Helena, 49
Hammond, Wm., 49
Handehon, Lawrence, 2635
Handley, Margareta, 1278
Handley, Maria, 1738
Handroson, Maria J. [or I.], 3918
Hanen, Jeremiah, 4715
Hankey, Luisa (Orndorf), 4142
Hankey, Antonium, 4912
Hankey, Antonius, 4141
Hankey, Antonius, 4142
Hankey, Mrs., 4141
Hanlan, John William, 2178
Hanlan, John, 2178
Hanlan, John, 4554
Hanlan, Mary, 2178
Hanley, Ann, 4692
Hanly, Michael, 5448

Hann, Henrietta, 4014
Hanna, M., 2729
Hannah, Mary, 4674
Hannan, Dominick, 2039
Hannan, Julia, 2039
Hannan, Rosanna, 2039
Hannon, Bernardus, 1360
Hannon, Opherebus Dominius, 4496
Hannon, William, 1367
Hansbury, Sarah Ann, 2569
Hansen, Anna, 3185
Hanson, Anna, 3223
Hanson, Ann, 2965
Hanson, Annie, 5541
Hanson, Annie, 5607
Hanson, Mary, 2374
Hanson, Mary, 5141
Hanson, Mary, 5793
Hanson, Owen Andrew, 2965
Hansucker, Anna Rebecca, 2063
Hansucker, Charles Henry, 2211
Hansucker, Elizabeth, 2062
Hansucker, Elizabeth, 2063
Hansucker, Elizabeth, 2064
Hansucker, Elizabeth, 2211
Hansucker, George Howard, 2062

Hansucker, Henry, 2062
Hansucker, Henry, 2063
Hansucker, Henry, 2064
Hansucker, Henry, 2211
Hansucker, Mary Frances, 2064
Hany, Johann, 1537
Hany, Edwardus, 1537
Hapelty, Catharinae, 1186
Hapet, Catherine, 4667
Hapet, Thos., 2782
Happel, Catharina, 4035
Happel, Catharine, 3975
Happel, Maria, 3975
Happel, Susanna, 4035
Happel, Annam Catharinam, 4905
Happel, Catharina, 3907
Happel, Louisam Rosam, 3480
Happel, Maria, 3911
Happel, Maria, 4040
Happel, Maria, 4120
Happel, Mariam S., 4776
Happel, Martin, 4776
Happel, Martiney, 4172
Happel, Martinis, 3693
Happel, Martino, 3480
Happel, Martino, 4894
Happel, Martino, 4905

Happel, Rosa, 3480
Happel, Rosa, 4118
Happel, Rosa, 4871
Happel, Susanna, 4118
Happel, Susanna, 4815
Happel, Susanna, 4844
Happell, M., 2922
Happell, Rosinse, 2922
Happell, Susan R., 4871
Happell, Susan, 2922
Happle, Annam Catharinam, 3198
Happle, Martino, 3198
Happle, Rosina, 3198
Happle, Henry, 5121
Happle, John Henry, 3086
Happle, Martin, 3086
Happle, Martinus, 3131
Happle, Rosa, 3131
Happle, Rosina, 3295
Happle, Rosine, 3086
Happol, Martimus, 3692
Harbaugh, Anna (Miss), 4561
Harbaugh, John C., 2507
Harbaugh, Lebeda, 3764
Harbaugh, Leila Ady, 3652
Harbaugh, Maria A., 3124
Harbaugh, Mary, 2507

Harbaugh, Sarah Jane, 2507
Harber, Philippi, 1506
Harber, Rosa Anna, 1506
Harber, Sophiae, 1506
Harbin, Franciscum Percival, 3983
Harbin, Jacobo T., 3983
Harbin, Jennie, 3983
Harbine, Anna, 2139
Harbine, Catharine A., 2447
Harbine, Catharine, 2139
Harbine, Catharine, 2260
Harbine, Catharine, 2320
Harbine, Catharine, 2512
Harbine, Catharine, 2546
Harbine, Catharine, 2546
Harbine, John Michael, 2447
Harbine, Kate, 2604
Harbine, Mary, 5795
Harbine, Mary, 2604
Harbine, Thomas, 2139
Harbine, Thomas, 2320
Harbine, Thomas, 2320
Harbine, Thomas, 2447
Harbine, Thomas, 2512
Harbine, Thomas, 2512
Harbine, Thomas, 2546
Harbine, Thomas, 4533

Harbine, Thomas, 4938
Harbine, Thos., 2604
Hardgrove, Eliza, 93
Harding, Emma B., 3830
Harding, Emmam, 4765
Hardy, Edith, 480
Hardy, Edith, 481
Hardy, Eliza Ellon, 481
Hardy, Elizabeth (Miss), 481
Hardy, George, 480
Hardy, George, 481
Hardy, Pryrilla, 480
Hardy, Thomas Edward, 480
Hare, Eliza Mariam, 3302
Hare, Jacob, 3302
Hare, Michl, 4249
Hare, Philemena, 3302
Hargan, Maria, 1357
Haris, Maria, 73
Harkan, Grce, 14
Harkin, Alice or Else, 14
Harkins, Carolus, 1408
Harkins, Catharina, 1739
Harkins, Catharinae, 1408
Harkins, Catharinae, 1730
Harkins, Catharinae, 909
Harkins, Daniel, 1730

Harkins, Joannes, 1408
Harkins, Joannes, 909
Harkins, Joannis, 1408
Harkins, Joannis, 1730
Harkins, Joannis, 909
Harley [or Hurley], Joannes, 1449
Harman, Charles W., 4563
Harman, Robertus, 1286
Ham, Ada, 2990
Ham, Eva, 4656
Harn, Maria Alphonsa, 3494
Harne, Ada, 2888
Harne, Ada, 3898
Harne, Maria, 3600
Harne, Maria, 3721
Harne, Mary Alphonsus Theresia, 2724
Harne, Mary, 2818
Harney, Arabella, 4707
Harper, Eliza Jane, 3456
Harper, Meredith, 3456
Harper, Priscilla, 3802
Harper, Sarah Ellen, 3456
Harrett, Catharine, 1890
Harrigan, Maria, 1509
Harrington, Geo. B., 3929
Harrington, Geo. B., 4119

Harris, Anna, 2067
Harris, Harriet, 2245
Harris, Harriet, 2252
Harris, John Thomas, 2252
Harris, Maria Anna, 1114
Harris, Robert, 4590
Harris, Thomas, 2245
Harris, William, 2245
Harris, William, 2252
Harris, Wm., 52
Harrison, Adam, 5579
Harrison, Abraham, 1871
Harrison, Amos, 1875
Harrison, Benjamin, 1874
Harrison, Catharine, 1877
Harrison, Clara, 1879
Harrison, Clara, 4067
Harrison, Cornelius Cassey, 2295
Harrison, Elbert, 2295
Harrison, Emilia, 3139
Harrison, Emmert, 4067
Harrison, George W., 159
Harrison, Henry, 1873
Harrison, James, 1881
Harrison, Joannis Thomae, 1134
Harrison, Joannis Thomae, 1376
Harrison, Joannis Thomae, 797

Harrison, Josua Dixson, 797
Harrison, Juliam Geneviefam, 4067
Harrison, Lawrence, 1872
Harrison, Louisa, 1880
Harrison, Margareta Elisabeth, 1376
Harrison, Margaretae, 1134
Harrison, Margaretae, 1376
Harrison, Margaretae, 797
Harrison, Maria Anna, 1134
Harrison, Maria, 1876
Harrison, Mary, 1878
Harrison, Mary, 2295
Harrison, Phebe, 159
Harrison, Sam Harrison, 159
Harrison, Sam, 160
Harrison, Saml, 5288
Harrison, Samuel, 1871
Harrison, Samuel, 1872
Harrison, Samuel, 1873
Harrison, Samuel, 1874
Harrison, Samuel, 1875
Harrison, Samuel, 1876
Harrison, Samuel, 1877
Harrison, Samuel, 1878
Harrison, Samuel, 1879
Harrison, Samuel, 1880

Harrison, Samuel, 1881
Harrison, William H., 4569
Harriss, Mary, 73
Harrit, Francena, 2288
Harrit, Mr., 4555
Harritt, Catharine, 2297
Harritt, Cecelia, 1890
Harritt, Cecilia, 4502
Harsh, Catherine, 4718
Harsh, Elizabeth A., 4718
Harsh, Jacob, 4718
Harsh, Maria C., 4789
Hart, Alexander Warford, 2067
Hart, Ann Ellen, 2229
Hart, Ann Josephine, 2342
Hart, Ann, 2341
Hart, Anna, 2067
Hart, Anna, 2211
Hart, Charles, 4541
Hart, Eugene Alphonsus, 2341
Hart, William, 2067
Hart, William, 2341
Harter, Anna, 2976
Hartley, Caroline, 1922
Hartmann, Mary, 2442
Hartmann, Elisabeth, 4462
Hartmann, Elleonora, 4470

Hartmann, Joannes, 4516
Hartmann, Josephus, 4498
Hartmann, Margareta, 4416
Hartmann, Maria Anna, 4420
Hartnet, Frances, 9
Hartshoge, George, 4205
Hasan, Gorge, 217
Haskin, Robert, 5150
Hasland, Catharinae, 1553
Hasland, Michael, 1553
Hasland, Michaelis, 1553
Hasset, Ann, 2955
Hasset, Anna Elizabeth, 2469
Hasset, Bridget, 2326
Hasset, Catharine, 2327
Hasset, Catharine, 2556
Hasset, Clarence Regina [sic], 2769
Hasset, Ellen, 2326
Hasset, Ellen, 2469
Hasset, Ellen, 2556
Hasset, Ellen, 2556
Hasset, Ellen, 2769
Hasset, John, 2469
Hasset, Michael, 2327
Hasset, Sarah Amelia, 2326
Hasset, Thomas, 2326
Hasset, Thomas, 2469

Hasset, Thomas, 2556
Hasset, Thos., 2768
Hasset, Thos., 2769
Hassett, Cathar., 2811
Hassett, Catharina, 3167
Hassett, Ellen, 2660
Hassett, Ellen, 2830
Hassett, Jno., 2657
Hassett, Kate, 2646
Hassett, Kate, 2830
Hassett, Kate, 2913
Hassett, Kate, 4627
Hassett, Lyda Belle, 2660
Hassett, Mary Ann, 2660
Hassett, Mary, 2811
Hassett, Thomas, 4553
Hassett, Thos, 2660
Hassett, Thos., 2830
Hassmann, Elisabeth, 1026
Hassmann, Guillelmi, 1026
Hassmann, Maria Wilhelmina, 1026
Hasting, Catharine Elizabeth, 2232
Hasting, David, 2230
Hasting, David, 2231
Hasting, David, 2232
Hasting, David, 2256

Hasting, John Henry, 2230
Hasting, Mary Ann, 2230
Hasting, Mary Ann, 2231
Hasting, Mary Ann, 2232
Hasting, Samuel, 2231
Hastings, Annam, 3757
Hastings, Mariom, 3756
Hasty, Joanne, 3611
Hasty, Rosam Lucindem, 3611
Hasty, Samuele, 3611
Hatain, Mary, 331
Hath, Birgittae, 919
Hath, Guillelmus, 919
Hath, Thomae, 919
Haugh, Margaret Catharine, 2390
Haughens, Elisabeth, 1670
Haukins, Anna, 812
Haule, James, 450
Haule, James, 451
Haule, James, 452
Haule, Lucy, 452
Haule, Lucy, 450
Haule, Lucy, 451
Haule, Mary, 452
Haule, Richard, 451
Haule, Rose, 450
Haurande, Christina, 2692

Haurande, Martin, 2692
Haurande, Wm. Henry, 2692
Haurende, Christina Catharine, 2440
Haurende, Martin, 2440
Haurende, Mary Christina, 2440
Hausley, Maria, 1601
Hauss?, Elizabeth (Miss), 4528
Havard, Catharinae, 1547
Havard, Maria Anna, 1547
Havard, Thomae, 1547
Havis, Cloe, 12
Hawken, Anna A., 3156
Hawken, Anna A., 3537
Hawken, Carolum Foster, 3537
Hawken, Catharine, 86
Hawken, Catharine, 2068
Hawken, George Thomas, 86
Hawken, Gulielmo W., 3156
Hawken, Gulielmum, 4728
Hawken, Jas. E., 2695
Hawken, Jas., 2835
Hawken, Kate, 5575
Hawken, Mary (Miss), 5021
Hawken, Mary E., 2695
Hawken, Mary Elizabeth, 2695
Hawken, Mary S., 2695

Hawken, Mary Susan, 2835
Hawken, Mary, 2068
Hawken, Mary, 2068
Hawken, Mary, 2243
Hawken, Mary, 2436
Hawken, Mary, 4540
Hawken, Mrs. May, 2100
Hawken, Nelly Lee, 2835
Hawken, Richardum Vincentium Whelan P., 3156
Hawken, Sarah Jane, 2436
Hawken, Thomas Robinson, 2243
Hawken, Wilfred E., 4540
Hawken, Wilfred, 2243
Hawken, William, 2436
Hawken, William, 2778
Hawken, Wm, 86
Hawken, Wm. H., 2695
Hawken, Wm. W., 3537
Hawken, Wm., 2667
Hawken, Wm., 5505
Hawkens, Anna Catharina, 646
Hawkens, Catherine (Mrs.), 567
Hawkens, Joannis, 645
Hawkens, Joannis, 646
Hawkens, Maria, 645

Hawkens, Sarah, 1935
Hawkens, Sarah, 2121
Hawkey, Catherin (widow), 4342
Hawkey, Julianna, 2398
Hawkin, William, 4180
Hawkins, Ann, 3222
Hawkins, Anna A., 3387
Hawkins, Benjamen Josephum, 3608
Hawkins, Catharine, 76
Hawkins, Catharine, 77
Hawkins, Catharine, 78
Hawkins, Catharine, 79
Hawkins, Catharine, 80
Hawkins, Catherine, 189
Hawkins, Catherine, 286
Hawkins, Catherine, 343
Hawkins, Catherine, 538
Hawkins, Frances, 3222
Hawkins, Gulielmo, 3608
Hawkins, Henry, 76
Hawkins, James, 78
Hawkins, Jenny, 77
Hawkins, Jesse, 79
Hawkins, Kate, 3069
Hawkins, Mary Am, 80
Hawkins, Mary Elissa, 286

Hawkins, Milton R., 4889
Hawkins, Wilfred, 189
Hawkins, Wilhelmam Edwinum, 3387
Hawkins, Wilhelmo H., 3387
Hawkins, William, 189
Hawkins, William, 343
Hawkins, Wilm, 286
Hawkins, Wilm, 343
Hawkins, Wm, 3069
Hawkins, Wm, 3222
Hawtherne, Sophiam, 4761
Hay, Elizabeth, 614
Hay, John, 4234
Hayden, Eleonorae, 1278
Hayden, Guillelmi, 1114
Hayden, Henriettae, 1114
Hayden, J.O. (Rev.), 3332
Hayden, Joannes Richardus, 1114
Hayden, Joannis, 1278
Hayden, John, 1911
Hayden, Petrus, 1278
Hayden, Richardus, 1114
Haydon, John, 1857
Hayet, Barbara, 1863
Hayet, Eva, 1863
Hayet, John, 1863

Hays, Elisabeth, 1652
Hays, Margaret R., 2383
Hayward, Wiliam H., 4563
Hazelet, Robert, 4523
Healy, Bernardus, 1276
Healy, Helena, 4398
Healy, Honora, 1276
Healy, J., 611
Healy, John (Fr.), 596
Healy, John (Rev.), 592
Heapley, Wm., 2902
Heard, Francisco S., 4841
Hearn, Eda, 2765
Hearn, Mary Regina, 5716
Heart, Elisabeth, 891
Heart, Joannis, 891
Heart, Michael, 4383
Heart, Thomas, 891
Heary, Harrietta, 418
Heary, James, 418
Heary, John, 418
Hebb (Heil), Anne, 5302
Hebb, Anna, 3999
Hebb, Anne (Mrs.), 3974
Hebb, Helenam Josephinam, 3999
Hebb, Ricardo J., 3999
Hebb, Richard J., 4867

Hebb, William A., 4867
Hedwidge, Maria, 4426
Hegan, Catharina, 656
Hegan, Catharinae, 656
Hegan, Terentii, 656
Hegert, Henricus, 4446
Heigel, Maria, 3131
Heigel, Philippo, 3131
Heigel, Rosam Annam, 3131
Heil, Jr., Alberto, 3589
Heil, Jr., Carolina, 3589
Heil, Jr., Gulielmum Oliver, 3589
Heil, Sr., Alberto, 4794
Heil, Alb. [Albert], 2949
Heil, Albert, 2395
Heil, Albert, 2396
Heil, Albert, 2576
Heil, Albert, 2795
Heil, Albert, 2909
Heil, Alberto, 3800
Heil, Albertus, 3622
Heil, Anna, 3999
Heil, Annam, 4867
Heil, Carolina, 2576
Heil, Carolina, 5747
Heil, Caroline, 2395
Heil, Caroline, 2795

Heil, Caroline, 2909
Heil, Caroline, 2949
Heil, Carrie, 3800
Heil, Catharina, 3527
Heil, Catharina, 3589
Heil, Catharina, 3800
Heil, Catharina, 3974
Heil, Catharinam Estellam, 3527
Heil, Catherina, 3759
Heil, Catherinam, 4840
Heil, Clara, 3527
Heil, Clara, 3528
Heil, Clara, 3759
Heil, Clara, 3760
Heil, Clara, 3798
Heil, Emiliam J., 4837
Heil, Emily Jane, 2949
Heil, Emlia I. [or J.], 3887
Heil, Emma, 3528
Heil, Henricum Milford, 3528
Heil, Howard Carolum, 3800
Heil, Joanne, 3759
Heil, Joanne, 3760
Heil, Joanne, 3798
Heil, Joannem, 3759
Heil, Joanni H., 3528
Heil, Joanni, 3527

Heil, John Henry, 2395
Heil, Margeret Ann, 2576
Heil, Mariam Magdalenam, 3798
Heil, Mary Ann, 2909
Heil, Mary Catharine, 2795
Heil, Maud Genefefuen, 3760
Heim, Anna Elizabeth, 3553
Heimel, Augustum, 4913
Heiser, Henrietta, 4505
Heit, Albert, 2570
Heit, Albert, 2570
Heit, Albert, 2571
Heit, Caroline, 2570
Heit, Caroline, 2570
Heit, Margaret, 2570
Heit, Margret, 2571
Helaine, Julia, 4047
Helaine, Julia, 4094
Helaine, Joanne, 4047
Helaine, Joannes, 4094
Helaine, Joannes, 4135
Helane, Johannes, 4755
Heldebrand, Elizabetha A.., 3680
Helene, Franciscus, 3106
Helene, Louisa Catharina, 3106
Helene, Philippo, 3106
Helferolay, Charles L., 4773

Helferstay, Carole L., 3561
Helferstay, Carolo L., 3654
Helferstay, Carolum Alphons, 3561
Helferstay, Carolum Joseph, 3654
Helferstay, Carolum L., 4788
Helferstay, Carolus A., 3578
Helferstay, Chas. Jos., 5088
Helferstay, Maria E., 3654
Helferstay, Rebecca A., 3561
Helfrick, John, 2158
Helgele, Mrs., 2881
Hellaine, Julia, 4122
Hellaine, Glen Joseph, 3897
Hellaine, Joanne, 3897
Hellaine, Joannes T., 4122
Hellaine, Julia, 3897
Hellane, Jack, 4764
Hellane, Joanne, 3821
Hellane, Joannem Thomam, 4828
Hellane, Johannes, 3463
Hellane, John, 5698
Hellane, Julia, 3821
Hellane, Mariam Helenam, 3821
Helsel, Mariem Lucindem, 3795
Helsely, Frid, 5167
Helsely, Frederick, 4546
Helsley, Anna Josephina, 2434

Helsley, Ferdinand, 2434
Helsley, Joseph, 2434
Helsley, Mrs., 5240
Helzele, Mrs., 2881
Helzele, Mrs., 2965
Hembach, Wm. D., 4682
Hemlsly, Mary, 399
Hemlsly, Nancy, 399
Hemlsly, Peter, 399
Hemmensley, James, 138
Hemmensley, John, 138
Hemmensley, Mary, 138
Hemmersley, Alice, 4857
Hemsley, Andrew J. C. R., 5759
Hemsley, Joseph, 46
Hemsley, Judith, 46
Hemsley, Jack, 438
Hemsley, Jack, 422
Hemsley, Jjohn, 227
Hemsley, John, 22
Hemsley, John Henery, 438
Hemsley, John Paul, 355
Hemsley, John, 22
Hemsley, John, 2408
Hemsley, John, 2431
Hemsley, Margaret, 2408
Hemsley, Margaret, 2520

Hemsley, Margaret, 2554
Hemsley, Margaret, 4574
Hemsley, Margret, 422
Hemsley, Mary, 22
Hemsley, Mary, 227
Hemsley, Mary, 2611
Hemsley, Mary, 355
Hemsley, Mary, 422
Hemsley, Mary, 5786
Hemsley, Nancy, 438
Hemsley, Paul, 22
Hemsley, Peter, 438
Hemsley, Sarah, 1982
Hemsley, Sarah, 2431
Hemsley, Sarah, 2431
Hemsley, Sarah, 2506
Hemsley, Sarah, 2549
Hemsley, Sarah, 355
Hemsley, Wilm, 227
Hemsly, Margareta, 3745
Hemsly, Sarah, 4590
Henek, Davidem L., 4797
Henessey, Bridget, 2382
Henessey, Peter, 2443
Henessey, Thomas, 2382
Henessey, Thomas, 2398
Henessy, Gulielmum Richard, 3529

Henessy, Helena, 3529
Henessy, Peter, 4612
Henessy, Thoma, 3529
Henley, Mary, 1922
Henneberger, Bernardinam, 3903
Henneberger, Emma, 3903
Henneberger, Emma, 4060
Henneberger, Henrico, 3903
Henneberger, Henrico, 4060
Henneberger, Henricum L., 4826
Henneberger, Henry C., 2848
Henneberger, Herbert Aloysium, 4060
Henneberger, Hiram, 2847
Henneberger, Hy Clay Morris, 2847
Henneberger, M. Eliz., 2847
Henneberger, Maria E., 3765
Hennegan, Joannes, 1359
Hennessey, Bridget, 2286
Hennessey, Bridget, 4582
Hennessey, Bridgett, 2523
Hennessey, Catharina, 3842
Hennessey, Catharina, 3946
Hennessey, Elisa I., 4054
Hennessey, Ellen, 3025
Hennessey, Ellen, 4752

Hennessey, Guliemum Aloysorem, 4054
Hennessey, Helena, 3842
Hennessey, Helena, 3858
Hennessey, Jeremia, 4054
Hennessey, Jeremiam, 4882
Hennessey, Joannem Leroy, 3858
Hennessey, John C., 5248
Hennessey, John, 3025
Hennessey, John, 3025
Hennessey, Joseph Omer, 3842
Hennessey, Maria L., 3858
Hennessey, Peter, 2286
Hennessey, Peter, 4582
Hennessey, Petro, 3858
Hennessey, Petrum, 4842
Hennessey, Raimundum Jeremiam, 3946
Hennessey, Thoma J., 3842
Hennessey, Thoma, 3946
Hennessey, Thomam, 4752
Hennessey, Thomas, 3842
Hennessy, Annam Lorettam, 3667
Hennessy, Catharina, 3789
Hennessy, Catharina, 3893
Hennessy, Ellen, 2646
Hennessy, Ellen, 2706

Hennessy, Ellen, 2787
Hennessy, Ellen, 3789
Hennessy, Helena, 3394
Hennessy, Henricum Jacobum, 3394
Hennessy, Henricum Jacobum, 3789
Hennessy, Jeremiah, 2787
Hennessy, Joanne, 4842
Hennessy, Joannem Cornelium, 3868
Hennessy, Joannem Murvey, 3893
Hennessy, Joseph Benedict, 2706
Hennessy, Joseph, 3868
Hennessy, Josepho, 3667
Hennessy, Margaret, 2146
Hennessy, Margareta, 3868
Hennessy, Mary, 2892
Hennessy, Mary, 3667
Hennessy, Peter, 2145
Hennessy, Peter, 2646
Hennessy, Peter, 2706
Hennessy, Peter, 2787
Hennessy, Peter, 2871
Hennessy, Peter, 2892
Hennessy, Peter, 2892
Hennessy, Peter, 5289

Hennessy, Thoma J., 3789
Hennessy, Thoma, 3394
Hennessy, Thoma, 3893
Hennessy, Thoma, 4842
Hennessy, Thomas, 2144
Hennessy, Thomas, 2646
Hennessy, Thomas, 3789
Hennessy, Thomas, 4582
Hennessy, Thos., 2664
Hennessy, Thoma, 4819
Hennessy, Henry, 5125
Hennessy, Thomas, 4270
Hennessy, Thomas, 4819
Hennessy, Timothius, 1234
Henney, Edwardus, 1131
Henniberger, Hiram, 3385
Henniberger, Joseph, 3385
Henniberger, Maria E., 3385
Henroty, Franciscus, 1117
Henroty, Mariae, 1117
Henroty, Owen, 1117
Henry, John, 48
Henry, Birgitta, 1239
Henry, blank, 1778
Henry, Geo., 2618
Henry, Georgius, 1239
Henry, James, 2618

Henry, Joannis, 1778
Henry, Kahleen [sic], 2618
Henry, Lucinda, 1778
Henry[?], Henny, 232
Henry[?], Peter, 232
Henry[?], Peter, 232
Henser, Mary, 3024
Hensley, John, 21
Henson, Anna, 3522
Henson, Anna, 3523
Henson, Annam A., 4734
Henson, Mary, 2263
Hepner, Mr., 5083
Heppel, Rosanna, 2949
Herbert, Bertha Regina, 2520
Herbert, C.H., 4785
Herbert, Dorsey, 3717
Herbert, Fealy, 4274
Herbert, Frederick Dorsey, 2554
Herbert, Helenam May, 3717
Herbert, James William, 2408
Herbert, Jane, 3322
Herbert, Margaret, 2408
Herbert, Margaret, 2520
Herbert, Margaret, 2554
Herbert, Philip, 2408
Herbert, Philip, 2520

Herbert, Philip, 2554
Herbert, Philip, 4574
Herbert, Susanna, 3717
Herely, David, 4667
Hererley, Nicholaus, 1498
Herlehy, David Thomas, 2800
Herlehy, David, 2800
Herlehy, Ellen, 2800
Herlehy, Richard, 2800
Herman, Anna, 3987
Herr, Mary, 2644
Herr, Elizabeth, 2416
Herr, John Henry, 2416
Herr, Sarah Ann, 2416
Hersberger, Jacob, 2086
Hersberger, John S., 2086
Hersberger, Mary Ann E., 2086
Heslan, Owen, 1176
Heslehan, Ellen, 4584
Hessberger, Elizabeth, 576
Hessberrgar, Elisabeth, 558
Hetzer, Alphonsum F., 4083
Hetzer, Anna J., 4083
Hetzer, Anne J., 4127
Hetzer, Carolo H., 4083
Hetzer, Carolo I. [or J.}, 4127

Hetzer, Cath., 2845
Hetzer, Chas., 2845
Hetzer, Jno. W., 2845
Hetzer, Minervam Elisabeth, 4127
Heven, Patrick, 137
Hevend, James Edward, 1827
Hevend, James, 1827
Hevend, May, 1827
Heverle, Christinae, 675
Heverle, Margareta, 675
Heverle, Nicolai, 675
Heverty, Mariae, 1091
Heverty, Michael, 1091
Heverty, Petri, 1091
Hicky, Catharinae, 1252
Hicky, Henrici, 1252
Hicky, Maria Christina, 1252
Hiel, Albert, 2726
Hiel, Carlisle, 2726
Hiel, Cath., 3760
Hiel, Joseph Herman, 2726
Hifleman, George, 4653
Hifton, Prudy (Miss), 314
Higans, Elisabeth, 795
Higans, Jacobus, 795
Higans, Ransom, 795
Higgans, Maria, 4511

Higgens, Birgitta, 1313
Higgens, E. Maria Ludovica, 1767
Higgens, Elisabeth, 1767
Higgens, Jacobus, 1373
Higgens, Ransom, 1767
Higgins, Eduardum A., 4858
Higgins, Eliza, 2040
Higgins, Eliza, 2071
Higgins, Eliza, 2154
Higgins, Eliza, 2215
Higgins, Eliza, 2283
Higgins, Jennie A., 4876
Higgins, Mary, 594
Higgins?, Bridget, 4314
Higgs, John Daniel, 2026
Higgs, John, 2026
Higgs, Margaret, 2026
Highbarger, Clara, 3815
Hight, "unknown", 3351
Hight, Jesse, 3351
Hight, Maria Helena, 3351
Hildebrand, [blank], 3680
Hildebrand, Elisabeth A., 3790
Hildebrand, Elisabeth, 3841
Hildebrand, Elisabeth, 3907
Hildebrand, Elizabetha, 3725
Hildebrand, Joanne, 4901

Hildebrand, John, 5319
Hildenbrand, Apollinae, 1165
Hildenbrand, Matheus, 1165
Hildenbrand, Michaelis, 1165
Hilderbrand [or Hildenbrand], Appoloniae, 787
Hilderbrand [or Hildenbrand], Michaelis, 787
Hilderbrand [or Hildenbrand], Theresia, 787
Hile, Albert, 2166
Hill, Carena, 4503
Hilldebrand, Apolinia, 621
Hilldebrand, Michl, 621
Hilldebrand, Michl, 621
Hillman, Maria, 4797
Hilsle, Anna Jos., 3497
Himes, Ada, 3088
Himes, Bell, 3088
Hines, Maria, 1546
Hines, Addore, 3732
Hines, Ann E., 3442
Hines, Annae, 1072
Hines, Annae, 1450
Hines, Birgitta, 1072
Hines, Mary, 19
Hines, Michael, 1450

Hines, Robert Ambrose, 3732
Hines, Thomae, 1072
Hines, Thomae, 1450
Hines, Thomas, 1546
Hinson, Mary A., 5393
Hipkins, Jennie, 3272
Hipkins, Jennie, 3329
Hipkins, Margaritam Helenam, 3329
Hipner, Maria, 3294
Hipner, Mariam Elisabeth, 4844
Hipner, Mary Elis., 2824
Hipner, Mary, 2824
Hipner, Thomas, 2824
Hipple, Rosa, 2993
Hippner, Mrs., 3273
Hippner, Elisabeth, 3872
Hippner, Elisabeth, 3945
Hippner, Elizabetha, 3722
Hippner, Elizabetha, 4823
Hippner, Elsiabeth, 4002
Hippner, Mrs., 3185
Hippner, Mrs., 3945
Hirshberger, Helena Catharina, 792
Hirshberger, Joannis Sebastiani, 792

Hirshberger, Mariae Annae Elisabeth, 792
Hirzelan, Ludovica, 4396
his sister, her brother, 4548
Hitzelbarger, Agnete Caecilia, 3882
Hitzelberger, Agneti R., 3556
Hitzelberger, Agnete, 3663
Hitzelberger, Agneti Caeilia, 3778
Hitzelberger, Baptisto, 3663
Hoarse, Joannes, 1237
Hoarse, Joannes, 1237
Hoarse, Mariae, 1237
Hoarse, Mariae, 1237
Hobbs, Maria, 3807
Hoelle, Agnetem Muriel, 4144
Hoelle, Elisabeth, 4144
Hoelle, Martino R., 4144
Hoeltzle, Joseph, 5626
Hoey, James, 32
Hofacker, Julia Anna, 4408
Hoffman, Barbara, 1791
Hoffman, Catharine, 2403
Hoffman, Elizabeth, 2404
Hoffman, Georgory, 4840
Hoffman, H. (Rev.), 4752
Hoffman, Joannem H., 4789

Hogan, Garret, 1204
Hogan, Garret, 4467
Hohel, Dyonisius, 1580
Hohenstein, Leinfard, 1577
Hohenstein, Leonardi, 1802
Hohenstein, Lienhard, 4489
Hohenstein, Margaretae, 1577
Hohenstein, Margaretae, 1802
Hohenstein, Maria Catharina, 1577
Hohenstein, Sara, 1802
Hohfacher, Joanna, 4421
Hoke, Maria A., 3792
Hoke, Maria A., 3883
Holbert, Archebald, 1074
Holbert, Catharinae, 1074
Holbert, Guillelmus, 1074
Holbert, Maria Anna, 1706
Holbert, 1466
Holbert, Archibol, 341
Holbert, Catherine, 341
Holbert, Joannes, 1706
Holbert, Margareta, 4472
Holbert, Mary Anna, 341
Holden, Catharina B., 3983
Holehen, Ellen, 2599
Holehen, Michael, 2599
Hollan, Mary, 515

Holland (Black), Mary, 434
Holland, Ann E., 2318
Holland, Catharine Hester, 2318
Holland, Dyonisii, 1319
Holland, Johanna, 1319
Holland, John W., 2318
Holland, John William, 4538
Holland, John, 4597
Holland, Juliae, 1319
Holland, Mary, 101
Holland, Mary, 138
Holland, Mary, 187
Hollaran, Ludovicam Helenam, 3533
Hollyday, Floyd Sprigg, 3383
Hollyday, Gullielmo, 3383
Hollyday, Louisa, 3383
Holm, Fredericus, 3824
Holm, Julia, 5051
Holmes, Charles Emmanuel, 2863
Holmes, Jno. 2863
Holmes, Margt., 2863
Holton, Annae, 745
Holton, Birgitta, 745
Holton, Michaelis, 745
Holtzapple, Harry, 4827
Homersby, Sarah Ann, 2514

Homsley, Mary, 79
Honodel, Maria, 3110
Hood, Laura E., 3309
Hook, Charles McGill, 2065
Hook, James (Capt.), 634
Hook, James D., 1929
Hook, James, 1912
Hook, James, 2065
Hook, Mary Elizabeth, 1912
Hook, Mary, 1912
Hook, Mary, 2065
Hoover, Benjamin, 3139
Hoover, Carolum Eduardum, 4830
Hoover, Carolum Gulielmum, 3837
Hoover, Charlottam Maud., 3680
Hoover, Chas. Edmund, 2947
Hoover, Eduardum Sylvestrum, 3592
Hoover, Edwardo, 3837
Hoover, Elisabeth (Mrs.), 5329
Hoover, Elisabeth A.., 3790
Hoover, Elisabeth, 3841
Hoover, Elisabeth, 3907
Hoover, Elizabeth, 3646
Hoover, Elizabetha A., 3680
Hoover, Elizabetha, 3725
Hoover, Elizabetha, 3730

Hoover, Ellen, 5611
Hoover, Emilia, 3139
Hoover, Francis, 5549
Hoover, Frank, 2774
Hoover, Geirgie, 3352
Hoover, George, 4676
Hoover, Georgeo, 3725
Hoover, Georgio D., 3790
Hoover, Georgio H., 3680
Hoover, Georgio, 3841
Hoover, Georgio, 3907
Hoover, Georgius, 3271
Hoover, Ginny, 5670
Hoover, Helen, 3271
Hoover, Helen, 4747
Hoover, Helena, 3352
Hoover, Helena, 3429
Hoover, Helena, 3555
Hoover, Helena, 3646
Hoover, Helena, 3765
Hoover, Helena, 3878
Hoover, Helena, 4037
Hoover, Jacobum Fredericum, 3907
Hoover, Jemmi, 4754
Hoover, Jennie T., 4783
Hoover, Jenny, 5618

Hoover, Jno., 4691
Hoover, Joannem Joseph, 3790
Hoover, John Elder, 5691
Hoover, Jos., 2675
Hoover, Jos., 2947
Hoover, Joseph, 4747
Hoover, Joseph, 5209
Hoover, L. Margaret, 3232
Hoover, Leonem R., 3841
Hoover, Lucind, 5193
Hoover, Lucinda (Mrs.), 3429
Hoover, Lucinda M., 2947
Hoover, Lucinda, 2675
Hoover, Lucinda, 2847
Hoover, Lucinda, 2856
Hoover, Lucinda, 3176
Hoover, Lucinda, 3385
Hoover, Lucindam Margaretan, 3725
Hoover, Lydia A., 3837
Hoover, Maria A., 3215
Hoover, Maria Anna, 3141
Hoover, Maria Anna, 3142
Hoover, Maria Anna, 3143
Hoover, Maria Anna, 3144
Hoover, Maria Anna, 3145
Hoover, Maria E., 3385

Hoover, Maria, 3352
Hoover, Maria, 3370
Hoover, Mariam Anna, 3140
Hoover, Mariam Annam, 3139
Hoover, Mary Annie, 5753
Hoover, Sarah Ann, 2675
Hoover, Sarah, 3592
Hopewell, Nancy, 430
Hopkins, Birgitta, 4375
Hopner, Elizabeth, 3798
Hoppo, John Igna[runs in to margin], 562
Hoppyse, John [middle initial illegible], 560
Horenda, Christina, 2496
Horenda, Martin, 2496
Horenda, Teresa Matilda, 2496
Horgan, Catherine, 4282
Horin, Michael, 4562
Horine, Catharina, 3157
Horine, Catharine (Miss.), 4589
Horine, Catharine, 2557
Horine, Catharine, 2558
Horine, Catharine, 2559
Horine, Emma, 3400
Horine, Emma, 3401

Horine, Eugeniam Franciscam, 3401
Horine, Johanne, 3400
Horine, Johanne, 3401
Horine, Johannem Francis, 3400
Horn, Ada, 3252
Horn, Maria, 1394
Horn, Maria, 3097
Horn, Maria, 3173
Horn, Maria, 3332
Hornbach, Jacobus, 1290
Hornbach, Maria, 1290
Hornbach, Clara May, 3059
Hornbach, Elizabeth Bernadettam, 3557
Hornbach, Josephina, 1538
Hornbach, Virginia, 3059
Hornbach, William D., 3059
Hornback, Chas., 2884
Hornback, Mrs., 2884
Hornback, Wm., 2884
Hornbeck, Josephine, 2093
Hornbeck, Lavinia, 2093
Hornbeck, Lavinia, 2178
Hornbeck, Mary (Miss), 4554
Horne, Bridget (Miss), 4568
Hornesby, Benj. Francis, 2893
Hornesby, Margt., 2893
Hornesby, Reuben, 2893
Hornesby, Reuben, 4690
Hornsby, Margaret, 3068
Hornsby, Reuben, 2851
Hornsby, Reuben, 4684
Horret, Lucinda, 2932
Horse, Maria, 4459
Hose, Carolum Eduardum, 3510
Hose, Elisabeth, 3804
Hose, Elisabeth, 3828
Hose, Gulielmum Henricum, 3509
Hose, Jennie, 3263
Hose, Jennie, 3327
Hose, Joanne, 3804
Hose, Joanne, 3805
Hose, Joanne, 3806
Hose, Joanni P., 3509
Hose, Joanni P., 3510
Hose, Johanne, 3263
Hose, Johannem P., 4750
Hose, Johanni, 3327
Hose, Joseph R., 3805
Hose, Lauram Virginiam, 3263
Hose, Mariam, 3806
Hose, Mary Ann, 3008
Hose, Mary R., 5279
Hose, Reinam May, 3327
Hose, Sara Johanna, 3509
Hose, Sara Johanna, 3510
Hose, Sarah, 3805
Hose, Sarah, 3806
Hose, Sarai J., 3804
Hoskinson, Mrs., 2743
Hoskinson, Sara, 3105
Hossett, Catherine, 2753
Hothel, Dyonisius, 1580
Hounay, Maria, 1601
Houp, Jennie, 4003
Houraty, Owen, 4435
Houser, Frederick, 4706
Houser, Hiram, 2698
Houser, Margaret, 2698
Houser, Mary, 2698
Howard, Mary Jane, 5754
Howard, Cath, 121
Howard, E., 5188
Howard, Mariam Emmam, 3582
Hoy, Lauram Catharinam, 3419
Hoy, annam Mariam, 3189
Hoy, Annam Mariam, 4883
Hoy, Annamaria, 4106
Hoy, Bertah, 4883
Hoy, Bertha, 4044
Hoy, Bertham Aloysiam, 3268
Hoy, Bertham, 4900
Hoy, Bridget, 2476
Hoy, Bridget, 2681
Hoy, Bridget, 4619
Hoy, Bridgitt, 2282
Hoy, Bridgitt, 2435
Hoy, Bridgitt, 2515
Hoy, Catarinam, 4742
Hoy, Cath., 3172
Hoy, Catharina, 3241
Hoy, Catharina, 3268
Hoy, Catharina, 3565
Hoy, Catharina, 3618
Hoy, Catharine, 2282
Hoy, Ellen, 2201
Hoy, Evam Aureliam, 3524
Hoy, George, 2282
Hoy, George, 2435
Hoy, George, 2515
Hoy, George, 2515
Hoy, George, 4608
Hoy, Helenam Catharinam, 3418
Hoy, James, 2201
Hoy, Katarina, 3413
Hoy, Kate, 3082
Hoy, Kate, 3189

Hoy, Kate, 3292
Hoy, Kate, 4709
Hoy, Kate, 5577
Hoy, L. Cath., 3418
Hoy, Laura C., 3524
Hoy, Laurence, 2201
Hoy, Laurence, 5576
Hoy, Laurentio, 3618
Hoy, Laurentio, 3189
Hoy, Laurentio, 3268
Hoy, Laurentio, 3418
Hoy, Laurentio, 3524
Hoy, Mariam Louisam, 3618
Hoy, Mary Ellen, 2435
Hoy, Matheus, 1238
Hoy, Petri, 1238
Hoy, Petri, 1788
Hoy, Petrus, 1788
Hoy, Rosae Annae, 1788
Hoy, Rosae, 1238
Hoyle, Elizabeth, 3649
Hubart, Mary, 1936
Hubert, Adamie, 1626
Hubert, Georgius, 1626
Hubert, Margaretae, 1626
Hubert, Ellen, 114
Hughes, Andreas, 1027

Hughes, Anna, 1414
Hughes, Anna Catharina, 870
Hughes, Anthony, 2015
Hughes, Antonii, 1011
Hughes, Antonii, 1349
Hughes, Antonius, 1168
Hughes, Antonius, 1652
Hughes, Bernardus Thomas, 700
Hughes, Birgitta, 1433
Hughes, Birgitta, 1585
Hughes, Bridget, 1986
Hughes, Bridget, 2121
Hughes, Carolum Clark, 3931
Hughes, Catharine, 2323
Hughes, Daniel, 2322
Hughes, Eduardum, 3411
Hughes, Edward, 2047
Hughes, Edwardi, 950
Hughes, Edwardus, 1497
Hughes, Eleonora, 1011
Hughes, Eleonora, 988
Hughes, Francescam G., 3668
Hughes, Guillelmi, 849
Hughes, Guillelinus, 849
Hughes, Guillelmi, 1027
Hughes, Helen Alice, 3612
Hughes, Helen Alice, 3613

Hughes, Helenem Alice, 3612
Hughes, Henrici, 1063
Hughes, Henriei, 700
Hughes, Jacobi, 1414
Hughes, Jacobi, 1687
Hughes, Jacobo, 3411
Hughes, Jacobo, 3478
Hughes, Jacobo, 3612
Hughes, Jacobo, 3613
Hughes, Jacobo, 3668
Hughes, Jacobo, 3750
Hughes, Jacobo, 3754
Hughes, Jacobo, 3931
Hughes, Jacobum Henricum, 3754
Hughes, Jacobus, 1063
Hughes, Jacobus, 3182
Hughes, Jacobus, 3481
Hughes, Jacobus, 3994
Hughes, Jacobus, 4728
Hughes, Jacobus, 950
Hughes, James, 4304
Hughes, James, 1825
Hughes, James, 1826
Hughes, James, 5465
Hughes, Jas. [James], 5501
Hughes, Joannane Francescam, 3750

Hughes, Joanne, 643
Hughes, John, 4559
Hughes, Kate, 2941
Hughes, Margaret, 3411
Hughes, Margareta, 3754
Hughes, Margaretae, 1027
Hughes, Margarethem Regimam, 3613
Hughes, Margaretus, 849
Hughes, Margarita, 3565
Hughes, Margarita, 3612
Hughes, Margarita, 3613
Hughes, Margarita, 3668
Hughes, Margarita, 3750
Hughes, Margarita, 3931
Hughes, Margaritta, 3478
Hughes, Maria, 1350
Hughes, Maria, 1414
Hughes, Maria, 1784
Hughes, Maria, 3097
Hughes, Maria, 3116
Hughes, Maria, 4728
Hughes, Mariae, 1349
Hughes, Mariae, 1011
Hughes, Mariae, 1063
Hughes, Mariae, 1433
Hughes, Mariae, 1687

Hughes, Mariae, 700
Hughes, Mariae, 950
Hughes, Mariae, 988
Hughes, Mariam, 3478
Hughes, Mary Anna, 2015
Hughes, Mary, 1966
Hughes, Mary, 2015
Hughes, Mary, 2047
Hughes, Mary, 2282
Hughes, Mary, 5155
Hughes, Michael, 1349
Hughes, Nellie, 4139
Hughes, Terrentii, 1433
Hughes, Terrentii, 988
Hughes, Theresia, 3864
Hughes, Tim, 3245
Hughes, William, 1687
Hughs, Anthony, 1936
Hughs, Mary, 1934
Hulahan, Catherine, 2776
Hulbert, S.S., 3795
Hulbert, S.S., 3846
Hulbert, Sidney S., 3883
Hulbert, Sidney S., 3895
Hull, Amanda L., 3533
Hull, Joanni Wm., 3533
Hull, Ludovicam Helenam, 3533

Hull, Anna R., 4101
Hull, Amnam R., 4892
Hull, Elizab, 133
Hull, Joannem T., 4850
Hull, Mathilda, 3439
Hull, Mrs., 4096
Hull, N. B., 3439
Hull, Othonem, 3439
Hull, Rosa, 4041
Hull, Rosa, 4096
Hull, Rosa, 4156
Humbach, Jennie, 5705
Humbrickhouse, Catharine, 1883
Humelsine, Catharina, 4121
Humelsine, Catharinam Reginem, 4121
Humelsine, Cather. Regina, 5353
Humelsine, Leonardo E., 4121
Humelsine, Leonardum E., 4885
Humelsine, Leonardum Eduardum, 4138
Humelsine, Manarias, 4138
Humerich-House, Catharine, 2160
Humerickhouse, Catharine M., 2526
Humerickhouse, Catharine Mari, 2432

Humerickhouse, Catharine, 2028
Humes, Ella T., 4173
Humes, Ella Thoma [or Thomas], 4095
Humrickhouse, Mr., 4199
Humrickhouse, Mrs., 4199
Humrickhouse, Eliza (Miss), 4199
Hundermark, Cristiana, 3653
Hunsteine, Gertrudam May, 3099
Hunsteine, Gulielmo, 3099
Hunsteine, Maria D., 3099
Hunt, George, 2172
Hunt, James, 2172
Hunt, Margaret, 2172
Hunt, Robert, 2172
Hunt, Robertus, 1352
Hunt, Thomas, 2071
Hunt, Thomas, 4560
Hunter, Anna Elisabeth, 1183
Hunter, Anna Elisabeth, 1183
Hunter, Elisabeth, 1183
Hunter, Morgan, 2609
Huntman, Ellen, 1841
Huntsberger, Harriet, 2485
Huntsberger, Harriet, 2486
Huntsberger, Harriet, 2487
Huntsberger, Harriet, 2488

Hupet, Catherine, 4667
Hurd, Leona, 3929
Hurerley, Nicholaus, 1498
Hurlehan, Mich., 2644
Hurlehan, Richd., 2661
Hurlehe, Richd., 2642
Hurlehee, Bridget, 4627
Hurlehee, Danl. Wm., 2894
Hurlehee, David, 2913
Hurlehee, Ellen, 2894
Hurlehee, Honora, 2913
Hurlehee, Kate, 2913
Hurlehee, Rich., 2894
Hurleheigh, Johanna, 2312
Hurleheigh, Mary, 2312
Hurlehey, Catherine, 2973
Hurlehey, Catherine, 2973
Hurlehey, David, 2973
Hurlehey, Ella Honora, 3090
Hurlehey, Ellen, 3090
Hurlehey, Ellen, 3221
Hurlehey, Joanna, 2483
Hurlehey, Johanna, 4610
Hurlehey, Ricardo, 3221
Hurlehey, Richard, 3090
Hurlehey, Susan, 3221
Hurlehy, Cathar., 2811

Hurlehy, David, 2471
Hurlehy, David, 2811
Hurlehy, David, 2811
Hurlehy, David, 5053
Hurlehy, Richard, 2811
Hurley, Jos., 4641
Hurley, Maria, 1691
Hurley, Sophia, 2686
Hurley, Annae, 810
Hurley, Annette, 4741
Hurley, Catherine, 554
Hurley, Cornelius, 5269
Hurley, Daniel, 3022
Hurley, Daniel, 4460
Hurley, Diomysius, 1691
Hurley, Gulielmus, 3109
Hurley, Henrietta, 3768
Hurley, J. [or I.], 4766
Hurley, Jacobi, 1140
Hurley, Jacobi, 1637
Hurley, Jacobi, 780
Hurley, Jacobo I., 4792
Hurley, Jacobus I., 3651
Hurley, Jacobus I., 3741
Hurley, Jacobus, 1482
Hurley, James, 628
Hurley, James Demetrius, 593

Hurley, James I., 2491
Hurley, James I. [or T.], 4602
Hurley, James I., 1889
Hurley, James I., 2397
Hurley, James I., 2432
Hurley, James I., 2447
Hurley, James I., 2500
Hurley, James I.[or T.], 4599
Hurley, James J. [or I.], 5245
Hurley, James, 2152
Hurley, James, 4278
Hurley, James, 554
Hurley, James, 593
Hurley, Jannette, 3382
Hurley, Jas. I., 5781
Hurley, Jas. I., 2686
Hurley, Jennette, 4792
Hurley, Joannes Otheus, 780
Hurley, Joannes, 1449
Hurley, Joannis, 810
Hurley, Joe (Dr.), 4763
Hurley, Josaphine, 2983
Hurley, Josaphine, 3029
Hurley, Josaphine, 3044
Hurley, Josaphine, 4705
Hurley, Josephene M. Agnes, 5406
Hurley, Josephina, 1140

Hurley, Josephina, 3133
Hurley, Josephina, 3134
Hurley, Josephina, 3138
Hurley, Josephina, 3139
Hurley, Josephina, 3140
Hurley, Josephina, 3141
Hurley, Josephina, 3142
Hurley, Josephina, 3143
Hurley, Josephina, 3144
Hurley, Josephina, 3145
Hurley, Josephina, 3152
Hurley, Josephina, 3159
Hurley, Josephina, 3168
Hurley, Josephina, 3173
Hurley, Josephina, 3179
Hurley, Josephina, 3272
Hurley, Josephina, 3300
Hurley, Josephina, 3315
Hurley, Josephina, 3339
Hurley, Josephina, 3340
Hurley, Josephina, 3513
Hurley, Josephina, 3768
Hurley, Josephina, 3856
Hurley, Josephine A., 2533
Hurley, Josephine, 2656
Hurley, Josephine, 2718
Hurley, Josephine, 3016

Hurley, Josephine, 3042
Hurley, Josephine, 3085
Hurley, Josephine, 3149
Hurley, Josephine, 3163
Hurley, Josephine, 3196
Hurley, Josephine, 3265
Hurley, Josephine, 3299
Hurley, Josephine, 3810
Hurley, Josephine, 3841
Hurley, Josephini, 3416
Hurley, Josephine, 2673
Hurley, Js., 4579
Hurley, Maria Catharina, 1637
Hurley, Maria, 3117
Hurley, Maria, 3138
Hurley, Maria, 3224
Hurley, Mariae, 748
Hurley, Mary C.C., 5377
Hurley, Mary, 2513
Hurley, Mary, 2788
Hurley, Mary, 2928
Hurley, Mary, 4700
Hurley, Michael, 810
Hurley, Mollie, 3039
Hurley, Mollie, 4714
Hurley, Nettie, 3034
Hurley, Nettie, 3651

Hurley, Nettie, 3709
Hurley, Nettie, 3941
Hurley, Nettie, 3969
Hurley, Nettie, 4762
Hurley, Nettie, 4764
Hurley, Nettie, 4765
Hurley, Nitty, 5613
Hurley, Otho, 4635
Hurley, Richard, 4622
Hurley, Sophia (Mrs.), 5073
Hurley, Sophia A. (Mrs.), 1826
Hurley, Sophia Antoinette, 1889
Hurley, Sophia J., 3824
Hurley, Sophia J., 3904
Hurley, Sophia Janette, 1889
Hurley, Sophia Jennette, 2397
Hurley, Sophia, 2152
Hurley, Sophia, 2397
Hurley, Sophia, 554
Hurley, Sophia, 593
Hurley, Sophiae, 1140
Hurley, Sophiae, 1637
Hurley, Sophiae, 780
Hurley, Thomae, 748
Hurley, Thomas, 748
Hurley, William, 2152
Hurley, Wm., 5067

Hurley, Wm., 5551
Hurley, Wm., 5602
Hurleyhe, Ricardus (Mrs.), 3664
Hurleyhe, Ricardus, 3664
Hurleyheath, Johanna, 2201
Hurleyhee, Helena, 3748
Hurleyhy, Catharina, 3167
Hurleyhy, Daniel, 2405
Hurleyhy, David, 3167
Hurleyhy, Davide, 3167
Hurleyhy, Davidem Patricium, 3167
Hurleyhy, Ellen, 2405
Hurleyhy, Johanna, 2398
Hurly, Josephine, 2998
Hurt, [blank], 4523
Huslein, Catharinae, 1366
Huslein, Catharinae, 1744
Huslein, Margareta, 1744
Huslein, Michaelis, 1366
Huslein, Michaelis, 1744
Huslein, Petrus, 1366
Hussong, Christianna, 62
Hussong, Ann Christianna, 62
Hussong, Elizabeth, 62
Hussong, George, 62
Hussong, John, 62

Hutton, Mary, 4676
Hutzell, Catharinam Helenam, 3399
Hutzell, E. C., 3410
Hutzell, Elizabeth C., 3397
Hutzell, Elizabeth C., 3398
Hutzell, Elizabeth C., 3399
Hutzell, Florentiam Virginiam, 3398
Hutzell, Jacob P. E., 3410
Hutzell, Josephum, 3397
Hutzell, Samuele, 3397
Hutzell, Samuele, 3398
Hutzell, Samuele, 3399
Hutzell, Samuele, 3410
Hyder, Adam, 2600
Hyder, Anna Maria, 2545
Hyder, Jno. Adam Theobald, 2600
Hyder, John A., 2545
Hyder, Mary, 2600
Hyder, Sarah, 2545
Hyenes, Mary, 217
Hyle, Albert, 2504
Hyle, Alberto, 3151
Hyle, Carolina, 3151
Hyle, Caroline, 2504
Hyle, Helenam Joannam, 3151

Hyle, William Edward, 2504
Hyles, Albert, 2700
Hyles, Francis, 2700
Hyles, Mrs, 2700
Hypp, Joe, 4340
Hyskins, Jinnie, 3036
Idelburgh, Sarah, 4647
Iler, Margaret, 2562
Ingram, Anna Elizabeth, 2375
Ingram, Charles Wm., 2375
Ingram, Charles, 2242
Ingram, Margaret, 2242
Ingram, Margaret, 2375
Ingram, Mary Ellen, 2242
Inlius, Mary, 5800
Irvin, Carrie, 3800
Irving, Willm. C., 4677
Irwin, Carolina, 3589
Iseminger, Albertus, 4712
J uch, Helen Cecelia, 5739
Jacbos, Martah, 3334
Jack, Ann (Miss), 4180
Jack, Ann, 155
Jack, Catharine, 155
Jack, John, 155
Jack, John, 4183
Jackson, John (Mrs.), 11

Jackson, Elizab, 66
Jackson, Elizab, 67
Jackson, Hanna, 48
Jackson, John, 11
Jackson, John C. W., 4179
Jackson, John, 66
Jackson, William, 66
Jacob, Gulielmus, 4903
Jacobs, [blank], 3366
Jacobs, [blank], 3367
Jacobs, [blank], 3368
Jacobs, Ann Maria, 4705
Jacobs, Ann, 3080
Jacobs, Annam Elizabeth, 3367
Jacobs, Edna L., 4903
Jacobs, Florence May, 3368
Jacobs, Johannem Michaelem, 3366
Jacobs, Maria, 3214
Jacobs, Martha, 3227
Jacobs, Matilda, 3367
Jacobs, Matilda, 3368
Jacobs, Matilda, 4758
Jacobs, R., 4758
Jacobs, T. R., 3366
Jacobs, T. R., 3368
Jacobs, Theodesia V., 4758

Jacobs, Theodoria, 3366
Jacobs, Theodosia Virginia, 3647
Jacobs, Theodosia, 3580
Jacobs, Thoma R., 3367
Jacson, Catharina, 1191
Jacson, Elisabeth, 1191
Jacson, Henriei, 1191
Jagel, Joannes, 1100
James, Catharina, 4043
James, Catharina, 4102
James, Catharinam, 4839
James, Henry, 358
James, John Erasmus, 2302
James, John, 2164
James, John, 2302
James, John, 2376
James, Mary Frances, 2376
James, Rachel, 358
James, Rosanna, 2164
James, Rosanna, 2376
James, Rose Ann, 2302
James, Sam, 358
James, William Henry Watkins, 2164
Jamison, Franciscus B., 1441
Jan, Jeremiae, 1419
Janner, Elisabeth, 1680

Janner, Franciscae, 1817
Janner, Georgii, 1817
Janner, Godlieb, 1680
Janner, Joannes Theophilus, 1817
Janner, Rosannae, 1680
Jarboe, Elizabeth, 3691
Jarboe, Frances E. E., 2319
Jarboe, Frances E.C. [or E.E.], 1981
Jarboe, Frances, 2117
Jarboe, Lethey Ann, 1981
Jarifert, Josephus, 1416
Jarifert, Serinae, 1416
Jasco, Rachael, 3619
Jeffers, Henricum Jacobum, 4905
Jeffrey, Catharina, 4124
Jeffrey, Henry James, 4124
Jeffrey, Jacobo E., 4124
Jefrey, Patrick, 531
Jegel, Catharina Elisabeth, 995
Jegel, Elisabeth, 995
Jegel, Jonnis, 995
Jekel, Catharina, 4446
Jenderman, Barbara, 2437
Jenderman, Lewis Peter, 2437
Jenderman, Samuel Francis Patrick, 2437

Jenkins, Elizabeth, 2194
Jenkins, R.A., 4086
Jessup, [blank], 3249
Jessup, Guglielmum, 3249
Jessup, Maria, 3249
Jiegner, Elisabeth, 1181
Johanigan, Catharinae, 785
Johanigan, Franciscus, 785
Johanigan, Francisii, 785
Johnes, Amorld, 1793
Johnes, Jeremias, 1163
Johnes, Theresia, 1804
Johnson, Jacob, 3281
Johnson, Margaret, 3281
Johnson, Susan, 3281
Johnson, Leva [or Lena], 1964
Johnson, Amanda L., 3533
Johnson, Ann Eliza, 1
Johnson, Benjamini, 845
Johnson, Catherinam Elizabeth, 3511
Johnson, David, 3262
Johnson, Dr., 4687
Johnson, Dr., 4695
Johnson, Elisabeth, 1685
Johnson, Elisabeth, 3865
Johnson, Elizabeth, 163

Johnson, Elizabeth, 3328
Johnson, Elizabeth, 3376
Johnson, Elizabeth, 3483
Johnson, Elizabeth, 3585
Johnson, Elizabeth, 4756
Johnson, Elizabetha, 3655
Johnson, Elizabetha, 3656
Johnson, Elizabetha, 3766
Johnson, Franciscus, 1225
Johnson, Geigio W., 3328
Johnson, George W., 3282
Johnson, Georgium Guglielmum, 3262
Johnson, Henrici, 1813
Johnson, Henrietta, 114
Johnson, Henrietta, 845
Johnson, I C, 1813
Johnson, Johanne, 3300
Johnson, John, 5048
Johnson, Judith, 1297
Johnson, Judith, 1530
Johnson, Judy, 1897
Johnson, Margatha, 3511
Johnson, Maria, 3262
Johnson, Maria, 3262
Johnson, Mariae, 845
Johnson, Mariam Catharina, 3282

Johnson, Mariam Claram, 3300
Johnson, Mary, 105
Johnson, Mary, 106
Johnson, Mary, 1
Johnson, Mary, 114
Johnson, Mary, 2151
Johnson, Pricilla, 3300
Johnson, Silvestra, 1813
Johnson, Susan, 3281
Johnson, Susan, 3307
Johnson, Susanna, 120
Johnson, Susannah, 3282
Johnson, Theresae, 1685
Johnson, Thomas H, 163
Johnson, Thomas, 1
Johnson, Thomas, 114
Johnson, Thomas, 163
Johnson, Thos., 4660
Johnson, Wm. A., 3511
Johnston, Abraham, 181
Johnston, Arthur John, 13
Johnston, Jack, 181
Johnston, James Wm., 2412
Johnston, John, 2130
Johnston, Judith, 1777
Johnston, Mary, 13
Johnston, Mary, 181

Johnston, Mr., 4542
Johnston, Phebe, 2412
Johnston, William, 13
Johston, Carolo F., 4873
Johston, Edwardus, 1777
Joice, Joannes, 1491
Joice, Michel, 4349
Joken, Maria, 140
Jones, Theresa, 5552
Jones, Theresa, 5593
Jones, D. (Mrs.), 4061
Jones, Johnson (Dr.), 5295
Jones, Mary, 363
Jones, Upton & Anna, 1778
Jones [sic], Anna Amelia, 3017
Jones [sic], Lucinda, 3016
Jones [sic], Lucinda, 3017
Jones [sic], Mary Janet, 3016
Jones, A.J., 3847
Jones, Abram, 73
Jones, Andrea J., 3786
Jones, Andrea Johnson, 3730
Jones, Andream J., 4813
Jones, Andream Johnsen, 3188
Jones, Andrew J. [or I.], 5219
Jones, Anna Sarah Elizabeth, 2457
Jones, Anna Sarah Elizabeth, 5469

Jones, Annam Mariam, 3349
Jones, Arah, 4059
Jones, Audream Johnson, 3730
Jones, Carolum Eduardum, 3343
Jones, David, 3188
Jones, David, 3191
Jones, Elizabeth, 74
Jones, Ellenora, 2424
Jones, Eric Ludovicum, 3457
Jones, Geirgium, 3342
Jones, George, 363
Jones, Gertrudem Rush, 3491
Jones, Guglielmum Albertum, 3346
Jones, Helena, 3341
Jones, Helena, 3342
Jones, Helena, 3343
Jones, Helena, 3344
Jones, Helena, 3345
Jones, James, 307
Jones, Jeremiah, 3341
Jones, Jeremiah, 3342
Jones, Jeremiah, 3343
Jones, Jeremiah, 3344
Jones, Jeremiah, 3345
Jones, Joanne, 4059
Jones, Johannem Hardie, 3348
Jones, Joseph C., 4059

Jones, Laurentio Scott, 3491
Jones, Letitiam Madelinam, 3344
Jones, Lilliam Mariam, 3345
Jones, Louis Resh, 3786
Jones, Ludovico, 3346
Jones, Ludovico, 3347
Jones, Ludovico, 3348
Jones, Ludovico, 3349
Jones, Ludovico, 3350
Jones, Ludovico, 3457
Jones, Ludovico, 3749
Jones, Margareta A., 3188
Jones, Margareta, 3730
Jones, Margaretha, 3491
Jones, Margarita, 3742
Jones, Margarita, 3786
Jones, Margarita, 3847
Jones, Maria, 3346
Jones, Maria, 3347
Jones, Maria, 3348
Jones, Maria, 3349
Jones, Maria, 3350
Jones, Maria, 3457
Jones, Maria, 3491
Jones, Maria, 3749
Jones, Mariam C., 3847
Jones, Mariam Helenam, 3341

Jones, Mary (widow), 4327
Jones, Mary, 73
Jones, Mary Elisa, 307
Jones, Mary Jane, 5472
Jones, Mary, 307
Jones, Mary, 5480
Jones, Michael, 73
Jones, Mrs., 561
Jones, Nelly, 362
Jones, Pearliam Agnetem, 3350
Jones, Rebecca, 2456
Jones, Robert, 2457
Jones, Ruth, 2457
Jones, Samuel L.C., 3347
jones, Sarah, 3023
Jones, Sarah, 4951
Jones, Sarah, 5479
Jones, Sophia (Mrs.), 617
Jones, Teresa, 2424
Jones, Theresa, 4703
Jones, Theresia, 1793
Jones, Thomas Wm., 4616
Jones, Vinton Augusterum, 3749
Jonson, Jack, 362
Jonson, James, 282
Jonson, John, 282
Jonson, Mary, 214

Jonson, Mary, 281
Jonson, Mary, 282
Jonson, Mary, 362
Jonson, Washington, 362
Jonston, James, 4310
Jonston, Beryamini, 1083
Jonston, Henricus, 4503
Jonston, Jacobi, 1338
Jonston, Jacobi, 819
Jonston, Jacobus, 1083
Jonston, Joannes, 1338
Jonston, Judith, 1338
Jonston, Judith, 819
Jonston, Mariae, 1083
Jonston, Matheus, 819
Jordan, Anna, 4110
Jordan, Ambrose, 378
Jordan, Annae, 827
Jordan, Annae, 828
Jordan, Henny, 176
Jordan, Joannes, 827
Jordan, Leady, 378
Jordan, Margarita, 3935
Jordan, Margarita, 3985
Jordan, Margarita, 4082
Jordan, Margarita, 4152
Jordan, Maria, 3935

Jordan, Mary, 459
Jordan, Michaelis, 827
Jordan, Michaelis, 828
Jordan, Timotheus, 828
Jordan, Wilm, 378
Jordon, John, 4526
Jourdain, Anna, 3436
Joy, Eleanor, 119
Joy, Elias Anna, 396
Joy, Jain, 396
Joy, John, 119
Joy, Susanna, 119
Joy, Wilm, 396
Judey, Rebecca, 2082
Julius, Mrs., 5514
Julius, Mrs., 4641
Julius, Mary, 2647
Julius, Mary, 4670
Julius, Mary, 5800
Julius, Mary, 5536
Jumper, Sarah, 2598
Justice, M. Maria, 3882
Justice, Catherine, 548
Justice, Francis, 491
Justice, Jacob, 548
Justice, John Jacob, 548
Justice, Joseph, 491

Justice, Kate, 2855
Justice, Lucratia, 491
Justice, Lucretia, 548
Justis, Andre, 19
Justis, Catharine (Mrs.), 61
Justis, Mary, 19
Justis, Sarah, 19
Juvet, Caroline, 377
Juvet, Catherine, 377
Juvet, Edmond, 377
Kail, Mary, 4608
Kain, Ishman, 120
Kain, Mary Ann, 120
Kain, Susama, 120
Kaiser, Maria Francesca, 3475
Kaiser, Maria Francesca, 3552
Kaisert, Carolina, 663
Kaisert, Jacobi Frediria, 663
Kaisert, Theresiae, 663
Kale, Mary, 2281
Kale, Mary, 2382
Kammarer, Charles, 5294
Kammarer, Frederico, 4115
Kammarer, Fredericum Joseph, 4115
Kammarer, Lawrence, 5369
Kammarer, Maria, 4115

Kammarer, Minnie, 3993
Kammarer, Minnie, 4049
Kammarer, Willhelmina, 3933
Kammarer, Willhelmina, 3905
Kammerer, Maria, 4798
Kammerer, Carolo, 4798
Kammerer, Carolus, 3782
Kammerer, Maria, 3782
Kammerer, Maria, 3831
Kammerer, Minnie, 3782
Kammerer, Minnie, 3831
Kammerer, Peter, 5194
Kammerer, Philomenam, 4798
Kammerer, Wilhelmina, 3722
Kammerer, Willhelmina, 3863
Kan, Anna, 743
Kan, Guillelmi, 743
Kan, Marcellae, 743
Kane, Catherine, 3033
Kane, Edward, 2218
Kane, Guillelmi, 1067
Kane, Jacobus, 4389
Kane, Markellae, 1067
Kane, Mary Jane, 2218
Kane, Mary Jane, 2218
Kane, Thomas, 1067
Kannedy, Catharina, 1651

Kannon, Annae, 912
Kannon, Carolus, 912
Kannon, Jacobi, 912
Kanoh, Catharina, 1514
Kany, Jacobus, 1417
Kappel, Rosa, 4172
Kappler, Antonius, 1707
Karbey, Francisii, 759
Karbey, Helenae, 759
Karbey, Jacobus, 759
Karnes, Charles, 4532
Karney, Jacobus, 1242
Karney, James, 2165
Karr, Sara, 1627
Karr, Elisabeth, 1821
Karr, Hanna, 169
Karr, Jacobi, 1243
Karr, Jacobi, 1821
Karr, John, 169
Karr, Margaret, 169
Karr, Rosa Anna, 1243
Karr, Sarae, 1243
Karr, Sarae, 1821
Kasekanom, Catharina, 4436
Kauffman, Maria, 3749
Kaufman, Maria, 3457
Kauker, Joannis, 1722

Kauker, Maria, 1722
Kauker, Mariae, 1722
Kavanagh, Caroli, 778
Kavanagh, Donnel, 2738
Kavanagh, Donnel, 2738
Kavanagh, Mary, 2738
Kavanagh, Michael, 778
Kavanagh, Rosae, 778
Kavelin, Margaret, 1927
Keady, Clarentium Lane, 3389
Keady, Henrico H., 3389
Keady, Julia M., 3389
Keany, Libby, 108
Kearney, Ann, 23
Kearney, Anne, 52
Kearney, Martin, 52
Kearney, Michael James, 52
Kechline, Joannem Leonem, 3678
Keedwik, Margareta, 3868
Keedy, Henry Horatio, 3000
Keedy, Elizabeth Lane, 3039
Keedy, Henrico H., 3122
Keedy, Henrico H., 3544
Keedy, Henricum H., 3122
Keedy, Henry H., 5273
Keedy, Henry, 3039
Keedy, Julia (Mrs.), 3846

Keedy, Julia, 3039
Keedy, Julia, 3122
Keedy, Julia, 3197
Keedy, Julia, 3544
Keedy, Richardum Daniel, 3544
Keefe, Frances, 2362
Keefe, Helena, 2361
Keefe, Helena, 2362
Keefe, Margaret, 15
Keefe, Margaret, 2361
Keefe, Nicholas, 2361
Keefe, Nicholas, 2362
Keefe, Patrick, 15
Keefe, Sarah, 15
Keefer, Elizabeth, 2122
Keefer, Elizabeth, 2276
Keefer, Elizabeth, 2276
Keefer, George, 2276
Keefer, George, 2409
Keefer, Joseph, 2122
Keefer, Joseph, 2122
Keefer, Maria Elizabeth, 2409
Keefer, Mary Magdalen, 2409
Keeffer, Elisabeth, 1739
Keeffer, Franciscus, 1337
Keeffer, Georgii, 1337
Keeffer, Georgii, 1739

Keeffer, Georgius, 1739
Keeffer, Mariae Elisabeth, 1337
Keegan, Winnie, 4163
Keenan, Andreas, 1146
Keenan, Annae, 1146
Keenan, Catharinae, 1605
Keenan, Eduardum Sylvestrum, 3592
Keenan, Jacobus, 1146
Keenan, Jane, 1952
Keenan, Joanne, 3592
Keenan, Johanna, 1413
Keenan, Michael, 1606
Keenan, Michaelis, 1605
Keenan, Patr, 5162
Keenan, Sarah, 3592
Keenan, Thomas, 1092
Keenan, Thomas, 1952
Keenan, Thomas, 1413
Keenan, Thomas, 1605
Keenan, Thomas, 1605
Kehoe, Am, 2072
Kehoe, Elizabeth, 2072
Kehoe, Thomas, 2072
Keil, Gertrudis, 4390
Keilemann, Anna Martha, 4498
Keiper, Margareta, 3233

Keitz, Conradi, 3576
Keitz, Maria Elizabeth, 3576
Keitz, Mariam Elizabeth, 3576
Keley, Francisci, 1716
Keley, Maria, 1716
Keley, Theodorae, 1716
Kelhoffer, Elisabeth (Mrs.), 3824
Kelhoffer, Elisabeth, 3827
Kellen, Nancy, 4359
Keller, Nancy (widow), 4359
Keller, Anna Margareta, 1745
Keller, Catharinae, 1745
Keller, Catherina, 3767
Keller, Grace, 5348
Keller, Hella, 4060
Keller, Joseph, 1745
Keller, Josephi, 1592
Keller, Maria, 1592
Keller, Mariae, 1592
Keller, Seikfinth?, 4242
Kelley, Mrs., 605
Kelley, [blank], 1973
Kelley, Anna, 3670
Kelley, Annae, 714
Kelley, Catharinae, 1824
Kelley, Catherin, 613
Kelley, Daniel, 1322

Kelley, Edward Joseph, 613
Kelley, Edward, 393
Kelley, Edward, 393
Kelley, Eleonora, 1320
Kelley, Guillelmi, 1320
Kelley, Guillelmus, 4392
Kelley, Henery, 506
Kelley, Henery, 507
Kelley, Henry B., 4213
Kelley, Honorae, 799
Kelley, Honorae, 1322
Kelley, Jacobi, 799
Kelley, Jennie, 5208
Kelley, Joanna, 681
Kelley, Joanne, 3670
Kelley, Joannis, 1322
Kelley, Joannis, 714
Kelley, Joseph [Henry crossed], 613
Kelley, Joseph, 4288
Kelley, Josephi, 1824
Kelley, Julianna, 393
Kelley, Ludovicum David, 3670
Kelley, Ludovicus M., 1824
Kelley, Ludovicus, 1824
Kelley, Margret (Mrs.), 443
Kelley, Margret, 506

Kelley, Margret, 507
Kelley, Maria, 4332
Kelley, Mariae, 1320
Kelley, Mariae, 681
Kelley, Mary Anna, 506
Kelley, Mias, 681
Kelley, Michael, 799
Kelley, Mr., 605
Kelley, Patricius, 714
Kelley, Patrick, 5084
Kelley, Thos, 4358
Kelley, Wilm Edward, 507
Kelly, Agnete, 3913
Kelly, Agnete, 4172
Kelly, Amelia, 3493
Kelly, Ann, 2116
Kelly, Anna, 1154
Kelly, Anna Rosina, 5706
Kelly, Anna, 1184
Kelly, Anna, 1541
Kelly, Anna, 2535
Kelly, Anna, 3631
Kelly, Anna, 3632
Kelly, Anna, 3633
Kelly, Anna, 855
Kelly, Annae, 1209
Kelly, Annae, 1412

Kelly, Annae, 917
Kelly, Birgitta, 1589
Kelly, Birgittae, 1184
Kelly, Birgittae, 1196
Kelly, Brigetta, 3720
Kelly, Carlottam Annam, 3913
Kelly, Carolina, 917
Kelly, Catharina, 1204
Kelly, Catharina, 1196
Kelly, Catharina, 1285
Kelly, Catharina, 4368
Kelly, Catharinae, 1222
Kelly, Catharinae, 1565
Kelly, Catharinae, 833
Kelly, Catharine, 2116
Kelly, Catherine, 564
Kelly, Charles Edward, 1960
Kelly, Charles, 3034
Kelly, Charles, 5453
Kelly, Christophori, 1285
Kelly, Christophori, 1671
Kelly, Chs., 2907
Kelly, Eleanora, 3109
Kelly, Elisabeth, 1106
Kelly, Elisabeth, 1247
Kelly, Elisabeth Mariam, 4172
Kelly, Elisabeth, 1246

Kelly, Elisabeth, 1517
Kelly, Eliz., 2697
Kelly, Eliza (Miss), 1955
Kelly, Elizabeth B., 3468
Kelly, Elizabeth, 5383
Kelly, Ellen, 2879
Kelly, Ellen, 5605
Kelly, Guillelmus, 1412
Kelly, H., 525
Kelly, Hanora, 1417
Kelly, Hanorae, 1471
Kelly, Helen, 5562
Kelly, Helena, 3150
Kelly, Helena, 3530
Kelly, Henery, 556
Kelly, Hieronimus Franciscus, 1565
Kelly, Honora, 1753
Kelly, Hugh, 5485
Kelly, Hugo, 1756
Kelly, Hugo, 3633
Kelly, Jacobi, 1184
Kelly, Jacobi, 1669
Kelly, Jacobus, 1081
Kelly, Jacobus, 1436
Kelly, Jacobus, 1524
Kelly, Jacobus, 1608

Kelly, James, 294
Kelly, James Wilm., 564
Kelly, James, 556
Kelly, Jane, 2079
Kelly, Joanna, 3710
Kelly, Joanna, 3711
Kelly, Joanna, 3713
Kelly, Joannae, 1081
Kelly, Joannae, 755
Kelly, Joannes, 1149
Kelly, Joannes, 1171
Kelly, Joannes Henricus, 1222
Kelly, Joannes, 1471
Kelly, Joannes, 1697
Kelly, Joannes, 4459
Kelly, Joannis, 1209
Kelly, Joannis, 1471
Kelly, Joannis, 1799
Kelly, Johanna, 3494
Kelly, John, 1951
Kelly, Joseph John, 2363
Kelly, Joseph John, 5697
Kelly, Joseph, 564
Kelly, Joseph, 833
Kelly, Josephi, 1222
Kelly, Josephi, 1565
Kelly, Josepho M., 3493

Kelly, Josephum, 3493
Kelly, K. [sic], 1799
Kelly, Lewis, 3866
Kelly, Lewis, 3913
Kelly, Lewis, 4172
Kelly, Lizzie, 4623
Kelly, Lizzie, 4642
Kelly, Lizzie, 4643
Kelly, Lizzie, 5790
Kelly, Lucas, 1669
Kelly, Mabel, 4140
Kelly, Margareta, 1145
Kelly, Margareta, 1209
Kelly, Margareta, 1223
Kelly, Margareta, 1318
Kelly, Margareta, 1608
Kelly, Margareta, 4495
Kelly, Margaretae, 1669
Kelly, Margaretae, 4438
Kelly, Margret, 556
Kelly, Maria Catharina, 833
Kelly, Maria Louisa, 2610
Kelly, Maria, 1137
Kelly, Maria, 1456
Kelly, Maria, 1470
Kelly, Maria, 1523
Kelly, Maria, 1799

Kelly, Maria, 3109
Kelly, Maria, 3225
Kelly, Maria, 755
Kelly, Mariae, 1148
Kelly, Mariae, 1223
Kelly, Mariae, 1246
Kelly, Mariae, 1285
Kelly, Mariae, 1671
Kelly, Mariae, 1692
Kelly, Mariae, 855
Kelly, Mary, 1917
Kelly, Mary, 1853
Kelly, Mary, 2213
Kelly, Mary, 2224
Kelly, Mary, 2705
Kelly, Mary, 2907
Kelly, Mary, 3018
Kelly, Mary, 4642
Kelly, Michael, 1184
Kelly, Michael, 2444
Kelly, Michael, 2535
Kelly, Morgan, 1223
Kelly, Morgan, 1692
Kelly, Morgan, 2213
Kelly, Mrs., 3458
Kelly, Mrs., 3459
Kelly, N., 1412

Kelly, Patrici, 1756
Kelly, Patricii, 1137
Kelly, Patricii, 1196
Kelly, Patricii, 1517
Kelly, Patricii, 917
Kelly, Patricius, 1192
Kelly, Patricius, 1064
Kelly, Patricius, 3493
Kelly, Patricius, 4429
Kelly, Patrick [Michael crossed out], 2610
Kelly, Patrick, 1960
Kelly, Patrick, 2363
Kelly, Patrick, 2535
Kelly, Patrick, 2708
Kelly, Patrick, 5443
Kelly, Regina Virginia, 2708
Kelly, Rich, 4623
Kelly, Sally, 2708
Kelly, Sally, 3327
Kelly, Sara, 1064
Kelly, Sarae, 1137
Kelly, Sarae, 1517
Kelly, Sarae, 1756
Kelly, Sarah (Mrs.), 5312
Kelly, Sarah P., 2610
Kelly, Sarah, 1960

Kelly, Sarah, 1963
Kelly, Sarah, 2363
Kelly, Sarah, 2535
Kelly, Sarah, 2818
Kelly, Susanna, 1692
Kelly, Thomaae, 1081
Kelly, Thomae, 1246
Kelly, Thomae, 755
Kelly, Thomae, 855
Kelly, Thomas, 1183
Kelly, Thomas, 1425
Kelly, Thomas, 1671
Kelly, Thomas, 1671
Kelly, Virginia, 3631
Kelly, Virginia, 4784
Kelly, William J., 4161
Keltey, Birgitta, 1018
Keltey, Catharinae, 1018
Keltey, Guillelmi, 1018
Kemmer, Maria, 3660
Kemmer, Wilhilmina, 3660
Kemp, Anastasia, 2759
Kemp, D., 2597
Kemp, David, 2691
Kemp, David, 2759
Kemp, David, 2831
Kemp, David, 2943

Kemp, David, 2943
Kemp, David, 3079
Kemp, Geo. Wm., 2597
Kemp, Ida [Ada?] Cecilia, 3079
Kemp, Jas. Day, 2831
Kemp, Laura Millicent, 2691
Kemp, Margaret, 2597
Kemp, Margaret, 2691
Kemp, Margaret, 2759
Kemp, Margaret, 3079
Kemp, Margt., 2831
Kemp, Margt., 2943
Kenden, Anna, 1283
Kenden, Annae, 1283
Kenden, Mauricii, 1283
Kenely, Ellenora, 2540
Kennedy, Cath., 2631
Kennedy, Anna, 1698
Kennedy, Bergittae, 839
Kennedy, Cath., 2599
Kennedy, Cornelisi, 839
Kennedy, Eliza (widow), 4317
Kennedy, Eliza, 2368
Kennedy, Elizabeth, 2337
Kennedy, Guillelim, 1698
Kennedy, Johanna, 4465
Kennedy, John, 2114

Kennedy, Marg., 3161
Kennedy, Margatha, 3511
Kennedy, Maria, 839
Kennedy, Mariae, 1698
Kennedy, Mary Ann, 2368
Kennedy, Mary, 2599
Kennedy, Michal, 5178
Kennedy, Thomas, 2368
Kennedy, Thos., 2599
Kennedy, Thos., 2631
Kennedy, Winfrod (widow), 4354
Kenner, Caroline, 2080
Kenney, Arthur, 2382
Kenney, Arthur, 2523
Kenney, Arthur, 2727
Kenney, Arthur, 4582
Kenney, Arthur, 4676
Kenney, Arthur, 5253
Kenney, Bridget, 2382
Kenney, Bridget, 2443
Kenney, Bridget, 2727
Kenney, Bridgett, 2523
Kenney, Catharine, 2523
Kenney, Easter, 566
Kenney, Elisabeth Ellen, 2727
Kenney, Joseph James, 2382
Kenney, Joseph James, 5649

Kenney, Mrs., 5017
Kenney, Mrs., 3893
Kenny, Arthur, 2706
Kenny, Arthur, 3132
Kenny, Bridget, 2651
Kenny, Briget, 2706
Kenny, Catharine, 115
Kenny, Jacobus, 1199
Kenny, John, 115
Kenny, John, 2651
Kenny, Jos, 5677
Kenny, Mary, 115
Kenny, Mary, 3132
Kenny, S.E., 4140
Kenny, Simon, 2651
Kennys, Catharinae, 894
Kennys, Margareta, 894
Kennys, Thomae, 894
Kensell, Martham, 4740
Keough, Bridget, 589
Keough, John, 589
Keough, Mary (widow), 4349
Keough, Mary, 589
Keper, Sarah Jane, 2105
Keper, Sarah Jane, 2106
Kerbay, Caha..., 781
Kerbay, Guillenmi, 781

Kerbay, Patricius, 781
Kerbey, Bernardus, 1013
Kerbey, Eleonorae, 1013
Kerbey, Francisci, 1013
Kerby, Anna, 1568
Kerby, Georgius, 1103
Kerby, Joannes, 1449
Kerby, Joannis, 1449
Kerby, Margareta, 1728
Kerby, Margaretae, 1449
Kerby, Maria Anna, 1281
Kerchener, Francis B. F., 5376
Kerker, Henricus, 1500
Kerkert, Elizabeth, 1993
Kerkert, George, 1993
Kerkert, Mary, 1993
Kerman, Joannis, 1190
Kerman, Maria, 1190
Kerman, Mariae, 1190
Kern, Maria, 1690
Kern, Carolus, 1690
Kerney, Dennis, 63
Kerney, Petrus, 1465
Kerney, Petrus, 1764
Kerry, Carolus, 1731
Kerr, Claram Virgeniam, 3501
Kerr, Elizabeth Mariam, 3502

Kerr, Maria Elizabeth, 3501
Kerr, Maria Elizabeth, 3502
Kerrigan, Catherine, 3045
Kerrigan, Margaret, 3045
Kerrigan, Patrick, 3045
Kerrney, Thomas, 23
Kerry, Jacobus, 1635
Kershner, Sr., Mrs., 4065
Kershner, Agnetem Teresiam, 3536
Kershner, Annam Laviniam, 3429
Kershner, Anne Lavinia, 5341
Kershner, Benjamin F., 4578
Kershner, Carolem Joseph, 3352
Kershner, Carolo, 4043
Kershner, Carolo, 4102
Kershner, Carolum C., 4839
Kershner, Carolum Joseph, 3878
Kershner, Catharina, 4043
Kershner, Catharina, 4102
Kershner, Charles Edward, 2989
Kershner, Chas., 5109
Kershner, Clarence Gulielmum, 4065
Kershner, Clemente, 4065
Kershner, Cyro, 3536
Kershner, Cyro, 3609
Kershner, Cyrus, 2989

Kershner, Cyrus, 4698
Kershner, Danielem Gregorium, 3269
Kershner, Emma, 4065
Kershner, Ezro, 3193
Kershner, Ezro, 3269
Kershner, Franciscum, 4037
Kershner, Georgium Guglielmums, 3271
Kershner, Gingunn Albertum, 3193
Kershner, Gulielmum David, 3646
Kershner, H. (Mrs.), 3786
Kershner, Helen (Mrs.), 3837
Kershner, Helen, 3271
Kershner, Helena, 3352
Kershner, Helena, 3429
Kershner, Helena, 3646
Kershner, Helena, 3765
Kershner, Helena, 3878
Kershner, Helena, 4037
Kershner, Henricum Raymundum, 3609
Kershner, Irvin McKinley, 4102
Kershner, Jonathan, 3275
Kershner, Jos, 4037
Kershner, Joseph, 3271

Kershner, Joseph, 3352
Kershner, Joseph, 3429
Kershner, Joseph, 3646
Kershner, Joseph, 3878
Kershner, Joseph, 4747
Kershner, Josepho, 3765
Kershner, Laura C., 1917
Kershner, Laura C., 2495
Kershner, Laura, 2074
Kershner, Laura, 2235
Kershner, Laura, 2385
Kershner, Mariam G., 4043
Kershner, Mariam Motter, 3765
Kershner, Mrs., 3790
Kershner, Mrs., 4038
Kershner, Mrs., 4092
Kershner, Mrs., 4102
Kershner, Sara A., 3536
Kershner, Sara Agneto, 3609
Kershner, Sara, 3193
Kershner, Sarah (Mrs.), 4043
Kershner, Sarah, 2989
Kershner, Sarah, 3269
Kershsner, Helena, 3555
Kershsner, Henricum Edmundum, 3555
Kershsner, Joseph, 3555

Kesfort, Olys, 3927
Keting, Catharina, 4376
Keven, Patrick, 137
Key, Catherine, 252
Key, Catherine, 338
Key, Henry, 338
Key, Lucinda, 338
Keyne, Margaret, 4697
Keys, Uncle Frank, 5362
Kheler, Matheus, 1303
Kiamp, John, 476
Kiamp, Rose Ann, 476
Kiamp, Rose Anna, 476
Kildogf, Patricius, 1151
Killdoff, Jacobus, 1521
Killdoff, Patricii, 1521
Killdoff, Rosae, 1521
Kilroy, Catharina, 1391
Kilroy, Catharinae, 1351
Kilroy, Patricii, 1351
Kilroy, Thomas, 1351
Kimble, Alice, 3068
Kimble, Wm. Arthur, 3068
Kimble, Wm., 3068
Kindle, Anne Elizabeth, 2585
Kindle, blank, 2585
Kindle, Jacob, 2585

Kinek, Albertem Clarentium, 3772
Kinek, Davide, 3772
Kinek, Elizabeth, 3772
Kiney, Thomas, 4376
King, Ellen, 2312
King, Bernardus, 1240
King, Bernardus, 1454
King, Birgitta Anna, 4768
King, Bridget, 2483
King, C.R. Ann, 5769
King, Effie R., 4008
King, Effie Rcahel, 4821
King, Effie, 3779
King, Effie, 3848
King, Effie, 3920
King, Effie, 4086
King, Effie, 4158
King, Ellen, 2405
King, Ellen, 2483
King, Ellen, 4630
King, Helena, 3707
King, James, 4192
King, Jennie, 3209
King, M.C. Heston, 5767
King, Maria, 3167
King, Mariam Ellen, 4768
King, Mary, 2405

King, Mary, 3090
King, Mary, 4719
King, Michael, 4927
King, Owen, 2312
King, Owen, 2405
King, Owen, 2483
King, Owen, 4584
King, Owen, 4928
King, Patrick, 4206
King, Patrick, 4209
Kingan, Mary, 110
Kinney, Mary (widow), 4294
Kirchmer, Helena, 3592
Kirshner, Maria, 3636
Kiser, Anna, 4846
Kleineibst, Adolpho, 3658
Kleineibst, Guleilmum Maxiunum, 3658
Kleineibst, Henrietta, 3658
Kleinmeyer, Josephus, 1575
Kline, Adam, 2455
Kline, George, 2455
Kline, George, 4600
Kline, Margaret, 2455
Kluch, Catharina, 4417
Klueh, Jacobus, 1686
Kluh, Flora, 1378

Kluh, Florae, 1272
Kluh, Jacobi, 1272
Kluh, Jacobus, 1272
Kluh, Elisabeth, 1783
Kluh, Florae, 1783
Kluh, Jacobi, 1783
Klunk, Joseph, 4547
Knackstedt, John Theodore, 4599
Knapp, Catharinae, 971
Knapp, Henrici, 971
Knapp, Henricus, 1327
Knapp, Henry, 1326
Knapp, Joannes Bernardus, 971
Knave, [blank], 2031
Knave, Jacob, 2031
Knave, William, 2031
Kneckstet, John T., 2404
Kneckstet, Mary A., 2404
Kneniss, Margaret Anna Amelia, 2493
Kniess, Adolphus Leopold, 2338
Kniess, Adolphus Leopold, 4566
Kniess, Adolphus, 2510
Kniess, Adolphus, 2510
Kniess, Emile, 2338
Kniess, Margaret, 2510
Kniess, Maria, 2338

Knight, Abraham, 181
Knight, Mary, 181
Knodle, Elisabetham, 4731
Knodle, Elizabeth, 3415
Knodle, J., 4731
Knott, Alexandrum, 4794
Knox, Richard, 4630
Knox, Ellen, 2659
Knox, Maria, 3707
Koehler, Cristiana, 3653
Koehler, Henricum Xaverium, 3653
Koehler, Mynolf, 3653
Kohlenberg, Caroline, 11
Konig, Bernardus, 4448
Kooperstine, Maria, 3889
Kooperstine, Mrs, 3889
Koppler, Mary, 2909
Kouck, Albertem Clarentium, 3772
Kouck, Davide, 3772
Kouck, Elizabeth, 3772
Kountz, Cremell, 3666
Kountz, Joannem Semmllen [Samuelem?], 3666
Kountz, Julia, 3666
Koyle, Edward A., 2478
Koyle, Edward, 2466

Koyle, Samuel, 2507
Koyle, Samuel, 2541
Koyle, Samuel, 2547
Koyle, Samuel, 2560
Koyle, Samuel, 2563
Koyle, Samuel, 2578
Koyle, Stanislaus, 5429
Koyle, Thomas, 5486
Kraft, Mary, 2803
Krakom, Adrian (Rev.), 4115
Kramer, Annie (Miss), 5059
Kramer, Genevieve, 2538
Kramer, Henry, 2538
Kramer, Josephine, 5427
Kramer, Mary, 2538
Kraus, Bernardus, 1129
Kraus, Bernardus, 4447
Krauss, Bernardy, 1290
Krauss, Maria Elisabeth, 1290
Krauss, Mariae Annae, 1290
Krebs, Eugenium Josephum, 3638
Krebs, Henrico, 3638
Krebs, Theresaq, 3638
Kreigh, Luisa, 4659
Kreigh, Margaret, 2544
Kreigh, Margaret, 2622

Kreigh, Catharine Rebecca Regina, 2513
Kreigh, Catharinem, 3801
Kreigh, Franciscus, 3982
Kreigh, Frank, 2626
Kreigh, Franklin, 2383
Kreigh, Fredericum Spickler, 3822
Kreigh, Helena, 3822
Kreigh, John, 2383
Kreigh, Lomsa, 5497
Kreigh, Louisa, 5464
Kreigh, Louisa, 5540
Kreigh, Margaret R., 2383
Kreigh, Margaret, 2108
Kreigh, Margaret, 2513
Kreigh, Margaret, 5476
Kreigh, Margt., 2946
Kreigh, Maria Anna, 3195
Kreigh, Mary A., 2527
Kreigh, Mary An [sic], 4621
Kreigh, Mary Ann, 2383
Kreigh, Mary Am, 2912
Kreigh, Mary Jane, 2383
Kreigh, Mary, 2676
Kreigh, Mary, 2984
Kreigh, Mary, 4606
Kreigh, Maud, 3374

Kreigh, Miss, 2710
Kreigh, Modie [sic], 3248
Kreigh, Monroe, 4610
Kreigh, Mrs, 2102
Kreigh, Peter, 5547
Kreigh, Petro, 3822
Kreigh, Petro, 4726
Kreigh, Petrum Henricum, 4825
Kreigh, Regina, 5444
Kreigh, Sallie, 3959
Kreigh, Sara, 3801
Kreigh, Sara, 4769
Kreigh, Sarah, 2545
Kreigh, Sarah, 4659
Kreigh, William, 2513
Kreigh, Wm., 2544, 2622, 2912, 4659, 4598
Kreighs, "whole family of", 4621
Kreitz, Maria, 4028
Kreitz, Aliciam, 3639
Kreitz, Condrad, 3727
Kreitz, Conrad, 4016
Kreitz, Conradio, 3639
Kreitz, Conradus, 3940
Kreitz, Conradus, 3792
Kreitz, Conradus, 4028
Kreitz, Edgar Aloysium, 4016

Kreitz, Francisus, 4016
Kreitz, Joseph Ernestum, 3940
Kreitz, Maria E, 3792
Kreitz, Maria, 3727
Kreitz, Maria, 3886
Kreitz, Maria, 3940
Kreitz, Maria, 4016
Kreitz, Marion [or Marian?], 3639
Kreitz, Mrs., 3832
Kreitz, Mrs., 3973
Kreitz, Mrs., 3989
Kreitz, Mrs., 3991
Kreitz, Mrs., 3993
Kreitz, Stellam Amandam, 3727
Kreitzer, Mr., 4103
Kreitzer, Mrs., 4103
Kreitzs, Mrs., 4037
Kreiz, Agnetem Catharinam, 3825
Kreiz, Conrado, 3825
Kreiz, Maria E., 3825
Krichton, Catharinam Margaretam, 4068
Krichton, Gulielmo A., 4068
Krichton, Maria, 4068
Krichton, Christina, 2710
Kriegh, Cristina, 2771
Kriegh, Elisabeth, 2749

Kriegh, Ella J., 3875
Kriegh, Georg, 2771
Kriegh, George Wm., 2710
Kriegh, Gulielmum Franciscum, 3875
Kriegh, Margaret, 2772
Kriegh, Margaret, 4655
Kriegh, Miss, 2772
Kriegh, Petro, 3875
Kriegh, Robt., 2771
Kriegh, Sarah Scholastica, 2710
Kriegh, Wm., 2771
Krigh, Sallie, 2609
Krish, Wm, 5810
Kroon, Maria, 3447
Kroone, Maria Eliz., 3573
Krugh, T., 5179
Kunell, Catherinam Magdalenam, 3686
Kunell, Jacobo, 3684
Kunell, Jacobo, 3685
Kunell, Jacobo, 3686
Kunell, Joannem Henricum, 3684
Kunell, Josaphina, 3685
Kunell, Josephina, 3684
Kunell, Josephina, 3686
Kunell, Josephinam Ethel, 3685

Kurley, Catharinae, 1242
Kurley, Jacobus, 1242
Kurley, Patricii, 1242
Kushner, Cyro, 3108
Kushner, David Clemens, 3108
Kushner, Sara Agneto, 3108
Kushner, Sara, 3146
Kushner, Sara, 3147
Kuz, Conrado Adolpho, 3846
Kyne, Mathias C., 4565
Kyper, Christianna, 2801
Kyper, Geo., 2934
Kyper, Geo., 2935
Kyper, George M., 2934, 2935
Kyper, George, 2801
Kyper, George, 2801, 4670, 5633
Kyper, Georgius, 3200
Kyper, John, 2801
Kyper, Margaret, 2977
Kyper, Margaritam, 4764
Kyper, Margt., 2934, 2935
Kyper, Mrs., 3075
Laby, Evy, 211
Lachenmeyer, Eleonorae, 1693
Lachenmeyer, Jacobus, 1693
Lachenmeyer, Josiphi, 1693
Ladden, Elisabeth, 1336

Laedver, Mary, 4977
Laesure, Danielem, 3259
Laghan, Maria, 1184
Laghty, Catharinae, 1073
Laghty, Jacob, 1073
Laghty, Maria, 1073
Lahey, Daniel, 4280
Laikin, Mary, 1925
Laikin, Michale, 1925
Laird, Georgius H., 3099
Lake, Jas. Edwd., 2649
Lake, Kate, 2649
Lake, Saml., 2649
Lallay, Guillelmus, 4402
Lalley, Birgetta, 969
Lalley, Guillelini, 969
Lalley, Maria, 1254
Lalley, Mariae, 969
Laly, Aree, 196
Lamar, Louisa, 3383
Lamasney, Bridget, 90
Lamasney, Eleanor, 90
Lamasney, Garratt, 90
Lamasney, Mrs., 89
Lamber, Catherine, 471
Lamber, John (Mrs.), 473
Lamber, John, 471

Lambert, Michal, 471
Lambert, Catherine Emmilia, 407
Lambert, Catherine, 407
Lambert, Jenny, 4682
Lambert, John, 618
Lambert, John, 407
Lambert, Virginia, 3059
Lambride, Allis Sophia, 1755
Lambride, Mariae, 1755
Lambride, William, 1755
Lambright, George William, 1978
Lambright, Mary, 1978
Lambright, William, 1978
Lanagan, Richard, 4259
Lanan, Hanora, 1371
Lancaster, Anna, 3319
Lancaster, Anna, 3320
Lancaster, Anna, 3321
Lancaster, Henriettam Myers, 3321
Lancaster, Jacob, 3319
Lancaster, Jacob, 3320
Lancaster, Jacob, 3321
Lancaster, Mariam Blanche, 3319
Lancaster, Ricardeum McCardell, 3320
Land, Joannes, 1451
Land, Judith, 1451

Land, Michael, 4466
Land, Michaelis, 1451
Landenslager, Leteie, 3917
Lander, Nelly, 334
Landers, Elonora, 328
Landrigan, Charoli, 865
Landrigan, Jacobus, 865
Landrigan, Mariae, 865
Lane, Agnetem Myrtle Mantz, 3581
Lane, Frances C., 92
Lane, Helena V., 3581
Lane, Henny, 4198
Lane, Horatio M., 3581
Lane, Julia M., 3389
Lane, Julia, 2741
Lane, Julia, 3039
Lane, Julia, 3122
Lane, Julia, 3544
Lane, Margareta, 4442
Lane, Mary, 4207
Lanet, Philippus, 1271
Lang, Maria Catharina, 4440
Lanless, Annae, 1313
Lanless, Catharina, 1313
Lanless, Patricii, 1313
Lann, Christophors, 641

Lanon, Birgitta, 1270
Lanon, Honorae, 1270
Lanon, Mathei, 1270
Lanret, Joannes, 1432
Lantz, David, 2446
Lantz, Mary Catharine, 2446
Lantz, Mary Ellen, 2446
Lapole, Angustimam, 3700
Lapole, Anna C., 3489
Lapole, Bernardum Edwardum, 3615
Lapole, Carolum Guglielmum, 3454
Lapole, David, 3525
Lapole, Ericum Vinton, 3489
Lapole, Guglielmo, 3455
Lapole, Guglielum, 3454
Lapole, Guilelmo, 3700
Lapole, Gulielmo L., 3489
Lapole, Gulielmo, 3615
Lapole, Harry Rutherford, 3455
Lapole, Helena Cath., 3615
Lapole, Hubertum Russel, 3525
Lapole, Laura, 3525
Lapole, Lena C., 3455
Lapole, Lena Catherina, 3454
Lapole, Lena, 3700

Lapole, Lena, 3700
Lapole, Martha E., 3453
Lapole, Martha Ellen, 3452
Larber, Philippi, 1506
Larber, Rosa Anna, 1506
Larber, Sophiae, 1506
Larguery, John, 4282
Largy, Joannes, 4494
Larkin, Birgittae, 888
Larkin, Elisabeth, 888
Larkin, Guillelini, 888
Larkin, Maria, 3628
Larkin, Maria, 3629
Larkin, Michael, 2343
Larris, Francena, 2288
Larver, Mary, 4977
Lary, Dionysii, 826
Lary, Helenae, 826
Lary, Jeremias, 826
Lasley, Catharina, 1235
Lasley, Catharinae, 1235
Lasley, Richardi, 1235
LaStrange, Bridget, 497
LaStrange, Cahterine, 497
LaStrange, Patrick, 497
LaStrange, Thoms., 497
Latmann, Georgii, 1571

Latmann, Matilda, 1571
Latmann, Serinae, 1571
Lauber, Annae, 1046
Lauber, Guillelmus Henricus, 1046
Lauber, Henrici, 1046
Lauber, Mary, 2010
Lauber, Mary, 2429
Laudenslager, Lutie, 3970
Laudenslager, Lutie, 4074
Lauderslager, Lettie, 4137
Lauer, Caroline, 4382
Laughlin, Birgittae, 1432
Laughlin, Elisabeth, 1432
Laughlin, Jacobi, 1432
Laughlin, Michael, 1180
Laughlin, Stephanus, 1179
Laughlin, Stephanus, 1238
Laurence, Anna, 3369
Laurence, Magdalen, 3364
Laurence, Maria, 3460
Laurence, Mary, 2607
Laurence, Laurentium (Johannem), 4755
Laurence, [blank], 3490
Laurence, Aannam Bernedettam, 3726
Laurence, Aaron A., 4820

Laurence, Andreas, 3369
Laurence, Andrew C., 3032
Laurence, Andrew C., 3194
Laurence, Andrew, 2607
Laurence, Ann, 2982
Laurence, Ann, 2995
Laurence, Anna M., 3194
Laurence, Anna, 2607
Laurence, Anna, 5679
Laurence, Annam Mariam, 3490
Laurence, Cath., 5564
Laurence, Catharina, 3490
Laurence, Catharine, 4753
Laurence, Catherina, 3726
Laurence, Catherina, 3743
Laurence, Catherina, 3746
Laurence, Catherine, 3032
Laurence, Gregorium Sylvestrem, 3369
Laurence, Gregory, 5133
Laurence, Gul., 4814
Laurence, Jannes, 3726
Laurence, Jerenimo, 3490
Laurence, Jerome M., 3032
Laurence, Jno. M., 5137
Laurence, Joanne P., 3682
Laurence, Johanne, 3369

Laurence, Johanne, 3460
Laurence, Johannem Martinum, 3460
Laurence, Johannes, 3364
Laurence, Johannes, 3187
Laurence, John, 5570
Laurence, Margareta, 3726
Laurence, Maria F., 3682
Laurence, Maria, 3260
Laurence, Maria, 3364
Laurence, Maria, 3469
Laurence, Maria, 3469
Laurence, Maria, 3652
Laurence, Maria, 3763
Laurence, Maria, 3764
Laurence, Maria, 5674
Laurence, Mariam Margaretam, 3682
Laurence, Mary Agnes, 3032
Laurence, Mary J., 3194
Laurence, Mary, 5675
Laurence, Michael Joachim, 2607
Laurence, Michael, 2607
Laurence, Michael, 3460
Laurence, Mr., 3371
Laurence, Mr., 4753
Laurence, Mrs., 3363

Laurence, Noah, 3652
Laurence, Noah, 3682
Laurence, Noah, 3764
Laurence, Noah, 5574
Laurence, Rebecca, 2971
Laurence, Sarah Cath., 3682
Laurence, Sarah, 3369
Laurence, Sarah, 3460
Laurence, Virginia, 5186
Laurens, Maria Anna, 3103
Laurens, Maria Josephina, 3103
Laurens, Michael, 3103
Laurens, Rebecca, 3153
Lausburgh, Laura, 5608
Laver, Carolinae, 709
Lawber, Mary, 189
Laweet, Joannes, 1432
Lawet, Philippus, 1271
Lawler, Mary, 12
Lawless, Annae, 1313
Lawless, Catharina, 1313
Lawless, Patricii, 1313
Lawless, Anna, 1721
Lawrenc, Andreas C., 3567
Lawrence, Elisabeth, 3828
Lawrence, Jacobo, 3828

Lawrence, Lauram Lucretiam, 3828
Lawrence, Jerome, 3785
Lawrence, Joannes (Mrs.), 4056
Lawrence, Maria, 3791
Lawrence, Noah (Mrs.), 4886
Lawrence, Sarai, 4050
Lawrence, Aaron, 3866
Lawrence, Aaron, 5643
Lawrence, Agnete, 3977
Lawrence, Andrea, 4907
Lawrence, Andreas C., 4774
Lawrence, Ann, 2662
Lawrence, Anne M., 5354
Lawrence, Carolo L., 4159
Lawrence, Catharina, 3622
Lawrence, Catharina, 3856
Lawrence, David Henricum, 3791
Lawrence, Elisabeth, 1482
Lawrence, Elisabeth, 3866
Lawrence, Florence (Mrs.), 3947
Lawrence, Florence (Mrs.), 3957
Lawrence, Florence (Mrs.), 4159
Lawrence, Florentiam Louisam, 4159
Lawrence, H.P., 5241

Lawrence, Helenam Paulinam, 3856
Lawrence, Hieronimo, 3622
Lawrence, Huronimus, 3639
Lawrence, Jerome, 3856
Lawrence, Jerome, 4833
Lawrence, Joannam Gertrudim, 3622
Lawrence, Joanne P., 3791
Lawrence, Joanne, 3922
Lawrence, Joanne, 4050
Lawrence, Joannes, 3966
Lawrence, Joannes, 3997
Lawrence, Joannes, 4056
Lawrence, Joanni Patritio, 3567
Lawrence, Joseph Leonem, 3567
Lawrence, Lila A., 4159
Lawrence, Louisa C.M.A., 5773
Lawrence, Lucia, 3567
Lawrence, Magdalenem L., 4907
Lawrence, Margarita, 4838
Lawrence, Maria Agnes, 3937
Lawrence, Maria Agnes, 4851
Lawrence, Maria F., 3621
Lawrence, Maria F., 3626
Lawrence, Maria F., 3809
Lawrence, Maria F., 3833

Lawrence, Maria, 3908
Lawrence, Maria, 5644
Lawrence, Mariam Agnetem, 4855
Lawrence, Mariam Ednam, 3866
Lawrence, Mariam Theresiam, 3876
Lawrence, Mary Francy, 3860
Lawrence, Mary Jos., 5645
Lawrence, Mary M. (Mrs.), 5246
Lawrence, Mary, 4047
Lawrence, Matilda, 4318
Lawrence, Michael C.J., 5762
Lawrence, Michael, 5266
Lawrence, Michaelem, 4836
Lawrence, Noah (Mrs.), 3796
Lawrence, Noah (Mrs.), 3916
Lawrence, Noah (Mrs.), 3943
Lawrence, Noah (Mrs.), 3980
Lawrence, Noah F., 3621
Lawrence, Noah F., 3626
Lawrence, Noah F., 3791
Lawrence, Noah Franciscum, 4774
Lawrence, Noah, 3796
Lawrence, Noah, 3833
Lawrence, Noah, 3860
Lawrence, Noah, 3876
Lawrence, Noah, 4886

Lawrence, Sarah C., 3567
Lawrence, Sarah C., 3791
Lawrence, Sarai C., 3966
Layzari, Ausilia, 4030
Lazzari, Andrea, 4030
Lazzari, Ausilia, 4099
Lazzari, Ausilia, 4150
Leach, Margareta, 4046
Leaman, Jacobum, 4909
Leamey, James, 250
Lechleider, Franciscum A., 4841
Lechleider, M.C., 4841
Lechlider, Francisco A., 3942
Lechlider, Margaritam Rebeccam, 3942
Lechliter, Maria C., 3942
Lechliter, Francisco A., 4011
Lechliter, Franciscum M., 4011
Lechliter, Maria, 4011
Lecord, Maria Elizabeth, 3584
Lecord, Mariam Eliza Cath., 3584
Lecord, Wilhelm, 3584
Ledan, [blank], 660
Ledan, Annae, 661
Ledan, Joannes, 660
Ledan, Joannis, 660
Ledan, Joannis, 661

Ledan, Maria Ludovica, 661
Ledwidge, Guilelinus, 1236
Lee, Aunt Sally, 4965
Lee, Caeciliae, 1396
Lee, Caeciliae, 1794
Lee, Catharina, 1396
Lee, Cornelii, 1174
Lee, Daniel, 1358
Lee, Eleonora, 1174
Lee, Guillelini, 931
Lee, H [sic], 1488
Lee, Ignatius, 239
Lee, James, 1855
Lee, Joannes, 708
Lee, Joannis, 1488
Lee, John, 239
Lee, John, 2424
Lee, Joseph Arnold, 2424
Lee, Josephus, 931
Lee, Lucenta, 1488
Lee, Lucia, 843
Lee, Margareta, 1488
Lee, Margaretae, 708
Lee, Maria, 1174
Lee, Old Uncle, 5004
Lee, Patricii, 708
Lee, Priscilla, 2292

Lee, Rebeccae, 843
Lee, Robert, 4414
Lee, Roberti, 1396
Lee, Roberti, 1794
Lee, Salley, 104
Lee, Sally, 173
Lee, Sara A.R., 1794
Lee, Sara, 1794
Lee, Sarah, 2292
Lee, Sarah, 2292
Lee, Sarah, 239
Lee, Silviae, 931
Lee, Teresa, 2424
Lee, Thomae, 843
Lee, William, 2292
Lefevere, Anna, 3168
Lefevre, Francisco, 4877
Lefvre, Gulielmum H., 4877
Leffer, Margret, 602
Lefferman, Carolem Fredriem, 3664
Lefferman, Geirgio, 3312
Lefferman, George, 3064
Lefferman, Georgio, 3664
Lefferman, Lucretia, 3064
Lefferman, Lucretia, 3312
Lefferman, Michael Amos, 3064
Leffermann, Samuelem C., 3312
Leffermann, George, 2982
Leffermann, John Franklin, 2982
Leffermann, Lucretia, 2982
Leffleman, Ann Amanda, 2910
Leffleman, Geo., 2836
Leffleman, Geo., 2910
Leffleman, Lucretia, 2836
Leffleman, Lucretia, 2910
Leffleman, Wm. Hy., 2836
Leiner, Barbara, 1625
Leiser, Cath., 5651
Leiser, Martha Ann, 5636
Leixner, Doratheae, 1268
Leixner, Dorothea, 1564
Leixner, Dorotheae, 1801
Leixner, Jacobus, 1801
Leixner, Joannes, 1268
Leixner, Philippi, 1268
Leixner, Philippi, 1801
Leizer, Joseph Francis, 5692
Leman, Helena, 3177
Leman, Mariam Helenam, 3177
Leman, Petro, 3177
Lemen, Eliza Monahan, 3030
Lemen, Helen, 3030
Lemen, Peter, 3030
Lemen, Helena, 3177
Lemen, Mariam Helenam, 3177
Lemen, P. (Mr.), 5061
Lemen, Petro, 3177
Lemen, Sallie, 5061
Lemon, Helena M., 3095
Lemon, Jane, 336
Lemon, Petro L., 3095
Lemon, Saml, 336
Lemon, Saml, 336
Lemon, Saram Alicem, 3095
Lenis, Alexander, 1640
Lenis, Mariae, 1640
Lennen, Eliza Monahan, 3030
Lennen, Helen, 3030
Lennen, Peter, 3030
Lenner, Dorothea, 2115
Lenner, Philip, 2115
Lennon, Helan, 2956
Lennon, Peter, 2956
Lennon, Robert Eli, 2956
Lens, Jacobo, 3506
Lens, Sharam Annam Matildam, 3506
Lens, Susanna, 3506
Leoles, Betsy, 353
Leonard, Margaret, 2399
Lepold, E. C., 3410
Lepold, Elizabeth C., 3397
Lepold, Elizabeth C., 3398
Lepold, Elizabeth C., 3399
Lepold, Maria, 3409
Lestrange, Thomas, 1759
Leuxner, Dorothea, 1939
Leuxner, Ignatius, 1939
Leuxner, Philip, 1939
Levin, Mary, 2821
Lewis [or Lewin], Johann, 2871
Lewis, Annae, 1087
Lewis, Catharina, 1532
Lewis, Cora M., 4861
Lewis, Elisabeth, 1532
Lewis, Elisabeth, 648
Lewis, Eliza, 4686
Lewis, Elizabeth, 3220
Lewis, Elizabeth, 4954
Lewis, Georgio, 3220
Lewis, Helena Elizabeth, 2398
Lewis, Isabella, 2663
Lewis, Joannes, 4367
Lewis, Joannis, 1532
Lewis, Joannis, 648
Lewis, Julian, 2130
Lewis, Julianna, 2398

Lewis, Margaret, 2524
Lewis, Margaret, 2804
Lewis, Margaret, 3220
Lewis, Margaret, 4629
Lewis, Maria Elisabeth Anna, 1087
Lewis, Mariam Catharinam, 3220
Lewis, Mary Catherine, 2713
Lewis, Mathildis Anna, 648
Lewis, Perry, 1087
Lewis, Robert, 2130
Lewis, Robert, 2398
Lewis, Robert, 4296
Lewis, Robert, 5085
Lewis, Robt, 2663
Lewis, Robt., 4631
Lewis, William Henry, 2130
Lewis, Wm, 5572
Lewis?, Elisabeth, 924
Lewis?, Joannis, 924
Lewis?, Maria, 924
Ley, Sara, 1225
Liba, Eva, 4205
Liberg, Theodore, 2411
Liberman, Dorothea, 2087
Lice, Catherene (widow), 4352
Lichty, Catharinae, 750

Lichty, Henricus, 750
Lichty, Jacobi, 750
Liddy, Helena D., 4028
Liddy, Jeremiah, 4028
Liddy, Mariam, 4028
Liddy, Mary, 5361
Lidy, Mrs., 340
Ligon, Gulielano Andrea, 3652
Lile, Basil, 181
Lile, Dianna, 181
Linam, Anna, 1205
Linam, Michael, 1313
Linch, Antonius, 1524
Linch, Birgitta, 1458
Linch, Birgitta, 1490
Linch, Birgitta, 957
Linch, Birgittae, 1473
Linch, Birgittae, 1587
Linch, Birgittae, 1609
Linch, Catharinae, 1524
Linch, Catharinae, 976
Linch, Catharinae, 977
Linch, Catharinae, 978
Linch, Catharinae, 979
Linch, Catharinae, 980
Linch, Catharinae, 981
Linch, Eleonora, 978

Linch, Elisabeth, 980
Linch, Hiram, 976
Linch, Hiram, 977
Linch, Hiram, 978
Linch, Hiram, 979
Linch, Hiram, 980
Linch, Hiram, 981
Linch, Jacobus Patricius, 981
Linch, Joanna, 976
Linch, Joannes, 1195
Linch, Joannes, 1472
Linch, Joannes, 1490
Linch, Joannes, 4512
Linch, Joannis, 1473
Linch, Margareta, 1587
Linch, Margareta, 1609
Linch, Michael, 1473
Linch, Owen, 1195
Linch, Own[Owen?], 957
Linch, Patricias, 1458
Linch, Patricii, 1524
Linch, Patricii, 1587
Linch, Patricii, 1609
Linch, Patricius, 1375
Linch, Patricius, 4490
Linch, Rosa Anna, 979
Linch, Rosae, 1195

Linch, Rosae, 957
Linch, Sara, 977
Lindon, Joannem J., 4916
Lingg, Bernadettam Josephinam, 4168
Lingg, Catharina, 3940
Lingg, Catharina, 3978
Lingg, Catharina, 4048
Lingg, Catharina, 4103
Lingg, Catharina, 4168
Lingg, Joseph F., 4168
Lingg, Joseph, 3940
Lingg, Joseph, 3978
Lingg, Joseph, 4048
Lingg, Joseph, 4103
Lingg, Margaritam Virginiam, 3978
Lingg, Mariam Ruth, 4048
Lingg, Paulinam Catherinam, 4103
Link, Christian, 4593
Linn, Margaret, 2192
Linn, Mary Ann, 2192
Lintz, Bernard, 2261
Lintz, James Henry, 2261
Lintz, Louisa, 2261
Liones, Betsey, 320
Lismen, Peter L., 4695

Lithco, Jnoss, 4701
Little, Kate, 3245
Little, Alverta Gertrude, 2971
Little, Anna Catharine, 2238
Little, Carolo, 3153
Little, Carolum Alphonsum, 3153
Little, Catharina, 3156
Little, Charles Albert, 2008
Little, Charles, 2971
Little, Charles, 3076
Little, Charles, 4717
Little, Chs., 2833
Little, David, 93
Little, Eliza, 93
Little, Elizabeth, 2416
Little, Guglielmum Thomam, 3266
Little, Ida Kate, 2833
Little, Ignatius Joseph Wm, 93
Little, Isabella, 1856
Little, Isabella, 2008
Little, Isabella, 2238
Little, John, 1856
Little, Kate, 3069
Little, Maria, 4464
Little, Mary Loreta, 3069
Little, Patricius, 1364
Little, Patricius, 4504

Little, Patrick, 1856
Little, Patrick, 2008
Little, Patrick, 2238
Little, Rebecca, 2833
Little, Rebecca, 2971
Little, Rebecca, 3076
Little, Rebecca, 3153
Little, Rebecca, 5108
Little, Wm. Henry, 3076
Little, Wm., 3069
Littleton, Charlotte, 2439
Littleton, Charlotte, 2552
Lively, Catharinae, 825
Lively, Jacobi, 825
Lively, Joannes, 825
Lively, Johanna, 1697
Lively, Mary Jane, 2119
Lizer, Wesley, 4548
Lizer, Ann, 3203
Lizer, Bernardum, 3853
Lizer, Catharina A., 3514
Lizer, Catharine, 3203
Lizer, Catherina A., 3657
Lizer, Catherina, 3416
Lizer, Catherine, 3810
Lizer, Eleonora, 3862

Lizer, Eleonoram Catharinam, 3645
Lizer, Elisabeth, 3853
Lizer, Eliza, 3710
Lizer, Eliza, 3710
Lizer, Elizabetha, 3711
Lizer, Elizabetha, 3711
Lizer, Elizabetha, 3712
Lizer, Elizabetha, 3712
Lizer, Elizabetha, 3746
Lizer, Elizabetha, 3746
Lizer, Gulielmune Emory, 3712
Lizer, Honoram, 3710
Lizer, Idam May, 3711
Lizer, Jacobum Henricum, 3746
Lizer, Joseph Francisco, 3645
Lizer, Joseph Franciscum, 4782
Lizer, Joseph, 3416
Lizer, Joseph, 3644
Lizer, Joseph, 4012
Lizer, Maria E., 3844
Lizer, Maria Elizabeth, 4782
Lizer, Maria, 3644
Lizer, Maria, 3729
Lizer, Mariam Elisabeth, 4012
Lizer, Mariam, 4790
Lizer, Martha Ann, 2161

Lizer, Martha Anna, 3898
Lizer, Martha, 3844
Lizer, Martha, 4701
Lizer, Martham A., 4864
Lizer, Mary Elizabeth, 2161
Lizer, Samuel, 3710
Lizer, Samuel, 3711
Lizer, Samuel, 3712
Lizer, Samuel, 3746
Lizer, Samuele, 3853
Lizer, Susanna R., 4012
Lizer, Susannah R., 3645
Lizer, Wesley, 2161
Lizer, Catharine Alveretto, 2370
Lizor, Daniel, 3008
Lizor, Joseph Francis, 2478
Lizor, Joseph T., 3738
Lizor, Martha A., 3009
Lizor, Martha, 3738
Lizor, Mary A., 2478
Lizor, Mary Elizabeth, 2624
Lizor, Mary, 2370
Lizor, Mary, 2624
Lizor, Samuelem Clifford, 3738
Lizor, Susan Rebecca, 3738
Lizor, Wesley, 2370
Lizor, Wesley, 2478

Lizor, Wesley, 2624
Lizzer, Samuel Wm., 4996
Lloyd, Gulielmo, 4848
Lloyd, Joanne, 3120
Lloyd, Joanne, 3121
Lloyd, Joannem, 3120
Lloyd, Mariam Catharinam, 3121
Lloyd, Mrs., 4074
Lloyd, Mrs., 4137
Lloyd, Sara, 3120
Lloyd, Sara, 3121
Loan, Anna, 4463
Locher, Elizabeth, 4323
Loftus, Antonius, 1556
Loftus, John, 1788
Loftus, Owen, 1569
Logan, James, 70
Logan, Joannes, 1669
Logan, Margaret, 70
Logan, Mary Jane, 2025
Logan, Mary Jane, 2118
Logan, Mary Jane, 2270
Logan, Mary Jane, 2420
Logan, Susan, 2025
Logan, Susanna, 2420
Logee, John, 349
Logee, Martha, 349

Logee, Wilm, 349
Loghan, Maria, 1184
Loghan, Birgittae, 1126
Loghan, Joannis, 1126
Loghan, Maria Anna, 1126
Loghan, Birgitta, 1333
Loghan, Catharina, 1110
Loghan, Joannis, 1110
Loghan, Joannis, 1459
Loghan, Mariae, 1110
Loghan, Mariae, 1459
Loghan, Patricius, 1459
Loghan, Petrus, 1459
Logue, Martha, 162
Logue, Rachel, 162
Logue, William, 162
Logun, Mary Jane (Miss), 4525
Lolley, Birgittae, 1207
Lolley, Joannis, 1207
Lolley, Michaelis, 1207
Lombi, M____, 4196
Lon, Anna Catharina, 1347
Londergen, Patrick, 4214
Long,, 4979
Long, Abraham Augustimm, 3602
Long, Adam A., 3925
Long, Adamo A., 3835

Long, Adamo A., 3836
Long, Catharina, 3835
Long, Catharina, 3836
Long, Catharina, 3925
Long, Dan., 2952
Long, Daniel, 5695
Long, Ellen, 2680
Long, Ellen, 2952
Long, Ellen, 3238
Long, Franklin Jeremiam, 3836
Long, Georgium B., 3925
Long, Hannah, 3692
Long, Maria, 1527
Long, Mary E. (Miss), 4540
Long, Mary, 2068
Long, Mary, 2243
Long, Mary, 2436
Long, Michael, 5685
Long, Rebeccam Lucindam, 3835
Longstaff, Joannes M., 639
Lonny, Robert, 226
Lord, Maria, 3884
Lord, Protase M., 4874
Lord, Protasia, 4062
Lorgy, Johanna, 1545
Lorsbaugh, Frances, 2360
Lorsbaugh, George Edward, 2360

Lorsbaugh, George, 2360
Lorsbaugh, Charles Howard, 2524
Lorsbaugh, Charles Romanus, 2467
Lorsbaugh, Claget, 5127
Lorsbaugh, Frances, 2194
Lorsbaugh, Frances, 2467
Lorsbaugh, Frances, 2479
Lorsbaugh, Frances, 2524
Lorsbaugh, George, 2194
Lorsbaugh, George, 2467
Lorsbaugh, George, 2524
Lorsbaugh, Laura Catharine, 2194
Lorschbaugh, Fanny, 2890
Lorschbaugh, Frances [See Notes], 2693
Lorschbaugh, Frances Elizabeth, 2693
Lorschbaugh, Geo, 2693
Lorschbaugh, Geo, 2890
Lorschbaugh, Sarah Berry, 2890
Lorshbaugh, Carolo H., 3578
Lorshbaugh, Carolo, 4075
Lorshbaugh, Carrolum H., 4773
Lorshbaugh, Dora, 3995
Lorshbaugh, Gulielmum Herman, 3995
Lorshbaugh, Jacobo, 3995

Lorshbaugh, Laura, 5621
Lorshbaugh, Laurentium Claggett, 3578
Lorshbaugh, Margaretta V., 3578
Lorshbaugh, Margaritam Helenam, 4075
Lorshbaugh, Maria V., 4075
Lorshbough, George, 4542
Losler, Joannem Henricum, 4846
Loterzo, Maria, 3891
Loudenslager, Letie, 4848
Loudeslager, Pollie, 2714
Lough, Martha, 268
Lough, Wilm, 268
Lough, Wilm, 268
Loughrey, Anna, 3596
Loughrey, Gulielmo, 3596
Loughrey, Mariam Gertrudim, 3596
Louis, Redmond, 2288
Louman, Jacobo, 3420
Louman, Louisa, 3420
Louman, Mariam Johannam, 3420
Lout, Flora, 4830
Louvson, Annie, 5498
Love, Susana, 4771
Lovell, Thomas, 1410

Lover, Maria, 1600
Lover, Mary (Mrs.), 75
Lover, Mary, 206
Lover, Mrs., 442
Lover, Mrs., 343
Lover, Mrs., 389
Lover, Mrs., 536
Low, Mr., 4545
Lowe, Laura, 4848
Lowery, Catharine, 2364
Lowery, Catharine, 2365
Lowery, Catharine, 2366
Lowery, Catharine, 2367
Lowery, John, 2364
Lowery, John, 2365
Lowery, John, 2366
Lowery, John, 2367
Lowery, Robert, 4239
Lowery, Sarah Ann, 2364
Lowery, Sarah Ann, 2365
Lowery, Sarah Ann, 2366
Lowery, Sarah Ann, 2367
Lowman, Elizabeth (Miss), 4529
Loyd, James Wm., 2960
Loyd, John, 2960
Loyd, John, 2997
Loyd, Sarah, 2960

Loyd, Sarah, 2997
Loyd, Stonewall Jackson, 2997
Loynes, Catharinae, 719
Loynes, Guillelmus, 719
Loynes, Patricii, 719
Luay, Cornelii, 809
Luay, Dionisius, 809
Luay, Mariae, 809
Lucas, Catharine, 47
Lucas, Terresa, 47
Luce, Nathan F., 3623
Luck, Jacob A., 4629
Lucket, Eliza, 117
Lucket, Hanna, 2757
Lucket, Hanna, 2764
Lucket, Hester, 117
Lucket, Hurriet, 187
Lucket, John, 117
Luckett, Hannah, 2521
Ludders, Catharine, 1892
Ludders, Mary Elizabeth, 1892
Ludders, Thomas, 1892
Luhy, Magareta, 4411
Lulain, Catharenae, 1009
Lulain, Hugonis, 1009
Lulain, Rosa, 1009
Lularn, Catharenae, 1009

Lularn, Hugonis, 1009
Lularn, Rosa, 1009
Lundragen, Charles, 4271
Luschbaugh, B.F., 4785
Lushbaugh, Catherina, 3767
Lushbaugh, Margaretam, 3767
Lushbaugh, Windel, 3767
Lushbaugh, Carolo, 3694
Lushbaugh, Carolo, 3819
Lushbaugh, Fannie (Mrs.), 3819
Lushbaugh, Frances, 2565
Lushbaugh, George, 2565
Lushbaugh, Georgium Vendel, 3819
Lushbaugh, Honoram Leola, 3694
Lushbaugh, Joanne H., 3647
Lushbaugh, Joannem Franciscum, 3580
Lushbaugh, Joanni, 3580
Lushbaugh, Lawrence Clegget, 2565
Lushbaugh, Louis Bernard, 5243
Lushbaugh, Ludovicum Bernardum, 3647
Lushbaugh, Margarita, 3694
Lushbaugh, Maria Virginia, 3819
Lushbaugh, Theodesia, 3577

Lushbaugh, Theodosia Virginia, 3647
Lushbaugh, Theodosia, 3580
Lusk, Patricius, 1463
Luthringer, Theresiae, 663
Luttman, Mariae, 638
Lutz, Rosanna, 2540
Lyands, Rosa, 4415
Lyddam, Anna, 3773
Lyddam, Joanne G., 3773
Lyddam, Mariem Virginam, 3773
Lyddem, Joannem W., 4810
Lyddy, Helenard [or Helen D.], 4085
Lyddy, Jacobum Willson, 4085
Lyddy, Jeremiah, 4085
Lydelaine, Margt, 4681
Lydelane, Jas. Q., 4681
Lydy, Marian, 3677
Lyles, Betsy, 4223
Lymbach, Catharinam, 3126
Lymbach, Catharinam, 3126
Lymbach, Francisca, 3126
Lymbach, Francisca, 3126
Lynch, Bernard, 4563
Lynch, Bridget, 2180
Lynch, Catharina, 3211

Lynch, Catharina, 3290
Lynch, Catharine, 2000
Lynch, Catharine, 3412
Lynch, Ellen A., 1984
Lynch, Harriet, 3088
Lynch, Jacob, 2456
Lynch, Jane, 71
Lynch, John, 4339
Lynch, Lucia, 903
Lynch, Margaret, 4339
Lynch, Margaret, 4944
Lynch, Margret, 4311
Lynch, Mary Catharine, 2456
Lynch, Mary Catharine, 5468
Lynch, Mary, 1991
Lynch, Patrick, 71
Lynch, Patrick, 2329
Lynch, Philippi, 903
Lynch, Rebecca, 2456
Lynch, Sarah B., 119
Lynch, Susannae, 903
Lyndca, Joseph, 4155
Lyon, John, 1361
Lyons, Bridget, 2938
Lyons, Catharina, 1145
Lyons, Danl., 2938
Lyons, Eliza, 2938

Lyons, Hannora, 2671
Lyons, Jno., 2938
Lyons, John, 3010
Lyons, Kate, 2670
Lyons, Kate, 2671
Lyons, Mariae, 1145
Lyons, Mary, 3010
Lyons, Mes, 4662
Lyons, Michael, 2670
Lyons, Michael, 2670
Lyons, Michael, 2671
Lyons, Nicolai, 1145
Lyons, Rosa Anna, 3010
Lyttle, Cecie, 2843
Lyttle, Hy, 2843
Lyttle, Ida Kate, 2843
Lyttle, Mary, 2843
Lyzer [or Lzzer], Mary, 2689
Lyzer [or Lzzer], Saml. W., 2689
Lyzer [or Lzzer], Wesley, 2689
M. [blank], Jacobus, 1688
M___ [blank], Jos., 3566
MacCoskey, Peter, 1916
MacDonald, Mary, 2294
Macginty, Elizabeth, 40
Macginty, Elizabeth, 40
Macken, Jas. (Rev.), 4172

MacLain, Margaretha, 4412
Maclain, Annae Elisabeth, 1768
Maclain, Martha Susanna, 1768
MaClain, Martha, 1768
Maclain, Upton, 1768
MacMahon, Richardum Randolph, 4778
Madan, Sara, 1153
Madden, Birgitta, 1359
Madden, Birgitta, 1418
Madden, Eleonora, 1230
Madden, Hanora, 1404
Madden, Joannis, 1230
Madden, Mariae, 1230
Madden, Michael, 1404
Madden, Patricius, 1473
Maddoc [or Maddoe], Emma Eliza, 2415
Maddoc [or Maddoe], Emma, 2415
Maddoc [or Maddoe], Wm., 2415
Maddon, Edwardus, 1170
Maddon, Joannis, 1170
Maddon, Sarae, 1170
Made, Anna, 1088
Mades, Jeremiah, 4264
Madison, Maria Francesca, 3470
Madison, Maria Francesca, 3471

Madison, Maria Francesca, 3479
Madison, Maria Francesca, 3515
Maffatt, Hermione, 3204
Maffatt, Hermione Virginiam, 3205
Maffatt, Hermione, 3205
Maffatt, Isaac, 3204
Maffatt, Isaac, 3205
Maffatt, Mariam, 3204
Magee, Hugh, 241
Magee, Joseph Henery, 241
Magee, Mary, 241
Mager, Peter, 311
Magguire, Jane, 2761
Magher, Martinus, 1543
Magher, Guillelimus, 1761
Magher, John, 4251
Magonigle, Margaret, 4618
Magonigle, James, 2536
Maguire, Cathar, 2820
Maguire, Ann S., 2563
Maguire, Ann, 2857
Maguire, Anna, 2497
Maguire, Barbara, 2234
Maguire, Cath., 2601
Maguire, Catharina, 3555
Maguire, Catharine, 2437
Maguire, Catharine, 4583

Maguire, E. (Miss), 4519
Maguire, E. (Miss), 4520
Maguire, E. (Miss), 4527
Maguire, E. (Miss), 4532
Maguire, Elizabeth M., 2168
Maguire, Elizabeth, 2321
Maguire, J. I.[or J.] (Rev.), 4583
Maguire, James Augustine, 2234
Maguire, James, 2234
Maguire, Jane B., 2735
Maguire, Jane, 2536
Maguire, Jane, 2643
Maguire, Jane, 2652
Maguire, Jane, 2833
Maguire, Jane, 2857
Maguire, Jane, 3076
Maguire, Julia, 2039
Maguire, Kate, 5799
Maguire, Mary Elizabeth (Miss), 4535
Maguire, Mary Elizabeth, 2038
Maguire, Mary S. (Miss), 1948
Maguire, Matthew, 2120
Maguire, Rev. J, 4580
Maguire, Susan, 4576
Mahany, Ellen, 2577
Maheny, Margaret, 149

Maher, Andrew, 42
Maher, Christina, 193
Maher, Christina, 42
Maher, Elisabeth, 193
Maher, Nicholas D., 3571
Maher, Patk., 42
Maher, Patrick, 193
Maher, Robert, 4161
Mahew, Maria, 4130
Mahon, Ellen, 3060
Mahon, Anna, 1352
Mahon, Annae, 1455
Mahon, Bernardus, 1343
Mahon, Bernardus, 1775
Mahon, Catharina, 3132
Mahon, Catherine, 3060
Mahon, Jacobi, 1455
Mahon, Joanne, 3132
Mahon, John, 3060
Mahon, John, 4317
Mahon, Patricius, 1455
Mahon, Patricius, 1785
Mahon, Philippum, 3132
Mahon, Sarah, 3060
Mahon, William, 3060
Mahoney, Arabella Frances, 2980
Mahoney, Danial, 4316

Mahoney, Ellan, 4413
Mahoney, Elmira, 2187
Mahoney, Elmira, 2188
Mahoney, Elmira, 2189
Mahoney, Elmira, 2190
Mahoney, Francis Marshall, 2980
Mahoney, George, 2187
Mahoney, Johanna, 4638
Mahoney, Margaret, 2189
Mahoney, Martha, 2190
Mahoney, Mary, 4703
Mahoney, Mary, 85
Mahoney, Rebecca, 3560
Mahoney, Stephen, 3560
Mahoney, Stephen, 4693
Mahoney, Thomas, 2188
Mahoney, Thomem Sylvestrem, 3560
Mahoney, William, 2187
Mahoney, William, 2188
Mahoney, William, 2189
Mahoney, William, 2190
Mahoney, Wilm, 4286
Mahoney, Wm., 2980
Mahony, Arrabella Frances, 2764
Mahony, Charles William, 2764
Mahony, Esther, 4992

Mahony, Johanna, 2664
Mahony, Mary Ann, 2664
Mahony, Mary, 32
Mahony, Patr., 2664
Mahony, Patr., 4633
Mahony, William, 2764
Mahony, Wm., 4658
Main, Philip, 167
Maines, Thomas, 1217
Maines, Thomas, 1532
Maines, Thomas, 4539
Mains, Catharine, 167
Mains, P., 59
Mains, Philip, 127
Mains, Philip, 156
Mains, Philip, 33
Mains, Philip, 85
Mains, Philip, 4
Mains, Philip, 57
Mains, Philip, 58
Mains, Thomas, 126
Mains, Thomas, 1621
Mains, Thomas, 248
Mains, Thomas, 54
Mains, Thos, 166
Mains, Thos, 179
Mains, Thos, 34

Mains, Thos, 29
Mains, Thos, 30
Makay [or Nakay], Charlotte (Mrs.), 580
Makens, Anna Elisabeth, 1550
Makens, Eliae, 1550
Makens, Elisabeth, 1550
MaKenzy, Catharina, 1129
MaKenzy, Eliae, 1129
MaKenzy, Elisabeth, 1129
Makes, William, 1928
Mallery, Patricii, 1171
Mallery, Patricius, 1171
Mallery, Sarae, 1171
Mallon, Birgettae, 1293
Mallon, Elisabeth, 1293
Mallon, Jaannes, 4481
Mallon, Neale, 1293
Mallon, Patricius, 1444
Malone, Maria, 3267
Malone, Bessie, 3892
Malone, Catherine, 3018
Malone, Ellen, 2942
Malone, Hugh (Mrs.), 4643
Malone, Hugh, 2907
Malone, Hugh, 3018
Malone, Hugh, 3225

Malone, Hugh, 4642
Malone, Hugh, 4643
Malone, Hugone, 3109
Malone, Jacobo, 4855
Malone, Jacobus (Mrs.), 3412
Malone, Jacobus Patricius, 3109
Malone, Jacobus, 3267
Malone, Jacobus, 3412
Malone, Jacobus, 3918
Malone, James P., 5367
Malone, James, 2942
Malone, James, 3018
Malone, James, 5323
Malone, Jas., 2942
Malone, Margaretha, 3524
Malone, Maria, 3109
Malone, Maria, 3225
Malone, Maria, 3522
Malone, Maria, 3523
Malone, Maria, 3594
Malone, Maria, 3640
Malone, Maria, 4878
Malone, Mariam Joseph, 3225
Malone, Mary Eliz., 2907
Malone, Mary, 2907
Malone, Mary, 3018
Malone, Mary, 5345

Malone, Mrs., 4057
Maloney, Margaritem, 4802
Maloney, Maria, 3599
Malony, Emma J., 2790
Maloon, Benjamin, 64
Maloon, Catharine, 64
Maloon, Wm, 64
Malot, Elias, 2648
Malot, Jno., 2648
Malot, Margaret Ann, 2648
Malott, Margaret A., 4684
Maloy, Robertus, 1523
Man, Joannes, 1389
Manford, J.S., 4884
Mangen, John, 24
Maniou, Mary (Miss), 4247
Manley, D., 3681
Manley, D., 3684
Manley, D., 3685
Manley, D., 3686
Manley, Domenicus, 3721
Manley, Domincus, 3740
Manley, Joannes, 3653
Manning, James, 4341
Mannon, Elisabeth, 1236
Mannon, Joannes son, 1236
Mannon, Richardi, 1236

Mansfield, Joannes, 1369
Mansfield, Ellen, 1369
Mantague, Sara, 3804
Manuel, Maria Anna, 670
Manuel, Mariae, 670
Manuel, Thomas, 670
Manwarren?, Elisabeth, 967
Manwarren?, Patricius, 967
Manwarren?, Richardi, 967
March, Jacobo, 3956
March, Jacobo, 4013
March, Lillie (Mrs.), 3878
March, Lillie Magdalenam, 4013
March, Lillie, 3956
March, Lillie, 4013
March, Paulum Lesley, 3956
Marco, Elizabeth, 2530
Mardam, Elisabeth, 774
Mardam, Michael, 774
Mardam, Richardi, 774
Marellues, Saml, 532
Mark, Blanche, 4914
Marken, Margaretae, 1275
Markin, Rebecca, 4000
Marko, Elizabeth, 2560
Markoe, Elizabeth (Miss), 4596
Markoe, Elizabeth, 2464

Marks, Carolina, 649
Marks, Carolina, 649
Marks, Joannis, 649
Marks, Benjamin, 4652
Marlot, Jno. Stillwell, 2841
Marlot, John, 2841
Marlot, Margt., 2841
Marlot, Margt., 2893
Marlow, Emma, 3944
Marlow, Emma, 4123
Marony, Mary, 2327
Marony, Patrick, 2327
Marony, Thomas, 2327
Marren, [blank], 678
Marren, Joannes, 678
Marren, Patricii, 678
Marsh, Rosa, 3483
Marshal, Agnes Emelina, 993
Marshal, Agnetis Emelinae, 993
Marshal, Elizabeth (Miss), 4226
Marshal, Joannis, 993
Marshall, Elizab., 117
Marshall, Elizabeth, 163
Marshbay, Elizabeth, 600
Marten, David, 2036
Marten, Rosanna, 2133
Martil, Jacob, 2205

Martil, John Joseph, 2205
Martil, Mary, 2205
Martin, Ann R., 4609
Martin, Anna F., 3583
Martin, Anna F., 3689
Martin, Anna F., 3742
Martin, Anna, 2035
Martin, Anna, 3640
Martin, Anna, 3803
Martin, Anna, 3871
Martin, Amam F., 4770
Martin, Christina, 2710
Martin, Clarence V., 3915
Martin, Clarence, 4048
Martin, Clarence, 4121
Martin, Clifford P., 3845
Martin, Clifford R., 4835
Martin, Cristina, 2771
Martin, David (Mrs.), 4081
Martin, David, 2352
Martin, David, 3978
Martin, David, 4014
Martin, David, 4588
Martin, Ednam Mariam, 3845
Martin, Eduardum Allen Alexander, 4147
Martin, Elizabeth, 2352

Martin, Emery, 3392
Martin, Ernestum Austin, 3915
Martin, Gertrude, 3932
Martin, Henricus, 4168
Martin, Henrietta, 4014
Martin, Isabel, 2352
Martin, Jennie, 4850
Martin, Jno. S. (Rev.), 3742
Martin, Joanne D., 3915
Martin, John H., 2328
Martin, John Henry, 4577
Martin, John, 2170
Martin, Joseph H., 4875
Martin, Joseph H., 4906
Martin, Joseph, 4147
Martin, Joseph, 4152
Martin, Josephina, 3392
Martin, Loretta, 2036
Martin, Lorretta, 1822
Martin, Lorretto, 2287
Martin, Lucy, 2328
Martin, Ludovicum Augustinum, 4014
Martin, Margareta, 3832
Martin, Maria, 4109
Martin, Maria C., 4856
Martin, Maria C., 4875

Martin, Maria H., 3915
Martin, Maria, 3845
Martin, Maria, 4014
Martin, Maria, 4147
Martin, Maria, 4906
Martin, Mariam Cecilliam, 3392
Martin, Mary (Mrs.), 3978
Martin, Mary Loretto, 2328
Martin, Mary Loretto, 2328
Martin, Mary, 2230
Martin, Mary, 2655
Martin, Michael, 1256
Martin, Minnie A., 4868
Martin, Nicholem B., 4796
Martin, Sophia, 3932
Martin, Susanna, 3919
Martin, Susanna, 3965
Martin, Susanna, 4036
Martin, Virginia, 4147
Martiney, Sarah, 4677
Martinez, Sara, 3096
Martini, Sallie, 3062
Martini, Sallie, 3230
Martiny, Sallie, 5502
Martiny, Sallie, 2614
Martiny, Sallie, 2650
Martiny, Sallie, 5466

Martiny, Sallie, 5523
Martiny, Sallie, 5791
Martiny, Sally, 2840
Martiny, Sally, 2865
Martiny, Wm. Carroll, 2840
Marton, Clarence, 4014
Martz, Anna, 3111
Martz, Anna, 3111
Martz, Benjamin, 3111
Martz, Carolus E., 3111
Mashuk, Christina, 42
Masom, Elisabeth, 710
Mason, John T., 4611
Mason, John, 4295
Mason, Judge [John T.], 2772
Mason, Judge, 5054
Mason, Mr., 4569
Mason, Mrs., 203
Mass, Peter, 4177
Masterson, Michael, 1202
Maten, Mary I., 2821
Matheus, Henriettae, 1219
Matheus, Jannis, 1219
Matheus, Johanna Rebecca, 1219
Mathew, Jacobus, 1305
Mathews, Alys Virginia, 1765

Mathews, Eleonora, 1430
Mathews, Elleonorae, 1820
Mathews, Henriettae, 1430
Mathews, Henriettae, 1765
Mathews, Joannis, 1430
Mathews, Joannis, 1765
Mathews, Patricii, 1820
Mathews, Patricius, 1814
Mathews, Thomas, 1820
Matheyly, Margret (Miss), 335
Mathinging, Mary, 352
Mattewes, Patricius, 4501
Matthews, Ann, 1899
Matthews, Annam Rachelem, 4135
Matthews, Francisco, 4872
Matthews, Harriet Ann, 1942
Matthews, Harriet his wife, 1942
Matthews, Harriet, 1899
Matthews, Harriet, 2126
Matthews, Jacobo, 4135
Matthews, Jacoburn Gulielmum, 4872
Matthews, John, 1899
Matthews, John, 1942
Matthews, John, 2126
Matthews, Maria, 1846
Matthews, Maria, 4135

Matthews, Mary Martha, 2126
Matthews, Preston, 4137
Mattingby, Elisabeth Catharine, 4479
Mattingly, Henrietta, 1687
Mattingly, Helena Eugenia, 1485
Mattingly, Mary (Miss), 367
Mattingly, Williamson, 1687
Matton, Birgitta Matton, 1133
Maudy, Mary, 5192
Mauley, Joannes, 3653
Maurice, Birgitta, 1573
Maurice, Anna, 1237
Maurice, Birgita, 1280
Maurice, Birgita, 1280
Maurice, Birgitta, 4500
Mauricy, Annae, 1131
Mauricy, Birgittae, 1193
Mauricy, Catharina, 1191
Mauricy, Catharina, 1574
Mauricy, David, 1131
Mauricy, Maria, 1131
Maurs, Elizabeth, 3713
Maurs, Elizabetha, 3731
Maus, Catharina, 647
Maus, Elisabeth Johanna, 1393
Maus, Joannae, 647

Maus, Margaretae, 1393
Maus, Petri, 647
Mause, J.M., 4787
Mausfield, Eleonorae, 1259
Mausfield, Joannes, 1259
Mausfield, Joannis, 1259
Mavier, Catharine, 2567
Maxwell, Catharinae, 644
Maxwell, Guillelini, 644
Maxwell, Guillellarus, 644
Maxwell, Margareta, 4450
May, Catharine, 2125
May, Elizabeth, 614
May, Elizabeth, 1910
May, Elizabeth, 1911
May, Elizabeth, 2055
May, Elizabeth, 2125
May, James Henry, 2055
May, James, 1910
May, James, 1911
May, James, 2055
May, James, 2125
May, M.W.L., 4755
May, Mary, 1910
May, Mary Mercy, 592
May, Mercy, 2112
May, Mercy (Miss), 2284

May, Mercy (Miss), 4583
May, Mercy, 2028
May, Mercy, 2077
May, Mercy, 2251
May, Mercy, 2321
May, Mercy, 2385
May, Mercy, 2425
May, Mercy, 4586
May, Mercy, 4587
May, Miss, 3519
May, Simon, 1911
May, Sophia, 4445
May, W. L., 3148
May, W. L., 3285
May, W.L., 3286
May, W.L., 3287
May, W.L., 4699
May, Wilhelmina Amelia Louisa, 3274
May, Wilhelmina L., 3289
May, Wilhelmina L., 3313
May, Wilhelmina L., 3677
May, Wilhelmina Louisa, 3234
May, Wilhelmina Maria Louisa, 3255
May, Wilhelmina, 2992
May, Wilhelmina, 3215

May, Wilhelmina, 3298
May, Wilhelmina, 3376
May, Wilhelmina, 5310
Mayar [or Magarn], Patrick, 4419
Mayberry, Margaret (Mrs.), 5225
Mayberry, Margt, 2921
Mayberry, Maria C., 3942
Mayberry, Maria, 4011
Mayberry, Mariam C., 4841
Mayberry, Mary Cath., 2921
Mayberry, Peter Justinian, 4673
Mayberry, Peter, 2921
Maygher, Martinus, 1543
Mayhew, Anna E., 3690
Mayhew, Anna E., 3788
Mayhew, Anna E., 3890
Mayhew, Anna E., 3988
Mayhew, Anna, 4134
Mayhew, Annam E., 4786
Mayhew, Clement, 3365
Mayhew, Clemente, 3769
Mayhew, Clyde Vincintium, 3365
Mayhew, Frances, 3365
Mayhew, Frances, 5715
Mayhew, Francisca, 3769
Mayhew, Georgium Earl, 3769
Mayhew, Irene, 3877

Mayhew, Irenes, 3769
Mayhew, Irenes, 3865
Mayhew, William, 5221
Mayhue, Clemento, 3486
Mayhue, Francesca, 3486
Mayhue, Gulielmum Francis, 3486
Mayhugh, Anna, 3961
Mayhugh, Clement, 2996
Mayhugh, Francis, 2996
Mayhugh, Lydia, 3475
Mayhugh, Mary Irene, 2996
Maynon, Eleonorae, 1192
Maynon, Franciscus Thomas, 1192
Maynon, Patricii, 1192
Maysinger, Margareta, 1666
Maysinger, Jacob, 1666
Maysinger, Jacob, 4456
McAafferty, Annae, 1000
McAafferty, Joannes, 1000
McAafferty, Joannis, 1000
McAdam, Catharina, 1782
McAdams, Jacobus, 1339
McAdams, Jacobus, 1485
McAdams, James, 9
McAffrey, Elisabeth, 4422
McAffrey, Arthur, 1329
McAffrey, Birgittae, 1329

McAffrey, Jacobus, 1329
McAleny, Frances Ann, 146
McAleny, Mary, 146
McAleny, Michael, 146
McAleny, Michael, 4189
McAlister, Eleonora, 899
McAlister, Emilia, 1460
McAlister, Margaretae, 899
McAlister, Patricii, 899
McAlleaney, Letitia, 2762
McAlleny, Laetitia, 2745
McAllister, Elizabeth, 9
McAltee, Edwardus, 1786
McAltee, Maria, 1788
McAltee, Mariae, 1786
McAltee, Walter, 1786
McAnally, Joannes, 1721
McAnally, Joannis, 1721
McAnally, Johanna, 1454
McAnally, Maria, 1721
McAnaly, Bernardus, 989
McAnaly, Joannae, 989
McAnaly, Thomae, 989
McAnaney, Franciscus, 1325
McAnaney, Johannae, 1325
McAnaney, Mary, 2267
McAnaney, Thomae, 1325

McAnany, Ann, 2703
McAnany, Francisci, 1572
McAnany, Margareta Anna, 1572
McAnany, Mariae, 1572
McAneny, Francis, 2096
McAneny, John Patrick, 2096
McAneny, Mary, 2096
McAnnally, Patricius, 1324
McAnneny, Francisa, 1012
McAnneny, Franciscus, 1012
McAnneny, Mariae, 1012
McAnnis, Joannes, 1028
McAnnis, Joannis, 1028
McAnnis, Mariae, 1028
McAnony, Annae, 1374
McAnony, Joannes Bop (Owen), 1374
McAnony, Patricii, 1374
McAntere, Rosanna, 152
McAnulty, Daniel, 486
McAnulty, Margaret, 88
McAnulty, William, 88
McAnulty, Edward, 149
McAnulty, Margaret, 171
McAnulty, Mary (Mrs.), 108
McArdele, Alice Johanna, 1656
McArdele, Mariae, 1656

McArdele, Richardi, 1656
McArdell, Ambrose, 4657
McArdell, Ann, 148
McArdell, Anna, 1656
McArdell, Courtney, 4586
McArdell, Thomas, 148
McArdell, Thos (Mrs.), 86
McArdell, Ulton F., 4586
McArdle, Ambrose D., 2816
McArdle, Anna, 2357
McArdle, Anna, 5375
McArdle, Catharine, 2308
McArdle, Cecilia, 2816
McArdle, Rolin Eugene, 2816
McArdle, Wilfred D., 2308
McArdle, Wilfred D., 2425
McArdle, Wilfred H., 2308
McAtee, Ann, 95
McAtee, Ann, 96
McAtee, Bennet, 96
McAtee, Wm, 95
McAtee, Cassandra, 2066
McAtee, Cassandra, 1966
McAtee, Georgius, 1179
McAtee, James Walter, 1966
McAtee, Jonathan, 1966

McAtee, Jonathan, 2066
McAtee, Mary, 84
McAtee, Polly, 95
McAtee, Samuelis, 1179
McAtee, Samuelis, 1180
McAtee, Sarae, 1179
McAtee, Sarae, 1180
McAtee, Thomas Jefferson, 2066
McAtee, Thomas, 84
McAtee, Walter, 84
McAtee, Walterius, 1180
McAtee, Waltr., 96
McAttee, Cassandra, 2283
McAttee, Elizabeth Rebecca, 2283
McAttee, Jacobus, 1796
McAttee, Johnathan, 2283
McAttee, Maria, 1796
McAttee, Maria, 1797
McAttee, Maria, 1797
McAttee, Samuel, 1796
McAttee, Samuel, 1797
McAttee, Sara, 1796
McAttee, Sara, 1797
McAttie, Casanae, 1607
McAttie, Franciscus, 1607
McAttie, Jonathan, 1607
McAvoy, Bridget, 4749

McAvoy, Catharine, 2323
McAvoy, David, 2250
McAvoy, Edward, 2323
McAvoy, Maria, 3105
McAvoy, Mary, 2073
McAvoy, Mary, 2331
McAvoy, Patrick, 2073
McAvoy, Patrick, 2323
McAvoy, Rosa, 2835
McAvoy, Rosa, 5573
McAvoy, Thomas, 2073
McAvoy, William, 2331
McBride, Maria, 1700
McBride, William J., 4603
McCabe, Anna, 1477
McCabe, blank, 730
McCabe, Elizabeth, 1865
McCabe, Franciscus, 1080
McCabe, James, 2143
McCabe, Jane, 2193
McCabe, Jdudy [sic], 4310
McCabe, Joannes, 730
McCabe, Juliae, 1080
McCabe, Maria, 1731
McCabe, Mariae, 1477
McCabe, Mariae, 1731
McCabe, Mary, 1865
McCabe, Mary, 2143
McCabe, Mary, 4435
McCabe, Patricii, 1080
McCabe, Patricii, 730
McCabe, Rosa Anna, 1619
McCabe, Rosa, 643
McCabe, Rosanna, 1932
McCabe, Terence, 2143
McCabe, Terrenticie, 1731
McCabe, Terrentii, 1477
McCabe, Tevens [sic], 1865
McCadden, Patrick, 1966
McCafferty, [blank], 199
McCafferty, [blank], 199
McCafferty, John Francis, 199
McCafferty, Margret (widow), 4269
McCafferty, Mrs., 388
McCafferty, Mrs., 339
McCafferty, Mrs., 406
McCafferty, Mrs., 484
McCaffrey, Rev. Th., 4598
McCaffrey, Thos. A., 2416
McCain, Charles, 4461
McCain, Margaret, 2309
McCall, Anna, 3851
McCall, Carolum Victorem, 3851
McCall, Jacobo, 3851
McCall, Jacobum, 4833
McCalleen, Martha, 2852
McCallen, Augustin, 2987
McCallen, Martha, 2987
McCallesten, Arahy?, 250
McCallesten, Arthur, 250
McCallesten, Catharine, 250
McCallion, Joseph, 5228
McCallion, Martha, 3154
McCallon, Martha, 3375
McCameron, Clagett Nelson, 2602
McCameron, Ellen, 2602
McCameron, Nelson, 2602
McCameron, Wm. Thos. Alex., 4968
McCan, Annae, 1438
McCan, Barnay, 2413
McCan, Cordelia, 2412
McCan, Cordelia, 2413
McCan, Elizabeth, 2413
McCan, Joanni, 1438
McCan, Michael, 1438
McCan, Sarah (Mrs.), 270
McCane, Mary Ellon, 577
McCane, Sarah, 577
McCane, Thos., 577
McCane?, Georgeris Alexander Fox, 928
McCane?, Sarae, 928
McCane?, Thomae, 928
McCann, George, 1949
McCann, John, 1949
McCann, Rosanna, 1949
McCann, Ann, 2029
McCann, Ann, 2202
McCann, Ann, 2203
McCann, Ann, 2238
McCann, Annae, 1116
McCann, Ella, 4085
McCann, Frances, 263
McCann, Francis, 264
McCann, Francis, 265
McCann, Geo, 5558
McCann, Geo. 5597
McCann, Hugh, 2029
McCann, Hugh, 263
McCann, Jane, 264
McCann, Joannes, 4409
McCann, Joannis, 1116
McCann, John, 2029
McCann, John, 2082
McCann, John, 2203
McCann, John, 4518

McCann, Julia, 2602
McCann, Lucenda, 263
McCann, Margaret, 2203
McCann, Maria Anna, 1116
McCann, Mary Catharine, 2082
McCann, Mary Hanna, 265
McCann, Mary, 5563
McCann, Mary, 5598
McCann, Mrs., 309
McCann, Peter, 2202
McCann, Rosanna, 2082
McCann, Sarah, 263
McCann, Sarah, 264
McCann, Sarah, 265
McCann, Thomas, 2202
McCanna, Elizabeth, 2
McCardal, Miss Lucreatia, 251
McCardel, Alfred Henry Myers, 2173
McCardel, Ann E., 2733
McCardel, Anna Ada, 2274
McCardel, Anna Maria, 2274
McCardel, Belinda Mary Eugenia, 2173
McCardel, Belinda, 2049
McCardel, C., 4564
McCardel, Catharine, 2160

McCardel, Edmund Didier, 2733
McCardel, Elizabeth, 3669
McCardel, Evelina, 2733
McCardel, Guleilmo, 3669
McCardel, Lucreatia (Miss), 286
McCardel, Mariam Golden, 3669
McCardel, Mary Alverta, 2160
McCardel, Mary Laura, 2049
McCardel, Richard, 2274
McCardel, Thomas C., 2173
McCardel, Thomas C., 2259
McCardel, Timon Wetleby, 2173
McCardel, Ulton, 2733
McCardel, Wilfred, 2160
McCardel, Williby, 2049
McCardell, Ann, 2555
McCardell, Anna, 4897
McCardell, Georgius (Mrs.), 4108
McCardell, Georgio, 4897
McCardell, Addie Eugeniam, 3848
McCardell, Albertus Melito, 2639
McCardell, Alfred, 3238
McCardell, Alfredo, 3643
McCardell, Alfredo, 4799
McCardell, Alfredun Earl Morrill, 3643
McCardell, Alice Eve, 3019

McCardell, Alice, 2924
McCardell, Aliciam Ryan, 4136
McCardell, Ambr. [Ambrose], 2944
McCardell, Ann (Mrs.), 3014
McCardell, Ann (Mrs.), 3019
McCardell, Ann (Mrs.), 4987
McCardell, Ann E., 2503
McCardell, Ann Maria, 2056
McCardell, Ann, 2361
McCardell, Ann, 2362
McCardell, Ann, 2828
McCardell, Ann, 4760
McCardell, Anna, 109
McCardell, Anna Cecilia, 2696
McCardell, Anna E., 3549
McCardell, Anna M., 4077
McCardell, Anna M., 4132
McCardell, Anna, 1441
McCardell, Anna, 2555
McCardell, Anna, 2924
McCardell, Anna, 3218
McCardell, Anna, 3319
McCardell, Anna, 3320
McCardell, Anna, 3321
McCardell, Anna, 3669
McCardell, Anna, 4136

McCardell, Anna, 5477
McCardell, Annam Helenam, 3920
McCardell, Annam Margaritam, 3588
McCardell, Anne, 2923
McCardell, Annie, 2828
McCardell, Belinda Mary E., 2401
McCardell, Belinda, 2056
McCardell, Belinda, 2502
McCardell, Belinda, 2579
McCardell, Belinda, 2614
McCardell, Belinda, 2656
McCardell, Belinda, 2761
McCardell, Belinda, 3188
McCardell, Belinda, 3191
McCardell, Belinda, 3218
McCardell, Belinda, 5111
McCardell, Blair, 4760
McCardell, Brazilia, 2579
McCardell, Catharine M., 2526
McCardell, Catharine Mari, 2432
McCardell, Catharine, 2567
McCardell, Catharine, 2639
McCardell, Cecilia, 2944
McCardell, Ceciliam Agnetem, 4112
McCardell, Charles D., 2502

McCardell, Charles, 4981
McCardell, Chas., 2696
McCardell, Effie R., 4008
McCardell, Effie, 3848
McCardell, Effie, 3920
McCardell, Effie, 4086
McCardell, Effie, 4158
McCardell, Elizabeth Francescam, 3541
McCardell, Elizabeth, 3881
McCardell, Ernesto F., 4064
McCardell, Ernesto F., 4112
McCardell, Ernesto, 4883
McCardell, Ernestum F., 4884
McCardell, Eugenio, 4158
McCardell, Eugenio, 3848
McCardell, Eugenio, 4086
McCardell, Eugenis, 3920
McCardell, Eugenius, 1441
McCardell, Eugenius, 3755
McCardell, Eva Maria, 5286
McCardell, Evam Mariam, 3960
McCardell, Francis Ernest, 2944
McCardell, Franciscum Eugenium, 4064
McCardell, Frederick Brien, 2567
McCardell, Genevef Regina, 2761

McCardell, Geo. Adrian, 2828
McCardell, George Willoughby, 2056
McCardell, George, 4161
McCardell, Georgio W., 4136
McCardell, Georgium W., 4888
McCardell, Georgius, 4108
McCardell, Gulielmum Ernestum, 4008
McCardell, Helena S., 3588
McCardell, Helena, 3623
McCardell, Helena, 3695
McCardell, Helena, 3737
McCardell, Helena, 3960
McCardell, Helena, 4021
McCardell, Irenes, 3854
McCardell, Irenam Juliam, 3623
McCardell, Jacobo B., 3588
McCardell, Jacobo B., 3737
McCardell, Jacobo Percy, 4077
McCardell, Jacobo, 3623
McCardell, Jacobo, 3695
McCardell, Jacobo, 3960
McCardell, Jacobo, 4021
McCardell, Jacobum B., 4781
McCardell, Jacobum Percy, 4897
McCardell, Jacobum Riorden, 4077

McCardell, Jacobus, 3599
McCardell, James Buchanan, 2555
McCardell, Janettie C.A., 5764
McCardell, Jean, 4086
McCardell, Jesse Sorrel, 2924
McCardell, John Roy Larcunbe, 3019
McCardell, Jonas Spielman, 2923
McCardell, Joseph, 4021
McCardell, Kate, 2696
McCardell, L. (Mrs.), 3931
McCardell, Laurence Willibey, 2401
McCardell, Lillie Gertrude, 5771
McCardell, Lillie, 3956
McCardell, Lillie, 4013
McCardell, Lilly Josephine, 2656
McCardell, Lucretia Parthenia, 2526
McCardell, Lucretia, 109
McCardell, Mariae, 1441
McCardell, Mariae, 949
McCardell, Mariam Amandam, 4132
McCardell, Mariam Angellam, 3695
McCardell, Mrs., 4186

McCardell, Mrs., 94
McCardell, Nettie R., 4799
McCardell, Norman Rollin, 4086
McCardell, O'Dellon Dubois, 2432
McCardell, Olton F., 3623
McCardell, Percey, 4132
McCardell, R. Eugeneo, 4008
McCardell, Riccardum King, 4158
McCardell, Richard, 163
McCardell, Richard P., 2056
McCardell, Richardi, 1441
McCardell, Richardi, 949
McCardell, Rina [sic], 3643
McCardell, Rina, 4799
McCardell, Rollini Eugene, 4821
McCardell, Thomam Flynn, 3737
McCardell, Thomas G. [or J.], 949
McCardell, Thomas, 109
McCardell, Thomas, 3019
McCardell, Thos, 4186
McCardell, Thos., 2924
McCardell, Ultan, 109
McCardell, Ultim, 2923
McCardell, Ulton F., 2503
McCardell, Ulton, 2555
McCardell, Ulton, 2828
McCardell, Vertie, 4064

McCardell, Vertie, 4112
McCardell, Wilfred D., 2432
McCardell, Wilfred D., 2567
McCardell, Wilfred, 2526
McCardell, Wilfrid, 2639
McCardell, Wilfrid, 4990
McCardell, Willabee, 2656
McCardell, Willebee, 2761
McCardell, Willebey, 2502
McCardell, William Blair Morin, 2503
McCardell, Willibey, 2401
McCardell, Williby, 2579
McCardle, Irenem Adelaidem, 3736
McCardle, John Henry, 3736
McCardle, Julia, 3736
McCardle, Adrian Ceolfrid, 1883
McCardle, Ambrose, 3228
McCardle, Ambrose, 3229
McCardle, Ambrose, 3617
McCardle, Ambrosius, 3779
McCardle, Ann, 1883
McCardle, Anna E., 3486
McCardle, Anna Virginia, 1918
McCardle, Anne, 2425
McCardle, Annie, 5788

McCardle, Belinda, 1918
McCardle, Bettie, 3388
McCardle, Bettie, 3485
McCardle, Blair, 3388
McCardle, Blair, 3485
McCardle, C., 4616
McCardle, Catharine, 1883
McCardle, Cecilia, 3228
McCardle, Cecilia, 3229
McCardle, Dne?[ne is superscript] Anna, 3388
McCardle, Effie, 3779
McCardle, Elizabeth F., 3779
McCardle, Elizabeth, 3594
McCardle, Elizabeth, 3781
McCardle, Eugenio, 3779
McCardle, Eugenio, 4803
McCardle, Georgium Alvey, 3388
McCardle, Gulielmo Blair, 3594
McCardle, Gulielmum Earl, 3485
McCardle, Jacobum Lee Roy, 3594
McCardle, James Percy, 3229
McCardle, Joseph Maguire, 2425
McCardle, L., 4810
McCardle, Latitia, 3618
McCardle, Margaritem Caceilliam, 3779

McCardle, Simon W., 1918
McCardle, Thom F., 5215
McCardle, Ulton F., 2425
McCardle, Upton Franciscum, 3484
McCardle, Wilfrid D., 1883
McCardle, William Walsh, 3228
McCarr, Annae, 1713
McCarr, Elisabeth, 1713
McCarr, Joannis, 1713
McCarrol, Anna, 1489
McCarrol, Mariae, 1489
McCarter, Georgim, 3627
McCarter, Georgius, 3468
McCarter, Maria J., 3672
McCarter, Maria J., 3673
McCartey, Barnay, 1886
McCartey, Barnay, 1999
McCartey, Barnay, 2137
McCartey, Barnay, 2233
McCartey, Barney, 2489
McCartey, Catharine, 2444
McCartey, Catharine, 5482
McCartey, Catherine, 545
McCartey, David, 2233
McCartey, Edward, 545
McCartey, Edward, 545

McCartey, Harriet, 1886
McCartey, Harriet, 1999
McCartey, Harriet, 2137
McCartey, Harriet, 2233
McCartey, Harriet, 2489
McCartey, John Alexander, 2137
McCartey, Levi, 2489
McCartey, Margaret Ann, 1886
McCartey, Mary, 1999
McCartey, William, 2155
McCarthey, Barney, 2346
McCarthey, Catharine Elizabeth, 2346
McCarthey, Harriet, 2346
McCarthy, Dan, 5099
McCarthy, Giorgium, 3428
McCarthy, Jerome, 54
McCarthy, Joannes, 1333
McCarthy, Joannes, 1619
McCarthy, John, 2503
McCarthy, Joseph, 3428
McCarthy, Julia, 2315
McCarthy, Margaret, 54
McCarthy, Margaret, 54
McCarthy, Margaret, 55
McCarthy, Maria, 3359
McCarthy, Maria, 3360

McCarthy, Maria, 3361
McCarthy, Maria, 3363
McCarthy, Maria, 3428
McCarthy, Maria, 3441
McCarthy, Patrick, 5424
McCartin, Catharinae, 1667
McCartin, Edward, 4189
McCartin, Edwardi, 1667
McCartin, Edwd, 114
McCartin, Margareta, 1667
McCartin, Mary, 2963
McCartney, Catharinae, 1578
McCartney, Catharinae, 893
McCartney, Catharine, 2045
McCartney, Catherine, 505
McCartney, Catherine, 606
McCartney, Edward, 2045
McCartney, Edward, 505
McCartney, Edward, 606
McCartney, Edwardi, 1578
McCartney, Edwardi, 893
McCartney, Henry, 2045
McCartney, Henry, 5635
McCartney, Jacobas, 893
McCartney, John, 606
McCartney, Maria Anna, 1578
McCartney, Mary, 5151

McCartney, Mr., 5158
McCartney, Patricia, 5428
McCartney, Wilm, 505
McCarty, Alexr, 131
McCarty, Alexr, 132
McCarty, Anna, 1351
McCarty, Catharinae, 1136
McCarty, Catharinae, 696
McCarty, Catharine, 131
McCarty, Catharine, 132
McCarty, Edwardi, 1136
McCarty, Honora (Mrs.), 498
McCarty, James, 5413
McCarty, Maria Helena, 696
McCarty, Mary, 131
McCarty, Michaelis, 696
McCarty, Robert, 1136
McCaughan, Mary, 2450
McCauley, Anna, 1409
McCauley, Anna, 1605
McCauley, Annae, 1115
McCauley, Annae, 1409
McCauley, Annae, 1606
McCauley, Caroli, 1115
McCauley, Caroli, 1409
McCauley, Charoli, 1606

McCauley, Charolus, 4510
McCauley, Joanna, 1606
McCauley, Joannes, 4482
McCauley, Maria Anna, 1115
McCauley, Samuelem, 4758
McCavoy, Jane, 1996
McCavoy, Margaret, 2053
McCavoy, Mary, 1907
McCavoy, Mary, 1907
McCavoy, Patrick, 1907
McCavoy, Terence, 1907
McCavoy, Thomas, 1996
McCawley, Anna, 775
McCawly, Annae, 775
McCawly, Thomae, 775
McCelollane, Charlotte (widow), 4316
McClain, Ann, 3305
McClain, Anna, 3217
McClain, Wm. B. (Mrs.), 2846
McClain, Ambrose, 427
McClain, Am, 2514
McClain, Anna, 4691
McClain, Anna, 5580
McClain, Clara, 2626
McClain, Clara, 2627

McClain, Clarissa, 2037
McClain, Clarissa, 2462
McClain, Clarissa, 2547
McClain, Elesa, 482
McClain, Eliaza, 483
McClain, Elisa, 427
McClain, Elizab, 66
McClain, Elizab, 65
McClain, Elizabeth, 4179
McClain, Ellen Jane, 3571
McClain, Guglielmus, 3217
McClain, Henny, 172
McClain, James (Mrs.), 174
McClain, James (Mrs.), 65
McClain, James, 65
McClain, James A., 2462
McClain, James A., 4531
McClain, James B., 2627
McClain, James Buchanan, 2547
McClain, James, 111
McClain, James, 112
McClain, James, 2037
McClain, James, 2547
McClain, Jas., 2627
McClain, John Elie, 2462
McClain, John, 4208
McClain, John, 64

McClain, John, 65
McClain, Josia, 482
McClain, Josiah, 483
McClain, Josiah, 427
McClain, Lewis, 4298
McClain, Lucretia, 65
McClain, Lucy, 172
McClain, Magdalena, 5434
McClain, Margaret, 112
McClain, Margret (Mrs.), 427
McClain, Margrt. (Mrs.), 482
McClain, Maria, 66
McClain, Maria, 3781
McClain, Maria, 3812
McClain, Maria, 3813
McClain, Maria, 68
McClain, Martha Ann, 2037
McClain, Martha S., 3164
McClain, Martha S., 3118
McClain, Martha, 2272
McClain, Martha, 2273
McClain, Martha, 2517
McClain, Martha, 2667
McClain, Martha, 2736
McClain, Martha, 3258
McClain, Martha, 3305
McClain, Martha, 4655

McClain, Martha, 4700
McClain, Martin, 4691
McClain, Mary A.J. (Miss), 4238
McClain, Mary Ann J., 2517 (Miss), 4601
McClain, Mary Am, 2736
McClain, Mary D., 2568
McClain, Mary, 4715
McClain, Matilda, 3217
McClain, Mr., 2568
McClain, Mrs., 2568
McClain, Otho, 4301
McClain, Patsy, 4969
McClain, Peter (of John), 172
McClain, Rachel Ann, 2037
McClain, Sophia, 483
McClain, Tho., 482
McClain, Ultan, 112
McClain, Upton, 4509
McClain, W., 4558
McClain, William, 2139
McClain, William, 2517
McClain, William, 2736
McClain, William, 4236
McClain, Wm, 4601
McClain, Wm. B. (Mrs.), 2887
McClain, Wm. B., 2846

McClain, Wm. B., 2859
McClain, Wm. B., 2887
McClain, Wm. B., 2910
McClain, Wm., 2390
McClain, Wm., 3305
McClain, Wm., 4589
McClain, Wm., 5683
McClaine, Mrs., 2569
McClairy, Margaret A., 2572
McClanahan, Catharine, 2473
McClanahan, Catharine, 2474
McClane, Anna, 190
McClane, Elisa, 365
McClane, Elizabeth, 574
McClane, James, 190
McClane, Jessey, 365
McClane, Margret, 190
McClane, Martha Eliza Jane, 2655
McClane, Mary, 191
McClane, Mary, 2654
McClane, Mary, 2655
McClane, Mrs., 257
McClane, Mrs., 365
McClane, Nancy, 4204
McClane, Patr. Jas. Hogan, 2655
McClane, Sarah Anna, 190
McClane, Timy., 240

McClane, Upton, 365
McClane, Wilm (Mrs.), 542
McClaskey, Catharine (Mrs.), 2
McClearey, Jerome, 4619
McClearey, Margaret, 2472
McClearey, Catherine, 2763
McCleary, Eva (Mrs.), 3093
McCleary, Eva (Mrs.), 3899
McCleary, Eva, 2870
McCleary, Eva, 2921
McCleary, Eva, 3560
McCleary, Eva, 3681
McCleary, Eva, 3687
McCleary, F.B. (Mrs.), 4693
McCleary, F.B, 4693
McCleary, Jerome B., 2604
McCleary, Jerome, 2748
McCleary, Jerome, 2758
McCleary, Jerome, 4649
McCleary, Jerome, 4658
McCleary, Jerome, 4666
McCleary, John, 4189
McCleary, Kate, 2860
McCleary, Margaret, 2513
McCleary, Margaret, 2690
McCleary, Margt, 2860
McCleary, Maria, 1848

McCleery, Eva (Mrs.), 3467
McCleery, Eva, 3248
McCleery, Eva, 3433
McCleery, Jerome B., 4679
McCleery, Kate, 4679
McCleery, Kate, 4680
McCleery, Margaret Ann, 2532
McClenlen, Anna, 559
McClenlen, Catherine, 559
McClenlen, John, 559
McClery, Jerome B., 2704
McClery, Kate, 2572
McClosker, Charles, 149
McClosker, Fargus, 149
McClosker, Rosanna, 149
McCloskery, Margareth, 3020
McCloskey, Catharinae, 1008
McCloskey, Elisabeth, 1008
McCloskey, Mary Ann, 2580
McCloskey, Peter, 1977
McCloskey, Petrii, 1008
McClosky, Catharine, 53
McClosky, Charles, 53
McClosky, Maria Elisabeth, 1186
McClosky, Marthae, 1186
McClosky, Petri, 1186
McClosky, Petrus, 1400

McClosky, Philip, 53
McCloughlen, Margret, 222
McCoane, Jacobus, 1145
McComas, Bridget, 2299
McCondres, Bridget, 2070
McCondres, Bridget, 2070
McCondres, Mark, 2070
McConmal, Joannes M., 4381
McConster, Hugh, 2302
McCord, James, 299
McCord, Mary (Miss), 299
McCord, Nancy, 299
McCordel, Catharine, 2028
McCordel, Thomas C., 2028
McCordel, Thomas Edward William, 2028
McCordel, Wilfred, 2028
McCormack, Catharina, 1523
McCormack, Catharinae, 1556
McCormack, Dominicus Augustinus, 1556
McCormack, Edward, 1721
McCormack, Joannis, 1523
McCormack, Maria, 1524
McCormack, Mariae, 1523
McCormack, Patricius, 1493
McCormack, Thomae, 1556

McCormack, Thomas, 4480
McCormack, Wilm, 4307
McCormack, Mariae, 1250
McCormick, Anna (Mrs.), 4251
McCormick, Anna, 943
McCormick, Annae, 692
McCormick, Bridgett, 2489
McCormick, Francis, 4668
McCormick, Franciscis Michael, 939
McCormick, Guillelmi, 939
McCormick, Jacobus, 1323
McCormick, John, 4265
McCormick, Maatheus, 1197
McCormick, Margaret, 2300
McCormick, Mariae, 1323
McCormick, Mariae, 943
McCormick, Martini, 692
McCormick, Matheldis, 692
McCormick, Patricii, 1323
McCormick, Patricii, 943
McCormick, Patricius, 1088
McCormick, Patricius, 1250
McCormick, Rebecca, 2299
McCormick, Rebecca, 2300
McCormick, Rebecca, 2301
McCormick, Rebecca, 2525

McCormick, Rebeccae, 939
McCormick, Samuel, 2299
McCormick, Sarah, 2301
McCormick, William, 2299
McCormick, William, 2300
McCormick, William, 2301
McCormick, William, 2525
McCormick, William, 2525
McCoshar, Hugo, 1293
McCoskar, Margareta, 1548
McCoskar, Margarita, 1294
McCoskar, Catharina, 1668
McCoskar, Hugo, 1312
McCoskar, Hugo, 1294
McCoskar, Hugo, 1548
McCoskar, Hugo, 1576
McCoskar, Hugo, 1750
McCoskar, Hugonis, 1665
McCoskar, Hugonis, 958
McCoskar, Margareta Johanna, 1665
McCoskar, Margareta, 1576
McCoskar, Margareta, 1814
McCoskar, Margaretae, 1665
McCoskar, Margaretae, 958
McCoskar, Maria Anna, 958
McCosker, Anna, 390

McCosker, Bernard, 387
McCosker, Catherine, 429
McCosker, Ellon, 484
McCosker, Fergus, 396
McCosker, Fr., 336
McCosker, Hugh, 347
McCosker, Hugh, 361
McCosker, Hugh, 387
McCosker, Hugh, 4215
McCosker, Hugh, 4377
McCosker, Hugh, 4556
McCosker, Hugh, 462
McCosker, Hugh, 484
McCosker, Hugh, 886
McCosker, Jacobus, 886
McCosker, Margaret, 1856
McCosker, Margaret, 2732
McCosker, Margret, 4264
McCosker, Margret, 432
McCosker, Margret, 486
McCosker, Mariae, 886
McCosker, Mary Jane, 389
McCosker, Micl, 627
McCosker, Mr? Teryl?, 383
McCosker, Mrs., 342
McCosker, Mrs., 424
McCosker, Old Tergus, 612

McCosker, Pantos [or Fanios], 484
McCosker, Peter, 289
McCosker, Peter, 387
McCosker, Peter, 389
McCosker, Peter, 390
McCosker, Peter, 429
McCosker, Peter, 486
McCosker, Sally, 429
McCosker, Sally, 486
McCosker, Sarah, 387
McCosker, Sarah, 389
McCosker, Sarah, 390
McCoskey, Catherine, 2717
McCoskey, Mary, 2717
McCoslar, Joannes, 4418
McCoy, Caroline, 2433
McCoy, Edmond, 2433
McCoy, Edward, 4585
McCoy, William James, 2433
McCray, Elisabeth, 3857
McCray, Isabella, 3849
McCrea, Elisabeth, 3902
McCready, William, 1986
McCrey, Mary, 2985
McCristal, Patrick, 2
McCue, Ann, 2372
McCue, Birgitta, 1338

McCue, Birgitta, 1587
McCue, Birgitta, 1609
McCue, Edwardus, 1297
McCue, Elisabeth, 1297
McCue, Elisabeth, 1731
McCue, Elisabeth, 1816
McCue, Elisabeth, 1816
McCue, Elizabeth, 1857
McCue, Jacobi, 1367
McCue, Joannes, 1367
McCue, Maria, 1536
McCue, Mariae, 1367
McCue, Mary, 2204
McCue, Patricii, 1297
McCue, Patricii, 1816
McCue, Thomas, 1297
McCue, Thomas, 2018
McCulloff, Ann, 2805
McCullogh, Bernard, 4640
McCullogh, Bernard, 5499
McCullogh, Bernard, 5804
McCullogh, Elizabeth, 2106
McCullogh, James Henry, 2105
McCullogh, Sarah Elizabeth, 2106
McCullogh, Sarah Jane, 2105
McCullogh, Sarah Jane, 2106
McCullogh, William, 2105

McCullogh, William, 2106
McCumssy, Margaret, 107
McCune, Margret (Mrs.), 4252
McCurdy, Jacobum C., 4816
McCurdy, Mariae Annae, 1710
McCurdy, Thomas, 1710
McCusker, Hugh, 2427, 2376
McCusker, John T., 4702
McCusker, John, 2483
McCusker, Joseph, 5063
McCusker, Josephum, 3591
McCusker, Marg., 2810
McCusker, Margar, 2810
McCusker, Margaret, 1919, 1945, 2171, 2209, 2435, 2515, 4676
McCusker, Mary P., 4675
McCusker, Rosanna, 2069
McCusker, Rosanna, 2376
McCusker, Sarah, 2031
McCuskery, Mary, 2961
McCuskery, Mary, 2961
McDaniel, Maria Elisab., 4042
McDeomath, Nancy (Miss), 298
McDeomoth, Mrs., 233
McDeomoth, Nancy, 285
McDeomoth, Patrick, 285
McDeomoth, Thomas, 285

McDeritt, Cornelio, 3181
McDeritt, Daniel, 3181
McDeritt, Margaret, 3181
McDermet, James, 2113
McDermot, Thomas, 1182
McDermot, Thomas, 1093
McDermoth, Catherine (Miss), 4237
McDermoth, Michl, 4297
McDermoth, Tho., 260
McDermoth, Thoms, 4274
McDermott, [blank], 694
McDermott, Ann Mary (Mrs.), 4616
McDermott, Anna, 1015
McDermott, Cornelius, 567
McDermott, Helena Catharina, 694
McDermott, Margaretae, 1015
McDermott, Maria, 567
McDermott, Mariae, 694
McDermott, Mary E., 2049
McDermott, Mary Ellen, 3092
McDermott, Mary Ellen, 3092
McDermott, Michl, 567
McDermott, Patricii, 1015
McDermott, Patricius, 1233
McDermott, Richard, 3092

McDermott, Rosanna, 137
McDermott, Rosanna, 149
McDev___?, Mrs., 4209
McDevitt, Brosnin, 2902
McDevitt, Cath, 2902
McDevitt, Catherine, 2988
McDevitt, Catherine, 3078
McDevitt, Hugh, 2988
McDevitt, Maria, 3937
McDevitt, Maria, 4135
McDevitt, Mariam E., 4872
McDevitt, Mary Elizabeth, 3078
McDevitt, Moses, 2988
McDevitt, Moses, 3078
McDevitt, Owen, 2902
McDevt, James Barnet, 457
McDevt, James, 457
McDevt, Mary Anna, 457
McDonald, Louisa, 4641
McDonald)), Louisa, 5521
McDonald, Aaron, 2966
McDonald, Alice Elizabeth, 2966
McDonald, Alice Virginia, 2371
McDonald, Alice, 5668
McDonald, Alicia, 3414
McDonald, Aliciam, 4759
McDonald, Anna Elizabeth, 2475

McDonald, Anna, 2206
McDonald, Anna, 2966
McDonald, Anna, 3464
McDonald, Anna, 5669
McDonald, Annam, 4766
McDonald, Charles, 2304
McDonald, Ida, 5077
McDonald, James, 5214
McDonald, Joannem, 4795
McDonald, John, 16
McDonald, Louisa, 2677
McDonald, Louisa, 2304
McDonald, Louisa, 2371
McDonald, Louisa, 2475
McDonald, M.D., 5527
McDonald, Margaret (widow), 2206
McDonald, Margaret (widow), 2207
McDonald, Margaret (widow), 2208
McDonald, Margaret (widow), 2209
McDonald, Margaret, 2209
McDonald, Michael, 2304
McDonald, Michael, 2371
McDonald, Michael, 2475

McDonald, Michael, 3437
McDonald, Michael, 4759
McDonald, Michaelem, 4732
McDonald, Mr. D., 5506
McDonald, Mr., 4641
McDonald, Nancy, 16
McDonald, Philip T., 4605
McDonald, Richard, 16
McDonald, Rosa, 2208
McDonald, William, 2207
McDonald, Wm. H., 4744
McDonel, Patrick, 2111
McDonnal, Charles, 470
McDonnal, Lovenia Anna, 470
McDonnal, Margret Eliza, 470
McDonnal, Maria Virginia, 1798
McDonnal, Michael, 1739
McDonnel, Angus, 1798
McDonnel, Anis, 1025
McDonnel, Anna, 883
McDonnel, Annae, 698
McDonnel, Augusti, 883
McDonnel, Dorothea, 864
McDonnel, Juliae, 1335
McDonnel, Juliae, 864
McDonnel, Mariae, 1025
McDonnel, Mary Anna, 331

McDonnel, Michael, 1025
McDonnel, Michael, 1426
McDonnel, Michael, 698
McDonnel, Michaeliis, 698
McDonnel, Morgan Patricius, 1335
McDonnel, Morgan, 1335
McDonnel, Morgan, 864
McDonnel, Nancy, 331
McDonnel, Richard, 331
McDonnel, Rosa, 638
McDonnel, Sara Elmira, 1798
McDonnel, Sarae, 1798
McDonnel, Sarae, 883
McDonnell, Julia, 1547
McDonnell, Alexander, 1647
McDonnell, Alice, 5620
McDonnell, Anna, 1606
McDonnell, Annae, 1157
McDonnell, Annae, 1581
McDonnell, Annie, 5619
McDonnell, Caecilia, 1157
McDonnell, Catharina, 1323
McDonnell, Daniel, 1098
McDonnell, Elleonora, 1679
McDonnell, Helena, 1495
McDonnell, Honora, 1258
McDonnell, Julia, 1269

McDonnell, Juliae, 1098
McDonnell, Juliae, 1679
McDonnell, Maria Elisabeth, 1111
McDonnell, Maria, 1380
McDonnell, Mariae, 1495
McDonnell, Mariae, 1647
McDonnell, Mary L., 3880
McDonnell, Michaelis, 1157
McDonnell, Michaelis, 1581
McDonnell, Morgan, 1098
McDonnell, Morgan, 1269
McDonnell, Morgan, 1547
McDonnell, Morgan, 1679
McDonnell, Patricii, 1495
McDonnell, Patricii, 1647
McDonnell, Patricius, 1581
McDonnell, Patricius, 4471
McDonnol, Nancy, 330
McDonnol, Richard, 330
McDonnol, Saml, 330
McDote?, Patricii, 1315
McDote?, Sara, 1315
McDote?, Susannae, 1315
McDrade, Patricius, 4386
McEenrue, Terrentis, 1087
McElhany, Letty, 4669
McElhener, Lethsia, 337

McElhener, Mary, 337
McElhener, Michal, 337
McElhenny, Letitia, 3095
McElhenny, Letitia, 3164
McElhenny, Lotitia, 3107
McElroy, Maria, 4399
McElroy, Miss, 627
McEnerry, Anna, 985
McEnerry, Annae, 985
McEnerry, Patricii, 985
McEnrue?, Gullillmus Henricus, 1086
McEnrue?, Rosae Annae, 1086
McEnrue?, Terrentii, 1086
McEntee, Cassandrae, 1460
McEntee, Joannes, 1460
McEntee, Jonathan, 1460
McEntey, Charolus, 1243
McEntier, Francisia, 1192
McEntire, Bridget, 4309
McEntire, Elisabeth, 1752
McEntire, Francisca, 1667
McEntire, Mary, 4265
McEntye, Birgitta, 1201
McEnulty, Bridget, 462
McEnulty, Danl., 462
McEnulty, John, 462

McEvoy, Birgitta, 1364
McEvoy, Mariae, 1364
McEvoy, Patricii, 1364
McEvoy, Maria, 1166
McEvoy, Maria, 639
McEvoy, Mariae, 1712
McEvoy, Mariae, 892
McEvoy, Mary, 2915
McEvoy, Patricii, 1712
McEvoy, Patricii, 892
McEvoy, Rosa Anna, 892
McEvoy, Rosa, 3919
McEvoy, Rosa, 4087
McEvoy, Terrentius Joannes, 1712
McFadden, Anna, 1760
McFadden, Ann, 1953
McFadden, Ann, 1885
McFadden, Ann, 2000
McFadden, Ann, 2085
McFadden, Anna, 1226
McFadden, Anna, 1400
McFadden, Anna, 1427
McFadden, Anna, 1759
McFadden, Daniel, 3053
McFadden, Daniel, 3054
McFadden, Francis Daniel, 3053
McFadden, James, 4246

McFadden, Joannes, 1760
McFadden, Joannes, 1226
McFadden, Joannes, 1427
McFadden, Leila May, 3054
McFadden, Mary, 3053
McFadden, Mary, 3054
McFarrel, Thomas, 1433
McFaul, Felig, 3041
McFaul, Thomas, 3042
McGafferty, Dennis, 110
McGafferty, Dennis, 111
McGafferty, James Joseph, 111
McGafferty, Margaret, 111
McGahan, James, 4551
McGamley, Mary, 92
McGamley, Thomas, 92
McGann, Ann, 2155
McGann, James, 2155
McGann, William Henry, 2155
McGar, Patrick, 1914
McGarry, Maria, 4320
McGarvey, Thomas, 243
McGary, Guillelmi, 1032
McGary, Maria, 1032
McGary, Peter J., 2449
McGary, Rose, 2641
McGary, Rose, 2829

McGary, Sarae, 1032
McGaulin, Patrick, 4665
McGeaham, J.J., 3127
McGeary, Eliza, 2794
McGeary, Rose, 2823
McGee, Peter, 10
McGee, Ann Maria (Mrs.), 20
McGee, Anna Maria, 10
McGee, Birgitta, 1132
McGee, Birgitta, 4441
McGee, Bridget, 1826
McGee, Hugh, 10
McGee, Jacobus, 1600
McGee, Jacobus, 1751
McGee, James, 1826
McGee, James, 1826
McGee, James, 1870
McGee, James, 4203
McGee, Jas., 5553
McGee, Martha, 10
McGee, Nancy, 1870
McGee, Patrick, 1870
McGeehaw, Mary, 1
McGeehee, Elizabeth, 163
McGeehee, Thomas H., 163
McGeeher, Mary, 114
McGeery, Peter, 4602

McGeeve?, Elleonorae, 1426
McGeeve?, Margareta, 1426
McGeeve?, Martini, 1426
McGerem, Maria, 3662
McGerry, Birgitta, 1016
McGerry, Margareta, 1279
McGerry, Margaretae, 1016
McGerry, Margaretae, 1254
McGerry, Maria, 1254
McGerry, Patricii, 1016
McGerry, Patricii, 1254
McGiff, Patrick, 2368
McGill, [blank], 4777
McGill, Dr., 4658
McGill, Henricum, 4777
McGinley, Emma Catherinam, 3776
McGinley, Gulielmo H., 3776
McGinley, Sarah Elis., 3776
McGinley, Anna (Mrs.), 518
McGinley, Anna, 6
McGinley, Edwardo, 3820
McGinley, Edwardum Guliemum, 3820
McGinley, Edwardum J., 4823
McGinley, Emma Catharina, 3820
McGinley, John, 6

McGinly, Rosa Anna, 4457
McGinnis, Anna, 1490
McGinnis, Bridget, 1913
McGinnis, Catharine, 1892
McGinnis, Catharine, 2122
McGinnis, Daniel, 1923
McGinnis, Daniel, 1923
McGinnis, Daniel, 1924
McGinnis, Daniel, 1992
McGinnis, Danielis, 1490
McGinnis, Ellen, 1924
McGinnis, Mariae, 1490
McGinnis, Mary, 1923
McGinnis, Mary, 1924
McGinnis, Mary, 1993
McGinty, Catharine, 100
McGinty, Elizabeth, 100
McGinys, Birgitta, 1766
McGinys, Daniel, 1766
McGinys, Mariae, 1766
McGirey, Margt., 3964
McGirr, Catharine, 1857
McGirr, Maria, 1062
McGirr, Mariae, 1062
McGirr, Patricii, 1062
McGlannan, Sarae, 550
McGlaughlen, Wilm, 492

McGlenan, Anna Allosius, 474
McGlenan, Patrick, 474
McGlenan, Sarah, 474
McGlenman, Isabell, 563
McGlenman, Patrick, 563
McGlenman, Sarah, 563
McGlonagel, Francis, 5391
McGlone, Mary E., 4620
McGloughlen, Catherine, 218
McGloughlen, Catherine, 219
McGloughlen, Henritta Maria, 298
McGloughlen, Henry, 219
McGloughlen, Jane, 298
McGloughlen, Jane, 368
McGloughlen, John, 298
McGloughlen, Mary, 219
McGloughlen, Mary, 341
McGloughlen, Mechal, 368
McGloughlen, Michal, 298
McGloughlen, Michl, 432
McGloughlen, Mrs., 382
McGloughlen, Phile, 218
McGloughlen, Sarah Anna, 368
McGloughlen, Susan (Miss), 313
McGloughlen, Susamna, 271
McGloughlen, Susamna, 304
McGloughlen, Willm, 218

McGloughlen, Willm, 219
McGlouglen, Bridget, 4206
McGlouglen, Mrs., 229
McGnee, Birgitta, 1248
McGnee, Elionorae, 1248
McGnee, Martini, 1248
McGnives [sic], Anna, 1727
McGoath, Mrs., 451
McGonicle, Susan, 1578
McGonigal, Birgitta, 1756
McGonigal, John R., 4647
McGonigal, John, 2045
McGonigal, Margaret, 2045
McGonigal, Mrs., 5792
McGonigle, Guillelmus Franciscus, 1119
McGonigle, Jacobi, 1119
McGonigle, James, 2021
McGonigle, James, 2722
McGonigle, James, 4967
McGonigle, Joannes, 1565
McGonigle, John, 2321
McGonigle, John, 2360
McGonigle, John, 2722
McGonigle, John, 5012
McGonigle, Margaret, 2084
McGonigle, Margaret, 2130

McGonigle, Margaret, 2235
McGonigle, Margaret, 2360
McGonigle, Margaret, 2402
McGonigle, Margaret, 2444
McGonigle, Margaret, 2502
McGonigle, Margaretae, 1119
McGonigle, Sarah, 2722
McGonnagal, Trms, 199
McGonnagal, Augustin, 582
McGonnagal, Ellon (Mrs.), 440
McGonnagal, Ellon (Mrs.), 479
McGonnagal, Ellon, 293
McGonnagal, Ellonora, 266
McGonnagal, Elon, 279
McGonnagal, J. Sherty (Mr.), 278
McGonnagal, James (Mrs.), 545
McGonnagal, James (Mrs.), 564
McGonnagal, James (Mrs.), 613
McGonnagal, James, 4225
McGonnagal, James, 443
McGonnagal, James, 475
McGonnagal, James, 525
McGonnagal, James, 525
McGonnagal, James, 582
McGonnagal, Magy, 199
McGonnagal, Margret (Miss), 4213
McGonnagal, Margret, 295

McGonnagal, Margret, 4219
McGonnagal, Margret, 443
McGonnagal, Mrs., 262
McGonnagal, Mrs., 349
McGonnagal, Mrs., 525
McGonnagal, Susan, 525
McGonnagal, Susan, 582
McGonnagal, Susanna, 443
McGonnagal, Susanna, 475
McGonnagal, Wilm Henery, 475
McGonnal, James, 502
McGonnal, John Robert, 502
McGonnal, Susan, 502
McGonnegal, James (Mrs.), 506
McGonnegal, Hugh, 246
McGonnegal, James, 262
McGonnegal, James, 506
McGonnegal, Margret, 277
McGonnigal, James, 502
McGonnigal, Margret, 2574
McGonnigle, Bridget, 1842
McGonnigle, James, 1825
McGonnigle, Susan, 1825
McGonnigle, James, 1825
McGonnogal, Cornelius, 4309
McGoughlin, Mary, 402
McGovenor, Jacobus, 1231

McGovern, Anna, 1306
McGovern, Annae, 1318
McGovern, Annae, 872
McGovern, Birgittae, 1306
McGovern, Catharina, 1270
McGovern, Catharina, 968
McGovern, Elisabeth, 968
McGovern, Joannes, 872
McGovern, Michaelelis, 1318
McGovern, Michaelis, 1306
McGovern, Michaelis, 968
McGovern, Patricii, 1306
McGovern, Susan, 4353
McGovern, Thomae, 872
McGovern, Thomas, 1318
McGow, Jacobus, 1363
McGowan, Mary, 2143
McGrakin, Ellen, 2942
McGran, Regina, 2942
McGran, Bernard, 2275
McGran, Catharine, 2113
McGran, John, 2113
McGran, Mary Ann, 2202
McGran, Patrick, 2113
McGrane, Catharina, 1236
McGrane?, Patricius, 4394
McGrath, Catherine, 246

McGrath, James, 246
McGrath, James, 424
McGrath, John, 383
McGrath, John, 383
McGrath, John, 424
McGrath, Maria, 3377
McGrath, Maria, 3420
McGrath, Maria, 3431
McGrath, Rose, 383
McGrath, Rose, 424
McGrath, Sarah, 246
McGrath, Thomas, 2348
McGratte, Maria Margarita Josephina, 3396
McGraw, John, 1914
McGraw, Maria, 1914
McGraw, Teresa, 1914
McGret [?], Honora, 509
McGron, Cornelius, 1186
McGrow, Bernardus, 1728
McGrow, Elisabeth, 1631
McGrow, Jacobi, 1631
McGrow, Jacobus, 1401
McGrow, Jacobus, 4491
McGrow, Thomas Edwardus, 1631
McGuchen, Jacobo, 3127
McGuchen, Johanna, 3127

McGuchen, Richardum, 3127
McGuern, Anna, 3607
McGuigan, Edwardus, 1668
McGuigan, Hugo, 2165
McGuigan, Mariae, 1668
McGuigan, Mary, 2165
McGuigan, Terence, 2165
McGuigan, Terentius, 4399
McGuigan, Terrentii, 1668
McGuigan, Terrentius, 1772
McGuire, Alexander, 1740
McGuire, Joannes, 1203
McGuire, William, 4384
McGuire, Wm., 1475
McGunnigle, James, 162
McGunnigle, Macilla, 162
McGurg, Guillelini, 1308
McGurg, Maria, 1484
McGurg, Petrus, 1308
McGurg, Sarae, 1308
McGurk, Guillelmus, 4406
McGurke, Sara, 1476
McGury, Maria, 1113
McGusker, Mrs., 198
McHenry, [blank], 3026
McHenry, Grace, 3026
McHenry, James, 3026

McHoy, Anne, 4044
McIlhaney, Lotitia, 1902
McIlhany, Letitia, 3073
McIlhany, Letitia, 3074
McIlhany, Letitia, 3053
McIlhany, Letitia, 3224
McIlhany, Letitia, 4721
McIlhany, Letty, 2997
McIlhany, Letty, 3017
McIlheney, Frances Ann, 2141
McIlheney, Latitia, 2397
McIlheney, Latitia, 2432
McIlheney, Latitia, 2141
McIlheney, Lettie, 3041
McIlheney, Letty, 2534
McIlhenney, Frances Ann, 2332
McIlhenney, Frances, 2032
McIlhenney, Frances, 2448
McIlhenney, Frances, 2509
McIlhenney, Francisca, 1497
McIlhenney, Latitia, 2032
McIlhenney, Letitia, 2332
McIlhenney, Mary, 523
McIlhenney, Michl, 523
McIlhenney, Sarah Ellon, 523
McIlhenny, Carolus, 1552
McIlhenny, Francisca, 1381

McIlhenny, Francisca, 4508
McIlhenny, Let, 3004
McIlhenny, Let, 3001
McIlhenny, Let, 3005
McIlhenny, Let., 3006
McIlhenny, Letitia, 2786
McIlhenny, Lettie, 2653
McIlhenny, Letty, 2868
McIlhenny, Mary, 4579
McIlheny, L., 4699
McIlheny, Mary Elisa, 201
McIlheny, Mary, 201
McIlheny, Micl., 201
McIlvaugh, James, 5663
McIntere, John, 4529
McIntire, Charles, 1960
McIntire, Fanny, 1843
McIntire, Frances (Miss), 4542
McIntire, Frances, 1960
McIntire, Frances, 2194
McIntire, Frances, 2360
McIntire, Frances, 2467
McIntire, Frances, 2524
McIntire, Mrs., 4950
McIvoy, Anna, 4379
McKaig, F. T., 3569
McKaig, F.T., 4780

McKaig, Frisby Tilghman, 3354
McKaig, Gen., 3354
McKaig, Gen., 3355
McKaig, Margaret (Mrs.), 3336
McKaig, Margaret, 3353
McKaig, Margaret, 3354
McKaig, Margarita, 3355
McKaig, Margarita, 3590
McKaig, Margt., 3702
McKaig, Nina L., 3529
McKaig, Nina, 3337
McKaig, Nina, 3394
McKaig, Nina, 3590
McKaig, Nina, 3702
McKaig, Ninam Lamar, 4780
McKaig, Ninam, 3355
McKaig, Thos. J., 5176
McKaig, Tilghman F., 3529
McKaig, Tilghman, 3394
McKaig, Tilghman, 3590
McKaig, Tilgman, 3338
McKale, Hugh, 4918
McKalvey, Anna M., 4139
McKalvey, Jacobo N., 4139
McKalvey, Jesse Virginiam, 4139
McKalving, Jacoburn N., 4901
McKanah, Hugo, 1823

McKanah, Hugonis, 1822
McKanah, Jacobus, 1477
McKanah, Maria Anna P., 1822
McKanah, Maria, 1823
McKanah, Mariae, 1822
McKane, Scott, 4093
McKann, Joannes, 1409
McKann, Mary, 4572
McKarnan, Hugo, 926
McKarnan, Huyonis, 926
McKarnan, Margaretae, 926
McKearnan, Alice, 122
McKee, Dr., 4660
McKee, Jas., 2927
McKee, Joseph, 2927
McKee, Maria, 3491
McKee, Rebecca, 2927
McKelecker, Catherine, 293
McKelecker, James, 293
McKelecker, James, 293
McKern, Henrius, 1461
McKenna, Hugh, 2200
McKenna, Hugonis, 1400
McKenna, Jacobus, 1400
McKenna, Maria, 3311
McKenna, Maria, 3461
McKenna, Mariae, 1400

McKenna, Mary, 2200
McKennedy, Hughey, 2300
McKenney, Hugh, 1930
McKenney, Hugh, 2335
McKenney, Mary, 1930
McKenney, Peter, 1930
McKenny, Edward, 496
McKenny, Elizabeth, 496
McKenny, Nichls, 496
McKenny, Barney, 504
McKenny, Hugh, 2525
McKenny, Joseph, 3025
McKern, Patrick, 161
McKessick, Mary, 145
McKewn, Henrico A., 4837
McKey, Annae, 770
McKey, Jacobi, 770
McKey, Joannes, 770
McKey, Birgitta, 1367
McKneeve, Elleonora, 1703
McKneeve, Ellionorae, 1703
McKneeve, Martini, 1703
McKneff, Anna, 1410
McKnight, Bridget A., 2218
McKnight, Bridget, 2123
McKnight, Bridget, 2343
McKnight, Sophia, 1581

McKnight, Sophia, 2063
McKnight, Sophia, 2170
McKnight, Sophia, 2217
McKosker, Rosanna, 161
McKune, Elizabeth, 2966
McKune, Hugh, 2966
McKuskar, Johanne, 3380
McKuskar, Margaretta, 3380
McKuskar, Martha, 3380
McKuskar, Mary Jane, 3380
McKusker, Hugh, 5037
McKusker Jr., Marg., 2591
McKusker Sr., Margaret, 2593
McKusker, Anna Martha, 3114
McKusker, Anna Martha, 3115
McKusker, Anna, 2592
McKusker, Daisie Mariam, 3532
McKusker, Elizabeth M., 2221
McKusker, Hugh, 2164
McKusker, Joanne Thoma, 3115
McKusker, Joanni, 3532
McKusker, Johannam Albertam, 3114
McKusker, Johanne, 3264
McKusker, Johannem, 3264
McKusker, Kate, 2886
McKusker, Margaret, 2164

McKusker, Margaret, 4663
McKusker, Margaret, 5123
McKusker, Maria, 3114
McKusker, Maria, 3115
McKusker, Martha, 3264
McKusker, Martha, 3532
McKusker, Mary, 2619
McKusker, Mary, 2867
McKusker, Mary, 4663
McKusker, Mrs., 3264
McKusker, Rosanna, 2164
McKusker, Sara Anna, 3115
McKusker, Th. Jno., 3114
McKuskery, Hugh Francis, 2978
McKuskery, John, 2978
McKuskery, Margaret, 2978
McKuskery, Margaret, 2979
McKuskery, Martha, 2978
McLafferty, Birgitta, 1368
McLafferty, Franciscae, 1368
McLafferty, Joannis, 1368
McLain, Amelia, 3013
McLain, Ann (Miss), 5
McLain, Eliza, 3021
McLain, Guilielmus, 1644
McLain, Sara, 1644
McLaine, Martha, 1630

McLane, Patricius, 1453
McLane, Sara, 1385
McLane, Sara, 1751
McLane, William, 1385
McLane, Willm, 5661
McLary, Joannes, 1675
McLaughlen, John, 475
McLaughlen, Susan (Miss), 4225
McLaughlin, James R., 4604
McLaughlin, Amelia, 3003
McLaughlin, Anna, 1231
McLaughlin, Anna, 1513
McLaughlin, Annae, 1512
McLaughlin, Birgettae, 1151
McLaughlin, Birgitta, 1151
McLaughlin, Birgittae, 1372
McLaughlin, Catharina, 1183
McLaughlin, Catharina, 1409
McLaughlin, Catharina, 3942
McLaughlin, Catharine, 2045
McLaughlin, Catharine, 2077
McLaughlin, Catherine (Mrs.), 5309
McLaughlin, Cecilia, 3969
McLaughlin, Eleonora, 1558
McLaughlin, Eleonorae, 1253
McLaughlin, Emily, 2809

McLaughlin, Emily, 4666
McLaughlin, Geneviefe, 3941
McLaughlin, Geo, 14
McLaughlin, Helena, 1512
McLaughlin, Honora, 1171
McLaughlin, Honora, 1925
McLaughlin, Honora, 2012
McLaughlin, Honora, 2154
McLaughlin, Jacobus R., 3382
McLaughlin, Jacobus, 1387
McLaughlin, Jacobus, 3768
McLaughlin, James [John crossed out], 2477
McLaughlin, James R., 3003
McLaughlin, James, 3003
McLaughlin, James, 5247
McLaughlin, Joannes, 1253
McLaughlin, Joannes W., 1372
McLaughlin, Joannis, 1372
McLaughlin, John T., 2096
McLaughlin, Julianae, 1569
McLaughlin, Kate, 2477
McLaughlin, Lewis, 4700
McLaughlin, Ludovicus, 4738
McLaughlin, Maria Anna, 1569
McLaughlin, Maria C., 3709
McLaughlin, Maria, 3362

McLaughlin, Martha, 935
McLaughlin, Martini, 1151
McLaughlin, Martinus, 4375
McLaughlin, Mary A.., 2522
McLaughlin, Mary Ann, 2096
McLaughlin, Mary Louisa, 2477
McLaughlin, Mary, 2165
McLaughlin, Mary, 5617
McLaughlin, matrina fuit Maria, 1735
McLaughlin, Michael, 1169
McLaughlin, Michael, 1253
McLaughlin, Michael, 4451
McLaughlin, Michaelis, 1569
McLaughlin, Molly, 5667
McLaughlin, Patricii, 1253
McLaughlin, Patricii, 1481
McLaughlin, Patricii, 935
McLaughlin, Philip, 5249
McLaughlin, Rebecca, 1481
McLaughlin, Rosa, 1121
McLaughlin, Sara, 1348
McLaughlin, Sara, 1387
McLaughlin, Sara, 1480
McLaughlin, Sara, 1554
McLaughlin, Sara, 1820
McLaughlin, Sarae, 1481

McLaughlin, Sarae, 935
McLaughlin, Sarah, 1702
McLaughlin, Timotheus, 1505
McLaughlin, William, 1495
McLaughllin, Ludovico, 3117
McLaughllin, Maria, 3117
McLaughllin, Mariam Caeiliam, 3117
McLaughtin, Jennie, 5157
McLaughtin, Mary, 5165
McLauglin, Rosa Anna, 4451
McLeary, Matheus, 1809
McLeary, Timothei, 1809
McLeary, Mr., 2775
McLeary, Rose (Miss), 2781
McLeary, Sally (Miss), 2782
McLeary, Timotheus, 4515
McLee, Hugh, 234
McLeer, Hugh, 272
McLeer, Margret (Miss), 322
McLeney, Mickey, 4189
McLenny, Attiliae, 954
McLenny, Lucretia Anna, 954
McLeod, Fredericus, 1374
McLofferty, Francisca, 1522
Mcloughlen, Jane, 440
Mcloughlen, Michal, 440

Mcloughlen, Philip, 440
McLoughlen, Henrietta, 504
McLoughlen, Jane, 504
McLoughlen, Mary, 502
McLoughlen, Michael, 4210
McLoughlen, Michl., 504
McLoughlen, Wilm, 443
McLoughlin, Birgittae, 933
McLoughlin, Francisce, 933
McLoughlin, Jacobus, 3224
McLoughlin, Joannis, 933
McLoughlin, Louis, 4714
McLoughlin, Ludovico, 3224
McLoughlin, Maria, 177
McLoughlin, Maria, 3180
McLoughlin, Maria, 3224
McLoughlin, Mariam Genevieve, 3224
McLoughlin, Peggy, 177
McLoughlin, Thomas, 146
McLoughlin, Thos, 94
McLoughlin, Thos, 177
McLoughlin, Susan, 1825
McLouhlen, Mary, 606
McMahan, Brigistta, 4365
McMahan, Eliza, 1937
McMahon, Andreae, 1534

McMahon, Andrias, 1085
McMahon, Antonius, 1820
McMahon, Daniel, 1370
McMahon, deceased, 2095
McMahon, Eleonora, 1534
McMahon, Joannes, 1534
McMahon, Maria, 2095
McMahon, Mariae, 1534
McMahon, Mary, 2095
McMahon, Patricius, 1478
McMahon, Patrick J., 4237
McMannany, Patrick, 623
McManum, Mary, 4389
McManus, A., 638
McManus, Margaret, 4623
McMememm, Mrs. Mary, 5809
McMullan, Bridget, 1958
McMullan, Mary Ann, 1958
McMullen, A Ellon, 313
McMullen, Annae, 863
McMullen, Bridget, 153
McMullen, Bridget, 154
McMullen, Bridget, 244
McMullen, Bridget, 313
McMullen, Dionysius, 863
McMullen, Frances, 153
McMullen, Frances, 154

McMullen, Frances, 4212
McMullen, Francis, 244
McMullen, Francis, 268
McMullen, Francis, 313
McMullen, Joamis, 863
McMullen, John (twin), 154
McMullen, Mary Anna, 244
McMullen, Peter (twin), 153
McMullen, Rose, 4295
McNamara, Daniel, 2012
McNamara, Daniel, 2124
McNamara, Daniel, 2177
McNamara, Daniel, 2266
McNamara, John, 5250
McNamara, Margaret, 1980
McNamarcy, John, 1937
McNamarcy, Mary, 1864
McNamee, Francis, 1950
McNeal, Alex. (Dr.), 4662
McNeal, Dr. Alexander V., 2472
McNeal, Martha A., 2472
McNealy, Mary, 2929
McNeney, Patrick, 4328
McNulty, Arthur, 1316
McNulty, Henrici, 666
McNulty, Margaretae, 666
McNulty, Maria, 666

McNulty?, Henry, 4306
McOwen, Terrence, 4187
McPherson, Preston L., 4899
McQuade, Anna, 406
McQuade, Edw., 429
McQuade, Edward, 406
McQuade, Hanna, 289
McQuade, Honora, 88
McQuade, James, 289
McQuade, James, 289
McQuade, James, 406
McQuade, Mrs., 390
McQuade, Sasake Anna, 289
McQuaid, Catharina, 4394
McQuichan, John, 1937
McQuichan, Mary, 1937
McQuichan, Terence, 1937
McQuickgan, Mary, 1950
McQuickgan, Mrs., 1911
McQuigan, Mariae, 1294
McQuigan, Terentii, 1294
McQuigan, Thomas, 1294
McRainey, Annae, 973
McRainey, Franciscus, 973
McRainey, Patricii, 973
McShenney, Mrs., 505
McSherry, Denis L., 4191

McSweany, Juliae, 1580
McSweany, Maria, 1580
McSweany, Miles, 1580
McSweeney, Patritium, 4761
McTigert, Arter, 233
McWilliams, Andrias, 900
McWilliams, Annae, 900
McWilliams, Michaelis, 900
Mead, Benedict, 5144
Mead, T.D., 3702
Mead, Theo. (Rev.), 3658
Meade, Jeremias, 2011
Meade, Jeremias, 2011
Meade, Margaret, 2011
Meades, Jeremiah, 4264
Meades, Margret, 627
Meades, Martin, 627
Meades, Terrencr, 627
Meads, C. Elisabeth, 951
Meads, Catharine, 4640
Meads, Ed, 5010
Meads, Jeremiae, 951
Meads, John, 5006
Meads, Margaretae, 951
Meads, Mrs., 4984
Mealene, Hugh, 2705
Mealene, Mary, 2705

Mealene, Sarah, 2705
Means, 1227
Means, Thomas, 1709
Means, Thomas, 648
Meath, Anna, 1195
Meats, Jeremiae, 1382
Meats, Margaretae, 1382
Meats, Sara Adelaidis, 1382
Medcalf, Clarissa, 2037
Medcalf, Clarissa, 2547
Medcalf, James Lewis, 2569
Medcalf, Sarah Ann, 2569
Medcalf, William E, 4607
Medcalf, Wm., 2569
Medcalff, Sarah Ann, 5511
Medcalff, Sarah Ann, 2650
Medcalff, Sarah, 5525
Medcalff, Wm. Hy Myers, 2650
Medcalff, Wm., 2650
Meeds, Amelia, 3013
Meeds, Benedict, 3013
Meeds, Josiah, 3013
Meginly, Anna, 1120
Mehan, Ann, 2203
Mehan, Bridget, 2179
Mehan, James Edward, 1936
Mehan, Mary, 1934

Mehan, Mary, 1936
Mehan, Patrick, 1936
Mehen, Jeremy, 4355
Mehlman, Mariae, 1210
Mehlman, Thomas, 1210
Mehlmann, Elisabeth, 1540
Meinan, Elisabeth, 4410
Meisner, Jacob, 2594
Meisner, Peggy, 5130
Meisner, Rabecca, 2594
Meisonner, Margareta, 1383
Mellon, Neel, 4285
Mells, Annae, 904
Mells, Arthur, 904
Mells, Margareta, 904
Melman, Margaret W., 2166
Melman, Welhelma, 2298
Melony, Birgitta, 1472
Meloy, Robertus, 1150
Meloy, Robertus, 1285
Melton, Frances (Mrs.), 48
Melton, Francisca, 1140
Melton, Mrs., 269
Melton, Philip, 1837
Melus, Charles A., 4753
Memmigh, Eugenius, 1455
Menall, Anna, 2878

Mendenhall, Mary S., 2695
Menge, M. Regina, 1612
Menkey, Angelinae, 1130
Menkey, Joannis Josephi, 1130
Menkey, Josephus, 1130
Mense, Joanne E., 3781
Mense, Maria, 3781
Mense, Thomen Edwardum, 3781
Meraban, Eliza, 2930
Merko, John, 576
Merlight, James, 367
Merlight, Mary, 367
Merlight, Susanna, 367
Memmigh, Eugenius, 1455
Merrick, A.D., 5796
Merrick, Alfred D., 2500
Merrick, Alfred W., 5363
Merrick, Alfred, 5496
Merrick, Alfred, 5526
Merrick, Winfred (widow), 4324
Merz, Anna Margareta, 796
Merz, Catharinae, 796
Merz, Georgii, 796
Mesisinger, Jacobus, 1550
Mesisinger, Margareta, 1550
Mesman, Maria Evae, 1716
Messer, Margareta, 1757

Messman, Joseph, 1903
Messman, Maria E., 2493
Messman, Maria Eva, 1903
Messman, Maria Eva, 1976
Messman, Maria, 2338
Messman, Maria, 4942
Messman, Mary Eva, 1829
Messman, Mary, 2464
Messmann, Adelin, 581
Messmann, Anna Adelin, 581
Messmann, Henery, 581
Messner, Maria, 2434
Metcaff, Ann C.M., 5765
Metcalf, Wm. C., 4725
Mettegin?, Elizabeth (Mrs.), 579
Mettony, Frances, 4973
Metz, Anna Elisabaeth, 558
Metz, Casper, 608
Metz, Casper, 558
Metz, Elisabeth, 558
Metz, Elizabeth, 608
Metzer, Cathrine, 3135
Metzler, Catharine, 2020
Metzler, Catharine, 2396
Metzs, Henry, 110
Metzs, James, 110
Metzs, Mary, 110

Mevrin, Ann E., 2733
Meyer, Guillelmus, 1395
Meyer, Joannis, 1395
Meyer, Joannis, 1707
Meyer, Joannis, 800
Meyer, Maria Anna, 800
Meyer, Samuel Henricus, 1707
Meyer, Theresiae, 1707
Meyer, Theresiae, 800
Meyer, Therisae, 1395
Meyham, Anna, 853
Meyham, Mariae, 853
Meyham, Patricii, 853
Meyler, Michael, 2201
Michael, Mariae, 1655
Michan, Catharine, 2071
Michan, Mary, 2071
Michan, Patrick, 2071
Michel, Henrice, 3702
Michel, Meoniam Stephenuem, 3702
Michel, Nina, 3702
Mickle, Eduardus, 4780
Mickle, Henricum, 4780
Midcalf, Anna (Miss), 4236
Midcalf, Anna Elizabeth, 2514
Midcalf, Clarissa, 2462

Midcalf, Sarah Ann, 2514
Midcalf, William, 2514
Middcalf, Clarissa C. (Miss), 4531
Middlecaff, Sarah, 4656
Middlekauf, Lawrence, 5734
Middlekauff, Annie, 5742
Middlekauff, Charles, 3015
Middlekauff, Elias, 3015
Middlekauff, Gulielmo, 4914
Middlekauff, Martha, 3015
Middlekauff, Mrs., 4753
Middlekoff, Anna, 3006
Middlekoff, E., 3005
Middlekoff, Elias, 3004
Middlekoff, Elias, 3006
Middlekoff, Lawrence, 3004
Middlekoff, M. M., 3005
Middlekoff, Margarite, 3005
Middlekoff, Martha M., 3004
Middlekoff, Martha M., 3006
Middleton, Matilda, 2060
Middleton, Matilda, 2061
Miehan, Catharine, 2071
Miehan, Mary, 2071
Miehan, Patrick, 2071
Migham, Anna, 853
Migham, Mariae, 853

Migham, Patricii, 853
Mighan, Maria, 1363
Mighan, Maria, 1754
Mighan, Mariae, 1363
Mighan, Mariae, 1753
Mighan, Michael, 1753
Mighan, Patricii, 1363
Mighan, Patricii, 1753
Mighan, Patricius, 1308
Mikle, Henrico, 3590
Mikle, Nina, 3590
Mikle, Thomam McKaig, 3590
Miles, Ann, 2202
Miles, Carolum Matth. Bern., 3539
Miles, Chas., 5181
Miles, Joannem Thomam Sandford, 3540
Miles, Joanni, 3539
Miles, Joanni, 3540
Miles, John, 5168
Miles, Lucia, 3539
Miles, Lucia, 3540
Miller &c, Mrs., 4605
Miller, Alice, 4867
Miller, Ann, 1916
Miller, Ann, 3365
Miller, Anna Maria, 10

Miller, Anna Mary, 3077
Miller, Anna, 1620
Miller, Anna, 3650
Miller, Anna, 4497
Miller, Annae, 1620
Miller, Annae, 1701
Miller, Apolona, 516
Miller, Carolo, 4038
Miller, Carolo, 4092
Miller, Catharina, 4124
Miller, Catharine, 100
Miller, Elisabeth May, 4092
Miller, Elisabeth, 1701
Miller, Elisabeth, 198
Miller, Eliza, 2306
Miller, Elizabeth, 40
Miller, Elizabeth, 100
Miller, Elizabeth, 40
Miller, Emmam Theresiam, 4038
Miller, Frances, 3365
Miller, Francis, 2996
Miller, Francisca, 3769
Miller, George Valentine, 1968
Miller, Georgia W., 3650
Miller, Gul., 4801
Miller, Gulielmum Franciscum, 3650

Miller, Gulielmum V., 4799
Miller, Gulielmus, 3820
Miller, Israel J. [or I.], 3735
Miller, Jacob, 1599
Miller, Jacobi, 1620
Miller, Jesse J., 4893
Miller, John Adam, 1836
Miller, John, 198
Miller, John, 516
Miller, Joseph, 1896
Miller, Lucy Ann, 1900
Miller, Lucy Ann, 1901
Miller, Lucy Ann, 1901
Miller, Lydia M.C., 5417
Miller, Margaret, 1836
Miller, Margaret, 1896
Miller, Margaret, 1968
Miller, Margaret, 2097
Miller, Margaret, 2195
Miller, Mariam Ruth, 3735
Miller, Mary Ann, 2310
Miller, Mary Anna, 4724
Miller, Mary Frances, 2097
Miller, Mary, 1847
Miller, Mary, 2058
Miller, Mary, 2205
Miller, Mary, 2241

Miller, Mary, 2330
Miller, Mary, 2423
Miller, Mary, 604
Miller, Matthew, 2003
Miller, Nettie (Mrs.), 4915
Miller, Nettie, 3820
Miller, Nettie, 3956
Miller, Nettie, 4801
Miller, Rebecca, 2516
Miller, Sallie, 3735
Miller, Sarah, 4092
Miller, Sarai, 4038
Miller, Sickfried, 516
Miller, Sophia, 4628
Miller, Teresa, 1956
Miller, Teresa, 2290
Miller, Tobias, 198
Miller, Tobias, 100
Miller, Tobias, 40
Miller, Valentine, 1836
Miller, Valentine, 1968
Miller, Valentine, 2097
Miller, Valentine, 2195
Miller, Valentine, 2199
Miller, W. (Mrs.), 3896
Miller, William, 5332
Millor [sic], Mary Ann, 2279

Mills, 624
Mills,, 625
Mills, Annae, 1375
Mills, Arthur, 1375
Mills, Carolum Eduardum, 3402
Mills, Catharina Anna, 1022
Mills, Eduardo, 3402
Mills, Francesca, 3486
Mills, Guillelmi, 1022
Mills, Guillelmi, 1217
Mills, Lavinia (Miss), 4519
Mills, Lavinia, 1933
Mills, Lavinia, 2041
Mills, Maria Anna, 1375
Mills, Mariae, 1022
Mills, Mariae, 1217
Mills, Martha (Mrs.), 5072
Mills, Matilda (Miss), 4595
Mills, Robert, 622
Mills, Robert, 623
Mills, Sally, 3402
Mills, Thomas, 1217
Mills, William, 5075
Milton, Frances (Mrs.), 4193
Milton, Frances, 135
Milton, Frances, 93
Milton, Francis (Mrs.), 41

Milton, Francis (Mrs.), 81
Milton, Mrs., 325
Milton, Mrs., 212
Milton, Mrs. Frances, 139
Milton, Mrs., 210
Milton, Mrs., 301
Milton, Mrs., 325
Milton, Mrs., 4175
Milton, Mrs., 4182
Milton, Mrs., 4186
Milton, Mrs., 4200
Milton, Mrs., 4579
Milton, Mrs., 508
Milton, Philippus, 1799
Mindrum?, Henery, 596
Mindrum?, Mary Catherine, 596
Mindrum?, Mary Catherine, 596
Mink, Dorothea, 2087
Mink, Michael, 2087
Mink, William, 2087
Minor, James, 2258
Minor, Margaret, 2246
Misener, Margaret, 2005
Mishner, Jacob Michael, 3240
Mishner, Mrs., 3240
Misiner, Margaret, 2508
Mitchel, Auguston, 612

Mitchel, Augustus, 549
Mitchel, Birgitta, 1155
Mitchel, Caroline, 11
Mitchel, Elisabeth, 549
Mitchel, Ignatius, 11
Mitchel, Patricius, 1155
Mitchel, Robert, 549
Mitchel, William, 11
Mitchell, Susanna, 3699
Mitchell, Susan, 3538
Mitchell, Anna, 3851
Mitchell, Annam, 4833
Mitchell, Archie John, 3406
Mitchell, Carleton Eugene Smith, 3407
Mitchell, Carlton E., 4032
Mitchell, Carolum W., 3405
Mitchell, Georguim Henricum, 3404
Mitchell, Jennie, 3983
Mitchell, Johanne R., 3404
Mitchell, Johanne R., 3405
Mitchell, Johanne R., 3406
Mitchell, Johanne R., 3407
Mitchell, Johanne R., 3408
Mitchell, Josia Ray, 4032
Mitchell, Lydia, 3408

Mitchell, Lydia, 3404
Mitchell, Lydia, 3405
Mitchell, Lydia, 3406
Mitchell, Maria Eliz., 4032
Mitchell, Mariam Sally, 3408
Mitchell, Pearli Ireniam Placidiam, 3538
Mitchell, Pearli Ireniam Placidiam, 3538
Mitchell, Susan, 3407
Mitchell, Susan, 3538
Mitterer, Johanna, 4606
Mitx, Antony, 576
Mitx, Clare, 576
Mitx, Danial, 576
Mo___ [blank], Birgittae, 1334
Mo___ [blank], Henria, 1334
Mo___ [blank], Margaretta Anna, 1334
Moates, Helena, 1840
Moates, Samuel, 1840
Moates, William Henry, 1840
Moats [or Moatz], Anna, 4007
Moats [or Moatz], Georgio, 4007
Moats [or Moatz], Mariam Josephinam, 4007
Moats, Adelinam Elisabeth, 4056

Moats, Anna E., 4169
Moats, Anna, 4056
Moats, Edwin M., 4169
Moats, Edwin M., 4907
Moats, Genevefam Catharinam, 4169
Moats, Georgio, 4056
Moats, Jeremiae, 1382
Moats, Margaretae, 1382
Moats, Sara Adelaidis, 1382
Moatz, Anna, 3966
Moatz, Edmun M., 4860
Moatz, Edwin M., 4865
Moatz, Georgio, 3966
Moatz, Gulielmum Alonzo, 3966
Mobley, Ann, 4760
Mobley, Anna V., 3485
Mobley, Anna V., 3643
Mobley, Anna, 3218
Mobley, Carver, 3218
Mobley, Ellen, 5087
Mobley, Harry H., 4783
Mobley, Helenam May, 3218
Mobley, Mrs., 4013
Moellenkamp, Frederici, 858
Moellenkamp, Fredericus, 858

Moellenkamp, Mariae Catharinae, 858
Moge, Hugh, 311
Moge, John, 311
Moge, Mary, 311
Moher, Christianna, 94
Moher, Patrick, 94
Moher, William, 94
Mohler, J., 4847
Moine, Mary, 1952
Molatt, Mrs. Mary A., 5647
Moller [or Miller], Lea, 3886
Moller [sic], Nettie (Mrs.), 3736
Moller, Jesse J. [or I.], 4104
Mollow, Neel, 4285
Monaghahn, Elisabeth, 1637
Monagham, Catharina, 1493
Monagham, Cornelius, 1617
Monagham, Cornelius, 1784
Monaghan, Catharinae, 1002
Monaghan, Catharinae, 1218
Monaghan, Catharinae, 1390
Monaghan, Elisabeth, 1551
Monaghan, Elisabeth, 1618
Monaghan, Eliza, 593
Monaghan, Jacobus, 1002
Monaghan, Joannes, 1390

Monaghan, Joannis, 1002
Monaghan, Joannis, 1218
Monaghan, Joannis, 1390
Monaghan, Maria, 1218
Monaghan, Patricius, 1133
Monaghan, Thomas, 1107
Monahan, Alice E., 148
Monahan, Anna, 970
Monahan, Bryne, 4378
Monahan, Charles T., 93
Monahan, Charles, 20
Monahan, Cornelias, 2015
Monahan, Eleanor (Miss), 6
Monahan, Eleanor, 39
Monahan, Elisa (Miss), 247
Monahan, Eliza, 2160
Monahan, Eliza, 2634
Monahan, Eliza, 4180
Monahan, Elizabeth, 4182
Monahan, Ellen, 10
Monahan, Ellen, 22
Monahan, Ellen, 4180
Monahan, Ellen, 4186
Monahan, Hugh J. (Rev.), 4137
Monahan, John, 4193
Monahan, Margaretae, 970
Monahan, Mary, 43

Monahan, Mary Ann, 4189
Monahan, Mary Ann, 4189
Monahan, Mary, 146
Monahan, Michaelis, 970
Monahan, Terrence, 4261
Monde, Sophia, 2369
Mondy, Peter, 4204
Money, Thos, 74
Money, Elizabeth, 74
Money, Philip, 74
Mong, Anna, 294
Mong, Anna, 500
Mong, Anne, 213
Mong, Elisa Anne, 213
Mong, Jacob, 213
Mong, Jacob, 294
Mong, Jacob, 500
Mong, Jos. P., 4616
Mong, Josaphean, 500
Mong, Thomas, 294
Monohan, Bridget, 2476
Monohan, Patrick, 584
Monsey, Mary, 220
Monsey, Phillip, 220
Monsey, Wilm, 220
Monsil, James, 215
Monsil, Mary, 215

Monsil, Mary, 216
Monsil, Philip, 215
Monsil, Philip, 216
Monsil, Wilm, 216
Monsy, James, 221
Monsy, Mary, 221
Monsy, Philip, 221
Montague, Anna C., 3912
Montague, Anna C., 3962
Montague, Anne, 5220
Montague, Gulielmus, 3825
Montague, Joanne, 3912
Montague, Joannem Oscar, 4853
Montague, Maria, 3683
Montague, Mariam Willhelminam, 3962
Montague, Martha, 3243
Montague, Mrs., 3883
Montague, Mrs., 3905
Montague, Mrs., 3977
Montague, Oscar, 3962
Montague, Sara, 3805
Montague, Sara, 3806
Montague, Sarah (Mrs.), 3825
Montague, Sarah (Mrs.), 3933
Montague, Sarah (Mrs.), 4016
Montague, Sarah, 3243

Montague, Sarah, 3280
Montague, Sarah, 3624
Montague, Sarah, 3683
Montague, Sarah, 3688
Montague, Sarah, 3740
Montague, Stellam [or Hellam] Ceciliam, 3912
Montague, William, 5236
Montaigue, Sarah, 3169
Montgomery, Victore, 4851
Moody, Adam, 1997
Moody, Maria, 1997
Moody, William, 1997
Mooney, Catharina, 4507
Mooney, Maria, 1137
Mooney, Maria, 1035
Mooney, Michael, 2061
Mooney, Mrs., 5007
Mooney, Sara, 4429
Mooney, Sarah, 1960
Mooney, Sarah, 2363
Mooney, Sarah, 2535
Moony, Sally, 2708
Moor, Alexander, 31
Moor, Anna, 648
Moor, Eliz., 2346
Moor, Levi, 2352

Moore, Adam, 3808
Moore, Idam Virginiam, 3809
Moore, Isabellam Susannam, 3808
Moore, Jacobo, 3809
Moore, Mary, 1951
Moore, Ida, 3902
Moore, Joanne, 3832
Moore, Albertum Lawrence, 3943
Moore, Alexander, 156
Moore, Alexander, 2256
Moore, Alexander, 4538
Moore, Alexander, 4595
Moore, Alexandro, 4127
Moore, Alx, 319
Moore, Alx, 455
Moore, Ann E. (Miss), 4538
Moore, Anna, 1242
Moore, Anna E., 3957
Moore, Anna J., 4083
Moore, Anna, 1388
Moore, Anna, 1621
Moore, Anna, 449
Moore, Annam V., 3796
Moore, Anne J., 4127
Moore, Birgitae, 862
Moore, Catharina, 1217
Moore, Catharina, 1532

Moore, Catharina, 4121
Moore, Catharinae, 1020
Moore, Catharinae, 1621
Moore, Catharinam L., 4885
Moore, Catharine, 2232
Moore, Catharine, 2254
Moore, Catharine, 2254
Moore, Catharine, 2255
Moore, Catharine, 2269
Moore, Catharine, 2369
Moore, Catharine, 2388
Moore, Catharina, 4024
Moore, Cecilia, 4145
Moore, Daniele A., 3957
Moore, Danielem A., 4854
Moore, David Gulielmum, 3919
Moore, Eduardo, 3872
Moore, Edwardo, 3945
Moore, Edwardo, 4002
Moore, Edwardus, 4817
Moore, Elisa, 319
Moore, Elisabeth (Mrs.), 3855
Moore, Elisabeth, 1485
Moore, Elisabeth, 3857
Moore, Elisabeth, 3872
Moore, Elisabeth, 3902
Moore, Elisabeth, 3945

Moore, Elisabeth, 4036
Moore, Elisabeth, 4115
Moore, Elizabeth (Mrs.), 4885
Moore, Elizabeth ., 156
Moore, Elizabeth, 156
Moore, Elizabeth, 2024
Moore, Elizabeth, 2051
Moore, Elizabeth, 2137
Moore, Elizabeth, 2185
Moore, Elizabeth, 2255
Moore, Elizabeth, 2271
Moore, Elsiabeth, 4002
Moore, George, 5022
Moore, Georgium Edwardum, 3872
Moore, Guillelini, 862
Moore, Helena V., 3581
Moore, Helenam Matildam, 3833
Moore, Henricum Leonem, 3965
Moore, Honora, 1503
Moore, Ida (Mrs.), 3876
Moore, Ida V., 3796
Moore, Ida V., 3860
Moore, Ida V., 3916
Moore, Ida V., 4022
Moore, Ida Virginia, 3833
Moore, Ida Virginia, 3980
Moore, Ida, 3868

Moore, Ida, 3943
Moore, Isaac, 2035
Moore, Isaac, 2118
Moore, Isaac, 4595
Moore, Isaac, 4909
Moore, Isaak, 5314
Moore, Isabaella (Mrs.), 4033
Moore, Isabella, 3849
Moore, Isac?, 319
Moore, James B., 4525
Moore, James, 2025
Moore, James, 2118
Moore, James, 2234
Moore, James, 2270
Moore, James, 2420
Moore, James, 4536
Moore, Jennie (Mrs.), 3917
Moore, Joannes Alexander, 1621
Moore, Joannes, 1170
Moore, Joannis, 1503
Moore, John (Mrs.), 4059
Moore, John Alexander, 2270
Moore, John, 5255
Moore, Jos., 4084
Moore, Joseph Cornelium, 3916
Moore, Joseph, 3919
Moore, Joseph, 3965

Moore, Joseph, 4036
Moore, Joseph, 4083
Moore, Josephine, 5296
Moore, Leonardi, 1485
Moore, Leonardus, 4479
Moore, Levi Eduardum, 4844
Moore, Levi, 1597
Moore, Levi, 1598
Moore, Levi, 1621
Moore, Levi, 1999
Moore, Levi, 2025
Moore, Levi, 2137
Moore, Levi, 2232
Moore, Levi, 2233
Moore, Levi, 2254
Moore, Levi, 2255
Moore, Levi, 2334
Moore, Levi, 2369
Moore, Levi, 2388
Moore, Levi, 4525
Moore, Levi, 4536
Moore, Levi, 4538
Moore, Levi, 4595
Moore, Levy, 1020
Moore, Lilian Joannam, 3902
Moore, Louisa, 4670
Moore, Lucia S., 4093

Moore, Lucia, 3970
Moore, Lucia, 4024
Moore, Lucia, 4055
Moore, Lucia, 4145
Moore, Lucia, 4817
Moore, Luciam E., 4875
Moore, M., 4670
Moore, Margaret (Mrs.), 4093
Moore, Margaret, 2150
Moore, Margaret, 2271
Moore, Margareta, 3832
Moore, Margaritam Josephinam, 4022
Moore, Margt, 2934
Moore, Margt, 2935
Moore, Mariam Geneviefam, 3832
Moore, Mariam Josephinam, 3945
Moore, Mariam V., 4818
Moore, Mariam Violam, 3860
Moore, Martha Eugenia, 1485
Moore, Mary Ann, 2024
Moore, Mary Jane, 2025
Moore, Mary Jane, 2118
Moore, Mary Jane, 2234
Moore, Mary Jane, 2270
Moore, Mary Jane, 2420
Moore, Mr., 450

Moore, Mrs., 4055
Moore, Mrs., 4082
Moore, Nora Elisabeth, 3957
Moore, Philippus, 1020
Moore, Philomena, 2255
Moore, Praxedes, 2025
Moore, Regina, 2118
Moore, Sara, 862
Moore, Sarae, 1503
Moore, Sebastium Grant, 3980
Moore, Susan (Miss), 4614
Moore, Susan, 2254
Moore, Susanna Frances, 2420
Moore, Susanna, 2289
Moore, Susanna, 3919
Moore, Susanna, 3965
Moore, Susanna, 4036
Moore, Thoma, 3849
Moore, Thomam Alexandum, 3857
Moore, Thomam Ricardum, 4002
Moore, Thoman Alexandum, 3849
Moore, Thomas, 2136
Moore, Thomas, 2270
Moore, Thomas, 2289
Moore, Thomas, 319
Moore, Thomas, 3857
Moore, Thomas, 3902

Moore, Thomas, 4138
Moore, Thomas, 4145
Moore, Thomas, 4614
Moore, Thos, 444
Moore, Ulton (Mrs.), 4543
Moore, Ulton C., 3796
Moore, Ulton, 2024
Moore, Ulton, 2185
Moore, Ulton, 2255
Moore, Ulton, 2271
Moore, Ulton, 3902
Moore, Ulton, 3916
Moore, Ulton, 3943
Moore, Ulton, 4022
Moore, Ulton, 4536
Moore, Ulton, 4543
Moore, Upton, 3833
Moore, Upton, 3860
Moore, Upton, 3868
Moore, Upton, 3980
Moorhead, Anna, 3134
Moorhead, Anna, 3134
Moorhead, Jacobo, 3134
Moorhead, Joannem, 3134
Mooty, Birgitta, 1288
Mooty, Joannes, 1672
Moran, Jacobus (Mrs.), 4134

Moran, Jacobus (Mrs.), 4164
Moran, Amanda, 3727
Moran, Annam Ceciliam, 3883
Moran, Birgitta, 1648
Moran, Birgitta, 859
Moran, Birgittae, 1632
Moran, Catharina, 3241
Moran, Catharinae, 859
Moran, Eleonorae, 823
Moran, Gul., 3727
Moran, Gulielmus F., 4851
Moran, Henrici, 1632
Moran, Henricus, 1403
Moran, Henricus, 1648
Moran, Iva (Mrs.), 3972
Moran, Jacobi, 1099
Moran, Jacobo H., 3792
Moran, Jacobo H., 3883
Moran, Jacobus, 3775
Moran, Jacobus, 4134
Moran, Jacobus, 4164
Moran, James (Mrs.), 4034
Moran, Joannes, 823
Moran, Joannes, 1099
Moran, Joannes, 1591
Moran, Joannes, 4735
Moran, Julian, 496

Moran, M, 1591
Moran, M. (Rev., 2773
Moran, M., 4653
Moran, Malachy, 5609
Moran, Margarite, 4735
Moran, Margaritta, 3127
Moran, Maria (MRs.), 3906
Moran, Maria A., 3792
Moran, Maria A., 3883
Moran, Maria Anna, 4735
Moran, Maria E., 3825
Moran, Maria Elizabeth, 3576
Moran, Maria, 1632
Moran, Maria, 3727
Moran, Maria, 3775
Moran, Maria, 3940
Moran, Maria, 4016
Moran, Mariae, 1099
Moran, Mariam Catharinam, 3792
Moran, Marion [or Marian?], 3639
Moran, Mattew, 3883
Moran, Mr., 5307
Moran, Mrs., 4113
Moran, Mrs., 497
Moran, P., 2710
Moran, P., 4644
Moran, Patricii, 823

Moran, Petri, 1591
Moran, Thomae, 859
Moran, Thomas, 1099
Moran, Wilm, 496
Morarty, Daniel, 1283
Morarty, Jacobi, 1369
Morarty, Jacobus, 1259
Morarty, Maria, 1259
Morarty, Mariae, 1369
Morarty, Mary, 2125
Morarty, Thomas, 1369
Morarty, Timotheus, 1174
Morco, John, 600
More, Catharine, 2318
More, Levi (Mrs.), 1886
More, Ann, 1831
More, Catharine, 1933
More, Catharine, 4525
More, Joannis, 1153
More, Joannis, 729
More, Leonard More, 1915
More, Levi, 1930
More, Levi, 1933
More, Levi, 1886
More, Levi, 2318
More, Levi, 4597
More, Margaret, 1882

More, Margareta, 1153
More, Maria, 1096
More, Michael, 729
More, Sarae, 1153
More, Sarae, 729
More, Ulton, 1831
More, Ulton, 1833
Morearty, Jacobi, 1728
Morearty, Jacobi, 767
Morearty, Jacobus, 1728
Morearty, Joanna dau., 767
Morearty, Joannia, 658
Morearty, Margarethae, 658
Morearty, Mariae, 1728
Morearty, Mariae, 767
Morearty, Thomae, 658
Moreland, Susan, 3426
Morenam, Joannae, 716
Morenam, Joannis, 716
Morenam, Timotheus, 716
Morgan, Anna, 803
Morgan, Annae, 803
Morgan, Annae, 804
Morgan, Catharina, 1155
Morgan, Catharina, 804
Morgan, Guillelmi, 1155
Morgan, Guillelmi, 1567

Morgan, Guillelmus, 1406
Morgan, Guillelmus, 1584
Morgan, Jacobi, 803
Morgan, Jacobi, 804
Morgan, James, 4359
Morgan, Margaret, 2393
Morgan, Margret (Miss), 4234
Morgan, Maria, 1406
Morgan, Maria, 1584
Morgan, Mariae, 1155
Morgan, Mariae, 1567
Morgan, Mary Jane, 2393
Morgan, Thomas, 1567
Morganstern, Wm. R., 3695
Moriartey, Bridget, 1979
Moriartey, James, 1979
Moriartey, Mary, 1979
Moriarty, Catharine, 1864
Moriarty, Jacobus, 1582
Moriarty, James, 1864
Moriarty, Joanne, 3707
Moriarty, Maria, 1582
Moriarty, Mary, 1864
Morin, Ann E., 2503
Morin, Ann E., 4586
Morin, Anne, 2425
Morissey, Patrick, 2008

Morissey, Patrick, 2556
Morne, Anna, 2555
Morris, Rosa, 3585
Morrison, Brown, 2867
Morrison, David, 4428
Morrison, Doris Josephinam, 4173
Morrison, Ella T., 4173
Morrison, Ella Thoma [or Thomas], 4095
Morrison, G. W. Brown, 2961
Morrison, George W.B., 4675
Morrison, Gulielmo, 4095
Morrison, Gulielmo, 4173
Morrison, Lillie, 4173
Morrison, Lillie, 4908
Morrison, M [rest blank], 946
Morrison, M. Daisy, 4908
Morrison, Maria, 946
Morrison, Mary Daisy, 2961
Morrison, Mary, 2867
Morrison, Mary, 2961
Morrison, Patricii, 946
Morrison, Violetta, 4095
Morrison, Vivian Geneviefam, 4095
Morrison, Wm. Baker, 2867
Morrow, Mary, 84

Mortaugh, Anna, 814
Mortaugh, Catharinae, 814
Mortaugh, Michaelis, 814
Mortial, Elisa (Miss), 329
Morton, "F.P., 4844
Moser, Bertha E., 4066
Moser, Bertha, 4165
Mosser, Apolonia, 4242
Mosthial, Louisa, 501
Mosthial, Michl., 501
Mosthial, Sarah Anna, 501
Motter, George, 2803
Motter, Lucinda M., 2947
Motter, Lucinda Margaret, 2803
Motter, Lucinda, 2675
Motter, Mary, 2803
Mourer, Benjamen, 3693
Mourer, Georgia, 3693
Mourer, Gul., 4815
Mourer, Gulielmum L., 3693
Mourer, Margret, 269
Mous, Catharina Maria, 1021
Mous, Joannae, 1021
Mous, Petri, 1021
Mouse, Gulielmen Edwardum, 3812
Mouse, Joanne, 3812

Mouse, Maria, 3811
Mouse, Maria, 3812
Mouse, Samuelem Ludovicum, 3811
Mouse, Themati, 3811
Mouse, Ann Jane, 2862
Mouse, Catharine, 30
Mouse, Danl., 2863
Mouse, Isabella, 2136
Mouse, Isabella, 4588
Mouse, Jacob, 125
Mouse, Jane, 1930
Mouse, Jane, 1954
Mouse, Jane, 125
Mouse, Jane, 1888
Mouse, Jane, 2135
Mouse, Jane, 2163
Mouse, Jane, 2257
Mouse, Jane, 235
Mouse, Jane, 2352
Mouse, Jane, 2768
Mouse, Joanne, 3813
Mouse, John, 235
Mouse, June, 29
Mouse, Lucy, 4577
Mouse, Margaret, 2026
Mouse, Maria, 3813

Mouse, Mariem Catharinem, 3813
Mouse, Martha Eliz., 2861
Mouse, Mary Amanda, 2638
Mouse, Mary Catharine, 2638
Mouse, Mary Catharine, 2861
Mouse, Mary Catharine, 2862
Mouse, Mr., 4577
Mouse, Mrs., 236
Mouse, Mrs., 4577
Mouse, Mrs., 4614
Mouse, Old Uncle, 5008
Mouse, Peter, 235
Mouse, Peter, 125
Mouse, Peter, 4539
Mouse, Philip, 30
Mouse, Philip, 30
Mouse, Sophia, 1916
Mouse, Sophia (Miss), 4539
Mouse, Sophia, 2036
Mouse, Sophia, 2136
Mouse, Sophia, 2544
Mouse, Thos., 2638
Mouse, Thos., 2861
Mouse, Thos., 2862
Mousfeel, Catharina, 4387
Moxley, Cecelia Iris, 2506
Moxley, Johanne, 3247

Moxley, Johannem Franciscum, 3247
Moxley, John Robert, 2431
Moxley, Joseph Perry, 2549
Moxley, Julia, 3247
Moxley, Perry, 2431
Moxley, Perry, 2506
Moxley, Perry, 2549
Moxley, Sarah, 2431
Moxley, Sarah, 2506
Moxley, Sarah, 2549
Moxly, Perry, 4590
Moyers, John, 514
Muladoon, Annae, 1509
Muladoon, Michael, 1509
Muladoon, Michaelis, 1509
Mulhargan, Anna, 1687
Mulharon, Anna, 1273
Mulharon, Anna, 1293
Mulharon, Anna, 1408
Mulharon, Catharina, 1363
Mulharon, Catharina, 4493
Mulharon, Maria, 1607
Mulharon, Thomas, 1390
Mulharon, Maria, 1339
Mulholland, Catherine, 4335
Mulhoron, Catharine, 4451

Mullan, Elizabeth, 2461
Mullan, Gilbert, 2461
Mullan, Henry, 2461
Mullan, Lucy, 2461
Mullegan, Birgitta, 1723
Mullen, Carolum B., 4804
Mullen, Patricius, 1196
Mullen, [blank], 4769
Mullen, Carolo A., 3758
Mullen, Carolo A., 3840
Mullen, Carolo, 3879
Mullen, Carolo, 3928
Mullen, Carolo, 3996
Mullen, Carolus, 4166
Mullen, Catharine, 137
Mullen, Georgius, 1111
Mullen, Jacobi, 1111
Mullen, Johanna, 1229
Mullen, Ludovicam Clementinam, 3840
Mullen, Lutie, 3879
Mullen, Lutie, 3928
Mullen, Lutie, 3996
Mullen, Lutie, 5368
Mullen, Margaritam Annam, 3879
Mullen, Maria Ludivico, 3758
Mullen, Maria Ludovica, 3840

Mullen, Mariae Annae, 1111
Mullen, Mariam Josephinam, 3758
Mullen, Nellie Rosalie, 3996
Mullen, Saraim Jennie, 3928
Muller, Gaspar, 1720
Muller, Maria, 1694
Muller, Maria, 1108
Mulligan, Birgittae, 1263
Mulligan, Birgittae, 1474
Mulligan, Catharina, 1474
Mulligan, Jacobi, 1263
Mulligan, Joannes, 1263
Mulligan, Joannes, 4438
Mulligan, Joannis, 1474
Mulligan, Mary, 2096
Mulligan, Naty, 1176
Mulligan, Thomas, 1318
Mulon, Nancy, 4260
Mulryan, Catharine, 171
Mulryan, James, 171
Mulryan, Margaret, 171
Mulvana, Anna, 1240
Mulvana, Anna, 1493
Mulvana, Jacobus, 1493
Mulvana, Thomae, 1493
Mulvana, Annae, 1177
Mulvana, Christophorus, 1177

Mulvana, Thomae, 1177
Mumma, Allen H., 4914
Mumma, Allen Joseph Hartzler, 4157
Mumma, Henrico C., 4157
Munday (widow), Mrs., 4532
Munday, Anna, 1146
Munday, Anna, 1411
Munday, Catharinae, 671
Munday, Patricii, 671
Munday, Patricius, 671
Munday, Peter, 1416
Mundenhall, Am, 4651
Mundey, [child], 3363
Mundey, Bernardum, 3361
Mundey, Georgio, 3359
Mundey, Georgio, 3361
Mundey, Georgio, 3363
Mundey, Giergio, 3360
Mundey, Giorgio, 3441
Mundey, Johannem Guglielmum, 3359
Mundey, Laurentium Sylvestrem, 3441
Mundey, Maria, 3359
Mundey, Maria, 3360
Mundey, Maria, 3361

Mundey, Maria, 3363
Mundey, Maria, 3441
Mundey, Mary, 3049
Mundey, Norman Scott, 3360
Mundy, Denis, 400
Mundy, Ann Cath., 2963
Mundy, Anna (Mrs.), 431
Mundy, Anna, 260
Mundy, Anna, 445
Mundy, Catherine, 360
Mundy, Catherine, 400
Mundy, Catherine, 400
Mundy, Catherine, 4263
Mundy, Catherine, 447
Mundy, Catherine, 462
Mundy, Catherine, 474
Mundy, Denis, 445
Mundy, George, 2963
Mundy, M____, 260
Mundy, Margret, 360
Mundy, Mary Anna, 447
Mundy, Mary, 2963
Mundy, Nancy (widow), 4328
Mundy, Patrick, 260
Mundy, Patrick, 360
Mundy, Patrick, 400
Mundy, Patrick, 447

Mundy, Patrick, 555
Mundy, Peter Wilem, 400
Mundy, Thomas, 445
Mung, [blank], 4817
Munsen, Ellsworth, 4061
Munsen, Helenam Emiliam, 4061
Munsen, Maria, 4061
Munson, Maria Elizabeth, 3584
Munson, Maria, 4895
Munson, Sarah Ann, 2630
Muntha, Bridget, 3926
Murphey, Anastasia, 1086
Murphey, Anastasia, 1308
Murphey, Birgittae, 1233
Murphey, Birgittae, 1359
Murphey, Birgittae, 1520
Murphey, Edwardus, 1573
Murphey, Eleonora, 1119
Murphey, Eleonora, 1445
Murphey, Guilelini, 1234
Murphey, Guilielmus, 944
Murphey, Guillelumi, 1573
Murphey, Guilllmi [sic], 944
Murphey, Hugh, 1932
Murphey, Hugh, 2029
Murphey, Jacobi, 1688
Murphey, Jacobi, 1689

Murphey, Jacobus, 1234
Murphey, Jeremias, 1229
Murphey, Joannes son, 1233
Murphey, Johanna Murphey, 1104
Murphey, Johanna, 4494
Murphey, John, 2169
Murphey, Margaret, 2034
Murphey, Margaretae, 1573
Murphey, Margaretae, 944
Murphey, Maria Anna, 1375
Murphey, Maria, 1328
Murphey, Mariae Ambo, 1688
Murphey, Mariae Ambo, 1689
Murphey, Mariae, 1234
Murphey, Mary Ellen, 2034
Murphey, Mary, 2078
Murphey, Mary, 2169
Murphey, Maurice, 2169
Murphey, Michael, 1359
Murphey, Patricii, 1233
Murphey, Patricii, 1520
Murphey, Patricius, 1520
Murphey, Patricius, 1688
Murphey, Patricius, 4441
Murphey, Rosa Anna, 1689
Murphey, Thomae, 1359
Murphey, William, 2034

Murphy, Choft (Mrs.), 467
Murphy, Christophor, 575
Murphy, Chrty ("Old Mrs."), 582
Murphy, Bridget, 1865
Murphy, Catharine, 2344
Murphy, Catherine, 590
Murphy, Chotf, 467
Murphy, Clara J., 3487
Murphy, Eleanor, 17
Murphy, Eleonorae, 1446
Murphy, Ellen, 2751
Murphy, Francescum Patritium, 4847
Murphy, Genefeffa, 3815
Murphy, Guillelmas, 1446
Murphy, Guillelmi, 1446
Murphy, Honora, 4257
Murphy, Hugh, 2323
Murphy, Hugh, 2580
Murphy, Hugh, 2894
Murphy, Hugh, 5114
Murphy, Jeremiah, 4704
Murphy, Joanne, 3487
Murphy, Joanne, 3815
Murphy, Joannem Thematem, 3815
Murphy, John, 4262
Murphy, Julia, 3605

Murphy, Julia, 3634
Murphy, Julia, 3706
Murphy, Julia, 3794
Murphy, M., 3605
Murphy, Margaret (widow), 4262
Murphy, Margaret, 590
Murphy, Maria, 3794
Murphy, Mariam Agnetem, 3487
Murphy, Mrs., 241
Murphy, Richd. H., 4188
Murphy, Sara Joanna, 3128
Murphy, Sarah Ann Caroline, 1861
Murphy, Susanna, 145
Murphy, Wm, 590
Murphyq, Hugh, 2663
Murray, Lizzie, 5503
Murray, [blank], 2969
Murray, [blank], 652
Murray, Agatha, 1849
Murray, Agatha, 1850
Murray, Agatha, 1851
Murray, Amelia E. (Miss), 4549
Murray, Amelia, 2033
Murray, Andrew, 2714
Murray, Ann, 123
Murray, Ann, 157
Murray, Ann, 1909

Murray, Ann, 1990
Murray, Ann, 2248
Murray, Anna, 4403
Murray, Annae, 1544
Murray, Brown, 984
Murray, Catharina Anna, 652
Murray, Catharinae, 640
Murray, Catharinae, 972
Murray, Charolus, 1790
Murray, Daniel, 972
Murray, Danienil, 652
Murray, Edward Ross, 1935
Murray, Eleonorae, 1527
Murray, Elisabeth, 984
Murray, Elisabeth, 984
Murray, Elizabeth, 2616
Murray, Ellen, 2248
Murray, Ellen, 2249
Murray, Ellen, 2250
Murray, Elleonora, 1704
Murray, Emelia, 1929
Murray, Emilia, 1792
Murray, Hanora, 1560
Murray, Helena, 1511
Murray, Henriei, 972
Murray, Henrii, 640

Murray, Jacobus, 1649
Murray, Jeremiae, 1527
Murray, Jeremias, 1642
Murray, Joannis, 1544
Murray, John Jackson, 1849
Murray, Juliae, 1148
Murray, Laurence, 1935
Murray, Laurentii, 1154
Murray, Laurentii, 1670
Murray, Lawrence, 2121
Murray, Lawrence, 2248
Murray, Lizzie, 5467
Murray, Lizzie, 5537
Murray, Lizzie, 5807
Murray, M., 4732
Murray, Margaret Matilda, 2121
Murray, Margaret, 1991
Murray, Maria Anna, 1154
Murray, Maria, 1473
Murray, Maria, 1544
Murray, Martin Van Buren, 1850
Murray, Mary (Mrs.), 5315
Murray, Mary Ann, 123
Murray, Mary Ann, 1851
Murray, Mary, 1991
Murray, Mathilda, 1314
Murray, Matilda, 2340

Murray, Matilda, 2737
Murray, Michael, 1144
Murray, Patricius, 1148
Murray, Patricus, 1177
Murray, Pollie, 2714
Murray, R. [blank], 1670
Murray, Rd., 123
Murray, Richard (Mrs.), 4549
Murray, Richard, 2249
Murray, Richard, 4549
Murray, Richardi, 1789
Murray, Richardi, 1790
Murray, Richardus Leonidas, 1670
Murray, Richardus Leonidas, 1789
Murray, Sara Anna, 1527
Murray, Sarae, 1154
Murray, Sarae, 1670
Murray, Sarae, 1789
Murray, Sarae, 1790
Murray, Sarah Agnes, 2714
Murray, Sarah Agnes, 5600
Murray, Sarah Agnes, 5664
Murray, Sarah, 1935
Murray, Sarah, 2121
Murray, Saram Agnetem, 4775
Murray, Silvester, 1372
Murray, Stephen, 1849

Murray, Stephen, 1850
Murray, Stephen, 1851
Murray, Susan, 156
Murray, Susanna, 126
Murray, Susanna, 167
Murray, Sydney, 5005
Murray, Thomas, 1991
Murray, Timothei, 1148
Murrey, John, 539
Murrey, Patricius, 788
Murrey, Richardis, 788
Murrey, Stephaninom, 788
Murry, Alma, 357
Murry, Elisa, 238
Murry, Ellon (Miss), 4356
Murry, Emilia Elisa, 238
Murry, Margret Matilda, 357
Murry, Mrs., 452
Murry, Nancy, 238
Murry, Richard, 238
Murry, Richard, 357
Murry, Suan, 4289
Murry, Susanna, 82
Murth, Bridget, 2060
Mutter, Matheus, 1395
Myer, Joannes, 1038
Myer, Joannis, 1038

Myer, Theresae, 1038
Myers [the priest] H., 1861
Myers [the priest], Henry, 1862
Myers, [blank], 3563
Myers, [blank], 3563
Myers, Agnes, 3778
Myers, Agnete Cacelilia, 3882
Myers, Agnete, 3663
Myers, Agneti Caeilia, 3778
Myers, Agneti R., 3556
Myers, Ann E. Isabella, 2237
Myers, Charles James, 2236
Myers, Eli, 158
Myers, Eliza Ilda [ILDA], 2237
Myers, Elizabeth, 2024
Myers, Elizabeth, 2255
Myers, Elizabeth, 4536
Myers, Eugeniam Allen, 3663
Myers, George, 2290
Myers, Gulielmum Herman Jos., 3563
Myers, H., 1931
Myers, H., 2038
Myers, H., 2065
Myers, H., 2197
Myers, H., 2210
Myers, H., 2339

Myers, H., 2422
Myers, H., 2430
Myers, H., 2465
Myers, H., 2468
Myers, H., 2533
Myers, H., 2534
Myers, H., 2549
Myers, H., 2562
Myers, H., 2566
Myers, Henriettam Baptistem, 3556
Myers, Henry, 1946
Myers, Henry, 2264
Myers, Henry, 2397
Myers, Henry, 2441
Myers, Henry, 2495
Myers, Henry, 2512
Myers, James, 2236
Myers, James, 2237
Myers, John, 1956
Myers, John, 2290
Myers, Ludovicum Vincentium, 3778
Myers, Margoret [sic] Ann, 2236
Myers, Margoret [sic] Am, 2237
Myers, Maria, 611
Myers, Mariam Agnetem, 3882
Myers, Mary, 115

Myers, Mary, 2388
Myers, Mr., 4663
Myers, Peggy, 158
Myers, R.M., 3778
Myers, R.M., 3882
Myers, Ricardo M., 3663
Myers, Stephen, 158
Myers, Susan, 1956
Myers, Teresa, 1956
Myers, Teresa, 2290
Myres, Wm., 5182
Myres, Ellen, 4340
N egal, Jacob, 345
N. [rest of name is blank], Petrus & Anna Margareta, 1663
N. [rest of name is blank], Petrus, 1663
Naason, Uncle, 5802
Nagle, Anna, 109
Nalley, William, 2075
Nasy, Uncle, 5504
Nathan, Margaratae, 1447
Nathan, Margareta, 1463
Nathan, Maria, 1447
Nathan, Petri, 1447
Nathan, Petrus, 4475
Naughton, Anna, 1315

Naughton, Honora, 2341
Naughton, Catharina, 1269
Naughton, Hanora, 1335
Naughton, Honorae, 1269
Naughton, Honorae, 1464
Naughton, Joannes, 1247
Naughton, Joannis, 1269
Naughton, Margareta, 1464
Naughton, Michael, 1270
Naughton, Timothei, 1464
Naughton, Timotheus, 1315
Naughton, Timothy, 2341
Neanes, Thom, 236
Nearman, Auguste, 3232
Nebbles, Elizabeth, 3031
Nebbles, Patrick, 3031
Nebbles, Patrick, 3031
Neberlen, Chrissintia, 2688
Neberlen, Chrissontia, 2687
Neberlen, Johanna, 2688
Neberlen, Joseph, 2688
Needy, Catharina, 3175
Needy, Catharina, 3393
Needy, Catharine, 3279
Needy, Catherin, 2986
Needy, Catherine, 2739
Needy, Catherine, 3057

Needy, Clara Virginia, 2866
Needy, David, 3256
Needy, David, 4723
Needy, Edwardum Ludovicum, 3256
Needy, Florence Ceciliam, 3279
Needy, Gulielmum, 3393
Needy, Isaac, 2739
Needy, Isaac, 2866
Needy, Isaac, 2986
Needy, Isaac, 3057
Needy, Isaac, 3175
Needy, Isaac, 3279
Needy, Isaac, 3393
Needy, Jacob Henry, 2986
Needy, Joannem Everitt, 3175
Needy, Kate, 2866
Needy, Maria Elizabeth, 3568
Needy, Maria, 3256
Needy, Mary Eliza, 2739
Needy, Sarah Jane, 3057
Neibert, Joannes, 4397
Neibert, Nettie, 4845
Neikirk, Clarentium Carolum, 3545
Neikirk, M. Agneti, 3705
Neikirk, Maria Agnete, 3545
Neikirk, Silas, 3545

Neikirk, Silas, 3705
Neikirk, Susannem Mariem, 3705
Nelegan, Ann, 2314
Nelligan, Anna, 4777
Nelligan, Annam A., 4784
Nelligan, Ellen Anastasia, 5708
Nelligan, Ellen, 3065
Nelligan, Jeremiah, 5218
Nelligan, Josephinam, 4777
Nelligan, Nellie, 3949
Nelligan, Patrick, 3065
Nelligan, Nellie, 4834
Nelson, Gulielmo, 4858
Nelson, Joannem W., 4876
Nerejan, Patrick, 2665
Nerman, Elizabeth, 2019
Nerman, Margaret, 2019
Nevel, Guillelimus, 651
Nevel, Michaelis, 651
Nevel, Rosae, 651
Neville, Pat, 2975
Newcomer, May, 4806
Newcomer, Sybilla, 2837
Newcummer, Barbara, 184
Newcummer, Daniel, 183
Newcummer, Elizabeth, 182
Newcummer, Elizabeth, 183

Newcummer, Elizabeth, 184
Newcummer, Elizabeth, 185
Newcummer, Michael, 182
Newhart, Carolina, 4243
Newsome, Augustus, 2826
Newsome, Emila Hugheshew, 2826
Newsome, Mary Olivia, 2826
Nicely, Jennie, 3299
Nicely, Jennie, 3438
Nicely, Johanna, 3530
Nicely, Virginia Anna, 3174
Nicely, Virginia, 3234
Nicely, Virginia, 3599
Nichols, Johannae, 1257
Nichols, W. Thomas, 1257
Nickerson, James, 2226
Nickerson, James, 2228
Nickerson, Sarah, 2226
Nickerson, Sarah, 2228
Nickerson, Sarah, 2228
Nickerson, Susanna Catharine, 2226
Nicodemus, Anna Elisabeth, 1075
Nicodemus, Barbara, 2528
Nicodemus, Barbara, 2529
Nicodemus, Edwd. M., 2626

Nicodemus, Elizabeth Catharine, 2528
Nicodemus, Elizabeth Catharine, 2529
Nicodemus, Fred., 2626
Nicodemus, Frederici, 1075
Nicodemus, Frederici, 783
Nicodemus, Jacob, 2528
Nicodemus, Jacob, 2529
Nicodemus, James Sylvester, 2529
Nicodemus, Jeremias, 783
Nicodemus, John Jacob, 2528
Nicodemus, Laura, 5578
Nicodemus, Maria Anna, 1439
Nicodemus, Mariae Annae, 1075
Nicodemus, Mariae, 783
Nicodemus, Mary A., 2626
Nicodemus, Mary Ann, 2002
Nicodemus, William, 5473
Nierman, Amelia, 4119
Nierman, August, 3043
Nierman, August, 5080
Nierman, Augusto, 3113
Nierman, Augusto, 3242
Nierman, Augusto, 3339
Nierman, Augusto, 4079
Nierman, Augusto, 4119

Nierman, Augustum Henricum, 3242
Nierman, Augustum, 4896
Nierman, Augustus, 3154
Nierman, Clara Elizabeth, 3043
Nierman, Clara, 5355
Nierman, Daisy, 4079
Nierman, Daisy, 4119
Nierman, Joannem Augustinum, 4119
Nierman, Lulam May Catharinam, 4079
Nierman, Maria Ameliam, 3113
Nierman, Mariam Teresiam, 3339
Nierman, Mrs., 4011
Nierman, Philamena, 3043
Nierman, Philamena, 3079
Nierman, Philemena, 3339
Nierman, Philomena, 3113
Nierman, Philomena, 3154
Nierman, Philomena, 3242
Nierman, Rosa, 4079
Niermann, Augusto, 3473
Niermann, Philomena, 3473
Niermann, Rosam Bernadettam, 3473
Nikirk, Maria Agneto, 3474

Nikirk, Mariam Josephnam, 3474
Nikirk, Silas A., 3474
Nilis, Annae, 930
Nilis, Georgii, 930
Nilis, Joannes, 930
Nimmy, John Henry, 2468
Nimmy, Louisa, 2468
Nipe, Georgium W., 4740
Nocton, Ellenora, 2154
Nocton, Honora, 2012
Nocton, Honora, 2066
Nocton, Honora, 2154
Nocton, Honora, 2186
Nocton, Mary, 2177
Nocton, Thomas, 2012
Nocton, Timothy, 2012
Nocton, Timothy, 2154
Noel, Anna L., 4034
Noel, Elisabeth, 4034
Noel, Jacobo H., 4034
Noeton, Honora, 2012
Noeton, Thomas, 2012
Noeton, Timothy, 2012
Nolan, Eduardum I., 4894
Nolan, Danniel, 1583
Nolan, Ellen, 1992
Nolan, Elleonora, 1425

Nolan, Elleonorae, 1425
Nolan, James R. Polk, 1992
Nolan, Jeremiah, 1938
Nolan, Mariae, 1583
Nolan, Martini, 1583
Nolan, Martinus, 1727
Nolan, Michael, 1992
Nolan, Michaelis, 1425
Nolan, Sallie K., 4097
Nolan, Theresia, 4097
Nollman, John, 4195
Nonan, Danielis, 1522
Nonan, Elisabeth, 1522
Nonan, Michael, 1522
Noon, Catharina, 1220
Noon, Joannis, 1220
Noon, Mariae, 1220
Noonan, James, 2261
Noonan, Maria, 1432
Noonan, Mary, 4388
Noose, John, 145
Noose, John, 145
Noose, Mary, 145
Noran, Eleonorae, 1446
Norris, Catharine Lucinda, 2007
Norris, Catherina, 3752
Norris, Mary Ann, 1929

Norris, Mary Jane, 2470
Norris, Mary, 1972
Norris, May Jane, 2090
Norris, Melean [or Wiliard?], 3752
Norris, Paulum, 3752
Norton, Honora, 1925
Norton, Mariae, 824
Norton, Michael, 1925
Norton, Thomae, 824
Norton, Thomas, 824
Norton, Timothy, 1925
Noughton, Agnes Cecilia, 2342
Noughton, Honora, 2342
Noughton, Timothy, 2342
Nowell, Jacoburn R., 4088
Nufskel, Eva Catharina, 2180
Nufskel, Ludwick, 2180
Nufskel, Mary Anna, 2180
Nufskel, Eva, 2181
Nugent, Michael, 1624
Nugent, Thomas, 1113
Nugent, Thomas, 1462
Null, Anna Elizabeth, 2439
Null, Charlotte, 2217
Null, Charlotte, 2439
Null, Charlotte, 2552
Null, George Buchanan, 2552

Null, George J., 2552
Null, George, 2217
Null, George, 2439
Null, Mary (Mrs.), 471
Null, Mary Virginia, 2217
Nusskel, Eva, 2181
Nusskel, Eva Catharina, 2180
Nusskel, Ludwick, 2180
Nusskel, Mary Anna, 2180
O Taly, Henerietta, 405
O Taly, Isiac, 405
O Taly, Leo Ruben, 405
Oak, Berta C., 4033
Oak, Bertha C., 4129
Oaster, Emma Martha, 2518
Oaster, Lewis, 2518
Oaster, Lewis, 2570
Oaster, Louisa, 2518
Oaster, Luisia, 2571
O'beca, Agathae, 874
O'beca, Ferdinandi, 874
O'beca, Josephus, 874
O'Boyle, Mary Anne (Miss), 213
O'Brian, [blank], 650
O'Brian, [blank], 650
O'Brian, Birgitta, 650
O'Brian, Caroles, 1357

O'Brian, Caroli, 724
O'Brian, Catharine, 2018
O'Brian, Dyonisius, 1078
O'Brian, Edwardi, 1055
O'Brian, Edwardi, 1273
O'Brian, Eleonorae, 1055
O'Brian, Eleonorae, 1273
O'Brian, Elisabeth Anna, 1055
O'Brian, Jacobus Alexander, 1273
O'Brian, Jacobus, 1487
O'Brian, Jacobus, 712
O'Brian, John, 2186
O'Brian, Judith, 1197
O'Brian, Julia, 4466
O'Brian, Margaretae, 1078
O'Brian, Margaretae, 1487
O'Brian, Margaretae, 712
O'Brian, Maria, 724
O'Brian, Mariae, 724
O'Brian, Mary, 4449
O'Brian, Patricii, 1078
O'Brian, Patricii, 1487
O'Brian, Patricii, 712
O'Brian, Patricius, 1488
O'Brian, Phebe, 1977
O'Brian, Phoebe, 4514
O'Brien, Cath., 2610

O'Brien, Cornelius, 3839
O'Brien, Francis, 5433
O'Brien, Geneveffam, 3794
O'Brien, Helenem Mariam, 3706
O'Brien, James, 24
O'Brien, Jas., 2680
O'Brien, Joannes, 1332
O'Brien, John Thomas, 3066
O'Brien, John, 1907
O'Brien, Julia, 3605
O'Brien, Julia, 3634
O'Brien, Julia, 3706
O'Brien, Julia, 3794
O'Brien, Laurence, 23
O'Brien, Laurence, 24
O'Brien, Maria Josephinam, 3634
O'Brien, Maria, 4109
O'Brien, Mariam, 3605
O'Brien, Mary Ann, 23
O'Brien, Mary, 23
O'Brien, Mary, 24
O'Brien, Mary, 2670
O'Brien, Mary, 3066
O'Brien, Matheo, 3605
O'Brien, Matteo, 3634
O'Brien, Mattheo, 3706
O'Brien, Mattheo, 3794

O'Brien, Matthew, 2868
O'Brien, Matthew, 5436
O'Brien, Michel, 2752
O'Brien, Miles Benedict, 2868
O'Brien, Patrick, 4945
O'Brien, Rebecca, 2868
O'Brien, Rebecca, 2868
O'Brien, Timothy, 3066
O'Brist, Anna R., 4101
O'Brist, Joanne R., 4101
Obrist, Joannem R., 4892
O'Brist, Veronicam Ohiliam, 4101
Obritt, Anna, 4156
O'Connell, Anne, 5371
O'Conner, Margarrita, 3211
O'Conner, Flora, 2785
O'Conner, Jacobus, 3211
O'Conner, James Remar J.[or Remard], 5732
O'Conner, James, 2785
O'Conner, Mary, 2785
O'Conner, Bernard, 4269
O'Conner, Birgitta, 3948
O'Conner, Catharine, 3948
O'Conner, Margareta, 3233
O'Conner, Margaretta, 3575
O'Conner, Margarita, 3317

O'Conner, Margaritam, 4749
O'Conner, Patritius, 3948
O'Conner, Thos., 4627
O'Connor, Anna, 3575
O'Connor, Catharina, 3472
O'Connor, Eileen [sic], 2617
O'Connor, Ellen, 2617
O'Connor, Felix Michael, 5731
O'Connor, Jane, 2543
O'Connor, Jane, 3055
O'Connor, Jane, 3056
O'Connor, Jane, 4690
O'Connor, Jas, 169
O'Connor, Jno, 2617
O'Connor, Margareta, 3723
O'Connor, Margaritta, 3151
O'Connor, Maria Johanna, 3627
O'Connor, Maria, 3723
O'Connor, Michael, 2617
O'Connor, Morris, 2753
O'Connor, Patrick, 5091
O'Connor, Richard (Rev.), 4529
O'Connor, Thomas, 3723
Ocpherin, Joseph, 373
Ocpherin, Mary, 373
Ocpherin, Peter, 373
O'Donnal, Joannes, 1445

O'Donnal, Joannis, 1445
O'Donnal, Margaretae, 1445
O'Donnel, Anna, 318
O'Donnel, Dominius Augustus, 975
O'Donnel, Joannes, 742
O'Donnel, Joannis, 742
O'Donnel, John (Mrs.), 4211
O'Donnel, John, 259
O'Donnel, John, 318
O'Donnel, John, 4211
O'Donnel, Margaretae, 742
O'Donnel, Margaretae, 952
O'Donnel, Maria, 1316
O'Donnel, Maria, 952
O'Donnel, Mary Anna, 259
O'Donnel, Paatricii, 952
O'Donnel, Susanna, 259
O'Donnel, Susanna, 318
O'Donnel, Susanna, 4386
O'Donnell, Anna, 1649
O'Donnell, Augustinus Dominicus, 1314
O'Donnell, Columbus, 3895
O'Donnell, Columbus, 4818
O'Donnell, Dominius Augustus, 4370
O'Donnell, Franciscus, 1528

O'Donnell, James, 157
O'Donnell, Jane, 4313
O'Donnell, Jno, 164
O'Donnell, John, 4190
O'Donnell, John, 4334
O'Donnell, Maria Anna, 4439
O'Donnell, Patricius, 1479
O'Donnell, Susanna, 164
O'Donnelly, Margaret, 193
O'Donnelly, Patrick, 193
O'Donohue, Daniel, 3181
O'Donohue, Margaret, 3181
Oesterman, Joseph, 4754
O'Farrell, Alice, 122
O'Farrell, James, 4289
O'Farrell, John, 122
O'Farrell, Peter, 122
O'Ferrel, John, 4199
O'Flynn, E. (Rev.), 3898
O'Forbes, Catherine, 188
O'Forbes, Edward, 188
O'Forbes, Henry, 188
Ogle, Louisa, 5197
Ogle, Luisa, 3463
O'Hara, Catherine, 3045
O'Hara, Wm. A., 4646

O'Harran, Danielis, 1332
O'Harran, Johannae, 1332
O'Harran, Maria, 1332
O'Hay, Catharinae, 1515
O'Hay, Johanna, 1515
O'Hay, Thomae, 1515
O'Henan, Joanna E., 5735
O'Huran, Annie Cecelia, 5755
O'Huran, Catherine Lillie, 5756
O'Huran, Ellen Emelia, 5736
O'Keefe, Anna, 4110
O'Keefe, Danielem, 4110
O'Keefe, Nicholas, 4537
O'Keefe, Thoma, 4110
O'Keeffe, Helena, 2153
O'Keeffe, Isabella, 2153
O'Keeffe, Nicholas, 2153
Oker, Caroline, 2373
Oker, Elizabeth, 5425
Oker, Mary A., 2373
Oker, Mary A., 2597
Oker, Mary Ann, 2498
Oker, Mary C., 4725
Oker, Mary Elizabeth, 2373
Oker, Mary, 5495
O'Kerran, Joannes, 4379
O'Kief, Anna Luiza, 2417

O'Kief, Helena, 2417
O'Kief, Nicholas, 2417
Older, Georgiin, 1718
Older, Maria, 1718
Older, Mariae, 1718
Oldman, Mariae, 878
Oldman, Own [Owen?], 878
Oldman, Patricius, 878
O'Learey, Daniel, 4517
O'Learey, Elizabeth, 2404
O'Learey, Thomas Theodore, 2404
O'Learey, Thomas, 2404
O'Leary, Daniel, 1897
O'Leary, Daniel, 2168
O'Leary, Daniel, 2284
O'Leary, Daniel, 2284
O'Leary, Elizabeth, 2284
O'Leary, Elizabeth, 5379
O'Leary, Thomas, 2284
Oliver, Cecelia, 2574
Oliver, A. (Mrs.), 5044
Oliver, Cath., 5569
Oliver, Catharina, 3158
Oliver, Catherine, 4711
Oliver, Cecelia, 2737
Oliver, Cecilia, 2696
Oliver, Cecilia, 2816

Oliver, Cecilia, 2944
Oliver, Cecilia, 4657
Oliver, Ella, 2895
Oliver, Ella, 2944
Oliver, Ella, 3319
Oliver, Ella, 3320
Oliver, Ella, 3321
Oliver, Ella, 3541
Oliver, Ella, 3612
Oliver, Ella, 3613
Oliver, Ella, 3616
Oliver, Ella, 3848
Oliver, Ella, 3920
Oliver, Ella, 3951
Oliver, Ella, 4027
Oliver, Ella, 4158
Oliver, Ella, 4711
Oliver, Ella, 4880
Oliver, Ellen S., 2816
Oliver, Ellen, 2645
Oliver, Ellen, 2840
Oliver, Ellen, 3112
Oliver, Ellen, 3228
Oliver, Ellen, 3292
Oliver, Ellen, 3418
Oliver, Ellen, 5513
Oliver, Ellen, 5566

Oliver, Fannie, 3012
Oliver, Fanny, 2895
Oliver, Frances, 3112
Oliver, Helena, 3158
Oliver, Helena, 3177
Oliver, Helena, 3817
Oliver, Kate, 2872
Oliver, Maria, 2140
Oliver, Maria, 2649
Oliver, Maria, 2872
Oliver, Mary F., 4648
Oliver, Mary S., 2011
Oliver, Mary, 2208
Oliver, Mary, 2259
Oliver, Mary, 2324
Oliver, Mary, 3012
Oliver, Percy Costello, 2872
Olvier, Cecilia, 3228
Olvier, Cecilia, 3229
Olvier, Eda, 4064
Olvier, Ellen, 3069
O'Mara, Elizabetha, 4814
O'Neal, Annam, 4744
O'Neal, Birgittae, 1275
O'Neal, Gulielmum, 4802
O'Neal, Hugonis, 1275
O'Neal, Rosa Anna, 1275

O'Neal, William, 5462
O'Neale, Margaret, 99
O'Nealle, Henry, 161
O'Nealle, Margaret, 161
O'Neil, Ann, 2974
O'Neil, Catherine, 3081
O'Neil, Ellen, 2577
O'Neil, James, 3081
O'Neil, John, 2577
O'Neil, Margarita, 3829
O'Neil, Margt., 3708
O'Neil, Margt., 3795
O'Neil, Miss, 3081
O'Neil, Patrick, 2577
O'Neil, Thomas, 3081
O'Neill, Catherine (Mrs.), 5357
O'Neill, Edw., 5244
O'Neill, Edward, 2941
O'Neill, Frederico, 3728
O'Neill, Joannes, 3156
O'Neill, Kate, 2941
O'Neill, Margarita (Mrs.), 3963
O'Neill, Margarita (Mrs.), 4008
O'Neill, Maria, 3728
O'Neill, Mariam Selma, 3728
O'Neill, Thomam, 4735
O'Neill, Thos., 2941

O'Neill, Thos., 5149
O'Neill, William, 4991
Oner, [blank], 2774
Oner, [blank], 2774
Oner, Joseph, 2774
Ooster, Emma Martha, 2518
Ooster, Lewis, 2518
Ooster, Louisa, 2518
Oppe, John [possible middle name but illegible], 554
Ordner, Anna, 2897
Ordner, Geo., 2897
Ordner, Wm. Benj., 2897
O'Reiley, John, 4351
O'Reilly, M., 2513
O'Rieley, Bridget, 4351
O'Rielly, James, 4353
O'Riely, Patrick, 4336
O'Riely, Rebecca, 609
Orndorf, Maria, 4006
Orndorf, Agnel Euladiam, 3681
Orndorf, Agnes, 5200
Orndorf, Dna [na is superscript] Romana, 3382
Orndorf, Francescum S., 3855
Orndorf, Francis, 5104
Orndorf, Franciscum B., 3119

Orndorf, Franciscum Henrieum, 3313
Orndorf, Guglielmo, 3313
Orndorf, Guglielmum, 4741
Orndorf, Guglielmus, 3265
Orndorf, Guglieluco, 3216
Orndorf, Gulielmo F., 3119
Orndorf, Gulielmo F., 3382
Orndorf, Gulielmo F., 3598
Orndorf, Gulielmo, 3681
Orndorf, Gulielmo, 3855
Orndorf, Gulielmum J., 4832
Orndorf, Harriet Louisam, 3265
Orndorf, Isaac, 5693
Orndorf, Jno. Wm., 2932
Orndorf, Jr., Gulielmus, 3555
Orndorf, L. Harriet, 4912
Orndorf, M. (Mrs.), 5052
Orndorf, Maria J., 3119
Orndorf, Maria, 3855
Orndorf, Maria, 4141
Orndorf, Maria, 4142
Orndorf, Mariam H., 4902
Orndorf, Mariam Helenam, 3216
Orndorf, Mary Jane, 2932
Orndorf, Robertum Carrole, 3382
Orndorf, Romana, 3598

Orndorf, Romana, 3681
Orndorf, Romanus, 3216
Orndorf, Romanus, 3265
Orndorf, Romanus, 3313
Orndorf, Rosam Mariam, 3598
Orndorf, Rose, 5086
Orndorf, Wm., 2932
Orndorfe, Charles, 5337
Orndorff, Geneviefe, 3873
Orndorff, Gulielmo, 3873
Orndorff, Gulielmo, 4824
Orndorff, Mary J., 2947
Orndorff, Mary, 2856
Orndorff, Mrs., 3735
Orndorff, W. F., 3097
Orndorff, Wm. F., 5196
Orndorff, Wm., 2856
O'Rourk, Mary, 4346
O'Rourke, Anna, 2199
O'Rourke, Bernard, 2197
O'Rourke, Bernard, 2198
O'Rourke, Bernard, 2199
O'Rourke, Charles, 2197
O'Rourke, Hannah, 2197
O'Rourke, Hannah, 2198
O'Rourke, Hannah, 2199

O'Rourke, Louisa, 2198
Osborn, Jas, 5596
Osborn, Jas., 5595
Osborn, Jas., 5556
Oster, Sophia, 4483
Osterman, Rosam E., 4899
O'Toole, Maria, 4009
O'Toole, Maria, 4010
Ott, Josephum W., 4737
Otte, Garret, 557
Ottman, Frances E. E., 2319
Ottman, Frances E., 2166
Ottman, Frances E., 2223
Ottman, Frances E., 2372
Ottman, Frances E.C. [or E.E.], 1981
Ottman, Frances, 2117
Ottman, Frances, 2196
Ottman, James Dallas, 1981
Ottman, John, 1981
Ottman, John, 2117
Ottman, John, 2319
Ottman, Joseph Marian Campbell, 2117
Ottman, Mary Frances Virginia, 2319
Ourey, Mary, 196
Ourey, Peter, 196
Ourey, Teresa, 196
Ourough, Elisa, 291
Ourough, Mary, 291
Ourough, Peter, 291
Over, [blank], 2774
Over, [blank], 2774
Over, Joseph, 2774
Overbeck, Romadne V., 4029
Owens, Dan, 4276
Owens, Sarah (widow), 4341
Owner, 3676
Owner, Emma B., 3830
Owner, Gratiam Geneviefam, 3830
Owner, Jos. S., 3709
Owner, Joseph L., 4765
Owner, Joseph, 3830
Owner, Joseph, 4762
Owner, Joseph, 5623
Owner, Mrs. Mary, 5630
Owner, Mrs., 4686
Paddon, Elis., 2825
Paddon, Mary, 2825
Paden, Elizabeth, 3183
Paden, John, 4327
Page, Augustin, 356
Page, Catherine, 356

Page, Jeremy, 356
Painey, William, 2123
Painter, Jacob, 174
Painter, Jacob, 174
Painter, Jacob, 257
Painter, Jacob, 257
Painter, Jacob, 258
Painter, Jacob, 366
Painter, Margret, 366
Painter, Mary, 174
Painter, Mary Anna, 257
Painter, Mary Anna, 258
Painter, Mary, 366
Painter, Rosana, 258
Palmer, John, 473
Palmer, Marietta, 473
Palmer, Richard, 473
Panafather, John, 4245
Pap, Barbara, 2920
parents are Black, Lucy, 452
parents are Black, Lucy, 450
parents are Black, Lucy, 451
Parker, Anna A., 3156
Parker, Anna A., 3387
Parker, Anna A., 3537
Parker, Anna Anderson, 2428
Parker, Anna Virginia, 1677

Parker, Annam A., 4728
Parker, Archibald Ensminger, 2426
Parker, Catharine, 2426
Parker, Catharine, 2427
Parker, Catharine, 2428
Parker, Catharine, 2429
Parker, Emililam J., 4894
Parker, Frances, 2429
Parker, John, 2426
Parker, John, 2427
Parker, John, 2428
Parker, John, 2429
Parker, Mary, 2754
Parker, Samuel Culberson, 2427
Parker, Susannae, 1677
Parker, Thomae, 1677
Parkes, Ann, 3222
Parks, C.E. (Rev.), 4085
Parks, Helena D., 4028
Parks, Helenard [or Helen D.], 4085
Parks, T.E. (Rev.), 4085
Parsons, Ann, 150
Parsons, Ann, 56
Parsons, Mary, 123
Pass, Barbara, 2920
Paster, Christiamna, 2571

Paster, Lewis, 2571
Paster, Luisia, 2571
Paten, Chambers, 128
Paten, Chambers, 129
Paten, Chambers, 130
Paten, John, 128
Paten, Louisa, 129
Paten, Mary, 128
Paten, Mary, 129
Paten, Mary, 130
Paten, Mary, 131
Paten, Mary, 132
Paten, Rosanna, 130
Paterson, Caroli, 1231
Paterson, Edwardus, 1231
Paterson, Mariae Anarr, 1231
Paton, Jacobus, 1655
Paton, Joannes, 1041
Paton, Joannis, 1041
Paton, Joannis, 1655
Paton, Maria, 1214
Paton, Mariae, 1041
Paton, Mariae, 1655
Patritii, H., 3924
Paulr?, Ellon, 4245
Paulus [sic], Paulus, 1366
Paulus [sic], Paulus, 1811

Paulus, Angline, 4997
Paulus, Doretheae, 1428
Paulus, Eva Catharina, 1428
Paulus, Guilelmus, 1244
Paulus, Magdalen, 1828
Paulus, Maria, 2220
Paulus, Mary, 2479
Paulus, N., 1244
Paulus, Peter, 1828
Paulus, Petry, 1428
Paulus, Sophia, 1828
Paw, Clarissa, 121
Payne, Annam Mariam, 4100
Payne, Cecilia, 4100
Payne, Joanne, 4100
Payne, Mary Ellen, 4626
Peak, Bennet, 1
Peak, Elizabeth, 1
Peake, Bent (Mrs.), 469
Peake, Mr., 4956
Pearl, Bertam Mariam, 3948
Pearl, Catharina (Mrs.), 4165
Pearl, Catharine, 3948
Pearl, Cornelio, 3948
Pearl, Cornelius, 4109
Peck, Eliza, 1860
Peck, Jacob, 1860

Peck, Jacob, 2042
Peck, Jacob, 2135
Peck, Jacob, 2299
Peck, Jacob, 4185
Peck, Jacobus, 1810
Pecker, Joseph, 2122
Peekins, Jane Elen, 4358
Peltz, Rebecca A., 3561
Pembrook, Peggy, 4220
Pembrook, Basil, 458
Pembrook, Nelley, 458
Pembrook, Richard, 458
Pembrooke, Basil, 335
Pembrooke, Daniel, 335
Pembrooke, Nelly, 335
Pentz, Arnelia, 3493
Perkins, Eliza Jane, 3456
Perkinson, H. (Rev.), 3289
Peters, Jno. (Mrs.), 2906
Peters, Jno., 2906
Peters, Maria Sophia, 2016
Petre, John W., 4820
Petri, Jacobus, 4401
Petticord, Annam H. Florentiam, 3924
Petticord, Eduardus, 3924
Petticord, Jacobo A., 3924

Petticord, Maria E., 3924
Peugh, Dr., 4534
Peugh, Dr., 4557
Phenig, Maria, 2240
Philipps, Birgitta, 1230
Philips, Birgitta, 4481
Philips, Jeremiae, 1725
Philips, Joannes, 1725
Philips, John, 2171
Philips, Mariae, 1725
Philips, Robertus, 1725
Phillips, Hugh, 2013
Pic, Ada Maria L., 3984
Pickens, Jane E., 631
Picket, William, 2577
Piegut, Joseph, 4437
Pierce, Josiah, 3929
Pierce, Josiah (Mrs.), 3929
Pierce, Josiah Dahlgren, 3929
Pierce, Josiah, 4029
Pierce, Jr., Josiah, 4852
Pierce, Ulrica, 3929
Pierce, Ulrica, 4029
Pierce, Ulricum Vinton Dalgreen, 4029
Pile, Ada Maria L., 3984
Pile, Catharine, 76

Pile, Catharine, 77
Pile, Catharine, 78
Pile, Francisci, 3984
Pile, Henry, 76
Pile, James, 78
Pile, Jenny, 77
Pile, Naas, 76
Pile, Naas, 77
Pile, Naas, 78
Pilz, Al., 2803
Pine, Ann, 97
Pine, Michael, 97
Pine, Wm, 97
Pith, Mary J., 2604
Pith, Ada Maria L., 3984
Pitt, Annie, 5560
Pitt, Mary I. [or J.], 2704
Planaet, Catharinae, 1391
Planaet, Patricii, 1391
Planaet, Petrus, 1391
Planke, Catharinae, 1391
Planke, Patricii, 1391
Planke, Petrus, 1391
Pleek, Annae, 1115
Pleek, Maria Anna, 1115
Plunke, Catharinae, 1391
Plunke, Patricii, 1391

Plunke, Petrus, 1391
Plunkett, Thomas, 2340
Po [rest blank], Catherine, 265
Poffenberger, Benjamin, 2407
Poffenberger, Elizabeth, 4684
Poffenberger, Louisa Jane, 2407
Poffenberger, Louisa, 2407
Poffenberger, Lucy A., 2452
Poffenberger, Lucy A., 2453
Poffenberger, Lucy A., 2454
Poffenberger, Margaret Ann, 2452
Poffenberger, Margaret Ann, 2453
Poffenberger, Margaret Ann, 2454
Poffenberger, Mrs., 5153
Poffinbarger, Lucy, 2648
Polito, Anthony, 3289
Pomme De Terre [sic], Emily, 2948
Pool, Garret F., 581
Pool, Margaretha F., 3551
Poole, Annam, 3333
Poole, Catharina, 3636
Poole, Jacobo F., 3333
Poole, Maria, 3333
Poper, Mary (Mrs.), 5334
Poper, Ann, 2911
Poper, Anna, 4692
Poper, Byron H., 5317

Poper, Byron Henricum, 4010
Poper, Carolo J., 4010
Poper, Carolo, 4009
Poper, Carolum Jacob, 4009
Poper, Carolum Jacob, 4046
Poper, Jacob, 4046
Poper, Margareta, 4046
Poper, Maria, 4009
Poper, Maria, 4010
Portel, Hannah (Miss), 5234
Porter, Carolem Eugenium, 4031
Porter, Cath, 5101
Porter, Gulielmo, 4031
Porter, Gulielmo, 4830
Porter, Gulielmum Geary, 3923
Porter, Gulielmum, 4849
Porter, Gulielum, 3923
Porter, Joanna, 3923
Porter, Joanna, 4031
Porter, Lydia A., 3837
Porter, Lydiam Agnetem, 4830
Porter, Mrs., 4889
Porter, Thomas, 4849
Post, George W., 2553
Post, Mrs., 4685
Postetter, David [H crossed out after David], 2516

Postetter, Dorothea Sylvesta, 2516
Postetter, Rebecca, 2516
Pouer, Cecilia, 2767
Pouer, William Charles, 2767
Pouer, William, 2767
Powell, [blank], 2991
Powell, Catherine May, 2991
Powell, Ceceilia, 2720
Powell, Cecilia, 2720
Powell, Cecilia, 2991
Powell, H. Angelo, 2814
Powell, Wm. Angelo, 4624
Powell, Wm, 2720
Power, Anastasiae, 910
Power, Richardis, 910
Power, Richardis, 910
Power, McNamora, 1173
Power, Anastasia, 1109
Power, Catherine, 404
Power, Daniel, 1451
Power, Elisabeth, 1337
Power, Elizb, 63
Power, George, 404
Power, John, 404
Power, Margareta, 1173
Power, Richardus, 1380
Powers, Anastasiae, 1355

Powers, Elisea, 1092
Powers, Joannes, 1355
Powers, Richardi, 1355
Preston, Guglielmum Weston, 3235
Preston, Maria, 3235
Preston, Samuel, 3235
Price, Ann, 3014
Price, Anna A., 3166
Price, Anna A., 4697
Price, Anna Amelia, 3094
Price, Anna Amelia, 3476
Price, Anna, 3239
Price, Anna, 3274
Price, Anna, 3549
Price, Anna, 3627
Price, Anna, 3719
Price, Anna, 3894
Price, Annam, 3426
Pridy?, Maria, 584
Pridy?, Mary, 584
Pridy?, Thos, 584
Prier, Hugo, 1296
Primas, Basilie, 1187
Primas, Dianae, 1187
Primas, Theresia, 1187
Prince, Delilah, 4793
Prinston, Philip, 603

Prior, Hugh, 1952
Prior, Jacob, 2751
Prior, Margaret Elisabeth, 2751
Prior, Margaret Jane, 1952
Prior, Mary, 2751
Prior, Rosa, 1952
Prior, Rosa, 1952
Prior, Rosanna (Mrs.), 4556
Prior, Rosanna, 2067
Pritner, Julia, 2844
Proctor, Rosalia, 4794
Proctor, Rosalie, 4793
Proer, Elleonora, 1729
Proer, Hugonis, 1729
Proer, Rosae, 1729
Protastinger, Georgius, 4407
Protzman, Mr., 4603
Provence, Edmundum Ephraim, 3818
Provence, Ephradm, 3818
Provence, Helena, 3818
Provence, Maria, 3818
Provert, Alexander, 524
Provert, Alexander, 524
Pryer, Catharina, 1513
Pryer, Hugo, 1512
Pryer, Hugonis, 1513

Pryer, Rosa, 1512
Pryer, Rosae, 1513
Puffenburger, Anna Elisabeth, 1042
Puffenburger, Annae Elisabeth, 1042
Puffenburger, Annae Elisabeth, 1043
Puffenburger, Annae Elisabeth, 1044
Puffenburger, Guillelmus Henricus, 1044
Puffenburger, Samuelis, 1042
Puffenburger, Samuelis, 1043
Puffenburger, Samuelis, 1044
Puffenburger, Sara Anna, 1043
Pulmann, Catharinae, 1377
Pulmann, Frederici, 1377
Pulmann, Henricus Jacobus, 1377
Pultz, Jacob, 1224
Purcel, Patricius, 1588
Purcel, Patricius, 1610
Purcel, Patricius, 4500
Purl, Catharine Elizabeth, 27
Purl, Catharine Elizabeth, 28
Purl, Charles, 28
Purl, Charles, 25

Purl, Charles, 26
Purl, Charles, 26
Purl, Charles, 27
Purl, Elizabeth, 25
Purl, James Philip, 27
Purl, Nancy, 25
Purl, Nancy, 26
Purl, Thomas, 28
Putz, Jacobus, 1693
Putz, Jacobus, 1801
Putz?, Jacobi, 1251
Putz?, Margaretae, 1251
Putz?, Maria, 1251
Qannen, Thomas, 4350
Qucgley, Annae, 1291
Qucggley, Joannis, 1291
Qucggley, Susanna, 1291
Quegh, Margt, 59
Quicgley, Margareta, 1147
Quicgley, Maria, 1354
Quicgley, Mariae, 1291
Quicgley, Mariae, 1147
Quicgley, Mariae, 1354
Quicgley, Patricii, 1147
Quicgley, Petri, 1354
Quicgly, Mariae, 1673
Quicgly, Michael Henricus, 1673

Quicgly, Petrii, 1673
Quick, George, 2711
Quick, Jacob, 2711
Quick, Margaret, 2711
Quiegly, Anna, 1673
Quiegly, Joannis, 1673
Quiegly, Maria, 1675
Quig, Jacobi, 1429
Quig, Margaretae, 1429
Quig, William, 1429
Quigley, Mariae, 956
Quigley, Petrii, 956
Quigley, Rosa, 956
Quigley, Hugo, 757
Quigley, Mariae, 757
Quigley, Patricii, 757
Quigly, Annae, 1650
Quigly, Elisabeth, 1650
Quigly, Joannis, 1650
Quigly, John Andrew, 31
Quigly, Margaret, 31
Quigly, Moses A., 31
Quin, Ann, 2029
Quin, Anna, 4409
Quin, Annae, 896
Quin, Bernardus, 1394
Quin, Bernardus, 1713

Quin, Birgittae, 1453
Quin, Diyonysii, 896
Quin, Eleonorae, 1113
Quin, Ellen, 1264
Quin, Hanora, 1349
Quin, Jacobi, 1113
Quin, Jacobi, 1453
Quin, Jesse, 2458
Quin, Maria Johanna, 1182
Quin, Maria Johanna, 1453
Quin, Maria, 1713
Quin, Martinus, 1113
Quin, Mary Ann, 2458
Quin, Mary Olivia, 2458
Quin, Michael, 1397
Quin, Michael, 1554
Quin, Owen, 1241
Quin, Patricius, 1264
Quin, Rosa Annae, 1182
Quin, Thomae, 1182
Quin, William, 896
Quinlivin?, John, 4252
Quinn, Anna, 3987
Quinn, Anna, 4155
Quinn, Franciscum Joseph, 4155
Quinn, Jacobo, 3987
Quinn, Jacobo, 4155

Quinn, Joannes, 850
Quinn, Mariam Margaritam, 3987
Quinn, Mary Olivia, 5470
Quinn, Mrs., 3997
Quinn, Rosae, 850
Quinn, Thomae, 850
Quirellan, Jacobi, 2613
Quitney, Hanorae, 1733
Quitney, Jacobus, 1733
Quitney, Patricii, 1733
Rabbit, Michael, 2094
Rabit, Mary, 2707
Rabit, Mary, 2780
Radger, Catharina, 1143
Radger, Catharinae, 1143
Radger, Patricii, 1143
Rafferty, Catharine, 4745
Rafferty, Mary, 2085
Rafter, Maria, 1452
Ragan, Birgitta, 1429
Ragan, Catharinae, 1741
Ragan, Daniel, 1741
Ragan, Joannes, 1429
Ragan, Patricii, 1741
Ragney, George Edw., 5624
Ramacciotti, Ausilia, 4099
Ramacciotti, Ausilia, 4150

Ramacciotti, Bianca, 4099
Ramacciotti, Domenico, 4099
Ramacciotti, Domenico, 4150
Ramacciotti, Idam Mariam, 4150
Ramacciotti, Mariam Ednam, 4099
Ramaciotti, Ausilia, 4030
Ramaciotti, Domenico, 4030
Ramaciotti, Louisam, 4030
Rammacciotti, Bianca, 4150
Ramsburg, Carolum H., 4859
Ramsburg, Mariam Bernardinam, 4859
Randall, Isaac, 2979
Randall, Martha Ann, 2979
Randall, Martha, 2978
Randall, Martha, 2979
Raney, Maria, 1265
Ranney, Mariae, 1321
Ranney, Mariae, 1321
Ranney, Patricii, 1321
Ranney, Joannes, 1360
Ranney, Margaretae, 1360
Ranney, Michaelis, 1360
Rauth, Annam, 3906
Rauth, Anne Dorothea, 5272
Rauth, Carolo, 3974
Rauth, Carolum W., 4840

Rauth, Carroll Martinum, 3973
Rauth, Catharina, 3887
Rauth, Catharina, 3974
Rauth, Catharina, 3999
Rauth, Francis A., 5318
Rauth, Franciscum Augustinum, 4023
Rauth, Georgium Albertum, 3972
Rauth, Gulielmo, 3718
Rauth, Gulielmo, 3775
Rauth, Gulielmo, 3869
Rauth, Gulielmo, 3906
Rauth, Gulielmo, 3939
Rauth, Gulielmo, 3972
Rauth, Gulielmo, 3973
Rauth, Gulielmo, 4023
Rauth, Gulielmo, 4113
Rauth, Gulielmo, 4171
Rauth, Gulieslmum Franciscum, 3869
Rauth, Helenam Dorotheam, 4171
Rauth, Jacob Franc., 5280
Rauth, Jacob Franciscum, 3939
Rauth, Jacobum Riccardum, 4113
Rauth, Joannem Gul, 3718
Rauth, Lucia, 3718
Rauth, Lucia, 3775

Rauth, Lucia, 3869
Rauth, Lucia, 3906
Rauth, Lucia, 3939
Rauth, Lucia, 4023
Rauth, Lucia, 4113
Rauth, Lucia, 4171
Rauth, Lucy, 3973
Rauth, Mariam Catharinam, 3974
Rauth, Mariam Mabel, 3775
Rauthraff, Maria, 3333
Ravelin, Margaret, 1927
Ray, Ann, 83
Ray, Ann, 83
Ray, Elizabeth Ann, 82
Ray, Joseph, 82
Ray, Joseph, 83
Ray, William, 83
Raynalds, Catharinae, 640
Rayney, Maria, 1344
Raynolds, Birgittae, 1404
Raynolds, Catharina, 1353
Raynolds, Catharina, 932
Raynolds, Catharinae, 1071
Raynolds, Catharinae, 1331
Raynolds, Catharinae, 873
Raynolds, Elisabeth, 1331
Raynolds, Elisabeth, 1353

Raynolds, Francisa, 1331
Raynolds, Francisci, 1071
Raynolds, Francisci, 873
Raynolds, Jacobi, 1353
Raynolds, Jacobi, 932
Raynolds, Jacobus, 1331
Raynolds, Joannes, 1404
Raynolds, Maria, 1671
Raynolds, Maria, 873
Raynolds, Mariae, 1353
Raynolds, Mariae, 932
Raynolds, Michael, 1555
Raynolds, Patricii, 1404
Raynolds, Thomas, 1071
Raynolds, Thomas, 4478
Read, Elizabeth, 2027
Read, Antonii, 1410
Read, Catharinae, 1410
Read, Elisa, 237
Read, John, 237
Read, Maria, 1410
Reader, Joannes, 1154
Reading, Joannes, 4090
Reading, Maria, 4090
Reading, Susanna, 4090
Ready, Antonius, 4468
Ready, Catharina, 1426

Reagen, David, 4324
Reamer, Carolum Samuelem, 3932
Reamer, Georgio, 3932
Reamer, Gertrude, 3932
Reardon, Daniele, 3254
Reardon, Margaritta, 3563
Reardon, Maria, 3254
Reardon, Maria, 3578
Reardon, May, 2138
Reardon, Michaelem Aloysium, 3254
Reardon, Mrs., 3543
Reardon, Timotheus, 3561
Reariden, Michael, 4217
Reckert, Andrea, 3843
Reckert, Andream J. [or T.], 4814
Reckert, Eleonoram, 3843
Reckert, Ella E., 3843
Recket, Eleonora, 3843
Redding, Maria, 3885
Redding, Maria, 3955
Reddlemoser, W.A. (Dr.), 5154
Reddy, Ann, 56
Redmond, Fr., 25
Redmond, Fr., 26
Redmond, Fr., 27
Redmond, Fr., 28

Redmond, Geo, 125
Redmond, George, 231
Redmond, George, 237
Redmond, J., 124
Redmond, James (Rev.), 107
Redmond, James (Rev.), 41
Redmond, James, 153
Redmond, James, 154
Redmond, Jas. (Rev.), 109
Redmond, Patrick, 50
Redmond, Patrick, 4214
Redmond, Revd James, 81
Reed, Alicia, 4872
Reed, Benjamin Ernestum, 3930
Reed, Edwardum Maremn, 3616
Reed, Elizabeth, 2027
Reed, Elizabeth, 2042
Reed, Elizabeth, 2421
Reed, Francisco, 3322
Reed, Georgium, 3829
Reed, Guglielmo, 3417
Reed, Guilielmo, 3616
Reed, Gulielmo, 3829
Reed, Gulielmo, 3930
Reed, Gulielmum G., 3748
Reed, Jane, 3322
Reed, Johanneam, 3322

Reed, Marg. Ellen, 3748
Reed, Maria, 3417
Reed, Maria, 3616
Reed, Maria, 3829
Reed, Maria, 3930
Reed, Mary, 3061
Reed, Mary, 4430
Reed, Sara, 4406
Reed, Sarah Agnetem, 3417
Reed, Thomas, 1376
Reed, Thomas, 1529
Reed, Thomas, 1634
Reed, W. W., 3748
Reed, Wm., 4709
Reeder, Alice, 3068
Reeder, Annam Isabellam, 3190
Reeder, Emelia Alice, 2454
Reeder, Margaret Ann, 2452
Reeder, Margaret Ann, 2453
Reeder, Margaret Ann, 2454
Reeder, Maria A., 3701
Reeder, Maria A., 3701
Reeder, Maria, 3235
Reeder, Mary Elizabeth, 2453
Reeder, Samuelen Vincentium, 3701
Reeder, Wash., 3701

Reeder, Zacharias, 2452
Reeder, Zacharias, 2452
Reeder, Zacharias, 2453
Reeder, Zacharias, 2454
Reel, Barbara, 184
Reel, Daniel, 183
Reel, Elizabeth, 182
Reel, Elizabeth, 183
Reel, Elizabeth, 184
Reel, Joseph, 182
Reel, Joseph, 183
Reel, Joseph, 184
Reel, Michael, 182
Reerden, Michael, 309
Reese, Joannem N.[or W.] H., 4793
Regel, Andrew, 1985
Regel, Margaret, 2019
Regle, Margaret, 1985
Regler, Andrew, 2227
Regler, Margaret, 2227
Rehenny, Michael, 1471
Rehill, Catharine, 2387
Rehill, Mary, 2387
Rehill, Patk., 2316
Rehmeier, Guillelenni Hermanis, 835

Rehmeier, Henricus Guillelmus, 835
Rehmeier, Mariae, 835
Reichter, Caroline, 5718
Reichter, Emma, 4087
Reickert, Andrew, 5282
Reid, Catharine, 147
Reid, Catherina, 3481
Reid, Elizabeth, 1915
Reid, Ellen, 3257
Reid, Guglielmo, 3182
Reid, Guglielmo, 3257
Reid, Gulielmo, 3517
Reid, Henry, 147
Reid, James, 3089
Reid, Johannam, 4729
Reid, John, 147
Reid, Maria Ellen, 3182
Reid, Maria, 3241
Reid, Maria, 3257
Reid, Maria, 3517
Reid, Mariam Aliciam, 3182
Reid, Mariam Elizabeth, 3481
Reid, Mary, 3089
Reid, Thoma A. (Rev.), 3204
Reid, Victorem Franciscum, 3517
Reid, Wm, 3089

Reidout, Sarah, 2791
Reidy, Honora, 51
Reidy, Mary Ann, 51
Reihal, Patrick, 2337
Reilly, Bridget, 2880
Reilly, Elizabeth, 3713
Reilly, Gertrude, 3713
Reilly, Joanne, 3713
Reilly, John, 3023
Reilly, Mary, 3023
Reilly, Sarah, 3023
Reinhand, Elisabeth, 1416
Reinhard, Elisabeth K., 1769
Reinhard, Elisabeth, 1097
Reinhard, Elisabeth, 1549
Reinhard, Elisabeth, 1636
Reinhard, Jacobus Leonardus, 1636
Reinhard, Josephus, 4417
Reinhard, Samuelis, 1097
Reinhard, Samuelis, 1636
Reinhard, Thomas Joannes B., 1097
Reinhart, Samuel, 4423
Reinholder, Annam Elizabeth, 3307
Reinholder, Lemuel, 3307
Reinholder, Mary E., 3307

Reister, Maria, 4530
Relly, Mrs., 4338
Renden, Anna, 1283
Renden, Annae, 1283
Renden, Mauricii, 1283
Renner, Caroline, 2080
Renner, Aloysia Ernest, 1987
Renner, Aloysia Walburg, 1988
Renner, Aloysii, 1776
Renner, Aloysius, 1987
Renner, Andreas Aloysius, 1776
Renner, Andrew, 1985
Renner, Barbara, 1985
Renner, Barbara, 2147
Renner, Barbara, 4546
Renner, Carolina, 1516
Renner, Carolina, 1776
Renner, Caroline (Miss), 4552
Renner, Caroline, 1987
Renner, Caroline, 2088
Renner, Catharina, 1516
Renner, Evelina, 1748
Renner, Eveline, 1866
Renner, Eveline, 2088
Renner, Eveline, 2092
Renner, Guillelmus, 1101
Renner, Herman, 2088

Renner, Herman, 4552
Renner, Ignatii, 1135
Renner, Ignatii, 1516
Renner, Ignatii, 720
Renner, Ignatis, 600
Renner, Ignatius, 1939
Renner, Ignatius, 1415
Renner, Ignatius, 1866
Renner, Ignatius, 1988
Renner, Ignatius, 2088
Renner, Josephus Albertus, 720
Renner, Maria, 1101
Renner, Maria, 1531
Renner, Maria, 1800
Renner, Maria, 2147
Renner, Mariae Annae, 1135
Renner, Mariae Annae, 720
Renner, Mariae, 1516
Renner, Mariae, 1776
Renner, Mary Anna, 1988
Renner, Mary Ellen, 1963
Renner, Mary, 1866
Renner, Mary, 600
Renner, Mary, 600
Renner, Mr., 4575
Renner, Mrs., 4575
Renner, Nicholas, 1866

Renner, Syriacus, 1987
Renner, Syriacus, 1988
Renner, T [or I.] (Mr.), 4552
Renner, T [or I.]'s (Mrs.), 4552
Renner, Theresia, 1135
Renner, Valentine, 1985
Renner, Valentine, 2147
Renner, Valentine, 4546
Renner, William, 1867
Renny, Mariae, 1228
Renny, Matheus, 1228
Renny, Patricii, 1228
Rent, Anna C., 3489
Rent, Helena Cath, 3615
Rent, Lena C., 3455
Rent, Lena Catherina, 3454
Reordan, Elizabeth, 3254
Reordan, Maria, 3213
Reppey, Luciam, 4732
Reriden, Mich., 369
Reriden, Micl, 348
Reynolds, Ann (widow), 2114
Reynolds, Ann (widow), 4557
Reynolds, Ann, 1951
Reynolds, deceased, 2114
Reynolds, Emma C., 4767
Reynolds, Francis, 4348

Reynolds, James, 2066
Reynolds, Lucy, 2114
Reynolds, Sarah Elis., 3776
Reynolds, Sylvester, 1951
Reynolds, Thomas, 1951
Rhinehart (white), Eliza, 1884
Rhinehart, Eliza, 1912
Rhodes, Arthur, 4457
Rhodes, Arthuri, 1659
Rhodes, Joannes, 1659
Rhodes, Rosa Annae, 1659
Ribley, Alexander, 1467
Ribley, Francisca Virginia, 1467
Ribley, Joannis, 1467
Ribley, Mariae Annae, 1467
Rice, Annam C., 4854
Rice, Anna E., 3957
Rice, Bridget, 153
Rice, Bridget, 154
Rice, Elisabeth, 4486
Rice, Lillie, 4854
Rice, Mary (widow), 4272
Richard, Catharine, 2300
Richards, Elizabeth, 1895
Richards, John, 4187
Richards, Mary A., 5256
Richards, Mary, 4187

Richey, Mr., 324
Richter, Carolina (Mrs.), 3835
Richter, Carolina (Mrs.), 3836
Richter, Caroline, 2842
Richter, Cath., 3814
Richter, Cath., 4811
Richter, Charles, 5023
Richter, Chas., 2842
Richter, Emma C. Ann L., 5766
Richter, Emma, 3814
Richter, Emmam, 4811
Richter, Wm. Edwd. Chas., 2842
Rickter, Eliz., 2842
Riddle [or Riddler or Riddles], Margaret, 2698
Riddle, Margaret, 2623
Riddlemoser, Anna E., 3521
Riddlemoser, Annam Elizabeth, 677
Riddlemoser, M.D, Josepho, 3677
Riddlemoser, Marian, 3677
Rideout, O' George, 416
Rideout, Sarah, 416
Rideout, Wilm, 416
Rideout, Maria, 4431
Rideout, Sara, 1298
Rideout, Sara, 1654

Rideout, Sarah, 458
Rideout, Sarah, 2408
Rideout, Sarah, 2422
Rideout, Sarah, 3007
Rideout, Sarah, 3206
Rideout, Sarah, 3207
Rideout, Wilm, 255
Rider, Catharina, 3102
Rider, Charles, 205
Rider, David, 3101
Rider, Edgar S., 3101
Rider, Gulielmo, 3101
Rider, Gulielmus, 3129
Rider, Joanna, 3129
Rider, Louisa, 3101
Rider, Lucia, 3099
Rider, Maria D., 3099
Rider, Maria, 3101
Rider, Sarah, 205
Rider, Wel, 205
Ridgely, Martha, 2129
Ridount, O' George, 416
Ridount, Sarah, 416
Ridount, Wilm, 416
Ridout, Ann Carlisle, 103
Ridout, Rachel, 102
Ridout, Sarah, 101

Ridout, Sarah, 102
Ridout, Sarah, 103
Ridout, Sarah, 5116
Ridout, Wm Henry, 101
Ridout, Wm, 101
Ridout, Wm, 102
Ridout, Wm, 103
Riedout, Sarah, 380
Riedy, Mr., 5032
Riegel, Margareta, 1744
Rieley, Mary (widow), 4248
Rielly, Clarencum Franciscum, 3731
Rielly, Elizabetha, 3731
Rielly, Joanne, 3731
Rierdan, Terry, 4720
Riffsnyder, Mary A. (Mrs.), 4599
Rigan, Catharina, 866
Rigan, Catharina, 866
Rigan, Catharinae, 866
Rigan, Catharinae, 866
Rigan, Rick, 866
Rigan, Rick, 866
Rigler, Andrew, 4939
Rigney, Margaret, 3212
Rigney, Margaret, 3719
Rigney, Margareta, 3239

Rigney, Mary (Mrs.), 5366
Riley, Johanna, 1743
Riley, Anna, 1233
Riley, Anna, 1307
Riley, Anna, 4476
Riley, Antonius, 1142
Riley, Birgitta, 1499
Riley, Birgitta, 4488
Riley, Catharina, 1526
Riley, Catharinae, 713
Riley, Ellen, 2606
Riley, Gertrude, 4026
Riley, Guielelmus, 1588
Riley, Guillelmas, 1610
Riley, Guilelmo, 4787
Riley, Helenae, 791
Riley, Hug [or Huy], 791
Riley, Jacobis, 1116
Riley, Jacobus, 1103
Riley, Joannes, 1732
Riley, Joannes, 791
Riley, Joannis, 1142
Riley, Joannis, 1286
Riley, Joannis, 1574
Riley, Johannae, 1103
Riley, Johannae, 1588
Riley, Johannae, 1610

Riley, Johannae, 1732
Riley, John, 4556
Riley, Margaret, 2387
Riley, Maria, 1390
Riley, Maria, 1399
Riley, Mariae, 1142
Riley, Mariae, 1286
Riley, Mariae, 1574
Riley, Mariae, 840
Riley, Mary Alice, 2057
Riley, Mary, 2057
Riley, Mary, 2387
Riley, Mary, 4713
Riley, Michael Henricus, 1574
Riley, Michael, 2387
Riley, Michael, 713
Riley, Michaelis, 713
Riley, Miles, 1539
Riley, Owen, 2351
Riley, Patricius, 1633
Riley, Patricius, 1730
Riley, Patrick, 2606
Riley, Patrik, 5268
Riley, Petri, 1103
Riley, Petri, 1588
Riley, Petri, 1610
Riley, Petri, 1732

Riley, Petrus, 1743
Riley, Philip, 2057
Riley, Philippi, 840
Riley, Rachel, 3378
Riley, Rosa Anna, 1286
Riley, Rosa, 840
Riley, Thomas Antonius, 1142
Riley, Thos., 2606
Riley, William, 1724
Rinebaugh, George, 2501
Rinehart, Eliza (Mrs.), 1957
Rinehart, Eliza, 2117
Rinehart, Eliza, 2175
Rinehart, Eliza, 2339
Rinehart, Eliza, 2350
Rinehart, James Edgar, 2175
Rinehart, Mr., 4573
Rinehart, Mrs., 4573
Rinehart, Samuel, 2175
Rinehart, Samuel, 2339
Rinehart, Sarah Anna, 2339
Ringgold, Mrs., 4194
Ringgold, Georgeihe, 1423
Ringgold, Georgii, 1424
Ringgold, John J. Fayette, 1424
Ringgold, Mariae, 1423
Ringgold, Mariae, 1424

Ringold, Mary Antoinette, 1424
Ringold, Rebecca, 1423
Ringold, Walter, 1423
Riordan, Dan, 3161
Riordan, M.J. (Rev.), 3852
Riordan, Margarita, 4788
Riordan, Maria E., 3654
Riordan, Maria, 3448
Riordan, Maria, 4788
Riordan, Mariam E., 4788
Ripple, Catharina, 3789
Ripple, Catharina, 3893
Ripple, Catharina, 3946
Ripple, Catharinam, 4819
Riser, Catharine, 4672
Rister, Annie, 2618
Rister, Caroline, 5398
Rister, James, 2618
Rister, Kahleen [sic], 2618
Ritchie, Archibald, 145
Ritz, John, 4243
Roa, Richardus, 4507
Roach, Anne, 2781
Roach, Catharine, 2582
Roach, Catherine, 2734
Roach, Catherine, 2781
Roach, Elisabeth Mary, 2734

Roach, Jacobus, 1089
Roach, Joanna, 2939
Roach, Joannae, 1089
Roach, Margaret, 2582
Roach, Maria, 3126
Roach, Mary, 626
Roach, Michaelis, 1089
Roach, Patrick, 2281
Roach, William, 2781
Roach, Wm, 2582
Roach, Wm, 2659
Roach, Wm, 2734
Roache, M., 3757
Roache, Margt, 3784
Roache, Margt, 3813
Roads, Arthur, 1120
Roane, Edward, 4257
Roarke, Daniel, 50
Roarke, Elizabeth, 50
Roarke, John, 50
Robe?, Mary Elizabeth, 1944
Roberson, Eleonorae, 813
Roberson, Franciscae, 1189
Roberson, Joannis, 1189
Roberson, Joannis, 813
Roberson, Letitia, 813
Roberson, Maria, 1189

Roberts, Joannes, 4451
Robertson, Anitam Mateer, 3838
Robertson, Anna E., 3648
Robertson, Anna, 3838
Robertson, Franciscae, 1533
Robertson, Franciscae, 1793
Robertson, Harold Key Mauritium, 3648
Robertson, Joannes G., 1533
Robertson, Joannes, 1794
Robertson, Joannis, 1533
Robertson, Joannis, 1793
Robertson, Mauricio, 3838
Robertson, Robert Morris, 4771
Robertson, Roberto W., 3648
Robertson, William, 1793
Robinson, C, 4550
Robinson, C, 4562
Robinson, Cath, 4561
Robinson, Catharinae, 2173
Robinson, Catharine, 2285
Robinson, Catharine, 4547
Robinson, Catharine, 4565
Robinson, Catharine, 4566
Robinson, Catharine, 4568
Robinson, Eliza, 4635

Robinson, Elizabeth, 62
Robinson, Luisa, 4678
Robinson, Mary Ann, 4537
Robinson, Mary Ann, 4547
Robinson, Mary, 2057
Roche, James, 4339
Rock, Hugo, 4464
Rockhold, Mrs., 237
Rockhole, Elisa, 248
Rockhole, Eliza, 179
Rockhole, Elizab, 179
Rockhole, Elizabeth, 34
Rockhole, John, 179
Rockhole, John, 248
Rockhole, John, 34
Rockhole, John, 34
Rockhole, Joseph Solomon, 248
Rodenheiser, Maria, 4744
Rodes, Louisa, 2745
Rodes, Arthur, 4455
Rodger, Cathainae, 1405
Rodger, Catharinae, 1787
Rodger, Elisabeth, 1405
Rodger, Joannae, 1144
Rodger, Joannes, 1787
Rodger, Maria, 1330
Rodger, Patricii, 1405

Rodger, Patricii, 1787
Rodgers, Bridget, 2841
Rodgers, Bridget, 2890
Rodgers, Bridget, 3018
Rodgers, Bridget, 5206
Rodgers, Catharinae, 897
Rodgers, Jacobus, 897
Rodgers, John Edward, 1932
Rodgers, Joseph, 1932
Rodgers, Joseph, 4521
Rodgers, Maria, 1932
Rodgers, Patricii, 897
Rodgers, Patrick, 4283
Rodney, Catharina, 3950
Rodney, David, 3950
Rodney, Georgium, 3950
Rodrigues, Eulalia, 3898
Rody, Anna, 1598
Roe, Anna A., 4383
Rogan, Catharinae, 1048
Rogan, Joannes (son), 1048
Rogan, Patricii, 1048
Rogan, Annae, 1754
Rogan, Joannes, 1754
Rogan, Maria, 1194
Rogan, Maria, 4425
Rogan, Michael, 1194

Rogan, Patricii, 1754
Rogan, Patricius, 4463
Rogers, Birgitta, 3425
Rohe, John H., 1848
Rohe, Ann, 1944
Rohe, Ann, 2083
Rohe, Elizabeth (Miss), 4550
Rohe, John Henry, 1944
Rohe, John Henry, 4520
Rohe, John, 2083
Rohe, Mary Elizabeth, 1944
Rohe, Sarah Ann, 2083
Roland, Martha, 3264
Roland, Martha, 3532
Rollins, Milly, 116
Roman, Mr. D., 4542
Roman, Theresia, 4397
Ronalds, Milly, 21
Ronan, Honarae, 1448
Ronan, Laurentius, 1448
Ronan, Mauritii, 1448
Roner, Alice, 4819
Roof, John, 4211
Roof, John (Mrs.), 291
Roof, John, 404
Roof, John (Mrs.), 373
Roof, John (Mrs.), 4211

Roof, John (Mrs.), 466
Roof, John (Mrs.), 476
Roof, John, 291
Roof, John, 317
Roof, John, 408
Roof, John, 439
Roof, Joseph Henry, 317
Roof, Mary Anna Catherine, 439
Roof, Rosanna, 317
Roof, Rosanna, 439
Rooney, Bartholomew, 1913
Rooney, Bridget, 1913
Rooney, Margaret, 1913
Rooney, Sarah Jane, 1913
Rooney, Thomas, 368
Roony, Joannes Thomas, 1678
Roony, Mariae, 1678
Roony, Patricii, 1678
Root, Terresa Anna, 583
Root, Terresa Hanna, 4325
Roperstein, Mariam, 4827
Ropple, Catharina, 3842
Rose, Allen, 3168
Rose, Anna, 3168
Rose, Arthur, 1399
Rose, Carolus, 1399
Rose, Hugonem Alexandrum, 3168

Rose, Rosae Annae, 1399
Roser, Garrott, 208
Roser, Mary, 208
Roser, Prisilla, 208
Rosier, Jarret, 251
Rosier, Joseph, 251
Rosier, Mary, 251
Ross, Ann, 123
Ross, Arthur, 1399
Ross, Carolus, 1399
Ross, Rosae Annae, 1399
Roughan, Mary (Miss), 4249
Rouscoulp, Catharina, 3968
Rouscoulp, Gulielmum J., 3968
Rouscoulp, Henrico, 3968
Rouskulp, Ann M., 5386
Rouskulp, Ann Maria, 2358
Rouskulp, Catharina, 3823
Rouskulp, Catharina, 3896
Rouskulp, Catharina, 4006
Rouskulp, Catharinam Louise, 4006
Rouskulp, Gabriellam Ruth, 3896
Rouskulp, Henrico W., 3823
Rouskulp, Henrico W., 3896
Rouskulp, Henrico W., 4006
Rouskulp, Henricum W., 4824

Rouskulp, Mariam, 3823
Routh, Carolina, 557
Routh, Gulielmo, 3826
Routh, Joe, 557
Routh, Lucia, 3826
Routh, Luciam Barbaram, 3826
Routh, Theodora, 557
Rover [or Roner], Alice, 4819
Row, Mary (widow), 4266
Rowland, Anna Martha, 3114
Rowland, Anna Martha, 3115
Rowland, Isaac, 4256
Rowland, Kesia, 4443
Rowland, Kesiah, 1835
Rowland, Kesiah, 1836
Rowland, Kesiah, 1837
Rowland, Kesiah, 2213
Rowland, Martha, 3380
Rowland, Martha, 4702
Rowland, Martha, 5043
Rowland, Mary, 2065
Rowland, Resiah, 1984
Rubey, deceased, 2128
Rubey, Isaac (widower), 2128
Rubey, Jacob, 2128
Rudisill, George Washington, 2365
Rudisill, George, 2364

Rudisill, George, 2365
Rudisill, George, 2366
Rudisill, George, 2367
Rudisill, John Michael, 2364
Rudisill, Mary Catharine, 2366
Rudisill, Sarah Ann, 2364
Rudisill, Sarah Ann, 2365
Rudisill, Sarah Ann, 2366
Rudisill, Sarah Ann, 2367
Rudisill, Sarah Ellen, 2367
Rudy, Anna L., 3938
Rudy, Anna Lee, 3884
Rudy, Annam Lee, 4845
Rufcut, John, 2501
Rufcut, Joseph, 2501
Rufcut, Mary Ann, 2501
Rumley, Carolo, 3601
Rumley, Maria, 3601
Rumley, Mariam, 3601
Runney, Eleonora, 1361
Runney, Margaretae, 1361
Runney, Maria, 1321
Runney, Mariae, 1321
Runney, Michaelis, 1361
Runney, Patricii, 1321
Rush?, Eleonorae, 831
Rush?, Maria Anna, 831

Rush?, Martini, 831
Russel, Christophorus, 1405
Russel, Johanna, 1405
Russel, Mary, 19
Russell, Catharina, 1288
Russell, Christophori, 1288
Russell, Ellen, 2661
Russell, Jno., 2661
Russell, Johannae, 1288
Russell, Margaret, 2661
Russell, Mary, 2661
Russtte, Misses, 4356
Ryan, Bridget, 4455
Ryan, [blank], 844
Ryan, Ann, 2703
Ryan, Ann, 2925
Ryan, Anna Maria, 3573
Ryan, Anna Mary, 2703
Ryan, Anna, 4136
Ryan, Anna, 734
Ryan, Annam M., 4888
Ryan, Birgitta, 1701
Ryan, Catherene (widow), 4348
Ryan, Catherine, 585
Ryan, Danl., 4804
Ryan, Elisabeth, 1177
Ryan, Eliza, 4714

Ryan, Elizabeth, 2
Ryan, Father T., 614
Ryan, Georgio, 4888
Ryan, Georgium Mertin, 3447
Ryan, Georgius, 3447
Ryan, Guillelini, 734
Ryan, James, 2958
Ryan, James, 88
Ryan, Jas., 2869
Ryan, Jno., 4802
Ryan, Joannes, 1302
Ryan, Joannis, 782
Ryan, John, 2
Ryan, Julia, 2958
Ryan, M.A. (Rev.), 3879
Ryan, M.A. (Rev.), 4098
Ryan, Margaret, 88
Ryan, Maria Eliz., 3573
Ryan, Maria, 3447
Ryan, Mariae, 734
Ryan, Mariae, 782
Ryan, Mariam Franciscam, 3396
Ryan, Mary Elizabeth, 2
Ryan, Mary Malvina A., 2053
Ryan, Mary, 4345
Ryan, Mary, 585
Ryan, Mathei, 844

Ryan, Matheus Abraham, 844
Ryan, Mattheo, 3573
Ryan, May [or Mary] Ellen, 2869
Ryan, Mich. H., 2849
Ryan, Michaele, 3447
Ryan, Mrs., 2869
Ryan, Patr., 4665
Ryan, Patricius, 782
Ryan, Patrick, 4626
Ryan, Peter, 4960
Ryan, Rilam Elsie, 3573
Ryan, Rody, 4209
Ryan, T., 218
Ryan, T., 407
Ryan, T., 499
Ryan, T., 541
Ryan, T., 601
Ryan, T., 609
Ryan, Timotheus, 595
Ryan, Timotheus, 524
Ryan, Timothy, 223
Ryan, Timothy, 2703
Ryan, Timy, 264
Ryan, Timy, 270
Ryan, Timy, 299
Ryan, Timy, 306
Ryan, Timy, 264

Ryan, William H., 4615
Ryan, William, 88
Ryan, Wilm, 585
Ryan, Wm. Flora, 2849
Ryan, Wm. Henry, 2958
Ryder, David, 3124
Ryder, Louisa, 3124
Ryder, Lucy, 5711
Ryder, Mary, 5703
Rye, Henry, 4218
Rynolos, James, 4332
Sackenhour, Catharine, 147
Sackenhour, Catharine, 30
Sackenhour, Catharine, 30
Sackenhour, Henry, 29
Sackenhour, Philip, 30
Sahey, Daniel, 4280
Sallade', Andream M., 3569
Sarner, Charles (Rev.), 4710
Sander, Nelly, 334
Sanders, Catharina, 3100
Sanders, James, 297
Sanders, James, 297
Sanders, Jane, 297
Sanders, Margaret, 2994
Sanders, Margaret, 3044
Sanders, Mary Susan, 2994

Sanders, Sophia Agnes, 3044
Sanders, Wm, 2994
Sanders, Wm, 3044
Sanderson, Eleonora, 1142
Sands, Margaret, 2430
Sands, Maria, 177
Sands, Peggy, 177
Sane, Guillelmi, 1067
Sane, Markellae, 1067
Sane, Thomas, 1067
Saners, Marg., 2807
Sanner, Catharina, 1003
Sanner, Margaretae, 1003
Sanner, Thomas, 1003
Sansford, Danl., 2581
Sansford, Danl., 2589
Sansford, Geo. W., 2581
Sansford, Susanna, 2581
Sarracco, Mr., 5055
Sauer, Lucia, 3826
Sauer, Lucia, 3775
Sauer, Lucia, 3869
Sauer, Lucia, 3906
Sauer, Lucia, 3939
Sauer, Lucia, 4023
Sauer, Lucy, 3973
Saunders, Georginna, 2623

Saunders, Georginna, 2623
Saunders, Nancy, 2623
Saunders, Nancy, 2623
Saunders, Saml., 2623
Saur, Lucia, 3718
Saur, Maria, 3718
Sawer, Lucia, 4023
Sawer, Lucia, 4113
Sawers, Lucia, 4171
Scanlin, Mary, 1992
Scantling, Annae, 1582
Scantling, Jacobus, 1582
Scantling, Mauricii, 1582
Scarrlan, Antonii, 1122
Scarrlan, Bryan, 1122
Scarrlan, Sarae, 1122
Schaefer, Birgitta, 3498
Schaefer, Birgitta, 3499
Schaefer, Birgitta, 3500
Schaefer, Birgitta, 3501
Schaefer, Birgitta, 3502
Schaefer, Elisabeth, 1482
Schaefer, Elizabeth B., 3468
Schafer, Jahanne, 3468
Schafer, Jonathan, 1482
Schafer, Jonathan, 1482
Schafer, Norman Bruce, 3468

Schaffer, Catharinae, 867
Schaffer, Joannes, 867
Schaffer, Joannis, 867
Schafner, Frances, 2310
Schannon, Joannes, 1587
Schatzer, Catharinam, 3331
Schatzer, Eva, 3331
Schatzer, Roberto, 3331
Schatzer, Catharina, 3330
Schatzer, Francisco, 3330
Schatzer, Margaret Eve, 3330
Schealer, Catharinam, 3395
Scheiner, Barborae, 1791
Scheiner, Joannes, 1791
Scheiner, Josephi, 1791
Scheller, Maria, 3101
Schields, James, 1868
Schilemp, Mary, 4706
Schilemp, Sophia, 4706
Schilhass, Elisabeth, 4407
Schilling, Bernardum G., 3309
Schilling, Carolina, 3621
Schilling, Carolina, 3626
Schilling, Carolina, 3688
Schilling, Carolina, 3783
Schilling, Caroline, 4750
Schilling, Catharine, 1833

Schilling, Catharine, 3309
Schilling, David, 4815
Schilling, Eliz., 2952
Schilling, Franciscae, 842
Schilling, Henricus, 842
Schilling, Henry, 5201
Schilling, Jennie, 3263
Schilling, Jennie, 3327
Schilling, Jennie, 4750
Schilling, Joachim, 4971
Schilling, Joachim, 842
Schilling, none, 4999
Schilling, none, 5030
Schilling, Romana, 3598
Schilling, Romanus, 3216
Schilling, Romanus, 3265
Schilling, Romanus, 3313
Schilling, Sarah J., 5750
Schipers, Elizabeth, 2225
Schircliff, Honorius, 1870
Schleigh, Elizabeth (Miss), 4522
Schleigh, Mary Elizabeth, 2081
Schleigh, Mr. & Mrs., 4522
Schlick, Elisabeth, 1181
Schlick, Flora, 1181
Schlick, Joannis, 1181
Schlosser, J.W., 4629

Schlotterbeck, Elisabeth, 2824
Schlotterbeck, Elizabeth, 3192
Schlotterbeck, Catherina Maria, 3762
Schlotterbeck, Elizabeth, 3273
Schlotterbeck, Elizabeth, 3377
Schlotterbeck, Elizabetha, 3294
Schlotterbeck, Elizabetha, 3295
Schlotterbeck, Elizabetha, 3762
Schlotterbeck, Guglielmo, 3294
Schlotterbeck, Guglielmo, 3295
Schlotterbeck, Guglielmo, 3377
Schlotterbeck, Guglielmum Thomam, 3294
Schlotterbeck, Guglielmus, 3273
Schlotterbeck, Gul., 3660
Schlotterbeck, Louisa Regina, 3480
Schlotterbeck, Louisam, 4809
Schlotterbeck, Louisam, 3377
Schlotterbeck, Maria Catharina, 3554
Schlotterbeck, Mariam C., 4815
Schlotterbeck, Mariam Catharinam, 3273
Schlotterbeck, Mrs., 3198
Schlotterbeck, Rosinam Elizabetham, 3295

Schlotterbeck, Wm., 3192
Schneider, Mary E., 3307
Schneider, Susan, 3281
Schneider, Susannah, 3282
Schnell, Helenam, 3467
Schober, Josephina, 2020
Schockey, Susan (Mrs.), 5198
Schoeffer, Catharinae, 676
Schoeffer, Joannae Rebecca, 676
Schoeffer, Joannis, 676
Schoeffer, John Augustine, 2766
Schoeffer, Teresa Rebecca, 2766
Schofer, Mary Ann, 2766
Schour, Catharinae, 1663
Schour, Hugonis, 1663
Schour, Petrus, 1663
Schover, Theresia, 3497
Schow, Catharinae, 1663
Schow, Hugonis, 1663
Schow, Petrus, 1663
Schreiber, Josephus, 4427
Schuber, Anna Josephinae, 1628
Schuber, Laurentii, 1628
Schuber, Theresa, 1628
Schuck, Catharine, 1867
Schuck, Charles, 1867
Schuck, Hugo, 1866

Schuck, Hugo, 1867
Schueler, Carolum F., 4862
Schuh, Catharinae, 1415
Schuh, Edwardus Ignatius, 1415
Schuh, Hugonis, 1415
Schuh, Catharinae, 905
Schuh, Guillelmus, 905
Schuh, Hugo, 1346
Schuh, Hugoni, 905
Schultz, Carolina, 649
Schwartz, Joanne, 4778
Schwartz, Susanna, 4778
Schweitzer, Maria, 3260
Schweitzer, Maria, 3364
Schweitzer, Mariam Emmam, 3260
Schweitzer, Mariam Isabel, 3364
Schweitzer, Samuele, 3260
Schweitzer, Samuele, 3364
Schwitzer, Maria Cathar., 3103
Schwitzer, Maria Josephina, 3103
Schwitzer, Samuele, 3103
Scot, Maria, 642
Scot, Mariae, 642
Scot, Patricii, 642
Scott, N. (Mrs. Dr.), 4530
Scott, Augusta C.G., 1096
Scott, Augusti W., 1096

Scott, Clara Reginam, 3277
Scott, Eisabeth [sic], 1096
Scott, Emma, 1806
Scott, Emma, 1807
Scott, Josue B., 1807
Scott, Josue, 1806, 1807
Scott, Mariae, 1161
Scott, Michael, 1161
Scott, N. (Dr.), 4530
Scott, Patricii, 1161
Scott, Patrick, 4294
Scott, Sara Anna, 1806
Sculley, John, 4930
Scwope, Joseph, 2325
Seachrist, Maria J., 4052
Sechrist, Mariam Jane, 4889
Secondhour, [blank], 237
Sedan, Carolina, 4433
Sedon, Carolina, 962
See, Naason, 5529
Seffer, [blank], 601
Seffer, Jonnothan, 601
Seffer, Margret, 601
Seifert, Cunegunda, 1961
Sell, Elizabeth (Mrs.), 4119
Sellner, Barbara, 5060
Selmer, Mary, 2824

Selner, Elizabetha, 3294
Selner, Elizabetha, 3295
Semler, Clara, 4873
Semler, Margareta, 3730
Semler, Margarita, 3786
Semler, Margarita, 3847
Semler, Margaritam R., 4813
Senecal, Augusto, 3885
Senecal, Augusto, 3955
Senecal, Augusto, 4090
Senecal, Augustum Leonem, 4090
Senecal, Maria, 3885
Senecal, Maria, 3955
Senecal, Maria, 4090
Senecal, Mauritium Augustum, 3885
Senecal, Paulum, 3955
Sengstack, Edward Charles, 41
Sengstack, Edward Charles, 81
Sengstack, Eliza (Mrs.), 4193
Sengstack, Eliza Mary, 41
Sengstack, Eliza Mary, 81
Sengstack, Henry, 41
Sengstack, Henry, 81
Sery, Thomas, 4369
Sewel, Ann Eliza, 168
Sewel, Philis, 168

Seyfert, Kunegunda (Miss), 4527
Sgarkotich, Elise, 4646
Shacy [or Shaey], Elisabeth, 4042
Shadrach, Jacobum, 4817
Shadrich, Sophia, 5305
Shafer, Amelia, 3728
Shafer, Amilia, 4816
Shafer, Brigetta, 3720
Shafer, Elizabeth, 2534
Shafer, Frances, 2167
Shafer, Franciscum E., 3981
Shafer, Isabella, 4631
Shafer, Jacobum Aloysium, 3720
Shafer, Joanne W., 3720
Shafer, Joanne, 3981
Shafer, Joannem L., 4861
Shafer, John P., 5308
Shafer, Louisam Romaine, 4142
Shafer, Margaret Elizabeth, 1931
Shafer, Maria, 3981
Shafer, Maria, 4141
Shafer, Maria, 4142
Shafer, Mary E. (Miss), 4598
Shafer, Mary Elizabeth, 2449
Shafer, Mary, 3040
Shafer, Ricardum Orndorf Antonium, 4141

Shafer, Roberto, 4141
Shafer, Roberto, 4142
Shaffer, Robertum F., 4902
Shaffer, Catharinae, 1818
Shaffer, Charles E., 499
Shaffer, Edward, 551
Shaffer, Eleonora Elisabeth, 1818
Shaffer, Elisabeth Victorina, 885
Shaffer, Eliza (Mrs.), 500
Shaffer, Eliza, 499
Shaffer, Frances, 1847
Shaffer, Francisca, 2003
Shaffer, Joannis, 1818
Shaffer, Johnathen (Mrs.), 511
Shaffer, Jonathan, 499
Shaffer, Jonnathan, 551
Shaffer, Margret (Mrs.), 499
Shaffer, Mrs. Johnathen Shaffer, 4253
Shahen, Cornelius, 2952
Shahen, Ellen, 2952
Shahen, Mary Ann, 2952
Shaker, Maria E., 3384
Shanaghan, Birgittae, 1208
Shanaghan, Birgittae, 1585
Shanaghan, Christopheri, 1208

Shanaghan, Christophori, 1585
Shanaghan, Jacobus, 1208
Shanaghan, Joannes, 1585
Shanaham, Birgittae, 731
Shanaham, Christophori, 731
Shanaham, Margareta, 731
Shanahan, John, 5074
Shane, Edward, 1902
Shane, Frances, 1902
Shane, George, 1658
Shane, Georgeus, 1594
Shane, Henricus C., 1810
Shane, Joannis, 1118
Shane, Joannis, 1356
Shane, Joannis, 1594
Shane, Joannis, 1658
Shane, Joannis, 1810
Shane, Laura Birgitta, 1356
Shane, Margaret, 1902
Shane, Margaretae, 1118
Shane, Margaretae, 1594
Shane, Margaretae, 1658
Shane, Margaritae, 1810
Shane, Margereta Isabella, 1118
Shane, Maria, 1356
Shane, Susanna, 1657
Shaneck, Anna, 1494

Shaneck, Mariae, 1494
Shaneck, Michaelis, 1494
Shank, Elie, 3199
Shank, Maria, 3199
Shank, Mariam Protis, 3199
Shank, Adam Roberto, 3884
Shank, Adam, 2497
Shank, Adam, 2563
Shank, Adam, 2652
Shank, Adam, 2750
Shank, Adam, 2857
Shank, Alicem Catharinam, 3938
Shank, Alverta J., 5520
Shank, Alverta, 2971
Shank, Andrew, 2494
Shank, Andrew, 4609
Shank, Ann S., 2563
Shank, Ann Sophia, 2563
Shank, Ann, 2652
Shank, Ann, 2857
Shank, Anna L., 3938
Shank, Anna Lee, 3884
Shank, Anna, 2497
Shank, Anne Sophia, 2750
Shank, Cora, 3179
Shank, Cora, 3232
Shank, Cora, 3315

Shank, George, 2750
Shank, Jane Agora, 2652
Shank, Maria, 3199
Shank, Maria, 3938
Shank, Maria, 4062
Shank, Mariam Protis, 3199
Shank, Mary Catharine, 2497
Shank, Roberto, 3938
Shank, Robertum Clifford, 3884
Shank, Robertum F., 4845
Shank, Robt. Franklin, 2857
Shamen [or Shaman], Michael, 2608
Shannon, Catharina, 1052
Shannon, Catharina, 1588
Shannon, Catharina, 1610
Shannon, Catharinae, 1052
Shannon, Catharinae, 1478
Shannon, Catharinae, 1690
Shannon, Catharinae, 1857
Shannon, Dominici, 1676
Shannon, Edward, 1857
Shannon, Edwardi, 1052
Shannon, Edwardi, 1478
Shannon, Edwardi, 1690
Shannon, Gertrudam, 4737
Shannon, Jacobus, 1690

Shannon, Jane, 1857
Shannon, Joannes, 1609
Shannon, Juliae, 1676
Shannon, Margareta, 1676
Shannon, Michael, 1478
Shannon, Michael, 2654
Sharen, Maria, 1355
Sharen, Maria, 4471
Sharidan, Joannae, 690
Sharidan, Mathei, 690
Sharidan, Thomas, 690
Shaten, Christina, 2692
Shaw, David Silvester, 2335
Shaw, Elis, 2815
Shaw, Elizabeth, 2334
Shaw, Elizabeth, 2335
Shaw, Jacob, 2333
Shaw, Jacob, 2334
Shaw, Jacob, 2334
Shaw, Jacob, 2335
Shay, Elisabeth, 5333
Shea, Catherine, 3027
Shea, Thomas, 4326
Shearan, Anna, 2177
Shearan, Anna, 2177
Shearan, Edward, 2177
Sheddrick, Jacob Ulroy, 2637

Shedrick, Michael, 2637
Sheddrick, Sophia, 2637
Shedrick, Mrs., 4588
Shedrick, Ann Jane, 2036
Shedrick, Benjamin Franklin, 2544
Shedrick, Isabella Agnes, 2136
Shedrick, John Michael, 2369
Shedrick, Michael, 2036
Shedrick, Michael, 2136
Shedrick, Michael, 2257
Shedrick, Michael, 2369
Shedrick, Michael, 2544
Shedrick, Michael, 4539
Shedrick, Mr., 4588
Shedrick, Peter, 2257
Shedrick, Sophia, 2036
Shedrick, Sophia, 2136
Shedrick, Sophia, 2257
Shedrick, Sophia, 2369
Shedrick, Sophia, 2544
Sheean, Catherine, 3508
Sheean, Maria, 3576
Sheean, Wm, 3576
Sheedy, Fanny, 2940
Sheedy, Margaret (Mrs.), 5039
Sheedy, Mike, 2940
Sheehan, Patricius, 3098

Sheehan, Agnes, 3678
Sheehan, Ann Elizabeth, 2620
Sheehan, Anna Jeannette, 2448
Sheehan, Annam C., 4895
Sheehan, Carolina, 3852
Sheehan, Carolus R. E., 3176
Sheehan, Catharina, 3098
Sheehan, Catharina, 3162
Sheehan, Charles, 5239
Sheehan, David Willibee, 2620
Sheehan, Edward, 2032
Sheehan, Edward, 2448
Sheehan, Edward, 2509
Sheehan, Edward, 2509
Sheehan, Elisabeth, 3176
Sheehan, Ellen, 2987
Sheehan, Eulichmo, 3098
Sheehan, Frances, 2032
Sheehan, Frances, 2448
Sheehan, Frances, 2509
Sheehan, Guilielmo, 3162
Sheehan, Jeremiah, 3678
Sheehan, Joannem Leonem, 3678
Sheehan, John Patrick, 2032
Sheehan, Josephum Patricium, 3162
Sheehan, Margaret, 5324

Sheehan, Maria, 4061
Sheehan, Mariam Honoram, 3098
Sheehan, Marias, 3161
Sheehan, Marten, 2620
Sheehan, Martino, 3176
Sheehan, Mary, 2509
Sheehan, Maurie, 2509
Sheehan, Mrs., 3503
Sheehan, Mrs., 5304
Sheehon, Anna C., 4116
Sheely, M., 2926
Sheely, Margaret, 2926
Sheely, Margaret, 2926
Sheffer, Elizabeth, 602
Sheffer, Jonothen, 602
Sheffer, Upton Otho, 602
Shefton, Prudy (Miss), 4212
Sheghran, Maria, 1248
Shehan, Ann, 2955
Shehan, Annam Ceciliam, 3238
Shehan, Catherine, 3033
Shehan, Cornelis, 3238
Shehan, Cornelius, 2955
Shehan, Cornelius, 3071
Shehan, Cornelius, 5297
Shehan, Ed., 4558
Shehan, Edward, 2141

Shehan, Edward, 2332
Shehan, Edward, 2526
Shehan, Edwardus, 4508
Shehan, Elizabeth, 2332
Shehan, Elizabeth, 3468
Shehan, Ellen, 3071
Shehan, Ellen, 3238
Shehan, Frances Ann, 2141
Shehan, Frances Ann, 2332
Shehan, Frances Letitia, 2141
Shehan, Henry Lee, 2955
Shehan, John Michael, 3033
Shehan, Margaret, 3071
Shehan, Martin, 2955
Shehan, Martin, 4710
Shehan, Mary Susan, 5455
Shehan, Mary, 2975
Shehan, Peter, 3033
Shehan, Schilling (Mrs.), 3263
Shehan, Sm, 3033
Shelburn, Elizabeth, 2276
Sheling, Francis, 568
Sheling, Jochim, 568
Sheling, Leonard, 568
Shellhouse, Maria Elizabeth, 2409
Shelling, Franciscae, 1694
Shelling, Joachim, 1694

Shelling, Joannis, 837
Shelling, Maria, 1694
Shelling, Mariae, 837
Shephan, John, 5066
Sheppard, James V., 4812
Sheppard, Sarah E., 4812
Shepperd, John, 4575
Sherbown, Maggie, 3395
Shercliff, Francis, 4174
Sherdan, Patrick, 4619
Sherden, Anna, 4802
Shergan, Maria, 488
Shergan, Mary Anna, 488
Shergan, Wilm, 488
Sheridan, Ann, 3268
Sheridan, Anna, 1007
Sheridan, Anna, 2580
Sheridan, Anna, 3478
Sheridan, Anna, 3773
Sheridan, Annae, 1007
Sheridan, Annam M., 4810
Sheridan, Bernardi, 889
Sheridan, Bernardus, 889
Sheridan, Bridget, 2580
Sheridan, Bridget, 2681
Sheridan, Bridget, 2817

Sheridan, Ellan, 889
Sheridan, Ellen Genevieve, 2817
Sheridan, Joannis, 1007
Sheridan, Mary Elizabeth, 2681
Sheridan, Patr, 2817
Sheridan, Patrick, 2580
Sheridan, Patrick, 2681
Sheridon, Elisabeth C.H., 5774
Sheriff, Elizabeth (Miss), 4573
Sherkery, Margaretta, 4301
Sherley, Elizabeth, 2616
Sherley, Lizzie, 2693
Sherley, Wm?/Mrs.?, 268
Sherlock, John, 4338
Sherlock, Robert, 4745
Sherran, Mary, 4296
Shervan, Isabellae, 1708
Shervan, Samuel Eccleston, 1708
Shervan, Thom, 1708
Shervin, Bell, 3223
Shervin, Bell, 3415
Shervin, Belle, 3214
Shervin, Cath., 2585
Shervin, Catharina, 3372
Shervin, Catharine J., 2496
Shervin, Catharine J., 2566
Shervin, Catharine, 2486

Shervin, Catherine, 2754
Shervin, Elizabeth, 3415
Shervin, Henry J., 4617
Shervin, Henry, 1840
Shervin, Henry, 2082
Shervin, Henry, 2566
Shervin, Henry, 2754
Shervin, Henry, 2896
Shervin, Hy., 2838
Shervin, Isabella, 1840
Shervin, Isabella, 2145
Shervin, James, 4617
Shervin, Jas. Clarke, 2754
Shervin, Johannem Hampton, 3415
Shervin, Kate Clark, 2896
Shervin, Kate, 2838
Shervin, Kate, 2896
Shervin, M., 3356
Shervin, Margaret (Miss), 4617
Shervin, Margaret, 1949
Shervin, Margaret, 2144
Shervin, Margaret, 3080
Shervin, Margaret, 3370
Shervin, Margaret, 3441
Shervin, Margaret, 4722
Shervin, Margaret, 4745
Shervin, Margaret, 4752

Shervin, Margaret, 4756
Shervin, Margaret, 4757
Shervin, Margaret, 4767
Shervin, Margareta, 4751
Shervin, Margaretta, 3428
Shervin, Maria, 3186
Shervin, Mary Aloysia, 2566
Shervin, Mary Jos., 5707
Shervin, Mr. & Mrs., 4518
Shervin, Mrs. Henry, 5024
Shervin, Mrs., 5036
Shervin, Rosanna (Miss), 4518
Shervin, Rosanna, 1949
Shervin, Rosanna, 2082
Shervin, Samuel, 4715
Shervin, Samuel, 5494
Shervin, Samuele, 3415
Shervin, Samuelem, 4731
Shervin, Thomas, 2146
Shervin, Thomas, 2426
Shervin, Thomas, 2523
Shervin, Thomas, 5041
Shervin, Thos., 2838
Shervin, Wm., 2838
Shervins, Miss, 4715
Shervins, James, 5277
Shervin, Kate, 5283

Sherwin, Margarita, 3767
Shevan, Edward, 2343
Shevan, Isabellae, 1064
Shevan, Mary Ellen, 2343
Shevan, Nancy, 2343
Shevan, Thomae, 1064
Shevan, Thomas, 1064
Shevin, Margaret, 2482
Shevin, Thomas, 2482
Shields, Anna M., 4139
Shields, Annam M., 4901
Shields, Elizabeth, 1891
Shields, Elizabeth, 1991
Shields, Elizabeth, 2253
Shields, James, 1891
Shields, James, 2253
Shields, James, 2253
Shields, James, 2253
Shields, Michael, 1891
Shillen, Elizabeth, 2955
Shiller, Franciscae, 1164
Shiller, Joachim, 1164
Shiller, Joannes (son), 1164
Shiller, Sara Johanna, 3509
Shiller, Sara Johanna, 3510
Shilling (widower), Joachim, 4596
Shilling, Anna, 5439

Shilling, Antony, 604
Shilling, Barbara Catharine, 1847
Shilling, Carolina Victoria, 2530
Shilling, Carolina, 3936
Shilling, Carrie, 3503
Shilling, Catherina Maria, 3762
Shilling, David C., 3692
Shilling, David, 3762
Shilling, Dnacum, 604
Shilling, Elisabeth, 3176
Shilling, Elizabeth, 2464
Shilling, Elizabeth, 2530
Shilling, Elizabeth, 2560
Shilling, Elizabeth, 2578
Shilling, Elizabeth, 4710
Shilling, Ellenora, 4596
Shilling, Frances Elizabeth, 2167
Shilling, Frances, 1847
Shilling, Frances, 2167
Shilling, Frances, 2310
Shilling, Francesca, 604
Shilling, Francisca, 2003
Shilling, Guleilmo, 3692
Shilling, Hannah, 3692
Shilling, Henricum, 3716
Shilling, Joacam, 2578
Shilling, Joachim Edward, 2560

Shilling, Joachim, 1847
Shilling, Joachim, 2003
Shilling, Joachim, 2167
Shilling, Joachim, 2310
Shilling, Joachim, 2464
Shilling, Joachim, 2530
Shilling, Joachim, 2560
Shilling, Joseph Peter, 2003
Shilling, Mariam Bernardinam, 3762
Shilling, Martha Anna, 2310
Shilling, Mary, 5454
Shilling, Romana, 3681
Shilling, Sarah Jane, 2578
Shilling, Theodore Ulrick, 2464
Shillong, Sarah, 3805
Shillong, Sarah, 3806
Shillong, Sarai J., 3804
Shilton, Nelly, 158
Shilton, Nelly, 159
Shine, Joseph, 1836
Shipley, Eleonora Elisabeth, 1249
Shipley, Elisabeth, 1249
Shipley, Elizabeth, 1965
Shipley, James Monroe, 1965
Shipley, Richard A., 4303
Shipley, Richard, 1965

Shipley, Richardi, 1249
Shipply, Edwardus Richardus, 963
Shipply, Elisabeth, 963
Shipply, Richardi, 963
Shipton, Prud, 142
Shipton, Prudentia, 146
Shirchlify, Chloe, 2055
Shircliff (white), Mary Ann, 1899
Shircliff, Ann, 2128
Shircliff, L, 2188
Shircliff, L, 2190
Shircliff, L, 4544
Shircliff, Mary Ann (Miss), 4544
Shircliff, Mary Ann, 1942
Shircliff, W., 2105
Shircliff, W, 4544
Shircliff, William, 2128
Shirdan, Eleonorae, 793
Shirdan, Jacobi, 793
Shirdan, Margareta, 793
Shiremon, Emelia, 1976
Shiremon, Maria Eva, 1976
Shirkey, Margaret, 122
Shirlagh, Joannis, 1431
Shirley, Mrs., 377
Shirley, Elisabeth, 1392
Shirley, Elisabeth, 1517

Shirley, Elisabeth, 1715
Shirley, Elizabeth (Mrs.), 1959
Shirley, Elizabeth, 175
Shirley, Elizabeth, 2576
Shirley, Elizabeth, 4545
Shirley, Elizabeth, 61
Shirley, Elizabeth, 61
Shirley, Elizabetha, 3674
Shirley, Elizabetha, 3675
Shirley, Henrietta (Miss), 4524
Shirley, Joseph, 175
Shirley, Joseph, 175
Shirley, Joseph, 61
Shirley, Lizzie, 2994
Shirley, Lizzie, 5784
Shirley, Mary Ann, 1897
Shirley, Mary Ann, 2285
Shirley, Mary Ann, 2402
Shirley, Mary Anna, 4300
Shirley, Mary Anna, 490
Shirley, Mary Anna, 540
Shirley, Mrs., 517
Shirley, Mrs., 423
Shirley, Mrs., 284
Shirley, Mrs., 570
Shirmer?, Isable, 279
Shirmer?, Rose, 279

Shirmer?, Thomas, 279
Shirran, Edwardi, 1398
Shirran, Edwardus, 1398
Shirran, Susannae, 1398
Shirren, Edwardi, 1675
Shirren, Jacobus, 1675
Shirren, Susannae, 1675
Shisven?, Isabela, 277
Shisven?, James, 277
Shisven?, Thomas, 277
Shlotterbeck, Elisabeth, 3863
Shlotterbeck, Elisabeth, 4002
Shlotterbeck, Lizzie, 4049
Shlotterbeck, Mrs., 3776
Shnenick, Joannes, 1070
Shnenick, Mariae, 1070
Shnenick, Michaelen, 1070
Shnider, Anne, 2421
Shnider, Bessie, 4166
Shnider, Elizabeth, 2421
Shnider, Henry, 2421
Shobe [or Shober?], Anna Josephina, 2434
Shober, Ann (widow), 4546
Shober, Michael, 5449
Shober, Rebecca, 5423
Shoch, Gulielmum W., 4800

Shockert, Adelin T, 581
Shoise, Mariae, 701
Shoise, Michael, 701
Shoise, Michaelis, 701
Shonecx, Maria, 1332
Shonor, Annae Josephinae, 1774
Shonor, Joannes D., 1774
Shonor, Laurentii, 1774
Shoop, Maria, 3676
Shopaerd, Mary (Mrs.), 635
Shorb, Augustus, 5328
Shordan, Bernardi, 1373
Shordan, Ellen, 1373
Shortan, Bernardi, 1373
Shortan, Ellen, 1373
Shorter, Catherine, 413
Shorter, Charles, 413
Shorter, Emmelia, 413
Shorter, "not known", 392
Shorter, Aaroli [or Naroli or Maroli], 908
Shorter, Alice, 3395
Shorter, Aliciam, 3308
Shorter, Anna Lucia, 1159
Shorter, Annae, 846
Shorter, Cath., 1964
Shorter, Catharina, 1384

Shorter, Catharinae, 908
Shorter, Catharine, 2386
Shorter, Catharine, 2549
Shorter, Catharine, 79
Shorter, Catharine, 80
Shorter, Cather, 578
Shorter, Catherine, 5171
Shorter, Catherine, 465
Shorter, Catherine, 520
Shorter, Catherine, 520
Shorter, Charles, 187
Shorter, Charles, 273
Shorter, Charles, 391
Shorter, Charles, 520
Shorter, Charls, 465
Shorter, Clara Ellen, 2854
Shorter, Dolly, 36
Shorter, Edwardi, 846
Shorter, Eiza[Eliza?], 520
Shorter, Elisa, 204
Shorter, Elisa, 321
Shorter, Elisabeth, 1187
Shorter, Elisabeth, 391
Shorter, Elisabeth, 465
Shorter, Eliza, 117
Shorter, Elizabeth, 87
Shorter, Elizabeth, 118

Shorter, Elizabeth, 36
Shorter, Elizabeth, 77
Shorter, Frances, 2854
Shorter, George, 392
Shorter, Guillelmus Henricus, 908
Shorter, Harietta, 273
Shorter, Harietta, 391
Shorter, Harriet, 16
Shorter, Harriet, 45
Shorter, Harriet, 78
Shorter, Hurriet, 187
Shorter, Jesse, 79
Shorter, Jesse, 79
Shorter, Jesse, 80
Shorter, Joannes, 846
Shorter, John, 391
Shorter, Joseph, 465
Shorter, Kitty, 2826
Shorter, Kitty, 3308
Shorter, Kitty, 3318
Shorter, Lucia, 4437
Shorter, Lucretea Elizabeth, 187
Shorter, Lucretiae, 1159
Shorter, Lucy, 87
Shorter, Marcella, 273
Shorter, Mary Ann, 80
Shorter, Matilda, 392

Shorter, Mrs., 413
Shorter, Nathan, 2854
Shorter, Nathan, 5094
Shorts, Ada Maria L., 3984
Shorts, Henrico, 3984
Shoup, Christianna, 94
Shour, Catharinae, 1663
Shour, Hugonis, 1663
Shour, Petrus, 1663
Shover, Annae Josephinae, 1774
Shover, Elisabeth, 3152
Shover, Joannes D., 1774
Shover, John, 5484
Shover, Laurentii, 1774
Shover, Mary Ann, 2882
Shover, Teresa, 4738
Shover, Teresa, 5483
Shover, Teresia, 3152
Shover, Theresa, 2882
Shover, Theresa, 3780
Shover, Theresia R., 3554
Shreiner, Roy P., 3850
Shriner, Davide, 4170
Shriner, Joannem Francescum, 4170
Shriner, Maria, 4170
Shubll, Mary, 2133

Shue, Catharine, 1988
Shue, Catharine, 2219
Shue, Catharine, 2349
Shue, Francisca Theresia, 2349
Shue, Hugo, 640
Shue, Hugo, 2219
Shue, Hugo, 2349
Shue, Laurettam, 4910
Shue, Maria, 4910
Shue, Mary Margaret, 2219
Shue, Mrs., 4130
Shueler, Carolo F., 3954
Shueler, Carolo F., 4015
Shueler, Carolo F., 4078
Shueler, Carolo, 4133
Shueler, Carolum Petrum, 4133
Shueler, Maria, 3954
Shueler, Maria, 4015
Shueler, Maria, 4078
Shueler, Maria, 4133
Shueler, Mariam Vincentiam, 4078
Shueler, Pearl Anastasiam, 3954
Shueler, Phoebe Laurentinam, 4015
Shuhe, [blank], 654
Shuhe, Henricus, 654
Shuhe, Hugonis, 654
Shunei, Albert (Mrs.), 4725

Shuten, Christina Catharine, 2440
Shwink, Anna Daley, 3979
Shwink, Anna, 3834
Shwink, Anna, 3892
Shwink, Amam Reginam, 3892
Shwink, Decatur, 3834
Shwink, Decatur, 3892
Shwink, Decatur, 3979
Shwink, Mariam Bertam, 3834
Shwink, Vera Margaritam, 3979
Siegler, Elisabeth, 1783
Sigler, Adam, 2115
Sigler, Elizabeth, 2115
Sigler, Philip, 2115
Sigler, Franciscam Magdalenam, 4062
Sigler, Henrico A., 4062
Sigler, Otho O., 4874
Sigler, Protasia, 4062
Silas, Betsy, 385
Siler, Echart, 2223
Siler, Mary Elizabeth, 2223
Siler, Nancy, 2223
Silis, Annae, 930
Silis, Georgii, 930
Silis, Joannes, 930
Silvers, Ellen (Miss), 4553

Silvers, Ellen, 2469
Silvers, Ellen, 2769
Simler, [blank], 4163
Simler, Jacobum Eduardum, 4163
Simler, Winnie, 4163
Simmon, Elizabeth, 44
Simmon, Jacob, 44
Simmon, James, 44
Simmons, Cyrus, 4809
Simmons, Ruby, 4818
Simms, Susanna, 4018
Simmy, Susanna, 3901
Sims, Catharine, 2392
Sims, Joannem M., 4736
Sims, Mary Louisa, 2392
Sims, Thomas, 2392
Singer, Isaac, 1245
Singer, Maria Anna, 2167
Singer, Mariannae, 1245
Singer, Theresa, 1245
Sinon, Henry, 51
Sinon, Honora, 51
Sinon, Mary Ann, 51
Skelly, Jannis, 1237
Skelly, Joannes, 1237
Skelly, Mariae, 1237
Skelly, Anna, 1286

Skelly, Jacobus, 1672
Skelly, Joannes, 1218
Skelly, Joannis, 1672
Skelly, John, 4528
Skelly, Mariae, 1672
Slater [or Stakes], Catherine, 4305
Sleet, Catharina, 1117
Sleete, Maria, 1477
Sleets, Maria, 1329
Sleighk [sic], Elizabeth, 2251
Sleight, [blank], 3366
Sleight, [blank], 3367
Sleight, [blank], 3368
Slephun, Rachel, 4644
Sloe, Hugo, 1086
Slowe, Hugonis, 1529
Slowe, Maria, 1529
Slowe, Mariae, 1529
Slowie, Hugo, 4430
Slye, Mary, 4192
Slye, Robt A., 4192
Small, Robertus, 1201
Smidy, John, 188
Smisth, Erasmo, 3566
Smisth, Henrietta, 3566
Smisth, Violettam Mariam, 3566
Smith, Betty, 3389

Smith, Catharina, 1681
Smith, Danl. Florence, 2674
Smith, Emma, 3986
Smith, Mary, 2674
Smith, Mrs. C., 4589
Smith, Rosa, 4870
Smith, Wm., 2674
Smith (Black), Lucinda, 2445
Smith, Catharine E., 2447
Smith, Cathrine, 2320
Smith, Cornelia, 3058
Smith, Edward, 4712
Smith, Elizabeth, 3562
Smith, John, 4723
Smith, Josia, 503
Smith, Maria J., 3512
Smith, Philips, 364
Smith, Sophia (Miss), 521
Smith, Sophia Antoinette, 1889
Smith of M. Smith, Catharine, 1921
Smith, Sr., M., 2110
Smith, Jenette, 1921
Smith, [blank], 3075
Smith, Adam, 1997
Smith, Albertum C., 3129
Smith, Alfrid B., 1715
Smith, Anaslusia, 1982

Smith, Anastasia, 1645
Smith, Anastasia, 1819
Smith, Anastasiae, 1386
Smith, Anastasiae, 1630
Smith, Anastatia, 2542
Smith, Anastia, 412
Smith, Anna (widow), 4355
Smith, Anna Elisabeth, 1629
Smith, Anna, 3587
Smith, Anna, 4652
Smith, Anna, 5588
Smith, Annae, 1483
Smith, Annae, 1645
Smith, Anne Lee, 2794
Smith, Anne, 3028
Smith, Annie, 5543
Smith, Augustine, 5435
Smith, Bernard, 4560
Smith, Bernardi, 773
Smith, Betsey, 334
Smith, Birgitta, 1489
Smith, Birgittae, 1461
Smith, Birgittae, 1736
Smith, Brigitae, 665
Smith, Brigittae, 4374
Smith, Caroli, 1618
Smith, Carolum D., 4733

Smith, Carolum Matth. Bern., 3539
Smith, Carolum, 3136
Smith, Carolus F., 3671
Smith, Carrie, 3885
Smith, Cath., 2582
Smith, Cath., 2672
Smith, Cath., 2690
Smith, Cath., 2917
Smith, Cath., 2918
Smith, Cath., 2943
Smith, Cath., 4805
Smith, Cath., 5582
Smith, Catharina Ludovica, 1736
Smith, Catharina, 1090
Smith, Catharina, 1262
Smith, Catharina, 1325
Smith, Catharina, 1386
Smith, Catharina, 1440
Smith, Catharina, 1629
Smith, Catharina, 1662
Smith, Catharina, 3100
Smith, Catharina, 3136
Smith, Catharina, 3137
Smith, Catharina, 3542
Smith, Catharina, 3545
Smith, Catharina, 3550
Smith, Catharina, 3636
Smith, Catharinae, 1049
Smith, Catharinae, 1618
Smith, Catharinae, 1629
Smith, Catharinae, 773
Smith, Catharinam, 3157
Smith, Catharine (Miss), 4533
Smith, Catharine, 167
Smith, Catharine A., 2447
Smith, Catharine E., 2390
Smith, Catharine E., 1889
Smith, Catharine, 2046
Smith, Catharine, 2139
Smith, Catharine, 2512
Smith, Catharine, 2546
Smith, Catharine, 2557
Smith, Catharine, 2558
Smith, Catharine, 2559
Smith, Catharine, 5532
Smith, Catherina E., 3474
Smith, Catharina, 3488
Smith, Catherine (Mrs.), 346
Smith, Catherine, 2741
Smith, Catherine, 2741
Smith, Catherine, 2742
Smith, Catherine, 411
Smith, Catherine, 414
Smith, Catherine, 4712
Smith, Catherine, 472
Smith, Catherine, 5001
Smith, Catherine, 521
Smith, Charels Jessie, 2809
Smith, Charles Aloyisius, 2572
Smith, Charles, 2977
Smith, Charles, 5374
Smith, Daniel, 4319
Smith, Donnielis, 1537
Smith, Dr. Frank, 5033
Smith, Dr. J., 4602
Smith, Dr. Josiah F., 2557
Smith, Dr. Josiah F., 2558
Smith, Dr. Josiah F., 2559
Smith, Dr. Josiah F., 4589
Smith, Dr. Otho, 5038
Smith, Edgar Thomas, 3028
Smith, Edmond, 9
Smith, Edmund Didier, 2823
Smith, Edmundum Franklin, 3170
Smith, Eduardo, 3624
Smith, Edw., 2977
Smith, Edw., 3170
Smith, Edward John, 5700
Smith, Edward, 3070
Smith, Edward, 5696
Smith, Edwd., 2905
Smith, Edwd., 5678
Smith, Elisabeth Johanna, 1645
Smith, Elisabeth, 1050
Smith, Elisabeth, 1214
Smith, Elisabeth, 1715
Smith, Elisabeth, 3137
Smith, Elisabeth, 4017
Smith, Elisabeth, 4107
Smith, Elisabeth, 4873
Smith, Elisobeth, 1552
Smith, Eliza, 537
Smith, Elizabeth Laura Virginia, 2481
Smith, Elizabeth, 2742
Smith, Elizabeth, 3505
Smith, Elizabeth, 5491
Smith, Elizabetha, 3671
Smith, Ella Teresa, 2558
Smith, Ella, 3544
Smith, Ella, 3895
Smith, Emily, 2809
Smith, Emma Florence, 2756
Smith, Emma, 3400
Smith, Emma, 3401
Smith, Emma, 5202
Smith, Emman Linden, 3624
Smith, Esau, 124

Smith, Eugene E., 4689
Smith, Eugenio Eduardo, 3495
Smith, Eustasiae, 697
Smith, Fanny Eliz. Julia, 2844
Smith, Frances, 5459
Smith, Francis, 3184
Smith, Francisca Emilia, 1618
Smith, G. A. (Mrs.), 2760
Smith, Geneveva, 3495
Smith, Geneviva, 3624
Smith, Genoveffa, 3170
Smith, Geo Alexander, 124
Smith, George, 3075
Smith, Guillelmes Edwardus, 1049
Smith, Gulielmo H., 3100
Smith, Gulielmus F., 3630
Smith, Helen J., 2558
Smith, Helen Jenette, 1921
Smith, Helena, 3630
Smith, Helena, 3651
Smith, Henny, 124
Smith, Henrici, 702
Smith, Henricum Bernardum, 3636
Smith, Henricus, 1630
Smith, Henry Edwd., 2905
Smith, Henry Stanislaus, 2755
Smith, Hugo, 773

Smith, Infant, 5046
Smith, Infrasanptus, 3562
Smith, Irenam Agnetem, 3495
Smith, J.A. (Rev.), 3762
Smith, J. M., 2569
Smith, Jacob, 412
Smith, Jacob, 334
Smith, Jacobum Sheridan, 3546
Smith, Jacobus Samuel, 3100
Smith, Jacobus, 1387
Smith, Jacobus, 665
Smith, James Alois, 521
Smith, Jane, 334
Smith, Jane, 2377
Smith, Jane, 3070
Smith, Jennie (Mrs.), 5207
Smith, Jennie, 2977
Smith, Jennie, 3332
Smith, Jenny, 2905
Smith, Jesse, 3157
Smith, Jno. W., 2844
Smith, Jno. W., 2901
Smith, Joachim, 1386
Smith, Joanna, 3102
Smith, Joanna, 3129
Smith, Joanne, 3129
Smith, Joanne, 3136

Smith, Joanne, 3137
Smith, Joannem Thomam Sandford, 3540
Smith, Joannes K., 4400
Smith, Joannes Michael, 1763
Smith, Joannes T., 1552
Smith, Joannes, 1819
Smith, Joannis K., 1715
Smith, Joannis, 1552
Smith, Johanne W., 3636
Smith, John D., 2559
Smith, John H., 2957
Smith, John H., 4649
Smith, John Jacob, 2399
Smith, John K., 1214
Smith, John M., 2150
Smith, John Michael, 2377
Smith, John Michael, 2690
Smith, John Michal, 411
Smith, John Michl, 414
Smith, John, 2399
Smith, John, 2756
Smith, John, 2823
Smith, John, 3029
Smith, John, 3075
Smith, John, 4645
Smith, John, 537

Smith, Jos. M., 2641
Smith, Jos. M., 2690
Smith, Jos. M., 2860
Smith, Jos. M., 4693
Smith, Joseph, 1949
Smith, Joseph Edward, 2532
Smith, Joseph M., 2472
Smith, Joseph Maines, 2532
Smith, Joseph N. [or M.], 2794
Smith, Joseph, 1629
Smith, Joseph, 1921
Smith, Joseph, 2572
Smith, Joseph, 2755
Smith, Joseph, 4531
Smith, Joseph, 4553
Smith, Joseph, 4665
Smith, Josephus, 1630
Smith, Josephus, 1724
Smith, Joshae, 697
Smith, Josia, 412
Smith, Josiah (Dr.), 5069
Smith, Josiah, 4339
Smith, Josiah, 2741
Smith, Josiah, 2742
Smith, Josias, 1050
Smith, Josias, 3117
Smith, Josua, 1819

Smith, Josua, 1630
Smith, Julia Kate, 3029
Smith, Julia, 3666
Smith, Kate, 3029
Smith, Laetitiae, 1050
Smith, Louis, 3058
Smith, Lucia, 3539
Smith, Lucia, 3540
Smith, Lucinda Susanna, 2481
Smith, Lucinda, 2621
Smith, Lucinda, 3335
Smith, Lucy, 2461
Smith, Lucy, 364
Smith, Margaret A., 2572
Smith, Margaret A., 2641
Smith, Margaret Ann, 2532
Smith, Margaret, 2399
Smith, Margaret, 2472
Smith, Margaret, 2690
Smith, Margaret, 2755
Smith, Margaret, 2794
Smith, Margaret, 2809
Smith, Margaret, 3067
Smith, Margaret, 4666
Smith, Margaret, 75
Smith, Margt, 2860
Smith, Maria, 1196

Smith, Maria (Mrs.), 3995
Smith, Maria (Mrs.), 4120
Smith, Maria (Mrs.), 4126
Smith, Maria (Mrs.), 4129
Smith, Maria (Mrs.), 4901
Smith, Maria (Mrs.), 4909
Smith, Maria (Mrs.), 4915
Smith, Maria Anna, 1461
Smith, Maria Anna, 1483
Smith, Maria J., 3671
Smith, Maria J., 3739
Smith, Maria J., 3774
Smith, Maria L., 3858
Smith, Maria, 1360
Smith, Maria, 1386
Smith, Maria, 1537
Smith, Maria, 1632
Smith, Maria, 1997
Smith, Maria, 3293
Smith, Maria, 3384
Smith, Maria, 3505
Smith, Maria, 3562
Smith, Maria, 3630
Smith, Maria, 3827
Smith, Maria, 3874
Smith, Maria, 3953
Smith, Maria, 4009

Smith, Maria, 4010
Smith, Maria, 4098
Smith, Maria, 4111
Smith, Maria, 4392
Smith, Maria, 4581
Smith, Maria, 4850
Smith, Maria, 4859
Smith, Maria, 4864
Smith, Maria, 4874
Smith, Maria, 4876
Smith, Mariae, 1262
Smith, Mariae, 1537
Smith, Mariae, 1724
Smith, Mariae, 702
Smith, Mariam I., 4763
Smith, Mariam L., 4842
Smith, Marie, 1387
Smith, Mary, 138
Smith, Mary (Mrs.), 3998
Smith, Mary (Mrs.), 4001
Smith, Mary (Mrs.), 4003
Smith, Mary (Mrs.), 4023
Smith, Mary (Mrs.), 4036
Smith, Mary (Mrs.), 4069
Smith, Mary (Mrs.), 4151
Smith, Mary (Mrs.), 4167
Smith, Mary (Mrs.), 4171

Smith, Mary (Mrs.), 4881
Smith, Mary (Mrs.), 4894
Smith, Mary (Mrs.), 4899
Smith, Mary (widow), 4344
Smith, Mary, 22
Smith, Mary A. (Miss), 4619
Smith, Mary A., 2512
Smith, Mary A., 2557
Smith, Mary A., 4662
Smith, Mary Ann, 167
Smith, Mary Ann, 2139
Smith, Mary Ann, 4553
Smith, Mary Anna, 472
Smith, Mary C. (Mrs.), 4107
Smith, Mary Catharine, 2472
Smith, Mary Catharine, 4940
Smith, Mary Elizabeth, 3070
Smith, Mary G. [or J.], 3047
Smith, Mary Jane, 2481
Smith, Mary Jane, 2542
Smith, Mary Jane, 2621
Smith, Mary Josephina, 2557
Smith, Mary, 170
Smith, Mary, 2112
Smith, Mary, 2871
Smith, Mary, 4200
Smith, Mary, 4208

Smith, Mary, 4712
Smith, Mary, 4853
Smith, Mary, 5474
Smith, Mary, 5673
Smith, May [Mary?] Ann, 1882
Smith, May [or Mary], 2874
Smith, Mechl, 472
Smith, Mechl. (Mrs.), 483
Smith, Michael, 1681
Smith, Michael, 1388
Smith, Michael, 75
Smith, Michael, 1440
Smith, Michael, 1460
Smith, Michael, 1661
Smith, Michael, 167
Smith, Michael, 1882
Smith, Michael, 1889
Smith, Michael, 2320
Smith, Michael, 4531
Smith, Michael, 4589
Smith, Michaelis, 1049
Smith, Michaelis, 1461
Smith, Michaelis, 1629
Smith, Michaelis, 1736
Smith, Michaelis, 665
Smith, Michl, 411
Smith, Michl, 414

Smith, Michl, 4343
Smith, Michl, 521
Smith, Micl (Mrs.), 366
Smith, Missoura, 4843
Smith, Missouri, 3706
Smith, Mr. Jos., 4615
Smith, Mr., 4533
Smith, Mrs. (widow), 177
Smith, Mrs. Catharine Elizabeth, 2532
Smith, Mrs. Dr. J., 5057
Smith, Mrs., 3446
Smith, Mrs., 3546
Smith, Mrs., 3566
Smith, Mrs., 4533
Smith, Otho B., 3487
Smith, Otho, 1921
Smith, Otho, 3706
Smith, Otho, 4805
Smith, Otho, 5359
Smith, Owen, 537
Smith, Patricii, 1724
Smith, Patrick, 2203
Smith, Petrus, 697
Smith, R. (Mr.), 5046
Smith, Sallie (Mrs.), 4026
Smith, Sara Anna, 1214

Smith, Sarah A., 2844
Smith, Sarah A., 2901
Smith, Sarah A., 4698
Smith, Sarah Washington, 2901
Smith, Sarah, 4092
Smith, Sarai, 4038
Smith, Sofia Smith, 411
Smith, Sopha, 464
Smith, Sophia (Miss), 437
Smith, Sophia (Miss), 472
Smith, Sophia, 414
Smith, Sophia, 2152
Smith, Sophia, 2397
Smith, Sophia, 4278
Smith, Sophia, 503
Smith, Sr., Cath., 2110
Smith, Sr., Catharine, 2546
Smith, Susan R., 2822
Smith, Susan R., 3046
Smith, Susan R., 4645
Smith, Susan, 2760
Smith, Susan, 2874
Smith, susan, 2954
Smith, Suzanna, 3123
Smith, Sylvester, 1982
Smith, Teresa, 2823
Smith, Teresa, 415

Smith, Theresa, 2756
Smith, Theresa, 2957
Smith, Theresam, 3635
Smith, Thomas, 702
Smith, Thos. McCleary, 2641
Smith, Toho, 3028
Smith, Uriah, 4707
Smith, William Adolphus, 2532
Smith, William Francis, 2559
Smith, William Henry, 2542
Smith, William, 1262
Smith, William, 2377
Smith, William, 2481
Smith, William, 2542
Smith, William, 2809
Smith, William, 2957
Smith, William, 4592
Smith, William, 4666
Smith, William, 5350
Smith, Wm. Francis, 2860
Smith, Wm, 2621
Smith, Wm, 4655
Smyth, Edwd., 63
Smyth, Elizb, 63
Smyth, John, 63
Smyth, Sophia, 593
Snayne, Genefeffa, 3815

Sneider, Elisabeth, 1709
Sneider, Henrici, 1709
Sneider, Henricus Thomas, 1709
Sneider, Jacobus, 1181
Sneider, Jacobus, 1377
Sneidor, Jacobus, 1272
Snell, John, 301
Snell, John, 301
Snell, Rachel, 301
Snevel, Margaretha, 3516
Snider, Catharine, 2185
Snider, Elizabeth, 2185
Snider, Henry, 2185
Snider, Margaret, 4921
Snovell, Margaret, 3261
Snyder, Anna, 2897
Snyder, Elizabeth, 1915
Snyder, Elizabeth, 2027
Snyder, Elizabeth, 2042
Snyder, Gertrude, 3864
Snyder, Henry, 1915
Snyder, Henry, 2027
Snyder, Henry, 2042
Snyder, Martha (widow), 4543
Snyder, Mary, 2048
Snyder, Philip, 2027
Snyder, Philip, 2042

Snyder, Susan (Miss), 4603
Snyder, Susanna, 1915
Sogee, John, 349
Sogee, Martha, 349
Sogee, Wilm, 349
Somerville, Rebecca, 2632
Sonner, Catharina, 1003
Sonner, Margaretae, 1003
Sonner, Thomas, 1003
Souder, Margaret (Miss), 4575
Souders, Anna, 1570
Souers, Annie, 5652
Souers, Annie, 2819
Souers, Daniel, 2819
Souers, Mary, 2819
Soupe, Catherine, 2419
Soupe, Dolly, 2419
South, Elisabeth, 4290
South, [blank], 2773
South, [blank], 2773
South, Benj., 2908
South, Benjamin, 2748
South, Benjamin, 2790
South, Cath., 2908
South, Catharine, 2790
South, Catherine, 2748
South, Elisabeth, 2748

South, Eliz. May, 2908
South, Julian Lee, 2790
South, Mally, 5628
South, Mary Alice, 2773
South, Mary, 2957
South, Richd, 5629
Spalding, Dora, 3995
Spalding, Gulielmus, 3995
Spalding, Johannes, 3110
Spalding, Sara, 3110
Spangler, Ada, 3255
Spangler, Adelaide V., 4739
Spangler, M. L., 4739
Spechman, Philamena, 3043
Spechman, Philemena, 3339
Speckman, Philomena, 3242
Speckman, Philomena, 3113
Speckmann, Philomena, 3473
Spelohan, Donel, 4411
Spense, Anna, 718
Spense, Jacobi, 718
Spense, Jacobus, 718
Spickler, Ella J., 3875
Spickler, Helena, 3822
Spickler, Helenem, 4825
Spidzing, Amilia, 3877
Spielman, Cora, 3854

Spielman, Evam Estellam, 3854
Spielman, Henrico, 3854
Spittler, Henrietta, 4434
Spohn, Gertrude, 4076
Spohn, Gertrude, 4108
Spohn, Gertrude, 4146
Spoilan, Catharinae, 911
Spoilan, Michael, 911
Spoilan, Petri, 911
Spolan, Margaretae, 881
Spolan, Maria, 881
Spolan, Michaelis, 881
Spolen, Catharina, 1505
Spollen, Catharina, 1131
Spollen, Anna, 1674
Spollen, Catharina, 1672
Spollen, Margareta, 1143
Spollen, Margaretae, 1324
Spollen, Margaretae, 1674
Spollen, Michael, 1324
Spollen, Michael, 1678
Spollen, Michaelis, 1324
Spollen, Michaelis, 1674
Spollen, N., 1143
Spollen, Petrus, 1237
Sponsi, Patre, 4763
Spor, Harrison, 2212

Spor, Mary Frances, 2212
Spor, Mary, 2212
Spotts, James Thompson, 2441
Sprague, Julia, 3462
Sprague, Julia, 3548
Sprig, Antonius, 1496
Sprigg, Julia, 3335
Spriggs, Julia, 3247
Spriggs, Julia, 3625
Spriggs, Rachel, 3247
Springer, Margret Ann, 2573
Springer, Martha Jane, 2573
Sprout, Mech, 621
Squire, Helena H., 3929
Sreiner, Matheus, 1165
Srymbersly, Maria, 4094
Sshuber, Annae, 1638
Sshuber, Laurentii, 1638
Sshuber, Theresa, 1638
St. Clair, David Vinton, 3453
St. Clair, Henri, 3452
St. Clair, Henri, 3453
St. Clair, Joseph Alvey, 3452
St. Clair, Martha E., 3453
St. Clair, Martha Ellen, 3452
St. John, Bridget, 1826
Stabb, Maria, 566

Stabb, Olatius, 566
Stabb, Wilm. Peter, 566
Stabues, Jacob, 316
Stadt, William D., 4195
Stake, Ellen, 2099
Stake, Helen (Mrs.), 2812
Stake, Mary Josephine, 2384
Stake, Eli (Mrs.), 2836
Stake, Eli (Mrs.), 397
Stake, Eli (Mrs.), 435
Stake, Eli (Mrs.), 457
Stake, Ellen, 112
Stake, Georges, 1601
Stake, Guillelmi, 1601
Stake, Harim, 286
Stake, Hiram (Mrs.), 409
Stake, Mariae, 1601
Stake Sr., Ellen, 2484
Stake, Alice E., 148
Stake, Amelia (Miss), 4564
Stake, Amelia, 2259
Stake, Amelia, 2511
Stake, Amelia, 2889
Stake, Atariane [or Stasiane], 397
Stake, Catharina Elisabeth, 918
Stake, Catharina Geneva, 1381
Stake, Catharinae, 1341

Stake, Catharinae, 918
Stake, Catharine (Mrs.), 4986
Stake, Catharine, 86
Stake, Catharine, 4180
Stake, Catharine, 435
Stake, Catherine Anna, 397
Stake, Catherine, 397
Stake, Cathrinae, 1198
Stake, Charels Aughtan, 314
Stake, Eleanor (Mrs.), 111
Stake, Elei, 148
Stake, Eli, 435
Stake, Eli, 112
Stake, Eli, 2099
Stake, Eli, 2836
Stake, Eli, 2956
Stake, Eli, 339
Stake, Eli, 397
Stake, Eli, 409
Stake, Eli, 4564
Stake, Eli, 457
Stake, Elia, 247
Stake, Elia, 314
Stake, Eliae, 1381
Stake, Eliae, 693
Stake, Elias, 3095
Stake, Elie, 2391

Stake, Elie, 2462
Stake, Elie, 3231
Stake, Elie, 3310
Stake, Elie, 3330
Stake, Elie, 3331
Stake, Elie, 3461
Stake, Elie, 4186
Stake, Elie, 4743
Stake, Elisa Francis, 409
Stake, Elisa, 460
Stake, Elisa, 442
Stake, Eliza F., 1918
Stake, Eliza F., 2533
Stake, Eliza F., 4602
Stake, Eliza, 2391
Stake, Eliza, 2686
Stake, Eliza, 2762
Stake, Eliza, 2930
Stake, Elizabeth, 2308
Stake, Ellan, 2912
Stake, Ellen, 2898
Stake, Ellen M., 2436
Stake, Ellen, 1381
Stake, Ellen, 2009
Stake, Ellen, 2048
Stake, Ellen, 2368
Stake, Ellen, 2462

Stake, Ellen, 2503
Stake, Ellen, 2605
Stake, Ellen, 2633
Stake, Ellen, 2676
Stake, Ellen, 2817
Stake, Ellen, 3013
Stake, Ellen, 3222
Stake, Ellen, 4651
Stake, Ellen, 5124
Stake, Ellon, 409
Stake, Ellon, 247
Stake, Ely, 5270
Stake, Emelia, 2384
Stake, Emmilia, 435
Stake, Franciscus Thomas, 1341
Stake, Genevieve, 5565
Stake, George Thomas, 86
Stake, H___ (rest of the name is blank), 918
Stake, Helan, 2956
Stake, Helen M., 4695
Stake, Helen, 3030
Stake, Helen, 4687
Stake, Helena M., 3095
Stake, Helena, 3177
Stake, Helena, 693
Stake, Helena, 693

Stake, Hellen, 2428
Stake, Hierom, 155
Stake, Hiram, 1341
Stake, Hiram, 409
Stake, Hiram, 435
Stake, Hugonis, 1198
Stake, James Elie, 2391
Stake, John M., 2099
Stake, John, 2391
Stake, John, 247
Stake, Josephine, 4917
Stake, Juliana, 1198
Stake, Lem, 442
Stake, M., 649
Stake, Maria, 3379
Stake, Mary Ellen, 2099
Stake, Mary Ellon, 442
Stake, Mary J., 2526
Stake, Mary J., 2588
Stake, Mary J., 2642
Stake, Mary Jane, 2448
Stake, Mary L. [or Q.], 2639
Stake, Mary Q., 4687
Stake, Mr., 379
Stake, Mr., 4657
Stake, Mrs., 379
Stake, Mrs., 4657

Stake, N. (Mrs.), 535
Stake, Nelly, 2837
Stake, Slsn, 314
Stake, Susan, 2099
Stake, Susan, 2391
Stake, Susanna Emma, 2210
Stake, Thomas Hierom, 148
Stakenius?, Godfried, 841
Stakenius?, Maria Cecilia, 841
Stakenius?, Wilhelminae, 841
Stalh, Louisa, 2518
Stallon, Abrahami, 1342
Stallon, Catharina, 1341
Stallon, Catharinae, 1342
Stallon, Richardus Whealan, 1342
Stanlan, Antonii, 1122
Stanlan, Bryan, 1122
Stanlan, Sarae, 1122
Stanton, Michael, 1602
Stanton, Michael, 4437
Starling, Abraham, 4342
Starling, Catharine, 2104
Starling, Mrs., 2100
Starling, Richard, 2801
Stashm, E. (Mrs.), 554
Staub, Amelia, 2488
Staub, Amelia, 2485

Staub, Amelia, 2487
Staub, Harriet, 2485
Staub, Harriet, 2486
Staub, Harriet, 2487
Staub, Harriet, 2488
Staub, James, 2485
Staub, James, 2486
Staub, James, 2487
Staub, James, 2488
Staub, Joseph Frisby Tilgman, 2486
Staub, Josias Francis, 2485
Staub, Margaret Anna, 2488
Staub, Thomas Maddox, 2487
Stauch, Elizabeth, 3669
Staulbert, Arch John, 394
Staulbert, Catherine, 394
Staulbert, Elias Jana, 394
Stauntan, Michael, 1158
Steal, Petrus, 4436
Steamer, Salley, 416
Steel, Syn, 4427
Steele, Ann, 1887
Steele, John S., 1887
Steele, Sarah Jane, 1887
Steele, Sarah Jane, 1888
Steffey, Gertrude, 4809

Steffey, Joannem L., 4809
Steffey, L. (Mrs.), 3872
Steimtmiyer, Sophia, 3638
Stein, Catharina A., 3514
Stein, Catharine, 3203
Stein, Henricum Franklin, 3203
Stein, Howard Benjamin, 3514
Stein, Jacob, 3203
Stein, Jacobo L., 3514
Steinmichel, Anreas, 715
Steinmichel, Francisae, 715
Steinmichel, Joannes Philipus, 715
Steintneyer, Theresaq, 3638
Stekenius, Guellelmina, 1210
Stekenius [sic], Frederick, 1968
Stekenius, Amelia, 1957
Stekenius, Ellen Virginia, 1957
Stekenius, Frances Amelia Catharine, 2298
Stekenius, Frederick, 1957
Stekenius, Frederick, 2298
Stekenius, Welhelma, 2298
Stembly, John, 399
Stemner, Andrias Franciscus, 1327
Stemner, Eberhardi, 1327
Stemner, Magdalenae, 1327
Stephan, Antonii, 1100

Stephan, Magdalenae, 1100
Stephan, Stephanus, 1100
Sterling, Anna, 2778
Sterling, Anna, 2878
Sterling, Bertrand, 2878
Sterling, Jno., 2878
Sterling, John F., 2778
Sterling, John, 4651
Sterling, Maria, 611
Sterling, Matilda, 2737
Sterling, R., 2852
Sterling, Rd., 4690
Sterling, Rd., 2858
Sterling, Rd., 4689
Sterling, Richard W., 2787
Sterling, Richd. W., 4682
Sterling, Richd., 2849
Sterling, Richd., 4683
Sterling, Sally, 611
Sterling, Sarah Ellen, 2737
Sterling, Whelan, 2645
Sterling, William Edgar, 2778
Sterling, William, 2737
Sterling, Wm, 611
Stern, Hattie B., 4879
Stemner, Andrias Franciscus, 1327
Sternner, Eberhardi, 1327

Stemner, Magdalenae, 1327
Stevens, Arthur, 4672
Steward, Hester Ann, 2484
Steward, Joannes, 1141
Steward, Joannes, 1481
Steward, William Adam, 2484
Steward, Wm., 2484
Stewart, [blank], 2891
Stewart, [blank], 2891
Stewart, Augustine, 2757
Stewart, Eliza, 179
Stewart, Eliza, 2715
Stewart, Eliza, 2715
Stewart, Eliza, 2757
Stewart, Elizab, 179
Stewart, Emma Etta, 2891
Stewart, Henry, 2715
Stewart, Henry, 2757
Stewart, Hy., 4635
Stewart, John, 4980
Stewart, Maria E., 3155
Stewart, Maria, 3210
Stewart, Maria, 3314
Stewart, Maria, 3450
Stewart, Maria, 3558
Stewart, Maria, 3859
Stewart, Mariam E., 4730

Stexenius, Mina, 1653
Stey, Conradus, 4395
Steyet, Carolinae, 764
Steyet, Conradi, 764
Steyet, Henricus, 764
Stickenius, 1540
Stickenius, Anna, 1541
Stickenius, Godfried, 1540
Stickenius, Godfried, 1541
Stickenius, Wilhelminae, 1540
Stickenius, Wilhelminae, 1541
Stienberger, Catherine, 4812
Stienberger, Franciscum, 4812
Stikenius, Godfrey, 2166
Stikenius, James Albert, 2166
Stikenius, Margaret W., 2166
Stindor, Catharine Elizabeth, 27
Stindor, Catharine Elizabeth, 28
Stine, Catharina, 3645
Stine, Catherina A., 3657
Stine, Catherina, 3416
Stine, Catherine, 3810
Stine, Charles, 5213
Stine, Charolum Wesley, 3657
Stine, Jacob L., 3416
Stine, Jacobo L., 3657
Stine, Jacobo L., 3810

Stine, Joseph Victorum, 3416
Stine, Mary Elisabeth, 3810
Stipes, Mirandam, 4757
Stock, Bettie, 3485
Stonebraker, John, 2001
Stonebraker, John, 2313
Stonebraker, John, 4919
Stonebreak, Maria, 1437
Stoner, Cecilia, 2303
Stoner, Francis Xavier, 2303
Stoner, Joannes Edwardus, 3178
Stoner, John, 2303
Stoner, Margaritta, 3178
Stoner, Roberto, 3178
Stonesiefer, Catharinam S., 4779
Stonton, Thomas, 1347
Stopps, Henrietta, 39
Stopps, Mary Ellen, 39
Stopps, Peter, 39
Stopps, Mary Ann, 180
Stopps, Mary Magdalene, 135
Stopps, Mary, 180
Stopps, Peter, 180
Storck, Elizabeth, 3594
Storm, Sarah, 3431
Stoss, Joseph Jackson, 302
Stoss, Mary Magdalene, 17

Stoss, Mary, 302
Stoss, Peter, 302
Stoter, [blank], 3568
Stoter, Emory Clarence Joseph, 3568
Stoter, Maria Elizabeth, 3568
Stots, Catharine, 2345
Stottelmeyer, Jane, 2229
Stottelmeyer, Lucy Ellen, 2229
Stottelmeyer, Peter, 2229
Stouck, Bettie, 3388
Stoudt, Aaron, 4250
Stouffer, Andr., 2899
Stouffer, Andrew, 2603
Stouffer, Emory Edwd., 2603
Stouffer, Kate, 2603
Stouffer, Kate, 2899
Stouffer, Margt. Alice, 2899
Stoullper, Georgio W., 4790
Stout, Elizabeth, 4760
Stout, Mary (Mrs.), 546
Stouter, Henrico, 4835
Stover, Frederico, 4836
Stover, Mr. & Mrs., 4523
Street, Margaretta, 3451
Streit, Reuben, 4561
Strite, Daniel, 3449

Strite, Daniele, 3226
Strite, Danielem Deurie, 3449
Strite, Jennie, 3226
Strite, Jennie, 3449
Strite, Nettie Virginia, 3226
Stroubel, Anna Catharine, 2239
Stroubel, John, 2239
Stroubel, Mary, 2239
Strovinger, John, 4628
Stuart, Elizabeth, 34
Stuart, Maria, 3770
Stubel, Mary, 2133
Stuck, Jane C., 4660
Stuckart, Carolinae, 1066
Stuckart, Fredericus, 1066
Stuckart, Philippi, 1066
Stughy, Peter, 357
Stuk, C. F., 2806
Stuk, Jane C., 2806
Stuk, Mary, 2806
Stump, Antony, 211
Stump, Antony, 217
Stump, George, 217
Stump, Mary, 4196
Stump, Regina, 317
Stump, Teresa, 197
Stump, Teresa, 217

Stymmates, Margret, 557
Suce, Catherene, 4352
Suckgen, Christina, 2496
Suddenly, Ulerick, 4959
Sulbert, Archobold (Mrs.), 559
Sulbert, Archobold, 561
Sulbert, Catherine, 561
Sulbert, Henery Francis, 561
Sulbert, Mary, 387
Sullavan, Mary (widow), 4270
Sullavan, Wilm, 4279
Sullen, Archy, 492
Sullen, Catherine, 492
Sullen, James, 492
Sullevan, Bridget, 2176
Sullivan, Mary, 2702
Sullivan, Mary, 2738
Sullivan, Bridget, 2120
Sullivan, C.., 1476
Sullivan, Cath., 2879
Sullivan, Catharina, 1127
Sullivan, Catharina, 3213
Sullivan, Catharina, 3381
Sullivan, Catharinae, 1185
Sullivan, Catharine, 2176
Sullivan, Catharine, 2315
Sullivan, Catherine, 2702

Sullivan, Catherine, 2776
Sullivan, Catherine, 2972
Sullivan, Catherine, 3051
Sullivan, Daniel, 1185
Sullivan, Daniel, 1281
Sullivan, Danielis, 1185
Sullivan, Damiel, 1643
Sullivan, David, 1175
Sullivan, Eliza, 2176
Sullivan, Elleonora, 1741
Sullivan, Guillelimi, 1172
Sullivan, Guillelmus, 1172
Sullivan, Guillelmus, 1641
Sullivan, Guillemas, 687
Sullivan, Hellenae, 687
Sullivan, Honora, 2315
Sullivan, Jeremia, 2315
Sullivan, Jeremia, 5223
Sullivan, Jeremiah, 1104
Sullivan, Jeremias, 1641
Sullivan, Jeremias, 4455
Sullivan, Joannes, 1185
Sullivan, Joannes, 1456
Sullivan, John, 2702
Sullivan, Johnna [sic], 2775
Sullivan, Margaretae, 1281
Sullivan, Maria A., 1565

Sullivan, Maria A., 1595
Sullivan, Maria Ann, 1812
Sullivan, Maria Anna, 1467
Sullivan, Maria, 1643
Sullivan, Maria, 3381
Sullivan, Mary Am, 2522
Sullivan, Mary, 2522
Sullivan, Mary, 2707
Sullivan, Mary, 2780
Sullivan, Mary, 2780
Sullivan, Mary, 2805
Sullivan, Patrick, 2522
Sullivan, Patrick, 3051
Sullivan, Rodger, 2176
Sullivan, Sara, 1543
Sullivan, Sarae, 1172
Sullivan, Sarae, 1641
Sullivan, Thomas, 2707
Sullivan, Thos., 2707
Sullivan, Thos., 2738
Sullivan, Thos., 2780
Sullivan, Timotheas, 1281
Sullivan, Timotheas, 4398
Sullivan, Timothei, 1281
Sullivan, Timothei, 687
suman, Alberto H., 3477
suman, Barbara A., 3477

Suman, Elizabeth, 4774
Suman, Mariam Florentam, 4774
suman, Mariam Florentiam, 3477
Sumann, Maria F., 3490
Summer, Alice, 4122
Summers, Mary, 2156
Summers, Michael, 2156
Sunderman, Maria, 4373
Sunding, Susanna, 2014
Suoup, Mr., 2779
Suter, Catharine Mary, 2359
Suter, Catharine, 2407
Suter, Mary C., 5380
Sutter, Catharenae, 1639
Sutter, Guillelmus, 1639
Sutter, Thomai, 1639
Swab, Lizzie, 5650
Swab, Anna Dorothea, 1719
Swain, Ann Maria, 1905
Swain, Charlotte, 1906
Swain, Nancy, 1905
Swain, Nancy, 1906
Sweaney, Caroli, 1036
Sweaney, Elisabeth, 1036
Sweaney, Elisabeth, 1036
Sweany, Annae, 1702
Sweany, Birgitta, 1438

Sweany, Birgitta, 1775
Sweany, Catharina, 1816
Sweany, Catharinae, 1777
Sweany, Dionysius, 1229
Sweany, Francisci, 1702
Sweany, Franciscus, 1822
Sweany, Garret, 1438
Sweany, Joannis, 1777
Sweany, Johanna, 1777
Sweany, Julianae, 1229
Sweany, Maria Anna, 1702
Sweany, Miles, 1229
Sweany, Rosa Anna, 1478
Sweeney, Ann, 1916
Sweeney, Ann, 2098
Sweeney, Bernardus, 1121
Sweeney, Catharine, 2018
Sweeney, Charles, 533
Sweeney, Charley, 359
Sweeney, Charley, 401
Sweeney, Charly, 571
Sweeney, David, 3693
Sweeney, David, 3084
Sweeney, David, 3085
Sweeney, David, 3692
Sweeney, deceased, 2098
Sweeney, Eduardum Hurley, 3969

Sweeney, Elisa, 359
Sweeney, Elisa, 401
Sweeney, Elisabeth, 571
Sweeney, Francis, 1916
Sweeney, Francis, 2098
Sweeney, Fredericum Gulielmum, 3824
Sweeney, Helena, 3600
Sweeney, Helena, 4792
Sweeney, Henrietta, 3768
Sweeney, J. B., 3830
Sweeney, J., 3339
Sweeney, J.B., 3293
Sweeney, J.B., 3304
Sweeney, J.B., 4756
Sweeney, J.B., 4765
Sweeney, Jacobum Holton, 3709
Sweeney, James, 571
Sweeney, Jeannette, 5275
Sweeney, Jennette (Mrs.), 4162
Sweeney, Joanne B., 3651
Sweeney, Joanne B., 3709
Sweeney, Joanne B., 3768
Sweeney, Joanne B., 3824
Sweeney, Joanne B., 3904
Sweeney, Joanne B., 3941
Sweeney, Joanne B., 3969

Sweeney, Joannem B., 4792
Sweeney, Joannem Jones, 3651
Sweeney, John B., 3971
Sweeney, John B., 3976
Sweeney, John B., 4162
Sweeney, John B., 4902
Sweeney, John, 2018
Sweeney, John, 2018
Sweeney, John, 401
Sweeney, Mariam Josephinam, 3768
Sweeney, Martha Ellen, 1916
Sweeney, Mary Ellon, 359
Sweeney, Nettie, 3651
Sweeney, Nettie, 3709
Sweeney, Nettie, 3941
Sweeney, Nettie, 3969
Sweeney, Riccardum Hurley, 3941
Sweeney, Rosa, 1940
Sweeney, Sophia J., 3824
Sweeney, Sophia J., 3904
Sweeney, Sophiam Joannettam, 3904
Sweeny, Birgitta, 1190
Sweeny, Brian, 1172
Sweeny, Daniel, 3063
Sweeny, David, 3077

Sweeny, David, 4721
Sweeny, David, 4722
Sweeny, David, 4724
Sweeny, Franciscus, 4497
Sweeny, G., 1190
Sweeny, John, 2962
Sweeny, John, 2963
Sweeny, John, 4705
Sweeny, Rosa Anna, 1099
Sweitzer, Annam A., 4789
Sweitzer, Annam E., 4860
Sweitzer, Annam Elizabeth, 3194
Sweitzer, Ceciliam Virginiam, 3469
Sweitzer, Maria, 3469
Sweitzer, Maria, 3647
Sweitzer, Mary J., 3194
Sweitzer, Samuel, 3194
Sweitzer, Samuele, 3469
Sweitzer, Charly, 494
Sweney, Eliza, 494
Sweney, Margret, 494
Swinger, Henrico, 4860
Swinger, Mary Ann, 2537
Swinger, Mary, 4694
Swink, Anna, 3892

Swink, Annam Reginam, 3892
Swink, Decatur, 3892
Swink, Anna Daley, 3979
Swink, Decatur, 3979
Swink, Vera Margaritam, 3979
Swink, Anna, 3761
Swink, Decatur, 3761
Swink, Joannam, 3761
Swink, Vera, 5344
Swisser, Catherine, 295
Swisser, George, 295
Swisser, Peggy, 295
Switzer, Anna, 3947
Switzer, Joannem Alphonsum, 3947
Switzer, N., 3947
Switzer, Anna E., 4169
Switzer, Anna, 3947
Switzer, Anna, 3966
Switzer, Anna, 4007
Switzer, Anna, 4056
Switzer, Annam E., 4865
Switzer, Bertham Josephenam, 3763
Switzer, Cecilia, 4112
Switzer, Cecilia, 4117
Switzer, Emma, 4865

Switzer, Gulielmum Henricum, 4047
Switzer, Irenem M., 3908
Switzer, Isabella, 4117
Switzer, Joannem Alphonsum, 3947
Switzer, M. Isabella, 4050
Switzer, Maria, 3763
Switzer, Maria, 3763
Switzer, Maria, 3861
Switzer, Maria, 3908
Switzer, Maria, 3922
Switzer, Mariam Isabellam, 4886
Switzer, Mariam, 4838
Switzer, Mary, 4047
Switzer, Mrs., 3922
Switzer, Mrs., 4007
Switzer, Samuel, 3763
Switzer, Samuele, 3908
Switzer, Samuele, 4047
Swob, Margarita, 4516
Swop, [blank], 1646
Swop, Andreas, 1646
Swop, Gasparis, 1646
Swope, Dolly, 2904
Swope, Anna Margaret, 1975
Swope, Casimirus, 2225

Swope, Caspar, 1975
Swope, Caspar, 4934
Swope, Casper, 2089
Swope, Casper, 2904
Swope, Casper, 2904
Swope, Catharine (Miss), 4567
Swope, Catharine, 2225
Swope, Catharine, 2499
Swope, Catharine, 2551
Swope, Dorothea, 1975
Swope, Dorothea, 2089
Swope, Dorothea, 2474
Swope, Dorotheae, 1805
Swope, Elizabeth, 2225
Swope, Elizabeth, 3772
Swope, Elizabetha, 4797
Swope, Gasparis, 1805
Swope, Ino., 2904
Swope, Joannes M., 1805
Swope, Jos., 3559
Swope, Jos., 3772
Swope, Joseph, 5415
Swope, Joseph, 5475
Swope, Margarita, 3559
Swope, May Jane, 2089
Swope, Mr., 2779
Swope, Nelly, 2904

Swope, Theodora, 2317
Sylvis, Ellen, 2556
Syphon, Sarah, 2992
Tadden, Grace, 2709
Tafe, Birgittae, 1454
Tafe, Patricius, 1454
Tafe, Petri, 1454
Tagen, Patrick, 4211
Tagent, Mary, 2565
Tagert, Mary, 2573
Taggar, Maria, 1821
Taggaret, Mary, 2722
Taggart, Eliz, 2708
Taggart, E. (Miss), 2783
Taggart, Ella, 2907
Taggart, Ella, 3225
Taggart, Ella, 3317
Taggart, Ella, 3414
Taggart, Ella, 4629
Taggart, Ellen (Miss), 2784
Taggart, Ellenora J., 3581
Taggart, Helena, 3106
Taggart, Helena, 3160
Taggart, Helena, 3518
Taggart, Helena, 3679
Taggart, Hugh, 2708
Taggart, Hugh, 2796

Taggart, Hugh, 2798
Taggart, Margaret, 4923
Taggart, Mary, 2152
Taggart, Mary, 4632
Taggart, Mary, 4642
Taggart, Mary, 5252
Taggart, Thomas, 3547
Taggart, Thomas, 4618
Taggart, Thomas, 5293
Taggarty, Ellen, 2596
Tailor, Michael, 67
Tailor, Nathaniel, 67
Tailor, Terry, 67
Talbott, Anna, 2926
Talbott, Mrs., 403
Tancy, Catharine (Miss), 4517
Taney, Brook, 2053
Taney, Catharine, 1926
Taney, Catharine, 2030
Taney, Catharine, 2033
Taney, Catharine, 2184
Taney, Catharine, 4554
Taney, Eliza, 1926
Taney, Ethelbert, 4543
Taney, Mary Ellen, 2023
Taney, Mary Ellen, 2184
Tanner, Helena, 4143

Tanner, Helenam, 4143
Tanner, Thoma H., 4143
Tanny, Elisabeth M., 1799
Tanny, Maria Elisabeth, 1577
Tanny, Philbert, 1577
Tany, Elisabeth, 1082
Tany, Ethelbert, 1082
Tany, Maria Eleonora, 1082
Tarlton, Stephen, 4222
Tarr, Frederico C., 3676
Tarr, Maria, 3676
Tarr, Xavieruim Wallace, 3676
Tarrel, Anna Elisabeth, 1183
Tarrel, Elisabeth, 1183
Tarrel, Jacobi, 1183
Tarry, Benjamin, 68
Tarry, Hanna, 68
Tarry, Martha, 68
Tarton, Edmond, 186
Tarton, Susanna Cassandra, 186
Tarton, Teresa, 186
Tasco, Rachel, 3802
Tasea, Frederick Augustus, 2791
Tasea, Julias, 2791
Tasea, Rachel, 2791
Tasker (Black), Rachel, 2980
Tasker, Harriet, 5616

Tasker, Cath, 5615
Tasker, Julius, 4644
Tasman, Birgittae, 1057
Tasman, Maria, 1057
Tasman, Michaelis, 1057
Tayler, Frances, 3208
Tayler, Mariam Grace Reginam, 3208
Tayler, Ottone, 3208
Taylo, Mary, 170
Taylo, Phebe, 170
Taylor (Black), Judith, 4677
Taylor, Peter, 4198
Taylor, Andrew, 3016
Taylor, Andrew, 3017
Taylor, Anna Amelia, 3017
Taylor, Beatricem, 4071
Taylor, Charlie, 3250
Taylor, Daisy, 4880
Taylor, Frances, 3208
Taylor, Francesco, 4004
Taylor, Francis, 3184
Taylor, Francisco, 4071
Taylor, Francisco, 4125
Taylor, Franciscum D., 4880
Taylor, Franciscum, 4004

Taylor, George W., 159
Taylor, Hanna, 118
Taylor, Henny, 287
Taylor, Inig, 4635
Taylor, Jesse, 4004
Taylor, Jesse, 4071
Taylor, Jesse, 4125
Taylor, Joannes Thomas, 1274
Taylor, John Owen, 287
Taylor, Jordan, 69
Taylor, Judith, 4672
Taylor, Judy, 4661
Taylor, Judy, 4664
Taylor, Judy, 4703
Taylor, Julia, 4730
Taylor, Lauran Beatricum, 3250
Taylor, Levi, 326
Taylor, Lizzie, 3250
Taylor, Lizzie, 3250
Taylor, Lucinda, 3016
Taylor, Lucinda, 3017
Taylor, Margareta, 1243
Taylor, Mariam Aureliam, 4125
Taylor, Mariam Jane Rebeccam, 3184
Taylor, Mary Janet, 3016
Taylor, Maud Maria, 3963

Taylor, Nanie, 4025
Taylor, Nanie, 4161
Taylor, Nammie, 4070
Taylor, Nathal, 288
Taylor, Nathaniel, 143
Taylor, Otho, 3184
Taylor, Peter, 287
Taylor, Phebe, 159
Taylor, Phobe, 69
Taylor, Saml, 326
Taylor, Sarae Anna, 1274
Taylor, Teaby, 326
Taylor, Terry, 172
Taylor, Terry, 160
Taylor, Terry, 69
Tedrick, Anna, 4019
Tedrick, Jacob, 4019
Tedrick, Liza Jane, 4019
Tedrick, Mary, 3667
Tee, Thos. J. (Rev.), 3905
Teeney, Julian, 534
Teeny, Julian, 531
Teff, Anna, 1169
Teff, Birgittae, 1169
Teff, Peetri, 1169
Teilly, Hugh, 4330
Teiman, Jacobi, 941

Teirnan, Mariae, 941
Teirnan, Patricias, 941
Teirnan, Adalaide, 2632
Teirnan, L., 2632
Teirnan, Virginia, 2632
Templeton, Beatrice, 3799
Templeton, Beatrice, 3914
Templeton, Fremciscum Allen, 3799
Templeton, Gulielmum Burns, 3914
Templeton, Jacobo, 3799
Templeton, Jacobo, 3914
Templeton, Mrs., 4154
Templeton, S., 3668
Tenderman, Barbara, 2437
Tenderman, Lewis Peter, 2437
Tenderman, Samuel Francis Patrick, 2437
Tendery, Rosa B., 3738
Tenery?, Arthur, 4260
Tengary, Aanna (widow), 4315
Tenley, Ann, 12
Tenley, Cloe, 12
Tenley, Dennis, 166
Tenley, Nancy, 166
Tenley, Thomas, 12

Tenley, William, 166
Teoney, Elisa, 272
Teoney, John, 272
Teoney, Mary, 272
Termey, Michael, 5686
Terney, John, 4211
Terney, John (Mrs.), 401
Terney, John (Mrs.), 4211
Terney, John, 386
Terney, John, 401
Terney, John, 410
Terney, Mary, 410
Terney, Michal, 410
Terny, Birgittae, 1759
Terry, Birgittae, 906
Terry, Bridget, 1953
Terry, Bridget, 2200
Terry, Bridget, 2270
Terry, Brigittae, 1343
Terry, Catharina, 1343
Terry, Jacobi, 906
Terry, Jacobus, 906
Terry, Margaret Elizabeth, 2200
Terry, Maria Johanna, 1759
Terry, Michael, 4371
Terry, Robert, 1953
Terry, Robert, 1953

Terry, Robert, 2200
Terry, Roberti, 1343
Terry, Roberti, 1759
Terry, Robertus, 4380
Teterick, Margaret, 2174
Teuley, Ann, 12
Teuley, Cloe, 12
Teuley, Thomas, 12
Tgel?, George, 4527
Thank, Verdy, 5648
Thirven?, Henry, 278
Thirven?, Isabela, 278
Thirven?, Thomas, 278
Thomas, Alenda, 141
Thomas, Anna, 3596
Thomas, Anne, 3028
Thomas, Barney, 141
Thomas, Cloe, 136
Thomas, Cloi, 45
Thomas, Guglielmum Arthurum, 3291
Thomas, Guglielmum Arthurum, 3291
Thomas, James, 239
Thomas, Joannem R., 4900
Thomas, Mary, 141
Thomas, Mrs., 305

Thomas, Mrs., 344
Thomas, Susan, 3291
Thomas, Susan, 3291
Thomas, Susanna, 3641
Thomas, Susanna, 3717
Thomas, Tany (Miss), 259
Thomaswc, Susanna, 3642
Thompson, Anges, 3112
Thompson, Anges, 3930
Thompson, Annam Helenam, 3881
Thompson, Carlottam, 4057
Thompson, Catharina, 3698
Thompson, Catharina, 3817
Thompson, Catharina, 3881
Thompson, Catharinam Hazel, 3951
Thompson, Catharini Agnes, 3951
Thompson, Catherina, 3755
Thompson, Clara, 5581
Thompson, Elizabeth, 2984
Thompson, Fanney, 4687
Thompson, Fannie (Mrs.), 4125
Thompson, Fannie, 3012
Thompson, Fannis M., 2812
Thompson, Fanny, 2895
Thompson, Fanny, 3229
Thompson, Frances, 3112

Thompson, Francesca, 3316
Thompson, Francesca, 3316
Thompson, Francesca, 3537
Thompson, Georgina Leenen, 3698
Thompson, Henrico, 4057
Thompson, Isaac, 2104
Thompson, Isaac, 2104
Thompson, James Isaac, 2574
Thompson, Jas. Zellers, 2832
Thompson, Jesse F., 2812, 4648
Thompson, Jesse, 2574
Thompson, Jesse, 2696
Thompson, Jesse, 2895
Thompson, Jesse, 3012
Thompson, Jesse, 3112
Thompson, Jesse, 3316
Thompson, Jesse, 3925
Thompson, Jesse, 4004
Thompson, Jesse, 4071
Thompson, Jesse, 4125
Thompson, Jesse, 4880
Thompson, Jesse, 5100
Thompson, Jessi Louisam, 3316
Thompson, John Wm., 2645
Thompson, Joseph Motter, 3012
Thompson, Leone, 3817
Thompson, Leone, 3881

Thompson, Leone, 3951
Thompson, Leone, 4027
Thompson, Leonem, 4803
Thompson, Loene D., 3698
Thompson, Ludivico, 3755
Thompson, Margaret (Mrs.), 4684
Thompson, Margaret, 2645
Thompson, Margret, 2574
Thompson, Margt., 2832
Thompson, Mariam, 4027
Thompson, Mariane Evam, 3755
Thompson, Mrs., 2813
Thompson, Netty Amelia, 2895
Thompson, Rebecca, 2104
Thompson, Rebecca, 4936
Thompson, Susan, 2813
Thompson, Susan, 3323
Thompson, Susan, 3324
Thompson, Tanny [Fanny?], 2778
Thompson, Victorem Bernardum, 3817
Thompson, William H., 4618
Thompson, William Henry, 2574
Thompson, Wm, 5585
Thompson, Wm, 2645
Thompson, Wm, 2832
Thompson, Wm, 5018

Thompson, Wm, 5538
Thoms, Bernard, 332
Thoms, Mary, 332
Thoms, Mrs., 381
Thoms, Shexious?, 332
Thomson, David Lucian, 3659
Thomson, David, 3659
Thomson, Sarah, 3659
Thomson, Agnetem Caeciliam, 4160
Thomson, Ann, 95
Thomson, Ann, 96
Thomson, Bennet, 96
Thomson, Catharina, 4160
Thomson, Elias, 95
Thomson, Elias, 96
Thomson, Elleonora, 1216
Thomson, Fannie (Mrs.), 4071
Thomson, Fannie (Mrs.), 4161
Thomson, Fannie, 3994
Thomson, Georges, 1600
Thomson, Helena, 777
Thomson, Henrici, 777
Thomson, Isaac, 1216
Thomson, Isaak, 1600
Thomson, Isacc [or Dfeu], 538
Thomson, John Mills, 243

Thomson, Leone, 4160
Thomson, Mary, 243
Thomson, Mrs, 308
Thomson, Rebecca, 538
Thomson, Rebeccae, 1216
Thomson, Rebeccae, 1600
Thomson, Sarae, 777
Thomson, Susanna, 3659
Thomson, William, 1752
Thomson, Wilm, 538
Thomson, Wm, 95
Thornbury, Elisabeth, 1023
Thornbury, Georgii, 1023
Thornbury, Maria Elisabeth, 1023
Thornton, Ellen, 4330
Tice, Ann Elizabeth, 1882
Tice, Anna, 4019
Tice, Daniel, 1882
Tice, Daniel, 2150
Tice, Daniel, 2271
Tice, Danielis, 1388
Tice, Danielis, 1681
Tice, Danielis, 869
Tice, Joannes Thomas, 1388
Tice, John, 433
Tice, Josephus Ludovicus, 1681
Tice, Louisa Virginia, 2271

Tice, Margaret, 1882
Tice, Margaret, 2150
Tice, Margaret, 2271
Tice, Margaretae, 1388
Tice, Margaretae, 1681
Tice, Margaretae, 869
Tice, Maria Anna, 869
Tice, Maria, 433
Tice, Otho, 433
Tice, William Albert, 2150
Tidball, Mary (Mrs.), 595
Tidball, Maria Ann, 1424
Tidball, Maria, 1436
Tidrich, Elisa J., 4054
Tidrick, Elisam J., 4882
Tidwick, Ida V., 3796
Tidwick, Ida V., 3860
Tidwick, Ida V., 3916
Tidwick, Ida Virginia, 3833
Tidwick, Ida Virginia, 3980
Tidwick, Ida, 3943
Tidwik, Ida V., 4022
Tierney, Anna Eccleston, 2074
Tierney, Anna Eccleston, 3595
Tierney, Anna, 3178
Tierney, Anna, 4757
Tierney, Annie, 5604

Tierney, Benjamin Franklin, 2235
Tierney, Benjamin Franklin, 5601
Tierney, Edward, 1917
Tierney, Elizabeth, 5438
Tierney, Franty, 4669
Tierney, Joannes, 1708
Tierney, John A., 4946
Tierney, John G., 2495
Tierney, John, 1917
Tierney, John, 2074
Tierney, John, 2235
Tierney, John, 2385
Tierney, John, 4599
Tierney, Johrna [sic], 2775
Tierney, Laura C., 1917
Tierney, Laura C., 2495
Tierney, Laura Regina, 2495
Tierney, Laura, 2074
Tierney, Laura, 2235
Tierney, Laura, 2385
Tierney, Leo, 2235
Tierney, Leo, 2385
Tierney, Maria, 3304
Tierney, Maria, 3766
Tierney, Martin, 2775
Tierney, Martin, 2776
Tierney, Mary, 2775

Tierney, Mary Virginia Seaton, 1917
Tierney, Mary, 2750
Tierney, Michael, 2385
Tierney, Mollie, 4683
Tierney, Mrs., 2780
Tierney, Mrs., 90
Tierney, Anna S. [or E.], 3535
Tierny, Catharine Laura, 1894
Tigart, Hugh, 271
Tigart, Margret, 271
Tigart, Mary, 271
Tigart, Ellon, 467
Tigert, Hugh, 369
Tigert, Hugh, 467
Tigert, Hugh, 494
Tigert, Hugh, 528
Tigert, Leonides, 369
Tigert, Margareta, 1136
Tigert, Margret, 369
Tigert, Margret, 467
Tigert, Margret, 528
Tigert, Margret, 528
Tigert, Maria, 1708
Tigh, Anna, 1156
Tigh, Birgittae, 1069
Tigh, Birgittae, 1380

Tigh, Danielis, 1514
Tigh, Jacobi, 1156
Tigh, Jacobi, 1069
Tigh, Jacobi, 1380
Tigh, Jacobus, 1069
Tigh, Jacobus, 1157
Tigh, Johanna, 1380
Tigh, Margareta, 1515
Tigh, Margaretae, 1514
Tigh, Maria Anna, 1514
Tigh, Patricus, 1109
Tighlman, Mary, 597
Tighlman, Simean [or Simcan], 597
Tighlman, Thoms, 597
Tigue, Anna, 1149
Tihlman, David, 526
Tihlman, Mary, 526
Tihlman, Thos, 526
Tilghman, Thomas, 4221
Tilghman, Christophorus, 1138
Tilghman, George, 423
Tilghman, Margaret, 3354
Tilghman, Margaret, 3355
Tilghman, Maria, 1138
Tilghman, Maria, 779
Tilghman, Mariae, 779
Tilghman, Mary, 423

Tilghman, Mary, 478
Tilghman, Thomae, 779
Tilghman, Thomas, 1138
Tilghman, Thomas, 423
Tilghman, Thomas, 478
Tilghman, Thomas, 478
Tilhman, Mary, 547
Tim, Catharinae, 1005
Tim, Joannes, 1005
Tim, Thomae, 1005
Timmonds, Ann, 97
Timmons, Elisabeth, 1734
Timmons, Eliza, 2417
Timmons, Eliza, 2418
Timmons, Elizabeth, 2153
Timple, Catharina, 1150
Timple, Catharina, 4467
Tims, Margarita, 1712
Tims, Joannes, 1484
Tims, Margaret, 2375
Tims, Margareta, 1732
Tinderman, Barbara, 2244
Tinderman, Barbara, 2508
Tinderman, Barbary [sic], 2744
Tinderman, George Wm., 2744
Tinderman, John Cornelius, 2244
Tinderman, Leuis [Lewis?], 2744

Tinderman, Lewis Daniel, 2508
Tinderman, Lewis, 2244
Tinderman, Lewis, 2508
Tinges, Philippus, 4420
Tinken [sic], Catharina, 3137
Tinken, Andrea, 3135
Tinken, Catharina, 3135
Tinken, Cathrine, 3135
Tinterman, Lewis, 4558
Tinterman, Barbara, 2347
Tinterman, Barbara, 2594
Tinterman, Barbary [sic], 2684
Tinterman, Jacob Edward, 2347
Tinterman, Jos. Danl., 2684
Tinterman, Lewis, 2684
Tinterman, Louis Benjamin, 2594
Tinterman, Louis, 2347
Tinterman, Louis, 2594
Tinterman, Louis, 5389
Tippet, Catharina, 1678
Tippet, Georgii, 1750
Tippet, Samuel, 1750
Tippet, Sara, 1810
Tippet, Sarae, 1750
Tirns, Margarita, 1713
Tiva, Anna, 4455
Toben, Mary C., 3051

Toben, Cath., 5546
Toben, Cath., 5591
Toben, Kate, 2651
Togan, Cath., 2608
Tojan, Patrick, 235
Tolan, Alice or Else, 14
Tolan, Eleanor, 14
Tolan, John, 14
Toland, John, 164
Toland, Susanna, 164
Toland, Jane, 4210
Toland, Jane, 63
Toland, Mary, 164
Toland, Susanna, 4190
Tollen, Ellon, 479
Tollen, John, 479
Tollen, Margret, 479
Tollen, Charles, 531
Tollen, Elie, 432
Tollen, Ellon, 531
Tollen, Ellonora, 432
Tollen, John (Mrs.), 504
Tollen, John, 259
Tollen, John, 432
Tollen, John, 531
Tollen, Mary (Miss), 359
Tollen, Mrs., 494

Tombi, M___, 4196
Toohey, Anna Elisabeth, 4428
Toohy, Birgittae, 1316
Toohy, Michael, 1316
Tool, Bridget, 15
tooney, John, 351
tooney, Leonidas, 351
tooney, Mary, 351
Topper, Margaret, 2994
Topper, Margaret, 3044
Tornay, Patricius, 4465
Tosman, Birgittae, 1057
Tosman, Maria, 1057
Tosman, Michaelis, 1057
Toy, Daniel, 4450
Toy, Maria I., 3119
Toy, S. Daniel, 5687
Tracey, Ann, 2124
Tracey, Anna, 2275
Tracey, Elsie, 3905
Tracey, Mary, 2507
Tracy, Annae, 737
Tracy, Joannes, 737
Tracy, Michaelis, 737
Tracy, Mrs., 4082
Trainor, Helenam, 4042
Trainor, Jacobo, 4042

Trainor, Maria Elisab., 4042
Trainor, Annae, 1634
Trainor, Michael, 1634
Trainor, Owen, 1634
Tranan, Catharinae, 1499
Tranan, Daniel, 1499
Tranan, Thomae, 1499
Traner, Bridget, 2047
Traner, Bridget, 2170
Traner, Ellen, 2072
Traner, John, 2039
Traner, Rosa, 2113
Traner, Rosanna, 2039
Travers, Margareta, 1374
Tray, Owen, 238
Tremble, Jacobus, 1146
Trenner, Catharina, 898
Trenner, Joannis, 898
Trenner, Patrick, 4322
Trenner, Rosae, 898
Trexell, Elizabeth, 3187
Trice, Daniel Weisel, 2048
Trice, Mary, 2048
Trice, Thomas, 2048
Tritch, Alicia, 3414
Tritch, Franklin, 3414
Tritch, Franklin, 4759

Tritch, Lulam Reginam, 3414
Tritch, Mrs., 4759
Trone, Annam Ruth, 4018
Trone, Carolo, 3901
Trone, Carolo, 4018
Trone, Catharinam Lucindam, 3901
Trone, Jennie, 3901
Trone, Jennie, 4018
Troupe, D. (Mrs.), 5056
Troupe, Infant, 5056
Troupe, Maria, 4736
Trout, Emma, 4065
Trout, Julia, 3736
Trueman, Agnes Johanna, 1298
Trueman, Carolina Regina, 1654
Trueman, David, 1298
Trueman, Elisa, 236
Trueman, Joannes, 1813
Trueman, Joannes, 733
Trueman, Joannis, 1298
Trueman, Joannis, 1654
Trueman, John, 126
Trueman, John, 236
Trueman, Joseph, 126
Trueman, Margareta Anna, 733
Trueman, Sara, 1138
Trueman, Sarae, 1298

Trueman, Sarae, 1654
Trueman, Sarae, 733
Trueman, Sarah, 126
Trueman, Sarah, 236
Truman, [blank], 2044
Truman, Betty, 430
Truman, Cecelia Irene, 2521
Truman, Charles [or Charlot], 526
Truman, Jack, 599
Truman, Janck, 598
Truman, John (deceased), 2521
Truman, John Pius, 2311
Truman, John, 1839
Truman, John, 2044
Truman, John, 2245
Truman, John, 2252
Truman, John, 2311
Truman, John, 430
Truman, John, 4570
Truman, John, 4587
Truman, John, 4948
Truman, John, 515
Truman, Margaret, 2520
Truman, Martha Angelina, 1839
Truman, Mary (widow), 2521
Truman, Mary F., 4957
Truman, Mary Frances, 599

Truman, Mary, 2311
Truman, Mary, 5787
Truman, Matt, 430
Truman, Sarah Ann, 1839
Truman, Sarah, 599
Trumpour, George, 2388
Trumpour, Mary Magdalen, 2388
Trumpour, Mary, 2388
Trumpower [?], George, 2035
Trumpower [?], Margaret, 2035
Trumpower [?], Mary, 2035
Trumpower, George, 2287
Trumpower, Mary, 2287
Trumpower, Susan Elizabeth, 2287
Trunpour, George, 2035
Trunpour, Margaret, 2035
Trunpour, Mary, 2035
Trussel, Elisabeth Sauerbeer J.A., 4727
Trussel, Josephus, 4727
Trussell, Catharina, 3147
Trussell, Catharinam, 3146
Trussell, Ebenezer, 3146
Trussell, Savannah, 3146
Tully, James, 4330
Tully, Owen, 4330
Tunberger, Adam, 2227

Tunberger, Andrew, 2227
Tunberger, Elizabeth, 2227
Turberger, Adam, 2227
Turberger, Andrew, 2227
Turberger, Elizabeth, 2227
Turner, Ann (Mrs.), 5058
Turner, Ann Amelia, 5717
Turner, Ann, 2917
Turner, Ann, 2918
Turner, H., 2087
Turner, H., 4740
Turner, Henry, 2086
Turner, Joannes, 4740
Turner, John D., 4579
Turner, John Jas., 2779
Turner, Joseph E., 3880
Turner, Joseph Edwd., 2918
Turner, Joseph, 2779
Turner, Joseph, 2807
Turner, Joseph, 2917
Turner, Joseph, 2918
Turner, Marg., 2807
Turner, Margaret, 2779
Turner, Mary A. Catharine, 2807
Turner, Mary L., 3880
Turner, Rosam Mariam, 3880
Turner, Sarah, 2917

Turner, Thomas, 1125
Turney, John, 89
Turney, John, 89
Turney, Mary, 89
Twigg, Casandra, 2066
Tydrick, Saml., 2303
Tyerney, Joannes, 1708
Tygert, Hugh, 348
Tygert, Leonides, 348
Tygert, Margret, 348
Tygh, Anna, 1194
Tygh, Annae, 1194
Tygh, Patricii, 1194
Tyler, Ann, 1951
Tyler, Dionysium Tyler, 3378
Tyler, Sarah, 3007
Tyman, Michael, 1510
Tyme, Daniel, 1639
Tyrney, Michael, 1258
Ulerich, Gaspar, 1720
Ulgry, Jacob, 4228
Ullepstsip [or Ullepstssih], Philippina, 2491
Ulrich, Johan Peter, 4196
Ulrich, John Peter, 4196
Unseld, [blank], 5260
Unseld, John H., 5254

Upton, Elisabaeth, 807
Upton, Elisabeth, 1348
Upton, Joannes, 1480
Upton, Joannis, 1348
Upton, Joannis, 807
Upton, John, 4323
Upton, Maria, 807
Upton, William, 1348
V erner, Catharine, 2392
V erner, Mary Louisa, 2392
Vantz, Berta C., 4033
Vantz, Bertha C., 4129
Vantz, Carolum Herbertum, 4129
Vantz, Jacob P., 4033
Vantz, Jacob R., 4129
Vantz, Thomam Andream, 4033
Vartz, Berta C., 4033
Vartz, Jacob P., 4033
Vartz, Thomam Andream, 4033
Veifel, Margaret, 1836
Velslager, Elisa Magdallen, 242
Velslager, Mary, 242
Velslager, Saml, 242
Vernon, deceased, 2286
Vernon, Elizabeth Ellen, 2286
Vernon, Mrs., 2286
Vincendeeffiner, Anastasa, 425

Vincendeeffiner, Mary Elosia, 425
Vincendeeffiner, Vincen, 425
Virtz, Charles Franklin, 2505
Vogt, Georgius, 1626
Volgomet, John, 134
Volgomet, Juliann, 134
Volgomet, Rosanna, 134
Volke, John Wesley, 1841
Volkey, Vesley, 1944
Volz, Henricus, 3595
Voud, John Augustine, 2766
Voud, John, 2766
Voud, Teresa Rebecca, 2766
Wade, Mathilda, 3439
Waese, Caecilia, 1594
Waese, Josephus, 1594
Wagner, Annam Margaretam, 4114
Wagner, Jacobo, 4114
Wagner, Jacobum A., 4856
Wagner, James, 5356
Wagner, Sarah, 4114
Wagoner, Christopher, 2562
Wagoner, Margaret, 2562
Wagoner, William, 2562
Waid, Mary, 2389
Waise, Cecilia, 1658
Waise, Josephus, 1658

Walder, Maria, 2280
Walder, George, 2043
Walder, George, 2183
Walder, George, 2220
Walder, Georges, 1722
Walder, Joshua, 2280
Walder, Maria, 2043
Walder, Maria, 2183
Walder, Maria, 2220
Walder, Mary (widow), 4594
Walgamoth, Mrs., 258
Walhs, Elizabeth, 42
Walk, Mary, 2770
Walk, Mary, 4654
Walker, Allen, 3107
Walker, Anna, 3107
Walker, Ludovicus, 3107
Walker, Allen, 3037
Walker, Allen, 3303
Walker, Allen, 4678
Walker, Anna, 3206
Walker, Anna, 3303
Walker, Anna, 3745
Walker, Annie, 3037
Walker, Guglielmum, 3303
Walker, Joanne Franciscum, 3206
Walker, Mary Elizabeth, 3037

Wall, Berta, 3997
Wall, David, 509
Wall, Gratiam Catharinam, 3997
Wall, James Patrick, 509
Wall, Mary, 509
Wall, Mary, 510
Wall, Michaele, 3997
Wallace, Annae, 1330
Wallace, Danielis, 1439
Wallace, Elisabeth, 1439
Wallace, Guillelmus, 1330
Wallace, Joannis, 1330
Wallace, Maria Susanna, 1439
Wallas, Ellon, 284
Wallas, Lawrence, 284
Wallas, Otho, 284
Wallasse, Anna, 1285
Wallslager, Mary, 552
Wallslager, Saml., 552
Wallslager, Wilm Charls., 552
Wals, Cecelia, 4414
Walsh, Richard, 4235
Walsh [wife of Barney Halpin], Widow, 2892
Walsh, Anne, 2763
Walsh, Charles, 489
Walsh, Elisa (Miss), 310

Walsh, Elisa Anna, 518
Walsh, Elisa, 242
Walsh, Elisabeth, 2727
Walsh, Elizabeth, 40
Walsh, Elizabeth, 5561
Walsh, Elizabeth, 5599
Walsh, Ellon, 518
Walsh, John, 549
Walsh, Kate, 2659
Walsh, Marg., 2658
Walsh, Marg., 2658
Walsh, Marg., 2659
Walsh, Marg., 2734
Walsh, Margaret Catherine, 610
Walsh, Margaret, 2763
Walsh, Margaret, 610
Walsh, Margret, 463
Walsh, Margret, 489
Walsh, Margret, 553
Walsh, Martin, 617
Walsh, Mary Elisa, 463
Walsh, Mary, 617
Walsh, Mary, 617
Walsh, Nancy, 2658
Walsh, P., 3703
Walsh, P., 3704
Walsh, P., 3705

Walsh, Patrick, 518
Walsh, Richard, 463
Walsh, Richard, 489
Walsh, Richard, 553
Walsh, Richard, 610
Walsh, Robt., 2659
Walsh, Susanna, 553
Walsh, Wm, 42
Walsh, Wm., 2658
Walshlear, Mrs., 4235
Walshlear, Mrs., 463
Walshler, Anna Cecilia, 490
Walshler, Mary, 490
Walshler, Mrs., 489
Walshler, Saml., 490
Walter, George, 1846
Walter, George, 2147
Walter, Joseph, 1846
Walter, Maria Agneto, 3474
Walter, Maria, 1846
Walter, Maria, 2147
Walter, Mary, 2698
Walters, Adleid, 3519
Walters, Domina, 3752
Walters, Eliz., 5164
Walters, Elizabeth, 5445
Walters, Georgio, 3519

Walters, M. Agneti, 3705
Walters, Maria Agnete, 3545
Walters, Mariam Elizabeth, 3519
Walters, Mary, 5457
Walters, Rebeccam, 4787
Walton, Ann, 2897
Warner, Rosa, 3611
Waner, Joseph, 2043
Waner, Mary, 2043
Waner, Michael, 2043
Wanner, Francisca, 1311
Wanner, Rubertus, 1311
Ward, Ann, 4
Ward, Annae, 760
Ward, Aquella, 4
Ward, Aquila, 85
Ward, Berthem Lorrettem, 3603
Ward, Catharina, 3603
Ward, Dr., 4611
Ward, Eleanor, 4
Ward, Elis., 2815
Ward, Elizabeth (Mrs.) (widow), 605
Ward, Elizabeth (widow), 4347
Ward, Elizabetham Helenam, 3751
Ward, Geneveva, 3495
Ward, Genevieve, 5638

Ward, Genoveffa, 3170
Ward, Henry Peter, 85
Ward, Jacobo A., 3603
Ward, Jennie A., 4689
Ward, Jennie, 2977
Ward, Joannes, 760
Ward, Maria, 1597
Ward, Mariam Gertrudem, 3572
Ward, Mary (Miss), 300
Ward, Mary, 85
Ward, Mary Ward, 1915
Ward, Mary, 1832
Ward, Mary, 1999
Ward, Mary, 2231
Ward, Mary, 5185
Ward, Michaelis, 760
Ward, Samuel, 2815
Ward, Virginia, 2815
Warmir, Rosa, 4829
Warner, Mrs. Robt., 5508
Warner, Adam Dellam, 3384
Warner, Adam Rebeccam, 3871
Warner, Addie, 5145
Warner, Anna F., 3583
Warner, Anna F., 3689
Warner, Anna F., 3742
Warner, Anna, 3640

Warner, Anna, 3803
Warner, Anna, 3871
Warner, Berthem Mariem, 3697
Warner, Elisabeth, 2777
Warner, Elizabeth, 2534
Warner, Francisca, 2226
Warner, Frederico, 3697
Warner, George, 3803
Warner, George H., 5301
Warner, George Howan, 2584
Warner, Georgio H., 3583
Warner, Georgio H., 3640
Warner, Georgio H., 3689
Warner, Georgio, 3871
Warner, Georgium H., 4770
Warner, Georgius Howard, 3583
Warner, Gorgio H., 3742
Warner, Grace, 3742
Warner, Harry M., 5688
Warner, Henry Myers, 2534
Warner, Illsworth, 5026
Warner, John Frederick, 2777
Warner, John, 2716
Warner, Julia Elizabeth, 5741
Warner, Julia, 2668
Warner, Juliam Vidier, 3803
Warner, Leo, 3040

Warner, Maria E., 3384
Warner, Mariam Elizabetham, 3689
Warner, Mary Elisabeth, 2716
Warner, Mary Eliz., 2584
Warner, Mary Eliz., 2850
Warner, Mary Elizabeth, 2449
Warner, Mary Elizabeth, 2628
Warner, Mary, 2668
Warner, Mary, 2850
Warner, Mary, 3040
Warner, Mary, 5528
Warner, Mrs., 2797
Warner, Philip, 5481
Warner, Phillip, 5014
Warner, Robert E., 5641
Warner, Robert Ellsworth, 2449
Warner, Robert, 2449
Warner, Robert, 2534
Warner, Robert, 2716
Warner, Robert, 2777
Warner, Robert, 3040
Warner, Robert, 4598
Warner, Robert, 5316
Warner, Roberto, 3384
Warner, Robertum, 3640
Warner, Robertus, 3583

Warner, Robertus, 3640
Warner, Robt., 2584
Warner, Robt., 2668
Warner, Robt., 2850
Warner, Robt., 5782
Warner, Ros., 5016
Warner, Rosa, 3697
Warren, Geneviva, 3624
Warren, P. (Rev.), 3846
Warthen, Dolley, 204
Warthen, Joseph, 204
Warthen, Joseph, 204
Warther?, Dolly, 280
Warther?, Joseph, 280
Warther?, Michal, 280
Warton, Dorethea, 1813
Warton, Fannie Elisab. (Mrs.), 5227
Washington, Abraham Lincoln, 3446
Washington, Emmam, 4846
Washington, Emmerikas Mariam, 3446
Washington, Harriet, 3446
Washington, John, 2148
Washington, Mary Ann, 2148
Washington, Philip Emory, 2148

Wassum, Maria, 3100
Wastler, Maria, 4911
Wastler, Carolo A., 4911
Wastler, Carolum Albertum, 4904
Wastler, Maria, 4904
Wastler, Mariam, 4911
Waters, Eliza, 3021
Waters, Ellon, 206
Waters, James, 3021
Waters, Jeffery, 321
Waters, Jeffery, 426
Waters, Jeffrey, 206
Waters, Jefrey, 140
Waters, Maria, 140
Waters, Maria, 426
Waters, Marian, 3061
Waters, Martha, 426
Waters, Mary, 206
Waters, Mary, 3061
Waters, Mary, 3089
Waters, Mary, 321
Waters, Richard, 140
Waters, Rosan, 321
Waters, Susan, 3373
Waters, William Thomas, 3021
Waters, William, 3061
Waters, William, 4708

Watkins, Carolus Henricus, 1770
Watkins, E W [sic], 1770
Watkins, Ed W [sic], 1769
Watkins, Edgart Augustinus, 1549
Watkins, Ellen, 1838
Watkins, Elleonorae, 975
Watkins, Georgius S., 1769
Watkins, Helenae, 1549
Watkins, Helenae, 1769
Watkins, Helenae, 1770
Watkins, Roberti W., 1549
Watkins, Roberti White, 975
Watkins, Robertus W., 4391
Watkins, Thomas Wilson, 975
Watson,, 1365
Watson, [blank], 4603
Watson, Amanda, 3245
Watson, Amanda, 3246
Watson, Anna, 305
Watson, Anna, 784
Watson, Donold, 305
Watson, F? Wilm, 305
Watson, Geo. Wm., 2662
Watson, George W., 5758
Watson, Jacobi, 1657
Watson, Jacobi, 784
Watson, James, 4312

Watson, Jane, 2662
Watson, Jno., 2605
Watson, Jno. Joseph, 2662
Watson, Maria Catharina, 1657
Watson, Mary Damanda [sic], 2605
Watson, Mary J., 2605
Watson, Mary S., 5768
Watson, Sarae, 1657
Watson, Sarae, 784
Watts, Joanna, 3558
Watts, Helena Cindry, 3209
Watts, Jennie, 3209
Watts, Jennie, 3539
Watts, Jennie, 3540
Watts, Jennie, 4793
Watts, Joannes W., 3539
Watts, Joannes W., 3540
Watts, Joannes, 3558
Watts, Johannem, 3422
Watts, John W., 3209
Watzler, Albertus, 4110
Watzler, Carolo A., 4153
Watzler, Georgium Carlton, 4153
Watzler, Maria E., 4153
Weast, Suzanna, 3117
Weast, Emma Mariem, 3550
Weast, Emma, 3634

Weast, Emmem K., 4805
Weast, Homey, 5146
Weast, Horine, 4736
Weast, Susan, 2742
Weast, Susan, 3028
Weast, Susannam M., 4736
Weaver, Anna Catharine, 1958
Weaver, Anna, 347
Weaver, Anna, 361
Weaver, Anna, 388
Weaver, Belend, 347
Weaver, Belend, 361
Weaver, Belinda Mary E., 2401
Weaver, Belinda, 1918
Weaver, Belinda, 2049
Weaver, Belinda, 2502
Weaver, C. Mary E., 5751
Weaver, Catharine, 2353
Weaver, Catharine, 5404
Weaver, David, 347
Weaver, David, 361
Weaver, David, 388
Weaver, Francisca, 2473
Weaver, Georgius, 1779
Weaver, Georgius, 1780
Weaver, Georgius, 1781
Weaver, Joannes Henricus, 1780

Weaver, John, 5395
Weaver, Lucinda Francisca, 1779
Weaver, M., 2561
Weaver, Margaret, 1968
Weaver, Maria, 2220
Weaver, Martin, 2636
Weaver, Mary Ann, 1958
Weaver, Mary Elizabeth, 2479
Weaver, Mary, 1959
Weaver, Mary, 2463
Weaver, Mary, 2479
Weaver, Mary, 2490
Weaver, Michael, 2220
Weaver, Michael, 2220
Weaver, Michael, 2463
Weaver, Michael, 2479
Weaver, Patientia, 1779
Weaver, Patientia, 1780
Weaver, Patientia, 1781
Weaver, Philip D., 1958
Weaver, Upton A., 1781
Weaver, Wilm, 388
Webb, Margaritta, 3178
Weber, Joannes, 1563
Weber, Mariae, 1563
Weber, Mariae, 1811
Weber, Michael, 1553

Weber, Michaelis, 1563
Weber, Michaelis, 1811
Weber, Paulus, 1811
Weedon, Alfredo, 3802
Weedon, Carrie May, 3802
Weedon, Priscilla, 3802
Weider, Anna Maria, 2575
Weighand, Adam, 947
Weighand, Helenae, 947
Weighand, Margareta, 947
Weight, Jacobus, 1126
Weirich, Idam [sic] Robertam, 3253
Weirich, Isaac, 3253
Weirich, Lucretia, 3253
Weirich, Lucretia, 3253
Weirich, Maria, 3253
Weiser, Emmam Maud, 4053
Weiser, Maud Emma, 4081
Weiser, Rachele, 4053
Weiser, Samuel H., 4053
Weiss, Carolus Guillelmus, 4396
WeissMuller, Rosalia, 4385
Welch, Anna, 1962
Welch, Elizabeth, 2787
Welch, Jennie, 4722
Welch, Judith, 1973

Welch, Margarita, 3564
Welch, Margarita, 3564
Welch, Margarita, 3784
Welch, Maria, 3607
Welch, Patritio, 3607
Welch, Peter, 1962
Welch, Robertum Petrem, 3607
Welch, Rosa, 1962
Weldon, Bridgitt, 2282
Weldon, Bridgitt, 2515
Weldon, Michael, 3926
Welhnzer, Anna C., 3912
Well Slager, Mary, 550
Well Slager, Richard Thomas, 550
Well Slager, Saml, 550
Weller, Catharine, 131
Weller, Catharine, 132
Wellesleger, Emmilia Corolina, 310
Wellesleger, Mary, 310
Wellesleger, Saml, 310
Wellinger, Anna C., 3962
Wellinger, Annam Catherinam, 4853
Wells, Anna Maria, 2265
Wells, Elizabeth Virginia, 2264
Wells, Emelia Isabella, 2305

Wells, Mary E., 2305
Wells, Mary Elizabeth, 2264
Wells, Mary Elizabeth, 2265
Wells, Michael Harrison, 2410
Wells, Minor Francis, 2264
Wells, Minor Francis, 2265
Wells, Minor, 2305
Wells, Sophia Jane, 2410
Welsh, "name not remembered", 2443
Welsh, Anna, 1402
Welsh, Anna, 966
Welsh, Barbara, 4924
Welsh, Benjamin, 3201
Welsh, Birgettae, 726
Welsh, Birgitta, 1109
Welsh, Birgittae, 997
Welsh, Birgittai, 997
Welsh, Catharina, 1742
Welsh, Catharina, 987
Welsh, Eleonorae, 1434
Welsh, Elizabeth, 2145
Welsh, Ellen, 877
Welsh, Ellionorae, 1121
Welsh, Fanney, 2123
Welsh, Guillelmus, 877
Welsh, Henricus, 1197

Welsh, Henry, 2144
Welsh, Henry, 2145
Welsh, Henry, 2146
Welsh, Henry, 2322
Welsh, Henry, 2443
Welsh, Henry, 4929
Welsh, Honora, 1260
Welsh, Jacobi, 1109
Welsh, Jacobi, 1492
Welsh, Jacobi, 1742
Welsh, James, 2123
Welsh, James, 2144
Welsh, Joannae, 1109
Welsh, Joannae, 1492
Welsh, Joannes, 1121
Welsh, Joannes, 1611
Welsh, Johanna, 1853
Welsh, Johanna, 2079
Welsh, Johannae, 1611
Welsh, Johannae, 1742
Welsh, Julia, 2465
Welsh, Juliana, 1530
Welsh, M. Elisabeth, 1530
Welsh, M. Franklin, 1530
Welsh, Margaret Ann Missouri, 2465
Welsh, Margaret, 2606

Welsh, Margaret, 4665
Welsh, Margarita, 3665
Welsh, Maria, 1172
Welsh, Maria, 1647
Welsh, Maria, 3662
Welsh, Maria, 3753
Welsh, Maria, 3967
Welsh, Mariae, 987
Welsh, Mariam Elizabeth, 3662
Welsh, Martini, 726
Welsh, Martini, 997
Welsh, Mary (Mrs.), 5233
Welsh, Mary Ann, 2123
Welsh, Mary Ann, 2322
Welsh, Mary, 2144
Welsh, Mary, 2145
Welsh, Mary, 2146
Welsh, Mary, 2322
Welsh, Michael J. [or I.], 1492
Welsh, Michael, 1434
Welsh, Michaelis, 1121
Welsh, Michaelis, 1434
Welsh, Michaelis, 877
Welsh, Patricii, 987
Welsh, Patrick, 2202
Welsh, Patritio, 3662
Welsh, Petri, 1197

Welsh, Petri, 966
Welsh, Rosae, 1197
Welsh, Rosae, 966
Welsh, Sarah, 2146
Welsh, Thomas, 2443
Welsh, Thomas, 726
Welsleider, Mary, 610
Wenerler, Catharinae, 1124
Wenerler, Marci, 1124
Wenerler, Maria, 1124
Werverler, Catharinae, 1124
Werverler, Marci, 1124
Werverler, Maria, 1124
Wesley, Anna Josephine, 2263
Wesley, Frederick, 2278
West, Matilda, 4298
Westenhaver, Stewart, 4822
Wethiger, Anna C., 3912
Wetmuller, Catharina Maria, 1287
Wetmuller, Catharinae, 1287
Wetmuller, Dyonisii, 1287
Wetzel, Albertus, 1139
Wetzel, Margaretae, 1139
Wetzel, Sara Joanna, 1139
Wewerler, Catharinae, 1124
Wewerler, Marci, 1124
Wewerler, Maria, 1124

Weynih, Maria, 376
Whalen, Edwd., 2933
Whalen, Margaret (widow), 4306
Whaley, John, 4699
Wharton, Dolly, 35
Wharton, Dolly, 36
Wharton, Elizabeth, 36
Wharton, Joe, 36
Whealan, Anastasia, 915
Whealan, Anna, 1334
Whealan, Anna, 1566
Whealan, Annae, 1403
Whealan, Annae, 1695
Whealan, Bernardi, 1403
Whealan, Bernardi, 1695
Whealan, Bernardus, 1566
Whealan, Bernardus, 1632
Whealan, Bernardus, 1695
Whealan, Edwardus, 1792
Whealan, Guillelmi, 1162
Whealan, Jacobi, 1475
Whealan, Jacobi, 1476
Whealan, Jacobi, 1792
Whealan, Jacobi, 915
Whealan, Jacobus, 1403
Whealan, Jacobus, 1475

Whealan, James, 1328
Whealan, Joannes, 1162
Whealan, Joannes, 1476
Whealan, Johannae, 1475
Whealan, Johannae, 1476
Whealan, Johannae, 1792
Whealan, Johannae, 915
Whealan, Josephus, 1792
Whealan, Mariae, 1162
Whealan, Mary, 4333
Whealen, Andrias, 1132
Whealen, Jacobi, 1132
Whealen, Judith, 1132
Wheeler, "unknown", 350
Wheeler, George, 350
Wheeler, Louisa, 350
Whelan, Birgittae, 965
Whelan, Catharine, 2355
Whelan, Guillelmi, 752
Whelan, James, 1853
Whelan, James, 1973
Whelan, James, 2079
Whelan, Johanna, 1853
Whelan, Johanna, 2079
Whelan, Judith, 1973
Whelan, Judith, 1974
Whelan, Lewis, 4678

Whelan, Margareta, 752
Whelan, Mariae, 752
Whelan, Michael, 2079
Whelan, Michaelis, 965
Whelan, Thomas, 1973
Whelan, Thomas, 965
Whelan, William, 1853
Whetstone, Elizabeth, 2334
Whetstone, Elizabeth, 2335
Whigfield, Elizabeth, 1910
Whigfield, Mary, 1910
Whigfield, Elizabeth, 1911
Whigfield, Simon, 1911
Whily, Patricius, 1486
Whipp, Frances, 2999
Whipp, Franey, 5267
Whipple, F., 3122
White, Kate (Mrs.), 3424
White, Carolum Eduardum, 3402
White, Cath., 2945
White, Cath., 2967
White, Catharina, 3165
White, Catharine (Miss), 4565
White, Cecelia, 456
White, Charles Frederick, 2967
White, Jacobum Franciscum, 3165
White, Joannes, 1643

White, Joseph, 4000
White, Julia, 2958
White, Mariae, 1643
White, Mariam Catharinam Wise, 4000
White, Mauricii, 1643
White, Mich., 2967
White, Mich., 2968
White, Michael, 3424
White, Michael, 3530
White, Michael, 4674
White, Michaele, 3165
White, Rebecca, 4000
White, Sally, 3402
Whitney, Jacobem, 4829
Whitney, John, 4626
Whitney, Mary, 2807
Whitney, Michel, 4626
Wi nkelman, Bernard, 1980
Wi nkelman, Elizabeth, 1980
Wi nkelman, Henry, 1980
Wi nkelman, Mary Ellen, 1980
Wieley, Ella, 3570
Wigus, Sara Anna, 4432
Wigus, Sara Anna, 964
Wihand?, Catharina, 4395
Wiles, Carolum Eduardum, 4898

Wiley, Maria Johanna, 3559
Wilhand, Carolinae, 764
Wilhand, Henricus, 764
Wilhide, Catharine, 5490
Wilhide, Louisa, 5426
Wilhyde, Marg. Elfrida, 3577
Wilhyde, Mary Jane A. [or O.] [Margaret has been overwritten by Mary Jane], 5408
Wilkinson, Adeline, 1838
Wilkinson, Catharine, 1838
Willace, Eleanor, 155
Willard, Johanna, 3127
Williams, [blank], 5132
Williams, Catherine, 3024
Williams, Edwd., 2853
Williams, Edwd., 4686
Williams, Eliza, 5065
Williams, Ellen, 3458
Williams, Ellen, 3459
Williams, F. C., 3458
Williams, F. C., 3459
Williams, George Anne, 3125
Williams, George, 3024
Williams, Georgia, 3492
Williams, Georgiana, 3250
Williams, Georgianna, 3189

Williams, Georgianna, 3604
Williams, Gulielmo, 3617
Williams, Jennie, 3459
Williams, Jno, 4195
Williams, John, 4195
Williams, Lilia, 3492
Williams, Lilia, 4742
Williams, Lillie C.T., 5763
Williams, Lillie F., 5152
Williams, Lillie, 3249
Williams, Maria, 3617
Williams, Mariae, 642
Williams, Mariam Louisam, 3617
Williams, Mariam, 3458
Williams, Mary (Mrs.), 297
Williams, Mary, 3024
Williams, Sallie, 4846
Williams, Susan, 4797
Williamson, David, 3310
Williamson, Giorgium D., 3310
Williamson, Matilda, 4590
Williamson, Sarah, 3310
Willis, Mary, 4271
Wills, Carrie, 4898
Wills, Clara, 5299
Wills, Claran Louisam, 3217
Wills, Edw., 5105

Wills, Edwardum Guistini, 3305
Wills, Gertrude, 3258
Wills, Gulielmo J., 3941
Wills, Gulielmo, 4908
Wills, Gulielmus, 3580
Wills, Infant, 5045
Wills, Jacob H., 3002
Wills, Jacob H., 4700
Wills, Jacob J. [or I.], 4898
Wills, Jacob, 3053
Wills, Jacob, 3217
Wills, Jacob, 3258
Wills, Jacob, 3305
Wills, Jacob, 3743
Wills, Jacob, 3744
Wills, Jacobo H., 3118
Wills, Jacobus H., 3579
Wills, Jacobus, 3620
Wills, Joanne F., 3164
Wills, Joannem F., 3118
Wills, Laura, 3440
Wills, Margaritam Laetitiam, 4898
Wills, Margaritta Letitia, 3164
Wills, Maria, 4140
Wills, Maria, 4144
Wills, Martha S., 3164
Wills, Martha S., 3118

Wills, Martha, 3137
Wills, Martha, 3258
Wills, Martha, 3305
Wills, Martha, 3334
Wills, Martha, 3506
Wills, Matilda, 3217
Wills, Mr., 5045
Willson, Riccardum Cole, 4162
Willson, Bessie, 4166
Willson, Carolo, 4166
Willson, Francisca R., 4162
Willson, Henricus, 4085
Willson, Joseph Carolum, 4166
Willson, Walter D., 4162
Willy, William, 4869
Wilsen, Betty, 4693
Wilsen, Charles William, 2279
Wilson, Harriet, 4707
Wilson, Henrietta, 3566
Wilson, Joshua, 2279
Wilson, Lucia Anna, 1159
Wilson, Nathaniel J., 3983
Wilson, Rebecca, 2279
Wilson, Rebecca, 3560
Wilson, Robertus, 4437
Wilson, Sarah Ann, 60
Wilson, Sarah Ann, 36

Wilson, Sarah Ann, 21
Winch, Jacob Jos., 4080
Winch, Jacob Joseph, 4080
Windle, Emmilia, 449
Windle, Isaac Thomas, 455
Windle, John, 449
Windle, John, 455
Windle, Sarah, 449
Windle, Sarah, 455
Wingarty, Anna Maria, 2575
Wingarty, Eve Margret, 2575
Wingarty, Theobold, 2575
Wingelman, Bernardus, 1705
Winger, Henrico, 4865
Winkelman, Ellen Mary, 2307
Winkelman, Henry, 2307
Winkelman, John B., 2307
Winkelman, John B., 4571
Winkelman, John William, 2307
Winortgy, Theobald, 2600
Winslon, Maria, 1263
Winslon, N., 1263
Winters, Margret (widow), 4214
Winzer, Elisabeth, 776
Winzer, Joannis, 776
Winzer, Mariae, 776
Winzfeld, M., 2167

Wire, Jacob, 3998
Wire, Mariam Josephinam, 3998
Wire, Sarai, 3998
Wise, Elisabeth, 4017
Wise, Elisabeth, 4107
Wise, Franciscam Irenem, 4107
Wise, Henricum Scott, 4873
Wise, Jerome, 1929
Wise, Jesse Paulinam, 4017
Wise, Maria Angela, 2743
Wise, Maria, 3845
Wise, Mariam, 4835
Wise, Mary Ann, 1929
Wise, Mary, 2653
Wise, Mary, 2743
Wise, Peter, 1929
Wise, Richard H., 4620
Wise, Richard, 2653
Wise, Richard, 2743
Wise, Sarah Virginia, 2653
Wise, Sarah, 5096
Wise, Walter S., 4017
Wise, Walter S., 4107
Wiser, Maria E., 4890
With, Victoria, 4224
Witney, Dionysius, 1397
Witney, Johannae, 1397

Witney, Patricii, 1397
Witsin, Alberti, 808
Witsin, Margaretae, 808
Witsin, Maria Anna, 808
Witt, Maria, 1124
Witt, Mariae, 868
Witt, Melchiori, 868
Witt, Michael, 1124
Witt, Therisia, 868
Wittmuller, Catharinae, 902
Wittmuller, Henrici, 902
Wittmuller, Henricus, 902
Witty, Cararie, 3787
Wlaker, Allan, 2962
Wlaker, Ann, 2962
Wlaker, Margaret Ann, 2962
Woeford, Lucretia, 4653
Wolf, Henry, 4601
Wolf, Anna, 4509
Wolf, Edgar Willm. Leonem, 3861
Wolf, Emlia I. [orI.], 3887
Wolf, Georgio H., 3887
Wolf, Georgium H., 4837
Wolf, Henrico, 3861
Wolf, Henricum, 4838
Wolf, Henry Stanislaw, 2846
Wolf, Henry, 2517

Wolf, Henry, 2568
Wolf, Henry, 2736
Wolf, Hy, 2667
Wolf, Hy, 2846
Wolf, J. Upton, 3435
Wolf, Jennie, 3901
Wolf, Jennie, 4018
Wolf, Jennie, 4843
Wolf, Joanne, 3705
Wolf, John, 3191
Wolf, Margareta A., 3188
Wolf, Margaretam, 3191
Wolf, Margaretha, 2667
Wolf, Maria, 3435
Wolf, Maria, 3435
Wolf, Maria, 3861
Wolf, Maria, 3908
Wolf, Maria, 3981
Wolf, Mariam M., 4861
Wolf, Mary (Mrs.), 4066
Wolf, Mary Ann J., 2517
Wolf, Mary Ann, 2736
Wolf, Mary Ann, 2846
Wolf, Mary Catharine, 2736
Wolf, Mary D., 2568
Wolf, Mary Genero, 2517
Wolf, Mary, 2667

Wolf, Phoebem Genevefam, 3887
Wolf, Sarah Josephine, 5772
Wolf, William Bernard, 2568
Wolfe, Hopkin, 3922
Wolfe, Joannam Catherinem, 3614
Wolfe, John, 4601
Wolfe, Joseph, 2324
Wolfe, Maria, 3922
Wolfe, Martha, 2324
Wolfe, Mary Eugene, 2324
Wolfe, Samuelem Henricum, 3922
Wolff, Anna Laucenia, 2887
Wolff, Henry, 2887
Wolff, Maria, 4169
Wolff, Mary Ann, 2887
Wolford, Lucretia, 2910
Wolgamoth, John, 540
Wolgamoth, Julian, 540
Wolgamoth, Thoms, 540
Wolgumoth, Augusten, 381
Wolgumoth, John, 381
Wolgumoth, Julianna, 381
Wolke, Wesley, 4550
Wolls, Martha, 3135
Wolls, Martha, 3136
Wolse, Catherine, 2717
Wolse, John, 2717

Wolse, Mary Enna, 2717
Woltz, Amelia, 2259
Woltz, Amelia, 2511
Woltz, Amelia, 2889
Woltz, Anna Minerva, 2591
Woltz, Cath., 3020
Woltz, Catharina, 3517
Woltz, Catharine, 2511
Woltz, Catharine, 2591
Woltz, Catharine, 2592
Woltz, Catharine, 2593
Woltz, Catherine E., 5320
Woltz, Charles W., 4564
Woltz, Charles Wm., 2259
Woltz, Charles Wm., 2384
Woltz, Chs. W., 2889
Woltz, Emelia, 2384
Woltz, Geo. Hyner, 2889
Woltz, John Van Buren, 2593
Woltz, John, 2591
Woltz, John, 2592
Woltz, John, 2593
Woltz, Mary Emma, 2384
Woltz, Mrs., 3532
Woltz, Thomas Courtney, 2259
Woltz, Wm., 2511

Wolvington, James W., 4555
Wood, Anna Elizabeth, 3553
Wood, Idam Helenam, 3553
Wood, Joseph, 3553
Woods, Ann E., 3442
Woods, Anna, 3283
Woods, Anna, 3283
Woods, Johanne F., 3442
Woods, Johannem Guglielmum, 3442
Woods, Joseph, 3283
Woods, Mariam Elizabeth, 3283
Woods, Sarah, 2262
Woolrich, Emma F., 3498
Woolrich, Emma F., 3499
Woolrich, Emma F., 3500
Woolrich, Florentiam Violam, 3500
Woolrich, Gulielmum A. Ludovicam, 3498
Woolrich, Joanni, 3498
Woolrich, Joanni, 3499
Woolrich, Joanni, 3500
Woolrich, Mariam Rebeccam, 3499
Woolts, Cath., 5631
Wooltz, James Elie, 2619
Wooltz, Jno., 2619

Wooltz, Kate, 2619
Wooltz, [blank], 3035
Wooltz, Am., 2647
Wooltz, Amelia, 2647
Wooltz, Amelia, 2786
Wooltz, Caroline, 2786
Wooltz, Catharinam, 4746
Wooltz, Geo. Wm., 2886
Wooltz, Jno., 2886
Wooltz, John William, 2647
Wooltz, Kate, 2886
Wooltz, Kate, 5666
Wooltz, William, 2786
Wordon, Gulielmum Everest, 3543
Wordon, Julia, 3543
Wordon, Richardo, 3543
Worley, Barbary, 374
Worth, Barbary, 358
Wright, Mrs., 2711
Wright, Ann Eliza, 2601
Wright, Anna, 3653
Wright, Annie Elisabeth, 5740
Wright, Bernardum Alexium, 3656
Wright, Carolum Gregorium, 3585
Wright, Charles (Dr.), 5204
Wright, Charles, 5554
Wright, Charles, 5594

Wright, Elisabeth, 3847
Wright, Elisabeth, 3865
Wright, Elizabeth R., 5174
Wright, Elizabeth Reginam, 3483
Wright, Elizabeth, 3376
Wright, Elizabeth, 3483
Wright, Elizabeth, 3585
Wright, Elizabetha, 3655
Wright, Elizabetha, 3656
Wright, Elizabetha, 3766
Wright, Fannie, 4640
Wright, Fanny, 4683
Wright, Frances M., 5458
Wright, Frances, 2970
Wright, Frances, 4634
Wright, Harry, 5136
Wright, Helen, 4978
Wright, Henricum Augustinum, 3376
Wright, Infant, 5089
Wright, Irena A., 3691
Wright, Irene A., 3839
Wright, Irene A., 4785
Wright, J. A., 3119
Wright, J.A., 2601
Wright, Jacob A., 2536
Wright, Jacob P., 2804

Wright, Jacob, 2735
Wright, Jacob, 4618
Wright, Jacob, 5222
Wright, James A., 5653
Wright, Leonem Aloysirem, 3865
Wright, Marg. Mary, 5704
Wright, Margaret Agnes, 2536
Wright, Maria Francisca, 3163
Wright, Mary Geneva, 2735
Wright, Mary Geneva, 5015
Wright, Mary, 5422
Wright, Mr., 2711
Wright, Mrs., 4775
Wright, Paulum Joseph, 3655
Wright, Sara R., 3119
Wright, Sarah R., 2536
Wright, Sarah R., 2601
Wright, Sarah R., 2675
Wright, Sarah R., 2735
Wright, Sarah, 2804
Wright, Sarah, 4800
Wright, Susan, 5403
Wright, Urbanum Alphonsum, 3766
Wright, V., 4681
Wright, Victor, 5625
Wright, Wilfred G., 3376

Wright, Wilfred Gergory, 3483
Wright, Wilfredo, 3766
Wright, Wilfredo, 3865
Wright, Wilfrid, 3655
Wright, Wilfrid, 3656
Wright, Wilfrid, 5559
Wright, Wilfrido G., 3585
Wright, Wilfridum G., 4756
Wroe, Anitam Eulaliam, 3160
Wroe, Anna E., 3648
Wroe, Anna, 3838
Wroe, Anna, 3989
Wroe, Anna, 3990
Wroe, Annam E., 4771
Wroe, Annita, 3288
Wroe, Daisie, 3990
Wroe, Daisy Paulitam, 3288
Wroe, Dr., 3285
Wroe, Dr., 3286
Wroe, Dr., 3287
Wroe, Dr., 3288
Wroe, Dr., 3289
Wroe, Dr., 4697
Wroe, Francisco, 4771
Wroe, Joanne, 3160
Wroe, Johannem L., 3285
Wroe, Martha J. [or I.], 3285

Wroe, Martha J. [or I.], 3286
Wroe, Martha J. [or I.], 3287
Wroe, Martha J. [or I.], 3288
Wroe, Martha J. [or I.], 3289
Wroe, Martha, 3160
Wroe, Martha, 3476
Wroe, Martha, 3648
Wroe, Martha, 3838
Wroe, Martham J. [or I.], 3284
Wroe, Mrs. Dr., 4697
Wroe, Ninam Carlotam, 3289
Wroe, Ninam Eulaliam, 3990
Wroe, Ricardem E., 3286
Wroe, Ricardo E., 3989
Wroe, Ricardo, 3990
Wroe, Riccardum Liton, 3989
Wroe, Samuel C., 3287
Wultz, Maria, 3617
Wultz, Mrs., 3617
Wye, Francesca, 3553
Wyland, Ann (Miss), 4520
Wyland, Ann, 1944
Wyland, Ann, 2083
Wyman, Julian, 2004
Yasuxor, Catharina, 1162
Yates, Danieles, 3886
Yates, Evam Mariam, 3886

Yates, Lea, 3886
Yeager, Mary E., 2561
Yeakle, Carolum, 4907
Yeates, Evam B., 4851
Yingling, Mrs., 3557
Yingling, Rosa, 3580
Yinglon, Rosa, 3807
Yohn, Annam Reginam, 3163
Yohn, Carolo, 4847
Yohn, Charles Ragan, 2970
Yohn, Frances, 2970
Yohn, J.[or I.] M., 5098
Yohn, Maria Francisca, 3163
Yohn, Mrs., 4775
Yohn, Philip, 2970
Yohn, Philip, 4683
Yohn, Philippo, 3163
Yohn, Sallie, 4847
Yost, Lila A., 4159
Young, Barbara, 2920
Young, Benjamin F., 4886
Young, Benjamin, 4117
Young, Benjamon F., 4050
Young, Claram A. Ednam, 3542
Young, Daisy Agnetem, 3488
Young, David, 3409
Young, David, 3488

Young, David, 3542
Young, Davide, 3390
Young, Davide, 3391
Young, Davidem Cadwile, 3390
Young, Emma, 3449
Young, Emmam S., 4778
Young, Emmam, 3197
Young, Guglielmum C., 3409
Young, Helenam Misouri, 3391
Young, Henry, 4661
Young, Henry, 4664
Young, Hermione, 3204
Young, Hermione Moffatt, 3196
Young, Hermione, 3205
Young, Indiana Blanche, 2920
Young, Inez Ceciliam, 4117
Young, Isabella, 4117
Young, Jennie, 3226
Young, Jennie, 3449
Young, Jerome, 3196
Young, Jerome, 3197
Young, Jos., 2920
Young, M. Isabella, 4050
Young, Maria E., 3488
Young, Maria E., 3542
Young, Maria, 3196
Young, Maria, 3196

Young, Maria, 3197
Young, Maria, 3197
Young, Maria, 3390
Young, Maria, 3391
Young, Maria, 3409
Young, Mariam Violam, 4050
Zeller, Margaret E., 3673
Zeller, Margaretham E., 4772
Zeller, Margarita E., 3672
Zeller, Sara, 4772
Zellers, Raisin, 3431
Zellers, Maria, 3431
Zellers, Sarah, 3431
Zickler, Elizabeth, 2276
Ziegler, Adami, 1686
Ziegler, Elisabeth, 1686
Ziegler, Jacobus, 1686
Zieler, Adami, 1378
Zieler, Elisabeth, 1378
Zieler, Elisabeth, 1379
Zieler, Flora M., 1378
Zincant, Ulrick, 2530
Zinkand, Franciscus Martinus, 4421
Zinkant, Andrew, 2020
Zinkant, Andrew, 2396
Zinkant, Andrew, 2396

Zinkant, Anna Rebecca, 2020
Zinkant, Catharine, 2020
Zinkant, Catharine, 2396
Zinkant, Laurence, 2537
Zinkant, Marcella, 2537
Zinkant, Mary Ann, 2537
Zinkant, Ulrick, 2464
Zinkant, Ulrick, 2537
Zinke [or Zinken], Andrew, 5662
Zinken, Catharina, 3136
Zittle, Claram Melissam Violam J., 3403
Zittle, Johanna, 3526
Zittle, Lydia, 3403
Zittle, Maria Eliz., 4032
Zittle, Pearli Ireniam Placidiam, 3539
Zittle, Sallie, 3735
Zittle, Samuele, 3403
Zittle, Susan, 3838
Zoken, Maria, 140
Zonk, Jacob A., 2643
Zonk, Margaret, 2643
Zonk, Sarah Helen, 2643
Zook, [blank], 5159
Zook, Catharina, 3623
Zook, Catharina, 4791

Zook, Georgium A., 4791
Zook, Helena S., 3588
Zook, Helena, 3623
Zook, Helena, 3695
Zook, Helena, 3960
Zook, Helena, 4021
Zook, Helenam S., 4781
Zook, Jacobo, 4791
Zook, Jacobum Henricum, 3547
Zook, Jacobum Henricum, 4779
Zook, Margaret, 3302
Zooke, Helena, 3737
Zroderick, Romana E., 5743
Zuck, Charles Henry, 2804
Zuck, Jacob, 2804
Zuck, Margaret, 2804
Zuck, Susan, 2802
Zuck, Susan, 2808
Zwoke, Edward Franklin, 5726

NO LAST NAMES:

_ay, 8
_elly, 7
_rma Mary, 8
Alexander, 4244
Alinda, 143

Alinda, 144
Amanda, 4212
Ambrose, 104
Anasastia, 485
Anastasia, 1998
Anastasia, 415
Ann, 143
Anna Elisabeth, 1616
Anna, 1459
Anna, 3206
Anna, 4255
Apolinae, 1031
Arnold, 165
Arnold, 7
Aunt Nancy, 5034
Barnar[?] Rosier, 224
Basil, 214
Basil, 384
Basil, 43
Bayley, 3642
Ben, 4182
Ben, 4292
Bernardus, 1014
Bridget, 2119
Catherine, 276
Cathurina, 1615
Celia, 106

Celia, 173
Charles, 113
Claram Virgeniam, 3501
Cleofas M, 4084
Cloe "of John Harry", 113
Congregation, 4612
Daniel, 1614
Danielem Josephem, 3606
Darcas, 33
David, 43
Delia, 4188
Develbis, 914
Dianna, 283
Dianna, 281
Dianna, 282
Dominii, 1590
Ebberts, 1031
Elisabeth Annae, 768
Elisabeth Hellena, 657
Elisabeth, 1680
Elisabeth, 3152
Elisabeth, 711
Elisabetha, 756
Eliza Ann, 58
Elizabeth, 87
Elizabeth Mariam, 3502
Estatia, 2103

Eustatia, 2109
Francis Horris, 384
Fredericus, 1310
George Scott, 2482
Georgius, 1054
Hanna, 253
Hanna, 105
Hanna, 43
Hanna, 76
Harriet, 4569
Henry, 315
Henry, 4182
Henry, 87
Henrietta, 2103
Henrietta, 2109
Henriettae, 1010
Hilarius, 1010
Ignatius, 173
Iris, 4194
Jacob, 415
Jacobi, 768
Jacobus, 1613
Jane, 59
Jareth, 756
Jesse, 104
Jesse, 105
Jesse, 113

Jesse, 165
Jesse, 8
Joanne Franciscum, 3206
Joannes, 836
Joannes, 1591
Joannes, 756
Joannis, 1010
Joannis, 657
Joe, 415
John Sweeney, 509
John, 2119
John, 290
Jortue [sic], 1998
Jose, 485
Joseph, 1969
Joseph, 33
Joshua, 2103
Joshua, 2109
Josue, 4212
Jude, 4193
Judith, 1590
Judith, 1591
Julianna, 290
Julianna, 326
Lenny, 4240
Louisa, 5420
Lucy, 104

Lucy, 105
Lucy, 165
Lucy, 232
Lucy, 87
Ludovicus, 751
Magdalena, 1531
Mardam, 774
Margaret, 1884
Margaret, 1998
Margareta, 1590
Margareta, 3219
Maria Anna, 1222
Maria Elizabeth, 3501
Maria Elizabeth, 3502
Maria, 4292
Mariae, 1014
Mariae, 657
Mariam Bernardum, 3466
Mary Jane, 2460
Mary, 2076
Mary, 315
Mary, 8
Matilois, 4244
Monica Anna, 230
Mrs., 226
Naas, 173
Nancy, 4227

Ned, 4188
Nelly, 7
Nn_[?], 4227
O'Donnell, 1014
Old Aunt Dolley, 4947
Old Aunt Nelly, 5019
Patience, 4201
Peggy, 113
Pembrooke, 384
Philip, 33
Polley, 4287
Prince, 4255
Rachel Ann, 1969
Rachel, 106
Rachel, 2132
Ralph, 106
Rebecca, 165
Richard, 281
Richard, 57
Robert, 2460
Robertum Henricum, 3867
Ruth, 2460
Sally, 173
Samll, 281
Samuel Johannem Joseph, 3340
Samuelem Hubertem, 3703
Sarah Anna, 485

Sarah, 142
Sarah, 225
Simon, 1031
Sofia, 192
Somerset, 4194
Sophia Mary (Mrs.), 541
Stephen, 4240
Susan, 2731
Susanna, 3699
Syrena, 1884
Telientas, 292
Terasa, 7
Teresia, 3152
Terrentius, 1334
Terresa, 287
Terresa, 327
Terresa, 412
Thomas, 143
Thomas, 144
Thomas, 1651
Thomson, 279
Ullricam Mariem, 3699
Ullricem Mariam, 3704
Uncle Arnold, 4952
Unnamed Slave of E. Taney, 1969
Violettam Franciscam, 3991
William, 144, 1538, 2132

www.ingramcontent.com/pod-product-compliance
Lightning Source LLC
Chambersburg PA
CBHW060905300426
44112CB00011B/1354